D1546069

Bibliography

of

Captain James Cook

R.N., F.R.S., Circumnavigator

Bibliography
of
Captain James Cook

R.N., F.R.S., Circumnavigator

THE LIBRARY OF NEW SOUTH WALES

Editor: M. K. BEDDIE

2ND EDITION

SYDNEY
1970

First edition published by the Trustees of the Public
Library of New South Wales, Mitchell Library, Sydney.

© The Council of the Library of New South Wales, Sydney, 1970.

National Library of Australia card number and SBN.
SBN 7240 9999 9

Printed in Australia by Waite & Bull Pty. Limited, Sydney.

LIST OF CONTENTS

(Following the general entries, references are arranged alphabetically by the name of the associate, and where necessary further subdivided as under Banks)

PREFACE

T HE *Bibliography of Captain James Cook* was first published by the Trustees of the Public Library of New South Wales in 1928 as a catalogue of the exhibition then held in the Mitchell Library to celebrate the bicentenary of Captain Cook's birth. The first edition contained entries for items in the Mitchell Library and the General Reference Library and in the private collections of the late Sir William Dixson and the late Sir John Ferguson, with some items of special interest from other collections.

This second edition has been compiled at the direction of the Council of the Library of New South Wales—the successor to the former Trustees—as part of the celebrations commemorating the bicentenary of Captain Cook's discovery of the east coast of Australia. It has been much extended in scope in an attempt to record all relevant items in the various collections of the Library of New South Wales and the National Library of Australia, and to include important items in other Australian libraries. It does not, however, purport to be a union list of Cook material in Australia. The Council expresses its warm thanks to the institutions named in the Introduction, and especially to the National Library of Australia, for their contributions to the *Bibliography*.

Compilation and editing fell mainly to Miss M. K. Beddie, B.A., who carried out those arduous and exacting tasks in addition to her normal duties as librarian in charge of cataloguing for the Mitchell Library. The Council hopes that this second edition of the *Bibliography of Captain James Cook* will, like its predecessor, be a valuable bibliography and reference work on the three voyages of the great navigator.

A. J. DUNSTON
President of the Council

G. D. RICHARDSON
Principal Librarian and Secretary
April 1970

INTRODUCTION

SOME major changes have taken place since the first edition of this Bibliography was published in 1928. The Australian Museum has transferred many of its written and pictorial records to the Mitchell Library; the private collections of Sir William Dixson and Sir John Ferguson now form special collections in the Library of New South Wales and the National Library of Australia respectively; and items located in the galleries of the Library of New South Wales (designated "Art Gallery" in the first edition) have now been given individual call numbers.

The present Bibliography contains entries for items held by the Library of New South Wales (Mitchell Library, Dixson Library and Galleries, General Reference Library) which were catalogued by May 1969, together with selected entries from other Australian institutions. The following institutions were asked to send entries for important material in their collections for inclusion in this revised edition.

The National Library of Australia, the Public Library of Queensland, the State Library of South Australia, the State Library of Tasmania, the State Library of Victoria, the State Library of Western Australia, the Parliamentary Library, Sydney, the Parliamentary Library, Melbourne, the Queensland Parliamentary Library, the Australian Museum, the Australian National University, Flinders University, La Trobe University, Macquarie University, Monash University, the University of Adelaide, the University of Melbourne, the University of New England, the University of New South Wales, the University of Newcastle, the University of Queensland, the University of Sydney, the University of Tasmania, and the University of Western Australia.

Also represented are the holdings of the Australasian Pioneers' Club, Sydney, the Art Gallery of New South Wales (these items having been copied from the 1928 edition), the Basser Library of the Australian Academy of Science, and Captain Cook's Landing Place Trust whose Director gave valuable held in the listing of documents in the Museum at Kurnell.

Entries were also selected from the Guide to Collections of Manuscripts Relating to Australia, and from Australian Public Affairs Information Service: a subject index to current literature, 1964–8.

An attempt has been made to record information about Cook material when it has been offered for sale, with the thought that this information would be a useful guide to students. However, many references to this type of information are contained in the official correspondence of the Library of New South Wales, and it has not been practicable to index these.

The documents held in institutions other than the Library of New South Wales have not been examined, but have been listed from information supplied by those institutions. The National Library of Australia provided copies of cards from relevant sections of its catalogue of printed books, and revised entries for its manuscripts and pictures. Items in the State Library of Victoria have been taken from its list Material relating to Captain James Cook in the Reference Library, 1960.

As a general rule, original documents have been listed with only the name of the institution which holds the original, since, under the Australian Joint

Copying Project, photographic copies of those documents held overseas will eventually be available in the major libraries in Australia. The Library of New South Wales plans to photograph the original documents in its possession; photographic copies of these documents have therefore not always been noted.

Many illustrations published in books were indexed for the 1928 edition of the *Bibliography*. This indexing has been done very selectively in the Mitchell Library since 1928. Analytical entries in the 1970 edition of the *Bibliography* do not show complete holdings by libraries, of the items analysed.

Items listed in the first edition have been omitted from the second edition if they were not found in 1969, or if they had been mistakenly included. For example, the entry on p.79 of the 1928 edition for *Remarks on a passage from the River Balise, in the Bay of Honduras, to Merida . . . Jucatan* has been omitted because previously it had been wrongly attributed to Captain James Cook, the circumnavigator. It has been established that this document was written by Captain James Cook, Master of the *Mercury*, 1759–60. The autograph letter from Sir Phillip Stephens to Captain Cook, 20th July, 1776, shown as the last entry on p.62 of the 1928 edition, could not be traced in the National Library of Australia, and so this entry has not been included.

The scheme of arrangement for the present edition is shown in the List of Contents. Where practicable, the arrangement is chronological, but in many sections containing illustrative material, alphabetical arrangement by title or artist has been used.

The index covers titles of publications, compilers, editors, artists, engravers, printers, publishers and important names mentioned on the title-pages; it is not a subject index. A system of running numbers gives quick reference from the index to the items included in the *Bibliography*.

The symbol NPL has been used throughout this second edition of the *Bibliography* to represent the Library of New South Wales which was known as the Public Library of New South Wales prior to 1st July, 1969.

My colleagues in the Library of New South Wales have given me much help and advice, for which I would like to express my thanks and appreciation.

M. K. BEDDIE

AUTHORITIES, CONTRIBUTING LIBRARIES AND ABBREVIATIONS

Beaglehole	The Journals of Captain James Cook on his voyages of discovery. Ed. by J. C. Beaglehole . . . Pub. for the Hakluyt Society. Cambridge, U.P., 1955–67.
Du Rietz	Du Rietz, Rolf. Captain James Cook. A bibliography of literature printed in Sweden before 1819. Upsala, 1960.
Holmes	Holmes, *Sir* Maurice. Captain James Cook, R.N., F.R.S. A bibliographical excursion. London, Francis Edwards, 1952.
Jackson	Jackson, James. James Cook, oct.27,1728-fév.14,1779: cartographie et bibliographie. Paris, 1879. (*Bulletin de la Société de Géographie.*)
Roberts	Roberts, Stanley. Captain Cook's voyages: a bibliography of the French translations, 1772–1800. (*Journal of Documentation* vol.III, no.3, Dec. 1947.)
Spence	Spence, S.A. Captain James Cook, R.N., 1728–1779. A bibliography. Mitcham, Sy., England, 1960.

ANL	National Library of Australia, Canberra
ANL(EAPetherick)	National Library of Australia, Petherick Collection
ANL:F	National Library of Australia, Ferguson Collection
ANL(Nan Kivell)	National Library of Australia, Nan Kivell Collection
NAuM	Australian Museum, Sydney
NNcU	University of Newcastle, N.S.W.
NPL:D	Dixson Library, Library of New South Wales, Sydney
NPL:M	Mitchell Library, Library of New South Wales, Sydney
NPL:R	General Reference Department, Library of New South Wales
NParl	The Library, Parliament of New South Wales, Sydney
NUN	University of New South Wales, Kensington, N.S.W.
QOM	Oxley Memorial Library of Queensland, Public Library of Queensland, Brisbane
QParl	Queensland Parliamentary Library, Brisbane
QU	University of Queensland, St. Lucia, Queensland
SPL	State Library of South Australia, Adelaide
VMoU	Monash University Library, Clayton, Victoria
VParl	The Library, Parliament of Victoria, Melbourne
VSL	State Library of Victoria, Melbourne
VU(Baillieu)	University of Melbourne, Baillieu Library, Parkville, Victoria
TSL	State Library of Tasmania, Hobart
WU	University of Western Australia, Reid Library, Nedlands, W.A.

Australasian Pioneers' Club, Sydney
Captain Cook's Landing Place Trust, Kurnell, N.S.W.

A. & R.	Angus & Robertson
A.J.C.P.	Australian Joint Copying Project
ALS	autograph letter, signed
Adm.	Admiralty
app.	appendix, appendices
Aufl.	Auflage
B.M.	British Museum
B.M.Add.MSS.	British Museum Additional Manuscript
b./wh.	black and white
Bd.	Band
bearb.	bearbeitet
bibl.	bibliography
br./wh.	brown and white

AUTHORITIES, CONTRIBUTING LIBRARIES AND ABBREVIATIONS – *Continued*

c., ca.	circa
ch.	chapter
cm	centimetre(s)
col.	coloured
Coll.	Collection
cols	colours
comp.	compiled, compiler
Dept.	Department
ed.	edited, edition, editor
f., ff.	folio, folios
facs.	facsimile(s)
fasc.	fascicle, fascicule
frontisp.	frontispiece
Govt.Pr.	Government Printer
H.M.S.O.	Her Majesty's Stationery Office, London
hrsg.	herausgegeben
illus.	illustration(s), illustrated
intro.	introduction
LS	letter, signed
M.L.	Mitchell Library
MS., MSS.	manuscript, manuscripts
meas.	measurement
n.d.	no date of publication
n.p.	no place of publication
n.s.	new series
neg.	negative
no.	number
O.U.P.	Oxford University Press
p., pp.	page, pages
P.R.O.	Public Record Office, London
pl.	plate
port.	portrait(s)
pr.	printer
pseud.	pseudonym
pt.	part
pub.	publication, published, publisher
reprod.	reproduced, reproduction
S.C.	General Reference Department, Library of New South Wales, Special Collections
TLS	typescript letter, signed
trad.	traduction, traduit
trans.	translation, translated, translator
U.P.	University Press
W. & T.	Whitcombe & Tombs
Zeit.	Zeitschrift

VOYAGES

Manuscripts

1764–79 BONWICK TRANSCRIPTS.—Cook Papers.

4 cases.

Copies of State papers and official records preserved in the Public Record Office, the Admiralty and other Departments of State, and the British Museum; collected by James Bonwick, who, in 1891, was authorized by the Government of New South Wales, on the recommendation of the History Board, to search for all official records relating to Captain Cook and his connection with Australian discovery. These were published, with introduction, notes and index, as vol. 1, pt. 1 of the *Historical Records of New South Wales*. Bonwick also included in the Transcripts all the material which he could gather, after an exhaustive search, from unofficial sources, such as copies of manuscripts, extracts from books, pamphlets, periodicals and newspapers, and miscellaneous biographical information. They cover all phases of Cook's career from his survey of the coast of Newfoundland, in 1764, to his death in 1779. They contain:

(a) Extracts from the Log of the *Grenville*, and the logs and journals of Cook and his officers in the *Endeavour*, with notes and reports by Bonwick, notes on logs of the *Resolution*, Cook's last journal, and reviews and criticisms of various accounts of his voyages, chiefly those of Hawkesworth and Forster.

(b) Copies of the official correspondence between Cook, Palliser, the Admiralty and the Navy Board concerning his survey of Newfoundland, the equipment of his ships, and the conduct of his three voyages. Also correspondence between Cook, the Viceroy of Brazil, Banks, Clerke, Furneaux, and others.

(c) Accounts of Cook's death and memorials.

(d) Biographical material, chiefly concerning his early days, family, and descendants.

Copies: NPL:M(B.T. ser.2; Cook, boxes 1–4).   1

[176–] COOK DOCUMENTS from the Australian Museum, Sydney.

pp.195.

Original manuscripts, with a manuscript copy of each document.

Copies: NPL:M(Safe 1/83).   2

1768–79 FACSIMILE COPIES of original manuscripts re voyages of Captain James Cook, 1768–1779; with charts.

1 portfolio.

This collection was made up from material formerly kept in Basement Cabinet, and prior to that in Drawer 46.

CONTENTS:

1. Pages from Cook's Log, 1768–1771. Photocopy. Original in Safe 1/83.
2. Rules to be observed by every person on the *Endeavour*, drawn up by Cook, 1768+. Photocopy. Original in Safe 1/83.
3. Pages from Cook's Log book, 1768–1771, with Admiralty chart. Photocopies. Originals in possession of R. Milbank Hudson, 1928.
4. Page from Cook's Journal showing change of name from Stingray Bay to Botany Bay, May 1770. Lithographic facsimile and photostat.
5. Pages from Cook's Log, 19–22 Apr. 1770. Photocopy.
6–7. Pages from Sir Joseph Banks' Journal, 1769–1770. Photocopies. Original of Item 6 is in Safe 1/12–13 and of Item 7 in Auckland Public Library.
8. ALS to Lord Sandwich from Cook, 6 Feb. 1772 with enclosure of his opinion of the route to be taken by the *Resolution* and *Adventure*. Photocopy. Original in Safe 1/82.

9. Pages from Cook's Journal, Nov. 1778– Jan. 17, 1779; with chart. Photostat copies. Original in the British Museum.
10. Page of unidentified journal, Feb. 1779 re Cook's death. Photocopy and photostat copy. Original in National Library of Australia.
11. Page from James Burney's Journal 13 Feb. 1779. Original in Safe 1/64.
12. 'Directions for sailing' and 'Descriptions of the Harbour of Halifax & the Coast Adjacent' written by Cook. Photocopies. Originals in the Museum of the Royal United Service Institution, Whitehall, London.

Copies: NPL:M(MS.1285X). 3

[177–] THOMSON, Charles
Commonplace-book. Late 18th century.

pp.c.170.

MS. Commonplace book of Charles Thomson, an American, containing transcripts of Cook's voyages with notes of letter from *Spanish Mercury*, 7 January 1780 concerning Cook's death. Also extract of a letter from Mr. Pallas, professor at Petersburg to Mr. Busching, Counsellor at Berlin, dated 21 December 1778, re Cook's death and Capt. Clerke's call at Kamschatka.

Copies: ANL (Nan Kivell 4229). 4

1771–8 COOK, James
Letter book, 1771–1778.

pp.161.

Contains chiefly orders to and from the Admiralty, Navy Commissioners and Victualling Commissioners, and Cook's orders to his officers during his second and third voyages. Gives many interesting details relating to the second and third voyages.

Copies: ANL(MS.6). 5

1891 COPIES OF DOCUMENTS relating to Captain Cook, R.N., the originals in the Grey Collection at the Public Library of Auckland, New Zealand.

ff.291.

Manuscript copy made by Mrs. Davies, 1891. Includes a copy of part of Banks' journal and letters.

Copies: NPL:M(C697). 6

1893 [CORRESPONDENCE between Cook, Palliser, the Admiralty and the Navy Board, also between Cook, Banks, Clerke, Furneaux, and others, concerning . . . the equipment of his ships and the conduct of his three voyages, Dec. 30, 1762–Feb. 2, 1780; with notes and facsimiles of letters.]

(*Historical Records of New South Wales*. Sydney, Govt. Pr., 1893. Vol. 1, pt. 1, pp. 299–432.)

Copies: NPL:M(991/N); NPL:D(89/267); NPL:R(994.4/44). 7

1928 GREAT BRITAIN—Admiralty
Instructions to Captain Cook for his three voyages [from the original in the P.R.O., Adm. 2/1332].

(Navy Records Society—*Naval miscellany*; ed. by W. G. Perrin. London, 1928. Vol. 3, pp. 339–64.)

Copies: NPL:M(359.05/N); NPL:R(DS359.06/2); ANL; VSL. 8

Printed Accounts

Entries for the various editions of Cook's own journals and logs are filed here. For books written about the voyages *see* the subheadings: *Books about* and *Articles*.

1778 NEW DISCOVERIES concerning the world and its inhabitants. In two parts, Pt I containing a circumstantial account of all the islands in the South-Sea . . . Comprehending all the discoveries made in the several voyages of Commodore . . . Byron, Captain Wallis, Carteret and Cook. Related by Mr Hawkesworth, Sydney Parkinson, Mr Forster and Captain Cook . . . Pt II containing a summary account of Captain Cook's attempt to discover a southern continent in 1773, 1774 and 1775. London, J. Johnson, 1778.

Illus. maps, pp. xviii, 408.

Copies: NPL:M(980/N); NPL:D(77/23); NPL:R(09:S909·8A/114); ANL; VSL.   9

1780–86 La Harpe's Edition

Abrégé de l'histoire générale des voyages, par M. de La Harpe. Paris, Hôtel de Thou, 1780–86.

A rearrangement and abridgement of Prévost d'Exiles, A. F. *abbé*—Histoire générale des voyages. Vols. 19–23 contain Cook's voyages. *See also* nos. 23, 88, 99, 104.

Copies: VSL.   10

[1783] London Edition

The British navigator; containing Captain Cook's three voyages round the world. The first in the *Endeavour*, begun in the year 1768 and finished in 1771. The second in the *Resolution*, accompanied by the *Adventure*, commanded by Capt. Furneaux; begun in 1772 and finished in 1775. And the third in the *Resolution* and *Discovery*, the latter being commanded by Capt. Clerke; begun in 1776 and finished in 1780. Including every interesting particular in the course of those voyages, and an account of the unfortunate death of Capt. Cook. Pt. 1–2. London, John Fielding, [1783].

Illus. 2 vols.
(*The Polite traveller and British navigator*, vol. 5–6.)

Copies: NPL:M(910·8/43A5–6).   11

1783–4 PABST, Johann Georg Friedrich

Die Entdeckungen des fünften Welttheils; oder, Reisen um die Welt. Ein Lesebuch für die Jugend. Nürnberg, Felsseckerische Buchhandlung, 1783–84.

Frontisp. 2 vols.
Vol. 2 deals with Cook's voyages. *See also* no. 13.

Copies: NPL:M(980/P, vol. 2 only); ANL.   12

COLLECTED VOYAGES – *Printed Accounts – continued*

1783-8 PABST, Johann Georg Friedrich

Die Entdeckungen des fünften Welttheils; oder, Reisen um die Welt. Ein Lesebuch für die Jugend. 2e.Aufl. Nürnberg, Felsseckerische Buchhandlung, 1783-8.

4 vols. in 2.

Vols. 2–4 deal with Cook's voyages. *See also* no. 12.

Copies: NPL:M(980/P). 13

1784 THE HISTORY of Captain Cook's three voyages round the world. The first in the *Endeavour* begun in the year 1768 and finished in 1771; the second in the *Resolution* accompanied by the *Adventure* . . . begun in 1772 and finished in 1775; and the third in the *Resolution* & *Discovery* begun in 1776 and finished in 1780. Containing every interesting particular in the course of these voyages, and an account of the unfortunate death of Captain Cook. London, Hodges and Pain, pr., 1784.

2 vols.

Copies: NPL:M(980:Col/1A1-2); VSL. 14

1784 Kearsley's Edition

A Compendious history of Captain Cook's first and second voyages. The first performed in the years 1768, 1769, 1770, 1771 in the *Endeavour*; the second in 1772, 1773, 1774 and 1775 in the *Resolution* and *Adventure*. Including an abridgement of Capt. Furneaux's narrative of his proceedings during the separation of the two ships. [Ed. by G. Kearsley.] London, printed for G. Kearsley, 1784.

pp.iv, 308.

Adapted from the quarto editions published by the Admiralty. Published uniformly with this: *A Compendious history of Captain Cook's last voyage*, and *An Abridgement of Captain Cook's last voyage*. *See also* nos. 30, 31, 60.

Copies: NPL:R(09:S990A/80); ANL:F; SPL; VSL. 15

1784-5 Italian Edition

Storia de'viaggi intrapresi per ordine di S.M. Brittannica dal Capitano Giacomo Cook, ricavata dalle autentiche relazioni del medesimo, e dalle osservazioni di varj filosofi inglesi compagni di tali spedizioni. Con una introduzione generale, contenente la notizia de'più celebri viaggi precedenti, colla vita di questo celebre navigatore, il tutto arricchito di note e di altre interessanti osservazioni. Napoli, La Nuova Societa' Letteraria e Tipografica, 1784-5.

13 vols.

General introduction, volume 1, p. 6, states that this does not follow La Harpe's *Compendio della Storia generale dei viaggi*. For a later edition *see* no. 45.

Copies: NPL:M(980:Col/2A1-13). 16

[1784-6] ANDERSON, G. W.

A New, authentic and complete collection of voyages round the world, undertaken and performed by royal authority. Containing a new, authentic, entertaining, instructive, full and complete historical account of Captain Cook's first, second, third and last voyages, undertaken by order of his present Majesty, for making new discoveries in . . . the southern and northern hemispheres, &c. &c. &c. His first voyage [etc.] . . . Together with a narrative of Capt. Furneaux's proceedings in the *Adventure* during the separation of that ship from the *Resolution*; in which period several of his people were destroyed by the natives of Queen Charlotte's Sound in New Zealand. To which will be added complete and genuine narratives of other voyages . . . viz. . . . Lord Byron, Capt. Wallis, Capt. Carteret, Lord Mulgrave, Lord Anson &c. &c. &c. Including a faithful relation of . . . important travels and journeys . . . The whole of these voyages of Capt. James Cook, &c. being newly written by the editors from the authentic journals of several principal officers and other gentlemen . . . who sailed in the various ships, and now publishing under the . . . direction of G. W. Anderson . . . assisted . . . by a principal officer who sailed in the *Resolution*, sloop, and by other gentlemen of the Royal Navy. London, printed for Alex. Hogg, [1784–86].

Maps, plates, ports. pp. iv + [ii], 5–655 + [i].
Bound in kangaroo, with blind tooling by F. Heyner, M.L., 1918.
Previously in the possession of Charles Hellmrich, Mayor of Paddington, and owned by Mrs Rachel Barrington, descendant of Captain Cook. MS letters, documents, newscuttings, etc. have been inserted. With MS annotations, and note re engravings of Cook's arms and crest on the plate entitled *A Night dance of women in Hapaee*, bound opposite p. 452. Published weekly in 80 six-penny numbers, later bound together. List of subscribers (2pp) bound after p.iv, carries imprint, dated 1784.
Further date from British Museum General catalogue.
Title on p. [5] reads: *A New, genuine and complete history of the whole of Capt. Cook's voyages*, [*etc.*]
Title on p. 108 reads: *Capt. Cook's second voyage towards the South Pole* [*etc.*]
Title on p. 399 reads: *A New, authentic and complete history of Captain Cook's third and last voyage* [*etc.*]
Frontispiece is portrait of Cook, engraved as follows at foot of plate: *Accurately drawn from an original painting & engraved by Mr Noble*. At top of plate: *Frontispiece to Anderson's Large folio edition of the whole of Capt. Cook's voyages, &c, complete*. Photograph of Mrs Barrington is pasted onto this plate.
See also nos. 18, 19, 21, 22, 25, 26, 29, 39, 44, 46, 49, 61, 68, 69, 76, 83, 95, 97.

Copies: NPL:M(A346); ANL:F; QOM.　　　　　　　　　　　　17

[1784–6] ANDERSON, G. W.

A New, authentic and complete collection of voyages round the world, undertaken and performed by royal authority. Containing an authentic, entertaining, full and complete history of Capt. Cook's first, second, third and last voyages, undertaken by order of his present Majesty, for making discoveries in . . . the southern and northern hemispheres, &c. &c. &c. and successively performed in the years 1768 . . . 1780. The first voyage [etc.] . . . together with Capt. Furneaux's narrative of his proceedings in the *Adventure* during the separation of the ships in the second voyage. To which will be added genuine narratives of other voyages . . . viz. . . . Lord Byron, Capt. Wallis, Capt. Carteret, Lord Mulgrave, Lord Anson, Mr Parkinson . . . &c. Likewise a faithful relation of . . . travels and journeys . . . The whole of these voyages of Capt. Cook, F.R.S. &c.

now publishing under the . . . direction of G. W. Anderson . . . assisted by a principal officer who sailed in the *Resolution,* sloop, and by many other gentlemen of the most distinguished naval abilities. London, printed for the proprietors and pub. by Alex Hogg, 1784–[1786].

Maps, plates, pp. iv, 5–655 + [v].

D.S. Mitchell's copy.

Published weekly in 80 six-penny numbers, later bound together. List of subscribers (4pp) bound at end of volume, without imprint and not dated.

Title on p. [5] reads: *A Genuine and complete history of the whole of Capt. Cook's voyages [etc.]*

Title on p. 108 reads: *Capt. Cook's second voyage towards the South Pole [etc.]*

Title on p. 399 reads: *A New, authentic and complete history of Captain Cook's third and last voyage.*

Frontispiece is portrait of Cook, engraved, as follows, at foot of plate: *Accurately drawn from an original painting & engraved by Mr Thornton . . . Sept. 11, 1784.* At top of plate: *Frontispiece to Anderson's Large folio edition, etc.*

In copy held by Captain Cook's Landing Place Trust frontispiece is dated 1781, and illustration of the death of Cook is dated 1785. Date 1786 taken from British Museum General catalogue.

See also no. 17.

Copies: NPL:M(F980/5A1); NPL:R(09:F990A/11); ANL; Captain Cook's Landing Place Trust. 18

[1784–6] ANDERSON, G. W.

A New, authentic and complete collection of voyages round the world, undertaken and performed by royal authority. Containing a new, authentic, entertaining, instructive, full and complete historical account of Captain Cook's first, second, third and last voyages, undertaken by order of his present Majesty, for making new discoveries in . . . the southern and northern hemispheres, &c. &c. &c. and successively performed in the years 1768 . . . 1780 . . . His first voyage [etc.] . . . Together with a narrative of Capt. Furneaux's proceedings in the *Adventure* during the separation of the ships in the second voyage, during which period several of his people were destroyed by the natives of Queen Charlotte's Sound. To which will be added complete and genuine narratives of other voyages . . . viz . . . Lord Byron, Capt. Wallis, Capt. Carteret, Lord Mulgrave, Lord Anson, Mr Parkinson . . . &c. Including a faithful relation of . . . travels and journeys . . . The whole of these voyages of Capt. James Cook, &c. being newly written by the editors from the authentic journals of several principal officers and other gentlemen . . . who sailed in the various ships; and now publishing under the . . . direction of G. W. Anderson . . . assisted . . . by a principal officer who sailed in the *Resolution,* sloop, and by many other gentlemen of the Royal Navy. London, printed for Alex. Hogg, [1784–86].

Maps, plates, pp. iv, 5–655, [v].

Published weekly in 80 six-penny numbers, later bound together. List of subscribers without imprint and not dated.

Title on p. [5] reads: *A New, genuine and complete history [etc.].* Other titles and frontispiece as in D. S. Mitchell's copy at F980/5A1, no. 18.

In copy held by Captain Cook's Landing Place Trust frontispiece dated 1781. *See also* no. 17.

Copies: NPL:M(F980/5A2); Captain Cook's Landing Place Trust; NAuM. 19

[1785] THE BEAUTIES of Captain Cook's voyages; or, A selection of interesting narratives. Being a circumstantial and entertaining account of all the curious and extraordinary occurrences which happened in his voyages round the world, and to the Pacific Ocean. Selected from the voluminous performances that have been published, etc. [Vol.1]. London, G. Lister, [1785].

Frontisp. pp. iv, 127.
Consists mainly of accounts of the manners and customs of native races described by Cook.
Publication date from advertisement at end, dated 14th Feb. 1785, which says the second volume will be published in about fourteen days. Preface makes it clear that the work is to be complete in two volumes. *See also* no. 53.

Copies: NPL:M(980/B); NPL:D(78/61). 20

[1785] Hogg's Edition
A New, authentic and complete collection of voyages round the world, undertaken and performed by royal authority. Containing a new, authentic, entertaining, instructive, full and complete historical account of Captain Cook's first, second, third and last voyages, undertaken by order of his present Majesty . . . to which will be added genuine narratives of other voyages . . . This octavo edition of Cook's Voyages, &c. newly written by the editors, from the authentic journals of several principal officers and other gentlemen . . . The whole now revised, corrected and improved by Capt. John Hogg. London, printed for Alex. Hogg, [1785].

Maps, plates, ports. 6 vols.
Also issued in eighty sixpenny parts.
Date from frontispiece to volume 1, which is entitled *Frontispiece to Hogg's Cheap & elegant octavo edition of Cook's Voyages &c. complete.*
Taken from G. W. Anderson's edition, for which *see* no. 17.

Copies: NPL:M(980/H); NPL:D(78/25–30); QOM. 21

[1785] Hogg's Edition
New, authentic and complete edition of Captain Cook's first, second, third and last voyages round the world. Ed. by Capt. John Hogg. London, [1785–95].

Illus. maps, 3 vols.
Volume 1 undated; volume 2, 1795; volume 3, 1785. ANL copy has some plates and maps damaged. *See* no. 21.

Copies: ANL. 22

1785 Italian Edition
For edition of thirteen volumes published Napoli, 1784–5, *see* no. 16.

1785 La Harpe. Italian Edition
Storia dei viaggi di Cook: opera di M. De La Harpe . . . tradotta dal Francese. Venezia, Vincenzio Formaleoni, 1785.

Illus. maps, 7 vols.
See also nos. 10, 88, 99, 104.

Copies: NPL:M(980:Col/3B1–7); VSL. 23

1785–89 SAMMLUNG der besten Reisebeschreibungen. Troppau, J. G. Trassler, 1785–89.

33 vols.

Imprint varies. Bd. 11–33 published in Brünn. Bd 7–10, *Reise um die Welt des Lieutenants J. Cook . . . 1768 . . . 1771.* Bd. 11–14, *J. R. Forster's und seines Sohns G. Forster's Reise um die Welt unternommen und während den Jahren 1772 bis 1775.* Bd. 17–18, *Dritte und letzte Reise um die Welt des J. Cook Befehlshaber der königlichen Korvette die Resoluzion, in den Jahren 1776 bis 1778.*

Copies: NPL:M(980:Co2/3A1–4, Bd. 7–10 only); VU(Baillieu).   24

1786 A NEW, AUTHENTIC COLLECTION of Captain Cook's voyages round the world; undertaken by order of His Present Majesty, for making new discoveries, &c. &c. . . . Written by several principal officers, and other gentlemen who sailed in the various ships. Manchester, printed by G. Swindells & Co., 1786.

Illus. port. pp. 620 [i.e. 600].

Page 536 is erroneously numbered 556, and the error is continued to the end of the volume.

Bound in full Kangaroo, with Cobb ends and blind tooling floral design by F. Heyner in the Mitchell Library bindery. From G. W. Anderson's edition, originally published in 1784, *see* no. 17.

Copies: NPL:M(980:Co1/4A1).   25

1787 ANDERSON, George William

A New, authentic and complete collection of voyages round the world, undertaken and performed by royal authority. Containing an authentic . . . account of Captain Cook's first, second, third and last voyages . . . now publishing under the direction . . . of G. W. Anderson, assisted . . . by a principal officer who sailed in the *Resolution* sloop, and by many other gentlemen. London, A. Hogg, 1787.

Illus. pp. 655.

Pages 1–10 missing. *See also* no. 17.

Copies: VU(Baillieu).   26

1787 HISTORY OF NEW HOLLAND, from its first discovery in 1616 to the present time; with a particular account of its produce and inhabitants and a description of Botany Bay. Also a list of the naval, marine, military and civil establishment. [*Anon.*] To which is prefixed an introductory Discourse on banishment by . . . W. Eden [1st Baron Auckland]. London, John Stockdale, 1787.

Maps, pp. xxiv, 254.

Compiled from the published journals *etc.* of Cook, Dampier, Sydney Parkinson, *etc.* For later editions *see* nos. 28, 43, 71.

Copies: NPL:M(991/31A1); NPL:D(78/54); VSL.   27

1787 HISTORY OF NEW HOLLAND, from its first discovery in 1616 to the present time; with a particular account of its produce and inhabitants and a description of Botany Bay. Also a list of the naval, marine, military and civil establishment. [*Anon.*] To which is prefixed an introductory Discourse on banishment by . . . W. Eden [1st Baron Auckland]. 2nd ed. London, John Stockdale, 1787.

Maps in colour, pp. xxxv, 254.
Compiled from the journals of Cook, Dampier, S. Parkinson, etc. *See also* nos. 27, 43, 71.
Copies: NPL:M(991/31B1); NPL:D(78/55); VSL.   28

1787 A NEW, AUTHENTIC COLLECTION of Captain Cook's voyages round the world; undertaken by order of His Majesty, for making new discoveries . . . comprehending the life and death of Captain Cook. Together with Captain Furneaux's narrative in the *Adventure*, during the separation of the ships in the second voyage, during which period several of his people were destroyed by the natives of Queen Charlotte's Sound. Written by the principal officers who sailed in the various ships. London, William Lane, 1787.

Port. pp. 576.
From G. W. Anderson's edition, originally published 1784, *see* no. 17.
Copies: NPL:M(980:Col/4B1).   29

1788 Kearsley's Edition
An Abridgment of Captain Cook's first and second voyages. [Ed. by G. Kearsley.] 4th. ed London, G. Kearsley, 1788.

See also no. 15.
Copies: VSL.   30

1788 Kearsley's Edition
An Abridgment of Captain Cook's first and second voyages. The first performed in the years 1768, 1769, 1770, 1771; the second in 1772, 1773, 1774 and 1775, for making discoveries in the northern hemisphere, by order of His Majesty. Extracted from the quarto edition, in five volumes . . . including an abridgment of Capt. Furneaux's narrative of his proceedings during the separation of the two ships, to which is added a narrative of Commodore Phipps's, now Lord Mulgrave, Voyage to the North Pole; also an Extract from Forster's Introduction to his history of the northern discoveries on the progress of navigation. [Ed. by G. Kearsley.] The sixth edition, ornamented with several plates. London, printed for G. Kearsley, 1788.

Illus. map, port. pp.viii, 448.
See also no. 15.
Copies: NPL:M(980:Col/5A1).   31

1788 KIPPIS, *Rev.* Andrew
The Life of Captain James Cook, by A. Kippis. London, G. Nicol, G. G. J. & J. Robinson, 1788.

Port. pp. xvi, 527.
Appendix 2 is *The Morai, an ode*, by Miss Helen Maria Williams. As well as the ordinary edition, the Dixson Library holds two copies in special bindings, both of which are

grangerized and one has an original miniature of Cook inset on cover. *See also* nos. 33–8, 55, 81, 90, 92, 102–3, 106–8, 113, 120, 126, 128, 129, 131–2, 136–7, 141, 144, 148, 153, 159, 161–2, 172, 178, 185, 188, 196, 216.

Copies: NPL:M(Q980:Col/K1A1); NPL:D(Q77/13,Q78/8,9); NPL:R(09:Q990A/49); SPL; VParl; VU(Baillieu).   32

1788 KIPPIS, *Rev.* Andrew

The Life of Captain James Cook. Basil, J. J. Tourneisen, pr., 1788.

2 vols.
Paris, sold by Pissot, also in imprint. *See also* no. 32.

Copies: NPL:M(980:Col/K2B1–2); NPL:R(09:S990A/92); ANL:F.   33

1788 KIPPIS, *Rev.* Andrew

The Life of Captain James Cook. Dublin, H. Chamberlaine, W. Colles [and others], 1788.

Port. pp. xvi, 527.
See also no. 32.

Copies: NPL:M(980:Col/K2A1); ANL; VMoU.   34

1789 KIPPIS, *Rev.* Andrew

Leben des Capitain James Cook, von Andreas Kippis . . . Aus dem Englischen. Hamburg, B. G. Hoffmann, 1789.

Port. 2 vols.
Volume 1 has additional title-page. *See also* no. 32.

Copies: NPL:M(980:Col/K2E1–2); NPL:D(78/7–8).   35

1789 KIPPIS, *Rev.* Andrew

Vie du Capitaine Cook; traduite de l'anglois du Docteur Kippis . . . par M.[J. H.] Castera. Paris, Hôtel de Thou, 1789.

2 vols.
See also no. 32.

Copies: NPL:M(980:Col/K2C1–2); QOM.   36

1789 KIPPIS, *Rev.* Andrew

Vie du Capitaine Cook; traduite de l'anglois du Docteur Kippis . . . par M. [J. H.] Castera. Paris, Hôtel de Thou, 1789.

pp. [xxxiv], 546, [ii].
See also no. 32.

Copies: NPL:M(Q980:Col/K1B1); NPL:R(09:S990A/67).   37

1789 KIPPIS, *Rev.* Andrew

Vie du Capitaine Cook; traduite de l'anglois du Docteur Kippis, [by J. H. Castera]. Paris, Hôtel de Thou, 1789.

2 vols.
Lettre du traducteur . . . à M. Garat precedes Preface, pp. i–xlviii; signed at end, Castera.
See also no. 32.

Copies: NPL:M(980:Col/K2D1–2); VU(Baillieu).   38

1790 ANDERSON, G. W.

A Collection of voyages round the world . . . containing a complete historical account of Captain Cook's first, second, third and last voyages . . . to which are added . . . narratives of other voyages . . . round the world . . . viz. those of Lord Byron, Capt. Wallis, Capt. Carteret, Lord Mulgrave, Lord Anson, Mr Parkinson, Capt. Lutwidge, Mess. Ives, Middleton, Smith &c &c. including the substance of all the . . . important travels and journeys . . . Comp [by G. W. Anderson] from the . . . journals of several principal officers and other gentlemen . . . who sailed in the various ships. London, A. Millar, W. Law and R. Cater, 1790.

Maps, plates, ports. 6 vols.
Large folio edition published 1784–86, *see back*, no. 17.
This edition originally issued in 80 weekly parts, and also called Large octavo edition.
Volume 1, 4 and 6 want title-pages, and volume 6 wants pp. 1940–4, and directions to the binder, p. 2243 et seq.
Title on p. 11, volume 1, reads: *A New, genuine, and complete history of the whole of Capt. Cook's voyages.*
Title on p. 373, volume 2, reads: *A New, genuine, full, satisfactory and complete history of Capt. Cook's second voyage.*
Title on p. 1185, volume 4, reads: *A New, authentic and complete history of Capt. Cook's third & last voyage . . . taken, by permission, verbatim from Mr Anderson's folio edition.*
Copies: NPL:M(980:Col/6A1–6); NPL:D(79/37–42); NPL:R(09:S990A/68–73); ANL; QOM.   39

1790 BANKES, *Rev.* Thomas, *and others*
[New discoveries.]

(*In their* New, royal, authentic and complete system of universal geography . . . including (every discovery throughout Captain Cook's voyages round the world.) London, J. Cooke, [1790].)
See also nos. 59, 62–3, 84.
Copies: VSL.   40

1790 Bérenger. French Edition

Collection abrégée des voyages faits autour du monde. Paris, Lejay fils, 1790.

Vols. 7–9 of this set give account of Cook's voyages. *See also* nos. 47–8, 50, 51, 56.
Copies: VSL.   41

1790 Birmingham Edition

A New, authentic collection of Captain Cook's voyages round the world. Birmingham, R. Martin, 1790.
Copies: VSL.   42

1790 HISTORY OF NEW HOLLAND from its first discovery in 1616 to the present time; and A discourse on banishment . . . by Lord Aukland (*sic*).

Map.
(*In* Phillip, Arthur—Voyage of Governor Phillip to Botany Bay. 2nd ed. London, John Stockdale, 1790. Vo. 2, pp. lxxv–clxxv.)
An abridgement of no. 27. Also published in 3rd edition, 1790.
Copies: NPL:M(Q991/P); NPL:D(Q79/47, 3rd ed.); NPL:R(09:Q991A/8).   43

1790 Newcastle Edition

Captain Cook's voyages round the world. The first performed in the years 1768, 1769, 1770, 1771; the second in 1772, 1773, 1774, 1775; the third and last in 1776, 1777, 1778, 1779, and 1780, for making discoveries in the northern and southern hemispheres, by order of His Present Majesty. Containing a relation of all the interesting transactions which occurred in the course of the voyages, including Captain Furneaux's journal of his proceedings during the separation of the ships. With a narrative of Commodore Phipps's voyage to the North Pole and an abridgement of Foster's (*sic*) Introduction to his History of northern discoveries on the progress of navigation, to which is added Governor Phillip's Voyage to Botany-Bay, with an account of the establishment of the colonies of Port Jackson and Norfolk Island, &c. &c. Newcastle, M. Brown, 1790.

Illus. maps, port. 2 vols.
Resembles G. W. Anderson's edition (*see* no. 17 and nos. 39, 69). Title-page to Vol. 2 covers only Cook's third voyage (*see* no. 1574). The narrative is written partly in the first person, following Cook's journal, and partly in the third person, paraphrased from the official account. Illustrated with engravings by Bewick, Beilby and others, including the Death of Captain James Cook, D. Lizars, sculpt. Spence lists as being issued in two or four volumes. NPL:R set bound in three volumes, with title-page to Vol. 2 bound out of place as title-page to "second volume".

Copies: NPL:M(980:Col/7A1–2); NPL:D(79/33–4); NPL:R(S990A/74–6); ANL; SPL; VU(Baillieu). 44

1791–2 Italian Edition

Storia dei viaggi intrapresi per ordine di S.M. Britannica dal Capitano Giacomo Cook, ricavata dalle autentiche relazioni del medesimo. Con una introduzione generale, contenente la notizia dei più celebri viaggi precedenti. Torino, I. Soffietti e F. Prato, 1791–2.

Illus. map, port. 8 vols.
For an earlier edition *see* no. 16.

Copies: NPL:M(980:Col/8A1–8). 45

[1794?] ANDERSON, G. W.

A New, complete and universal collection of authentic and entertaining voyages and travels to all parts of the world; containing . . . complete narratives of the . . . most important journals . . . and including A New, authentic, entertaining, instructive, full and complete historical account of the whole of Captain Cook's . . . voyages . . . Now published under the . . . direction of G. W. Anderson. Rev., corrected and improved by W. H. Portlock; assisted by many officers and gentlemen. London, printed for A. Hogg, [1794?].

Frontisp. maps, plates, pp. 234, 5–836 + [iv].
First published in 1784–86, *see* no. 17. Pagination is in two sequences. Some plates are dated 1794, but Preface states it is "near twenty years" since any collection of voyages has been published. The British Museum lists a different edition, dated [1794]. Issued in 90 separate parts, now bound in one volume.
Frontispiece entitled: *Portlock's New collection of voyages and travels.* Title on p. 5 (second sequence) reads: *A New, complete and genuine history of a voyage round the world in . . . the*

Endeavour. Title on p. 108 (second sequence) reads: *Capt. Cook's second voyage towards the South Pole.* Title on p. 399 (second sequence) reads: *A New, authentic and complete history of Captain Cook's third and last voyage.*

Copies: NPL:D(F79/1); ANL; VSL.   46

1794 Bérenger. Italian Edition

Raccolta di tutti i viaggi fatti intorno al mondo da diverse nazioni dell'Europa; compilata in Francese da Signor Berenger. Tradotta in Italiano. Venezia, A. Zatta, 1794–6.

Charts, plates, 16 vols.
Some plates hand-coloured. An account of the three voyages of Cook is contained in vols. 4–7. For a separate issue of these four volumes, with a different title-page, *see* no. 48. *See also* nos. 41, 50, 51, 56.

Copies: NPL:M(910.8/B).   47

1794 Bérenger. Italian Edition

Viaggi intorno al mondo, fatti dal Capitano Giacomo Cook. Venezia, A. Zatta, 1794–5.

Charts, plates, 4 vols.
Some plates missing. These four volumes are vols. 4–7 of Bérenger's *Raccolta di tutti i viaggi fatti intorno al mondo* (Venezia, 1794–6 no. 47), issued with separate title-page. (Compare publisher's declaration at end of each volume.)
See nos. 41, 50, 51, 56.

Copies: NPL:M(980:Col/9A1–4); ANL:F.   48

[1794] Wilson's Edition

A New, complete and universal collection of authentic and entertaining voyages and travels to all parts of the world . . . Including a new, authentic, entertaining . . . account of the whole of Captain Cook's first, second, third and last voyages . . . The whole compiled from the original journals of the respective voyagers, &c and now published under . . . direction of P. Wilson. Assisted by G. W. Anderson and W. H. Portlock. London, Alex. Hogg, [1794].

Maps, plates, pp. iv, [5]–234, 5–836.
An abridged edition of Anderson's 1784–86 work. *See* no. 17. Pagination is in two sequences, as in the other folio editions, and also indicates abridgement (e.g. p. 29 labelled p. 29–39; p. 57 labelled p. 72 on verso, with signatures P–S on recto). Date of publication taken from *A New . . . chart of the discoveries of Capt. Cook*, and those plates which are from Portlock's edition, no. 46. Other plates are undated. Preface, entitled *Wilson's New collection of voyages and travels*, states "Near twenty years have elapsed since any collection of voyages and travels has been published". Originally issued in parts. Titles on pp. [5], 108 (second sequence) as in no. 46.
Title on p. 381 (second sequence) reads, *Captain Cook's third and last voyage to the Pacific Ocean.*

Copies: NPL:M(F980/W).   49

1795 Bérenger. French Edition

Collection de tous les voyages faits autour du monde, par les différents nations de l'Europe; rédigée par Bérenger. Paris, Dufart, 1795.

Plates, 9 vols.
Second edition. Previously published by Poinçot, 1788–90. Vol. 5 of Mitchell Library set is first edition. Vols. 7–9 deal with Cook's voyages. *See also* nos. 41, 47–8, 51, 56.
Copies: NPL:M(910.8/B).

50

1795 Bérenger. French Edition

Histoire abrégée des premier, second et troisième voyages autour du monde, par Cook. Mise à la portée de tout le monde par Bérenger. Basle, J. J. Thurneysen, 1795.

3 volumes in 1.
See also nos. 41, 47–8, 50, 56.
Copies: NPL:M(980:Col/10A1).

51

1795 Dutch Edition

Reizen rondom de waereld door J. Cook; vertaald door J. D. Pasteur. [With] (Bladwijzer) [i.e. index]. Leyden, Honkoop, Allart en Van Cleef, 1795–1809.

Illus. maps, port. tables, 14 vols. and atlas.
The Atlas, without title-page, contains portrait, 133 (i.e. 134) plates and 51 (i.e. 52) charts, engraved by J. S. Klauber, A. Klauber and C. van Baarsel: two different plates being numbered XX, and two different charts XXX. It was published in thirteen separate parts, but the copy at NPL:M F980:Col/1A1 has been bound in one volume. Bladwijzer, compiled by Rev. W. Chevallerau, was published at Amsterdam, J. Allart, 1809. Volumes 1 and 2 have title: *Reize rondom de waereld, etc.*, and half-titles vary throughout the set. Library of Congress catalogue gives imprint, Leyden, Amsterdam en s'Haage, 1797–1809. Volumes 1–3 include *Reize rondom de waereld 1768–1771* [*komp. door J. Hawkesworth*]. Volumes 4–7, *Reize naar de zuid-pool en rondom de waereld, 1772–1775* [*door J. Cook; met*] *Aantekeningen getrokken uit het dagverhaal van G. Forster*. Volumes 8–13, *Reize naar den Stillen Oceaan, 1776–1780* [*door J. Cook en J. King*]. Volume 14, *Bladwijzer door W. Chevallerau*.
Copies: NPL:M(980:Col/12A1–14, F980:Col/1A2–14, F980:Col/1A1); ANL.

52

[1795?] French Edition

Beautés des voyages du Capitaine Cook; ou, Relation historique du premier et du plus intéressant des voyages de cet illustre marin. Paris, Librairie Enfantine et Juvénile de Pierre Maumus, n.d.

Title-page and frontispiece only. *Inserted in* no. 54.
See also no. 20.
Copies: NPL:M(980:Col/11A1).

53

[1795?] French Edition

Le Cook du jeune âge; ou, Abrégé des voyages de ce célèbre navigateur. Besançon, Imprimèrie de Ch. Deis, n.d.

pp. 388.
This version may be a further abridgement of Bérenger's *Histoire abrégée des premier, second et troisiéme voyages autour du monde par Cook*, 1795. A title-page and frontispiece on different paper from the book and apparently belonging to another work, have been tipped in. This work is: *Beautés des voyages du Capitaine Cook; ou, Relation historique du premier et du plus intéressant des voyages de cet illustre marin*. Paris, Libairie Enfantine et Juvénile de P. Maumus. *See also* nos. 70, 80.
Copies: NPL:M(980:Col/11A1).

54

1795 Hogg's Edition
See no. 22.

1795 KIPPIS, *Rev.* Andrew

Historia de la vida y viages del Capitan Jaime Cook; obra escrita en
Ingles por A. Kippis . . . y traducida al Castellano por . . . Cesareo de
Nava Palacio. Madrid, En la Imprenta Real, 1795.

2 vols.
See also no. 32.

Copies: NPL:M(980:Col/K2F1–2); ANL:F.   55

1796 Bèrenger. French Edition

Histoire des premier, second et troisième voyages autour du monde,
par Cook. Mise à la portée de tout le monde, par Bérenger. Avec figures
et une grande mappe-monde en deux hémisphères, ou sont marquées
les decouvertes les plus récentes et les routes des trois voyages de Cook;
dressée par Henisson. Paris, Dufart, 1796.

3 vols.
Wanting map. Volume 2 has title-page bearing briefer title in different type, and date
1795. *See also* nos. 41, 47–8, 50, 51.

Copies: NPL:M(980:Col/10B1–3).   56

1796 Mavor's Edition

Historical account of the most celebrated voyages, travels and discoveries,
from the time of Colombus to the present period. By W. Mavor. London,
E. Newbery, 1796–1801.

25 vols.
Wanting plates? Volumes 6–7, dated 1796, deal with Cook's three voyages. *See also*
nos. 67, 73–4, 78–9.

Copies: NPL:M(910.8/28A1–25).   57

1797 CAPTAIN COOK'S three voyages to the Pacific Ocean. The first
performed in the years 1768, 1769, 1770, and 1771; the second in 1772,
1773, 1774, and 1775; the third and last in 1776, 1777, 1778, 1779, and
1780. Faithfully abridged from the quarto editions. Containing a particular relation of all the interesting transactions during the several
voyages, to which is prefixed the Life of Captain Cook. Boston, Thomas
and Andrews and D. West, 1797.

Illus. port. 2 vols.
See also no. 82.

Copies: NPL:M(980:Col/13A1–2).   58

1797 Dutch Edition
See back no. 52.

1798 BANKES, *Rev.* Thomas, *and others*
New discoveries.

Illus. maps.
(*In their* New, royal and authentic system of universal geography. London, C. Cooke, [1798]. pp. 1–106.)
Wanting pp. 1–2. British Museum lists 1st edition, 1790. *See also* nos. 40, 62–3, 84.
Copies: NPL:M(X910/11A).   59

1798 Kearsley's Edition
An Abridgment of Captain Cook's first and second voyages. The first performed in the years 1768, 1769, 1770, 1771; the second in 1772, 1773, 1774 and 1775 for making discoveries in the northern hemisphere, by order of His Majesty. Extracted from the quarto edition, in five volumes; containing a relation of all the interesting transactions, including an abridgement of Captain Furneaux's narrative. [Ed. by G. Kearsley.] 7th. ed. London, printed for G. Kearsley, 1798.

Illus. pp.iii, 328.
See also no. 15.
Copies: ANL.   60

1799 COOK'S VOYAGES ROUND THE WORLD for making discoveries towards the North and South Poles. Manchester, Sowler & Russell, 1799.
Illus. port. pp. viii, 567.
British Museum lists as abridgement by G. W. Anderson, previous edition 1794. *See also* no. 17.
Copies: NPL:M(980:Co1/14A1); ANL:F.   61

1799 Dutch Edition
See back no. 52.

[1800?] BANKES, *Rev.* Thomas, *and others*
New discoveries.

(*In their* Modern, authentic and complete system of universal geography. London, C. Cooke, [1800?]. pp. 1–106.)
Wanting pp.1–2. Running title: A New, royal and authentic system of universal geography. *See also* nos. 40, 59, 63, 84.
Copies: NPL:R(09:F909.9A/2).   62

1800 BANKES, *Rev.* Thomas, *and others*
New discoveries.

Illus.
(*In their* New and authentic system of universal geography. London, C. Cooke, [1800]. pp. 1–106.)
Running title: New, royal and authentic system of universal geography. *See also* nos. 40, 59, 62, 84.
Copies: NPL:M(X910/11).   63

1800 Dutch Edition
See back no. 52.

1801 Dutch Edition
See back no. 52.

1802 Dutch Edition
J. Cook's drie reizen rondöm de waereld, 1768–1780, verkort. Amsterdam, W. Holtrop, 1802.

Port. 3 vols.
Copies: NPL:M(980:Col/15A1–3).   64

1803 Austrian Edition
Jakob Cook's sämmtliche Reisen um die Welt. Wien, in der Camesinaischen Buchhandlung, 1803.

Illus. port. 3 vols.
Volume 2 has on p. [1] . . . beschrieben von Georg Forster.
Copies: NPL:M(980:Col/16A1–3).   65

1803 Dutch Edition
See back no. 52.

1804 Breton's Edition. French
Premier (second [and] troisième) voyage[s] de James Cook autour du monde . . . precédé[s] des relations de MM Byron, Carteret et Wallis. Traduction nouvelle par J. B. J. Breton. [With] (Atlas). Paris, chez la veuve Lepetit, an xii, 1804.

15 vols, in 9.
(*Bibliothèque Portative des Voyages.*)
Text in 12 volumes, bound in 6. Atlas in 3 volumes. For later edition *see* no. 87.
Copies: NPL:M(980:Col/17A1–9).   66

1805 Mavor's Edition
An Historical account of the voyages of Captain James Cook to the southern and northern hemispheres. London, pr. for J. Harris, 1805.

Illus. folded map, 2 vols.
Newspaper cuttings concerning Cook Cottage inserted.
See also nos. 57, 73–4, 78–9.
Copies: ANL.   67

1806 Wilson's Edition
Voyages of discoveries round the world successively undertaken by . . . Commodore Byron in 1764, Captains Wallis and Carteret in 1766, and Captain Cook in the years 1768 to 1789 [*sic*] inclusive. Comprehending authentic and interesting accounts of countries never before explored . . .

The whole carefully selected from the journals of the respective commanders, by R. Wilson. London, J. Cundee, 1806.

Plates, 3 vols.
Volumes 2–3 deal with Cook's voyages. Title-page of volume 2 has date 1780 in place of 1789. British Museum lists as an abridgement of G. W. Anderson's edition. *See* no. 17.
Copies: NPL:M(980/W); QOM; QU(vol.3 only); VSL.   68

[1807] London, A. Lemoine and J. Roe
See no. 72.

1807–9 Glasgow Edition

Captain Cook's voyages round the world . . . including Captain Furneaux's journal of his proceedings during the separation of the ships. Glasgow, W. D. & A. Brownlie, 1807–9.

Illus. maps, port. 3 vols.
Another edition of nos. 39 and 44. This edition lacks the additional matter, except for a short account of animals in New South Wales. Form of printers' and publishers' names varies on each of the title-pages.
Copies: NPL:M(980:Col/6B1–3).   69

1808 LE COOK DE LA JEUNESSE; ou, Extrait des voyages les plus récens dans les régions les plus éloignées. Suivi de l'abrégé de la vie du Capitaine Cook par M. le Capitaine B** [i.e. J. P. Bérenger]. Paris, 1808.

Illus. 2 vols.
Binder's title: Cook de la jeunes. *See also* nos. 54, 80.
Copies: NPL:D(80/88–9).   70

1808 THE HISTORY OF NEW HOLLAND from its first discovery in 1616, to the present time; with a particular account of its produce and inhabitants and a description of Botany Bay . . . by Geo. Barrington. 2nd ed. London, John Stockdale, 1808.

Maps in colour, pp. xxv, 254.
Reprint of 2nd ed. 1787, erroneously attributed to Barrington by the publisher. Compiled from the journals of Cook, Dampier, S. Parkinson. *See also* nos. 27–8, 43.
Copies: NPL:M(991/31C1); NPL:D(80/69); VSL.   71

[1808] Lemoine and Roe Edition

The Voyages of Captain James Cook round the world; with an account of his unfortunate death at Owhyhee, one of the Sandwich Islands. London, Ann Lemoine and J. Roe, [1808].

Illus. pp. 322.
(*The Pocket Navigator*, consisting of a collection of the most select voyages. Vol. 4, containing the three voyages of Captain James Cook.)
Mitchell Library copy lacks series title-page. One plate is dated 1808, the others 1807. Title-page undated. Dixson Library copy lacks title-page to volume 4. *See also* no. 96.
Copies: NPL:M(980:Col/18A1); NPL:D(80/106); ANL.   72

1809 Dutch Edition

See back no. 52.

1809 Phillips Edition

The Voyages of Captain James Cook round the world. Printed verbatim from the original editions, and embellished with a selection of the engravings. London, Richard Phillips, 1809.

Maps, ports. 7 vols.
Separate accounts of the first, second and third voyages, transcribed from the edition authorized by the Admiralty, and now published under a covering title. *See also* nos. 57, 67, 74, 78–9.

Copies: NPL:M(980:Col/19A1–7); NPL:R(S990A/47–53); ANL:F.   73

1809–10 Mavor's Edition

A General collection of voyages and travels, from the discovery of America to the commencement of the nineteenth century. 2nd ed. London, printed for Phillips, 1809–1810.

Illus. maps, 28 vols.
Volumes 1, 13, 15, 21, 22, 23, 28 have date 1810. *See also* nos. 57, 67, 73, 78–9.

Copies: ANL.   74

1811 French Edition

Voyages du Capitaine Cook dans la mer du sud, aux deux poles, et autour du monde, premier, second et troisième, accompagnés des relations de Byron, Carteret et Wallis, et d'une notice, ou nouveaux détails extraits de différens voyages plus récens, sur la Nouvelle-Hollande, la Nouvelle-Zélande, les Iles de la Société, les Iles des Amis, les Iles Sandwich, l'Indien Omaï, et la révolte de l'équipage d'un vaisseau pour se fixer à Taïti. De 1764 à 1804. Traduction nouvelle . . . par M. G . . . . . t [J. B. Gouriet]. Ornée de la carte générale et de 30 figures. Paris, Lerouge, 1811.

6 vols.
Copies: NPL:M(980:Col/20A1–6).   75

1811 Manchester Edition

Captain Cook's voyages round the world, for making discoveries towards the North and South Poles. With an appendix. Manchester, Russell and Allen, pr., 1811.

Illus. port. pp. viii, [567].
Abridgement by G. W. Anderson. Previous edition 1799. *See also* no. 17.

Copies: NPL:M(980:Col/14B1); VSL.   76

1812 PINKERTON, John

Abstract of Captain Cook's first, (second [and] last) voyages.

Illus.
(*In his* A General collection of the best and most interesting voyages and travels in all parts of the world. London, Longman, Hurst, Rees and Orme, 1812. Vol. 11, pp. 498–738.)

Copies: NPL:M(Q910.8/P); NPL:D(Q80/31); NPL:R(DQ909.8A/64); ANL; VSL. 77

1813 London Edition

The Voyages of Captain James Cook round the world; printed verbatim from the original editions, and embellished with a selection of the engravings. London, Sherwood, Neely and Jones, 1813.

Maps, ports. 7 vols.
Separate accounts of the first, second and third voyages, transcribed from the edition authorized by the Admiralty, and now published under a covering title. These seven volumes were also issued as vols. 4–10 of a general collection of voyages by W. F. Mavor (*see* nos. 74, 79) but are here republished as a set of Cook's voyages, vols. 1–7, with title-pages differing from the general collection. The contents list to vol. 1 of the Mitchell Library set is entitled *Contents of the fourth volume,* and bears signature vol. IV, b. Plates bear reference to both numberings of the volumes, e.g. Cook vol.7, Voyages vol.10.
The Mitchell Library holds another copy of vol.3, with authograph of Helenus Scott.
See also nos. 57, 67, 73.
Copies: NPL:M(980:Co1/21A1–7; 980:Co1/21A10).　78

1813 Mavor's Edition

A General collection of voyages. London, 1813.

Volumes 4–10 deal with Cook's voyages. For earlier editions *see* nos. 57, 67, 73–4, 78.
Copies: VSL.　79

1814 LE COOK DE LA JEUNESSE; ou, Extrait des voyages les plus récens dans les régions éloignées. Paris, Giguet et Michaud, 1814.

Illus. 2 vols.
Taken from J. P. Bérenger's account. *See also* nos. 54, 70.
Copies: ANL.　80

1814 KIPPIS, *Rev.* Andrew

A Narrative of the voyage round the world performed by Captain James Cook. With an account of his life during the previous and intervening periods. London, Carpenter and Son, 1814.

Illus. 2 vols.
See also no. 32.
Copies: QU.　81

1814 New York Edition

Captain Cook's three voyages to the Pacific Ocean . . . faithfully abridged from the quarto editions . . . to which is prefixed the Life of Captain Cook. New York, E. Duyckinck, 1814.

Ports. 2 vols.
Previously published 1797, *see* no. 58.
Copies: NPL:M(980:Co1/13B1–2).　82

[1815] CAPTAIN COOK'S ORIGINAL voyages round the world, performed by royal authority, containing the whole of his discoveries in geography, navigation, astronomy, etc., with memoirs of his life and particulars relative to his unfortunate death. Woodbridge, B. Smith & Co., [1815].

Illus. port. pp. [iv], 798.
See no. 17; for reprint *see* no. 97.
Copies: NPL:M(Q980:Col/2A1); ANL; VSL.   83

1815 NEW DISCOVERIES [by Captain Cook and others].

Port.
(*In* New historical and commercial system of geography. Manchester, Russell and Allen, 1815. pp. 565–691.)
Resembles Bankes, *Rev.* Thomas, *and others*—New royal and authentic system of universal geography. *See* nos. 40, 59, 62–3.
Copies: NPL:M(F910/N).   84

1815 A VOYAGE round the world in the years 1768, 1769, 1770, 1771, (Second voyage round the world) [and] (Third voyage round the world).

Illus.
(*In* The World displayed; or, A collection of voyages and travel. Dublin, J. Christie, 1815. Vol. 10, pp. 69–416.)
Copies: NPL:M(910.8/24).   85

1816–17 Italian Edition

Navigazioni di Cook pel grande oceano e intorno al globo per servire d'introduzione alla raccolta de' viaggi più interessanti eseguiti dopo quel celebre navigatore nelle varie parti del mondo. Milano, Sonzogno e Comp., 1816–17.

Illus. map, port. 7 vols.
See also nos. 110–11.
Copies: NPL:M(980:Col/22A1–7); ANL:F.   86

1817 Breton's Edition

Premier (second [and] troisième) voyage[s]. (Trad. de l'anglais par MM Henry et Breton.) [With] (Atlas). Paris, chez Mme Ve Lepetit, 1817.

Illus. maps, port. 15 vols. in 7.
(*Bibliothèque Portative des Voyages.*)
For earlier edition *see* no. 66.
Copies: NPL:M(980:Col/23A1–7).   87

1817 Italian Edition

See no. 86.

1817 La Harpe's Edition

Abrégé des trois voyages du Capitaine Cook. Précédé d'un extrait des voyages de Byron, Wall [i.e. Wallis], Carteret et Bougainville autour du monde. Par J.-F. Laharpe. Nouvelle éd., revue et corrigée. Paris, Ledoux et Tenré, 1817.

Map, 6 vols.
See also nos. 10, 23, 99, 104.
Copies: NPL:M(980:Col/3C1–6).   88

1819 Lisbon Edition

Viagem do Capitão Cook á roda do mundo no navio de sua majestade, a diligencia. Lisboa, Na typografia Rollandiana, 1819.

pp. 203.

(*Nova e completa collecão de viagens, e jornadas às quarto partes do mondo, secunda parte.*)

Copies: ANL.

89

[182—?] KIPPIS, *Rev.* Andrew

A Narrative of the voyages round the world, performed by Captain James Cook, with an account of his life, during the previous and intervening periods, by A. Kippis. London, J. F. Dove, [182–?].

Frontisp. pp. viii, 416.

(*Dove's English classics.*)

With additional engraved title-page with vignette depicting Death of Cook, and entitled *Cook's Voyages and life*. London, engraved for Dove's English Classics. *See also* no. 32.

Copies: NPL:M(980:Col/K2L1); NPL:D(82/27).

90

1820 German Edition

Des Capitäns James Cook Beschreibung seiner Reise um die Welt; ein nützliches Lesebuch für die Jugend. Nach Campe's [i.e. J. H. Campe's] Lehrart bearbeitet von F. W. von Schütz. New ed. Wien, B. Ph. Bauer, 1820.

Frontisp. 3 vols. in 1.

German version of Cook's voyages, translated by J. H. Campe, and re-told in dialogue form by F. W. von Schütz. *See also* no. 1654.

Copies: NPL:M(980:Col/49A1).

91

1820 KIPPIS, *Rev.* Andrew

A Narrative of the voyages round the world, performed by Captain James Cook; with an account of his life during the previous and intervening periods, by A. Kippis. Chiswick, C. Whittingham, pr., 1820.

2 vols.

Each volume has additional engraved title-page, with vignette, with title: Narrative of Captn. Cook's three voyages, by A. Kippis. *See also* no. 32.

Copies: NPL:M(980:Col/K2G1–2); ANL:F.

92

1820 London Edition

Voyages round the world, performed by Captain James Cook, F.R.S., by royal authority. Containing the whole of his discoveries in geography, navigation, astronomy, etc.; with memoirs of his life and particulars relative to his unfortunate death. London, J. Robins, and Sherwood, Neely and Jones, 1820.

Illus. port. pp. [iv], 798.

With four additional engraved title-pages. Abridged from Anderson's edition. *See also* no. 17.

Copies: NPL:D(Q82/7).

93

1821 Longman's Edition

The Three voyages of Captain James Cook round the world. London, Longmans, Hurst, Rees, Orme and Brown, 1821.

Illus. map, 7 vols.
Separate accounts of the first, second and third voyages, transcribed from the edition authorised by the Admiralty, and now published under a covering title.

Copies: NPL:M(980:Col/24A1–7); NPL:R(S990A/54–60); Captain Cook's Landing Place Trust (vols. 5–6 only); SPL; VSL. **94**

1821 Robins' Edition

Voyages round the world; performed by Captain James Cook, F.R.S. London, J. Robins, 1821.

1 vol. in 2.
Taken from Anderson's edition. *See* no. 17.

Copies: VSL. **95**

1822 Hughes' Edition

The Voyages of Captain James Cook round the world; with an account of his unfortunate death at Owhyhee, one of the Sandwich Islands. London, pr. for T. Hughes, 1822–[23].

Illus. pp. 324.
Previously published 1808, London, Lemoine and Roe, *see* no. 72. Dated on title-page 1822. Plates dated 1823.

Copies: NPL:M(980:Col/25A1); ANL. **96**

1822 Robins' Edition

Voyages round the world; performed by Captain James Cook . . . by royal authority. Containing the whole of his discoveries in geography, navigation, astronomy, &c.; with memoirs of his life and particulars relative to his unfortunate death. London, J. Robins and Co., Albion Press, 1822.

Illus. port. pp. [iv], 798, [i].
Taken from Anderson's edition. The text is reprinted from the edition published in 1815 by B. Smith at Woodbridge (*see* no. 83) with extra plates and four engraved title-pages with varying titles. The British Museum Catalogue lists an 1820 abridgement. Mitchell Library copy previously owned by Richard Jones.

Copies: NPL:M(Q980:Col/3A1). **97**

1823 London, T. Hughes

See back no. 96.

1824 Limbird's Edition

The Three voyages of Captain Cook round the world with . . . a memoir of his life. New ed. London, J. Limbird, 1824.

Illus. map, port. pp. ii, 637.
A criticism of this edition by a former owner, Guy Stone, is written on back of plate facing page 1. For later edition *see* no. 105.

Copies: NPL:M(980:Col/26A1). **98**

1825 La Harpe's Edition

Abrégé de l'histoire générale des voyages . . . par J. F. La Harpe; [continued by V. Delpuech de Comeiras] . . . Accompagnée d'un atlas (dressé par A. [F.] Tardieu). Nouvelle éd. Paris, Ledentu, 1825.

Illus. vols. 19–24.

A rearrangement and abridgement of Prévost d'Exiles, A. F., *abbé*—Histoire générale des voyages. Volumes 19–24 contain Cook's voyages. *See also* nos. 10, 23, 88, 104.

Copies: NPL:R(S909.8A/61–66).

99

1825 London Edition

The Voyages of Captain James Cook round the world, comprehending a history of the South Sea islands, &c. &c. London, Jaques and Wright, 1825.

Illus. port. 2 vols.

See also nos. 109, 116, 121, 127, 134–5, 145–6.

Copies: NPL:M(980:Col/27A1–2); QOM; QU.

100

1826 Italian Edition

Navigazioni di Cook pel grande oceano e intorno al globo. Livorno, Tipografia Vignozzi, 1826–7.

Plates, 6 vols.

(*Biblioteca Istruttiva e Piacevole ovvera Raccolta dei più Interessanti Viaggi*. Tomo 3–8.)
Mitchell Library set bound in two volumes. Some plates hand-coloured.

Copies: NPL:M(980:Col/28A1–2); ANL:F; VSL(Wanting vol. 5).

101

1826 KIPPIS, *Rev.* Andrew

A Narrative of the voyages round the world, performed by Captain James Cook; with an account of his life during the previous and intervening periods, by A. Kippis. Chiswick, C. and C. Whittingham, 1826. 2 vols.

Each volume includes additional engraved title-page dated 1820, *see* no. 90. *See also* no. 32.

Copies: NPL:M(980:Col/K2H1–2).

102

1826 KIPPIS, *Rev.* Andrew

Voyages round the world, performed by Capt. James Cook; with an account of his life, during the previous and intervening periods, by A. Kippis. London, Cowie, Low & Co., 1826.

2 vols.

See also no. 32.

Copies: NPL:M(980:Col/K2J1–2).

103

1826 La Harpe's Edition

Choix des traits les plus intéressans des voyages du Capitaine Cook autour du monde.

(*In his* Abrégé de l'histoire générale des voyages, par Laharpe. Reduit . . . par A. Caillot. 3rd ed. Paris, Ledentu, 1826. Vol. 2, pp. 306–[460].)

See also nos. 10, 23, 88, 99. An abridgement of Prévost d'Exiles, A. F., *abbé*—Histoire générale des voyages.

Copies: NPL:M(910.4/183C2).   104

1827 Italian Edition

See 1826 Italian Edition, no. 101.

1827 Limbird's Edition

The Three voyages of Captain Cook round the world with . . . a memoir of his life. New ed. London, J. Limbird, 1827.

2 vols.
Previous edition 1824. *See* no. 98.

Copies: ANL:F.   105

1828 KIPPIS, *Rev.* Andrew

A Narrative of the voyages round the world, performed by Captain James Cook; with an account of his life, during the previous and inter-vening periods, by A. Kippis. Boston. N. H. Whitaker, 1828.

Illus. ports. 2 vols.
Each volume has an additional engraved title-page. Frontispiece to volume 2 is Death of Captain Cook. *See also* no. 32.

Copies: NPL:M(980:Col/K2K1–2).   106

[183–] Allman's Edition

A Narrative of Captain Cook's voyages round the world; with an appendix detailing the progress of the voyage after the death of Captain Cook. London, T. Allman & Son, n.d.

Frontisp. pp. 320.
Mitchell Library copy wanting pp. 295–8. Taken from Kippis' account. *See also* nos. 32, 120, 126, 129, 132, 136, 144, 153, 159, 161, 194.

Copies: NPL:M(980:Col/29A1).   107

[183–?] Smith's Edition

Cook's voyages round the world, containing the whole of his discoveries. London, J. Smith, [183–?].

Frontisp. pp. [i], 478.
Engraved title-page. Caption title: *A Narrative of the voyages round the world performed by Captain James Cook*. Spine title: *Cook's three voyages round the world*. Taken from Kippis' account. *See* no. 32.

Copies: NPL:M(980:Col/30A1); NPL:D(83/226).   108

[183–?] Wright's Edition

Captain Cook's voyages round the world, containing the whole of his discoveries. London, Wright, n.d.

See also nos. 100, 116, 121, 127, 134–5, 145–6.

Copies: VMoU.   109

1830 Italian Edition

Navigazioni di Cook pel grande oceano ed intorno al globo, per servire d'introduzione alla raccolta de' viaggi più interessanti eseguiti dopo quel celebre navigatore nelle varie parti del mondo. Torino, Dalla Stamperia Alliana, 1830.

Port. 15 vols. in 5.
See also nos. 86, 111.

Copies: NPL:M(980:Col/31A1–5); ANL:F.   110

1830 Italian Edition

Navigazioni di Cook pel grande oceano ed intorno al globo, per servire d'introduzione alla raccolta de' viaggi piu interessanti eseguiti dopo quel celebre navigatore nelle varie parti del mondo. Torino, Dalla Stamperia Alliana, 1830.

Port. 15 vols.
In original cloth covers. *See also* nos. 86, 110.

Copies: NPL:M(980:Col/31B1–15).   111

1831 COOLEY, William Desborough

Cook's . . . [three] voyage[s].

Illus.
(*In his* History of maritime and inland discovery. London, Longman, Rees, Orme, Brown & Green, 1831. Vol. 3, pp. 28–92.)
See also no. 115.
With additional title-page, with title *The Cabinet cyclopaedia*, conducted by the Rev. D. Lardner . . . 1831.
The section on Cook's voyages was abridged and published in D. L. Purves, *The English circumnavigators*, 1874, *see* no. 169.

Copies: NPL:M(910.9/C).   112

1832 KIPPIS, *Rev.* Andrew

A Narrative of the voyages round the world, performed by Captain James Cook; with an account of his life, during the previous and intervening periods, by A. Kippis. Philadelphia, L. Johnson, 1832.

2 vols.
Each volume has an additional engraved title-page, with title *Narrative of Captain Cook's three voyages*, and vignette. Both these title-pages have been cut down, that for volume 1 having been cut into the title. *See also* no. 32.

Copies: NPL:M(980:Col/K2M1–2).   113

1833–34 Montemont's Edition

Bibliothèque universelle des voyages. Paris, 1833–34.

Cook, 1769–80, in vols. 5–11.
See also nos. 118, 154.

Copies: VSL.   114

1834 COOLEY, William Desborough
Cook's . . . [three] voyage[s].

Illus.
(*In his* History of maritime and inland discovery. London, Longman, Rees, Orme, Brown & Green, 1831. Vol. 3, pp. 28–92.)
See also no. 112.
With additional title-page, with title *The Cabinet cyclopaedia, conducted by the Rev. D. Lardner* . . . New ed. London, 1834.
Copies: NPL:R(S909A/26).   115

1834 Wright's Edition
Voyages round the world, comprehending a history of the South Sea islands, etc. etc. London, W. Wright, 1834.

2 vols.
See also nos. 100, 109, 121, 127, 134–5, 145–6.
Copies: VSL.   116

[1835] Fairburn's Edition
Voyages of Captain James Cook round the world, with an account of his unfortunate death at Owhyhee, one of the Sandwich Islands. London, pr. by J. Fairburn, [1835].

Illus. map, 28 pts in 1 vol.
Published weekly. No. 6–7 issued as one part. Date from Edwards' catalogue.
Copies: NPL:M(980:Col/32A1).   117

1835–7 Montémont's Edition. Italian
Biblioteca universale dei viaggi.
Venezia, G. Antonelli, 1834–9.

The three voyages of Captain Cook are given in vols. 5–10, 1835–7.
See also nos. 114, 154.
Copies: NPL:M(910.8/M).   118

1836 Edinburgh Edition
An Historical account of the circumnavigation of the globe, and of the progress of discovery in the Pacific Ocean, from the voyage of Magellan to the death of Cook. Illustrated by a portrait of Cook, engraved by Horsburgh after Dance, a facsimile of his Observations on the transit of Venus in 1769, and twenty-one highly-finished engravings by Jackson. Seventh thousand. Edinburgh, Oliver & Boyd, [1836].

pp. 423.
(*Edinburgh Cabinet Library*, new ed.)
With additional engraved title-page, with title *Circumnavigation of the globe*. Date taken from Preface. Section (pp. 241–423) entitled *Cook*, deals with Cook's life and voyages. For later editions *see* nos. 123, 130, 150.
Copies: NPL:M(910.4/H).   119

1836 Tegg's Edition

Narrative of Captain James Cook's voyages round the world; with an account of his life during the previous and intervening periods. London, pr. for Thomas Tegg & Son, 1836.

Illus. pp. 378.

A later edition of no. 107, which *see* for other editions. Taken from Kippis' account, *see* no. 32.

Copies:NPL:M(980:Col/29B1).   120

[1836] Wright's Edition

The Voyages of Captain James Cook round the world, comprehending a history of the South Sea islands, &c. &c. London, W. Wright, [1836?].

Illus. ports. 2 vols.

Volume 1 has engraved title-page. Lacks printed title-page. Date from volume 2. *See also* nos. 100, 109, 116, 127, 134–5, 145–6.

Copies: NPL:M(980:Col/27B1–2).   121

1836 YOUNG, *Rev.* George

The Life and voyages of Captain James Cook; drawn up from his journals and other authentic documents, and comprising much original information. By the Rev. G. Young. London, Whittaker, Treacher, 1836.

Illus. port. pp. xii, 466.

The Mitchell Library has another 1836 edition, with 472 pages, the additional pages being a list of subscribers. *See also* nos. 147, 156.

Copies: NPL:M(980:Col/Y1A1); NPL:D(83/194); ANL; VSL.   122

1837 Edinburgh Edition

An Historical account of the circumnavigation of the globe, and of the progress of discovery in the Pacific Ocean, from the voyage of Magellan to the death of Cook. Illustrated by a portrait of Cook, engraved by Horsburgh after Dance, a facsimile of his Observations on the transit of Venus in 1769, and twenty-one highly-finished engravings by Jackson. 2nd ed. Edinburgh, Oliver & Boyd, 1837.

pp. 496.

With additional engraved title-page, with title *Circumnavigation of the globe*. Section (pp. 281–490) entitled *Cook*, deals with Cook's life and voyages. *See also* nos. 119, 130, 150.

Copies: NPL:M(910.4/H); NPL:R(MD3P13); ANL:F.   123

1837 Lebrun's Edition

Voyages et aventures du Capitaine Cook. Bruxelles, Meline, Cans, 1837.

See also nos. 143, 151, 157, 180.

Copies: VSL.   124

1837 Parker's Edition

The Life, voyages and discoveries of Captain James Cook. London, J. W. Parker, 1837.

Illus. port. pp. 220.
See also nos. 133, 158.

Copies: NPL:M(980:Col/34A1); NPL:D(83/466).   125

1838 Milner's Edition

Narrative of Captain James Cook's voyages round the world; with an account of his life during the previous and intervening periods. Also an appendix detailing the progress of the voyage after the death of Captain Cook. London, William Milner, 1838.

Illus. pp. 384.
Halifax also mentioned in imprint. A later edition of no. 107, which *see* for other editions.
Taken from Kippis' account, no. 32.

Copies: ANL.   126

1838 Wright's Edition

The Voyages of Captain James Cook round the world; comprehending a history of the South Sea islands, etc. etc. London, William Wright, 1838.

Illus. ports. 2 vols. in 1.
See also nos. 100, 109, 116, 121, 134–5, 145–6.

Copies: QOM.   127

1839 KIPPIS, *Rev.* Andrew

A Narrative of the voyages round the world, performed by Captain James Cook; with an account of his life, during the previous and intervening periods, by A. Kippis. London, Scott, Webster and Geary, 1839.

Frontisp. pp. [ii], x, 445.
Additional title-page includes engraving of Cook's death and the title, Cook's voyages and life. *See also* no. 32.

Copies: NPL:R(S990A/66).   128

1839 Milner's Edition

Narrative of Captain James Cook's voyages round the world, with an account of his life during the previous and intervening periods; also an appendix. London, Pub. by the booksellers, William Milner, Halifax, 1839.

pp. xvi, 368.
A later edition of no. 107, which *see* for other editions. Taken from Kippis' account, *see* no. 32. With newscutting dated May 1835, relative to the death of Mrs Cook, and an inscription in the handwriting of Mrs Cook's man-servant, Doswell, to whom the book belonged.

Copies: ANL:F.   129

1839 New York Edition

An Historical account of the circumnavigation of the globe, and of the progress of discovery in the Pacific Ocean, from the voyage of Magellan to the death of Cook. Illustrated by numerous engravings. New York, Harper, 1839.

pp. 366.
(*The School District Library*, no. 31.)
With two additional title-pages entitled *The School district library*, and *Circumnavigation of the globe*. Includes section on Cook's life and voyages. For other editions *see* nos. 119, 123, 150.

Copies: NPL:M(910.4/H).

130

[184—?] KIPPIS, *Rev.* Andrew

A Narrative of the voyages round the world, performed by Captain James Cook; with an account of his life during the previous and intervening periods. Philadelphia, Henry T. Coates, [184–?].

Illus. pp.424.
See also no. 32.

Copies: QOM.

131

1840 Milner's Edition

Narrative of Captain James Cook's voyages round the world; with an account of his life during the previous and intervening periods. Also an appendix detailing the progress of the voyage after the death of Captain Cook. Halifax, William Milner, 1840.

Frontisp. pp. xvi, 368.
Taken from Kippis' account, first published 1788, no. 32. Contains additional engraved title-page, entitled *Cook's Voyages round the world*, London. A later edition of no. 107, which *see* for other editions.

Copies: NPL:M(980:Co1/29G1).

132

1840 Parker's Edition

Life, voyages and discoveries of Captain James Cook. 2nd ed. London, J. W. Parker, 1840.

See also nos. 125, 158.

Copies: VSL.

133

1840 Smith's Edition

The Voyages of Captain James Cook round the world, comprehending a history of the South Sea islands. London, Joseph Smith, 1840.

2 vols. in 1.
Volume 1 has additional engraved title-page, with vignette and title *Captain Cook's voyages round the world, containing the whole of his discoveries. See also* nos. 100, 109, 116, 121, 127, 135, 145–6.

Copies: NPL:M(980:Co1/33A1).

134

1840 Wright's Edition

The Voyages of Captain James Cook round the world; comprehending a history of the South Sea islands. Peoples ed. London, W. Wright, 1840.

Illus. ports. 2 vols. in 32 pts.
The 32 parts have cloth wrapper and slip case. *See also* nos. 100, 109, 116, 121, 127, 134, 145–6.

Copies: NPL:D(84/232). 135

1841 Barr's Edition

Narrative of Captain James Cook's voyages round the world; with an account of his life during the previous and intervening periods; also an appendix. London, J. Barr, 1841.

pp. viii, 352.
With an additional title-page, with imprint, London, I. S. Pratt. Taken from Kippis' account, *see* no. 32. A later edition of no. 107, which *see* for other editions.

Copies: NPL:M(980:Co1/29C1). 136

1841 KIPPIS, *Rev.* Andrew

A Narrative of the voyages round the world, performed by Captain James Cook; with an account of his life, during the previous and intervening periods, by A. Kippis. Philadelphia, Haswell, Barrington & Haswell, 1841.

2 vols. in 1.
A reprint of 1832 edition (no. 113). Engraved title-pages with vignettes as in 1832 edition "Philadelphia, published by L. Johnson" bound in front of volume 1. *See also* no. 32.

Copies: NPL:M(980:Co1/K2N1). 137

1841 Pratt's Edition

See 1841 Barr's Edition, no. 136.

[1841?] Smith's Edition

Voyage autour du monde [1768–1771]; (Voyage au Pôle austral et autour du monde) [1772–1775; and] (Troisième voyage) [1776–1780]. Paris, Société Bibliophile, [1841?].

Maps, plates, 4 vols.
(Smith, William—Voyages autour de monde . . . mis en ordre par W. Smith. Vols. 2–5.)
With biographical note on Cook. Translated from the edition authorised by the Admiralty. *See also* nos. 139–40, 142, 149, 152, 1240.

Copies: NPL:M(910.4/253A2–5). 138

[1841] Smith's Edition

Voyage autour du monde en 1768, 1769, 1770 et 1771; (Voyage au Pole austral et autour du monde . . . en 1772, 1773, 1774 et 1775; [and] Troisième voyage du Capitaine Cook). Paris, P. Duménil, [1841].

Illus. 4 vols.
(Smith, William—Nouvelle bibliothèque des voyages; [with intro. by A. Duponchel]. Tome 2–5.)
Dixson Library copy wanting pp. 3–6 and plate 3 of Tome 5. Translated from the edition authorised by the Admiralty. *See also* nos. 138, 140, 142, 149, 152, 1240.

Copies: NPL:D(84/531–4); VSL. 139

[1841 ?] Smith's Edition

Voyage autour du monde [1768–1771]; (Voyage au Pôle austral et autour du monde) [1772–1775; and] (Troisième voyage) [1776–1780]. Paris, Bureau de la Publication, [1841 ?].

Maps, plates, 4 vols.
(Smith, William—Collection choisie des voyages autour de monde . . . Mis en ordre par W. Smith. Vols. 2–5.)
With biographical note on Cook. Translated from the edition authorised by the Admiralty. *See also* nos. 138-9, 142, 149, 152, 1240.

Copies: NPL:M(910.4/253B2–5). 140

1842 KIPPIS, *Rev.* Andrew

A Narrative of the voyages round the world, performed by Captain James Cook; with an account of his life during the previous and intervening periods, by A. Kippis. London, Scott, Webster and Geary, 1842.

Frontisp. pp. [ii], x, 445.
Additional title-page includes engraving of Cook's death and the title, Cook's voyages and life. *See also* no. 32. SPL copy is undated.

Copies: ANL:F; SPL. 141

1842 Smith's Edition. English

Voyages of Captain James Cook; illustrated with maps and numerous engravings on wood. With an appendix giving an account of the present condition of the South Sea islands. London, W. Smith, 1842.

Illus. maps, port. 2 vols.
Consists of separate accounts of the first, second and third voyages, transcribed from the edition authorised by the Admiralty, and now published under a covering title. Volume 1 has an additional engraved title-page, with title, *Three voyages of Captain Cook round the world*. Mitchell Library copy with bookplate of F. R. Hagner. For other editions *see* nos. 138, 139, 140, 149, 152, 1240.

Copies: NPL:M(Q980:Col/4A1–2); NPL:R(S990A/61–2); VSL. 142

1843 Lebrun's Edition

Voyages et aventures du Capitaine Cook. New ed. Tours, Mame, 1843.

Frontisp. pp. 288.
(*Bibl. des Écoles Chrétiennes.*)
See also nos. 124, 151, 157, 180.

Copies: NPL:D(84/231). 143

1843 Pratt's Edition

Narrative of Captain James Cook's voyages round the world; with an account of his life during the previous and intervening periods. Also an appendix detailing the progress of the voyage after the death of Captain Cook. London, J. S. Pratt, 1843.

pp. viii, 319.
A later edition of no. 107, which *see* for other editions. Taken from Kippis' account, *see* no. 32.

Copies: NPL:M(980:Col/29D1). 144

1843 Wright's Edition

The Voyages of Captain James Cook round the world, comprehending a history of the South Sea islands. London, W. Wright, 1843.

Plates, 2 vols.
Volume 1 contains additional engraved title-page, with vignette. *See also* nos. 100, 109, 116, 121, 127, 134–5, 146.

Copies: ANL.

145

1843 Wright's Edition

The Voyages of Captain James Cook round the world, comprehending a history of South Sea islands. London, W. Wright, 1843.

Plates, 2 vols. in 1.
A re-issue of no. 145. Wanting title-pages and seventeen plates.

Copies: ANL.

146

1843 Young. Dutch Edition

Het Leven en de reizen van Kapitein J. Cook; beschreven naar naauwkeurige berigten, in zijne dagboeken en andere bescheiden voorhanden door G. Young. Uit het engelsch; [trans. by C.]. Amsterdam, M. H. Binger, 1843.

Illus. map, 2 vols.
The Mitchell Library copy has holograph notes by the publisher and the engravers. *See also* nos. 122, 156.

Copies: NPL:M(980:Col/Y1C1–2).

147

1844 KIPPIS, *Rev.* Andrew

A Narrative of the voyages round the world, performed by Captain James Cook; with an account of his life during the previous and intervening periods, by A. Kippis. Philadelphia, Henry F. Anners, 1844.

Port. 2 vols. in 1.
Similar to 1832 Philadelphia edition (no. 113) but does not have additional title-pages. *See also* no. 32.

Copies: NPL:M(980:Col/K2P1).

148

1846 Smith's Edition

Voyages of Captain James Cook; illustrated with maps and numerous engravings on wood. With an appendix giving an account of the present condition of the South Sea islands, etc. London, W. Smith, 1846.

Port. 2 vols.
A reprint of no. 142, which *see* for other editions. Volume 1 with additional engraved title-page, with title *The Three voyages of Captain James Cook*.

Copies: NPL:M(Q980:Col/4B1–2); ANL:F; VMoU(vol. 2 only).

149

1852 CIRCUMNAVIGATION OF THE GLOBE, and progress of discovery in the Pacific Ocean, from the voyage of Magellan to the death of Captain Cook. London, Nelson, 1852.

Facs. illus. port. pp. 423.
(*Edinburgh Cabinet Library*, new ed.)
With additional engraved title-page, 1837 edition, entitled *An Historical account of the circumnavigation etc. See also* nos. 119, 123, 130.
Copies: ANL.

150

1852 Lebrun's Edition

Voyages et aventures du Capitaine Cook, par H. Lebrun, [pseud.] Nouvelle éd., revue et approuvée par une société d'ecclésiastiques. Tours, Mame, 1852.

Illus. pp. [ii], 236.
See also nos. 124, 143, 157, 180.
Copies: NPL:M(980:Col/35A3).

151

[1852] Tallis Edition

The Voyages of Captain James Cook round the world; illustrated with maps and numerous engravings on wood and steel. London, John Tallis, [1852].

Illus. maps, port. 2 vols.
Separate accounts of the first, second and third voyages, transcribed from the edition authorised by the Admiralty, and now published under a covering title. Both volumes have additional illustrated title-page, engraved, with title *The Three voyages of Captain Cook round the world* surrounded by vignettes. For other editions *see* nos. 138–40, 142, 149.
Copies: NPL:M(Q980:Col/4C1–2);NPL:R(Q990A/10–11); QU;VSL.

152

1853 Milner and Sowerby's Edition

Narrative of Captain James Cook's voyages round the world; with an account of his life during the previous and intervening periods. Also an appendix. Halifax, Milner and Sowerby, 1853.

pp. xvi, 368.
(*Cottage Library.*)
A later edition of no. 107, which *see* for other editions. Taken from Kippis' account, *see* no. 32.
Copies: NPL:M(980:Col/29E1).

153

1853 Montémont's Edition

Voyages autour du monde et en Océanie par Bougainville, Cook, etc. . . . Illus. par Ch. Mettais et Bocourt. Revus et traduits par M. Albert-Montémont. Paris, J. Bry, Ainé, 1853.

Illus., some hand-coloured, map, ports. pp. [ii], 160.
Forms vol.2 of the author's Histoire des voyages. *See also* nos. 114, 118.
Copies: NPL:M(Q910.8/M); ANL.

154

1853 Spanish Edition

Historia de los viajes del Capitan Cook por mar y tierra; trad. al Castellano por Don J.M.Y.P.Y. Dons C. Madrid, Imprenta de Dona Teresa Martinez é Hijo, 1853.

pp. 232.
Wrapper has title as *Viajes del Capitan Cook alrededor del mundo*, and date as 1855, and publisher as *Imprenta de M. Gonzalez.*
Copies: ANL:F.

155

1854 YOUNG, *Rev.* George

Het Leven en de reizen van Kapitein J. Cook. Utrecht, Van der Post, 1854.

See also nos. 122, 147.
Copies: VSL.

156

1855 Lebrun's Edition

Voyages et aventures du Capitaine Cook, par Henri Lebrun. Nouvelle édition, revue et approuvée par une société d'ecclésiastiques. Tours, Mame, 1855.

Illus. pp. 236.
(Bibliothèque des Écoles Chrétiennes.)
In original board covers. Copy awarded to Francis Burgess, 1856. *See also* nos. 124, 143, 151, 180.
Copies: NPL:M(980:Co1/35A1); ANL.

157

1855 Parker's Edition

The Life, voyages and discoveries of Captain James Cook. 5th ed. London, J. W. Parker, 1855.

Illus. pp. 220.
See also nos. 125, 133.
Copies: NPL:R(S990A/78).

158

1855 Spanish Edition

See no. 155.

1856 Allman's Edition

A Narrative of Captain Cook's voyages round the world, with an appendix dealing with the progress of the voyage after the death of Captain Cook. London, Allman, 1856.

Ports. pp. 320.
Taken from Kippis' account, *see* no. 32. *See also* no. 107.
Copies: QOM.

159

1857 Charton's Edition. French

James Cook, navigateur anglais: [the voyages, with introductory notes and bibl. by E. Charton].

Illus.
(Charton, Edouard—Voyageurs anciens et modernes. Paris, Bureau du *Magazin Pittoresque*, 1857. Tome 4, pp. 351–438.)
Abridged edition. *See also* no. 163.
Copies: NPL:M(Q910.8/C).

160

1857 Milner and Sowerby's Edition

Narrative of Captain James Cook's voyages round the world, with an account of his life during the previous and intervening periods; also an appendix. Halifax, Milner and Sowerby, 1857.

pp. xvi, 368.

A later edition of no. 107, which *see* for other editions. Taken from Kippis' account, *see* no. 32.

Copies: ANL:F.

161

1858 KIPPIS, *Rev.* Andrew

Narrative of the voyages around the world; with an account of his life, by A. Kippis. New York, 1858.

See also no. 32.

Copies: ANL.

162

1861 CHARTON, Edouard

James Cook, navegante inglès, 1769–78.

Illus.

(*In his* Viajeros antiguos y modernos. Madrid, J. T. Ponzano, 1861. Vol. 2, pp. 173–95.)
See also no. 160.

Copies: NPL:M(910.8/C).

163

1864 Mueller's Edition

Cook der Weltumsegler: Leben, Reisen und Ende des Kapitän James Cook, insbesondere Schilderung seiner drei grossen Entdeckungsfahrten nebst einem Blick auf die heutigen Zustände der Südsee-Inselwelt. Herausgegeben von . . . K. Müller. Leipzig, Otto Spamer, 1864.

Illus. pp. xxiv, 288.

(*Das Buch der Reisen und Entdeckungen*, Aeltere Reisen [no.] 1).
See also no. 181.

Copies: NPL:M(980:Col/M5A1).

164

1865 Barrow's Edition

Cook's voyages of discovery; ed. by J. Barrow. Edinburgh, Black, 1865.

First published in 1860. *See also* nos. 166, 168, 174, 195, 200, 205, 208–9, 211, 215, 217, 219–20, 226, 230, 234.

Copies: VSL.

165

[1869] Barrow's Edition

Voyages of Captain Cook. Edinburgh, [1869].

See no. 165 for other editions.

Copies: ANL.

166

1870 Chapman's Edition

Chapman's Centenary memorial of Captain Cook's description of New Zealand one hundred years ago. Auckland, Geo. T. Chapman, 1870.

Facs. illus. charts, pp. 160, [iv].
A condensed account of Cook's three voyages, with a short biography and reprints of Cook's charts of New Zealand.

Copies: NPL:M(987/84A1); NPL:D(87/138); NPL:R(S997A/73); ANL; QOM; QU; VSL.

167

1874 Barrow's Edition

Cook's voyages of discovery. Ed. by J. Barrow. Edinburgh, A. and C. Black, 1874.

Facs. illus. map, port. pp. viii, 417.
First published 1860. *See* no. 165 for other editions.

Copies: NPL:R(S990A/63); ANL.

168

1874 Purves' Edition

The English circumnavigators: the most remarkable voyages round the world by English sailors. With a preliminary sketch of their lives and discoveries. Edited with notes, etc., by David Laing Purves. London, William P. Nimmo, 1874.

Illus. maps, ports. pp.831.
With additional engraved title-page. Includes a section, pp.475–823, entitled *Cook's voyages round the world*, 1768–1780, abridged from W. D. Cooley's *History of maritime and inland discovery* (*see* nos. 112, 115). *See also* nos. 173, 175–6, 183–4.

Copies: NPL:M(910.4/P); ANL:F.

169

1874 Steger's Edition

James Cook; drei Reisen um die Welt; neu herausgegeben von F. Steger. Dritte Ausgabe. Leipzig, Verlag von G. Senf's Buchhandlung, 1874.

2 vols.
Copies: NPL:M(980:Co1/48C1–2).

170

1876 Low's Edition

Captain Cook's three voyages round the world; with a sketch of his life. Ed. by C. R. Low. London, Routledge, 1876.

2 plates in colour, pp. 512.
Plates in Mitchell Library second copy differ from those in the first. First published 1875. *See also* nos. 179, 182, 186, 192–3, 198, 201–3.

Copies: NPL:M(980:Co1/37A1; 37A2); ANL:F.

171

1878 KIPPIS, *Rev.* Andrew

A Narrative of the voyages round the world, performed by Captain James Cook; with an account of his life during the previous and intervening periods, by A. Kippis. London, Bickers and Son, 1878.

Illus. pp. x, [ii], 404.
With twelve illustrations reproduced in exact facsimile from drawings made during the voyages. Fly leaf and half-title are missing from Mitchell Library copy. Cover title, Cook's Voyages and life. *See also* no. 32.
Copies: NPL:M(980:Co1/K2Q1); Captain Cook's Landing Place Trust; QOM. 172

1878 Purves' Edition
The English circumnavigators; [ed. by D. L. Purves and R. Cochrane]. Edinburgh, W. P. Nimmo, 1878.
Includes a section, pp. 475–823 on Cook's voyages. *See also* nos. 169, 175–6, 183–4.
Copies: VSL. 173

1879 Barrow's Edition
Cook's voyages of discovery; ed. by J. Barrow. Edinburgh, A. and C. Black, 1879.
Facs. illus. map, port. pp. viii, 417.
Facsimile damaged. The Mitchell Library also holds a reprint, wanting title-page and preliminary pages. First published 1860. *See* no. 165 for other editions.
Copies: NPL:M(980:Co1/36D1,D2); ANL; QOM. 174

[188–] Purves' Edition
Captain Cook's voyages round the world. Edinburgh, W. P. Nimmo, Hay and Mitchell, [n.d.].
Frontisp. pp. 351.
See also nos. 169, 173, 176, 183–4.
Copies: ANL:F. 175

[188–?] Purves' Edition
Voyages round the world [1768–1780] by Captain James Cook. Ed. with notes by D. Laing Purves. Edinburgh, W. P. Nimmo, Hay & Mitchell, [n.d. 188–?].
Frontisp. pp. 351.
Mainly from account in *Lardner's Cabinet Cyclopaedia* Book 5, Chapters 3 & 4. *See also* nos. 169, 173, 175, 183–4.
Copies: NPL:M(980:Co1/38A1). 176

[188–?] THE VOYAGES of Captain James Cook round the world, illustrated with maps and numerous engravings on wood and steel. London, London Printing and Publishing Co. [188–?].
Illus. maps, ports. 2 vols.
Copies: QOM. 177

1880 KIPPIS, *Rev.* Andrew
A Narrative of the voyages round the world, performed by Captain James Cook; with an account of his life during the previous and intervening periods, by A. Kippis. London, Bickers and Son, 1880.

Illus. pp. x, [ii], 404.
A reprint of the 1878 edition. *See also* no. 32.
Copies: NPL:M(980:Col/K2R1); QOM.   178

[1880?] Low's Edition
Captain Cook's three voyages round the world; with a sketch of his life.
Ed. by C. R. Low. London, Routledge, [1880?].

pp. 512.
Wanting illustrations. First published 1875. *See also* nos. 171, 182, 186, 192-3, 198, 201–3.
Copies: NPL:R(DS990A/77).   179

1882 Lebrun's Edition
Voyages et aventures du Capitaine Cook, par H. Lebrun. Nouvelle éd., revue. Tours, Mame, 1882.

Frontisp. pp. [191].
(*Bibliothèque de la jeunesse.*)
See also nos. 124, 143, 151, 157.
Copies: NPL:M(980:Col/35B1).   180

1882 Leipzig Edition
Cook, der Weltumsegler: Leben, Reisen und Ende des Kapitän James Cook. Nebst einem Blick auf die heutigen Zustände der Südsee-Inselwelt. Ursprunglich herausgegeben von K. Müller, in den späteren Auflagen bearbeitet von der Redaktion des Buchs der Reisen. Dritte verbesserte Auflage. Leipzig, Otto Spamer, 1882.

Illus. pp.xxiv, 276.
(*Das Buch der Reisen und Entdeckungen.*)
See also no. 164.
Copies: NPL:M(980:Col/M5C1).   181

1882 Low's Edition
Captain Cook's three voyages round the world; with a sketch of his life.
Ed. by C. R. Low. London, Routledge, 1882.

Frontisp. in colour, pp. 512.
First published 1875. *See also* nos. 171, 179, 186, 192–3, 198, 201–3.
Copies: NPL:M(980:Col/37F1).   182

1882 Purves' Edition
The English circumnavigators: the most remarkable voyages round the world by English sailors, with a preliminary sketch of their lives and discoveries. Edited . . . by David Laing Purves and R. Cochrane. Edinburgh, William P. Nimmo, 1882.

Illus. maps, pp. 831.
See also nos. 169, 173, 175–6, 184.
Copies: ANL; VSL.   183

1882 Purves' Edition

Voyages round the world by Captain James Cook; ed. with notes by
D. Laing Purves. Edinburgh, W. P. Nimmo, 1882.

See also nos. 169, 173, 175–6, 183.

Copies: VSL.

184

1883 KIPPIS, *Rev.* Andrew

A Narrative of the voyages round the world, performed by Captain
James Cook; with an account of his life during the previous and intervening periods, by A. Kippis. London, Bickers and Son, 1883.

Illus. pp. x, [ii], 404.
A reprint of the 1878 edition. *See also* no. 32.

Copies: NPL:M(980:Col/K2S1).

185

[1883] Low's Edition

Three voyages round the world . . . With a sketch of his life. Ed. by Lieut.
Charles R. Low. London, [1883].

Illus.
First published 1875. *See also* nos. 171, 179, 182, 192–3, 198, 201–3.

Copies: ANL.

186

1887 French Edition

Voyages du Capitaine Cook; extraits publiés avec une introduction,
des notes et un glossaire des termes nautiques, par A. Angelier. Paris,
Hachette, 1887.

First published 1880, held by WU.

Copies: VSL.

187

1889 KIPPIS, *Rev.* Andrew

A Narrative of the voyages round the world, performed by Captain
James Cook; with an account of his life during the previous and intervening periods, by A. Kippis. London, Bickers and Son, 1889.

Illus. pp. x, [ii], 404.
See also no. 32. Apparently a reprint of the 1878 and 1883 editions, with different title-leaf
and different imprint at foot of p. 404; also with one less preliminary page, the list of
plates being printed on the verso of the Contents list. For later reprint, *see* no. 196.

Copies: NPL:M(980:Col/K2T1); ANL:F.

188

[189–?] Hawkesworth's Edition

The Three famous voyages of Captain James Cook round the world,
narrating his discoveries and adventures in Tierra del Fuego . . . *etc.*,
together with the account of his murder at Hawaii and the subsequent
voyage of Captain King to Kamtschatka, Japan and China. London,
Ward, Lock, Bowden and Co., [189–?].

Illus. maps, ports, pp. xx, 1176.
With MS inscription, dated Dec. 1894. *See also* nos. 190–1.

Copies: NPL:M(Q980:Col/5B1); QU.

189

[189–?] Hawkesworth's Edition

The Three famous voyages of Captain James Cook, *etc.* London, Ward, Lock and Co., [189–?].

Illus. maps, ports. pp. xx, 1152.
With appendix further abridged.
Presentation label dated 1891. *See also* nos. 189, 191.

Copies: NPL:M(Q980:Co1/5C1).   190

[189–?] Hawkesworth's Edition

The Voyages of discovery of Captain James Cook, describing his discoveries and adventures in Tierra del Fuego, Tahiti, New Zealand, Van Diemen's Land, Australia, the Friendly Islands, New Hebrides, New Caledonia, the Sandwich Islands, Western North America, etc., partly narrated by the great navigator himself, and partly compiled from his notes and journals by Dr. Hawkesley. London, Ward Lock, Bowden & Co., [189–?].

Illus. maps, port. 2 vols.
The Dr. Hawkesley referred to here is evidently intended for Dr. Hawkesworth, this edition being a reprint of Hawkesworth's edition of Cook's Voyages. *See also* nos. 189–90.

Copies: NPL:M(Q980:Co1/5A1–2); QU;VSL.   191

[189–?] Low's Edition

Captain Cook's three voyages round the world; with a sketch of his life. Ed. by C. R. Low. London, Routledge, [189–?].

Illus. pp. 512.
First published 1875. *See also* nos. 171, 179, 182, 186, 193, 198, 201–3.

Copies: ANL:F.   192

[189–?] Low's Edition

Captain Cook's three voyages round the world; with a sketch of his life. Ed. by C. R. Low. London, Routledge, [189–?].

Illus. in colour, pp. 512.
First published 1875. *See also* nos. 171, 179, 182, 186, 192, 198, 201–3.

Copies: NPL:M(980:Co1/37E1).   193

[189–] Milner's Edition

Narrative of Captain James Cook's voyages round the world; with an account of his life during the previous and intervening periods. Also an appendix. London, Milner, [n.d.].

Frontisp. in colour, pp. xvi, 368.
A later edition of no. 107. Inscription on fly leaf dated 1893.

Copies: NPL:M(980:Co1/29F1).   194

1893 Barrow's Edition

Voyages of discovery. Ed. by John Barrow. London, A. C. Black, 1893.

Illus. pp. 417.
See no. 165 for other editions.

Copies: QU.   195

1893 KIPPIS, *Rev.* Andrew

A Narrative of the voyages round the world, performed by Captain James Cook; with an account of his life during the previous and intervening periods, by A. Kippis. London, Bickers & Son, 1893.

Illus. pp. x, [ii], 404.
Apparently a reprint of the 1889 edition. *See also* no. 32.
Copies: NPL:M(980:Col/K2U1). 196

1894 Synge's Edition

Cook's voyages; the text reduced, with introduction and notes, by M. B. Synge. London, Rivington, Percival, 1894.

First published 1892. For a different abridgement by Synge *see* nos. 199, 204.
Copies: VSL. 197

1895 Low's Edition

Captain Cook's three voyages round the world; with a sketch of his life. Ed. by . . . C. R. Low. With plates in colours from designs by G. Browne and twenty-eight illustrations. New ed. London, Routledge, 1895.

pp. 512.
With Alfred Lee's book-plate. First published 1875. *See also* nos. 171, 179, 182, 186, 192–3, 201–3.
Copies: NPL:M(980:Col/37B1). 198

1897 Synge's Edition

Captain Cook's voyages round the world; with an intro. life by M. B. Synge. London, T. Nelson and Sons, 1897.

Illus. maps, ports. pp. xiv, ix, 11–512.
See also nos. 197, 204. This is a different abridgement from no. 197.
Copies: QOM. 199

1899 Barrow's Edition

Cook's voyages of discovery; ed. by J. Barrow. London, A. and C. Black, 1899.

Facs. illus. map, port. pp. viii, 417.
A re-issue of 1879 Edinburgh edition. *See* no. 165 for other editions.
Copies: ANL. 200

[190–?] Low's Edition

Captain Cook's three voyages round the world; with a sketch of his life. Ed. by C. R. Low. London, Routledge, and New York, E. P. Dutton, [190–?]

Illus. some in colour, pp. 512.
From the Knox Collection. First published 1875. *See also* nos. 171, 179, 182, 186, 192–3, 198, 202–3.
Copies: NPL:M(980:Col/37C1); VMoU. 201

[190–?] Low's Edition

Three voyages round the world, by Captain Cook. Ed. with a sketch of his life, by C. R. Low. Melbourne, E. W. Cole, [190–?].

Frontisp. in colour, pp. 512.
(*Cole's Popular Library.*)
First published 1875. *See also* nos. 171, 179, 182, 186, 192–3, 198, 201, 203.
Copies: NPL:M(980:Col/37D1).   202

[190–?] Low's Edition

Three voyages round the world, made by Captain James Cook, R.N. With a sketch of life. Ed. by C. R. Low. New York, A. L. Burt, [190?].

Port. as frontisp. pp. 472.
(*Burt's Home Library.*)
First published 1875. *See also* nos. 171, 179, 182, 186, 192–3, 198, 201–2.
Copies: NPL:M(980:Col/37G1).   203

1903 Synge's Edition

Captain Cook's voyages round the world; with an intro. life by M. B. Synge. London, T. Nelson and Sons, 1903.

Illus. maps, port. pp. xv, ix, 11–512.
See also nos. 197, 199. This abridgement differs from no. 197.
Copies: NPL:M(980:Col/40A1).   204

1904 Barrow's Edition

Cook's voyages of discovery; ed. by J. Barrow. With eight illustrations in colour by J. Williamson. London, A. and C. Black, 1904.

Facs. illus. map, pp. viii, 417.
See no. 165 for other editions.
Copies: NPL:M(980:Col/36G1); VSL.   205

[1905] Cash's Edition

The Life and voyages of Captain James Cook; selections, with intro. and notes by C. G. Cash. London, Blackie & Son, [1905].

Frontisp. pp. vi, 7–192.
Date from British Museum General catalogue.
Copies: NPL:M(980:Col/39A1); ANL; QOM; VSL.   206

[1905?] Leipzig Edition

Cook der Weltumsegler. Leben, Reisen und Ende des Kapitäns James Cook, für Jugend und Volk erzählt, von J. März. Zweite Aufl. Leipzig, Otto Spamer, [1905?].

Illus. ports. pp.261, [xi.].
Copies: NPL:M(980:Col/50B1).   207

1906 Barrow's Edition

Captain Cook's voyages of discovery. [Ed. by J. Barrow.] 2nd ed. London, J. M. Dent, 1906.

pp. ix, 479.
(*Everyman's Library.*)
First issued February, 1906. *See* no. 165 for other editions.
Copies: NPL:M(980:Col/36K1). 208

1906 Everyman's Library
See no. 208.

1908 Barrow's Edition

Captain Cook's voyages; [ed. by J. Barrow]. London, Cassell, 1908.

pp. 446.
(*The People's Library.*)
See no. 165 for other editions.
Copies: NPL:M(980:Col/36H1). 209

1908 Cassell's Edition
See no. 209.

1908 German Edition

Die Weltumsegelungsfahrten des Kapitäns James Cook: ein Auszug aus seinen Tagebüchern: bearbeitet und übersetzt von Dr. Edwin Hennig. [With bibl.] Hamburg, Gutenberg, 1908.

Illus. fold. map, pp. 554.
(*Bibliothek denkwürdiger Reisen:* Bd. 1.)
Mitchell Library copy wanting map.
Copies: NPL:M(980:Col/41A1); ANL. 210

1910 Barrow's Edition

Cook's voyages of discovery; ed. by J. Barrow . . . illus. by J. Williamson. London, A. & C. Black, 1910.

Facs. illus. some in colour, pp. viii, 418.
Reprint of 1904 edition. *See* no. 165 for other editions.
Copies: NPL:M(980:Col/36J1). 211

[1911?] Dent's Edition

Captain Cook's voyages of discovery; [ed. by G. C. Dent]. London, J. M. Dent & Sons, [1911?].

pp. 128.
(*Temple Continuous Readers.*)
See also no. 215.
Copies: NPL:M(980:Col/42A1). 212

[1913?] Strang's Edition

Captain Cook's voyages; [ed. by H. Strang]. London, Henry Frowde, [1913?].

Illus. pp. 255.
(*Herbert Strang's Library.*)
Copies: NPL:M(980:Col/43A1).   213

1914 [RECORDS RELATING TO COOK'S VOYAGES.]

(McNab, Robert—Historical records of New Zealand. Wellington, Govt. Pr., 1914.
Vols 1–2, various pp.)
Copies: NPL:M(997/M); NPL:D(90/387–8).   214

1915 CAPTAIN COOK'S voyages of discovery. London, J. M. Dent and Sons, Ltd., 1915.

pp. x, 480.
(*Everyman's Library.*)
First published 1906. *See also* nos. 165, 212.
Copies: ANL:F.   215

1924 KIPPIS, *Rev.* Andrew

Captain Cook's voyages; with an account of his life, during the previous and intervening periods. By A. Kippis. New York, Alfred Knopf, 1924.

Illus. pp. x, [ii], 404.
Apparently an American reprint of the 1889 edition, with differing title-page. *See also* no. 32.
Copies: NPL:M(980:Col/K2V1); NPL:D(92/173).   216

[1925] Barrow's Edition

Captain Cook's voyages of discovery. London, J. M. Dent, [1925].

pp. ix, 479.
(*Everyman's Library.*)
Taken from Barrow's edition. Reprint of 1906 edition. *See* no. 165 for other editions.
Copies: NPL:M(980:Col/36N1); ANL; WU.   217

1925 Everyman's Edition

See no. 217.

[1925?] French Edition

Les Trois voyages du Capitaine Cook autour du monde; racontés par lui-même. Paris, Albin Michel, [1925?].

Illus. port. pp. 448.
Illustrations are by C.M. Date supplied by Edwards.
Copies: NPL:M(Q980:Col/6A1).   218

1929 Everyman's Edition

Captain Cook's voyages of discovery; (ed. by E. Rhys). London, J. M. Dent & Sons, 1929.

pp. ix, 479.
(*Everyman's Library.*)
First published 1906. *See also* no. 165.

Copies: NPL:D(92/238). 219

1930 Barrow's Edition

Cook's voyages of discovery; ed. by J. Barrow. London, A. & C. Black, 1930.

Illus. some in colour, pp. viii, 418.
Reprinted. *See* no. 165 for other editions.

Copies: NPL:M(980:Col/36Q1). 220

1949 Lloyd's Edition

Voyages of Captain James Cook round the world. Selected from his journals and ed. by C. Lloyd. London, Cresset Press, 1949.

Maps, pp. [xxiv], 384.
(*The Cresset Library.*)
Endpapers are reproductions of Cook's sketch of track of the *Endeavour*, and coasts discovered on first voyage, reproduced for the first time from Bougainville's Voyage autour du monde, belonging to Dr Burney, in which Cook sketched it. The volume is now in the British Museum. *See also* nos. 222, 224.

Copies: NPL:M(980:Col/44A1); NPL:R(E910.4); ANL; Captain Cook's Landing Place Trust; QU; VMoU; VSL; WU. 221

1949 Lloyd's Edition

The Voyages of Captain James Cook round the world. Selected from his journals, and ed. by C. Lloyd. Paris, Chanticleer Press, 1949.

pp. xxiii, 384.
Maps as endpapers.
See also nos. 221, 224.

Copies: ANL. 222

1950 Zagreb Edition

[The Voyages of Captain James Cook round the world]: Putovanja oko svijets: 12 bor. Zagreb, Novo Pokoljenje, 1950.

Diags. illus. map as endpapers, ports. pp. 413.

Copies: ANL. 223

1951 Lloyd's Edition

Voyages autour du monde; choix [from his journals, ed. with] introduction, notes par C. Lloyd. Traduction de l'anglais par G. Rives. Paris, R. Julliard, [1951].

Map, pp. 403, [2].
See also nos. 221-2.

Copies: NPL:D(95/13); ANL. 224

1951 Reed's Edition

Captain Cook in New Zealand: extracts from the journals of Captain Cook giving a full account . . . of his adventures and discoveries in New Zealand. Ed. [with intro., biog. and notes] by A. H. Reed and A. W. Reed. [With] (Note on the literature, by C. R. H. Taylor). Wellington, A. H. & A. W. Reed, 1951.

Illus. maps, port. pp. 262.
Text of first voyage is from Wharton's edition, 1893, and of second and third voyages from *Three famous voyages of Captain Cook*, published by Ward Lock Bowden, undated. *See also* no. 238.

Copies: NPL:M(980:Col/45A1); ANL; QParl; VSL. 225

[1954] Barrow's Edition

Voyages of discovery; ed. by J. Barrow. Intro. by G. N. Pocock. [With bibl.] London, Dent, [1954].

(*Everyman's Library*.)
See no. 165 for other editions.

Copies: ANL; VMoU. 226

1955–68 Hakluyt Society Edition

The Journals of Captain James Cook on his voyages of discovery . . . Ed. [from the original MSS., with intro. notes and appendices] by J. C. Beaglehole, *and others*. [With] (Charts & views drawn by Cook and his officers, and reproduced from the original MSS.; ed. R. A. Skelton). [And] (Addenda and corrigenda to vol. 1) . . . Pub. for the Hakluyt Society. Cambridge, U.P., 1955–68.

Frontisp. in colour, illus. maps, ports. 3 vols. in 4, portfolio and addenda.
(Hakluyt Society—Extra series nos. 34–6.)
CONTENTS:
[Vol.] 1 The Voyage of the *Endeavour*, 1768–1771; with Addenda.
[Vol.] 2 The Voyage of the *Resolution* and *Adventure*, 1772–1775.
[Vol.] 3 The Voyage of the *Resolution* and *Discovery*, 1776–1780; pts. 1–2.
Portfolio. Charts & views.
Vol. 4, still to be published, will contain a "series of essays on particular aspects of Cook's life and achievement and on the scientific results of the voyages, together with a bibliography and lists of the original charts, drawings and paintings made on the voyages." For Russian translation of vols. 1–2, *see* no. 233.
The various volumes have been reviewed as follows:
E. S. Dodge—Captain Cook's first voyage. (*American Neptune* vol. 16, pp. 281–5, Oct. 1956).
M. H. Ellis—Captain Cook's own story. (*Bulletin*, Sydney. Vol. 77, May 2–9, 1956, *various pp.*)
D. Glover—[Review]. (*Landfall* vol. 11, pp. 60–67, Mar. 1957.)
B. Smith—The Journals of Captain James Cook. (*Historical Studies* vol. 7, pp. 480–82, May, 1957.)
A. P. Elkin—[Review]. (*Oceania*, vol. 27, pp. 320–23, 1957.)
The Journals of Capt. James Cook on his voyages of discovery. (*Geographical Review* vol. 48, pp. 143–4, Jan. 1958.)
The Voyages of Captain Cook. (*Alexander Turnbull Library Bulletin* no. 15, pp. 3–4, [1959].)
A. P. Elkin—Captain Cook's Journal, vol 2. (*Oceania* vol. 32, pp. 191–7. Mar. 1962.)

C. Lloyd—The Journals of Captain James Cook . . . Vol.III. (*Mariner's Mirror* vol. 53, pp. 390–91, Nov. 1967.)

G. S. Ritchie—Review of third voyage. (*Institute of Navigation, London—Journal* vol. 21, no. 3, pp. 250–55, July 1968.)

Copies: NPL:M(980:Col/46A1–4,X980/25); NPL:D(95/54–7,F95/1); NPL:R (S990A/215E,F990A/47); ANL; Captain Cook's Landing Place Trust; QOM; QParl; QU; VSL; WU.   227

1957 Limited Editions Club Edition
See no. 228.

1957 Price's Edition
The Explorations of Captain James Cook in the Pacific, as told by selections of his own journals, 1768–1779; ed. by A. G. Price . . . Illus. by G. C. Ingleton; [edition designed by D. A. Dunstan]. New York, Limited Editions Club, 1957.

Map as endpapers, port. pp. xii, 297.
With connecting narrative by the editor. Boards bound in tapa cloth. Spine of kangaroo leather, into which are bound sacred designs of the Australian aborigines. Printed at the Griffin Press, Adelaide. Edition limited to 1500 copies signed by the illustrator and designer, this being no. "M.L." *See also* nos. 231–2.

Copies: NPL:M(C956); NPL:R(09:LQ8C); ANL; SPL.   228

[1957] Spanish Edition
Viajes. Traducción integra y directa des ingles por Elena Garcia Ortiz. Barcelona, Fama, [1957].

pp. 519.
(*Serie junco.*)

Copies: ANL.   229

1958 Barrow's Edition
Capitan James Cook: viajees. Barcelona, Editorial Mateu, 1958.

pp. 221.
(*Colleccion de Bolsillo.*)
Translated into Spanish from Barrow edition 1904. *See* no. 165 for other editions.

Copies: NPL:M(980:Col/36T1).   230

1958 Price's Edition
The Explorations of Captain James Cook in the Pacific, as told by selections of his own journals, 1768–1779; ed. by A. G. Price . . . Illus. by G. C. Ingleton; [edition designed by D. A. Dunstan]. Melbourne, Georgian House, 1958.

Map as endpapers, port. in colour as frontisp. pp. xii, 297.
For other editions *see* nos. 228, 232.

Copies: NPL:M(Q980:Col/7B1); NPL:R(Q990A/120); QU; VMoU; VSL; WU. 231

[1958?] Price's Edition
The Explorations of Captain James Cook in the Pacific, as told by selections of his own journals, 1768–1779; ed. by A. G. Price . . . Illus. by G. C. Ingleton; [edition designed by D. A. Dunstan]. New York, Heritage Press, [1958?].

Map as endpapers, port. in colour as frontisp. pp. xii, 297.
For other editions *see* nos. 228, 231.
Copies: NPL:M(Q980:Col/7C1); ANL.   232

1958 Spanish Edition
See no. 230.

1960–64 Russian Edition
Pervoe krugosvetnoe plavanie kapitana Dzhemsa Kuka; [trans. by A. V. Shalygina.] Moskva, Gos. Izd-vo Geografićheskoĭ Literatury, 1960–4.

Facs. illus. maps, ports. 2 vols.
Russian edition of vols. 1–2 of no. 227. Title transliterated.
Copies: NPL:M(980:Col/46B1–2); ANL; VU(Baillieu).   233

1961 Barrow's Edition
Captain Cook's voyages of discovery; ed. by J. Barrow . . . introd. by G. N. Pocock. [With bibl.] London, Dent, 1961.

Maps, pp. 20, 485.
(*Everyman's library.*)
See no. 165 for other editions.
Copies: NPL:M(980:Col/36U1).   234

1963 German Edition
Cooks Fahrten um die Welt; Bericht nach seinen Tagebüchern. Herausgegeben von P. Beyer. Leipzig, Brockhaus, 1963.

Illus. some in colour, map, pp. 404.
See also no. 237.
Copies: NPL:M(980:Col/47A1).   235

[1965] Jackdaw Series
The Voyages of Captain Cook: a collection of contemporary documents; comp. by S. Lewenhak. London, Jonathan Cape, [1965].

Diags. facs. illus. map, port.
(*Jackdaw Series*, no. 20.)
Separate sheets in a folder.
CONTENTS:
1. Cook's ships.
2. Letter from the Office for Sick and Hurt Seamen, describing the effects of measure against scurvy.
3. A chart of New Zealand, drawn by Cook in 1770.
4. A report on the state and condition of the *Endeavour* in 1771.

5. Admiralty secret orders for Cook's second voyage.
6. Pages from the log of Cook's first voyage, and the journal of his Antarctic voyage.
7. Eye-witness report of the death of Captain Cook.
8. Incidents on Cook's voyages, drawn by the artists who accompanied him.
9. Seven broadsheets.

Copies: NPL:M(Q980:Col/L1A1); NPL:R(NQ909.088/1); ANL.   236

1965 Leipzig Edition

Cooks Fahrten um die Welt; Bericht nach seinen Tagebüchern. Herausgegeben von P. Beyer. Leipzig, Edition Leipzig, 1965.

Illus. some in colour, map, pp. 404.
For earlier edition *see* no. 235.

Copies: NPL:M(980:Col/47B1).   237

1969 Reed's Edition

Captain Cook in New Zealand: extracts from the journals of Captain James Cook giving a full account in his own words of his adventures and discoveries in New Zealand. Ed. [with intro., biog. and notes] by A. H. & A. W. Reed; [with note on the literature by C. R. H. Taylor, and bibl.]. 2nd ed. Wellington, N.Z., A. H. & A. W. Reed, 1969.

Illus. maps, port. pp.262.
Folding facsimile of *Chart of New Zealand explored in 1769 and 1770 by Lieut. I. Cook*, published 1772, at back. Text for first voyage is from Wharton's edition 1893, and for second and third voyages, from *Three famous voyages of Captain Cook*, published by Ward, Lock, Bowden, n.d.
Includes part of Capt. Furneaux's *Narrative*, and Mr. Anderson's *Remarks on the country near Queen Charlotte Sound*.
See also no. 225.

Copies: NPL:M(980:Col/45B1).   238

Books about the Voyages

1777 A LETTER to the English nation on the present war with America. London, G. Corrall, 1777.

pp. iv, 59.
Contains a criticism of Cook's discoveries, and claims he would have been more usefully employed charting the American coast.

Copies: NPL:D(77/32).   239

1777 MODERN TRAVELLER. London, 1777.

Vols. 4-5.

Copies: VSL.   240

1780 NACHRICHTEN VON DEM LEBEN und den Seereisen des berühmten Capitain Cook. Reval, Albrecht und Compagnie, 1780.

pp.48.
Photographic copy only in the State Library of Victoria.

A rare work published in Revel (*sic*, Tallinn) in Estonia. Jackson, item 91 is probably a record of it. Undoubtedly the first account of Cook's death to be published in book form. The volume gives a short account of Cook's life, voyages and death, with many inaccuracies on his early career. Mainly taken from a letter, *Auszug des Briefes von Kensington den 4ten Febr. 1780 die Nachrichten von Kapitain Cook betressend.* (Note from Nan Kivell copy.) *See also* Spence, p.20, where he describes the pamphlet and records a French edition (no. 242); possibly from the pen of J. R. or G. Forster.

Copies: ANL (Nan Kivell); VSL. 241

[1780?] PRÉCIS DE LA VIE & des voyages du Capitaine Cook.
Ecrit de Kensington ce 4 Février 1780. Reval & Leipsic, Albrecht & Co., [1780?].
pp.47.
For note *see* no. 241, and *see also* Spence, p.20, who records another copy in the collection of B.Kroepelien, Oslo.
Copies: NPL:M(Safe 1/99); ANL(Nan Kivell). 242

[1782] MILLER, George Henry
The New and universal system of geography . . . including all the valuable discoveries made in the most remarkable voyages and travels made to different parts of the world, by Captain Cook [and others. London, 1782.]
See also no. 244.
Copies: ANL. 243

[1782] MILLER, George Henry
The New, complete, authentic and universal system of geography . . . including . . . the most remarkable voyages and travels . . . Comprising every interesting circumstance . . . in Captain Cook's voyages round the world [etc.] . . . by G. H. Miller . . . assisted by . . . William Langford . . . who accompanied Capt Cook. London, Alex. Hogg, [1782].
Illus. pp. viii, 5–812, [6].
Issued also in separate parts. *See also* nos. 243, 255–6.
Copies: NPL:R(09:F909.9A/1). 244

1783 WALL, Martin
Observations on the diseases prevalent in the South Sea Islands, particularly the Lues Venera, with some remarks concerning its first appearance in Europe.
(*In his* Dissertations on select subjects in chemistry and medicine. Oxford, D. Prince and J. Cooke, 1783. Tract no.III, pp.135–66.)
Mitchell Library copy has an additional title-page, entitled *Dissertations, letters, &c. &c.*, Oxford, Clarendon Press, 1786. Dixson Library copy extracted. The author examines the accounts of Hawkesworth, Cook and J. R. Forster.
Copies: NPL:M(540/W); NPL:D(78/2, 78/3). 245

1786 FORSTER, Johann Georg Adam
Dissertatio inauguralis botanico-medica de plantis esculentis insularum Oceani Australis. Quam ex Decreto ordinis, gratiosi speciminis gratia

pro adipiscendis summis in Medicina Honoribus publicavit Auctor Georgius Forster, Phil.D. et LL.A.A.M.Sereniss. Halae ad Salam. 1786. pp.80.

Thesis for the author's M.D.degree, on the edible plants of the South Pacific islands. The preface gives a brief account of the characteristics and customs of the various islanders. *See also* no. 248.

Copies: ANL. 246

1786 FORSTER, Johann Georg Adam

Florulae insularum Australium prodromus. Auctore Georgio Forster. Gottingae, J. C. Dieterich, 1786.

pp.8, 103.

Contains descriptions of New Zealand and Pacific Islands plants. Dedicated to A. Sparrman.

Copies: NPL:M(581.99/F); ANL. 247

1786 FORSTER, Johann Georg Adam

Georgii Forster, Medic. Doct. Sereniss. Poloniae Regi A Consiliis Intimis, etc. De plantis esculentis insularum Oceani Australis commentatio botanica. Berolini, Haude et Spener, 1786.

pp.80.

Thesis for the author's M.D.degree, on the edible plants of the South Pacific islands. *See also* no. 246.

Copies: NPL:M(581.99/F); ANL. 248

1786 FORSTER, Johann Reinhold

History of the voyages and discoveries made in the north; translated from the German of J. R. Forster, and elucidated by several new and original maps. London, G. G. J. and J. Robinson, 1786.

pp.399–407: Captain Cook. Refers to Cook's three voyages and to his death. From the German edition published 1784 (*see* Holmes, nos. 48, 59).

Copies: NPL:M(Bayldon); VU(Baillieu). 249

1791 LABORDE, Jean Benjamin de

Histoire abrégée de la Mer du Sud. [With bibl. notes, and Atlas.] Paris, P. Didot, l'aîné, 1791.

Illus. 3 vols. and atlas.
Volumes 2–3 deal with Cook's voyages.

Copies: NPL:M(980/L, X980/4 Atlas); NPL:R(09:S990A/121–3, 09:Q990A/85); VSL. 250

1791 MORTIMER, George

Des Lieutenants Georg Mortimer Bemerkungen auf seiner Reise in der Brigantine *Merkur*.

(*In* Forster, J.G.A.—Geschichte der Reisen die seit Cook an der Nordwest- und Nordost-Küste von Amerika, vol. 3, pp. 165–224. 1791.)
See also nos. 252–4, 257, 259.

Copies: NPL:M(Q910.4/F). 251

1791 MORTIMER, George
Observations and remarks made during a voyage to the islands of Teneriffe, Amsterdam, Maria's Islands near Van Diemen's Land, Otaheite, Sandwich Islands, Owhyhee, the Fox Islands on the north west coast of America, Tinian, and from thence to Canton, in the brig *Mercury*, commanded by J. H. Cox . . . By Lieut. George Mortimer. London, the author, 1791.

Illus. maps, pp. [xvi], 71, [i].
Pp. ix–xvi give List of subscribers. Contains references to Captain Cook's voyages, and to Omai and Potatow, and a description of the village of Kowrowa, the spot where Cook was killed. *See also* nos. 251, 253–4, 257, 259.

Copies: NPL:M(Q989.5/5A1).   252

1791 MORTIMER, George
Observations and remarks made during a voyage to the islands of Teneriffe, Amsterdam, Maria's Islands near Van Diemen's Land, Otaheite, Sandwich Islands, Owhyhee, the Fox Islands on the north west coast of America, Tinian and from thence to Canton, in the brig *Mercury*, commanded by J. H. Cox . . . By Lieut. George Mortimer. London, the author, 1791.

Maps 2, plate 1, pp. viii, 71, [i, viii].
List of subscribers inserted at end of volume. *See also* nos. 251–2, 254, 257, 259.

Copies: NPL:M(Q989.5/5A2).   253

1791 MORTIMER, George
Observations and remarks made during a voyage to the islands of Teneriffe, Amsterdam, Maria's Islands near Van Diemen's Land, Otaheite, Sandwich Islands, Owhyhee, the Fox Islands on the north west coast of America, Tinian and from thence to Canton, in the brig *Mercury*; commanded by J. H. Cox . . . By Lieut. George Mortimer. Dublin, P. Byrne, J. Moore, A. Grueben, W. Jones and K. White, 1791.

pp. [xvi], 118, [2].
See also nos. 251–3, 257, 259.

Copies: NPL:M(989.5/26A1); NPL:D(79/100).   254

1793 ADAMS, Michael
New, royal system of universal geography . . . including every interesting discovery in the narratives of Capt. Cook's voyages. 1793.

See also nos. 243–4, 256.

Copies: ANL.   255

[1793] ADAMS, Michael
The New, royal geographical magazine; or, A modern, complete, authentic and copious system of universal geography. Containing a complete . . . history and description of all the several parts of the whole world . . . including every interesting discovery and circumstance in the

narratives of Captain Cook's voyages round the world . . . Carefully written and compiled . . . by Michael Adams. London, Alex. Hogg, [1793].

Maps, plates, pp.iv, [9]—960.
See also nos. 243–4, 255. Date from frontispiece. With additional engraved title-page, with varying title.
Copies: NPL:M(Q910.8/A).   256

1793 MORTIMER, George

Waarneemingen en Aanmerkingen aangetekend geduurende eene Reize . . . in het Brigantijn-schip de *Mercurius* . . . uitgegeeven door G. Mortimer . . . uit het Engelsch vertaald door J. D. Pasteur. Leyden, A. en J. Honkoop, 1793.

pp. viii, 132, [4].
English edition entitled *Observations and remarks, etc. See also* nos. 251–4, 259.
Copies: NPL:M(989.5/26B1); NPL:R(S990A/93).   257

[1797] GRASSET DE SAINTE-SAUVEUR, Jacques

Histoire abrégée des découvertes des Capitaines Cook, Wilson, La Perouse, etc. Paris, the author, An VI, [1797].

pp. 60.
Running title: *Découvertes de Cook et La Pérouse.*
Copies: NPL:D(Q79/65); VSL.   258

1798 MORTIMER, George

Engelsmannen Joh. Hindric Cox Resa genom Söderhafvet till ön Amsterdam, Marien-Öarna, O-Taheiti, Sandvichs-och Räf-Öarna, Tinian, Unalaska och Canton i China. Uitgifnen af G. Mortimer. Nyköping, Peter Winge, 1798.

pp. 77.
English edition entitled *Observations and remarks, etc. See also* nos. 251–4, 257.
Copies: NPL:M(C980).   259

1832 VERREAUX, Jules

L'Océanie en estampes; ou, Description géographique et historique de toutes les îles du Grand Océan et du continent de la Nouvelle Hollande. Notasie, Polynésie, Australie . . . Ouvrage destiné à l'instruction et à l'amusement de la jeunesse; orné d'une carte et de cent huit gravures . . . rédigé d'après les documens tant anciens que recens, et des notices inédites de voyageurs français et étrangers, M.M. Lesson, Sainson, Ellis, Marsden, etc. Par J. et E. Verreaux. Paris, Librairie Nepvue, 1832.

pp. xvi, 437, [iii].
Copies: NPL:M(980/V).   260

1835 BAJOT, Louis Marie—Abrégé historique.
See 1836, no. 261.

1836 BAJOT, Louis Marie

Abrégé historique et chronologique des principaux voyages de découvertes par mer, depuis l'an 2000 avant Jésus-Christ jusqu'au commencement du XIXe siécle. 2nd ed. Paris, l'Imprimerie Royale, 1836.

pp. 156.
Cover dated 1835.
Copies: NPL:M(910.9/B); ANL; VSL.   261

[186–] HORN, W. O. von, *pseud.*

James Cook; Leben und Thaten des weltberühmten Seefahrers und Erdumseglers. Der Jugend und dem Volke erzählt. Wiesbaden, Niedner, [186–?].

4 plates, pp. 136.
See also nos. 263, 271.
Copies: NPL:M(980:Col/H3B1).   262

1867 HORN, W. O. von, *pseud.*

James Cook, den namnkunnige verldsomseglaren hans lefnad och bedrifter. Skildrade för ungdomen af W. O. von Horn. Stockholm, Ebeling, [1867].

4 plates, pp. [ii], 130.
Cover title: *James Cook's Lefnad och Bedrifter. See also* nos. 262, 271.
Copies: NPL:M(980:Col/H3A1).   263

[187–?] BALLANTYNE, Robert Michael

The Cannibal Islands; or, Captain Cook's adventures in the South Seas. London, James Nisbet & Co., [187–?].

Illus. pp. 120.
(*Ballantyne's miscellany* no. 9.)
Copies: NPL:M(989.5/B).   264

[187–] JONES, M.

The Story of Captain Cook's three voyages round the world. Told by M. Jones. 3rd ed. London, Cassell, Petter and Galpin, [187–].

Illus. pp. viii, 264.
See also no. 266.
Copies: NPL:M(980:Col/J2C1).   265

[1870] JONES, M.

The Story of Captain Cook's three voyages round the world. Told by M. Jones. London, Cassell, Petter & Galpin, [1870].

Illus. pp. viii, 264.
See also no. 265.
Copies: NPL:M(980:Col/J2A1).   266

[1871] KINGSTON, William Henry Giles
Captain Cook, his life, voyages and discoveries. London, Religious Tract Society, [1871].
Listed in British Museum catalogue, which also lists [1890] and [1926] editions. *See also* no. 274.
Copies: QU; VSL.

267

1881 VERNE, Jules
Die Vorläufer des Kapitän Cook; [with accounts of the three voyages].
Illus. port.
(*In his* Bekannte und unbekannte Welten. Wien, A. Hartleben, 1881. Vol. 33–4.)
Copies: NPL:R(N843.8/V531).

268

1884 H., A. F.
James Cook's resor på Stilla Hafwet. Helsingfors, Folkupplysnings–sällskapets Förlag, 1884.
Illus. map, port. pp. 58.
Copies: NPL:M(980:Col/H1A1).

269

[1886] MEISSNER, H.
James Cook, oder dreimal um die Erde: ein Lebensbild für die reifere Jugend, von H. Meissner. Stuttgart, Gebrüder Kröner, [1886].
Illus. maps, pp. iv, 286.
Illustrations, by Fritz Bergen, include coloured plates. For Swedish edition *see* no. 272.
Copies: NPL:M(980:Col/M2A1).

270

1894 HORN, W. O. von, *pseud.*
James Cook: Leben und Thaten des weltberühmten Seefahrers und Erdumseglers. Der Jugend und dem Volke erzählt. 4th ed. Altenburg, Geibel, 1894.
4 plates, pp. 116.
(*Horn'sche Volks- und Jugenbibliothek*, no. 58.)
See also nos. 262–3.
Copies: NPL:M(980:Col/H3C1).

271

1894 MEISSNER, H.
James Cook, eller jorden rundt tre gånger; bearbetning från Tyskan [of H. Meissner] af D. S. Hector. Stockholm, P. A. Norstedt, 1894.
Illus. pp. 296.
(*P.A. Norstedt & Söners Ungdomsböcher*, nr. 18.)
Slightly abridged. Illustrations in black and white. For Stuttgart edition *see* no. 270.
Copies: NPL:M(980:Col/M2B1).

272

[19–?] Whitcombe and Tombs, Ltd.
Under Cook's flag; [with chronology of Cook's life]. Auckland, W. & T., [19–?].

Illus. maps, port. pp. 148.
(*Whitcombe's Hist. Story Books.*)
Written for children.
Copies: NPL:M(980:Col/W2A1). 273

[1904] KINGSTON, William Henry Giles
Captain Cook, his life, voyages and discoveries. London, Religious Tract Society, [1904].

Illus. pp. 319.
British Museum catalogue lists [1871], [1890], and [1926] editions. *See also* no. 267.
Copies: NPL:M(980:Col/K1A1). 274

[1908?] CAPTAIN COOK'S voyages of discovery. Leeds, E. J. Arnold, [1908?].

Illus.
(*A. L. Bright story readers;* ed. by A. Gardiner. No. 146.)
Copies: QU. 275

1913 BATEREAU, Alfred
Captain James Cook, life and voyages . . . bearbeitet von . . . A. Batereau; [with] (Wörterbuch . . . von . . . B. Koeppen). Berlin, Weidmannsche Buchhandlung, 1913.

2 vols.
(*Schulbibliothek Französischer und Englischer Prosaschriften*, Abt. 2, Band 61.)
Copies: NPL:D(91/240–1); ANL:F. 276

[1918] BEST, Elsdon
The Discovery & re-discovery of Wellington Harbour, with remarks by early voyagers on the local natives, etc., by E. Best. (Pub. by the Wellington Harbour Board.) Wellington, N.Z., Palmer & Mahood, pr., [1918].

Maps, pp. [i], 44.
Copies: NPL:M(997.1/B); NPL:D(91/1097); ANL. 277

1926 VERNE, Jules
Premier voyage du Capitaine Cook. Edited by H. Wiltshire. Sydney, the Author, 1926.

pp.74.
Reprint of the author's *Les Grands navigateurs du dix-huitième siècle*. Chapter 3. *See also* nos. 268, 362.
Copies: ANL. 278

1927 MITTON, Geraldine Edith
Captain Cook. London, A. and C. Black, 1927.
Illus. map, port. pp. vi, 90.
(*Peeps at Great Explorers [Ser.].*)
Copies: NPL:M(980:Col/M4A1); ANL.

279

[1928] AUSTRALIA—High Commissioner for Australia in London
Capt. Cook: the greatest of English navigators. [1928].
Copies: ANL.

280

[1929] THIÉRY, Maurice
The Life and voyages of Captain Cook, by M. Thiéry. [Trans. from the French by C. J. C. Street.] London, Bles, [1929].
Illus. map, port. pp. ix, 238.
Map showing voyages as endpapers. *See also* nos. 282, 285.
Copies: NPL:M(980:Col/T1B1); NPL:D(92/246); NPL:R(S920/C771/10); ANL; QU; WU.

281

[1929] THIÉRY, Maurice
La Vie et les voyages du Capitaine Cook; illus. par A. Zaccagnino. Paris, P. Roger, [1929].
Map, port. pp. 238.
(*La Vie des Grands Navigateurs.*)
See also nos. 281, 285.
Copies: NPL:M(980:Col/T1A1); ANL; VSL.

282

1930 CARRUTHERS, *Sir* Joseph Hector McNeil
Captain James Cook, R.N. London, Murray, [1930].
Facs. illus. map, port. pp. xx, 316.
See also no. 284. Reviewed in the *Times Literary Supplement*, July 3, 1930, p. 549; and by H. Palmer in the *Geographical Journal* volume 77, May 1931, pp. 491–6.
Copies: NPL:M(980:Col/C2A1); NPL:D(93/37); NPL:R(S920/C771/2); ANL; Captain Cook's Landing Place Trust; QParl; QU; VMoU; VSL.

283

1930 CARRUTHERS, *Sir* Joseph Hector McNeil
Captain James Cook, R.N. New York, E. P. Dutton, 1930.
Facs. illus. map, port. pp. xx, 316.
See also no. 283. Reviewed in the *Times Literary Supplement*, July 3, 1930, p. 549; and by H. Palmer in the *Geographical Journal* vol. 77, May 1931, pp. 491–6.
Copies: NPL:M(980:Col/C2B1).

284

1930 THIÉRY, Maurice
Captain Cook, navigator and discoverer, by M. Thiéry. [Trans. from the French by C. J. C. Street.] New York, R. M. McBride, 1930.
Facs. illus. port. pp. [x], 265.
Map showing voyages as endpapers. *See also* nos. 281–2.
Copies: NPL:M(980:Col/T1C1).

285

[1935] GOULD, Rupert Thomas
Captain Cook; [with bibl. notes]. London, Duckworth, [1935].

Maps, pp. 144.
(*Great Lives*, no. 49.)

Copies: NPL:M(980:Co1/G2A1); NPL:D(93/627); NPL:R(920/C771/3); ANL;
VSL.   286

1936 CAMPBELL, Gordon
Captain James Cook, R.N., F.R.S. London, Hodder and Stoughton, 1936.

Illus. maps, port. pp. 320.

Copies: NPL:M(923.9/C771.2/19A1); NPL:D(93/126); NPL:R(DS990A/128); ANL;
QParl; VSL; WU.   287

1939 CARRINGTON, Arthur Hugh
Life of Captain Cook, by A. H. Carrington. [With bibl.] London,
Sidgwick & Jackson, 1939.

Illus. maps, port. pp. ix, 324.
See also no. 317.

Copies: NPL:M(980:Co1/C1A1); NPL:D(93/127); ANL; QU; VSL; WU.   288

1939 MUIR, John Reid
The Life and achievements of Captain James Cook . . . explorer, navigator,
surveyor and physician. [With bibl.] London, Blackie, 1939.

Illus. map, port. pp. [ix], 310.

Copies: NPL:M(980:Co1/M6A1); NPL:D(93/626); NPL:R(DS990A/195); ANL;
QParl; QU; VMoU; VSL.   289

1940 LEMONNIER, Leon
Le Capitaine Cook et l'exploration de l'Océanie. Paris, Gallimard, 1940.

Illus. maps, port. pp. 251.
(*La Découverte du Monde*.)

Copies: NPL:M(980/109A1); ANL.   290

1945 BELLINGSHAUSEN, Thaddeus von
Voyage of Captain Bellingshausen to the Antarctic Seas, 1819–1821;
trans. from the Russian. Edited by F. Debenham. London, Hakluyt
Society, 1945.

Illus. maps, ports. 2 vols.
(Hakluyt Society—*Works*, ser.2, vols.91,92.)
Contains references to Cook.

Copies: NPL:M(980/156B1–2); NPL:R(S909.6A/7).   291

1946 WILLIAMSON, James Alexander
Cook and the opening of the Pacific; [with bibl.] London, Hodder &
Stoughton for E.U.P., 1946.

Illus. maps, port. pp. xii, 251.
(*Teach Yourself History.*)
Maps as endpapers.
For reprint, 1948 *see* no. 294.
Copies: NPL:M(980:Col/W4A1); NPL:R(E990/Wil); ANL; QParl; QU; VSL; WU.

292

1947 WOOD, David

Cook, the explorer: [an account for children]. London, Peter Lunn, 1947.
Illus. maps, pp. 217.
Copies: NPL:M(980:Col/W5A1); NPL:R(DS990A/208); ANL; VSL.   293

1948 WILLIAMSON, James Alexander

Cook and the opening of the Pacific; [with bibl.] London, Hodder &
Stoughton for E.U.P., 1948.
Illus. maps, port. pp. xii, 251.
(*Teach Yourself History.*)
Maps as endpapers. Reprinted from 1946 edition, *see* no. 292.
Copies: NPL:M(980:Col/W4B1).   294

1951 VANDERCOOK, John Womack

Great sailor: a life of the discoverer Captain James Cook. [With] (note
on sources). New York, Dial Press, 1951.
Frontisp. pp. viii, 339.
Frontispiece is portrait of Cook after James Webber from National Portrait Gallery.
Map of voyages forms endpapers.
Copies: NPL:M(980:Col/V1A1); NPL:R(920/C771/11); ANL.   295

1952 LLOYD, Christopher

Captain Cook: [a biography]. London, Faber and Faber, 1952.
Illus. maps, port. pp. 172.
Copies: NPL:M(980:Col/L2A1); NPL:R(920/C771/12); ANL; QParl; VMoU; VSL.

296

1952 SWENSON, Eric Pierson

The South Sea shilling: voyages of Captain Cook, R.N., by E. Swenson.
Illus. by C. M. Daugherty. New York, Viking Press, 1952.
pp. 224.
Written for children. *See also* no. 312.
Copies: NPL:M(980:Col/S3A1); ANL.   297

1954 MERRILL, Elmer Drew

The Botany of Cook's voyages and its unexpected significance in relation
to anthropology, biogeography and history. Waltham, Mass., Chronica
Botanica Co., 1954.
Facs. illus. ports. pp. [iv, 224].
A cloth bound edition of *Chronica Botanica*, vol. 14, no.5/6.
Copies: NPL:M(Q581.999/M); ANL; QU.   298

1955 SPERRY, Armstrong
  Captain Cook explores the South Seas. New York, Random House, 1955.
  Illus. pp. 184.
  (*World Landmark Books.*)
  Written for children. *See also* nos. 301, 311.
  Copies: NPL:M(980:Col/S2A1); ANL.   299

1956 TAYLOR, Eva Germaine Rimington
  The Haven-finding art: a history of navigation from Odysseus to Captain
  Cook. [With bibliography.] London, Hollis & Carter, 1956.
  Facs. illus. maps, pp.xii, 295.
  Copies: NPL:M(527.09/T).   300

1960 SPERRY, Armstrong
  All about Captain Cook. Rev. ed. London, W. H. Allen, 1960.
  Illus. map as endpapers, pp. [iv], 147.
  (*All About Books.*)
  Written for children. *See also* nos. 299, 311.
  Copies: NPL:M(980:Col/S2B1); ANL.   301

1960 SYME, Ronald
  Captain Cook, Pacific explorer; [written for children], by R. Syme.
  Illus. by W. Stobbs. New York, W. Morrow, 1960.
  Illus. pp. 96.
  (*Morrow Junior Books.*)
  Copies: NPL:M(980:Col/S4A1); ANL.   302

1960 ZAVATTI, Silvio
  I Viaggi del capitano James Cook. Milano, Schwarz editore, 1960.
  Illus. port. pp. 206.
  See also no. 304.
  Copies: NPL:M(980:Col/Z1A1).   303

1961 ZAVATTI, Silvio
  I Viaggi del capitano James Cook. Milano, Schwarz, 1961.
  Illus. port. pp. 206.
  See also no. 303.
  Copies: ANL.   304

1963 WARNER, Oliver Martin Wilson
  Captain Cook and the South Pacific, by the editors of *Horizon* Magazine;
  author, O. Warner, consultant . . . J. C. Beaglehole. New York, American
  Heritage Pub. Co., 1963.
  Illus. some in colour, maps as endpapers, ports. pp. 153.
  (*Horizon Caravel Book.*)
  See also no. 308.
  Copies: NPL:M(980:Col/W1A1); ANL.   305

1964 CAMERON, Roderick William

The Golden haze: with Captain Cook in the South Pacific. London, Weidenfeld and Nicolson, 1964.

Illus. some in colour, maps, ports, pp. 301.
For U.S. edition *see* no. 307.

Copies: NPL:M(990/16A1); NPL:R(996.1/2); ANL; QU.   306

1964 CAMERON, Roderick William

The Golden haze: with Captain Cook in the South Pacific. Cleveland, U.S.A., World Publishing Co., 1964.

Illus. some in colour, maps, ports. pp. xvii, 283.
For London edition *see* no. 306.

Copies: NPL:M(990/16B1).   307

1964 WARNER, Oliver Martin Wilson

Captain Cook and the South Pacific, by the editors of *Horizon* Magazine; author O. Warner, consultant . . . J. C. Beaglehole. London, Cassell, 1964.

Illus. some in colour, maps as endpapers, ports. pp. 153.
(*Cassell Caravel Book*, [no.] 6.)
First British edition. For New York edition *see* no. 305.

Copies: NPL:M(980:Col/W1B1).   308

1965 PRESTON, C.

Captain James Cook, R.N., F.R.S., and Whitby, by C. Preston. Pub. by Whitby Literary and Philosophical Society. Whitby, Horne, pr., 1965.

Facs. illus. maps, port. pp. 48.

Copies: NPL:M(980:Col/P 1A1); ANL; Captain Cook's Landing Place Trust.   309

1965 QUILICI, Folco

Sui mar del Capitano Cook. Firenze, Vallecchi Editore, 1965.

Facs. illus. some in colour, maps, pp. 191, vi.
(*Avventure nella storia*. Enciclopedia monografica diretta da Piero Pieroni.)
Photographed in 1956–7 and 1961–2, whilst the author was making a television series, *Le avventure del Capitano Cook*.

Copies: NPL:M(Q980:Col/Q1A1).   310

1965 SPERRY, Armstrong

Le Capitaine Cook explore le Pacifique, [by] (A Sperry); adapté [from the English] par J. Petrus. Paris, F. Nathan, 1965.

Illus. maps, ports. pp. 157.
(*Histoire et Documents* ser.)
See also nos. 299, 301.

Copies: NPL:R(N920/C771/2).   311

1965 SWENSON, Eric Pierson

The South Sea shilling: voyages of Captain Cook, R.N., by E. Swenson. Illus. by C. M. Daugherty. New ed. Sydney, A. & R., 1965.

Maps as endpapers, pp. 224.
Written for children. *See also* no. 297.

Copies: NPL:M(980:Col/S3B1); ANL.   312

1966 BROSSARD, Maurice Raymond de, *Admiral*

Moana, océan cruel: les dieux meurent à la grande mer du sud. [With bibl.] Paris, France-Empire, 1966.

Maps, plates, pp. 382.

Copies: NPL:M(910.45/32A1).   313

[1966] COPLEY, Roger

Dampier and Cook, by R. Copley. Illus. by C. Kivinen. Croydon, Vic., Longmans, [1966].

Illus. some in colour, maps, ports. pp. [ii], 30.
(*Great people in Australian history.*)
For young readers.

Copies: NPL:M(990.1/121A1); NPL:R(E994.01/Cop).   314

1966 MOOREHEAD, Alan McCrae

The Fatal impact: an account of the invasion of the South Pacific, 1767–1840. [With bibl.] London, Hamilton, 1966.

Illus. maps, ports. pp. xiv, 230.
Maps as endpapers. *See also* nos. 316, 322.

Copies: NPL:M(999.5/13A1); NPL:R(990/5); ANL; QParl; QU.   315

1966 MOOREHEAD, Alan McCrae

The Fatal impact: an account of the invasion of the South Pacific, 1767–1840. [With bibl.] New York, Harper and Row, 1966.

Illus. maps, ports. pp. xiv, 230.
See also nos. 315, 322.

Copies: NPL:M(999.5/13B1); ANL.   316

1967 CARRINGTON, Arthur Hugh

Life of Captain Cook; [with bibl.] New ed. London, Sidgwick & Jackson, 1967.

Maps, pp. [vii], 324.
(*Watergate editions.*)
See also no. 288.

Copies: NPL:M(980:Col/C1B1).   317

1967 CARRISON, Daniel J.
Captain James Cook: genius afloat. [With bibl.] New York, Franklin Watts, 1967.

Map, pp. vii, 194.
(*Immortals of History.*)
Copies: NPL:M(980:Col/C3A1); ANL. 318

1967 MUSMAN, Richard
Captain Cook, [by] R. Musman. Illus. by Biro, pseud. Maps by K. Dance. [With bibl.] London, Hutchinson Educational, 1967.

Port. pp. [96].
(*Men of mark.*)
For children.
Copies: NPL:M(980:Col/M7A1). 319

1967 VILLIERS, Alan John
Captain Cook, the seamen's seaman: a study of the great discoverer. [With bibl.] London, Hodder and Stoughton, 1967.

Illus. maps, ports. pp. 256.
Reviewed by Charles H. Cotter in the *Mariner's Mirror*, vol. 54, pp. 104–5, Feb. 1968. *See also* no. 321.
Copies: NPL:M(980:Col/V2A1); NPL:R(910.0942/1). 320

1967 VILLIERS, Alan John
Captain James Cook: [a biography. With bibl.] New York, Charles Scribner's Sons, 1967.

Illus. maps, port. pp. xii, 307.
Maps also as endpapers. Published also with title *Captain Cook, the seamen's seaman.* London, 1967. *See* no. 320.
Copies: NPL:M(980:Col/V2B1). 321

1968 MOOREHEAD, Alan McCrae
The Fatal impact: an account of the invasion of the South Pacific 1767–1840. [With bibl.] Harmondsworth, England, Penguin Books, 1968.

Illus. maps, ports. pp.283.
See also nos. 315, 316.
Copies: NPL:M(999.5/13C1). 322

[1968] NATIONAL MARITIME MUSEUM, *Greenwich*
Cook's voyages; [questionnaire for children. Comp. by National Maritime Museum. Greenwich, the Museum, 1968.]

Illus. maps, pp.9.
Cover title. Processed.
Issued to commemorate the bi-centenary of Cook's first voyage round the world.
Copies: NPL:M(Q980:Col/N3A1). 323

1968 RIENITS, Rex

The Voyages of Captain Cook, [by] R. & T. Rienits. London, Paul Hamlyn, 1968.

Facs. illus., many in colour, maps, ports. pp. 157.
Sydney also mentioned in imprint. Includes reproductions of drawings and maps by Cook.
Copies: NPL:M(Q980:Co1/R1A1); NPL:R(NQ910.4/4).   324

1968 WIGGINS TEAPE LIMITED

Captain Cook on orbit round the world, 1768–1968: [collection of coloured facsimile documents in a folder]. London, Wiggins Teape, 1968.

CONTENTS:
Plan of the *Endeavour*.
A Letter from Cook to the Admiralty.
Part of the complement of the *Endeavour*.
Map of Tahiti.
Page from the ship's log.
Drawings of the dancer and the chief.
French map of the world.
Drawing of ship's officer.
Description of a kangaroo.
Issued to commemorate bi-centenary of Cook's first voyage.
Copies: NPL:M(Q980:Co1/W2A1).   325

n.d. Whitcombe and Tombs, Ltd.

Captain James Cook, for ages 12 to 14 years. Auckland, Whitcombe & Tombs, n.d.

Illus. maps, port. as frontisp. pp. 59.
(*Whitcombe's Story Books*, no. 653.)
Written for children.
Copies: NPL:M(923.9/C771.2/31A).   326

Articles, etc., about the Voyages

1780 DESPERRIÈRES, Poissonnier

Observations sur le discours de M. Pringle qui termine la relation des voyages de M. Cook lûes à la Société Royale de Médecine; [with] (Rapport de Mrs les commissaires de la Société).

(*In his* Traité des fièvres de l'Isle de St. Domingue. Paris, L'Imprimerie Royale, 1780. pp. 243–312.)
Copies: NPL:M(980:Co1/D2B1).   327

1781 *UNIVERSAL MAGAZINE*

A Succinct account of the life and voyages of Captain James Cook; with an exact representation of the death of that celebrated navigator; communicated by respectable authority, and elegantly engraved on copper. London, 1781.

Illus. port.
Extract from the *Universal Magazine*, vol. 68, no. 476, June 1781, pp. 281–5. Bound with other magazine extracts. *Cover title:* Magazine articles, Cook, Banks, Dalrymple, etc.
Copies: NPL:M(910.4/122). 328

1784 AN AMERICAN, *pseud.*
New Holland and isles in the Pacific Ocean.

(*In* Geography epitomized; or, A tour round the world . . . description . . . in verse . . . for the use of schools. By An American. Philadelphia, J. Crukshank, 1784. pp. 45–8.)
Copies: NPL:M(910.7/G). 329

1790 ADAMS, *Rev.* John
Of Captain Cook.

(*In his* Modern voyages. London, G. Kearsley, 1790. Vol. 1, pp. 283–326.)
See also no. 331.
Copies: NPL:M(910.8/A); NPL:R(MD3:P14). 330

1790 ADAMS, *Rev.* John
Of Captain Cook.

(*In his* Modern voyages. Dublin, Chamberlaine & Rice, etc., 1790. Vol.1.)
See also no. 330.
Copies: VSL. 331

1793 PARIS, P. L.
Lofreden over den engelschen scheepsbevelhebber J. Cook.

(Cook, James—2nd voyage—Printed accounts—[1793. Dutch Ed.] Reis naar de Zuidpool. Utrecht, G. T. Pattenburg en Zoon, Schalekamp, 1793. pp. 1–72.)
Copies: NPL:M(980:Co3/7B1). 332

1801 RICHARD, Jerome F., *Abbé*
Vols faits par les insulaires, procédés des Anglais avec eux, sévérité outrée de Cook [Society Islands].

(*In his* Voyages chez les peuples sauvages. Paris, Laurens, aîné, 1801. Vol. 2, pp. 371–95.)
Copies: NPL:M(*989/R). 333

1805 DUFOUR, Joseph, et Cie
Les Sauvages de la Mer Pacifique: tableau pour décoration, en papier peint. Macon, de l'Imprimerie de Moiroux, an xiii, [i.e. 1805].
pp. [3]–48.
Descriptions of 20 pictures based on the voyages of Cook, La Pérouse and others, manufactured by J. Dufour et Cie. With historical accounts of the peoples and places depicted.
Copies: NPL:M(980/D). 334

1806 PELHAM, Cavendish
Strictures on the life of Captain James Cook, and on his first and second (and third) voyages.

(In his The World. London, J. Stratford, 1806. Vol. 1.)
See also no. 337.

Copies: NPL:R(09:Q909.8A/13); VSL.   335

[1810?] COOKE, George Alexander
New discoveries in the great Pacific Ocean.

Illus. maps.
(In his Modern and authentic system of universal geography. London, C. Cooke, [1810?] Vol. 1, pp. 5–364.)

Copies: NPL:M(Q910/18); NPL:R(DQ909.9A/4); ANL:F; VSL.   336

1810 PELHAM, Cavendish
Strictures on the life of . . . Cook, and on his first and second voyages, [and account of his] Voyage to the Pacific Ocean . . . in the years 1776– 1780.

Illus. map.
(In his The World. London, J. Stratford, 1810. Vol. 1, pp. 141–344.)
See also no. 335.

Copies: NPL:M(Q910.8/7A1).   337

1818 BINGLEY, *Rev.* William
[Cook.]

(In his Biographical conversations on the most eminent voyagers. London, 1818. pp. 239–348.)
See also nos. 339, 342.

Copies: NPL:R(MD3R36).   338

1818 BINGLEY, *Rev.* William
[Cook.]

(In his Biographical conversations on the most eminent voyagers. 2nd ed. London, Sharpe, 1818.)
See also nos. 338, 342.

Copies: ANL; QU.   339

[182–?] KELLY, Christopher
Captain James Cook's voyages.

Illus.
(In his Selection of voyages and travels. London, T. Kelly, [182–?]. pp. 207–374.)
See also no. 345.

Copies: NPL:R(MD7:P14).   340

1820 PRIOR, Samuel, *pseud.* (*John Galt*)
Captain Cook, 1768–(1780).
Illus.
(*In his* All the voyages round the world. London, Sir Richard Phillips, 1820. pp. 326–426.)
See also no. 343.
Copies: NPL:M(910.4/P); ANL.   341

1826 BINGLEY, *Rev.* William
[Cook.]
(*In his* Biographical conversations on the most eminent voyagers. 3rd ed. London, C. & J. Rivington, 1826. pp. 248–365.)
See also nos. 338–9.
Copies: NPL:M(A923.9/B).   342

1827 PRIOR, Samuel, *pseud.* (*John Galt*)
Captain Cook, 1768–(1780).
Illus.
(*In his* All the voyages round the world. New ed. London, Sir Richard Phillips, 1827. pp. 326–426.)
See also no. 341.
Copies: NPL:M(910.4/P); NPL:D(82/181).   343

1831 CAPTAIN COOK'S VOYAGES.
(*The Phrenological Journal*, vol. 7, no. 27, 1831. pp. 36–45. London, Phrenological Society.)
Copies: ANL.   344

1840 KELLY, Christopher
Captain James Cook's voyages.
Illus.
(*In his* Selection of voyages and travels. London, T. Kelly, 1840. pp. 207–374.)
See also no. 340.
Copies: NPL:M(910/55A1).   345

1843 JAMES COOK, 1768–1771, 1772–1775, 1776–1779. Precis de ses voyages; sa mort.
(*In* Voyages autour du monde, de 1484 a nos jours. 10e ed. Bruxelles, n.p., 1843. Vol. 2, pp. 76–92.)
Published anonymously.
Copies: NPL:M(910.8/39K2).   346

[1847] CAPTAIN COOK.
(*In* Ocean scenes; or, The Perils and beauties of the deep. New York, Leavitt & Allen, [1847]. pp. 113–38.)
Copies: NPL:M(910.4/0).   347

1850 FIRST VOYAGE and discoveries of Lieutenant Cook; (Captain Cook's second voyage), [and] (Captain Cook's third voyage).

Illus.
(*In* Sailings over the globe. London, John Cassell, 1850. pp. 35–79.)
Copies: NPL:M(910.8/25). 348

1857 EDWARDS, Bela Bates
James Cook.

Port.
(*In his* Biography of self-taught men. London, T. Nelson, 1857. pp. 1–31.)
Copies: NPL:M(920.8/1B1). 349

[1859] GOODRICH, Frank Boott
[Cook's voyages.]

(*In his* The Sea and her famous sailors. London, Hogg, [1859]. pp. 208–36.)
Abridged edition of the author's *Man upon the sea*, 1858, which was also published as *The History of the sea* (*see* no. 354), and *The Ocean's story*, 1873. *See also* no. 353.
Copies: NPL:M(910.9/3A1). 350

1860 COGGESHALL, George
[Captain Cook's voyages.]

(*In his* Historical sketch of commerce, etc. New York, Putnam, 1860. pp. 39–72.)
Copies: NPL:M(910.4/C). 351

1868 CAPTAIN COOK: his voyages and the places he visited. [Anon.] 1868.

(*In* [Various magazine articles relating to Australia: vol. 2].)
Copies: ANL. 352

[187–?] GOODRICH, Frank Boott
[Cook's voyages.]

(*In his* The Sea and her famous explorers. London, Gall & Inglis, [187–?]. pp. 206–36.)
Abridged edition of the author's *Man upon the sea*, 1858, which was also published as *The History of the sea* (*see* no. 354), and *The Ocean's story*, 1873. *See also* no. 350.
Copies: NPL:M(Bayldon). 353

[187–?] GOODRICH, Frank Boott
[Cook's voyages.]

Illus. ports.
(*In his* History of the sea. London, Hubbard Bros., [187–?]. pp. 461–511.)
Reprint of the author's *The Ocean's story*, 1873, which was first published 1858 as *Man upon the sea*. *See* nos. 350, 353 for abridged editions. *See also* no. 355.
Copies: NPL:R(S909.9A/157). 354

[187–?] GOODRICH, Frank Boott

[Cook's voyages.]

Illus. ports.

(*In his* The History of the sea. Guelph, Ontario, J. W. Lyon, [187–?]. pp. 461–511.)
Reprint of the author's *The Ocean's story*, 1873, which was first published 1858 as *Man upon the sea. See* nos. 350, 353 for abridged editions. *See also* no. 354.

Copies: NPL:M(910.9/2C1); Captain Cook's Landing Place Trust. 355

1873 BEETON, Samuel Orchart

Captain Cook and his discoveries.

(*In his* Beeton's famous voyages, brigand adventures. London, Ward, Lock, [1873]. pp. 143–200.)

Copies: NPL:M(910.8/40A1). 356

1874 TIELE, Pieter Anton

(James Cook, 1768–79.)

(*In his* De ontdekkingsreizen sedert de vijftiende eeuw. Leiden, S. C. van Doesburgh, 1874. pp. 215–36.)

Copies: NPL:M(910.9/T). 357

1877 COLENSO, *Rev.* William

Notes, chiefly historical, on the ancient dog of the New Zealanders; [with bibl.] Wellington, N.Z., Lyon and Blair, pr., [1878].

pp. 135–55.

Extract from New Zealand Institute—*Transactions* vol. 10, 1877. Bound with the author's *On the day in which Captain Cook took . . . possession of New Zealand.*

Copies: NPL:M(980:Co2/C1A1); NPL:D(9/82); NPL:R(DS506/8). 358

1878 BLAIR, David

Cook's discoveries.

Facs. port.

(*In his* History of Australasia. Glasgow, McGready, Thomson and Niven, 1878. pp. 38–83.)

See also no. 360.

Copies: NPL:M(Q990/B); NPL:R(MB1U1). 359

1879 BLAIR, David

Cook's discoveries.

Facs. port.

(*In his* History of Australasia. Glasgow, McGready, Thomson and Niven, 1879. pp. 38–83.)

See also no. 359.

Copies: NPL:M(Q990/B); NPL:D (Q87/28). 360

1879 ROSMEAD, Hercules George Robert Robinson, *1st Baron*

Unveiling of statue of Captain Cook, Feb. 25, 1879.

(*In his* Speeches. Sydney, Gibbs, Shallard, 1879. pp. 214–30.)

Copies: NPL:M(308); QParl. 361

[1880?] VERNE, Jules
[Voyages of Captain Cook.]
Illus. maps.
(*In his* Les Grands navigateurs du XVIIIe siècle. Paris, Bibliothèque d'éducation et de récréation, [1880?]. pp. 108–226.)
Histoire générale des grands voyages et de grands voyageurs.
See also nos. 268, 278.
Copies: ANL.   362

1884 MARKAHM, *Sir* Clements Robert
[James Cook.]
(*In his* The Sea fathers: a series of lives of great navigators of former times. London, Cassell, 1884. pp. 192–7.)
See also no. 366 entitled *Famous sailors of former times.*
Copies: NPL:M(926.56/2A1).   363

1885 HUNTINGTON, Henry William Hemsworth
Captain Cook's discoveries in Australasia [and] (Subsequent visits of Cook, Furneaux, etc.)
(*In his* History of Australasia. n.p., 1885. pp. 19–49.)
Copies: NPL:M(Q990.1/H); NPL:R(Q990.1/1).   364

1886 GARRAN, Andrew
Captain Cook; [with port. and autograph].
Illus. map.
(*In his* Picturesque Atlas of Australasia. Sydney, Picturesque Atlas Pub. Co., 1886. Vol. 1, frontisp. and pp. 7–14.)
Copies: NPL:M(F990/G); NPL:R(F990A/6).   365

1886 MARKHAM, *Sir* Clements Robert
[James Cook.]
(*In his* Famous sailors of former times. 2nd ed. London, Cassell, 1886. pp. 192–7.)
See also no. 363 entitled *The Sea fathers.*
Copies: NPL:M(926.56/2B1).   366

1888 HYDROGRAPHY. No. IV–VI, The works of the late Capt. James Cook, R.N.
(*United Service Journal*, pt. 1, 1888, pp. 726–9; pt. 2, pp. 88–94, 209–16.)
Copies: NPL:R(355.05/U).   367

1888 MÉTENIER, J.
Episodes remarquables des trois voyages du Capitaine Cook.
(*In his* Taïti. Tours, Catteer, 1888. pp. 107–220.)
Copies: NPL:M(Q989.5/M).   368

1890 SHERRIN, Richard A. A.

Cook's first voyage [and] (Cook's visits on his second and third voyages).
Illus.
(*In* Early history of New Zealand . . . by R. A. A. Sherrin . . . [and] J. H. Wallace. Ed. by T. W. Leys. Auckland, H. Brett, 1890. pp. 14–57.)
Copies: NPL:M(Q997/12A1); NPL:R(Q997/2).   369

1893 RAINAUD, Armand

La Dernière controverse au sujet du continent austral: A. Dalrymple et J. Cook.
(*In his* Le Continent austral: hypothèses et découvertes. Paris, Armand Colin, 1893. pp. 437–74.)
See also no. 480.
Copies: NPL:M(Q980/29A1).   370

1895 CAPTAIN COOK; [with port.]

(*In* Columbus and Cook: the story of their lives, voyages and discoveries. London, W. & R. Chambers, 1895. pp. 88–152).
Copies: NPL:M(910.4/120A1).   371

1895 GAUNT, Mary

Captain Cook in New Zealand.
Illus. map, port.
(*In* Cassell & Co.—Pictorial New Zealand. London, Cassell, 1895. pp. 285–93.)
Copies: NPL:M(987/C).   372

1895 IN THE WAKE OF CAPTAIN COOK.

(*Macmillan's Magazine*, Feb. 1895, pp. 294–301.)
Copies: NPL:R(S050/M167); QParl.   373

[1896] SAUNDERS, Alfred

Captain Cook and his journal, etc.; [with port.]
(*In his* History of New Zealand. Christchurch, W. & T., [1896]. Vol. 1, pp. 1–47.)
Copies: NPL:M(997/S); NPL:D(89/188).   374

1898 STORY, Alfred Thomas

[Voyages of Captain Cook; with port.]
Illus.
(*In his* Building of the Empire. London, Chapman & Hall, 1898. pp. 168–74.)
Copies: NPL:M(942/S); NPL:R(S909/61).   375

1899 JACOBS, Joseph

Australia and the South Seas: Tasman and Cook.
Map.
(*In his* The Story of geographical discovery. London, Newnes, 1899. pp. 156–70.)
Later editions have title *Geographical discovery, see* nos. 383, 385.
Copies: NPL:M(910.9/J); NPL:R(S909.9A/15).   376

1899 MARKHAM, *Sir* Clements Robert
Voyages and discoveries, 1763–1792; [with bibl.]
Illus.
(*In* Clowes, William Laird—Royal Navy. London, Sampson Low, Marston, 1899. Vol. 4, pp. 117–49.)
Copies: NPL:M(Bayldon); NPL:R(Q359.0942/13).   377

[1899?] YATES, Matthew Thompson
Captain Cook.
Illus. port.
(*In his* Graphic stories of sailors. London, Collins' Clear-Type Press, [1899?] pp. 181–9.)
Copies: NPL:M(923.9/5B1).   378

1900 BANCROFT, Hubert Howe
Notable voyages into the Pacific.
(*In his* New Pacific. London, Kegan Paul, Trench, Trübner, 1900. pp. 616–59.)
New York edition, 1900, filed at NPL:R(S327.9/17). *See also* no. 391.
Copies: NPL:M(980/B).   379

1900 MORRIS, Edward Ellis
On the tracks of Captain Cook.
(New Zealand Institute—*Transactions*, 1900. Vol. 33, pp. 499–514.)
Copies: NPL:M(506/N); NPL:D(90/197); NPL:R(DS506/8).   380

1902 DUNCAN, Russell
Following the tracks of Captain Cook [in New Zealand; with plates].
(New Zealand Institute—*Transactions*, 1902, pp. 32–45.)
Copies: NPL:M(506/N); NPL:D(9/107); NPL:R(DS506/8).   381

1902 HASZARD, H. D. M.
Foot-tracks of Captain Cook [in the vicinity of Mercury Bay, N.Z.; with bibl. and plates].
(New Zealand Institute—*Transactions*, 1902, pp. 24–32.)
Copies: NPL:M(506/N); NPL:D(9/107); NPL:R(DS506/8).   382

1909 JACOBS, Joseph
Australia and the South Seas: Tasman and Cook.
Map.
(*In his* Geographical discovery. London, Hodder and Stoughton, 1909. pp. 156–70.)
Previously published with title *The Story of geographical discovery, see* no. 376. *See also* no. 385.
Copies: NPL:M(910.9/J).   383

1909 McNab, Robert
Cook explores, 1770 . . . Cook's last visit [1777].
(*In his* Murihiku: a history. Wellington, N.Z., Whitcombe & Tombs, 1909. pp. 13–76.)
Copies: NPL:M(997.9/M); NPL:D(90/182); NPL:R(DS997/16).   384

[191–?] JACOBS, Joseph

Australia and the South Seas: Tasman and Cook.

Map.

(*In his* Geographical discovery. Rev. ed. London, Hodder and Stoughton, [191–?]. pp. 156–70.)

Previously published with title *The Story of geographical discovery, see* no. 376. *See also* no. 383.

Copies: NPL:M(Bayldon).   **385**

1910 ADRIAN, F. G.

What do we owe to Captain Cook?

(*Lone Hand*, April, 1910. pp. 626–8.)

Copies: NPL:M(059/L); NPL:D(90/376); NPL:R(DQ050/L847).   **386**

[1910?] GILLIES, William

Cook and the discovery of Australasia.

Maps, port.

(*In his* Stories in English history. Melbourne, Whitcombe and Tombs, [1910?] pp. 214–27.)

Copies: NPL:M(942/G).   **387**

[1910?] LONG, Charles Richard

Captain James Cook.

Illus. map, port.

(*In his* Stories of Australian exploration. Melbourne, Whitcombe & Tombs, [1910?]. pp. 39–59.)

(*Austral history readers.*)

A revised edition was published in 1913, *see* no. 395.

Copies: NPL:M(980/L).   **388**

[1910?] MARSHALL, Patrick

Discovery and exploration of New Zealand.

Maps.

(*In his* The Geography of New Zealand. Christchurch, Whitcombe & Tombs, [1910?]. pp. 23–30.)

Copies: NPL:M(987/M).   **389**

1910 *The Register*, Adelaide

Foundation Day, Australia's birthday: what we owe to Captain Cook.

Illus. port.

(*The Register*, Adel., Jan. 22, 1910. p. 6.)

Copies: NPL:M(MDQ079/79); NPL:R(F079/R337).   **390**

1912 BANCROFT, Hubert Howe
Notable voyages into the Pacific.
(*In his* New Pacific. New York, Bancroft Co., 1912. pp. 436–79.)
See also no. 379.
Copies: NPL:M(980/B). 391

1912 HEAWOOD, Edward
A History of geographical discovery in the seventeenth and eighteenth centuries, by E. Heawood. Cambridge, U.P., 1912.
Facs. illus. maps, ports. pp.xii, 475.
(*Cambridge geographical series*.)
See also no. 477.
Copies: NPL:M(910.9/19A1); NPL:D(91/455); NPL:R(S909.9A/3). 392

1913 KELTIE, John Scott
James Cook and his successors.
(*In his* History of geography, by J. S. Keltie and O. J. R. Howarth. London, Watts & Co., 1913. pp. 87–9.)
Copies: NPL:M(910.9/K). 393

1913 KER, Alfred J.
Heroes of exploration, by A. J. Ker and C. H. Cleaver. London, Blackie, 1913.
Illus. maps, ports. pp. 208.
Includes chapters on Captain Cook.
Copies: NPL:M(910.8/37A1). 394

[1913] LONG, Charles Richard
Captain James Cook.
Illus. map, port.
(*In his* Stories of Australian exploration. Rev. ed. [1913]. pp. 36–54.)
See also no. 388.
Copies: NPL:M(980/L). 395

[192–?] DIXSON, *Sir* William
'Notes re Captain Cook.' Compiled by Sir William Dixson.
pp. 60.
With index. Includes copies of extracts from periodicals and manuscripts, of items concerning Cook and his associates, in particular accounts of Cook's death and the introduction of venereal disease to the Pacific Islands. Several press cuttings inserted.
Copies: NPL:D(WD3). 396

1923 ANDERSON, G. H.
1757–1775. Early life and first voyage with Cook, [and] 1776–1780. Second voyage with Cook.
(*In his* Vancouver and his great voyage. King's Lynn, Thew & Son, pr., 1923. Chapter 1–2).
Copies: NPL:M(923.9/V223/1A1); NPL:D(92/817); ANL. 397

1924 DENTON, V. L.
Captain James Cook, the great circumnavigator.
(*In his* The Far West Coast [of America]. Toronto, Dent, 1924. pp. 47–160.)
Copies: NPL:M(910.4/D); VSL.   398

1925 COOK, James, 1728–79.
(*In* The Australian encyclopaedia; ed. by A. W. Jose and H. J. Carter. Sydney, A.&R., 1925. Vol. 1, pp. 304–9.)
Copies: NPL:M(Q039/A Ref Shelf); NPL:D(Q92/44); NPL:R(Q990.1A/21).   399

1925 DORLING, Henry Taprell
Captain James Cook.
Illus. map.
(*In his* Sea venturers of Britain, by Taffrail, pseud. [i.e. H. Taprell Dorling.] Illus. by C. King. London, Collins, 1925. pp. 176–207.)
See also nos. 409, 412.
Copies: NPL:M(Nichols); NPL:R(S909.8A/10).   400

[1925?] WHALL, W. B.
Some eighteenth century navigators.
Port.
(*In his* The Romance of navigation, by W. B. Whall . . . ed. by F. E. McMurtie. London, Sampson Low, [1925?]. pp. 125–6.)
Copies: NPL:M(656.509/5A1).   401

1925 WILLIAMSON, James Alexander
Captain James Cook, the pioneer of the Pacific Ocean.
Illus. maps, port.
(*In his* Builders of the Empire. Oxford, Clarendon Press, 1925. Chapter 4, pt. 2.)
See also no. 440.
Copies: ANL.   402

[1926] COAD, Nellie Euphemia
Captain Cook, 1728–79.
Illus. map, port.
(*In her* History of the Pacific. Wellington, N.Z. Book Depot, [1926]. pp. 53–64.)
Copies: NPL:M(990/C).   403

1927 HILDEBRAND, J. R.
Columbus of the Pacific.
Illus.
(*National Geographic Magazine*, Jan. 1927, pp. 84–132.)
Copies: NPL:R(S050/N277).   404

1928 BAYLDON, Francis Joseph
Captain Cook.
Illus.
(*Navy League Journal* Dec. 1928, pp. 24–7.)
Copies: NPL:M(359.06/N); NPL:D(92/1555).   405

1928 GIBLIN, Robert W.
[Captain Cook's first, second and last voyages.]
Maps.
(*In his* Early history of Tasmania. Melbourne, U.P., 1928. [Vol. 1] pp. 25–34, 43–70.)
Copies: NPL:M(996/G); NPL:R(DS996/5); ANL.   406

1929 BRENDON, John Adams
James Cook.
Illus. maps, port.
(*In his* Great navigators & discoverers. London, Harrap, 1919. pp. 214–26.)
See also no. 483.
Copies: NPL:M(923.9/B).   407

1929 CAPTAIN JAMES COOK, R.N., the great navigator and discoverer.
Illus. one in colour, map, pp. 70–88.
Extracted from *Smith's Dock Journal* vol. 10, no. 73, Ap. 1929. The concluding article.
Copies: NPL:D(Q92/138).   408

1929 DORLING, Henry Taprell
Captain James Cook.
(*In his* Sea venturers of Britain, by Taffrail, pseud., [i.e. H. Taprell Dorling]. London, P. Allan, 1929. pp. 167–94.)
See also nos. 400, 412.
Copies: NPL:M(Nichols).   409

1929 DOUGLAS, Henry Percy
Cook as an hydrographical surveyor; [with discussion].
(*Geographical Journal*, London, vol. 73, Feb. 1929, pp. 110–16, 119–20.)
Copies: NPL:M(980:Col/G1A1); NPL:R(DS909.6A/2).   410

1929 DYSON, *Sir* Frank
Captain Cook as an astronomer; [with discussion].
(*Geographical Journal*, London, vol. 73, Feb. 1929, pp. 116–22.)
Copies: NPL:M(980:Col/G1A1); NPL:R(DS909.6A/2).   411

[193–?] DORLING, Henry Taprell
Captain James Cook.
(*In his* Sea venturers, [by] Taffrail, pseud. . . . H. Taprell Dorling. London, Collins Clear-Type Press, [193–?]. pp. 177–208.)
See also no. 400, 409.
Copies: NPL:M(923.9/3C1).   412

1930 GODWIN, George Stanley
With Cook in the Antarctic, 1771-1775; with Cook to Hawaii, 1776–1780; [and] Thomas Edgar's Story [of Cook's death] Feb. 14–22, 1779.
(*In his* Vancouver. London, Philip Allan, 1930. pp. 4–19, 289–96.)
Copies: NPL:M(923.9/V223/2A1); NPL:D(93/842); NPL:R(S909.8A/V223); ANL. 413

[1930] JACKSON, George Gibbard
Discoveries of Captain Cook [and] (Last voyage).
(*In his* Romance of exploration. London, Sampson, Low, Marston, [1930]. pp. 156–81.)
Copies: NPL:M(910.8/J).   414

1931 ENGLISH, Thomas H.
[Cook's career and the vessels he sailed in.]
(*In his* Introduction to the collecting and history of Whitby prints. n.p., Horne & Son, 1931. Vol. 2, S.12.)
Copies: NPL:M(Q942.7/E); NPL:D(Q93/119).   415

1931 MANWARING, George Ernest
Round the world with Captain Cook; (With Captain Cook in southern seas; [and] Cook's last voyage).
Illus.
(*In his* My friend the admiral: the life, letters and journal of . . . James Burney. London, G. Routledge, 1931. pp. 15–47, 64–154.)
Copies: NPL:M(A923.9/B); NPL:D(93/509); NPL:R(920/B965.4/1); ANL.   416

1932 ANDERSEN, Johannes Carl
Observations during Cook's first . . . second [and] third voyages.
Illus.
(Polynesian Society—*Memoir* no. 10.)
Published in the Polynesian Society journal, vol. 41, Mar. 1932, Supp. pp. 1–30. Reprinted in 1934 in the author's *Maori music with its Polynesian background*, for which *see* no. 423.
Copies: NPL:M(Q572.9/P); ANL.   417

1932 DIXSON, *Sir* William
Notes on the crews on Captain Cook's voyages.
(Royal Australian Historical Society—*Journal and Proceedings*, vol. 18, 1932. pp. 153–5.)
Copies: NPL:M(991/R,Ref.Books); NPL:D(93/129); NPL:R(S991.06/1A,Ref.Books).
                                                                 418

1932 WOOD, *Rev.* Alfred Harold
Cook's first visit to Tonga, 1773 . . . 2nd visit . . . 1774 [and] 3rd . . . visit, 1777.
(*In his* History and geography of Tonga. Nuku'alofa, Tonga, Govt. Pr., 1932. pp. 18–23.)
Copies: NPL:M(999.3/W).   419

1933 BAYLDON, Francis Joseph
Remarks on criticisms of explorers in the Pacific Ocean.
(Royal Australian Historical Society—*Journal and proceedings*, vol. 19, 1933, pp. 158–174.)
Copies: NPL:M(991/R,Ref Books); NPL:D(9/69); NPL:R(S991.06/1,Ref Books). 420

1933 HENDERSON, George Cockburn
The Discoverers of the Fiji Islands: Tasman, Cook, Bligh, Wilson, Bellingshausen. [With bibl.] London, John Murray, 1933.
Illus. maps, ports. pp. xviii, 324.
See also no. 431.
Copies: NPL:M(988.8/13A1); ANL. 421

1933 ROSE, John Holland
Discovery and exploration [Pt.] 1, Captain Cook. [With bibl. notes.]
(*In his* Cambridge history of the British Empire. Vol. 7, pt. 2, New Zealand. Cambridge, U.P., 1933. pp. 22–30.)
Copies: NPL:M(997/7); NPL:R(DS909/221); ANL. 422

1934 ANDERSEN, Johannes Carl
Observations during Cook's voyages.
Illus.
(*In his* Maori music with its Polynesian background. New Plymouth, N.Z., Avery, pr., 1934. pp. 1–78.)
Polynesian Society—Memoir, no. 10.
See also no. 417.
Copies: NPL:M(572.997/A); NPL:D(93/58); ANL. 423

1934 BEAGLEHOLE, John Cawte
Cook . . . 1768–1780.
Map.
(*In his* Exploration of the Pacific. London, A. & C. Black, 1934. pp. 274–381.)
See also nos. 444, 481.
Copies: NPL:M(980/16A1); NPL:D(93/299,Ref Bks); NPL:R(DS990A/151); ANL; VMoU. 424

1934 SYKES, *Sir* Percy Molesworth
Captain Cook explores the Pacific Ocean.
Illus.
(*In his* A History of exploration. London, Routledge, 1934. pp. 171–80.)
See also no. 448.
Copies: NPL:R(S909.9A/28); ANL. 425

[1935] OUTHWAITE, Leonard
Captain James Cook, 1728–1779.
Illus.
(*In his* Unrolling the map. London, Constable, [1935]. pp. 229–31, 308–9.)
See also no. 427.
Copies: NPL:M(Q910.9/0). 426

[1935] OUTHWAITE, Leonard
Captain James Cook, 1728–1779.
Illus.
(*In his* Unrolling the map. New York, Reynal & Hitchcock, [1935]. pp. 229–31, 308–9.)
See also no. 426.
Copies: NPL:R(Q909.8A/11).   427

[1935] ROSE, John Holland
Early man in the Pacific, etc.; [with bibl. notes].
Illus. maps, port.
(*In his* Man and the sea. Cambridge, W. Heffer, [1935]. pp. 161–218.)
Copies: NPL:M(910.4/R); NPL:R(S909.8A/32).   428

1935 WATSON, Elspeth J. Boag-
Captain James Cook.
Map.
(*In* Beyond the sunset. By E. J. Boag-Watson and J. I. Carruthers. London, O.U.P., 1935.
pp. 113–19.)
Copies: NPL:M(910.9/W).   429

1936 WOLLSCHLAEGER, Alfred (*A. E. Johann, pseud.*)
James Cook.
Map.
(*In his* Känguruhs, Kopra und Korallen. Berlin, Im Verlag Ullstein, 1936. pp. 222–42.)
See also no. 433.
Copies: NPL:M(980/144A1).   430

1937 HENDERSON, George Cockburn
The Discoverers of the Fiji Islands: Tasman, Cook, Bligh, Wilson,
Bellingshausen. [With bibl.] London, John Murray, 1937.
Facs. illus. map, ports. pp. 342.
See also no. 421.
Copies: NPL:M(988.8/13B1); NPL:R(DS998.8/5).   431

[1937] TAYLOR, Alan Carey
[Cook.]
(*In his* Le Président de Brosses et l'Australie. Paris, Ancienne Librairie Furne, Boivin,
[1937]. pp. 162–70.)
Copies: NPL:M(980/T); NPL:D(93/93).   432

1937 WOLLSCHLAEGER, Alfred (*A. E. Johann, pseud.*)
James Cook; [with bibl. notes; map].
(*In his* Känguruhs, Kopra och Korallen. Stockholm, Lindquists, 1937. pp. 247–68.)
See also no. 430.
Copies: NPL:M(980/144B1).   433

[1938] LA RONCIÈRE, Charles de
Cook, 1769–1779.

Illus. maps, port.
(*In his* Histoire de la découverte de la terre. Paris, Lib. Larousse, [1938]. pp. 200–4.)
Copies: NPL:M(Q910/L); NPL:R(Q909.9A/20).   434

1939 BEAGLEHOLE, John Cawte
James Cook.

Illus. map.
(*In his* The Discovery of New Zealand. Wellington, N.Z., Dept. of Internal Affairs, 1939. pp. 38–103.)
See also no. 467.
Copies: NPL:M(987/16A1); NPL:D(93/225); ANL; QU.   435

[1939] WILSON, James G.
Captain Cook.

(Wilson, J. G., *and others.* History of Hawke's Bay. Dunedin, A. H. and A. W. Reed, [1939]. pp. 115–25.)
Copies: NPL:M(997.5/W).   436

[1940] RIESENBERG, Felix
Captain James Cook, explorer extraordinary.

Maps.
(*In his* Pacific Ocean. New York, Whittlesey House, [1940]. pp. 183–225.)
Copies: NPL:M(910.9/R); NPL:D(94/257); NPL:R(990/17).   437

1940 VAN LOON, Hendrik Willem
Captain James Cook, R.N.

(*In his* The Story of the Pacific. New ed. London, Harrap, 1949. pp. 245–310.)
See also no. 449.
Copies: NPL:M(980/28F1).   438

1942 WILLIAMSON, James Alexander
Captain James Cook: the pioneer of the Pacific Ocean.

Illus. maps, port.
(*In his* Builders of the Empire. Oxford, Clarendon Press, 1942. pp. 125–41.)
Reprint of 1925 edition, no. 402.
Copies: NPL:M(923.9/W).   439

1944 BUCK, *Sir* Peter Henry
Cook's discovery of the Hawaiian Islands; [with bibl.].

(Bernice Pauahi Bishop Museum, Honolulu—*Report of the director*, 1944. pp. 26–44.)
Copies: NPL:M(Q507/B).   440

1944 WROTH, Lawrence Counselman
Captain Cook and the Terra Australis; [and] A last word on Captain Cook.

(*In his* Early cartography of the Pacific. New York, 1944. pp. 176–9, 227–30.)
(Bibliographical Society of America—*Papers*, vol. 38, no. 2.)
Copies: NPL:M(980/W).   441

1945 BUCK, *Sir* Peter Henry
Cook; [with bibl.]

(*In his* An Introduction to Polynesian anthropology. Honolulu, 1945. Bernice Pauahi Bishop Museum—*Bulletin*, no. 187, pp. 23–6.)
Copies: NPL:M(989/B).   442

1945 GREAT BRITAIN—*Admiralty*—Naval Intelligence Division
Achievement of Cook.

Map.
(*In its* Pacific Islands. London, H.M.S.O., 1945. Vol. 1, pp. 254–61.)
Copies: NPL:M(988/G,Ref.Books).   443

1947 BEAGLEHOLE, John Cawte
Cook . . . 1768–1780.

Map.
(*In his* Exploration of the Pacific. 2nd ed. London, A. & C. Black, 1947. pp. 274–381.)
See also nos. 424, 481.
Copies: NPL:M(980/16B1).   444

1947 STEFANSSON, Vilhjalmur
Discovery of Australia [and] The Great Southland.

(*In his* Great adventures and explorations from the earliest times to the present as told by the explorers themselves; ed. . . . by V. Stefansson [and] . . . O. R. Wilcox . . . Maps designed by R. E. Harrison. [With bibl.] New York, Dial Press, 1947. pp. 658–713.)
Copies: NPL:M(910.9/S); NPL:R(E910.9).   445

1948 KUYKENDALL, Ralph Simpson
Captain Cook, the discoverer.

(*In* Hawaii: a history. From Polynesian kingdom to American commonwealth, by R. S. Kuykendall and A. Grove Day. New York, Prentice Hall, 1948. pp. 13–19.)
See also no. 468.
Copies: NPL:M(999.6/19A1); NPL:R(999.6/10).   446

1949 HOLMES, *Sir* Maurice
Captain James Cook, R.N., F.R.S.

Illus. in colour, port.
(*Endeavour* vol. 8, pp. 11–17, Jan. 1949.)
Copies: NPL:R(Q506/38).   447

1949 SYKES, *Sir* Percy Molesworth
Captain Cook explores the Pacific Ocean.

Illus. map.
(*In his* A History of exploration from the earliest times to the present day. 3rd ed. London, Routledge & Kegan Paul, 1949. pp. 171–80.)
See also no. 425.

Copies: NPL:M(910.9/4C1).   448

1949 VAN LOON, Hendrik Willem
Captain James Cook, R.N.

(*In his* The Story of the Pacific. London, Harrap, 1949. pp. 245–310.)
Reprint of no. 438.

Copies: NPL:M(980/28A1).   449

1952 HARLOW, Vincent Todd
James Cook and the Spanish reactions.

Maps.
(*In his* Founding of the second British Empire, 1763–1793. London, Longmans Green, 1952. Vol. 1, pp. 42–55.)

Copies: NPL:R(325.342/51).   450

1955 BUTCHER, T. K.
Captain Cook's voyages in the South Seas.

(*In his* Asia and Australasia. London, Dobson, [1955]. pp. 83–98.)
Written for children.

Copies: NPL:M(910.8/B).   451

1956 LEITHEAUSER, Joachim Gustave
The Discovery of the oceans.

Illus.
(*In his* Worlds beyond the horizon. London, Allen & Unwin, 1956. pp. 131–40.)

Copies: NPL:M(910.4/86B1); NPL:R(910.9/3).   452

1957 NATIONAL TRUST OF AUSTRALIA, Victoria
The Voyages of Captain James Cook.

(*In its* The History of Cook's cottage; and, Voyages of Captain James Cook. Compiled by the National Trust of Australia, Victoria, by direction of the Parks, Gardens and Recreations Committee of the Melbourne City Council. Melbourne, 1957. pp. 18–20.)

Copies: NPL:M(923.9/C771.2/23A1).   453

1958 APPLETON, Marjorie Irene
Captain Cook comes to New Zealand; Captain Cook in New Zealand; Places named by Cook; [and] James Lind and James Cook find the cure for scurvy.

Illus. port.
(*In her* They came to New Zealand. London, Methuen, 1958. pp. 89–95; 96–139; 281; 283–5.)

Copies: NPL:M(997/2).   454

1958 FREUCHEN, Peter
All for science.

(*In his* Peter Freuchen's Book of the seven seas. London, Cape, 1958. pp. 255–64.)
Copies: NPL:M(910/12A1).   455

1958 SCHOLES, William Arthur
Columbus of the south.

Illus. port.
(*In his* The Sixth continent. London, Allen & Unwin, 1958. pp. 26–35.)
Copies: NPL:M(990.1/16A1).   456

1958 WARNER, Oliver Martin Wilson
Cook.

(*In his* English maritime writing. Pub. for the British Council and National Book League.
Longmans, Green, 1958. pp. 29–31.)
British Book News Bibl. series of supps., no. 105.
Copies: NPL:M(910.4/74A1); NPL:R(S909.8A/104).   457

1959 BODI, Leslie
Georg Forster: the Pacific expert of eighteenth-century Germany. [With
bibl. notes.]

(*Historical Studies*, Melbourne. Vol. 8: pp. 345–63, May 1959.)
Copies: NPL:M(990.05/1).   458

1959 EMMANUEL, Marthe
La Fin de deux chimères. La Pérouse: complément aux voyages de Cook.

(*In her* La France et l'exploration polaire. Paris, Nouvelles Editions Latines, 1959.
pp. 347–83.)
Copies: NPL:M(989/3A1).   459

1959 FORCE, Roland W.
The Varied peoples of thousands of Pacific Isles.

(Chicago Natural History Museum—*Bulletin*, vol. 30. pp. 6, 8, May, 1959.)
Copies: NPL:M(Q570.7/2).   460

1959 FORSYTH, John Walter
Latouche-Tréville and his proposal to explore the south coast of New
Holland. [With two letters from Cook to Latouche, 6 Sept. 1775 and
10 Feb. 1776, and bibl. notes.]

(*Mariner's Mirror* vol. 45, pp. 115–29, May, 1959.)
Copies: NPL:D(9/72); NPL:R(DS656.506/7).   461

1959 SPENCER, Albert Henry
Captain James Cook, F.R.S.

(*In his* The Hill of Content. Sydney, A. & R., 1959. pp. 135–40.)
Copies: NPL:M(655.56/1A1); NPL:D(95/53); NPL:R(655.56/14).   462

1960 ANDERSON, Bern
Cook's first and second voyages, [and] Cook's third voyage.
(*In his* Surveyor of the sea: the life of Captain George Vancouver. Seattle, Washington U.P., 1960. pp. 7–18.)
Copies: NPL:M(923.9/V223/3A1); NPL:R(N920/V223/1).   463

1960 AUROUSSEAU, Marcel
Cook's voyages; [with bibl.].
(Geographical Society of New South Wales—*Paper*, Oct. 1960. pp. 10.)
Copies: NPL:M(Q981.06/4); ANL.   464

1960 FORCE, Roland W.
Discovery of Pacific Isles: it all started with spice and ended with science.
Illus.
(Chicago Natural History Museum—*Bulletin*, vol. 31, pp. 4–5, Mar. 1960.)
Copies: NPL:M(Q570.7/2).   465

1960 MARSHALL, James Stirrat
Captain James Cook.
Port.
(*In* Pacific voyages: selections from *Scots Magazine*, 1771–1808. Compiled and annotated by J. S. Marshall and C. Marshall. Portland, Oreg., Binfords & Mort, 1960. pp. 1–31.)
Copies: NPL:M(980/27A1).   466

1961 BEAGLEHOLE, John Cawte
James Cook.
Illus. map.
(*In his* The Discovery of New Zealand. 2nd ed. London, O.U.P., 1961. pp. 24–85.)
See also no. 435.
Copies: NPL:M(987/16B1); NPL:R(919.31/1).   467

1961 KUYKENDALL, Ralph Simpson
Captain Cook, the discoverer.
(*In* Hawaii: a history. From Polynesian kingdom to American commonwealth, by R. S. Kuykendall and A. Grove Day. New York, Prentice Hall, 1961. pp. 13–19.)
See also no. 446.
Copies: NPL:M(999.6/19B1); NPL:R(E999.6).   468

1961 WARNER, Oliver Martin Wilson
Cook.
Port.
(*In his* Great seamen. London, Bell, 1961. pp. 82–115.)
Copies: NPL:M(926.56/1A1); NPL:R(920/1196).   469

1961 WARNER, Oliver Martin Wilson
New light on Captain Cook's discoveries; [with port.].
(*The Listener*, Sept. 18, 1961.)
Copies: NPL:R(NQ384.5406/2).   470

1962 DEACON, George Edward Raven
Captain James Cook in search of a continent; [with illus., some in colour, and map and portrait in colour].
(*In his* Oceans: an atlas history of man's exploration of the deep. 1962. pp. 36–45.)
Copies: NPL:R(NQ551.46/4).   471

1962 GROSSECK, Joyce, *Mrs*
Captain James Cook, 1728–1779.
Illus. map, port.
(*In his* Great explorers, [by] J. Grosseck [and] E. Attwood. Grand Rapids, Mich., Fideler, 1962. pp. 110–20.)
Written for children.
Copies: NPL:M(Q910.9/4B1).   472

1962 VILLIERS, Alan John
Captain Cook and the seagoing clock; [with illus. port. in colour].
(*In his* Men, ships and the sea. Washington, National Geographic Society, 1962. pp. 154–9.)
Copies: NPL:M(Q623.82/1A1); NPL:R(NQ910.45/1).   473

1964 KNIGHT, Frank
Captain Cook and the men of science [and] (Remarkable occurrences on board H.M.S. *Endeavour*).
Illus.
(*In his* Stories of famous explorers by sea. London, Oliver & Boyd, 1964. pp. 80–100.)
Copies: NPL:M(910.9/18A1).   474

1965 CAMERON, Ian
Venus, sauerkraut and Yorkshire grit: James Cook delineates the Pacific, 1768–71.
Illus. maps, port.
(*In his* Lodestone and evening star. London, Hodder & Stoughton, 1965. pp. 174–99.)
Copies: NPL:M(910.9/15A1); NPL:R(E910.4/Cam).   475

1965 DODGE, Ernest Stanley
[Captain James Cook.]
(*In his* New England and the South Seas. Cambridge, Mass., Harvard U.P., 1965.)
Copies: NPL:M(999/5A1).   476

1965 HEAWOOD, Edward

A History of geographical discovery in the seventeenth and eighteenth centuries. New York, Octagon Books, 1965.

Facs. illus. maps, ports. pp. xii, 475.
See also no. 392.

Copies: NPL:M(910.9/19B1). 477

1965 RABLING, Harold

A New era dawns.

Illus.
(*In his* Pioneers of the Pacific: the story of the South Seas. Sydney, A. & R., 1965. pp. 38–54.)
For young readers. Also published under title *The Story of the Pacific. See* no. 479.

Copies: NPL:M(999/4B1). 478

1965 RABLING, Harold

A New era dawns.

Illus.
(*In his* The Story of the Pacific. New York, Norton, 1965. pp. 58–79.)
For young readers. Also published under title *Pioneers of the South Seas. See* no. 478.

Copies: NPL:M(999/4A1). 479

1965 RAINAUD, Armand

La Dernière controverse au sujet du continent austral: A. Dalrymple et J. Cook.

(*In his* Le Continent austral: hypothèses et découvertes. Amsterdam, Meridian Pub. Co., 1965. pp. 437–74.)
See also no. 370.

Copies: NPL:M(980/146A1). 480

1966 BEAGLEHOLE, John Cawte

Cook . . . 1768–1780.

Map.
(*In his* Exploration of the Pacific. 3rd ed. London, A. & C. Black, 1966. pp. 229–324.)
See also nos. 424, 444.

Copies: NPL:M(980/16C1); NPL:R(919/11). 481

1966 SVET, Iakov Mikhailovich

Kuk: [an account of his voyages].

Illus. map, port.
(*In his* Istoriia otkrytiia i issledovaniia Avstralii i Okeanii. Moskva, Mysl', 1966. pp. 160–89.)
Transliterated title.

Copies: NPL:M(980.1/258A1). 482

1967 BRENDON, John Adams
James Cook.

Illus. map, port.
(*In his* Great navigators & discoverers. Freeport, N.Y., Books for Libraries Press, 1967. pp. 214–26.)
See also no. 407.
Copies: NPL:R(910.092/2).   483

1967 RITCHIE, George Stephen
The Admiralty chart: British naval hydrography in the nineteenth century. [With bibl.] London, Hollis & Carter, 1967.

Facs. illus. maps, ports. pp. [x], 388.
Copies: NPL:M(526.99/1A1); NPL:R(N526.99/2).   484

1968 THE EXTRAORDINARY EXPLORATIONS of Capt. James Cook, during which he discovered New South Wales. [With] (An appraisal of his voyages . . . by . . . Manning Clark).
Illus. ports.
(*The Australian* Aug. 17–24, 1968, *various pp.*)
Copies: NPL:M(NA111); NPL:R(F079/A938); ANL.   485

1968 LANGDON, Robert
Captain Cook's debt to Tahiti and the Tahitians.
Illus. port.
(*P.L.A. Monthly* vol.43, Aug. 1968, pp.305–10.)
Copies: NPL:R(N387.129421/2); ANL.   486

1968 LOCKETT, Alison
That untravell'd world, pt. 1–2.

Facs. illus. maps, ports.
(*P.L.A.Monthly* vol.43, July–Aug.1968, pp.244–7, 264–70.)
Copies: NPL:R(N387.129421/2); ANL.   487

1968 MOORHOUSE, Geoffrey
Voyages of Captain Cook.

(*In* Plymouth City Museum & Art Gallery—Captain James Cook bi-centenary exhibition, 8th–28th August 1968: [souvenir programme]. pp. [4–8] 1968.)
Copies: NPL:M(980:Co1/P3A1).   488

1968 PRICE, *Sir* Archibald Grenfell
Captain Cook: a remarkable record.
Illus. in colour, port.
(*International Nickel*, 1968, no.2, pp.12–17.)
Contains extracts from Cook's journal, and coloured illustrations of Cook's timekeeper.
Copies: NPL:M(Q673.73305/1).   489

1968 RICKARD, Lawrence Sandston
Tasman and Cook.
(*In his* Historic place names of New Zealand. Auckland, Minerva, 1968. pp. 1–14.)
Copies: NPL:M(997/61A1).   490

n.d. DULCKEN, Henry W.
Captain Cook and his discoveries.
Illus.
(*In his* World's explorers. London, Ward, Lock & Tyler, n.d. pp. 143–200.)
Copies: NPL:M(980/D).   491

n.d. HAAS, Hugo
James Cook: der Weltumsegler, Forscher und Entdecker. [Zürich, Orell
Füssli, n.d.]
pp.7.
Reprinted from *Schweizerischen Evangelischen Schulblatt*, Jahrg. 80, Nr.15/16.
Copies: ANL.   492

n.d. JAMES COOK in de Nederlandsche Oost-Indische bezittingen: [by
C. v.d.B.]. n.d.
pp. 96.
(*Reis-bibliotheek* no. 27.)
Copies: ANL.   493

[n.d. NEWSPAPER CUTTINGS, relating to Captain Cook's voyages,
journals, memorials, etc. 187- —1935.]
Illus. 3 vols.
Copies: NPL:M(Q980:Co1/N1A1–3).   494

Charts
Manuscripts

n.d. COOK, Elizabeth, *Mrs.*
[Photograph of a chart of the western hemisphere, embroidered in silk
by Mrs. James Cook, n.d.]
No scale given, ca 16 cm in diam. on 1 sheet, cm 22 x 17, photograph, b./wh.
Shows tracks of Cook [1769–79].
Copies: NPL:M (M1 120/1769–79/1).   495

n.d. E., I.
'The Southernmost ISLAND bearing from SE b S to W b S distant two
Mile.' Profile sketch of an island, probably in the South Pacific.
Watercolour.
'I.E. delint'.
THE SAME photocopy, MS.F1 p. 99
Copies: NPL:D(MS.F1, pp. 51–2.)   496

[1763–80] SMITH, Isaac

Original sketches, drawings, maps, etc., [1763–80] collected by Admiral Isaac Smith, who served as an officer under Captain James Cook, the circumnavigator, in his first & second voyages. A.D. 1768–1775.

ff.49, 97 drawings.

Title is in the hand of Canon Bennett, a relative of Isaac Smith, from whom the volume was acquired by the Government of New South Wales. MS. contents list is from Isaac Smith's papers. A new contents list and an index have been made and are inserted. Some of the drawings are signed "H. Roberts", "Hen^y Roberts" one is signed "W.H.", others are ascribed in Canon Bennett's hand to W. Hodges; presumably this was on the back of the drawings (now pasted down) or may have been noted in pencil, as still apparent in some cases, on the leaves of the volume, as it is not on the MS. contents list. A note at the beginning in Canon Bennett's hand, suggests that some of the unsigned drawings may be by Isaac Smith. Some of the drawings appear to be the originals of the plates to Cook's second voyage. With the exception of two of the first voyage, the drawings probably all belong to the second voyage but some may be of the third. The charts include two by Cook of Newfoundland 1763, one of Charlestown 1780, one of the track of H.M.S. *Perseverance* etc. The drawings are listed separately at no. 1379, the maps, charts and coastal profiles at no. 1331.

Copies: NPL:M(PXD11). 497

Charts
Reproductions

1774–85 [ATLAS DE BANCK: 206 charts and plates illustrating French translations of the accounts of Cook's three voyages, including Hawkesworth's account of the first voyage.] Paris, 1774–1785.

cm 26.

Spine lettered Atlas de Banck.

CONTENTS:

A No. [1] see below C.
B No. [2–54, with 34 omitted from the numbering].
Lettered Tome 1, pl.1–16; tome 2, pl.1–16; tome 3, pl.1–17; and tome 4, pl.1–3.
From Relations des voyages . . . rédigée . . . par J. Hawkesworth. Paris, Saillant et Nyon. 4 vols.
Hawkesworth's account included the voyages of Commodore Byron, Captain Wallis and Captain Carteret so some of these plates do not relate to Cook's voyage.
C No. [1] and [55–120], with 94 omitted from the numbering.
Lettered Pl.1–65.
From Voyage dans l'Hémisphère austral et autour du monde . . . écrit par Jacques Cook. Paris, Hôtel de Thou, 1778. 5 vols.
D T.–p. and prefatory note, pp. [4].
Title reads Cartes et figures du troisième voyage de Cook. Paris, Hôtel de Thou, 1785.
E No. [121–208].
Lettered Pl.1–87 and 1 plate titled Mort de Cook. Plates are bound out of order and no. 51 has been incorrectly lettered 52.
From Troisième voyage de Cook. Paris, Hôtel de Thou, 1785, 4 (or 5) vols. 4to.
Where bound in four volumes the plates are distributed according to directions printed as vol.4 pp.549–552. When bound in five volumes the accompanying title-page (see item D) becomes the title-page to vol.5. QOM set bound in three volumes: vols. 1 and 2 lack title-page, and that for vol. 3 reads "Cartes et figures du troisième voyage de Cook".

Copies: NPL:D(Q77/38); QOM. 498

1778 JOHNSON, J.

A Map of the new discoveries in the South Sea, with the tracks of the navigators. (1778). [Engraved by] Mw. Smith. London, I. Johnson, January 1st 1778.

No scale given, 1 sheet, cm 17 x 32, engr., b./wh.
Area: Includes the whole of Australasia and the East Indies.
Shows tracks of Byron, 1765, Carteret, 1767, Wallis, 1767, Cook, 1769, 1773–4, Furneaux, 1773–4.
The Same.
(*In* New discoveries concerning the world, and its inhabitants. London, J.Johnson, 1778. Part 1, facing p.1. NPL:M 980/N; NPL:R 09:S909.8A/114.)
Copies: NPL:M(M1 910/1765–74).   499

[178–?] DROÜET, Santiago

Carta esferica del Globo terraqüeo. (Escrita por Sgo. Drüet; T.Prolo g.) [178–?]

No scale given, 1 sheet cm 29 x 38.
Shows routes of J. Cook (all three voyages) and other navigators 1766–80.
Copies: NPL:D(Cb 78/2).   500

1780 KITCHIN, Thomas, *the elder*

A Chart of the discoveries made by the late Capt. Cook, & other European navigators, in the great Pacific Ocean between Asia & America. By T. Kitchin, Senr. London, R. Baldwin, July 1780.

No scale given, 1 sheet, cm 41 x 34, engr., b./wh.
Area: Excludes Central and South America.
Shows coastlines and islands without any ships' tracks.
Extracted from the *London Magazine*, July 1780.
Bound with Williams, R.–Extract of a journal [1789].
THE SAME, showing the route of Cook, 1777–79.
(*In* the *London Magazine*, December 31, 1780 [A summary account of Cook's third voyage], at NPL:M 980:Co4/P1A1.)
Copies: NPL:M(Q991/W).   501

1782 LOTTER, Mathieu Albert

Mappemonde, ou carte générale de l'univers, sur une projection nouvelle d'une sphère ovale . . . avec le tour du monde du Lieut. Cook et tous les découvertes nouvelles . . . par Mathieu Albert Lotter. Augsbourg, 1782.

No scale given, 1 sheet, cm 45 x 91, litho. cols. A flattened, oval projection is used.
Shows routes of Cook, 1768–1771; Cook and Furneaux, 1772–1775; Cook and Clerke, 1777–1780 by cols.
Copies: NPL:M(M4 100at /1782/1).   502

[1784] ROBERTS, Henry

A General Chart; Exhibiting the Discoveries made by Captn. James Cook in this and his two preceding Voyages; with the Tracks of the Ships under his Command. By Lieut. Henry Roberts of His Majesty's Royal Navy. [Engraved by] W. Palmer. [London, G. Nicol . . . and T. Cadell, 1784.]

No scale given, 1 sheet, cm 54 x 90.
(*In* Cook, James *and* King, James—A Voyage to the Pacific Ocean . . . for making discoveries in the Northern Hemisphere. London, G. Nicol and T. Cadell, 1784. Atlas, [p. 1].)
This has not been listed for other copies and editions.
Copies: NPL:M(X980/24A). 503

1785 GUTHRIE, William

A Chart of the world, according to Mercators projection, showing the latest discoveries of Capt. Cook. Engraved for Guthries New system of geography, by W. Darton, Tottenham. London, C. Dilly and G. Robinson, June 15, 1785.

No scale given, 1 sheet, cm 36 x 47, engr., hand cols.
Shows tracks of the *Endeavour*, 1768–71, and the *Resolution*, 1772–80; rivers, place names, coastlines in colours.
(*In* An untitled atlas, 1783–5, map 1.)
Copies: NPL:M(F912/D). 504

[179–?] LODGE, John

A New and accurate chart of the discoveries of Capn. Cook, and other later circumnavigators. Engrav'd by J. Lodge, Junr. Bedford Street. London, [179–?].
Copies: VSL. 505

1790 ARROWSMITH, Aaron

A Chart of the world upon Mercators projection, shewing all the new discoveries to the present time with the tracts of the most distinguished navigators, since the year 1700 carefully collected from the best charts, maps, voyages &c. extant. And regulated from the accurate astronomical observations made in three voyages perform'd under the command of Capt. James Cook in the years 1768, 69, 70, 71,—72, 73, 74, 75,—76, 77, 78, 79, & 1780. Compiled and published by A. Arrowsmith, Geographer. London, April 1st 1790.

ca1: 19,000,000 at equator, 1 sheet, cm 122 x 197, engr., col. outlines.
Shows navigators' routes 1400–1790, dates, bearings; hachures.
Copies: NPL:M(M4 100/1400–1800/1). 506

[1790] BOWEN, Thomas

A New and complete chart of the world; displaying the tracks of Captn. Cook, and other modern navigators. Drawn and engraved by T. Bowen for Bankes's New System of Geography. Published by Royal Authority. [London, C. Cooke, 1790.]

No scale given, 1 sheet, cm 32 x 44, engr., b./wh.
Shows tracks of the *Endeavour*, 1768–71, the *Resolution* and the *Adventure*, 1772–5, the *Resolution* and *Discovery*, 1776–80, the *Racehorse* and the *Carcass*, 1773.
(*In* Bankes, T.– A New and authentic system of universal geography. London, C. Cooke, [1790]. Facing p.69.)

Also published in the [1798?] edition, facing p.100 (NPL:M X910/11A); and in the [1800] edition, facing p.68 (NPL:R 09: F909.9A/2).
An enlarged facsimile edition was published by the *Australian* 26 Aug 1968 and is filed at NPL:M(M3 100/1768–80/2) and NPL:R(C3 100/1768–80/1), *see* no. 534.

Copies: NPL:M(X910/11).   507

[1792?] WEIGEL UND SCHNEIDER

Karte von Australien oder Polynesien, nach den Zeichnungen, Reisebeschreibungen und Tagebücher der vorzüglichsten Seefahrer bis 1789 entworffen im Jahr 1792. Nürnberg, Weigel und Schneider, [1792?]

No scale given, 1 sheet approx. 18¼″ x 25⅞″. Slightly mutilated. Measurements taken from inside heavy border line.
Shows routes of Cook's voyages. Republished in [1796?]

Copies: NPL:M(F2/p.5; F2/p.7).   508

[1794–1806] ROBERTS, Henry

A General chart exhibiting the discoveries made by Captn. James Cook in this and his two preceeding voyages; with the tracks of the ships under his command. By Lieut. Roberts of His Majesty's Royal Navy. [London, W. Faden, 1794–1806.]

No scale given, 1 sheet, cm 53 x 88, engr., hand cols.
Shows the tracks of the *Endeavour*, 1768–1771, and the *Resolution*, 1772–1780; the discoveries of the British in the Pacific Ocean and of the Russians in Asia and North America. Coloured by continents.
See also Faden, W. —[General atlas of the world. London, 1794–1806, Map no. 5], at NPL:M(X912/27).

Copies: NPL:M(M3 100/1786–1780/1).   509

1798 ARROWSMITH, Aaron

Chart of the Pacific Ocean [in nine sheets]; drawn from a great number of printed and MS journals. [With] (Reduced chart of the Pacific Ocean from the one published in nine sheets). Engraved by T. Foot. London, A. Arrowsmith, 1798.

No scale given, 10 sheets each approx. 24⅝″ x 31¾″, folded.
Shows navigators' routes, including those of Cook's three voyages. Measurements taken from fine line inside heavy border line, but map breaks through the border in several places. Some edges cut into degree border. Title within large engraved view.

Copies: NPL:M(X980.01/2).   510

1799 ANVILLE, Jean Baptiste Bourguignon D'

Asia and its islands according to D'Anville; divided into empires, kingdoms, states, regions, &ca. with the European possessions and settlements in the East Indies and an exact delineation of all the discoveries made in the eastern parts by the English under Captns. Cook, Vancouver & Peyrouse. London, Laurie & Whittle, Feby. 2d., 1799. (Shs 45–47).

No scale given, 3 sheets, cm 143 x 118 fold. to 36 x 54, engr., cols.
Insets: The Discoveries made by the Ship *Duke* on the south extremity of New Holland in 1791 *(sic)*. Sketch of King Geo IIIds Sound.

Area: from North Pole to Tasmania, from Greece to New Guinea.
Shows countries, internat. bdries, place names with historical & topo. notes; rs. lakes mtns.
Copies: NPL:M(MF400/1799/1).   511

c.1810 KELLY, Thomas, pr.

Pacific Ocean on Mercators Projection. London, Thomas Kelly, [c.1810].
cm 23·5 x 17.
Shows tracks of Cook's voyages.
Copies: NPL:D(MS.Q144 pp.343-4).   512

[1814?] ARROWSMITH, Aaron

Chart of the world on Mercator's projection, exhibiting all the new
discoveries to the present time: with the tracks of the most distinguished
navigators since the year 1700, carefully collected from the best charts,
maps, voyages, &c. extant. And regulated from the accurate astronomical
observations, made in three voyages, perform'd under the command of
Captn. James Cook, in the years 1768, 69, 70, 71,— 72, 73, 74, 75,— 76,
77, 78, 79, & 80. Compiled and published by A. Arrowsmith, Hydrographer to His Royal Highness the Prince of Wales. London, April 1st
1780. [1814?]

ca1: 19,000,000 at equator, 1 sheet, cm 123 x 199, engr., cols.
Shows navigators' routes 1400–1800, dates, bearings; hachures.
Copies: NPL:M(M4 100/1400–1800/2).   513

1814 ARROWSMITH, Aaron

Map of the world on a globular projection exhibiting particularly the
nautical researches of Capn. James Cook, F.R.S. with all the recent
discoveries to the present time, carefully drawn by A. Arrowsmith;
[dedicated to A. Dalrymple]. Plan work by T. Foot, writing by I. Puke,
Wigzell and Mozeen. London, A. Arrowsmith, January 1 1794, corrected
to 1814.

No scale given, 4 sheets (incl.2 hemispheres 91 cm diam.) fold. to 60 x 51, engr., hand cols
t.p. and dedication, with ports. of J. Cook and A. Dalrymple on two separate sheets.
Shows the routes of Captain J. Cook, 1768–79, place names, rivers, hachures, boundaries
in colours.
Accompanied by his *Companion to a map of the world.* London, 1794. 25pp. *See also* no. 519.
Copies: NPL:M(MX 100/1814/1).   514

[1818?] PURDY, John

Chart of the world, on Mercator's projection reduced from the large
chart . . . on four similar sheets. 2nd ed. London, J. Whittle and R. H.
Laurie, [1818?].

1 sheet approx. 24½″ x 37¾″.
"Scale for the exact measurement of distances in every direction" is given, with an
example of how to use it. From this example scale of the map itself can be calculated as
approx. 600 nautical miles (or 690 statute miles) to an inch. The map was first published
in this reduced size in 1816, the 2nd ed. brings the additions up to 1818. Measurements
taken from fine inside heavy line of outer degree border.
Shows navigators' routes, including those of Captain Cook.
Copies: NPL:M(Fl/p.52).   515

[182–?] BETTS, John

The Western Hemisphere. London, J. Betts, [182–?].

No scale given, 1 sheet diameter cm 32½.
Shows routes of James Cook's voyages.
(Betts, J.—Betts's school atlas.)
Copies: NPL:D(Ca 82/3).   516

[1820–30?] GUTHRIE, William

Chart of the world according to Mercators projection shewing the tracks & discoveries of Captn. Cook, Russell Junior sculpt. Engraved for Guthries New system of geography. London, Wilkie & Robinson, J. Mawman and the other Proprietors, [1820–30?].

No scale given, 1 sheet, cm 32 x 46, engr., cols.
Shows tracks of the *Endeavour*, 1768–71, the *Resolution*, 1772–5 and 1776–80, coastlines in colours.
Copies: NPL:M(M2 100/1820–30?/1).   517

1821 TARDIEU, Ambroise

Carte de l'océanie ou cinquième partie du monde, dréssée pour l'intelligence de l'histoire générale des voyages de Laharpe. Paris, chez Ledentu, 1821.

No scale given, 1 sheet approx. $15^{11}/_{12}''$ x $21\frac{1}{4}''$.
Measurements taken from fine line inside black border line.
Shows routes of the discoverers, including those of Capt. Cook.
(*In his* Atlas pour . . . l'histoire générale des voyages de Laharpe, plate 6. 1825.)
Copies: NPL:R(F909.8A/11).   518

1827 ARROWSMITH, Aaron

[Map of the world on a globular projection, exhibiting the nautical researches of Capt. J. Cook.] London, A. Arrowsmith, 1827.

No scale given, 4 sheets each approx. $19\frac{1}{2}''$ x $37\frac{5}{8}''$. Wanting title-page. Title from British Museum Catalogue of Maps, World col.74. This lists also the first edition, 1794, with Companion. Measurements taken from inside heavy border line. *See also* no. 514.
Copies: NPL:M(F1/55).   519

1827 THOMSON, John

Chart of the world on Mercator's projection; (drawn by J. Wyld, engraved by Sidy Hall). [Edinborough, J. Thomson & Co., 1827.]

No scale given, 1 sheet cm 48 x 58½.
(Thomson, J.—Thomson's New general atlas, [map]1.)
Copies: NPL:D(Cb 82/11).   520

[1827] THOMSON, John

Eastern hemisphere. [Edinborough, J. Thomson & Co., 1827.]

No scale given, 1 sheet diameter cm 48½.
(Thomson, J.—Thomson's New general atlas, [map]4.)
Copies: NPL:D(Cb 82/8).   521

[1827] THOMSON, John

Northern hemisphere, projected on the plane of the horizon of London. [Edinborough, J. Thomson & Co., 1827.]

3,000 miles to 4⅝″, 1 sheet diameter cm 48½.
(Thomson, J.—Thomson's New general atlas, [map]6.)
Copies: NPL:D(Cb 82/6).   522

[1827] THOMSON, John

Southern hemisphere, projected on the plane of the horizon of London. [Edinborough, J. Thomson & Co., 1827.]

3,000 miles to 4⅝″, 1 sheet diameter cm 48½.
(Thomson, J.—Thomson's New general atlas, [map]7.)
Copies: NPL:D(Cb 82/5).   523

[1827] THOMSON, John

Western hemisphere. [Edinborough, J. Thomson & Co., 1827.]

No scale given, 1 sheet diameter cm 48½.
(Thomson, J.—Thomson's New general atlas, [map]5.)
Copies: NPL:D(Cb 82/7).   524

[1827–8] NORIE, John William

A New chart of the world on Mercator's projection, drawn for William Heather by J. W. Norie, London, 1812, new ed. [1827–8.]

No scale given, 1 sheet, cm 59 x 97, engr., b./wh.
Shows mtns, rivers, &c. unexplored land, route of Ritchie and Lyons, Denham and Clapperton (1824) in Northern Africa.
Routes of Commodore James (1754–1755) Cook (1772–1777) Gore (1780) etc.
Copies: NPL:M(M4 100/1827–8/1).   525

1830 LAPIE, Pierre

Océanie ou Australasie et Polynésie; [engraved by J. A. Cancrin]. Amsterdam, F. J. Weygand, 1830.

No scale given, 1 sheet approx. 18⅜″ x 28¹/₁₂″. Measurements taken from the fine line immediately outside the degree space.
Shows routes of Cook's voyages.
Copies: NPL:M(F3/p.8).   526

[184–?] BETTS, John

The Eastern hemisphere. London, J. Betts, [184–?].

No scale given, 1 sheet diameter cm 32½.
(Betts, J.—Betts's school atlas.)
Copies: NPL:D(Ca 84/3).   527

[1911?] VIDAL DE LA BLACHE, Paul

Découvertes, 17ᵉ et 18ᵉ siècles: [a chart]. Paris, Librairie A. Colin, [1911?]

1: 92,500,000, 1 sheet approx. $11^5/_{12}''$ x $17\frac{1}{3}''$.
Shows routes of Cook's voyages.
(*In his* Atlas général. 1911. pp.46d–e.)
Copies: NPL:R(F912/38).   528

[1919?] CRAMP, Karl Reginald
Voyages in the Pacific, Magellan to Cook.
No scale given, $7\frac{5}{8}''$ x 10''.
(*In* Bartholomew, J. G. *and* Cramp, K. R.—Australasian school atlas. Melbourne,
Humphrey Milford, [1919?]. p.49.)
See also no. 531.
Copies: NPL:M(Q912/B).   529

1939 FADEN, William
A New general chart of the world, exhibiting the whole of the discoveries
made by the late Captain James Cook, F.R.S. with the tracks of the
ships under his command. Selections [by J. W. Ross?] from World map
by Wm. Faden, published 1787, from the original in the Cruising
Association Library.
No scale given, 1 sheet, cm 28 x 40, pr., b./wh.
Shows tracks of the *Endeavour*, 1768–71, the *Resolution*, 1772–80, and the *Discovery*, 1776–80.
(*In* Muir, J. R.—The Life and achievements of Captain James Cook. London, Blackie,
1939. Facing p.1.)
Copies: NPL:M(980:Co1/M6A1).   530

1961 CRAMP, Karl Reginald
[Voyages in the Pacific, Magellan to Cook.]
(*In* Bartholomew, J. G. *and* Cramp, K. R.—Australasian school atlas. 4th ed. Melbourne,
1961. p.49.)
See also no. 529.

Copies: NPL:M(MAQ 100.804/1961/2).   531

1963 ROBERTS, Henry
Part of a general chart by Lieutenant Henry Roberts . . . pub. in London
in 1784 . . . redrawn with additions up to 1792 by G. C. Ingleton.
Sydney, 1963.
No scale given, 1 sheet, cm 15 x 25 on 23 x 25, pr., b./wh.
Insets: Settlements of Sydney N.S.W., and Sydney Norfolk Is. the latter showing location
of wreck of H.M.S. *Sirius*.
Area: From the Moluccas to S. of N.Z., from W. of Sumutra to E. of N.Z.
Shows routes of the *Endeavour* (1770), the *Resolution* (1777), the *Sirius* (1787–9), the
Discovery (1791), the *Waaksamheyd* (1791), the *Providence* (1792).
Copies: NPL:M(M2 800/1792/1).   532

1967 A CHART of the southern hemisphere, showing the tracks of some of
the most distinguished navigators, by Captain James Cook, 1777.
[Melbourne, Hill of Content Archive, 1967.]

1 sheet
Issued with Jennings, Margaret Jean—The Discovery of Australia. 1967.
Original published by W. Strahan, London, 1777, in Cook's *A Voyage towards the South Pole.*
Copies: NPL:M(Q990.1/15A1).   533

1968 *THE AUSTRALIAN*

A New and complete chart of the world; displaying the tracks of Captn Cook and other modern navigators. [An enlarged facsimile edition of the chart by T. Bowen published in 1790.] Sydney, *The Australian*, 26 August, 1968.

No scale given, 1 sheet, cm 54 x 76, pr., cols.
Shows tracks of the *Endeavour*, 1768–71, the *Resolution* and the *Adventure*, 1772–5, the *Resolution* and the *Discovery*, 1776–80, the *Racehorse* and the *Carcass*, 1773. *See also* no. 507.
Copies: NPL:M(M3 100/1768–80/2); NPL:R(C3 100/1768–80/1).   534

Charts
Bibliography

1879 JACKSON, James

James Cook, 27 oct. 1728—14 fév. 1779: cartographie et bibliographie. Paris, 1879.

pp.43.
From the *Bulletin de la Société de Géographie*, May 1879.
Copies: NPL:M(980:Col/J1A1); NPL:D(87/120); NPL:R(S920/C771/9); VSL.   535

1925 LIST OF CHARTS of Captain Cook at the British Museum . . .
1892; [and] List of Manuscripts of and relating to . . . Cook, 1890 with additions to 1925.

(Captain Cook Miscellanea, vol.1, pp.3–8.)
Copies: NPL:M(MS.A1713⁻¹).   536

1950 GREAT BRITAIN—Hydrographic Department
Manuscript charts by Capt. Cook's assistants of parts of Australia and New Zealand: [list].

(*In its* Summary of selected manuscript documents of historic importance, preserved in the Archives of the Department. London, 1950. pp. 43–8. Great Britain—Hydrographic Department—Prof. papers, no. 13.)
Copies: NPL:M(Q980.01/G, Ref. Books).   537

Charts
Printed Books and Articles

1955 SKELTON, Raleigh Ashlin
Explorers' maps: James Cook and the mapping of the Pacific.
Facs. illus. maps.
(*Geographical Magazine* vol. 28, pp. 95–106, June 1955.)
Copies: NPL:R(S909.5A/5).   538

1958 SKELTON, Raleigh Ashlin
James Cook and the mapping of the Pacific.

Illus. maps.
(*In his* Explorers' maps. London, Routledge and Kegan Paul, 1958. pp.228–50.)
Reprint issued 1960.
Copies: NPL:M(912/3A1).   539

1960 COPYRIGHT AND PIRACY in eighteenth-century chart publication.
(*Mariner's Mirror* vol. 46, pp. 207–9, Aug.1960.)
Copies: NPL:R(DS656.506/7).   540

Films about the Voyages

1963 AUSTRALIAN BROADCASTING COMMISSION
Remarkable occurrences. 1963.

30 minutes.
A record of the life and journeys of Captain James Cook, illustrated from old engravings.
Producer, K. L. Porteous; script, Lionel Hudson; commentators, Ron Haddrick, Gordon
Scott.
Copies: ANL.   541

Illustrations, General

Originals, Including Photocopies of Originals

[1763–80] SMITH, Isaac
Original sketches, drawings, maps etc. [1763–80] collected by Admiral
Isaac Smith who served as an officer under Captain James Cook, the
circumnavigator, in his first & second voyages. A.D. 1768–1775.

ff.49, 97 drawings.
Title is in the hand of Canon Bennett, a relative of Isaac Smith, from whom the volume
was acquired by the Government of New South Wales. MS. contents list is from Isaac
Smith's papers. A new contents list and an index have been made and are inserted.
Some of the drawings are signed "H. Roberts", "Hen^y Roberts" one is signed "W.H.",
others are ascribed in Canon Bennett's hand to W. Hodges; presumably this was on
the back of the drawings (now pasted down) or may have been noted in pencil, as still
apparent in some cases, on the leaves of the volume, as it is not on the MS. contents
list. A note at the beginning in Canon Bennett's hand, suggests that some of the unsigned
drawings may be by Isaac Smith. Some of the drawings appear to be the originals of
the plates to Cook's second voyage. With the exception of two of the first voyage, the
drawings probably all belong to the second voyage but some may be of the third. The
charts include two by Cook of Newfoundland 1763, one of Charlestown 1780, one of
the track of H.M.S. *Perseverance* etc. The drawings are listed separately at no. 1379,
the maps, charts and coastal profiles at no. 1331.
Copies: NPL:M(PXD11).   542

Illustrations, General
Reproductions

[177– —COLLECTION of various editions of engravings of Cook's three voyages.]
21 engravings.
Copies: NPL:M(PX *D79). 543

[177– —] ILLUSTRATIONS to Captain Cook's voyages, in a series of one hundred and fifteen engravings from the original drawings. London, W. and S. Graves, printers.
8vo.
Plates, of various dates and by various engravers extracted from different editions of Cook's voyages; many plates published by Alex. Hogg. A printed title-page has been added to the collection of plates, which are mounted.
Copies: NPL:M(980:Col/I1A1). 544

[177––ILLUSTRATIONS to the voyages of Captain Cook, *and others.* 1703–1846.]
Fol.
A scrap-book, containing a large number of illustrations to Cook's voyages, various publishers and dates. Some plates are hand-coloured.
Copies: NPL:M(X980/17). 545

[177– SOUTH SEA VOYAGES: atlas, comprising maps and views to illustrate Captain Cook's three voyages round the world. London, 177–.]
pp. [4], ff.155.
Ff.1–39 contain maps and views to illustrate Hawkesworth's *Account of the voyages . . . by Commodore Byron, Captain Wallis, Captain Carteret and Captain Cook;* ff. 40–91 contain charts and views to illustrate Cook's second voyage, the views and a portrait of Captain Cook being by W. Hodges; ff.92–155 contain charts and views to illustrate Cook's third voyage, the views being by J. Webber. A coloured print by R. Laurie entitled *The Poa,* and a print of *The Death of Captain Cook,* by J. Webber are also included.
The Webber views are printed on thick folio paper, all the other plates are mounted. The first four pages comprise a hand-written title-page with title *Plates to South Sea voyages,* and a contents list. Many of the plates are titled and annotated by hand.
The whole bound in full calf with two coloured lettering pieces. Lettered *South Sea voyages. Atlas.* With bookplate of Joseph W. Pease, Hutton Hall, Gisborough.
Copies: NPL:D(F77/5). 546

[177– —Three voyages round the world, being a complete set of the plates of the three voyages, comprising fine proofs of the engravings, many in two states, two original drawings, four cancelled plates and six coastal profiles. 169 plates, by J. Webber, W. Hodges and others; engraved by F. Bartolozzi and others. With separate portfolio of 8 plates extracted from the above, comprising 4 originals and 4 engravings.]

2 vols.

The cancelled plates are those accompanying plates no. 40, 47, 54 and 64. Many of the plates are inscribed, either on recto or verso, with titles and description in a contemporary hand.

In the main volume there are 15 plates on thin paper, attached in each case to the verso of the preceding plate. The plates in the portfolio are nos. 1, 52 (a), 115, and 123–125 (originals) and nos. 126–129 (engravings).

ORIGINALS:

No.1, [Death of Cook, by J. Webber].
Watercolour, 14″ x 21″, pasted on mount. Unsigned and undated. (PXD 59⁻², f.1).
No. 2 is the corresponding engraving by Bartolozzi and Byrne, and nos.126–129, the same engraving in 4 states.

No.52(a), [Landing at Middleburgh, one of the Friendly Islands, drawn from nature by W. Hodges].
Unfinished watercolour 7″ x 18¼″, pasted on mount. Unsigned and undated.
No.52(b) is the engraving of the completed view by J. K. Sherwin.

No.115, [Sledge scene]. Unfinished watercolour, probably by J. Webber, 13⅝″ x 20 5/16″, pasted on mount. Unsigned and undated. Similar to nos. 114(a) and 114(b), Man of Kamtschatka travelling in winter, engraved by S. Middiman, drawn by J. Webber.

No.123, [View of St. Peter and St. Paul in Kamtschatka. Unpublished watercolour, probably by J. Webber.] 11¾″ x 21″, pasted on mount. Unsigned and undated. The view is very close in details and style, except that it is drawn from a slightly different angle, to the drawing by Webber in the British Museum, (Add. MS. 17277. 30), "The village of Petropavlosk, Avacha Bay". (PXD 59⁻², f.6).

No.124, [View in Vaitepiha Bay, Tahiti]. Unpublished watercolour. 12¼″ x 17⅝″, pasted on mount. Unsigned and undated.
This has been ascribed to Webber, but it shows the same view, with minor variations, as the signed and dated watercolour by W. Ellis, 1777, "View in Oitapeeah Bay in the Island Otaheite", which is in the Bernice P. Bishop Museum, Honolulu. (PXD59⁻², f.7).

No.125, [Ship anchored near a pine-covered shore]. Unpublished watercolour, possibly by J. Webber. 10 9/16″ x 18¾″, pasted on mount. Unsigned and undated.
The view is almost certainly of Resolution, (or Ship) Cove, Nootka, or King George's Sound, and the ship the *Resolution* which anchored there for repairs in April, 1778.
Cf. watercolour by William Ellis in the National Library of Australia, "A view of Ships Cove in King George's Sound". (PXD 59⁻², f.8).

Fuller descriptions of these 6 originals and of the corresponding engravings will be found under the following sub-headings:

No.1—*Personal*—Death—Illustrations—Webber group
No.52—*Second Voyage*—Illustrations
No.115—*Third Voyage*—Illustrations
No.123–5—*Third Voyage*—Illustrations

Copies: NPL:M(PXD59⁻¹⁻²).   547

1774–85 [ATLAS DE BANCK: 206 charts and plates illustrating French translations of the accounts of Cook's three voyages, including Hawkesworth's account of the first voyage.] Paris, 1774–1785.

cm 26.

Spine lettered *Atlas de Banck.*

CONTENTS:

A No. [1] see below C.
B No. [2–54, with 34 omitted from the numbering].
    Lettered Tome 1, pl.1–16; tome 2, pl.1–16; tome 3, pl.1–17; and tome 4, pl.1–3.
    From *Relation des voyages . . . rédigée . . . par J. Hawkesworth.* Paris, Saillant et Nyon.

4 vols.

Hawkesworth's account included the voyages of Commodore Byron, Captain Wallis and Captain Carteret so some of these plates do not relate to Cook's voyage.

C   No. [1] and [55–120], with 94 omitted from the numbering. Lettered pl.1–65.
From *Voyage dans l'Hémisphère austral et autour du monde . . . écrit par Jacques Cook*. Paris, Hôtel de Thou, 1778. 5 vols.

D   Title-page and prefatory note, pp. [4].
Title reads *Cartes et figures du troisième voyage de Cook*. Paris, Hôtel de Thou, 1785.

E   No. [121–208].
Lettered pl.1–87 and 1 plate titled *Mort de Cook*. Plates are bound out of order and no. 51 has been incorrectly lettered 52. From *Troisième voyage de Cook*. Paris, Hôtel de Thou, 1785, 4 (or 5) vols. 4to.

When bound in four volumes the plates are distributed according to directions printed in vol.4 pp.549–552.

When bound in five volumes, the accompanying title-page (see item D) becomes the title-page to vol.5. QOM set bound in three volumes: vols. 1 and 2 lack title-page, and that for vol. 3 reads *Cartes et figures du troisième voyage de Cook*.

Copies: NPL:D(Q77/38); QOM.   548

1960 SMITH, Bernard William

[Cook's first, second and third voyages]: plates.

(*In his* European vision and the South Pacific, 1768–1850. Oxford, Clarendon Press, 1960. pp.8–95.)

Copies: NPL:M(Q759.09/1A1); NPL:R(Q759.09/23).   549

1965 QUILICI, Folco

Sui mar del Capitano Cook. Firenze, Vallecchi Editore, 1965.

Facs. illus., some in colour, maps, pp.191, vi.

(Avventure nella storia. Enciclopedia monografica diretta da Piero Pieroni.) Photographed in 1956–7 and 1961–2, whilst the author was making a television series, Le avventure del Capitano Cook.

Copies: NPL:M(Q980:Co1/Q1A1).   550

[1968] CENTREGRAPHIC LIMITED

1969 calendar of original illustrations from the books first published 1790 of Captain Cook's voyages of discovery, 1768–1780. London, Centregraphic, [1968].

Port. ff.15.
Spiral binding.

Copies: NPL:M(F980:Co1/C1A1).   551

1968 RIENITS, Rex

The Voyages of Captain Cook, [by] R. & T. Rienits. London, Paul Hamlyn, 1968.

Facs. illus., many in colour, maps, ports. pp.157.

Sydney also mentioned in imprint. Includes reproductions of drawings and maps by Cook.

Copies: NPL:M(Q980:Co1/R1A1); NPL:R(NQ910·4/4).   552

1968 WHITEHEAD, Peter James Palmer

Forty drawings of fishes made by the artists who accompanied Captain James Cook on his three voyages to the Pacific, 1768–71, 1772–75, 1776–80, some being used by authors in the description of new species: [36 plates, some in colour. Comp. under the direction of and with] text by P. J. P. Whitehead . . . [Pub. by] the British Museum, Natural History; [with bibl.] London, 1968.

Facs. ports. pp.xxviii, xxix–xxxi.
(British Museum—Natural History—*Publication* no. 670.)
Includes information on the artists and naturalists.

Copies: NPL:M(F597.084/1A1); NPL:R(NF597·0022/1).   553

Illustrations Arranged by Artist

BROWNE, GORDON
Originals

TWELVE illustrations to Cook's voyages: [watercolour drawings. Prepared to illustrate C. R. Low's edition of Captain Cook's voyages. 187–?]

$5\frac{5}{8}''$ x $3\frac{7}{8}''$ meas. of views on mounts $12\frac{5}{8}''$ x $10\frac{5}{8}''$.

Copies: NPL:M(MS.A560).   554

CHARVET, J. C.
Reproductions

VOYAGES du Capitaine Cook. Wallpaper designed by J. C. Charvet, and made by Joseph Dufour, depicting scenes from Cook's voyages.

1805. Photographs (5).
Not to be reproduced without the permission of the National Monuments Record, London.
The wallpaper is hanging in Laxton Hall, Northants, England. Descriptions of the wallpaper by the National Monuments Record, and by David Watkin in an article "Some Dufour wallpapers" (*Apollo*, June 1967, pp.432–6), and a photograph of Laxton Hall, are filed with the photographs.
Another roll of the wallpaper is in the Pennsylvania Museum of Art. A panel from this set is reproduced in colour in Warner, O.—Captain Cook and the South Pacific. 1963, p.114. *See also* no. 334.

Copies: NPL:M(Small Picture File: Cook—Miscellanea).   555

NOVELLI
Reproductions

ARRIVÉE du navigateur anglois Capitaine Cook à l'Ile d'Otaiti.
See forward Arrivo del navigatore Inglese Cook all'Isola di Taiti, no. 556.

ARRIVO del navigatore Inglese Cook all'Isola di Taiti. Ap. Antonio Zatta e Figli Venezia. G.Z. sc. Novelli del.

Engraving. Meas. within frame lines 11¼" x 14⅞". In upper right corner "10". Title also in French.

Copies: NPL:M(V* Cook 33B). 556

ST. SAVEUR
Reproductions

TABLEAU des découvertes du Cap^{ne} Cook, & de la Pérouse. T.G.St.Saveur fecit, Phelipeau sculp. A Paris, chez l'auteur, Rue Coqueron, M^{on} de France. Et à Bordeaux chez la C^{ne} S. Sauveur sous le peristile de la grande Comédie. Ecrit par Malbeste.

Hand-coloured engraving, border gilt.
Meas. within frame lines 11$\frac{7}{16}$" x 17". Meas. of plate mark 16¾" x 20⅝".
Contains 24 groups of inhabitants of countries visited. The frame contains figures of natives and flora and fauna.

Copies: NPL:M(V* Cook 24); NPL:D(DL.Pf60). 557

also See 2 5 8

Illustrations
Printed Books and Articles about the Illustrations

1899 SHILLINGLAW, John Joseph
Notes on an original chart of the south and east coasts of Tasmania . . . by T. Furneaux; [also Cook pictures, etc.].

(Royal Geographical Society of Australasia—Victorian Branch—*Transactions*, vol.16, 1899, pp.38–42.)
Copies: NPL:M(980/R); NPL:D(9/227); NPL:R(DS992A/3). 558

1924 DIXSON, *Sir* William
Rare pictures relative to Australia: notes of a lantern lecture.

(Royal Australian Historical Society—*Journal and proceedings*. Vol. 10, 1924, pp.207–10.)
Copies: NPL:M(991/R, Ref. Books); NPL:D(9/69); NPL:R(S991.06/1). 559

1932 ANDERSEN, Johannes Carl
Observations during Cook's first and second voyages.

Illus. pp.30.
(Polynesian Society—*Journal*, vol. 41, Mar. 1932. Supp.)
Published as Polynesian Society—*Memoirs*, no. 10, and reprinted in 1934 in the author's *Maori music*.
Copies: NPL:M(Q572.9/P). 560

1932 DIXSON, *Sir* William
Cook's voyages: illustrations. [Note on Cook's artists.]

(*Mariner's Mirror* vol. 18, Oct. 1932, p.425.)
Copies: NPL:R(DS656.506/7). 561

1950 SMITH, Bernard William
European vision and the South Pacific; [with bibl.]

Illus.
Reprinted from the *Journal of the Warburg and Courtauld Institutes*, vol.13, pp.65–100. 1950. Illustrations are reproductions from early artists.

Copies: NPL:M(Q759.29/2A1).   562

1964 AUCKLAND CITY ART GALLERY
Captain James Cook: his artists and draughtsmen. [Catalogue of an exhibition held at] Auckland City Art Gallery, October-December, 1964. Auckland, 1964.

Illus. ports. pp.40.
Copies: NPL:M(756/2A1).   563

Ships

1908 WEATHERILL, Richard
Captain Cook; [with list of ships in which Capt. Cook sailed, and their later history].

(*In his* Ancient port of Whitby. Whitby, Horne & Son, 1908. pp.383–9.)
Copies: NPL:M(339.7/W); NPL:R(S656.509/5); VSL.   564

1925 JEFFREY, Walter James
Cook's ships.

(*In* The Australian encyclopaedia. Sydney, A. & R., 1925. Vol.1, pp.307–8.)
Also included in second and third editions, 1925 and 1927.

Copies: NPL:M(Q039/A. Ref. Shelf); NPL:D(Q92/44); NPL:R(Q990.1A/21).   565

1927 CLOWES, Geoffrey Swinford Laird
Ships of early explorers: (Captain Cook's ships).

Illus.
(*Geographical Journal* pp. 216–35, 555–7, Mar., June, 1927.)
Copies: NPL:M(Q910.6/G); NPL:R(DS909.6A/2).   566

1956-7 NAISH, George Prideaux Brabant *and* SKELTON, Raleigh Ashlin
Explorers' ships.

Facs. illus., some in colour.
(*Geographical Magazine* vol.29, pp.374–87, 436–46, Dec.1956, Jan.1957.)
Copies: NPL:R(S909.5A/5).   567

[1965] COOK'S ships: draught plans of the *Resolution*, Cook's report on the *Endeavour's* sailing qualities and pictures of both ships.

pp.2.
(*In* Cook, J.—Collected Voyages—Printed Accounts [1965] Jackdaw ser.—The Voyages of Captain Cook: a collection of contemporary documents. London, J.Cape, 1965. No.1.)

Copies: NPL:M(Q980:Co1/L1A1); NPL:R(NQ909.088/1); ANL.   568

1967 JENKS, Robert W.

Cook's *Endeavour*. Extract from *Providence Journal*, Rhode Island, Dec. 17, 1834: ship *Endeavour* again.

(*Mariner's Mirror* vol.53, pp.183–4, May, 1967.)

Reprint of the letter describing the author's visit to London in 1825 and meeting sailors at Greenwich Hospital who had sailed with Cook. He states that the ship moored in the Thames was the *Endeavour*. A note by A. Villiers says it was Cook's *Discovery*. A further note by J.E.Roberts published in *Mariner's Mirror* vol.53, Nov.1967, p.370, says this was Vancouver's ship *Discovery*, not Cook's, and cites references correcting the mistake.

Copies: NPL:R(N387.06/2).   569

1967 ROBERTS, J. E.

Note the *Endeavour*. [Letter in reply to article in *Mariner's Mirror* vol. 53, p.183, May 1967, stating that the ship moored in the Thames in 1825, and drawn by E. W. Cooke with title: *Discovery convict ship, Deptford, 1825*, is not the *Endeavour*, nor is it Cook's *Discovery*, but Vancouver's ship *Discovery*.]

(*Mariner's Mirror* vol.53, p.370, Nov.1967.)

Copies: NPL:R(N387.06/2).   570

Publication

n.d. BANKS, *Sir* Joseph

Autograph list of persons who received, by order of the Admiralty, presentation copies of Captain Cook's voyages. MS. fo. 1p. and list of views and charts.

pp.7.

Copies: ANL(MS.9, item 27).   571

n.d. MEMORANDUM for the division of the profits arising from the sale of Captain Cook's late voyages; agreed in the presence of Lord Sandwich, Lord Howe, Sir Joseph Banks, and Mr. Stephens.

MS. copy.

(Copies of documents relating to Captain James Cook, R.N., from originals in the Grey Collection, Auckland Public Library, f.238.)

Copies: NPL:M(C697).   572

1820 DOUGLAS, John, *successively Bishop of Carlisle and of Salisbury*

Select works of the Right Rev. J. Douglas . . . with a biographical memoir by . . . Rev. W. Macdonald. Salisbury, Brodie and Dowding, 1820.

Facs. port. as frontisp. pp. [viii], 99, [579].

Biographical memoir contains references to the publication of Cook's journals.

Copies: NPL:M(Q081/1A1).   573

Manuscript Journals and Logs

COOK, James

1768–71 Journal of H.M.S. *Endeavour*, 1768–71.

Folio, pp.753.

Holograph journal of the voyage of H.M.S. *Endeavour* during which Cook discovered Eastern Australia and circumnavigated New Zealand. Bound in with the journal is a copy of a report from John Hutchinson, surgeon of the *Dolphin*, to Captain Samuel Wallis, 16 May 1768, of observations on the effects of saloop, portable soup, mustard and vinegar, distilled water and beef fat on scurvy. The journal was acquired by the Commonwealth Government in 1923 when it was auctioned by Sotheby's as part of the Cook collection from Marton Hall. Sotheby's described the journal as having been the property of the late H. W. F. Bolckow. For further details *see* Beaglehole, vol.1, pp.cxciv–cci. There is a photostat copy at NPL:M(A3388–89).

Copies: ANL(MS.1). 574

COOK, James

1768–71 A Journal of the Proceedings of His Majesty's Bark the *Endeavour* in a Voyage Round the World Performed In the Years, 1768, 69, 70 & 71 By Lieutenant James Cook Commander.

pp.362 +2.

A.J.C.P. Microfilm. P.R.O. *Ships Logs Supplementary*, Ser. II, Adm.55/40.

See Beaglehole, vol.1, pp.ccxxiii–ccxxv.

MS. copy of journal of Cook's voyage in the *Endeavour*, the only complete fair copy in existence, runs from May 27, 1768 to July 13, 1771. This is apparently the copy handed over to the Admiralty at the end of the voyage, and is possibly that from which Hawkesworth worked. It appears to be in Orton's hand, and is corrected by Cook throughout and signed at end "Jam^s Cook". The journal is divided into books, each with a separate title-page, and attached to the fly-leaves of the first volume are a letter from Bolckow and a note by Wharton. It was from this MS. that Wharton completed his text.

575

COOK, James

1768–71 Log of H.M.S. *Endeavour*, May 27, 1768–June 11, 1771.

Negative microfilm.

Microfilm of MS. copy of the log of the *Endeavour*. Virtually a complete copy of the log, this was a gift from Cook to Sir Hugh Palliser, and is now in the possession of Lieut.-Commander Palliser Hudson. *See* Beaglehole, vol.1, p.ccxxvii. A report on this copy, by James Bonwick, 1890, is filed in the Mitchell Library at *B.T. ser.2, Cook box* 3a, no.227. Extracts were printed in the *Historical Records of New South Wales*, Sydney, Govt. Pr., 1893. Vol.1, pt.1, pp.289–98.

Copies: ANL(G508). 576

COOK, James

1768–70 Journal of H.M.S. *Endeavour*, 1768–1770.

MS. copy of journal of Cook's voyage in the *Endeavour*. At top of title-page is the signature of Charles Paget, 1797, and at the bottom is written: 'The best Naval Journal I ever read. A. Hervey'. This copy of the journal is in three or four different hands, and is not complete, ending on 10 October, 1770. It is a composite of Cook's log and his journal, the log entries covering the whole 24 hours and not being summarized, and alternating with the journal entries until November, 1769. From 8 December, 1769 this manuscript is a straightforward copy of Cook's journal. Presented in 1935 to the National Maritime Museum, Greenwich, by His Majesty the King. A.J.C.P. Microfilm. *See* Beaglehole, vol.1, pp.ccxxi–ccxxiii.

Copies: NPL:M(FM4/9); ANL(G16).   577

COOK, James

1768–70 A Journal of the proceedings of His Majestys Bark *Endeavour* on a Voyage round the World by Lieutenant James Cook Commander commencing the 25th of May 1768 [i.e. May 27, 1768–Oct. 23, 1770]. pp.[323].

The MS. is divided into four books, with engraved charts of the voyage bound at the end of the journal. It is written in the hand of Richard Orton, Cook's clerk, signed in full "James Cook", and appears to be the copy sent home to the Admiralty from Batavia. The journal was appropriated by Sir Philip Stephens, secretary to the Admiralty, and seems to have come into the possession of Lord Ranelagh whose son the 7th and last Viscount sold it sometime prior to 1885 to F. W. Cosens of Lewes. In 1890 it passed into the possession of John Corner, and was bought from his executors by F. H. Dangar in 1895 for presentation to the Australian Museum, Sydney, whose Trustees handed it over to the Mitchell Library in 1935. The *King Papers* in the Mitchell Library contain reports on the journal, 1892–5, by J. Bonwick, Wharton and A. McFarland (*King Papers* vol.2, pp.758, 774; vol.5, pp.80–2, 86–92. A1977, A1980.) Wharton used this journal for his edition of 1893 and completed the account from the Admiralty copy, also adding certain paragraphs from it throughout. For further history and details *see* Beaglehole, vol.1, pp.ccxviii–ccxxi. Negative microfilm (FM4/1757) and xerox copies held in the Mitchell Library.

Copies: NPL:M(Safe 1/71).   578

COOK, James

1768–70 Log of the *Endeavour*: 2 holograph portions. Nov.5, 1768–May 8, 1769; Feb.18–Sept.23, 1770.

Originals held in the British Museum, Add. MSS.27955, 27885. The first bears on the fly-leaf the note "Purchased of Mr. C. J. Smith 12 Decr. 1868". It is headed in a hand not Cook's *Continuation of the Endeavours Log Book*, and may be a rough or draft log. The closing pages are printed in an appendix to Beaglehole. In Add. MS. 27885 the log is preceded by a page of calculations and two receipts, inserted, from William Perry. The logbook finishes with a printed form of *Computations for finding the longitude*. See Beaglehole, vol.1, pp.ccxxvi–ccxxvii. Photostat copies held by the Mitchell Library.

Copies: NPL:M(A3391, 3390).   579

COOK, James

1768 Oct.19 'Computations for finding the Longitude by Observations taken': fragment of printed form, with MS. observations for 19 Oct. 1768, entered in Cook's hand.

Copies: NPL:D(MS.F1, pp.55–6).   580

COOK, James

1769 Oct.9–Nov.27 [Draft journal and notes, Oct.9–Nov.27, 1769; in Cook's handwriting, giving his experiences in Poverty Bay, N.Z.]

pp.13.
(Cook Documents from the Australian Museum, pp.51–63.)
Numbered H 504.
There are no entries for Oct.11–24, Nov.5–25. A copy in manuscript is filed in the same volume on pp.65–99. *See* Beaglehole, vol.1, p.ccx.
Copies: NPL:M(Safe 1/83).   581

COOK, James

1769 Oct.11 Journal: photocopy of entry for Wed.11 Oct.1769, referring to the naming of Poverty Bay.
Copies: NPL:D(MS.Q143, p.75).   582

COOK, James

1770 May 5 Journal: Lithographic facsimile of entries 5 & 6 May 1770, referring to the naming of Botany Bay.
(The 'Huntingdon Draft Leaf' *see* Beaglehole's ed. of Cook's Journals, vol.1, p.ccix.)
Copies: NPL:D(MS.Q143, p.77).   583

OFFICIAL LOG

1768–71 [Official log of the *Endeavour*, May 27, 1768–July 18, 1771.]

Original in the British Museum, Add. MS. 8959. This appears to be the official ship's log. In dates it is the most inclusive document of all. It is kept in two different hands, and is followed at the end by "An Acc^t of the *Endeavour* Barks's Way from August 1768 . . ." This however breaks off at Nov.13, 1768. The MS. was left to the British Museum by Sir Joseph Banks on his death. *See* Beaglehole, vol.1, pp.ccxxviii–ccxxix. Photostat copy held in the Mitchell Library.
Copies: NPL:M(A3392).   584

ANONYMOUS

1768–70 Journal. May 27, 1768–Sept.28, 1770.

A.J.C.P. Microfilm, P.R.O. Adm. 51/4547/153.
See Beaglehole, vol.1, p.ccxxxvi.

585

ANONYMOUS

1768–70 Log of H.M.S. *Endeavour*, 1768–1770.

Folio, pp.192.
Although attributed to Charles Green in the 1928 edition of this bibliography (p.26), this verion is considered anonymous. *See* Beaglehole, vol.1, pp.ccxxxvii–ccxxxviii. The connection with Green is not impossible, but must be held unproven.
The log may be said to be almost entirely a copy of the ship's log, and seems to be a fair copy done sometime after the original. It was kept in astronomical time and runs from May 26, 1768 to Oct.6, 1770, when the ship was off Batavia.
Pencilled title-page reads: A log of a Voyage round the WORL (*sic*) in HIS BRITANNIC MAIEST (*sic*) BARK ENDEAVOUR PERFORM'D in the YEARS 1768, 9, 70 & 71 IS COOK LIEUT & PURSER COMANDER (*sic*).
Original is in the National Library of Australia, Canberra, and bears the trade card of the stationer who supplied the book (Bate of Birchin Lane, Cornhill). The Mitchell Library holds a photostat copy.
Copies: NPL:M(A3401); ANL(MS3).   586

ANONYMOUS
1768–70 Log. Aug.26, 1768–Sept.27, 1770.

A.J.C.P. Microfilm. P.R.O. Adm. 51/4548/155.
See Beaglehole, vol.1, p.ccxxvi.

587

ANONYMOUS
1768–9 Log. Aug.26, 1768–July 18, 1769.

A.J.C.P. Microfilm. P.R.O. Adm. 51/4548/154.
See Beaglehole, vol.1, p.ccxxxvi.

588

BANKS, *Sir* Joseph
1768–71 Journal of Sir Joseph Banks on the *Endeavour*.

Document in the possession of Dowager Lady Brabourne, a MS. copy by Miss Sophia
Banks of the original journal held by the Mitchell Library. *See* Beaglehole, vol.1,
p.ccxxix. Negative microfilm held by the Mitchell Library.
Copies: NPL:M(FM4/62).

589

BANKS, *Sir* Joseph
1768–71 Journal of Sir Joseph Banks on the *Endeavour*.

A MS. copy held by the Alexander Turnbull Library, Wellington, N.Z., of the original
MS. in the Mitchell Library. Bears the bookplate of the "Honble Constantine John
Phipps", later Lord Mulgrave. *See* Beaglehole, vol.1, p.ccxxxix.

590

BANKS, *Sir* Joseph
1768–71 Journal of Sir Joseph Banks on the *Endeavour*.

MS. copy of the original journal held by the Mitchell Library, on loan to the National
Maritime Museum, Greenwich, from Lord Stanley of Alderley. *See* Beaglehole, vol.1,
p.ccxxxix. Positive microfilm held by the Mitchell Library.
Copies: NPL:M(FM4/65).

591

BANKS, *Sir* Joseph
1768–71 Original manuscript journal, kept by Banks on H.M.S. *Endeavour*
from Aug.25, 1768 to July 12, 1771.

2 vols.
Includes lists of the plants and fish of the Madeira, and notes entitled "Electricity",
"Plantes Brasiliensis" and "Plants of Terra del Fuego". A letter from N. Hulme to
James (*sic*) Banks, Esq. re orange and lemon juice is inserted.
After the death of Sir Joseph Banks in 1820, this journal, together with other papers,
was placed in the hands of Robert Brown, who agreed to write a biography of his patron;
but on account of his infirmities he was unable to do so. The material was then passed
on to Dawson Turner, who had a copy made of the journal, but did nothing further
towards the biography. In 1873 the manuscripts were deposited in the British Museum,
where they remained until about 1885, when they were claimed and removed by Lord
Brabourne. This journal became the property of [Sir] J. Henniker Heaton, who later

sold it to Mr. Alfred Lee, of Sydney, from whom Mr. D. S. Mitchell acquired it when he bought the Lee Collection.

The journal was edited by Sir J. D. Hooker and published in London by Macmillan in 1892. In 1962 it was published by the Trustees of the Public Library of New South Wales in association with Angus and Robertson, Sydney, and edited by Dr. J. C. Beaglehole.

Copies: NPL:M(Safe1/12–13). 592

BANKS, *Sir* Joseph
1769–71 [Banks material in the Auckland Public Library, N.Z. Grey MS. 48, 49, 51, 52.]

See Beaglehole, vol. 1, pp.ccxl–ccxli. A copy is MS. held in the Mitchell Library in *Copies of documents relating to Captain James Cook, R.N., from originals in the Grey collection, Auckland Public Library*, pp.32–180 (C697); also a photographic copy at A3394.

CONTENTS:

Grey MS.48: Folio, 4pp. A description of Tahiti, possibly a draft outline.

Grey MS.49: Small quarto, 3ff. Notes on the Society Islands and the Tuamotus.

Grey MS.51: Small quarto, 40ff. Referred to traditionally as a journal of Banks, this covers the dates Oct.9, 1769–Oct.10, 1770. It is in Banks' handwriting, but is simply an abstract of Cook's journal.

Grey MS.52: 6ff. Dec.26, 1770–July 9, 1771. This seems to be a continuation of the above.

593

BANKS, *Sir* Joseph
1770 Extracts from journal, May 1, 4–6, 1770.

pp.2.

(Banks Papers, vol.16, pp.29–30.)

In Banks' handwriting, describing an excursion from Botany Bay on May 1, a catch of large stingrays and a dinner from stingray and leaves of tetragonia cornuta.

Copies: NPL:M(MS.A80⁻⁴). 594

BOOTIE, John
1768–70 Journal. May 27, 1768–Nov. 24, 1769; Nov. 26, 1769–Sep. 3, 1770.

A.J.C.P. Microfilm. P.R.O. Adm. 51/4546/134–5.

See Beaglehole, vol.1, pp.ccxxxiv–ccxxxv.

595

BOOTIE, John
1768–70 Log. June 1, 1768–June 22, 1769; Aug. 26, 1768–Mar. 8, 1769; Mar. 9, 1769–Oct. 22, 1769; Oct. 9, 1769–Mar. 1, 1770.

A.J.C.P. Microfilm. P.R.O. Adm. 51/4546/136–9.

See Beaglehole, vol.1, pp.ccxxxiv–ccxxxv.

596

BRISCOE, Peter
1768–70 'A Journal of His Majesties Bark *Endeavour* by Gods Permishon Bound to the South Seas Lieut. James Cook Commander 27th May 1768 Peter Briscoe'.

pp.131, 1, cm 25.
May 27, 1768–May 14, 1770. Paged in Library. Spine sticker: '17111'. Cover title (painted
out): 'The Account of Mr. Robert Haswhitle Senior Church Warden of the Parish of
Saint James Westminster for the year 1767'. Inside front cover: 'Phillipps MS 17111'
and bookplate of T. Jolley.
CONTENTS:
Lists: 'A List of the Officers and Company Majesty's Bark *Endeavour* 27th May 1768'.
pp. 2–3.
'Detachments of Marines Embark'd at Plymo. as part of her Compliment 16th
Augus 1768'. p.3.
'Gentlemen and Servants Supernumaries.' p.3.
Log & Journal: The journal is mainly a navigational and weather record, although there
are descriptions of the coasts of New Zealand and New Holland, in particular Queen
Charlotte Sound, Dromedary Bay and Stingray Bay, and remarks of the expedition's
relations with the Maoris. The journal ends in the lat. 30° 22'S during the ship's passage
along the coast of New Holland. pp. 4–133.
Recipe: 'To Make Reason Wine'. Written in another hand? Last page.
Negative microfilm of this journal filed in Mitchell Library at FM4/222. Loose notes
found inside cover have been removed to W. Dixson Correspondence File and MS.Q158.
Copies: NPL:D(MS.96). **597**

CLERKE, Charles
1768–70 Journal. Aug. 26, 1768–Oct. 31, 1769; Nov. 1, 1769–June 8, 1770.
A.J.C.P. Microfilm. P.R.O. Adm. 51/4548/143–4.
See Beaglehole, vol.1, p.ccxxxvi.

598

FORWOOD, Stephen
1768–70 Journal. May 27, 1768–Sept. 26, 1770.
A.J.C.P. Microfilm. P.R.O. Adm. 51/4545/133.
See Beaglehole, vol.1, p.ccxxxiv.

599

GORE, John
1768–9 Journal. July 3, 1768–Dec. 7, 1769.
A.J.C.P. Microfilm. P.R.O. Adm. 51/4548/145–6.
See Beaglehole, vol.1, pp.ccxxx–ccxxxi.

600

GREEN, Charles
1768–9 Journal. May 27, 1768–Oct.3, 1770.
A.J.C.P. Microfilm. P.R.O. Adm. 51/4545/151.
See Beaglehole, vol.1, pp.ccxli–ccxlii.
Bears the signature of John Ibbetson, Secretary to the Board of Longitude. A copy of
portion of the log is in the *King Papers*, vol.2, pp.713–41 (NPL:MA1977). This copy
was used by the Hon.P.G. King in preparing his comments on Cook's log, published
in 1891. Discussion by Capt. Wharton on the log, is also contained in this volume.

601

HICKS, Zachery

1768–71 Journal. May 27, 1768–Nov. 19, 1769; Nov. 20, 1769–Mar. 14, 1771.

> A.J.C.P. Microfilm. P.R.O. Adm. 51/4546/147–8. *See* Beaglehole, vol.1, p.ccxxix. An extract, 13 Ap.–22 Aug. 1770 is published in *Historical Records of New South Wales*. Sydney, Govt. Pr., 1893. Vol.1, pt.1, pp.177–90.

602

HICKS, Zachary

1768–70 Log. Dec. 8, 1768–June 22, 1770.

> Alexander Turnbull Library. *See* Beaglehole, vol.1, pp.ccxxix–ccxxx. Fair copy. At the beginning of the volume is an inserted leaf containing copies of two letters from Cook to the Admiralty about the *Grenville*, one dated 13 Dec. 1764, the other undated; and of three letters to him in reply from the Admiralty Office, the Navy Office and the Victualling Office.

603

MOLYNEUX, Robert

1768–70 Journal. May 27, 1768–Jan.10, 1770. (Last complete entry 9 Jan. 1770.)

> A.J.C.P. Microfilm. P.R.O. Adm. 51/4546/152. P.R.O.List erroneously notes it as anonymous. *See* Beaglehole, vol.1, p.ccxxii.

604

MOLYNEUX, Robert

1768–9 Log. Aug.26, 1768–Oct.20, 1769.

> A.J.C.P. Microfilm. P.R.O. Adm. 55/39. *See* Beaglehole, vol.1, p.ccxxxii. Noted as a log in the P.R.O. List, and as conjecturally Molyneux's, but a large part of it is a journal, and from internal evidence it is clearly his. Called on first page "The master's Logg". Tahitian portion printed in Beaglehole as App. IV, 2.

605

MOLYNEUX, Robert

1769 Log of H.M.S. *Endeavour*, Captain Cook, 25th July, 1769 to 6th Oct. 1769.

> A.J.C.P. Microfilm. P.R.O. Adm. Ships Logs II Supp. 55/41. Photostat copy in the Mitchell Library, (B1357), ff.35, with title in ink: *Endeavour* Log between the 25th July 1769 & 6th Oct. 1769, by Robert Molineux. No.111.

606

MONKHOUSE, Jonathan

1768–9 A Logg kept on board his Majesties ship the *Endeavour*, Jas. Cooke Commander. May 27, 1768–Nov.19, 1769. [Original MS.]

pp.[361].

In original vellum binding. The log finishes on p.352. It is followed by Dimensions of Masts and Yards, pp.358–61. The writer himself, to judge by his title-page, spelt his name Munkhouse. The log, previously in Sir Leicester Harmsworth's collection, was acquired by the Mitchell Library in 1932. *See* Beaglehole, vol.1, pp.ccxxxv–ccxxxvi.

Copies: NPL:M(Safe 1/29).

607

MONKHOUSE, Jonathan
1769 Journal. May–Aug. 1769.

Alexander Turnbull Library. (Miscellaneous material relating to Cook's voyages.) Anonymous fragment. *See* Beaglehole, vol.1, p.ccxxxvii. Possibly by J. Monkhouse. Printed in Beaglehole, vol.1, App.IV,1.

608

MONKHOUSE, William Brougham
1769 Journal. 6–21 Oct. 1769. Transcript only.

B.M. Add. MS27889, ff.83–96. *See* Beaglehole, vol.1, pp.ccxxxi–ccxxxii. Printed in Beaglehole as App.IV, 3.

609

PICKERSGILL, Richard
1768–70 Journal. June 10, 1768–Oct.6, 1769; Oct.7, 1769–Aug.20, 1770.

A.J.C.P. Microfilm. P.R.O. Adm. 51/4547/140–1. *See* Beaglehole, vol.1, pp.ccxxxii–ccxxxiii.

610

PICKERSGILL, Richard
1768–70 Log. June 10, 1768–Sept. 29, 1770.

A.J.C.P. Microfilm. P.R.O. Adm. 51/4547/142. Fair copy. *See* Beaglehole, vol.1, p.ccxxxiii.

611

ROBERTS, James
1768–70 A Journal of His Majesty's Bark *Endeavour* round the world, Lieut. James Cook, Commander. May 27, 1768–May 14, 1770.

pp.[vi],78.
Original MS. In original vellum binding. A list of the officers and ship's company precedes the journal. Roberts was servant to Sir Joseph Banks. His information is taken mainly from Pickersgill's log.

Copies: NPL:M(Safe1/65).

612

WILKINSON, Francis
1768–70 Journal. June 22, 1768–Oct.8, 1769; Oct.9, 1769–Aug.3, 1770.

A.J.C.P. Microfilm. P.R.O. Adm. 51/4547/149–50. *See* Beaglehole, vol.1, pp.ccxxxiii–ccxxxiv.

613

EXTRACTS
1893 Extracts from the log-book of Lieutenant James Cook in the *Endeavour* (from the [official] logbook of the *Endeavour*) [and] (the Palliser copy of Cook's log); [also extracts from the journals of Hicks, Forwood, Pickersgill, Clerke, Wilkinson, Bootie and an anonymous log]. Being the portion wherein the discovery of the eastern coast of Australia is recorded; [with notes and facsimiles of entries in the logs and journals].

(*In* Historical Records of New South Wales, Sydney, Govt. Pr., 1893. Vol.1, pt.1, pp. 1–298, 494–502.)

Copies: NPL:M(991/N); NPL:D(89/267); NPL:R(994.4/44).

614

Manuscript Correspondence, Instructions, etc.

n.d. DOCUMENTS relating to James Cook, and letter from Sir James Bruce to Sir Joseph Banks and from Banks to Davies Gilbert.

Grey Collection, Auckland Public Library, 1955.
1 reel, positive microfilm.
Filmed by Auckland Public Library, 1955.
Copies: NPL:M(FM3/186).   615.

COOK, James
1768-78 Letterbook and Admiralty Secret Instructions, 1768-1778.

2 vols, and pp.58, pp.4.
CONTENTS:
MS.2:   Contemporary MS. copies of Cook's correspondence with the Admiralty,. Victualling Office, etc., relating to the first voyage of H.M.S. *Endeavour*. Including the Secret Instructions and Additional Instructions to him from the Admiralty. The Secret Instructions are bound in with the correspondence. Cover is titled *Cook's Voyage 1768-71. Copies of Correspondence etc.* (1 vol.).
MS.6:   Letterbook 1771-8. Chiefly orders to and from the Admiralty, Navy Commissioners and Victualling Commissioners; Cook's orders to his officers and alterations to his staff caused by officers' deaths. (1 vol.) Also a typescript list comparing the letterbook with *The Historical Records of N.S.W.* (pp.58).
MS.108: Typescript extracts from the Secret Instructions, from the Instruction concerning the Observation of the Transit of Venus, 30 Jul. 1768. (pp.4.)

Copies: ANL(MS.2,MS.6,MS.108).   616.

COOK, James
1768 July 4 Cook to Victualling Board. LS in R. Orton's hand, dated Victualling Office, ordering supplies of wine and watercasks, arrack and saloup for HM Bark *Endeavour*.
Copies: NPL:D(MS.Q140,pp.13-16).   617

COOK, James
1768 Sep.17 Cook to Victualling Board. LS in R. Orton's hand, dated Funchal Road Off Madeira, advising that Cook has drawn bills on the Commissioners for the purchase of fresh beef, onions and water as supplies for HMS *Endeavour*.
Copies: NPL:D(MS.Q140,pp.17-20).   618.

COOK, James
1768 Nov.30 Cook to Victualling Board. LS in R. Orton's hand, dated Rio de Janeiro, that he has drawn a bill for the purchase of provisions for HMS *Endeavour*, and commission is charged because the Vice Roy compelled him to employ an agent for the purchase.
cm 32.
Copies: NPL:D(MS.Q140,pp.21-4).   619.

COOK, James

1768 Nov.30 Autograph letter, Rio, Nov.30, 1768, to the Commissioners for Victualling, stating that he has drawn on them for the value of provisions for the use of H.M. Bark *Endeavour*.

p.1.
(Cook Documents from the Australian Museum, p.169.)
Unsigned and incomplete draft.

Copies: NPL:M(Safe1/83).   620

COOK, James

1768 Nov.30 Autograph letter, Rio, Nov.30, 1768, to the Secretary of the Admiralty. Describing the conduct of the Vice-Roy of Brazil towards the Captain and crew of the *Endeavour*: draft.

pp.20.
(Cook Documents from the Australian Museum, pp.129–48.)
Letter printed in the *Historical Records of New South Wales*, vol.1, pt.1, pp.316–22. A copy in manuscript of the draft is filed following it in the volume on pp.149–67.

Copies: NPL:M(Safe1/83).   621

COOK, James

[1769] Rules to be observed by every person belonging to His Majesty's Bark *Endeavour* for the better establishing a regular and uniform trade for provision, etc., with the inhabitants of Georges Island.

pp.5.
(Cook Documents from the Australian Museum pp.175–7.)
An unsigned and undated draft in Cook's handwriting, probably written on the arrival of the *Endeavour* at Tahiti, June 1, 1769. A copy in manuscript is filed in the same volume on pp.181–3.

Copies: NPL:M(Safe1/83).   622

COOK, James

1770 Oct. Photocopy of letter to Governor General of Netherlands India from Batavia, 9 or 10 Oct. 1770, written for Captain Cook in Dutch by Notary Blonhert at Batavia, requesting shelter for the *Endeavour* and re-stocking of stores before the return voyage to Europe; with typescript copy of translation and of covering letter from T. A. Coghlan, 11 June 1924.

p.1.
Original held by the Netherlands Historical Shipping Museum, Amsterdam.

Copies: NPL:M(Doc.1311).   623

COOK, James

1770 Oct.16 Autograph letter written in the third person to His Excellency [the Governor of Batavia] requesting him to furnish money for refitting the *Endeavour*, for bills of exchange on the Admiralty.

p.1.
(Cook Documents from the Australian Museum, p.103.)
Copy in manuscript filed in the same volume on p.105.

Copies: NPL:M(Safe1/83).   624

COOK, James
1770 Oct.23 ALS to the President and Council of the Royal Society, from Batavia, Oct.23, 1770, reporting success in observing the transit of Venus. [Draft.]

p.1.
(Cook Documents from the Australian Museum, p.123.)
Copy in manuscript filed in the same volume on pp.125–7.

Copies: NPL:M(Safe1/83).   625

COOK, James
1770 Oct.23 Letter to the Secretary of the Admiralty, from Batavia, Oct.23, 1770, reporting the course of his voyage since leaving Rio, the observation of the Transit of Venus, and discoveries made in New Zealand and New Holland; forwarding a copy of his journal and some charts.

pp.5.
(Cook Documents from the Australian Museum, pp.109–13.)
Draft holograph. A copy in manuscript is filed in the same volume on pp.115–21.

Copies: NPL:M(Safe1/83).   626

COOK, James
1771 Aug.17 Copy of letter to Capt. J. Walker, Aug.17, 1771; mentions his audience with the King on his return, and outlines the course of his voyage of discovery.

pp.3.
(Cook, James—Miscellaneous primary and secondary source material. B, items i–ii.)
With typescript copy. Original is in the Records Office, Clerk of the Council's Dept., Gloucestershire, England.

Copies: NPL:M(MS.A1713⁻²).   627

COOK, James
1771 Sep.13 Cook to Capt. John Walker, Whitby. ALS No.2 dated Mile end, London, describing his voyage to the South Sea Islands, his circumnavigation of New Zealand, the Maoris, his exploration of the east coast of New Holland naming it New South Wales, the Australian Aborigines, and his passage through (Endeavour) strait.

cm 30.
Other copies in the Dixson Library include a typescript with corrections in MS. by Sir William Dixson (Q143, pp.17–20), and a MS. transcript by Sir William Dixson (Q143, pp.33–50).

Copies: NPL:D(MS.Q140,pp.25–8).   628

COOK, James
1771 Sept.13 Holograph letter to Capt. J. Walker of Whitby, Sept.13, 1771, describing part of the voyage to the South Seas; with information relating to New Zealand and New South Wales. [Photographic copy, with another copy in manuscript.]

pp.4,4.
(Cook, James—Miscellaneous primary and secondary source material. B. item i.)
Original held in the Dixson Library. Notes on the original letter are included in Sotheby,
Wilkinson & Hodge—Catalogue of . . . letters & MSS . . . sale July, 1914.
Copies: NPL:M(MS.A1713⁻²).

629

COOK, James

1771 Dec.10 ALS to Joseph Cockfield, Dec.10, 1771, offering to accompany
him to Mr. Banks, where he may obtain some of the rare plants he is
so anxious to have.
p.1.
(Papers in the Autograph of Capt. James Cook, 1728–1779. p.11.)
Copies: NPL:M(Safe1/80).

630

COOK, James

1776 Apr.22 Signed certificate in Cook's hand of the good behaviour of
Thomas Jones seaman, of the *Endeavour* May 1768–Aug.3, 1771.
f.1, cm 22·5.
Copies: NPL:D(MS.Q140,p.83).

631

COOK, James

n.d. [Instructions to crews of boats sent to examine any coast, with code
of signals arranged.]
pp.2.
(Cook Documents from the Australian Museum, pp.178–9.)
A copy in manuscript is filed in the same volume on pp.185–7.
Copies: NPL:M(Safe1/83).

632

BANKS, *Sir* Joseph

1766 Autograph extract from the transactions of the Royal Society relative
to the sending out people to observe the transit of Venus in 1769. June
5–9, 1766.
pp.8.
Copies: ANL(MS.9,item 1).

633

BANKS, *Sir* Joseph

1768 Autograph memorials to the Viceroy of Brazil requesting permission
to make natural history observations in the neighbourhood of Rio de
Janeiro, dated 17th and 18th Nov., 1768. MS.
pp.14.
These MSS. comprise the rough drafts by Banks of the memorials to the Viceroy, with
fair copies of them, also rough draft for a memorial which evidently was not submitted.
The replies by the Viceroy are originals, that of the 18th November being in Spanish
only with translation by Banks, that of the 20th November is in Spanish and English,
and is accompanied by a contemporary transcript of the English versions. The MSS.
throw additional light on the episode of the Viceroy's refusal of permission to the scientists
to land.
Copies: ANL(MS.9,item 2).

634

BANKS, *Sir* Joseph

1768 Dec.1 ALS to Earl of Morton, written from Rio de Janeiro, describing the voyage and the hostility of the Portuguese. Dec.1st, 1768.

pp.8, 40.

Copies: ANL(MS.9,item 3.Nan Kivell 32).   635

BANKS, *Sir* Joseph

1768 Dec.1 ALS to ? Thomas Pennant, dated Rio de Janeiro: Commenting on their efforts to collect specimens, describing 'Molluca', fish, 'Pisos' and various bird species; relating their difficulties with the Viceroy and authorities in obtaining specimens and supplies.

ff.2, cm 23.5.

Inserted in Hawkesworth, J.—An Account of the voyages . . . for making discoveries in the Southern Hemisphere. 1773. Vol.2, Thomas Pennant's set (Q77/31 opp. p.38).

Typed transcript. ff.2. Filed in manilla folder and *placed with* Hawkesworth, J. Vol.1, Thomas Pennant's set (Q77/30,ff.4–5).

Copies: NPL:D(Q77/31,opp.p.38).   636

BANKS, *Sir* Joseph

1771 Jy.13 ALS to Thomas Pennant, dated London: Reporting his and Dr. Solander's return, the deaths which have occurred, mostly from disease contacted in the East Indies; and that the collection contains few quadrupeds but includes a 'Gerbua'. Expressing anxiety to see Pennant again.

ff.2, cm 20.

Inserted in Hawkesworth, J.—An Account of the voyages . . . for making discoveries in the Southern Hemisphere. 1773. Vol.3, Thomas Pennant's set. Typed transcript. f.1. Filed in manilla folder and *placed with* Hawkesworth, J. Vol.1, Thomas Pennant's set (Q 77/30, f.6).

Copies: NPL:D(Q77/32,opp.p.798).   637

BIGGE, John Thomas

1823 Feb.27 Visit to New Zealand recollected by many old Maoris. Bigge to Earl Bathurst, Feb.27, 1823.

(Bigge, J.T.—Report, Appendix, p.7192.)

Copies: NPL:M(B.T.ser.2, box28).   638

CROŸ, *duc de*

1775–6 [Letters, written in French, July 24, 1775, Mar.15, 1776, concerning Cook's recent discoveries.]

(Copies of MSS. in the Bibliothèque Nationale, Paris, relating to Australasia. Vol.1, pp.1–3, 5–8.)

Copies: NPL:M(MS.B1191).   639

GREAT BRITAIN—Admiralty

1930 [Account of the Admiralty Secret Instructions to Cook, and research in connection with them.]

(*In* Carruthers, *Sir* Joseph Hector McNeil—Captain James Cook, R.N. London, J. Murray, 1930. pp.28–38.)

Copies: NPL:M(980:Co1/C2A1); NPL:D(93/37); NPL:R(S920/C771/2); Captain Cook's Landing Place Trust; QParl; QU; VMoU; VSL. 640

GREAT BRITAIN—Admiralty

1955 The Instructions, secret; [with Additional Instructions, and instruction to commanders of other vessels. 30th July, 1768].

(*In* Cook, James—The Journals of Captain James Cook . . . ed. by J. C. Beaglehole . . . for the Hakluyt Society. Cambridge, U.P., 1955. Vol.1, pp.cclxxix–cclxxxiv.)
Printed from the Canberra Letter Book, after collation with P.R.O. Adm.2/1332, pp. 160ff., as printed in Navy Records Society, *Naval Miscellany*, III (1928) pp.343–50. The appended instruction to the commanders of other vessels is not entered in the Canberra Letter Book.

Copies: NPL:M(980:Co1/46A1); NPL:D(95/54); NPL:R(S990A/215). 641

MATRA, James Maria

1790 Copy of letter from J. M. Matra, at Tangier, to Sir Joseph Banks, 7th May, 1790, in which he states that a mutiny similar to that of the *Bounty* had been planned by most of the people on board the *Endeavour*, and that he had given up his own plan of remaining at Tahiti in order to help to dissuade them.

(Bonwick Transcripts: Matra, No. 58.)
Copies: NPL:M(B.T.ser.1,Box 37). 642

MORTON, James Douglas, *14th Earl*

1768 Aug.10 Manuscript hints offered to the consideration of Captain Cooke, Mr. Bankes, Doctor Solander and other gentlemen who go upon the expedition on Board the *Endeavour*. 10 Aug. 1768.

pp.16.
The Earl of Morton was President of the Royal Society in 1764.

Copies: ANL(MS.9,item 113). 643

NORRIS, Henry

1775 Letter to Sir James Wright, 1775, thanking him for an original MS. account of Tasman's voyage, and commenting on differences as to latitude and longitude between this and Cook's account, which latter he estimates to be much more accurate.

pp.4.
(Copies of documents relating to Captain James Cook, R.N., from originals in the Grey Collection, Auckland Public Library, pp.208–212.)

Copies: NPL:M(C697). 644

STEPHEN, *Sir* Alfred

1890 May 24 The Name Port Jackson, Sydney, N.S.W. Typescript memorandum by Sir Alfred Stephen, May 24, 1890.

(Parkes Correspondence, vol.35, pp.300–302.)
Copies: NPL:M(MS.A905). 645

WATKINS, *Rev.* J.
1842 Visit of Cook remembered by Korako, an aged chief.

(Rev. J. Watkin's journal, July 5, 1842, p.38.)

Copies: NPL:M(MS.A835). 646

Printed Accounts

This section includes entries for printed editions of Cook's own account. For the printed journals of others on the voyage, *see* the subheading *Printed Accounts of Associates*. Books written about the voyages are entered under the subheadings *Books About* and *Articles*. For a description of the plates in the official account *see* the subheadings *Illustrations* and *Charts*.

1771 VARIATION OF THE COMPASS as observed on board the *Endeavour* Bark in a voyage round the world. London, [1771].

pp. 422–32.

Magazine extract. *Issued with* Green, C. & Cook, J.—Observations made . . . at King George's Island in the South Sea. 1771. *See also* no. 719.

Copies: NPL:M(524/G); ANL. 647

1773 Hawkesworth's Edition

An Account of the voyages undertaken by the order of His Present Majesty for making discoveries in the southern hemisphere, and successively performed by Commodore Byron, Captain Wallis, Captain Carteret and Captain Cook, in the *Dolphin*, the *Swallow* and the *Endeavour*. Drawn up from the journals which were kept by the several commanders, and from the papers of J. Banks, by J. Hawkesworth. London, W. Strahan & T. Cadell, 1773.

Charts, plates, 3 vols.

Vol.1 ends on p.676, and includes 21 charts and plates. Page 139 is numbered 139–360. Vols.2–3 contain *An Account of a voyage round the world in the years MDCCLXVIII, MDCCLXIX, MDCCLXX and MDCCLXXI*, by Lieutenant James Cook, and pagination is recommenced. Vol.2 consists of pp. [i–xvi,1]–410, and 22 charts and plates. Page 189 is misnumbered 191. Vol.3, paginated [i–vi,411]–710, contains 9 charts and plates. The earliest issues of the first edition lack the directions for placing the cuts and the *Chart of the Streight of Magellan* which faces p.1. *See also* Holmes no.5. The second edition differs in that it contains a Preface to the second edition, in which Hawkesworth replies to the charges made against him by Alexander Dalrymple, and in that each volume is separately paginated. A typescript index to Hawkesworth's Account is included in W. J. Jeffery's indexes in the Dixson and Mitchell Libraries. The Dixson Library holds three sets of the first edition, the first of which has hand-coloured plates. The second set bears the inscription *The gift of Capt. Cook to J. Walker, 1773*, and the third forms part of a set of Cook's voyages which formerly belonged to Thomas Pennant, and includes extra illustrations some of which are hand-coloured, and two holograph letters from Sir Joseph Banks. *See also* nos. 649–54, 656–62, 665, 670–71, 676.

Copies: NPL:M(Q980/38A1–3); NPL:D(a.Q77/5–7; b.Q77/22–4; c.Q77/30–32); NPL:R(Q990A/13–14); ANL:F; NUN; QOM; QParl; QU; VMoU; VSL. 648

1773 Hawkesworth's Edition

An Account of the voyages undertaken by the order of His Present Majesty for making discoveries in the southern hemisphere, and successively performed by Commodore Byron, Captain Wallis, Captain Carteret and Captain Cook in the *Dolphin*, the *Swallow* and the *Endeavour*. Drawn up from the journals which were kept by the several commanders and from the papers of J. Banks, by J. Hawkesworth. Dublin, A. Leathley, etc., 1773.

3 vols.

A general chart of the voyages folded at back of vol.1. Vols.2–3 contain *An Account of a voyage round the world* . . . by Lieutenant James Cook. *See also* no. 648.

Copies: NPL:M(980/172A1–3); NPL:D(77/9–11); ANL:F; VParl.   649

1773 Hawkesworth's Edition

An Account of the voyages undertaken by the order of His Present Majesty for making discoveries in the southern hemisphere, and successively performed by Commodore Byron, Captain Wallis, Captain Carteret and Captain Cook in the *Dolphin*, the *Swallow* and the *Endeavour*. Drawn up from the journals which were kept by the several commanders, and from the papers of J. Banks, by J. Hawkesworth. 2nd ed. London, W. Strahan & T. Cadell, 1773.

Charts, plates, 3 vols.

Vols.2–3 deal with Cook's voyages. The Preface to the second edition contains a reply by Hawkesworth to A Letter from Mr. Dalrymple to Dr. Hawkesworth occasioned by some groundless and illiberal imputations in his account of the late voyages to the South Seas. The Dixson Library set, with spine title Cook's First Voyage, forms part of a set of Cook's voyages once belonging to Viscount Sydney. *See also* no. 648.

Copies: NPL:M(Q980/38B1–3,Q980/38A4–6); NPL:D(Q77/14–16); QOM; QU; SPL; VMoU; VSL; VU(Baillieu).   650

1773 LIEUTENANT COOK'S DESCRIPTION of the inhabitants of New Zealand, their habitations, apparel, ornaments, food, cookery and manner of life. From an account of the voyages . . . drawn up . . . by Dr. Hawkesworth.

2 sheets.

Extracted from *London Chronicle*, vol.34, July 6–8, 8–10, 1773. *See also* no. 648.

Copies: NPL:M(Q980:Co2/3A1).   651

1773 Hawkesworth's Edition

A Letter from Mr. Dalrymple to Dr. Hawkesworth, occasioned by some groundless and illiberal imputations in his account of the late voyages to the south. London, J. Nourse and others, 1773.

Folding chart, pp.[iv],35.

See Holmes, no.6. There are two issues of this rare pamphlet, the first on thick paper containing no chart, and the second on ordinary paper containing a *Chart of the South Pacifick Ocean*. The Mitchell and Dixson copies both contain this chart. After Hawkesworth's reply in the preface to the second edition of his Voyages, Dalrymple prepared another pamphlet (*see* no. 4360) which however was not published because of the death of Hawkesworth.

Copies: NPL:M(Q980/36A1); NPL:D(77/4).   652

1773 Hawkesworth's Edition

Review and summary of Dr. Hawkesworth's account of Cook's first voyage.

(*Monthly Review* vol.49, 1773, pp.457–67, 479–98.)

Copies: NPL:R(DSO50/M789). 653

1773 Hawkesworth's Edition

Review of An account of Voyages, etc., by John Hawkesworth, in the *Universal Catalogue*, June 1773.

(Bonwick Transcripts: Cook, case 1, no. 115.)

Copies: NPL:M(B.T.Ser.2,box 1). 654

1773 Henry's Edition

Captain Cook's voyage round the world in 1768, 1769, 1770 and 1771.

Map.
(*In* Henry, David—Historical account of all the voyages round the world. London, F. Newbery, 1773. Vol. 3, pp. 165–470; vol. 4, pp. 1–122.)
Account compiled from Cook's journal, and that of Sydney Parkinson.

Copies: NPL:M(980/H); NPL:D(77/21–22); NPL:R(MD8R50–51); QOM(vol.4 only); VU(Baillieu). 655

1774 Hawkesworth's Edition

A New voyage round the world, in the years 1768, 1769, 1770 and 1771; undertaken by order of His Present Majesty. Performed by Captain James Cook in the ship *Endeavour*; drawn up from his own journal and from the papers of Joseph Banks . . . and published by the special direction of the . . . Lords of the Admiralty, by J. Hawkesworth. New York, James Rivington, pr., 1774.

Chart, illus. 2 vols.
See Holmes no.9. The first American edition of Cook's first voyage. The frontispiece to vol.1 is engraved by Paul Revere, and is signed "P.Revere". The chart in vol.1 was "Protracted by B:Romans". *See also* no. 648.

Copies: NPL:M(980:Co2/2A1–2); NPL:D(77/12–13); ANL:F; VSL. 656

1774 Hawkesworth's Edition

Geschichte der See-Reisen und Entdeckungen im Süd-Meer welche auf Befehl Sr Grosbrittannischen Majestät unternommen und von Commodore Byron, Capitain Wallis, Capitain Carteret und Capitain Cook, im *Dolphin*, der *Swallow* und dem *Endeavour* . . . ausgeführet worden sind; aus den Tagebüchern der verschiedenen Befehlshaber und den Handschriften J. Banks . . . verfasst von J.Hawkesworth . . . aus dem Englischen übersetzt von J.F. Schiller. Berlin, A. Haude und J.C.Spener, 1774.

Charts, plates, 3 vols.
Vols. 2–3 contain *Des Lieutenant Cook's Reise um die Welt in den Jahren 1768, 1769, 1770 und 1771.* From the original English edition; *see* no. 648.

Copies: NPL:M(980/172C1–3); VMoU(Vols. 1, 3 only). 657

1774 Hawkesworth's Edition

Reizen rondom de weereld ondernomen op bevel van Zyne Majesteit den tans regeerenden Koning van Groot-Brittanje tot het doen van ontdekkingen in het zuider halfrond en volvoert door den Kommandeur Byron, Kaptein Wallis, Kaptein Carteret en den Luitenant Cook, met de schepen de *Dolphyn*, de *Zwaluw* en de *Ondernemer*; uit de dagregisters der gemelde Bevelhebberen en uit de papieren van . . . J. Banks in orde gebragt door . . . J. Hawkesworth. Uit het Engelsch vertaalt. Rotterdam, Reiner Arrenberg, 1774.

Frontisp. pp.[lv],351.

Abridged edition. pp.167–351 contain *Verkort verhaal eener reize rondom de weereld, gedaan in de jaaren 1769, 1770 en 1771, door den Luitenant James Cook, etc.* From the original English edition, for which *see* no. 648.

Copies: NPL:M(980/172D1); VSL. 658

1774 Hawkesworth's Edition

Relation des voyages entrepris par ordre de Sa Majesté britannique actuellement regnante; pour faire des découvertes dans l'hémisphère méridional, et successivement exécutés par le Commodore Byron, le Capitaine Carteret, le Capitaine Wallis & le Capitaine Cook, dans les vaisseaux le *Dauphin*, le *Swallow* & l'*Endeavour*. Rédigée d'après les journaux tenus par les différens commandans, & les papiers de M. Banks, par J. Hawkesworth . . . Traduite de l'anglois [by J. B. A. Suard]. Paris, Saillant et Nyon, 1774.

Charts, plates, 4 vols.

From the English 1773 edition entitled *An Account of the voyages undertaken by order of His Present Majesty, see* no. 648. Vols.2–4 contain *Relation d'un voyage fait autour du monde, dans les années 1769, 1770 & 1771, par Jacques Cook.*

Copies: NPL:M(Q980/38C1–4); NPL:R(Q990A/88–90); VSL(vols.2–4 only). 659

1774 Hawkesworth's Edition

Relation des voyages entrepris par ordre de Sa Majesté britannique, et successivement exécutés par le Commodore Byron, le Capitaine Carteret, le Capitaine Wallis & le Capitaine Cook, dans les vaisseaux le *Dauphin*, le *Swallow* & l'*Endeavour*. Traduite de l'anglois [by J. B. A. Suard]. Paris, Saillant et Nyon, 1774.

Charts, plates, 9 vols.

In the Mitchell Library set, vol. [9] is Atlas, and is placed at Q980/38C5. Vols.3–5 include *Relation d'un voyage fait autout du monde, dans les années 1768, 1769, 1770 & 1771, par le Lieutenant James Cook.* The Mitchell Library's second set (transferred from the Australian Museum) wants Atlas and vol.3–4. Text bound eight volumes in four, with spine title *Voyage de Banck. See also* no. 648.

Copies: NPL:M(980/172B1–8,Q980/38C5; 980/172B9,11–12). 660

1775 Hawkesworth's Edition

An Account of the voyages undertaken by the order of His Present Majesty for making discoveries in the southern hemisphere, and successively performed by Commodore Byron, Captain Wallis, Captain Carteret and Captain Cook, in the *Dolphin*, the *Swallow* and the *Endeavour*. Drawn up from the journals which were kept by the several commanders, and from the papers of J. Banks, by J. Hawkesworth. To which is added A Voyage to the North Pole, by Commodore Phipps. Dublin, James Williams, 1775.

Charts, plates, 2 vols.
Section on Cook entitled *An Account of a voyage round the world . . . by Lieutenant James Cook. See also* no. 648.

Copies: NPL:M(980/172E1–2).   661

1775 Hawkesworth's Edition

Ausführliche und glaubwürdige Geschichte der neuesten Reisen um die Welt, welche auf Befehl . . . des Königs von England . . . unternommen worden sind . . . aus den Tagebüchern derer Schiffs-Capitains . . . welche zu diesen Expeditione gebraucht worden, namentlich des Commodore Byron, Capitain Wallis, Capitain Carteret, Capitain Cook, und . . . Herren Banks und D. Solander . . . zusammen getragen . . . von J. J. Hawkesworth. In vier Bänden . . . Aus dem Englischen übersetzt durch J. F. Schiller. Berlin, Haude und Spener, 1775.

Charts, plates, vols.1,3.
Contains *Beschreibung einer Reise um die Welt welche der Lieutenant J. Cook . . . gethan hat.* Spine title: *Banks Reisen um die Welt.* From the original English edition, *see* no. 648.

Copies: NPL:M(980/172F1,3).   662

1776 German Edition

[Erste Reise um die Welt des Lieutenants J. Cook.] Berlin, August Mylius, 1776.

Folded map, plate.
(*In* Sammlung der besten und neuesten Reisebeschreibungen, vol.16, pp.3–205, 1776.)

Copies: NPL:M(980:Co2/8A2).   663

1776 Leipzig Edition

Hauptmanns Cooks Fahrt um die Welt, von 1768 bis 1771.

(Historischer Bericht von den sämmtlichen, durch Engländer geschehenen, Reisen um die Welt, und den neuesten, dabey gemachten Entdeckungen, in einem getreuen Auszuge aus der Seefahrer Tagebüchern. Aus dem Englischen. Leipzig, J. F. Junius, 1776. Vols. 3–4.)

Copies: NPL:M(910.4/H); ANL.   664

1785 Hawkesworth's Edition

An Account of the voyages undertaken by the order of His Present Majesty for making discoveries in the southern hemisphere, and successively performed by Commodore Byron, Captain Wallis, Captain Carteret and Captain Cook, in the *Dolphin*, the *Swallow* and the *Endeavour*. Drawn up from the journals which were kept by the several commanders and from the papers of Sir Joseph Banks, by J. Hawkesworth. 3rd ed. London, W. Strahan and T. Cadell, 1785.

Charts, plates, 4 vols.
Vols. 2–4 contain *An Account of a voyage round the world . . . by Lieutenant James Cook. See also* no. 648.

Copies: NPL:M(980/172G1–4); NPL:R(S990A/124–7); NNcU.   665

1785–6 REISE UM DIE WELT des Lieutenants J. Cook, Befehlshabers des englischen Schiffs der *Endeavour* in den Jahren 1768, 1769, 1770, 1771. Troppau, J. G. Trassler, 1785–6.

4 vols.

(Sammlung der besten Reisebeschreibungen, Bd. 7–10.)

Copies: NPL:M(980:Co2/3A1–4); VU(Baillieu).   666

[1787] THE HISTORY OF BOTANY BAY in New Holland. Containing a full account of the inhabitants, description of the soil and produce of the Bay. Of the animals, fish and fowl. To which is added the number and equipment of the fleet sailed there. Bristol, printed and sold by L. Nayler, [1787].

pp. iv, 5–23.

CONTENTS:

pp. iii–iv, The Preface.

pp. 5–6, Description of New Holland by Captain Cook.

pp. 7–16, Description of Botany Bay in New Holland.

pp. 17–20, Description of the soil and productions of the country round Botany Bay.

pp. 21–3, [Number and equipment of the fleet.]

Date from British Museum catalogue. On verso of title-page is the picture of a ship in full sail. *See also* nos. 668, 672–3.

Copies: NPL:M(991/H); NPL:D(78/59); NPL:R(09:S991.1/3).   667

[1787?] THE HISTORY OF BOTANY BAY in New Holland. Containing a full account of the inhabitants, description of the soil and produce of the Bay. Of the animals, fish and fowl. Together with the number and equipment of the fleet sailed there. Printed and sold in London, [1787?]

pp. 24.

CONTENTS:

pp. 2–3,   A Description of New Holland by Captain Cook.

pp. 4–14,   A Description of Botany Bay in New Holland.

pp. 15–21, A Description of the soil and produce round Botany Bay.

pp. 22–24, [Number and equipment of fleet.]

Mitchell Library copy bound as *Chapbooks. See also* nos. 667, 672–3.

Copies: NPL:M(398.5/C); VSL.   668

1788 VARIATIONS OF THE COMPASS, observed on board His Majesty's Bark, the *Endeavour,* in her voyage round the world, under the command of James Cook, in the years 1768, 1769, 1770 and 1771.

Tables.

(In Wales, William—Astronomical observations made in the voyages . . . for making discoveries in the southern hemisphere. London, C. Buckton, pr., 1788. pp. 87–92.)

See also no. 647.

Copies: NPL:M(Q524/W); ANL; VSL.   669

1789 Hawkesworth's Edition

An Account of the voyages undertaken by the order of His Present Majesty for making discoveries in the southern hemisphere, and successively performed by Commodore Byron, Captain Wallis, Captain

Carteret and Captain Cook, in the *Dolphin*, the *Swallow* and the *Endeavour*.
Drawn up from the journals which were kept by the several commanders
and from the papers of Sir Joseph Banks, by J. Hawkesworth. 4th ed.
Perth, R. Morison, 1789.

Charts, plates, 4 vols. in 2.
Vols.2–4 contain *An Account of a voyage round the world . . . by Lieutenant James Cook. See*
also no. 648.

Copies: NPL:M(980/172H1–2); NPL:D(78/17–20, in 4 vols); ANL(in 4 vols).   670

1789 Hawkesworth's Edition

Relation des voyages entrepris par ordre de Sa Majesté britannique, et
successivement exécutés par le Commodore Byron, le Capitaine Carteret,
le Capitaine Wallis & le Capitaine Cook, dans les vaisseaux le *Dauphin*,
le *Swallow* & l'*Endeavour*; traduite de l'anglois. Paris, Nyon, 1789.

8 vols.
Vols. 3–8 contain *Relation d'un voyage fait autour du monde, dans les années 1768, 1769, 1770*
& 1771, par . . . Jacques Cook. From the original English edition *see* no. 648.

Copies: NPL:M(980/172J1–8).   671

[1789] THE HISTORY OF BOTANY BAY in New Holland. Containing
a full account of the inhabitants, description of the soil and produce of
the Bay. Of the animals, fish and fowl. To which is added the number
and equipment of the fleet sailed there . . . [and] the unfortunate and
lamentable death of Captain Cook. Liverpool, printed by R. Ferguson,
[1789].

pp. 31.
CONTENTS:
pp. 2–9,   Description of Botany Bay in New Holland.
pp. 9–12,   Description of the soil and produce of the country round Botany Bay.
pp. 12–13, [Number and equipment of the fleet.]
pp. 13–16, An Account of the convicts landing.
pp. 16–31, The Remarkable life and death of Captain Cook.
On verso p. 31 is a rough engraving of a man and a ship. *See also* nos. 667–8, 673.

Copies: NPL:D(78/60).   672

[1789?] THE HISTORY OF BOTANY BAY in New Holland. Containing
a full account of the inhabitants, description of the soil and produce of
the Bay. Of the animals, fish and fowl. To which is added the number
and equipment of the fleet which sailed there . . . [and] the unfortunate
and lamentable death of Captain Cook. Sheffield, printed by J. Gales,
[1789?].

pp. 32.
CONTENTS:
pp. 3–9,   Description of Botany Bay in New Holland.
pp. 10–13, Description of the soil and produce of the country round Botany Bay.
pp. 13–14, [Number and equipment of the fleet.]
pp. 14–17, An Account of the convicts landing.
pp. 17–32, The Remarkable life and death of Captain Cook.
Note about date, by P. Mander Jones, is attached. *See also* nos. 667–8, 672.

Copies: NPL:M(C898).   673

1793 Brorson's Edition

J. Cook's Reise omkring jorden i aarene 1768, 69, 70 og 71. Oversat af Mag. A. W. Brorson. Kiobenhavn, Gyldendals Forlag, 1793.

pp. xii, 3–752, [i].

Copies: NPL:M(980:Co2/10A1). 674

1793 UTRAG af Capitainens Jacop Cooks Dagbok, Hållen under dess Segling vid Nya Hollands Kust, år 1770.

(*In* White, John—Resa till Nya Holland, åren 1787 och 1788. Upsala, J.Edmansenka, 1793. pp.115–47.)

Copies: NPL:M(991/16A1); ANL. 675

1796 Hawkesworth's Edition

Relation des voyages entrepris par ordre de Sa Majesté britannique, et successivement exécutés par le Commodore Byron, le Capitaine Carteret, le Capitaine Wallis et le Capitaine Cook, dans les vaisseaux le *Dauphin*, le *Swallow* et l'*Endeavour*; traduit de l'anglois. Lausanne, Hignou, 1796.

8 vols.

Vols. 3–8 contain *Relation d'un voyage fait autour du monde, dans les années 1769, 1770 & 1771, par Jacques Cook.* From the original English edition, *see* no. 648.

Copies: NPL:M(980/172K1–8). 676

1814–15 KERR, Robert

A General history and collection of voyages. London, 1814–15.

Vols. 12–15 deal with Cook's voyages. *See also* no. 679.

Copies: VSL. 677

1819 Portuguese Edition

Viagem do Capitano Cook, à roda do mundo no navio de sua magestade, a Diligencia. Lisbon, Na typografia Rollandiana, 1819.

pp. 203.

Copies: NPL:M(980:Co2/4A1); ANL. 678

1824 KERR, Robert

Account of Lieutenant Cook's voyage in 1768, 1769 and 1770.

Maps.

(*In his* General history and collection of voyages. Edinburgh, W. Blackwood, 1824. Vol. 12, pp. 359–503; vol. 13, pp. 1–476.)

Account taken from the third edition of Hawkesworth's account.

See also no. 677.

Copies: NPL:M(910.8/K); NPL:R(DS909.8A/83). 679

1832 Spanish Edition

Viaje al rededor del mundo, hecho en los años 1768, 69, 70 y 71 por el célebre Santiago Cook . . . Traducido des francés por D. Santiago de Alvarado y de la Peña. Madrid, Tomas Jordan, 1832.

Plates 6, 6 vols.
(*Nueva Biblioteca de Viajes Modernos.*)
ANL set six volumes in three.
Copies: NPL:M(980:Co2/5A1–6); ANL. 680

1886 CAPTAIN COOK'S first voyage round the world. Pt. 1, Madeira, Rio Janeiro, Tierra de Fuego, Otaheite, Society Islands, New Zealand. London, Ward Lock and Co., 1886.

pp. iv, 16.
(*Popular Library of Literary Treasures.*)
Pt. 2 issued 1887, *see* British Museum General catalogue.

Copies: ANL:F; VSL. 681

1888 [EXTRACTS from Cook's Journal.]

Facs. maps.
(Russell, H.S.—Genesis of Queensland. Sydney, Turner & Henderson, 1888. pp. 513–42.)

Copies: NPL:M(Q994/R). 682

1893 Wharton's Edition

Captain Cook's Journal during his first voyage round the world, made in H.M. Bark *Endeavour*, 1768–71. A literal transcription of the original MSS.; with notes and intro. Ed. by W. J. L. Wharton. London, Elliot Stock, 1893.

Facs. illus. maps, port. pp. lvi, 400.
Edited from the Corner copy, with additions from the Admiralty copy. Another copy with marginal notes in pencil by R. F. B. May, 1893, is filed in Mitchell Library at Q980:Co2/2A1. Another copy, bound in wood from "Cook's Tree" is filed in Mitchell Library at Q980:Co2/2A3, (No.1 of 50 copies), and others of this issue at NPL:R (S990A/64) and in VSL. Dixson Library copy presented by Rev. Mr. Corner 1894, and has presscuttings, etc., inserted. *See also* no. 691.

Copies: NPL:M(Q980:Co2/2A2); NPL:D(Q89/10); NPL:R(S990A/64); ANL; QOM; QParl; QU; VSL. 683

1922 Spanish Edition

James Cook, Comandante del *Endeavour*: Relación de su primer viaje alrededor del mundo durante los años 1768, 1769, 1770 y 1771. Trad. de Inglés por M. Ortega y Gasset. Madrid, Calpe, [1922].

Illus. maps, 3 vols.
(*Grandes Viajes Clasicos.*)
Copies: NPL:M(980:Co2/6A1–3); ANL:F. 684

1929 Edition

In New Zealand [and] Discovery of Eastern Australia: [extract from journals].

Map.
(*In* Scott, *Sir* Ernest—Australian discovery. London, Dent, [1929]. Vol. 1, pp. 116–230.)
Copies: NPL:M(980.1/31A1). 685

1929 Harlow's Edition
First voyage round the world.
(*In* Harlow, Vincent Todd—Voyages of great pioneers. London, O.U.P., 1929. Chapter 9.)
Copies: ANL.

686

1940 [EXTRACTS from logs of members of Cook's expedition in H.M.S. *Endeavour* for the period Mar.5–11, 1770, containing references to Foveaux Strait; with composite Cook chart of southern New Zealand showing names from both the Bayly and the Pickersgill versions.]
(*In* Howard, Basil—Rakiura, a history of Stewart Island. Published for the Stewart Island Centennial Committee. Dunedin, Reed, 1940. pp.7, 327–33.)
The originals of the logs are in the P.R.O. London.
Copies: NPL:M(997.9/H).

687

1962 Hungarian Edition
Utazások a világ Körül: elsö utaz ás. [Trans. from the French.] 2nd ed. Budapest, Gondolat, 1962.
Illus. maps, ports. pp. 394.
(*Klasszikus Uteírások*, 1.)
Copies: NPL:M(980:Co2/7B1).

688

1967 EXTRACTS from the journals of Abel Tasman, William Dampier, James Cook. [Melbourne, Hill of Content Archive, 1967.]
Issued with Jennings, Margaret Jean—The Discovery of Australia. Melbourne, 1967.
Copies: NPL:M(Q990.1/15A1).

689

1968 Knight's Edition
Captain Cook & the voyage of the *Endeavour*, 1768–1771. [Ed. with introductory chapters by] F. Knight. Sydney, Nelson, 1968.
Facs. illus. maps, port. pp.[viii],174.
Decorative endpapers. With glossary.
Copies: NPL:M(980:Co2/9A1).

690

1968 Wharton's Edition
Captain Cook's journal during his first voyage round the world, made in H.M. Bark *Endeavour*, 1768–71. A literal transcription of the original MSS., with notes and intro. Ed. by W. J. L. Wharton. [Reproduced by the Libraries Board of South Australia, with foreword by A. G. Price.] Adelaide, the Board, 1968.
Facs. illus. maps, port. pp.[vi], 1vi, 400.
(*Australiana Facsimile Editions*, no.188.)
See also no. 683.
Copies: NPL:M(Q980:Co2/2B1).

691

1969 Reed's Edition

Captain Cook in Australia: extracts from the journals of Captain James Cook giving a full account in his own words of his adventures and discoveries in Australia. Ed., [with intro. and notes] by A. W. Reed; [with, Going back to the manuscripts, by C. R. H. Taylor]. Wellington, N.Z., A. H. & A. W. Reed, 1969.

Illus. maps, port. pp.192.

Text for first voyage is from Wharton's edition, 1893; other extracts, including text of Furneaux's and Cook's visits to Tasmania on second and third voyages, are from *The Three famous voyages of Captain Cook*, published by Ward, Lock, Bowden, n.d. Also includes Mr. Anderson's *Remarks on Van Dieman's Land*. Companion volume to *Captain Cook in New Zealand*, edited by A.H. & A.W.Reed, 1969.

Copies: NPL:M(980:Co2/11A1).   692

Printed Accounts of Associates

1771 Becket's Edition

A Journal of a voyage round the world in His Majesty's Ship *Endeavour*, in the years 1768, 1769, 1770 and 1771; undertaken in pursuit of natural knowledge at the desire of the Royal Society. Containing all the various occurrences of the voyage, with descriptions of several new discovered countries in the southern hemisphere . . . to which is added a concise vocabulary of the language of Otahitee. London, T. Becket and P. A. de Hondt, 1771.

pp. ii, 130, [iii].

Published anonymously, nearly two years before Hawkesworth's account. This copy bears a dedication to the Lords of the Admiralty and to Banks and Solander. The dedication was withdrawn on Banks' and Solander's request. (For copies without the dedication, *see* no. 694, and *see also* Holmes no. 3, and the *Gentleman's Magazine* Nov. 1771, p. 509.) Professor G. A. Wood in his *Discovery of Australia* attributed the Journal to James Magra or Matra, a midshipman on the *Endeavour*. Authorship has been variously attributed to Banks and Solander, Richard Orton, William Perry, and the publisher, Thomas Becket. Beaglehole favours Matra as author.

See also nos. 694–700. For facsimile reprint of London 1771 edition *see* no. 701. Roberts (p. 162) mentions two other French editions (Jackson, no. 50, 1777, and no. 118, 1782) and an edition of Bougainville including this published in Paris, 1793.

Copies: NPL:M(C685; Q980:Co2/1A1 2nd copy); NPL:D(Q77/2); NPL:R(S990A/79); ANL; QOM; SPL; VSL.   693

1771 Becket's Edition

A Journal of a voyage round the world in His Majesty's Ship *Endeavour*, in the years 1768, 1769, 1770 and 1771; undertaken in pursuit of natural knowledge at the desire of the Royal Society. Containing all the various occurrences of the voyage, with descriptions of several new discovered countries in the southern hemisphere . . . to which is added a concise vocabulary of the language of Otahitee. *Anon.* London, T. Becket and P. A. de Hondt, 1771.

pp. ii, 130, [iii].

Lacks the dedication, suppressed after the protest of Banks and Solander. For other editions *see* no. 693.

Copies: NPL:M(Q980:Co2/1B1).

694

1772 Becket's Edition

A Journal of a voyage around the world in His Majesty's Ship *Endeavour*, in the years 1768, 1769, 1770 and 1771; undertaken in pursuit of natural knowledge at the desire of the Royal Society. Containing all the various occurrences of the voyage, with descriptions of several new discovered countries in the southern hemisphere . . . to which is added a concise vocabulary of the language of Otahitee. *Anon.* Dublin, J. Exshaw, H. Saunders, etc., 1772.

pp. iv, 193, [vi].

For other editions *see* no. 693.

Copies: NPL:M(C979); ANL(Nan Kivell); TSL(Allport).

695

1772 Becket's Edition. French

Journal d'un voyage autour du monde en 1768, 1769, 1770, 1771. Contenant les divers événemens du voyage; avec la relation des contrées nouvellement découvertes dans l'hémisphère méridional, une description de leur sol & de leurs productions, & plusieurs singularités dans les habits, les coutumes, les moeurs, la police & les manufactures de leurs habitans. Traduit de l'Anglois, par M. de Fréville. Paris, Saillant & Nyon, 1772.

pp. xvi, 362, [iii].

For other editions *see* no. 693. Published anonymously. *See* Roberts, no. 1(a). The first appearance of the voyage in French. With Lettre de M. de Commerson, pp. 251–86, and Lettre de M. le B. de G., pp. 287–362; these letters do not appear in the English edition (no. 693).

Copies: NPL:M(980:Co2/1A1); VSL.

696

1772 Becket's Edition. French

Supplément au voyage de M. de Bougainville; ou, Journal d'un voyage autour du monde, fait par MM. Banks & Solander, Anglois, en 1768, 1769, 1770, 1771. Traduit de l'Anglois, par M. de Fréville. *Anon.* Paris, Saillant & Nyon, 1772.

pp. xvi, 362, [iii].

For other editions *see* no. 693. *See* Roberts, no. 1(b). The same edition as no. 696, issued with a new title and half-title, as a supplement to the second edition of Bougainville's *Voyage autour du Monde*, 2 vols. Paris, 1772.

Copies: NPL:M(980:Co2/1C1).

697

1772 Becket's Edition. German

Nachricht von den neuesten Entdeckungen der Engländer in der Süd-See: oder, Auszug aus dem Tagebuch des Königl. Schiffs *The Endeavour*, welches in den Jahren 1768 bis 1771, eine Reise um die Welt gethan, und auf derselben verschiedene bisher unbekannte Länder in der südlichen Hemisphäre entdeckt hat, nebst einer kurzen Beschreibung dieser Länder, deren vorzüglichen Seltenheiten, Beschaffenheit der Einwohner, und einer kleinen Probe von der Sprache die in jenem Theil der Welt üblich ist. Berlin, Haude & Spener, 1772.

pp. xvi, [ii], 232.
For other editions *see* no. 693.
Copies: NPL:M(980:Co2/1E1); ANL:F. 698

1773 Becket's Edition. French
Journal d'un voyage autour du monde en 1768, 1769, 1770, 1771 . . . traduit de l'Anglois par M.de Fréville. *Anon.* Paris, Saillant & Nyon, 1773.

pp.288.
A reprint of no. 696. For other editions *see* no. 693. *See* Roberts, no. 1(c).
Copies: NPL:M(980:Co2/1B1); ANL:F. 699

1773 Becket's Edition. French
Supplément au voyage de M. de Bougainville; ou, Journal d'un voyage autour du monde, fait par MM. Banks & Solander, Anglois, en 1768, 1769, 1770, 1771. Traduit de l'Anglois, par M. de Fréville. *Anon.* Nouvelle édition, augmentée. Neuchâtel, Société Typographique, 1773.

pp. 254.
Added on pp. 239–54, Observations de M. de la Condamine sur le jeune insulaire de l'isle de Taiti. For other editions *see* no. 693. *See* Roberts 1(d). Forms the supplement to the two-volume edition of Bougainville published at Neuchâtel in 1773.
Copies: NPL:M(980:Co2/1D1). 700

1967 Becket's Edition.
A Journal of a voyage round the world in H.M.S. *Endeavour,* 1768–1771. Amsterdam, N. Israel, 1967.

pp. [iv, 133.]
(*Bibliotheca Australiana,* vol. 14.)
Facsimile reprint of London edition, 1771, *which see back* for note re authorship (no. 693).
Copies: NPL:M(Q910.8/9A14). 701

BANKS, *Sir* Joseph
[1773? Letter] to the Count Lauraguais (London, December 6, 1772). N.p. [1773?]

pp.[7]–18.
A manuscript note signed E.S. 1889 gives the following information: The letter, containing a brief account of Cook's first voyage was written at the request of Count Lauraguais who had it printed. Sir Joseph procured all available copies and destroyed them. The initials are probably those of Edward Stanhope whose book plate appears in the volume, as also does that of James Edge-Partington. A manuscript note appended to p.18 says "for December 6, 1772 read December 6, 1771."
"Banks 1773" appears on p.[7], evidently written by the same hand as note on p.18. There appears also to be a gather missing at the beginning of this printed work; the pagination begins at [7] and the signature on this page is B.
Copies: NPL:M(C922). 702

BANKS, *Sir* Joseph

1896 Journal of the Rt. Hon. Sir Joseph Banks . . . during Captain Cook's first voyage in H.M.S. *Endeavour*, in 1768–71, to Terra (*sic*) del Fuego, Otahite (*sic*), New Zealand, Australia, the Dutch East Indies, etc. Ed. by Sir J.D. Hooker. London, Macmillan & Co., Ltd., 1896.

Charts, port. pp.ii, 466.

Copies: NPL:M(980/B); NPL:D(89/88); NPL:R(S990A/21); ANL; QParl; VSL.　703

BANKS, *Sir* Joseph

19— Extracts from Sir Joseph Banks' journal on board the *Endeavour*, 1770; the voyage up the east coast of Australia, and some account of New Holland.

Typed extracts from the Mitchell Library manuscript, for the use of students. Five copies.

Copies: NPL:M(F980.1/B/A–E).　704

BANKS, *Sir* Joseph

1962 The *Endeavour* journal of Joseph Banks, 1768–1771; ed. by J. C. Beaglehole. [Illus. mainly by S. Parkinson. Pub. by] . . . the Trustees of the Public Library of New South Wales, in association with Angus and Robertson. Sydney, 1962.

Facs. illus., some in colour, maps, ports. 2 vols.
Published from the original manuscript in the Mitchell Library. *See also* no. 706.

Copies: NPL:M(A925.8/B); NPL:R(919/2–3); ANL; Captain Cook's Landing Place Trust.　705

BANKS, *Sir* Joseph

1963 The *Endeavour* journal of Joseph Banks, 1768–1771; ed. by J. C. Beaglehole. [Illus. mainly by S. Parkinson. Pub. by] . . . the Trustees of the Public Library of New South Wales, in association with Angus and Robertson. 2nd ed. Sydney, 1963.

Facs. illus., some in colour, maps, ports. 2 vols.
Published from the original manuscript in the Mitchell Library. *See also* no. 705.

Copies: NPL:M(A925.8/B. Ref. Shelf.); Captain Cook's Landing Place Trust.　706

CLERKE, Charles

1893 Journal of the voyage in the *Endeavour*; [extract]. Sydney, Government Printer, 1893.

(*Historical Records of New South Wales*. Vol.1, part 1, pp.230–5.)

Copies: NPL:M(991/N Ref.Books); NPL:R(994.4/44).　707

GILBERT, George

1926 Captain Cook's first visit to the Hawaiian Islands.

(Hawaiian Historical Society—*Annual report*, 1926. pp.69–72.)
Extract from British Museum Add. MS. 38, 530, pp.107–15, of MS. narrative of Cook's last voyage.

Copies: NPL:M(999.6/H).　708

GREEN, Charles

1788 Astronomical observations made on board His Majesty's bark the *Endeavour*, in her voyage round the world, under the command of James Cook. By Mr. C. Green, Capt. Cook and Mr. Clerke.

Tables.
(*In* Wales, William—Astronomical observations made in the voyages . . . for making discoveries in the southern hemisphere. London, C. Buckton, pr., 1788. pp.15–65.)

Copies: NPL:M(Q524/W); ANL; VSL.   709

GREEN, Charles

1788 Observations on the state of the air, winds, weather, &c. at Otaheite, from May the 10th to July the 6th, 1769. By Charles Green.

Tables.
(*In* Wales, William—Astronomical observations made in the voyages . . . for making discoveries in the southern hemisphere. London, C. Buckton, pr., 1788. pp.67–71.)

Copies: NPL:M(Q524/W); ANL; VSL.   710

PARKINSON, Sydney

1773 Captain Cook's voyage round the world in 1768, 1769, 1770 and 1771.

(Henry, David—Historical account of all the voyages round the world. London, F. Newbery, 1773. Vol.3, pp.163–470; vol.4, pp.1–122.)

Copies: NPL:M(980/H); NPL:D(77/21–22); NPL:R(MD8R50–51); QOM(vol.4); VSL.   711

PARKINSON, Sydney

1773 A Journal of a voyage to the South Seas, in His Majesty's ship, the *Endeavour*, faithfully transcribed from the papers of the late Sydney Parkinson, draughtsman to Joseph Banks, Esq., on his late expedition with Dr. Solander, round the world; embellished with views and designs, delineated by the author, and engraved by capital artists. London, printed for S. Parkinson, sold by Richardson, Urquhart, Evans, Hooper, Murray, Leacroft, Riley, 1773.

Illus. map, ports. pp.xxii, 212, [2].
Printed for the author. The Mitchell Library has also thirteen duplicate plates in proof state, filed in a portfolio, another copy of the Journal printed on larger paper, and a copy with hand-coloured plates which are reversed.
Parkinson was the natural history draughtsman on the *Endeavour*. He died at Batavia of dysentery on January 26, 1771, on the homeward voyage. His brother Stanfield, to anticipate Hawkesworth's account, hurriedly published this journal. After a few copies had appeared, the further issue was stopped by an injunction in Chancery, on the ground of infringement of Hawkesworth's rights and of material belonging to Banks. Dr. Fothergill, a friend of the Parkinsons, afterwards bought the remainder, which appeared in 1784 as the reissue, with an appendix added.

Copies: NPL:M(Q980/P); NPL:D(Q77/54-55); NPL:R(Q990A/40); VU(Baillieu. Large paper edition).   712

PARKINSON, Sydney

1784 A Journal of a voyage to the South Seas, in H.M.S. the *Endeavour*; faithfully transcribed from the papers of the late Sydney Parkinson, draughtsman to Sir Joseph Banks, Bart., in his expedition with Dr. Solander round the world; and embellished with twenty-nine views and designs . . . To which is now added Remarks on the Preface, by the late John Fothergill, and an appendix, containing an account of the Voyages of Commodore Byron, Captain Wallis, Captain Carteret, Monsieur Bougainville, Captain Cook and Captain Clerke. London, C. Dilly, J. Phillips, 1784.

Illus. maps, port. pp.xxiii, 22, 4, 212, xxi, 213–353 +[2].
This edition has four extra pages comprising a letter of the author, October 16, 1770, to Mrs. Jane Gomeldon, her reply May 28, 1771, and poem to him and his friends 1771.

Copies: NPL:M(Q980/P).   713

PARKINSON, Sydney

1784 A Journal of a voyage to the South Seas, in H.M.S. the *Endeavour*; faithfully transcribed from the papers of the late Sydney Parkinson, draughtsman to Sir Joseph Banks, Bart., in his expedition with Dr. Solander round the world; and embellished with twenty-nine views and designs . . . To which is now added Remarks on the Preface, by the late John Fothergill, and an appendix, containing an account of the Voyages of Commodore Byron, Captain Wallis, Captain Carteret, Monsieur Bougainville, Captain Cook and Captain Clerke. London, Charles Dilly, James Phillips, 1784.

pp.xxiii, 22, 212 + [2], lxxi, 213–353.

Copies: NPL:M(Q980/P); NPL:D(Q78/10,11,12); NPL:R(Q990A/42,S.C.).   714

PARKINSON, Sydney

1797 Voyage autour du monde sur le vaisseau de Sa Majesté britannique l'*Endeavour*, par Sidney Parkinson, dessinateur attaché à M. Banks. Précédé d'un discours en forme d'introduction sur les principaux navigateurs anglais et français . . . suivi d'un abrégé des deux derniers voyages du Capitaine Cook, avec les planches de l'auteur. Ouvrage traduit de l'Anglais par le C. Henri. Paris, Imprimerie de Guillaume, 1797.

2 vols. in 1.

Copies: NPL:M(Q980/P); NPL:R(S990A/135–6); QOM.   715

PICKERSGILL, Richard

1893 Journal of the proceedings of His Majesty's Bark *Endeavour*: [extract]. Sydney, Government Printer, 1893.

(*Historical Records of New South Wales*. Vol.1, part 1, pp.212–229.)

Copies: NPL:M(991/N,Ref.Books); NPL:R(994.4/44).   716

PICKERSGILL, Richard

1907 Pickersgill's journal.

(*In* McNab, Robert—Murihiku and the southern islands. Invercargill, William Smith, 1907. pp.294–300.)

Copies: NPL:M(997.9/M); NPL:R(S997/15).   717

PICKERSGILL, Richard

1914 Lieutenant Pickersgill's log.

(*In* McNab, Robert—Historical records of New Zealand. Wellington, Government Printer, 1914. Vol.2, pp.183–96.)

Copies: NPL:M(997/M).   718

WALES, William

1788 Astronomical observations made in the voyages which were undertaken by order of His Present Majesty, for making discoveries in the southern hemisphere, and successively performed by Commodore Byron, Captain Wallis, Captain Carteret and Captain Cook, in the *Dolphin, Tamer, Swallow* and *Endeavour.* Drawn up and published by order of the Commissioners of Longitude, from the journals which were kept by the several commanders, and from the papers of Mr. Charles Green, by W. Wales. Illustrated with maps of New Zealand and the eastern coast of New Holland from the original drawings by Captain Cook. London, printed by C. Buckton, 1788.

Maps, tables, pp.[iv], xii, 4,146.

Copies: NPL:M(Q524/W); ANL; VParl; VSL.   719

Books about the First Voyage

1774 FRÉVILLE, Anne François Joachim de

Histoire des nouvelles découvertes faites dans la Mer du Sud en 1767, 1768, 1769 et 1770; rédigée d'après les dernières relations, par M. de Fréville. Paris, De Hansy le jeune, 1774.

2 vols.
Half-title: Hydrographie de la Mer du Sud.
Folding map at back. Includes account of Cook's first voyage. *See also* no. 721.

Copies: NPL:M(980/197A1–2); VSL.   720

1776 FRÉVILLE, Anne François Joachim de

Berättelse om de nys Uptäckter, som blifwit gjorde i Söderhafwet Aren 1767, 1768, 1769 och 1770; författad, enlight sednaste under-rättleser af Hr.de Freville. [Trans. from the French.] Upsala, J. Edman, 1776.

2 vols. in 1.
Folding map at back.
See also no. 720.

Copies: NPL:M(980/197B1).   721

1786–1790 CAMPE, Joachim Heinrich

Sammlung interessanter und durchgängig zweckmässig abgefasster Reisebeschreibungen für die Jugend. N.p., 1786–1790.

Map, 8 vols. in 4.
See also no. 724.

Copies: NPL:M(910.4/209A1–4).   722

1789 PRÉVOST D'EXILES, Antoine François, *Abbé*

Continuation de l'histoire générale des voyages; ou, Collection nouvelle des relations des voyages par mer, découvertes, observations, descriptions . . . [et] des voyages par terre . . . [Livre V]. Paris, Maradan, 1789.

Illus. maps, 2 vols.

Vols. 79 and 80 only, containing Cook's first voyage. Supplement to Prévost d'Exiles, A.F., *Abbé*—Histoire générale des voyages.

Copies: NPL:M(910.8/35A79–80).   723

1808 CAMPE, Joachim Heinrich

Berättelse om en resa kring jorden, ifrån 1768 till 1771, of James Cook, Löjtnant i Engelsk tjenst, samt Hir Banks och Solander, ryktbara Naturkännare. Stockholm, 1808.

pp. [ii], 180.

Series title: Geografikst bibliotek för ungdom. [Vol. 11].

A Swedish translation by D. Krutmejer, of J.H.Campe's German compilation for children on Cook's first voyage. Vols. 11–13 of the series form the Cook abridgement. *See* Du Rietz, R.—Captain James Cook: a bibliography. 1960. pp. 25–6. *See also* no. 722.

Copies: ANL.   724

1863 MOORE, Joseph Sheridan

Captain Cook and Botany Bay; with numerous illustrations from the original sketches [of J.R. Roberts] by W. Mason. Comp. and ed. by J.S. Moore. Sydney, J. Cole, 1863.

pp. 16.

The Mitchell Library holds another edition, wanting title-page.

Copies: NPL:M(991.1/M); NPL:D(86/152); SPL; VSL.   725

1901 BONWICK, James

Captain Cook in New South Wales; or, The mystery of naming Botany Bay. London, Sampson Low, Marston & Co. Ltd., 1901.

pp. 31.

Copies: NPL:M(991.1/B); NPL:R(S991.1A/12); ANL; VSL.   726

1903 GRASSO, Gabriele

Toponomastica per battesimo ufficiale e toponomastica per spontanea tradizione popolare: saggio comparativo sui nomi imposti da G. Cook alla costa orient. d'Australie nel 1770. Roma, Presso la Società Geografica Italiana, 1903.

Maps, pp. 40.

Reprinted from Bollettino della Società Geografica Italiana, fasc. 9–10, 1903.

Copies: NPL:M(980:Co2/G2A1).   727

1920 WALES, William

Captain James Cook and Australasia. (Excerpts from the original journal.) London, 1920.

Copies: VSL.   728

1925 WOOD, George Arnold
The Voyage of the *Endeavour*. Melbourne, Macmillan, 1925.
Prepared for the use of schools. *See also* nos. 730, 734, 736.
Copies: QU.   729

1926 WOOD, George Arnold
The Voyage of the *Endeavour*. Melbourne, Macmillan, 1926.
Facs. illus. maps, pp. vi, 116.
Prepared for the use of schools. *See also* nos. 729, 734, 736.
Copies: NPL:M(980:Co2/W3A1); ANL; QU; VSL.   730

1932 WATSON, James Frederick William
Lieutenant James Cook and his voyage in the *Endeavour*, 1768–71.
ff.1, 25.
A critical essay by J. F. Watson with covering letter, 6 Jan. 1932, to Mr. Robertson,
Angus & Robertson.
Copies: NPL:D(MS.100).   731

[1933] ALANSON, A. G.
Kurnell, the birthplace of Australia. Sydney, G.B. Philip, [1933].
Illus. map, pp. 95.
Copies: NPL:M(991.1/30A1); ANL; Captain Cook's Landing Place Trust.   732

1933 WATSON, James Frederick William
Lieutenant James Cook and his voyage in H.M. bark *Endeavour*. By
Frederick Watson. Sydney, A.&R., 1933.
pp. 37.
An examination of original documents relating to the voyage.
Copies: NPL:M(980:Co2/W2A1); ANL.   733

1933 WOOD, George Arnold
The Voyage of the *Endeavour*. Melbourne, Macmillan, 1933.
Facs. illus. maps, ports. pp. 126.
Prepared for the use of schools. *See also* nos. 729–30, 736.
Copies: NPL:R(S990A/3).   734

1934 WAGNER, Paula
James Cook's erste Entdeckungsreise in die Südsee, 1768–1771, in ihrer
Beziehung zu Winden und Strömungen; [with bibl.] Emsdetten, Heinr.
& J. Lechte, 1934.
Maps, pp. viii, 123.
Inaugural dissertation for the degree of Doctor of Philosophy at Westfälische Wilhelms-
Universität.
Copies: NPL:M(980:Co2/W1A1); ANL.   735

1944 WOOD, George Arnold

The Voyage of the *Endeavour*. Melbourne, Macmillan, 1944.

Facs. illus. maps, pp. x, 116.
(*Australian Pocket Library*.)
Prepared for the use of schools. *See also* nos. 729–30, 734.

Copies: NPL:M(980:Co2/W3D1); NPL:R(E919); Captain Cook's Landing Place Trust;
QU; VSL.   736

[195–?] CORNER, Sylvia

[Articles, compiled and written by S. Corner.]

Typescript.
CONTENTS:
Extracts from Banks' journal, Apl 27–May 6, 1770.
Modern botanical names of flora. Banks' collection from Botany Bay.
The Flora and fauna of eastern Australia and Tasmania, as observed by Cook, Banks
and others. By S. Corner.
Van Diemen's Land, by S. Corner.
The Story of Pacific voyaging before Cook's time, by S. Corner.
Captain Cook and Botany Bay. Extracts from the Royal Australian Historical Society—
Journal and proceedings, vol.10, pp.233–78; vol.11, pp.32–48; vol.14, pp.281–98.

Copies: Captain Cook's Landing Place Trust.   737

1954 GWYTHER, John

First voyage; being the full & authentic story of the great discoveries
made by Lt. James Cook, R.N., commanding H.M. Bark, *Endeavour*,
in the great South Seas . . . 1768–1771. (By J. Gwyther); [with bibl. and
extracts from Cook's own writings]. London, Melrose, 1954.

Facs. illus. maps, ports. pp. 208.
See also no. 740.

Copies: NPL:M(980:Co2/G1A1); NPL:R(E910.4); ANL; QU; VSL.   738

1954 ROBERTS, Lynette

The *Endeavour*: Captain Cook's first voyage to Australia. [With selected
bibl.] London, Owen, 1954.

Facs. illus. ports. pp. 280.

Copies: NPL:M(910.4/R); NPL:R(DS990A/213); ANL; QParl; QU.   739

1955 GWYTHER, John

Captain Cook and the South Pacific: the voyage of the *Endeavour*, 1768–
1771, by J. Gwyther. [With bibl. and extracts from Cook's own writings.]
Boston, Houghton Mifflin, 1955.

Facs. illus. map as endpapers, port. pp. xvi, 269.
See also no. 738.

Copies: NPL:M(980:Co2/G1B1); QU; WU.   740

[1960?] FORSYTH, John Walter

Cook's debt to Torres: some notes on the history of the exploration and
cartography of the Torres Straits. [1960?]

1 folder.
Negative photostat.
Copies: NPL:M(MSS.574).   741

1962 MITCHELL, Lorna Mary Maltravers
Pacific picture: stories of Pacific peoples, selected by L. M. M. Mitchell.
Sydney, A. & R., 1962.
pp. xii, 212.
A collection of writings, fiction and non-fiction, by various authors.
See also nos. 743, 747.
Copies: NPL:M(980/58A1).   742

1963 MITCHELL, Lorna Mary Maltravers
Pacific picture: stories of Pacific peoples, selected by L. M. M. Mitchell.
New ed. Sydney, A. & R., 1963.
Plates, ports. pp. xii, 212.
A collection of writings, fiction and non-fiction, by various authors. *See also* nos. 742, 747.
Copies: NPL:M(980/58B1).   743

1964 LEYDEN, Peter
Life aboard the *Endeavour*. Sydney, Peter Leyden Publishing House, 1964.
Illus. in colour, ports. pp. 8.
(*Australian Visual Books, History*, no. 3.)
For children. Cover title: The *Endeavour*.
Copies: NPL:M(Q990.1/10).   744

[1965] CORNER, Sylvia
Captain Cook and Australia; written and ed. by S. Corner. [Issued by
Captain Cook's Landing Place Trust.] Sydney, Govt. Pr., [1965].
Illus. maps, port. pp. 63.
Copies: NPL:M(980:Co2/C2A1); Captain Cook's Landing Place Trust.   745

1966 BEGG, Alexander Charles
Dusky Bay: [in the steps of Captain Cook], by A.C. Begg and N.C. Begg.
[With bibl.] Christchurch, N.Z., Whitcombe & Tombs, 1966.
Facs. illus., some in colour, maps, ports. pp. 239.
Copies: NPL:M(987.6/23A1).   746

1966 MITCHELL, Lorna Mary Maltravers
Pacific picture: stories of Pacific peoples, selected by L. M. M. Mitchell.
New ed. Sydney, A. & R., 1966.
Plates, ports. pp. xii, 212.
A collection of writings, fiction and non-fiction, by various authors. *See also* nos. 742, 743.
Copies: NPL:M(980/58C1).   747

1968 THE BRITISH MUSEUM—The King's Library

An Exhibition to commemorate the bi-centenary of Captain Cook's first voyage round the world: [catalogue. London, the Museum, 1968].

ff.vi,35.

Photocopy. Presentation copy to Mitchell Library from Map Room of British Museum. Photographs and colour transparencies of the exhibition placed at M.L. Pic. Acc.1582. Cased with the catalogue are two prospectuses of the exhibition.

Copies: NPL:M(Q980:Col/B1).   748

1968 RAUSCHENBERG, Roy Anthony

The Voyage of the *Endeavour*, 1768–1771.

(*In his* Daniel Carl Solander, naturalist on the *Endeavour*. Philadelphia, 1968. pp. 27–44.) American Philosophical Society—*Transactions*, n.s. vol. 58, pt. 8.

Copies: NPL:R(NQ506/5).   749

Articles, etc., about the First Voyage

1772–9 BONWICK, James

Collection of extracts from the *Monthly Review*, dealing with works on Cook and accounts of Botany Bay, 1772–9.

(Bonwick Transcripts: Cook, case 3, no.229b.)

Copies: NPL:M(B.T.ser.2 Box 32).   750

1778 MOORE, John Hamilton

Voyage of Captain Cook round the world in H.M. ship the *Endeavour* . . . 1768.

Illus.

(*In his* New and complete collection of voyages and travels. London, Alexander Hogg, 1778. Vol. 1, pp.170–236.)

Copies: NPL:M(F910.8/M); NPL:R(SC).   751

1779 CAMPBELL, John

Captain Cook's voyage round the world in 1768.

(*In his* Lives of the British Admirals. London, A. Donaldson, 1779. Vol. 4, pp. 288–325.) *See also* no. 753.

Copies: NPL:M(359.0942/C).   752

1813 CAMPBELL, John

[Naval history.]

(*In his* Lives of the British admirals. New ed. London, C. J. Barrington and others, 1813. Vol. 5, pp. 207–441.) *See also* no. 752.

Copies: NPL:M(Bayldon Collection).   753

1814 SYRACH, J.

Reize van Cook rondom de wereld.

(Maatschappij tot Nut van 't Algemeen—Korte uittreksels uit merkwaardige land- en zeereizen. Leiden, D. du Mortier en Zoon, 1814. pp. 117–51.)

Copies: NPL:M(910.8/M).   754

1838 MARTIN, *Sir* James

Botany Bay.

(*In his* The Australian sketch book. Sydney, James Tegg, 1838. pp. 43–58.)

Copies: NPL:M(A824/M); ANL.   755

1849 BARROW, *Sir* John

[Captain Cook.]

(*In his* Sketches of the Royal Society. London, J. Murray, 1849. pp. 18–26.)

Copies: NPL:M(925/B).   756

1854 TANIWHA, *Maori Chief*

[Recollections of Captain Cook's visit to New Zealand in 1769, by Taniwha (Taimoha), a Maori Chief. Statement made by him on 15th Nov. 1852, enclosed in despatch no. 80, 4th Jan. 1853, from Governor Sir George Grey to Sir John S. Pakington.]

(*In* Great Britain—New Zealand. Further papers relative to the affairs of New Zealand, in continuation of papers presented on the 7th Aug. 1851 and 3d and 14th May, 1852. Presented to both Houses of Parliament . . . Ap. 10, 1854. London, Eyre and Spottiswoode for H.M.S.O., 1854. pp. 180–1.)

Copies: NPL:M(Q997/Pa12).   757

1862 FLANAGAN, Roderick

Cook explores the coast of New South Wales.

(*In his* The History of New South Wales. London, Sampson Low, 1862. Vol.1, pp. 3–20.)
See also nos. 787–8.

Copies: NPL:M(991/F).   758

1865 HOWITT, William

Discoveries of Captain Cook in Australia, Van Diemen's Land, and New Zealand from 1768 to 1770.

(*In his* History of discovery in Australia. London, Longmans, Green, 1865. Vol. 1, pp. 76–103.)

Copies: NPL:M(980/127A1); NPL:R(S990A/147).   759

1873 COOK'S first voyage.

Illus.

(*In* Monarchs of ocean, Columbus and Cook. Edinburgh, Nimmo, 1873. pp. 123–227.)

Copies: NPL:M(910.4/119A1).   760

1878 COLENSO, *Rev.* William

On the day in which Captain Cook took formal possession of New Zealand; [with bibl.] Wellington, N.Z., Lyon and Blair, pr., [1878]. pp. 99–108.

Extracts from New Zealand Institute—*Transactions*, vol. 10, 1877.

Copies: NPL:M(980:Co2/C1A1); NPL:R(DS506/8).   761

1880 BATTLE of Botany Bay.

Illus.

(*Australian Pictorial Almanac*, 1880. pp. 38–9.)

Copies: NPL:M(Q990.1/A).   762

1880 VERNE, Jules

Captain Cook's first voyage.

Illus. maps, port.

(*In his* Great navigators of the eighteenth century. London, Sampson, Low, Marston, etc., 1880. pp. 100–205.)

Copies: NPL:M(910.45/18B1).   763

1885 HUNTINGTON, Henry William Hemsworth

History of Australasia. [Pt. 1] 1885.

Copies: NPL:M(Q990.1/H); NPL:R(Q990.1/1).   764

1888 WILLIAMS, *Rev.* William Leonard

On the visit of Captain Cook to Poverty Bay and Tolaga Bay.

Illus.

(New Zealand Institute—*Transactions*, vol. 21, 1888, pp. 389–97.)

Copies: NPL:M(506/N); NPL:R(DS506/8).   765

1890 STEPHEN, *Sir* Alfred

The Name Port Jackson, Sydney, N.S.W. May 24, 1890.

ff.3.

[Typescript.]

Copies: NPL:M(Q991.1/S).   766

1890 STEPHEN, *Sir* Alfred

The Name Port Jackson, Sydney, N.S.W. May 24, 1890.

pp.2.

(Parkes Correspondence, vol. 35, pp. 300–2, 304–5.)

Printed copy.

Copies: NPL:M(A905 MSSDept).   767

1892 CALVERT, Albert Frederick

The Early discovery of Australia.

Illus. maps, ff.16.

Extracted from the *British Australasian* vol. 10, no. 428, 8 Dec. 1892. With MS. annotations.

Copies: NPL:D(MS.Q146).   768

[1893] MARTIN, Arthur Patchett
Story of the *Endeavour*.
(*In his* True stories from Australasian history. London, Griffith Farran, [1893]. pp. 45–51.)
Copies: NPL:M(990/M).   769

1895 GAUNT, Mary
Captain Cook in New Zealand.
Illus. map, port.
(Cassell & Co.—Pictorial New Zealand, pp. 285–93. 1895.)
Copies: NPL:M(987/C).   770

1895 KIRK, Thomas William
Notes on MS. descriptions of collection made during Captain Cook's first voyage.
(New Zealand Institute—*Transactions*, vol. 28, 1895, pp. 491–3.)
Copies: NPL:M(506/N); NPL:R(DS506/8).   771

1895.6 NORMAN, *Sir* Henry Wylie
Captain Cook and his first voyage round the world, 1768 to 1771, with special reference to his exploration of the Queensland coast.
(Royal Geographical Society of Australasia—Queensland Branch—*Proceedings*. Vol. 11, 1895.6, pp. 1–30.)
Copies: NPL:M(980/R); NPL:R(S994A/5).   772

[1896] SAUNDERS, Alfred
Captain Cook and his journal.
(*In his* History of New Zealand. Christchurch, Whitcombe & Tombs, [1896]. pp. 1–17.)
Copies: NPL:M(997/S).   773

1897 MACDONALD, Alexander Cameron
Notes on the discovery of the eastern coast of New Holland, Australia, by Captain Cook.
Map, port.
(Royal Geographical Society of Australasia—Victorian Branch—*Transactions*, vol. 14, 1897. pp. 20–28.)
Copies: NPL:M(980/R); NPL:R(DS992A/3).   774

1899 CAPTAIN COOK'S LANDING at Botany Bay. [Extract from *Daily Telegraph*, Apr.28, 1899.]
Illus. port.
(Watson, J.H.—Scrap book, vol. 1, p. 76.)
Copies: NPL:M(F990.1/W).   775

1899 MORRIS, Edward Ellis
The Name Botany Bay: [extract from the *Sydney Morning Herald*, May 24, 1899].
(Newspaper cuttings, vol. 114, pp. 22–3.)
Copies: NPL:M(Q991/N); NPL:R(F079/S982).   776

1900 MORRIS, Edward Ellis
On the tracks of Captain Cook.
(New Zealand Institute—*Transactions*, vol.33, 1900. pp. 499–514.)
Copies: NPL:M(506/N); NPL:D(90/197); NPL:R(DS506/8).   777

1902 DUNCAN, R.
Following the tracks of Captain Cook.
Illus. map.
(New Zealand Institute—*Transactions*, vol. 35, 1902. pp. 32–45.)
Copies: NPL:M(506/N); NPL:R(DS506/8).   778

1902 HASZARD, H.D.M.
Foot-tracks of Captain Cook.
Illus.
(New Zealand Institute—*Transactions*, vol. 35, 1902. pp. 24–32.)
Copies: NPL:M(506/N); NPL:R(DS506/8).   779

1907 FOWLER, Thomas Walker
Captain Cook's Australian landfall.
Map.
(*Victorian Geographical Journal*, vol. 25, 1907. pp. 8–12.)
Copies: NPL:M(980/R); NPL:R(DS992A/3).   780

1907 McNAB, Robert
Discovery by Cook.
(*In his* Murihiku and the southern islands. Invercargill, W. Smith, pr., 1907. pp. 3–12.)
Also published in the author's *Murihiku: a history*, 1909.
Copies: NPL:M(997.9/M); NPL:R(S997/15).   781

1908 WATTS, Ebenezer John Moore
Cook discovers New South Wales.
Illus. port.
(*In his* Stories from Australian history. Sydney, William Brooks, 1908. pp. 36–47.)
Brooks's Australian School Series. See also no. 795.
Copies: NPL:M(990.1/W).   782

1909 McNAB, Robert
Cook explores, 1770.
(*In his* Murihiku: a history. Wellington, N.Z., Whitcombe & Tombs, 1909. pp. 13–30.)
Copies: NPL:M(997.9/M); NPL:R(DS997/16).   783

1909 WICHMANN, Arthur
Entdeckungsgeschichte von Neu-Guinea (bis 1828). Leiden, E. J. Brill, 1909.
(*Nederlandsche Nieuw-Guinea-Expeditie*, 1903. Vol. 1.)
Copies: NPL:M(Q988.4/W); NPL:R(Q998.4A/1).   784

1910 FALCON, *pseud.*
Conquest of the South Pacific: Cook's empire-making first voyage.
Maps.
(Newspaper cuttings, 1910.)
Copies: NPL:M(Q980:Col/N1A3).   785

[1910–11] HARGRAVE, Lawrence
Facing Island, why not charted by Captain Cook?
Map.
(Newspaper cuttings, vol. 186, ff. 12–13, 1910–11.)
Copies: NPL:M(990/N).   786

[1912] FLANAGAN, Roderick
First voyage of Captain Cook.
Illus. in colour.
(*In* Early days in Australia; ed. by Herbert Strang. London, H. Frowde & Hodder & Stoughton, [1912]. pp. 92–114.)
From Flanagan's *History of New South Wales. See also* nos. 758, 788.
Copies: NPL:M(980.1/S).   787

[1912?] FLANAGAN, Roderick
First voyage of Captain Cook.
Illus. in colour.
(*In* The Romance of Australia; ed. by Herbert Strang. London, H. Frowde & Hodder & Stoughton, [1912?]. pp.92–114.)
From Flanagan's *History of New South Wales. See also* nos. 758, 787.
Copies: NPL:M(980.1/S).   788

1912 SCOTT, *Sir* Ernest
English and French navigators on the Victorian coast; [with bibl.].
(*Victorian Historical Magazine*, vol. 2, 1912, pp. 145–76.)
Copies: NPL:M(992/V); NPL:R(S992.06/1).   789

[1912] STRANG, Herbert, *pseud.*
First voyage of Captain Cook.
Illus. in colour.
(*In his* Early days in Australia. London, H. Frowde & Hodder & Stoughton, [1912]. pp. 92–114.)
Copies: NPL:M(980.1/S).   790

1912 SYNGE, Margaret Bertha
Cook discovers New Zealand.
Illus. map.
(*In her* A Book of discovery. London, Jack, 1912. pp. 319–29.)
See also nos. 800, 846.
Copies: NPL:M(910.9/10A1).   791

1913 FITCHETT, *Rev.* William Henry
Man who discovered Australia, etc.
Port.
(*In his* New world of the south: Australia in the making. London, G. Bell, 1913. pp. 43–70.)
Copies: NPL:M(990.1/F); NPL:R(DS990/3).   792

1913 JOHNSTON, *Sir* Harry Hamilton
James Cook's first voyage; [and] (New South Wales).
Illus.
(*In his* Pioneers in Australasia. London, Blackie, 1913. pp. 178–251.)
Written for children.
Copies: NPL:M(980/J); NPL:R(S990/8).   793

1914 McNAB, Robert
Cook on the east coast, 1769; [and] (Cook completes his survey, 1769 and 1770). [With bibl.]
(*In his* From Tasman to Marsden. Dunedin, J. Wilkie, 1914. pp. 16–32, 46–58.)
Copies: NPL:M(997/M); NPL:R(DS997/5).   794

1914 WATTS, Ebenezer John Moore
Cook discovers New South Wales.
Illus. port.
(*In his* Stories from Australian history. 2nd ed. Sydney, William Brooks, 1914. pp. 38–46.)
See also no. 782.
Copies: NPL:M(990.1/W).   795

1915 JACK, Robert Logan
Exploration of Cape York Peninsula . . . Cook.
(Royal Australian Historical Society—*Journal and Proceedings*. Vol. 3, pp. 184–5. 1915.)
Copies: NPL:M(991/R,Ref.Books); NPL:D(9/69); NPL:R(S991.06/1,Ref.Books).   796

1916 CAMBAGE, Richard Hind
Captain Cook's Pigeon House and early South Coast exploration. Sydney, S.E. Lees, pr., 1916.
pp.24.
Copies: NPL:M(981.8/C); ANL.   797

[1917] MURDOCH, *Sir* Walter
Cook; [with port. after Dance].
Illus.
(*In his* Making of Australia. Melbourne, W.&T., [1917]. pp. 36–42.)
Copies: NPL:M(990.1/M); NPL:R(990.1/43).   798

[1919?] FINCH, Robert J.
First voyage of Captain Cook.
(*In his* Kingsway book of famous explorers. London, Evans, [1919?]. pp. 73–8.)
Copies: NPL:M(910.9/F).   799

1920 SYNGE, Margaret Bertha
Cook discovers New Zealand.
Illus. map.
(*In her* A Book of discovery. New York, Putnam, 1920. pp. 319–29.)
See also nos. 791, 846.
Copies: NPL:M(910.9/10B1).   800

1922 JACK, Robert Logan
Cook in *Endeavour*, 1770; [with port.].
(*In his* Northmost Australia. Melbourne, Robertson, 1922. Vol. 1, pp. 82–91.)
Copies: NPL:M(984.6/13A1); NPL:R(S994A/38); ANL.   801

1922 WOOD, George Arnold
Voyage of the *Endeavour*, etc. [With bibl.]
Illus. maps, ports.
(*In his* Discovery of Australia. London, Macmillan, 1922. pp. 380–479.)
Copies: NPL:M(980/125A1); NPL:R(DS990.1/19).   802

1922–5 BERTIE, Charles Henry
Captain Cook and Botany Bay; [with bibl. and] (comments).
(Royal Australian Historical Society—*Journal and Proceedings*. Vol. 10, 1922, pp. 233–74; vol. 11, 1925, pp. 47–8.)
Copies: NPL:M(991/R,Ref.Books); NPL:D(9/69); NPL:R(S991.06/1,Ref.Books).   803

1923 CAPTAIN COOK'S LANDING. (Anniversary studies, no. 3.)
(*Country Journal*, Apr. 1923, pp. 16–17.)
Copies: NPL:M(Q630.5/C).   804

1925 AARONS, F.
Cook's artists: [*Sydney Morning Herald*, May 16, 1925].
(Newspaper cuttings, vol. 166, pp. 170–2.)
Copies: NPL:M(Q991/N); NPL:R(F079/S982).   805

1925 CARRUTHERS, *Sir* Joseph Hector McNeil
Captain Cook and Botany Bay: comments on the paper by Mr C.H. Bertie.
(Royal Australian Historical Society—*Journal and Proceedings.* Vol. 11, 1925, pp. 32–8.)
Copies: NPL:M(991/R,Ref.Books); NPL:D(9/69); NPL:R(S991.06/1,Ref.Books). 806

1925 DUNLOP, N.J.
James Cook and the Australian medical harbingers.
(*Medical Journal of Australia*, Sept. 1925, pp. 362–73.)
Copies: NPL:M(Q610.5/M); NPL:R(DQ610.6/2). 807

1925 KIPPIS, *Rev.* Andrew
Captain Cook's visit to New Zealand; (Australia in the time of Cook [and] With Cook in New Guinea, New Hebrides and New Caledonia).
Port. as frontisp., illus.
(*In* Ridgway, Athelstan—The World revealed, Australasia. London, Nelson, 1925. pp. 21–45.)
Frontispiece is portrait of Cook, from a pen-drawing by E. Heber Thompson, after the National Gallery portrait.
Copies: NPL:M(980/143A1). 808

1925 SUTTOR, Horace Melbourne
Captain Cook's voyage.
(*In his* Australian milestones. Sydney, John Andrews, 1925. Vol. 1, pp. 4–9.)
Copies: NPL:M(990.1/S). 809

1926 BARR, John
Rediscovery of the Waitemata and Manukau Harbours.
Map, port.
(*In his* Ports of Auckland. Auckland, Unity Press Ltd., 1926. pp. 14–16.)
Copies: NPL:M(Q627.3/B); NPL:R(S656.52/2). 810

1928 COLES, S.F.A.
The *Endeavour* in New Zealand: [extract from the *Nineteenth Century*, vol. 104, Oct. 1928. pp. 521–7].
(Newspaper Cuttings: Captain Cook, vol. 2, pp. 151–7.)
Copies: NPL:M(Q980:Co1/N1A2); NPL:R(S050/N714). 811

1928 MEMORIAL to Captain Cook at Bustard Bay.
Illus.
(Historical Society of Queensland—*Journal.* Mar. 1928, pp. 159–88, 191.)
Copies: NPL:M(994/H); NPL:R(S994.06/1). 812

1928 STADLER, Hans
Kapitän Cooks erster Aufenthalt auf Otaheite. (Kapitän Cooks letzte Fahrt.)
Illus. port.
(*In his* Reisebilder aus Australien und Ozeanien. Wien, Deutscher Verlag für Jugend und Volk, 1928. Chapters 1 and 5.)
Copies: NPL:M(980/51A1); ANL.   813

1929 ROSE, John Holland
Captain Cook and the founding of British power in the Pacific; [with bibl. and discussion].
Map.
(*Geographical Journal*, London, vol. 73, Feb. 1929, pp. 102–9, 119–22.)
Copies: NPL:M(980:Col/G1A1); NPL:R(DS909.6A/2).   814

1930 JACKSON, Ernest Sandford
Early visitors to Moreton Bay.
(Royal Australian Historical Society—*Journal and Proceedings*. Vol. 15, 1930, pp. 311–12.)
Copies: NPL:M(991/R,Ref.Books); NPL:D(9/69); NPL:R(S991.06/1,Ref.Books).   815

1931 JACKSON, Ernest Sandford
[Mortality . . . aboard Cook's *Endeavour*.]
(*Medical Journal of Australia*, Dec. 1931, pp. 746–7.)
Copies: NPL:M(Q610.5/M); NPL:R(DQ610.6/2).   816

1931 WHITE, David Renfrew, *the younger*
[Captain Cook in Otakou.]
(*In his* Tidemarks at Otakou. Dunedin, J. McIndoe, 1931, pp. 8–14.)
Copies: NPL:M(997.4/W).   817

[1933] REED, Alfred Hamish
[Cook.]
Illus. map.
(*In* First New Zealand Christmases, by A.H. and A.W. Reed. Dunedin, Reed, [1933]. pp. 15–17.)
Copies: NPL:M(997/R).   818

1933 WILLIAMSON, James Alexander
Exploration and discovery; [including early exploration of Australia].
(*In* Turberville, Arthur Stanley—Johnson's England . . . life and manners of his age. Chapter 5.)
Copies: ANL.   819

1934 INGLETON, Geoffrey Chapman
H.M. Bark *Endeavour:* souvenir of an exhibition of models constructed
during Victoria's centenary year, 1934. Melbourne, *The Argus,* 1934.
Illus. pp.7.
Copies: NPL:M(623.8/I). 820

1935 OLSEN, Örjan
Le Premier voyage de Cook.
Illus. port.
(*In his* La Conquête de la terre. Paris, Payot, 1935. Vol. 4, pp. 246–69.)
Copies: NPL:M(910.4/0). 821

1936 MACKANESS, George
Banks and Cook; [with port.].
(*In his* Sir Joseph Banks. Sydney, A.&R., 1936. pp. 1–13.)
Copies: NPL:M(A925.8/B218/17A1); ANL. 822

[1936] ROBINSON, Gregory
The *Endeavour*: how Captain Cook opened up the Pacific and discovered
the north-western coast of America.
Illus. in colour. plan.
(*In his* Ships that have made history. London, P. Davies and L. Dickson, [1936]. pp.
137–53.)
Copies: NPL:M(656.509/R); NPL:R(DS656.509/55,Ref.Books); ANL. 823

1939 VEXED HISTORY: date of Captain Cook's first voyage.
(*N.Z. Centennial News*, Jan. 1939, p. 8.)
Copies: NPL:M(Q997.06/1). 824

1941 CURREY, Charles Herbert
James Cook . . . the voyage of the *Endeavour*.
Map, port.
(*In his* Notable pathfinders to new regions. Sydney, W. & T., 1941. pp. 78–84.)
For school children.
Copies: NPL:M(910.9/C). 825

1941 WOLSKEL, Augustus
Captain Cook and Point Hicks.
Maps.
(*Victorian Historical Magazine*, vol.19, June 1941, pp.17–30.)
Copies: NPL:M(992/V); NPL:R(S992.06/1). 826

1944 LOHSE, Charlotte

For James Cook.

Illus. map.
(*In* The Mysterious continent: the story of the adventurous sailors who discovered the south Pacific Islands. By C. Lohse and J. Seaton. Indianapolis, Bobbs-Merril, 1944. pp.141–57.)

Copies: NPL:M(980/L); ANL.   827

1944 MEARNS, David C.

Captain Cook's autograph journal of the voyage in the *Endeavour*; [photographic copy presented to Mrs Roosevelt for the Library of Congress, Sept. 4th, 1943].

(Library of Congress—*Quarterly Journal*. Jan.–Mar. 1944, pp. 24–9.)
Letter from W.H. Ifould with comments on the article bound with Mitchell Library copy.

Copies: NPL:M(980:Co2/M1A1); NPL:R(S010.6/7).   828

1946 JARVIS, Henry Wood

Captain Cook's first voyage.

(*In his* Let the great story be told: the truth about British expansion. [With note on sources, and bibl.] London, Sampson Low, Marston, [1946]. pp. 109–17.)

Copies: NPL:M(909/J); NPL:R(DS909/289).   829

1946 PARKER, Ferdinand Lucas

Cook's log and journal dates, particularly relating to the discovery of Whitsunday Passage and consequently of other points in New Zealand and the east coast of Australia. By F.L. Parker and J.D. Somerville.

(Royal Geographical Society of Australasia—South Australian Branch—*Proceedings*. Vol. 47, 1945–6. pp. 97–118.)
Reprinted in the Society's Historical Memorials Committee *Annual report*, 1945–6, pp. 22–43.)

Copies: NPL:M(980/R); ANL(reprint).   830

1947 ROSE, Frederica Dorothy Violet, *Lady*

Captain Cook's journal during his first voyage round the world, made in H.M. Bark *Endeavour*, 1768–71.

(*In her* The Traveller's eye. [With commentaries and bibl. notes. Ed.] by Dorothy Carrington, [i.e. Lady F.D.V. Rose]. New York, Pilot Press, 1947. pp. 360–76.)

Copies: NPL:M(910.4/R); NPL:R(S909A/199).   831

1950 MACKAY, Joseph Angus

Cook's historic landfall at Poverty Bay, etc.

Facs. illus. map.
(*In his* Historic Poverty Bay and the East Coast, N.I., N.Z., by J.A. Mackay . . . Pub. as a centennial memorial on behalf of the Poverty Bay-East Coast Centennial Council. Gisborne, J.A.Mackay, 1949, [i.e. 1950]. pp. 16–61.)
See also no. 850.

Copies: NPL:M(997.5/34A1).   832

1951 LLOYD, H. Alan
A Link with Captain Cook and H.M.S. *Endeavour*. [John Shelton's clock.]
Illus. map.
(*Endeavour*, vol. 10, pp. 200–4, Oct. 1951.)
Copies: NPL:R(Q506/38).   833

1952 BERRILL, Norman John
Venus observed.
(*In his* Journey into Wonder. New York, Dodd, Mead, 1952. pp. 148–59.)
See also no. 835.
Copies: NPL:M(910/B).   834

1953 BERRILL, Norman John
Venus observed.
(*In his* Journey into wonder. London, Gollancz, 1953. pp. 147–57.)
See also no. 834.
Copies: NPL:R(S570.9/8).   835

1954 REID, Frank
Cook's voyage inside the Reef.
(*In his* The Romance of the Great Barrier Reef. Sydney, A.&R., 1954. pp. 9–17.)
Copies: NPL:M(994.8/R); NPL:R(N994.3/1).   836

1956 HAWKESWORTH, John
Lieutenant James Cook's discovery of Moreton Bay, 1770; [with intro. and bibl.].
(*In* Mackaness, George—The Discovery and exploration of Moreton Bay and the Brisbane River. Sydney, D.S. Ford, pr., 1956. Pt. 1, pp. 6–7.)
Australian Historical monographs, no. 35.
Copies: NPL:M(994.1/M); NPL:R(S994/2).   837

1959 BORLAND, H. A.
East coast exploration: Captain Cook.
(*North Queensland Register*, Jan. 31, 1959, pp.24.)
Copies: ANL.   838

1959 CHARLIAT, Pierre-Jacques
Le Premier voyage de Cook, 1768–1772.
(*In his* Le Temps des grands voiliers. Paris, Nouvelle Librarie de France, 1959. pp. 178–81.)
Parias, L.H.—Histoire universelle des explorations, vol. 3.
Copies: NPL:M(910.9/9A1).   839

1959 CILENTO, *Sir* Raphael West
Cook's hundred days on the Queensland coast.

Illus. port.
(*In* Triumph in the tropics; comp. and ed. by Sir Raphael Cilento . . . with the assistance
of C. Lack . . . For the Historical Committee of the Centenary Celebrations Council of
Queensland. Brisbane, Smith & Paterson, 1959. pp. 22–32.)
Copies: NPL:M(994/3A1); NPL:R(994.3/2).   840

1959 LENNARD, Leslie Maurice Wynn
Cook lands at Motuarohia.

Illus. map.
(*In his* Motuarohia: an island in the Bay of Islands. Auckland, Pelorus Press, 1959.
pp. 5–10.)
Copies: NPL:M(997.5/8A1).   841

1959 WOOLF, Harry
[James Cook.]

(*In his* The Transits of Venus. Princeton, U.P., 1959. pp. 167–8.)
Copies: NPL:M(523.96/1A1); NPL:R(N523.42/2).   842

[1960?] SIMMONS, H.G.
The Discovery of Keppel Bay and related events. A paper presented to
the Rockhampton Historical Society. [Rockhampton, Queensland.,
Rockhampton Historical Society, 1960?]

pp. 11.
Cover title. Processed.
Copies: ANL.   843

1962 BERIOT, Agnes
Premier voyage: L'*Endeavour*, 1768–1771.

(*In her* Grands voiliers autour du monde: les voyages scientifiques, 1760–1850. Paris,
Editions du Pont Royal, 1962. pp. 41–54.)
Copies: NPL:M(Q910.4/14A1); NPL:R(NQ910.4/1).   844

1962 DANIELL, David Scott
James Cook: the discovery of New Zealand, 1768–71.

Illus. map.
(*In his* Explorers & exploration. London, Batsford, 1962. pp. 72–90.)
Copies: NPL:M(910.8/27A1).   845

1962 SYNGE, Margaret Bertha
Cook discovers New Zealand.

Illus. map.
(*In her* A Book of discovery. New ed. Edinburgh, Nelson, 1962. pp. 221–8.)
See also nos. 791, 800.
Copies: NPL:M(910.9/10C1).   846

1963 DAUGHERTY, Charles Michael
A Party of scientific gentlemen.
(*In his* Searches of the sea. London, Phoenix House, 1963. pp. 30–42.)
Copies: NPL:M(910.4/125B1); NPL:R(551.46/12).   847

1963 MILLER, Robert
James Cook, *Endeavour*, 1770.
(*Medical Journal of Australia*, pp. 303–4, Aug.24, 1963.)
Copies: NPL:M(Q610.5/M); NPL:R(DQ610.6/2).   848

1964 BEALE, Edgar
Cook's first landing attempt in New South Wales.
(Royal Australian Historical Society—*Journal and Proceedings*, vol.50, Aug. 1964, pp. 191–204.)
Copies: NPL:M(991/R); NPL:D(9/69); NPL:R(S991.06/1A); ANL.   849

1966 MACKAY, Joseph Angus
Cook's historic landfall at Poverty Bay, etc.
Facs. illus. map.
(*In his* Historic Poverty Bay. 2nd ed. Gisborne, N.Z., J.G. Mackay, 1966. pp. 16–61.)
See also no. 832.
Copies: NPL:M(997.5/34B1).   850

1968 [COLLECTION of articles published in *Australia & New Zealand Weekly* and *The Australian News*, July–Sep. 1968, to commemorate the bi-centenary of Captain Cook's first voyage round the world. London.]
Illus. 5 sheets.
Copies: NPL:M(Q980:Co2/C1).   851

1968 [COLLECTION of pamphlets and newspaper articles issued to mark the celebrations held at Whitby, August 1968, to commemorate the bi-centenary of Captain Cook's first voyage round the world.]
12 articles.
CONTENTS:
Whitby Museum—Notes on exhibits.
Shell-Mex Ltd.—Yorkshire, East and North Ridings.
Captain Cook: [biographical leaflet].
English, B.—The Rising tide: [prospectus about the play].
Leaflet giving programme of the bi-centenary celebrations.
Whitby Regatta—Souvenir programme.
St. Mary's Parish Church, Whitby—Captain James Cook bi-centenary service of thanksgiving . . . August 25th 1968.
Whitby, *parish*—Events during August 1968.
Captain James Cook, R.N., his Pacific explorations and circumnavigation of New Zealand [and] New Zealand today.
Whitby: [tourist guide].
Captain James Cook bicentenary: [souvenir programme].
Whitby Gazette, 30th August 1968.
Copies: NPL:M(Q980:Co2/C2).   852

1968 PRICE, F.C.
Cook's first voyage.
Illus. port.
(*Yorkshire Life*, vol.22 no.8, Aug. 1968, pp.18–19.)
Copies: NPL:M(Q914.274/1).   853

1968 STEARN, William Thomas
The Botanical results of the *Endeavour* voyage.
Plates, some in colour.
(*Endeavour*, London, Jan.1968. Vol.27, pp.3–10.)
Copies: NPL:R(NQ505/7).   854

Charts

Manuscripts

[1769?] COOK, James
A Plan of King Georges Island or Otaheite lying in the South Sea, by
Lieutenant I.Cook; discovr'd by Captn. Wallice [i.e. Wallis] the 19th
June, 1767: [ms. map 1769?].
1 sheet, cm 63½ x 88 [Scale *8 miles = 8″*.] Ink and wash. B./wh.
South to top of sheet. Watermarked, D. & C. Blauw IV, The name "[Point Venus]"
added in pencil. The spelling "Wallice" which appears on the map is that consistently
used by Cook throughout the Journal (c.f. Beaglehole's ed.).
Copies: NPL:D.   855

[1769?] COOK, James
A Plan of King Georges Island or Otaheite lying in the South Sea, by
Lieutenant I. Cook. Discover'd by Captn. Wallice, the 19th June 1767.
[1769?]
The original plan, in sepia and ink, drawn 1 mile to an inch. 34″ x 24½″. Enclosed in
buckram case.
Copies: NPL:D.   856

1770 COOK, James
A Chart of part of New Zealand, or the island of Aeheinomowe [i.e.
North Island] lying in the South Seas, by Lieut. I.Cook, commander of
His Majesty's Bark the *Endeavour*, 1770.
1 sheet, cm 97½ x 75½ [Scale not given.] Ink and wash. B./wh.
Two sheets joined as one. Watermarked, D. & C. Blauw IV. Pencilled notes in an
unidentified hand, around Mercury Point and Mercury Bay, read "Stony place for
holding position against natives, transit of Mercury observed 9 Nov. 1769. Excellent
and abundant oysters." Some draft lines in pencil. Red sticker in lower right corner
reads "6 Cook".
Copies: NPL:D.   857

1770 COOK, James

A Chart of part of New Zealand or the island of Tovypoenammu [i.e. South Island] lying in the South Sea, by Lieutenant J.Cook, commander of His Majestys Bark, the *Endeavour*, 1770.

1 sheet, cm 110 x 90½ [Scale not given.] Ink and wash. B./wh.
Two sheets joined as one. Watermarked, D. & C. Blauw IV. Has many draft lines in pencil. Red sticker in lower right corner reads "7 Cook".
Copies: NPL:D.

858

1770 COOK, James

A Chart of the sea coast of New South Wales or the east coast of New Holland, by Lieut. J.Cook, Commander of His Majesty's Bark the *Endeavour*, who discovered and explored this coast in 1770.

No scale given, 1 sheet, 22½" x 35¾".
(*Brabourne Papers.*)
Extends several degrees further E. and N. than the map published in Hawkesworth's account.)
Copies: NPL:M(MT4805/1770/1).

859

Charts

Reproductions

The following charts relating to Cook's voyage are contained in the first edition of Hawkesworth, John—*An Account of the voyages undertaken . . . for making discoveries in the southern hemisphere*. London, 1773. The charts have been indexed from the copy in the Mitchell Library at Q980/38A1–3(no.648), and have not been listed for other copies and editions.

Chart of part of the South Sea, shewing the Tracts & Discoveries made by His Majestys Ships *Dolphin*, Commodore Byron, & *Tamer*, Capn Mouat, 1765. *Dolphin*, Capn. Wallis, & *Swallow*, Capn. Carteret, 1767, and *Endeavour*, Lieutenant Cook, 1769. Engrav'd by W. Whitchurch. [London, 1773].

No scale given. 1 sheet, cm 34 x 64.
Area: from China to Terra (*sic*) del Fuego, from Sumatra to Falkland Islands.
Shows tracks of ships with dates, coastlines, newly discovered lands by shading, place names. *Vol. 1, facing title-page.*

A Chart of Captn. Carteret's Discoveries at New Britain, with part of Captn. Cooke's Passage thro Endeavour Streights, & of Captn. Dampier's Tract & Discoveries in 1699, & 1700, at New Guinea and New Britain. Engraved by W. Whitchurch . . . [London, 1773].

No scale given. 1 sheet, cm 20 x 60.
Shows tracks of Dampier, Carteret, Cook; coastlines, depths in fathoms, place names. *Vol. 1, facing p. 595.*

A Chart of the S.E. part of Terra (*sic*) del Fuego including Strait le Maire and part of Staten-Land. By Lieutenant J. Cook 1769. [Engraved by] T. Bowen & J. Gibson. [London, 1773].

No scale given. 1 sheet, cm 14 x 16 on cm 31 x 35.
Insets: A plan of Success Bay in Strait le Maire. [Four coastal views in profile of Terra (*sic*) del Fuego and Strait le Maire].
Shows coastlines, depths in fathoms, track of *Endeavour*, anchorages, dates; place names, rivers, hill shading. *Vol. 2, facing p. 39.*

Chart of the Island Otaheite, by Lieut. J. Cook 1769. [Engraved by] J. Cheevers. [London, 1773].

1:190,080. 1 sheet, cm 22 x 39.
Shows coastlines, depths in fathoms, anchorages; place names, rivers, forests, hill shading. *Vol. 2, facing p. 79.*

A Chart of the Islands discover'd in the Neighbourhood of Otaheite, in the Course of several Voyages round the World, made by the Capns. Byron, Wallis, Carteret, & Cooke, in the years 1765, 1767, 1769. [Engraved by] Whitchurch. [London, 1773].

No scale given. 1 sheet, cm 24 x 51.
Area: from Island of Disappointment to Ohetiroa, from Scilly Island to Whitsunday Island.
Shows tracks of ships; islands, place names. *Vol. 2, facing p. 249.*

Chart of the Society Isles, discovered by Lieut. J. Cook, 1769. [Engraved by] J. Cheevers. [London, 1773].

1:285,120. 1 sheet, cm 27 x 41.
Area: from Tubai to Ulietea, from Maurua to Huaheine.
Shows coastlines, depths in fathoms, anchorages; place names, hill shading. *Vol. 2, facing p. 249.*

[Charts of four harbours in Otaheite, Huaheine and Ulietea. Engraved by] J. Cheevers. [London, 1773].

Various scales. 1 sheet, cm 22 x 35.
Shows coastlines of: Matavia Bay, Owharre Harbour, Ohamaneno Harbour, Oopoa Harbour; depths in fathoms, anchorages; place names. *Vol. 2, facing p. 249.*

Chart of New Zealand, explored in 1769 and 1770, by Lieut: I. Cook, Commander of His Majesty's Bark *Endeavour*. Engrav'd by I. Bayly. [London, 1773].

No scale given. 1 sheet, cm 47 x 36.
Shows coastlines, track of *Endeavour*, depths in fathoms, anchorages; place names, hill shading. *Vol. 2, facing p. 281.*

[Charts of River Thames and Mercury Bay, Bay of Islands, Tolaga Bay in New Zealand. London, 1773.]

Various scales. 1 sheet, cm 28 x 42. *Vol. 2, facing p. 323.*

Chart of Cook's Strait in New Zealand. [Engraved by] John Ryland. [London, 1773].

1:380,160. 1 sheet, cm 26 x 26.
Shows coastlines, depths in fathoms; hill shading, trees, place names. *Vol. 2, facing p. 385.*

Botany Bay, in New South Wales. Lat: 34° 00.Sth. [Engraved by] J. Gibson & T. Bowen. [London, 1773].

ca1:126,720. 1 sheet, cm 14 x 17.
Shows anchorage, depths in fathoms, coastlines; place names, vegetation, creeks. *Vol. 3, facing p. 481. See also no. 891.*

A Chart of New South Wales, or the East Coast of New Holland. Discover'd and Explored by Lieutenant J. Cook, Commander of his Majesty's Bark *Endeavour* in the year MDCCLXX. Engraved by W. Whitchurch. [London, 1773].

1:190,080. 1 sheet, cm 35 x 77.
Area: coastline from Prince of Wales's Isles to Point Hicks.
Shows track of *Endeavour:* anchorages, depths in fathoms, coastline; place names. *Vol. 3, facing p. 481.*

Entrance of Endeavour River, in New South Wales. Lat: 15° 26′ Sth. [Engraved by] J. Gibson & T. Bowen. [London, 1773].

1:31,680. 1 sheet, cm 14 x 17.
Shows landing place, spot where *Endeavour* was repaired, depths in fathoms, coastline, place names, vegetation, hill shading. *Vol. 3, facing p. 481.*

Chart of part of the Coast of New South Wales, from Cape Tribulation to Endeavour Straits. By Lieut. J. Cook, 1770. [Engraved by] J. Cheevers. [London, 1773].

No scale given. 1 sheet, cm 28 x 32.
Shows track of *Endeavour*, anchorages, depths in fathoms, coastline; place names. *Vol. 3, facing p. 589.*

860

[177–?] DE L'ISLE, Guillaume

L'Hemisphere meridional pour voir plus distinctement les terres australes. New ed. Amsterdam, chez Jean Covens et Corneille Mortier, [177–?].

No scale given, 1 sheet diameter cm 43.
The map has been extensively revised to take account of the discoveries of Bougainville, 1766–9 and Cook, 1768–71.
Copies: NPL:D(Cb77/4).

861

1770 PICKERSGILL, Richard

A Plan of Sting-ray Bay on the Et. Coast of New Holland, by R.Pickersgill (from the original plan by Captain James Cook 1770, Hydrographic Office no 541/5).

ca1:42,240, 1 sheet, cm 34 x 26, pos. photostat, b./wh.
Shows soundings, shoals, anchorages.
See also no. 863.
Copies: NPL:M(M2811.1801/[1770]/2).

862

[1770] PICKERSGILL, Richard

A Plan of Stingray Bay on the Et. Coast of New Holland.

Photograph.
See also no. 862.
Copies: Captain Cook's Landing Place Trust.

863

1772 CHART of New-Zealand, explored in 1769 and 1770 by Lieut. I.Cook, commander of His Majesty's Bark *Endeavour*. Engraved by I.Bayly. Publish'd 1st Jan 1772. London.

No scale given, 1 sheet, 20¾″ x 15⅛″.
([Views of Australasia.])
Clipped at sides. Copy also in Hawkesworth 1st ed. *see* no. 860.
Copies: NPL:D.   864

1774 ZATTA, Antonio
Il Mappamondo o sia descrizione generale del globo ridotto in quadro.
Venezia, A.Zatta, 1774.
No scale given, 1 sheet, 11⅝″ x 16⅞″.
Measurements taken from plate mark; several borders containing further calculations
are added outside the degree border.
Shows route of Cook's first voyage.
(Atlante novissimo. Vol. 1. [no.6]. 1775.)
Copies: NPL:M(F912).   865

1775 ZATTA, Antonio
Il Mappamondo o sia descrizione generale del globo; [engraved by
G.Zuliani]. Venezia, A.Zatta, 1774.
No scale given, 1 sheet, 11 3/16″ x 15¾″.
Maps are in the form of two hemispheres, surrounded by coloured decorations.
Shows route of Cook's first voyage. Measurements taken from plate mark. Coloured
engravings as corner decorations.
(Atlante novissimo. Vol. 1, [no.7]. 1775.)
Copies: NPL:M(F912).   866

1776 ZATTA, Antonio
L'America divisa né suoi principali stati di nuova projezione; [engraved
by G.Zuliani]. Venezia, A.Zatta, 1776.
No scale given, 1 sheet, 12″ x 15⅞″.
Shows route of Cook's first voyage. Title is surrounded by coloured decoration. Measure-
ments taken from heavy border line. Map dated 1776 although title-page of volume is
dated 1775.
(Atlante novissimo. Vol. 1, [no.14]. 1775.)
Copies: NPL:M(F912).   867

1776 ZATTA, Antonio
Nuove scoperte fatte nel 1765, 67, e 69 nel Mare del Sud; [engraved by
G.Zuliani]. Venezia, A.Zatta, 1776.
No scale given, 1 sheet, 11⅝″ x 15 13/16″.
Measurements taken from outside border line; title is surrounded by a coloured marine
view and foliage.
Shows navigators' tracks, including Cook's first voyage.
(Atlante novissimo. Vol. 1, [no.12]. 1775.)
Copies: NPL:M(F912).   868

1778 ZATTA, Antonio
La Nuova Zelanda trascorsa nel 1769 c 1770 dal Cook commandante
dell'*Endeavour* vascello di S.M.Britannica; [engraved by G.Zuliani].
Venezia, A.Zatta, 1778.

No scale given, 1 sheet, 17½" x 14".
Title surrounded by small coloured engraving.
Shows Cook's route around New Zealand. Map dated 1778 although title-page of volume dated 1775.
(Atlante novissimo. Vol.1, at end.)
Copies: NPL:M(F912). 869

[1779] BOWEN, Thomas

The World, including the late discoveries, by Captn. Cook and other circum navigators. Carefully laid down to the present time by Thos. Bowen. Engraved for Middleton's New (and) complete system of geography. [London, J.Cooke, 1779].

No scale given, 1 sheet (Eastern and Western hemispheres 22 cm diam. each), cm 36 x 48, engr., b./wh.
Inset: The North Pole. Ornamental border.
Shows tracks of Anson, 1740–44, and Cook, 1768–71.
(*In* Middleton, C.T.—*A New and complete system of geography.* London, J.Cooke, [1779]. Vol.1, facing p.vii.)
Copies: NPL:M(F910.7/M). 870

1779 ZATTA, Antonio

Emisfero terrestre meridionale tagliato su l'Equatore; [engraved by G.Zuliani]. Venezia, A.Zatta, 1779.

No scale given, 1 sheet, 12⅜" x 16 1/16".
Map in circular form showing routes of Cook's first voyage and that of Bougainville. Measurements taken from inner border line. 1779 on map although title-page of volume is dated 1775.
(Atlante novissimo. Vol. 1, [no.8]. 1775.)
Copies: NPL:M(F912). 871

1780 DJURBERG, Daniel

Karte över Polynesien eller Femte Delen af Jordklotet. [Engraved by C.Berggvist.] Stockholm, 1780.

No scale given, 1 sheet, 18⅝" x 24¼".
Shows the routes of the early voyagers in the Pacific, including those of Capt. Cook's first and second voyages. Australia is called Ulimaroa. The title of the map is also given in French.
Copies: NPL:M(F18/84). 872

1786 [MAP of the Eastern Hemisphere, mutilated, title wanting, except the following: verfasst vo . . . von Frankreich. Shows Australia with an inscription written along the east coast, which translated from the German reads as follows:—"coast discovered by the English in 1770 who named this land New South Wales." Engraved by A. Amon.] Wien, 1786.

1 sheet, 24" x 24".
Copies: NPL:M(F2). 873

[1787?] BONNE

Carte de la Nouvelle Zéelande; [engraved by André].

No scale given, 1 sheet, 13 $\frac{5}{16}$″ x 9$\frac{1}{8}$″.
Four inset maps.
Shows route of Cook's voyage around New Zealand.
(*In* Bonne *and* Desmarest—Atlas encyclopédique. Paris, Hôtel de Thou, 1787. Plate 133.)
Copies: NPL:M(Q912/B).   874

[1787] BONNE

Carte des découvertes du Capite.Carteret dans la Nlle. Bretagne, avec
une partie du passage du Capite.Cook par le Détroit de l'*Endéavour* et les
découvertes du Capite.Dampierre dans ces parages.

ca103 miles=1″, 1 sheet 9$\frac{1}{8}$″ x 13^7/$_{12}$″.
Five inset maps.
Shows Cook's route to the south of New Guinea.
(*In* Bonne *and* Desmarest—Atlas encyclopédique. Paris, Hôtel de Thou, 1787. Plate 136.)
Copies: NPL:M(Q912/B).   875

[1787?] BONNE

Nlle. Galles Mridle.; ou, Côte Oriental de la Nouvelle Hollande.

No scale given, 1 sheet, 13″ x 9″.
Four inset maps.
Shows route of Cook's first voyage.
(*In* Bonne *and* Desmarest—Atlas encyclopédique. Paris, Hôtel de Thou, 1787. Plate 137.)
Copies: NPL:M(Q912/B).   876

1788 COOK, James

Chart of New Zealand explored by Capt. James Cook in 1769 & 1770
in His Majesty's Bark the *Endeavour*, from the original drawings of Capt.
Cook); [engraved by—Basire].

No scale given, 1 sheet, 19$\frac{3}{4}$″ x 14$\frac{1}{4}$″.
Measurements taken from fine line inside heavy border line.
(Wales, W.—Astronomical observations made in the voyages . . . performed by
Commodore Byron, Captain Wallis, Captain Carteret and Captain Cook, p.xii, 1788.)
Copies: NPL:M(Q524/W).   877

1788 COOK, James

Chart of the eastern coast of New Holland discovered & explored in
1770 by Captain James Cook, Commander of his Majesty's Bark *Endeavour*.
(From the original drawings of Capt.Cook); [engraved by—Basire].

No scale given, 1 sheet, 13$\frac{1}{4}$″ x 14$\frac{3}{8}$″.
Measurements taken from fine line inside heavy border line.
(Wales, W.—Astronomical observations made in the voyages . . . performed by
Commodore Byron, Captain Wallis, Captain Carteret and Captain Cook. Frontisp.
1788.)
Copies: NPL:M(Q524/W).   878

1798 CHART of Torres Strait from the surveys of Capt. Cook in 1769, and Capt. Bampton in 1793. (Published . . . by A.Arrowsmith.) London, 1798.

No scale given, 1 sheet, cm 61½ x 78, engr. b./wh.
Mercator's projection.
Shows the track of the *Endeavour.*
Copies: NPL:D(Cc79/2).

879

1801 FLINDERS, Matthew
Chart of part of the coast of New South Wales, from Ram Head to Northumberland Isles, by M.Flinders, 1800. London, Arrowsmith, 1801.

No scale given, 1 sheet, cm 76½ x 59½, engr. b./wh.
Mercator's projection. Published in Association with Flinders' pamphlet Observations on the coasts of Van Diemen's Land. Based largely on J.Cook's chart as modified by later discoveries, and showing the *Endeavour's* track.
Copies: NPL:D(Cc80/4).

880

1803 DE LA ROCHETTE, L.S.
Chart of the Indian Ocean improved from the chart of M.d'Après de Mannevillette with the addition of a part of the Pacific Ocean as well as of the original tracks of the principal discoverers or other navigators to India and China, and in which it has been attempted to give a chronological indication of the successive discoveries. London,W.Faden, 1803.

No scale given, 1 sheet approx. 23½″ x 44½″.
Two inset maps showing monsoon directions. East coast of Australia is marked "New South Wales explored and named by Cook, 1770."
Measurements taken from inside heavy line next to degree border.
Copies: NPL:M(M4110/1803/1).

881

1832 NORIE, John William
New chart of the China Sea and East India Archipelago comprehending the Sunda, Molucca, Phillipine Islands in which are exhibited the . . . straits and passages to Canton and between the India and Pacific Oceans: [sheet 3, from 23° 50′N.Lat. to 15°S.Lat. and from 129° 40′ to 145° E.Lat.]. Engraved by—Stephenson. London, J.W. Norie & Co., 1832.

No scale given, 1 sheet, 61½″ x 24½″, folded.
Two inset maps. First published in 1821.
Measurements taken from fine line inside heavy degree border line.
Shows Cook's track through Torres Straits in 1770.
(*In his* Country trade; or, Free mariners' pilot. 9th ed. 1833. Plate 143.)
Copies: NPL:M(X912/22).

882

1833 NORIE, John William
Chart of part of New South Wales, Van Diemen's Land, New Zealand and adjacent islands with the principal harbours. London, J.W.Norie & Co., 1833.

No scale given, 1 sheet, 24½" x 36½", folded.
Three inset maps. First published in 1819.
Measurements from fine line inside heavy degree border line.
Shows Cook's tracks through Cook's Strait, and round Stewart's Island, New Zealand in 1770.
This is sheet 3 of the New chart of part of the Pacific Ocean . . . from . . . observations . . . of Cook, Flinders, [and others] published with a separate title.
(*In his* Country trade; or, Free mariners' pilot, pl.26b, 9th ed. 1833.)
Copies: NPL:M(X912/22). 883

1833 NORIE, John William

New chart of part of the Pacific Ocean, exhibiting the various straits, islands and dangers . . . drawn . . . from the astronomical observations and surveys of Cook, Flinders, D'Entrecasteaux, Bougainville, Bligh, Kotzebue, Freycinet & other . . . navigators. Engraved by—Stephenson. London, J.W.Norie & Co., 1833.

No scale given, 1 sheet, 24 11/16" x 36½", folded.
Sheet 2 only. Two inset maps. First published in 1820.
Measurements taken from fine line inside heavy degree border line.
Shows Cook's track in 1770 along the coast of Queensland to Torres Straits.
(*In his* Country trade; or, Free mariners' pilot, pl.26a. 9th ed. 1833.)
Copies: NPL:M(X912/22). 884

[1891] COOK, James

A Chart of part of the sea coast of New South Wales on the East Coast of New Holland . . . By Lieut. J.Cook, Commander of His Majesty's Bark the *Endeavour*, 1770. [MS. copies from the originals in the British Museum by an expert in London under the supervision of Mr. James Bonwick. 1891.]

No scale given, 4 sheets, various sizes, ms. b./wh.
Area: from Cape York to Point Hicks.
Shows tracks of the *Endeavour*, coastline with names, soundings, shoals.
Copies: NPL:M(MT4/805/1770/1). 885

The Same. 4 sheets, cm 25 x 40 ea, pr., b./wh.

(*In* The Historical Records of New South Wales, Cook, 1762–80, facsimiles of charts to accompany vol.1, pt.1. Sydney, Govt.Pr., 1893, nos.3–6.)
Copies: NPL:M(Q991/N); NPL:D; NPL:R(Q991/8). 886

The Same [entitled] A Chart of the sea coast of New South Wales or the east coast of New Holland . . . 1770.

1 sheet, cm 34 x 53, photoengr., b./wh.
(*In* Beaglehole, J.C.—The Journals of Captain James Cook on his voyages of discovery . . . Charts and Views; ed. by R.A.Skelton. Pub. for the Hakluyt Society. Cambridge, U.P., 1955. Plate no.XX.)
Copies: NPL:M(X980/25). 887

The Same [entitled] A Chart of part of the sea coast of New South Wales on the east coast of New Holland from Cape Tribulation to Endeavours Streights . . . 1770.

1 sheet, cm 34 x 41, photoengr., b./wh.
(*In* Beaglehole, J.C.—The Journals of Captain James Cook on his voyages of discovery . . . Charts and Views; ed. by R.A.Skelton. Pub. for the Hakluyt Society. Cambridge, U.P., 1955. Plate no.XXIV.)
Copies: NPL:M(X980/25).   888

1893 HISTORICAL RECORDS of New South Wales: Cook, 1762–1780. (Photo-lithographic) facsimiles of charts to accompany vol.1, pt.1. Sydney, Govt. Printer, 1893.

12 maps, folded.
The majority of these charts were copied in London, under the personal supervision of J.Bonwick, from the originals in the British Museum, where they are preserved in a volume entitled: Charts, plans, views and drawings taken on board His Majesty's Bark *Endeavour* . . . by Lieutenant Jas. Cook, Commander.
Copies: NPL:M(Q991/N); NPL:D; NPL:R(Q991/8).   889

1893 PICKERSGILL, Richard
Charts of the east coast of New Holland.

(*Historical Records of New South Wales*—Cook: facsimiles of charts. Sydney, Govt.Pr., 1893.)
Copies: NPL:M(Q991/N); NPL:D; NPL:R(Q991/8).   890

[1905] COOK, James
Sketch of Botany Bay in New South Wales: [facsimile of . . . original chart of Botany Bay, copies by W.Woodrow, Feb., 1905]. N.p., [1770].

1 mile = 1″ approx., 1 sheet, 12¼″ x 13¼″.
Measurements taken from inside outer border line. Original in the British Museum, Add.7085. *See also* no. 860.
Copies: NPL:M(M2 811.1801/1770/1); Captain Cook's Landing Place Trust.   891

1913 ROBINSON, Hector E.C.
Map of the south-eastern coast of Australia including Tasmania, showing the routes taken by the early discoverers, Captn. James Cook, R.N., George Bass and Matthew Flinders. Sydney, H.E.C. Robinson, 1913.

20 statute miles = 1″, 1 sheet, 37⅝″ x 24⅓″.
Map was compiled from original data in the Public Library of New South Wales.
Copies: NPL:M(M3 806p/1770–1803/1).   892

1931 EMERY, James
Chart of part of the celebrated voyage thro. unknown austral seas within the South Pacific Ocean, made by Captain James Cook in the years 1769–1770; together with parts of the routes traversed by Luiz Vaez de Torres, 1606, and Abel Iansz Tasman, 1642–3. [Printed by E.H. Shea for Sunnybrook Press.] Sydney, 1931.

ca1:14,256,000, 1 sheet, cm 40 x 54, litho., water cols.
Area: from New Guinea to New Zealand, from 124°E to 172°E.
Signed "James Emery". Portrait of Cook as inset. Reproduced as endpapers of Slessor, Kenneth *and others*—Trio. The Mitchell Library also holds a reproduction in black and white, and an autographed pull of the endpapers of Trio.
Copies: NPL:M(M3 800/1606–1770/1); NPL:R(C3 800/1606–1700/1).   893

1955 A CHART of Cooks Strait in New Zeland (*sic*). [Reprod. from orig. MSS. in British Museum.]
No scale given, 1 sheet, cm 30 x 41, photoengr. b./wh.
Area: from Cape Farewell to S. of Cape Campbel.
Shows coastline, incomplete in some places; depths, reefs, names of capes and bays.
(*In* Beaglehole, J.C.—The Journals of Captain James Cook on his voyages of discovery . . . Charts and Views; ed. by R.A. Skelton. Pub. for the Hakluyt Society. Cambridge, U.P., 1955. Plate no.XVIII.)
Copies: NPL:M(X980/25).   894

1955 A CHART of part of the East Coast of New Zealand. [Reprod. from orig. MSS. in British Museum.]
No scale given, 1 sheet, cm 29 x 47, photoengr. b./wh.
Area: Cape Kidnappers to East Cape.
Shows coastline, track of ship with soundings, bearings; place names, mountains, rivers.
(*In* Beaglehole, J.C.—The Journals of Captain James Cook on his voyages of discovery . . . Charts and Views; ed. by R.A. Skelton. Pub. for the Hakluyt Society. Cambridge, U.P., 1955. Plate no.XIII.)
Copies: NPL:M(X980/25).   895

1955 [CHART of Polynesian islands drawn by Tupaia for Cook 1769. Reprod. from orig. MSS. in British Museum.]
No scale given, 1 sheet, cm 19 x 31, photoengr. b./wh.
Shows 74 islands with Tahiti at centre; Polynesian names of islands.
(*In* Beaglehole, J.C.—The Journals of Captain James Cook on his voyages of discovery . . . Charts and Views; ed. by R.A. Skelton. Pub. for the Hakluyt Society. Cambridge, U.P., 1955. Plate no.XI.)
Copies: NPL:M(X980/25).   896

1955 COOK, James
A Chart of New zeland (*sic*) or the Islands of Aeheinomouwe and Tovypoenammu lying in the South Sea. By Lieut. J.Cook . . . 1770. [Reprod. from orig. MSS. in British Museum.]
No scale given, 1 sheet, cm 33 x 35, photoengr. b./wh.
Shows coastline and mtns of both islands, track of ship with bearings and depths in fathoms; place names.
(*In* Beaglehole, J.C.—The Journals of Captain James Cook on his voyages of discovery . . . Charts and Views; ed. by R.A. Skelton. Pub. for the Hakluyt Society. Cambridge, U.P., 1955. Plate no.XII.)
Copies: NPL:M(X980/25).   897

1955 COOK, James

A Chart of the Great South Sea or Pacific Ocean shewing the Track and Discoveries made by the *Endeavour* Bark in 1769 and 1770. By Lieut.J. Cook, Commander. [Reprod. from orig. MSS. in British Museum.]

No scale given, 1 sheet, cm 23 x 60, photoengr. b./wh.
Area: From N. of New Guinea to S. of Lat. 60°S, from Java to E. of Rio de Janeiro.
Shows track of *Endeavour*, bearings, coastline of land discovered by *Endeavour* shaded, other coastlines copied from charts; place names.
(*In* Beaglehole, J.C.—The Journals of Captain James Cook on his voyages of discovery . . . Charts and Views; ed. by R.A. Skelton. Pub. for the Hakluyt Society. Cambridge, U.P., 1955. Plate no.I.)
Copies: NPL:M(X980/25). 898

1955 COOK, James

A Chart of the S.East Part of Terra (*sic*) del Fuego including Straits Le Maire and Part of Staten Land. By Lieut. J.Cook. Jany 1769. [Reprod. from orig. MSS. in British Museum.]

ca1:1,520,640, 1 sheet, cm 17 x 34, photoengr. b./wh.
4 coastal profiles.
Inset: A Plan of Success Bay.
Shows ship's track with soundings; place names.
(*In* Beaglehole, J.C.—The Journals of Captain James Cook on his voyages of discovery . . . Charts and Views; ed. by R.A. Skelton. Pub. for the Hakluyt Society. Cambridge, U.P., 1955. Plate no.III.)
Copies: NPL:M(X980/25). 899

The Same engr., cm 14 x 16.
(*In* Smith, Isaac—Original sketches, drawings, maps etc. [1763–80]. f.ii.)
Copies: NPL:M(D11). 900

1955 COOK, James

A Chart of the Society Isles in the South Sea. By Lieut. J.Cook . . . Discovered the 16th of July 1769. [Reprod. from orig. mss. in the British Museum.]

ca1:253,440, 1 sheet, cm 30 x 46, photoengr., b./wh.
Shows Huahine, Ulietea [Raiatea], Otaha [Tahaa], Bolaboia [Borabora] and Maurua [Maupiti] islands with surrounding reefs and islands, depths, bearings.
(*In* Beaglehole, J.C.—The Journals of Captain James Cook on his voyages of discovery . . . Charts and Views; ed. by R.A. Skelton. Pub. for the Hakluyt Society. Cambridge, U.P., 1955. Plate no.IX.)
Copies: NPL:M(X980/25). '901

1955 COOK, James

A Plan of King Georges Island or Otaheite. By Lieutenant J.Cook, 1769. Discover'd by Captn Wallis the 19th June 1767. [Reprod. from orig. MSS. in the British Museum.]

ca1:126,720, 1 sheet, cm 31 x 37, photoengr. b./wh.
Shows coastlines, anchorages, depths; rivers, creeks, vegetation, hill shading.
(*In* Beaglehole, J.C.—The Journals of Captain James Cook on his voyages of discovery
. . . Charts and Views; ed. by R.A. Skelton. Pub. for the Hakluyt Society. Cambridge,
U.P., 1955. Plate no.V.)
Copies: NPL:M(X980/25).   902

The Same. cm 10 x 16.

(*In* Robertson, George—Discovery of Tahiti: a ournal. London, Hakluyt Soc., 1948.)
Copies: NPL:M(980/R).   903

1955 COOK, James
A Sketch of part of the Bay of Rio de Janeiro situated on the Coast of
Brasil . . . By Lieut. J. Cook, Decr. 1768. [Reprod. from orig. MSS. in
British Museum.]

ca1:101,300, 1 sheet, cm 23 x 30, photoengr., b./wh.
Shows coastline, depths, anchorages; public bldgs. place names; hill shading, vegetation.
(*In* Beaglehole, J.C.—The Journals of Captain James Cook on his voyages of discovery
. . . Charts and Views; ed. by R.A. Skelton. Pub. for the Hakluyt Society. Cambridge,
U.P., 1955. Plate no.II.)
Copies: NPL:M(X980/25).   904

1955 COOK, James
Sketches of the Islands, Lagoon, Thrum-cap, Bow-Island, the two
Groups, Bird-Island and Chain-Island, lying in the South Sea. By
Lieut.J.Cook. Discovered in Apl. 1769. [Reprod. from orig. MSS. in
British Museum.]

ca1:475,200, 6 plans on 1 sheet, var. sizes, photoengr., b./wh.
Area: Tuamotu Archipelago.
Shows ship's track, outlines of islands, bearings.
(*In* Beaglehole, J.C.—The Journals of Captain James Cook on his voyages of discovery
. . . Charts and Views; ed. by R.A. Skelton. Pub. for the Hakluyt Society. Cambridge,
U.P., 1955. Plate no.IV.)
Copies: NPL:M(X980/25).   905

The Same. MSS. ink.

(*In* Smith, Isaac—Original sketches, drawings, maps, etc. [1763–80]. f.iii.).
Copies: NPL:M(D11).   906

1955 COOK, James
A View of part of the West side of Georges Island taken from the Ship
at anchor in Royal Bay. [Apl–Jy 1769. Reprod. from orig. MSS. in
British Museum.]

cm 10 x 35, photoengr., b./wh.
(*In* Beaglehole, J.C.—The Journals of Captain James Cook on his voyages of discovery
. . . Charts and Views; ed. by R.A.Skelton. Pub. for the Hakluyt Society. Cambridge,
U.P., 1955. Plate no.VI.)
Copies: NPL:M(X980/25).   907

1955 COOK, James

A View on the East side of Huaheine [and] A view of the N.E. side of
Bolabola. [Reprod. from orig. MSS. in British Museum.]

cm 11 x 39, photoengr., b./wh.

(*In* Beaglehole, J.C.—The Journals of Captain James Cook on his voyages of discovery
. . . Charts and Views; ed. by R.A.Skelton. Pub. for the Hakluyt Society. Cambridge,
U.P., 1955. Plate no.VIII.)

Copies: NPL:M(X980/25).   908

1955 COOK, James

A View of the Land about Endeavour River taken when the entrance
bore WSW distant 1 mile. [Aug.4, 1770. Reprod. from orig. MSS. in
British Museum.]

cm 25 x 38, photoengr., b./wh.

(*In* Beaglehole, J.C.—The Journals of Captain James Cook on his voyages of discovery
. . . Charts and Views; ed. by R.A.Skelton. Pub. for the Hakluyt Society. Cambridge,
U.P., 1955. Plate no.XXIII.)

Copies: NPL:M(X980/25).   909

1955 COOK, James

A View of the Watering Place in Queen Charlottes Sound. [Ship Cove.
Jan.16–Feb.6, 1770.] (A View of the Snowey Mountains Distant 6
Leagues. The seaward Kaikouras. [Feb.14, 1770.] A View of Five
Fingers Point bearing ESE Distant 2 Leagues. [Mar.14, 1770. Reprod.
from orig. MSS. in British Museum.])

3 views on 1 sheet, cm 25 x 38, photoengr., b./wh.

(*In* Beaglehole, J.C.—The Journals of Captain James Cook on his voyages of discovery
. . . Charts and Views; ed. by R.A.Skelton. Pub. for the Hakluyt Society. Cambridge,
U.P., 1955. Plate no.XIX.)

Copies: NPL:M(X980/25).   910

1955 COOK, James

A View of ye Land about Tolaga [and] A View of the Island Motuaro
lying in the Bay of Islands. [Nov.29–Dec.5 1769. Reprod. from orig.
MSS. in British Museum.]

cm 25 x 38, photoengr., b./wh.

(*In* Beaglehole, J.C.—The Journals of Captain James Cook on his voyages of discovery
. . . Charts and Views; ed. by R.A.Skelton. Pub. for the Hakluyt Society. Cambridge,
U.P., 1955. Plate no.XVI.)

Copies: NPL:M(X980/25).   911

1955 COOK, James

Views of the Low Islands in the South Sea. Lagoon Island, Thrum Cap,
Bird Island, Bow Island, Tethuroa seen from the hill of Otaheite. [Apl
4–9 1769. Reprod. from orig. MSS. in British Museum.]

cm 14 x 22, photoengr., b./wh.
(*In* Beaglehole, J.C.—The Journals of Captain James Cook on his voyages of discovery
. . . Charts and Views; ed. by R.A.Skelton. Pub. for the Hakluyt Society. Cambridge,
U.P., 1955. Plate no.IV.)
Copies: NPL:M(X980/25). 912

1955 COOK, James
The West elevation of the Fort. [Fort Venus at Matavai Bay, Tahiti.
Apl–Jy 1769. Reprod. from orig. MSS. in British Museum.]
cm 10 x 35, photoengr., b./wh.
(*In* Beaglehole, J.C.—The Journals of Captain James Cook on his voyages of discovery
. . . Charts and Views; ed. by R.A.Skelton. Pub. for the Hakluyt Society. Cambridge,
U.P., 1955. Plate no.VI.)
Copies: NPL:M(X980/25). 913

1955 THE ISLAND of Ohetiroa in the South Sea. [Reprod. from orig.
MSS. in British Museum.]
1:110,880, plan D. of 4 on 1 sheet, cm 10 x 12, photoengr., b./wh.
Area: Rurutu, Tubuai Islands.
Shows coastline, reefs, bearings.
(*In* Beaglehole, J.C.—The Journals of Captain James Cook on his voyages of discovery
. . . Charts and Views; ed. by R.A. Skelton. Pub. for the Hakluyt Society. Cambridge,
U.P., 1955. Plate no.X.)
Copies: NPL:M(X980/25). 914

1955 PICKERSGILL, Richard
A Plan of Port and River Mercury, call'd by the natives Apuragge.
[Reprod. from orig. MSS. in the Hydrographic Dept. of the Admiralty.]
ca1:47,520, 1 sheet, cm 22 x 33, photoengr., b./wh.
Shows outline of bay and river estuaries with depth soundings, reefs, anchorage.
(*In* Beaglehole, J.C.—The Journals of Captain James Cook on his voyages of discovery
. . . Charts and Views; ed. by R.A. Skelton. Pub. for the Hakluyt Society. Cambridge,
U.P., 1955. Plate no.XV.)
Copies: NPL:M(X980/25). 915

1955 PICKERSGILL, Richard
A Plan of the Bay of Oamonenno on the West Side of Uliateah. [Reprod.
from orig. MSS. in the Hydrographic Dept. of the Admiralty.]
ca1:18,100, plan A. of 4 on 1 sheet, cm 15 x 15, photoengr., b./wh.
Area: Rautoanui, in Raiatea.
Shows coastline, depths, anchorages.
(*In* Beaglehole, J.C.—The Journals of Captain James Cook on his voyages of discovery
. . . Charts and Views; ed. by R.A. Skelton. Pub. for the Hakluyt Society. Cambridge,
U.P., 1955. Plate no.X.)
Copies: NPL:M(X980/25). 916

1955 PICKERSGILL, Richard
Plan of the Bay of Oapoa on the N° side of Uliateah. [Reprod. from the
orig. MSS. in the Hydrographic Dept. of the Admiralty.]

ca1:19,550, plan B. of 4 on 1 sheet, cm 12 x 20, photoengr., b./wh.
Area: Opoa, Raiatea.
Shows coastlines, reefs, depths, anchorage.
(*In* Beaglehole, J.C.—The Journals of Captain James Cook on his voyages of discovery
. . . Charts and Views; ed. by R.A. Skelton. Pub. for the Hakluyt Society. Cambridge,
U.P., 1955. Plate no.X.)
Copies: NPL:M(X980/25).   917

1955 A PLAN of Mercury Bay on the N.E. Coast of New Zeland (*sic*).
[Reprod. from orig. MSS. in British Museum.]
ca1:119,000, 1 sheet, cm 15 x 22, photoengr., b./wh.
Shows coastline, depths, anchorages, rivers, vegetation, hill shading.
(*In* Beaglehole, J.C.—The Journals of Captain James Cook on his voyages of discovery
. . . Charts and Views; ed. by R.A. Skelton. Pub. for the Hakluyt Society. Cambridge,
U.P., 1955. Plate no.XIV.)
Copies: NPL:M(X980/25).   918

1955 A PLAN of Queen Charlottes Sound in New Zeland (*sic*). [Reprod.
from orig. MSS. in British Museum.]
ca1:103,000, 1 sheet, cm 24 x 36, photoengr., b./wh.
Area: incl. part of Admiralty Bay.
Shows coastline, bays, islands, reefs, depths in fathoms, anchorage, place names.
(*In* Beaglehole, J.C.—The Journals of Captain James Cook on his voyages of discovery
. . . Charts and Views; ed. by R.A. Skelton. Pub. for the Hakluyt Society. Cambridge,
U.P., 1955. Plate no.XVII.)
Copies: NPL:M(X980/25).   919

1955 A PLAN of Royal Matavie (*sic*) Bay in Georges Islands [and] A Plan of
Fort Venus in Royal Bay. [Reprod. from orig. MSS. in British Museum.]
ca1:23,000 and 1:480, cm 13 x 18 and 13 x 15 on 16 x 36, photoengr., b./wh.
Area: Matavai Bay, Dolphin's Bank, Pt. Venus; Fort Venus.
Shows depths, reefs, river entrance, creeks, hill shading, bldgs with ref. list.
(*In* Beaglehole, J.C.—The Journals of Captain James Cook on his voyages of discovery
. . . Charts and Views; ed. by R.A.Skelton. Pub. for the Hakluyt Society. Cambridge, U.P.,
1955. Plate no.VII.)
The Same. [Matavai Bay] cm 10 x 11.
(*In* Robertson, George—Discovery of Tahiti: a journal. London, Hakluyt Soc., 1948,
at NPL:M980/R).
Copies: NPL:M(X980/25).   920

1955 A PLAN of the Harbour of Ohwarhe in the Island of Huaheine.
[Reprod. from orig. MSS. in British Museum.]
ca1:54,000, plan C. of 4 on 1 sheet, cm 10 x 14, photoengr., b./wh.
Area: Fare, in Huaheine.
Shows coastline, reefs, depths, anchorage, hill-shading, vegetation.
(*In* Beaglehole, J.C.—The Journals of Captain James Cook on his voyages of discovery
. . . Charts and Views; ed. by R.A.Skelton. Pub. for the Hakluyt Society. Cambridge, U.P.,
1955. Plate no.X.)
Copies: NPL:M(X980/25).   921

1955 A PLAN of Tolaga Bay in New Zeland (*sic*). [Reprod. from orig. MSS. in British Museum.]

ca1:147,520, 1 sheet, cm 15 x 21, photoengr., b./wh.
Shows coastline, anchorage, depths; watering place, hill shading, vegetation.
(*In* Beaglehole, J.C.—The Journals of Captain James Cook on his voyages of discovery ... Charts and Views; ed. by R.A.Skelton. Pub. for the Hakluyt Society. Cambridge, U.P., 1955. Plate no.XIV.)
Copies: NPL:M(X980/25).   922

1955 SPÖRING, H. D.

A View from the Point at Otaheite. [The view, taken from Point Venus, extends from Fort Venus on the left to Moorea on the right. Reprod. from orig. MSS. in British Museum.]

cm 12 x 51, photoengr., b./wh.
(*In* Beaglehole, J.C.—The Journals of Captain James Cook on his voyages of discovery ... Charts and Views; ed. by R.A.Skelton. Pub. for the Hakluyt Society. Cambridge, U.P., 1955. Plate no.VIII.)
Copies: NPL:M(X980/25).   923

1966 COOK, James

Chart of New-Zealand, explored in 1769 and 1770, by Lieut.I.Cook, Commander of His Majesty's Bark *Endeavour*; engrav'd by I.Bayly. Originally published 1772. Facs. pub. by Avon Fine Prints. Christchurch, 1966. (no.607).

Scale varies with latitude, 1 sheet, cm 44 x 33, pr., cols.
Shows track of *Endeavour* with bearings & dates, depths; place names, mountains, decorated with a sailor, ship and sea monsters.
Copies: NPL:M(M2980/1769–1770/1).   924

1969 COOK, James

Chart of New-Zealand, explored in 1769 and 1770, by Lieut.I.Cook, Commander of His Majesty's Bark *Endeavour*; engrav'd by I.Bayly. (Publish'd as the Act directs 1st Jany 1772.) [Facsimile.]

Folded.
(*In* Cook, James—Collected Voyages—Printed Accounts [1969 Reed's edition]— Captain Cook in New Zealand ... Ed. by A.H. & A.W.Reed. 2nd ed. Wellington, N.Z., A.H. & A.W.Reed, 1969. Pasted in at back.)
Copies: NPL:M(980:Co1/45B1).   **925**

n.d. WHITCHURCH, W.

Chart of part of the South Sea showing the tracts & discoveries made by . . . *Dolphin*, Commodore Byron, and *Tamer*, Capn. Mouat, 1765, *Dolphin*, Capn. Wallis, and *Swallow*, Capn. Carteret, 1767, and *Endeavour*, Lieutenant Cooke, 1769; engraved by W.Whitchurch. Islington, [n.d.]

No scale given, 1 sheet, approx. 14″ x 26″.
A copy of the chart included in the fourth edition of Hawkesworth's account.
Copies: NPL:M(F2/4).   926

Charts

Bibliography

1893 KING, Philip Gidley

Charts in British Museum regarded as copies; set issued by J. Dalrymple "with the Hydgrophical (*sic*) notices upon them", considered to be originals.

(Hon. P. G. King to A. Oliver, Ap.10, 1893. *King Papers*, vol. 5, pp. 71–2.)

Copies: NPL:M(MS.A1980). 927

Films about the First Voyage

1959 SHELL COMPANY OF AUSTRALIA, LTD.

Captain James Cook. 1959.

45 minutes, colour.

(*In the Steps of the Explorers Ser.*, no.3.)

Retraces the voyage of Captain Cook along the eastern coast of Australia from Point Hicks to Possession Island in 1770, contrasting Cook's comments in his journal with modern scenes of cities and industries. Producer, Bern Gandy; director, photographer, Geoffrey Collings; assistant director, Douglas White; production assistants, Ray Webster, George Brice; sound, John Heath; music, Raymond Hanson.

Copies: ANL. 928

1964 AUSTRALIAN BROADCASTING COMMISSION

Prelude to glory. 1964.

29 minutes, including 2½ minutes on Cook's explorations.

(*The Anzac Story*, no.1.)

Made by Supreme Sound Studios. Producer, Frank Hunter; sound, Cliff Curll; art and graphics, Nancy Phillips, Werner Wallais; production liaison, Rob McAuley; production assistant, Norman Smidt; editor, Doc. K. Sternberg; commentator, Peter Whitchurch.

Copies: ANL. 929

Illustrations

Originals cannot be reproduced without the permission of the owner.

A View of Endeavour River.

See forward under the subhead *Ships—Illustrations—Reproductions.*

Illustrations, General

Originals, Including Photocopies of Originals

ILLUSTRATIONS to Cook's first voyage: British Museum Add. MSS.7085, 9345, 15507–8, 23920–1, Print Room A45.

1 reel. Negative microfilm.
List of contents by J.D. Hine of all these volumes, except Add. MSS.7085, filed at B1489.
Other copies in the Mitchell Library:
FM2/115 Half-plate negs. of 54 illustrations selected from 9345, 15508, 23920–1.
B1489^{-2} A set of prints numbered 1–54 following the negs; with descriptive list supplied by J.D. Hine.
FM2/139 Negs. of 3 illustrations from Add. MSS.7085.
Glass negs. 12/4–9 Glass negs. of Add. MSS.9345, f.57, 23920, ff.43b, 50, 54 and 15508, f.41; with list of contents.

Copies: NPL:M(FM4/222).   930

ILLUSTRATIONS to Cook's first voyage in the British Museum (Natural History) being 3 vols of Zoological drawings and 18 vols of Botanical drawings.

129 reels.
CONTENTS:
FM2/191–319, Glass negs. 29/1–8 Negatives (half-plate and glass) and coloured transparencies of selected illustrations.
B1489^{-3} Prints of most of the above negatives. Descriptive list (3) of illustrations copied, by J.D. Hine and P. Mander Jones, 1957 and 1959.

Copies: NPL:M(FM2/191-319; Glass negs. 29(1-8); B1489^{-3}).   931

Illustrations, General

Reproductions

The first official publication of the first voyage is the section in Hawkesworth's *Account of the voyages undertaken . . . for making discoveries in the Southern Hemisphere*, vol. 2–3, 1773. This contains the plates listed and described hereunder; all are line engravings and all are untitled, the titles in each case being taken from pp. xxxv–xxxvi of Vol. 1. The set from which the listing has been made is no. 648 in this Bibliography, Dixson Library set no. Q77/22–4.
Plates in subsequent editions and translations have often been redrawn and engraved by different artists. These are not described in this Bibliography. Plates held by the Mitchell and Dixson Libraries, which are extracted from the various editions and translations, are not listed except in the case of ships, for which *see* the subhead *Ships*.

No. 1 A view of the Indians of Terra (*sic*) del Fuego in their hut. A. Cipriani, del. F. Bartolozzi sculp.

Meas. of engraved surface 8⅛″ x 10⅞″. Meas. of plate mark 9″ x 11¾″. *Vol. 2 bet. pp. 54 & 55.*

No. 2 A view of Matavia (*sic*) Bay in Otaheite . . . from One Tree Hill.

Meas. of view 7¾″ x 9⅞″. Meas. of plate mark 9¼″ x 10¾″. *Vol. 2, bet. pp. 80 & 81.*

No. 3 A view of the Island of Ulietea, with a double canoe and a boat-house. E. Rooker sculp.

Meas. of view 8 13/16″ x 18″. Meas. of plate mark 9 7/16″ x 18¾″. *Vol. 2, bet. pp. 258 & 259.*

No. 4 A view of the Island of Otaheite, with several vessels of that island. E. Rooker sculp.

Meas. of view 7⅞″ x 15 11/16″. Meas. of plate mark 9 5/16″ x 16⅞″. *Vol. 2, bet. pp. 184 & 185.*

No. 5 A view in the Island of Otaheite; with the house or shed called tupapow, under which the dead are deposited, and a representation of the person who performs the principal part in the funeral ceremony in his peculiar dress. W. Woollett sculp.

Meas. of engraved surface $7\frac{7}{8}''$ x $13\frac{1}{8}''$. Meas. of plate mark $9\frac{3}{8}''$ x $14\frac{1}{4}''$. *Vol. 2, bet. pp. 234 & 235.*

No. 6 A view in the Island of Huaheine; with the Ewharra no Eatua, or House of God. W. Woolett sculp.

Meas. of view $7\frac{7}{8}''$ x $14\frac{1}{2}''$. Meas. of plate mark $9\frac{1}{2}''$ x $14\frac{1}{2}''$. *Vol. 2, bet. pp. 252 & 253.*

No. 7 A view of the inside of a house in the Island of Ulietea, with the representation of a dance to the music of the country. I. B. Cipriani del. F. Bartolozzi sculp.

Meas. of engraved surface $8\frac{1}{16}''$ x 13″. Meas. of plate mark 10″ x $14\frac{1}{4}''$. *Vol. 2, bet. pp. 264 & 265.*

No. 8 A military gorget worn in the South Sea Islands. James Roberts. Delin et Sculpsit.

Meas. inside frame lines $7\frac{7}{8}''$ x $6\frac{5}{8}''$. Meas. of plate mark $8\frac{13}{16}''$ x $7\frac{1}{2}''$. *Vol. 2, facing p. 185.*

No. 9 [Native implements.] The first two figures, reckoning from the left hand, are chissels (*sic*) or gouges; the third an adze of the smaller kind; the fourth, the instrument with which the bread-fruit is beaten into a paste; the fifth, the nasal flute; the sixth, a thatching needle; the seventh, the instrument used for beating the cloth. Record sculp.

Meas. inside frame lines $6\frac{5}{8}''$ x $8\frac{1}{16}''$. Meas. of plate mark $7\frac{5}{8}''$ x $9\frac{1}{16}''$. *Vol. 2, facing p. 212.*

No. 10 [Native implements.] The first figure, reckoning from the left hand, is an adze of the larger size; the second and third are different representations of the upper part of it . . . the smaller figures are tattowing (*sic*) instruments . . . the last is the instrument with which they are struck. Record sculp.

Meas. inside frame lines 8″ x $6\frac{3}{8}''$. Meas. of plate mark 9″ x $7\frac{3}{8}''$. *Vol. 2, facing p. 191.*

No. 11 A branch of the bread-fruit tree with the fruit. I. Miller fecit.

Meas. of plate mark $14\frac{1}{4}''$ x $11\frac{13}{16}''$. Plate surface and engraved mark correspond. *Vol. 2, bet. pp. 80 & 81.*

No. 12 [Native implements.] The middle figure represents a fly-flap of the Island Ohiteroa; the two side figures, handles of the same instrument made in Otaheite.

Meas. inside frame lines $7\frac{15}{16}''$ x $6\frac{3}{8}''$. Meas. of plate mark $8\frac{3}{4}''$ x $7\frac{1}{8}''$. *Vol. 2, facing p. 185.*

No. 13 The head of a New Zealander, with a comb in his hair, an ornament of green stone in his ear, and another of a fish's tooth round his neck.

Meas. of engraved surface $7\frac{7}{8}''$ x $6\frac{1}{4}''$. Meas. of plate mark $8\frac{3}{4}''$ x $7\frac{1}{4}''$. *Vol. 3, facing p. 453.*

No. 14 Bludgeons, used as weapons by the New Zealanders, and called patoo-patoos, as seen on the side, the edge and the end. Record sculp.

Meas. inside frame lines $6\frac{5}{16}''$ x $7\frac{7}{8}''$. Meas. of plate mark $7\frac{3}{8}''$ x $8\frac{15}{16}''$. *Vol. 3, facing p. 466.*

No. 15 A chest of New Zealand, as a specimen of the carving of the country.

Meas. inside frame lines 8″ x $6\frac{3}{8}''$. Meas. of plate mark $8\frac{7}{8}''$ x $7\frac{5}{16}''$. *Vol. 3, facing p. 463.*

No. 16 A war canoe of New Zealand, with a view of Gable End Foreland.

Meas. of view 7¾″ x 21¾″. Meas. of plate mark 9⅜″ x 22¾″. *Vol. 3, bet. pp. 462 & 463.*

No. 17 A view of a perforated rock in Tolaga Bay in New Zealand.

Meas. of engraved surface 7¾″ x 9¾″. Meas. of plate mark 9 3/16″ x 10½″. *Vol. 2, bet. pp. 318 & 319.*

No. 18 A fortified town or village, called a Hippah, built on a perforated rock at Tolaga, New Zealand.

Meas. of engraved surface 7¾″ x 9¾″. Meas. of plate mark 9¼″ x 10½″. *Vol. 2, bet. pp. 340 & 341.*

No. 19 A view of Endeavour River, on the coast of New Holland, where the ship was laid on shore, in order to repair the damage which she received on the rock. Will Byrne scul^p.

Meas. of view 7 5/16″ x 18⅝″. Meas. of plate mark 9¾″ x 19¼″. *Vol. 3, facing p. 557.*

No. 20 An animal found on the coast of New Holland called Kanguroo.

Meas. of engraved surface 7¾″ x 9½″. Meas. of plate mark 9″ x 10 9/16″. *Vol. 3, facing p. 561.*

932

[177– COLLECTION of various editions of engravings of Cook's first voyage.]

15 engravings.

Copies: NPL:D(DL PX 21).

933

1901–5 BANKS, *Sir* Joseph, *and* SOLANDER, Daniel Carl

Illustrations of Australian plants, collected in 1770 during Captain Cook's voyage round the world in H.M.S. *Endeavour*. [The plants collected and classified] by . . . Sir Joseph Banks . . . and D. Solander . . . With determinations by J. Britten . . . Printed by order of the Trustees of the British Museum. London, 1901–5.

Maps, plates [319], 3 vols.

Part 1 contains plate 45A; last plate numbered 318. Part 1 published 1900, part 2 published 1901, part 3 published 1905. The title as given above first appeared in part 3, which carried instructions that it was to replace the temporary titles of parts 1–2, which read: *Illustrations of the botany of Captain Cook's voyage round the world in H.M.S. Endeavour in 1768–71.* (*See* Holmes, no.127*.) Part 1 reviewed by E. E. Morris in the *Victorian Naturalist* vol. 17, 1900, pp. 148–51.

Copies: NPL:M(X581.9901/2); NPL:D(F90/43–5); NPL:R(F581.9901/3–5); ANL; VSL.

934

1968 CAPTAIN COOK'S florilegium: a selection of engravings from the drawings of plants collected by J. Banks and D. Solander, on Captain Cook's first voyage to the islands of the Pacific. With an intro. by W. Blunt and botanical notes by . . . W. T. Stearn. [30 hand-engravings from original plates in the British Museum, Natural History. Drawn by S. Parkinson and others. Prospectus of book to be published, 1968, for the Royal College of Art.] London, Lion & Unicorn Press, 1966.

Plate 1, pp.3.
Prospectus only.

Copies: NPL:M(X980:Co2/1A1).

935

Illustrations Arranged by Artist

BARRALET, J.

Originals, Including Photocopies of Originals

[A WAR canoe of New Zeland (*sic*).]

Watercolour. 13⅝″ x 20½″, within frame lines.
Signed "J. Barralet" [or Barrulet] on bow of canoe. Undated. Engraved as plate no. 16 in Hawkesworth's Account (item no. 932 in this Bibliography) though whether it is a copy of the engraving or the original from which the plate was engraved is doubtful. Title above is taken from the corresponding engraving in Hawkesworth's Account. *See also* nos. 982–5.
(*In* Webber, J.—[Watercolours illustrating Captain Cook's last voyage], plate no. 15.)
Copies: NPL:D(PXX2).   936

CIPRIANI, G. B.

[A VIEW of the Indians of Terra (*sic*) del Fuego in their hut, possibly by G. B. Cipriani.]

Watercolour. 8 3/16″ x 11¼″, within frame lines.
Unsigned and undated. Engraved as plate no. 1 in Hawkesworth's Account (item no. 932 in this Bibliography) though whether a copy of the engraving or Cipriani's own original is uncertain. Title above taken from engraving in Hawkesworth's Account.
(*In* Webber, J.—[Watercolours illustrating Captain Cook's last voyage], plate no. 43.)
Copies: NPL:D(PXX2).   937

[A VIEW of the inside of a house in the Island of Ulietea, with the representation of a dance to the music of the country, possibly by G.B. Cipriani.]

Watercolour. 8⅜″ x 13¼″ within frame lines. Engraved as plate no. 7 in Hawkesworth's Account (item no. 932 in this Bibliography), though whether it is a copy of the engraving or Cipriani's own original is doubtful. Title above is taken from the engraving in Hawkesworth's Account.
(*In* Webber, J.—[Watercolours illustrating Captain Cook's last voyage], plate no. 14.)
Copies: NPL:D(PXX2).   938

FOX, EMANUEL PHILLIPS

Originals, Including Photocopies of Originals

LANDING of Captain Cook at Botany Bay, 1770.

Oil painting.
Commissioned in 1902.
Copies: National Gallery of Victoria, Melbourne.   939

CAPT. COOK landing at Botany Bay.

1902. Photographic reproduction. 7¼″ x 10″ inside mount.
Original is in possession of the National Gallery of Victoria.
Copies: NPL:M(P3/42B).   940

Reproductions

CAPTAIN COOK landing at Botany Bay: [reproduced from the painting
in the National Gallery, Melbourne].

(*In* Long, Charles Richard—Stories of Australian exploration. 2nd ed. Melbourne,
Whitcombe & Tombs, [1910?]. p.49.)
Copies: NPL:M(980/L).   941

CAPTAIN COOK'S landing: the great navigator landing at Botany Bay;
[reproduced from a painting by E.P. Fox. Extracted from the *Sydney
Morning Herald*, May 1, 1926].

(*In* Newspaper cuttings: Captain Cook. Vol.1, p.97.)
Copies: NPL:M(Q980:Col/N1A1).   942

THE LANDING of Captain Cook: [reproduced from the painting in the
National Gallery, Melbourne].

(*In* Watts, Ebenezer John Moore—Stories from Australian history. Sydney, W. Brooks
& Co., 1908. p.8.)
Copies: NPL:M(990.1/W); NPL:D(91/164).   943

THE LANDING of Captain Cook: [reproduced from the painting in the
National Gallery, Melbourne].

(*In* Watts, Ebenezer John Moore—Stories from Australian history. Sydney, W. Brooks
& Co., 1914. p.8.)
Copies: NPL:M(990.1/W).   944

THE LANDING of Captain Cook; [reproduced from the painting in the
National Gallery, Melbourne].

(*In* Murdoch, Walter Logie Forbes—Making of Australia. Melbourne, Whitcombe and
Tombs, [1917]. Frontisp.)
Copies: NPL:M(990.1/M).   945

LANDING of Captain Cook at Botany Bay: [reproduced from the painting
in the National Gallery, Melbourne].

(*In* Wood, George Arnold—The Discovery of Australia. London, Macmillan, 1922.
p.417.)
Copies: NPL:M(980/125A1); NPL:D(92/153); NPL:R(DS990.1/19).   946

179

LANDING of Captain Cook at Botany Bay: [reproduced from the painting in the National Gallery, Melbourne].

(*In* Wood, George Arnold—The Voyage of the *Endeavour*. Melbourne, Macmillan, 1926. p.86.)

Copies: NPL:M(980:Co2/W3A1); NPL:D(92/172).   947

THE LANDING of Captain Cook at Botany Bay, April 28, 1770: [reproduced from the painting in the National Gallery, Melbourne].

(*In* Long, Charles Richard—Stories of Australian exploration. Rev. ed. Melbourne, Whitcombe and Tombs, [1913].)

Copies: NPL:M(980/L).   948

GILFILLAN, JOHN ALEXANDER
Originals, Including Photocopies of Originals

CAPTAIN COOK taking possession of Botany Bay, 1770.

n.d. Oil. 42″ x 51¾″.
Unsigned and undated. This is a copy by an unknown artist of the original oil by Gilfillan in possession of the Royal Society of Victoria.

Copies: NPL:M(ML647).   949

Reproductions

CAPTAIN COOK taking possession of the Australian Continent on behalf of the British Crown, A.D. 1770. From a painting by Gilfillan in the possession of the Royal Society of Victoria. Calvert [sculp.].

Coloured lithograph 12½″ x 17¾″ inside mount.
This seems to be a reproduction of the copy of the oil painting now in the Mitchell Library (ML 647).
(Supplement to the *Illustrated Melbourne Post*, Dec.1865.)
Damaged.

Copies: NPL:M(V*Cook43).   950

Another print.

Cut to omit mount and title. Edges torn.

Copies: NPL:M(SV*Cook3).   951

The Same. Col. reproduction made by the N.S.W. Govt.Pr., 1919.

Copies: NPL:M(Small Picture File: Cook 1st Voyage 1).   952

CAPTAIN COOK formally taking possession of Botany Bay 1770.

n.d. Pencil and wash. 11½″ x 19¼″ inside mount.
This is probably after Gilfillan's painting, and was made for reproduction in Garran's *Picturesque Atlas of Australasia*, 1886, by one of the artists working for this publication. Presented by Sir William Dixson, 1951.

Copies: NPL:D(DGV*Cook2).   953

CAPTAIN COOK'S landing at Botany Bay; adapted from the painting presented to the Philosophical Institute of Victoria by the artist T. (*sic*) A. Gilfillan.

(*In* McFarland, Alfred—Captain Cook. Sydney, Govt.Pr., [1899]. Opp. p.27.)

Copies: NPL:M(923.9/C771.2/12A1); ANL.   954

CAPTAIN COOK proclaiming New South Wales a British possession. Botany Bay, 1770. [Adapted from the painting by J.A. Gilfillan. Extract from the *Sydney Mail*, Apr.28, 1926.]

(Newspaper cuttings: Captain Cook. Vol.1, p.98.)

Copies: NPL:M(Q980:Co1/N1A1).   955

CAPTAIN COOK proclaiming New South Wales a British possession, Botany Bay 1770; adapted from the painting by J.A. Gilfillan.

(New South Wales—Govt. Printer—Photographs illustrating the earliest times of New South Wales. n.d. p.3.)

Copies: NPL:M(F981/N).   956

CAPTAIN COOK taking possession of the Australian continent on behalf of the British Crown, A.D. 1770. Coloured reproduction by Calvert, from a painting by Gilfillan in the possession of the Royal Society of Victoria.

Copies: VSL.   957

CAPTAIN COOK proclaiming New South Wales a British possession, Aug.23, 1770: [reproduced from the painting by J.A. Gilfillan].

(*In* Phillips, H.—Picturesque Sydney Harbour. Sydney, [1924]. p.1.)

Copies: NPL:M(F981.1/P).   958

KUYPER, I
Reproductions

LANDING van Capt. Cook op de Oostkust van Nieuw Holland. I. Kuyper inv. et del. L.A.Claessons sculp.

Engraving. Meas. of engraved surface $3\frac{11}{16}''$ x $2\frac{5}{8}''$.

Copies: NPL:M(P3/41E).   959

LINDSAY, RAYMOND
Reproductions

CAPTAIN COOK at Botany Bay: [reproduction in colour, from the painting by R. Lindsay].

(*B.P. Magazine* vol. 3, no. 3, June 1931, cover.)

Copies: NPL:M(Q059/B).   960

MUGGINS, THOMAS
Originals, Including Photocopies of Originals

[THE CANOE scene, with verse referring to Banks.]

Watercolour. Signed Thomas Muggins.
Presented by J. J. Shillinglaw.
Copies: VSL.   961

PARKINSON, SYDNEY
Reproductions

A NATIVE of Otaheite, in the dress of his country. S. Parkinson del. R.B. Godfrey Sc.

Engraving. Meas. inside frame lines $9\frac{7}{16}''$ x $7\frac{7}{16}''$.
Cut to omit plate mark. "Plate III" in upper right corner.
Copies: NPL:M(SSV*Cook12).   962

SMITH, ISAAC
Originals, Including Photocopies of Originals

NATURAL arch, 75' long 27' broad, 45' high, Tegadoo Bay, New Zealand.

1769. Pencil drawing. $10\frac{3}{4}''$ x $16\frac{7}{8}''$ inside ruled frame lines.
Unsigned. Titled as above and dated '23. Oct. 1769' in ink on mount in Canon Bennett's hand, with note 'vide Kippis Life of Cook, pp.67.68'. Note by Bennett at beginning of volume attributes this drawing to Smith.
(*In* Smith, Isaac—Original sketches . . . [etc., relating to Cook's voyages]. f.v.)
Copies: NPL:M(PX D11).   963

TEGADOO Bay, New Zealand, 23 Octr 1769.

1769. Pencil drawing. $9\frac{1}{2}''$ x $15\frac{1}{4}''$ inside ruled frame lines.
Unsigned. Titled and dated in ink in Canon Bennett's hand on mount, with note 'vide Kipp's Life of Cook p.67'. Note by Bennett at beginning of volume attributes this drawing to Smith.
(*In* Smith, Isaac—Original sketches . . . [etc., relating to Cook's voyages]. f.iv.)
Copies: NPL:M(PX D11).   964

STOTHARD, THOMAS
Originals, Including Photocopies of Originals

Notes compiled Feb. 1966, on the Stothard drawing in the Mitchell Library, depicting an incident on Cook's visit to Botany Bay are filed at NPL:M(PXn70). The drawing was reproduced in colour in Warner, O.M.W.—Captain Cook and the South Pacific. New York, American Heritage Pub. Co., 1963, p.55. (NPL:M980:Co1/W1A1.)

[EPISODE at the landing of Captain Cook at Botany Bay, April 1770; drawn by Thomas Stothard.]

Sepia sketch. Meas. within frame lines 3″ x 2¼″, on a sheet 5″ x 4″.

Signed "T. Stothard." Undated. Has pencil inscription at bottom of sheet: "At the same time they brandished their spears and seemed resolved to defend their coast to the utmost."

Copies: NPL:M(SSV*/Cook2). 965

The Same: [engraving, with letters "H. Corbould. W. Finden", and quotation].

(*In* Kippis, *Rev.* Andrew—Narrative of the voyages round the world performed by Captain Cook. London, J.F.Dove, [182–?]. Frontisp.)

Copies: NPL:M(980:Co1/K2L1). 966

The Same: [engraving, with letters as above].

(*In* A Narrative of Captain Cook's voyages round the world. London, Allman, [183–?]. Frontisp.)

Copies: NPL:M(980:Co1/29A1). 967

STUBBS, GEORGE

Originals, Including Photocopies of Originals

A KANGAROO.

1771 or 1772. Photo. of oil on panel.

The original measures 23¼″ x 27½″ and is signed 'Geo. Stubbs'. It was painted for Sir Joseph Banks from whom it passed to the Knatchbull Family. In 1957 known to be in the possession of Mrs. W.P.Keith née Knatchbull-Hugessen, who told Public Library Liaison Officer that her grandfather bought it and a painting of a dingo (which she also owns) from his cousin, who had inherited them from Sir Joseph Banks.

Exhibited at the Society of Artists 1773, at Liverpool 1951, and at an exhibition of George Stubbs' works, Whitechapel Art Gallery Feb.–Ap.1957. A catalogue of the 1957 exhibition is filed in NPL:M Pam. File 759.2/S. Filed with the photo. is an illustrated article by Dr. A. Lysaght entitled *Captain Cook's kangaroo*, extracted from the *New Scientist* Mar. 14, 1957. Three coloured slides of the original painting are filed at NPL:M(FM5/123,198–9).

Copies: NPL:M(Small Picture File). 968

The Same. Engraving, proof before letters.

Meas. of engraved surface 7¾″ x 9½″.

The engraving was first published in 1773 as plate 20 in Hawkesworth's *Account of . . . voyages . . . in the southern hemisphere*, and is there entitled "An animal found on the coast of New Holland, called Kanguroo", according to the list of plates in vol.1. For a description of the engraving *see* item no. 932 in this Bibliography.

Copies: NPL:M(PXD 59⁻²). 969

The Same; [entitled] A Remarkable Animal found on one of the Hope Islands in Captn. Cook's first voyage. Rennoldson sculp.

London. Published by Alex^r Hogg.
Engraving. Meas. of engraved surface inside border 4⅝″ x 6⅛″. Meas. of plate mark
11½″ x 7¼″. Also on sheet is engraving The Vari . . . of Madagascar.
Copies: NPL:M(SV*Cook4). 970

Another Print.

(Anderson, G.W.—A New, authentic and complete collection of voyages. London,
Alex. Hogg, 1784–6. Opp. p.65.)
Copies: NPL:M(F980/5A1). 971

WILLIAMSON, JOHN
Reproductions

[COLOURED reproduction of painting entitled: I now took possession . . .
by the name of New South Wales.]
(*In* Cook's voyages of discovery; ed. by J. Barrow. London, Black, 1904. Frontisp.)
Copies: NPL:M(980:Col/36G1); VSL. 972

ARTIST UNKNOWN
Originals, Including Photocopies of Originals

[A VIEW in Matavia (*sic*), Bay in Otaheite.]
Watercolour. 7 3/16″ x 10 7/16″ within frame lines.
Unsigned and undated. Engraved as plate 2 in Hawkesworth's Account (item no.932
in this Bibliography), though whether it is a copy of the engraving or the original is
uncertain. Title above is taken from the corresponding engraving in Hawkesworth's
Account.
(*In* Webber, J.—[Watercolours illustrating Captain Cook's last voyage], plate no.44.)
Copies: NPL:D(PXX2). 973

[A VIEW in the Island of Huaheine; with the Ewharra no Eatua, or
House of God.]
Watercolour. 7⅞″ x 14⅝″ within frame lines.
Unsigned and undated. Engraved as plate 6 in Hawkesworth's Account (item no.932
in this Bibliography), though whether it is a copy of the engraving or the original is
doubtful. Title above is taken from the engraving in Hawkesworth's Account.
(*In* Webber, J.—[Watercolours illustrating Captain Cook's last voyage], plate no.46.)
Copies: NPL:D(PXX2). 974

[A VIEW in the Island of Otaheite; with the shed called tupapow . . . and a
representation of the person who performs the principal part in the
funeral ceremony in his peculiar dress.]
Watercolour. 7⅞″ x 13 7/16″ within frame lines.
Unsigned and undated. Engraved as plate no.5 in Hawkesworth's Account, though
whether it is a copy of the engraving or the original is uncertain. Title above taken from
the engraving in Hawkesworth's Account.
(*In* Webber, J.—[Watercolours illustrating Captain Cook's last voyage], plate no.45.)
Copies: NPL:D(PXX2). 975

[WATERCOLOUR of the Tasmanian coastline. 177–? Claimed to be by the surgeon of the *Endeavour*.]
Copies: VSL. 976

Reproductions

CAPTAIN Cook's landing at Botany, A.D. 1770.
n.d. Col. print. 14½″ x 18¼″.
Copies: NPL:M(V*Cook44). 977

CAPTAIN James Cook, R.N., landed at Botany Bay April 28, 1770: [a reproduction of portrait of Cook by Hall after Dance, surrounded by colour print of H.M.S. *Endeavour* in Botany Bay and natives opposing Cook's landing, portraits of Tasman and Dampier and Letterpress.] Photos & design by Chas. Whiting.
1928. Peacock Bros. Pty. Ltd., Melb. 18″ x 14½″.
Copies: NPL:M(P3/40). 978

THE VARI, or Maucauco, a native of Madagascar. Rennoldson sculp.
London. Published by Alexʳ Hogg.
Engraving. Meas. of engraved surface 4¼″ x 6¼″. Meas. of plate mark 11½″ x 7⅝″.
On sheet with engraving of *A Remarkable animal found on one of the Hope Islands*.
(*In* Anderson, G.W.—A New . . . collection . . . of voyages round the world. London, Alex. Hogg, [1784–6]. Opp. p.65.)
Copies: NPL:M(F980/5A1). 979

The Same.
Background sky is more detailed.
Copies: NPL:M(SV*Cook4). 980

VIEW of Captain Cook's first landing near Gisborne.
(Cylopedia of New Zealand. Wellington, 1902. Vol.2, p.88.)
Copies: NPL:M(Q997/C). 981

[A WAR canoe of New Zealand, with a view of Gable End Foreland.]
The engraving was first published as plate no.16 in Hawkesworth's Account, 1773. For a description *see* no.932, and *see also* no.936.

The Same. Proof before letters.
Meas. of engraved surface 7¾″ x 21¾″.
Copies: NPL:M(PXD59⁻²). 982

The Same. A War canoe of New Zealand with Gable End Foreland. F.Bannerman sculp.

Meas. of engraved surface $4\frac{5}{16}''$ x $7\frac{7}{8}''$. Plate mark $5\frac{1}{4}''$ x $8\frac{1}{8}''$.

Copies: NPL:M(SSV*Cook1). 983

The Same; [entitled] War canoe of New Zealand. Grieg sculp[t].

Meas. within frame lines $7\frac{5}{8}''$ x $10\frac{5}{8}''$.

This shows the same canoe as in the previous engravings, but there are no figures in it, no view, and the background and foreground are only sketched.

Copies: NPL:M(SSV*Cook10). 984

The Same; [entitled] A New Zealand War canoe. Engraved for *Middleton's Complete System of Geography.* [Engraving.]

Meas. of engraved surface $3\frac{5}{8}''$ x $10\frac{9}{16}''$. Meas. of plate mark $7\frac{3}{4}''$ x $11\frac{3}{8}''$.

Also on sheet is engraving of heads of New Zealand chiefs.

Copies: NPL:D(DL PX20). 985

Illustrations

Printed Books and Articles about the Illustrations

1925 IREDALE, Tom, *and* TROUGHTON, Ellis Le Geyt
Captain Cook's kangaroo.

Illus.

(*Australian Zoologist* vol. 3, pp. 311–16, Jan. 1925.)

Copies: NPL:M(Q590.5/A); NPL:D(MS.Q144, extract). 986

1950 SCOTT, T.C.S.Morrison-, *and* SAWYER, F.C.
Identity of Captain Cook's kangaroo. [With bibl.] London, 1950.

Facs. illus. pp. 43–50, plates 3–5.

(British Museum, Natural History—*Bulletin, Zoology.* Vol. 1, no. 3, Mar. 1950.)

With account of the drawings by Sydney Parkinson and Sir Nathaniel Dance.

Copies: NPL:M(Q599.2/S). 987

1966 PALMER, G.
Duplication of folio numbers depicting fishes in Parkinson's unpublished drawings of animals from Cook's first voyage, 1768–1771.

(Society for the Bibliography of Natural History—*Journal.* Vol. 4, pt. 5, pp. 267–8, Feb. 1966.)

Copies: NPL:R(S570.306/1). 988

Ships

Plans, Originals and Reproductions

Originals cannot be reproduced without the permission of the owner.
See also accounts of the first voyage.

1768 THE DRAUGHT of His Majesty's Bark *Endeavour*, as fitted out at this port, her body taken off in the single dock. Deptford Yard, 17 July 1768. Woolwich Yard 16 Oct. 1771.

27″ x 42½″.
Original in the Hydrographic Office. Copy by a draughtsman.
Copies: Captain Cook Landing Place Trust.   989

The Same.
Photograph. 24¾″ x 40⅛″.
Copies: NPL:M(XV*Ships/End9).   990

Another 3 Copies.
Photograph, reduced. 8½″ x 13¾″.
Copies: NPL:M(SSV*Ships/End1–3).   991

Another Copy.
Photograph, reduced. 5⅜″ x 8″.
Copies: NPL:M(Ships File:End8).   992

Another Photocopy.
Copies: NPL:M(V*Ships/End4D).   993

1768 DRAUGHT of His Majesty's Bark *Endeavour*, her body being taken off in the Single Dock, April 25, 1768: the original plan.

14⅝″ x 40″.
This plan has been mounted and framed. The mount bears the inscription, "This plan (the only one known to exist) is the master shipwright's copy from which the alterations were made to the cat-built bark purchased by the Admiralty, April 1768; registered afterwards in the Royal Navy as the *Endeavour*. She was thus altered by this plan to enable her to suitably accommodate Capt. Jas. Cook, Sir Joseph Banks, Dr. Solander & party for the voyage to Tahiti to observe the Transit of Venus. Purchased by the Committee of Australasian Pioneers' Club, Sep.21st, 1911."
Copies: Australasian Pioneers' Club, Sydney.   994

The Same: [photograph].
7 5/16″ x 19 11/16″.
Copies: NPL:M(F623.8/E).   995

1911 PLANS of the *Endeavour:* [extract from the *Daily Telegraph* November 14, 1911, relating how the Australasian Pioneers' Club came into possession of the plans].

Illus.
(Newspaper cuttings, vol.25, pp.70–73.)
Copies: NPL:M(Q991/N).   996

1934 MOTT, G.

Blueprints. Rigging plans, etc., H.M. Bark *Endeavour*. By G. Mott, Willoughby, 1934.

Copies: Captain Cook's Landing Place Trust. 997

[1948?] UNDERHILL, Harold Alonso

Endeavour Bark, 1768: [plans. Glasgow, Brown, Son and Ferguson Ltd. 1948?]

Helios? 5 sheets.

Copy negs. are at NPL:M FM2/337–341. *See also* no. 1001.

CONTENTS:

Drawing no.887: Lines for scale model. cm 32 x 47.
Drawing no.888: General arrangement drawing. cm 57 x 95½.
Drawing no.889: Sail and rigging plan. cm 63¼ x 93.
Drawing no.890: Cross sections, details and accommodation plan. cm 53 x 79½.
Drawing no.891: Spar construction and rigging details. cm 69½ x 85.

Copies: NPL:M(XV*Ships/End4–8). 998

1952 CLOWES, Geoffrey Swinford Laird

[Description of a] photograph of contemporary draught of the *Endeavour* Bark in 1768.

(*In his* Sailing ships, their history & development. London, H.M.S.O., 1930–52. Part II, p.63.)

Copies: NPL:M(623.822/3); NPL:R(S623.822/2). 999

1965 H.M. BARK *Endeavour:* a diagrammatic section of the interior, after the original dockyard plans in the National Maritime Museum. [With description.]

(*In* Australian Encyclopaedia. Sydney, A. & R., 1958. Vol.3, p.45.)

Copies: NPL:M(Q039/A); NPL:R(NQ994.003/23A); NPL:D(Q95/17 Ref. Bks.). 1000

1967 UNDERHILL, Harold Alonso

The *Endeavour:* [reproduction of plans by Harold A. Underhill, from the collection in the Mitchell Library. Melbourne, Hill of Content Archive Ser., 1967.]

Folded sheet.

Issued with Jennings, Margaret Jean—The Discovery of Australia, 1967. *See also* no. 998.

Copies: NPL:M(Q990.1/15A1). 1001

n.d. GREAT BRITAIN—Admiralty

[Copies of draft plans of H.M.S. *Endeavour* sent out by the Admiralty, c.1924.]

Copies: Captain Cook's Landing Place Trust. 1002

n.d. HIS MAJESTY'S BARQUE *Endeavour*, built at Whitby, Yorkshire 1764: [blueprints for a model].

CONTENTS:
1. Rigging plan. 30″ x 38¾″. Scale: full-size.
2. Deck fittings. 22¾″ x 28¾″. Scale: full-size.
3. Hull plan. 22¾″ x 28¾″. Scale ¼″ to 1″.
Presented by L.J.Finn, 1952.
The Trustees of the Public Library of New South Wales do not own the original plans and cannot grant permission for their reproduction. Microfilm copies filed at NPL:M (FM2/408–10).
Copies: NPL:M(XV*Ships/End1–3).   1003

Ships

Illustrations

Original Illustrations, Including Photocopies of Originals

CRAWSHAW, Lionel T.
[Photograph of L.T.Crawshaw's painting of the *Endeavour* leaving Whitby.]
Meas. on photo, within frame 2¾″ x 4⅛″.
Copies: NPL:M(Ships File).   1004

CRAWSHAW, Lionel T.
The *Endeavour* 1768 Leaving Whitby for the Thames.
Etching. Meas. of plate mark 7⅜″ x 10⅜″.
Signed "Lionel T. Crawshaw" below plate mark.
Copies: NPL:M(V*Ships/End6B).   1005

LUNY, Thomas
The *Earl of Pembroke*, later Captain Cook's *Endeavour*, outward bound from Whitby.
Oil painting. 31″ x 57″. Untitled; unsigned.
Attributed to Thomas Luny (1759–1837).
Copies: ANL.   1006

LUNY, Thomas
Endeavour leaving Whitby.
Photograph of oil painting. 11½″ x 22″.
Uncoloured. Attributed to Thomas Luny.
Copies: Captain Cook's Landing Place Trust.   1007

LUNY, Thomas
H.M. Bark *Endeavour* leaving Whitby Harbour 1768.
Colour reproduction. 4¾″ x 6¾″.
Attributed to Thomas Luny (1759–1837).
Original in National Library of Australia, Canberra.
Copies: NPL:M(Ships File).   1008

CLEVELEY, J.
[H.M. Bark *Endeavour*. Ships in a harbour, one with sails set.]
1768. Photograph. $3\frac{7}{8}''$ x $4\frac{7}{8}''$.
Caption below reads "Said to be the "*Endeavour*", from a painting by J.Cleveley dated 1768".
Copies: NPL:M(V*Ships/End4A). 1009

PARKINSON, Sydney
Sketches (3) of the *Endeavour*.
1768? Photographs (3). $6\frac{1}{4}''$ x $8\frac{1}{8}''$.
Originals are in the British Museum(Add. MSS.9345).
Copies: NPL:M(Ships File/End4–6). 1010

PARKINSON, Sydney
H.M.S. *Endeavour* in Matavi (*sic*) Bay: [reproduction of a brush and ink sketch . . . in the British Museum].
(*In* Carrington, Arthur Hugh—Life of Captain Cook. London, Sidgwick & Jackson, 1939. Opp. p.90.)
Copies: NPL:M(980:Col/C1A1); NPL:D(93/127); ANL; QU; VSL; WU. 1011

MUGGINS, Thomas
H.M.Bark *Endeavour* coming to anchor in Port Royal, Otaheite, 13 April 1769.
Watercolour. Signed Thomas Muggins.
Presented by J.J.Shillinglaw.
Copies: VSL. 1012

ROBINS, J.F.
H.M.S. *Endeavour* leaving N.Z. for N.S.W., 1770. Compiled and drawn from the most accurate data, and presented to the Mitchell Library by Commander J.F.Robins, R.N.
Watercolour. Oval. $6\frac{1}{4}''$ x $8\frac{5}{8}''$.
Signed "J.F.Robins".
Copies: NPL:M(SV*Ships/End). 1013

THE "*ENDEAVOUR*" entering Botany Bay. April 28th 1770.
Photograph. $5\frac{7}{8}''$ x $7\frac{7}{8}''$.
Photograph of sketch in King, P.G.—Comments on Cook's log. Opp. p.7.
Copies: NPL:M(V*Cook 42A). 1014

ALLCOT, John
John Allcot's oil painting of the *Endeavour* entering Botany Bay.
Coloured reproduction of the original donated to the H.M.S. *Endeavour* Trust for the Australian Maritime Museum.
Copies: NPL:M(Ships File). 1015

ALLCOT, John

The Ship that put Australia on the Map. H.M.S. "*Endeavour*", (366 tons) commanded by Captain James Cook, R.N. entering Botany Bay, Sunday 29th April, 1770, where the famous Navigator first landed on Australian Shores. Painted by John Allcot, December, 1924.

1924. Photo-reproduction. Meas. of view 8″ x 11¼″.
Signed "John Allcot. 1924".
Copies: NPL:M(V*Ships/End5). 1016

ALLCOT, John

Endeavour entering Botany Bay. [Reproduction of a painting.]
Copies: Captain Cook's Landing Place Trust. 1017

ALLCOT, John

The Ship that put Australia on the map . . . H.M.S. *Endeavour* . . . entering Botany Bay, Sunday April 29, 1770. [Reproduction of a painting.]

(*In* Philip, Geo. B. & Son—Australian historical pictures. Sydney, 1930. Plate 2.)
Copies: NPL:M(F990.1/P). 1018

INGLETON, Geoffrey Chapman

H.M.Bark *Endeavour*, Botany Bay Welcome.

1936–7? Original etching numbered 9/50. Meas. of plate mark 9″ x 11½″.
(*In his* Etchings. [1936–7?].)
Copies: NPL:M(D148). 1019

INGLETON, Geoffrey Chapman

H.M.Bark *Endeavour* The First Voyage 1768–1771.

1957. Reprod. of drawing.
(*In* Cook, J.—Collected Voyages—Printed Accounts [1957. Price's Edition] The Explorations of Captain James Cook in the Pacific. New York, 1957. p.[13].)
Copies: NPL:M(C956). 1020

PIGUENIT, W.C.

The *Endeavour* Capt Cook passing Sydney Heads, on the 6th May 1770.

Pencil drawing.
(*In his* Collection of views, no.37.)
Copies: NPL:D(DG*D16). 1021

H.M.S. "*ENDEAVOUR*". (The vessel in which Cap. Cook explored the East Coast of New Holland—1770.) From a pencil sketch by Buchan.

Watercolour. Meas. inside mount 7½″ x 10″.
This sketch has been erroneously ascribed to Buchan.
Copies: NPL:M(SV*Ships/End1). 1022

The Same. Electro of woodblock, probably by W.F. Chambers. 4½″ x 7″.
Copies: NPL:M(R 160). 1023

The Same.

Reproduced in Historical Records of New South Wales. Sydney, Govt.Pr., 1893. Vol.1,
pt.1. Opp. p.308.
Notes by F.J. Bayldon on this reproduction are at NPL:M PXn 187, p.3.

1024

The Same; [entitled] The *"Endeavour's"* work done.

Photographs (2). 4½″ x 6⅜″. Copied from a view in the Whitby Museum.
Title below view reads "The *Endeavour's* work done. Reproduced from a photograph
taken by the Australian Government's Printer from a watercolour in the Mitchell Gallery
Sydney".

Copies: NPL:M(Ships File/Endeavour 12–13); Captain Cook's Landing Place Trust.
1025

BAYLDON, Francis Joseph
Dimensional sketch of "Ye cat-built Bark", H.M.S. *Endeavour.* Captain
James Cook. 1768–1771. Scale: ½ inch = 1 foot.

1923. Col. photocopy of sketch of ship with sails set. Meas. within mount 14″ x 17¼″.
Signed 'Francis J. Bayldon Commd^r. R.N.R. 1923.' Typescript notes by Bayldon 1924,
part of which were used as letterpress on the print below, and other notes on the *Endeavour,*
are at NPL:M PXn 187.

Copies: NPL:M(V*Ships/End1); ANL; Captain Cook's Landing Place Trust; VSL.
1026

The Same; [with title]. Dimensional sketch of H.M.S. *Endeavour.* Captain
James Cook. 1768–1771.

1923. Full colour relief print. Meas. of sketch c.10¼″ x 12¼″. Meas. of sheet 15⅛″ x 21¼″.
With letterpress.
Copies: NPL:D(DL Pf51). 1027

Another Print.
Copies: NPL:M(V*Ships/End2). 1028

The Same.

Reproduced in Wood, G.A.—Voyage of the *Endeavour.* Melbourne, Macmillan, 1926.
Frontisp.
Copies: NPL:M(980:Co2/W3A1); NPL:D(92/172); NPL:R(S990A/3); ANL. 1029

BAYLDON, Francis Joseph
Dimensional sketch of "Ye cat-built Bark", H.M.S. *Endeavour.* Captain
James Cook. 1768–1771. Scale 1″ = 12 feet.

1924. Col. photocopy of sketch of ship with sails furled. Meas. inside mount 14″ x 17⅜″.
Signed 'Francis J. Bayldon Commd! R.N.R. 1924'.
Copies: NPL:M(V*Ships/End3); ANL; Captain Cook's Landing Place Trust. 1030

ROBINS, J.F.
H.M.S. *Endeavour* and Cook's coat-of-arms.
Original sketch. Meas. inside frame 11½″ x 17″. Signed in lower right-hand corner.
Copies: Captain Cook's Landing Place Trust.   1031

Photograph.
(*In* James Cook Papers—Biography and Bibliography. p.347.)
Copies: NPL:D(MS.Q144).   1032

Ships

Illustrations

Reproductions

[THE *EARL OF PEMBROKE* under construction in Whitby Harbour.]
Photograph of a print in the possession of the Whitby Literary and Philosophical Society.
5″ x 9⅝″.
Copies: NPL:M(SSV*Cook6).   1033

EARL OF PEMBROKE, built at Whitby 1764; taken over by the Admiralty
and renamed *Endeavour* 1768. From a print formerly in the possession
of Mr. T.H.Woodward, retired solicitor, of Whitby . . .
Half-tone. 4¼″ x 5¹⁵⁄₁₆″.
Title from inscription below view.
Copies: NPL:M(V*Ships/End6A).   1034

WEATHERILL, Richard
Earl of Pembroke, 1764: [illustration].
(*In his* The Ancient port of Whitby. Whitby, Horne and Son, 1908. p.46.)
Copies: NPL:M(339.7/W); NPL:R(S656.509/5); Captain Cook's Landing Place Trust.
                    1035

THE *ENDEAVOUR* approaching Otaheite: [an engraving], Huggins del.,
Watkins sculp.
(*In* Cook, James—Voyages of Captain James Cook. London, W. Smith, 1846. Vol.1,
engraved title-page: *The three voyages of Captain James Cook.*)
Copies: NPL:M(Q980:Col/4B1).   1036

THE *ENDEAVOUR* off Tahiti: [illustration].
(*In* Story, Alfred Thomas—The Building of the Empire. London, Chapman & Hall,
1898. Vol.2, p.171.)
Copies: NPL:M(942/S); NPL:R(S909/62).   1037

THE *ENDEAVOUR* off Tahiti: [illustration].
(*In* Kingston, William Henry Giles—Captain Cook, his life, voyages and discoveries.
London, Religious Tract Society, [1904]. p.61.)
Copies: NPL:M(980:Col/K1A1).   1038

CLAYTON, Matthew Thomas

Captain Cook in the *Endeavour* off the east coast of New Zealand, A.D. 1769: [a reproduction] (from the painting by . . . M.T. Clayton.)

(*In* Cowan, James—New Zealand. Wellington, N.Z., Govt. Pr., 1907. p.5.)

Copies: NPL:M(987/C); NPL:D(90/297). 1039

CLAYTON, Matthew Thomas

Captain Cook in the *Endeavour* off the east coast of New Zealand, A.D. 1769: [a reproduction] (from the painting by . . . M.T. Clayton.)

(*In* Cowan, James—New Zealand. Wellington, N.Z., Govt.Pr., 1908. p.4.)

Copies: NPL:M(987/C); NPL:D(90/298). 1040

ROBINS, John

Endeavour, 1770.

1921. Print of pen and ink sketch.

Copies: Captain Cook's Landing Place Trust; VSL. 1041

GRIBBLE, Bernard

The *"Endeavour"* passing Sydney Harbour, 1770. From the original by Bernard Gribble. Reproduced . . . from the original in the possession of . . . the Duke and Duchess of York.

Col. reproduction. 8½" x 11¾".

Copies: NPL:M(SSV*Ships/End4). 1042

ELLIOTT, Fred

The *"Endeavour"* off Moreton Bay, by Fred Elliott.

Col. reproduction. Meas. of view 7 15/16" x 8 1/16". Signed "F.Elliott".

Copies: NPL:M(V*Ships/End4C). 1043

[A VIEW of Endeavour River, on the coast of New Holland, where the ship was laid on shore, in order to repair the damage which she received on the rock.]

The engraving was first published as plate 19 in Hawkesworth's Account 1773. For a description *see* item no. 932 in this Bibliography.

The Same. [Proof.] Will Byrne sculp[t].

Meas. of engraved surface 7⅞" x 18⅜". Meas. of plate mark 9 7/16" x 19 7/16".

(*In* [Three voyages round the world]. Plate no.19.)

Copies: NPL:M(PXD59⁻¹). 1044

[CAPTAIN COOK'S vessel beached at the entrance of the Endeavour River: an engraving], I.C.G. Fritzsch, sc.

(*In* Hawkesworth, John—Geschichte der See-Reisen und Entdeckungen im Süd-Meer. Berlin, A. Haude und J.C. Spener, 1774. Vol.3, p.152.)

Copies: NPL:M(980/172C3). 1045

VUE de la rivière d'Endeavour sur la côte de la Nouvelle Hollande ou le vaiseau fut mis à la bande: [an engraving], Duret, sculp.

(*In* Hawkesworth, John—Relation des voyages . . . Paris, Saillant et Nyon, 1774. Vol. 9, Atlas, 3rd plate from end.)

Copies: NPL:M(Q980/38C5); NPL:R(09:Q990A/90). 1046

A VIEW in Endeavour River, in New South Wales: with the *Endeavour* Bark laid up, after a wonderful escape from shipwreck. No.15. Page sc. Engraved for Payne's *Universal Geography*, vol.1, p.557.

7⅛″ x 10⅛″. Coloured.
(Views in Australasia.)

Copies: NPL:D(DLPd677). 1047

VIEW of Endeavour River, on the Coast of New Holland, where Captain Cook had the Ship laid on Shore in order to repair the Damage which she received on the Rock. Rennoldson, sculp. London. Published by Alex^r. Hogg.

Reversed plate, with ship on the left. Meas. within frame lines 6¼″ x 10⅜″. Meas. of plate mark 7$\frac{7}{16}$″ x 11½″.

Copies: NPL:M(SSV4B/EndR1). 1048

VIEW of Endeavour River on the coast of New Holland, where Captain Cook had the ship laid on shore & repaired: [a copper engraving], eng. by J.G. Wooding.

(*In* Illustrations to Captain Cook's voyages. London, Graves, pr., [n.d.] p.41.)

Copies: NPL:M(980:Col/I1A1). 1049

VIEW of Endeavour River, on the coast of New Holland, where Captain Cook had the ship laid on shore, in order to repair the damage which she received on the rock: [an engraving], Rennoldson sculp.

(*In* Anderson, George William—A New, authentic and complete collection of voyages˙ London, printed for Alex. Hogg, [1784–86]. Opp. p.64.)
Also contained in other editions of this work.

Copies: NPL:M(A346); NPL:R(09:F990A/11). 1050

GEZIGT van de Rivier Endeavour op de Kust van Nieuw-Holland: [an engraving], I.S. Klauber, sculps.

(*In* Cook, James—Reizen rondom de waereld. Amsterdam & Leyden, Honkoop, Allart en Van Cleef, 1795–1809. Atlas, pl.XIX.)
Not indexed for other copies.

Copies: NPL:M(F980:Col/1A1). 1051

REPAIRING of Captain Cook's ship in Endeavour River: [engraving].

(*In* Wilson, Robert—Voyages of discoveries. London, J. Cundee, 1806. Vol.2, p.13.)

Copies: NPL:M(980/W). 1052

RIVIÈRE D'ENDEAVOUR: [copper engraving], Brion direxit.

(*In* Cook, James—Premier, (second) [and] (troisième) voyage. Paris, Chez Mme. Ve Lepetit, 1817. Atlas, plate 22. *Bibliothèque portative des voyages, tome XVIII.*)
Copies: NPL:M(980:Co1/23A7). 1053

SOUTER, David Henry
The *Endeavour* on the reef: [illustration].

(*In* Watts, Ebenezer John Moore—Stories from Australian history. Sydney, W. Brooks, 1908. p.42. *Brooks Aust. School Ser.*)
Copies: NPL:M(990.1/W); NPL:D(91/164). 1054

CAPTAIN COOK'S vessel beached at the entrance of Endeavour River . . . from an engraving in the Atlas to Cook's first voyage.

(*In* Synge, Margaret Bertha—A Book of discovery. London, Jack, 1912. p.327.)
Also contained in the 1920 edition.
Copies: NPL:M(910.9/10A1). 1055

SOUTER, David Henry
The *Endeavour* on the reef: [illustration].

(*In* Watts, Ebenezer John Moore—Stories from Australian history. 2nd ed. Sydney, W. Brooks, 1914. p.44. *Brooks Aust. School Ser.*)
Copies: NPL:M(990.1/W). 1056

COOK'S SHIP careened at Endeavour River: [illustration].

(*In* Jose, Arthur Wilberforce—History of Australasia. 6th ed. Sydney, A. & R., 1918· p.13.)
Also contained in other editions of this work.
Copies: NPL:M(990/1F1); NPL:R(S990/3); NPL:D(90/489). 1057

THE *ENDEAVOUR* in Endeavour River, beached for repair.

(*In* Wood, George Arnold—The Voyage of the *Endeavour.* Melbourne, Macmillan, 1926. p.99.)
Copies: NPL:M(980:Co2/W3A1); NPL:R(S990AE/3); NPL:D(92/172). 1058

VIEW of the Endeavor (*sic*) River.

(*In* Coad, N.E.—A History of the Pacific. Wellington, N.Z. Book Depot, 1926. Opp. p.50.)
Copies: NPL:M(990/C). 1059

H.M.S. *ENDEAVOUR,* Lieut Cook, A.D.1770 in the river he called Endeavour River.

11½″ x 18½″ inside mount.
Undated. Engraver's name not given. Supp. to the *Sydney Mail.*
Copies: NPL:M(V4B/EndR1). 1060

THE *ENDEAVOUR* [in full sail: illustration].
(*In* Gillies, William—Simple studies in English history:(for fifth class). Rev. ed. Melbourne, Whitcombe & Tombs, [1910?]. p.205. *Austral History Readers*.)
Copies: NPL:M(942/G).   1061

THE *ENDEAVOUR* in full sail: [illustration].
(*In* Long, Charles Richard—Stories of Australian exploration. 2nd ed. Melbourne, W. & T., [1910?]. p.56. *Austral History Readers*.)
See also no. 1063.
Copies: NPL:M(980/L).   1062

THE *ENDEAVOUR* in full sail: [illustration].
(*In* Long, Charles Richard—Stories of Australian exploration. Rev. ed. Melbourne, W. & T., [1913]. p.51.)
See also no. 1062.
Copies: NPL:M(980/L).   1063

THE ENDEAVOUR in full sail: [illustration].
(*In* Murdoch, Walter Logie Forbes—Making of Australia . . . Melbourne, Whitcombe & Tombs, [1917]. p.38.)
Copies: NPL:M(990.1/M).   1064

CAPTAIN COOK'S ship *Endeavour:* [newspaper extract dated Nov.11, 1924].
(Newspaper cuttings, vol.3, p.133.)
Copies: NPL:M(Q991/N).   1065

THE BARQUE *ENDEAVOUR:* [illustration].
(*Endeavour:* a quarterly review. Vol.1, no.1, Jan.1942. Front cover.)
Copies: NPL:M(Q980:Co2/E1A1); NPL:R(Q506/38).   1066

ROBINSON, Gregory
The *Endeavour:* [reproduction of a painting].
(*In* Lloyd, Christopher—Captain Cook. London, Faber and Faber, 1952. Opp. p.36.)
Copies: NPL:M(980:Co1/L2A1); NPL:R(920/C771/12); ANL; QParl; VMoU; VSL.
1067

LANGMAID, R.
Endeavour: [reproduction in colour of painting].
(*Endeavour* vol.27, p.39, Jan.1968.)
Copies: NPL:R(NQ505/7).   1068

ELLWOOD, C.E.

His Majesty's Bark *"Endeavour"*. From a watercolour by C.E.Ellwood, 1969.

1969. Col. reproduction. Printed in Australia by W.C.Penfold & Co. Pty. Ltd. 19¼″ x 22″. Legend below title.

Copies: NPL:M(V*Ships/End7). 1069

Another Print.

Copies: NPL:M(V*Ships/End8). 1070

Ships

Models and Illustrations of Models

1911 MODEL of H.M.S. *Endeavour* in silver-plate, forming a table centre, presented to H.M.S. *Commonwealth* by the people of Australia, June 22, 1911: [reproduction of photograph].

(*In* Ward, W.F.—Commonwealth shield and table centre. Sydney, 1911. Plate 2.)

Copies: NPL:M(739/W). 1071

[191–?] A MODEL of Captain Cook's *"Endeavour"*.

Constructed by Norman Lindsay. Photo. A. Hall.

Half-tone. 5⅛″ x 4″.

Copies: NPL:M(V*Ships/End4B). 1072

1913 *THE ENDEAVOUR* bark: a model of Captain Cook's famous vessel, [constructed] by Norman Lindsay. [Illustration.]

(*Lone Hand*, Ap. 1913, p. 488.)

Copies: NPL:M(059/L); NPL:D(90/382); NPL:R(Q050/L847). 1073

[c.1917 MODEL of the *Endeavour*, made by Norman Lindsay. Acquired by the Museum in 1917.]

Copies: Museum of Applied Science, Melbourne. 1074

1930–32 BROOKS, Cecil

Model of H.M.S. *Endeavour* built by Commander Cecil Brooks, 1930–1932.

Scale ⅕″ = *1″.* 22″ overall, height of main mast from deck = 21″.

Presented by Mrs. Cecil Brooks, widow of Commander Brooks, to the people of N.S.W. 1947, to be placed with other Cook relics in the Australian Museum, Sydney, and transferred to the Mitchell Library Oct. 1955, with other Cook relics.

Three photographs of the model, two photographs of the presentation ceremony and a copy of part of an article about the model written by Commander Brooks in the *Sydney Morning Herald* Dec.21, 1932, are mounted together and filed in the Ships File, with newscutting of the article. Copy of the correspondence from the Australian Museum Correspondence Files, about the gift of the model is in NPL:MA3936⁻².

Copies: NPL:M(XR13.Mitchell Galleries). 1075

[c.1932] PHOTOGRAPH of a model of the *Endeavour*, made at Chatham Dock by C.W. Whitaker and C. Knight, c.1932.

8½″ x 6½″.
See also nos. 1077, 1079, 1100.
Copies: NPL:M(Ships File). 1076

1934 CAPTAIN COOK'S *Endeavour*, 1768: [reproduction of a photograph of a model, constructed by C.W. Whitaker. With historical description.]

(*In* Chatterton, Edward Keble—Sailing models, ancient and modern. London, Hurst & Blackett, 1934. pp.62–3, fig.67.)
See also nos. 1076, 1079, 1100.
Copies: NPL:R(*Q623.82/4). 1077

1934 INGLETON, Geoffrey Chapman

H.M. Bark *Endeavour:* souvenir of an exhibition of models constructed during Victoria's centenary year, 1934. Melbourne, the *Argus*, 1934.
Illus.
Copies: NPL:M(623.8/1); NPL:D(93/288, MS.Q144). 1078

1939 MODEL of H.M.S. *Endeavour*, [by C.W. Whitaker], in the Science Museum South Kensington: [reproduction of a photograph].

(*In* Carrington, Arthur Hugh—Life of Captain Cook. London, Sidgwick & Jackson, 1939. Opp. p.66.)
See also nos. 1076–7, 1100.
Copies: NPL:M(980:Co1/C1A1); NPL:D(93/127); ANL; QU; VSL; WU. 1079

[196–?] SCALE MODEL of Captain Cook's *Endeavour*, made by Finecraft Scale Models Pty. Ltd. [Illustration extracted from the *Sydney Morning Herald* 16.1.67.)

The model is to be on display at the Roxy Restaurant at Sans Souci, N.S.W.
Copies: NPL:M(Ships File/Endeavour). 1080

1966 LINDSAY, Norman Alfred William

[Account of his model of Cook's *Endeavour*, now in the Melbourne National Gallery.]

(*In his* Norman Lindsay's ship models. Sydney, A. & R., 1966. pp.13–14.)
Copies: NPL:M(Q623.82/6A1); NPL:R(EQ623.822/Lin). 1081

1969 QANTAS EMPIRE AIRWAYS LTD.

Model of the *Endeavour* in Cooktown Museum: [reproduction of a photograph].

(*In* Cook, James—First Voyage—Printed Accounts [1969 Reed's Edition]—Captain Cook in Australia . . . Ed. by A.W. Reed. Wellington, N.Z., Reed, 1969. Between pp.96 and 97.)
Copies: NPL:M(980:Co2/11A1). 1082

Ships

Printed Books, Articles, etc. about the Endeavour

1775 GREAT BRITAIN—Admiralty
Cost of the upkeep of the *Endeavour* for 1775.

(*In its* The Ordinary estimate of His Majesty's Navy for 1775. p.56.)
Copies of documents formerly in the possession of Lord North.
Copies: NPL:M(MS.A1692).   1083

1884 MASON, George Champlin
Cook's ship *Endeavour*.

(*In his* Reminiscences of Newport. Newport, R.I., C.E. Hammett, *Jr.*, 1884. pp.300–301.)
Copies: NPL:M(974.57/M).   1084

1899 CAPTAIN COOK'S *Endeavour:* [extract from the *Sydney Morning Herald* April 8, 1899. Letter to the Editor from John W. Deering, quoting letter from the Mayor, City of Newport, R.I., U.S.A., re the *Endeavour* and relics from her held in Newport].

(*Newspaper cuttings*, vol.114, p.22.)
Copies: NPL:M(Q991/N).   1085

[1899?] DEERING, John W.
Captain Cook's *Endeavour*.

Formerly in *Newspaper cuttings*, vol.177, p.134.
Copies: NPL:M(Cuttings File).   1086

[1899?] MORRIS, Edward Ellis
H.M. Barque, *Endeavour*.

Formerly in *Newspaper cuttings*, vol.177, p.134.
Copies: NPL:M(Cuttings File).   1087

1899 MORRIS, Edward Ellis
His Majesty's Bark *Endeavour:* the fate of Cook's exploring ship. [Extracted from the *Argus*, Ap.22, 1899.]
Copies: NPL:M(359/M).   1088

1904 BLADEN, Frank Murcott
Captain Cook's ship *Endeavour:* [notes by F.M. Bladen. Published for the N.S.W. Legislative Assembly]. Sydney, Govt. Pr., [1904.].
pp.3.
Copies: NPL:M(Q623.826/B); ANL.   1089

1904 BLADEN, Frank Murcott
Captain Cook's ship *Endeavour*. Sydney, Govt. Pr., 1904.
pp.4.
(New South Wales—Legislative Assembly—*Votes and Proceedings,* 2nd sess. 1904, vol.2,
pp.911–13.)
Copies: NPL:D(MS.Q144).   1090

1904 CAPTAIN COOK'S ship *Endeavour.* [Extracted from the *Hobart
Mercury,* Nov.19, 1904.]
(*Newspaper cuttings relating to Tasmania,* vol.1, p.4.)
Copies: NPL:M(Q996/N).   1091

1907 McNAB, Robert
[The *Endeavour;* and] (Cook's *Endeavour* controversy.)
(*In his* Murihiku and the southern islands. Invercargill, William Smith, pr., 1907.
pp.9–12, 276–93.)
Copies: NPL:M(997.9/M); NPL:D(90/180); NPL:R(S997/15).   1092

1913 LINDSAY, Norman Alfred William
The Rig of the *Endeavour.*
Illus.
(*Lone Hand,* Nov.1912–Ap.1913, pp.451, 488–94.)
Copies: NPL:M(059/L); NPL:D(90/382); NPL:R(Q050/L847).   1093

1913 MOORE, Arthur
H.M.S. *Endeavour.* [Extracted from the *Daily Telegraph,* Dec.27, 1913.]
(*Newspaper cuttings,* vol.35, p.69.)
Copies: NPL:M(Q991/N).   1094

1913 S., B.
H.M.S. *Endeavour* and what became of her.
(*Lone Hand,* Nov.1912–Ap.1913, various pp.)
Copies: NPL:M(059/L); NPL:D(90/382); NPL:R(Q050/L847).   1095

1926 WOOD, George Arnold
Voyage of the *Endeavour.* Melbourne, Macmillan, 1926.
Illus.
Not indexed for other editions.
Copies: NPL:M(980:Co2/W3A1); NPL:D(92/172); NPL:R(S990AE/3); ANL.   1096

1927 BAYLDON, Francis Joseph
[The *Endeavour,* with sketch.]
(*In* Australian encyclopaedia. 3rd ed. Sydney, A. & R., 1927. Vol.1, pp.308–9.)
Copies: NPL:M(Q039/A); NPL:D(Q92/48); NPL:R(Q990.1A/35 Ref.Bks.); ANL. 1097

1927 LOST GUNS of Cook's *Endeavour.* [Extracted from the *Labor Daily,*
Ap.27, 1927.]
Illus.
(*In* Newspaper cuttings: Captain Cook. Vol.1, p.122.)
Copies: NPL:M(Q980:Co1/N1A1). 1098

1930 CLOWES, Geoffrey Swinford Laird
[The *Endeavour* Bark.]
(*In his* Sailing ships, their history & development. London, H.M.S.O., 1930–52. Part 1,
p.92.)
Copies: NPL:M(623.822/3); NPL:R(S623.822/2). 1099

1933 KNIGHT, C.
H.M. Bark *Endeavour.*
Illus. plans.
(*Mariners Mirror,* Jy. 1933, pp.292–302.)
A description of the *Earl of Pembroke* and its refit, etc., and reproductions of one plan and
two draughts of the *Endeavour,* from the Admiralty. With reproductions of photographs
of a model of the *Endeavour,* constructed by C.W. Whitaker, for which *see also* nos. 1076,
1077, 1079.
Copies: NPL:D(9/72); NPL:R(DS656.506/7); ANL. 1100

[1936] ROBINSON, Gregory
The *Endeavour:* how Captain Cook opened up the Pacific and discovered
the north-western coast of America.
Illus. in colour, plan.
(*In his* Ships that have made history. London, P. Davies and L. Dickson, [1936]. pp.
137–53.)
Copies: NPL:M(656.509/R); NPL:R(DS656.509/55, Ref. Books); ANL. 1101

1937 RHODES, F.
[Cook's *Endeavour.*]
(*In his* Pageant of the Pacific. Sydney, F.J. Thwaites, [1937]. Vol.1, pp.271–2.)
Copies: NPL:M(980/R); NPL:D(93/594). 1102

1961 ARGYLE, E.W.
[New Zealand postage stamp depicting Cook's *Endeavour.*]
Illus.
(*Sea Breezes,* n.s. vol.31, Feb. 1961. p.132.)
Copies: NPL:M(656.50905/1). 1103

[1965] A REPORT on the state and condition of the *Endeavour* in 1771.
p.1.
(*In* Cook, J.—Collected Voyages—Printed Accounts [1965 Jackdaw ser.]—The Voyages
of Captain Cook: a collection of contemporary documents. London, J.Cape, 1965, no.4.)
Copies: NPL:M(Q980:Co1/L1A1); NPL:R(NQ909.088/1); ANL. 1104

[1966] H.M.S. *ENDEAVOUR* TRUST
1770–1790: voyage into history. Sydney, Conpress pr., [1966].
Illus. one in colour, map, plan, ports. pp.8. Without title-page. Title from cover.
Copies: NPL:M(Q980:Col/H1A1); ANL. 1105

1967 VILLIERS, Alan John
The Replica *Endeavour* plan.
(*In his* Captain Cook. London, Hodder & Stoughton, 1967. p.250.)
Copies: NPL:M(980:Col/V2A1); NPL:R(910.0942/1). 1106

Publication

[177–] HAWKESWORTH, John
Letter from Dr. Hawkesworth to David Garrick, undated, re terms made
with publishers for account of Garrick.
(Bonwick Transcripts—Biography, vol.2, pp.487–9.)
Copies: NPL:M(MS.A2000⁻²). 1107

1773 LETTERS to Dr. Hawkesworth, published in the *Morning Chronicle*,
May 15 and June 19, 1773, and the *Public Advertiser*, June 14th and 15th,
1773, attacking his account of Cook's first voyage.
(Bonwick Transcripts: Cook, case 1, no. 114, 117–19.)
Copies: NPL:M(B.T.ser.2,box 1). 1108

1773 SCHILLER, Johann Christoph Friedrich von
Letter from John Frederick Schiller to Banks and Solander, Nov. 14,
1773, appealing to them to refute Mr. Ferber's allegations against Dr.
Hawkesworth, as they are ruining the sale of his German translation of
Dr. Hawkesworth's book.
(Bonwick Transcripts: Cook, case 2, no. 122.)
Copied from the Banks correspondence in the British Museum.
Copies: NPL:M(B.T.ser.2,box 2). 1109

1774 Feb.26 SPENER, J.C., *the younger*
Letter from Spener to Sir Joseph Banks, re contemplated printing of a
German edition of Sir Joseph Banks' account of Cook's first voyage.
(Bonwick Transcripts—Biography, vol.2, pp.492–9.)
Copies: NPL:M(MS.A2000⁻²). 1110

1890-92 CORRESPONDENCE and papers re editorship of the Cook
Journal, 1890–92, including letters to A.H. Bell from J. Corner and
Elliott Stock.
Copies: NPL:M(MS.A1713⁻⁵). 1111

1893 KING, Philip Gidley, *the younger*

Literary men, without nautical experience, were appointed by N.S.W. Government to publish Cook's Logs and Charts, resulting in some erroneous statements and needless repetition. Hon. P.G. King to Capt. Wharton, July 22, 1893.

(King Papers, vol.2, p.789.)
A reference to the publication of *Historical Records of New South Wales* vol.1, pt.1.
Copies: NPL:M(MS.A1977). 1112

1897–1901 A WORK on the voyage of the *Endeavour* being prepared by E.E. Morris.

(Letters to Alfred Lee, 1897–1906.)
Professor Morris died before completing the work.
Copies: NPL:M(MS.A1808). 1113

SECOND VOYAGE

Manuscript Journals and Logs

COOK, James
1771–5 Journal. 1771–5.

ff.367.
Original in the British Museum, Add. MSS. 27888. *See* Beaglehole, vol.2, pp.cxv–cxxiii. Numerous sections have been lost. Used by Cook as a draft for the text of his printed account of the second voyage. The journal is kept in civil time.

1114

COOK, James
1771–4 Log. Nov.30, 1771–Dec.28, 1774.

Charts, ff.135.
B.M.Add. MSS. 27887. *See* Beaglehole, vol.2, p.cxxx. Fair copy. The fly-leaf has a note re the log's purchase from Boone after Puttick's sale Lot 647. Pasted in at the end, ff.136–41, are a number of sheets giving daily ships' positions and meteorological observations.

1115

COOK, James
1771–4 Log-Book and Journal of Capt. Cook, Nov.1771–Nov.1774.

ff.323.
Original in the British Museum, Add. MSS. 27886. *See* Beaglehole, vol.2, pp.cxv–cxx. Title erroneous. This journal was written in seven folio books, originally of 45 leaves each, bound in thick marbled paper, but now rebound. With a few interpolations: calculations, observations, etc., and notes mainly by Gilbert. Covers period Nov.28, 1771–Nov.10, 1774. Furneaux's journal for Feb.8–May 15, 1773 is copied out in a clerk's hand in Book 3. Used as the text for Beaglehole, vol.2. The journal is kept in ship time.

1116

COOK, James

1772–5 Journal of H.M.S. *Resolution,* 1772–1775.

Sm. fol., pp.473, 24 maps of which 10 are double folio.
This version was written by Cook's clerk, William Dawson. Title-page reads: Captn
James Cook's Voyage from The Year 1772 to July 1775 Given to me by Himself, Bristol.
Original in the National Maritime Museum, Greenwich. *See also* Beaglehole, vol.2,
p.cxxvii. A.J.C.P. Microfilm. The copy in the National Library of Australia is a bound
photographic reproduction which was presented by Queen Elizabeth on the occasion
of her first visit to Australia in 1954. It had originally been prepared for presentation
by Princess Elizabeth, on behalf of her father King George VI, and bears the following
inscription:
Presented by His Majesty King George VI . . . to commemorate the visit of their Royal
Highnesses the Princess Elizabeth, Duchess of Edinburgh, and the Duke of Edinburgh
to Australia March 1st–May 1st, 1952.
The gift was not made in this manner for King George VI died and the proposed visit
was postponed until 1954.

Copies: ANL(MS.1153).   1117

COOK, James

1772–5 A Journal of the proceedings of His Majesty's Sloop the *Resolution*
in a voyage on discoveries towards the South Pole and round the world,
by Captain James Cook. 1772, 3, 4, and 5.

2vols.
A.J.C.P. Microfilm. Original held by the National Library of Ireland, Dublin (MS.
J7–8). *See* Beaglehole, vol.2, Addenda and Corrigenda. The journal begins Apl 9, 1772,
and ends with the entry for July 1775. Of Cook's other journals, it most closely resembles
the Greenwich manuscript. The handwriting (after comparison with Adm. 55/111–13)
appears to be that of Cook's clerk on the *Resolution* (third voyage). The journal is part
of the collection of Dr. Jaspar Robert Joly (1819–92), given to the Royal Dublin Society
under an indenture dated Apl 8, 1863, and forming with the library of the Royal Dublin
Society the foundation of the National Library of Ireland. For references to the Joly
Collection *see* the *Library Association Record* March–April, 1902, pp.95–109, and the
Irish Book Lover, March–April, 1921, pp.99–101.

                                                      1118

COOK, James

1772–5 Journal of the Proceedings of His Majesty's Sloop *Resolution* In
Exploring the South Atlantic, Indian & Pacific Oceans by James Cook
Commander.

pp.302.
A.J.C.P. Microfilm. P.R.O. Adm. 55/108. *See* Beaglehole, vol.2, pp.cxxv–cxxvii. The
extract from Furneaux's journal is compressed into a summary. Vocabularies drawn
up by William Anderson are on pp.243–302. The journal originally included fourteen
charts, of which ten have been removed to the P.R.O. Map Room. Note by J. Bonwick
in NPL:M B.T.ser.2, Cook case 2, no.128.

                                                      1119

COOK, James

1772–5 Journal of the Proceedings of His Majesty's Sloop *Resolution* In
Exploring the South Atlantic, Indian & Pacific Oceans by James Cook
Commander.

pp.361.

Original in the possession of Lieut. Commander Palliser A. Hudson. MS. journal given by Cook to Sir Hugh Palliser. Begins differently from the other MS. copies of the journal. Copied partly by Dawson, and partly perhaps by Daniel Clark. The engraved portrait of Cook by Basire after Hodges is bound in at the beginning. The title-page bears the signatures Graham Palliser and E.W. Palliser.

At the end of the journal is bound in Sir John Pringle's Discourse upon some late improvements on the Means of Preserving the Health of Mariners.

See Beaglehole, vol.2, pp.cxxviii–cxxix. Negative microfilm filed in the National Library of Australia.

Copies: ANL(G508, neg.microfilm). 1120

COOK, James

1773–5 Log. Oct.16, 1773–July 28, 1775.

ff.164.

B.M. Add. MSS. 27956. *See* Beaglehole, vol.2, pp.cxxix–cxxx. Holograph. The fly-leaf is inscribed "Purchased of Mr C.J.Smith 12 Decr 1868". The log appears to have been originally in two volumes, later taken to pieces and the separate folios pasted into a guard book. The log occupies ff.1–139, and is followed by "Describtions of the Bearings and Harbours within Trinity Bay" not in Cook's hand, and notes and figures, etc. There is no complete holograph log by Cook extant.

1121

COOK, James

1773, 1774 Fragment. 1773, Mar.26–29; 1774, Nov.12–Dec.4. Two stray leaves from the original Cook log (B.M.Add.MSS.27956).

ff.2.

(Papers in the autograph of Captain James Cook, 1728–1779, pp.7–10.) Holograph.

Copies: NPL:M(Safe 1/80). 1122

COOK, James

1773 Log-book, March 1773.

p.1.

National Library of Australia.

Half leaf from the original log-book kept on Cook's second voyage in the *Resolution*, containing his observations and remarks for Thursday 18th and Saturday 20th March, 1773.

Copies: ANL(Nan Kivell 7432). 1123

COOK, James

1773 Oct. [Fragments held in the Mitchell Library. Estrays from Cook's journal in the British Museum, Add. MSS. 27888.]

Two sets of 8 pp. each, and one isolated page.

a.) Description of Tonga, Oct. 1773. Acquired in 1935, after a long sojourn in America. Safe 1/70.

b.) Description of Tonga, Oct. 1773. (Cook documents from the Australian Museum, pp.23–30.) Safe 1/83.

c.) Isolated page, numbered 76. Oct. 1773. (Papers in the Autograph of Captain Cook, 1728–1779, p.19.) Safe 1/80.

See Beaglehole, vol.2, p.cxxiv.

Copies: NPL:M(Safe 1/70; 1/83; 1/80). 1124

COOK, James

1774 Dec.18–28 Journal of HMS *Resolution:* Fair copy in Cook's hand of part of his journal, describing the passage from Cape Descado to Cape Horn.

ff.6, cm 32.

Some pp. headed in a different hand. Photocopy of p.7 is at p.91. 'This MS. is the original of the corresponding part of the Palliser Hudson MS.' (Beaglehole, vol.2, p.cxxiv: and *see* note in MS. F1n.) A single leaf with 'From C C Janell' in ink at top l.h., and 'Writing of Captain Cook' in another hand on r.h. side, precedes this item. It has a different watermark.

Copies: NPL:D(MS.F1, pp.3–16). 1125

COOK, James

[177–] Cook's second voyage. Fragments.

ff.138.

Original in British Museum, Add. MSS. 27889. Contents extremely varied, and some items do not refer to Cook. Contains some of the sections missing from Add. MSS. 27888. *See* Beaglehole, vol.2, pp.cxxiii–cxxiv.

1126

COOK, James

[c.1776] Draft of the General Introduction for the published account of Cook's second voyage: (a copy in a clerk's hand of Add. MS. 27889, ff.11–21v); with further deletions and alterations both by Cook and his editor Douglas.

ff.36.

See notes at MS.F1n. MS. is in two sections: 'General Introduction' (pp.33–50) probably not by Cook, but with marginal critical comments by him. The second part 'Introduction' (pp.17–32) has the last five pages in Cook's hand, which include comments on the conventions of time and position adopted, Hodges' views, a tribute to his friends, and a brief summary of his career.

Copies: NPL:D(MS.F1, pp.17–50). 1127

ANONYMOUS

1772–4 Log. Nov.23, 1772–Feb.20, 1774.

A.J.C.P. Microfilm. P.R.O. Adm. 51/4524/3–4, (labelled 17–18). *See* Beaglehole, vol.2, p.cxl.

1128

ANONYMOUS

1772–3 Log. Nov.22, 1772–Dec.31, 1773.

A.J.C.P. Microfilm. P.R.O. Adm. 51/4555/218. *See* Beaglehole, vol.2, p.cxxxvii.

1129

ANONYMOUS

1773–5 Log. July 1, 1773–Mar.9, 1775.

A.J.C.P. Microfilm. P.R.O. Adm. 51/4557/219. *See* Beaglehole, vol.2, p.cxxxvii.

1130

ANONYMOUS

1774 Memoire abrégé sur une partie du dernier voyage des Anglais vers les terres australles.

(Copies of MSS. in Service Hydrographique, Paris, relating to Australasia, pp. 515–519.)

Copies: NPL:M(MS.B1190).   1131

BAYLY, William

[1772–5?] Observations.

A.J.C.P. Microfilm. Royal Greenwich Observatory, Herstmonceux. Board of Longitude Papers, vol. XLV. *See* Beaglehole, vol.2, p.cxliii. Astronomical observations and calculations, daily record of the winding of the watches signed by Furneaux, Bayly and one of the lieutenants.

1132

BAYLY, William

1772–4 Log. July 1, 1772–July 13, 1774.

A.J.C.P. Microfilm. Royal Greenwich Observatory, Herstmonceux. Board of Longitude Papers, vol. XLIV. *See* Beaglehole, vol.2, pp.cxlii–cxliii.

1133

BAYLY, William

1773–4 Journal. June 23, 1773–July 14, 1774.

pp.135.

The New Zealand entries have been printed by McNab in the *Historical Records of New Zealand*, vol.2, pp.201–18. *See* Beaglehole, vol.2, p.cxli.

Copies: Alexander Turnbull Library, Wellington, N.Z.   1134

BROWNE, Robert

1772–4 Journal. Mar.18, 1772–Mar.16, 1774.

A.J.C.P. Microfilm. P.R.O. Adm. 51/4521/9–10. *See* Beaglehole, vol.2, p.cxxxix.

1135

BURNEY, James

1772–4 Journal. Nov.19, 1772–May 20, 1774.

A.J.C.P. Microfilm. P.R.O. Adm. 51/4523/3–4. *See* Beaglehole, vol.2, p.cxxxviii.

1136

BURNEY, James

1772–4 Log. Nov.18, 1772–Jan.23, 1774. With chart of Van Diemen's Land. Pasted into the log is a copy of the report Burney made to Furneaux on his expedition to East Bay in search of the massacred boat's crew.

A.J.C.P. Microfilm. P.R.O. Adm. 51/4523/1–2.

See Beaglehole, vol.2, p.cxxxviii. Extracts of the log, including the report on the massacre are printed in Beaglehole, vol.2, pp.746–52. A copy of this report in Burney's hand, and another of his chart are in the Alexander Turnbull Library, Wellington, N.Z., *Holograph Letters and Documents of and relative to Captain James Cook*. There is a copy of the chart in the Ferguson MS. (*see* no. 1138). The chart is reproduced in the Portfolio accompanying Beaglehole's edition of the journals as Chart XXVII.

1137

BURNEY, James

1772–3 Journal made during Capt. Cook's second voyage, 1772–3, from Plymouth to Madeira, and then in search of the southern continent, to New Zealand, Tasmania and Friendly Islands. June 22, 1772–Dec.22, 1773.

Charts, illus. ff.35.
A journal-letter to the author's family. Includes a copy of his chart of Van Diemen's Land, and New Zealand and Tongan tunes in music notation. *See* Beaglehole, vol.2, pp.cxxxviii–cxxxix. The journal was described in the *Sydney Morning Herald*, 4 Mar. 1922.

Copies: ANL:F; NPL:M(FM3/793microfilm). 1138

BURR, John Daval

1771–5 Log. Dec.24, 1771–Mar.15, 1775.

A.J.C.P. Microfilm. P.R.O. Adm. 55/106. *See* Beaglehole, vol.2, p.cxxxiv.

1139

CLERKE, Charles

1771–5 Log of the proceedings of, and occurrences onboard His Majesty's Ship *Resolution*, upon a voyage of discovery towards the South Pole, by C^s Clerke. Nov.28, 1771–Mar.21, 1775.

A.J.C.P. Microfilm. P.R.O. Adm. 55/103. Fair copy. Original is in the British Museum, Add. MSS. 8951–3, and another fair copy, Add. MSS. 8961–2. Both the original and the British Museum copy have Banks' name-stamp in them. Extracts from Adm.55/103 printed in App.IV, vol.2, Beaglehole. *See also* Beaglehole, vol.2, pp.cxxxi–cxxxii.

1140

CONSTABLE, Love

1771–4 Journal. Dec.6, 1771–Mar.14, 1774.

A.J.C.P. Microfilm. P.R.O. Adm. 51/4520/7–8. *See* Beaglehole, vol.2, p.cxxxix.

1141

COOPER, Robert P.

1771–4 A Journal of the Proceedings of His Majesty's Sloop *Resolution*, on a Voyage upon Discovery, Towards the South-Pole. Commencing from her first fitting out at Deptford [i.e. 30 Nov. 1771] to the 22 of April 1774 . . . kept by Robt P. Cooper.

More of a log than a journal.
A.J.C.P. Microfilm. P.R.O. Adm. 55/104,109. *See* Beaglehole, vol.2, p.cxxxi.

1142

DYKE, Thomas

1772–4 Log. June 4, 1772–July 12, 1774.

A.J.C.P. Microfilm. P.R.O. Adm. 51/4521/12. *See* Beaglehole, vol.2, p.cxl.

1143

ELLIOTT, John

1772–5 Log. Nov.23, 1772–Mar.2, 1775.

A.J.C.P. Microfilm. P.R.O. Adm. 51/4556/208. *See* Beaglehole, vol.2, p.cxxxvi.

1144

ELLIOTT, John

n.d. Memoirs of the early life of John Elliott, of Elliott House, near Mission, Yorkshire, Esqr and Lieut^t of the Royal Navy, written by himself at the request of his wife for the use and amusement of his children only.

B.M. Add. MSS. 42714. *See* Beaglehole, vol.2, p.cxxxvi. Typescript summary with extracts from the original, filed in the Mitchell Library in *Captain Cook Miscellaneous*, vol.1, pp.21–4 at A1713⁻¹.

1145

FALCONER, John Richard

1772–4 Log. Nov.23, 1772–July 11, 1774.

A.J.C.P. Microfilm. P.R.O. Adm. 51/4524/1–2. *See* Beaglehole, vol.2, p.cxl. The writer's own spelling of his name is Falconar.

1146

FURNEAUX, Tobias

1771-4 [Journal, headed] Remarks onboard His Majesty's Sloop the *Adventure* (late called the *Raleigh*). Nov.28, 1771–July 10, 1774. Fair copy.

A.J.C.P. Microfilm. P.R.O. Adm. 55/1. *See* Beaglehole, vol.2, p.cxxxvii, and printed extracts, pp.143–61.

1147

FURNEAUX, Tobias

1771–4 The Logg of His Majesty's Sloop *Adventure*.

A.J.C.P. Microfilm. P.R.O. Adm. 55/1. *See* Beaglehole, vol.2, p.cxxxvii.

1148

FURNEAUX, Tobias

1772–4 Account of the *Adventure's* voyage, written by Furneaux. July 13, 1772–Mar.3, 1774.

B.M. Add. MS.27890. *See* Beaglehole, vol.2, pp.cxxxvii–cxxxviii; extracts printed as App.IV. A fair copy of portion of this narrative, 8 Feb.–19 May, 1773, is in the Alexander Turnbull Library, Wellington, N.Z., in *Holograph Letters and Documents of and relating to Captain James Cook*.

1149

GILBERT, Joseph

1772–5 A Log of the proceedings of His Majesty's Sloop *Resolution* on discoveries in the Pacific and Southern Ocean, containing such astronomical and nautical observations as may be usefull to navigation. Jan.3, 1772–Mar.21, 1775.

Illus. plans.
A.J.C.P. Microfilm. P.R.O. Adm. 55/107. *See* Beaglehole, vol.2, pp.cxxxiii–cxxxiv.

1150

GREAT BRITAIN—Board of Longitude

1772–5 Papers of the Board of Longitude, 1714–1830.

Positive microfilm. Originals in the Royal Greenwich Observatory.
CONTENTS:
P.R.O. Reel 1756 Observations on board the *Resolution*, 1772–1775.
Captain Cook's journal of the voyage of 1776.
Observations of variation of the compass and chronometer rates, etc.
Astronomical observations on Cook's last voyage.
FM4 1559 Log book of the *Resolution*, 1772–5.

Copies: NPL:M(P.R.O. Microfilm Reel 1756; FM4/1559). 1151

HARVEY, William
1771–5 Journal. Dec.17, 1771–Mar.7, 1775.

A.J.C.P. Microfilm. P.R.O. Adm. 51/4553/184–7. A log rather than a journal. *See* Beaglehole, vol.2, p.cxxxv.

1152

HAWKEY, William
1772–4 Log. Jan.8, 1772–Mar.14, 1774.

A.J.C.P. Microfilm. P.R.O. Adm. 51/4521/11. *See* Beaglehole, vol.2, p.cxl.

1153

HERGEST, Richard
1772–4 Journal. July 13, 1772–July 12, 1774.

A.J.C.P. Microfilm. P.R.O. Adm. 51/4522/13. *See* Beaglehole, vol.2, p.cxxxix.

1154

HOOD, Alexander
1772–5 Journal. Mar.5, 1772–Mar.10, 1775.

A.J.C.P. Microfilm. P.R.O. Adm. 51/4554/181–3. *See* Beaglehole, vol.2, p.cxxxv.

1155

KEMPE, Arthur
1772–4 Journal. Jan.3, 1772–July 13, 1774.

A.J.C.P. Microfilm. P.R.O. Adm. 51/4520/4–5. *See* Beaglehole, vol.2, p.cxxxviii.

1156

KEMPE, Arthur
1772–4 Journal. Jan.3, 1772–July 13, 1774.

A.J.C.P. Microfilm. P.R.O. Adm. 51/4520/1–3. *See* Beaglehole, vol.2, p.cxxxviii.

1157

LIGHTFOOT, Henry
1772–3 Log. Nov.23, 1772–May 14, 1773.

A.J.C.P. Microfilm. P.R.O. Adm. 51/4523/5. *See* Beaglehole, vol.2, p.cxxxix.

1158

LOGGIE, Charles
1772–3 Journal. Jan.18, 1772–July 26, 1773.

A.J.C.P. Microfilm. P.R.O. Adm. 51/4554/207. *See* Beaglehole, vol.2, p.ccxxxv.

1159

MAXWELL, James

1772–5 Log. Nov.22, 1772–Mar.13, 1775.

A.J.C.P. Microfilm. P.R.O. Adm. 51/4555/2–6. *See* Beaglehole, vol.2, p.cxxxv.

1160

MITCHEL, Bowles

1772–5 Log. Nov.23, 1772–Mar.14, 1775.

A.J.C.P. Microfilm. P.R.O. Adm. 51/4555/194–5. *See* Beaglehole, vol.2, p.cxxxv.

1161

PICKERSGILL, Richard

1771–4 Logg of the proceedings of His Majesty's Sloop *Resolution*, on discoveries in 1772, 1773 and 1774. [Nov.28, 1771–June 7, 1773; June 8, 1773–June 4, 1774.]

Charts.

A.J.C.P. Microfilm. P.R.O. Adm. 51/4553/205–6. A fragmentary journal.

1162

PICKERSGILL, Richard

1771–3 Journal.

National Maritime Museum, Greenwich (57/038). Purchased 1957. Previously owned by the Enderby Family. A fragmentary journal, finishing 3 Oct. 1773. Extracts printed in Beaglehole, vol.2, App.IV. *See also* Beaglehole, vol.2, p.cxxxii–cxxxiii.

1163

PRICE, Joseph

1772–5 Journal. Dec.18, 1772–Mar.15, 1775.

A.J.C.P. Microfilm. P.R.O. Adm. 51/4556/188–9. *See* Beaglehole, vol.2, pp.cxxxvi–cxxxvii.

1164

PRICE, Joseph

1773–5 Log. Sept.1, 1773–Mar.15, 1775.

A.J.C.P. Microfilm. P.R.O. Adm. 51/4556/190. *See* Beaglehole, vol.2, pp.cxxxvi–cxxxvii.

1165

SMITH, Isaac

1771–5 Log. Dec.17, 1771–Mar.11, 1775.

Illus. charts.

A.J.C.P. Microfilm. P.R.O. Adm. 55/105. *See* Beaglehole, vol.2, p.cxxxiv.

1166

WALES, William

1772–5 Journal of a voyage made by order of the Commissioners of Longitude, on board of his Majesty's Sloop *Resolution*, 1772, 1773, 1774, 1775.

A.J.C.P. Microfilm. Royal Greenwich Observatory, Herstmonceux. Board of Longitude Papers, vol.XLVII. *See* Beaglehole, vol.2, p.cxlii, "appears to be the rough draft of the log".

1167

WALES, William
1772–5 Log-book of the *Resolution.* July 21, 1772–Aug.1, 1775.

Charts.
A.J.C.P. Microfilm. Royal Greenwich Observatory, Herstmonceux. Board of Longitude
Papers, vol.XLVI. *See* Beaglehole, vol.2, pp.cxli–cxlii.

1168

WALES, William
1772–5 Observations.
Record of the winding of the chronometers, signed by Cook, Wales, and
one of the officers.
Astronomical observations made at different places on shore.
Observations on the variation of the compass; rates of the clocks; tides;
dip of the magnetic needle.
Lunar observations and observations of the solar eclipse.

A.J.C.P. Microfilm. Royal Greenwich Observatory, Herstmonceux. Board of Longitude
Papers, vol.XLVII. *See* Beaglehole, vol.2, p.cxlii. The first item is the astronomical
observations made by Wales on the voyage, entered in tabular form, with some notes
on the instruments used and calculations of longitude.

1169

WALES, William
1772–4 Journal. June 21, 1772–Oct.7, 1774.

Charts, pp.376.
Incomplete. *See* Beaglehole, vol.2, pp.cxl–cxli. Printed in Beaglehole, vol.2, App.V,
with some omissions.
Copies: NPL:M(Safe 1/84).

1170

WHILBY, John
1772–4 Journal. July 14, 1772–July 13, 1774.

A.J.C.P. Microfilm. P.R.O. Adm. 51/4522/14. *See* Beaglehole, vol.2, p.cxxxix.

1171

WILLIS, Thomas
1772–5 Journal. Jan.3, 1772–Dec.23, 1773; Dec.24, 1773–Mar.13, 1775.

A.J.C.P. Microfilm. P.R.O. Adm. 51/4554/199–200. *See* Beaglehole, vol.2, p.cxxxv.

1172

WILLIS, Thomas
1772–5 Log. Nov.23, 1772–Oct.18, 1774; Oct.19, 1774–Feb.6, 1775.

A.J.C.P. Microfilm. P.R.O. Adm. 51/4554/201–2. *See* Beaglehole, vol.2, pp.cxxxiv–cxxxv.

1173

WILLIS, Thomas
1775 Log. Feb.7–Mar.13, 1775.

A.J.C.P. Microfilm. P.R.O. Adm. 55/106. *See* Beaglehole, vol.2, p.cxxxv.

1174

Manuscript Journals and Logs

Works about the Journals

1879 HET LOGBOEK van Cook gedurende zijn reis in 1772.

(Aardrijkskundig Genootschap—Tijdschrift, vol.3, p.315, 1879.)
Refers to the discovery of the copy of part of a log-book kept by J. R. Forster on the *Resolution*.

Copies: NPL:M(Q910.6/6).   1175

Manuscript Correspondence, Instructions, etc.

COOK, James

1771–8 Letter book, 1771–1778.

pp.161.
Contains chiefly orders to and from the Admiralty, Navy Commissioners andVictualling
Commissioners, and Cook's orders to his officers during his second and third voyages.
Gives many interesting details relating to the second and third voyages.

Copies: ANL(MS.6).   1176

COOK, James

1772–6 [Autograph letters to Sir Joseph Banks, dated June 2, 1772, Nov.18,
1772, May 24, 1776 and July 10, 1776. Facsimile reproductions.]

pp. [12].
Facsimiles of the original letters at NPL:M(Safe 1/68). NPL:M facsimile set is from the
collection of books associated with the name of Sir Henry Parkes, and housed in the
N.S.W. Chief Secretary's Department until 1956. Privately printed; without title-page.
These letters were printed and reproduced in facsimile in *Historical Records of New South
Wales*. Sydney, Govt. Pr., 1893. Vol.1, pt.1.

Copies: NPL:M(980:Co3/1A1); ANL; SPL.   1177

COOK, James

1772–5 Ship's husband's bill for HMS *Resolution* and HMS *Adventure* kept
in Cook's hand, Aug.1, 1772–Apr.27, 1775.

f.1, cm 38.5.
Copies: NPL:D(MS.F1,pp.67–8).   1178

COOK, James

[177–?] ALS to Joseph Banks, Esqr., relating to furnishing the cabin with
a stove, baize, brass locks and hinges, for the second voyage. n.d.

A passage reads "Whenever it is certain that Dr. Lynd goes with us I beg you will let
me know by the Penny Post."
See also no. 1191.

Copies: NPL:M(Safe 1/11).   1179

COOK, James

1772 Jan.3 ALS to Captain William Hammond, stating that the Admiralty
has altered the names of the ships from *Drake* to *Resolution* and from *Raleigh*
to *Adventurer* (*sic*). With MS. notes by Col. T.Hammond and E.B.G.

pp.2.
Photoprint.
Reduced facsimile published in J.R. Muir—The Life and achievements of Captain James Cook. 1939. p.167. NPL:M(980:Col/M6A1).

Copies: NPL:M(Doc.830,A1713⁻²B, item iii); NPL:D(Q143,pp.25,27); VSL.   1180

COOK, James

1772 Jan.13   Cook to Victualling Board. LS stating that the *Resolution* and *Adventure* will take all the sour krout and salted cabbage that has been prepared for them; that they will victual more men than their present complements. With minutes of action overleaf.

31 cm.

Copies: NPL:D(MS.Q140,pp.29–30).   1181

COOK, James

1772 Feb.6   Holograph letter to the Earl of Sandwich, Feb.6, 1772, enclosing a map and his Opinion of the proposed route for the second voyage.

Bound with enclosures in a volume entitled *Original manuscripts in the handwriting of Captain Cook relating to his second voyage.*

Copies: NPL:M(Safe 1/82).   1182

COOK, James

1772 Feb.10   Cook to Victualling Board. ALS ordering water casks for the *Resolution.*

23.5 cm.

Copies: NPL:D(MS.Q140,pp.33–6).   1183

COOK, James

1772 Feb.21   Cook to Victualling Board. ALS requesting that the *Resolution* be supplied with coopers tools noted in the enclosed list, which he is informed will be necessary for his intended voyage; with 'Coopers Tools Necessary to be taken on a Long Voyage' in another hand, initialled 'JW'.

23 cm., 32.5 cm.

Copies: NPL:D(MS.Q140,pp.37–42).   1184

COOK, James

1772 Mar.2   Cook to Victualling Board. ALS asking that *Resolution* be supplied with the remaining part of the provisions demanded, except bread in bags, beer, butter, cheese and spirit.

30.5 cm.

Copies: NPL:D(MS.Q140,pp.43–6).   1185

COOK, James

1772 Mar.9   Cook to Victualling Board. ALS ordering bread, sea beer, and the undermentioned provisions for the *Resolution;* with list at foot of page.

30.5 cm.

Copies: NPL:D(MS.Q140,pp.47–50).   1186

COOK, James

1772 Mar.9   Cook to Victualling Board. ALS requesting strong pickle with which to fill up the casks of beef and pork after they are stored on board the *Resolution.*

32 cm.

Copies: NPL:D(MS.Q140,pp.51–4).   1187

COOK, James

1772 Mar.10   Cook to Victualling Board. ALS stating that the saloup supplied to the *Endeavour* on her late voyage was of great use to the sick, and requesting *Resolution* and *Adventure* be supplied with proportional quantities.

30.5 cm.

Copies: NPL:D(MS.Q140,pp.55–8).   1188

COOK, James

1772 Mar.13   Cook to Victualling Board. ALS asking for the remaining bags of bread which would not fit in the Bread Room and were returned on shore, be repacked in butts and sent on board again.

31 cm.

Copies: NPL:D(MS.Q140,pp.59–62).   1189

COOK, James

1772 Mar.18   Cook to Victualling Board. ALS ordering additional butter and the usual complement of tongues for the *Resolution.*

30 cm.

Copies: NPL:D(MS.Q140,pp.63–6).   1190

COOK, James

1772 Apr.3   Receipt. London, Apl.3, 1772, Recd. of Joseph Banks, Esqr., on Accot. the sum of Three hundred pound. *Signed* Jams. Cook.

Respecting the stove for the *Resolution.*

Copies: NPL:M(Safe1/11).   1191

COOK, James

1772 May 26   Cook to Victualling Board. ALS dated Sheerness, that the bread room of the *Resolution* will be ready to receive bread in two days and ordering 21,280 pounds to replace what had been taken out. Minute overleaf orders care to be taken to avoid bread getting damp or wet.

33 cm.

Copies: NPL:D(MS.Q140,pp.67–70).   1192

COOK, James

1772 May 28 Cook to Capt. William Hammond, Hull. ALS dated Sheerness, asking for full details of his opinion and discussion in the town as to the seaworthiness of the *Resolution*, and stating 'I am in no doubt of her answering now she is stripped of her superfluous top hamper.'

22.5 cm.

Copies: NPL:M(MS.Q140,pp.71–4).   1193

COOK, James

1772 May 30 ALS to the Commissioners of the Victualling, Sheerness, May 30, 1772. [Print and facsimile.]

(*In* Triggs, A.B.—Catalogue of the collection of . . . letters. 1924. pp.60–61.)

Copies: NPL:M(091/T).   1194

COOK, James

1772 June 2 ALS to Joseph Banks, Esq., from Sheerness, in reference to the Removal of goods belonging to Banks from the *Resolution*.

pp.2.

(Letters of Capt. James Cook, R.N., p.1.) The removal of Banks' property from the *Resolution* was the result of his decision not to take part in the expedition. This letter was part of the Brabourne Papers. Facsimile filed at NPL:M(980:Co3/1A1).

Copies: NPL:M(Safe1/68).   1195

COOK, James

1772 June 15 Cook to Victualling Board. ALS dated Victualling Office, ordering one thousand pounds of stockfish for the *Resolution*. Minute overleaf requests stockfish be brought from Plymouth on first available vessel.

32.5 cm.

Copies: NPL:D(MS.Q140,pp.75–8).   1196

COOK, James

1772 July 11 ALS to George Perry, Esq., Victualling Office, London. Plymouth Sound, 11th July 72. Concerning the accuracy of Cook's charts, and relating to Perry's request to take on Madeira wine. The P.S. refers to Cook's intention of sailing the following day.

p.1.

Photostat copy at ANL MS.7A.

Copies: ANL(Nan Kivell 33).   1197

COOK, James

1772 Nov.18 ALS to Joseph Banks, Esq., from the Cape. Has heard the French from Mauritius have discovered land in Lat.48'.

pp.2.

(Letters of Capt. James Cook, R.N., p.5.) This letter was part of the Brabourne Papers. Facsimile filed at NPL:M(980:Co3/1A1).

Copies: NPL:M(Safe1/68).   1198

COOK, James

1772 Nov.20 Cook to Capt. John Walker, Whitby. Copy: That breaking his connection with the civilised world is like leaving it, but his fears of the dangerous voyage are allayed by his trust in 'the divine protection' and his two good ships 'well provided and well man'd'. He has never set foot in a finer ship than the *Resolution*.

f.1.

Facsimile.

Reproduced in *The New Zealander*, Mar. 1923, and in *N.Z. Centennial News*, Aug. 1938, p.15.

Copies: NPL:D(MS.Q143,p.29). 1199

COOK, James

1772 Nov.20 Writing of Captain James Cook: letter to Captain James Walker, Whitby, England, 20 Nov.1772. [Facsimile of letter written by Cook from the Cape of Good Hope; original held in the National Historical Collection, Wellington, N.Z.]

(*NZFS Bulletin*, issued by the New Zealand Founders Society, Wellington. No.12, p.3, Dec. 1956.)

Copies: NPL:M(997.06/3). 1200

COOK, James

1775–6 Letters, in French, Sep.6, 1775, and Feb.10, 1776, on his recent discoveries.

(Copies of MSS. in Bibliothèque Nationale, Paris, relating to Australasia, vol.2. pp.348–59.)

Copies: NPL:M(B1192). 1201

COOK, James

1775 Aug.19 Letter to John Walker, Aug.19, 1775, after his return from the second voyage: [facsimile].

f.1.

(Miscellaneous primary and secondary source material re the life and voyages of Captain James Cook.)

Copies: NPL:M(MS.A1713⁻²B,item iv). 1202

COOK, James

1775 Sep.14 Cook to Capt. John Walker, Whitby. ALS dated from Mile End, London, giving account of Cook's second voyage with *Resolution* and *Adventure*, reporting his visit to Dusky Bay & Queen Charlotte Sound, N.Z., Tahiti, Huaheine, Ulitea, Amsterdam I., Easter I., and the Marquesas; his discovery of New Caledonia and several other islands; and his satisfaction that no Southern Continent exists. He concludes that he had hoped to 'put an end to all voyages . . . to the Pacific Ocean, . . . but the sending home Omiah will occasion another Voyage which I expect will soon be undertaken.'

23 cm.
With typescript copy (MS.Q141,pt.B), and MS. transcript by Sir William Dixson (MS.Q143, pp.51–68).
Copies: NPL:D(MS.Q141,pp.1–8); NPL:M(MS. A1713⁻¹,pp.45–54,copy).   1203

COOK, James
1776 May 24 Letter from Cook to Banks, Mile End, May 24th 1776, re the drawing of the New Zealand spruce and the stove which was in the *Resolution*. Printed, with intro. note by H.C.Cameron, from the transcript in the Dawson Turner collection, British Museum (Natural History).

Author states that this letter had not previously been published.
(*Geographical Journal* vol.116, pp.50–51, Sept. 1950.)
Copies: NPL:R(DS909·6A/2).   1204

COOK, James
1776 July 10 ALS to Sir Joseph Banks, relating to descriptions of plants and engravings for his journal of the second voyage, and preparations for departure on the third. He expresses gratification at being awarded a prize medal by the Royal Society.

pp.2.
(Letters of Capt. James Cook, R.N.,p.11.)
This letter was part of the Brabourne Papers. Facsimile filed at NPL:M(980:Co3/1A1).
Neg. photostat filed at NPL:M(MS.A1713⁻²B,item vii).
Copies: NPL:M(Safe1/68).   1205

BANKS, *Sir* Joseph
[177–] Volume of Banks's Papers lettered "Voluntiers, Instructions, Provision for 2d. Voyage."

The volume contains rough drafts by Sir Joseph Banks of his letters to Lord Sandwich and to "The printer of the *Gazeteer*," explaining his reasons for not accompanying Capt. Cook on the second voyage; also a large number of receipted accounts for articles bought for the use of Banks and his assistants, and for presents for exchange purposes with the South Sea islanders; letter from Capt. Cook to Jos. Banks, Esq., undated, relative to furnishing the ship's cabin; receipt dated Apl. 3, 1772, written and signed by "Jams." Cook for £300 received from Joseph Banks; applications from, and testimonials relating to, persons who wished positions on the second voyage; directions for preserving meat, for collecting and preserving specimens; list of scientists and servants with proposed salaries, &c. The volume was in the Alfred Lee collection and was purchased by D.S. Mitchell.
Copies: NPL:M(Safe1/11).   1206

CLERKE, Charles
1772 May 13 ALS to Sir Joseph Banks referring to the dangerous condition of the *Resolution*. *Resolution in Sea Reach*, May 13, 1772.

pp.2.
(Brabourne Papers.)
Copies: NPL:M(A78⁻¹).   1207

CLERKE, Charles

1772 May 31 ALS to Joseph Banks, thanking him for calling upon Lord Rochford on his behalf, stating that he (Clerke) will hold to the expedition (Cook's second voyage), and discussing Cook's plan of stowage, which has been kept secret. *Resolution at Sheerness*, May 31st, 1772.

pp.2.
(Brabourne Papers.)
Copies: NPL:M(A78⁻¹).   1208

CLERKE, Charles

1772 June 7? ALS to Sir Joseph Banks stating that he is ready for the South Seas and expressing his regret at not being able to visit Banks. *H.M.S. Resolution, Sheerness*, June 7th (?), 1772.

pp.4.
(Brabourne Papers.)
Copies: NPL:M(A78⁻¹).   1209

CLERKE, Charles

[1775] July 30 ALS to Sir Joseph Banks on return from second voyage, stating that they will anchor at Spithead in a few hours and expressing his devotion to Sir Joseph. *H.M.S. Resolution*, July 30th, [1775].

pp.2.
(Brabourne Papers.)
Copies: NPL:M(A78⁻¹).   1210

GREAT BRITAIN—Admiralty

1961 Secret instructions for Capt Cook, Commander of His Majesty's Sloop *Resolution*. (By the Commissioners for executing the Office of Lord High Admiral of Great Britain & Ireland &c^a [25th June, 1772].)

(Cook, James—The Journals of Captain James Cook on his voyages of discovery . . . Ed. by J.C.Beaglehole . . . for the Hakluyt Society. Cambridge, U.P., 1961. Vol.2, pp. clxvii–clxx.)

Printed from the Canberra Letter Book, after collation with P.R.O.Adm. 2/1332,pp. 196–203, as printed in Navy Records Society—*Naval Miscellany*, vol.3, 1928, pp.351–6.

Copies: NPL:M(980:Col/46A2).   1211

GREAT BRITAIN—Admiralty

[1965] Admiralty secret orders for Cook's second voyage.

pp.2.
(*In* Cook, J.—Collected Voyages—Printed Accounts [1965 Jackdaw ser.]—The Voyages of Captain Cook: a collection of contemporary documents. London, J.Cape, 1965. No.5.)

Copies: NPL:M(Q980:Col/L1A1); NPL:R(NQ909.088/1); ANL.   1212

SOLANDER, Daniel Carl

[1771 Dec.] AL to Dr. James Lind: that a better-equipped expedition comprising the *Drake* and *Raleigh*, with Cook & Furneaux commanding and many members of the first voyage, will sail next March for New Holland, New Zealand & further south than any other European navigator, spending 2 or 3 summers in the high latitudes and wintering in the tropics to complete 'our former discoveries'. Banks and Solander who are advising re personnel and equipment wish Lind to go as one of the two astronomers.

pp. 6, cm 23.
Incomplete, lacks signature. Dated from internal evidence.
Copies: NPL:D(MS.Q161). 1213

SOLANDER, Daniel Carl

1774 July 27 ALS to Dr. James Lind dated London, describing Capt. Furneaux's voyage with Cook (1772–1776); their various separations; the vain search for Cape Circumcision and La France Meridionale; the discovery of Dusky Bay; relations with the Maoris, a native battle fought at Otaheite before their arrival; the embarkation of Omai; the massacre of some of *Adventure's* crew at Charlotte Sound; the conclusion that no great southern continent exists. Promises more account of Omai in next letter. Postscript: the late French discoveries are not as considerable as supposed.

pp. 8, 1; cm 23, 22.5.
Paginated in pencil 7–15. Postscript is possibly part of another letter.
Copies: NPL:D(MS.Q161). 1214

WATSON, *Sir* William

1775 Sep.19 ALS to Edward Wortley Montagu dated London, —he has dined twice with Cook since his return; Cook's latest discoveries; publication of the voyages is being prepared by Cook and Forster; Clark (*sic*) is to get a command to take Omay home; Omay has ridden unaccompanied to visit Baron Dimsdale; Cook has been made post captain and a captain of Greenwich Hospital.

pp.4, cm 22.5.
Copies: NPL:D(MS.Q161; typescript copy MS.Q160). 1215

Printed Accounts

This section includes entries for printed editions of Cook's own account. For the printed journals of others on the voyage, *see* the subheading *Printed Accounts of Associates*. Books written about the voyage are entered under the subheadings *Books About* and *Articles*. For a description of the plates in the official account *see* the subheadings *Illustrations* and *Charts*.

1777 London Edition

A Voyage towards the South Pole and round the world, performed in His Majesty's Ships the *Resolution* and *Adventure*, in the years 1772, 1773, 1774 and 1775; written by James Cook, Commander of the *Resolution*. In which is included Captain Furneaux's narrative of his proceedings in the *Adventure* during the separation of the ships. In two volumes. Illustrated with maps and charts, and a variety of portraits . . . and views . . . drawn during the voyage by Mr. Hodges, and engraved by the most eminent masters. London, W. Strahan and T. Cadell, 1777.

2 vols.

Vol.2, pp.317–63, A Vocabulary of the language of the Society Isles; p.365, A Table . . . of different languages spoken in the South Sea; pp.367–8, Letter from J. Ibbetson . . . to Sir John Pringle, Mar.15, 1777; pp.369–96, A Discourse upon some late improvements of the means of preserving the health of mariners . . . by Sir John Pringle.

A typescript index by W. J. Jeffery is filed at NPL:D(MS.Q61 and Q74), and in Vol.2 of Jeffery's indexes at NPL:M(Q991/J, Ref Books). The Dixson Library set (Q77/25–6) is bound as vols.4–5 of a set of Cook's voyages which was formerly the property of John Walker of Whitby. Another set in the Dixson Library (Q77/33–4) is part of a nine-volume set of Cook's voyages, which formerly belonged to Thomas Pennant, a scientist and friend of Sir Joseph Banks. The latter set has additional illustrations, some coloured. The Mitchell Library holds another set of the charts and plates (incomplete) bound in a folio volume with spine title *Plates to Cook's voyages* (NPL:M F980:Co3/1A1), and another two-volume set of the Voyage with which is bound *A Second voyage round the world*, London, 1776 (*see* no. 1245).

See also nos. 1217–18, 1221–4, 1226, 1229–30, 1232–5.

Copies: NPL:M(Q980:Co3/2A1–2); NPL:D(Q77/25–6); NPL:R(09:Q990A/15–16); ANL; NUN; QOM; QU; SPL; VSL; VU(Baillieu). 1216

1777 London Edition

A Voyage towards the South Pole, and round the world, performed in His Majesty's Ships the *Resolution* and *Adventure*, in the years 1772, 1773, 1774 and 1775; written by James Cook, Commander of the *Resolution*. In which is included Captain Furneaux's narrative of his proceedings in the *Adventure* during the separation of the ships. In two volumes. Illustrated with maps and charts, and a variety of portraits . . . and views . . . drawn during the voyage by Mr. Hodges, and engraved by the most eminent masters. 2nd ed. London, W. Strahan and T. Cadell, 1777.

2 vols.

For other editions *see* no. 1216.

Copies: NPL:R(Q990A/17–18); VSL. 1217

1777 Dublin Edition

Voyage round the world, performed in His Britannic Majesty's Ships the *Resolution* and *Adventure* . . . 1772, 1773, 1774, and 1775; written by J. Cook . . . and [J.]G.[A.] Forster. Dublin, printed for W. Whitestone, S. Watson, etc. 1777.

Illus. map, ports. 4 vols.

Binder's title: Cook and Forster's Voyage. Consists of the two-volume Dublin editions of Cook's *Voyage towards the South Pole, etc.* 1777, and Forster's *Voyage round the world, etc.* 1777, each volume having two title-pages. With the book-plate of Deburgh, Earl of Clanricarde, inserted.

Copies: NPL:M(980:Co3/2A1–4); ANL(Dame Mabel Brookes' Collection); VSL. 1218

1777 Dublin Edition

Voyage towards the South Pole and round the world, performed in H.M.S. the *Resolution* and *Adventure* . . . 1772, 1773, 1774 and 1775;

written by J. Cook. In which is included Captain Furneaux's Narrative of his proceedings in the *Adventure* during the separation of the ships. Dublin, printed for W. Whitestone, S. Watson, etc. 1777.

Illus. map, ports. 2 vols.
(Cook, James—Voyage round the world . . . in . . . *Resolution* and *Adventure* . . . 1772 . . . [to] 1775; written by J. Cook . . . and [J.] G. [A.] Forster. 1777. Vols.1–2.)
The errata of the London 1777 edition have been corrected in the text. Illustrations are fewer than in the London edition, and smaller.

Copies: NPL:M(980:Co3/2A1–2); ANL(Dame Mabel Brookes' Collection); VSL.   1219

1778 NEW DISCOVERIES concerning the world and its inhabitants. In two parts. Pt.I containing a circumstantial account of all the islands in the South-Sea . . . Comprehending all the discoveries made in the several voyages of Commodore . . . Byron, Captain Wallis, Carteret and Cook. Related by Mr. Hawkesworth, Sydney Parkinson, Mr. Forster, and Captain Cook . . . Pt.II containing a summary account of Captain Cook's attempt to discover a southern continent in 1773, 1774 and 1775. London, J. Johnson, 1778.

Illus. maps, pp.xviii, 408.

Copies: NPL:M(980/N); NPL:D(77/23); NPL:R(09:S990A/114); VSL.   1220

1778 Dutch Edition

Reis naar de Zuidpool en rondom de weereld, gedaan, op bevel van zyne Brittannische Majesteit, met de schepen, de *Resolution* en de *Adventure*, in de jaren 1772, 1773, 1774 en 1775 . . . waarby gevoegt is, Kapitein Furneaux's verslag van deszelfs reize met het schip de *Adventure*, na dat het zelve van de *Resolution* was afgeraakt. Uit het Engelsch vertaalt. Rotterdam, A. Bothall, D. Vis en P. Holsteyn, 1778.

Frontisp. pp.xii, 371.
For other editions *see* no. 1216.

Copies: NPL:M(980:Co3/4A1).   1221

1778 French Edition

Voyage au Pôle Austral et autour du monde, fait sur les vaisseaux de roi l'*Aventure* & la *Résolution* en 1772, 1773, 1774 & 1775. Écrit par J. Cook . . . dans lequel on a inséré la relation du capitaine Furneaux & celle de messieurs Forster. Traduit de l'anglois. Paris, 1778.

6 vols. and atlas.
Lacking the observations of the elder Forster. For other editions *see* no. 1216.

Copies: NPL:M(980:Co3/5B1–6, Q980:Co3/3B2).   1222

1778 French Edition

Voyage dans l'hémisphère austral, et autour du monde, fait sur les vaisseaux de Roi, l'*Aventure* & la *Résolution* en 1772, 1773, 1774 & 1775. Ecrit par Jacques Cook, commandant de la *Résolution* . . . dans lequel on a inséré la relation du Capitaine Furneaux, & celle de MM. Forster. Traduit de l'Anglois. Ouvrage enrichi de plans, de cartes, de planches, de portraits & de vues de pays, dessinés pendant l'expédition par M. Hodges. Paris, Hôtel de Thou, 1778.

5 vols.

The translator, Suard, explains in his introduction that he has used, as well as Cook's account, the account in two volumes quarto published by the younger Forster. He has drawn from the latter material that is not included in Cook, and has indicated the Forster extracts by inverted commas. These dovetailed accounts occupy four volumes. The fifth volume has a separate title-page as follows: *Observations faites, pendant le second voyage de M. Cook, dans l'hémisphère austral, et autour du monde, sur la géographie, l'histoire naturelle, et la philosophie morale . . . par M. Forster, père . . . Tome cinquième.* His introduction to this volume states that it serves as an appendix to the four preceding ones, that it forms, in English, a separate work from the account of the voyage published by the captain, and also from that by the younger Forster, and that he has omitted from it the material already given in those two accounts, save for a very few repetitions.

NPL:R copy has the plates bound separately, forming a sixth volume.

For other editions *see* no. 1216.

Copies: NPL:M(Q980:Co3/3A1–5); NPL:R(Q990A/23–8); ANL; VSL.   1223

1778 French Edition

Voyage dans l'hémisphère austral, et autour du monde; fait sur les vaisseaux de roi l'*Aventure* & la *Résolution*, en 1772, 1773, 1774 & 1775. Écrit par Jacques Cook . . . dans lequel on a inséré la relation du Capitaine Furneaux & celle de MM Forster. Traduit de l'anglois. Paris, Hôtel de Thou, 1778.

6 vols. and atlas.

See no. 1216 for other editions.

Copies: NPL:M(980:Co3/5A1–6, Q980:Co3/3B1).   1224

1778–80 Leipzig Edition

Des Hauptmanns Cook zweite Fahrt um die Welt in den Jahren 1772 bis 1775.

(Historischer Bericht von den sämmtlichen, durch Engländer geschehenen, Reisen um die Welt, und den neuesten, dabey gemachten Entdeckungen, in einem getreuen Auszuge aus der Seefahrer Tagebüchern. Aus dem Englischen. Leipzig, J. F. Junius, 1778–80. Vols. 5–6.)

Copies: NPL:M(910.4/H).   1225

1779 London Edition

A Voyage towards the South Pole and round the world, performed in His Majesty's Ships the *Resolution* and *Adventure* in the years 1772, 1773, 1774 and 1775; written by James Cook, Commander of the *Resolution*. In which is included Captain Furneaux's narrative of his proceedings in the *Adventure* during the separation of the ships. In two volumes. Illustrated with maps and charts, and a variety of portraits . . . and views . . . drawn during the voyage by Mr. Hodges, and engraved by the most eminent masters. 3rd ed. London, W. Strahan and T. Cadell, 1770.

2 vols.

See also no. 1216. Mitchell Library copy lacks title-page to vol.1. ANL also holds copy presented by H.M. the Queen. Dixson Library copy bound in three volumes, the plates coloured and bound separately.

Copies: NPL:M(Q980:Co3/2C1–2); NPL:D(Q77/8–9,F77/1); NPL:R(Q990A/19–20); ANL; QParl; VParl(vol.1 only).   1226

1783 Swedish Edition

Sammandrag af Capitain Jacob Cooks åren 1772, 73, 74 och 1775, omkring Södra Polen förrättade resa; hwarwid Herrar Forsters och Furneaux Journaler blifwit jämnförde och nyttjade. Innehållande det hufwudsakeligaste af de på denna resa gjorda nya uptäckter i Söderhafwet, rörande Södra Polens Ishaf, etc. Upsala, Johan Edman, 1783.

pp.[20], 366, [10].
Binder's title: Cooks Senare-resa.
Copies: NPL:M(980:Co3/6A1).   1227

1784 ACCOUNT of Captain Cooke's second voyage.
(*In* Parkinson, Sydney—Journal of a voyage to the South Seas. London, Charles Dilly, 1784. pp.213–313.)
See also no. 1236.
Copies: NPL:M(Q980/P); NPL:R(Q990A/42); ANL.   1228

1784 London Edition

A Voyage towards the South Pole, and round the world, performed in His Majesty's Ships the *Resolution* and *Adventure*, in the years 1772, 1773, 1774 and 1775; written by James Cook, Commander of the *Resolution*. In which is included Captain Furneaux's narrative of his proceedings in the *Adventure* during the separation of the ships. In two volumes. Illustrated with maps and charts, and a variety of portraits . . . and views . . . drawn during the voyage by Mr. Hodges, and engraved by the most eminent masters. 4th ed. London, W. Strahan and T. Cadell, 1784.

2 vols.
See also no. 1216. Dixson Library copy belonged to Viscount Sydney.
Copies: NPL:M(Q980:Co3/2D1–2); NPL:D(Q77/17–18); NPL:R(Q990A/21–22); QOM; VMoU; VParl(vol.2 only).   1229

1784 Dublin Edition

A Voyage towards the South Pole, and round the world, performed in His Majesty's Ships the *Resolution* and *Adventure*, in the years 1772, 1773, 1774 and 1775; written by James Cook, Commander of the *Resolution*. In which is included Captain Furneaux's narrative of his proceedings in the *Adventure* during the separation of the ships. Dublin, T. Williams, etc., 1784.

2 vols.
Not seen. Octavo edition. For other editions *see* no. 1216.
Copies: ANL:F.   1230

1793 Dutch Edition

Reis naar de Zuidpool en rondom de weereld, gedaan . . . met de schepen de *Resolution* en de *Adventure* in de jaren 1772, 1773, 1774 en 1775 . . . waarbij gevoegt is Kaptein Furneaux's verslag van deszelfs reize met het Schip de *Adventure*, na dat het zelve van de *Resolution* was afgeraakt.

Uit het Engelsch vertaald . . . met eene lofrede over J. Cook door . . . P.L.Paris. 2nd ed. Utrecht, G.T. Pattenburg en Zoon, en M. Schalekamp, 1793.

Illus. port. pp.xii, 498, [i].

Copies: NPL:M(980:Co3/7B1). 1231

1794 Bérenger's Edition
Secondo viaggio del Capitano Giacomo Cook.

Illus.

(*In* Bérenger, Jean Pierre—Raccolta di tutti i viaggi fatti intorno al mondo. Venezia, A. Zatta, 1794. Tomo 5, pp.129–282; tomo 6, pp.3–292.)
See also no. 1233.

Copies: NPL:M(910.8/B). 1232

1795 Bérenger's Edition
Second voyage de Jaques Cook.

(*In* Bérenger, Jean Pierre—Collection de tous les voyages faits autour du monde. 2nd ed. Paris, F. Dufart, 1795. Tome 8; tome 9, pp.3–41.)
See also no. 1232.

Copies: NPL:M(910.8/B). 1233

1796 Lausanne Edition
Voyage dans l'hémisphère austral et autour du monde, fait sur les vaisseaux de roi l'*Aventure* et la *Résolution*, en 1772, 1773, 1774 et 1775. Écrit par J.Cook . . . dans lequel on a inséré la relation du capitaine Furneaux, et celle de Messieurs Forster. Traduit de l'anglois. Ouvrage enrichi de plans, de cartes, de planches, de portraits, et de vues de pays, dessinés pendant l'expédition par M. Hodges. Lausanne, Hignou, 1796.

6 vols. in 3, and atlas.

Mitchell Library holds another set, bound in six volumes, without illustrations. For other editions *see* no. 1216.

Copies: NPL:M(980:Co3/5C1–3,Q980:Co3/3B3). 1234

1796–1800 Russian Edition
Puteshestvie v iuzhnoi polovine zemnago shara i bokrug onago utchinennoe v prodolzhenie 1772, 73, 74 i 75 godov, Anglinskimi korolevskimi sudami *Rezoluitsieiu* i *Adventuirom* pod natchaloshvom Kapitana Iakova Kuke s Frantouzskago perevel Loggin Golensishchev Kushuzov. Sanktpeterbufge, Morskago Shliakheshnago Keleshskago, 1796–1800.

Illus. maps, 6 vols. in 3.

Translation of title: The Voyage to the southern hemisphere and round the world made during 1772, 73, 74 & 75, by the English Royal ships *Resolution* and *Adventure* under command of Captain Jacob Cook. From the French, translated by L.G.Kutuzov. Part 1. Published by order of His Majesty. In the printing works of the Naval Cadet Corps for the Nobles, in 1796. *See also* no. 1216.

Copies: NPL:M(Q980:Co3/4A1–3); ANL:F. 1235

1797 ABRÉGÉ du second voyage du capitaine Cook, sur le vaisseau de Sa Majeste la *Resolution*, faisant suite à la relation de Sidney Parkinson.

(*In* Parkinson, Sydney—Voyage autour du monde. Paris, Imprimerie de Guillaume, 1797. Vol.2, pp. 7–234.)
See also no. 1228.
Copies: NPL:M(Q980/P); ANL. 1236

1814–15 KERR, Robert
A General history and collection of voyages. London, 1814–15.

Vols. 12–15 deal with Cook's voyages. *See also* no. 1238.
Copies: VSL. 1237

1824 KERR, Robert
Account of a voyage towards the South Pole and round the world performed in His Majesty's Ships the *Resolution* and *Adventure*, 1772–5.

(*In his* General history and collection of voyages and travels. Edinburgh, W. Blackwood, 1824. Vol. 14–15.)
See also no. 1237.
Copies: NPL:M(910.8/K); NPL:R(D10:S17–18). 1238

1832–3 Spanish Edition
Viaje al polo austral ó del sur, y al rededor del mundo, hecho en los navíos del Rey la *Resolucion* y la *Aventura* en . . . 1772 al 1775 por . . . Santiago Cook . . . en el que se inserta la relacion del capitan Furneaux y la de los señores Forster. Trad. al castellano con algunas notas por . . . S. de Alvarado y de la Peña. Madrid, T. Jordan, 1832–3.

Illus. 8 vols.
(*Nueva Bibliot. de Viajes Modernos*, tom.8–15.)
Copies: NPL:M(980:Co3/8A1–8). 1239

1880 Abridged French Edition
Deuxième voyage du Capitaine Cook autour du monde, 1772–1775; raconté par lui-même. Paris, Maurice Dreyfous, 1880.

pp. [iii], x, 271.
Abridged from W. Smith's edition, *see* no. 138.
Copies: NPL:M(980:Co3/3B1). 1240

[190–?] Rouse's Edition
Captain Cook's second voyage. London, Blackie, [190–?].

pp.128.
(*Highways and byways of English literature*. Blackie's English texts; ed. by W.H.D. Rouse.)
Reprinted from the folio edition of G. W. Anderson.
Copies: QU. 1241

[192–?] French Edition

Voyage du Capitaine Cook dans l'hémisphère austral 1772–1774; avec 8 planches hors texte d'après les vues dessinées par M. Hodges pendant l'expédition. Paris, Ed. P. Roger, [192–?].

Map, port. pp.254.
(*Coll. Voyages de Jadis et d'Aujourd'hui.*)
Copies: NPL:M(980:Co3/9A1); ANL:F.   1242

[1921–2] Spanish Edition

Viaje hacia el polo sur y alrededor del mundo realizado a bordo de los navios reales *Resolution* y *Adventure* . . . 1772, 1773, 1774 y 1775. Trad. del inglés por M. Ortega y Gasset. Madrid, Calpe, [1921–2].

Illus. 3 vols.
(*Viajes Clásicos.*)
Copies: NPL:M(980:Co3/10A1–3).   1243

1965 [EXTRACT from The Journals of Captain James Cook, vol.2, ed. by J. C. Beaglehole, 1961.]

(*In* Chapman, Walker—Antarctic conquest. Indianapolis, Bobbs-Merrill, 1965. pp.26–37.)
Copies: NPL:M(999.8/12A1).   1244

Printed Accounts of Associates

1776 A SECOND voyage round the world, in the years MDCCLXXII, LXXIII, LXXIV, LXXV; by James Cook, Esq. Commander of His Majesty's Bark the *Resolution*. Undertaken by order of the King, and encouraged by a parliamentary grant of four thousand pounds. Drawn up from authentic papers. London, printed for the editor, 1776.

pp. [iv], 102, [i].
Sold by J. Almon, Piccadilly, and Fletcher & Hodson, Cambridge.
A surreptitious account of Cook's second voyage from the journal of one of the officers, published anonymously, a year before the official account. In the prospectus of George Forster's account of Cook's second voyage, it is stated that the author of the present account was a student of Cambridge University (Holmes, no.21). Reviewed in *The Monthly Review*, Oct.1776, pp.270–3.
The Mitchell Library holds another two copies, one bound with the official account of the voyage (NPL:M Q980:Co3/2A4).
See also no. 1246.
Copies: NPL:M(Q980:Co3/S1A1); VSL.   1245

1781 A VOYAGE round the world in the years MDCCLXXII, LXXIII, LXXIV, LXXV, by Captain James Cook, Commander of His Majesty's Bark the *Resolution*. Undertaken by order of the King, and encouraged by a parliamentary grant of four thousand pounds. Drawn up from authentic papers, by an Officer on board. London, printed for W. Lane, 1781.

pp. [iv], 102, [i].
In spite of the statement that this work was printed for W. Lane, it is a remainder issue of no. 1245, the only new matter being the title-page. Like the first issue it is of extreme rarity. (Holmes, no.39.)
See also no.1245.
Copies: NPL:M(Q980:Co3/S1B1).   1246

FORSTER, Johann Georg Adam
1777 A Voyage round the world in His Britannic Majesty's Sloop, *Resolution*, commanded by Capt. James Cook, during the years 1772, 3, 4 and 5. London, B.White, J.Robson, P.Elmsby and G.Robinson, 1777.

Map, 2 vols.
This account was published some months before Cook's account of his second voyage. Dixson copy belonged to Viscount Sydney.

Copies: NPL:M(Q980/F); NPL:D(Q77/46–7); NPL:R(Q990A/68–9); ANL; Captain Cook's Landing Place Trust; QOM; SPL; VSL.   1247

FORSTER, Johann Georg Adam
1777 A Voyage round the world, performed in His Britannic Majesty's Ships the *Resolution* and *Adventure* in the years 1772, 1773, 1774 and 1775. Written by James Cook . . . and George Forster. Illustrated with a chart of the southern hemisphere . . . and a variety of portraits . . . and views . . . drawn during the voyage by Mr. Hodges. Dublin, pr. for W.Whitestone, S.Watson and others, 1777.

Illus. ports. 2 vols.
(Cook, James—Second Voyage—Printed Accounts—Voyage round the world . . . in . . . *Resolution* and *Adventure* . . . 1772 [to] 1775; written by J.Cook . . . [J.] G. [A.] Forster. 1777. Vols. 3–4.)
Copies: NPL:M(980:Co3/2A3–4); NPL:D(77/2–3).   1248

FORSTER, Johann Georg Adam
1778–80 Geschichte de See-Reisen und Entdeckungen im Sud-Meer, welche auf Befehl Sr: Grossbrittannischen Majestät George des Dritten unternommen worden sind. Aus den Tagebüchern der Schiffs-Befehlshaber und den Handschriften der Gelehrten Herren J. Banks, Dr. Solander, Dr. J.R. Forster und Herrn G. Forster, welche diesen Reisen als Naturkundiger beygewohnt haben herausgegeben. Aus dem Englischen übersetzt vom Verfasser . . . Mit Zusätzen fur den deutschen Leser vermehrt und durch Kupfer erläutert. Berlin, Haude und Spener, 1778–[1780].

Illus. folded map, 2 vols.
Vol. 5 has added title-page: Dr. Johann Reinhold Forster's und seines Sohnes Georg Forster's Reise um die Welt auf Kosten der Grossbrittanischen Regierung zur Erweiterung der Naturkenntniss unternommen und während den Jahren 1772 bis 1775 in dem von Capitain J. Cook commandierten Schiffe *The Resolution* ausgeführt. Vols.4–5 of a set of 5 volumes, vols. 1–3 written by John Hawkesworth.
Copies: ANL; VSL; VU(Baillieu).   1249

FORSTER, Johann Georg Adam

1778–80 Johann Reinhold Forster's . . . Reise um die Welt während den Jahren 1772 bis 1775, in dem von Seiner itztregierenden Grossbrittanischen Majestät auf Entdeckungen ausgeschickten und durch den Capitain Cook geführten Schiffe *The Resolution* unternommen. Berlin, Haude und Spener, 1778–80.

Illus. 2 vols.

Copies: QOM. 1250

FORSTER, Johann Georg Adam

1778 Reply to Mr. Wales' remarks. London, B. White, J. Robson, P. Elmsley, 1778.

pp.53.

Copies: NPL:M(Q980/F); NPL:D(Q77/61); ANL; VSL; VU(Baillieu). 1251

FORSTER, Johann Georg Adam

1780 Johann Reinhold Forster's . . . Reise um die Welt während . . . 1772 bis 1775 . . . beschrieben und herausgegeben von dessen Sohn und Reisegefährten G. Forster . . . von Verfasser selbst aus dem Englischen übersetzt. Berlin, Haude und Spener, 1780.

Illus. map, 2 vols.
For English edition *see* no. 1247.

Copies: NPL:M(Q980/F). 1252

FORSTER, Johann Georg Adam

1784 Geschichte der See-Reisen und Entdeckungen im Süd-Meer welche auf Befehl Sr. Grosbrittannischen Majestät George des Dritten unternommen worden sind. Aus den Tagebüchern der Schiffs Befehlshaber und den Handschriften der Gelehrten Herren J. Banks Esq. Dr. Solander, Dr. J.R. Forster und Herrn G. Forster welche diesen Reisen als Naturkundiger beygewohnt haben herausgegeben . . . Aus dem Englischen übersetzt vom Verfasser Herrn Georg Forster . . . Mit Zusätzen für den deutschen Leser vermehrt und durch Kupfer erläutert. Band 5–7. Berlin, Haude und Spener, 1784.

Plates, 3 vols.
Each volume has an additional title-page as follows: Johann Reinhold Forster's . . . Reise um die Welt während den Jahren 1772 bis 1775 in dem von Sr. itztregierenden grosbrittannischen Majestät auf Entdeckungen ausgeschichten und durch den Capitain Cook geführten Schiffe *The Resolution* unternommen. Beschrieben und herausgegeben Georg Forster . . . Vom Verfasser selbst aus dem Englischen übersetzt, mit dem Wesentlichsten aus des Capitain Cooks Tagebüchern und andern Zusätzen für den deutschen Leser vermehrt und durch Kupfer erläutert. Band 1–3.

Copies: NPL:M(980/F). 1253

FORSTER, Johann Georg Adam

1785–9 J.R.Forster's und seines Sohns G.Forster's Reise um die Welt unternommen und während den Jahren 1772 bis 1775. Troppau, J.G. Trassler, 1785–9.

(*Sammlung der besten Reisebeschreibungen*. Troppau, 1785–9. Bd. 11–14.)
Copies: VU(Baillieu).   1254

FORSTER, Johann Georg Adam
1793 J. Cook's anden reise omkring jorden i aarene 1772 til 1775; [by
J.G.A. Forster and J.R. Forster.] Oversat af Mag. A.W. Brorson.
Kiøbenhavn, Gyldendals Forlag, 1793.
pp.vi, 553.
Copies: NPL:M(980:Co3/11A1).   1255

FORSTER, Johann Georg Adam
1922 James Cook: die Suche nach dem Südland, nach den Aufzeichnungen
[J.] G. [A.] Forsters. Bearb. von . . . H.Damm. Leipzig, F.A.Brockhaus,
1922.
Illus. maps, port. pp.157.
(*Alte Reisen und Abenteuer*, [no.] 3.)
See also no. 1257.
Copies: NPL:M(980/F); ANL.   1256

FORSTER, Johann Georg Adam
1926 James Cook: die Suche nach dem Südland, nach den Aufzeichnungen
[J.] G. [A.] Forsters. Bearb. von . . . H.Damm. 2 Aufl. Leipzig, F.A.
Brockhaus, 1926.
Illus. maps, port. pp.157.
(*Alte Reisen und Abenteuer*, [no.] 3.)
See also no. 1256.
Copies: NPL:M(980/F); ANL.   1257

FORSTER, Johann Georg Adam
1960 Reise um die Welt, [by] (G. Forster) [and J. R. Forster. Hrsg. von B.
Neubauer. Mit einem Nachwort von G. Steiner.] Berlin, Rütten &
Loening, 1960.
Map, pp. [667].
Copies: NPL:M(980:Co3/F1A1); ANL.   1258

FORSTER, Johann Georg Adam
1963 Weltumsegelung mit Kapitän Cook. [With a preface by H.E.
Rubesamen.] München, F.Bruckmann, 1963.
Illus. port. pp.299.
(*Bruckmann Querschnitte.*)
Illustrations are from etchings in earlier German edition reproduced photomechanically.
Abridged edition of J.R.Forster's and G.Forster's *Reise um die Welt in den Jahren 1772–
1775*. For English edition *see* no. 1247.
Copies: NPL:M(980/F).   1259

FORSTER, Johann Georg Adam
1965–6 Reise um die Welt; bearb. von G. Steiner. Teil 1–(2). Berlin, Akademie–Verlag, 1965–6.

Facs. illus. map, 2 vols.
(Forster, Johann Georg Adam—Georg Forsters Werke. Sämtliche Schriften, Tagebücher, Briefe. Hrsg. von der Deutschen Akademie der Wissenschaften zu Berlin. Band 2–3.)
First published 1778.
Copies: NPL:M(925.8/F733.1/8A2–3); ANL.   1260

FORSTER, Johann Reinhold
1778 Observations faites, pendant le second voyage de M. Cook, dans l'hémisphère austral.

(*In* Cook, James—Voyage dans l'hémisphère austral. Paris, Hôtel de Thou, 1778. Vol.5.)
Copies: NPL:M(Q980:Co3/3A5); VSL.   1261

FORSTER, Johann Reinhold
1778 Observations made during a voyage round the world, on physical geography, natural history and ethic philosophy; especially on 1, The Earth and its strata; 2, Water and the ocean; 3, The Atmosphere; 4, The Changes of the globe; 5, Organic bodies; and 6, The Human species. With table of languages and map. London, G. Robinson, 1778.
pp.649,[2].
Copies: NPL:M(Q980/F); ANL; VSL; VU(Baillieu).   1262

FORSTER, Johann Reinhold
1783 Johann Reinhold Forster's . . . Bemerkungen über Gegenstände der physischen Erdbeschreibung; Naturgeschichte und sittlichen Philosophie auf seiner Reise um die Welt gesammlet (*sic*). Uebersetzt und mit Anmerkungen vermehrt von dessen Sohn und Reisegefährten, Georg Forster. Berlin, Haude und Spener, 1783.

Maps, tables, pp.vi, [22], 560.
First published in English in 1778, with title *Observations made during a voyage round the world.*
Copies: NPL:M(551/4A1).   1263

FORSTER, Johann Reinhold
1785–7 Beskrifning om Människo-Slägtet uti Söderländerne, af Hr J.R. Forster.

(*Historiska Biblioteket*, no.88, Jan.4, 1785 — no.51, June 29, 1789, Stockholm.)
Extracts only. A translation of chapter 6 on the Polynesian peoples in J.R.Forster's Observations, made from the German edition, Bemerkungen über Gegenstände der physischen Erdbeschreibung, Naturgeschichte und sittlichen Philosophie auf seiner Reise um die Welt. Berlin, 1783.
From 1787 the above title changed to: "Berättelse om Söderländarnes Religion . . ." and to "Berättelse om Söderländarnes Beskaffenhet i almänhet . . ."
See Du Rietz, Rolf— Captain James Cook: a bibliography. Upsala, 1960.

The journal was edited by Carl Christoffer Gjörwell, who presumably translated this article. The title of the journal was changed in 1786 to *Upfostrings-Sälskapets Historiska Bibliothek*. Almost the whole set was printed at Kumblinske Tryckeriet; in 1786 the printer was Johan A.Carlbohm; in 1787 And.J.Nordstrom.

Copies: NPL:M(980:Col/H4A1). 1264

FORSTER, Johann Reinhold

1785 Osservazioni naturli fatti de Renaldo Forster nell' emisfero Australe. Pt.1–4.

(*In* Cook, James—Storia de' viaggi intrapressi . . . dal Capitano Giacomo Cook. Naples, La Nuova Societa' Letteraria et Tipografica, 1785. Vols.9–10.)

Copies: NPL:M(980:Col/2A9–10); VSL. 1265

FORSTER, Johann Reinhold

1787 Johann Reinhold Forster's . . . Bemerkungen über Gegenstände der physischen Erdbeschreibung; Naturgeschichte und sittlichen Philosophie auf seiner Reise um die Welt gesammelt. Uebersetzt und mit Anmerkungen vermehrt von dessen Sohn und Reisegefährten, Georg Forster. New ed. Wien, J.T.Edlen von Trattnern, 1787.

Maps, tables, pp.vi, 20, 531.

Copies: NPL:M(551/4B1); VU(Baillieu). 1266

FORSTER, Johann Reinhold

1832–3 Observaciones . . . hechas por el senor Forster, padre.

(*In* Cook, James—Second Voyage—[1832–3 Spanish edition]—Viaje al polo austral. Madrid, T. Jordan, 1832–3. Vol.8, pp.91–304.)

Copies: NPL:M(980:Co3/8A8). 1267

FURNEAUX, Tobias

1969 Captain Furneaux's Narrative, from the time the two ships were separated to their joining again in Queen Charlotte's Sound, [and] concerning the massacre in Queen Charlotte (*sic*) Sound: [extracts].

(*In* Cook, James—Collected Voyages—Printed Accounts [1969. Reed's Edition]—Captain Cook in New Zealand . . . Ed. by A.H. & A.W. Reed. 2nd ed. Wellington, N.Z., Reed, 1969. pp.183–6, 209–12.)
See also no. 225.

Copies: NPL:M(980:Col/45B1). 1268

FURNEAUX, Tobias

1969 Captain Furneaux's Narrative of a brief visit to Van Dieman's Land, 9 Mar. 1773–19 Mar. 1773.

Map.
(*In* Cook, James—First Voyage—Printed Accounts [1969. Reed's Edition]—Captain Cook in Australia . . . Ed. by A.W.Reed. Wellington, N.Z., Reed, 1969. pp.159–64.)

Copies: NPL:M(980:Co2/11A1). 1269

MARRA, John
1775 Journal of the *Resolution's* voyage in 1772, 1773, 1774 and 1775, on discovery to the southern hemisphere, by which the non-existence of an undiscovered continent between the equator and the 50th degree of southern latitude is demonstratively proved. Also a journal of the *Adventure's* voyage in the years 1772, 1773, and 1774; with an account of the separation of the two ships and the most remarkable incidents that befel each. Interspersed with historical and geographical descriptions of the islands and countries discovered in the course of their respective voyages. Illustrated with a chart in which the tracks of both vessels are accurately laid down, and other cuts. [By John Marra. Ed. by D. Henry.] London, F. Newbery, 1775.

Plates 5, folding map, pp.[xiv], 328.
Running title: Capt. Cooke's (*sic*) second voyage to the southern hemisphere. Published anonymously and surreptitiously about 18 months before Cook's own account. For information re authorship *see* Cook's letter to Secretary Stephens, Sept.18, 1775 and enclosure (*Historical Records of New South Wales*, vol.1, part 1, pp.383–4).
See also Hocken's Bibliography and Holmes (no.16). The Mitchell Library holds another copy with two additional charts. NPL:R copy has one extra chart.
See also nos. 1271–3.

Copies: NPL:M(980:Co3/M1A1); NPL:D(77/33); NPL:R(09:S990A/81); ANL:F; QOM; SPL; VSL.   1270

MARRA, John
1776 Dublin Edition
Journal of the *Resolution's* voyage in 1772, 1773, 1774 and 1775 on discovery to the southern hemisphere; also a journal of the *Adventure's* voyage in the years 1772, 1773 and 1774. Dublin, Caleb Jenkin, 1776.
Map.
Published anonymously.
Listed in the British Museum General catalogue.
See also no. 1270.

Copies: ANL (Nan Kivell); VSL.   1271

MARRA, John
1777 French Edition
Journal du second voyage du Capitaine Cook, sur les vaisseaux la *Résolution* et l'*Aventure*. Entrepris par ordre de S.M.Britannique dans les années 1774 & 1775. [Trans. by A. F. J. Fréville.] Amsterdam, et se trouve à Paris, Pissot, Nyon, 1777.
Map, pp.[ii],mxix,546.
Published anonymously. Translated from the English edition of 1775, *see* no. 1270.
Copies: NPL:M(980:Co3/M1B1); ANL:F.   1272

MARRA, John
1967 Journal of the *Resolution's* voyage in 1771–1775. Amsterdam, N. Israel, 1967.

Map, plates, pp.[xvi], 328.
(*Bibliotheca Australiana*, vol.15.)
Facsimile reprint of London edition, 1775.
Copies: NPL:M(Q910.8/9A15); NPL:R(E919/Coo).   1273

SPARRMAN, Anders
1783–1802 Resa till Goda Hopps-Udden, Sôdra Pol-kretschen och omkring
   Jordklotet samt till Hottentott och Caffer-Landen, aren 1772–76.
   Stockholm, Anders J. Nôrdstrom, 1783–1802.

Illus. map, 2 vols. in 1.
Vol.2, part 1, 1802 was published by Carl Delén, and has additional title-page. Wanting
two engravings and specimen of bark cloth. Wanting vol.2, part 2.
See also nos. 1275–85.
Copies: NPL:M(C908).   1274

SPARRMAN, Anders
1784 Reise nach dem Vorgebirge der guten Hoffnung, den südlichen
   Polarländern und um die Welt, hauptsächlich aber in den Ländern der
   Hottentotten und Kaffern in den Jahren 1772 bis 1776; aus dem
   Schwedischen frey übersetzt von C. H. Groskurd, hrsg. und mit einer
   Vorrede begleitet von [J.] G. [A.] Forster. With chart and illus. Berlin,
   Haude und Spener, 1784.

pp. xxviii, 626.
See no.1274 for other editions.
Copies: NPL:M(980:Co3/S2B1).   1275

SPARRMAN, Anders
1785 A Voyage to the Cape of Good Hope, towards the Antarctic polar
   circle, and round the world; but chiefly into the country of the Hottentots
   and Caffres, from the year 1772 to 1776. By Andrew Sparrman. Translated
   from the Swedish original. Dublin, White, Cash and Byrne, 1785.

Plates, map, 2 vols.
See no. 1274 for other editions.
Copies: NPL:M(980:Co3/S2C1-2).   1276

SPARRMAN, Anders
1786 A Voyage to the Cape of Good Hope, towards the Antarctic polar
   circle, and round the world; but chiefly into the country of the Hottentots
   and Caffres, from the year 1772 to 1776. By Andrew Sparrman. Translated
   from the Swedish original. 2nd ed., corrected. London, G.G.J. and
   J. Robinson, 1786.

Plates, map, 2 vols.
Frontispiece to vol.1 is printed in reverse, cf. no. 1276. *See* no. 1274 for other editions.
Copies: NPL:M(Q980:Co3/S2A1-2); VSL.   1277

SPARRMAN, Anders

1787 Reize naar de Kaap de Goede Hoop, de landen van den Zuidpool, en rondom de waereld; doch voornaamlijk in de landen der Hottentotten en Kafferen, in de jaaren 1772 tot 1776 gedaan door Andreas Sparman. Met eene voorreede en aantekeningen van den Heer [J.] G. [A.] Forster. Leyden, S. en J.Luchtmans, 1787.

Map, plates, 2 vols.
See no. 1274 for other editions.
Copies: NPL:M(980:Co3/S2E1–2).   1278

SPARRMAN, Anders

1787 Voyage au Cap de Bonne-Espérance, et autour du monde, avec le capitaine Cook, et principalement dans le pays des Hottentots et des Caffres. Par André Sparrman. Traduit par M. Le Tourneur. Paris, Buisson, 1787.

Map, plates, 2 vols.
See no. 1274 for other editions.
Copies: NPL:M(Q980:Co3/S2B1–2).   1279

SPARRMAN, Anders

1787 Voyage au Cap de Bonne-Espérance, et autour du monde, avec le capitaine Cook, et principalement dans le pays des Hottentots et des Caffres. Par André Sparrman . . . Traduit par M. le Tourneur. Paris, Buisson, 1787.

Maps, plates, 3 vols.
See no. 1274 for other editions.
Copies: NPL:M(980:Co3/S2D1–3); NPL:R(S968A/28–30); VSL.   1280

SPARRMAN, Anders

1789 A Voyage to the Cape of Good Hope, towards the Antarctic polar circle, and round the world; but chiefly into the country of the Hottentots and Caffres, from the year 1772 to 1776. By Andrew Sparrman. Translated from the Swedish original. Perth, R.Morison and Son, 1789.

Map, plates, 2 vols.
Vol.2 undated.
Frontispiece to vol.1 is engraved in reverse, cf. no. 1276.
See no. 1274 for other editions.
Copies: NPL:M(980:Co3/S2F1–2); VU(Baillieu).   1281

SPARRMAN, Anders

1939 James Cook's second expedition to the Pacific in 1772–1775: [a brief résumé taken from Sparrman's Voyage, part 2].

(*In* Söderström, Jan Georg Karl—A. Sparrman's ethnographical collection. Stockholm, Bokförlags Aktiebolaget Thule, 1939. pp.15–18.)
Copies: NPL:M(Q572.99/S); ANL; VSL.   1282

SPARRMAN, Anders

1939 Un Compagnon suédois du Capitaine James Cook au cours de son deuxième voyage: [narrative of the voyage, from June 7, 1773 to June 16, 1774. Trans. from the Swedish; with introduction by Bjarne Kroepelien.] Oslo, La Coquille Qui Chante, 1939.

Illus. pp.91, [iii].
Limited edition, no.24/100 with signature of translator on title-page. This is a translation of part of the original Swedish edition, Stockholm 1802, and was translated into English by A. Mackenzie-Grieve in Sparrman's *A Voyage round the World with Captain James Cook*, 1944, *see* no. 1284.

Copies: NPL:M(980:Co3/S1A1).   1283

SPARRMAN, Anders

1944 A Voyage round the world with Captain James Cook in H.M.S. *Resolution*, by A. Sparrman; [translated from the Swedish by H.Beamish and A.Mackenzie-Grieve. With] introduction & notes by O.Rutter. Wood-engravings by P.Barker-Mill. London, Golden Cockerel Press, 1944.

Map, pp.218.
First English translation of the second part of Sparrman's *Resa Till Goda Hopps . . . aren 1772–6*, published in two volumes in Swedish, 1802–1818. Limited edition, no.240/350. *See* no. 1274 for other editions.

Copies: NPL:M(Q980:Co3/S2C1); SPL; VSL.   1284

SPARRMAN, Anders

1953 A Voyage round the world with Captain James Cook in H.M.S. *Resolution*. By Anders Sparrman. Translated by H.Beamish and A. Mackenzie-Grieve. Introduction and notes by O.Rutter. Illustrated by C. W. Bacon, London, Robert Hale, 1953.

Map, pp.xx, 214.
First general edition, a reprint of the Golden Cockerel Press edition of 1944.
See no. 1274 for other editions.

Copies: NPL:M(980:Co3/S2G1); QParl; VMoU; VSL.   1285

SPARRMAN, Anders

n.d. Un Compagnon suédois du capitaine James Cook au cours de son deuxième voyage. [Extracts from the narrative of A. Sparrman; translated and edited by B. Kroepelien. English translation by Sir William Dixson, entitled Anders Sparrman.]

ff.71.
Copies: NPL:D(WD30).   1286

WALES, William

1777 The Original astronomical observations made in the course of a voyage towards the South Pole, and round the world, in his Majesty's ships the *Resolution* and *Adventure* in the years 1772, 1773, 1774, and 1775; by W. Wales and W. Bayly. Pub. by order of the Board of Longitude. London, W. & A. Strahan, pr., 1777.

pp.lv, 385.
Copies: NPL:M(Q524/W); ANL; VSL.   1287

Books about the Second Voyage

1776 COOK, James

The Method taken for preserving the health of the crew of His Majesty's Ship the *Resolution* during her late voyage round the world. By Captain James Cook, F.R.S. Addressed to Sir John Pringle. [Letter, dated March 5, 1776, and extract of letter from Captain Cook to Sir John Pringle, dated July 7, 1776.] London, 1776.

Extract from the Royal Society of London—*Philosophical transactions*, vol.66, 1776, pp. 402–6.

For this paper Cook was awarded the Copley Medal. *See also* no. 1289, 1293.

Copies: NPL:M(613.69/C); NPL:D(77/35); NPL:R(N506/16, reprint).   1288

1776 COOK, James

The Method taken for preserving the health of the crew of His Majesty's Ship the *Resolution* during her late voyage round the world. By Captain James Cook . . . Read at the [Royal] Society, March 7, 1776. [Letter] to Sir John Pringle . . . March 5, 1776, [and extract of a letter from Captain Cook to Sir John Pringle, July 7, 1776].

(*In* Pringle, Sir John—A Discourse upon some late improvements of the means of preserving the health of mariners. London, the Royal Society, 1776. pp.39–44.)

For this paper Cook was awarded the Copley Medal. *See also* no. 1288, 1290, 1291, 1293.

Copies: NPL:M(613.68/1A1); NPL:D(77/1); ANL; VSL.   1289

1776 PRINGLE, *Sir* John

A Discourse upon some late improvements of the means for preserving the health of mariners. Delivered at the anniversary meeting of the Royal Society, November 30, 1776, by Sir John Pringle. London, the Royal Society, 1776.

pp.[ii], 44.

Presidential address prior to the presentation to Mrs. Cook (in Captain Cook's absence) of the Copley Medal. Cook's paper (no.1289) is printed on pp.39–44. *See* Holmes, no.20. *See also* no.1291.

Copies: NPL:M(613.68/1A1); NPL:D(77/1); ANL; VSL.   1290

1777 PRINGLE, *Sir* John

A Discourse upon some late improvements of the means for preserving the health of mariners. Delivered at the anniversary meeting of the Royal Society, November 30, 1776, by Sir John Pringle . . . Corrected by the author.

(*In* Cook, James—Second Voyage—Printed Accounts [1777 London Edition]—A Voyage towards the South Pole. London, W. Strahan and T. Cadell, 1777. pp.369–96.)

Presidential address prior to the presentation to Mrs. Cook (in Captain Cook's absence) of the Copley Medal. *See* Holmes, no.20.

See also no.1290.

Copies: NPL:M(Q980:Co3/2A2); NPL:D(Q77/26); NPL:R(09:Q990A/16); ANL; NUN; QOM; QU; SPL; VSL; VU(Baillieu).   1291

1778 WALES, William

Remarks on Mr. Forster's Account of Captain Cook's last voyage round the world in the years 1772, 1773, 1774, and 1775. London, J. Nourse, 1778.

pp.[i], 110.

Copies: NPL:M(980/W); VSL. 1292

1795 PRINGLE, *Sir* John

Methodo do Capitao Cook, com o qual preservava a saude dos seus marinheiros, traduzido do original Inglez, e offerecido ao illustrissimo e excellentissimo Senhor Conde de S.Vicente. Lisboa, Na Regia Officina Typografica, 1795.

pp.16.

See also nos. 1288–91.

Copies: NPL:M(613.68/2B1). 1293

1803–4 CAMPE, Joachim Heinrich

Capitain James Cooks Reise omkring Jorden: en Láèsebog for Ungdommen, efter Campes, Láèremaade . . . Oversat af H.C. Lund. Kiøbenhavn, Mathew Johan Sebbelom, 1803–4.

Illus. in colour, 3 vols. in 1.

Copies: NPL:M(980/Co4/C2A1). 1294

1844 FORSTER, Johann Reinhold

Descriptiones animalium quae in itinere ad Maris Australis terras per annos 1772, 1773, et 1774; suscepto, collegit, observavit et delineavit Ioannes Reinoldus Forster . . . nunc demum editae . . . Henrico Lichtenstein. Berolini, ex officina academica, 1844.

pp.xiv, 424, [ii].

Latin descriptions of 305 animals observed during Cook's second voyage.

Copies: NPL:M(591.9901/F); ANL. 1295

1926 BIRMINGHAM—Assay Office

Matthew Boulton's Otaheite medal, distributed by Captain Cook on his second voyage to the Pacific Ocean, 1772. Birmingham, Assay Office, 1926.

Illus. pp.11.

Copies: NPL:M(Q980:Co3/B1A1); NPL:D(Q92/161); ANL. 1296

Articles, etc., about the Second Voyage

1778 CAPTAIN COOK'S attempts to discover a southern continent in 1773–5.

Illus.

(New discoveries concerning the world. London, J. Johnson, 1778. pp.369–408.)

Copies: NPL:M(980/N); NPL:D(77/23); NPL:R(09:S909.8A/114). 1297

1779 CAMPBELL, John

Voyage of Captain Cook and Captain Fourneaux round the world.

(*In his* Lives of British admirals. London, A. Donaldson, 1779. Vol. 4, pp.347–65.)

Copies: NPL:M(359.0942/C). 1298

1780 DESPERRIÈRES, Poissonier

Observations sur le discours de M. Pringle qui termine la relation des voyages de M. Cook; lûes à la Société Royale de Médecine. [With] (Rapport de Mrs. les Commissaires de la Société.)

(*In his* Traité des fièvres de l'Isle de St. Domingue. Paris, l'Imprimerie Royale, 1780. pp.243–312.)

Copies: NPL:M(980:Col/D2B1). 1299

1790 CLARET DE FLEURIEU, Charles Pierre, *Comte*

New Caledonia ou Nouvelle Calédonie découverte par Cook en 1774.

(*In his* Découvertes des François en 1768 & 1769. Paris, l'Imprimerie Royale, 1790. pp. 243–7.)
See also no. 1303.

Copies: NPL:M(Q988/F); NPL:R(09:Q998A/6). 1300

1790 CLARET DE FLEURIEU, Charles Pierre, *Comte*

Reconnoissance complette de la Terre Australe du Saint-Esprit de Quiros, sous le nom de Nouvelles Hebrides, par le Capitaine Cook en 1774.

Map.
(*In his* Découvertes des François en 1768 & 1769. Paris, l'Imprimerie Royale, 1790. pp.155–69.)
See also no. 1302.

Copies: NPL:M(Q988/F); NPL:R(09:Q998A/6). 1301

1791 CLARET DE FLEURIEU, Charles Pierre, *Comte*

The Complete recognition of the Tierra Austral de Espiritu Santo, of Quiros, under the name of the New Hebrides, by Captain Cook in 1774.

(*In his* Discoveries of the French in 1768 and 1769. London, J.Stockdale, 1791. pp. 164–79.)
See also no. 1301.

Copies: NPL:M(Q988/F); NPL:R(09:Q998A/7). 1302

1791 CLARET DE FLEURIEU, Charles Pierre, *Comte*

New Caledonia discovered by Captain Cook in 1774.

(*In his* Discoveries of the French in 1768 and 1769. London, J. Stockdale, 1791. pp. 255–8.)
See also no. 1300.

Copies: NPL:M(Q988/F); NPL:R(09:Q998A/7). 1303

1854 BRAINNE, Charles
Voyage de Cook et de Forster.
(*In his* La Nouvelle-Calédonie. Paris, Hachette, 1854. pp.1–20.)
Copies: NPL:M(998.7/1A); ANL.   1304

1865 HOWITT, William
Voyage of Cook and Furneaux, Jan. 1772 to 1774.
(*In his* History of discovery in Australia. London, Longman, Green, Longman, Roberts & Green, 1865. Vol.1, pp.110–22.)
Copies: NPL:M(980/127A1); NPL:R(S990A/147).   1305

1905 MILL, Hugh Robert
The Achievement of James Cook; [with bibl.].
Illus. maps, port.
(*In his* The Siege of the South Pole. London, A. Rivers, 1905. pp.56–90.)
Copies: NPL:M(989.8/M); VSL.   1306

1907 McNAB, Robert
Cook Surveys Dusky, 1773.
(*In his* Murihiku and the southern islands. Invercargill, W. Smith, pr., 1907. pp.13–25.)
Also published in the author's *Murihiku; a history*, 1909.
Copies: NPL:M(997.9/M); NPL:R(S997/15).   1307

1909 McNAB, Robert
Cook's second visit, 1773.
Illus.
(*In his* Murihiku. Wellington, N.Z., W. & T., 1909. pp.31–46.)
Copies: NPL:M(997.9/M); NPL:R(DS997/16).   1308

1909 McNAB, Robert
Cook's third and fourth visits, 1773 and 1774.
(*In his* Murihiku. Wellington, N.Z., W. & T., 1909. pp.47–61.)
Copies: NPL:M(997.9/M); NPL:R(DS997/16).   1309

1913 JOHNSTON, *Sir* Harry Hamilton
Cook's second and third voyages.
Illus.
(*In his* Pioneers in Australasia. With eight coloured illustrations by Alec Ball. London, Blackie, 1913. pp.252–77.)
Pioneers of Empire.
Copies: NPL:M(980/J); NPL:R(S990/8).   1310

[1919?] FINCH, Robert J.
Second voyage of Captain Cook.
(*In his* Kingsway book of famous explorers. London, Evans, [1919?]. pp.79–84.)
Copies: NPL:M(910.9/F).   1311

1925 IREDALE, Tom

Captain Cook's artists.

Illus.

(*Australian Museum Magazine*, vol. 2, 1924–5, pp.224–30.)

Copies: NPL:M(507/A); NPL:R(S590.6/17). 1312

[1936] FILDES, H.

The Last of the Ngati Mamoe, the wild people of the New Zealand mountain and bush. Dunedin, Reed, [1936].

Illus. map, pp. [ii], 15.

Describes Captain Cook's meeting with members of this almost extinct tribe, when the *Resolution* called at Dusky Sound in 1773.

Copies: NPL:M(572.997/F). 1313

1937 FOX, Lorene K.

[The First Antarctic expedition: Captain James Cook's expedition with *Resolution* and *Adventure*, 1772–5.]

(*In her* Antarctic icebreakers. New York, Double Day, Doran, 1937. pp.4–9.)
Junior Books.

Copies: NPL:M(989.8/F). 1314

1937 HARRISSON, Thomas Harnett

Great Englishman; [with bibl. notes].

Illus.

(*In his* Savage civilisation. London, Gollancz, 1937. pp.116–23.)

Copies: NPL:M(572.9986/7A1); NPL:R(572.9986/1). 1315

1939 CARRINGTON, Arthur Hugh

A Note by Captain James Cook on the Tahiti creation myth, [in Captain Cook's holograph MS. in the British Museum. With extract.]

(Polynesian Society—*Journal*, March 1939, pp.30–1.)

Copies: NPL:M(Q572.9/P). 1316

1943 ALLISON, Richard Sydney

The Beginnings of reform: [the effect of Lind's teachings on naval hygiene on Captain Cook's second voyage].

(*In his* Sea diseases. London, John Bale Medical Publications, 1943. pp.145–9.)

Copies: NPL:M(359.9/A); NPL:R(S359.9/11). 1317

1950 CAMERON, Hector Charles

Failure of the philosophers to sail with Cook in the *Resolution*. [With letters from Cook to Banks and from Banks to First Lord of the Admiralty; and bibl. notes.]

(*Geographical Journal*, London, vol.116, pp.49–54, Sept. 1950.)
The natural philosophers referred to were Banks, Solander and party. A reprint of the article is filed in the Mitchell Library.
Copies: NPL:M(980:Co3/C1A1); NPL:R(DS909.6A/2). 1318

1951 CHRISTIE, Eric William Hunter
Captain Cook.
(*In his* Antarctic problem: an historical and political study. [With app. of documents and bibl.] London, Allen and Unwin, 1951. pp.47–59.)
Copies: NPL:M(999.8/C); NPL:R(DS999.8/2). 1319

1952 BERRILL, Norman John
Where the winds blow, [and] (Venus observed) etc.
(*In his* Journey into wonder. New York, Dodd, Mead, 1952. pp.130–200.)
See also no. 1321.
Copies: NPL:M(910/B). 1320

1953 BERRILL, Norman John
Where the winds blow, [and] (Venus observed) etc.
(*In his* Journey into wonder. London, Gollancz, 1953. pp.131–96.)
See also no. 1320.
Copies: NPL:R(S570.9/8). 1321

1956 BROWN, Roderick Langmere Haig Haig-
Boy seaman; [with Cook on his second voyage].
(*In his* Captain of the *Discovery*: the story of Capt. George Vancouver. London, Macmillan, 1956. pp.1–17.)
Copies: NPL:M(910.4/B). 1322

1956 SMITH, Bernard
Coleridge's Ancient mariner and Cook's second voyage.
(*Journal of the Warburg & Courtauld Institute*, vol. 19, pp.117–54 Jan.Je 1956.)
Copies: NPL:R(Q062/5); QU. 1323

1959 CHARLIAT, Pierre Jacques
Le Second voyage de Cook; ou, La démolition du continent australe, 1772–1775.
(*In his* Le Temps des grands voiliers. Paris, Nouvelle Librairie de France, 1959. pp. 191–9.)
Parias, L.H.—Histoire universelle des explorations, vol. 3.
Copies: NPL:M(910.9/9A1). 1324

1959 HERDMAN, H.F.P.

Some notes on sea ice observed by Captain James Cook, R.N., during his circumnavigation of Antarctica, 1772–75. [With bibl.].

Map.

(*Journal of Glaciology*, Cambridge, vol.3, pp.534–41, Oct. 1959.)

Copies: NPL:M(980:Co3/H1A1, extract); NPL:R(N551.3106/1).   1325

1960 FURNEAUX, Rupert

The *Adventure:* [Furneaux on Cook's second voyage].

(*In his* Tobias Furneaux, circumnavigator. London, Cassell, 1960. pp.86–143.)

Copies: NPL:M(923.9/F987/2A1); NPL:R(S909.4A/113); ANL.   1326

1961 PRICE, Archibald Grenfell

Captain James Cook's discovery of the Antarctic continent?

(*Geographical Review*, N.Y., vol.51, pp.575–77, Oct. 1961.)

Copies: NPL:R(N910.6/8).   1327

1962 BERIOT, Agnes

Le Second voyage: l'*Adventure* et le *Resolution*, 1772–1775.

(*In her* Grands voiliers autour du monde: les voyages scientifiques 1760–1850. Paris, Editions du Pont Royal, 1962. pp.54–65.)

Copies: NPL:M(Q 910.4/14A1); NPL:R(NQ 910.4/1).   1328

1968 DOLAN, Edward F., *the younger*

The Unseen continent: [Antarctica].

(*In his* Explorers of the Arctic and Antarctic. New York, Crowell-Collier Press, 1968. pp.96–100.)

Copies: NPL:M(999.8/18A1).   1329

1968 RAUSCHENBERG, Roy Anthony

Early plans for the second Cook voyage [and] (Withdrawal from the second Cook voyage) [by Banks and Solander].

(*In his* Daniel Carl Solander, naturalist on the *Endeavour*. Philadelphia, 1968, pp.44–7.)

American Philosophical Society—*Transactions* n.s. vol. 58, pt. 8.

Copies: NPL:M(NQ506/5).   1330

Charts

Manuscripts

Originals cannot be reproduced without the permission of the owner.

[1763–80] SMITH, Isaac

Original sketches, drawings, maps etc. [1763–80] collected by Admiral Isaac Smith who served as an officer under Captain James Cook, the circumnavigator, in his first & second voyages, A.D. 1768–1775.

ff.49, 97 drawings.

Title is in the hand of Canon Bennett, a relative of Isaac Smith, from whom the volume was acquired by the Government of New South Wales. MS. contents list is from Isaac Smith's papers. A new contents list and an index have been made and are inserted. Some of the drawings are signed "H.Roberts", "Hen^y Roberts", one is signed "W.H.", others are ascribed in Canon Bennett's hand to W.Hodges; presumably this was on the back of the drawings (now pasted down) or may have been noted in pencil, as still apparent in some cases, on the leaves of the volume, as it is not on the MS. contents list. A note at the beginning in Canon Bennett's hand, suggests that some of the unsigned drawings may be by Isaac Smith. Some of the drawings appear to be the originals of the plates to Cook's second voyage. With the exception of two of the first voyage, the drawings probably all belong to the second voyage but some may be of the third. The charts include two by Cook of Newfoundland 1763, one of Charlestown 1780, one of the track of H.M.S. *Perseverance* etc. The drawings are listed separately at no. 1378.

CONTENTS:

f.ia   Cook, James—A Plan of the Harbou^r of St Johns in Newfoundland. 1763. Ink and watercolour chart. 7¾″ x 10″ inside ruled frame lines. Titled and signed in ink in upper right corner with a list of references. Scale in lower right corner.

f.ib   Cook, James—A Plan of the Harbour of Croque in Newfoundland. 1763. Ink and wash chart. 11⅞″ x 15¾″ inside ruled frame lines. Titled and dated in pencil outside ruled frame lines. Ruled insert along upper edge is blank. Notes in pencil on map. In ink on mount in Canon Bennett's hand 'Maps of Newfoundland Drawn by Captain Cook. 1763'.

f.ii   Cook, James—[Four profiles of the coast of] Terra del Fuego, a Plan of Success Bay in Strait le Maire [and] A Chart of the S.E. part of Terra del Fuego . . . by Lieut. J.Cook. 1769? Printed charts. 12″ x 14¼″ inside ruled frame lines. Plate from Hawkesworth's voyages, vol.2.

f.iii   Cook, James—Sketches of the islands Lagoon, Thrum-Cap, Bow-Island, the Two Groups, Bird Island and Chain-Island, lying in the South-Sea . . . discovered in Apl 1769 (by Lieut. J.Cook). 1769. Pen and ink. 16¾″ x 21⅞″ inside ruled frame lines. Unsigned. Titled and dated as above along upper edge, with a scale of leagues to all islands. Note in ink under title 'Note. the prick'd line shews the ship track in which she Passed the Islands'. Each island is sketched separately and latitude and longitude are given.

f.1   Hodges, William—Profile of the coast of the Isle of Mayo, Cape Verde Islands. 1772. Wash drawing. 6⅝″ x 18⅜″ meas. to the pencil line below title. Unsigned. Titled 'Isle of Mayo distant 2 miles and the hill B west'. 'N 1—' in ink upper right corner. 'W.Hodges' in pencil on mount in Canon Bennett's hand.

f.2   Hodges, William—Profile of the Isle of Mayo. 1772. Wash drawing. 6¾″ x 19″ from pencil line beneath title of upper drawing. Unsigned. Titled 'Isle Mayo when the hill C. bears NWBN distance 1 league'. Signed 'W.Hodges' in pencil on mount in Canon Bennett's hand. Similar to view at f.1 but scale is smaller.

f.2   Hodges, William—Profile of the coast of the Isle of Mayo. 1772. Wash drawing. 5¼″ x 19″ to the pencil line below title. Unsigned. Titled 'Isle of Mayo distant 2 miles and the hill B west'. 'N°2—' in ink upper right corner. 'W.Hodges' signed in pencil on mount in Canon Bennett's hand. Similar to view at f.1 but scale is smaller and the hill marked 'B' is completed.

f.3   Hodges, William—Profile of the Island of St. Jago, Cape Verde Island. 1772. Wash drawing. 12″ x 18⅞″. Unsigned. Titled in ink below view 'The Island of St Jago where the point D bears WSW distant 3 leagues. AA joins'. In ink in upper right corner 'N° 3—'.

f.3a   Hodges, William—Chart of Port Praya in the Island of St Jago, Cape Verde Islands. 1772. Watercolour. 5⅝″ x 10½″ inside ruled frame lines. Unsigned.

Titled 'Port Praya in the Island St Jago one of the Cape de Verds (*sic*). A scale of [2″ to] $\frac{1}{2}$ a mile.' Attributed to William Hodges.

f.3b Hodges, William—View of unidentified island. 177–?. Wash sketch. 5″ x 14$\frac{3}{4}$″. Unsigned and untitled. In ink on left hand side 'N by E' and on right hand side 'E by N'. Attributed to William Hodges.

f.4 Hodges, William—View of Porto Santo extending from NNW to WBN distant 5 miles. 1772? Watercolour. 5″ x 18″. Unsigned and undated. Titled in ink along lower edge of view. In ink in upper right corner 'N. 4'. In pencil on mount in Canon Bennett's hand 'W. Hodges'.

f.5 Hodges, William—View of Porto Santo bearing North distant 2 Leagues. 1772? Watercolour. 6$\frac{1}{4}$″ x 18$\frac{1}{4}$″. Unsigned and undated. Titled as above in ink along lower edge of view. 'No 5' written in ink in upper right corner. 'W.Hodges' in pencil on mount in Canon Bennett's hand.

f.6 Hodges, William—Island of Bonavista: 2 profiles. 1772. Wash drawings. 4$\frac{1}{4}$″ x 15$\frac{1}{4}$″; 3$\frac{1}{2}$″ x 15$\frac{5}{8}$″ inside ruled frame lines. Unsigned and undated. Titled in ink along lower edges of profiles 'Island of Bonavista S.W. distant 5 leagues' and 'The Island of Bonavista when the hill A, off which lies a ledge of rocks bears west 2 leagues.' Attributed to Hodges. In ink in upper right corner of top view 'N°. 6'.

f.7 Hodges, William—View of the Deserters. 1772? Wash drawing. 4$\frac{1}{4}$″ x 20$\frac{5}{8}$″ inside ruled frame lines; 21″ outside. Unsigned and undated. Titled in ink lower edge 'View of the Deserters'.

f7 Hodges, William—View of Porto Santo bearing north. 1772? Wash drawing. 3$\frac{3}{4}$″ x 20$\frac{7}{8}$″ inside ruled frame lines; 4″ x 21$\frac{3}{16}$″ outside. Unsigned and undated. Titled in ink lower edge 'View of Porto Santo bearing north distant 2 leagues'.

f.7 Hodges, William—View of Porto Santo. 1772? Wash drawing. 3$\frac{1}{2}$″ x 20$\frac{7}{8}$″ inside ruled frame lines; 3$\frac{3}{4}$″ x 21$\frac{3}{16}$″ outside. Unsigned and undated. Titled in ink along lower edge 'View of Porto Santo extending from NNW to WBN distant 5 miles'. In upper right corner in ink 'N° 7—'.

f.8 Hodges, William—View of the Deserters. 1772? Watercolour sketch. 3$\frac{1}{4}$″ x 20$\frac{3}{8}$″ inside ruled pencil lines. Unsigned and undated. Titled in ink lower edge of view and in pencil near right hand edge.

f.8 Hodges, William—View of Porto Santo bearing north. 1772? Wash drawing. 3$\frac{1}{4}$″ x 20$\frac{1}{4}$″ inside ruled pencil lines. Unsigned and undated. Titled in ink below view 'View of Porto Santo bearing north distant 2 leagues'. Title also faintly in pencil along upper edge of view.

f.8 Hodges, William—View of Porto Santo. 1772? Wash drawing. 4$\frac{3}{4}$″ x 20$\frac{3}{8}$″ inside ruled pencil lines. Unsigned and undated. Titled in ink below view 'View of Porto Santo extending from NNW to WBN distant 5 miles'. Title also written faintly in pencil along upper edge. 'N°.8' upper edge. Similar to view at f.7.

f.19 Roberts, Henry—Profile of Middleburg Island. 1773. Wash drawing. 3$\frac{5}{8}$″ x 12$\frac{5}{8}$″ below title. Signed 'Hen^y Roberts' in ink lower right corner. Undated. Title printed in ink below view 'Middleburg Island bearing W by S distant 3 leagues'. 'N 19' in ink upper right corner.

f.19 Roberts, Henry—Pylstuart Island: two profiles. 1774? Watercolour washes. 4″ x 12$\frac{5}{8}$″ below title. Signed 'Hen^y Roberts' in ink lower right corner. Undated. Titles printed below views 'Pylstuart Island SW distant nine leagues' and 'Pylstuart NWbN distant six leagues'.

f.19 Roberts, Henry—Middleburg Island: profile. 1773? Watercolour. 3″ x 12$\frac{5}{8}$″ below title. Signed 'Hen^y Roberts' in ink lower right corner. Undated. Title printed in ink below view 'Middleburg E by S distant five miles.'

f.19 Roberts, Henry—Amsterdam Island: profile. 1773. Watercolour. 2$\frac{7}{8}$″ x 12$\frac{3}{4}$″ below title. Signed 'Hen^y Roberts' in ink lower right corner. Undated. Title printed in ink below view 'Amsterdam Island when the south point bears west distant four miles'.

f.25a/b Profile of Osnabrug (*sic*) Island. 1769? Watercolour. $6\frac{1}{8}''$ x $13\frac{1}{4}''$. Unsigned. Titled in ink lower edge of view 'Osnabrug (*sic*) Island. Bearing S. by W. 5 leagues distant'. In pencil in upper right corner 'No 18'.

f.25a/c Profile of Dominica Island. 1774. Wash drawing. $5\frac{1}{8}''$ x $15\frac{3}{4}''$. Unsigned and undated. Titled in ink lower edge 'I. Dominica bearing from N by W to ESE distant $1\frac{1}{2}$ mile.' In pencil beneath title 'Marquesas' with query on mount '?Canaries'. In pencil upper right corner 'No 9'.

f.25b/a Map and profile of Palmerston Island. 1774. Wash drawing. Map meas. $4''$ x $9\frac{5}{8}''$. Profile meas. $2\frac{5}{8}''$ x $9\frac{5}{8}''$. Unsigned and undated. Titled in pencil upper left corner 'Palmerston Island Lat.18 S Long 163.5 W.' 'Palmerston' written faintly in pencil in middle of view.

f.25b/b Profile of unidentified Pacific Island showing a lagoon. 177–? Watercolour. $4\frac{1}{2}''$ x $13\frac{1}{2}''$. Unsigned, untitled and undated. 'North' printed in ink above horizon.

f.25b/c Profile of unidentified island. 177–? Wash drawing. $3''$ x $14\frac{3}{4}''$. Unsigned. 'W' in ink left hand side, 'N' on right hand side. 'A league off shore' written faintly in pencil along lower edge.

f.25b/d Profile of unidentified island. 177–? Wash sketch. $4\frac{3}{4}''$ x $14\frac{3}{4}''$. Unsigned, untitled and undated. 'E' printed in ink left hand side and 'SSW' on right.

f.37a Sketch of Block Island. 177–? Sketch map. $11\frac{1}{4}''$ x $7\frac{3}{4}''$. Unsigned and undated. Titled in ink upper left corner 'Sketch of Block Island. Lat^d of the South Head 41.9H'.

f.37b [Map of] Charles Town and state of the Kings troops March 11 1780. 1780. Pen and ink and watercolour. $8\frac{3}{4}''$ x $7\frac{3}{16}''$. Unsigned and undated. Titled as above in pencil along lower edge. Key in pencil lower left corner.

f.37c Plan of the harbour of St Lucia. Pen and ink. $12\frac{5}{8}''$ x $17\frac{7}{8}''$ inside ruled frame lines. Unsigned and undated. Titled in ink upper right corner with 'West Indies' written below in pencil. Scale of fathoms in lower left corner.

f.38a Map of S.Andheman Island. 1775. Pen and ink. $15\frac{1}{4}''$ x $9\frac{3}{4}''$. Unsigned and undated. Titled 'S. Andheman Island' in pencil upper left edge. Gives latitude and longitude.

f.38b The Track of His Majesty's ship *Perseverance* between Rutland and the Cinque Islands. Pen and ink. $11\frac{1}{4}''$ x $14\frac{3}{4}''$. Unsigned and undated. Titled in ink along upper edge. Scale of $5'' = 10$ nautical miles.

Copies: NPL:M(PXD11). 1331

[1771?] MAP of the Southern Hemisphere showing the discoveries made in the Southern Ocean up to 1770.

1 sheet, $12''$ x $12''$.
Original map, with Capt. Cook's proposed route of the *Resolution* and *Adventure* marked in yellow. This map and an autograph account by Capt. Cook of his proposed route were submitted by him, with a covering letter, to the Earl of Sandwich. Bound with letter and the other MS. in a volume entitled—Original manuscript in the handwriting of Captain Cook relating to his second voyage.

Copies: NPL:M(Safe1/82). 1332

1772-5 FANNIN, Peter

A Collection of drawings and charts made by Peter Fannin, Master of the *Adventure* during Capt. Cook's second voyage, 1772–1775, with the addition of an anonymous drawing of Adventure Bay, Van Diemen's Land, during Capt. Cook's third voyage 1776–1780. [11 photocopies, some in colour, of originals in the Naval Historical Branch, Ministry of Defence, London.] Stewkely, Bedfordshire, Eng., A.L.Faber (Microfilm) Ltd., 1965.

10 sheets in portfolio, 16″ x 11½″.

CONTENTS: CHARTS

Photocopy no. 3. A Plan of the Bay of Porto Praja in the Island of St. Jago, [1772]. *ca1:15,840*. 1 sheet, cm 34 x 39. *Shows* coastline with hills, palm trees, bldgs; sandflats, reefs, soundings.

Photocopy no.6. Adventure Bay, Van Diemens Land, [1773]. *1:63,360*. 1 sheet, cm 28 x 18. *Shows* bay outline with profile of hills; soundings, reefs, anchorage with bearings.

Photocopy no.7. Van Diemens Land on the South Coast of New Holland surveyed by Peter Fannin, Master of His Majesty's Bark *Adventure*, Tobias Furneaux Commander . . . March 1773. *No scale given*. 1 sheet, cm 10 x 47. *Area:* S.W.Cape to Furneaux Islands. *Shows* ship's track, bays and capes with names, latitudes and longitudes. Note on Banks' Strait descr. as a river, bay or entrance.

Photocopy no.8. Cooks Straits New Zealand, [1773]. *No scale given*. 1 sheet, cm 27 x 23, *Shows* coastal outline, islands, names of coves, bays, capes; anchorage in Jacksons Bay, soundings.

Photocopy no.9, sketch no.5. Matavia (*sic*) Bay, [1773]. *No scale given*. 1 sheet, cm 12 x 23. *Shows* coast, reefs, soundings, watering place, Dolphin Bank.

Photocopy no.9, sketch no.2. [Island at Lat.17 00'S. and Long. 142 30'W. 1773.] *No scale given*. 1 sheet, cm 11 x 19. *Area:* Tuamotu Archipelago. *Shows* reef circle with some land, trees; latitude and longitude.

Photocopy no.10, sketch no.2. Isl^d Amsterdam, [1773]. *ca1:177,480*. 1 sheet, cm 21 x 22. *Area:* Tongatapu Island in the Tonga Group. *Shows* island with palms, reef belt, small surrounding islands. Northern part of island not drawn.

Photocopy no.10, sketch no.3. Island of Middleburgh when at anchor here, [1773]. *ca1:177,480*. 1 sheet, cm 21 x 27. *Area:* Eua Island, and Kallau Is., Tonga Group. *Shows* outline of island with mountain ridge, palms, reef belt, anchorage.

CONTENTS: COASTAL PROFILES

Photocopy no.7
- (1.) Thus appear'd the Land to NW of the Mewstone, [Tasmania].
- (2.) The Extreame of the Land in sight appear'd thus as we stood in between the Mewstone and the Main ab^t 3 leag^s of Shore.
- (3.) This shows the Land to E^t of the Mewstone Toward the SE Cape ab^t 3 leag^s Off Shore.
- (4.) Thus appears Maria's Islands and Hills on the Main between them and Schout Islands. [Schouten Is.]
- (5.) Thus appears Furneaux Islands.

Photocopy no. 9
- (1.) [Island at] lat. 17 30' S, long. 141 07' W.
- (3.) The Isl^d from the Mast Head bearing NBW 4 leag: Lat 17 10' S Long. 143 55' W.
- (4.) Island Osnaburgh [Mururoa, Tuamotu Archipelago].
- (6.) The Remarkable appearance of the Little Otahita as you stand into Otapia bay ab^t 3 miles off Shore. [Tahiti].
- (7.) Thus shows Uhena [Huaheine] about 3 leags off Shore.
- (8.) Thus shows Ulitea 3 or 4 miles off Shore. [Raiatea].
- (9.) Otahaw. [Taha].
- (10.) Bolabola. Thus shows both these Islands ab^t 3 leag: Dist from each.
- (11.) Thus shows these 2 small Islands from the Masthead.

Photocopy no. 10
- (1.) Thus appears the Island of Middleburgh ab^t 6 or 7 miles off Shore. [Eua I. Tonga Group].

Copies: NPL:M(PX*D54); ANL.   1333

1776–9 ROBERTS, Henry, *mate*

Prince Edward I. and Marion I., Indian Ocean
Chart: showing tracks of HMS *Resolution* and HMS *Discovery*, 1777, (i.e. 1776).
Coloured. cm 14·5 x 12·5. MS.Q151 p. 7.

Profile: Prince Edward I.
Ink and watercolour. MS.Q151 p. 7.

Kerguelen Island
'Chart of the NE Coast of the Island of Desolation' Dec.1776. showing ship's track, signed 'H.Roberts'.
cm 32·5 x 30. MS.F2 p. 1.

Baie de l'Oiseau, Kerguelen I.
Chart: 'Christmas Harbour, in the Island of Desolation.' Dec.1776. Initialled 'H.R.'
cm 20 x 14·5. MS.Q151 p. 16.

Port Palliser, Kerguelen I.
Chart: 'Sketch of Port Palliser.' 1776.
cm 20 x 17·5. MS.Q151 p. 16.

Mewstone Rock, Tasmania
Profile: 'A View of Van Diemans Land when the Mewstone bears NW b W dist 3 Leagues.' 30 Jan.1777.
Watercolour. MS.Q151 p. 32.

Cape Palliser, New Zealand
Profile: 'Sketch of Cape Palliser bearᵍ. NW by N 3½ leagues' Feb.1777.
Watercolour. MS.Q151 p. 43.

Mangaia, island, Cook Islands
Profile: of Mangaia island, showing two natives in a canoe.
Watercolour. MS.Q151 p. 61.

Chart: Mar.1777.
Coloured. Initialled 'H.R.' cm 18 x 11. MS.Q151 p. 61.

Cook Islands
Chart: showing Manuae ('Hervey's Isles'), Takutea ('Mangea') and Atiu ('Watieu'), with the track of HMS *Resolution* and *Discovery*, Apr.1777.
cm 18·5 x 22·5. MS.Q151 p. 65.

Profile: of island, showing native in outrigger canoe.
Watercolour. MS.Q151 p. 65.

Palmerstone Islands
Rough sketch of a group of islands, 16 Apr. 1777.
Watercolour. MS.Q151 p. 72.

Tonga Islands
Chart: 'Chart of the Friendly Isles.' Signed 'H. Roberts', showing tracks of HMS *Resolution* and *Adventure*, 1777.
Coloured. cm 31 x 19. MS.Q151 p. 95.

Moorea, harbour, Society Islands
Chart: 'Mooreea Harbour in Eimao' Oct.1777.
Coloured. cm 16 x 13. MS.Q151 p. 117.

Kauai, island, Hawaiian Islands
Profile: 'A View of the Anchoring Place at A'toui.' Feb.1778?
Watercolour. MS.Q151 p. 147.

Niihau, island, Hawaiian Islands
Profile: 'View of the Anchoring Place at Oneehow.' Feb.1778. Signed 'Hen^y. Roberts.'
Watercolour. MS.Q151 p. 147.

Nootka Sound, Vancouver Island
Chart: 'Sketch of King George's Sound,' Mar.1778.
Coloured. cm. 21 x 20·5. MS.Q151 p. 179.

Prince Williams Sound and Cook Inlet, Alaska
Chart: showing ship's track, May–June 1778.
cm 44 x 37. MS.F2 p. 2.

Norton Sound, Alaska
Chart: 'Norton Sound'. Sep.1778. Showing track of HMS *Resolution* (?). Initialled 'H.R.'
MS.Q151 p. 249.
Profile: 'Bald Head Bear^g North 2 leagues.'
Watercolour. MS.Q151 p.249.

English Bay, Unalaska, Aleutians
Chart: Shamganooda Harbour in the Island of Oonalascka.' Oct.1778.
Coloured. cm 16 x 19. MS.Q152 p. 2.

Kealakekua Bay, Hawaii, Hawaiian Is.
Chart: 'Ka'ra'ca'ooo'a Bay, in the Island of O'Why'he.' Feb.1779, showing settlements. Initialled 'H.R.'
Coloured. cm 21 x 18·5. MS.Q152 p. 45.

Avacha Bay, Kamchatka
Chart: 'Awatscha Bay.' Oct.1779. Initialled 'H.R.'
cm 21 x 21. MS.Q152 p. 119.

Iwo Jima, island, Kazan Islands
Chart: 'Sulphur Island.'
Nov.1779. cm 13·5 x 12. MS.F2 p. 3.

Bangka Strait, East Indies
MS. copy of 'Plain Chart of Strait of Banca by Capt. Charles Gustavus Ekeberg.'
MS.F2 p. 4.
Copies: NPL:D.

1334

n.d. 'ISLAND of Bonavista, S.W. distant 5 Leagues.' and 'The Island of Bonavista when the Hill A, off which lies a ledge of Rocks bears West 2 Leagues.' Two profile sketches in watercolour wash, possibly by Hodges.

Copies: NPL:D(MS.F1, pp. 53–4; photocopy,MS.F1p.101.)   1335

Charts

Reproductions

The following charts relating to Cook's voyage are contained in his *A Voyage towards the South Pole*. London, W. Strahan and T. Cadell, 1777. The charts have been indexed from the copy in the Mitchell Library at Q980:Co3/2A1–2, and have not been listed for other copies and editions.

A Chart of the Southern Hemisphere; shewing the Tracks of some of the most distinguished Navigators: By Captain James Cook, of his Majesty's Navy. [Engraved by] Gulielmus Whitchurch, 1776. London, Wm. Strahan . . . & Thos. Cadell, Feb.1, 1777. (*Plate No. I*).

No scale given. 1 sheet, cm 50 in diam.
Tables of latitudes and longitudes.
Shows tracks of explorers with dates, coastlines, place names. *Vol. 1, facing p. 1.*

A Chart of the Southern Extremity of America 1775. London, Wm. Strahan . . . & Thos. Cadell, Feb.1, 1777, (*Plate No. II*).

No scale given. 1 sheet, cm 41 x 49.
Inset: Part of Staten Land.
Area: from Cape Blanco to I. Diego Ramirez, from Islands of Direction to Cape Pembroke.
Shows track of *Resolution* with dates, depths in fathoms, anchorage; place names. *Vol.2, facing p. 198.*

Chart of Discoveries made in the South Pacific Ocean in His Majesty's Ship *Resolution* Under the Command of Captain Cook. 1774. Published as the Act directs Feby.12, 1776. Engraved by W. Palmer. London, Wm. Strahan . . . & Thos. Cadell, Feb.1, 1777. (*Plate No. III*).

No scale given. 1 sheet, cm 35 x 45.
Area: from Sandy Is. to Erronan, from Isle of Pines to Cape Cumberland.
Shows coastlines, track of *Resolution*, depths in fathoms, anchorages; place names, hill shading. *Vol. 2, facing p. 210.*

Chart of the Discoveries made in the South Atlantic Ocean, in His Majestys ship *Resolution*, under the Command of Captain Cook in Jany. 1775. [Engraved by] J. Russell. London, Wm. Strahan . . . & Thos. Cadell, Feb.1, 1777. (*Plate No. IV*).

No scale given. 1 sheet, cm 31 x 33.
Area: from Thule to the Isle of Georgia, from Sandwich Land to Willis's Is.
Shows track of *Resolution* with dates, coastlines, depths in fathoms; place names, hill shading. *Vol. 2, facing p. 25.*

Sketch of the Marquesas de Mendoça. [Engraved by] J. Russell. London, Wm. Strahan . . . & Thos. Cadell, Feb.1, 1777. (*Plate No. V*).

ca1: 64,000. 1 sheet, cm 18 x 15.
Inset: Resolution Bay or Port Madre de Dios.
Shows track of *Resolution* with date, depths in fathoms; rivers, hill shading. *Vol. 1, facing p. 305.*

Norfolk Isle. Lat. 29°02′30″S. Longit. 168°16′00″ @ Greenwich. London, Wm. Strahan . . . & Thos. Cadell, Feb.1, 1777. (*Plate No. VI*).

No scale given. 1 sheet, cm 20 x 18.
Shows coastlines, depths in fathoms, track of *Resolution* with date. *Vol. 2, facing p. 147.*

Christmas Sound on the S.W. Coast of Terra (*sic*) del Fuego. London, Wm. Strahan . . . & Thos. Cadell, Feb.1, 1777. (*Plate No. VII*).

1:126,720. 1 sheet, cm 23 x 17.
Area: from Devils Bason (*sic*) to Point Nativity, from Port Clerke to Goose Cove.
Shows coastlines, depths in fathoms, anchorages; place names. *Vol. 2, facing p. 177.*

Sketch of Van Diemen Land, Explored by Captn. Furneaux, in March 1773. [Engraved by] J. Russell. London, Wm. Strahan . . . & Thos. Cadell, Feb.1, 1777. (*Plate No. VIII*).

No scale given. 1 sheet, cm 20 x 13.
Area: from Point Hicks to Swilly Isles, from W. of S.W. Cape to Schoutens Isles.
Shows coastline, track of *Adventure*, depths in fathoms; place names, notes. *Vol. 1, facing p. 115.*

Easter Island. Latitude 27°05′30″S, Longitude 109°46′20″ Wt of Greenwich. [Engraved by] W. Whitchurch, 1776. London, Wm. Strahan . . . & Thos. Cadell, Feb.1, 1777. (*Plate No. IX*).

ca1:108,600. 1 sheet cm 22 x 20.
Shows coastline, depths in fathoms, anchorage; hill shading. *Vol. 1, facing p. 277.*

Port Praya in the Island of St. Jago, one of the Cape de Verds. London, Wm. Strahan . . . & Thos. Cadell, Feb.1, 1777. (*Plate No. X*).

1:15840. 1 sheet, cm 19 x 18.
Shows coastline, depths in fathoms, anchorage, watering place. *Vol. 1, facing p. 8.*

[Charts of harbours in New Caledonia, Tanna and Mallicollo.] London, Wm. Strahan . . . & Thos. Cadell, Feb.1, 1777. (*Plate No. XI*).

Various scales. 1 sheet, 3 maps on cm 26 x 20.
Shows Harbour of Balade in New Caledonia, Port Resolution in the Isle of Tanna; Port Sandwich in Mallicollo; depths in fathoms, anchorages. *Vol. 2, facing p. 38.*

[Sketches of four islands.] London, Wm. Strahan . . . & Thos. Cadell, Feb.1, 1777. (*Plate No. XII*).

Various scales. 1 sheet, 4 maps on cm 25 x 21.
Shows coastlines of: Palmerston Isle, Savage Isle; Turtle Isle, Harvey's Isle, lat. & long. readings, hill shading. *Vol. 2, facing p. 2.*

Sketch of Dusky Bay in New Zealand; 1773. [Engraved by] W. Whitchurch, 1776. London, Wm. Strahan . . . & Thos. Cadell, Feb.1, 1777. (*Plate No. XIII*).

1:126,720. 1 sheet, cm 21 x 38.
Inset: Pickersgill Harbour.
Shows coastline, track of *Resolution*, depths in fathoms, anchorages; place names, lakes, rivers. *Vol. 1, facing p. 92.*

Chart of the Friendly Isles. London, Wm. Strahan . . . & Thos. Cadell, Feb.1, 1777. (*Plate No. XIV*).

No scale given. 1 sheet, cm 19 x 31.
Area: from N. of Comango to Van Diemens Road, from Oghao to Middleburg or Eaoowe.
Shows coastlines, tracks of *Resolution* and *Adventure*, depths in fathoms, anchorages; place names. *Vol. 1, facing p. 191.*

1336

Plate No.15 -"Draught, plan, and Section of the Brittania, a war canoe at Otaheite." (From List of Plates in Vol.I, Page 344 of Cook's 2nd Voyage.

Plate No.16 -"Draught, plan and section of an Amsterdam canoe." (From List of Plates in Vol.I, Page 215 of Cook's 2nd Voyage.

A Map of the world in three sections; describing the Polar Regions to the Tropic in which are traced the tracks of Lord Mulgrave and Captain Cook towards the North and South Poles and the torrid zone or tropical regions with the new discoveries in the South Sea; accurately laid down. London, I. Johnson, January 19, 1778.

No scale given, 1 sheet, cm 30 x 46 (incl.2 hemispheres, cm 14) engr., b./wh.
Inset: The Torrid Zone or tropical regions of the world; in which are accurately laid down the new discoveries in the Pacific Ocean or South Sea.
Shows tracks of Lord Mulgrave, 1775, Cook 1773, 1774 and 1775.
(*In* New discoveries concerning the world, and its inhabitants. London, I. Johnson, 1778, part 1. Frontisp.)
Copies: NPL:M(980/N); NPL:R(09:S909.8A/114). 1338

[1787?] BONNE

Carte des Isles des Amis; [engraved by—André]. Paris, Hôtel de Thou, [1787?].

ca 10 miles = 1″, 1 sheet, 9¼″ x 13½″.
(*In* Bonne *and* Desmarest—Atlas encyclopédique, 1787. Pl. 129.)
Four small inset maps. *Shows* track of Cook's second voyage.
Copies: NPL:M(Q912/B). 1339

[1816?] THOMSON, M.

World on Mercator's projection; [drawn and engraved by M. Thomson]. London, Printed by Barnard and Farley, [1816?].

No scale given, 1 sheet, 7¹/₁₂″ x 9¼″.
(Walker's Universal Atlas [no.26]. 1816.)
Measurements taken from fine line inside heavy border line.
Shows track of Cook's second voyage.
Copies: NPL:M(912/W). 1340

1911 VIDAL DE LA BLACHE, Paul

Pôle sud ou austral: [a chart].

ca1:70,000,000 = 1″, 5¹/₁₂″ x 8¼″.
(*In his* Atlas général. Paris, Librairie A. Colin, 1911. p.53, inset.)
Shows route of Cook's second voyage.

Copies: NPL:R(F912/38).   1341

1944 RUTTER, Owen

The World: tracks of H.M.S. *Resolution*, 1772–5. [Plotted on the outline of part of Admiralty Chart No.673 published in London, April 1944.]

No scale given, 1 sheet, cm 12 x 62, pr., b./wh.
(*In* Sparrman, A.—A Voyage round the world with Captain James Cook in H.M.S. *Resolution;* ed. by O. Rutter. London, Golden Cockerel Press, 1944. Facing p.206.)

Copies: NPL:M(Q980:Co3/S2C1).   1342

1955 BURNEY, James

Adventure Bay, Van Diemens Land. [Reprod. from orig. MSS. in Public Records Office.]

1:50,688, 1 sheet, cm 35 x 22, photoengr., b./wh.
Area: from Cape Frederick Henry to Cookville.
Shows outline of bay, depths, beach, mtns, trees, watering place.
(*In* Beaglehole, J.C.—The Journals of Captain James Cook on his voyages of discovery . . . Charts and Views; ed. by R.A. Skelton. Pub. for the Hakluyt Society. Cambridge, U.P., 1955. Plate no.XXVIII.)

Copies: NPL:M(X980/25).   1343

1955 BURNEY, James

[The SE coast of Van Diemens Land. Reprod. from orig. MSS. in Public Records Office.]

No scale given, 1 sheet, cm 37 x 21, photoengr., b./wh.
Area: from Flinders Is. to S.W. Cape.
Shows track of *Adventure* with depths and bearings, Bass Str. as "Suposd Streights or Passage", place names.
(*In* Beaglehole, J.C.—The Journals of Captain James Cook on his voyages of discovery . . . Charts and Views; ed. by R.A. Skelton. Pub. for the Hakluyt Society. Cambridge, U.P., 1955. Plate no.XXVII.)

Copies: NPL:M(X980/25).   1344

1955 CHART of the Friendly Isles. [Reprod. from orig. MSS. in the Public Records Office.]

No scale given, 1 sheet, cm 21 x 30, photoengr., b./wh.
Area: Tonga Islands excluding Vava'u Group.
Shows islands with names, reefs, islets, track of *Resolution* and *Adventure* in 1773, and track of *Resolution* in 1774, depths.
(*In* Beaglehole, J.C.—The Journals of Captain James Cook on his voyages of discovery . . . Charts and Views; ed. by R.A. Skelton. Pub. for the Hakluyt Society. Cambridge, U.P., 1955. Plate no.XXXV.)

Copies: NPL:M(X980/25).   1345

1955 CHART of the N.E.Coast of New Caledonia. Discovered the 4th Sept. 1774. [Reprod. from orig. MSS. in the British Museum.]

No scale given, 1 sheet, cm 30 x 33, photoengr., b./wh.
Area: incl. Isle of Pines.
Shows N.E. coastline, reefs, ship's track with depth meas.; supposed S.W. coastline; hill shading.
(*In* Beaglehole, J.C.—The Journals of Captain James Cook on his voyages of discovery . . . Charts and Views; ed. by R.A. Skelton. Pub. for the Hakluyt Society. Cambridge, U.P., 1955. Plate no.XXXVIII.)
Copies: NPL:M(X980/25).   1346

1955 CHART of the South Coast of Terra del Fuego and Staten Land. [Reprod. from orig. MSS. in the Public Records Office.]

No scale given, 1 sheet, cm 34 x 50, photoengr., b./wh.
Area: from N. of Desolation Island to Cape St.John.
Shows sketchy coastline with names of capes and bays; ship's track, with depths.
(*In* Beaglehole, J.C.—The Journals of Captain James Cook on his voyages of discovery . . . Charts and Views; ed. by R.A. Skelton. Pub. for the Hakluyt Society. Cambridge, U.P., 1955. Plate no.XL.)
Copies: NPL:M(X980/25).   1347

1955 EASTER Island. [Reprod. from orig. MSS. in British Museum.]

No scale given, 1 sheet, cm 20 x 22, photoengr., b./wh.
Shows ship's tracks, coastline, depths, hill-shading.
(*In* Beaglehole, J.C.—The Journals of Captain James Cook on his voyages of discovery . . . Charts and Views; ed. by R.A. Skelton. Pub. for the Hakluyt Society. Cambridge, U.P., 1955. Plate no.XXXI.)
Copies: NPL:M(X980/25).   1348

1955 GILBERT, Joseph
[Amsterdam, Middleburgh. Reprod. from orig. MSS. in Public Records Office.]

No scale given, 1 sheet, cm 12 x 14, photoengr., b./wh.
Area: Tongatabu and Eua in the Tonga (Friendly) Islands.
Shows ship's track, reefs, rocks, islets, depths.
(*In* Beaglehole, J.C.—The Journals of Captain James Cook on his voyages of discovery . . . Charts and Views; ed. by R.A. Skelton. Pub. for the Hakluyt Society. Cambridge, U.P., 1955. Plate no.XXX.)
Copies: NPL:M(X980/25).   1349

1955 GILBERT, Joseph
Dusky Bay in New Zealand. [Reprod. from orig. MSS. in the Public Records Office.]

ca1: 206,000, 1 sheet, cm 21 x 20, photoengr., b./wh.
Inset: Pickersgill Harbour.
Shows ship's track, coastline, islands in bay, depths.
(*In* Beaglehole, J.C.—The Journals of Captain James Cook on his voyages of discovery . . . Charts and Views; ed. by R.A. Skelton. Pub. for the Hakluyt Society. Cambridge, U.P., 1955. Plate no.XXIX.)
Copies: NPL:M(X980/25).   1350

1955 GILBERT, Joseph

[King George Islands, Tuamotu Archipelago. Reprod. from orig. MSS. in Public Records Office.]

No scale given, 1 sheet, cm 7 x 12, photoengr., b./wh.
Area: Takaroa and Takapoto atolls.
Shows ship's track.
(*In* Beaglehole, J.C.—The Journals of Captain James Cook on his voyages of discovery . . . Charts and Views; ed. by R.A. Skelton. Pub. for the Hakluyt Society. Cambridge, U.P., 1955. Plate no.XXXIII.)
Copies: NPL:M(X980/25).   1351

1955 GILBERT, Joseph

[The Marquesas Islands. Reprod. from orig. MSS. in the Public Records Office.]

No scale given, 1 sheet, cm 8 x 17, photoengr., b./wh.
Inset: Port Resolution, Tahuata Island.
Shows ship's track, hill-shading, place names.
(*In* Beaglehole, J.C.—The Journals of Captain James Cook on his voyages of discovery . . . Charts and Views; ed. by R.A. Skelton. Pub. for the Hakluyt Society. Cambridge, U.P., 1955. Plate No.XXXII.)
Copies: NPL:M(X980/25).   1352

1955 GILBERT, Joseph

[The Marquesas Islands.] Views of Dominica, [Santa] Christina [and] SW part of the Bay when at anchor, [Port Resolution. Apl 6–12 1774. Reprod. from orig. MSS. in the Public Records Office.]

cm 22 x 18, photoengr., b./wh.
(*In* Beaglehole, J.C.—The Journals of Captain James Cook on his voyages of discovery . . . Charts and Views; ed. by R.A. Skelton. Pub. for the Hakluyt Society. Cambridge, U.P., 1955. Plate no.XXXII.)
Copies: NPL:M(X980/25).   1353

1955 GILBERT, Joseph

Norfolk Island. [Reprod. from orig. MSS. in the Public Records Office.]

No scale given, 1 sheet, cm 12 x 17, photoengr., b./wh.
Shows coastline; ship's track; depths in fathoms, hill-shading.
(*In* Beaglehole, J.C.—The Journals of Captain James Cook on his voyages of discovery . . . Charts and Views; ed. by R.A. Skelton. Pub. for the Hakluyt Society. Cambridge, U.P., 1955. Plate no.XXXIX.)
Copies: NPL:M(X980/25).   1354

1955 GILBERT, Joseph

[The Tonga or Friendly Islands, Nomuka group. Reprod. from orig. MSS. in the Public Records Office.]

No scale given, 1 sheet, cm 14 x 18, photoengr., b./wh.
Area: incl. Ha'apai Group.
Shows ship's track, islands with names, reefs, islets.
(*In* Beaglehole, J.C.—The Journals of Captain James Cook on his voyages of discovery . . . Charts and Views; ed. by R.A. Skelton. Pub. for the Hakluyt Society. Cambridge, U.P., 1955. Plate no.XXVI.)
Copies: NPL:M(X980/25).   1355

1955 GILBERT, Joseph
[Two views of Middleburg Island and two views of Amsterdam Island. Oct.1–7 1773. Reprod. from orig. MSS. in the Public Records Office.]
cm 12 x 14, photoengr., b./wh.
(*In* Beaglehole, J.C.—The Journals of Captain James Cook on his voyages of discovery ... Charts and Views; ed. by R. A. Skelton. Pub. for the Hakluyt Society. Cambridge, U.P., 1955. Plate no.XXX.)
Copies: NPL:M(X980/25). 1356

1955 GILBERT, Joseph
[A View of King George Islands, Tuamotu Archipelago. Apl 18 1774. Reprod. from orig. MSS. in the Public Records Office.]
cm 3 x 13, photoengr., b./wh.
(*In* Beaglehole, J.C.—The Journals of Captain James Cook on his voyages of discovery ... Charts and Views; ed. by R.A. Skelton. Pub. for the Hakluyt Society. Cambridge, U.P., 1955. Plate no.XXXIII.)
Copies: NPL:M(X980/25). 1357

1955 GILBERT, Joseph
[A View of Nomuka Island, Tonga Islands. June 25–30 1774. Reprod. from orig. MSS. in the Public Records Office.]
cm 5 x 19, photoengr., b./wh.
(*In* Beaglehole, J.C.—The Journals of Captain James Cook on his voyages of discovery ... Charts and Views; ed. by R.A. Skelton. Pub. for the Hakluyt Society. Cambridge, U.P., 1955. Plate no.XXXVI.)
Copies: NPL:M(X980/25). 1358

1955 GILBERT, Joseph
[Views of the south and north entrances into Dusky Bay, New Zealand. Mar.26–May 11 1772. Reprod. from orig. engraving in the Public Records Office.]
cm 11 x 19, photoengr., b./wh.
(*In* Beaglehole, J.C.—The Journals of Captain James Cook on his voyages of discovery ... Charts and Views; ed. by R.A. Skelton. Pub. for the Hakluyt Society. Cambridge, U.P., 1955. Plate no.XXIX.)
Copies: NPL:M(X980/25). 1359

1955 HERVEY'S ISLES. [Anon. 23 Sept. 1773. Reprod. from orig. MSS. in British Museum.]
No scale given, 1 sheet, cm 6 x 14, photoengr., b./wh.
Area: Manuae and Auotu, Cook Islands.
Shows 2 islands surrounded by reef circle.
(*In* Beaglehole, J.C.—The Journals of Captain James Cook on his voyages of discovery ... Charts and Views; ed. by R.A. Skelton. Pub. for the Hakluyt Society. Cambridge, U.P., 1955. Plate no.XXX.)
Copies: NPL:M(X980/25). 1360

1955 [INSET VIEWS representing Resolution Harbour in the island of Tanna, New Hebrides, Aug.5–20 1774; Sandwich Island, New Hebrides, Jy 26 1774; and Freezeland Peak in the South Sandwich group, Feb.1 1775. Reprod. from orig. MSS. in British Museum.]

cm 36 x 60, photoengr., b./wh.
(*In* Beaglehole, J.C.—The Journals of Captain James Cook on his voyages of discovery . . . Charts and Views; ed. by R.A. Skelton. Pub. for the Hakluyt Society. Cambridge, U.P., 1955. Plate no.XXVI.)
Copies: NPL:M(X980/25).

1361

1955 ISLE OF GEORGIA. [Reprod. from orig. MSS. in British Museum.]

No scale given, 1 sheet, cm 16 x 27, photoengr., b./wh.
Area: South Georgia.
Shows ship's track, with depths, other islands.
(*In* Beaglehole, J.C.—The Journals of Captain James Cook on his voyages of discovery . . . Charts and Views; ed. by R.A. Skelton. Pub. for the Hakluyt Society. Cambridge, U.P., 1955. Plate no.XLI.)
Copies: NPL:M(X980/25).

1362

1955 [PALLISER ISLAND, Tuamotu Archipelago. Reprod. from orig. MSS. in British Museum.]

No scale given, 1 sheet, cm 14 x 22, photoengr., b./wh.
Area: Apataki, Toau, Kaukura and Arutua atolls.
Shows ship's track, reefs.
(*In* Beaglehole, J.C.—The Journals of Captain James Cook on his voyages of discovery . . . Charts and Views; ed. by R.A. Skelton. Pub. for the Hakluyt Society. Cambridge, U.P., 1955. Plate no.XXXIII.)
Copies: NPL:M(X980/25).

1363

1955 PALMERSTONE'S REEF ISLANDS. [Reprod. from orig. MSS. in British Museum.]

No scale given, 1 sheet, cm 7 x 17, photoengr., b./wh.
Area: Palmerston Atoll, Cook Islands.
Shows ship's track, islands with surrounding reefs.
(*In* Beaglehole, J.C.—The Journals of Captain James Cook on his voyages of discovery . . . Charts and Views; ed. by R.A. Skelton. Pub. for the Hakluyt Society. Cambridge, U.P., 1955. Plate no.XXXIV.)
Copies: NPL:M(X980/25).

1364

1955 PART of the Southern Hemispher showing *Resolution*'s track through the Pacific and Southern Ocean. [Reprod. from orig. MSS. in British Museum.]

No scale given, 1 sheet, cm 47 x 60, photoengr., b./wh.
Shows coastlines, track of *Resolution* 1772–1775 with bearings; northern limit of icebergs; place names.
(*In* Beaglehole, J.C.—The Journals of Captain James Cook on his voyages of discovery . . . Charts and Views; ed. by R.A. Skelton. Pub. for the Hakluyt Society. Cambridge, U.P., 1955. Plate no.XXVI.)
Copies: NPL:M(X980/25).

1365

1955 SAVAGE ISLAND. [Reprod. from orig. MSS. in British Museum.]

No scale given, 1 sheet, cm 13 x 14, photoengr., b./wh.
Shows ship's track, coastline.
(*In* Beaglehole, J.C.—The Journals of Captain James Cook on his voyages of discovery
. . . Charts and Views; ed. by R.A. Skelton. Pub. for the Hakluyt Society. Cambridge,
U.P., 1955. Plate no.XXXIV.)
Copies: NPL:M(X980/25). 1366

1955 [THE SOUTH SANDWICH ISLANDS. Reprod. from orig. MSS. in
the British Museum.]

No scale given, 1 sheet, cm 13 x 29, photoengr., b./wh.
Shows ship's track, south coast of islands, hill shading.
(*In* Beaglehole, J.C.—The Journals of Captain James Cook on his voyages of discovery
. . . Charts and Views; ed. by R.A. Skelton. Pub. for the Hakluyt Society. Cambridge,
U.P., 1955. Plate no.XLII.)
Copies: NPL:M(X980/25). 1367

1955 [THREE VIEWS of] Easter Island. [By Cook? Mar.11–17 1774.
Reprod. from orig. MSS. in British Museum.]

cm 12 x 22, photoengr., b./wh.
(*In* Beaglehole, J.C.—The Journals of Captain James Cook on his voyages of discovery
. . . Charts and Views; ed. by R.A. Skelton. Pub. for the Hakluyt Society. Cambridge,
U.P., 1955. Plate no.XXXI.)
Copies: NPL:M(X980/25). 1368

1955 TURTLE REEF AND ISLAND. [Reprod. from orig. MSS. in
British Museum.]

No scale given, 1 sheet, cm 8 x 10, photoengr., b./wh.
Area: Vatoa, Fiji Islands.
Shows outline of island with hill-shading surrounded by reef.
(*In* Beaglehole, J.C.—The Journals of Captain James Cook on his voyages of discovery
. . . Charts and Views; ed. by R.A. Skelton. Pub. for the Hakluyt Society. Cambridge,
U.P., 1955. Plate no.XXXVI.)
Copies: NPL:M(X980/25). 1369

1955 [A VIEW of Cape Bristol, South Sandwich Islands Jan.31–Feb.3
1775. Reprod. from orig. MSS. in British Museum.]

cm 9 x 30, photoengr.
(*In* Beaglehole, J.C.—The Journals of Captain James Cook on his voyages of discovery
. . . Charts and Views; ed. by R.A. Skelton. Pub. for the Hakluyt Society. Cambridge,
U.P., 1955. Plate no.XLII.)
Copies: NPL:M(X980/25). 1370

1955 [A VIEW of Cape Charlotte and Cooper's Isle South Georgia. Jan.16–
24 1775. Reprod. from orig. MSS. in the Public Records Office.]

cm 5 x 28, photoengr., b./wh.
(*In* Beaglehole, J.C.—The Journals of Captain James Cook on his voyages of discovery
. . . Charts and Views; ed. by R.A. Skelton. Pub. for the Hakluyt Society. Cambridge,
U.P., 1955. Plate no.XLI.)
Copies: NPL:M(X980/25). 1371

1955 [A VIEW of] Hervey's Isles [Sept.23 1773. Reprod. from orig. MSS. in British Museum.]

cm 3 x 15, photoengr., b./wh.
(*In* Beaglehole, J.C.—The Journals of Captain James Cook on his voyages of discovery . . . Charts and Views; ed. by R.A. Skelton. Pub. for the Hakluyt Society. Cambridge, U.P., 1955. Plate no.XXX.)
Copies: NPL:M(X980/25). 1372

1955 [A VIEW of Palliser Islands, Tuamotu Archipelago. By Cook? Apl 19 1774. Reprod. from orig. MSS. in British Museum.]

cm 3 x 23, photoengr., b./wh.
(*In* Beaglehole, J.C.—The Journals of Captain James Cook on his voyages of discovery . . . Charts and Views; ed. by R.A. Skelton. Pub. for the Hakluyt Society. Cambridge, U.P., 1955. Plate no.XXXIII.)
Copies: NPL:M(X980/25). 1373

1955 [A VIEW of] Palmestone's Reef Islands. [June 16 1774. Reprod. from orig. MSS. in British Museum.]

cm 5 x 17, photoengr., b./wh.
(*In* Beaglehole, J.C.—The Journals of Captain James Cook on his voyages of discovery . . . Charts and Views; ed. by R.A. Skelton. Pub. for the Hakluyt Society. Cambridge, U.P., 1955. Plate no.XXXIV.)
Copies: NPL:M(X980/25). 1374

1955 [A VIEW of Turtle Reef and Island, Fiji Islands. Jy 1–2 1774. Reprod. from orig. MSS. in British Museum.]

cm 5 x 11, photoengr., b./wh.
(*In* Beaglehole, J.C.—The Journals of Captain James Cook on his voyages of discovery . . . Charts and Views; ed. by R.A. Skelton. Pub. for the Hakluyt Society. Cambridge, U.P., 1955. Plate no.XXXVI.)
Copies: NPL:M(X980/25). 1375

1955 [VIEWS of New] Caledonia when at anchor in Ballarde Harbour; [and] The Isle of Pines the highest part being WbW one Mile. [Sept? 1774. Reprod. from orig. MSS. in British Museum.]

cm 12 x 22, photoengr., b./wh.
(*In* Beaglehole, J.C.—The Journals of Captain James Cook on his voyages of discovery . . . Charts and Views; ed. by R.A. Skelton. Pub. for the Hakluyt Society. Cambridge, U.P., 1955. Plate no.XXXIX.)
Copies: NPL:M(X980/25). 1376

n.d. PETERMANN, A.
Süd-Polar-Karte: [photographic facsimile of] Stieler's Hand-Atlas, No. 42a.

1:40,000,000, 1 sheet, approx. 11$\frac{3}{16}$″ x 13$\frac{5}{8}$″.
Fifteen small inset maps. Measurements taken from outside heavy border line.
Shows the route of Cook's second voyage.
Copies: NPL:M(F8/8). 1377

Illustrations, General
Originals, Including Photocopies of Originals

Originals cannot be reproduced without the permission of the owner.

[PAINTINGS of birds collected on Cook's second voyage; photoprints of originals in the Royal Scottish Museum and the British Museum Print Room.]

63 photoprints.

CONTENTS:

1. Thirty eight coloured Drawings of Birds of the Southern Hemisphere, executed from the Life, in the course of Captain Cook's second voyage.
   Original volume is in the possession of the Royal Scottish Museum, Edinburgh.
2. Natural History Drawings, Various Artists, Banks Collection (Vol.199* B4 ff.7–23, 61–4). [ff.61–4 are unsigned paintings by Gertrude Metz, copies or different versions of ff.17,15,23, and 20. The original volume is in the British Museum Print Room.] The drawings are described in Lysaght, Averil—Some eighteenth century bird paintings in the Library of Sir Joseph Banks (*Bulletin of the British Museum of Natural History, Historical Series*, vol.1, no.6, 1959, pp.310–322, 348.)

Microfilm is at FM3/397.

Copies: NPL:M(B1618).   1378

SMITH, Isaac

Original sketches, drawings, maps etc. [1763–80] collected by Admiral Isaac Smith who served as an officer under Captain James Cook, the circumnavigator, in his first & second voyages, A.D. 1768–1775.

ff.49, 97 drawings.

Title is in the hand of Canon Bennett, a relative of Isaac Smith, from whom the volume was acquired by the Government of New South Wales. MS. contents list is from Isaac Smith's papers. A new contents list and an index have been made and are inserted. Some of the drawings are signed "H.Roberts", "Hen^y Roberts", one is signed "W.H", others are ascribed in Canon Bennett's hand to W.Hodges; presumably this was on the back of the drawings (now pasted down) or may have been noted in pencil, as still apparent in some cases, on the leaves of the volume, as it is not on the MS. contents list. A note at the beginning in Canon Bennett's hand, suggests that some of the unsigned drawings may be by Isaac Smith. Some of the drawings appear to be the originals of the plates to Cook's second voyage. With the exception of two of the first voyage, the drawings probably all belong to the second voyage but some may be of the third. The charts include two by Cook of Newfoundland 1763, one of Charlestown 1780, one of the track of H.M.S. *Perseverance* etc.

The drawings are listed separately hereunder, with the exception of maps, charts and coastal profiles, for which *see* the subhead *Charts*.

CONTENTS:

f.iv   Smith, Isaac— Tegadoo Bay, New Zealand. 23.Octr 1769. Pencil drawing. 9½" x 15¼" inside ruled frame lines. Unsigned. Titled and dated in ink in Canon Bennett's hand on mount, with note 'vide Kipp's Life of Cook p.67'. Note by Bennett at beginning of vol. attributes this to Smith.

f.v   Smith, Isaac— Natural arch. 75' long, 28' broad 45' high, Tegadoo Bay, New Zealand. 1769. Pencil drawing. 10¾" x 16⅞" inside ruled frame lines. Unsigned. Titled as above and dated '23 Oct.1769' in ink on mount in Canon Bennett's hand, with note 'vide Kippis Life of Cook, pp.67.68'. Note by Bennett at beginning of vol. attributes this to Smith.

f.3a   Hodges, William— A View of Port Praya taken from the anchoring place. 1772. Watercolour. 4½" x 10⅞" inside ruled frame lines. Unsigned. Titled in ink below view. Ascribed to William Hodges.

f.10   Hodges, William— Table Mountain, Cape Town. 1771–5? Watercolour. 12¼″ x 18⅝″. Unsigned and undated. Titled in ink on mount and signed 'W.Hodges' in Canon Bennett's hand.

f.11   Hodges, William— Table Mountain, Cape Town. 1771–5? Watercolour. 9¾″ x 20⅞″. Unsigned and undated. Titled in ink on mount in Canon Bennett's hand. In ink upper right corner 'No 11'.

f.12   Hodges, William— Table Mountain, Cape Town. 1771–5? Watercolour. 9⅝″ x 17½″. Unsigned and undated. Titled as above in ink on mount in Canon Bennett's hand. 'No 12' in pencil upper right corner.

f.13   Roberts, Henry— Matavai Bay, Otaheite. 1773. Pen and ink and wash. 12¾″ x 21¼″. Unsigned and undated. Titled as above in ink on mount. 'N 13' in ink upper right corner. Seems to be by the same hand as f.16 which is signed.
        The Same [entitled] View of Matavai Bay and Point Venus Tahiti. Reprod. (*In* The Journals of Captain Cook on his voyages of discovery, ed. by J.C. Beaglehole, vol.2, opp. p.384.)

f.14   Hodges, William— The Otaheite fleet at Appany Bay. 1774. Wash drawing. 14½″ x 21¼″. Signed 'W.H.—74' in ink lower left corner. Titled as above in ink on mount. '14' in ink upper right corner. 'W.Hodges' in ink on mount in Canon Bennett's hand.
        The Same [entitled] War canoes of Tahiti, at Pare. Reprod. (*In* The Journals of Captain Cook on his voyages of discovery, ed. by J.C. Beaglehole, vol.2, opp. p.384.)

f.14b   Diagram of a double canoe seen at Amsterdam in the South Seas. 1774? Pen and ink. 10½″ x 21⅝″ inside ruled frame lines. Unsigned and undated. Explanation on a separate sheet below diagram. Lower left hand corner missing.

f.15   Hodges, William— War canoe, Otaheite. 1774? Wash drawing. 14½″ x 21⅝″. Unsigned and undated. Titled in ink on mount in Canon Bennett's hand. 'W. Hodges' also in ink on mount. In the upper right corner 'N 15'.

f.15a   Hodges, William— Canoes, Otaheite. 1774? Wash drawing. 10⅝″ x 15¾″. Unsigned and undated. Titled as above in ink on mount in Canon Bennett's hand. 'W.Hodges' also written on mount in ink.

f.16   Roberts, Henry— Otaheite, when Point Venus bears S.W. by W. 5 miles distant. 1774? Watercolour. 14¾″ x 21½″. Signed 'H.Roberts' in ink upper right corner. Undated. Titled as above in ink in centre of view. 'N 16' upper right.

f.17   Hodges, William— Potatow, the Otaheite admiral. 1773? Crayon and white drawing. 21″ x 14½″. Unsigned and undated. Titled in ink on mount in Canon Bennett's hand 'Potatow. "The Otaheite Admiral". The original sketch for the finished drawing. Engraved. Second voyage. W.Hodges.'
        The Same [entitled] Potatau, chief of Punaauia. Reprod. (*In* The Journals of Captain Cook on his voyages of discovery, ed. by J.C. Beaglehole, vol.2, opp. p.417, fig.62.)

f.18   Hodges, William— Otaheite native. 1774? Crayon and white drawing. 14¼″ x 10¼″. Unsigned and undated. Title in ink on mount in Canon Bennett's hand 'Otaheite. W.Hodges.'

f.19   Roberts, Henry— West point of Middleburg. 1773. Watercolour. 2⅞″ x 12⅝″ below title. Signed 'Henʸ Roberts' in ink lower right corner. Undated. Title printed in ink below view 'West point of Middleburg N by W four miles'.

f.19a   Hodges, William— Portrait of a native. 177–? Crayon drawing. 21¼″ x 14¾″. Unsigned, untitled and undated. 'W.Hodges' in ink on mount in Canon Bennett's hand.

f.20   Hodges, William— A Large sailing canoe of the Friendly Islands. 1774? Wash drawing. 14⅝″ x 21⅝″. Unsigned and undated. Titled in ink on mount in Canon Bennett's hand. 'W.Hodges' also in ink on mount. In ink upper right corner 'N 20.'

f.21   Hodges, William— A Fishing canoe of the Friendly Islands. 1774? Wash drawing. 10⅝″ x 14⅞″. Unsigned and undated. Titled in ink on mount in Canon Bennett's hand, also 'W.Hodges'. In upper right corner in ink 'N 21'.
        The Same [entitled] Fishing canoe of Tongatapu. Reprod.
        (*In* The Journals of Captain Cook on his voyages of discovery, ed. by J.C. Beaglehole, vol.2, bet. pp.256–7, fig.48.)

f.21a   Diagram of a native canoe. 177–? Pen and ink drawing. 7⅜″ x 21¼″. Unsigned and undated.

f.22   Roberts, Henry— Huaheine, one of the Society Islands. 1773. Wash drawing. 14½″ x 21⅛″. Unsigned and undated. Titled in ink on mount in Canon Bennett's hand.
        The Same [entitled] View of Huahine. Reprod.
        (*In* The Journals of Captain Cook on his voyages of discovery, ed. by J.C. Beaglehole, vol.2, bet. pp.224–5, fig.39.)

f.23   Roberts, Henry— Ulietea, one of the Society Islands. 1773? Wash drawing. 12⅛″ x 21¼″. Unsigned and undated. Titled in ink on mount in Canon Bennett's hand. In ink upper right corner 'N23' and in pencil upper left corner 'Ulietea'.
        The Same [entitled] View of Raiatea. Reprod.
        (*In* The Journals of Captain Cook on his voyages of discovery, ed. by J.C. Beaglehole, vol.2, bet. pp.224–5, fig.41.)

f.24   Roberts, Henry— The Bay of Amsterdam, Friendly Islands. 1773? Wash drawing. 12½″ x 21⅜″. Unsigned and undated. Titled in ink on mount in Canon Bennett's hand. In ink in upper right corner 'N24'.
        The Same. Reprod.
        (*In* The Journals of Captain Cook on his voyages of discovery, ed. by J.C. Beaglehole, bet. pp.256–7, vol.2, fig.46.)

f.24a   Hodges, William— Otago, chief of Amsterdam Island. 1774? Crayon drawing. 21⅛″ x 14¾″. Unsigned and undated. Titled in ink on mount in Canon Bennett's hand 'Otago Chief of Amsterdam Island. Original sketch. Engraved— Second voyage. W.Hodges'.
        The Same [entitled] Ataonga. Reprod.
        (*In* The Journals of Captain Cook on his voyages of discovery, ed. by J.C. Beaglehole, vol.2, opp. p.256, fig.50.)

f.25   Hodges, William— Resolution Bay in the Marquesas. 1774. Wash drawing. 14⅝″ x 21⅜″. Unsigned. Titled and dated in ink on mount 'Resolution Bay in the Marquesas March 1774' in Canon Bennett's hand; also in ink on mount 'Sketch for picture engraved in Second voyage. W.Hodges'. In ink upper right corner 'N25'.

f.25a/a Roberts, Henry— Eimeo as it appears from Matavia (*sic*) Bay, Otaheite. 1774? Watercolour. 8″ x 14¾″. Signed 'H Roberts' in ink lower right corner. Title printed in ink in centre of view.

f.26   Hodges, William— The *Resolution* and *Adventure*, 4 Jan. 1773, taking in ice for water, lat. 61.⁸. 1773. Wash drawing. 15″ x 21⅞″. Unsigned. Titled and dated in ink on mount with 'W.Hodges' in Canon Bennett's hand. 'N 26' in ink along right edge.
        The Same [entitled] H.M.S. *Resolution* taking in ice for water, in the Antarctic seas. Reprod.
        (*Australian Museum Magazine* vol.2, p.225, 1924–5.)

> *The Same* [entitled] The ships watering by taking in ice, in 61° S. Reprod. (*In* The Journals of Captain Cook on his voyages of discovery, ed. by J.C. Beaglehole, vol.2, bet. pp.64–65, fig.15.)

f.27   Hodges, William— Ice Islands, with the *Resolution* in the foreground. 1773–4. Watercolour drawing. 16⅞″ x 12″. Unsigned and undated. Titled 'Ice Islands' in ink on mount in Canon Bennett's hand. 'W.Hodges' also on mount in ink. 'N.–?' written in ink along right edge but partly blotted out.
        The Same [entitled] The *Resolution* in a stream of pack-ice. Reprod.
        (*In* The Journals of Captain Cook on his voyages of discovery, ed. by J.C. Beaglehole, vol.2, bet. pp.64–65. fig.16.)

f.27a   Hodges, William— Ice Island, [with *Resolution*]. 1773–4. Wash and watercolour. 12¾″ x 18¼″. Unsigned and undated. Titled as above and 'W.Hodges' written in ink on mount in Canon Bennett's hand. 'N 27A' in ink upper right corner.
        The Same [entitled] The *Resolution* passing a tabular berg. Reprod.
        (*In* The Journals of Captain Cook on his voyages of discovery, ed. by J.C. Beaglehole, vol.2, bet. pp.64–65, fig.17.)

f.28   Hodges, William— Ice Islands with the *Resolution* and the *Adventure*. 1773–4. Wash and watercolour. 14½″ x 21½″. Unsigned and undated. Titled 'Ice Islands' and signed 'W.Hodges' in ink on mount in Canon Bennett's hand. In upper right corner 'N 28' in ink.
        The Same [entitled] The *Resolution* and *Adventure* among berges. Reprod.
        (*In* The Journals of Captain Cook on his voyages of discovery, ed. by J.C. Beaglehole, vol.2, bet. pp.64–65, fig.18.)

f.29   Hodges, William— Ice Islands. 1773–4. Wash. 10¾″ x 14⅞″. Unsigned and undated. Titled as above and signed 'W Hodges' in ink on mount in Canon Bennett's hand. In ink in upper right corner 'N 29' and writing that is too faint to read.
        The Same [entitled] The *Resolution* in the Antarctic. Reprod.
        (*In* The Journals of Captain Cook on his voyages of discovery, ed. by J.C. Beaglehole, bet. pp.64–65, vol.2, fig.19.)

f.30   Hodges, William— Ice Islands. 1773–4. Watercolour. 13¾″ x 21¾″. Unsigned and undated. Titled as above and signed 'W Hodges' in ink on mount in Canon Bennett's hand. 'N 30' in ink upper right corner.

f.31   Hodges, William— In Dusky Bay, New Zealand. 1773. Watercolour. 15″ x 21⅞″. Unsigned and undated. Titled as above and signed 'W Hodges' in ink on mount in Canon Bennett's hand. In ink upper right corner 'N.32'.
        The Same [entitled] View of Dusky Sound from the sea. Reprod.
        (*In* The Journals of Captain Cook on his voyages of discovery, ed. by J.C. Beaglehole, vol.2, opp. p.128, fig.23.)

f.32a   Hodges, William— View, possibly of Dusky Bay, New Zealand. 1773. Wash. 9″ x 14¾″. Unsigned, untitled and undated. Similar to other views at f.31 and f.32. In ink at upper right corner 'N 32ᴬ'.

f.32b   Hodges, William— Portrait of a Maori. 1773? Crayon. 21¼″ x 14⅛″. Unsigned and undated. Titled 'New Zealand' and signed 'W.Hodges' in ink on mount in Canon Bennett's hand.
        The Same. Reprod.
        (*In* The Journals of Captain Cook on his voyages of discovery, ed. by J.C. Beaglehole, vol.2, bet. pp.128–9. fig.28.)

f.33   Hodges, William— The Island of South Georgia. 1775. Wash drawing. 14½″ x 21¼″. Unsigned and undated. Titled as above and signed 'W.Hodges' in ink on mount in Canon Bennett's hand. 'N33' in ink upper right corner.
        The Same [entitled] View South Georgia 19 January, 1775. Reprod.
        (*In* The Journals of Captain Cook on his voyages of discovery, ed. by J.C. Beaglehole, vol.2, bet. pp.576–7, fig.76.)

f.34   Roberts, Henry— The *Resolution*. 177–? Watercolour. 21¼″ x 15″. Signed 'H
Roberts' in ink in lower right hand corner. Undated. Title and 'H.Roberts' in
ink on mount in Canon Bennett's hand. 'N34' in ink upper right corner.
The Same [entitled] H.M.S. *Resolution*. Reprod.
(*Australian Museum Magazine* vol.2, p.220, 1924–5.)
The Same. Col. reprod.
(*In* The Journals of Captain Cook on his voyages of discovery, ed. by J.C.
Beaglehole, vol.2, frontis.)

f.35   Three native idols. 177–? Wash drawings. 11½″ x 19¾″. Unsigned, untitled and
undated.

f.36   Native weapons. 1770–75. Wash drawings. 14¼″ x 20⅛″ inside ruled frame lines.
Unsigned, undated and untitled.

Copies: NPL:M(PXD11).   1379

SMITH, Isaac

South Sea birds: drawings by Admiral Isaac Smith and others, in the
second voyage of Captain Cook, A.D.1772–1775.

55 plates in 1 vol.

Title is in the hand of Canon Bennett, a relative of Mrs. Cook and of Isaac Smith, from
whom the volume was acquired by the Government of New South Wales. Contents list is
from Isaac Smith's papers. The drawings are not signed. The birds are mostly New
Zealand birds, the remainder being from New Caledonia (*plates 6, 11, 12, 32*) Friendly
Is. (*plates 3, 10*) Norfolk Is. (*plate 3*) Tierra del Fuego (*plates 35, 48, 51-2*) High S. Lat.
(*plates 36-9, 42-4, 49*) Antarctic Regions (*plates 42, 53*) off Cape of Good Hope (*plate 45*)
and New Hebrides? (*plate 24*). Plate 22 is without location. There is also a fish of Cape
de Verde Is. (*plate 55*) and a spruce pine of Isle of Pines (*plate 54*).

T. Iredale ascribes some of the bird drawings to Georg Forster, and describes them all
in his article on Georg Forster's paintings (*Australian Zoologist* vol.4, pp.48-53). Dr. A.
Lysaght states that this attribution is incorrect: *see her* article *Some eighteenth century bird
paintings in the Library of Sir Joseph Banks* (British Museum, Natural History—*Bulletin . . .
Historical Series*, vol.1, no.6, pp.260–62, 310–11, 1959). She describes the bird drawings on
pp.317–22 of this article.

Copies: NPL:M(*D72).   1380

Illustrations, General

Reproductions

The first official publication of the second voyage is entitled, *A Voyage towards the South
Pole, and around the world, performed in His Majesty's Ships the* Resolution *and* Adventure, *in
the years 1772, 1773, 1774 and 1775, written by James Cook . . . In two volumes. Illustrated,
with maps and charts, and a variety of portraits . . . and views . . . drawn during the voyage by
Mr. Hodges and engraved by the most eminent masters*. London, W. Strahan and T. Cadell, 1777.
The set described hereunder (listed in this Bibliography as no.1216, NPL:M Q 980:Co3/
2A3–4) contains 63 engraved and numbered plates, as well as a frontispiece to Vol.1.
Plates nos.1–14 are charts and maps and are listed under the subhead *Charts*. All plates,
except nos.38, 45, 55 and 58, have the imprint "Published Feb.[ry] 1.st 1777 by W.[m]
Strahan in New Street Shoe Lane & Tho.[s] Cadell in the Strand London". These four
plates have been bled, but the imprint has been supplied from the set numbered 1216,
NPL:D Q 77/33–4 in this Bibliography, except for no.38; no set has been sighted
which shows the imprint for this plate.

Plate no.36 has been bled on the outside edge, so that the plate number and engraver's name do not show. These have been supplied from the set numbered 1216, NPL:M Q 980:Co3/2A1–2 in this Bibliography.
Plates nos.17–24 are untitled and titles have been taken from the List of the plates, on pp.xxxvii–xxxix of vol.1. In this list no.59 has been wrongly numbered as 54, but the plate itself has the correct numbering.
Plate no.25 in this set has been misplaced to face p.293 in vol.1, instead of p.291.
Plates in subsequent editions and translations have often been redrawn and engraved by different artists. These are not described in this Bibliography. Plates held by the Mitchell and Dixson Libraries which are extracted from these editions and translations are not listed here, except in the case of portraits, for which *see* the heading—*Personal—Portraits.*

Frontisp. to Vol.1 Captain James Cook, F.R.S. Painted by Wm. Hodges, engraved by J. Basire, 1777.

Oval, 7″ x $5\frac{5}{8}$″. Meas. of engraved surface $10\frac{3}{4}$″ x $5\frac{3}{4}$″. *Vol.1, frontisp.*

No. 15 A Draught plan and section of the Britannia Otehite war canoe, shewing two in the plan. W. Palmer sculp.

Meas. within frame lines $9\frac{3}{8}$″ x $17\frac{5}{8}$″. Meas. of plate mark $10\frac{1}{4}$″ x $18\frac{1}{2}$″. *Vol.1, bet. pp.344 & 345.*

No. 16 A Draught plan & section of an Amsterdam canoe, seen in the South Seas; shewing two in the plan. W. Palmer sculp.

Meas. within frame lines $9\frac{5}{8}$″ x $21\frac{1}{2}$″. Meas. of plate mark $10\frac{5}{16}$″ x $22\frac{1}{4}$″. *Vol.1, bet. pp.214 & 215.*

No. 17 [Ornaments and weapons at the Marquesas.] Chapman, Del. Record sculp.

Meas. of engraved surface and plate mark $8\frac{5}{8}$″ x $7\frac{5}{16}$″. *Vol.1, facing p.311.*

No. 18 [Weapons, &c. at Mallicollo and Tanna.] Cha.[s] Chapman del. Ja.[s] Roberts sculp.

Meas. of engraved surface and plate mark $8\frac{3}{4}$″ x $6\frac{7}{8}$″. *Vol.2, facing p.82.*

No. 19 [Specimens of New Zealand workmanship, &c.] Record, Sculp.

Meas. of engraved surface and plate mark $8\frac{5}{8}$″ x $6\frac{7}{8}$″. *Vol.1, facing p.245.*

No. 20 [Ornaments, weapons &c. at New Caledonia.] Chapman, Del. Record, Sculp.

Meas. of engraved surface and plate mark $8\frac{7}{8}$″ x $14\frac{5}{8}$″. *Vol.2, facing p.120.*

No. 21 [Ornaments, utensils and weapons at the Friendly Isles.] Chapman, Del. Record, Sculp.

Meas. of engraved surface and plate mark $9\frac{1}{8}$″ x 15″. *Vol.1, bet. pp.220 & 221.*

No. 22 [Tea plant of New Zealand.]

Meas. of engraved surface and plate mark $8\frac{5}{8}$″ x 7″. *Vol.1, facing p.100.*

No. 23 [Flax plant of New Zealand.]

Meas. of engraved surface and plate mark $14\frac{11}{16}$″ x $8\frac{7}{8}$″. *Vol.1, bet. pp.96 & 97.*

No. 24 [Plant used at Otaheite to catch fish by intoxicating them.]

Meas. of engraved surface and plate mark $14\frac{7}{8}$″ x $8\frac{15}{16}$″. *Vol.1, bet. pp.156 & 157.*

No. 25 Woman of Easter Island. Drawn from nature by W. Hodges. Engraved by J. Caldwall.

Meas. of engraved surface $8\frac{7}{8}''$ x $6\frac{15}{16}''$. Meas. of plate mark $10\frac{1}{8}''$ x $7\frac{1}{2}''$. *Vol.1, facing p.293.*

No. 26 Man of the Island of Tanna. Drawn from nature by W. Hodges. Engrav'd by J. Basire.

Meas. within frame lines $9\frac{1}{8}''$ x $7''$. *Vol.2, facing p.78.*

No. 27 Man in Christmas Sound, Tierra del Fuego. Drawn from nature by W. Hodges. Engrav'd by J. Basire.

Meas. within frame lines $9''$ x $7''$. *Vol.2, facing p.183.*

No. 28 Afia-too-ca, a burying place in the Isle of Amsterdam. Drawn from nature by W. Hodges. Engrav'd by W. Byrne.

Meas. of view $8\frac{9}{16}''$ x $15\frac{1}{16}''$. Meas. of plate mark $10\frac{1}{4}''$ x $15\frac{15}{16}''$. *Vol.1, bet. pp.200 & 201.*

No. 29 View in the Island of Tanna. Drawn from nature by W. Hodges. Engrav'd by W. Woollett.

Meas. of view $8\frac{3}{16}''$ x $14\frac{3}{4}''$. Meas. of plate mark $9\frac{1}{2}''$ x $15\frac{1}{4}''$. *Vol.2, facing p.63.*

No. 30 The Ice Islands, seen the 9th of Jan.ry 1773. Drawn from nature by W. Hodges. Engrav'd by B.T. Pouncy.

Meas. of view $8\frac{5}{8}''$ x $14\frac{7}{8}''$. Meas. of plate mark $9\frac{3}{4}''$ x $15\frac{7}{8}''$. *Vol.1, bet. pp.36 & 37.*

No. 31 View in the Island of Pines. Drawn from nature by W. Hodges. Engrav'd by W. Byrne.

Meas. of view $8\frac{7}{8}''$ x $15''$. Meas. of plate mark $10\frac{3}{8}''$ x $16\frac{1}{4}''$. *Vol.2, facing p.135.*

No. 32 Christmas Sound, Tierra del Fuego. Drawn from nature by W. Hodges. Engrav'd by W. Watts.

Meas. of view $8\frac{5}{8}''$ x $14\frac{3}{8}''$. Meas. of plate mark $9\frac{7}{8}''$ x $15\frac{1}{2}''$. *Vol.2, facing p.185.*

No. 33 Resolution Bay in the Marquesas. Drawn from nature by W. Hodges Engrav'd by B. T. Pouncy.

Meas. of view $8\frac{3}{4}''$ x $14\frac{3}{8}''$. Meas. of plate mark $9\frac{3}{8}''$ x $15\frac{3}{16}''$. *Vol.1, bet. pp.306 & 307.*

No. 34 Possession Bay in the Island of South Georgia. Drawn from nature by W. Hodges. Engrav'd by S. Smith.

Meas. of view $8\frac{3}{8}''$ x $14\frac{3}{4}''$. Meas. of plate mark $9\frac{3}{8}''$ x $15\frac{7}{16}''$. *Vol.2, facing p. 212.*

No. 35 O-Hedidee. Drawn from nature by W. Hodges. Engrav'd by J. Caldwall.

Meas. of engraved surface $9\frac{5}{8}''$ x $7''$. Meas. of plate mark $10\frac{3}{16}''$ x $7\frac{7}{8}''$. *Vol.1, facing p.375.*

[No. 36] The Chief at S.ta Christina. Drawn from nature by W. Hodges. Engrav'd [by J. Hall].

Meas. within frame lines $9''$ x $7\frac{15}{16}''$.
Plate number and engraver's name from the copy listed in this Bibliography as no. 1216, NPL:M Q 980:Co3/2A1–2. *Vol.1, facing p.310.*

No. 37 Woman of S.ta Christina. [Drawn from] nature by W. Hodges. Engrav'd by J. Hall.

Meas. within frame lines $9''$ x $7\frac{3}{16}''$. *Vol.1, facing p.309.*

No. 38 Otoo King of O-Taheite. Drawn from nature by W. Hodges. Engrav'd by J. Hall.

Meas. within frame lines 8 $\frac{13}{16}$" x 7 $\frac{1}{8}$". *Vol.1, facing p.154.*

No. 39 Man of New Caledonia. Drawn from nature by W. Hodges. Engrav'd by Aliamet.

Meas. within frame lines 9" x 7". *Vol.2, facing p.119.*

No. 40 Otago. Drawn from nature by W. Hodges. Engrav'd by J.K. Sherwin.

Meas. of engraved surface 9 $\frac{1}{16}$" x 7 $\frac{1}{4}$". *Vol.1, facing p.197.*

No. 41 Tynai-mai. Drawn from nature by W. Hodges. Engrav'd by J.K. Sherwin.

Meas. of engraved surface 8 $\frac{15}{16}$" x 6 $\frac{13}{16}$". Meas. of plate mark 10 $\frac{1}{4}$" x 7 $\frac{3}{4}$". *Vol.1, facing p.368.*

No. 42 Boats of the Friendly Isles. Drawn from nature by W. Hodges. Engraved by W. Watts.

Meas. of view 8 $\frac{5}{8}$" x 14 $\frac{3}{8}$". Meas. of plate mark 9 $\frac{7}{8}$" x 15 $\frac{13}{16}$". *Vol.2, facing p.18.*

No. 43 A View in the Island of Rotterdam. Drawn from nature by W. Hodges. Engrav'd by W. Byrne.

Meas. of view 9" x 15 $\frac{1}{16}$". Meas. of plate mark 10 $\frac{1}{2}$" x 15 $\frac{3}{4}$". *Vol.2, facing p.9.*

No. 44 A Toupapow with a corpse on it attended by the chief mourner in his habit of ceremony. Drawn from nature by W. Hodges. Engrav'd by W. Woollett.

Meas. of engraved surface 8 $\frac{7}{16}$" x 14 $\frac{3}{4}$". Meas. of plate mark 9 $\frac{3}{8}$" x 15 $\frac{1}{4}$". *Vol.1, bet. pp.184 & 185.*

No. 45 Woman of the Island of Tanna. Drawn from nature by W. Hodges. Engrav'd by J. Basire.

Meas. within frame lines 8 $\frac{15}{16}$" x 6 $\frac{15}{16}$". *Vol.2, facing p.80.*

No. 46 Man of Easter Island. Drawn from nature by W. Hodges. Engrav'd by F. Bartolozzi.

Meas. of engraved surface 8 $\frac{9}{16}$" x 7". *Vol.1, facing p.290.*

No. 47 Man of the Island of Mallicolo. Drawn from nature by W. Hodges. Engrav'd by J. Caldwall.

Meas. within frame lines 8 $\frac{13}{16}$" x 6 $\frac{15}{16}$". *Vol.2, facing p.34.*

No. 48 Woman of New Caledonia. Drawn from nature by W. Hodges. Engrav'd by J. Hall.

Meas. within frame lines 9" x 7". *Vol.2, facing p.120.*

No. 49 Monuments in Easter Island. Drawn from nature by W. Hodges. Engraved by W. Woollett.

Meas. of engraved surface 8 $\frac{7}{16}$" x 14 $\frac{13}{16}$". Meas. of plate mark 9 $\frac{1}{2}$" x 15 $\frac{1}{4}$". *Vol.1, bet. pp.294 & 295.*

No. 50 View in the Island of New Caledonia. Drawn from nature by W. Hodges. Engraved by W. Byrne.

Meas. of view $9\frac{1}{8}''$ x $15\frac{1}{4}''$. Meas. of plate mark $10\frac{11}{16}''$ x $16\frac{3}{8}''$. *Vol.2, facing p.110.*

No. 51 The Spruce fir of New Zealand.

Meas. within frame lines $8\frac{1}{16}''$ x $6\frac{3}{8}''$. Meas. of plate mark $9\frac{5}{16}''$ x $7\frac{3}{8}''$. *Vol.1, facing p.70.*

No. 52 Poe-bird, New-Zeeland.

Meas. of engraved surface $8\frac{1}{4}''$ x $6\frac{9}{16}''$. Meas. of plate mark $8\frac{5}{8}''$ x $6\frac{7}{8}''$. *Vol.1, facing p.97.*

No. 53 The Island of Otahiete bearing S.E. distant one league. Painted by W. Hodges. Engrav'd by W. Watts.

Meas. of view $9\frac{1}{4}''$ x $18\frac{7}{16}''$. Meas. of plate mark $10\frac{1}{2}''$ x $19\frac{9}{16}''$. *Vol.1, facing p.181.*

No. 54 The Landing at Middleburgh one of the Friendly Isles. Painted by W. Hodges. Engrav'd by J.K. Shirwin [i.e. Sherwin].

Meas. of view $9\frac{3}{16}''$ x $18\frac{5}{8}''$. Meas. of plate mark $10\frac{3}{4}''$ x $20\frac{5}{16}''$. *Vol.1, bet. pp.192 & 193.*

No. 55 Man of New Zealand. Drawn from nature by W. Hodges. Engrav'd by Michel.

Meas. within frame lines $9''$ x $8\frac{3}{16}''$. *Vol.2, facing p.152.*

No. 56 Potatow. Drawn from nature by W. Hodges. Engraved by I. Hall.

Meas. within frame lines $8\frac{15}{16}''$ x $7\frac{1}{16}''$. *Vol.1, facing p.159.*

No. 57 Omai. Drawn from nature by W. Hodges. Engraved by J. Caldwall.

Meas. of engraved surface $8\frac{15}{16}''$ x $6\frac{7}{8}''$. *Vol.1, facing p.169.*

No. 58 Woman of New Zealand. Drawn from nature by W. Hodges.

Meas. within frame lines $8\frac{13}{16}''$ x $6\frac{13}{16}''$. No engraver's name given. *Vol.2, facing p.152.*

No.59 The Landing at Tanna one of the New Hebrides. Painted by W. Hodges. Engraved by J.K. Sherwin.

Meas. of view $9\frac{1}{4}''$ x $18\frac{1}{2}''$. Meas. of plate mark $10\frac{3}{4}''$ x $19\frac{3}{16}''$. *Vol.2, facing p.54.*

No. 60 The Landing at Mallicolo, one of the New Hebrides. Painted by W. Hodges. Engrav'd by J. Basire.

Meas. of view $9\frac{15}{16}''$ x $18\frac{1}{4}''$. Meas. of plate mark $11\frac{1}{16}''$ x $19''$. *Vol.2, facing p.30.*

No. 61 The Fleet of Otaheite assembled at Oparee. Painted by W. Hodges. Engraved by W. Woollett.

Meas. of view $8\frac{3}{8}''$ x $14\frac{13}{16}''$. Meas. of plate mark $9\frac{5}{8}''$ x $15\frac{5}{8}''$. *Vol.1, bet. pp.342 & 343.*

No. 62 The Landing at Erramanga one of the New Hebrides. Painted by W. Hodges. Engraved by J.K. Sherwin.

Meas. of view $9\frac{5}{16}''$ x $18\frac{1}{4}''$. Meas. of plate mark $10\frac{15}{16}''$ x $19\frac{3}{8}''$. *Vol.2, facing p.46.*

No. 63 Family in Dusky Bay, New Zealand. Drawn from nature by W. Hodges. Engrav'd by Lerperniere.

Meas. of view $8\frac{1}{2}''$ x $13\frac{13}{16}''$. Meas. of plate mark $9\frac{3}{4}''$ x $14\frac{3}{4}''$. *Vol.1, bet. pp.74 & 75.*

1381

[177–] COLLECTION of various editions of engravings of Captain Cook's second voyage.

22 engravings

Copies: NPL:D(DLPX20). 1382

1947 REYNOLDS, Graham

Captain Cook's draughtsmen; [with reproductions of illustrations, and map].

(*Geographical Magazine* vol.19, pp.457–66, Feb. 1947.)

Copies: NPL:R(S909.5A/5). 1383

Illustrations Arranged by Artist

FANNIN, PETER

Originals, Including Photocopies of Originals

A COLLECTION of drawings and charts made by Peter Fannin, Master of the *Adventure* during Capt. Cook's second voyage, 1772–1775, with the additions of an anonymous drawing of Adventure Bay, Van Diemen's Land, during Capt. Cook's third voyage 1776–1780. [11 photocopies, some in colour, of originals in the Naval Historical Branch, Ministry of Defence, London]. Stewkley, Bedfordshire, Eng., A.L.Faber (Microfilm) Ltd., 1965.

10 sheets in portfolio, 16″ x 11½″.

Photocopy no. 1 gives cover title of original album.

Photocopy no. 2 gives facs. of a note found in the album, which reads in part: "Sketches and charts drawn on Cook: 2nd Voyage, by Fannin as Master of HMS *Adventure* (Captain T. Furneaux)."

The portfolio contains the following views, all by Fannin, except no. 11, which is anonymous.

Photocopy no. 4, A south side view of Porto Praja from the Island Port. Meas. within frame lines 10¼″ x 17¾″.

Photocopy no. 5, [Coloured drawing of the *Adventure* and *Resolution* with Icebergs in the background.] Meas. within frame lines 7⅛″ x 9⅝″.

Photocopy no. 6, [Adventure Bay, Van Diemen's Land. Map, and coloured drawings of Fauna.] Meas. within frame lines 10⅛″ x 18⅞″.

Photocopy no. 10d, [Coloured drawing of a flying fox.]

Photocopy no. 11, Captain Cook's interview with natives in Adventure Bay, Van Diemen's Land, January 29, 1777. Meas. of view 13¼″ x 18¾″.

For the maps and coastal profiles on photocopies nos. 6,7,8,9 and 10 *see back* under the subhead *Charts*.

Copies: NPL:M(PX*D54); ANL. 1384

FORSTER, JOHANN REINHOLD

Originals, Including Photocopies of Originals

CHARACTERES generum plantarum, quas in itinere ad insulas Maris Australis, collegerunt, descripserunt, delinearunt, annis MDCCLXXII–

MDCCLXXV. Joannes Reinoldus Forster et Georgius Forster. [Plates, with descriptive text.] Londini, B. White, T. Cadell, & P. Elmsly, 1776.

Plates 75 [i.e.78], pp.[xii], viii, [ii], 150, [ii]. A. Sparrman described the plants, G. Forster drew them and J.R. Forster supervised the whole. (*See* Holmes, nos.17,18.) The Mitchell Library holds a copy with hand-coloured plates. A folio edition was also issued in the same year, with collation: plates 75, [i.e. 78], pp.viii, viii [i.e. iv], [77]. *See also* no.1386.

Copies: NPL:M(Q 581.99; F581.99); NPL:D(Q 77/39); NPL:R(09:Q 581.99/7); ANL.

1385

JOHANN REINHOLD FORSTER'S und Georg Forster's Beschreibungen der Gattungen von Planzen, auf einer Reise nach den Inseln der Süd-see, gesammelt, beschrieben und abgezeichnet während den Jahren 1772 bis 1775. Stuttgardt, Mäntler, 1779.

1 vol. (various pagination), 18 plates. Translated from the Latin Characteres generum plantarum quas in itinere ad insulas Maris Australis, *see* no.1385.

Copies: ANL.

1386

HODGES, WILLIAM
Originals, Including Photocopies of Originals

[CRAYON drawings of the National Maritime Museum, Greenwich, on indefinite loan to the National Library of Australia.]

CONTENTS:

Man of Amsterdam.
Crayon drawing 21¾″ x 14¾″. Titled "Amsterdam"; unsigned.

Man of Easter Island.
Crayon drawing 21½″ x 14½″. Titled "Easter Island"; unsigned. Engraving by F. Bartolozzi in Cook's *A Voyage towards the South Pole* . . . London, 1777. pl.46.

Man of New Caledonia, full-face and profile.
Crayon drawing 21¼″ x 15″. Titled "New Caledonia"; unsigned. Engraving by Aliamet in Cook's *A Voyage towards the South Pole* . . . London, 1777. pl.39.

Man of New Caledonia, with pale head-dress.
Crayon drawing 21¾″ x 14¾″. Titled "New Caledonia"; unsigned.

Man of New Zealand, with long hair and cloak.
Crayon drawing 21¾″ x 14¾″. Titled "New Zeland" (*sic*); unsigned.

Man of New Zealand, tattooed.
Crayon drawing 21½″ x 14¾″. Titled "New Zeland" (*sic*); unsigned. Engraving by Michel in Cook's *A Voyage towards the South Pole* . . . London, 1777. pl.55.

Man of Otaheite, with long hair, beard and moustache.
Crayon drawing 21½″ x 14¾″. Titled "Otaheite"; unsigned.

Man of Otaheite, with white beard.
Crayon drawing 21½″ x 14¾″. Titled "Otaheite"; unsigned.

Man of Otaheite, clean-shaven.
Crayon drawing 21¾″ x 14¾″. Untitled; unsigned.

Man of Tanna.
Crayon drawing 21½″ x 14¾″. Titled "Tanna"; unsigned. Engraving by J. Basire in Cook's *A Voyage towards the South Pole* . . . London, 1777. pl.26.

Oedidee, Otaheite.
Crayon drawing 21½″ x 15″. Titled; unsigned. Engraving by J. Caldwall in Cook's *A Voyage towards the South Pole* . . . London, 1777. pl.35.

Old man of New Zealand.
Crayon drawing 21½″ x 15″. Titled "New Zeland" (*sic*); unsigned.

Otoo King of Otaheite.
Crayon drawing 21½″ x 14¾″. Titled; unsigned. Engraving by J. Hall in Cook's *A Voyage towards the South Pole* . . . London, 1777. pl.38.

Woman of Easter Island.
Crayon drawing 21½″ x 14¾″. Titled "Easter Island"; unsigned. Engraving by J. Caldwall in Cook's *A Voyage towards the South Pole* . . . London, 1777. pl.25.

Woman of New Caledonia.
Crayon drawing 21¾″ x 14¾″. Titled "New Caledonia"; unsigned. Engraving by J. Hall in Cook's *A Voyage towards the South Pole* . . . London, 1777. pl.48.

Woman of New Zealand.
Crayon drawing 21½″ x 14¾″. Titled "New Zealand"; unsigned.

Woman of Otaheite.
Crayon drawing 21¼″ x 14¾″. Titled "Otaheite"; unsigned.

Woman of the island of Tanna.
Crayon drawing 21½″ x 14¾″. Titled "Tanna"; unsigned. Engraving by J. Basire in Cook's *A Voyage towards the South Pole* . . . London, 1777. pl.45.

Copies: ANL.   1387

[LANDING at Middleburgh, one of the Friendly Islands.]

Unfinished watercolour. 7″ x 18⅛″ pasted on mount. Unsigned; undated. One section in the lower half of the drawing has been torn roughly, superimposed and pasted together. This section is more sketchy than the rest, the sky and background on the left being only faintly suggested. The tear has left two figures in the boat on the left without the upper parts of their bodies. There is no doubt, however, that this is a sketch, probably by Hodges, for the scene shown in plate no. 54 in the first official account *A Voyage towards the South Pole and around the world.* For a description of the engraving *see* item no.1381 in this Bibliography.
(*In* [Three voyages round the world]. Plate no.52a).
Copies: NPL:M(PXD59⁻¹).   1388

THE LANDING of Capt.ⁿ Cook &c. at Middleburgh, one of the Friendly Isles.

London, Published as the Act directs, by Alexʳ Hogg, at the Kings Arms, Paternoster Row. Engraving. Meas. of engraved surface 7 15/16″ x 12⅝″. Meas. of plate mark 9⅜″ x 14 5/16″. Hand-coloured.
Copies: NPL:D(DLPX20).   1389

MARQUESAS: [portrait of an islander, presumably by W. Hodges].

Photo of red chalk drawing. 9½″ x 7½″.
The original has red watercolour frame lines and measures 8⅞″ x 7 1/16″ (drawing) and 11⅛″ x 9⅛″ (with border). Title as above is lettered within frame lines.
The original owned by B.Weinreb, Esq., 1958, was offered at Sotheby's sale 10th November 1965 as lot 91. Appears to be the original of the engraving The Chief of Sta Christina, in the official account of Cook's second voyage, 3rd ed., vol.1, opp. p.310, and for this reason is attributed to Hodges.
Copies: NPL:M(Small Picture File: Marquesas Islands).   1390

NEGATIVES of paintings by Westall, Hodges and Webber at the Admiralty and the National Maritime Museum, Greenwich.

See no. 1826.

SOUTH SEA islander.

Pen-and-ink drawing. 4″ x 3¾″ pasted in mount.
Untitled; signed.
Copies: ANL.   1391

SOUTH SEA islanders.

3 oil paintings. 3⅞″ x 2 5/16″, 3⅞″ x 2½″, 5½″ x 4⅞″ on one mount. Note in blue pencil on back of mount states 'painted on ship's canvas'.
Title followed by 'Webber' written in pencil at bottom of mount and note re Cook reference on right-hand side. These two notes may be in a former library officer's hand. The largest painting has inscription in pencil in lower left-hand corner, which seems to read '434 (or 424 or 494) J. Webber.' It is similar to a plate in Cook's second voyage, vol.2, opp. p.152, titled 'Man of New Zealand' which is captioned 'Drawn from nature by W. Hodges'.
Also on back of mount in pencil '494'.
Copies NPL:M(SSV*/MAO/1).   1392

Photoprint; (Govt. Pr. neg. no.49646).

Copies: NPL:M(Small Picture File—Maoris).   1393

SOUTH SEA man and woman.

Pencil drawing. 9⅝″ x 6½″ pasted in mount. Untitled; signed.
Copies: ANL.   1394

TABLE BAY.

Negative of a painting in the residence of the First Lord of the Admiralty, Whitehall. Not to be reproduced without acknowledgement to the Trustees of the National Maritime Museum and to the Admiralty. *See* corres. 277/1955.
Copies: NPL:M(FM2/123).   1395

TONGATABU or Amsterdam.

Watercolour painting. 14⅞″ x 21½″. Titled; unsigned.
Engraving by W. Byrne in Cook's *A Voyage towards the South Pole* . . . London, 1777. Plate 43.
Copies: ANL (Nan Kivell).   1396

TWO STUDIES from life of South Sea islanders.

Oil painting. 4⅛″ x 5⅝″ pasted in mount. Untitled; signed.
Copies: ANL.   1397

[VIEW of William Fehr's home at Cape Town, 1958, showing to the left of the cupboard a painting by William Hodges of Table Bay, 1772.]
Photograph. 7¼″ x 9¾″.
NPL:M(Small Picture File). 1398

Reproductions

CANOES of Tahiti in 1773. [Reproduction in colour, from original in the National Maritime Museum, Greenwich.]
(*Geographical Magazine* Dec. 1956, p. 379.)
Copies: NPL:R(S909.5A/5). 1399

THE LANDING at Erramanga, one of the New Hebrides.
The engraving was first published as plate no.62 in A *Voyage toward the South Pole and around the world . . . 1772, 1773, 1774 and 1775*, pub. 1777. For a description *see* item no.1381 in this Bibliography.

The Same [entitled] Landing op het eiland Erramanga, een van de Nieuwe Hebriden.
Proof before letters. Meas. within frame lines 7 15/16″ x 17 11/16″.
Meas. of plate mark 9¼″ x 19¼″.
Copies: NPL:M(V*Cook 27). 1400

THE LANDING at Mallicolo, one of the New Hebrides.
The engraving was first published as plate no.60 in A *Voyage toward the South Pole and around the world . . . 1772, 1773, 1774 and 1775*, pub. 1777. For a description *see* item no. 1381 in this Bibliography.

The Same.
Proof before letters. Meas. of engraved surface 9¼″ x 17¾″. Meas. of plate mark 11″ x 16¼″.
Copies: NPL:M(V*Cook 25). 1401

The Same [entitled] The Landing of Captn Cook, &c. at Mallicolo, one of the New Hebrides.
London, Published as the Act directs, by Alex^r Hogg, at the Kings Arms N° 16 Paternoster Row. Engraving. Meas. of engraved surface 8⅛″ x 12 9/16″. Meas. of plate mark 9⅜″ x 14 5/16″.
Hand-coloured.
Copies: NPL:D(DLPX20). 1402

THE LANDING of Captn Cook &c. at Tanna, one of the New Hebrides.
Engraving. Meas. of engraved surface 8 1/16″ x 12 7/16″. Meas. of plate mark 9⅜″ x 14 5/16″.
Hand-coloured.
The engraving was first published as plate no.59 in A *Voyage toward the South Pole and around the world . . . 1772, 1773, 1774 and 1775*, pub. 1777. For a description *see* item no. 1381 in this Bibliography.
Copies: NPL:D(DLPX20). 1403

PLATES to Cook's second voyage, comprising a portrait and 35 views. London, 1776–7.

Plates 36.
Plates bear the imprint of W. Strahan and T. Cadell, or *Printed as the Act directs*, and are dated 1776 or 1777. Printed on large thick paper. Plates are titled but not numbered. The volume is bound half red leather with marbled boards. Spine lettered *Plates to Cook's second voyage*.
Copies: NPL:D(F77/2). 1404

Another Set; [comprising portrait, 37 views and 25 proofs of some of the views].

Plates 63, foliated 1-61.
Reputed to be one of six sets for persons connected with the Admiralty. The twenty-five proofs are mostly unlettered, and there are sometimes two proofs of the same print. All are mounted. The volume is bound in half-calf with marbled boards, and is lettered on spine *Cap. Cook. 2nd voyage*. Cuttings from the catalogues of Saville's sale 1833 and Baker's sale 1855 are inserted.
Copies: NPL:D(F77/3). 1405

Another Set; [comprising the Hodges portrait of Cook, and maps and plates numbered 1–63].

Bound in half-calf, with one coloured lettering-piece, lettered *Cook's voyages-plates*. Also included in the volume are the Dance portrait of Cook, a general chart, a set of the Webber views and one proof.
Copies: NPL:D(F77/4). 1406

Another Set; [comprising the Hodges portrait of Cook, and maps and plates numbered 1–63].

Bound in [South Sea voyages: atlas].
Copies: NPL:D(F77/5). 1407

RESOLUTION BAY, in the Marquesas. Engraved by G. Cooke.

London, published by Longman, Hurst, Rees, Orme & Brown Feb.ʸ 1, 1812.
Meas. within frame lines 5″ x 8″. Meas. of plate mark 8½″ x 10½″.
The engraving was first published as plate no.33 in *A Voyage towards the South Pole and around the world*, listed in this Bibliography as no. 1381.
Copies: NPL:M(SSV*Cook 5). 1408

1965 BRADLOW, Frank R.
The William Hodges picture of Table Bay; [With photographic reproduction of a water-colour in the William Fehr Collection, Rust en Vreugd, Cape Town, and of an aquatint in the Africana Museum.]
(*Africana Notes and News* vol. 16, no. 8, Dec. 1965, pp. 316-21.)
Xerox copy.
Copies: NPL:M(980:Co3/B1A1). 1409

ARTIST UNKNOWN
Reproductions

THE POA bird.

1776. Coloured mezzotint. Meas. of plate mark 13⅞" x 9⅞".

Titled on back with inscription "Given by Capt. Cook the Circumnavigator to Robt Laurie—who invented the art of Printing in Oil Colours—of which this plate was the first specimen—and he received from the Society of Arts in The Adelphi a premium and a medal for the same."

There are further MS. notes in a different hand on back, and also signature "A.W.F. Fuller 19 Novr 1936". Collector's mark of late 18th century in lower left-hand corner. Notes re mezzotint by P. Mander Jones 1960 and a letter from R.S. Arts filed at NPL:M PXn 122.

A copy of inscription and further MS. notes in pencil on the Lauries also filed at this number.

Presented by Mrs. E. Fuller in memory of her husband Capt. A.W.F. Fuller, 1963.

Plate no.52 in the first official account of the second voyage, (*see* no.1381) is titled Poebird, New Zealand. It differs markedly from the present mezzotint, which however could have been based on it or on a common original drawing.

Copies: NPL:M(SV*Birds- N.Z.2).   1410

Negs. of mezzotint and notes.

Copies: NPL:M(Glass Negs. 26 no.1–2).   1411

Photograph of mezzotint and notes.

Copies: NPL:M(Small Picture File: Turi).   1412

The Same [entitled] The Poa. From the bird which was brought back from New Zeeland (*sic*) by Capt Cook in his late voyage round the world. And which obtained of the Society of Artists a premium of 30 guineas. R. Laurie, del. et fec^t.

London, published by J.Sharpe . . . June 1; 1784. Engraving. Hand-coloured. Meas. of engraved surface and plate mark, 14" x 9$\frac{13}{16}$".

Copies: NPL:D(DLPf62).   1413

Ships
Illustrations
Originals, Including Photocopies of Originals

Originals cannot be reproduced without the permission of the owner.

Illustrations which show the *Resolution* alone are included under the above subheading, unless definitely connected with the third voyage.

A drawing of the *Resolution* and several other drawings which show the *Resolution* and the *Adventure* are contained in the volume of original sketches, maps, etc., compiled by Admiral Isaac Smith and numbered 1379 in this Bibliography. For descriptions of these drawings *see back* under the subhead *Second Voyage—Illustrations,General—Originals, Including Photocopies of Originals. See* no. 1384 for a coloured reproduction of a drawing by Peter Fannin of the *Adventure* and the *Resolution*.

[A FIGUREHEAD, possibly of the *Resolution* formerly in the possession of Viscount Galway.]

Photograph. 10⅜″ x 7⅜″.

Copies: NPL:M(Ships File). 1414

HOLMAN, Francis

Captain Cook's HMS *Resolution* and *Adventure* in the Long Reach 1772.

1772. Oil 34″x 58″ inside frame; 41½″x 65½″ framed. Unsigned. Title from mount.
Colour transparency filed at NPL:M FM5/210.

Copies: NPL:D(DG 22). 1415

The Same.

Coloured reproduction in Public Library of New South Wales Reproductions U.

1416

INGLETON, Geoffrey Chapman

Cook's *Resolution* approaching Ship Cove, Queen Charlotte Sound, N.Z.

195–. 1, Rough sketch, 6⅜″ x 8⅞″.
2, Pen and ink sketch, 6½″ x 8⅞″ inside border.
3–4, Two etchings: trial proof and artist's proof. 6⅞″ x 8¾″ meas. of plate.

Copies: NPL:D(DG A2pt.1). 1417

INGLETON, Geoffrey Chapman

H.M.S. *Resolution* The Second Voyage 1772–1775; [and] The *Resolution* arrives at Tahiti April 1774.

1957. Reprod. of drawings.
(*In* Cook, J.—Collected Voyages—Printed Accounts. [1957. Price's ed.] pp.93, 163.)

Copies: NPL:M(C956). 1418

LUNY, Thomas

The *Resolution* and *Adventure* in the Southern Ocean.

1781. Oil painting. 25¼″ x 38″ inside frame. 31½″ x 43⁴/₁₀″ framed.
Signed "T.Luny 1781" in lower left-hand corner. Colour transparencies filed at NPL:M (FM4/208,147).

Copies: NPL:M(402). 1419

SKETCH in Captain Cook's log book: the *Resolution* at anchor, 1773.

Pen and wash drawing. 12½″ x 7¾″. Untitled; signed J.E.
Artist unknown.

Copies: ANL(Nan Kivell). 1420

Ships
Illustrations
Reproductions

CAPTAIN COOK'S SHIPS.

(*The Geographical Journal*, vol.69, no.6, Je. 1927. pp.555–57.)

Copies: NPL:M(Q910.6/G); NPL:R(DS909.6A/2). 1421

HODGES, William

Cape of Good Hope, the *Adventure* inshore; [from the painting] . . . by W. Hodges [in] the National Maritime Museum, Greenwich.

(*United Empire*, Aug. 1937, p.451.)

Copies: NPL:R(DS320.6/1.)   1422

HODGES, William

H.M.S. *Resolution* . . . and H.M.S. *Adventure* . . . in Matavay (*sic*) Bay, Tahiti, Au.26, 1773. [Half-tone reproduction of detail from painting in the National Maritime Museum, Greenwich; lent by the Admiralty.]

(*In* Merrill, Elmer Drew—The Botany of Cook's voyages. Waltham, Mass., Chronica Botanica Co., 1954. Plate 83.)
Cloth bound edition of *Chronica Botanica* vol.14, no.5/6.

Copies: NPL:M(Q 581.9901/M); NPL:R(Q 581.99/11); ANL; QU.   1423

HODGES, William

Resolution and *Adventure* in Matavi (*sic*) Bay, Tahiti; from the painting in the National Maritime Museum, Greenwich.

(*United Empire* Aug. 1937, p.431.)

Copies: NPL:R(DS320.6/1).   1424

HODGES, William

The *Resolution* and *Adventure* lying in Matavai Bay, Tahiti, 1773. [Reproduction in colour of oil painting in the National Maritime Museum, Greenwich.]

(*Geographical Magazine* Dec. 1956, p. 384.)

Copies: NPL:R(S909.5A/5).   1425

THE OTHER SIDE of the monument, showing Captain Cook's vessel, *Resolution*: [illustration].

(*In* The Captain Cook monument, with biographical sketch of the great circumnavigator. Whitby, Horne & Son, [1912]. pp. 11.)

Copies: NPL:M(923.9/C771.2/16A1).   1426

Ships
Models and Illustrations of Models

MODEL of H.M.S. *Resolution* made by H.C. Burton of Nelson, N.Z.

Photographs (2). Size of model. c.2′ 3″ x 2′ 3″ x 10″.
Size of photographs 6 $\frac{5}{16}$″ x 7 $\frac{15}{16}$″.

Copies: NPL:M(Ships File/Resolution 4–5).   1427

MODEL of the '*Resolution*' shown standing on the "Cook Table" at the bicentenary Exn. Whitby. E.Hall, photographer.

Photograph. 4 $\frac{3}{8}$″ x 6 $\frac{1}{8}$″.

Copies: NPL:M(Ships File/Resolution 2).   1428

The Same. Postcard.

Photograph of model supposed to be of the *"Resolution"*, though experts say that ship was only pierced for 16 guns. The model has 26. The model is in the Whitby Museum.

Copies: NPL:M(Ships File/Resolution 3). 1429

The Same. Process plate.

Model of the *Resolution* made at Messrs. Fishburn's yards, and now in the Museum, Whitby.

(*In* Kitson, Arthur Captain James Cook. London, Murray, 1907. Opp. p.226.)

Copies: NPL:M(923.9/C771.2/14A1); NPL:D(90/206); NPL:R(S920/C771/4). 1430

THE RESOLUTION: [photograph of model in the Provincial Library, Victoria, B.C.].

$7\frac{5}{8}''$ x $9\frac{3}{8}''$.

Copies: NPL:M(Small Picture File). 1431

Ships
Printed Books and Articles about the Ships

1775–81 GREAT BRITAIN—Admiralty

Cost of the upkeep of the *Endeavour* for 1775 and the *Adventure* for 1777 and 1781, at Deptford.

(Gt.Brit.—Admiralty—Ordinary estimate of His Majesty's Navy for 1775, p.56, 1777, p.56, 1781, p.57.)

Copies: NPL:M(MS.A1692). 1432

1814 CIRCUMNAVIGATION RELIC: [loss of the *Adventure*, May 24, 1811].

(*Naval Chronicle*, vol. 32, p. 308, July-Dec. 1814.)

Copies: NPL:M(359.05/N); NPL:D(80/51); NPL:R(DS359.0942/24). 1433

1938 CULVER, Henry Brundage

The *Resolution*.

(*In his* Forty famous ships. 1938.)

Copies: ANL. 1434

1952 CLOWES, Geoffrey Swinford Laird

Autotype reproduction of oil-painting of Captain Cook's departure on his second voyage of discovery, 1772: [description only, of painting by Francis Holman, of Cook's ships in the Downs, with note on the ships].

(*In his* Sailing ships, their history and development, as illustrated by the collection of ship-models in the Science Museum. Pt. 2, Catalogue. 4th ed. London, H.M.S.O., 1952. pp. 63–4.)

Copies: NPL:M(623.822/3). 1435

Publication

1776 July 10 COOK, James

ALS to Sir Joseph Banks, relating to descriptions of plants and engravings for his journal of the second voyage, and preparations for departure on the third. He expresses gratification at being awarded a prize medal by the Royal Society.

pp.2.
(Letters of Capt. James Cook, R.N., p.11.)
This letter was part of the Brabourne Papers. Facsimile filed at NPL:M(980:Co3/1A1). Neg. photostat filed at NPL:M(MS.A1713–²B,item vii).

Copies: NPL:M(Safe 1/68). 1436

1776 Nov.5 COOK, James

Extract from a letter from Cook to W. Strahan, Nov.5, 1776, written from the Cape of Good Hope, from whence he is about to depart; mentions the forthcoming publication of his Voyages, states Dr. Forster has written to several people there about his own forthcoming book.

(Cook, J.—Miscellaneous primary and secondary source material. B, item vi.)
With typescript copy from description of the letter which was sold at Sotheby's, June 27, 1932 and bought by Maggs Bros. This extract with a description of the original letter is printed in Maggs Catalogue no. 576, 1932.

Copies: NPL:M(MS.A1713–²). 1437

1777–8 FORSTER, Johann Reinhold

Letter addressed to Sir Joseph Banks, 1777–8, setting out at length his grievances regarding the publication of his narrative of Cook's second voyage, complaining of Cook's treatment of him, and the breaking of agreements and promises made to him by Cook and others.

(Bonwick Transcripts: Cook, Case 2, No. 188.)
Copied from a manuscript in the York Gate Library.

Copies: NPL:M(BT.Ser.2.Cook Box 2). 1438

1778 FORSTER, Johann Georg Adam

A Letter to the Right Honourable the Earl of Sandwich . . . from George Forster [i.e. J. G. A. Forster]. London, G. Robinson, 1778.

pp. [ii], ii, 25, 6.
Complaining that the author's father, J. R. Forster, had been prevented from writing the official narrative of Captain Cook's second voyage around the world.
Bound as frontispiece in Mitchell Library copy is a sepia illustration entitled The German Doctor on his travels from England. Doctor Faustus delt., Robinson. At foot of illustration: The German Doctor with his family on his travels to England conducted by Mynheer Shinder Knecht.

Copies: NPL:M(Q 980/35A1); VSL. 1439

1781–3 BANKS, *Sir* Joseph *and* PANCKOUCKE, C.

Autograph correspondence regarding the paper to be used for publication of Cook's 2nd and 3rd voyages, with enclosures.

pp. 50, 40 and fo.
Various dates between Sept., 1781, and June, 1783.
Copies: ANL(MS.9, item16).   1440

n.d. PERRY, William
Autograph letters [2] to Sir Joseph Banks concerning the publication of
Captain Cook's journal. n.d.
pp. 4.
Copies: ANL(MS.9, item 143).   1441

THIRD VOYAGE
Manuscript Journals and Logs

COOK, James
1776–9 Journal. Feb.10, 1776–Jan.6, 1779.

ff.605.
BM.Dept.MSS. Egerton MS.2177A. *See* Beaglehole, vol.3, pt.1, pp.clxxi–clxxvi. In
Cook's hand, and headed "Journal". With note on fly-leaf "Purchased of W.Douglas
Esq. 13 July, 1872".

1442

COOK, James
1776–9 Log and proceedings. Feb.10, 1776–Jan.6, 1779.

3 vols.
A.J.C.P. Microfilm. P.R.O.Adm.55/111–13. *See* Beaglehole, vol.3, pt.1, pp.clxxi–clxxvi.
In a clerk's hand. The first two volumes cover the period Feb.10, 1776–Nov.27, 1778;
the third volume ends with the entry for Jan.6, 1779, overlapping the second volume,
and is presumably the second volume of another copy of Cook's log.
Adm.55/111 is headed "Journal or Log"; Adm.55/113 is headed "Proceedings"; Adm.55/
111 is illustrated by two charts (Prince Edward Islands and Christmas Harbour) and a
sketch of Port Palliser. The originals from which these were copied have disappeared.

1443

COOK, James
1779 Fragment of log. Jan.7–17, 1779.

B.M.Dept.MSS. Egerton MS.2177B, ff.1–4v. *See Beaglehole*, vol.3, pt.1, pp.clxxi–clxxvi.
In Cook's hand.   1444

ANONYMOUS
1776–9 Log. Aug.2, 1776–Nov.28, 1777, Nov.29, 1777–Dec.28, 1778, Dec.29,
1778–Aug.10, 1779, Aug.11–Nov.26, 1779. (*Discovery.*)

A.J.C.P. Microfilm. P.R.O.Adm.51/4530/65–6, 71–2. *See* Beaglehole, vol.3, pt.1, p.
clxxxviii. The first two volumes are vellum-bound quarto, the second two folios in marbled
paper, but all seem part of the same log. In appearance a copy of the ship's log.

1445

ANONYMOUS

1776–8 A Logg of the proceedings of his Majestys sloop *Resolution* James Cook Esquire Commander. Feb.10, 1776–Nov.15, 1778.

A.J.C.P. Microfilm. P.R.O.Adm.55/114. *See* Beaglehole, vol.3, pt.1, pp.clxxxviii–clxxxix. Possibly written by James Trevenen. No.1451 (P.R.O.Adm.55/123) is continuation.

1446

ANONYMOUS

1776–7 Log. Feb.10, 1776–May 29, 1777. (*Resolution.*)

A.J.C.P. Microfilm. P.R.O.Adm.51/4528/64. *See* Beaglehole, vol.3, pt.1, p.clxxxviii. Looks like a copy of the ship's log. The writing is not unlike P.R.O.Adm.51/4531/67–9, and 51/4532/70, (nos.1488–9) attributed by Beaglehole to Portlock.

1447

ANONYMOUS

1776–7 Log. Dec.2, 1776–July 17, 1777. (*Resolution.*)

A.J.C.P. Microfilm. P.R.O.Adm.51/4561/220. *See* Beaglehole, vol.3, pt.1, p.clxxxviii.

1448

ANONYMOUS

1777 Log. 15 May–30 Nov.1777. (*Resolution.*)

A.J.C.P. Microfilm. P.R.O.Adm.51/4561/221. *See* Beaglehole, vol.3, pt.1, p.clxxxviii.

1449

ANONYMOUS

1778–80 Astronomical observations in the *Discovery*, 1778–80.

A.J.C.P. Microfilm. Royal Greenwich Observatory, Herstmonceux. Board of Longitude records, vol.48. *See* Beaglehole, vol.2, pt.1, p.cxcv.

1450

ANONYMOUS

1778–9 A Logg of the proceedings of his Majestys sloop *Resolution* James Cook Esquire Commander, from Nov.16th 1778 to Feb.15th 1779 when Charles Clerke Esq took the command of her & from that time to Aug.23d 1779 when I left the ship.
Afterwards follows the logg of proceedings on board his Majesty's sloop *Discovery* James King Esq. Commander from the 23d of Aug. 1779 to Nov.29th 1779.

A.J.C.P. Microfilm. P.R.O.Adm.55/123. *See* Beaglehole, vol.3, pt.1, pp.clxxxviii–clxxxix. Possibly written by James Trevenen. A continuation of no. 1446 (P.R.O.Adm.55/114).

1451

ANONYMOUS

n.d. Astronomical observations made for the Board of Longitude by Cook and King.

A.J.C.P. Microfilm. P.R.O.Adm.55/119. *See* Beaglehole, vol.3, pt.1, p.cxcv. The astronomical observations continue to be recorded (*see* no. 1465).

1452

ANONYMOUS

n.d. Observations. Lunar and other observations made at places visited. Also record re chronometer.

A.J.C.P. Microfilm. P.R.O.Adm.55/118. *See* Beaglehole, vol.3, pt.1, p.cxcv.

1453

ANDERSON, William

1776–7 Genera Nova Plantarum, 1776–1777: with descriptiones seu Characteres Specificos.

pp.40.

Latin and English. *See* Beaglehole, vol.3, pt.1, p.cxci. B.M.(Natural History) Dept. of Botany.

1454

ANDERSON, William

1776–7 A Journal of a voyage made in his Majestys sloop *Resolution*, May 16th 1776, Wm Anderson. May 30, 1776–Sept.2, 1777.

2 vols.

A.J.C.P. Microfilm. P.R.O.Adm.51/4560/203–4. *See* Beaglehole, vol.3, pt.1, pp.cxccxci. Vol.3 lost.

1455

BAYLY, William

1776–9 Log, June 11, 1776–Ap.30, 1779. Journal, Aug.12, 1777–June 30, 1778.

Charts, 2 vols.

Alexander Turnbull Library, Wellington. *See* Beaglehole, vol.3, pt.1, pp.clxxxix–cxc.

1456

BAYLY, William

1776–9 A Log and journal, kept on board His Majesties sloop *Discovery* by Wm Bayly Astronomer. Aug.1, 1776–Dec.3, 1779.

A.J.C.P. Microfilm. P.R.O.Adm.55/20. *See* Beaglehole, vol.3, pt.1, p.clxxxix.

1457

BLIGH, William

1776–9 Marginal annotations to his copy of the printed Voyage, 1784.

Admiralty Library. *See* Beaglehole, vol.3, pt.1, p.cxcvii. The notes were published by R.T.Gould in Bligh's Notes on Cook's last voyage, *Mariner's Mirror* vol.xiv, 1928, pp.371–85.

1458

BURNEY, James

1776–80 Journal of Lieutenant James Burney with Captain Jas Cook 1776 to 1780. Feb.10, 1776–Aug.24, 1780.

B.M.Add.MS8955. *See* Beaglehole, vol.3, pt.1, p.clxxxiii.

1459

BURNEY, James

1776–9 Journal of the proceedings of His Majest's Sloop, the *Discovery*, Chas Clerke, Commander, in company with the *Resolution*, Captn James Cook. Feb.10, 1776–Oct.11, 1777; Oct.12, 1777–July 24, 1778; July 25, 1778–Feb.14, 1779; Feb.15–Aug.24, 1779.

Charts, illus. 4 vols. in 2.
The third volume contains an account of the manner in which Cook was killed. Vol.4 of the Journal was bought in Sydney in 1921, vols.1–3 in London about eighteen months later. *See* Beaglehole, vol.3, pt.1, p.clxxxiii, and H.H.Payne—Admiral Burney and the death of Cook (*Cornhill Magazine* Nov. 1914. NPL:M Q 980:Col/N1A2).
James Burney was born in 1750 and died in 1821. He was a brother of Fanny Burney, Mme. D'Arblay. He entered the Navy in 1764. He was on the *Resolution* with Cook, as midshipman, in 1772–75, on the second voyage. On the third voyage after the death of Capts. Cook and King, he was made Senior Lieutenant. In 1783 he retired with rank of Admiral.
Copies: NPL:M(Safe 1/64,79). 1460

BURNEY, James

1776–8 Journal of a voyage in the *Discovery* Ch^s Clerke Esqr Commander in company with the *Resolution* Captⁿ Ja^s Cook. Feb.10, 1776–Ap.26, 1778.

Charts.
A.J.C.P. Microfilm. P.R.O.Adm.51/4528/45. *See* Beaglehole, vol.3, pt.1, p.clxxxii–clxxxiii.

1461

CHARLTON, William

1776–9 Journal. Feb.10, 1776–Nov.28, 1779.

A.J.C.P. Microfilm. P.R.O.Adm.51/4557/191–3. *See* Beaglehole, vol.3, pt.1, p.clxxxvi. The writer calls it a journal "but it looks very much as if it is a copy of the 'remarks' in the ship's log".

1462

CLERKE, Charles

1776–9 Log and proceedings. Feb.10, 1776–May 17, 1778; May 18, 1778–Feb.12, 1779.

ff.174, 128.
A.J.C.P. Microfilm. P.R.O.Adm.55/22,23. Clerke's record whilst he was in command of the *Discovery*. *See* Beaglehole, vol.3, pt.1, p.clxxvii.

1463

CLERKE, Charles

1776–8 Log on board His Majesty's Sloop *Discovery*, March 28, 1776, to July 5, 1778.

Charts.
This appears to be a copy of Clerke's original journal, probably by the ship's clerk, as the handwriting on comparison with letters of Clerke in the possession of the Mitchell Library does not appear to be his.
Copies: NPL:M(MS.A559). 1464

CLERKE, Charles
1779 Log. 14 Feb.–26 July, 1779.

A.J.C.P. Microfilm. P.R.O.Adm.55/124. *See* Beaglehole, vol.3, pt.1, pp.clxxvii–clxxviii. Up to 29 April a transcript, probably by Gregory Bentham, of Clerke's journal, beginning with the account of the death of Cook. The log entries are followed by certificates, tables of courses and distances, positions and bearings, and astronomical tables.

1465

CLERKE, Charles
1779 Log and observations. 14 Feb.–24 May, 1779.

A.J.C.P. Microfilm. P.R.O.Adm.51/4561/217. Clerke's record whilst in command of the *Resolution*. Includes An Account of the Sandwich Islands; An Account of plants at Sandwich Islands; An Account of the birds of Sandwich Islands. *See* Beaglehole, vol.3, pt.1, p.clxxvii.

1466

CLERKE, Charles
1779 Extract from journal, February–March 1779.

1 reel, positive microfilm.
Extract from Journal of Captain Charles Clerke, R.N. from 14th February 1779, on which date he succeeded Captain James Cook in command of H.M.S. *Resolution* until 13th March 1779. Filmed by A.L.Faber 1963 (No.142 of A.L.Faber Microfilm Library), from the original in the Admiralty Library, London, MSS.74/8.
Copies: NPL:M(FM3/641); ANL(G755).

1467

EDGAR, Thomas
1776–80 Log. Feb.10, 1776–Aug.4, 1778; June 17–Nov.29, 1779; Nov.30, 1779–July 19, 1780.

Charts.
A.J.C.P. Microfilm. P.R.O.Adm.55/21. *See* Beaglehole, vol.3, pt.1, p.clxxxiv.
See also nos. 1469, 1470.

1468

EDGAR, Thomas
1776–8 A Journal of a voyage undertaken to the South Seas . . . Kept by Thomas Edgar, Master. Feb.10, 1776–June 6, 1779.

Charts.
A.J.C.P. Microfilm. B.M.Add.MS.37528. *See* Beaglehole, vol.3, pt.1, pp.clxxxiv–clxxxv.
Apparently a fair copy of portion of Adm.55/21, pt.1 (no.1468).

1469

EDGAR, Thomas
1778–9 Log. Aug.5, 1778–June 16, 1779.

A.J.C.P. Microfilm. P.R.O.Adm.55/24. *See* Beaglehole, vol.3, pt.1, p.clxxxiv.
See also no. 1468.

1470

GILBERT, George
[1776–80] Journal.

> B.M.Add.MS38530. *See* Beaglehole, vol.3, pt.1, p.clxxxvi. Called a journal, but is really a narrative of the voyage, written soon after the end of the voyage.

1471

GILBERT, George
1776–80 MS.Journal of Captain Cooks Last Voyage. 1776–1780.

> pp.128, 19.5cm.
> Bound in vellum, with cloth hinge repair to spine. Title written in ink on front cover. "85 Park St. Manchester Square" in ink inside front cover. Intermittent alterations have been made to the text by erasure or overwriting, to p.75. Watermark, Lay Jun[r].
> A copy, apparently contemporary or near-contemporary, of B.M.Add.MS38530 (*see* no. 1471). *See* Beaglehole, vol.3, pt.1, pp.clxxxvi–clxxxvii, and notes filed at NPL:D (MS.94n).
> Copies: NPL:D(MS.94).

1472

GILBERT, George
1776–9 Journal. Ap.9, 1776–Nov.29, 1779.

> A.J.C.P. Microfilm. P.R.O.Adm.51/4559/213–15. *See* Beaglehole, vol.3, pt.1, p.clxxxvi.

1473

GORE, John
1776–80 Log. July 12, 1776–May 21, 1780.

> A.J.C.P. Microfilm. P.R.O.Adm.55/120. *See* Beaglehole, vol.3, pt.1, pp.clxxviii–clxxix. Wanting entries from 25 April–9 December, 1777, 31 March–26 April, 1778, and June 27, 1778–August 22, 1779. There was originally a chart drawn by Roberts at the entry for 31 May, 1778, now in P.R.O. Map Room, M.P.I.82, and reproduced in Portfolio to Beaglehole as Chart LI.

1474

GORE, John
1779–80 Capt[n] Gore's logg book for the *Discovery* from 21 July, 1779 to the 23 Aug[t] 1779. And for the *Resolution* from the 24 Aug[t] to the 22 March, 1780.

> A.J.C.P. Microfilm. P.R.O.Adm.51/4532/49. *See* Beaglehole,vol.3, pt.1, p.clxxix.

1475

GREAT BRITAIN—Board of Longitude
1772–80 Papers of the Board of Longitude, 1714–1830.

> Positive microfilm. Originals in the Royal Greenwich Observatory.
> CONTENTS:
> P.R.O. Reel 1756. Observations on board the *Resolution*, 1772–1775.
> Captain Cook's journal of the voyage of 1776.
> Observations of variation of the compass and chronometer rates, etc.
> Astronomical observations on Cook's last voyage.
> FM4/1559. Log book of the *Resolution*, 1772–5.
> Copies: NPL:M(P.R.O.Microfilm Reel 1756:FM4/1559).

1476

GREAT BRITAIN—Board of Longitude
1776 Board of Longitude records, vol.47. A work and observation book,
16 July–18 Oct. 1776. Signed by Cook and King.

pp.24.
A.J.C.P. Microfilm. Royal Greenwich Observatory, Herstmonceux. *See* Beaglehole,
vol.3, pt.1, p.cxcv.

1477

GRIFFIN, William
1776–8 A Short narrative of a voyage undertaken in His Majestys Ship
Resolution, Captn James Cook, with the *Discovery* Captn Clerke. May 29,
1776–Oct.6, 1780.

pp.41. cm 23.
Sewn booklet without cover, in a green watered silk portfolio. Paper watermarked 1813.
The manuscript bears no direct evidence of authorship, although the hand resembles
that in Griffin's parish account book (NPL:D.MS.Q 155C). The Dixson Library holds
also a typed transcript, entitled Diary of Capt. Cook's Last Voyage by W. Griffin, in
Sir William Dixson's hand. (MS.Q 156). *See also* Beaglehole, vol.3, pt.1, pp.cxcvi–cxcvii.

Copies: NPL:D(MS.Q 155); NPL:M(FM4/2738, negative microfilm).   1478

HARVEY, William
1776–7 A Log . . . kept by Wm Harvey, Master's mate. Feb.10, 1776–
June 9, 1777.

A.J.C.P. Microfilm. P.R.O.Adm.55/110. *See* Beaglehole, vol.3, pt.1, p.clxxxv.
See also no. 1480.

1479

HARVEY, William
1777–9 Log. June 10, 1777–Nov.28, 1779.

A.J.C.P. Microfilm. P.R.O.Adm.55/121. *See* Beaglehole, vol.3, pt.1, p.clxxxv.
See also no.1479.

1480

HOME, Alexander
1777–9 Journals, 1777–1779.

ff.29, pp.61.
MS. 'Journal of the Account of Otaheite and our transactions there' (Sept. 1777–Jan.
1778), ff.28, also a page containing a chart of Trarabon. Typescript transcript of the
same, pp.36.
MS. 'Journal of the Account of the Death of Capt. James Cook at Owhyee in the Sand-
wich Islands, January 1779' and 'Description of the Country of Kamtschatka from
April 1779'. The journal ends abruptly (pp.61. 4to).
Typescript transcript of the same (pp.7).
Also an extract from sales catalogue printed c.1925.
See Beaglehole, vol.3, pt.1, pp.cxcv–cxcvi.

Copies: ANL(MS.7).   1481

KING, James
1776–9 Log and proceedings. Feb.12, 1776–Feb.1, 1778; Feb.4, 1778–Nov.29, 1779.

A.J.C.P. Microfilm. P.R.O.Adm.55/116, 122. *See* Beaglehole, vol.3, pt.1, pp.clxxix–clxxii.

1482

KING, James
1778 Log and Journal of HMS *Resolution*, 2 Jan.–5 Sep.1778. Signed James King.

pp.349, 23cm.
Bound in vellum. Spine title, Log of part of Cook's 3rd voyage. The manuscript, possibly a fair copy, has alterations and insertions throughout, some possibly in another hand. Beaglehole describes it (vol.3, pt.1, pp.clxxix–clxxxii) as "a very neat fair copy, with some minor variations of the text of the P.R.O. volumes" (Adm.55/116, 122).

Copies: NPL:D(MS.98); NPL:M(FM4/2738, negative microfilm).

1483

LANYON
1776–9 Log. Feb.10, 1776–Nov.29, 1779.

A.J.C.P. Microfilm. P.R.O.Adm.51/4558/196–8. *See* Beaglehole, vol.3, pt.1, p.clxxxv. "Looks very like a straight copy of the ship's log."

1484

LAW, John
1778–9 Journal.

A fragment. B.M.Add.MS.27327. *See* Beaglehole, vol.3, pt.1, p.cxc.

1485

MARTIN, John Henry
1776–9 Journal. Dec.1, 1776–Nov.28, 1779.

A.J.C.P. Microfilm. P.R.O.Adm.51/4531/47. *See* Beaglehole, vol.3, pt.1, p.clxxxvi.

1486

PAUL, Mathew
1776–8 Log. July 13, 1776–Aug.8, 1778.

A.J.C.P. Microfilm. P.R.O.Adm.51/4560/209. *See* Beaglehole, vol.3, pt.1, p.clxxxvii.

1487

PORTLOCK, Nathaniel
1777–8 Log. May 30–Oct.31, 1777; Nov.1, 1777–May 20, 1778; May 21–Oct.30, 1778.

A.J.C.P. Microfilm. P.R.O.Adm.51/4531/67–9. *See* Beaglehole, vol.3, pt.1, p.clxxxvii.
See also no.1447, classed as anonymous in P.R.O. list.

1488

PORTLOCK, Nathaniel
1778–9 Log. Mar.15, 1778–Oct.9, 1779.

Charts.
A.J.C.P. Microfilm. P.R.O.Adm.51/4532/70. *See* Beaglehole, vol.3, pt.1, p.clxxxvii.
Classed as anonymous in P.R.O. list.

1489

RICKMAN, John
1776–9 Log. Mar.16, 1776–Nov.29, 1779.
A.J.C.P. Microfilm. P.R.O.Adm.51/4529/46. *See* Beaglehole, vol.3, pt.1, p.clxxxiv.
1490

RIOU, Edward
1776–9 Log. Feb.22, 1776–Mar.5, 1778; Mar.6–Aug.3, 1778; Aug.4, 1778–Jan.17, 1779; July 26–Nov.29, 1779.
Charts, illus.
A.J.C.P. Microfilm. P.R.O.Adm.51/4529/41–4. The fourth book, 18 Jan.–25 July, 1779 is missing. *See* Beaglehole, vol.3, pt.1, p.clxxxviii.
1491

ROBERTS, Henry
1776–9 A Log of the proceedings of His Majesties Sloop *Resolution* on discoveries, towards the North Pole. James Cook, Esqr., Commander. By Hen^y. Roberts, Mate.
Charts, illus. 3 vols. 37 cm.
Journal bound in brown rough calf. Charts found loose in MS.Q 151–2 removed and mounted as MS.F2. Contents list of charts and coastal profiles is filed at NPL:D(MS. Q 151n). *See also* Third Voyage—Charts. The manuscript is in the form of a log-journal, two volumes, illustrated with coloured charts and sketches. *See also* Beaglehole, vol.3, pt.1, p.clxxxv.
Copies: NPL:D(MS.Q 151–2,MS.F2); NPL:M(FM4/222, negative microfilm of text).
1492

SAMWELL, David
1776–9 Some account of a voyage to South Sea's (*sic*) in 1776–1777–1778. Written by David Samwell, Surgeon of the *Discovery*. Feb.10, 1776–Nov. 29, 1779.
B.M.Egerton MS.2591. *See* Beaglehole, vol.3, pt.1, pp.cxcii–cxcv.
1493

SHUTTLEWORTH, William
1777–9 Proceedings. July 18, 1777–Feb.14, 1779.
A.J.C.P. Microfilm. P.R.O.Adm.51/4561/210–11. *See* Beaglehole, vol.3, pt.1, p.clxxxviii.
1494

SHUTTLEWORTH, William
1779 Journal of the proceedings of his Majesty's Sloop *Discovery* . . . by Wm Shuttleworth, Mid. 16 Feb.–28 Nov. 1779.
A.J.C.P. Microfilm. P.R.O.Adm.51/4531/48. *See* Beaglehole, vol.3, pt.1, p.clxxxviii.
1495

TAYLOR, William
1779 Log. 16 Ap.–29 Nov. 1779.
A.J.C.P. Microfilm. P.R.O.Adm.51/4561/216. *See* Beaglehole, vol.3, pt.1, p.clxxxviii.
1496

TREVENEN, James

1776–9 Annotations in a copy of the printed Voyage.

See Beaglehole, vol.3, pt.1, p.cxcvii. The volumes have disappeared, but the notes are extant in the National Maritime Museum and Alexander Turnbull Library MSS. of the Penrose Memoirs of James Trevenen. Some have been printed in the edition of Penrose edited by Christopher Lloyd and R.C.Anderson (Navy Records Society, 1959). A MS. copy of the original is in the Archives of British Columbia, Victoria, B.C.

1497

WATTS, John

1776–9 Proceedings. Ap.23, 1776–Nov.29, 1779.

3 vols. in 1.

A.J.C.P. Microfilm. P.R.O.Adm.51/4559/212. *See* Beaglehole, vol.3, pt.1, p.clxxxviii.

1498

WILLIAMSON, John

1776–8 Log and proceedings. Feb.23, 1776–June 28, 1778.

A.J.C.P. Microfilm. P.R.O.Adm.55/117. *See* Beaglehole, vol.3, pt.1, p.clxxxiii.

1499

Manuscript Correspondence, Instructions, etc.

COOK, James

1771–8 Letter book, 1771–1778.

pp.161.

Contains chiefly orders to and from the Admiralty, Navy Commissioners and Victualling Commissioners, and Cook's orders to his officers during his second and third voyages. Gives many interesting details relating to the second and third voyages.

Copies: ANL(MS.6).

1500

COOK, James

1776–8 Capt. Cookes letter: abstract [in the autograph of Sir Joseph Banks, and endorsed by him with the title as given].

pp.4.

(Brabourne Papers.)

This abstract consists of brief entries made during the third voyage, from Dec. 30, 1776, to Oct. 20, 1778.

Copies: NPL:M(MS.A78⁻¹).

1501

COOK, James

1776 Feb.14 Cook to Capt. John Walker, Whitby. ALS No. 5 dated Mile End, London, commenting on his projected voyage to the South Sea at the end of April, and its prospects for himself; with draft of Walker's reply (2 Apr.1776) overleaf.

cm 23.

Facsimile, in MS.Q 143.

Copies: NPL:D(MS.Q 140, pp. 79–82).

1502

COOK, James
1776 Apr.2 LS to the Commissioners of His Majesty's Navy. *Resolution,*
Deptford, 2nd April 1776.

p.1, folio.
Signed "James Cook". Presumably written by Alexander Dewar, clerk on the *Resolution*
requesting thirteen articles of clothing for use on the *Resolution.*

Copies: ANL(Nan Kivell 9528); NPL:M(FM4/1552,1707, pos. and neg. microfilm). 1503

COOK, James
1776 May 24 AL written in the third person to Mr. Banks, in reference to
an engraving of the New Zealand spruce, his sitting for Mr. Dance, and
the stove from the *Resolution* which has been returned to the store.

pp.2.
(Letters of Capt. James Cook, R.N., p.9.)
This letter was part of the Brabourne Papers. Facsimile filed at NPL:M(980:Co3/1A1).

Copies: NPL:M(Safe 1/68).   1504

COOK, James
1776 June 11 Cook to Victualling Board ALS ordering ten puncheons of
beer for the *Resolution.*

cm 30.
Copies: NPL:D(MS.Q 140, pp. 85–6).   1505

COOK, James
1776 July 10 ALS to Sir Joseph Banks, relating to descriptions of plants
and engravings for his journal of the second voyage, and preparations
for departure on the third voyage. He expresses gratification at being
awarded a prize medal by the Royal Society.

pp.2.
(Letters of Capt. James Cook, R.N., p.11.)
This letter was part of the Brabourne Papers. Facsimile filed at NPL:M(980:Co3/1A1).
Neg.photostat filed at NPL:M(MS.A1713⁻²B,item vii).

Copies: NPL:M(Safe 1/68).   1506

COOK, James
1776 Aug.3 Copy of letter from Cook, dated Teneriff. He has called here
to remedy the deficiency in his supplies; he saw in Plymouth a book of
MS. sketches of several ports on the west coast of South America, suggests
it be obtained for the Admiralty; is about to sail and will stop for water
at St Jago; expects Capt. Clerke is not far behind him.

Typescript from *Gentleman's Magazine,* 1836, pt.1, pp.484–5; original letter then in
possession of Mr. Lake, Uxbridge.

Copies: NPL:D(MS.Q 143, pp.72a–b).   1507

COOK, James

1776 Nov.5 Extract from a letter to W. Strahan, Nov.5, 1776, written from the Cape of Good Hope, from whence he is about to depart: mentions the forthcoming publication of his Voyage, states Dr. Forster has written to several people there about his own forthcoming book.

(Cook, J.—Miscellanea. Vol.1, p.26.)

Copies: NPL:M(MS.A1713⁻¹).

1508

COOK, James

1776 Nov.28 Bill of exchange, drawn on the Victualling Board, signed by Cook, dated Cape of Good Hope, for provisions for *Resolution* and *Discovery*; with endorsements.

f.1, cm 15.5.

Copy of transcript at NPL:D(MS.Q 143, pp.73–4).

Copies: NPL:D(MS.Q 140, pp.87–8).

1509

COOK, James

1778 Nov.26 Order signed Jams. Cook, Commander of HMS *Resolution* at Sea, prohibiting unauthorised barter by officers or crew with the natives (to preserve the barter value of items used to obtain provisions), the taking of firearms ashore, and the bringing of women aboard ship or the going ashore of any persons suffering disease (to prevent its communication to the natives). Endorsed 'Orders respecting Sandwich Isles 26 Novbr/78'.

f.1, cm 31.5.

Copies: NPL:D(MS.Q 140, pp.91–4).

1510

COOK, James

n.d. Instructions to his Captains in sailing from the Friendly Isles to the northern coast of America, in the event of being separated from him.

f.1.

Photostat copy. In Cook's handwriting, but incomplete and unsigned. The original is in the Provincial Library, Victoria, B.C.

(Captain Cook Miscellanea. Vol.1, p.60.)

Copies: NPL:M(MS.A1713⁻¹).

1511

COOK, James

n.d. Note directing certain officers of the *Resolution* and *Discovery* to take a survey of the bread on the *Discovery*, and if it is as bad as represented by Captain Clerke, to throw it into the sea, and report on the matter.

f.1.

Photostat copy. In Cook's handwriting, but unsigned. The original is in the Provincial Library, Victoria, B.C.

(Captain Cook Miscellanea. Vol.1, p.62.)

Copies: NPL:M(MS.A1713⁻¹).

1512

ANONYMOUS

1781 Jan.23 Account of part of the third voyage, describing discoveries in the North Pacific, the Sandwich Islands and the death of Captain Cook.

pp.20.

MS. copy of letter written to Mrs. Strachan, dated Spithead, Jan. 23, 1781. The writer was not an eyewitness of the death of Captain Cook, his being on board the *Discovery* at the time. The copy is unfinished, but gives a detailed statement concerning the conduct of Lieut. John Williamson.

Copies: NPL:M(Safe 1/67).   1513

BLIGH, William

1776 Letters, 1776–1811.

pp.24.

Nine MS. letters by Capt. William Bligh to Capt. Frank Bond; the first written from the Cape on a voyage in company with the *Discovery*, mentioning Capt. Cooke (*sic*). Typescript copy at NK 4237.

Copies: ANL(Nan Kivell 34, 4237).   1514

BLIGH, William

1776 Oct.23 Proposed course of voyage of the *Resolution* and *Discovery*. (Wm Bligh to J. Bond, Oct.23, 1776.)

Copies: NPL:M(MS.Ab60).   1515

BURNEY, Charles

1775 Aug.12 Burney, Charles, musician, to Dr. James Lind, Edinburgh. ALS dated St Martin's St. Leicester Fields, to 'Dr. John Lind', Edinburgh: Lord Sandwich says confidentially, that now Cook has returned from having made considerable discoveries, another expedition consisting of two ships, will leave before Xmas; that Burney's son, already a circumnavigator with Capt. Fourneaux (and at present in the *Cerberus* for Boston, due back in Nov.) will go as Lieutenant. Cook & Fourneaux have been made Post Captains. Postscript: his ill health prevents publication of the 1st vol. of his History of Music before Nov.

pp.4, cm 22.5.

Copies: NPL:D(MS.Q 161).   1516

CLERKE, Charles

[1776] ALS to Sir Joseph Banks, shortly before the departure of the *Discovery* relating his difficult position owing to fear of arrest by money-lenders. [Feb.? 1776.]

pp.2.

(Brabourne Papers.)

Copies: NPL:M(MS.A78⁻¹).   1517

CLERKE, Charles

[1776] ALS to Sir Joseph Banks, stating that the Bench of Justices had fallen out amongst themselves and that he was therefore decamping, and asking if Banks wished him to wait on him ere his departure. [1776.]

pp.2.

(Brabourne Papers.)

Copies: NPL:M(MS.A78⁻¹).   1518

CLERKE, Charles

1776 Nov.23 ALS to Sir Joseph Banks, describing journey to and stay at the Cape of Good Hope. H.M.S. *Discovery*, Cape of Good Hope, Nov.23, 1776.

pp.4.

(Brabourne Papers.)

Page 4 written Nov. 29th reporting their departure that evening or the next morning.

Copies: NPL:M(MS.A78⁻¹).   1519

CLERKE, Charles

1779 Aug.10 Letter signed to Sir Joseph Banks, written for him by Capt. King, stating that he did not expect to live much longer. H.M.S. *Resolution* "at sea", Aug.10, 1779.

pp.2.

(Brabourne Papers.)

Copies: NPL:M(MS.A78⁻¹).   1520

DIXSON, George

1776 Nov.24 ALS from Captain George Dixon, Cape of Good Hope 24 Nov. 1776, to George Atkinson re the departure of Captain James Cook on the last voyage of the *Resolution*.

pp.3.

Copies: NPL:M(MS.Doc.583).   1521

DU MAGELLAN, J.H.

1779 June 18 Letter to the Royal Geographical Society, enclosing one from the Governor of Calais, the duc de Croy, June 18, 1779, detailing the steps he has taken to prevent Cook from falling into the hands of privateers.

MS. copy.

(Copies of documents relating to Captain James Cook, R.N., from originals in the Grey Collection, Auckland Public Library, ff. 218–220.)

Copies: NPL:M(MS.C697).   1522

EAST INDIA COMPANY—Select Committee of Supra Cargoes at Canton

1779 Copy of the postscript of a letter from the Select Committee of Supra Cargoes at Canton to the Directors of the East India Company, re the arrival of the *Resolution* and *Discovery* at Macao. Dec.5, 1779.

p.1.

(Brabourne Papers.)

Copies: NPL:M(MS.A78⁻¹).   1523

GREAT BRITAIN—Admiralty

1776–77 Secret instructions issued to Captain Cook, July 6, 1776 by the Earl of Sandwich on behalf of the Admiralty, with regard to the voyage about to be undertaken in the *Resolution* and *Discovery*. With extracts of instructions to Lieutenant Pickersgill, May 14, 1776, and to Lieutenant Young, Mar.13, 1777.

ff.22.
Photostat copy. Original in the British Museum, Department of Manuscripts, Egerton MS.2177B.

Copies: NPL:M(MS.A3434).   1524

GREAT BRITAIN—Admiralty

1777 Fragment of possible instructions to Captain Cook, 1777.

Photocopy. Original in possession of Mr. Kenneth Webster, 1962.

Copies: NPL:M(MS.Doc.1186).   1525

GREAT BRITAIN—Admiralty

1953 Secret instructions for Captain James Cook's third voyage.

(*In* Harlow, V. *and* Madden, F.—British colonial developments, 1774–1834. Select documents. 1953. pp.1–4.)

Copies: NPL:M(325.342/H).   1526

GREAT BRITAIN—Admiralty

1967 Secret instructions for Capt. James Cook, Commander of His Majesty's Sloop the *Resolution*. July 6, 1776.

(*In* The Journals of Captain James Cook on his voyages of discovery . . . Ed. by J.C Beaglehole. Cambridge, U.P., 1967. Vol.3, pt.1, pp.ccxx–ccxxiv.)
Printed from the copy in the British Museum, Department of Manuscripts, Egerton MS.2177B, after collation with P.R.O.Adm.2/1332, pp.284–96.

Copies: NPL:M(980:Col/46A3).   1527

GREAT BRITAIN—Victualling Board

1777 June 14   Receipted imprest, signed by officials of the Victualling Board instructing the Treasury to pay the above bill.

f.1, cm 32.

Copies: NPL:D(MS.Q 140, pp. 89–90).   1528

HARRIS, *Sir* James

1779 Oct.29/Nov.9   ALS to Lord Weymouth, conveying a report received through Prince Potemkin from the Commandant of Kamschatka concerning the visit of the ships of Cook's third expedition. Petersburg, Oct.29/Nov.9, 1779.

pp.2.
Headed: "Copy". Endorsed in Banks' hand, "First letter from Sir James Harris to Lord Weymouth".
(Brabourne Papers.)

Copies: NPL:M(MS.A78⁻¹).   1529

HARRIS, *Sir* James

1779 Nov. Extract of a letter to Lord Weymouth, enclosing the report of the Commandant of Kamschatka, and correcting the date previously given as that of the visit of the ships of Cook's third expedition. Petersburgh, Nov., 1779.

p.1.

Endorsed in Sir Joseph Banks' hand, "Second letter from Sr. Jas. Harris to Ld. Weymouth."

(Brabourne Papers.)

Copies: NPL:M(MS.A78⁻¹).   1530

KAMCHATKA—Governor

[1778?] Report of the Commandant of Kamtchatka (*sic*) [on the visit of the ships of Cook's third expedition]: manuscript in French, endorsed by Sir Joseph Banks "Translation of the Report of the Command of Kamschatka" (*sic*). [With trans. into English.]

pp.4.

Original enclosed with letter from Sir James Harris to Lord Weymouth, Petersburgh, Nov. 1779.

The Governor was Major Magnus von Behm, a Livonian in the service of the Empress Catherine.

Also published *in* Historical Records of New South Wales, Sydney, Govt. Pr., 1893. Vol.1, pt.1, pp.427–8.

(Brabourne Papers.)

Copies: NPL:M(MS.A78⁻¹).   1531

KING, James

1779 June 10 Copy of letter enclosing tables of observations made by Capt. Cook and himself and referring to difficulties with instruments; the letter sent at Clerke's instigation owing to the death of Cook. Harbor of St. Peter & St. Paul, Kamchatska, June 10th, 1779. Observations dated 1778.

pp.2,3.

(Brabourne Papers.)

Copies: NPL:M(MS.A78⁻¹).   1532

NEWMAN, J.

1780 Jan.4 [MS. copy of letter to an un-named correspondent [Sir J. Banks?] Jan.4, 1780, enclosing portions of two letters sent from Russia in Nov. 1779, dealing with the arrival and stay in Kamtschatka of Cook's third expedition.]

(Copies of documents relating to Captain James Cook, R.N., from originals in the Grey Collection, Auckland Public Library, ff. 213–216.)

Copies: NPL:M(MS.C697).   1533

1778 OBSERVATIONS MADE by Capt. Cook and Capt. King enclosed by King in a letter from Kamchatska, June 10th, 1779.

pp.3.

(Brabourne Papers.)

Copies: NPL:M(MS.A78⁻¹).   1534

PALLASS

1779 Dec.15/26 Autograph letter from Mr. Pallass to Mr. Pennant giving a detailed account, from the letters of Capts. Cook and Clerke, of events on the third voyage, including the death of Cook and the visit of the ships to Kamschatka. St. Petersburgh 15–26 Dec., 1779.

pp.4.

A copy, possibly made by Pallass. The original letter which was held by Orion Booksellers in 1947, contains an extra paragraph.

(Brabourne Papers.)

Copies: NPL:M(MS.A78⁻¹).   1535

POULTON, Thomas H.M.

1888 Nov.22 List of names of persons appearing on the books of the *Discovery* as having transferred from *Resolution* after the death of Captain Clerke. 22 Nov.1888.

Copies: NPL:D(MS.95).   1536

ST. HELENA—Governor

1780 Apr.5 Extract of a letter from the Governor and Council of the Island St. Helena to the Court of Directors of the East India Company, giving news of the departure of the *Resolution* and *Discovery* from Macao for Europe, and of the deaths of Capts. Cook and Clerke. 5th April, 1780.

p.1.

(Brabourne Papers.)

Copies: NPL:M(MS.A78⁻¹).   1537

SANDWICH, John Montagu, *4th Earl*

1780 Jan.10 Sandwich, John Montagu, 4th Earl, to Sir Joseph Banks ALS dated Blackheath 10 Jan.1780: Informs that Capt. Cook has been murdered by the natives of an island where he had a more friendly reception than Otaheite; the news comes from Capt. Clerke at Kamschatzcha where he has received very friendly treatment from the Russians; the voyage has been successful, only three men had died; Omai was left safely at Huaheine, but no particulars given, in short letter from Cook by the same conveyance; horses, cattle and sheep were landed at Otaheita; Capt. Gower (Gore) takes command of the *Discovery* and Clerke of the *Resolution;* Clerke means to make another attempt for the northern passage.

[Paginated 409–10.]

Dealer's catalogue description in NPL:D MS.Q 159.

Copies: NPL:D(MS.Q 158).   1538

SOLANDER, Daniel Carl

1775 Aug.14 Letter to Sir Joseph Banks. Charles Clerke was promised the command of the *Resolution* to carry Mr. Omai home, Pickersgill to be his first lieutenant.

Copies: NPL:M(MS.As24).   1539

UNITED STATES OF AMERICA—Congress

1779 Mar.10   Copy of Pass by B. Franklin, Minister Plenipotentiary from
the Congress of the United States at the Court of France, requesting all
captains and commanders of armed ships acting by commission from
the Congress of the USA now in war with Great Britain, to allow Cook's
ships to proceed unmolested by them, in view of the laudable purpose
of his voyage.

ff.2, cm 31.5.

Copies: NPL:D(MS.Q 140, pp. 95–8).   1540

WALKER, John

1776 Apr.2   Capt. John Walker to Cook. Draft of reply dated Whitby, on
second leaf of Cook's letter (14 Feb.1776); that he has sent ale and hams,
and wishing him a good voyage and safe return; with additional comments
on his own age and family affairs.

Copies: NPL:D(MS.Q 140, p.81).   1541

Printed Accounts

This section includes entries for printed editions of Cook's own account. For the printed
journals of others on the voyage, *see* the subheading *Printed Accounts of Associates*. Books
written about the voyage are entered under the subheadings *Books about* and *Articles*.
For a description of the plates in the official account *see* the subheadings *Illustrations* and
Charts.

1781 London Edition

Journal of Captain Cook's last voyage. London, E. Newbery, 1781.

See no. 1607. The authorship of this anonymous publication was previously attributed
to John Ledyard, but F.W. Howay in his *Authorship of the anonymous account of Captain
Cook's last voyage*, has established John Rickman as the author.

1782 THE ORIGINAL astronomical observations made in the course of a
voyage to the Northern Pacific Ocean, for the discovery of a North East
or North West passage: wherein the North West coast of America and
North East coast of Asia were explored in His Majesty's ships the *Resolution*
and *Discovery*, in the years 1776, 1777, 1778, 1779 and 1780, by Captain
James Cooke, F.R.S., Commander of the *Resolution*, and Lieutenant
James King, and Mr William Bayly, late assistant at the Royal
Observatory. Pub. by order of the Commissioners of Longitude. London,
William Richardson, pr., 1782.

pp. vii, [i], 351, [i].

Copies: NPL:M(Q 524/C).   1542

1784 London Edition

A Voyage to the Pacific Ocean, undertaken by the command of His
Majesty, for making discoveries in the northern hemisphere, to determine
the position and extent of the west side of North America, its distance

from Asia, and the practicability of a northern passage to Europe, performed under the direction of Captains Cook, Clerke and Gore, in His Majesty's Ships, the *Resolution* and *Discovery*, in the years 1776, 1777, 1778, 1779 and 1780. In three volumes: vol.1 and 2 written by Captain J. Cook, vol.3 by Captain J. King. Illustrated with maps and charts, from the original drawings made by Lieut. Henry Roberts under the direction of Captain Cook; and with a great variety of portraits of persons, views of places and historical representations of remarkable incidents, drawn by Mr. Webber during the voyage, and engraved by the most eminent artists. Published by order of the Lords Commissioners of the Admiralty. [Ed. by Dr. Douglas, Bishop of Salisbury.] London, printed by W. & A. Strahan for G. Nicol and T. Cadell, 1784.

Illus. maps, 3 vols. and atlas.
See also nos.1544–6, 1549–60, 1562, 1565, 1567, 1568, 1572, 1575, 1577–80, 1582–6. See Holmes no.47. The first edition consists of three quarto volumes, and one folio atlas, the latter without title-page. The large plates which can be bound as the atlas are included in the List of the plates in vol.1. There are 87 plates in all, including the charts, and of these the atlas contains 63. The Mitchell Library holds several copies of the atlas (X980/ 24), but as these have no title-pages it is impossible to tell to which edition they belong. One copy contains an extra plate by Bartolozzi after Webber representing the death of Cook, and another copy contains the 87 plates.
The Dixson Library holds another set (Q 77/27–9), the text forming vols.6–8 of a set of eight volumes bearing the binder's title *Cook's voyages*, and formerly the property of Captain John Walker, Cook's former employer. ANL holds another set (Copy N2) with variant title-page, and a third copy (Copy N3) presented by Her Majesty the Queen. VSL set in three volumes and atlas. Reviewed in *The Monthly Review*, London, 1784, pp.460–74, of which Mitchell Library holds extract (980:Co4/R2A1). Also reviewed in *The Universal Magazine*, June–December 1784 and supplement to volume 75, of which the Dixson Library holds June 1784 and supplement (Pam 78/45). A typescript index by W.J. Jeffrey is held in the Dixson Library (MS.Q 61.74) and is included in volume 2 of the set of Jeffrey indexes in the Mitchell Library.

Copies: NPL:M(Q 980:Co4/1A1–3, X980/24); NPL:D(Q 77/10–12, F78/1); NPL:R (Q 990A/29–31); ANL; NAMu; NUN; Q OM; Q Parl; QU; VMoU; VSL; VU (Baillieu). 1543

1784 London Edition

Voyage to the Pacific Ocean, undertaken by the command of His Majesty, for making discoveries in the northern hemisphere, to determine the position and extent of the west side of North America, its distance from Asia, and the practicability of a northern passage to Europe, performed under the direction of Captains Cook, Clerke and Gore, in His Majesty's Ships, the *Resolution* and *Discovery*, in the years 1776, 1777, 1778, 1779 and 1780. In three volumes: vol.1 and 2 written by Captain J. Cook, vol.3 by Captain J. King . . . Published by order of the Lords Commissioners of the Admiralty. [Ed. by Dr. Douglas, Bishop of Salisbury.] London, G. Nicol and T. Cadell, 1784.

3 vols.
Resembles no. 1543, except for the omission of the words "printed by W. & A. Strahan" and for the addition of a medallion decoration on the title-page.

Copies: NPL:M(Q 980:Co4/1B1, vol.1, only); VMoU. 1544

1784 London Edition. Abridged

A Voyage to the Pacific Ocean, undertaken by command of His Majesty, for making discoveries in the northern hemisphere; performed under the direction of Captains Cook, Clerke and Gore, in the years 1776, 1777, 1778, 1779 and 1780. Being a copious, comprehensive and satisfactory abridgement of the voyage written by Capt. J. Cook and Capt. J. King. Illustrated with cuts. London, J. Stockdale, Scatcherd and Whitaker, John Fielding and John Hardy, 1784.

Maps 2, plates 49, 4 vols.
See also no. 1543; and no. 1579 for a reprint.
Copies: NPL:M(980:Co4/1A1–4); QOM; VMoU; VSL. 1545

1784 Dublin Edition

A Voyage to the Pacific Ocean, undertaken by the command of His Majesty, for making discoveries in the northern hemisphere to determine the position and extent of the west side of North America, its distance from Asia, and the practicability of a northern passage to Europe. Performed under the direction of Captains Cook, Clerke and Gore, in His Majesty's Ships the *Resolution* and *Discovery*. In the years 1776, 1777, 1778, 1779 and 1780. In three volumes. Vol.1 and 2 written by Captain J. Cook. Vol.3 by Captain J. King. Illustrated by maps and charts from the original drawings made by Lieut. Henry Roberts . . . Published by order of the Lords Commissioners of the Admiralty. Dublin, H. Chamberlaine [and others], 1784.

Illus. maps, port. 3 vols.
See also no. 1543. Baillieu Library copy lacks plates, except portrait.
Copies: NPL:M(980:Co4/2A1–3); ANL; NUN; QOM; VU(Baillieu). 1546

1784 Kearsley's Edition

An Abridgement of Captain Cook's last voyage, performed in the years 1776, 1777, 1778, 1779 and 1780, for making discoveries in the northern hemisphere, by order of His Majesty. Extracted from the 4to edition, in 3 volumes. Containing a relation of all the interesting transactions, particularly those relative to the unfortunate death of Captain Cook, with his life, by Captain King. [Ed. by G. Kearsley.] London, printed for G. Kearsley, 1784.

Frontisp. pp.xxiv, 441.
Frontispiece is an engraving of the Royal Society's medal by Mr. Pingo, engraved by T. Trotter, and is described in the Preface. *See also* nos. 15, 1548, 1564, 1576.
Copies: NPL:M(980:Co4/3A1); NPL:R(S990A/83); NUN. 1547

1784 Kearsley's Edition

A Compendious history of Captain Cook's last voyage, performed in the years 1776, 1777, 1778, 1779 and 1780. In which all the interesting transactions are recorded, particularly those relative to his unfortunate death. With a map of the new discoveries, and the track of the ships. [Ed. by G. Kearsley.] New ed. London, printed for G. Kearsley, 1784.

Frontisp. pp.xxiv, 315.

Includes A Short view of the life and public services of Captain James Cook, extracted from Captain King's sketches; to which is added An Inscription to his memory. Frontispiece is an engraving of the Royal Society's medal by Mr. Pingo, engraved by T. Trotter, and is described in the Preface. *See also* no.1547.

Copies: NPL:R(S990A/82.S.C.); ANL; VSL.   1548

1784–5 London Edition

A Voyage to the Pacific Ocean, undertaken by the command of His Majesty, for making discoveries in the northern hemisphere . . . Published by order of the Lords Commissioners of the Admiralty. London, G. Nicol and T. Cadell, 1784–5.

3 vols. and atlas.
Another issue of no. 1543.

Copies: VSL.   1549

1784–6 London Edition

A Voyage to the Pacific Ocean, undertaken by the command of His Majesty, for making discoveries in the northern hemisphere. Performed under the direction of Captains Cook, Clerke and Gore, in His Majesty's Ships, the *Resolution* and *Discovery*, in the years 1776, 1777, 1778, 1779 and 1780. London, printed for J. Fielding, 1784–6.

Illus. maps, 4 vols.
See also no. 1543.

Copies: NUN.   1550

1784–6 London Edition. Abridged

A Voyage to the Pacific Ocean undertaken by command of His Majesty for making discoveries in the northern hemisphere; performed under the direction of Captains Cook, Clerke and Gore in the years 1776, 1777, 1778, 1779 and 1780. Being . . . [an] abridgement of the voyage written by Captain James Cook . . . and Captain James King. London, printed for John Stockdale, Scatcherd and Whitaker, John Fielding and John Hardy, 1784–6.

Illus. maps, port. 4 vols.
See also no. 1550. Dixson Library holds another set (78/37–40). For both sets the imprint varies.

Copies: NPL:D(78/33–6, 78/37–40).   1551

1785 London Edition

Voyage to the Pacific Ocean, undertaken by the command of His Majesty, for making discoveries in the northern hemisphere. Performed under the direction of Captains Cook, Clerke and Gore, in His Majesty's Ships, the *Resolution* and *Discovery*, in the years 1776, 1777, 1778, 1779 and 1780. In three vols.: vol.1 and 2 written by Captain J. Cook, vol.3 by Captain J. King . . . Published by order of the Lords of the Admiralty. [Ed. by Dr. Douglas, Bishop of Salisbury.] 2nd ed. London, printed by H. Hughs for G. Nicol and T. Cadell, 1785.

Illus. maps, 3 vols. and atlas.

See also no.1543. The Dixson Library holds two sets. The first (Q 77/35–7, F78/3) forms part of a nine-volume set of Cook's voyages which formerly belonged to Thomas Pennant, a scientist and friend of Sir Joseph Banks. The second (Q 77/19–21, F78/2) lettered on back Cook's third voyage, vol.1–3, forms part of a nine-volume set of Cook's voyages which formerly belonged to Viscount Sydney, and each volume contains his bookplate. For note re atlas *see* no. 1543.

Copies: NPL:M(Q 980:Co4/1C1–3, X980/24); NPL:D(Q 77/35–7, F78/3; Q 77/19–21, F78/2); NPL:R(F990A/9); NAMu; NParl; SPL; VSL.   1552

1785 London Edition

A Voyage to the Pacific Ocean, undertaken by the command of His Majesty, for making discoveries in the northern hemisphere. Performed under the direction of Captains Cook, Clerke and Gore, in His Majesty's Ships, the *Resolution* and *Discovery*, in the years 1776, 1777, 1778, 1779 and 1780. In three volumes: vol.1 and 2 written by Captain J. Cook, vol.3 by Captain J. King . . . Published by order of the Lords Commissioners of the Admiralty. [Ed. by Dr. Douglas, Bishop of Salisbury.] 3rd ed. London, printed by H. Hughs for G. Nicol and T. Cadell, 1785.

3 vols. and atlas of 63 plates.

See also no.1543. Volume 3, pp.557–64 contains A Defence of the arguments advanced against the existence of Cape Circumcision, by W. Wales. The Mitchell Library holds another copy of the Atlas, with additional unnumbered plate entitled The Death of Captain Cook. For note *see* no. 1543.

Copies: NPL:M(Q 980:Co4/1D1–3, X980/24); NPL:R(Q 990A/32–4, F990A/10); QOM; VParl.   1553

1785 London Edition

A Voyage to the Pacific Ocean, undertaken by the command of His Majesty, for making discoveries in the northern hemisphere. Performed under the direction of Captains Cook, Clerke and Gore, in the years 1776, 7, 8, 9 and 80. Compiled from the various accounts of that voyage hitherto published. London, printed for John Fielding, 1785.

4 vols.

See also no. 1559.

Copies: ANL:F.   1554

[1785?] London Edition. Abridged

Captain Cook's third and last voyage to the Pacific Ocean in the years 1776, 1777, 1778, 1779 and 1780: faithfully abridged from the quarto edition published by order of His Majesty. London, John Fielding and John Stockdale, [1785?].

Illus. port. pp.[ii], xii, 372.

See also no. 1543. VSL gives date [1790?].

Copies: NPL:M(980:Co4/4A1); VSL.   1555

1785 Paris Edition

Troisième voyage de Cook; ou, Voyage à l'Océan Pacifique, ordonné par le Roi d'Angleterre, pour faire des découvertes dans l'hémisphère nord, pour déterminer la position & l'étendue de la côte ouest de l'Amérique septentrionale, sa distance de l'Asie, & résoudre la question du passage au nord. Exécuté sous la direction des Capitaines Cook, Clerke & Gore, sur les vaisseaux la *Résolution* & la *Découverte*, en 1776, 1777, 1778, 1779 & 1780. Traduit de l'Anglois par M. D[emeunier]. Ouvrage enrichi de cartes & de plans, d'après les relèvemens pris par le Lieutenant Henry Roberts, sous l'inspection du Capitaine Cook, & d'une multitude de planches . . . dessinés . . . par M. Webber. Les deux premiers volumes de l'original ont été composés par le Capitaine Jacques Cook. & le troisième par le Capitaine Jacques King. Paris, Hôtel de Thou, 1785.

4 vols.
See no. 1543 for original London edition, and nos. 1557–8, 1584 for other French editions.

Copies: NPL:M(Q 980:Co4/2A1–4); NPL:R(Q 990A/35–9); ANL; VSL.   1556

1785 Paris Edition

Troisième voyage de Cook; ou, Voyage à l'Océan Pacifique, ordonné par le roi d'Angleterre pour faire déterminer la position & l'étendue de la côte ouest de l'Amérique septentrionale, sa distance de l'Asie, & résoudre la question du passage au nord. Exécuté sous la direction des Capitaines Cook, Clerke & Gore, sur les vaisseaux la *Résolution* & la *Découverte* en 1776, 1777, 1778, 1779 & 1780. Traduit de l'Anglois par M. D[emeunier]. Paris, Hôtel de Thou, 1785.

4 vols.
Mitchell Library holds another set with binder's title, Voyage autour du monde, vols. 11–14. *See also* no. 1556.

Copies: NPL:M(980:Co4/6A1–4).   1557

1785 Paris Edition. Abridged

Troisième voyage abrégé du capitaine Cook, dans l'Océan Pacifique, avec une carte générale & l'estampe représentant la mort de ce capitaine. Ou, Histoire des dernières découvertes dans la Mer du Sud, pendant les années 1776, 1777, 1778, 1779 & 1780. [Octavo ed.] Paris, Hôtel de Thou, 1785.

Frontisp. map, 3 vols.
Volume 1 wanting pages after p.512. Abridged from Demeunier's translation. *See* no. 1556.

Copies: NPL:M(980:Co4/6B1–3).   1558

1785 Perth Edition

A Voyage to the Pacific Ocean, undertaken by the command of His Majesty, for making discoveries in the northern hemisphere. Performed under the direction of Captains Cook, Clerke and Gore, in the years 1776, 7, 8, 9 and 80. Compiled from the various accounts of that voyage hitherto published. Perth, R. Morison and Son, 1785.

Illus. map, 4 vols.
See also nos. 1554, 1565, 1572, 1583.

Copies: NPL:M(980:Co4/5A1–4); VSL.   1559

1785–8 London Edition

A Voyage to the Pacific Ocean, undertaken by command of His Majesty for making discoveries in the northern hemisphere; performed under the direction of Captains Cook, Clerke and Gore, in the years 1776, 1777, 1778, 1779 and 1780. Being a copious, comprehensive and satisfactory abridgement of the voyage. Written by Captain James Cook . . . and Captain James King. London, John Fielding, Scatcherd & Whitaker and C. Stalker, 1785–88.

Illus. maps, ports. 4 vols.
Imprint varies. *See also* no. 1543.
Copies: NPL:D(78/41–4); VSL. 1560

1786 German Edition

Neueste Reisebeschreibungen; oder, Jakob Cook's dritte und letzte Reise . . . in den Jahren 1776 bis 1780. Nuernberg, C. Weigel und Schneider, 1786.

Illus. maps, 2 vols.
See also no. 1573, entitled *Jacob Cook's . . . neueste Reise.*
Copies: NPL:M(980:Co4/7A1–2); ANL(vol.1 only). 1561

1787 Dutch Edition

Reis naar den Stillen Oceaan, ondernomen op bevel van zyne Brittannische Majesteit, George de Derde, tot het doen van ontdekkingen in het noorder halfrond, ter uitvoer gebragt onder 't bestuur van de Bevelhebbers Cook, Clerke en Gore in de jaaren 1776, 1777, 1778, 1779 en 1780. Met de schepen de *Resolution* en *Discovery* en beschreven door den Commandeur J. Cook, en door Kapitein J. King. Uit het Engelsch vertaald. Rotterdam, A. Bothall en D. Vis, 1787.

Frontisp. pp. xvi, 611.
See also no. 1543. The Mitchell Library holds another copy, with date altered by hand to 1788.
Copies: NPL:M(980:Co4/10A1); ANL. 1562

1787 German Edition

Dritte und letzte Reise um die Welt des Lieutenants J. Cook, Befehlshaber der königlichen Korvette die *Resoluzion*, in den Jahren 1776 bis 1778. Brünn, Joseph Georg Trassler, 1787.

2 vols.
(*Sammlung der besten Reisebeschreibungen*, 17–18.)
Copies: NPL:M(980:Co4/8A1–2); VU(Baillieu). 1563

1787 Kearsley's Edition

An Abridgment of Captain Cook's last voyage, 1776–80. [Ed. by G. Kearsley.] 5th ed. London, G. Kearsley, 1787.

See also no. 1547.
Copies: VSL. 1564

1787 Perth Edition
A Voyage to the Pacific Ocean. 2nd ed. Perth, R. Morison, 1787.
Vols. 2, 4 only.
See also no. 1559.
Copies: VSL.   1565

1787 Swedish Edition. Abridged
Sammandrag af Capitain Jacob Cooks tredje Resa, i Söderhafwet och
emot Norra Polen . . . ifrån Engelskan. Upsala, J. Edman, 1787.
Map, pp. [xii], 618, [12].
Copies: NPL:M(980:Co4/11A1).   1566

1787–1812 German Edition
Capitain Cooks dritte und letzte Reise; oder, Geschichte einer
Entdeckungsreise nach dem stillen Ocean . . . Eine Uebersetzung nach
der zwoten grossen Englischen Ausgabe in drey Bänden in Quart, mit
einigen Anmerkungen von J.L. Wetzel. Anspach, J.L. Wetzel, 1787–
1812.
Illus. maps, port. 5 vols.
See also no. 1543.
Copies: NPL:M(980:Co4/9A1–5).   1567

1788 Dublin Edition. Abridged
Captain Cook's third and last voyage to the Pacific Ocean, in the years
1776, 1777, 1778, 1779 and 1780; faithfully abridged from the quarto
ed. pub. by order of His Majesty. Dublin, J. Jones, 1788.
pp.xii, 372.
See also no. 1543.
Copies: NPL:M(980:Co4/12A1).   1568

1788 German Edition
Geschichte der See-Reisen und Entdeckungen im Süd-Meer . . . aus
den Tagebüchern der Schiffs-Befehlshaber und den Handschriften der
Gelehrten Herren J. Banks, Dr. Solander, Dr. J.R. Forster und Herrn
G. Forster . . . hrsg . . . Aus dem Englischen übersetzt vom . . . G. Forster.
Berlin, Haude und Spener, 1778 (*sic*)–88.
Illus. port. maps, vol.4–7, [in 2 vols].
Separate title-pages for Band 4–7: Des Capitain Jacob Cook's dritte Entdeckungs-Reise
. . . in das stille Meer und nach dem Nordpol . . . mit den Schiffen *Resolution* und *Discovery*
während der Jahre 1776 bis 1780 . . . Aus den Tagebüchern des Capitain Cook . . . Clerke,
Gore und King, imgleichen des . . . Herrn Anderson hrsg. Aus dem Englischen übersetzt
von G. Forster. Berlin, 1787–(88).
Issued with a German edition of Hawkesworth's account of Cook's first voyage.
Copies: NPL:M(Q 980:Co1/1A1–2).   1569

1788 Russian Edition. Abridged

Posliednee puteshestvie okolo svieta Kapitana Kuka s obstoiatelstvami o ego Zhizni i smerti. Nov. izd. v Sanktpeterburgie, *s pozvoleniia ukaznago*, 1788.

pp. [i], 411.
Title transliterated.
Copies: NPL:M(980:Co4/13A1). 1570

1789 Berlin Edition

Cooks dritter Entdeckungsreise: fünf und vierzig Kupfer und Charten zur deutschen Quart-Ausgabe . . . für die Käufer der Oktav-Ausgabe eben dieses Werks. Berlin, Haude und Spener, 1789.

pp.[iv], 38pp. of illus. folded charts.
(Geschichte der neuesten Seereisen und Entdeckungen im Südmeer, Bd. 6 und 7.)
Copy imperfect. 2 charts and 1 plate missing.
Copies: ANL. 1571

1789 Perth Edition

A Voyage to the Pacific Ocean, undertaken by the command of His Majesty, for making discoveries in the northern hemisphere. Performed under the direction of Captains Cook, Clerke and Gore, in the years 1776, 7, 8, 9 and 80. Compiled from the various accounts of that voyage hitherto published. 3rd ed. Perth, printed by R. Morison, jr. for R. Morison & Son, 1789.

Illus. port. 4 vols.
Volume 1 has additional title-page. *See also* no. 1559.
Copies: NPL:M(980:Co4/5B1–4). 1572

1790 German Edition

Jacob Cook's . . . neuste Reise um die Welt in den Jahren 1776 bis 1780 . . . aus dem Englischen übersetzt. 2te Auf. Leipzig, C. Weigel und U.G. Schneider, 1790.

Illus. maps, 2 vols. in 1.
See also no.1561 entitled *Neueste Reisebeschreibungen; oder, Jakob Cook's dritte und letzte Reise.*
Copies: NPL:D(79/43). 1573

1790 Newcastle Edition

A Voyage to the Pacific Ocean, undertaken by command of His Majesty, for making discoveries in the northern hemisphere. Performed under the direction of Captains Cook, Clerke and Gore in . . . 1776, 1777, 1778, 1779, 1780. Vol.2. Newcastle, M. Brown, 1790.

Forms vol. 2 of no. 44, but contains no general title-page.
Copies: NPL:M(980:Co1/7A2); NPL:D(79/34); NPL:R(S990A/75–6); ANL; SPL; VU(Baillieu). 1574

1793 London Edition. Abridged

Voyage to the Pacific Ocean . . . for making discoveries in the northern hemisphere, performed under the direction of Captains Cook, Clerke and Gore, in the years 1776, 1777, 1778, 1779, 1780, being a copious . . . abridgement of the Voyage written by Captain James Cook . . . and Captain James King. London, printed for Champante and Whitrow . . . and M. Watson, 1793.

Illus. maps, port. 4 vols.
See also no. 1543.

Copies: NPL:M(980:Co4/14A1–4).   1575

1794 Kearsley's Edition

An Abridgment of Captain Cook's last voyage performed in the years 1776, 1777, 1778, 1779 and 1780, for making discoveries in the northern hemisphere, by order of His Majesty. Extracted from the quarto edition, in three volumes. Containing a relation of all the interesting transactions, particularly those relative to the unfortunate death of Captain Cook. To which are added extracts from Captain King's Account of his life and public services. [Ed. by G. Kearsley.] 7th ed. London, printed for C. and G. Kearsley, 1794.

Illus. pp.xxiv, 442, [16].
Mitchell Library copy wanting chart.
See also no. 1547.

Copies: NPL:M(980:Co4/3G1); VSL.   1576

1794–5 Bérenger's Edition

Terzo viaggio del Capitan Giacomo Cook.

Illus.
(Bérenger, Jean Pierre—Raccolta di tutti i viaggi intorno al mondo. Venezia, A. Zatta, 1794–5. Tomo 6–7.)
Abridged account. *See also* no. 1556; and no. 1578 for French edition.

Copies: NPL:M(910.8/B).   1577

1795 Bérenger's Edition

Troisième voyage de Jaques Cook.

(Bérenger, Jean Pierre—Collection de tous les voyages fait autour du monde. 2nd ed. Paris, Poincot et F. Dufart. 1795. Vol.9, pp.59–447.)
Abridged account. *See also* no. 1556; and no. 1577 for Italian edition.

Copies: NPL:M(910.8/B).   1578

1796 New York Edition

Voyage to the Pacific Ocean for making discoveries in the northern hemisphere, performed under the direction of Captains Cook, Clerke and Gore in the years 1776, 1777, 1778, 1779, 1780. By Capt. J. Cook . . . and Capt. J. King. New York, printed by Tiebout and O'Brien for Benjamin Gomez, 1796.

Volume 3 wanting title-page. Apparently a reprint of no. 1545. Volume 4 contains a life of Cook not included in the other edition.

Copies: NPL:M(980:Co4/16A1–4).   1579

[1800] London Edition

A Voyage to the Pacific Ocean. [Vol.2 by James Cook, vol.3 by James King. London? 1800.]

2 vols.
Title from title-page of volume 2.
Copies: ANL. 1580

1813 Leith Edition

A Voyage to the Pacific Ocean for making discoveries in the northern hemisphere, under the direction of Capt. Cook, Clerke & Gore, in the the years 1776, 7, 8, 9 & 80. Carefully revised and corrected. Leith, printed Wm. Reid & Co. for Archibald Constable & Co., Edinburgh, 1813.

Illus. map, port. 3 vols.
See also no. 1587.
Copies: NPL:M(980:Co4/17A1–3). 1581

1814–15 KERR, Robert

A General history and collection of voyages. London, 1814–15.

Vols.12–15 deal with Cook's voyages. *See also* nos. 1543, 1586.
Copies: VSL. 1582

1818 Philadelphia Edition

A Voyage to the Pacific Ocean, undertaken by the command of His Majesty for making discoveries in the northern hemisphere. Performed under the direction of Captains Cook, Clerke and Gore, in the years 1776, 1777, 1778, 1779, 1780. Compiled from the various accounts of that voyage hitherto published. Philadelphia, Robert Desilver, 1818.

Illus. 2 vols.
Portrait as frontispiece to volume 2 is not Captain Charles Clerke of Cook's voyage.
See also no. 1559.
Copies: NPL:M(980:Co4/5C1–2). 1583

1819 Paris Edition

Troisième voyage de Cook; ou, Voyage à l'Océan Pacifique, ordonné par le Roi d'Angleterre pour faire des découvertes dans l'Hemisphère nord pour déterminer la position et l'étendue de la côte ouest de l'Amérique septentrionale, sa distance de l'Asie et résoudre la question du passage au nord. Exécuté sous la direction des Capitaines Cook, Clerke & Gore, sur les vaisseaux la *Résolution* et la *Découverte*, en 1776, 1777, 1778, 1779 et 1780. Traduit de l'Anglois par M. D[emeunier]. Paris, Raymond, 1819.

4 vols.
See also no. 1556.
Copies: NPL:M(980:Co4/6C1–4). 1584

1820 INTRODUCTION to the third voyage of Captain Cook; [with] (To the memory of Captain James Cook). [By Bishop J. Douglas.]

(*In his* Select works. Salisbury, Brodie and Dowding, 1820, pp. 269–349.)
See no. 1543.

Copies: NPL:M(Q 081/1A1). 1585

1824 Kerr's Edition
A Voyage to the Pacific Ocean, undertaken by the command of His Majesty, for making discoveries in the northern hemisphere, to determine the position and extent of the west side of North America, its distance from Asia, and the practicability of a northern passage to Europe. Performed under the direction of Captains Cook, Clerke and Gore, in His Majesty's Ships the *Resolution* and *Discovery*, in the years 1776, 1777, 1778, 1779 & 1780.

(Kerr, Robert—A General history and collection of voyages and travels. Edinburgh, William Blackwood, 1824. Vols.15–17.)
See also nos. 1543, 1582.

Copies: NPL:M(910.8/K); NPL:R(D10:S18–20). 1586

1831 Leith Edition
Voyage to the Pacific Ocean, for making discoveries in the northern hemisphere, under the direction of Captains Cook, Clerke and Gore, in the years 1776, 7, 8, 9 and 80. With an introductory review of maritime discovery down to the time of Captain Cook. With twenty-eight copper-plate engravings. Leith, William Reid & Son; Edinb., Henry Constable, 1831.

2 vols. in 1.
See also no. 1581.

Copies: ANL:F. 1587

1876 *THE NEW LONDON MAGAZINE:* being an universal and complete monthly repository of knowledge, instruction and entertainment. Vol. 2, and supp. London, 1876.

Illus.
Captain Cook's third voyage published serially during the year.

Copies: ANL. 1588

[188–] New York Edition
The Third and last voyage of Captain Cook; intro. by Rev. H.R. Haweis. New York, Hurst and Co., [188–].

pp.160.
From the abridgement by C.R. Low. Cover title: Captain Cook's voyages round the world. *See also* no.1590.

Copies: ANL. 1589

1886 Routledge Edition

The Third and last voyage of Captain Cook; with an intro. by Rev. H. R. Haweis. London, Routledge, 1886.

pp.160.
(*Routledge's World Library.*)
From the abridgement by C.R. Low. *See also* no.1589.
Copies: NPL:M(980:Co4/18A1); VSL. 1590

1959 Day and Stroven Edition

The Discovery of the Hawaiian Islands: [extract from Cook's A Voyage to the Pacific Ocean.]

(*In* Day, Arthur Grove *and* Stroven, Carl—A Hawaiian reader. New York, Appleton-Century-Crofts, 1959. pp.1–10.)
Copies: NPL:M(989.6/8A1). 1591

1969 Dale's Edition

Seventy north to fifty south: the story of Captain Cook's last voyage, wherein are discovered numerous South Pacific islands, the Hawaiian Islands, the coast of North America and Alaska. Condensed, ed. and annotated by P.W. Dale. [With bibl.] Englewood Cliffs, N.J., Prentice-Hall, 1969.

Charts, facs. illus. ports. pp.xii, 370.
Track chart of Cook's last voyage as endpapers.
Abridged from the Dublin 1784 edition.
Copies: NPL:M(980:Co4/19A1); NPL:R(E919/Coo). 1592

Printed Accounts of Associates

1784 AN ABRIDGEMENT of the narrative of a voyage performed by Captain Cook and Captain Clerke, in search of a North West Passage.

(*In* Parkinson, Sydney—A Journal of a voyage to the South Seas . . . and an Appendix. London, Charles Dilly, 1784. pp.314–53.)
See also no. 1594.
Copies: NPL:M(Q 980/P); NPL:D(Q 78/10). 1593

1797 ABRÉGÉ de la relation d'un voyage entrepris à la recherche d'un passage au nord-ouest . . . pendant les années 1776, 1777, 1778 et 1779, par le Capitaine Cooke et le Capitaine Clerke.

(*In* Parkinson, Sydney—Voyage autour du monde. Paris, l'Imprimerie de Guillaume, 1797. Vol.2, pp.235–309.)
See also no. 1593.
Copies: NPL:M(Q 980/P). 1594

ANDERSON, William
1969 Mr. Anderson's Remarks on the country near Queen Charlotte Sound.
Illus.
(*In* Cook, James—Collected Voyages—Printed Accounts [1969. Reed's edition]—
Captain Cook in New Zealand . . . Ed. by A.H. & A.W.Reed. 2nd ed. Wellington, N.Z.,
Reed, 1969. pp.241–54.)
See also no. 225.
Copies: NPL:M(980:Co1/45B1).   1595

ANDERSON, William
1969 Mr. Anderson's Remarks on Van Dieman's Land.
Illus.
(*In* Cook, James—First Voyage—Printed Accounts [1969 Reed's Edition]—Captain
Cook in Australia . . . Ed. by A.W. Reed. Wellington, N.Z., Reed, 1969. pp.176–83.)
Copies: NPL:M(980:Co3/11A1).   1596

BURNEY, James
1914 Burney's log: [extract].
(McNab, Robert—Historical records of New Zealand. Wellington, Govt.Pr., 1914.
Vol.2, pp.197–9.)
Copies: NPL:M(997/M).   1597

EDGAR, Thomas
1914 Edgar's log: [extracts].
(McNab, Robert—Historical records of New Zealand. Wellington, Govt.Pr., 1914.
Vol.2, pp.222–9.)
Copies: NPL:M(997/M).   1598

ELLIS, William
1781 Journal of Captain Cook's last voyage. London, E. Newbery, 1781.
See no.1607. F.W. Howay in his *Authorship of the anonymous account of Captain Cook's last
voyage* has established John Rickman as the author of this publication.

ELLIS, William
1782 An Authentic narrative of a voyage performed by Captain Cook and
Captain Clerke in His Majesty's ships *Resolution* and *Discovery*, during
the years 1776, 1777, 1778, 1779 and 1780, in search of a north-west
passage between the continents of Asia and America; including a faithful
account of all their discoveries, and the unfortunate death of Captain
Cook. Illustrated with a chart, and a variety of cuts. By W. Ellis. London,
G. Robinson, J. Sewell and J. Debrett, 1782.
2 vols.
See also nos. 1600, 1601.
Copies: NPL:M(980:Co4/E1A1–2); NPL:D(78/21–2); ANL; SPL; VParl; VSL.
                                                                           1599

ELLIS, William

1783 An Authentic narrative of a voyage performed by Captain Cook and Captain Clerke in His Majesty's Ships *Resolution* and *Discovery*, during the years 1776, 1777, 1778, 1779 and 1780, in search of a north-west passage between the continents of Asia and America; including a faithful account of all their discoveries, and the unfortunate death of Captain Cook. Illustrated with a chart, and a variety of cuts. By W. Ellis. 2nd ed. London, G. Robinson, J. Sewell and J. Debrett, 1783.

2 vols.
See also no. 1599.

Copies: NPL:M(980:Co4/E1B1–2); NPL:D(78/72–3); NPL:R(S990A/86–7); ANL; QOM.   1600

ELLIS, William

1784 An Authentic narrative of a voyage performed by Captain Cook and Captain Clerke in His Majesty's ships *Resolution* and *Discovery*, during the years 1776, 1777, 1778, 1779 and 1780, in search of a north-west passage between the continents of Asia and America; including a faithful account of all their discoveries, and the unfortunate death of Captain Cook. Illustrated with a chart and a variety of cuts. By W. Ellis. 3rd ed. London, G. Robinson, J. Sewell and J. Debrett, 1784.

2 vols.
See also no 1599.

Copies: NPL:M(980:Co4/E1C1–2); NPL:R(S990A/88–9); VMoU.   1601

KING, James

1824 Captain King's journal of the transactions on returning to the Sandwich Islands.

(Kerr, Robert—General history and collection of voyages and travels. Edinburgh, W. Blackwood, 1824. Vol.16–17.)

Copies: NPL:M(910.8/K); NPL:R(DS909.8A/86–7).   1602

LEDYARD, John

1781 Journal of Captain Cook's last voyage. London, E. Newbery, 1781.

See no. 1607. The authorship of this anonymous publication was previously attributed to Ledyard, but F.W. Howay in his *Authorship of the anonymous account of Captain Cook's last voyage*, has established John Rickman as the author.

LEDYARD, John

1783 A Journal of Captain Cook's last voyage to the Pacific Ocean, and in quest of a North-West Passage between Asia & America; performed in the years 1776, 1777, 1778 and 1779. Illustrated with a chart, shewing the tracts of the ships employed in this expedition. Faithfully narrated from the original ms. of Mr. John Ledyard. Hartford, Connecticut, Nathaniel Patten, 1783.

pp.208.
Mitchell Library copy wanting chart and title-page. Original front paper cover bound in as title-page. Cover title varies slightly, and is preceded by the words Number 1. C.T. Evans in his *American Bibliography*, vol.6, no.17998, states that this journal was first issued in parts to subscribers, no.1 in June and no.2 in July 1783. Listed in Holmes as no.45, where it is stated that parts of the work including the chart, are copied literally from Rickman's anonymous Journal published 1781; Holmes also points out that the account of the death of Cook is not a first-hand account.
See also Beaglehole, vol.3, pt.1, pp.ccviii–ix, and nos.1604–5.

Copies: NPL:M(C454); Hawaiian Mission Children's Society Library, Honolulu (No.1 only). 1603

LEDYARD, John

1963 John Ledyard's Journal of Captain Cook's last voyage; ed. by J.K. Munford . . . Intro. by S.H. Hitchings; [with bibl.]. Corvallis, Oregon, State U.P., 1963.

Charts, illus. maps as endpapers, pp.1, 264.
(*Oregon State Monographs: Studies in history*, no.3.)
Reprint of the author's *A Journal of Captain Cook's last voyage to the Pacific Ocean*, no.1603.

Copies: NPL:M(980:Co4/L1C1); ANL. 1604

LEDYARD, John

1963 A Journal of Captain Cook's last voyage to the Pacific Ocean, and in quest of a north-west passage, between Asia and America, performed in the years 1776, 1777, 1778, and 1779. Chicago, Quadrangle Books, 1963.

pp.208.
(*Americana Classics*, no.10.)
Facsimile edition of 1783 edition, no. 1603, with new title-page.

Copies: NPL:M(980:Co4/L1B1). 1605

PICKERSGILL, Richard

1907 Pickersgill's journal: [extract].

(McNab, Robert—Murihiku and the southern islands. Invercargill, William Smith, pr., 1907. pp.294–300.)
Copies: NPL:M(997.9/M). 1606

RICKMAN, John

1781 Journal of Captain Cook's last voyage to the Pacific Ocean on discovery; performed in the years 1776, 1777, 1778, 1779. Illustrated with cuts, and a chart shewing the tracts of the ships employed in this expedition. Faithfully narrated from the original ms. London, E. Newbery, 1781.

pp. [iv], xlvi, 388.
Previously attributed to John Ledyard, and to William Ellis. A surreptitious and anonymous publication anticipating the authorised account by more than two years. The question of authorship was established by F.W. Howay in his *Authorship of the anonymous account of Captain Cook's last voyage*. Pagination of the last four pages of this copy is misprinted; the final page should be numbered 396. *See* Holmes no.38. *See also* nos.1608–17.

Copies: NPL:M(980:Co4/R1A1); NPL:D(78/31); NPL:R(S990A/84); ANL; NUN; QOM; QU; VSL. 1607

RICKMAN, John

1781 Journal of Captain Cook's last voyage to the Pacific Ocean on discovery; performed in the years 1776, 1777, 1778, 1779. Illustrated with cuts, and a chart shewing the tracts of the ships employed in this expedition. Faithfully narrated from the original ms. Dublin, Messrs. Price [and others], 1781.

Illus. map, pp.[iv], xlvii, 396.
Published anonymously. *See also* no. 1607.
Copies: NPL:D(78/32).   1608

RICKMAN, John

1781 Tagebuch einer Entdekkungs Reise nach der Südsee in den Jahren 1776 bis 1780 unter Anführung der Capitains Cook, Clerke, Gore und King. Mit einer verbesserten Karte und Kupfer nach der originellen Handschrift getreulich beschrieben. Eine Uebersetzung nebst Anmerkungen von J.R. Forster. Berlin, Haude und Spener, 1781.

Illus. map, pp.[xvi], 357.
Published anonymously. *See also* no. 1607.
Copies: NPL:M(980:Co4/R1B1); VSL; VU(Baillieu).   1609

RICKMAN, John

1781 Journal of Captain Cook's last voyage to the Pacific Ocean on discovery, performed in the years 1776, 1777, 1778, 1779. 2nd ed. London, E. Newbery, 1781.

Carefully revised and compared with the original manuscript, the latitudes and longitudes throughout the northern course added, and some errors in the former edition corrected. Not seen. *See also* no. 1607.
Copies: QOM.   1610

RICKMAN, John

1782 Troisième voyage de Cook; ou, Journal d'une expédition faite dans la Mer Pacifique du sud & du nord, en 1776, 1777, 1778, 1779 & 1780. Traduit de l'Anglois [by J.N. Demeunier]. Paris, Pissot, 1782.

Illus. map, pp. x, 508.
Published anonymously. *See also* no. 1607.
Copies: NPL:M(980:Co4/R1G1); ANL.   1611

RICKMAN, John

1782 Troisième voyage de Cook; ou Journal d'une expédition faite dans la Mer Pacifique du sud et du nord, en 1776, 1777, 1778, 1779 & 1780. Traduit de l'Anglois [by J.N. Demeunier]. 2nd ed. Paris, Belin, Volant, 1782.

Frontisp. map, pp.x, 508.
Published anonymously. *See also* no. 1607.
Probably a reissue of no. 1611 with a new title-page.
Copies: NPL:M(980:Co4/R1C1); NPL:R(S990A/85).   1612

RICKMAN, John

1783 Troisième voyage de Cook; ou, Journal d'une expédition faite dans la Mer Pacifique du sud et du nord, en 1776, 1777, 1778, 1779 & 1780. Traduit de l'Anglois [by J.N. Demeunier]. 2nd ed. Paris, Belin, 1783.

pp. [i], 376, plates 2.
Published anonymously. *See* Roberts, no. 6. *See also* no. 1607.

Copies: NPL:M(980:Co4/R1D1).   1613

RICKMAN, John

1783 Troisième voyage de Cook; ou, Journal d'une expédition faite dans la Mer Pacifique du sud et du nord, en 1776, 1777, 1778, 1779 & 1780. Traduit de l'Anglois [by J.N. Demeunier]. 3rd ed. Versailles, Poinçot, et Paris, Belin, 1783.

Frontisp. map, pp.lxiv, 454.
Published anonymously. *See also* no. 1607.

Copies: NPL:M(980:Co4/R1E2); ANL; QOM; VSL.   1614

RICKMAN, John

1785 Journal of Captain Cook's last voyage to the Pacific Ocean on discovery. Performed in the years 1776, 1777, 1778, 1779 and 1780. Illustrated with cuts and a chart, shewing the tracks of the ships employed in this expedition. New ed., compared with and corrected from the voyage published by authority. London, E. Newbery, 1785.

pp.[viii], lvii, 376. *See also* no. 1607.

Copies: NPL:M(980:Co4/R1F1).   1615

RICKMAN, John

1966 Journal of Captain Cook's last voyage to the Pacific Ocean, by J. Rickman. Ann Arbor, Mich., University Microfilms, Inc., 1966.

Illus. maps, pp.[vi, vi], xlvi, [396].
(*March of America Facsimile Series*, no.47.)
Facsimile reprint of London 1781 edition, *see* no. 1607.

Copies: NPL:M(980:Co4/R1H1).   1616

RICKMAN, John

1967 Journal of Captain Cook's last voyage to the Pacific Ocean. Amsterdam, N. Israel, 1967.

Map, plates, pp.[lii], 388.
(*Bibliotheca Australiana*, vol.16.)
Facsimile reprint of London edition, 1781, *see* no. 1607.

Copies: NPL:M(Q 910.8/9A16).   1617

SAMWELL, David

1786 Détails nouveaux et circonstanciés sur la mort du Capitaine Cook; traduits de l'Anglois. Paris, chez Née de la Rochelle, 1786.

pp. 56 + [ii].
Published anonymously. *See also* no. 1620.

Copies: NPL:M(C759).   1618

315

SAMWELL, David

1786 Interesting particulars respecting the death of Captain Cook. [From the Narrative of David Samwell, surgeon of the *Discovery*.]

Extract from the *New Annual Register* 1786, pp.198–202. *See also* no. 1620.

Copies: ANL:F. 1619

SAMWELL, David

1786 A Narrative of the death of Captain James Cook; to which are added some particulars concerning his life and character, and observations respecting the introduction of the venereal disease into the Sandwich Islands. London, G.G.J. and J. Robinson, 1786.

pp.[iv], 34.
See also nos. 1618–19, 1621–7.

Copies: NPL:M(C694); ANL. 1620

SAMWELL, David

1786 A Narrative of the death of Captain James Cook.

(*Weekly Entertainer*, Sherborne, Sept.25, 1786, pp.298–304.)
Abridged, and with alterations. *See also* no. 1620.

Copies: NPL:M(923.9/C771.2/1B1). 1621

SAMWELL, David

1789 [Extract from Narrative of the death of Capt. James Cook.]

(Kippis, *Rev.* Andrew—Biographia Britannica. 2nd ed. London, printed by Rivington and Marshall for J. Rivington [and others], 1789. Vol.4, pp.230–34.)
See also no. 1620.

Copies: NPL:M(F920.042); NPL:R(C22:Q20‡). 1622

SAMWELL, David

1893 Some account of a voyage to South Seas in 1776, 1777, 1778: [extract, giving an account of Cook's death].

(*Historical Records of New South Wales*. Sydney, Govt. Pr., 1893. Vol.1, pt.1, pp.450–78.)
Copies: NPL:M(991/N, Ref.Books.); NPL:D(89/267); NPL:R(991/16). 1623

SAMWELL, David

1899 Extracts from the diary of Dr. Samwell . . . by J. Edge Partington.

(Polynesian Society—*Journal*, vol.8, Dec.1899, pp.250–63.)
Copies: NPL:M(Q572.9/P); NPL:R(S572.99/2). 1624

SAMWELL, David

[1916] A Narrative of the death of Captain James Cook. [Trans. by B. Cartwright, Jr. Honolulu, 1916.]

pp.26.
(Hawaiian Historical Society—*Reprint* no.2.) Edition limited to 500 copies. *See also* no. 1620.

Copies: NPL:M(923.9/C771.2/1C1). 1625

SAMWELL, David

1957 Captain Cook and Hawaii: a narrative by David Samwell. With an introduction by Sir Maurice Holmes. San Francisco, David Magee, 1957.

Illus. ports, pp.[xx], 42.
Limited edition, 750 copies.
With portrait of author, and reproduction of The Death of Captain Cook, from a painting by Webber, engraved by Bartolozzi and Byrne. *See also* no. 1620.
Copies: NPL:M(923.9/C771.2/1D1); ANL; WU.   1626

SAMWELL, David

1966 A Narrative of the death of Captain James Cook.

(*In* Day, Arthur Grove—True tales of the South Seas. New York, Appleton-Century, 1966. pp.304–20.) *See also* no. 1620.
Copies: NPL:M(808.83/2A1).   1627

ZIMMERMANN, Heinrich

1781 Reise um die Welt mit Capitain Cook. Mannheim, E.F. Schwan, 1781.

pp.110.
See also nos. 1629–36.
Copies: NPL:M(C749); NPL:D(78/66); ANL; VSL.   1628

ZIMMERMANN, Heinrich

1782 Dernier voyage du Capitaine Cook autour du monde, où se trouvent les circonstances de sa mort; publié en Allemand par Henri Zimmerman. Berne, Nouvelle Société Typographique, 1782.

pp.xvi, 200.
See also no. 1628.
Copies: NPL:M(980:Co4/Z1B1); ANL:F.   1629

ZIMMERMAN, Heinrich

1783 Dernier voyage du Capitaine Cook autour du monde, où se trouvent les circonstances de sa mort; publié en Allemand par Henri Zimmerman. Berne, Nouvelle Société Typographique, 1783.

pp.xvi, 200.
Reprint of no. 1629. *See also* no. 1628.
Copies: NPL:M(980:Co4/Z1C1); VSL.   1630

ZIMMERMANN, Heinrich

1784 H. Zimmermann. Reize rondom de waereld. Met Kapitein Cook. Uit het Hoogduitsch Vertaald. Te Leyden, by A. en J. Honkoop, 1784.

pp.[ii], 6, 116.
See also no. 1628.
Copies: ANL.   1631

ZIMMERMANN, Heinrich

1791 Reize rondom de Waereld met Kapitein Cook. Leyden, L. van der Spyk, 1791.

pp.6, 116.
See also no. 1628.

Copies: NPL:M(980:Co4/Z1D1).   1632

ZIMMERMANN, Heinrich

1926 Cook's last voyage, Zimmermann narrative: [translation, made in the Turnbull Library, Wellington, of extracts from Zimmermann's book, published at Mannheim in 1781. From the *Evening Post*, Feb.27, 1926.]

(Cook, J.—Captain Cook's Journals, memorials, etc.: Newspaper cuttings, pp.104–107, 1922–26.)

Copies: NPL:M(Q 980/Co1/N1A1).   1633

ZIMMERMAN, Heinrich

1926 Zimmermann's Account of the third voyage of Captain Cook, 1776–1780; trans. by U. Tewsley, under direction of J.C. Andersen, with a few explanatory notes. Wellington, N.Z., Govt. Pr., 1926.

Facs. illus. map, pp.49.
(Alexander Turnbull Library—*Bulletin*, no.2.)
From the Mannheim 1781 edition, *see* no. 1628.

Copies: NPL:M(980:Co4/Z1E1); NPL:D(92/227); ANL; QParl; VSL.   1634

ZIMMERMANN, Heinrich

1930 Zimmermann's Captain Cook: an account of the third voyage of Captain Cook around the world, 1776–1780 . . . trans. from the Mannheim ed. of 1781 by E. Michaelis and C. French. Ed. with an intro. and notes by F.W. Howay. [With bibl.] Toronto, Ryerson Press, 1930.

Facs. illus. maps, pp.xviii, 120.
(*Canadian Historical Studies*.)
Limited edition no.82/250. *See also* no. 1628.

Copies: NPL:M(980:Co4/Z1F1); NPL:D(93/141); VSL.   1635

ZIMMERMANN, Heinrich

1941 Extracts from Voyage round the world with Captain Cook, by Heinrich Zimmermann, from Wisslock in the Palatinate. Mannheim, 1781. Trans. by M.E. Webster.

(*Victorian Historical Magazine*, vol.19, June 1941, pp.27–30.)

Copies: NPL:M(992/V); NPL:D(9/57).   1636

Books about the Third Voyage

1780 BROOKE, Robert

Remarks and conjectures on the voyage of the ships *Resolution* and *Discovery*

. . . after the death of Capt. James Cook, with . . . an eulogism to the memory of that celebrated navigator. London, the author, 1780.

See Holmes no.34.

Copies: VSL. 1637

1781 ENGEL, Samuel

Remarques sur la partie de la relation du voyage du Capitaine Cook, qui concerne le détroit entre l'Asie et l'Amerique . . . tr. de l'allemand & augmentée. Berne, F. S. Fetscherin, 1781.

Another edition listed in Roberts (no. 11, b) published in Geneva, Didier, 1781. (Jackson no. 98.)

Copies: VSL. 1638

1781 FORSTER, Johann Georg Adam

Strödde underrättelser om Capitaine Cooks sista resa och olyckeliga död i Söderhafwet; öfwersättning utur *Göthingisches Magazin* af A. Sparrman. Stockholm, P.A. Brodin, 1781.

Map, pp.47.

Copies: NPL:M(980:Co4/F1B1). 1639

1787 COXE, *Rev.* William

Account of the Russian discoveries between Asia and America, to which are added the conquest of Siberia and the history of the transactions and commerce between Russia and China. 3rd ed. London, Cadell, 1787.

Illus. maps, pp.xxviii [i.e. xxx], 454.

Includes a supplement giving a comparison of the Russian discoveries with those of Captains Clerke and Cook. *See also* no. 1642, 1649, and *see* Holmes, nos. 64, 107. The supplement does not appear in the previous editions published in 1780.

Copies: NPL:M(980:Co4/C1C1); ANL; QOM. 1640

1794 KIRCHHOF, Nikolaus Anton Johann

Auszug aus Cook und Kings Reise in den Jahren 1776 bis 80 nebst einem Verzeichnisse ihrer beobachteten Breiten und Langen. Berlin, F. Nikolai, 1794.

pp.62 + [1].

Copies: NPL:M(980:Co4/K1A1). 1641

1803 COXE, *Rev.* William

Account of the Russian discoveries between Asia and America, to which are added the conquest of Siberia and the history of the transactions and commerce between Russia and China. By William Coxe. 4th ed. London, Cadell and Davies, 1803.

Illus. maps, pp.xxiv [i.e. xxvi], 500.

See also nos. 1640, 1649.

Copies: NPL:M(980:Co4/C1D1). 1642

1893–5 GIGLIOLI, Enrico Hillyer

Appunti intorno ad una collezione etnografica fatta durante il terzo viaggio di Cook e conservata sin dalla fine del secolo scorso nel R. Museo di Fisica, e Storia Naturale di Firenze. Firenze, 1839–5.

Illus.

Copies: NPL:M(Q 572.99/G); ANL; VSL.   1643

1916 DAHLGREN, Erik Wilhelm

Were the Hawaiian Islands visited by the Spaniards before their discovery by Captain Cook in 1778? [With bibl.] Stockholm, Almqvist & Wiksells Boktryckeri-A.-B, 1916.

Maps, pp.222.

(Kungl. Svenska Vetenskapsakademien—*Handlingar* Band 57, no.4.)

Copies: NPL:M(Q 989.6/D); ANL; VSL.   1644

1956 BUSHNELL, Oswald Andrew

The Return of Lono: a novel of Captain Cook's last voyage. Boston, Little Brown, 1956.

pp.290.

(*An Atlantic Monthly Press Book.*)

See also no. 1646.

Copies: ANL.   1645

1957 BUSHNELL, Oswald Andrew

The Last days of Captain Cook: a novel. London, Chatto & Windus, 1957.

pp.252.

Originally published as *Return of Lono: a novel of Captain Cook's last voyage. See* no. 1645.

Copies: NPL:M(813.5/B979/1B1); ANL; QParl; VSL; WU.   1646

1960 MIERS, Earl Schenk

Vitus Bering and James Cook discover Alaska and Hawaii; written by E.S. Miers. With maps . . . by E. Arno and with wood engravings by S. Martin . . . Pub. . . . for the friends of the Curtis Paper Co. Newark, Del., 1960.

pp.[32].

Cover title *Arctic sun and tropic moon.*

Copies: NPL:M(910.4/80A1); ANL.   1647

[1963] FRASER, Conon

With Captain Cook in New Zealand. Illus. by Harry Toothill. London, Muller, [1963].

Diag. illus. map, ports. pp.144.

(*Adventures in geography*, ed. by Robert Owen.)

Copies: NPL:M(997/28A1); ANL.   1648

1966 COXE, *Rev.* William

A Comparative view of the Russian discoveries with those made by Captains Cook and Clerke; and a sketch of what remains to be ascertained by future navigators. Ann Arbor, Mich., Univ. Microfilms Inc., 1966. pp.31.

A facsimile of London 1787 edition, issued as a supplement to the author's The Russian discoveries. *See also* nos. 1640, 1642.

Copies: NPL:R(N910.0947).   1649

Articles, etc., about the Third Voyage

[17—] PALLAS, Peter Simon, *Professor*

Some particulars concerning Captain Cook's last voyage, with an account of his death, in a letter from Professor Pallas at Petersburgh to Dr. Busching at Berlin. Translated from the original.

Reprinted in *A Short review of the principal transactions of the present reign* [17—], pp. 157–60.

Copies: QOM.   1650

1780 PERIPLUS, *pseud.*

A Summary account of the voyage undertaken by order of government, in His Majesty's ships, the *Resolution* and *Discovery*. Compiled from authentic papers, and revised by an officer returned from the voyage, and illustrated by a new . . . chart. London, Dec. 1780.

pp.307–12.

Extract from *London Magazine*, issued as an extra half-sheet. It is a republication, with corrections to both account and chart, from the July, 1780, number of the magazine.

Copies: NPL:M(980:Co4/P1A1).   1651

1788 COOK'S VOYAGE to the Pacific Ocean; undertaken by command of His Majesty.

(*Lady's Magazine*, vol.19, 1788. various pp.)

Copies: NPL:M(980/L).   1652

[1798] CLARET DE FLEURIEU, Charles Pierre, *Comte*
Cook.

(*In his* Voyage autour du monde . . . 1790, 1791 et 1792, par Etienne Marchand. Paris, Imprimerie de la Republique, [1798]. Tome 1, pp.xcii–cv.)

Copies: NPL:M(910.4/M); NPL:R(S990A/94).   1653

1803–4 CAMPE, Joachim Heinrich

Capitain James Cooks Reise omkring Jorden: en Laesebog for Ungdommen, efter Campes Laeremaade . . . Oversat af H.C. Lund. Kiobenhavn, Math. John. Sebbelom, 1803–4.

Illus. in colour, 3 vols. in 1.

See also no.91.

Copies: NPL:M(980:Co4/C2A1).   1654

1816 WALKER, —
Sandwich Islands.

(*In his* Key to . . . geographical tour through the . . . western hemisphere. London, W. Darton, 1816. pp. 38–43.)

Copies: NPL:M(910.7/W). 1655

1817 CAMPBELL, John
Account of the third and last voyage round the world, performed by Captain Cook, between the years 1776 and 1780.

(*In his* Lives of British admirals. New ed. London, 1817. Vol. 7, pp. 111–74.)

Copies: NPL:R(S359.0942/87). 1656

1819 BURNEY, James
Captain Cook on the north-west coast of America.

(*In his* Chronological history of north-eastern voyages. London, Payne & Foss, 1819. pp. 202–34.)

Copies: NPL:M(989.9/B); NPL:R(S.C.). 1657

1819 BURNEY, James
Captain Cook through Bering's Strait, and in the sea north of the strait; [and] (Sequel).

(*In his* Chronological history of north-eastern voyages. London, Payne & Foss, 1819. pp. 235–70.)

Copies: NPL:M(989.9/B); NPL:R(S.C.). 1658

1828 SPARKS, Jared
[Remarks on Cook's last voyage.]

(*In his* Memoirs of the life and travels of John Ledyard. London, H. Colburn, 1828. pp. 48–166.)
See also nos. 1660–62.

Copies: NPL:M(A923.9/L); NPL:R(S920/L476). 1659

1828 SPARKS, Jared
[Remarks on Cook's last voyage.]

(*In his* Life of John Ledyard. Cambridge, U.S.A., Halliard and Brown, 1828. pp. 37–116.)
See also nos. 1659, 1661–2.

Copies: NPL:M(A923.9/L). 1660

1834 SPARKS, Jared
[Remarks on Cook's last voyage.]

(*In his* Travels and adventures of John Ledyard. London, pub. for H. Colburn by R. Bentley, 1834. pp. 48–166.)
See also nos. 1659–60, 1662.

Copies: NPL:M(A923.9/L). 1661

1834 SPARKS, Jared
[Remarks on Cook's last voyage.]

(*In his* Travels and adventures of John Ledyard. 2nd ed. London, pub. for H. Colburn by R. Bentley, 1834. pp. 48–166.)
See also nos. 1659–61.

Copies: NPL:M(A923.9/L).   1662

1838 CHAMPAGNAC, Jean Baptiste Joseph de
Histoire du Capitaine Cook.

Illus.
(*In his* Le Petit matelot; ou, Voyage en Océanie . . . par C.-H. de Mirval. Paris, Lehuby, 1838. pp. 220–36.)
See also nos. 1664, 1668.

Copies: NPL:M(989/34A1).   1663

[1842] CHAMPAGNAC, Jean Baptiste Joseph de
Histoire du Capitaine Cook.

Illus.
(*In his* Le Petit matelot . . . par E.-H. de Mirval. New ed. Paris, Lehuby, [1842]. pp. 196–210.)
Bibliothèque spéciale de la jeunesse.
See also nos.1663, 1668.

Copies: NPL:M(989/34B1).   1664

1843 JARVES, James Jackson
[Visit to the Sandwich Islands.]

(*In his* History of the Hawaiian or Sandwich Islands. London, Moxon, 1843. pp.96–123.)
See also nos. 1666–7, 1670.

Copies: NPL:M(999.6/J); NPL:D(84/248); VSL.   1665

1843 JARVES, James Jackson
[Visit to the Sandwich Islands.]

Illus.
(*In his* History of the Hawaiian or Sandwich Islands. 2nd ed. Boston, Tappan and Dennet, 1843. pp.107–36.)
See also nos. 1665, 1667, 1670.

Copies: NPL:M(999.6/J); VSL.   1666

1847 JARVES, James Jackson
[Visit to the Sandwich Islands.]

Illus.
(*In his* History of the Hawaiian Islands. 3rd ed. Honolulu, Hitchcock, 1847. pp.56–71.)
See also nos. 1665–6, 1670.

Copies: NPL:M(999.6/J); VSL.   1667

1853 CHAMPAGNAC, Jean Baptiste Joseph de
Histoire du Capitaine Cook.
(*In his* Le Petit matelot; ou, Voyage en Océanie. Chapter 12.)
See also nos. 1663–4.
Copies: ANL.   1668

1862 MALO, David
Ka Mooolelo Hawaii. Histoire de l'Archipel Havaiien . . . Texte [by D.
Malo and others] et traduction précédés d'une intro. sur l'état physique,
moral et politique du pays, par J. Remy. Paris, Franck, 1862.
pp. [ii], lxxv, 254.
Parallel texts in Hawaiian and French.
Copies: NPL:M(999.6/47A1); ANL.   1669

1872 JARVES, James Jackson
[Visit to the Sandwich Islands.]
Illus.
(*In his* History of the Hawaiian islands. 4th ed. Honolulu, Whitney, 1872. pp.51–64.)
See also nos. 1665–7.
Copies: NPL:M(999.6/J); NPL:D(87/169); VSL.   1670

1880 GILL, *Rev.* William Wyatt
Captain Cook's visit to Mangaia; The drama of Cook; Captain Cook's
visit to Atiu.
(*In his* Historical sketches of savage life in Polynesia; with illustrative clan songs. Welling-
ton, Govt. Pr., 1880. pp. 174–90.)
See also no. 1672.
Copies: NPL:M(398.1/G); ANL.   1671

1894 GILL, *Rev.* William Wyatt
Captain Cook's visit to Mangaia; The drama of Cook; Captain Cook's
visit to Atiu.
(*In his* From darkness to light in Polynesia; with illustrative clan songs. London, Religious
Tract Society, 1894. pp. 243–64.)
See also no. 1671.
Copies: NPL:M(398.1/G).   1672

1896 EYKYN, *Rev.* Thomas
Cook's discovery of the [Hawaiian] Islands; [with account of his death].
(*In his* Parts of the Pacific, by a peripatetic parson. London, Swan Sonnenschein, 1896.
pp. 292–7.)
Copies: NPL:M(980/161A1).   1673

1898 HALSTEAD, Murat
Early history of the Sandwich Islands.
(*In his* The Story of the Philippines. Chicago, Our Possessions Pub. Co., 1898. pp. 375–
404.)
Copies: NPL:M(998.2/30A1).   1674

1905 LAUT, Agnes Christina
Captain Cook in America.
Illus. port.
(*In her* Vikings of the Pacific. New York, Macmillan, 1905. pp. 172–209.)
Copies: NPL:M(910.4/110A1).   1675

1909 McNAB, Robert
Cook's last visit, La Perouse and Bligh, 1776 to 1788.
(*In his* Murihiku. Wellington, N.Z., W. & T., 1909. pp. 62–76.)
Copies: NPL:M(997.9M); NPL:R(DS997/16).   1676

1912 SYNGE, Margaret Bertha
Cook's third voyage and death.
Illus. map.
(*In her* A Book of discovery. London, Jack, 1912. pp. 330–8.)
See also nos. 1683, 1709.
Copies: NPL:M(910.9/10A1).   1677

1913 JOHNSTON, *Sir* Harry Hamilton
Cook's second and third voyages.
Illus.
(*In his* Pioneers in Australasia. London, Blackie, 1913. pp. 252–77.)
Pioneers of Empire.
Copies: NPL:M(980/J); NPL:R(S990/8).   1678

1914 PAYNE, Harold H.
Admiral Burney and the death of Captain Cook: some unpublished manuscripts. London, [1914].
(Newspaper cuttings: Captain Cook, vol.2.)
Reprint from *Cornhill Magazine*, Nov. 1914, pp. 677–91. The manuscripts comprise part of the Log of the *Discovery*, written by Burney, and a narrative, not in Burney's handwriting, entitled An Account of the death of Capt. Cook, etc.
Copies: NPL:M(Q 980:Co1/N1A2); NPL:R(DS050/C817).   1679

1916 BRITTEN, James
William Anderson, 1778, and the plants of Cook's third voyage; [with note].
(*Journal of Botany*, vol.54, pp.345–52, Dec. 1916; vol.55, p.54.)
Photographic copy. Also in microfilm.
Copies: NPL:M(980:Co4/B1A1).   1680

[1919?] FINCH, Robert J.
Captain Cook's last voyage.
(*In his* Kingsway book of famous explorers. London, Evans Brothers, [1919?]. pp. 85–90.)
Copies: NPL:M(910.9/F).   1681

[1919] GOWEN, Herbert Henry
Coming of the white man, [etc.].
(*In his* Napoleon of the Pacific. New York, F.H. Revell Co., [1919]. pp. 55–106.)
Copies: NPL:M(999.6/G). 1682

1920 SYNGE, Margaret Bertha
Cook's third voyage and death.
Illus. map.
(*In her* A Book of discovery. New York, Putnam, 1920. pp. 330–8.)
See also nos. 1677, 1709.
Copies: NPL:M(910.9/10B1). 1683

1921 HOWAY, Frederic William
Authorship of the anonymous account of Captain Cook's last voyage.
Seattle, Washington University State Historical Society, 1921.
Extract from *Washington Historical Quarterly*, vol. 12, no. 1, Jan. 1921.
Copies: NPL:M(980:Co4/H1A1). 1684

1923 WESTERVELT, William Drake
Captain Cook.
(*In his* Hawaiian historical legends. New York, Fleming H. Revell, 1923. pp.100–13.)
Copies: NPL:M(999.6/29A1); ANL. 1685

1925 KIPPIS, *Rev.* Andrew
Tasmania in 1777.
(*In* Ridgway, Athelstan—The World revealed: Australasia. London, Nelson, 1925. pp. 35–7.)
Copies: NPL:M(980/143A1). 1686

1928 GOULD, Rupert Thomas
Bligh's notes on Cook's last voyage.
Illus.
(*Mariner's Mirror*, vol. 14, Oct. 1928, pp. 371–85.)
See also no. 1688.
Copies: NPL:R(DS656.506/7); ANL. 1687

1928 GOULD, Rupert Thomas
Bligh's notes on Cook's last voyage.
pp. 13.
Transcribed, with variations, by Sir William Dixson, from the *Mariner's Mirror*, vol. 14, no. 4, Oct. 1928. *See also* no. 1687.
Copies: NPL:D(MS.99). 1688

1928 STADLER, Hans
Kapitän Cooks erster Aufenthalt auf Otaheite. (Kapitän Cooks letzte Fahrt.)

(*In his* Reisebilder aus Australien und Ozeanien. Wien, Deutscher Verlag für Jugend und Volk, 1928. Chapters 1 and 5.)

Copies: NPL:M(980/51A1); ANL.   1689

1931 MACKANESS, George
A Voyage with Captain Cook; [with bibl.].

(*In his* Life of Vice-Admiral William Bligh. Sydney, A. & R., 1931. pp.12–34.)
See also nos. 1693, 1703.

Copies: NPL:M(A923.59/B648.1/1A1); NPL:R(920/B648/1).   1690

1934 ANDERSEN, Johannes Carl
Observations during Cook's third voyage and during subsequent French voyages. New Plymouth, N.Z., 1934.

Illus.
(Polynesian Society—*Memoir*, no.10, pp.31–73.)
Polynesian Society—*Journal* vol.41, Supplement.

Copies: NPL:M(572.997/A).   1691

[1935] ROSE, John Holland
Charges against Captain Cook in Hawaii; [with bibl. notes].

(*In his* Man and the sea. Cambridge, W. Heffer, [1935]. pp. 270–72.)

Copies: NPL:M(910.4/R); NPL:R(S909.8A/32); ANL.   1692

1936 MACKANESS, George
A Voyage with Captain Cook; [with bibl.].

(*In his* Life of Vice-Admiral William Bligh. New ed. New York, Farrar & Rinehart, 1936. pp. 12–34.)
See also nos. 1690, 1703.

Copies: NPL:M(A923.59/B648.1/1B1).   1693

1937 WAGNER, Henry Raup
The Voyage of Captain Cook, 1776–1780.

(*In his* The Cartography of the northwest coast of America to the year 1800, [by] H.R. Wagner; [with bibl. and descriptive lists of maps and place names still in use, and obsolete place names]. Berkeley, 1937. Vol. 1, pp. 183–90.)

Copies: NPL:R(Q 970A/10); ANL.   1694

1939 BURKE, Marie Louise
The Return of Lono.

Illus.
(*In her* Kamehameha, King of the Hawaiian Islands. San Francisco, Colt Press, 1939. pp. 17–37.)

Copies: NPL:M(Q 999.6/B); NPL:R(Q 999.6/1); ANL.   1695

1939 MUNFORD, James Kenneth

Bound for the South Seas [and other chapters on Cook's Third Voyage].

(*In his* John Ledyard: an American Marco Polo. Portland, Oregon, Binfords & Mort, 1939. pp. 64–156.)

Copies: NPL:M(A923.9/L). 1696

1940 WHICH WAS COOK'S MARAE? [Articles by A.C. Rowland and J.D. McCornish.]

Illus.

(*Pacific Islands Monthly*, 1940, May, pp.46–8; Jy. pp.34–5.)

Copies: NPL:M(Q 988.05/P). 1697

1941 CHICKERING, William H.

Discovery and *Resolution*.

(*In his* Within the sound of these waves. New York, Harcourt, Brace, 1941. pp. 113–202.)

Copies: NPL:M(999.6/C); ANL; VSL. 1698

1946 AUGUR, Helen

Account of John Ledyard's experiences on the *Resolution*.

pp. 58–111.

(*In her* Passage to glory: John Ledyard's America. [A biography of John Ledyard. With bibl.] N.Y., Doubleday, 1946.)

Copies: NPL:M(A923.9/L). 1699

1949 LUOMALA, Katharine

Cook and his crews: [their accounts of the Maui myth].

(*In her* Maui-of-a-thousand tricks: his Oceanic and European biographers. [With bibl.] Honolulu, The Museum, 1949. pp. 252–6.)

Bernice P. Bishop Museum—*Bulletin*, no.198.

Copies: NPL:M(Q 572.999/L). 1700

1949 MITCHELL, Mairin

The North Pacific: Captain Cook.

(*In his* The Maritime history of Russia, 848–1948. London, Sidgwick and Jackson, 1949. pp. 217–21.)

Copies: NPL:M(656.509/M); NPL:R(947/82). 1701

1951 [EXTRACT from a letter, June 1776, signed An Old Sailor, and printed in the *Scots Magazine*, 1776. Mentions Cook's third voyage.]

(*Australian Genealogist*, Sydney, vol. 6, p. 158, Nov. 1951.)

Copies: NPL:M(A929.06/A). 1702

1951 MACKANESS, George

A Voyage with Captain Cook; [with bibl.].

(*In his* Life of Vice-Admiral William Bligh. New ed. Sydney, A. & R., 1951. pp. 9–25.)

See also nos. 1690, 1693.

Copies: NPL:M(A923.59/B648.1/1C1); NPL:R(N920/B648/4). 1703

1956 BROWN, Roderick Langmere Haig Haig–
Death of a leader [Captain Cook].
(*In his* Captain of the *Discovery:* the story of Captain George Vancouver. London, Macmillan, 1956. pp. 18–30.)
Copies: NPL:M(910.4/B). 1704

1959 CHARLIAT, Pierre-Jacques
Le Troisième voyage de Cook dans le Pacifique: le grand nord et la guerre des fourrures.
(*In his* Le Temps des grands voiliers. Paris, Nouvelle Librairie de France, 1959. pp. 201–12.)
Parias, L.H.—Histoire universelle des explorations, vol. 3.
Copies: NPL:M(910.9/9A1). 1705

1959 GREENE, Carla
Captain Cook discovers the [Hawaiian] Islands.
(*In her* A Trip to Hawaii. New York, Lantern Press, 1959. pp. 38–41.)
For children.
Copies: NPL:M(989.6/3A1). 1706

1961 HALLIDAY, E.M.
Captain Cook's American.
Illus. some in colour, ports.
(*American Heritage*, pp. 60–72, 84–7, vol. 23, no. 1, Dec. 1961.)
Copies: NPL:M(Q 973.05/1). 1707

1962 BERIOT, Agnes
Le Troisième voyage et la mort d'un grand marin.
(*In her* Grands voiliers autour du monde: les voyages scientifiques, 1760–1850. Paris, Editions du Pont Royal, 1962. pp. 66–78.)
Copies: NPL:M(Q 910.4/14A1); NPL:R(NQ 910.4/1). 1708

1962 SYNGE, Margaret Bertha
Cook's third voyage and death.
Illus. map.
(*In her* A Book of discovery. New ed. Edinburgh, Nelson, 1962. pp. 229–35).
See also nos. 1677, 1683.
Copies: NPL:M(910.9/10C1). 1709

1962 WILLIAMS, Glyndwr
The Boffin Bay expedition, and the voyage of James Cook.
(*In his* The British search for the Northwest Passage in the eighteenth century. London, pub. for the Royal Commonwealth Society by Longmans, 1962. pp. 184–211.)
Copies: NPL:M(989.9/5A1); NPL:R(N971.018/4). 1710

1966 HAZLITT, William Carew
Expedition of Captain Cook in 1776.

(*In his* British Columbia and Vancouver Island. Wakefield, Eng., S.R.Pubs., 1966. pp.23–9.)

Copies: NPL:R(N971.102/1).   1711

n.d. DISCOVERY of the Sandwich Islands.
(National school reader. London, W. Wetton, n.d. pp. 46–8.)

Copies: NPL:M(428/N).   1712

Charts
Manuscripts

Originals cannot be reproduced without the permission of the owner.

[1763–80] SMITH, Isaac
Original sketches, drawings, maps etc. [1763–80] collected by Admiral Isaac Smith who served as an officer under Captain James Cook, the circumnavigator, in his first & second voyages. A.D. 1768–1775.

ff.49, 97 drawings.

Title is in the hand of Canon Bennett, a relative of Isaac Smith, from whom the volume was acquired by the Government of New South Wales. MS. contents list is from Isaac Smith's papers. A new contents list and an index have been made and are inserted. Some of the drawings are signed "H. Roberts", "Hen^y Roberts" one is signed "W.H.", others are ascribed in Canon Bennett's hand to W. Hodges; presumably this was on the back of the drawings (now pasted down) or may have been noted in pencil, as still apparent in some cases, on the leaves of the volume, as it is not on the MS. contents list. A note at the beginning in Canon Bennett's hand, suggests that some of the unsigned drawings may be by Isaac Smith. Some of the drawings appear to be the originals of the plates to Cook's second voyage. With the exception of two of the first voyage, the drawings probably all belong to the second voyage but some may be of the third. The charts include two by Cook of Newfoundland 1763, one of Charlestown 1780, one of the track of H.M.S. *Perseverance* etc. The drawings are listed separately at no. 1379, the maps, charts and coastal profiles at no. 1331.

Copies: NPL:M(PXD11).   1713

Charts
Reproductions

The following charts relating to Cook's voyage are contained in his *A Voyage to the Pacific Ocean . . . for making discoveries in the Northern Hemisphere*. London, G. Nicol . . . and T. Cadell, 1784. The charts have been indexed from the copy in the Mitchell Library at Q 980:Co4/ 1A1–2 and X980/24A, and have not been listed for other copies and editions.

A General Chart: Exhibiting the Discoveries made by Captn. James Cook in this and his two preceeding Voyages; with the Tracks of the Ships under his Command. By Lieut. Henry Roberts of His Majesty's Royal Navy. [Engraved by] W. Palmer. [London, G. Nicol . . . and T. Cadell, 1784.] (Plate No. I).

No scale given, 1 sheet, cm 54 x 90.
Shows tracks of Cook's ships with dates, place names, notes re discovery; town; rivers.
Atlas, [p.1]. X980/24A.

Kerguelen's Land called by C. Cook Island of Desolation . . . Decr. 1776. Writing by Harmar. [Drawn by Lieut. Henry Roberts. London, G. Nicol . . . and T. Cadell, 1784.] (Plate No. II).

No scale given, 1 sheet, cm 24 x 28.
Inset: Islands discovered by M. Marion du Fresne 1772 called by C. Cook in 1776 Prince Edward Isles.
Shows coastline, track of *Resolution* with dates, depths in fathoms, anchorages; place names. *Vol. 1, facing p. 51.*

Sketch of Port Palliser [and] Plan of Christmas Harbour on Kerguelen's-Land. [Copied by Lieut. Henry Roberts. London, G. Nicol . . . and T. Cadell, 1784.] (Plate No. III).

Various scales. 1 sheet, 2 maps on cm 14 x 21.
Shows coastlines, track of *Resolution*, depths in fathoms, anchorages; place names, hill shadings. *Vol. 2, facing p. 61.*

Chart of Van Diemen's Land. [Engraved by] Harmar. [Copied by Lieut. Henry Roberts. London, G. Nicol . . . and T. Cadell, 1784.] (Plate No. V).

No scale given, 1 sheet, cm 21 x 34.
Coastal profiles of Van Diemen's Land.
Shows coastlines, track of *Resolution*, depths in fathoms; place names, hill shading. *See also* no. 1777 Bligh, 3rd V. Charts. *Vol. 1, facing p. 91.*

Plan of Adventure Bay on Van Diemen's Land. [Copied by Lieut. Henry Roberts. London, G. Nicol . . . and T. Cadell, 1784.] (Plate No. IX).

ca1:91,000. 1 sheet, cm 14 x 20.
Coastal profile of South side of Adventure Bay.
Shows depths in fathoms, anchorage; rivers, lake, vegetation, place names, hill shading. *Vol. 1, facing p. 117.*

Charts of Wateeoo I. & Wanooaette I., Toobouai Island, Mangeea Island. [Copied by Lieut. Henry Roberts. London, G. Nicol . . . and T. Cadell, 1784.] (Plate No. XXIV).

ca1:182,400. 1 sheet, 3 maps on cm 22 x 17.
Shows coastlines, lat. and long. readings, reefs, depths; hill shading, vegetation. *Vol.2, facing p. 5.*

Sketch of the Harbours on the North Side of Eimeo. [Copied by Lieut. Henry Roberts. London, G. Nicol . . . and T. Cadell, 1784.] (Plate No. XXX).

ca1:46,700. 1 sheet, cm 19 x 22.
Shows coastlines, depths in fathoms, anchorages; place names, buildings, rivers, vegetation. *Vol.2, facing p.79.*

Christmas Island Latitude 1°58′N. Longitude 202°28′E. Discovered in the Ships *Resolution* and *Discovery* 1777. Variation 6°0′E. [Copied by Lieut. Henry Roberts. London, G. Nicol . . . and T. Cadell, 1784.] (Plate No. XXXII).

ca1:182,400. 1 sheet, cm 18 x 21.
Shows coastline, depths in fathoms, anchorages. *Vol. 2, facing p. 179.*

Chart of the N.W. Coast of America and N.E. Coast of Asia explored in the years 1778 & 1779 . . . Writing Engraved by T. Harmar. [Copied by Lieut. Henry Roberts. London, G. Nicol . . . and T. Cadell, 1784.] (Plate No. XXXVI).

No scale given, 1 sheet, cm 39 x 66.
Shows coastlines, track of *Resolution* with dates, depths in fathoms; place names, hill shading. *Atlas, [p. 2]. X980/24A*

Sketch of Nootka Sound . . . 1778. The Writing Engraved by Mr. Smith. [Copied by Lieut. Henry Roberts. London, G. Nicol . . . and T. Cadell, 1784.] (Plate No. XXXVII).

1:182,400. 1 sheet, cm 26 x 21.
Shows coastline, depths in fathoms, anchorage; hill shading, vegetation. *Vol.2, facing p. 279.*

Chart of Cooks River in the N.W. part of America. Writing by W. Harrison. [Copied by Lieut. Henry Roberts. London, G. Nicol . . . and T. Cadell, 1784.] (Plate No. XLIV).

No scale given, 1 sheet, cm 23 x 29.
Shows coastline, tracks of *Resolution* with dates, depths in fathoms, anchorages; place names, hill shading, vegetation. *Vol. 2, facing p. 353.*

Chart of Norton Sound and of Bherings Strait made by the East Cape of Asia and the West Point of America. [Copied by Lieut. Henry Roberts. London, G. Nicol . . . and T. Cadell, 1784.] (Plate No. LIII).

No scale given, 1 sheet, cm 26 x 38.
Area: from Cape Serdze Komen to Anderson's Is., Tschukotskoi Noss to Norton Sound.
Shows coastlines, tracks of *Resolution* with dates, depths in fathoms, anchorages; place names, hill shading. *Vol.2, facing p.467.*

Sketch of the Harbour of Samganooda on the Island Oonolaska. Lat. 53°55′N. Long. 193°30′E. Variation 20°3′E. 1778. [Writing by Harmar. Copied by Lieut. Henry Roberts. London, G. Nicol . . . and T. Cadell, 1784.] (Plate No. LV).

ca1:46,700. 1 sheet, cm 18 x 18.
Shows coastline, depths in fathoms, anchorage; hill shading, rivers. *Vol.2, facing p.424.*

1714

1777 BLIGH, William

A Chart of Van Diemens Land, by William Bligh. [MS. tracing from the original in the Admiralty, 497/2 Shelf XM.]

1″ = 1⅘″ league, 1 sheet, cm 45 x 66, tracing, black ink and colour. With view of coast between S.W. and Three Hill Cape.
Area: S.–S.E. coast of Tasmania from S.W. cape to Maria Is.
Shows the coast and route of the *Resolution* and *Discovery*.
Reduced reproduction from the Admiralty original, published as Plate 44 *in* Hakluyt Society Journals Capt. James Cook: Charts & views.
Negative photostat of original in Admiralty, cm 35 x 51 at NPL:M (M881/1777/1A).
Copies: NPL:M(M2 881/1777/1). 1715

1780 KITCHIN, Thomas

A Chart of the discoveries made by the late Capt. Cook & other European navigators in the great Pacific Ocean between Asia & America. [London], printed for R. Baldwin, 1780.

No scale given, 1 sheet, cm 41½ x 32½. Extracted from the *London Magazine*, Jy. 1780.
Copies: NPL:M(980:Co4/P1A1); NPL:D(Ca78/2).   1716

[1787?] BONNE,—
Carte de l'Entrée de Norton et du Détroit de Bhering; [engraved by— André]. Paris, Hôtel de Thou, [1787?].

No scale given, 1 sheet, 9¼″ x 13⁷/₁₂″.
(*In* Bonne *and* Desmarest—Atlas encyclopédique, 1787. Plate 130.)
Shows route of Cook's third expedition through Behring Strait.
Copies: NPL:M(Q 912/B).   1717

[1787?] BONNE,—
Carte des Isles Sandwich; [engraved by—André]. Paris Hôtel de Thou, [1787?].

ca 26 miles = *1″*, 1 sheet, 9⅛″ x 13½″.
(*In* Bonne *and* Desmarest—Atlas encyclopédique, 1787. Plate 128.)
One inset map. *Shows* route of Cook's third voyage.
Copies: NPL:M(Q 912/B).   1718

[1930?] ROBERTS, Henry
Ka'ra'ca'coo'a Bay. in the Island of O'why'he. Situated in Latd: 20: 27′N°. Longd: 204:00E. London, Francis Edwards, [1930?].

ca1:21,120, 1 sheet, cm 19 x 21, photo. brown/wh.
Shows depths in fathoms, reefs, anchorage; village, place names; mtns, vegetation.
(*In his* Eye witness account of the death of Captain Cook. Facsimile from the Log of Henry Roberts.)
Copies: NPL:M(F980:Co4/R1A1).   1719

1955 [BERING STRAIT and the adjoining coasts of America and Asia. Reprod. from orig. MSS. in the Hydrographic Dept. of the Admiralty.]

No scale given, 1 sheet, cm 37 x 69, photoengr., b./wh.
Shows tracks of *Resolution* and *Discovery* under Captain Cook July–Sept. 1778, and under Capt. Clerke July–August 1779, with depth soundings.
(*In* Beaglehole, J.C.—The Journals of Captain James Cook on his voyages of discovery . . . Charts and Views; ed. by R.A. Skelton. Pub. for the Hakluyt Society. Cambridge, U.P., 1955. Plate no.LIII.)
Copies: NPL:M(X980/25).   1720

1955 BLIGH, William
Chart of the N.E. Coast of the Island of Desolation. [Reprod. from orig. MSS. in the Hydrographic Dept. of the Admiralty.]

No scale given, 1 sheet, cm 35 x 55, photoengr., b./wh.
Area: Kerguélen Island.
Shows ship's track, depth measures; sketchy outline of coast, mtns by hill shading; names of islands, capes and bays.

(*In* Beaglehole, J.C.—The Journals of Captain James Cook on his voyages of discovery . . .
Charts and Views; ed. by R.A. Skelton. Pub. for the Hakluyt Society. Cambridge, U.P.
1955. Plate no.XLIII.)
Copies: NPL:M(X980/25). 1721

1955 BLIGH, William

A Chart of Van Diemens Land. [Reprod. from orig. MSS. in the Hydrographic Dept. of the Admiralty.]

No scale given, 1 sheet, cm 35 x 52, photoengr., b./wh.
Area: from S.W.Cape to Maria Island.
Shows ships' track, depths, coastline, mtn. ranges, names of capes, bays.
(*In* Beaglehole, J.C.—The Journals of Captain James Cook on his voyages of discovery . . .
Charts and Views; ed. by R.A. Skelton. Pub. for the Hakluyt Society. Cambridge, U.P.,
1955. Plate no.XLIV.)
Copies: NPL:M(X980/25). 1722

1955 BLIGH, William

[Three views of the Island of Desolation]: A view of the Arch'd Point
when bearing South distant $2\frac{1}{2}$ miles; A view of the Land when Mount
Campbel bears SSW $4\frac{1}{2}$ miles; A view when the Prince of Wales Foreland
bears WSW dist. 3 leagues. [Reprod. from orig. MSS. in the Hydrographic
Dept. of the Admiralty.]

cm 14 x 32, photoengr., b./wh.
(*In* Beaglehole, J.C.—The Journals of Captain James Cook on his voyages of discovery . . .
Charts and Views; ed. by R.A. Skelton. Pub. for the Hakluyt Society. Cambridge, U.P.,
1955. Plate no.XLIII.)
Copies: NPL:M(X980/25). 1723

1955 CHART of Kealakekua Bay, Hawaii. [Reprod. from orig. MSS. in the Vancouver City Museum.]

No scale given, 1 sheet, cm 18 x 18, photoengr., b./wh.
Shows spot where Cook was killed; anchorages of *Resolution* and *Discovery*; sand bank,
reefs, some buildings.
(*In* Beaglehole, J.C.—The Journals of Captain James Cook on his voyages of discovery . . .
Charts and Views; ed. by R.A. Skelton. Pub. for the Hakluyt Society. Cambridge, U.P.,
1955. Plate no.LIV.)
Copies: NPL:M(X980/25). 1724

1955 CHART of part of the N.W. Coast of America. Explored by Capt. J. Cook in 1778. [Reprod. from orig. MSS. in the Public Records Office.]

No scale given, 1 sheet, cm 28 x 43, photoengr., b./wh.
Area: from Icy Cape, Alaska to Portland. Does not incl. Andreanof Islands.
Shows part outline of coasts, tracks of *Resolution* and *Discovery* with dates, soundings, notes
on terrain.
(*In* Beaglehole, J.C.—The Journals of Captain James Cook on his voyages of discovery . . .
Charts and Views; ed. by R.A. Skelton. Pub. for the Hakluyt Society. Cambridge, U.P.,
1955. Plate no.XLIX.)
Copies: NPL:M(X980/25). 1725

1955 CHART of the Sandwich Islands. [Probably drawn by Roberts, from Bligh's survey. 1778–1779. Reprod. from an engraved copy of the original in the British Museum.]

No scale given, 1 sheet, cm 21 x 36, photoengr., b./wh.
Inset: Sketch of Karakakooa Bay.
Area: Hawaiian Islands.
Shows track of *Resolution* with dates, depths, reefs, place names, hill shading.
(*In* Beaglehole, J.C.—The Journals of Captain James Cook on his voyages of discovery . . . Charts and Views; ed. by R.A. Skelton. Pub. for the Hakluyt Society. Cambridge, U.P., 1955. Plate no.LV.) Original now missing.
Copies: NPL:M(X980/25).   1726

1955 EDGAR, Thomas
Discoverys Island. [Reprod. from orig. MSS. in the Public Records Office.]

No scale given, 1 sheet, cm 11 x 12, photoengr., b./wh.
Area: Mangaia Island, Cook Islands.
Shows ship's track, coastal outline, hill shading, reefs.
(*In* Beaglehole, J.C.—The Journals of Captain James Cook on his voyages of discovery . . . Charts and Views; ed. by R.A. Skelton. Pub. for the Hakluyt Society. Cambridge, U.P., 1955. Plate no.XLV.)
Copies: NPL:M(X980/25).   1727

1955 EDGAR, Thomas
A Plan of Christmas Island. By Edgar; in his log. Dec.24, 1777–Jan.2, 1778. [Reprod. from orig. MSS. in the Public Records Office.]

No scale given, 1 sheet, cm 16 x 17, photoengr., b./wh.
Shows track of *Resolution*, anchorages, depths, reefs, vegetation.
(*In* Beaglehole, J.C.—The Journals of Captain Cook on his voyages of discovery . . . Charts and Views; ed. by R.A. Skelton. Pub. for the Hakluyt Society. Cambridge, U.P., 1955. Plate no.XLVIII.)
Copies: NPL:M(X980/25).   1728

1955 EDGAR, Thomas
A Plan of Hippie Isles. [Reprod. from orig. MSS. in the Public Records Office.]

1:158,400, 1 sheet, cm 35 x 23, photoengr., b./wh.
Area: Haapai group, Tonga Islands.
Shows ship's track, depths, reefs.
(*In* Beaglehole, J.C.—The Journals of Captain James Cook on his voyages of discovery . . . Charts and Views; ed. by R.A. Skelton. Pub. for the Hakluyt Society. Cambridge, U.P., 1955. Plate no.XLVI.)
Copies: NPL:M(X980/25).   1729

1955 EDGAR, Thomas
A Plan of Indian Cove, King Georges Sound. [Reprod. from orig. MSS. in the Public Records Office.]

335

ca1:15,840, 1 sheet, cm 12 x 11, photoengr., b./wh.
Area: Nootka Sound, Vancouver.
Shows coastline, reefs, depths, buildings.
(*In* Beaglehole, J.C.—The Journals of Captain James Cook on his voyages of discovery . . .
Charts and Views; ed. by R.A. Skelton. Pub. for the Hakluyt Society. Cambridge, U.P.,
1955. Plate no.L.)
Copies: NPL:M(X980/25). 1730

1955 EDGAR, Thomas
A Plan of Oaiti Peha Bay, Otaheite Ete. [Reprod. from orig. MSS. in the
Public Records Office.]

1:31,680, 1 sheet, cm 18 x 22, photoengr., b./wh.
Area: Vaitepiha Bay, Tahiti.
Shows river estuary, reefs, buildings, depths.
(*In* Beaglehole, J.C.—The Journals of Captain James Cook on his voyages of discovery . . .
Charts and Views; ed. by R.A. Skelton. Pub. for the Hakluyt Society. Cambridge, U.P.,
1955. Plate no.XLVII.)
Copies: NPL:M(X980/25). 1731

1955 EDGAR, Thomas
A Plan of Ship Cove, King Georges Sound. [Reprod. from orig. MSS.
in the Public Records Office.]

ca1:5,900, 1 sheet, cm 13 x 11, photoengr., b./wh.
Area: Nootka Sound, Vancouver.
Shows coastline, depths.
(*In* Beaglehole, J.C.—The Journals of Captain James Cook on his voyages of discovery . . .
Charts and Views; ed. by R.A. Skelton. Pub. for the Hakluyt Society. Cambridge, U.P.,
1955. Plate no.L.)
Copies: NPL:M(X980/25). 1732

1955 EDGAR, Thomas
A Plan of the Harbours of Tah-row and Av,voi,ta Eimo. By Edgar; in
his log, 30 Sept.–11 Oct. 1777. [Reprod. from orig. MSS. in the Public
Records Office.]

ca1:67,500, 1 sheet, cm 17 x 24, photoengr., b./wh.
Area: Papetoai and Paopao Bays, Moorea.
Shows coastline, depths, reefs, hill shading.
(*In* Beaglehole, J.C.—The Journals of Captain James Cook on his voyages of discovery . . .
Charts and Views; ed. by R.A. Skelton. Pub. for the Hakluyt Society. Cambridge, U.P.,
1955. Plate no. XLVIII.)
Copies: NPL:M(X980/25). 1733

1955 EDGAR, Thomas
Plan of the Isl^d of Anamocka. [Reprod. from orig. MSS. in the Public
Records Office.]

No scale given, 1 sheet, cm 9 x 10, photoengr., b./wh.
Area: Nomuka, Tonga Islands.
Shows coastline, depths.

(*In* Beaglehole, J.C.—The Journals of Captain James Cook on his voyages of discovery . . .
Charts and Views; ed. by R.A. Skelton. Pub. for the Hakluyt Society. Cambridge, U.P.,
1955. Plate no.XLV.)

Copies: NPL:M(X980/25).   1734

1955 EDGAR, Thomas
A Plan of the Island of Otobui. [Reprod. from orig. MSS. in the Public
Records Office.]

No scale given, 1 sheet, cm 13 x 16, photoengr., b./wh.
Area: Tubuai Island.
Shows coastline, reefs, hill shading.
(*In* Beaglehole, J.C.—The Journals of Captain James Cook on his voyages of discovery . . .
Charts and Views; ed. by R.A. Skelton. Pub. for the Hakluyt Society. Cambridge, U.P.,
1955. Plate no.XLVII.)

Copies: NPL:M(X980/25).   1735

1955 EDGAR, Thomas
A Plan of Whatdew and Mo-du. [Reprod. from orig. MSS. in the Public
Records Office.]

No scale given, 1 sheet, cm 9 x 13, photoengr., b./wh.
Area: Atiu and Takutea Islands, Cook Islands.
Shows ship's track, outline of islands with trees all over, reefs.
(*In* Beaglehole, J.C.—The Journals of Captain James Cook on his voyages of discovery . . .
Charts and Views; ed. by R.A. Skelton. Pub. for the Hakluyt Society. Cambridge, U.P.,
1955. Plate no.XLV.)

Copies: NPL:M(X980/25).   1736

1955 RIOU, Edward
Isle Noo anna laska. [Reprod. from orig. MSS. in the Hydrographic
Dept. of the Admiralty.]

1:316,800, 1 sheet, cm 33 x 50, photoengr., b./wh.
Inset: Sammaganoo'da Harbour.
Area: Unalaska, Aleutian Islands.
Shows Cook's track to north, west and south with dates, coast showing mtns; depths,
anchorages.
(*In* Beaglehole, J.C.—The Journals of Captain James Cook on his voyages of discovery . . .
Charts and Views; ed. by R.A. Skelton. Pub. for the Hakluyt Society. Cambridge, U.P.,
1955. Plate no.LII.)

Copies: NPL:M(X980/25).   1737

1955 RIOU, Edward
A Plan of the Bay of A'watch'ka, by Edward Riou. [Reprod. from orig.
MSS. in the Hydrographic Dept. of the Admiralty.]

1:120,000, 1 sheet, cm 27 x 22, photoengr., b./wh.
Inset: The Harbour of St. Peter and St. Paul.
Area: Avatcha Bay, Kamchatka.
Shows coastline, depth soundings, rivers, hill shading, vegetation, reefs.
(*In* Beaglehole, J.C.—The Journals of Captain James Cook on his voyages of discovery . . .
Charts and Views; ed. by R.A. Skelton. Pub. for the Hakluyt Society. Cambridge, U.P.,
1955. Plate no.LVII.)

Copies: NPL:M(X980/25.)   1738

1955 RIOU, Edward

A Sketch of Kara'ka'kooah Bay in the Island of Hawhy'hee. [Reprod. from orig. MSS. in the Hydrographic Dept. of the Admiralty.]

ca1:15,840, 1 sheet, cm 17 x 20, photoengr., b./wh.
Area: Kealakekua Bay, Hawaii.
Shows coastline, depths, reefs, observatories, buildings, mountains.
(*In* Beaglehole, J.C.—The Journals of Captain James Cook on his voyages of discovery . . .
Charts and Views; ed. by R.A. Skelton. Pub. for the Hakluyt Society. Cambridge, U.P.,
1955. Plate no.LIV.)
Copies: NPL:M(X980/25). 1739

1955 RIOU, Edward

A Sketch of the Harbour of St Peter & St Paul with Mount A'wautchka, as taken from the spit. [Ap.28–June 1779. Reprod. from orig. MSS. in the Hydrographic Dept. of the Admiralty.]

cm 6 x 21, photoengr., b./wh.
(*In* Beaglehole, J.C.—The Journals of Captain James Cook on his voyages of discovery . . .
Charts and Views; ed. by R.A. Skelton. Pub. for the Hakluyt Society. Cambridge, U.P.,
1955. Plate no.LVII.)
Copies: NPL:M(X980/25). 1740

1955 ROBERTS, Henry

Prince William Sound and Cook Inlet. [Reprod. from orig. MSS. in the Public Records Office.]

No scale given, 1 sheet, cm 34 x 41, photoengr., b./wh.
Shows track of the *Resolution* and *Discovery;* outline with islands, mtns, place names, coastline, depths.
(*In* Beaglehole, J.C.—The Journals of Captain James Cook on his voyages of discovery . . .
Charts and Views; ed. by R.A. Skelton. Pub. for the Hakluyt Society. Cambridge, U.P.,
1955. Plate no.LI.)
Copies: NPL:M(X980/25). 1741

Illustrations, General
Originals, Including Photocopies of Originals

Originals cannot be reproduced without the permission of the owner.

See also the subhead *Personal—Death—Illustrations*

SMITH, Isaac

Original sketches, drawings, maps etc. [1763–80] collected by Admiral Isaac Smith who served as an officer under Captain James Cook, the circumnavigator, in his first & second voyages. A.D. 1768–1775.

ff.49, 97 drawings.
Title is in the hand of Canon Bennett, a relative of Isaac Smith, from whom the volume was acquired by the Government of New South Wales. MS. contents list is from Isaac Smith's papers. A new contents list and an index have been made and are inserted.

Some of the drawings are signed "H.Roberts", "Hen^y Roberts" one is signed "W.H.", others are ascribed in Canon Bennett's hand to W. Hodges; presumably this was on the back of the drawings (now pasted down) or may be have been noted in pencil, as still apparent in some cases, on the leaves of the volume, as it is not on the MS. contents list. A note at the beginning in Canon Bennett's hand, suggests that some of the unsigned drawings may be by Isaac Smith. Some of the drawings appear to be the originals of the plates to Cook's second voyage. With the exception of two of the first voyage, the drawings probably all belong to the second voyage but some may be of the third. The charts include two by Cook of Newfoundland 1763, one of Charlestown 1780, one of the track of H.M.S. *Perseverance* etc. The drawings are listed separately at no. 1379, the maps, charts and coastal profiles at no. 1331.

Copies: NPL:M(PXD11).   1742

Illustrations, General
Reproductions

The first official account of the third voyage is entitled *Voyage to the Pacific Ocean undertaken . . . for making discoveries in the Northern Hemisphere performed under the direction of Captains Cook, Clerke and Gore . . . in the years 1776, 1777, 1778, 1779, and 1780 . . . In three volumes* [*with atlas of prints*]. London, Nicol and Cadell, 1784./The edition described hereunder is listed as no.1553 in this Bibliography (NPL:M Q 980:Co4/1D1–3). The plates in the atlas are all line engravings. They are titled and numbered in accordance with the list of plates on pp.xci–xcvi, vol.1. Vols.1–3 contain only maps and charts, which are listed and described under the subhead *Charts*; the atlas contains 61 plates, which are listed and described hereunder, and 2 maps, which are listed and described under the subhead *Charts*.

The copy of the atlas from which this listing has been made is that numbered NPL:M X980/24B. In this copy plates 26, 43 and 68 have been misplaced after plates 27, 35 and 62 respectively. Plates in subsequent editions and translations have often been redrawn and engraved by different artists. These are not described in this Bibliography. Plates held by the Mitchell and Dixson Libraries, which are extracted from these editions and translations are not listed.

[No.] 4 A view of Christmas Harbour, in Kerguelen's Land. J. Webber del. Newton sculp.

Meas. of view 8 $\frac{11}{16}$″ x 14 $\frac{3}{8}$″. Meas. of plate mark 10 $\frac{5}{16}$″ x 15 $\frac{15}{16}$″.

[No.] 6 A man of Van Diemen's Land. J. Webber del. J. Caldwall sc.

Meas. of engraved surface 8 $\frac{3}{4}$″ x 6 $\frac{7}{8}$″. Meas. of plate mark 11 $\frac{3}{8}$″ x 8 $\frac{5}{8}$″.

[No.] 7 A woman of Van Diemen's Land. J. Webber del. J. Caldwall sc.

Meas. of engraved surface 9″ x 7″. Meas. of plate mark 11 $\frac{1}{8}$″ x 8 $\frac{3}{4}$″.

[No.] 8 An opossum of Van Diemen's Land. J. Webber del. P. Mazell sculp.

Meas. of engraved surface 5 $\frac{13}{16}$″ x 9 $\frac{3}{8}$″. Meas. of plate mark 8 $\frac{1}{4}$″ x 10 $\frac{1}{2}$″.

[No.] 10 The inside of a hippah, in New Zeeland (*sic*). J. Webber del. B.T. Pouncy sculp.

Meas. of view 8 $\frac{5}{8}$″ x 14 $\frac{7}{8}$″. Meas. of plate mark 9 $\frac{15}{16}$″ x 16″.

[No.] 11 A man of Mangea. J. Webber del. W. Sharp sculp.

Meas. of engraved surface 8$\frac{13}{16}$" x 6$\frac{15}{16}$". Meas. of plate mark 12" x 9$\frac{3}{8}$".

[No.] 13 A view at Anamooka. J. Webber del. W. Byrne sc.

Meas. of view 8$\frac{1}{2}$" x 9$\frac{11}{16}$". Meas. of plate mark 10$\frac{3}{8}$" x 20$\frac{1}{2}$".

[No.] 14 The reception of Captain Cook, in Hapaee. J. Webber del. Heath sculp.

Meas. of view 8$\frac{3}{4}$" x 14$\frac{7}{8}$". Meas. of plate mark 10" x 16".

[No.] 15 A boxing match, in Hapaee. J. Webber del. I. Taylor sc.

Meas. of engraved surface 9" x 7$\frac{1}{8}$". Meas. of plate mark 12" x 8$\frac{7}{8}$".

[No.] 16 A night dance by men, in Hapaee. J. Webber del. W^{m}. Sharp sculp.

Meas. of view 8$\frac{13}{16}$" x 15$\frac{3}{16}$". Meas. of plate mark 10$\frac{5}{8}$" x 16$\frac{1}{4}$".

[No.] 17 A night dance by women, in Hapaee. J. Webber del. W. Sharp sculp.[t]

Meas. of view 8$\frac{13}{16}$" x 15$\frac{1}{8}$". Meas. of plate mark 10$\frac{11}{16}$" x 16$\frac{3}{16}$".

[No.] 18 Poulaho, King of the Friendly Isles. J. Webber del. J. Hall sculp.

Meas. within frame lines 9$\frac{1}{16}$" x 7$\frac{1}{16}$". Meas. of plate mark 11$\frac{7}{16}$" x 8$\frac{7}{8}$".

[No.] 20 Poulaho, King of the Friendly Isles, drinking kava. J. Webber del. W. Sharp sculp.

Meas. of engraved surface 9$\frac{1}{16}$" x 15$\frac{1}{4}$". Meas. of plate mark 10$\frac{3}{8}$" x 16$\frac{3}{8}$".

[No.] 21 A fiatooka, or morai, in Tongataboo. J. Webber del. W. Ellis sculp.

Meas. of view 8$\frac{3}{4}$" x 15". Meas. of plate mark 10$\frac{1}{8}$" x 16".

[No.] 22 The natche, a ceremony in honour of the King's son, in Tongataboo. J. Webber del. Figures by J. Hall.

Meas. of view 9$\frac{3}{4}$" x 18$\frac{1}{4}$". Meas. of plate mark 12$\frac{5}{16}$" x 19$\frac{1}{4}$".

[No.] 23 A woman of Eaoo. J. Webber del. J. Hall sculp.

Meas. within frame lines 9$\frac{1}{16}$" x 7". Meas. of plate mark 11$\frac{3}{8}$" x 8$\frac{3}{4}$".

[No.] 25 A human sacrifice, in a morai, in Otaheite. J. Webber del. W. Woollett sc.

Meas. of engraved surface 9$\frac{5}{8}$" x 18$\frac{1}{4}$". Meas. of plate mark 11$\frac{5}{16}$" x 19$\frac{1}{4}$".

[No.] 26 The body of Tee, a chief, as preserved after death, in Otaheite. J. Webber del. W. Byrne sculp.

Meas. of engraved surface 8$\frac{3}{4}$" x 15". Meas. of plate mark 10$\frac{1}{16}$" x 16".

[No.] 27 A young woman of Otaheite, bringing a present. J. Webber del. F. Bartolozzi sc.

Meas. of engraved surface 8$\frac{13}{16}$" x 7$\frac{1}{16}$". Meas. of plate mark 13$\frac{5}{8}$" x 10$\frac{7}{8}$".

[No.] 28 A dance in Otaheite. J. Webber del. J.K. Sherwin sc.

Meas. of engraved surface 9" x 15". Meas. of plate mark 10$\frac{7}{16}$" x 16$\frac{3}{16}$".

[No.] 29 A young woman of Otaheite, dancing. J. Webber del. J.K. Sherwin sc.

Meas. of engraved surface $9\frac{1}{16}''$ x $7\frac{1}{16}''$. Meas. of plate mark 11″ x 9″.

[No.] 31 A view of Huaheine. J. Webber del. W. Byrne sculp.

Meas. of view 9″ x $18\frac{1}{2}''$. Meas. of engraved surface $10\frac{1}{4}''$ x $19\frac{3}{8}''$.

[No.] 33 A morai, in Atooi. J. Webber del. Lerpernere (*sic*) sc.

Meas. of engraved surface $8\frac{7}{8}''$ x $14\frac{7}{8}''$. Meas. of plate mark $10\frac{1}{2}''$ x $16\frac{1}{4}''$.

[No.] 34 The inside of the house, in the morai, in Atooi. J. Webber del. Scott sculp.

Meas. of engraved surface 7″ x $9\frac{5}{8}''$. Meas. of plate mark $8\frac{5}{16}''$ x $10\frac{7}{8}''$.

[No.] 35 An inland view, in Atooi. J. Webber del. S. Middiman sc.

Meas. of view $8\frac{5}{8}''$ x $18\frac{7}{16}''$. Meas. of plate mark $10\frac{3}{16}''$ x $20\frac{3}{16}''$.

[No.] 38 A man of Nootka Sound. J. Webber del. W. Sharp sculp.

Meas. of engraved surface $9\frac{3}{4}''$ x $6\frac{1}{4}''$. Meas. of plate mark $11\frac{15}{16}''$ x $9\frac{3}{8}''$.

[No.] 39 A woman of Nootka Sound. J. Webber del. W. Sharp sculp.

Meas. of engraved surface $9\frac{1}{16}''$ x $6\frac{7}{8}''$. Meas. of plate mark 12″ x $9\frac{3}{8}''$.

[No.] 40 Various articles, at Nootka Sound. J. Webber del. J. Record sculp.[t]

Meas. of plate mark 8″ x $10\frac{15}{16}''$.

[No.] 41 A view of the habitations in Nootka Sound. J. Webber del. S. Smith sculp.

Meas. of view $8\frac{1}{2}''$ x $14\frac{3}{4}''$. Meas. of plate mark $10\frac{1}{16}''$ x $15\frac{3}{4}''$.

[No.] 42 The inside of a house, Nootka Sound. J. Webber del. W. Sharp sculp.

Meas. of engraved surface $8\frac{3}{4}''$ x $14\frac{3}{4}''$. Meas. of plate mark $10\frac{11}{16}''$ x $15\frac{15}{16}''$.

[No.] 43 A sea otter. J. Webber del. Mazell sculp.

Meas. of engraved surface $5\frac{5}{8}''$ x $9\frac{1}{2}''$. Meas. of plate mark $7\frac{3}{4}''$ x $10\frac{1}{2}''$.

[No.] 45 View of Snug Corner Cove, in Prince William's Sound. J. Webber del. W. Ellis sculp.[t]

Meas. of view $8\frac{1}{2}''$ x $14\frac{1}{2}''$. Meas. of plate mark $9\frac{15}{16}''$ x $15\frac{15}{16}''$.

[No.] 46 A man of Prince William's Sound. J. Webber del. J. Basire sculp.[t]

Meas. within frame lines $8\frac{3}{8}''$ x $16\frac{15}{16}''$. Meas. of plate mark $12\frac{1}{4}''$ x $9\frac{1}{2}''$.

[No.] 47 A woman of Prince William's Sound. J. Webber del. J. Basire sculp.[t]

Meas. within frame lines $8\frac{15}{16}''$ x 7″. Meas. of plate mark $12\frac{1}{4}''$ x $9\frac{9}{16}''$.

[No.] 48 A man of Oonalashka. J. Webber del. W. Sharp. sc

Meas. of engraved surface $8\frac{3}{4}''$ x $6\frac{7}{8}''$. Meas. of plate mark $12\frac{1}{16}''$ x $9\frac{1}{2}$

[No.] 49 A woman of Oonalashka. J. Webber del. Delattre sc.
Meas. of engraved surface 9″ x 6⅞″. Meas. of plate mark 11⅛″ x 8 7/16″.

[No.] 50 Canoes of Oonalashka. J. Webber del. W. Angus sc.
Meas. within frame lines 6 11/16″ x 9½″. Meas. of plate mark 7 9/16″ x 10 5/16″.

[No.] 51 The Tschuktschi, and their habitations. J. Webber del. Lerpiniere sc.
Meas. of engraved surface 8 11/16″ x 14⅞″. Meas. of plate mark 10″ x 16″.

[No.] 52 Sea horses. Drawn by J. Webber. Engraved by E. Scott. The figures by J. Heath.
Meas. of engraved surface 8 11/16″ x 14¾″. Meas. of plate mark 10⅜″ x 15⅝″.

[No.] 54 Inhabitants of Northern Sound, and their habitations. J. Webber del. B.J. Pouncy sc.
Meas. of engraved surface 8⅝″ x 14 3/16″. Meas. of plate mark 10″ x 15⅞″.

[No.] 56 Caps of the natives of Oonalashka. J. Webber del. J. Record sculp.
Meas. of plate mark 10 15/16″ x 8⅛″.

[No.] 57 Natives of Oonalashka, and their habitations. J. Webber del. J. Hall & S. Middiman sc.
Meas. of engraved surface 8½″ x 14⅞″.

[No.] 58 The inside of a house, in Oonalashka. J. Webber del. W. Sharp sculp.
Meas. of engraved surface 8 9/16″ x 14 11/16″. Meas. of plate mark 10″ x 16″.

[No.] 60 An offering before Cap.ᵗ Cook, in the Sandwich Islands. Drawn by J. Webber. The landscape eng.ᵈ by Middiman. The figures by Hall.
Meas. of engraved surface 8 9/16″ x 14¾″. Meas. of plate mark 10¼″ x 16¼″.

[No.] 61 Tereoboo, King of Owyhee, bringing presents to Cap.ᵗ Cook. J. Webber del. B.T. Pouncy sc.
Meas. of engraved surface 8 9/16″ x 14¾″. Meas. of plate mark 10⅛″ x 15¾″.

[No.] 62 A man of the Sandwich Islands, dancing. J. Webber del. J. Grignion sc.
Meas. of engraved surface 9⅝″ x 7″. Meas. of plate mark 11 13/16″ x 8 3/16″.

[No.] 63 A young woman of the Sandwich Islands. J. Webber del. J.K. Sherwin sc.
Meas. of engraved surface 9″ x 7⅛″. Meas. of plate mark 11 7/16″ x 8⅞″.

[No.] 64 A man of the Sandwich Islands, with his helmet. J. Webber del. J.K. Sherwin sc.
Meas. within frame line 9″ x 7¼″. Meas. of plate mark 11 9/16″ x 9 1/16″.

[No.] 65 A canoe of the Sandwich Islands, the rowers masked. J. Webber del. G. Grignion sc.
Meas. of engraved surface 8 11/16″ x 14 13/16″.

[No.] 66 A man of the Sandwich Islands, in a mask. J. Webber del. T. Cook sculp.^{t}
Meas. of engraved surface 9⅝″ x 7″. Meas. of plate mark 11¼″ x 8 3⁄16″.

[No.] 67 Various articles, at the Sandwich Islands. J. Webber del. J. Record sculp.^{t}
Meas. of plate mark 8⅛″ x 11 1⁄16″.

[No.] 68 A view of Karakokooa, in Owyhee. J. Webber del. W. Byrne sculp.
Meas. of view 8 13⁄16″ x 19 15⁄16″. Meas. of plate mark 10¼″ x 20⅜″.

[No.] 70 A man of Kamtschatka, travelling in winter. J. Webber del. S. Middiman sc.
Meas. of engraved surface 8 9⁄16″ x 14⅞″. Meas. of plate mark 9⅞″ x 15⅞″.

[No.] 71 A sledge of Kamtschatka. J. Webber del. Woodyer sc.
Meas. of plate mark 7 5⁄16″ x 9 13⁄16″.

[No.] 72 A view at Bolcheretzkoi, in Kamtschatka. J. Webber del. P. Benezech (*sic*) sc.
Meas. within frame lines 8⅜″ x 12 7⁄16″. Meas. of plate mark 9 7⁄16″ x 13 9⁄16″.

[No.] 73 A white bear. J. Webber del. Mazell sculp.
Meas. of engraved surface 6 13⁄16″ x 9⅝″. Meas. of plate mark 8 7⁄16″ x 10⅝″.

[No.] 74 A view of the town and harbour of St Peter and St Paul, in Kamtschatka. J. Webber del. B.T. Pouncy sc.
Meas. of view 8⅝″ x 19⅞″. Meas. of plate mark 9⅞″ x 21 15⁄16″.

[No.] 75 A man of Kamtschatka. J. Webber del. W. Sharp sc.
Meas. of engraved surface 8 13⁄16″ x 6 13⁄16″. Meas. of plate mark 12″ x 9⅜″.

[No.] 76 A woman of Kamtschatka. J. Webber del. W. Sharp sc.
Meas. of engraved surface 8⅞″ x 6 13⁄16″. Meas. of plate mark 11 13⁄16″ x 9⅜″.

[No.] 77 Summer and winter habitations in Kamtschatka. J. Webber del. S. Smith sc.
Meas. of engraved surface 8¼″ x 14 13⁄16″. Meas. of plate mark 9⅝″ x 15⅞″.

[No.] 78 The inside of a winter habitation, in Kamtschatka. J. Webber del. W. Sharp sculp.
Meas. of engraved surface 8 13⁄16″ x 15⅜″. Meas. of plate mark 10¾″ x 16½″.   1743

COLLECTION of various editions of engravings of Cook's third voyage.
45 engravings.
Copies: NPL:D(DL PX22).   1744

Illustrations Arranged by Artist

CLEVELEY, JAMES
Originals, Including Photocopies of Originals

CHARLOTTE SOUND in New Zealand in the South Seas.
Watercolour painting. 16½″ x 23½″. Titled; unsigned.
Drawn on the spot by James Cleveley; painted by John Cleveley. Aquatint by F.Jukes published London, T. Martyn, 1788.
Copies: ANL (Nan Kivell).   1745

DRAWINGS relating to Cook's third voyage.

Four watercolours, probably after the aquatints by Jukes and Piringer.

CONTENTS:

DG XV*
Cook 12
Queen Charlotte Sound—New Zealand. $17\frac{1}{4}''$ x $24\frac{1}{4}''$ meas. of view, in mount $24''$ x $31\frac{1}{4}''$. Title lettered on mount. Probably after the aquatint by Jukes.

DG XV*
Cook 13
Huaheine—Society Islands. $17\frac{1}{2}''$ x $24''$ meas. of view. Title lettered on mount. This view shows similarities to both the Jukes and the Piringer aquatints.

DG XV*
Cook 14
Morea—Friendly Islands. Title lettered on mount but 'Friendly' crossed out and 'Society' added in pencil. $17\frac{5}{8}''$ x $24\frac{1}{8}''$ meas. of view, in mount $24''$ x $31\frac{1}{4}''$. Probably after an aquatint by Jukes.

DG XV*
Cook 15
Owhyee—Sandwich Islands [Death of Cook]. $17\frac{3}{8}''$ x $24''$ meas. of view, in mount $24''$ x $31\frac{1}{4}''$. Title lettered on mount. Probably after the aquatint by Jukes.

For four similar watercolours in the possession of Mrs. Upcher, 1958 and two in the possession of Mr. Sabin, 1958 *see* NPL:M PXn–163 and NPL:M PXn–164. *See also* NPL:D DG D27 for a set of original watercolours of similar views by James Cleveley. *See also* separate entries under Cleveley, James for the Jukes and Piringer prints.

Copies: NPL:D(DGXV* Cook12–15). 1746

DRAWINGS relating to Cook's third voyage attributed to John Cleveley, from sketches made by his brother James, and painted c.1786.

Watercolours. All are pasted down on card, on which in some cases frame lines are drawn.

CONTENTS:

f.1. The *Resolution* and *Discovery* anchored at the Nore, June 15, 1776 [possibly]. $15\frac{1}{2}''$ x $22\frac{5}{8}''$ meas. of view, on sheet $16''$ x $23\frac{1}{8}''$.

f.2. The *Resolution* anchored in the Downs, June 26, 1776 [possibly]. $16\frac{1}{4}''$ x $22\frac{1}{4}''$ meas. of view, on sheet $16\frac{1}{2}''$ x $22\frac{7}{8}''$.

f.3. The *Resolution* and *Discovery* anchored in Plymouth Sound, June 30, 1776 [possibly]. $15\frac{7}{8}''$ x $22\frac{3}{8}''$ meas. of view, on sheet $16\frac{1}{4}''$ x $22\frac{7}{8}''$.

f.4. View in Queen Charlotte's Sound, New Zealand. $17''$ x $23\frac{7}{8}''$ meas. of view, on sheet $17\frac{5}{8}''$ x $24\frac{3}{8}''$.

f.5. View of Huaheine, one of the Society Islands. $17\frac{1}{4}''$ x $23\frac{3}{4}''$ meas. of view, on sheet $17\frac{5}{8}''$ x $24\frac{1}{4}''$.

f.6. View of Morea, or Eimeo, Society Islands. $17\frac{1}{4}''$ x $23\frac{3}{4}''$ meas. of view, on sheet $17\frac{5}{8}''$ x $24\frac{1}{4}''$.

f.7. Captain Cook landing at Owyhee [Hawaii]. $12\frac{7}{8}''$ x $18\frac{1}{4}''$ meas. of view, on sheet $13\frac{1}{2}''$ x $18\frac{5}{8}''$.

The drawings are untitled and it is not now possible to say for certain which is which of the first three listed. Folio 1 is signed 'Is Green'.

See also notes at NPL:M PXn–166.

The remaining four are similar to four aquatints from drawings on the spot by James Cleveley, painted by John Cleveley, Jukes aquætt., published by T. Martyn 1787–1788, and to another set of four by Piringer (for which *see* separate entries for each view under Cleveley, James) except that folio 7 shows Capt. Cook leaving his vessel for the shore, just before the attack which resulted in his death, while the published plate shows the attack itself, taken from the same angle. For what are thought to be two of the sketches by James, in the possession of S.F. Sabin, 1968, *see* NPL:M PXn–163.

For photographs and notes on four similar watercolours in the possession of Mrs. Upcher 1958 *see* NPL:M PXn–164. For yet another set of four watercolours, slightly bigger in

scale than the prints by Jukes and probably copies of the prints and filed at DG XV*
Cook 12–15, *see* separate entry under Cleveley, James.
Folio 4 (Queen Charlotte Sound) is inscribed l.r. 'Har——Coppy'. Below this there is
a part of a cut off word. The remaining letters could be 'l' and possibly 'e' (perhaps
'Cleveley'?). The view is very close in most details to the aquatint by Jukes and to Mrs.
Upcher's watercolour by John Cleveley titled 'Otaheite, Society Islands'.
Folio 5 (Huaheine) and 6 (Morea) are very close in most details to the aquatint by Jukes
and to Mrs. Upcher's watercolour by John Cleveley titled 'Otaheite, Society Islands',
but folio 6, like Mr. Sabin's sketch and like Mrs. Upcher's watercolour, shows an extra
figure in the lower left foreground and is signed 'W.H.' lower left corner.

Copies: NPL:DG(DG D27).   1747

MOREA, one of the Friendly Islands in the South Seas.

Watercolour painting. 17″ x 23½″. Titled; unsigned.
Drawn on the spot by James Cleveley; painted by John Cleveley. Aquatint by F. Jukes
published in London, T. Martyn, 1787.

Copies: ANL (Nan Kivell).   1748

MOREA, one of the Friendly Islands in the South Seas.

Watercolour painting. 13¾″ x 22½″. Untitled; unsigned.
Attributed to John Cleveley; after a sketch by James Cleveley. Landscape identical with,
details differ from the larger watercolour listed above.

Copies: ANL (Nan Kivell).   1749

VIEW OF MOOREA, by John Cleveley, presumably after his brother James.

1784. Watercolour. 19¼″ x 28″ inside mount. Signed "Jnº Cleveley Delin 1784". Titled
by comparison with print published by Jukes from which it differs considerably. Notes
entitled *Cleveley drawings connected with the third voyage of Capt. J. Cook in the Dixson Library
and in the Mitchell Library*, are at NPL:M PXn–165.

Copies: NPL:M(101).   1750

VIEW OF MOREA, one of the Friendly Islands, from a painting by John Cleveley, presumably after his brother James.

Photograph, c.3½″ x c.6″ meas. of view.
The location of the original is not known.
This view differs from other views of Morea by Cleveley, but is closest to the watercolour
by John, 1784, at NPL:M 101.

Copies: NPL:M(Small Picture File/M).   1751

Reproductions

MORT du Capitaine Cook.

See View of Owhyhee, no. 1779.

VIEW of Charlotte Sound in New Zealand. Drawn on the spot by Ja.ˢ Cleveley. Painted by Jn.º Cleveley, London. F. Jukes Aquat.ᵗ

Feb.5, 1788. London, T. Martyn. Aquatint. $17\frac{1}{8}''$ x $23\frac{3}{4}''$ meas. of view, on sheet $19\frac{5}{8}''$ x $26\frac{1}{8}''$ which seems to be cut on plate mark. On rock, foreground lower right 'Etch by Jnº Wright'. Title is taken from the dedication.
This is possibly not Queen Charlotte Sound but Matavai Bay.
For similar watercolours in the possession of Mrs. Upcher, 1958, and of S.F. Sabin, 1958, *see* notes and photographs filed at PXn–163 and PXn–164, and *see also* DG D27 and DG XV*Cook 12–15. In each case the watercolour is part of a set, entries for which are given under Cleveley, James—*Drawings relating to Cook's third voyage.*
Copies: NPL:DG(DGXV* Cook5). 1752

Another print.

Mounted to show dedication including title, imprint trimmed off.
Copies: NPL:M(V*Cook3). 1753

Another print.

Hand-coloured, trimmed to edge of view. $16\frac{7}{8}''$ x $23\frac{5}{8}''$, pasted down on backing board.
Copies: NPL:M(V*Cook1). 1754

Another print.

A very faint impression. Hand-coloured. No lettering visible below view. $16\frac{3}{4}''$ x $23\frac{3}{4}''$ meas. of view, on sheet $18\frac{5}{8}''$ x c.$24\frac{1}{2}''$.
Signed in watercolour or ink 'Th. Martyn' in lower right. Underneath this there may be an etched 'W' (as in 'Etch by Jnº Wright' shown on DG XV* Cook 5).
Copies: NPL:M(V*Cook2). 1755

Another print.

A very faint impression. Hand-coloured. No dedication, aquatinter's or publishers name visible. On rock, foreground lower right 'Etch by Jnº Wright'. In pencil below view, lower right, 'Exᵗ at Mr. Martyn's Academy Great Marlborough Street London 1788'.
Titled in ink below view 'Charlotte Sound in New Zealand'. $17''$ x $23\frac{1}{2}''$ meas. of view, $19\frac{1}{2}''$ x $25\frac{5}{8}''$ meas. of plate mark, on slightly larger sheet.
Copies: NPL:DG(DGXV*Cook1). 1756

The Same; with title Vue du Détroit Charlotte Sound dans la Nouvelle Zélande dans la mer du Sud. Jasˢ Clevely [del.] Piringer [sc.]. Paris, Bance aîné.

Aquatint. $16\frac{7}{8}''$ x $23\frac{1}{8}''$ meas. of view, on sheet $19\frac{1}{8}''$ x $25\frac{1}{4}''$.
Title is followed by an explanatory note.
(*Voyage du Capᵉ Cook No.1*)
Copies: NPL:M(V*Cook5). 1757

Another print.

Copies: NPL:M(V*Cook4). 1758

Another print.

Copies: NPL:DG(DGXV*Cook8). 1759

VIEW OF HUAHEINE, one of the Society Islands. Drawn on the spot by Ja.ˢ Clevely. Painted by Jn.º Clevely, London. F. Jukes Aquat.ᵗ

May 26 1787. London, T. Martyn. Aquatint. 17⅛″ x 23⅝″ meas. of view, 19½″ x 26¼″ meas. of sheet which seems to be cut on plate mark.

Title is taken from the dedication.

For similar watercolours in the possession of Mrs. Upcher, 1958, and of S.F. Sabin, 1958, *see* notes and photographs filed at PXn–163 and PXn–164, and *see also* DG D27 and DG XV* Cook 12–15. In each case the watercolour is part of a set, entries for which are given under Cleveley, James—*Drawings relating to Cook's third voyage.*

Copies: NPL:DG(DGXV*Cook6). 1760

Another 2 prints.

Copies: NPL:M(V*Cook 6–7). 1761

Another print.

Imprint trimmed off.

Copies: NPL:M(V*Cook8). 1762

Another print.

A very faint impression. Hand-coloured. No dedication, aquatinter's or publisher's name visible. In pencil below view, lower right. Exᵗ at Mr. Martyn's Academy Great Marlborough Street London 1788'. 17″ x 23⅜″ meas. of view, 19¾″ x 26″ meas. of plate mark, on slightly larger sheet.

Copies: NPL:DG(DGXV*Cook2). 1763

The Same; with title Vue de l'Ile Huaheim dans la Mer du Sud. Jaˢ Clevely [del.], Piringer [sc.]. Paris, Bance aîné.

Aquatint. 17¼″ x 23⅜″ meas. of view, on sheet 19¼″ x 25½″.

Title is followed by an explanatory note.

(*Voyage du Capᵉ Cook No.2*)

Copies: NPL:M(V*Cook10). 1764

Another print.

Copies: NPL:DG(DGXV*Cook9). 1765

Another print.

Aquatint printed in two colours, with additional hand-colour.

Copies: NPL:M(V*Cook9). 1766

VIEW OF MOREA, one of the Friendly Islands. Drawn on the spot by Ja.ˢ Clevely. Painted by Jn.º Clevely, London. F. Jukes Aquat.ᵗ

Sepʳ 1787. London, T. Martyn. Aquatint. 17¾″ x 24″ meas. of view.

Title is taken from dedication.

For similar watercolours in the possession of Mrs. Upcher, 1958, and of S.F. Sabin, 1958, *see* notes and photographs filed at NPL:M PXn–163 and NPL:M PXn–164, and *see also* DG D27 and DG XV* Cook 12–15. In each case the watercolour is part of a set, entries for which are given under Cleveley, James—*Drawings relating to Cook's third voyage.*

Copies: NPL:M(V*Cook11). 1767

Another print.

Trimmed to first line of dedication.

Copies: NPL:M(V*Cook12).

1768

Another print.

Imprint trimmed off.

Copies: NPL:DG(DGXV*Cook7).

1769

Another print.

Trimmed to edge of view. Hand-coloured, with an additional buoy in the right foreground.

Copies: NPL:M(V*Cook13).

1770

Another print.

Probably a very faint impression of the Jukes aquatint.
Hand-coloured. No imprint or aquatinter's name visible. Dedication barely visible. In pencil, lower left below view 'Drawn on the Spot by Mr. Jn.º Clevely.' and in pencil, lower right below view 'Exᵗ at Mr. Martyn's Academy Great Marlborough Street London 1788'. Titled in ink above the faintly printed title 'Morea one of the Friendly Islands'. The word 'Friendly' has been corrected in pencil in a later hand to 'Society'. 17¼″ x 23¾″ meas. of view, 19¾″ x 26″ meas. of plate mark, trimmed at plate mark.

Copies: NPL:DG(DGXV*Cook3).

1771

The Same; with title Vue de l'Ile Maréa une des Iles des Amis la Mer du Sud. Ja.ˢ Clevely [del.] Piringer [sc.]. Paris, Bance aîné.

Aquatint. 16¾″ x 23⅝″ meas. of view. Title is followed by explanatory note. (*Voyage du Capitaine Cook No. 3.*)

Copies: NPL:DG(DGXV*Cook10).

1772

Another print.

Printed in two colours, with additional hand-colouring.

Copies: NPL:M(V*Cook14).

1773

VIEW OF OWHYHEE one of the Sandwich Islands. Drawn on the spot by Jas.ˢ Cleveley. Painted by Jn.º Cleveley, London. F. Jukes Aquatᵗ.

July 5, 1788. London, T. Martyn. Aquatint.
17¼″ x 23¾″ meas. of view, on sheet 19½″ x 26⅛″, which seems to be cut on plate mark. Title is taken from dedication.
For similar watercolours in the possession of Mrs. Upcher, 1958, and of S.F. Sabin, 1958, *see* notes and photographs filed at NPL:M PXn–163 and PXn–164, and *see also* DG D27 and DG XV* Cook 12–15. That filed at DG D27 differs from all the others as it shows Capt. Cook leaving his vessel for the shore, while the others show the attack on Cook. In each case the watercolour is part of a set, entries for which are given under Cleveley, James—*Drawings relating to Cook's third voyage.* For a reproduction of the Sabin watercolour see *Geographical Magazine*, Dec. 1956, p.385.

Copies: NPL:M(V*Cook18).

1774

Another print.
Partly hand-coloured.
Copies: NPL:M(V*Cook15).   1775

Another print.
Trimmed to edge of view, hand-coloured.
Copies: NPL:M(V*Cook16).   1776

Another print.
Hand-coloured. No lettering visible below view. c.16¾″ x 23½″ meas. of view, on sheet 19″ x c.24″.
Copies: NPL:M(V*Cook17).   1777

Another print.
Probably a very faint impression of the Jukes aquatint.
Hand-coloured. No dedication, aquatinter's or publisher's name visible. There is a very faint pencil inscription lower right which probably reads 'Ex^t at Mar. Martyn's Academy Great Marlborough Street London 1788' (cf. rest of set at DG XV* Cook 1–3).
Titled in ink below view 'Owyhee one of the Sandwich Islands. (The Death of Capt. Cook–'. 17″ x 23⅛″ meas. of view, 19¼″ x 25½″ meas. of plate mark, on slightly larger sheet.
Copies: NPL:DG(DGXV*Cook4).   1778

The Same, with title Mort du Capitaine Cook. Ja.^{s} Clevely [del.] Piringer [sc.]. Paris, Bance aîné.
Aquatint. 16⅞″ x 23⅞″ meas. of view, on sheet 19⅛″ x 25⅜″.
Title is followed by an explanatory note.
(*Voyage du cap^e Cook No.4*)
Copies: NPL:M(V*Cook22).   1779

Another print.
Copies: NPL:M(V*Cook20).   1780

Another print.
Copies: NPL:DG (DG XV* Cook11).   1781

Another print.
Aquatint printed in two colours, with additional hand-colour.
Copies: NPL:M (V* Cook 19).   1782

The Same. Cleveley [del.] Piringer [sc.].
In different style from above. Title as above.
No explanatory note, imprint or series.
Aquatint. 16¾″ x 23⅝″ meas. of view, on sheet 19¾″ x 27⅛″.
Copies: NPL:M(V*Cook21).   1783

VUE DE DÉTROIT CHARLOTTE.
See View of Charlotte Sound in New Zealand, no.1757.

VUE DE L'ILE HUAHEIM.
See View of Huaheine, no. 1764.

Articles about the Illustrations

1932 DIXSON, *Sir* William

Cook's voyages: illustrations. [Note on Cleveley's *View of Charlotte Sound in New Zealand*.]

(*Mariner's Mirror* vol.18, Oct.1932, p.425.)

Copies: NPL:R(DS656.506/7). 1784

CLEVELEY, JOHN

See back Cleveley, James

ECKSTEIN, I.

PLATE representing the arrival of the *Discovery* and *Resolution* under Captains Clerke and Gore, at St. Peter and St. Paul, in Kamschatka, the 29th of April. Dedicated by de la Garde. Designed and etched by I.Eckstein. Aqua Tinta by I.C. Stadler. Vide Captn Cook's third voyage.

Coloured aquatint. Meas. within frame lines $18\frac{3}{4}''$ x 25''.
Sheet trimmed so that imprint does not show.
Copies: NPL:D(DL Pf57). 1785

PLATE representing the departure of Captains Gore and King, accompanied by Major Behm, governor of Kamschatka, described in Capt. Cook's third voyage. Dedicated by de la Garde. Designed and etched by I. Eckstein. Aqua Tinta by I.C. Stadler. London, published as the Act directs.

Coloured aquatint. Meas. within frame lines $18\frac{3}{4}''$ x 25''.
Copies: NPL:D(DL Pf58). 1786

Another print..
Less highly coloured.
Copies: NPL:M(V*Cook23). 1787

ELLIS, WILLIAM
Originals, Including Photocopies of Originals

ANOTHER VIEW of the Astronomer's Rock, in Ship-Cove, King George's Sound, on the north-west coast of America.

1778. Watercolour and ink. 13" x 18½". Titled; signed.

Copies: ANL (Nan Kivell).   1788

CHRISTMAS HARBOUR in the Island of Desolation, or Kerguelan's Land.

1776. Watercolour and ink. 13" x 19½". Titled; signed.

Copies: ANL (Nan Kivell).   1789

INSIDE OF A HUT Unalaschka on the N.W. coast of America.

1778. Watercolour painting. 11¼" x 16". Titled; signed.

Copies: ANL (Nan Kivell).   1790

OUTSIDE OF THE HUTS at Unalaschka, N.W. coast of America.

1778. Watercolour painting. 10" x 13½". Titled; signed.

Copies: ANL (Nan Kivell).   1791

PART OF THE HARBOUR of St. Peter and St. Paul.

1779. Watercolour painting. 13" x 18½". Untitled; signed.

Copies: ANL (Nan Kivell).   1792

PRINCE WILLIAM'S SOUND, in Sandwich Sound on the N.W. coast of America. Snug corner, P.W. Henry's Sound, Capt.J.D.

1778. Watercolour and ink. 9" x 11". Titled; signed.

Copies: ANL (Nan Kivell).   1793

A ROCK, and a distant view in King George's Sound, N.W. coast of America.

1778. Watercolour and ink. 11" x 9½". Titled; signed.

Copies: ANL (Nan Kivell).   1794

A RUSSIAN HUT, in the harbour of St. Peter and St. Paul, in Kamtschatska.

1779. Watercolour painting. 9" x 12¼". Titled; signed.

Copies: ANL (Nan Kivell).   1795

[VIEW in Vaitepiha Bay, Tahiti.]

Watercolour. 12¼" x 17⅝" pasted on mount. Unsigned and undated.

This has been ascribed to Webber, but it shows the same view, with minor variations, as the signed and dated watercolour by W. Ellis, 1777, which is in the Bernice P. Bishop Museum, Honolulu, and a reproduction of which appears in the Journals of Captain Cook, ed. by J.C. Beaglehole, vol.3, plate 20.
([Three voyages round the world]. Plate no.124.)

Copies: NPL:M(PXD59⁻²f.7).   1796

VIEW of a singular tree in King George's Sound, N.W. coast of America.
1778. Watercolour painting. 9¾" x 12". Titled; signed.
Copies: ANL(Nan Kivell).   1797

VIEW of King George's Sound, N.W. coast of America.
1778. Watercolour painting. 12" x 17¼". Titled; signed.
Copies: ANL(Nan Kivell).   1798

VIEW of King George's Sound on the north-west coast of America.
1778. Watercolour and ink. 7" x 9". Titled; signed.
Copies: ANL(Nan Kivell).   1799

VIEW of Ship-Cove, in King George's Sound, on the N.W. coast of America.
Where the tents are fixed was called Astronomer's Rock.
1778. Watercolour and ink. 13" x 19". Titled; signed.
Copies: ANL(Nan Kivell).   1800

VIEW of Snug-Corner Harbour, Sandwich Sound, N.W. coast of America.
P. Willm. Henry's Sound. Capt.Dixon.
1778. Watercolour and ink. 10¼" x 13½". Titled; signed.
Copies: ANL(Nan Kivell).   1801

VIEW of the huts at Tschutschi Moss, Asia.
1778. Watercolour and ink. 10" x 13½". Titled; signed.
Copies: ANL(Nan Kivell).   1802

VIEW up the valley which goes from Matavai-Bay; with the river, in the
island Otaheiti, South Sea.
1777. Watercolour painting. 12" x 17¼". Titled; signed.
Copies: ANL(Nan Kivell).   1803

WINTER VIEW of Kamtschatska.
1779. Watercolour painting. 10" x 13½". Titled; signed.
Copies: ANL(Nan Kivell).   1804

WEBBER, JOHN
Originals, Including Photocopies of Originals

[BOATS of the Friendly Isles.]
Pen and ink drawing. 12¼" x 19¼". Unsigned and undated.
Engraved as plate no.2 in the 1808 Boydell edition of Webber's *Views in the South Seas*.
(Item no.1872). Title is taken from that plate.
Copies: NPL:D(DL Pf52).   1805

[THE BODY OF TEE, a chief as preserved after death, in Otaheite.]

Watercolour. 12¼″ x 19½″.
Unsigned and undated. Engraved as plate 26 in Atlas to Cook's third voyage (listed in
this Bibliography as no.1743). The engraving shows the same scene in reverse, with the
addition of a figure in the foreground and some alteration of detail. Title is taken from
the engraving.

Copies: NPL:D(DL Pf50). 1806

[CANOE and men of Tahiti.]

Ink and wash drawing. 12⅝″ x 19⅝″. Unsigned and undated.
Title from pencil note on back in an unknown hand.

Copies: NPL:D(DL Pf51). 1807

[CANOE, Mangaia.]

Wash drawing. 12¼″ x 18″. Unsigned and undated.
Title from pencil note on back in unknown hand.

Copies: NPL:D(DL Pe210). 1808

CANOE of Otaheite.

Watercolour painting. 12″ x 19″. Untitled; unsigned.
Col. aquatint in Webber's *Views in the South Seas*, London, 1808. Plate 2. (No.1872).

Copies: ANL (Nan Kivell). 1809

CEREMONIAL GROUND at Tongatabu at which was performed the
mourning kava ceremony for the king's son, witnessed by Captain Cook
27 June 1777.

Wash drawing. 16½″ x 25″. Untitled; unsigned.
Engraving by S. Middiman, with figures added by J. Hall, entitled The natche, a ceremony in honour of the king's son, in Tongatubu, in *Atlas to Cook's 3rd voyage*. Plate 22.

Copies: ANL. 1810

[A CHIEF lying in state, Matavi (*sic*), Otaheite.]

Watercolour. 16 11/16″ x 22⅞″, pasted down on mount.
Signed "J.Webber del." in lower right-hand corner. Title from ink inscription on back
of mount in an unknown hand. Engraved as plate no.6 in the 1808 Boydell edition of
Webber's *Views in the South Seas* (listed in this Bibliography as no. 1872). The view is
there entitled *Waheiadooa, Chief of Oheitepeha, lying in state*. Photograph (Govt. Pr. neg.
no.58406) is at NPL:M PX B1675, no.35.

Copies: NPL:D(DG28). 1811

A CHIEF of the Sandwich Islands.

1787. Oil painting. 58″ x 45″. Untitled; signed.
Copies: ANL(Nan Kivell). 1812

A DEER.

Watercolour painting. 11$\frac{1}{4}$" x 18$\frac{1}{2}$". Titled; unsigned.
Possibly a deer of Kamtschatka.
Copies: ANL(Nan Kivell). 1813

A FIATOOKA, or morai, in Tongatabu, 26 June 1777.

Wash drawing. 16$\frac{1}{2}$" x 25". Untitled; unsigned.
Engraving by W. Ellis in Atlas to Cook's third voyage, plate 21.
Copies: ANL. 1814

[FRIGATE bird.]

Watercolour. 12$\frac{1}{4}$" x 19$\frac{5}{8}$".
Signed in lower right-hand corner, "J. Webber f.1777." Title from pencil note on back
in an unknown hand.
Copies: NPL:D(DL Pf53). 1815

HEAD and shoulders of a man.

Crayon drawing. 14" x 10". Titled; unsigned.
Possibly Tschutski man.
Copies: ANL(Nan Kivell). 1816

HEAD and shoulders of a woman.

Crayon drawing. 14" x 10". Titled; unsigned.
Possibly Tschutski woman.
Copies: ANL(Nan Kivell). 1817

[HUT and three natives of Tonga.]

Pen and ink drawing. 12$\frac{1}{4}$" x 18".
Signed "Jno Web.^{r} del. 1778" in lower left-hand corner. Title from pencil note on back
in an unknown hand.
Copies: NPL:D(DL Pe211). 1818

THE INSIDE of a winter habitation, in Kamtschatka.

Watercolour painting. 9" x 15$\frac{1}{2}$". Titled; unsigned.
Engraving by W. Sharp in Atlas to Cook's third voyage, plate 78.
Copies: ANL(Nan Kivell). 1819

THE INSIDE of a winter habitation, in Kamtschatka.

Watercolour painting. 13" x 20". Titled; unsigned.
Preliminary sketch for larger work, listed above.
Copies: ANL(Nan Kivell). 1820

A MAN of Kamtschatka.

Pencil drawing. 9$\frac{1}{4}$" x 7". Untitled; unsigned.
Engraving by W. Sharp in Atlas to Cook's third voyage, plate 75.
Copies: ANL(Nan Kivell). 1821

A MAN in Kamtschatka, travelling in winter.

1779. Pen and wash drawing. 12½″ x 18″. Titled; signed.
Copies: ANL(Nan Kivell). 1822

[A MAN of Mangea.]

Pen and ink drawing. 17¼″ x 12¼″. Unsigned and undated.
Engraved as plate no.11 in Atlas to Cook's third voyage (item no.1743 in this Bibliography). Title is taken from the engraving.
Copies: NPL:D(DL Pe212). 1823

[NATIVE girl of Tahiti.]

Pencil drawing. 10⅞″ x 8⅝″. Unsigned and undated.
Title from pencil note on back in an unknown hand.
Copies: NPL:D(DL Pe213). 1824

NEGATIVES of original drawings by J. Webber in B.M.Add.MSS15513.

CONTENTS:
1. A man of New Holland (f.4).
2. A woman of New Holland (f.5).
3. Inside of a Hippah or Fort (f.6).
Copies: NPL:M(Glass Neg. Copies 12). 1825

NEGATIVES of paintings by Westall, Hodges and Webber at the Admiralty and the National Maritime Museum Greenwich.

44 glass negatives, each c.4½″ x 6½″.
The paintings include views by Hodges and Webber during Cook's voyages, including views of Tahiti and the Society Islands, Huahine and New Zealand.
Prints are filed at NPL:M B1672.
Lists of contents are filed with negs. and prints, and detailed descriptive list is at NPL:M An25⁻³.
Copies: NPL:M(Glass Neg. Copies 23). 1826

A NEW ZEALAND chief drawn from life.

Pencil drawing. 5½″ x 4½″. Titled by E.E. Petherick; unsigned.
Head and shoulders.
Copies: ANL(Petherick). 1827

[A NIGHT dance by men, in Hapaee.]

Wash drawing. 19½″ x 26½″. Unsigned and undated.
Engraved as plate no.16 in Atlas to Cook's third voyage (item no.1743 in this Bibliography). Title is taken from the engraving.
Copies: NPL:D(DL Pf54). 1828

[OHEITEPEHA Bay in Otaheite, 1784.]

Watercolour. 14¾″ x 21″, inside mount.
Signed "J. Webber del.1784" in lower right-hand corner.
Copies: NPL:D(DG189). 1829

[AN OPOSSUM of Van Diemen's Land.]

Watercolour. 12½″ x 19½″.
Signed "John. Webber f.1777" towards lower right-hand corner.
Engraved as plate no.8 in Atlas to Cook's third voyage (item no.1743 in this Bibliography.) Title is taken from the engraving.
Copies: NPL:D(DL Pf55). 1830

AN OPOSSUM (*sic*)

Watercolour painting. 6″ x 9½″. Titled; unsigned.
Animal not coloured. Engraving by P. Mazell, with title *An opossum of Van Diemen's Land*, in Atlas to Cook's third voyage, plate 8.
Copies: ANL(Nan Kivell). 1831

PACIFIC ISLAND beach scene.

Watercolour painting. 10″ x 7½″. Titled; unsigned.
Native craft in left foreground, fish spread on beach, native hut in background.
Copies: ANL(Nan Kivell). 1832

PACIFIC ISLAND scene.

Watercolour painting. 10″ x 7½″. Titled; unsigned.
Native habitation adorned with carved figures. British flag flying from flagstaff on left.
Copies: ANL(Nan Kivell). 1833

PACIFIC ISLAND scene.

Watercolour painting. 8″ x 10¾″. Titled; unsigned.
Native habitation surrounded by tall palms. Giant clam shell in right foreground.
Copies: ANL(Nan Kivell). 1834

PHOTOGRAPHS of paintings by J. Webber, in the possession of Sir Bruce Ingram, 1962.

1 portfolio.
CONTENTS:
1. Teneriffe.
2. The Island of Bola Bola.
3. Indians of Kamchatka, 1784.
4. Hamilton Bay, with Mitre Hill in the background, New Zealand. Said to be by John Webber. Title from label on back of painting, but owner is of the opinion that the artist is Hodges whose style it resembles. The view may possibly be of Moorea, not of New Zealand.
Copies: NPL:M(B1673). 1835

THE PLANTAIN TREE, in the island of Cracatoa.

Watercolour painting. 16½″ x 14½″. Titled; unsigned.
Col. aquatint in Webber's *Views in the South Seas*, London, 1808. Plate 4. (Item no.1872.)
Copies: ANL(Nan Kivell). 1836

[PORTRAIT of a New Zealander.]

Pen and ink drawing. $17\frac{1}{4}''$ x $12\frac{3}{8}''$. Unsigned and undated.
Title from pencil note on back in an unknown hand.
Copies: NPL:D(DL Pe214). 1837

PORTRAIT of Poedooa, daughter of Orea, King of Ulaitea, Society Islands.

1785? Oil painting. 57″ x 37″. Untitled; unsigned.
Exhibited at Royal Academy, 1785. Similar to that in the National Maritime Museum; *see* Moorehead, A.—*The Fatal impact*, London, Hamish Hamilton, 1966, opp. p.55.
Copies: ANL(Nan Kivell). 1838

PORTRAIT of Poedooa, daughter of Orea, King of Ulaitea, Society Islands.

Photograph of original oil painting. 57″ x 37″.
In the possession of R. de C. Nan Kivell Esq., 1961. Exhibited Royal Academy 1785, no.392.
Copies: NPL:M(P1). 1839

[SAILING CANOE of Otaheite.]

Watercolour. $12\frac{1}{4}''$ x $17\frac{15}{16}''$.
Signed "Jn.º Webber del.1777" in lower right-hand corner.
Title from pencil note on back in an unknown hand.
Copies: NPL:D(DL Pe215). 1840

A SAVAGE of New Caledonia in the attitude of throwing a spear.

n.d. Unfinished watercolour. $13\frac{3}{16}''$ x $9\frac{15}{16}''$. Unsigned and undated.
Titled faintly in pencil along lower edge. Background sketched in pencil. Above title in pencil is "Polynesia". The title is the same as that on the engraving of this by Webber (no.1865).
Copies: NPL:D(DL Pe227). 1841

A SEA OTTER.

Watercolour painting. $8\frac{3}{4}''$ x $17\frac{1}{4}''$. Titled; unsigned.
Engraving by Mazell in Atlas to Cook's third voyage, plate 43.
Copies: ANL(Nan Kivell). 1842

[SHIP anchored near a pine-covered shore. Watercolour, possibly by J. Webber.]

10″ x $18\frac{3}{4}''$ pasted on mount.
The view is almost certainly of Resolution (or Ship) Cove, and the ship the *Resolution* which anchored there for repairs in April 1778.
(Cf. watercolour by William Ellis in the National Library of Australia, "A view of Ships Cove in King George's Sound", which is reproduced in the *Journals of Captain Cook*, ed. by J.C. Beaglehole, vol.3, plate 34b.
([Three voyages round the world], plate no.125.)
Copies: NPL:M(PXD59⁻² f.8). 1843

[SLEDGE SCENE.]

Unfinished watercolour. $13\frac{5}{8}''$ x $20\frac{5}{16}''$ pasted on mount.
Unsigned and undated. Although differing in certain details, this seems to be a sketch,
probably by Webber, for the scene shown as plate no.70 in the Atlas to the third voyage
(item no.1743 in this Bibliography). There are five dogs in both scenes; the watercolour,
however, has two figures on the sledge, where there is only one in the engraving, and
there is a figure on skis drawn in pencil which is not in the engraving.
([Three voyages round the world], plate no.115.)
Copies: NPL:M(PXD59⁻¹).   1844

[SOUTH SEA ISLANDERS: 3 oil paintings by Webber or Hodges.]

*See the subhead Second Voyage – Illustrations Arranged by Artist – Hodges, William – Originals,
Including Photocopies of Originals.*

[A TOOPAPAOO of a chief, with a priest making his offering to the morai, in Huoheine.]

Watercolour. $12\frac{7}{16}''$ x $19\frac{1}{2}''$.
Inscription in lower right-hand corner in Webber's hand "drawn from nature at Huaina
1777". Engraved as plate no.8 in the 1808 Boydell edition of Webber's *Views in the South
Seas* (item no.1872 in this Bibliography). The engraving shows the same scene in reverse,
with the alteration of a few minor details.
Copies: NPL:D(DL Pf56).   1845

[VIEW in Oheitepeha Bay, Tahiti.]

Watercolour. $16\frac{1}{8}''$ x $23\frac{5}{8}''$ inside mount.
Signed "J. Webber 1786" in lower left-hand corner.
Copies: NPL:D(DG27).   1846

VIEW in the island of Atoui, Sandwich Island.

Pen and wash drawing. $13\frac{1}{2}''$ x $12\frac{1}{2}''$. Untitled; unsigned.
Unfinished drawing.
Copies: ANL(Nan Kivell).   1847

VIEW in the island Oonalaska.

Watercolour painting. $14''$ x $21''$. Untitled; signed (?) Webber R.A.
Copies: ANL(Nan Kivell).   1848

VIEW in Ulietea.

1786. Oil painting. $17\frac{1}{8}''$ x $24''$. Untitled; signed.
Polynesian canoe and natives in foreground.
Copies: ANL(Nan Kivell).   1849

[VIEW in Ulieta, Society Islands.]

Watercolour. $13\frac{1}{4}''$ x $22\frac{1}{8}''$ inside mount.
Signed "John Webber del." in lower right-hand corner.
Copies: NPL:D(DG23).   1850

VIEW of Hothaheita Piha drawn from nature by John Webber 1777.

Photograph of a painting in the British Museum. With it is a note on the picture by
P. Warren.

Copies: NPL:M(Small Picture File:Tahiti). 1851

[VIEW of St. Peter and St. Paul in Kamtschatka. Watercolour, probably
by J. Webber.]

11¾" x 21" pasted on mount. Unsigned and undated.
The view is very close in details and style, except that it is drawn from a slightly different
angle, to the drawing in the British Museum (Add. MSS. 17277.30) "The village of
Petropavlosk, Avacha Bay". This is reproduced in the *Journals of Captain Cook*, ed. by
J.C. Beaglehole, vol.3, plate 63. ([Three voyages round the world] plate no.123.)

Copies: NPL:M(PXD59⁻² f.6). 1852

[A VIEW of the Harbour of Aimeo, one of the Society Islands.]

Watercolour. 16⅝" x 25⁷⁄₁₆" pasted on mount.
Signed "J. Webber del. 1786" in lower left-hand corner. Title from ink inscription on
back of mount, in an eighteenth century hand, possibly Webber's.

Copies: NPL:D(DG24). 1853

VIEW on a coast with upright rocks making a cave.

Oil painting. 14¼" x 17¾". Untitled; unsigned.
Polynesian canoe, native with spear in foreground.

Copies: ANL(Nan Kivell). 1854

[WATERCOLOURS illustrating Captain Cook's last voyage: 40 drawings
by J. Webber. Together with 6 watercolours of the first voyage, including
one signed by J. Barralet, and 3 engraved portraits.]

ff.38.
Contained in large folio volume, bound in green morocco by Colnaghi.
Spine title: *Illustrations of Cook's voyages: original drawings by Webber.*
The drawings by Webber are unsigned and undated except nos. 9 and 16, which are
signed and dated, and nos. 19, 20 and 37, which are signed but not dated. The titles
are written in an unknown hand beneath the frame lines and follow the titles given to
the corresponding engravings in the Atlas to the third voyage, listed in this Bibliography
as no. 1743. Of the 6 watercolours of the first voyage, (nos. 14, 15, 43–6) no. 15 is signed
"J. Barralet" (or "Barrulet"). It corresponds exactly with the engraved plate no. 16 in
Hawkesworth's *Account of a voyage round the world*, which is the first official account of the
first voyage (listed in this Bibliography as no. 932). Plates 14, 43, 44, 45 and 46 (all
unsigned) similarly correspond with engraved plates nos. 7, 1, 2, 5 and 6 respectively
in Hawkesworth's *Account*, though whether they are copies of the engravings, or the
originals from which the engravings were made is uncertain. The titles in pencil beneath
the frame lines of these 6 watercolours are not taken from the corresponding engravings
in Hawkesworth's *Account* and are not used in the descriptions of these 6 plates given
hereunder.
A complete list and brief description of all 46 watercolours follows. All drawings are held
in mounts, and in each case measurement within frame lines is given.
For descriptions of the engravings *see Personal – Portraits (Dance Group) – Reproductions;
Personal – Portraits (Webber Group) – Reproductions*, and *Associates of Cook – King, James.*

CONTENTS:

1. A view of Christmas Harbour in Kerguelen's Land. $8\frac{3}{4}''$ x $14\frac{7}{8}''$.
2. The inside of a Hippah, in New Zealand. $8\frac{3}{4}''$ x $15''$.
3. A view at Annamooka. $8\frac{5}{8}''$ x $19\frac{5}{8}''$.
4. The reception of Captain Cook, in Hapaee. $8\frac{3}{4}''$ x $15''$.
5. A night dance by men in Hapaee. $8\frac{3}{4}''$ x $15\frac{1}{4}''$.
6. A night dance by women in Hapaee. $8\frac{3}{4}''$ x $15''$.
7. Poulaho, King of the Friendly Islands, drinking Kava. $9\frac{1}{8}''$ x $15\frac{1}{4}''$.
8. A fiatooka, or morai in Tongataboo. $8\frac{3}{4}''$ x $15''$.
9. A larger drawing, varying from the engraved view. Signed "J. Webber del. 1778" in lower right-hand corner. $16''$ x $25\frac{3}{4}''$.
10. A human sacrifice, in a morai, in Otaheite. $9\frac{3}{4}''$ x $18\frac{3}{8}''$.
11. The body of Tee, a chief, as preserved after death in Otaheite. $8\frac{5}{8}''$ x $14\frac{3}{4}''$.
12. A young woman of Otaheite bringing a present. $8\frac{7}{8}''$ x $7\frac{3}{16}''$.
13. A dance in Otaheite. $9''$ x $14\frac{7}{8}''$.
14. [A view of the inside of a house in the Island of Ulietea, with the representation of a dance to the music of the country, possibly by G.B. Cipriani.] $8\frac{5}{8}''$ x $13\frac{1}{4}''$.
15. [War canoe of New Zealand.] Signed "I. Barralet" [or Barrulet] on bow of canoe. $13\frac{5}{8}''$ x $20\frac{1}{2}''$.
16. A view of Huaheine. Slightly varying from the engraved view. Signed "J. Webber del. 1778" in bottom right-hand corner. $15\frac{1}{2}''$ x $25\frac{1}{4}''$.
17. A morai, in Atooi. $8\frac{3}{4}''$ x $14\frac{7}{8}''$.
18. The inside of the house in the morai, in Atooi. $7''$ x $9\frac{11}{16}''$.
19. An inland view, in Atooi. Signed "J. Webber del." in lower right-hand corner. $8\frac{3}{4}''$ x $18\frac{1}{2}''$.
20. An inland view, in Atooi. (Another view). Signed "J. Webber del." in lower right-hand corner. $12\frac{3}{4}''$ x $25\frac{7}{8}''$. Corresponds almost exactly with no.19.
21. A man of Nootka Sound. $9\frac{1}{8}''$ x $6\frac{7}{8}''$.
22. A woman of Nootka Sound. $9''$ x $7''$.
23. A view of the habitations in Nootka Sound. $8\frac{3}{4}''$ x $14\frac{7}{8}''$.
24. The inside of a house in Nootka Sound. $8\frac{7}{8}''$ x $14\frac{3}{4}''$.
25. A view of Snug Corner Cove, in Prince William's Sound. $8\frac{3}{4}''$ x $14\frac{7}{8}''$.
26. A man of Prince William's Sound. $9''$ x $7\frac{1}{8}''$.
27. A woman of Prince William's Sound. $9''$ x $7\frac{1}{8}''$.
28. A man of Oonalashka. $8\frac{7}{8}''$ x $6\frac{7}{8}''$.
29. A woman of Oonalashka. $9''$ x $7''$.
30. Canoes of Oonalashka. $7''$ x $8\frac{7}{8}''$.
31. The Tschuktschi and their habitations. $8\frac{7}{8}''$ x $15\frac{1}{8}''$.
32. Sea Horses. $8\frac{5}{8}''$ x $14\frac{7}{8}''$.
33. Inhabitants of Norton Sound and their habitations. $8\frac{3}{4}''$ x $15''$.
34. The inside of a house in Oonalashka. $8\frac{5}{8}''$ x $14\frac{13}{16}''$.
35. Tereoboo, King of Owyhee, bringing presents to Captain Cook. $8\frac{5}{8}''$ x $14\frac{7}{8}''$.
36. A man of the Sandwich Islands, dancing. $9\frac{5}{8}''$ x $7''$.
37. A canoe of the Sandwich Islands, the rowers masked. Signed "Jn° Webber del." in lower right-hand corner. $8\frac{11}{16}''$ x $15''$.
38. A man of the Sandwich Islands in a mask. $9\frac{3}{16}''$ x $6\frac{7}{8}''$.

39. A view of Karakakooa, in Owyhee. 8$\frac{15}{16}$" x 20$\frac{1}{16}$".
40. A sledge of Kamtschatka. 7$\frac{1}{8}$" x 8$\frac{3}{4}$".
41. A view of the town and harbour of St. Peter and St. Paul, in Kamtschatka. 8$\frac{7}{8}$" x 20$\frac{1}{8}$".
42. Summer and winter habitations in Kamtschatka. 8$\frac{3}{8}$" x 14$\frac{7}{8}$".
43. [A view of the Indians of Terra (*sic*) del Fuego in their hut, possibly by G.B. Cipriani.]
    8$\frac{3}{16}$" x 11$\frac{1}{4}$".
44. [A view in Matavia Bay in Otaheite.] Unsigned and undated. 7$\frac{13}{16}$" x 10$\frac{1}{16}$".
45. [A view in the Island of Otaheite; with the house or shed called Tupapow . . . and a
    representation of the person who performs the principal part in the funeral ceremony
    in his peculiar dress.] Unsigned and undated. 7$\frac{3}{8}$" x 13$\frac{7}{16}$".
46. A view in the Island of Huaheine; with the Ewharra no Eatua, or House of God.
    Unsigned. 7$\frac{1}{8}$" x 14$\frac{5}{8}$".

Copies: NPL:D(DL PXX2).   1855

A WHITE BEAR.

1779. Pen-and-ink drawing. 12$\frac{1}{4}$" x 18". Titled; signed.
Engraving by Mazell in Atlas to Cook's third voyage, plate 73.

Copies: ANL(Nan Kivell).   1856

A WOMAN of Kamtschatka.

Pencil drawing. 16$\frac{1}{8}$" x 12$\frac{1}{4}$". Untitled; unsigned.
Engraving by W. Sharp in Atlas to Cook's third voyage, plate 76.

Copies: ANL(Nan Kivell).   1857

[A YOUNG WOMAN of Otaheite, dancing.]

Pen drawing. 17" x 12$\frac{1}{2}$".
Engraved as plate no.29 in Atlas to the third voyage (item no. 1743 in this Bibliography).
Title is taken from the engraving.

Copies: NPL:D(DL Pe216).   1858

Reproductions

BOXING MATCH before Captain Cook at Owyhee, Sandwich Islands,
Thursday, January 18, 1770 [i.e. 1779], from an unpublished drawing
by James (*sic*) Webber, draughtsman to the expedition. London, F.
Edwards. Photogravure.

15$\frac{1}{4}$" x 26$\frac{3}{4}$", mounted 28" x 37$\frac{3}{4}$".
Printed description on back extracted from Cook's third voyage, and advertisement for
reproduction. Date 1770 is misprint.
Reproduction of plate no.16 in the Atlas to the third voyage, listed in this Bibliography
as no.1743.

Copies: NPL:M(XV*Cook1); NPL:D(DG XV*Cook22).   1859

CAP.^t COOK'S last voyage to the Pacific Ocean: [8 coloured engravings after Webber round a blank centre]. Printed and published by Edwd. Langley . . . London.

Meas. of plate mark 17¼″ x 14″.

Copies: NPL:D(DL Pf59).   1860

CAPTAIN COOK'S ships in Resolution Cove, Vancouver Island; 1778.

Reprod. of pen and wash drawing. c.3¼″ x 8½″.
The original is at the Admiralty.
(Lubbock, B.—Adventure by sea from out of old time. London, The Studio, 1925. Plate 18.)
Copies: NPL:M(Q656.5/2A1).   1861

CHRISTMAS HARBOUR, in Kerguelen's Land; engraved by G. Cooke. London, published by Longman, Hurst, Rees, Orme and Brown. Octr. 1811.

Meas. within frame lines 5″ x 8⅝″.
Meas. of plate mark 8 11/16″ x 10⅞″.
Engraving first published as plate no.4 in Atlas to the third voyage, listed in this Bibliography as no.1743.
Copies: NPL:M(SSV*Cook4).   1862

COOK'S BAY, Moorea, Society Islands. Watercolor. 17 x 24 in. Signed: John Webber, 1777. [Reproduced, not in colour.]

(*In* Brewington, Marion Vernon— The Marine paintings and drawings in the Peabody Museum, by M.V. and D. Brewington. Salem, Mass., the Museum, 1968. p.455.)
Copies: NPL:R(NQ 758.2/2).   1863

[LANDING of the coffin of one of the members of Cook's party.]

Col. reprod. of watercolour. c.5¼″ x c.7¾″.
The original is in the Victoria and Albert Museum.
(Lubbock, B.—Adventure by sea from out of old time. London, The Studio, 1925. Plate 20.)
Copies: NPL:M(Q656.5/2A1).   1864

A SAVAGE of New Caledonia in the attitude of throwing a spear. Drawn by J. Webber. Engrav'd by A.W. Warren.

Engraving. Meas. within frame lines 6¾″ x 4 13/16″.
Meas. of plate mark 8⅜″ x 6½″.
Copies: NPL:D(DL Pd680).   1865

The Same, entitled Man of New Caledonia throwing the spear. Davenport sc.

Engraving. Meas. of engraved surface 7½″ x 5 5/16″.
Copies: NPL:D(DL PX22).   1866

TAUTIRA VALLEY, Tahiti. Watercolor. 17½ x 25 in. Signed: John Webber, 1777. [Reproduced, not in colour.]

(*In* Brewington, Marion Vernon—The Marine paintings and drawings in the Peabody Museum, by M.V. and D. Brewington. Salem, Mass., the Museum, 1968. p.454.)

Copies: NPL:R(NQ758.2/2).   1867

VIEW probably in Kamchatka. Watercolor, 18 x 23 in. Attributed to John Webber. [Reproduced, not in colour.]

(*In* Brewington, Marion Vernon—The Marine paintings and drawings in the Peabody Museum by M.V. and D. Brewington. Salem, Mass., the Museum, 1968. p.455.)

Copies: NPL:R(NQ758.2/2).   1868

[VIEWS in the South Seas, each with imprint 'London, J. Webber

414. WEBBER, JOHN.

[Twelve aquatint views illustrating Captain Cook's third voyage.] Measuring between 43 x 31 and 28 x 41 cm.

[London, 1788-89]

Provenance: Francis Edwards, 1960.

Reference: Holmes 79 (the 1808 bound issue of 16 plates.)

Following are the titles of the views, numbered after the corresponding plates in the 1808 issue:

1. View of Queen Charlotte's Sound, New Zealand. Pubd. Octr. 1, 1790.
2. Boats of the Friendly Islands. Augt. 1, 1791.
4. The Plantain Tree in the Island of Cracatoa. Pubd. Novr. 1, 1788. [Creased.]
5. A View in Oheitepeha Bay, in the Island of Otaheite.
6. Waheiadooa, Chief of Oheitepeha, lying in State. Published July 1, 1789.
7. View of the Harbour of Taloo, in the Island of Eimeo. Pubd. July 1, 1789.
8. A Toopapaoo Chief; with a Priest making his offering to the Morai, in Huoheine. Pub. Oct. 1, 1789.
10. The Narta or Sledge for Burdens in Kamtchatka. NB not mentioned in Cooks, last Voyage. Pubd. July 1, 1789.
12. View in Macao, Including the residence of Camoens, when he wrote his Lusiade. Pubd. Augt. 1, 1788.
13. View in Macao. Pubd. Augt. 1, 1788.
15. View in the Island of Cracatoa. Pubd. July 1, 1789.
16. The Fan Palm, in the Island of Cracatoa. Pubd. Augt. 1, 1788.

Webber was draftsman on board the *Resolution* under Cook from 1776 to 1780; he died in 1793. The twelve views described here are the original views published separately by Webber in his lifetime. The plates all have an inscription that they were done by Webber [in one he is described a "J Webber R."], and a reference to the volume and chapter, and sometime also the page, from "Cook's Last Voyage," presumably the official edition of 1784, to which they refer. All have the imprint, London Pubd [with date] by J. Webber N. 312 Oxford Street.—TWS.

STREETER COLLECTION · APRIL 1968 – VOL. IV

VIEWS in the South Seas from drawings by . . . James (*sic*) Webber . . .
[16 hand-coloured aquatints, with letterpress reprinted from the official
account of the third voyage, with one extract each from the official
accounts of the first and second voyages.] London, Boydell & Co., 1808.
All the plates are dated 1809.

CONTENTS:

No. 1, View in Queen Charlotte's Sound, New Zealand.

No. 2, Boats of the Friendly Isles.

No. 3, A sailing canoe of Otaheite.

No. 4, The plantain tree, in the island of Cracatoa.

No. 5, A view in Oheitepeha Bay, in the Island of Otaheite.

No. 6, Waheiadooa, Chief of Oheitepeha, lying in state.

No. 7, View of the harbour of Taloo, in the Island of Eimeo.

No. 8, A toopapaoo of a chief, with a priest making his offering to the morai, in Huoheine.

No. 9, The *Resolution* beating through ice, with the *Discovery* in the most eminent danger
in the distance.

No. 10, The narta, or sledge for burdens in Kamtschatka.

No. 11, Balagans or summer habitations, with the method of drying fish at St. Peter
and Paul, Kamtschatka.

No. 12, View in Macao, including the residence of Camoens, when he wrote his Lusiad.

No. 13, View in Macao.

No. 14, A view in the Island of Pulo Condore.

No. 15, View in the Island of Cracatoa.

No. 16, The fan palm, in the Island of Cracatoa.

Copies of an issue in which the plates are on paper watermarked 1819 are at NPL:M
(X989/1B) and NPL:D(F81/1), and one in which some plates are watermarked 1820,
at NPL:M(X989/1C). Plates have been checked only for copies held in the Public
Library of New South Wales.

Copies: NPL:M(X989/1A); NPL:D(F80/1); NPL:R(F999A/2); ANL:F; VSL.   1872

13 PRINTS by J. Webber, including Owyhee, Oonalaska, Van Diemen's
Land; [from Views in the South Seas].

Copies: VSL.   1873

ARTIST UNKNOWN
Originals, Including Photocopies of Originals

1777 CAPTAIN COOK'S interview with natives in Adventure Bay,
Van Diemen's Land, January 29, 1777, [by an anonymous artist].

Photocopy of drawing. Meas. of view 13¼" x 18¾".
(Fannin, P.—A Collection of drawings and sketches. Photocopy no.11.)

Copies: NPL:M(PX*D54).   1874

Ships

Illustrations

CLEVELEY, James

Discovery and *Resolution* at an Island in the Pacific.

1777. Oil painting. 27″ x 48″. Untitled; unsigned.
Attributed to John Cleveley; after a sketch by his brother James.

Copies: ANL(Nan Kivell). 1875

CLEVELEY, James

Drawings relating to Cook's third voyage attributed to John Cleveley from sketches made by his brother James, and painted c.1786.

Items relating to the *Resolution* and *Discovery* are listed and described under the subheading *Illustrations*.

CLEVELEY, James

H.M.S. *Discovery*, Capt. Clerke: [process reproduction from original watercolour].

(*In* Muir, John Reid—The Life and achievements of Captain James Cook. London, Blackie, 1939. opp. p.231.)

Copies: NPL:M(980:Co1/M6A1); NPL:D(93/626); NPL:R(DS990A/195); ANL; QParl; QU; VMoU; VSL. 1876

CLEVELEY, James

Ships in harbour, South Pacific.

Oil painting. 19⅞″ x 24⅛″. Untitled; unsigned.
Attributed to John Cleveley; after a sketch by his brother James.
Discovery and *Resolution* at Morea?

Copies: ANL(Nan Kivell). 1877

EDGAR, Thomas

H.M. Ships *Resolution* and *Discovery* at anchor in Kealakekua Bay: from the contemporary drawings in the journal of T. Edgar.

(*Mariner's Mirror*, vol.14, Oct.1928, facing p.312.)

Copies: NPL:R(DS656.506/7). 1878

COOK'S *RESOLUTION* approaching Ship Cove, Queen Charlotte Sound, N.Z.

[195-]. 6¾″ x 8⅞″, 6½″ x 8⅞″ inside border, 6⅜″ x 8¾″ meas. of plate.
Two sketches and two etchings, being rough sketch, pen and ink sketch, trial proof and artist's proof A.

Copies: NPL:D(DG A2 pt.1). 1879

INGLETON, Geoffrey Chapman

H.M.S. *Discovery*, H.M.S. *Resolution* astern. The Third Voyage 1776–1780.

1957. Reprod. of drawings.
(Cook, J.—Collected Voyages—Printed accounts [1957. Price's ed.]—The Explorations
of Captain James Cook in the Pacific. p.[195].)
Copies: NPL:M(C956). 1880

THE SHIPS approaching York Island: [engraving]. Royce, sc.

(*In* Rickman, John—Journal of Captain Cook's last voyage. London, E. Newbery, 1781.
p.164.)
Copies: NPL:M(980:Co4/R1A1); NPL:D(78/31); NPL:R(S990A/84); ANL; NUN;
QOM; QU; VSL. 1881

WEBBER, John

Captain Cook's ships in Resolution Cove, Vancouver Island; 1778.

Reprod. of pen and wash drawing. c.3¼" x 8½".
The original is at the Admiralty.
(Lubbock, Basil—Adventure by sea from out of old time. London, The Studio, 1925.
Plate 18.)
Copies: NPL:M(Q656.5/2A1); NPL:R(Q758/15). 1882

WEBBER, John

H.M.S. *Resolution* and *Discovery* under command of Captain James Cook, 1779. Watercolor. 12" x 19". Attributed to John Webber. [Reproduced, not in colour.]

(*In* Brewington, Marion Vernon—The Marine paintings and drawings in the Peabody
Museum, by M.V. and D. Brewington. Salem, Mass., the Museum, 1968. p.454.)
Copies: NPL:R(NQ758.2/2). 1883

WEBBER, John

H.M. Ships *Resolution* and *Discovery* anchored in Resolution Cove, Nootka Sound . . . from the drawing in pen and wash . . . in the Library of the Admiralty: [illustration].

(*Geographical Journal* June 1927, p.556.)
Copies: NPL:M(Q910.6/G); NPL:R(DS909.6A/2). 1884

Printed Books and Articles about the Ships

1790 [THE *DISCOVERY* put into commission, in command of Capt. Roberts, to sail in June, 1790.]

(*Lady's Magazine*, 1790, pp.52, 222.)
Copies: NPL:M(052/L). 1885

1952 CLOWES, Geoffrey Swinford Laird

Autotype reproduction of wash-drawing [by J. Webber] of Captain Cook's ships at Vancouver Island, 1778: [description of drawing, with note on the ships].

(*In his* Sailing ships, their history and development as illustrated by the collection of
ship-models in the Science Museum. Pt.2, Catalogue. 4th ed. London, H.M.S.O.,
1952. p.64.)
Copies: NPL:M(623.822/3). 1886

Publication

n.d. BANKS, *Sir* Joseph

Autograph account of engravings for the publication of Cook's 3rd voyage.

pp.4, fo.

Gives the titles of the plates, the names of the engravers and the prices paid to them.

Copies: ANL(MS.9, item28). 1887

n.d. BANKS, *Sir* Joseph

Autograph statement of expenses in connection with the publication of Captain Cook's third voyage.

pp.5.

Copies: ANL(MS.9, item30). 1888

n.d. BANKS, *Sir* Joseph

Autograph statements for publication of plates and plans for Captain Cook's journal: estimates, costs and lists of illustrations.

pp.41.

Copies: ANL(MS.9, item29). 1889

n.d. BANKS, *Sir* Joseph

Manuscript copy of three letters sent from the Admiralty, on behalf of George III, accompanying presentation copies of the history of Captain Cook's last voyage, to the King of France, the Empress of Russia, and Dr. Benjamin Franklin.

p.1, fo.

In the letters to the King of France and Dr. Franklin, appreciative reference is made to the fact that, though these countries were at war with England, they forebade all molestation of Captain Cook on his return to Europe. In that to the Empress of Russia acknowledgement is made of the assistance rendered by the Russian settlements in Alaska.

Copies: ANL(MS.9, item26). 1890

1780 Oct.10 SANDWICH, John Montagu, *4th Earl*

ALS dated Admiralty to Sir Joseph Banks: Informs Banks that as he wished his gardener is discharged from *Resolution;* Capt. King & Webber were presented to the King at Windsor, & the charts and drawings were examined by HM with satisfaction; desires to consult Banks re publication of the journals & drawings of Cook's third voyage, and the preservation of such of the 200 drawings not selected for publication.

Paginated 411.

Typed transcript in MS.Q160, p.13.

Copies: NPL:D(MS.Q158, pp.139–40). 1891

1781 FORSTER, Johann Reinhold

Letter of J. R. Forster [to a publisher or bookseller in Leipzig], August 1781, in reference to his forthcoming publication of a German translation of Cook's third voyage; comments on reported objections to his terms, with some self-praise; requests a small advance on the work.

pp.4, 3.

Original German manuscript with English translation in typescript.

Copies: NPL:M(MSS.Af34).   1892

1781–3 Banks, *Sir* Joseph, *and* PANCKOUCKE, C.

Autograph correspondence regarding the paper to be used for publication of Cook's 2nd and 3rd voyages, with enclosures.

pp.50, 4o and fo.

Various dates between Sept., 1781, and June, 1783.

Copies: ANL(MS.9, item16).   1893

1782 Jan.13 NICOL, George

ALS to Sir Joseph Banks concerning the statement of expenses in connection with the publishing of the accounts of Cook's voyages. *Strand, Jan.13, 1782.*

pp.2.

Copies: ANL.   1894

1782 Sep.13 SANDWICH, John Montagu, *4th Earl*

ALS dated Hertford St to Sir Joseph Banks: Enclosing letter from Capt. King; he has seen Webber & it is clear unless a supply of the proper paper for engraving is obtained quickly the book will be much delayed; Webber is willing to go to Paris to obtain it unless Banks knows a better method; the sum of £1000 must be advanced for the paper; should this be paid by the recipients of the profits of the work or by the Admiralty?

ff.2, cm 24.

Paginated 517–19.

Typed transcript in MS.Q 160, p.15.

Copies: NPL:D(MS.Q158, pp.141–4).   1895

1782 Sep.16 SANDWICH, John Montagu, *4th Earl*

ALS dated Hertford St to Sir Joseph Banks: He thinks no steps can be taken to procure the paper until it is settled who is to pay for it; suggests that Banks should write to Stephens, and Stephens will meet him, but does not wish to put himself forward; he is now deeply engaged in the Rowleian controversy; thanks Banks on behalf of the Mayor of Huntingdon for his intended gift of venison; hopes that Banks will visit him at Hinchingbrook during the Mayor's feast.

ff.2, cm 24.

Paginated 521–523.

Typed transcript in MS.Q160, p.17.

Copies: NPL:D(MS.Q158, pp.145–8).   1896

1782 Sep.21 SANDWICH, John Montagu, *4th Earl*

ALS dated Hertford St to Sir Joseph Banks: He has forwarded Banks' letter to Stephens requesting an interview with him; has just returned from fishing at Shepperton. Postscript: He has no predeliction for Cadel or any other printer & is willing to trust Banks' judgment, expecting Banks will ascertain the Admiralty's particular wishes on the subject.

ff.2, cm 23.5.
Paginated 525–527.
Typed transcript in MS.Q160, p.19.
Copies: NPL:D(MS.Q158, pp.149–51).   1897

1782 Sep.23 SANDWICH, John Montagu, *4th Earl*

ALS dated Hertford St to Sir Joseph Banks: Has had a satisfactory interview with Stephens who says Lord Keppel will continue the publication along lines S. & B. intend; the Admiralty will advance the money for the paper, to be repaid from the profits; asks Banks views how the profits should be divided; his own view is that Cook's family should have at least $\frac{2}{3}$ or $\frac{3}{4}$; Capt. King is next claimant, but he is doubtful about Gore, Webber and Roberts. Anderson's executors already had a gratuity; King, Dalrymple & Roberts are speedily making a general map on one sheet; Stephens is helpful & anxious to promote the work & would endeavour to place the book in the hands of Nichols, but unfortunately Cadel had been employed to publish the advertisement.

ff.3, cm 23.5.
Paginated 529–533.
Copy in MS.Q160, p.21.
Copies: NPL:D(MS.Q158, pp.153–8).   1898

1782 Oct.6 SANDWICH, John Montagu, *4th Earl*

ALS dated Hinchingbrook to Sir Joseph Banks: Has communicated the contents of Banks letter to Dr. Douglas & will forward his answer immediately; though the Admiralty will advance the money, Banks & Sandwich must arrange to procure the paper; expects the division of the profits will be settled as soon as Banks returns to town; thinks Mr. Hodges received 2 yrs salary from the Admiralty in lieu of share of profits; urges Banks return from the country; conveys Mayor of Huntingdon's thanks for venison sent by Banks whose health was drunk at the feast.

ff.2, cm 24.
Paginated 535–537.
Typed transcript in MS.Q160, p.23.
Copies: NPL:D(MS.Q158,pp.159–62).   1899

1782 Oct.12 SANDWICH, John Montagu, *4th Earl*

ALS dated Hertford St to Sir Joseph Banks: Wishes Banks to manage the procurement of the paper; has no wish to send Webber but leaves it to Banks to employ any means he thinks proper; as Lord Keppel is likely to leave the Admiralty Board soon, it is desirable all arrangements be concluded before there is another change there.

ff.2, cm 23.5.
Paginated 539 (339?)–541.
Typed transcript in MS.Q160, p.25.
Copies: NPL:D(MS.Q158, pp.163–6).   1900

1782 Nov.5 DOUGLAS, John, *Bishop of Salisbury*

MS. copy of letter to Sir Joseph Banks, Nov.5, 1782, saying that he has arranged, numbered and written inscriptions for Captain Cook's book and requests to be apprized of any alterations necessary.

(Copies of documents relating to Captain James Cook, R.N., from originals in the Grey Collection, Auckland Public Library, ff.227–8.)
Copies: NPL:M(C697).   1901

1783 Oct.1 NICOL, George

Letter to Sir Joseph Banks, Oct.1, 1783, relating to printers' delay over Cook's book.

(Copies of documents relating to Captain James Cook, R.N., from originals in the Grey Collection, Auckland Public Library, ff.231–5.)
MS. copy.
Copies: NPL:M(C697).   1902

1783 Dec.5 BANKS, *Sir* Joseph

Autograph minutes of a meeting held at Lord Sandwich's house in order to facilitate the finishing of the charts supposed to be delayed by misunderstandings between Mr. Dalrymple, Capt. King and Lieut. Roberts, Decr.5, 1783.

pp.2, fo.
Copies: ANL(MS.9, item18).   1903

1784 Apr.26 WOLLASTON, *Rev.* Frederick

Memorandum to Mr Cadell from Rev. Fredrick Wollaston, Bury St. Edmunds, 26 Ap. 1784, re publication of Cook's last voyage.
Copies: NPL:M(MS.Doc.825).   1904

1784 May 13 SANDWICH, John Montagu, *4th Earl*

ALS dated Hinchingbrook to Sir Joseph Banks: He expects the paper mentioned by Banks by tonight's post from Dr. Douglas, and will bring it with him on Monday (or could send it on Saturday); is happy to hear 'our publication will be made at the fixed time'.

f.1, cm 24.
Paginated 399 (499?).
Typed transcript in MS.Q160, p.27.
Copies: NPL:D(MS.Q158, pp.167–8).   1905

1785 Jy.28 BANKS, *Sir* Joseph

'Memorandum for the division of the Profits arising from the Sale of Cap.^{tn} Cooks late voyage Agreed in the Presence of Ld Sandwich Ld Howe S^r. Jos. Banks & M^r. Stephens'. Draft in Banks' hand with revision in another ink.

f.1, cm 30.5.
Paginated in pencil, 244.
Typed transcript in NPL:D(MS.Q160, p.33).
Copies: NPL:D(MS.Q158, pp.3–4).   1906

1795 Jan.7 NICOL, George

Letter to Mrs. Cook, Jan.7, 1795, stating profits from sale of Captain Cook's Third Voyage to be £3,863 9s. 4d., with a number of copies still on hand.

(Copies of documents relating to Captain James Cook, R.N., from originals in the Grey Collection, Auckland Public Library, ff. 247–250.)
MS.copy.
Copies: NPL:M(C697).   1907

1795 Jan.16 BANKS, *Sir* Joseph

Banks to Henry Dundas, 1st Viscount Melville; ALS, dated Soho Sq: Forwards statement of the manner in which publication of Cook's third voyage was managed; notes misjudgments made in publishing first two voyages; the engraving of the present journal can be entrusted to the 'King's bookseller', though Banks is willing to advise. Only drawings made by the Embassy's draughtsmen should be engraved, as the public believe Chinese representations to be exaggerated.

Enclosure: Statement of the manner in which publication of Cook's third voyage was managed. Contemporary copy. (MS.Q158, pp.49–52).
ff.2, cm 24.
Typed transcript of letter only in MS.Q159.
Copies: NPL:D(MS.Q158, pp.45–52).   1908

[1795 Jan.16] BANKS, *Sir* Joseph

Statement of the manner in which publication of Cook's third voyage, was managed.

ff.2, cm 32.
Enclosure in ALS, Banks to Viscount Melville. 16 Jan.1795(MS.Q158, pp.45–48).
Contemporary copy.
Copies: NPL:D(MS.Q158, pp.49–52).   1909

1801 Jan.14 NICOL, George

Letter to Sir Joseph Banks, Jan.14, 1801, respecting profits from sale of Third Voyage, which were £4,000 clear.

(Copies of documents relating to Captain James Cook, R.N., from originals in the Grey Collection, Auckland Public Library, ff.277–9.)
pp.2.
MS. copy.
Copies: NPL:M(C697).   1910

1821 May 5 SMITH, Isaac, *naval officer*, to Dr Elliotson, *physician*.
ALS dated Clapham 5 May 1821: Forwarding four books of Cook's last voyage on behalf of Mrs. Cook, in return for his medical attention; noting that the plates, letterpress and papers are superior to that of the first edition specially presented to Mrs Cook by the Lords of the Admiralty.

Inserted in Webber's Atlas, Mrs. Cook's copy.

Copies: NPL:D(F78/6).   1911

WORKS BY COOK NOT RELATING TO THE THREE VOYAGES

Charts

Manuscripts

1758–62 A SKETCH of Harbour Grace and Carbonere in Newfoundland; together with other documents relating to the survey of Newfoundland, Nova Scotia, Gulf of St. Lawrence and adjacent waters. 1758–62.

CONTENTS:

1. A sketch of Harbour Grace and Carbonere in Newfoundland, by Jas. Cook 1762.
   Harbour Grace and Carbonere, now spelt Carbonear, are near St. John's on the east coast.

2. [Untitled chart, unsigned and undated. The area depicted believed to be the Saint John River, New Brunswick.]

3. Description of the Sea coast of Nova Scotia [and of the Island Cape Britain, and of Newfoundland. With index.] ff.13, folio, 2 double page maps.
   Three items in one volume. The handwriting appears to be that of Cook, and the document to have been compiled after 1760.

4. Descriptions for Sailing in and out of Ports [Gulf of St. Lawrence]; with Soundings for particular Rocks, Shoals, etc. With Latitudes, Longitudes, Tides etc. Variations of the Compass.

pp.4, folio.
Title at head of p.[1].
Cook's North American service: from 1758 to 1767 Cook served in North American waters, first in H.M.S. *Pembroke* then in the *Northumberland* and later in the *Grenville*. During this period he was engaged in making surveys of the St. Lawrence, and of the coasts of Newfoundland, Nova Scotia and adjoining islands. In 1766 and 1768 he laid his collection of charts before the Admiralty, and received permission to publish.

Copies: ANL(MS.5); NPL:M(A3387, photostat only).   1912

1763 A PLAN of the Harbour of Croque in Newfoundland [unfinished].
B[y] J. Cook, 1763.

No scale given, 1 sheet, cm 30 x 40, original ink and pencil MS., b./wh.
Shows soundings, coastline.
(*In* Smith, Isaac—Original sketches, drawings, maps, etc. [1763–80]. f.ib.)
Copies: NPL:M(D11).   1913

[1763] A PLAN of the Harbour of St. Johns in Newfoundland. By James Cook, [1763].

ca1: 21,100, 1 sheet, cm 20 x 26, original ink MS., hand cols.
Area: Includes St. John's Bay from [Quidi Vidi] to [Spriggs Point].
Shows soundings, sand banks, coastline; buildings, wharf, batteries.
(*In* Smith, Isaac—Original sketches, drawings, maps, etc. [1763–80]. f.ia.)
Copies: NPL:M(D11). 1914

1967 A PLAN of the River St. Laurence from Green Island to Cape
Carrouge, by Jam^s. Cook: [catalogue of a manuscript chart . . . the
property of the late R.W. Reford of Montreal . . . [to] be sold at auction
by Christie, Manson & Woods, Ltd. . . . July 5, 1967.] London, John
Wallace Printing, 1967.
Facs. pp.5.
Copies: NPL:M(917.4/1A1). 1915

1967 [A PLAN of the River St. Laurence: two cuttings from the *Times*,
London. 12.6.67 (announcing the sale on July 5) and 26.7.67 announcing
that the chart was bought by Mr. Harvey Macmillan to be presented to
Canadian Government Archives, Ottawa.]
Copies: NPL:M(Cuttings File). 1916

n.d. NOTES referring to chart showing the Straights of Magalhaenes,
with autograph signature of James Cook.
ff.2, cm 16.
In glass frame. Transferred from Australian Museum Oct. 1935, their number H57.
Copies: NPL:M(Safe1/69). 1917

Manuscripts and Autograph Letters

1755–62 'SAILING DIRECTIONS and Routes to the E. & W. Indies.'
?1755–1762.
Illus. pp.64, cm 32.
Includes course and distances, sailing directions, depth soundings, latitudes and coastal
profiles. The authorship of this MS. has been attributed to James Cook, principally
because of the similarity of the handwriting to that of Cook's autograph letters, and a
facsimile page of Cook's log of HMS *Eagle* Apr.1756. However, several apparent dis-
crepancies remain: a. The dates '2' and '4 May 1734' which appear to be in the same
hand as '24 Nov.1757' (p.32). [Possibly the first dates were copied as part of the text
from another authority with the author's later observation dated for comparison.]
b. The remarks prefaced 'from Mr. Cook' on p.64. The dates 1755–1762 represent the
period, between Cook's enlistment in HMS *Eagle* 1755 and the commencement of the
Newfoundland surveys 1763, when it is probable that the volume was compiled. *See
also* Maggs' sale catalogue, 1927.
Copies: NPL:D(MS.Q142). 1918

1758–62 DESCRIPTIONS for sailing in and out of ports [Gulf of St.
Lawrence].
See no. 1912, item 4.

1759 Dec.8 COOK TO Treasurer of His Majesty's Navy.
Certificate of discharge by death of John Grigg able seaman (at Halifax Hospital), signed Jas. Cook, Master of HMS *Northumberland*. Minute re payment overleaf.
f.1, cm 30.
Copies: NPL:D(MS.Q140, pp.1–2). 1919

1760–70 NAVIGATION NOTES relating to Cook, 1760–1770.
pp.4.
Description of Trinidad Harbour, with sketch maps, by John Kidd, who took it from the journal of a Dutch East India Company ship, 1760. This is enclosed in a letter to the Earl of Sandwich from [Proby] who suggests it 'may [be] of use to Cap^n Cook . . .' Contemporary MS.copy, pp.4 folio. Also a slip of paper containing navigational details for 25 Jan. 1770, signed Alexander Hood.
Copies: ANL(MS.108). 1920

1760+ DESCRIPTION of the Sea coast of Nova Scotia.
See no. 1912, item 3.

1763 ARITHMETICAL TRIGONOMETRY, [and] Arithmetical dialling. 1763.
Sm. folio. ff. [97].
Original MS. in brown paper covers. A carefully written MS., with elaborate and beautifully drawn diagrams. The handwriting cannot be identified with Capt. James Cook, the circumnavigator, and there is no signature in the book. The connection with Capt. James Cook is questionable. The name *James Cook* is written in Roman capitals on the page preceding the title-page, under the lines,
"If you by chance do find this book
Which in the same you now do look
I pray return it unto me
Whose name is underneath you see".
The date, Nov.10, 1763, is written at the foot of the page.
Copies: NPL:M(Safe1/81). 1921

1764–5 COPIES of instructions and correspondence between Cook and the Commissioners of the Victualling and of the Navy, 1764–Mar. 9, 1765, as listed below. Possibly leaves torn from the *Grenville's* letterbook.
ff.3.
CONTENTS:
[1764] Palliser, Sir Hugh to Cook.
Copy of Instructions by H. Palliser, Commander of HMS *Guernsey* requiring HMS *Grenville* to survey the coast of Newfoundland from St Lawrence Harbour to Cape Ray, with particular regard to navigation, trade and fisheries. Incomplete. cm 33.
1764 Dec.18 Admiralty Office to Cook, at Woolwich.
Signed Philip Stephens, giving Cook permission to bring the *Grenville* from Woolwich to Deptford for safety during Cook's absence making fair copies of the surveys he made last Summer.

The Same in another hand, with corrections and additions in Cook's hand, dated 18 Dec. 1765 (*sic*) and addressed to the *Grenville* schooner at Deptford.

1765 Jan.12 Cook to Victualling Board.
Stating that until the manner of fitting out the *Grenville* is determined, he will be unable to determine the quantity of provisions the ship can stow.

Jan.14 Cook to Navy Board.
Requesting conduct money due to seven men of HMS *Grenville* be paid at Deptford instead of Portsmouth.

[Jan.22] Cook to Navy Board.
Requesting that HMS *Grenville* whose present schooner rigging is condemned, be fitted and rigged instead as a brig in order that the Survey may be carried out with greater despatch and safety.

Feb.6 Navy Board to Cook.
The officers of Deptford Yard have been instructed to fit and rig *Grenville* schooner as a brig.

Mar.9 Cook to Admiralty Office.
Copy in Cook's hand, addressed to Philip Stephens, asking that F. Gathman and J. McKenzie two able seamen of HMS *Grenville* who have provided their replacements, be allowed their discharge.

Copies: NPL:D(MS.Q140, pp.3–8).   1922

1766–7 A JOURNAL of the proceedings of His Majesty schooner ye *Grenville* . . . by James Cook, Master, [Jan.14, 1764–Dec.31, 1766; Mar.22–Nov.23, 1766; Mar.3–Nov. 15, 1767.]

(Bonwick Transcripts: Cook, case 2, no.194.)
Extracts from the Log of the *Grenville*, copied from the Admiralty papers.

Copies: NPL:M(B.T. ser.2, case 2).   1923

1776 Oct.30 COOK TO Capt. Hugh Debbieg. Autograph memo, dated St Johns, Newfoundland, concerning the angle at the place of observation which the Gibet Hill makes with meridian. Lat. 47° 34′ 34″N.

cm 22.
With ownership stamp 'Everard Home'.

Copies: NPL:D(MS.Q140, pp.9–12).   1924

1776 Feb.24 ALS to Jno Harrison Esq., Attorney at Law, Guisbrough, Yorkshire. Mile End, London, 24th Feb. 1776.

pp.2.
Concerning a charge of defrauding the Customs, against his brother-in-law, James Fleck.

Copies: ANL(MS.7); NPL:M(A1713⁻²Bv, photostat).   1925

1776 July 11 COOK TO *Rev*. Dr. Richard Kaye, St. James Palace, London. ALS dated Plymouth Sound, thanking Kaye for his tender of service to Mrs. Cook during his absence, and that he will make acknowledgment as Kaye requests providing God spares him till he reaches 'the place for Discoveries'. 'P.S. I expect to sail today'.

ff.2, cm 23.
With Cook's seal.

Copies: NPL:D(MS.92).   1926

1760 A NEW chart of the River St. Laurence, from the Island of Anticosti to the Falls of Richelieu . . . also particular Directions for navigating the [Gulf and] River [of St. Laurence, both by J. Cook] . . . Engraved by T. Jefferys . . . pub. by command of the . . . Admiralty. [London, T. Jefferys, 1760.]

12 sheets, cm 42¼ x 39.
Scale 10 marine leagues = 5″. Engraved. B./wh. Simple cylindrical projection. No graticule. The sheets vary very slightly in size. No degrees border. Dated on sheet 8, Pall Mall, May 1st. 1760. When the map is displayed, the sheet numbers run 1–6 across the top and 7–12 across the bottom, in both cases from left to right. The title is on sheet 7. Inset:— Large scale reproduction in two sections of the upper course of the river, and detailed charts of Quebec Bason, Bay of the Seven Islands, Mingan Island, Mingan Harbour and Gaspee Bay. *See also* nos.1931, 1944.

Copies: NPL:D(Cb72/2–13). 1927

1766 A CHART of part of the south coast of Newfoundland, including the islands St. Peters and Miquelon, from an actual survey . . . by James Cook . . . Larken f[e]c[it]. Published by permission of the . . . Admiralty, by James Cook. London., sold by I. Mount, 1766.

1 sheet, cm 69 x 96.
Scale 5 English leagues, 20 to a degree = 5″. Engraved. B./wh. Simple cylindrical projection. Inscribed at top, 10. Part of left margin cut out. 2 sheets joined as 1. Part of the south east coast is only roughly sketched in. Note following imprint reads, N.B. With a book of directions. This seems to have been Cook's *Directions for navigating on part of the south coast of Newfoundland.* Lond., 1768. Insets, all of irregular shape, and with scale 3 miles = 6″:—1. Great Jervis Harbour, cm 12¼ x 18½; 2. Harbours of St. Laurence, cm 18½ x 23½; 3. Harbour Briton, cm 21 x 15½.
All insets lie on the right hand sheet; the left hand sheet was later reprinted as part of Cook. J.— *A Chart of part of the south coast of Newfoundland, including the islands of Langley, St. Peters and Miquelon.* The Dixson Library holds another copy, with pencil note wrongly dating the survey 1763 (Cc7617).

Copies: NPL:D(Cc76/6). 1928

[1766?] A CHART of the straights of Bellisle, with part of the coast of Newfoundland and Labradore, from actual surveys . . . by James Cook . . . 1766. Pub. by permission of the Admiralty, by James Cook . . . Larken sculp. London, [1766?]

1 sheet, cm 60½ x 77½.
Scale 5 English leagues, 20 to a degree = 4⅞″. Engraved. B./wh. Simple cylindrical projection. Sold with a book of directions, by I. Mount & T. Pabe. Inscribed at top, No. 9. Section cut out from left-hand margin, including part of border. Insets, all irregularly shaped:—
1. Red Bay, cm 9½ x 11, *scale 3 miles = 2⅞″;* 2. Old Ferolle Harbour, cm 7½ x 11½, *scale 3 miles = 3″;* 3. Quirpon Harbour [and] Griguet Bays, cm 14 x 21, *scale 3 miles = 3″;* 4. York or Chateaux Bay, cm 24 x 20, *scale 3 miles = 2¹⁵⁄₁₆″;* 5. Croque Harbour, cm 14 x 21, *scale 1 mile = 2⅝″.*
See also no.1933.

Copies: NPL:D(Cc76/8). 1929

1767 BEVIS, J.

An Observation of an eclipse of the sun at the island of New-found-land, Aug.5, 1766, by Mr. James Cook.

pp.215–16.

Extracted from the Royal Society—*Philosophical Transactions* 1767.

Copies: NPL:D(77/36); NPL:R(N506/16, reprint).   1930

1768 DIRECTIONS for navigating the west-coast of Newfoundland, with a chart thereof, and a particular account of the bays, harbours, rocks, sands, depths of water, latitudes, bearings and distances from place to place, the flowing of the tides, &c. from an actual survey, taken by order of Commodore Pallisser (*sic*). London, printed for the author, 1768.

pp.11.

For accompanying chart *see* no. 1935. For French edition published in 1784 *see* no. 1941.

Copies: NPL:M(Q971.8/C).   1931

[177–?] DE L'ISLE, Guillaume

Mappe monde a l'usage du Roy, par Guillaume Delisle . . . nouvellement corrigée après les dernières découvertes faite par l'Académie de Petersbourg. (I. Condet s[culpsit].) Amsterdam, par Jean Covens et Corneille Mortier, [177–?].

No scale given, 1 sheet, diameters cm 32.

Copies: NPL:D(Cb77/5).   1932

1770 A CHART of the straights of Bellisle, with part of the coast of Newfoundland and Labradore, from actual surveys, pub. by permission of the . . . Admiralty; surveyed by James Cook in 1766 and Michael Lane in 1769. London, R. Sayer & I. Bennett, 1770.

1 sheet, cm 59½ x 110½.

2 sheets joined as one. The main, right-hand, sheet is printed from the same plate as the 1766? edition, now extensively revised to include Lane's surveys. Additional inset:— Bradore Harbour, cm 13½ x 14, no scale given. Has engraved map number XVII in top right-hand corner.

See also no. 1929.

Copies: NPL:D(Cc77/1).   1933

1770 A CHART of the west coast of Newfoundland, surveyed . . . by James Cook . . . Larken sculpt. Pub. by permission of the . . . Admiralty, by Cook. [Lond.], printed for R.Sayer and I.Bennett, 1770.

1 sheet, cm 49 x 171.

Scale 6 English leagues = 5⅞″. Engraved, b./wh.

Simple cylindrical projection. ESE to top of sheet. 3 sheets joined as one. Engraved map number XVI. "Sold with a book of directions", i.e. Cook, J.—*Directions for navigating the west-coast of Newfoundland*. London, 1768. Insets, both of irregular shape:— 1. A plan of Hawkes Harbour, Port Saunders and Keppel Harbour, cm 15 x 17½, *scale 3 miles* = 3″; 2. A plan of York and Lark Harbours in the Bay of Islands, cm 14½ x 18, *scale 3 miles* = 3″. (*In* The North American pilot, 1775. Map 16.)

See also no.1935.

Copies: NPL:M(X917.1/1); NPL:D(F77/7).   1934

1770 A CHART of the west coast of Newfoundland, surveyed by order of Commodore Pallisser (*sic*), Governor of Newfoundland, Labradore &c. &c. By James Cook, surveyor. Larken Sculpt. London, R. Sayer & I. Bennett, pr., 10 May, 1770.

ca1:190,080. 1 sheet, cm 49 x 173, engr., b./wh. Coastal profiles.
Insets: A Plan of York and Lark Harbours, in the Bay of Islands; A Plan of Hawkes Harbour, Port Saunders, and Keppel Harbour.
Area: coastal strip from Pt. Ferolle to Cape Anguille.
Shows depths in fathoms, anchorages, rocks above water, rocks below water, coastlines; place names; hachures.
See also nos.1931, 1934.

Copies: NPL:M(M4 621/1770/1).   1935

1774 A CHART of part of the south coast of Newfoundland, including the islands of Langley, St. Peters and Miquelon, with the southern entrance into the Gulf of St. Laurence, from actual surveys . . . by James Cook . . . Pub. by permission of the . . . Admiralty, by James Cook. London, printed for R. Sayer and J. Bennett, 1774.

Scale 6 English leagues, 20 to a degree = 6″. 1 sheet, cm 62½ x 170. Engraved, b./wh. 3 sheets joined as one, plus an unbordered continuation piece, cm 21 x 19½, pasted on right-hand edge. The right-hand sheet is from the same plate, with numerous revisions, as the left-hand sheet of Cook's *A Chart of part of the South coast of Newfoundland, including the islands St. Peters and Miquelon.*
Inset:— 1. Port aux Basque, cm 12 x 12, *scale 1 mile = 3″*; 2. St. Peters Island, survey'd by engineer Fortlin in 1763, cm 11 x 14, *scale 1 English mile = ¾″*; 3. Great Jervis Harbour, cm 10½ x 15, *scale 1 mile = 2″*; 4. Harbour Briton, cm 12 x 10½, *scale 2 miles = 2⅝″*; 5. Harbours of St. Laurence, cm 11 x 9, *scale 2 miles = 2⅝″*.

Copies: NPL:D(Cc77/2).   1936

1775 A GENERAL CHART of the island of Newfoundland . . . drawn from surveys taken by order of the . . . Admiralty, by James Cook and Michael Lane . . . and others . . . Pub. . . . by Thomas Jefferys. London, printed for Robt. Sayer & Jno. Bennett, 1775.

Scale not given. 1 sheet, cm 53 x 54. Engraved. Colours. Simple cylindrical projection. Engraved map number I. There is a 1770 printing, the same except for the date and the colours, in *The North American pilot.*

Copies: NPL:D(Cb77/6).   1937

1775 THE NORTH-AMERICAN Pilot, for Newfoundland [etc.] . . . being a collection of sixty accurate charts and plans drawn from original surveys taken by James Cook and Michael Lane . . . and other officers . . . Pub. by permission of the . . . Admiralty; chiefly engraved by . . . Thomas Jefferys. London, R. Sayer and J. Bennett, 1775.

Vol.1, pp.[4], maps 22, cm 56.

Copies: NPL:M(X917.1/1); NPL:D(F77/7).   1938

1781 A PLAN of Quebec and environs . . . during the siege of that place in 1759. Surveyed . . . by Lieut. Coll. [H.] Debbieg . . . by Major [S.]

Holland . . . [and] by Captn. [J.F.W.] Des Barres . . . In the soundings . . .
the author [Des Barres] was assisted by the late celebrated Captain
Cook who attended him. London, 1781.

800 feet = 1″, 1 sheet cm 63½ x 149, cut and folded, engr. colours.
(Des Barres, J.F.W.— The Atlantic Neptune, 1781. Vol.2, map 5.)
Copies: NPL:D(Cc78/1).   1939

1784 INSTRUCTIONS nautiques, relatives aux cartes & plans du
pilote de Terre-Neuve; publié au Dépôt Général des Cartes, Plans &
Journaux de la Marine en 1784, pour l'usage des vaisseaux du roi & des
bâtimens particuliers employés à la pêche; extraites du recueil de divers
mémoires anglois, intitulé, Sailing directions for the North American
pilot. [Trans. from the English by M. de Granchain.] Paris, de
l'Imprimerie Royale, 1784.

4 vols. in 1.
Copies: NPL:M(Q971.8/C).   1940

1784 INSTRUCTIONS pour naviguer sur la côte occidentale de Terre-
Neuve. Paris, de l'Imprimerie Royale, 1784.

pp.26.
Without chart. Pages 3–7 are in part additional to the English edition, 1768. (no. 1931).
Published in the author's *Instructions nautiques . . . de Terre-Neuve,* 1784 (no. 1940).
Copies: NPL:M(Q971.8/C).   1941

1807 A NEW geographical and nautical chart of the Gulf and River
St. Lawrence, with considerable improvements . . . The part of Newfoundland, Straights of Bellisle, [and] Isles St. Pierre & Miquelon
. . . are from actual surveys made by . . . James Cook and Michael Lane
. . . The whole . . . compiled . . . and adjusted by astronomical observations,
by Thos. Wright . . . principal Assistant on the General survey of North
America . . . Engraved by J. Walker. [London], Thos. Wright, 1807.

Scale not given. 3 sheets, cm 105 x 72, 105 x 73½, 105 x 71½. Engraved. Colours. Mercator's
projection. Insets.
Copies: NPL:D(Cc80/5–7).   1942

[1864] BABINET, Jacques
Planisphère Babinet, physique et politique; (E. Picard, geographe,
gravé par Gérin, écrit par Langevin.) Paris, Imp. Lemercier, [1864].
No scale given. 1 sheet, ellipse cm 20 x 40.
Copies: NPL:D(Ca86/1).   1943

1885 A NEW CHART of the River St. Laurence, from the Island of
Anticosti to the Falls of Richelieu. New ed. London, printed for R. Sayer
& J. Bennett, 1885.

3 sheets, each cm 85 x 78.

12 sheets joined as 3, and numbered XX–XXII. No.XX is sheets 5,6,11,12 of the original map; no.XXI is sheets 3,4,9,10; and no.XXII is sheets i,2,7,8, including title. Printed from the same plates with no apparent erasures, and the following additions:— the new imprint; continuation of the dashed line running downstream from Quebec, forking into two, and terminating near Cape Roziere; an inscription near Isle Bic, A rock on which the *Alcides* struck in 1760; and two new insets, Havre St. Nicholas, and Pointe aux Alouettes. *See also* no.1927.

Copies: NPL:D(Cc77/3–5). 1944

1899 MORRIS, Edmund Ellis

Captain Cook's first log in the Royal Navy [from June 27, 1755–Dec.31, 1756].

(*Cornhill Magazine* Oct. 1899, pp.519–32.)

Copies: NPL:R(S050/C817). 1945

1965 JAMES COOK, surveyor of Newfoundland, being A collection of charts of the coasts of Newfoundland and Labradore, &c., drawn from original surveys taken by James Cook and Michael Lane, London, Thomas Jefferys, 1769–1770. Reproduced in facs. from the copy in the Library of the University of California in Los Angeles; with an intro. essay by R.A. Skelton. San Francisco, David Magee, 1965.

The illustrated text of 32pp. and the 10 charts, loose in a portfolio, are contained in a cloth bound case. Limited edition of 365 copies, printed at the Grabhorn Press, San Francisco.

Copies: NPL:R(NF912.718/1); ANL; SPL. 1946

PERSONAL

BIOGRAPHY

For references to the birthplace and residences, etc., of Captain Cook, *see* the heading *Personal—Illustrations, etc.*

1728 RECORD OF BAPTISM of James Cook, Nov.3, 1728, from the register of St. Cuthbert's Parish Church, Marton, Yorkshire, England.

Photocopy.

Copies: NPL:M(Doc.1409). 1947

[174–?] JAMES COOK in Whitby ships. Entries showing his name on the muster rolls, Seamen's Hospital, Whitby.

Photocopy.

(Miscellaneous primary and secondary source material re the life and voyages of Captain James Cook.)

Copies: NPL:M(MS.A1713⁻³Item 3A,no.iv). 1948

1755–1815 DOCUMENTS relating to James Cook and properties at Great Ayton, Yorkshire.

CONTENTS:
Conveyance, Thomas Skottowe to James Cook, 16 June 1755.
Conveyance re houses and land, James Cook to C. Jackson, 16 May 1772.
Conveyance by feoffment . . . George Carrick to John Appleton, 23 May 1808.
Mortgage by demise . . . John Appleton to Thomas Graham, 16 Jan. 1815.
Copies: VSL.   1949

1762 Dec.21 MARRIAGE CERTIFICATE, 21 Dec. 1762, of James Cook and Elizabeth Batts, at St. Margaret's Church, Barking, Essex.
(Cook, James—Miscellaneous letters, 1771–6.)
Copies: ANL(MS7).   1950

1776 COOK, James
Will, 14th June 1776.
pp.4.
Photographic copy of Will of Captain Cook made before his final voyage. Sworn and proved in London, 24th January, 1780 and 20th March, 1780. Original in the Public Record Office, London.
Copies: NPL:M(ML MSS826X); ANL(MS1050).   1951

1776–1926 FAMILY PAPERS. 1776–1926.
24 items.
A collection of manuscript material relating to Captain Cook, his widow and his family. One letter, signed by James Cook, from the *Resolution* at Deptford, dated April 2, 1776, to the Commissioners of His Majesty's Navy asking for a supply of clothing to the ship. Eight letters to Mrs. F. McAllister, cousin of Captain Cook, including one from Elizabeth Cook, concerning Cook family affairs. Other letters of later date are those of John McAllister, Mrs. McAllister's son, who actively sought letters and relics of his famous cousin. Copies of letters from Cook to Sir Joseph Banks. Biographical note on Cook; newspaper cuttings concerning Cook, 1858–1926; extract from parish register relating to baptism of James Cook. Detailed contents list in ANL and NPL:M.
Copies: ANL(Nan Kivell 9528); NPL:M(FM4/1552,1707,pos. and neg. microfilm). 1952

1780 LOGAN, Robert
ALS Ayton [Yorkshire] 22d Jany, 1780, to Mr. Reed, Grays Inn, London.
pp.2.
Stating that Captain Cook "was born either in the Parish of Marton, or in the Parish of Ormsby" and enclosing a copy of the certificate of baptism attested by Thomas Peacock, Curate of Marton.
Copies: ANL(Nan Kivell 9528); NPL:M(FM4/1552,1717,pos. and neg. microfilm). 1953

1780 NACHRICHTEN von dem Leben und den Seereisen des berühmten Capitain Cook. Reval, Albrecht und Compagnie, 1780.
pp.48.
Photographic copy only in State Library of Victoria.
A rare work published in Revel (*sic*, Tallinn) in Estonia. Jackson, item 91 is probably a record of it. Undoubtedly the first account of Cook's death to be printed in book form.

The volume gives a short account of Cook's life, voyages and death, with many inaccuracies on his early career. Mainly taken from a letter, *Auszug des Briefes von Kensington den 4ten Febr. 1780 die Nachrichten von Kapitain Cook betreffend*. (Note from Nan Kivell copy.) *See also* Spence, p.20, where he describes the pamphlet and records a French edition (no. 1956); possibly from the pen of J.R. or G. Forster.

Copies: ANL(Nan Kivell); VSL. 1954

1780 PLAN of a memorial to procure a pension for Capt. Cooke *(sic)*.

pp.2.
(Brabourne Papers.)
Manuscript, partly in the handwriting of Sir Joseph Banks. It is headed "The nation is indebted to Capt. Cook". Printed in the *Historical Records of New South Wales* vol.1, pt.1, p.432.

Copies: NPL:M(MS.A78⁻¹). 1955

1780 PRÉCIS de la vie & des voyages du Capitaine Cook. Ecrit de Kensington ce 4 Février 1780. Reval & Leipsic, Albrecht & Co., [1780?]

pp.47.
For note *see* no. 1954, and *see also* Spence, p.20, who records another copy in the collection of B. Kroepelien, Oslo.

Copies: NPL:M(Safe1/99); ANL. 1956

1785 GIANETTI, Michelangiolo

Elogio del Capitano Giacomo Cook letto da M. Gianetti nella pubblica adunanza della Reale Accademia Fiorentina. (Elogy of Captain James Cook . . . trans. into English by a member of the Royal Academy of Florence, [i.e. R.M.].) Firenze, Gaetano Cambiagi, 1785.

pp.[88].
With parallel texts in Italian and English. Engraved vignette of Cook on each title-page. The Mitchell Library holds another copy, with additional pages numbered 9–16 at end of volume, consisting of part of the dedication which was cancelled and altered.

Copies: NPL:M(Q923.9/C771.2/1A1); NPL:D(Q78/33); ANL:F; VSL. 1957

1784–95 BLADE, Sade *and* BLADE, Mary

Four autographed letters signed, Mile End, 1786–94, to Mrs. M'Allister.

pp.6.
Mentioning Mrs. Cook's moving to Surrey and the deaths of her two sons.
(Family papers. 1776–1926.)

Copies: ANL(Nan Kivell 9528); NPL:M(FM4/1552,1707,pos. and neg. microfilm). 1958

1787 BLANC GILLI, Mathieu

Éloge du Capitaine Cook, par M. Blanc Gilli, de Marseille. Amsterdam, Morin, 1787.

pp.viii, 117.

Copies: NPL:M(923.9/C771.2/2A1). 1959

1787–8 PABST, Johann Georg Friedrich
Die Entdeckungen des fünften Welttheils; oder, Reisen um die Welt.
Ein Lesebuch für die Jugend. 2e Aufl. Nürnberg, Felsseckerische
Buchhandlung, 1787.

Vols.2–4.

Copies: NPL:M(980/P).   1960

1788 KING, James
Extract from the journal of Lieut. King, at Sydney, Feb.1, 1788, giving
an account of his official visit to La Perouse at Botany Bay and repeating
La Perouse's tribute to Cook's work.

pp.4.
(Brabourne Papers.)

Copies: NPL:M(MS.A78⁻¹).   1961

1788 KIPPIS, *Rev.* Andrew
The Life of Captain James Cook, by A. Kippis. London, G. Nicol,
G.G.J. & J. Robinson, 1788.

Port. pp.xvi, 527.
Appendix 2 is The Morai, an ode, by Miss Helen Maria Williams. As well as the ordinary
edition, The Dixson Library holds two copies in special bindings, one of which is grangerized and has an original miniature of Cook inset on cover. *See also* no.17.

Copies: NPL:M(Q 980:Co1/K1A1); NPL:D(Q 77/13, Q 78/8,9); NPL:R(09:Q 990A/
49); SPL: VParl; VU(Baillieu).   1962

1788 KIPPIS, *Rev.* Andrew
The Life of Captain James Cook. Basil, J.J. Tourneisen, pr., 1788.

2 vols.
Paris, sold by Pissot, also in imprint. *See also* no.17.

Copies: NPL:M(980:Co1/K2B1–2); NPL:R(09:S990A/92); ANL:F.   1963

1788 KIPPIS, *Rev.* Andrew
The Life of Captain James Cook. Dublin, H. Chamberlaine, W. Colles
[and others], 1788.

Port. pp.xvi, 527.
See also no.17.

Copies: NPL:M(980:Co1/K2A1); ANL; VMoU.   1964

1789 KIPPIS, *Rev.* Andrew
Leben des Capitain James Cook, von Andreas Kippis . . . Aus dem
Englischen. Hamburg, B.G. Hoffmann, 1789.

Port. 2 vols.
Volume 1 has additional title-page. *See also* no.17.

Copies: NPL:M(980:Co1/K2E1–2); NPL:D(78/7–8).   1965

1789 KIPPIS, *Rev.* Andrew
Vie du Capitaine Cook; traduite de l'anglois du Docteur Kippis . . .
par M. [J.H.] Castera. Paris, Hôtel de Thou, 1789.
pp.[xxxiv], 546, [ii].
See also no.17.
Copies: NPL:M(Q980:Col/K1B1); NPL:R(09:S990A/67). 1966

1789 KIPPIS, *Rev.* Andrew
Vie du Capitaine Cook; traduite de l'anglois du Docteur Kippis . . .
par M. [J.H.] Castera. Paris, Hôtel de Thou, 1789.
2 vols.
See also no.17.
Copies: NPL:M(980:Col/K2C1–2); QOM. 1967

1789 KIPPIS, *Rev.* Andrew
Vie du Capitaine Cook; traduite de l'anglois du docteur Kippis, [by
J.H. Castera]. Paris, Hôtel de Thou, 1789.
2 vols.
Lettre du traducteur . . . à M. Garat precedes Preface, pp.i–xlviii; signed at end, Castera.
See also no.17.
Copies: NPL:M(980:Col/K2D1–2); VU(Baillieu). 1968

1789 WIEDMANN, Johann Heinrich
Leben und Schicksale des Capitains James Cook. Erlangen, W. Walther,
1789.
Port. pp.[xiv], 384.
Copies: NPL:M(923.9/C771.2/4A1). 1969

1790 INTERESTING ACCOUNT of the early voyages made by the
Portuguese, Spaniards, etc. . . . to which is perfixed (*sic*) The Life of
Captain Cook, with particulars of his death. Extracted from Dr Kipps's
(*sic*). London, Stalker, 1790.
Copies: VSL. 1970

1790 PARIS, Pierre Louis
Éloge de Cook. Riom, Landriot, 1790.
Copies: VSL. 1971

1792 LÉMONTEY, Pierre Edouard
Eloge de Jacques Cook avec des notes: discours qui a remporté le prix
d'éloquence au jugement de l'Academie de Marseille, le 25 Août 1789.
Paris, Imprimerie Nationale, 1792.
pp.86.
Bound with others as Lémontey—Opuscules. *See also* no.1990.
Copies: NPL:M(980:Col/L1A1). 1972

1792–4 HONEYCHURCH, Elizabeth, *Mrs.*
Three autograph letters signed, Mile End, 1792–94, to Mrs. M'Allister.
pp.6.
Mentioning Mrs. Cook at Clapham, and the deaths of her two sons.
Copies: ANL(Nan Kivell 9528); NPL:M(FM4/1552,1707,pos. and neg. microfilm). 1973

1795 KIPPIS, *Rev.* Andrew
Historia de la vida y viages del Capitan Jaime Cook; obra escrita en
Ingles por A. Kippis . . . y traducida al Castellano por . . . Cesareo de
Nava Palacio. Madrid, En la Imprenta Real, 1795.
2 vols.
See also no.17.
Copies: NPL:M(980:Co1/K2F1–2); ANL:F. 1974

1797 COOKS LEBEN. Tübingen, in der I.G. Cottaschen Buchhandlung,
1797.
pp.iv, 264.
Published anonymously.
Copies: NPL:M(923.9/C771.2/5A1). 1975

[18—? The Earl of Dundonald; and, The Life of Captain Cook.]
Illus. pp.[64].
Two pamphlets without title-pages or covers, bound in one volume.
Copies: ANL. 1976

1800 MAVOR, William Fordyce
The British Nepos; or, Mirror of youth, consisting of select lives of
illustrious Britons [including Captain Cook]. 2nd ed. London, R. Phillips,
1800.
Frontisp. ports. pp.x, [6], 462.
Copies: NPL:D(80/12). 1977

1808 LE COOK de la jeunesse; ou, Extrait des voyages les plus récens dans
les régions les plus éloignées. Suivi de l'abrégé de la vie du Capitaine
Cook par M. le Capitaine B** [i.e. J.P. Bérenger]. Paris, 1808.
Illus. 2 vols.
Binder's title: Cook de la jeunes (*sic*).
See also nos.54, 1979.
Copies: NPL:D(80/88–9). 1978

1814 LA COOK de la jeunesse; ou, extrait des voyage les plus récens dans
régions éloignées. Paris, Giguet et Michaud, 1814.
Illus. 2 vols.
Taken from J.P. Bérenger's account. *See also* nos.54, 1978.
Copies: ANL. 1979

1814 KIPPIS, *Rev.* Andrew

A Narrative of the voyage round the world performed by Captain James Cook. With an account of his life during the previous and intervening periods. London, Carpenter and Son, 1814.

Illus. 2 vols.
See also no.17.

Copies: QU.   1980

[182–?] KIPPIS, *Rev.* Andrew

A Narrative of the voyages round the world, performed by Captain James Cook; with an account of his life, during the previous and intervening periods, by A. Kippis. London, J.F. Dove, [182–?].

Frontisp. pp.viii, 416.
(*Dove's English Classics.*)
With additional engraved title-page with vignette depicting Death of Cook, and entitled Cook's Voyages and life. London, engraved for Dove's English Classics. *See also* no.17.

Copies: NPL:M(980:Col/K2L1); NPL:D(82/27).   1981

1820 KIPPIS, *Rev.* Andrew

A Narrative of the voyages round the world, performed by Captain James Cook; with an account of his life during the previous and intervening periods, by A. Kippis. Chiswick, C. Whittingham, pr., 1820.

2 vols.
Each volume has additional engraved title-page, with vignette, with title: Narrative of Captn. Cook's three voyages, by A. Kippis. *See also* no.17.

Copies: NPL:M(980:Col/K2G1-2); ANL:F.   1982

1820 THE LIFE of Captain James Cook. Dublin, Richard Grace, 1820.

Illus. pp.179.
Published anonymously. Abridged for young readers, from the biography by A. Kippis. Dixson Library copy lacks frontispiece.
See also nos.1984, 1986, 1991–2, 1994–6.

Copies: NPL:M(923.9/C771.2/6A1); NPL:D(82/45); NPL:R(S920/C771/5).   1983

1821 THE LIFE of Captain James Cook. Dublin, Richard Grace, 1821.

Illus. pp.179.
Published anonymously. Abridged for young readers, from the biography by A. Kippis.
See also nos.1983, 1986, 1991–2, 1994–6.

Copies: NPL:M(923.9/C771.2/6B1); ANL.   1984

1822–1934 MOWLE, Percival Conrad

Cutting books, 1822–1934.

With references to Captain Cook.

Copies: ANL(MS258).   1985

1824 THE LIFE of Captain James Cook. Dublin, printed by John Jones, 1824.

Frontisp. pp.179.
Published anonymously. Abridged for young readers, from the biography by A. Kippis.
See also nos.1983–4, 1991–2, 1994–6.

Copies: ANL.   1986

1826 KIPPIS, *Rev.* Andrew
A Narrative of the voyages round the world, performed by Captain James Cook; with an account of his life during the previous and intervening periods, by A. Kippis. Chiswick, C. and C. Whittingham, 1826.

2 vols.
Each volume includes additional engraved title-page dated 1820 *see* no.1981. *See also* no.17.

Copies: NPL:M(980:Col/K2H1–2).   1987

1826 KIPPIS, *Rev.* Andrew
Voyages round the world, performed by Capt. James Cook; with an account of his life, during the previous and intervening periods, by A. Kippis. London, Cowie, Low & Co., 1826.

2 vols.
See also no.17.

Copies: NPL:M(980:Col/K2J1–2).   1988

1828 KIPPIS, *Rev.* Andrew
A Narrative of the voyages round the world, performed by Captain James Cook; with an account of his life, during the previous and intervening periods, by A. Kippis. Boston, N.H. Whitaker, 1828.

Illus. port. 2 vols.
Each volume has an additional engraved title-page. Frontispiece to volume 2 is Death of Captain Cook. *See also* no.17.

Copies: NPL:M(980:Col/K2K1–2).   1989

1829 LÉMONTEY, Pierre Edouard
Éloge de Jacques Cook, célèbre navigateur anglais . . . Discours qui a remporté le priz d'éloquence au jugement de l'Académie de Marseille, le 25 août, 1789.

(*In his* Oeuvres. Paris, A. Sautelet, 1829. Vol.3, pp.145–228.)
See also no.1972.

Copies: NPL:M(980:Col/L3A1).   1990

[183–?] THE LIFE of Captain James Cook. Stereotype ed. Belfast, printed by Joseph Smythe, [c.1830?].

pp.iv, 5–144.
Published anonymously. Abridged for young readers, from the biography by A. Kippis. Title repeated on wrapper, with imprint: Dublin, printed by C.M. Warren. pp.143–4 are further condensed than the last pages of other editions of this title. No. 1996 is identical with this, except for addition of publication date. *See also* nos.1983–4, 1986, 1992, 1994–6.

Copies: NPL:M(923.9/C771.2/6D1); ANL.   1991

[1831] THE LIFE of Captain James Cook. New ed. London, W. Wetton, [1831].

Illus. pp.iv, 170, 6, 10.
Published anonymously. Abridged for young readers, from the biography by A. Kippis. The supplementary pages at the end of the volume are publishers' advertisements, of which the tenth last page is entitled Superior books . . . published by C.F. Cock, Jan. 1831. pp.9–10 give an advertisement for the National School Reader. Stamped June 1832 inside front cover. *See also* nos.1983–4, 1986, 1991, 1994–6.
Copies: NPL:M(923.9/C771.2/6Cl).   1992

1832 KIPPIS, *Rev.* Andrew
A Narrative of the voyages round the world, performed by Captain James Cook; with an account of his life, during the previous and intervening periods, by A. Kippis. Philadelphia, L. Johnson, 1832.

2 vols.
Each volume has an additional engraved title-page, with title Narrative of Captain Cook's three voyages, and vignette. Both these title-pages have been cut down, that for volume 1 having been cut into the title. *See also* no.17.
Copies: NPL:M(980:Col/K2M1–2).   1993

1834 THE LIFE of Captain James Cook. New ed. London, printed for the executrix of the late W. Wetton, 1834.

Frontisp. pp.iv, 170.
Published anonymously. Abridged for young readers, from the biography by A. Kippis. *See also* nos.1983–4, 1986, 1991–2, 1995–6.
Copies: ANL:F.   1994

1835 THE LIFE of Captain James Cook. New ed. London, printed for the executrix of the late W. Wetton, 1835.

Illus. pp.iv, 170.
Published anonymously. Abridged for young readers, from the biography by A. Kippis. *See also* nos.1983–4, 1986, 1991–2, 1994, 1996.
Copies: QOM.   1995

1835 THE LIFE of Captain James Cook. Stereotype ed. Belfast, printed by Joseph Smyth, 1835.

pp.iv, 5–144.
Wanting wrappers.
Published anonymously. Abridged, for young readers, from the biography by A. Kippis. No. 1991 is identical with this, except that it is undated. pp.143–4 are further condensed than the last pages of other editions of this title. *See also* nos.1983–4, 1986, 1991–2, 1994–5.
Copies: NPL:R(S920/C771/6).   1996

1836 CHAMPAGNAC, Jean Baptiste Joseph de
Le Cook de l'enfance et de la jeunesse; ou, Choix des particularités les plus intéressantes, des details les plus instructifs et les plus curieux contenus

dans les relations des trois voyages de ce célèbre navigateur autour du monde, précédé d'une notice sur sa vie. Paris, Fruger et Brunet, Libraires, 1836.

Illus. pp.[ii], 320.

Copies: ANL:F. 1997

1836 AN HISTORICAL ACCOUNT of the circumnavigation of the globe, and of the progress of discovery in the Pacific Ocean, from the voyage of Magellan to the death of Cook. Illustrated by a portrait of Cook, engraved by Horsburgh after Dance, a facsimile of his Observations on the transit of Venus in 1769, and twenty-one highly-finished engravings by Jackson. Seventh thousand. Edinburgh, Oliver & Boyd, [1836].

pp.423.

(*Edinburgh Cabinet Library*, new ed.)

With additional engraved title-page, with title Circumnavigation of the globe. Date taken from Preface. Section (pp.241–423) entitled Cook, deals with Cook's life and voyages. *See also* nos.2001, 2004, 2020.

Copies: NPL:M(910.4/H). 1998

1836 Tegg's Edition

Narrative of Captain James Cook's voyages round the world; with an account of his life during the previous and intervening periods. London, pr. for Thomas Tegg & Son, 1836.

Illus. pp.378.

A later edition of no. 107, which *see* for other editions. Taken from Kippis' account.

Copies: NPL:M(980:Col/29B1). 1999

1836 YOUNG, *Rev.* George

The Life and voyages of Captain James Cook; drawn up from his journals and other authentic documents, and comprising much original information. By the Rev. G. Young. London, Whittaker, Treacher, 1836.

Illus. port. pp.xii, 466.

The Mitchell Library holds another copy, identical with the copy held by Captain Cook's Landing Place Trust, with 472 pages the additional pages being a list of subscribers. *See also* nos.2015, 2023.

Copies: NPL:M(980:Col/Y1A1); NPL:D(83/194); ANL; Captain Cook's Landing Place Trust; VSL. 2000

1837 AN HISTORICAL ACCOUNT of the circumnavigation of the globe, and of the progress of discovery in the Pacific Ocean, from the voyage of Magellan to the death of Cook. Illustrated by a portrait of Cook, engraved by Horsburgh after Dance, a facsimile of his Observations on the transit of Venus in 1769, and twenty-one highly-finished engravings by Jackson. 2nd ed. Edinburgh, Oliver & Boyd, 1837.

pp.496.

With additional engraved title-page, with title Circumnavigation of the globe. Section (pp.281–490) entitled *Cook*, deals with Cook's life and voyages. *See also* nos. 1998, 2004, 2020.

Copies: NPL:M(910.4/H); NPL:R(MD3:P13); ANL:F. 2001

1837 Parker' Edition

Life, voyages and discoveries of Captain James Cook. London, J.W. Parker, 1837.

Illus. port. pp.220.
See also nos.2010, 2024.

Copies: NPL:M(980:Col/34A1); NPL:D(83/466).   2002

1838 Milner's Edition

Narrative of Captain James Cook's voyages round the world; with an account of his life during the previous and intervening periods. Also an appendix detailing the progress of the voyage after the death of Captain Cook. London, William Milner, 1838.

Illus. pp.384.
Halifax also mentioned in imprint. A later edition of no.107, which *see* for other editions.
Taken from Kippis' account.

Copies: ANL.   2003

1839 AN HISTORICAL ACCOUNT of the circumnavigation of the globe, and of the progress of discovery in the Pacific Ocean, from the voyage of Magellan to the death of Cook. Illustrated by numerous engravings. New York, Harper, 1839.

pp.366.
(*The School District Library*, no. 31.)
With two additional title-pages entitled *The School district library*, and *Circumnavigation of the globe*. Includes section on Cook's life and voyages. *See also* nos.1998, 2001, 2020.

Copies: NPL:M(910.4/H).   2004

1839 KIPPIS, *Rev.* Andrew

A Narrative of the voyages round the world, performed by Captain James Cook; with an account of his life, during the previous and intervening periods, by A. Kippis. London, Scott, Webster and Geary, 1839.

Frontisp. pp.[ii], x, 445.
Additional title-page includes engraving of Cook's death and the title Cook's voyages and life. *See also* no.17.

Copies: NPL:R(S990A/66).   2005

1839 Milner's Edition

Narrative of Captain James Cook's voyages round the world, with an account of his life during the previous and intervening periods; also an appendix. London, pub. by the booksellers, William Milner, Halifax, 1839.

pp.xvi, 368.
A later edition of no. 107, which *see* for other editions. Taken from Kippis' account.
With newscutting dated May 1835, relative to the death of Mrs. Cook, and an inscription in the handwriting of Mrs. Cook's man-servant, Doswell, to whom the book belonged.

Copies: ANL:F.   2006

[184–] KIPPIS, *Rev.* Andrew

A Narrative of the voyages round the world, performed by Captain James Cook; with an account of his life during the previous and intervening periods. Philadelphia, Henry T. Coates, [184–].

Illus. pp.424.
See also no.17.

Copies: QOM.   2007

[1840?] FOA, Eugenie, *Mme., pseud.*

Contes historiques pour la jeunesse. Paris, Desforges, [1840?].

Illus. pp.[vi], 349.
Includes a chapter on Captain James Cook.

Copies: NPL:M(920/6A1).   2008

1840 Milner's Edition

Narrative of Captain James Cook's voyages round the world; with an account of his life during the previous and intervening periods. Also an appendix detailing the progress of the voyage after the death of Captain Cook. Halifax, William Milner, 1840.

Frontisp. pp.xvi, 368.
Taken from Kippis' account, first published 1788. Contains additional engraved title-page, entitled Cook's Voyages round the world, London. A later edition of no. 107, which *see* for other editions.

Copies: NPL:M(980:Col/29G1).   2009

1840 Parker's Edition

Life, voyages and discoveries of Captain James Cook. 2nd ed. London, J.W. Parker, 1840.

See also nos.2002, 2024.

Copies: VSL.   2010

1841 Barr's Edition

Narrative of Captain James Cook's voyages round the world; with an account of his life during the previous and intervening periods; also an appendix. London, J. Barr, 1841.

pp.viii, 352.
With an additional title-page, with imprint, London, I.S. Pratt. A later edition of no. 107, which *see* for other editions. Taken from Kippis' account.

Copies: NPL:M(980:Col/29C1).   2011

1841 KIPPIS, *Rev.* Andrew

A Narrative of the voyages round the world, performed by Captain James Cook; with an account of his life, during the previous and intervening periods, by A. Kippis. Philadelphia, Haswell, Barrington & Haswell, 1841.

2 vols. in 1.
A reprint of 1832 ed. no. 1993. Engraved title-pages with vignettes as in 1832 edition "Philadelphia, published by L. Johnson" bound in front of volume 1. *See also* no.17.

Copies: NPL:M(980:Col/K2N1).   2012

1842 KIPPIS, *Rev.* Andrew

A Narrative of the voyages round the world, performed by Captain James Cook; with an account of his life during the previous and intervening periods by A. Kippis. London, Scott, Webster and Geary, 1842.

Frontisp. pp.[ii], x, 445.

Additional title-page includes engraving of Cook's death and the title, Cook's voyages and life. *See also* no.17. SPL copy is undated.

Copies: ANL:F; SPL.   2013

1843 Pratt's Edition

Narrative of Captain James Cook's voyages round the world; with an account of his life during the previous and intervening periods. Also an appendix detailing the progress of the voyage after the death of Captain Cook. London, J.S. Pratt, 1843.

pp.viii, 319.

A later edition of no.107, which *see* for other editions. Taken from Kippis' account.

Copies: NPL:M(980:Col/29D1).   2014

1843 YOUNG, *Rev.* George

Het Leven en de reizen van Kapitein J. Cook; beschreven naar naauwkeurige berigten, in zijne dagboeken en andere bescheiden voorhanden door G. Young. Uit het engelsch; [trans. by C.]. Amsterdam, M.H. Binger, 1843.

Illus. map, 2 vols.

The Mitchell Library copy had holograph notes by the publisher and the engravers. *See also* nos.2000, 2023.

Copies: NPL:M(980:Col/Y1C1–2).   2015

1844 KIPPIS, *Rev.* Andrew

A Narrative of the voyages round the world, performed by Captain James Cook; with an account of his life, during the previous and intervening periods, by A. Kippis. Philadelphia, Henry F. Anners, 1844.

Port. 2 vols. in 1.

Similar to 1832 Philadelphia edition, but does not have additional title-pages. *See also* no.17.

Copies: NPL:M(980:Col/K2P1).   2016

1845 CHAMBERS, William

Life of Captain Cook. Edinburgh, W. and R. Chambers, 1845.

Port. pp.[iii], 32.

(*Chambers's Miscellany of Useful and Entertaining Knowledge*, vol.5, no.40.)

Copies: NPL:M(923.9/C771.2/7A1); ANL; VSL.   2017

1848 WELD, Charles Richard

History of the Royal Society, with memoirs of the Presidents; compiled from authentic documents by C.R. Weld. London, John W. Parker, 1848.

Frontisp. 2 vols.
Contains material on Banks and Cook.
Copies: NPL:M(506/W). 2018

1849 THE LIFE of Captain James Cook, the celebrated navigator. London, Newman & Co., 1849.

pp.122.
Published anonymously.
Adapted for young readers, from the biography by A. Kippis.
Listed in advertisement on verso of half title-page, as being published by W. Tegg & Co.
Copies: NPL:M(923.9/C771.2/8A1). 2019

1852 CIRCUMNAVIGATION of the globe, and progress of discovery in the Pacific Ocean, from the voyage of Magellan to the death of Captain Cook. London, Nelson, 1852.

Facs. illus. port. pp.423.
(*Edinburgh Cabinet Library*, new ed.)
With additional engraved title-page, 1837 edition, entitled An Historical account of the circumnavigation etc. *See also* nos.1998, 2001, 2004.
Copies: ANL. 2020

1853 Milner and Sowerby's Edition

Narrative of Captain James Cook's voyages round the world; with an account of his life during the previous and intervening periods. Also an appendix. Halifax, Milner and Sowerby, 1853.

pp.xvi, 368.
(*Cottage Library*.)
A later edition of no.107, which *see* for other editions. Taken from Kippis' account.
Copies: NPL:M(980:Co1/29E1). 2021

1854 SLAUGHTER, William

ALS, South Shields, Nov.30th, 1854, to John M'Allister in Philadelphia.

pp.3.
With reference to the Cook family and setting out their pedigree. Gifts of relics etc. from Mrs. Cook to his father-in-law. Amount of money left to Mary Fleck. Frances Wardale was a cousin of Captain Cook. In 1770 she married Mr. Lieber and settled in Philadelphia in 1773. After the death of Lieber she married John M'Allister. She died in Philadelphia in 1814.
(Family papers. 1776–1926.)

Copies: ANL(Nan Kivell 9528); NPL:M(FM4/1552,1707, pos. and neg. microfilm). 2022

1854 YOUNG, *Rev.* George

Het Leven en de reizen van Kapitein J. Cook. Utrecht, Van der Post, 1854.

See also nos.2000, 2015.
Copies: VSL. 2023

1855 Parker's Edition
The Life, voyages and discoveries of Captain James Cook. 5th ed. London, J.W. Parker, 1855.

Illus. pp.220.
See also nos.2002, 2010.
Copies: NPL:R(S990A/78).   2024

1857 Milner and Sowerby's Edition
Narrative of Captain James Cook's voyages round the world, with an account of his life during the previous and intervening periods; also an appendix. Halifax, Milner and Sowerby, 1857.

pp.xvi, 368.
A later edition of no.107, which *see* for other editions. Taken from Kippis' account.
Copies: ANL:F.   2025

1858 KIPPIS, *Rev.* Andrew
Narrative of the voyages around the world; with an account of his life, by A. Kippis. New York, 1858.

See also no.17.
Copies: ANL.   2026

[186–?] HORN, W.O. von, *pseud.*
James Cook; Leben und Thaten des weltberühmten Seefahrers und Erdumseglers. Der Jugend und dem Volke erzählt. Wiesbaden, Niedner, [186–?].

4 plates, pp.136.
For Swedish edition and later German edition *see* nos.2030, 2048.
Copies: NPL:M(980:Col/H3B1).   2027

1863 MOORE, Joseph Sheridan
Captain Cook and Botany Bay; with numerous illustrations from the original sketches [of J.R. Roberts] by W. Mason. Comp. and ed. by J.S. Moore. Sydney, J. Cole, 1863.

Port. pp.16.
Mitchell Library holds another edition, wanting title-page.
Copies: NPL:M(991.1/M); NPL:D(86/152); SPL; VSL.   2028

1864 COOK, der Weltumsegler: Leben, Reisen und Ende des Kapitän James Cook, insbesondere Schilderung seiner drei grossen Entdeckungs-fahrten. Nebst einem Blick auf die heutigen Zustände der Südsee-Inselwelt. Herausgegeben von . . . K. Müller. Leipzig, Otto Spamer, 1864.

Illus. pp.xxiv, 288.
(*Das Buch der Reisen und Entdeckungen*, Aeltere Reisen [no.]1.) *See also* no.2037.
Copies: NPL:M(980:Col/M5A1).   2029

[1867] HORN, W.O. von, *pseud.*

James Cook den namnkunnige verldsomseglaren, hans lefnad och bedrifter; skildrade för ungdomen. Stockholm, Ebeling, [1867].

4 plates, pp.[ii], 130.
See also nos.2027, 2048.

Copies: NPL:M(980:Co1/H3A1).   2030

[1870] CAPTAIN COOK'S landing in Botany Bay, with fac-simile of Cook's Chart and view of monument to Captain Cook. Sydney, Gibbs, Shallard, n.d. [1870].

Illus. pp.12.
Extract from the *Illustrated Sydney News* and *Sydney Morning Herald.*

Copies: NPL:M(991.1/C); NPL:R(MJ2S3).   2031

[1871] KINGSTON, William Henry Giles

Captain Cook: his life, voyages and discoveries. London, Religious Tract Society, [1871].

Listed in British Museum catalogue, which also lists [1890] and [1926] editions. *See also* no.2065.

Copies: QU; VSL.   2032

1876 Low's Edition

Captain Cook's three voyages round the world; with a sketch of his life. Ed. by C.T. Low. London, Routledge, 1876.

2 plates in colour, pp.512.
Plates in Mitchell Library second copy differ from those in the first. First published 1875. *See also* nos.2036, 2038, 2040, 2043–4, 2051, 2059–61.

Copies: NPL:M(980:Co1/37A1; 37A2); ANL:F.   2033

1878 KIPPIS, *Rev.* Andrew

A Narrative of the voyages round the world, performed by Captain James Cook; with an account of his life during the previous and intervening periods, by A. Kippis. London, Bickers and Son, 1878.

Illus. pp.x, [ii], 404.
With twelve illustrations reproduced in exact facsimile from drawings made during the voyages. Fly leaf and half-title are missing from Mitchell Library copy. Cover title, Cook's Voyages and life. *See also* no.17.

Copies: NPL:M(980:Co1/K2Q1); Captain Cook's Landing Place Trust; QOM.   2034

1880 KIPPIS, *Rev.* Andrew

A Narrative of the voyages round the world, performed by Captain James Cook; with an account of his life during the previous and intervening periods, by A. Kippis. London, Bickers & Son, 1880.

Illus. pp.x, [ii], 404.
A reprint of the 1878 edition. *See also* no.17.

Copies: NPL:M(980:Co1/K2R1); QOM.   2035

[1880?] Low's Edition

Captain Cook's three voyages round the world; with a sketch of his life. Ed. by C.R. Low. London, Routledge, [1880?]

pp.512.
Wanting illustrations. First published 1875. *See also* no.2033.

Copies: NPL:R(DS990A/77). 2036

1882 COOK, der Weltumsegler: Leben, Reisen und Ende des Kapitän James Cook. Nebst einem Blick auf die heutigen Zustände der Südsee-Inselwelt. Ursprünglich herausgegeben von K. Müller; in den späteren Auflagen bearbeitet von der Redaktion des Buchs der Reisen. Dritte verbesserte Auflage. Leipzig, Otto Spamer, 1882.

Illus. pp.xxiv, 276.
(Das Buch der Reisen und Entdeckungen.)
See also no.2029.

Copies: NPL:M(980:Col/M5Cl). 2037

1882 Low's Edition

Captain Cook's three voyages round the world; with a sketch of his life. Ed. by C.R. Low. London, Routledge, 1882.

Frontisp. in colour, pp.512.
First published 1875. *See also* no.2033.

Copies: NPL:M(980:Col/37F1). 2038

1883 KIPPIS, *Rev.* Andrew

A Narrative of the voyages round the world, performed by Captain James Cook; with an account of his life during the previous and intervening periods, by A. Kippis. London, Bickers & Son, 1883.

Illus. pp.x, [ii], 404.
A reprint of the 1878 edition. *See also* no.17.

Copies: NPL:M(980:Col/K2S1). 2039

[1883] Low's Edition

Three voyages round the world . . . With a sketch of his life. Ed. by Lieut. Charles R. Low. London, [1883].

Illus.
First published 1875. *See also* no.2033.

Copies: ANL. 2040

[1886] MEISSNER, H.

James Cook; oder, Dreimal um die Erde Ein. Lebensbild für die reifere Jugend, von H. Meissner. Stuttgart, Gebrüder Kröner, [1886].

Illus. maps, pp.iv, 286.
Illustrations, by Fritz Bergen, include coloured plates. For Swedish edition see no.2049.

Copies: NPL:M(980:Col/M2A1). 2041

1889 KIPPIS, *Rev.* Andrew

A Narrative of the voyages round the world performed by Captain James Cook; with an account of his life during the previous and intervening periods, by A. Kippis. London, Bickers & Son, 1889.

Illus. pp.x, [ii], 404.

See also no. 17. Apparently a reprint of the 1878 and 1883 editions, with different title-leaf and different imprint at foot of p.404; also with one less preliminary page, the list of plates being printed on the verso of the Contents list. For later reprint *see* no.2046.

Copies: NPL:M(980:Col/K2T1); ANL:F.   2042

[189–?] Low's Edition

Captain Cook's three voyages round the world; with a sketch of his life. Ed. by C.R. Low. London, Routledge, [189–?].

Illus. pp.512.

First published 1875. *See also* no.2033.

Copies: ANL:F.   2043

[189–?] Low's Edition

Captain Cook's three voyages round the world; with a sketch of his life. Ed. by C.R. Low. London, Routledge, [189–?].

Illus. in colour, pp.512.

First published 1875. *See also* no.2033.

Copies: NPL:M(980:Col/37E1).   2044

1890 BESANT, *Sir* Walter

Captain Cook. London, Macmillan, 1890.

Port. pp.vi, 191.

(*English Men of Action.*)

See also nos.2047, 2062, 2064, 2073.

Copies: NPL:M(923.9/C771.2/11A1); NPL:R(S920/C771/1); ANL:F; QParl; QU. 2045

1893 KIPPIS, *Rev.* Andrew

A Narrative of the voyages round the world, performed by Captain James Cook; with an account of his life during the previous and intervening periods, by A. Kippis. London, Bickers & Son, 1893.

Illus. pp.x, [ii], 404.

Apparently a reprint of the 1889 edition, no.2042. *See also* no.17.

Copies: NPL:M(980/Col/K2U1).   2046

1894 BESANT, *Sir* William

Captain Cook. London, Macmillan, 1894.

See also nos.2045, 2062, 2064, 2073.

Copies: VSL.   2047

1894 HORN, W.O. von, *pseud.*

James Cook: Leben und Thaten des weltberühmten Seefahrers und Erdumseglers. Der Jugend und dem Volke erzählt. 4th ed. Altenburg, Geibel, 1894.

4 plates, pp.116.
(*Horn'sche Volks– und Jugendbibliothek*, no.58.)
For Swedish edition and earlier German edition *see* nos.2027, 2030.
Copies: NPL:M(980:Co1/H3C1).   2048

1894 MEISSNER, H.

James Cook, eller jorden rundt tre gånger; bearbetning från Tyskan [of H. Meissner] af D.S. Hector. Stockholm, P.A. Norstedt, 1894.

Illus. pp.296.
(*P.A. Norstedt & Söners Ungdomsböcker*, nr. 18.)
Slightly abridged. Illustrations in black and white. For Stuttgart edition *see* no.2041.
Copies: NPL:M(980:Co1/M2B1).   2049

1894 SYNGE, Margaret Bertha

Cook's voyages; the text reduced, with introduction and notes, by M.B. Synge. London, Rivington, Percival, 1894.

First published 1892. For a different abridgement by Synge, *see* nos.2054, 2063.
Copies: VSL.   2050

1895 Low's Edition

Captain Cook's three voyages round the world; with a sketch of his life. Ed. by . . . C.R. Low. With plates in colours from designs by G. Browne and twenty-eight illustrations. New ed. London, Routledge, 1895.

pp.512.
With Alfred Lee's bookplate. First published 1875. *See also* no.2033.
Copies: NPL:M(980:Co1/37B1).   2051

1895–6 [MS. COPY OF] Captain Cook's descendants: [abstracts of several letters received in response to enquiries by Mr. Bonwick, 1895–6].

(Bonwick Transcripts: Cook, case 2, no.192).
Copies: NPL:M(B.T.Ser.2, Box 2).   2052

1895–6 NOTES on Capt. Cook's descendants, from the Bonwick Transcripts, 1895–6.

(Miscellaneous primary and secondary source material re the life and voyages of Captain James Cook.)
Copies: NPL:M(MS.A1713⁻³Item 4B, no.v).   2053

1897 SYNGE, Margaret Bertha

Captain Cook's voyages round the world; with an intro. life by M.B. Synge. London, T. Nelson and Sons, 1897.

Illus. maps, ports. pp.xiv, ix, 11–512.
See also nos.2050, 2063. This is a different abridgement from no.2050.

Copies: QOM. 2054

1899 McFARLAND, Alfred

Captain Cook, his life and voyages, services to New Holland and to man: a biographical sketch, (28th April, 1770–28th April, 1899). Sydney, Govt. Pr., [1899].

Illus. port. pp.34.
Cover title: *Kurnell, the landing place of Captain Cook, 1770*. Also published in New South Wales—Dept. Lands—Dedication of Capt. Cook's landing, pp.39–70, 1899.

Copies: NPL:M(923.9/C771.2/12A1); ANL. 2055

[19—] JOHNSON, *Sir* William Elliott

Press cuttings and articles.

Four bundles of newspaper cuttings and typescript articles, including references to Captain Cook.

Copies: ANL(MS.961). 2056

[19–?] WHITCOMBE AND TOMBS, LTD.

Captain James Cook, for ages 12 to 14 years. Auckland, W. & T., n.d.

Illus. map, port. as frontisp. pp.59.
(*Whitcombe's Story Books*, no.653.)

Copies: NPL:M(923.9/C771.2/31A1). 2057

[19–?] WHITCOMBE AND TOMBS, LTD.

Under Cook's flag; [with chronology of Cook's life]. Auckland, W. & T., [19–?].

Illus. maps, port. pp.148.
(*Whitcombe's Hist. Story Books*.)
Written for children.

Copies: NPL:M(980:Col/W2A1). 2058

[190–?] Low's Edition

Captain Cook's three voyages round the world; with a sketch of his life. Ed. by C.R. Low. London, Routledge, and New York, E.P. Dutton, [190–?].

Illus., some in colour, pp.512.
From the Knox Collection. First published 1875. *See also* no.2033.

Copies: NPL:M(980:Col/37C1). 2059

[190–?] Low's Edition

Three voyages round the world, by Captain Cook. Ed. with a sketch of his life, by C.R. Low. Melbourne, E.W. Cole, [190–?].

Frontisp. in colour, pp.512.
(*Cole's Popular Library.*)
First published 1875. *See also* no.2033.

Copies: NPL:M(980:Co1/37D1).   2060

[190–?] Low's Edition

Three voyages round the world, made by Captain James Cook, R.N. With a sketch of his life. Ed. by C.R. Low. New York, A.L. Burt, [190–?].

Port. as frontisp. pp.472.
(*Burt's Home Library.*)
First published 1875. *See also* no.2033.

Copies: NPL:M(980:Co1/37G1).   2061

1903 BESANT, *Sir* Walter

Captain Cook. London, Macmillan, 1903.

Illus. port. pp.v, 191.
(*Prize Library.*)
See also nos.2045, 2047, 2064, 2073.

Copies: NPL:M(923.9/C771.2/11D1); ANL:F.   2062

1903 SYNGE, Margaret Bertha

Captain Cook's voyages round the world; with an intro. life by M.B. Synge. London, T. Nelson and Sons, 1903.

Illus. maps, port. pp.xv, ix, 11–512.
See also no.2054. For a different abridgement *see* no.2050.

Copies: NPL:M(980:Co1/40A1).   2063

1904 BESANT, *Sir* Walter

Captain Cook. London, Macmillan, 1904.

Illus. port. pp.v, 191.
Reprint of no.2062. *See also* nos.2045, 2047, 2073.

Copies: NPL:M(923.9/C771.2/11E1).   2064

[1904] KINGSTON, William Henry Giles

Captain Cook, his life, voyages and discoveries. London, Religious Tract Society, [1904].

Illus. pp.319.
British Museum catalogue lists [1871], [1890], and [1926] editions. *See also* no.2032.

Copies: NPL:M(980:Co1/K1A1); ANL:F.   2065

[1905] Cash's Edition
The Life and voyages of Captain James Cook; selections, with intro. and notes by C.G. Cash. London, Blackie, [1905].

Frontisp. pp.vi, 7–192.
Date from British Museum General Catalogue.
Copies: NPL:M(980:Co1/39A1); ANL; QOM; VSL.   2066

[1905?] COOK der Weltumsegler. Leben, Reisen und Ende des Kapitäns James Cook, für Jugend und Volk erzählt, von J. März. Zweite Aufl. Leipzig, Otto Spamer, [1905?].

Illus. ports. pp.261, [xi].
Copies: NPL:M(980:Co1/50B1).   2067

[1906] LANG, John
The Story of Captain Cook . . . with pictures by W.B. Robinson. London, T.C. and E.C. Jack, [1906].

pp.vii, 119.
(*Children's Heroes Series.*)
Copies: NPL:M(923.9/C771.2/13A1); ANL.   2068

1907 KITSON, Arthur
Captain James Cook, R.N., F.R.S., the circumnavigator. London, John Murray, 1907.

Facs. illus. map, pp.xvi, 525.
See also nos.2070–71.
Copies: NPL:M(923.9/C771.2/14A1); NPL:R(S920/C771/4); ANL; VSL.   2069

1911 KITSON, Arthur
The Life of Captain James Cook, the circumnavigator. 2nd ed. London, John Murray, 1911.

Map, port. pp.[iv], 334.
Abridged. *See also* nos.2069, 2071.
Copies: NPL:M(923.9/C771.2/14B1); ANL:F; QU.   2070

1912 KITSON, Arthur
The Life of Captain James Cook, the circumnavigator. 2nd ed. London, John Murray, 1912.

Map, port. pp.[vi], 334.
Abridged. *See also* nos.2069–70.
Copies: NPL:M(923.9/C771.2/14C1); QOM.   2071

1913 BATEREAU, Alfred
Captain James Cook, life and voyages . . . bearbeitet von . . . A. Batereau; [with] (Wörterbuch . . . von . . . B. Koeppen). Berlin, Weidmannsche Buchhandlung, 1913.

2 vols.
(*Schulbibliothek Französischer und Englischer Prosaschriften*, Abt. 2, Band 61.)
Copies: NPL:D(91/240–1); ANL:F.   2072

1914 BESANT, *Sir* Walter
Captain Cook. London, Macmillan, 1914.
Illus. pp.191.
See also nos.2045, 2047, 2062, 2064.
Copies: QU.   2073

1914 OFFICIAL guide to Whitby. 19th ed. Whitby, Horne & Son, 1914.
Illus. pp.29–32, 124.
Copies: NPL:M(914.274/O).   2074

[192–?] DIXSON, *Sir* William
Notes re Cook and his associates.
pp.24.
MS.
Copies: NPL:D(WD4).   2075

1924 KIPPIS, *Rev.* Andrew
Captain Cook's voyages; with an account of his life, during the previous
and intervening periods. By A. Kippis. New York, Alfred Knopf, 1924.
Illus. pp.x, [ii], 404.
Apparently an American reprint of the 1889 edition, with differing title-page. *See also*
no.17.
Copies: NPL:M(980:Col/K2V1); NPL:D(92/173).   2076

1927 MITTON, Geraldine Edith
Captain Cook. London, A. and C. Black, 1927.
Illus. map, port. pp.vi, 90.
(Peeps at Great Explorers.)
Copies: NPL:M(980:Col/M4A1); ANL.   2077

1928 AUSTRALIA—High Commissioner for Australia in London
Capt. Cook: the greatest of English navigators. [1928].
Copies: ANL.   2078

1928 CAPTAIN COOK BI-CENTENARY CELEBRATIONS, *Cleveland*
Souvenir of the . . . celebrations arranged in the Cleveland District . . .
September 8th, 1928 to . . . 27th October, 1928. Middlesbrough, Hood
& Co., pr., 1928.
Illus. map, port. pp.24.
Copies: NPL:M(Q923.9/C771.2/4A1); NPL:D(Q92/164); QOM; QU.   2079

[1928?] HORSLEY, *Mrs.* Robert Grey
Cook family: notes and family tree. [1928?]
(Miscellaneous primary and secondary source material re the life and voyages of Captain
James Cook.)
Copies: NPL:M(MS.A1713⁻³Item4B, no.xiv).   2080

1928 *THE MARINER'S MIRROR*, vol.14, no.4, October 1928: [Cook bicentenary number].

Copies: NPL:R(DS656.506/7); ANL.   2081

1928 ROWE, John Gabriel

Captain Cook, explorer and navigator; [with bibl. and port.]. London, J.A. Sharp, The Epworth Press, [1928].

Illus. pp.128.
(*Noble Life* ser. 17.)

Copies: NPL:M(923.9/C771.2/25A1); ANL.   2082

1928 SEDGWICK, T. E.

Biographical notes, Feb.1928.

(Miscellaneous primary and secondary source material re the life and voyages of Captain James Cook.)

Copies: NPL:M(MS.A1713⁻³Item4B, no.xii).   2083

[1929] THIÉRY, Maurice

The Life and voyages of Captain Cook, by M. Thiéry. [Trans. from the French by C.J.C. Street.] London, Bles, [1929].

Illus. map, ports. pp.ix, 238.
Map showing voyages as endpapers. *See also* nos.2085–6.

Copies: NPL:M(980:Col/T1B1); NPL:D(92/246); NPL:R(S920/C771/10); ANL; QU; WU.   2084

[1929] THIÉRY, Maurice

La Vie et les voyages du Capitaine Cook; illus. par A. Zaccagnino. Paris, P. Roger, [1929].

Map, port. pp.238.
(*La Vie des Grands Navigateurs.*)
See also nos.2084, 2086.

Copies: NPL:M(980:Col/T1A1); ANL; VSL.   2085

1930 THIÉRY, Maurice

Captain Cook, navigator and discoverer, by M. Thiéry. [Trans. from the French by C.J.C. Street.] New York, R.M. McBride, 1930.

Facs. illus. port. pp.[x], 265.
Map showing voyages as endpapers. *See also* nos.2084–5.

Copies: NPL:M(980:Col/T1C1).   2086

1931 GREAT AYTON, *Parish, Yorkshire*

Parish register . . . 1600–1812. Transcribed, edited . . . by W.J. Kaye. Leeds, the Society, 1931.

(Yorkshire Parish Register Society—*Publications*, vol.90.)
This register contains records of births and deaths of the Cook family.

Copies: NPL:R(N942.7406/1).   2087

1931 WADE, Mary Hazelton, *Mrs.*
The Boy who loved the sea: the story of Captain James Cook. 1931.
Copies: ANL.   2088

1932 MAIDIÈRES, Pierre
Le Destin tragique de James Cook. Paris, Editions Jules Tallandier, 1932.
Illus. pp.124.
(*A travers l'univers. Collection illustrée pour la jeunesse.*)
Copies: NPL:M(923.9/C771.2/38A1).   2089

1934 GILL, George Hermon
Captain Cook's cottage, by H. Gill; with drawings by E. Paterson.
Melbourne, Lothian, 1934.
pp.32.
See also no.2108.
Copies: NPL:M(923.9/C771.2/32A1); ANL; VSL.   2090

1935 FAMILY TREES of the Cook, 1693–1794, and Fleck, 1739–1934,
families made by the Whitby Literary and Philosophical Society, 1935.
MS. and typescript: xerox copies.
Margaret Cook, sister of Captain James Cook, married James Fleck, 1764.
Copies: NPL:M(Doc.1407).   2091

[1935] GOULD, Rupert Thomas
Captain Cook; [with bibl. notes]. London, Duckworth, [1935].
Maps, pp.144.
(*Great Lives*, no. 49.)
Copies: NPL:M(980:Col/G2A1); NPL:D(93/627); NPL:R(920/C771/3); ANL; VSL.
                                                                             2092

1936 CAMPBELL, Gordon
Captain James Cook, R.N., F.R.S. London, Hodder and Stoughton,
1936.
Illus. maps, port. pp.320.
The Mitchell Library also holds proof copy.
Copies: NPL:M(923.9/C771.2/19A1); NPL:D(93/126); NPL:R(DS990A/128); ANL;
QParl; VSL; WU.   2093

1939 CARRINGTON, Arthur Hugh
Life of Captain Cook, by A.H. Carrington. [With bibl.] London,
Sidgwick & Jackson, 1939.
Illus. maps, port. pp.ix, 324.
See also no.2130.
Copies: NPL:M(980:Col/C1A1); NPL:D(93/127); ANL; QU; VSL; WU.   2094

[1939?] KUEHNWALD, Gerd

Unter den Kannibalen der Südsee: Tatsachenbericht über James Cooks Leben und Reisen von G. Kühnwald. Mit Bildern von M. Wulff. Berlin, A. Weichert, [1939?].

Frontisp. pp.112.
Written for children.

Copies: NPL:M(923.9/C771.2/20A1). 2095

1939 MUIR, John Reid

The Life and achievements of Captain James Cook . . . explorer, navigator, surveyor and physician. [With bibl.] London, Blackie, 1939.

Illus. map, ports. pp.[ix], 310.

Copies: NPL:M(980:Col/M6A1); NPL:D(93/626); NPL:R(DS990A/195); ANL; Q Parl; Q U; VMoU; VSL. 2096

1949 DE SELINCOURT, Aubrey

Mr Oram's story, the adventures of Capt. James Cook, R.N.; [written for children, by] (A. de Selincourt). Illus. by J. Baynes. London, Methuen, 1949.

Illus. port. pp.142.
With decorative maps as endpapers.

Copies: NPL:M(980:Col/D1A1); VSL. 2097

1951 KENDALL, Hugh P.

Captain James Cook, R.N., F.R.S., by H.P. Kendall [and] C. Preston. Whitby, Eng., Whitby Literary and Philosophical Society, 1951.

Facs. illus. maps, pp.23.

Copies: ANL. 2098

1951 VANDERCOOK, John Womack

Great sailor: a life of the discoverer Captain James Cook. [With] (Note on sources). New York, Dial Press, 1951.

Frontisp. pp.viii, 339.
Frontispiece is portrait of Cook after James Webber from National Portrait Gallery.
Map of voyages forms endpapers.

Copies: NPL:M(980:Col/V1A1); NPL:R(920/C771/11); ANL. 2099

1952 HENNIG, Edwin

James Cook, Erschliesser der Erde; [with bibl.]. Stuttgart, Wissenschaftliche Verlagsgesellschaft M.B.H., 1952.

Illus. maps, port. pp.[vii], 141.
(*Grosse Naturforscher*, Band 9.)

Copies: NPL:M(923.9/C771.2/30A1). 2100

1952 LLOYD, Christopher
Captain Cook: [a biography]. London, Faber and Faber, 1952.
Illus. maps, port. pp.172.
Copies: NPL:M(980:Col/L2A1); NPL:R(920/C771/12); ANL; QParl; VMoU; VSL.
2101

1954 MERRETT, John
The True book about Captain Cook. London, Shakespeare Head Press, 1954.
Illus. maps, pp.142.
(*True Book* Ser.)
For children. *See also* nos.2103, 2109.
Copies: NPL:M(923.9/C771.2/21A1).
2102

1954 MERRETT, John
True book about Captain James Cook; illus. by F. Stocks May. London, Muller, [1954].
Illus. maps, pp.140.
See also nos.2102, 2109.
Copies: ANL.
2103

1954 SKELTON, Raleigh Ashlin
Captain James Cook as a hydrographer: [annual lecture to the Society for Nautical Research, 1953]. London, 1954.
Illus. maps, pp.92–119.
Reprinted from *The Mariner's Mirror*, vol.40, no.2, May 1954.
Copies: NPL:M(923.9/C771.2/35A1); NPL:R(DS656.506/7).
2104

1955 SPERRY, Armstrong
Captain Cook explores the South Seas. New York, Random House, 1955.
Illus. pp.184.
(*World Landmark Books*.)
See also nos.2111, 2125.
Copies: NPL:M(980:Col/S2A1); ANL.
2105

1955–68 Hakluyt Society Edition
The Journals of Captain James Cook on his voyages of discovery . . . Ed. [from the original MSS., with intro. notes and appendices] by J.C. Beaglehole, [and others. With] (Charts & views drawn by Cook and his officers, and reproduced from the original MSS.; ed. by R.A. Skelton). [And] (Addenda and corrigenda to vol.1) . . . Pub. for the Hakluyt Society. Cambridge, U.P., 1955–68.
Frontisp. in colour, illus. maps, ports. 3 vols. in 4, portfolio and addenda.
CONTENTS:
[Vol.] 1 The Voyage of the *Endeavour*, 1768–1771, with Addenda.
[Vol.] 2 The Voyage of the *Resolution* and *Adventure*, 1772–1775.
[Vol.] 3 The Voyage of the *Resolution* and *Discovery*, 1776–1780. Pts. 1–2.

Portfolio. Charts & views.

Vol. 4, still to be published, will contain a "series of essays on particular aspects of Cook's life and achievement and on the scientific results of the voyages, together with a bibliography and lists of the original charts, drawings and paintings made on the voyages". For further note and list of reviews, *see* no. 227.

Copies: NPL:M(980:Col/46A1–4, X980/25); NPL:D(95/54–7, F95/1); NPL:R(S990A/215E, F990A/47); ANL; Captain Cook's Landing Place Trust; QOM; Q Parl; QU; VSL.

2106

[1956] WYMER, Norman George

Captain James Cook. London, O.U.P., [1956].

Illus. maps, port. pp.32.
(*Lives of Great Men & Women.*)
Written for children.

Copies: NPL:M(923.9/C771.2/22A1); ANL.

2107

1957 GILL, George Hermon

The History of Cook's cottage.

(*In* National Trust of Australia, Victoria—The History of Cook's cottage and Voyages of Captain James Cook. Comp. by the National Trust of Australia, Victoria, by direction of The Parks, Gardens and Recreations Committee of the Melbourne City Council. Melbourne, 1957. pp.5–17.)
See also no.2090.

Copies: NPL:M(923.9/C771.2/23A1).

2108

1957 MERRETT, John

Captain James Cook; illus. by L. Hoffman. New York, Criterion Books, 1957.

Illus. map, pp.192.
(*Criterion Book for Young People.*)
See also nos.2102–3.

Copies: ANL.

2109

1958 PEACH, Lawrence du Garde

The Story of Captain Cook: an adventure from history. Illus. by J. Kenney. Loughborough, Eng., Wills & Hepworth, 1958.

Illus. in colour, pp.51.
(*Ladybird Book*, ser. 561.)

Copies: ANL.

2110

1960 SPERRY, Armstrong

All about Captain Cook. Rev. ed. London, W.H. Allen, 1960.

Illus. map as endpapers, pp.[iv], 147.
(*All About Books Series.*)
See also nos.2105, 2125.

Copies: NPL:M(980:Col/S2B1); ANL.

2111

1960 SYME, Ronald

Captain Cook, Pacific explorer; [written for children], by R. Syme. Illus. by W. Stobbs. New York, W. Morrow, 1960.

Illus. pp.96.
(*Morrow Junior Books.*)
Copies: NPL:M(980:Col/S4A1); ANL. 2112

1962 KENDALL, Hugh P.

The Streets of Whitby and their associations, by . . . H.P.Kendall; [text revised by P. Burnett. Pub. by the Kendall Memorial Fund Committee. Whitby, 1962.]

Illus. pp.[ii], 45.
Originally published in *Whitby Gazette*, 1938.
Copies: NPL:M(942.74/2A1). 2113

1962 LEYDEN, Peter

Capt. James Cook, R.N. Sydney, Australian Schools Press, [1962].

Illus., some in colour, pp.18.
(*Children's Australian Pictorial Biographies.*)
Copies: ANL. 2114

1962 SELSAM, Millicent Ellis

The Quest of Captain Cook, by M.E. Selsam; illus. by L.J. Ames. New York, Doubleday, 1962.

Map, port. pp.128.
Copies: NPL:M(923.9/C771.2/24A1). 2115

1963 CLAIR, Colin

Captain James Cook, the navigator; [with bibl.]. Watford, Herts., Bruce & Gawthorn, 1963.

Facs. illus. maps, ports. pp.112.
(*Figures of the Commonwealth.*)
Copies: NPL:M(923.9/C771.2/26A1); NPL:R(N920/C771/1); ANL; QU. 2116

1963 DE LEEUW, Adèle Louise

A World explorer, James Cook. Illus. by N. Goldstein. Champaign, Illinois, Garrard Pub. Co., 1963.

Illus. in colour, maps as endpapers, pp.96.
(*World Explorer Books.*)
For children. *See also* no.2126.
Copies: NPL:M(923.9/C771.2/29A1); ANL. 2117

1963 SVET, Ia M.

Moreplavatel' tumannogo Al'biona: Dzhems Kuk. [In Russian. The Seafarer from the misty Albion: James Cook.] Moskva, Gos. Izt-vo Geograficheskoi Literatury, 1963.

Illus. maps, pp.80.
(*Zamechatel'nye geografy i puteshestvenniki.*)
Copies: NPL:M(923.9/C771.2/33A1).   2118

1964 DINGWELL, Alexander

The Great captain: the story of Captain Cook. London, Lutterworth Press, 1964.

Frontisp. in colour, map, pp.94.
(*Courage and Conquest* ser. no.9.)
For young readers.
Copies: NPL:M(923.9/C771.2/27A1); ANL.   2119

1964 KNIGHT, Frank

The Young Captain Cook, [by] F. Knight; illus. by J. Howell. London, Parrish, 1964.

pp.127.
(*Famous Childhoods.*)
For young readers. *See also* no.2121.
Copies: NPL:M(923.9/C771.2/28A1); ANL.   2120

1964 KNIGHT, Frank

The Young Captain Cook, [by] F. Knight. Illus. by J. Howell. New York, Roy Pub., 1964.

pp.127.
For young readers. *See also* no.2120.
Copies: NPL:M(923.9/C771.2/28B1); ANL.   2121

[1965] CORNER, Sylvia

Captain Cook and Australia; written and ed. by S. Corner. [Issued by Captain Cook's Landing Place Trust.] Sydney, Govt. Pr., [1965].

Illus. maps, port. pp.63.
Copies: NPL:M(980:Co2/C2A1); Captain Cook's Landing Place Trust.   2122

1965 GREGORY, Olive Barnes

James Cook, by O.B. Gregory. Illus. by A. Oxenham. Exeter, Wheaton of Exeter, 1965.

Illus. in colour, pp.[24].
(*Read About It* ser., book no.45.)
Copies: NPL:M(980:Co1/G3A1).   2123

1965 PRESTON, C.

Captain James Cook, R.N., F.R.S., and Whitby, by C. Preston. Pub. by Whitby Literary and Philosophical Society. Whitby, Horne, pr., 1965.

Facs. illus. maps, port. pp.48.

Copies: NPL:M(980:Col/P1A1); ANL; Captain Cook's Landing Place Trust.   2124

1965 SPERRY, Armstrong

Le Capitaine Cook explore le Pacifique, [by] (A. Sperry); adapté [from the English] par J. Petrus. Paris, F. Nathan, 1965.

Illus. maps, ports. pp.157.
(*Histoire et Documents* ser.)
See also nos.2105, 2111.

Copies: NPL:R(N920/C771/2).   2125

1966 DE LEEUW, Adèle Louise

A World explorer, James Cook. By A. De Leeuw; illus. by N. Goldstein. London, Muller, 1966.

Illus. in colour, maps as endpapers, pp.96.
(*World Explorer Books*.)
For children. *See also* no.2117.

Copies: NPL:M(923.9/C771.2/29B1).   2126

1966 MITCHELL, Thomas Walter

Correspondence with Sir Alexander Downer, 4, 26 May 1966 re posthumous knighthood for Captain Cook; with enclosure of correspondence between the Prime Minister and T.W. Mitchell, 25 Mar., 4 May 1966.

Typescript and carbon typescript.

Copies: NPL:M(Doc.1090).   2127

1966 MITCHELL, Thomas Walter

Typescript letter from the Prime Minister, Canberra, 4 Aug.1966 re his suggestion of a posthumous knighthood for Captain Cook.

Copies: NPL:M(Doc.989).   2128

1967 BEAGLEHOLE, John Cawte

Captain Cook and Captain Bligh. Wellington, New Zealand, Victoria University of Wellington, 1967.

pp.27.
The *Dr. W. E. Collins Lecture* delivered at the Victoria University of Wellington, 3 August, 1967.

Copies: NPL:M(923.9/C771.2/37A1).   2129

1967 CARRINGTON, Arthur Hugh

Life of Captain Cook; [with bibl.]. New ed. London, Sidgwick & Jackson, 1967.

Maps, pp.[vii], 324.
(*Watergate Editions.*)
See also no.2094.
Copies: NPL:M(980:Col/C1B1). 2130

1967 CARRISON, Daniel J.
Captain James Cook: genius afloat. [With bibl.] New York, Franklin Watts, 1967.
Map, pp.vii, 194.
(*Immortals of History.*)
Copies: NPL:M(980:Col/C3A1); ANL. 2131

1967 DOWNER, *Sir* Alexander Russell
TLS to T.W. Mitchell from London, 27 Oct. 1967 re i.a. the proposal of a posthumous knighthood for Captain Cook.
Copies: NPL:M(Doc.1169). 2132

1967 VILLIERS, Alan John
Captain Cook, the seamen's seaman: a study of the great discoverer. [With bibl.] London, Hodder and Stoughton, 1967.
Illus. maps, ports. pp.256.
Reviewed by Charles H. Cotter in the *Mariner's Mirror*, vol.54, pp.104–5, Feb. 1968.
See also no.2134.
Copies: NPL:M(980:Col/V2A1); NPL:R(910.0942/1). 2133

1967 VILLIERS, Alan John
Captain James Cook: [a biography. With bibl.] New York, Charles Scribner's Sons, 1967.
Illus. maps, port. pp.xii, 307.
Maps also as endpapers. Published also with title *Captain Cook, the seamen's seaman*. London, 1967, *see* no.2133.
Copies: NPL:M(980:Col/V2B1). 2134

1968 CABOT, Thomas D.
TLS to T.W. Mitchell from Boston, Mass. 14 Nov. 1968, approving a posthumous knighthood for Captain James Cook and suggesting that the State of Hawaii endorse the petition.
Copies: NPL:M(Doc.1347). 2135

1968 MITCHELL, Thomas Walter
Copies of correspondence, 22 May, 19 Aug., 25 Sep. 1968 with Harold Wilson, Prime Minister of Great Britain, re posthumous knighthood for Captain Cook.
Xerox copies.
Copies: NPL:M(Doc.1277). 2136

1968 MITCHELL, Thomas Walter

Copy of letter to Harold Wilson, Prime Minister of Great Britain, May 22 1968, re a posthumous knighthood for Captain Cook.

Typescript.

Copies: NPL:M(Doc.1188). 2137

1968 RIENITS, Rex

The Voyages of Captain Cook, [by] R. & T. Rienits. London, Paul Hamlyn, 1968.

Facs. illus., many in colour, maps, ports. pp.157.
Sydney also mentioned in imprint. Includes reproductions of drawings and maps by Cook.

Copies: NPL:M(Q980:Col/R1A1); NPL:R(NQ910.4/4). 2138

1968 ROSKILL, Stephen W., *Capt.*

Address given by Captain S.W. Roskill to open the Bicentenary Exhibition in memory of Captain James Cook, 1728–1779, at Great St. Andrew's Church, Cambridge, Oct. 18, 1968.

Typescript: xerox copy.

Copies: NPL:M(Doc.1406). 2139

n.d. NAMES OF SHIPS that Capt. James Cook sailed in.

(Miscellaneous primary and secondary source material re the life and voyages of Captain James Cook.)

Copies: NPL:M(MS.A1713⁻³ Item4B, no.xix). 2140

n.d. ROTH, Theodor

Das Leben des Kapitän Cook; aus dem Englischen. Stuttgart, Scheible, Rieger & Sattler, [n.d.].

Port. pp.40.

Copies: NPL:M(980:Col/R2A1). 2141

Articles, etc.

1781 *UNIVERSAL MAGAZINE*

A Succinct account of the life and voyages of Captain James Cook; with an exact representation of the death of that celebrated navigator; communicated by respectable authority, and elegantly engraved on copper. London, 1781.

Illus. port.

Extract from the *Universal Magazine*, vol.68, no.476, June 1781, pp.281–5. *Bound with* other magazine extracts. *Cover title* Magazine articles, Cook, Banks, Dalrymple, etc.

Copies: NPL:M(910.4/122). 2142

1784 KING, James C.
'An Account of the late Captain Cook, and some memoirs of his life . . .'
Port. ff.6.
Extract from the *Universal Magazine* July 1784, pp.33–40.
Copies: NPL:D(MS.Q144). 2143

1786 SAMWELL, David
Détails sur la vie & caractère du Capitaine Cook.
(*In his* Détails nouveaux et circonstanciés sur la mort du Capitaine Cook. Traduits de l'anglois. Paris, chez Née de la Rochelle, 1786. pp.39–48.)
See also nos.2145, 2252, 2332.
Copies: NPL:M(C759). 2144

1786 SAMWELL, David
Some particulars concerning the life and character of Captain Cook.
(*In his* Narrative of the death of Captain James Cook. London, G.G.J. and J. Robinson, 1786. pp.21–7.)
See also nos.2144, 2252, 2332.
Copies: NPL:M(C694). 2145

1789 ANECDOTE of Captain Cook and O'too [i.e. Pomaré: how Webber painted the portrait of the latter].
(Phillip, Arthur—Voyage . . . to Botany Bay. London, John Stockdale, 1789. pp.292–4.)
Copies: NPL:M(Q991/P). 2146

1789 KIPPIS, *Rev.* Andrew
Cook.
(*In his* Biographia Britannica. London, Rivington, 1789. Vol.4, pp.101–245.)
Copies: NPL:M(F920.042/K); NPL:R(C22:Q20); VSL. 2147

1789 *LITERARY MAGAZINE AND BRITISH REVIEW*
Life of Captain James Cook: [extract, May 1789. pp.321–40].
Copies: NPL:M(923.9/C771.2/3A1). 2148

[1789] THE REMARKABLE LIFE and death of Captain Cook.
(*In* The History of Botany Bay in New Holland. Liverpool, printed R. Ferguson, [1789]. pp.16–31.)
See no.672 for full descriptions of this item, and for other editions.
Copies: NPL:D(78/60). 2149

[c.1789] THE REMARKABLE LIFE and death of Capt. Cook.
(*In* The History of Botany Bay in New Holland. *Anon.* Sheffield, J. Gales, pr., [c.1789].)
Copies: NPL:M(C898). 2150

1791 *ALMANAC DE GOTHA* 1791; [with an account of Cook and two engravings, his reception by the King of England and his death]. Gotha, C.G. Ettinger.
Illus.
Text in French.
Copies: NPL:M(980:Co1/A1A1).   2151

1794 BÉRENGER, Jean Pierre
Vita del Capitano Giacomo Cook.
(*In his* Raccolta di tutti i viaggi. Venezia, A. Zatta, 1794. Tomo 4, pp.3–56.)
See also no.2153.
Copies: NPL:M(910.8/B).   2152

1795 BÉRENGER, Jean Pierre
Appendice sur la vie de Jaques Cook.
(*In his* Collection de tous les voyages. Paris, Poinçot and F. Dufart, 1795. Tome 9, pp. 42–58.)
See also no.2152.
Copies: NPL:M(910.8/B).   2153

1796 LIFE OF Captain James Cook.
(Cook, James—Third Voyage—Printed Accounts [1796. New York Edition]—Voyages to the Pacific Ocean . . . 1776, 1777, 1778, 1779, 1780. New York, Gomez, 1796. Vol.4, pp.1–40.)
Copies: NPL:M(980:Co4/16A4).   2154

1797 ENCYCLOPAEDIA BRITANNICA
[Article on Captain Cook from Encyclopaedia Britannica.]
pp.389–427.
Extracted from Encyclopaedia Britannica. 3rd ed. Edinburgh, 1797.
Copies: NPL:M(Q923.9/C771.2/6A1).   2155

1802 AIKIN, John, *and others*
Cook.
(*In their* General biography. London, 1802. Vol.3, pp.127–33.)
Copies: NPL:R(09:DQ920/106).   2156

1803 BIOGRAPHICAL MEMOIRS of the late Captain James Cook; [with port.].
(*Naval Chronicle*, London, Jan.–July, 1803, pp.1–24.)
Copies: NPL:M(359.05/N); NPL:R(S359.0942/24).   2157

1806 FRANKLIN, Benjamin
Letter respecting Captain Cook.
(*In his* Complete works. London, J. Johnson, 1806. Vol.3, pp.515–17.)
Copies: NPL:M(508/F).   2158

1806 PELHAM, Cavendish
Strictures on the life of Captain James Cook, and on his first and second
(and third) voyages.
(*In his* The World. London, J. Stratford, 1806. Vol.1.)
See also no.2163.
Copies: NPL:R(09:Q909.8A/13); VSL.   2159

1808 GRAVES, *Rev.* John
[Life of Captain James Cook.]
(*In his* History of Cleveland. Carlisle, J. Jollie, pr., 1808. pp.455–64.)
Copies: NPL:M(Q942.74/G); VSL.   2160

1808 RICHARD, Jerome F., *Abbé*
Dispositions des naturels des îles Sandwich: mort funeste de Cook.
(*In his* Voyages chez les peuples sauvages. 2nd ed. Paris, Laurens aîné, 1808. Vol.2,
pp.106–16.)
Copies: NPL:M(*989/R).   2161

1808 RICHARD, Jerome F., *Abbé*
Vols faits par les insulaires . . . sévérité outrée de Cook.
(*In his* Voyages chez les peuples sauvages. 2nd ed. Paris, Laurens aîné, 1808. Vol.2,
pp.371–95.)
Copies: NPL:M(*989/R).   2162

1810 PELHAM, Cavendish
Strictures on the life of . . . Cook, and on his first and second voyages,
[and account of his] Voyage to the Pacific Ocean . . . in the years 1776–
1780.
Illus. map.
(*In his* The World. London, J. Stratford, 1810. Vol.1, pp.141–344.)
See also no.2159.
Copies: NPL:M(Q910.8/7A1).   2163

1813 CHALMERS, Alexander
Cook.
(*In his* General biographical dictionary. London, J. Nichols, 1813. Vol.10, pp.189–204.)
Copies: NPL:M(920/C); NPL:R(DS920/844).   2164

1813 COOK.
(Biographie universelle ancienne et moderne. Paris, 1813. Tome 9, pp.527–36.)
See also no. 2191.
Copies: NPL:R(DS920/607).   2165

1816 CENNI SOPRA Giacomo Cook; [with port.].
(Cook, James—Collected voyages [1816]—Navigazioni. Milano, Sonzogno & Comp.,
1816. Tomo 1, pp.xv–xl.)
Copies: NPL:M(980:Col/22A1).   2166

1817 YOUNG, *Rev.* George
Captain James Cook.
Port.
(*In his* A History of Whitby. Whitby, Clark & Medd, 1817. Vol.2, pp.850–63.)
Copies: NPL:M(942.7/Y); NPL:D(81/79); ANL:F.   2167

1819 CAPTAIN COOK: [a short biographical sketch].
Port.
(*Biographical Magazine;* containing portraits [engraved by W. Holl] of eminent and
ingenious persons of every age and nation, with their lives and characters. London,
1819. Vol.1, p.35.)
Copies: NPL:R(DS920/104).   2168

1820 PRIOR, Samuel, *pseud.*
Captain Cook, 1768–(1780), [by S. Prior, *pseud.* i.e. John Galt].
Illus.
(*In his* All the voyages round the world. London, Sir Richard Phillips, 1820. pp.326–426.)
See also no.2174.
Copies: NPL:M(910.4/P).   2169

[c.1822] CAPTAIN COOK.
pp.4.
Extracts from *The Leisure Hour*, 15th April, 1852, and Counties of England: History and
topography of Yorkshire, about 1822.
Copies: ANL:F.   2170

1824 BIOGRAPHICAL memoir of Captain James Cook.
pp.4.
Prefixed to Cook, James—Collected Voyages—Printed Accounts [1824]—Three voyages
of Captain Cook round the world. London, J. Limbird, 1824.
See also no.2172.
Copies: NPL:M(980:Col/26A1).   2171

1824 CAPTAIN James Cook.
Port. pp.6.
(*In* Smeeton, George—The Unique, [no.] 88. London, the author, [1824].)
Also prefixed to Cook, James—Collected Voyages—Printed Accounts [1824]—Three
voyages of Captain Cook round the world.
See no.2171.
Copies: NPL:M(920/S).   2172

1826 CAPTAIN James Cook: [a brief memoir].
(*Sailor's Magazine and Naval Miscellany.* London, W. Simpkin and R. Marshall. Vol.7,
pp.425–7, Nov.1826.)
Copies: NPL:M(656.505/1).   2173

1827 PRIOR, Samuel, *pseud.*

Captain Cook, 1768–1771; Captain Cook's second voyage, 1772–75; [and] Captain Cook's third voyage, 1776–80, [by S. Prior, *pseud.* i.e. John Galt].

Illus.
(*In his* All the voyages round the world. London, Sir Richard Phillips, 1827. pp.326–426.)
See also no.2169.
Copies: NPL:M(910.4/P); NPL:D(82/181). 2174

1830 COLMAN, George, *the younger*
Random records. London, 1830.

2 vols.
Vol.1, pp.153–98, contains an account of the author's visit to Mulgrave Castle in 1775, with Sir Joseph Banks and Omai, and reference is made, pp.201–2, to Captain Cook's father living at that time at Kirkleatham.
Copies: NPL:M(928.22/C); VSL. 2175

1830 HOWARD, A.
Cook.

Port.
(*In his* Biographical illustrations. London, 1830. pp.69–70.)
Copies: NPL:R(DS920/978). 2176

1832 LOCKER, Edward Hawke
Captain James Cook: [a memoir with portrait, engraving after painting by N. Dance].

(*In his* Naval Gallery of Greenwich Hospital. London, Harding and Lepard, 1831 [i.e. 1832]. pp.16.)
Additional title-page, entitled *Memoirs of celebrated naval commanders*, 1832. Sections have separate pagination.
Copies: NPL:M(Q359.0942/L); NPL:R(C1:W21); ANL. 2177

1832 OCTOBER 27, the birth-day of Captain Cook; [with port.].
(*Penny Magazine*, Oct. 1832, pp.287–8.)
Copies: NPL:R(Q050/P416). 2178

1832 VERREAUX, Jules
Vie de Jacques Cook.

(*In his* L'Océanie en estampes . . . par J. et E. Verreaux. Paris, Librairie Nepveu, 1832. pp.viii–xii.)
Copies: NPL:M(980/V). 2179

1833 COLERIDGE, Hartley
Captain James Cook.

(*In his* Biographia borealis. London, Whitaker, Treacher, 1833. pp.556–664.)
Copies: NPL:M(920.042/C); VSL. 2180

1833 KNIGHT, C.
Cook; [with port.].
(*In his* Gallery of portraits, with memoirs, vol.2, pp.165–74. 1833.)
Copies: NPL:R(C3:W24).   2181

1834 CRAIK, George Lillie
[Captain Cook.]
Port.
(*In his* The Pursuit of knowledge under difficulties. 3rd ed. London, Charles Knight, 1834. Vol.1, pp.131–4.)
See also nos.2193, 2207.
Copies: NPL:R(DS374/18).   2182

1835 MONTÉMONT, Albert
Vita del capitano Cook.
(*In his* Biblioteca universale dei viaggi. Venezia, G. Antonelli, 1835. Vol.5, pp.5–18.)
See also no.2192.
Copies: NPL:M(910.8/M).   2183

1837 CUNNINGHAM, George Godfrey
Captain Cook.
(*In his* Lives of eminent and illustrious Englishmen. Glasgow, 1837. Vol.5, pp.352–60.)
Copies: NPL:R(DS920/1019).   2184

1838 GORTON, John G.
Cook.
(*In his* General biographical dictionary. London. Vol.1, 1838.)
Copies: NPL:R(DS920/124).   2185

1844 HUNT, Robert M.
[Palliser and Cook.]
(*In his* Life of Sir Hugh Palliser. London, Chapman and Hall, 1844. pp.58–123.)
Copies: NPL:M(923.542/P); NPL:R(DS920/P168.4/1); VSL.   2186

1844 ROSE, *Rev.* H.J.
Cook.
(*In his* New general biographical dictionary, vol.6, pp.453–5. 1844.)
Copies: NPL:R(C11:U37).   2187

1846 ORD, J.W.
[Life, etc. of Captain James Cook.]
Port.
(*In his* History and antiquities of Cleveland. London, Simpkin & Marshall, 1846. pp.413. 415, 546–52.)
Copies: NPL:M(Q942.74/0); VSL.   2188

1850 PENROSE, *Rev.* John
From his [Trevenen's] birth to his return in 1780 from the voyage round
the world with Captain Cook.
(*In his* Lives of Sir C.V. Penrose and Captain J. Trevenen. London, J. Murray, 1850.
pp.183–202.)
Copies: NPL:M(923.542/P); ANL; VSL.   2189

1852 COLERIDGE, Hartley
Captain James Cook.
(*In his* Lives of northern worthies. New ed. London, Edward Moxon, 1852. pp.117–288.)
Copies: NPL:M(920.042/C); VSL.   2190

1852 ROSSEL,—
Cook.
(Biographie universelle. Nouvelle éd. Paris, 1852. Tome 9, pp.134–40.)
See also no.2165.
Copies: NPL:R(DS920/659).   2191

1853 MONTÉMONT, Albert
Vie du Capitaine Cook.
Illus. port.
(*In his* Histoire des voyages. Paris, J. Bry, Aîné, 1853. Vol.2, pp.1–3.)
See also no.2183.
Copies: NPL:M(Q910.8/M).   2192

1858 CRAIK, George Lillie
[Captain Cook.]
(*In his* The Pursuit of knowledge under difficulties. New ed. 1858. Vol.1, pp.141–5.)
See also nos.2182, 2207.
Copies: ANL.   2193

1859 SANTIAGO COOK.
(*In* Aventuras historicao-novelescas de un viajero. Madrid, Ayguals de Izeo, 1859.
pp.428–30.)
Copies: NPL:M(910.4/29A1).   2194

[186–] TAYLOR, *Rev.* J.
Cook.
Port.
(*In* Waller, John Francis—Imperial dictionary of universal biography. London, [186–].
Vol.1, [pt.2], pp.112–13.)
Copies: NPL:R(DS920/511).   2195

1866 LACAZE, A. de
Cook; [with bibl.].
(Nouvelle biographie générale, tome 11, pp.686–714. 1866.)
Copies: NPL:R(C7:U11). 2196

1867 SMALES, *Rev.* Gideon
Whitby authors and their publications, with the titles of all the books
printed in Whitby, A.D.670 to A.D.1867. Whitby, Horne & Son, 1867.
Illus. pp.viii, 248.
Contains an account of Cook and his publications, also portrait and other illustrations.
Copies: ANL:F. 2197

1868 MOSSMAN, Samuel
Captain Cook.
Port.
(*In his* Heroes of discovery. Edinburgh, Edmonston & Douglas, 1868. pp.67–135.)
See also no.2201.
Copies: NPL:M(A923.9/M); ANL; VSL. 2198

1869 HAILSTONE, E.
Captain James Cook.
Port.
(*In his* Portraits of Yorkshire worthies. London, 1869. Vol.2, no.143.)
Copies: NPL:R(DS920/980). 2199

[187– —1935 NEWSPAPER CUTTINGS relating to Captain Cook's
voyages, journals, memorials, etc. 187– —1935.]
Copies: NPL:M(Q980:Co1/N1A1–3). 2200

[187–] MOSSMAN, Samuel
Captain Cook.
Port.
(*In his* Heroes of discovery. New ed. Edinburgh, Oliphant, Anderson & Ferrier, [187–].
pp.215–85.)
See also no.2198.
Copies: NPL:M(A923.9/M). 2201

1870 *THE NEW MAGAZINE OF CHOICE PIECES*
Some account of the life and particulars of the death of the late circum-
navigator Captain James Cook; [with frontisp.].
(*In* Vol.2, 1870, pp.372–404.)
Copies: NPL:M(052/11). 2202

1870 SMALES, *Rev.* Gideon
Life of Captain James Cook.

Illus.
(*In* Chapman, George Thomson—Chapman's Centenary memorial of Captain Cook's description of New Zealand. Auckland, Geo. T. Chapman, 1870. pp.154–6.)
Copies: NPL:M(987/84A1).   2203

1873 COOK'S first voyage.

Illus.
(*In* Monarchs of ocean, Columbus and Cook. Edinburgh, Nimmo, 1873. pp.123–227.)
Copies: NPL:M(910.4/119A1).   2204

1873 STODDARD, Charles Warren
The Last of the great navigator.

(*In his* South-Sea idyls. Boston, James R. Osgood, 1873. pp.163–83.)
See also no.2206.
Copies: NPL:M(989/S).   2205

[1874] STODDARD, Charles Warren
The Last of the great navigator.

(*In his* Summer cruising in the South Seas. London, Chatto and Windus, [1874]. pp. 154–66.)
See also no.2205.
Copies: NPL:M(989/S).   2206

1876 CRAIK, George Lillie
[Captain Cook.]

Port.
(*In his* The Pursuit of knowledge under difficulties. New ed. London, George Bell, 1876. pp.91–5.)
See also nos.2182, 2193.
Copies: NPL:R(S374/25).   2207

1879 CAPTAIN COOK; [with port.].
(*Sydney University Magazine*, 1879, pp.193–6, 257–62.)
Copies: NPL:M(059/S).   2208

1879 CAPTAIN COOK'S ACCURACY.
(*Nature*, March 1879, vol.19, pp.408–9.)
Copies: NPL:M(Q505/N); NPL:R(DQ505/1).   2209

1879 COOK.
(Heaton, Sir John Henniker—Australian dictionary of dates. Sydney, George Robertson, 1879. pp.41–3.)
Copies: NPL:M(990.1/25A1); NPL:R(S990.1/10).   2210

1879 SOCIÉTÉ DE GÉOGRAPHIE, *Paris*

Centenaire de la mort de Cook, célébré le 14 février 1879 à l'Hotel de la Société de Géographie. [With bibl.] Paris, Delagrave, 1879.

Map, pp.401–540.

(Société de Géographie—*Bulletin*, Mai, 1879.)

Copies: NPL:M(923.9/C771.2/9A1); NPL:R(S920/C771/9); ANL; QOM; VSL. 2211

1879 WHITMEE, *Rev.* S.J.

Captain Cook's accuracy: [a letter].

(*Nature*, Mar., 1879, vol.19, pp.408–9.)

Copies: NPL:M(Q505/N); NPL:R(DQ505/1) 2212

1881 BLAIR, David

Cook.

(*In his* Cyclopaedia of Australasia. Melbourne, Fergusson & Moore, 1881. pp.86–8.)

Copies: NPL:M(Q990/B); NPL:R(Q990A/21A). 2213

1881 LOW, Charles Rathbone

Captain James Cook.

(*In his* Maritime discovery. London, Newman, 1881. Vol.2, pp.223–65.)

Copies: NPL:M(910.9/L); NPL:R(DS909.8A/91); ANL. 2214

1886 AUTHENTICITY OF SPEECH attributed to Cook by Roderick J. Flanagan.

(McGuanne, John Percy—Press contributions, pp.44–5, 1886–1916.)

Newspaper cutting from *Sydney Morning Herald*, Oct.23, 1886.

Copies: NPL:M(Q991/M). 2215

1887 COOK; [with bibl.].

(Dictionary of national biography. London, Smith Elder and O.U.P., 1887. Vol.12, pp.66–70.)

Copies: NPL:M(920.042/1); NPL:R(920/12). 2216

1890 COOPER, Thompson

Cook.

(*In his* Biographical dictionary. London, 1890. Vol.1, p.437.)

Copies: NPL:R(DS920/924). 2217

1890 SHERRIN, Richard A.A., *and* WALLACE, J. Howard

Captain Cook.

Facs. illus. map, port.

(*In their* Early history of New Zealand. Auckland, H. Brett, 1890. pp.9–13.)

Copies: NPL:M(Q997/12A1); NPL:R(Q997/2). 2218

1892 ROWE, Richard
James Cook.
(*In his* Famous British explorers and navigators. London, C.H. Kelly, 1892. pp.147–83.)
Copies: NPL:M(A923.9/R).   2219

1893 MARTIN, Arthur Patchett
Story of Captain Cook.
(*In his* True stories from Australian history. London, Griffith Farran, 1893. pp.41–56.)
Copies: NPL:M(990/M).   2220

1895 CAPTAIN COOK.
Illus. port.
(Columbus and Cook: the story of their lives, voyages and discoveries. London, W. and R.
Chambers, 1895. pp.82–152.)
Published anonymously.
Copies: NPL:M(910.4/120A1); VSL.   2221

1897 GRIFFITH, George Chetwynd
James Cook, circumnavigator.
Illus.
(*In his* Men who have made the Empire. London, C. Arthur Pearson Ltd., 1897. pp.
119–42.)
Copies: NPL:D(89/667); NPL:R(S920/481).   2222

1898 HALSTEAD, Murat
Early history of the Sandwich Islands.
(*In his* The Story of the Philippines. Chicago, Our Possessions Pub. Co., 1898. pp.375–
404.)
Copies: NPL:M(998.2/30A1).   2223

1899 BECKE, Louis, *and* Jeffrey, Walter
Captain Cook, the discoverer; [with port.].
(*In their* Naval pioneers of Australia. London, Murray, 1899. pp.45–72.)
Copies: NPL:M(990.1/B); NPL:R(S990A/121); ANL.   2224

1901 MAIDEN, Joseph Henry
Two historical notes in regard to Captain Cook the circumnavigator.
The club which, it is believed, partly contributed to his death. Inscriptions
on a mural tablet and gravestone [in the Church of St. Andrew the Great,
Cambridge] commemorating some of Captain Cook's family.
(Royal Society of New South Wales—*Journal*, vol.35, 1901, pp.47–52.)
Copies: NPL:M(506/R); NPL:D(90/213); NPL:R(DS506/9); ANL:F.   2225

[1902?] JAMES COOK.

(*In* Men who have made themselves. London, Blackwood, [1902?]. pp.66–96.)
Copies: NPL:M(920/12A1).   2226

1902 KIRKALDY, A.W.

A Pioneer of discovery: Captain Cook.

(Working Men's College, London—*Journal*, July, 1902, pp.336–9.)
Pam.—Biography, vol.1.
Copies: NPL:R(S920/286).   2227

1904 COOK.

(Encyclopedia Americana, vol.5, 1904.)
Later editions held.
Copies: NPL:R(DS031/60).   2228

1904 WALKER, Frank

Beginnings of history . . . Captain Cook.

(Royal Australian Historical Society—*Journal and Proceedings*, vol.1, pp.173–5, 1904.)
Copies: NPL:M(991/R,Ref.Books); NPL:D(9/69); NPL:R(S991.06/1,Ref.Books).   2229

1905 MILL, Hugh Robert

The Achievement of James Cook; [with bibl.].

Illus. maps, port.
(*In his* The Siege of the South Pole. London, A. Rivers, 1905. pp.56–90.)
Copies: NPL:M(989.8/M); NPL:R(DS999.8A/13); VSL.   2230

1906 COOK and Phillip.

Illus.
(*Chautauquan*, Oct. 1906, pp.172–82.)
Copies: NPL:R(DS050/C499).   2231

1906 HILL, Martha, *Mrs*

Captain Cook.

Map.
(*In* Happy hours for children, by M. Hill and friends. Ser. 4. New ed. Hampstead, Sydney C. Mayle, 1906. pp.78–105.)
Copies: NPL:M(820.8/4B1).   2232

1906 STRIDE, *Rev.* W.K.

James Cook, the discoverer.

(*In his* Empire-builders, 1906.)
Copies: ANL.   2233

1907 MACDONALD, Alexander Cameron
Beginning of Australia.
Map.
(*Victorian Geographical Journal*, vol.25, 1907, pp.13–15.)
Copies: NPL:M(980/R).   2234

1908 CAPTAIN Cook's last days.
(Newspaper cuttings, vol.9, pp.104–5.)
Brisbane Courier, Feb. 15, 1908.
Copies: NPL:M(Q991/N).   2235

1908 FITCHETT, *Rev.* William Henry
Strange pages in Australasian history . . . No. 3, The Man who discovered
Australia; [with port. by Dance].
Illus.
(*Life*, Feb. 1908, pp. 155–61.)
Copies: NPL:M(059/L); NPL:R(S050/L722).   2236

1908 WEATHERILL, Richard
Capt. Cook.
(*In his* Ancient port of Whitby. Whitby, Horne & Son, 1908. pp.383–9.)
Copies: NPL:M(339.7/W); VSL.   2237

1909 FITCHETT, *Rev.* William Henry
Capt. James Cook, the man who discovered Australia.
(*Cornhill Magazine*, Jan. 1909, pp.114–23.)
Copies: NPL:R(S050/C817).   2238

1909 HEAVISIDES, M.
[Career of Captain James Cook and his monument on Easby Heights.]
Illus. port.
(*In his* Rambles in Cleveland, and peeps into the Dales. 3rd ed. Stockton-on-Tees,
Heavisides & Son, 1909. pp.69–77.)
Copies: NPL:M(914.274/H).   2239

[191–?] PIONEERS of intellectual progress; their trials and labours,
and their legacy to the world. London, Ward, [191–?].
Illus. ports. pp.193–416.
(*Ward and Lock's national library of interesting and instructive reading.*)
Includes chapter on Cook.
Copies: ANL.   2240

[1910] COOK.
(Nelson's Encyclopaedia. London, [1910]. Vol.3, p.307.)
Copies: NPL:R(DS032/6).   2241

1910 COOK; [with bibl.].
(Encyclopaedia Britannica, 1910. Vol.7, pp.71–2.)
Copies: NPL:R(Q032/157).   2242

1910 GOSLING, W.
Captain Cook's survey of Newfoundland and Labrador.
(*In his* Labrador. London, 1910. pp.197–9, 257.)
Copies: NPL:R(S971.9A/5).   2243

1910 MORGAN, *Rev.* James
Cooke's charity: [bequest by Mrs Cook].
(*In his* Short history of the Church of St. Andrew the Great, Cambridge. Cambridge,
Daily News, 1910. pp.46–7.)
Copies: NPL:M(283.42/M).   2244

[1912] CAPTAIN Cook monument [Whitby], with biographical sketch of
the great circumnavigator and a short account of the unveiling ceremony,
[Oct.2, 1912]. Whitby, Horne and Son, Ye Abbey Press, [1912].
Illus. ports. pp.33.
Copies: NPL:M(923.9/C771.2/16A1); NPL:D(91/998); ANL:F; VSL.   2245

1912 LONG, Charles Richard
Cook, the greatest of English navigators.
(*In* Long, C.R. *and* Wallace, G.M.—Notable deeds of famous men and women.
Melbourne, George Robertson, 1912. pp.126–35.)
Written for Grade III children attending Victorian schools.
Copies: NPL:M(904/12A1).   2246

1913 FITCHETT, *Rev.* William Henry
The Man who discovered Australia; [and] Mapping the Australian
coast. [With port.]
(*In his* New world of the south. London, G. Bell, 1913. pp.43–70.)
Copies: NPL:M(990.1/F).   2247

[1913] MEE, *Sir* Arthur
Captain James Cook.
Illus.
(*In his* Popular science. London, Educational Book Co., [1913]. Vol.7, pp.4525–8.)
Harmsworth Popular Science.
Copies: NPL:R(S503/8).   2248

1914 ALLAN, H.O.
The Captain Cook statue, St. Kilda beach . . . unveiling ceremony,
Dec. 7, 1914 . . . With a short memoir of the great circumnavigator.
Melbourne, Osboldstone & Co., pr., [1914].
Copies: VSL.   2249

1914 COOK.
(New International Encyclopaedia. 2nd ed. New York, 1914. Vol.6, pp.28–9.)
Copies: NPL:R(DS031/81). 2250

1914 WATSON, James Henry
Captain James Cook and his officers. [Extract from *Sydney Morning Herald*, Ap. 25, 1914.]
(Newspaper cuttings, vol.36, pp.14–15.)
Copies: NPL:M(Q991/N). 2251

[1916] SAMWELL, David
Some particulars concerning the life and character of Captain Cook.
Port.
(*In his* Narrative of the death of Captain James Cook. [1916]. pp.18–21.)
Hawaiian Historical Society—*Reprints*, no.2.
See also nos.2144, 2145, 2332.
Copies: NPL:M(923.9/C771.2/1C1). 2252

1917 HUNTER, Percy
Captain Cook and Australia.
Illus.
(*Mid-Pacific Magazine*, Aug. 1917, pp.112–17.)
Copies: NPL:M(Q059/6). 2253

[1918] COURTNEY, William Leonard, *and* COURTNEY, J.E.
Captain James Cook and the early explorers.
(*In their* Pillars of empire. London, Jarrolds, [1918]. pp.193–200.)
Copies: NPL:M(923.2/C); VSL. 2254

[192–] MISCELLANEOUS manuscript and printed biographical articles about Cook; collected by Sir William Dixson.
Illus. ports. maps, pp.376.
Volume compiled in Library. Includes notes and comments by Hugh Gunn, G. F. Jeanes, W. Basil Worsfeld and others, from the *United Empire Journal* 1928–1935, and the *Navy League Journal* Feb. 1927.
Copies: NPL:D(MS.Q144). 2255

[1920] COOK: [biographical sketch].
Port.
(Harmsworth's Universal Encyclopedia, vol.3, p.2241. [1920].)
Copies: NPL:R(S030/8). 2256

1920 RHODES, *Rev. B.*
Captain Cook at Great Ayton.
(Newspaper cuttings, vol.17, p.21. *Sydney Morning Herald*, June 18, 1920.)
Copies: NPL:M(Q991/N). 2257

1921 MARKHAM, *Sir* Clements Robert
Captain Cook; Bellingshausen.
(*In his* The Lands of silence: a history of Arctic and Antarctic exploration. Cambridge,
U.P., 1921. pp.394–6.)
Copies: NPL:M(989.8/M); ANL.   2258

1922 WOOD, George Arnold
Voyage of the *Endeavour*, etc.; [with bibl. and port.].
Illus. maps.
(*In his* Discovery of Australia. London, Macmillan, 1922. pp.380–479.)
Copies: NPL:M(980.1/125A1).   2259

1923 BROOMFIELD, Frederick John
The Tragic story of Captain Cook's family.
Illus.
(*Pacific*, Sept.14, 1923, pp.28–9.)
Copies: NPL:M(MDQ079/124).   2260

1923 FILDES, Horace Edward Manners
Some common errors concerning Captain Cook.
(*Pacific*, Nov.2, 1923, p.31.)
Copies: NPL:M(MDQ079/124).   2261

[1923] MOERNER, Carl Birger, *Count*
Cook.
Illus. port.
(*In his* Söderhavet. Uppsala, J.A. Lindblads Förlag, [1923]. Del. 1, pp.40–53.)
Copies: NPL:M(980/M).   2262

1924 ADRIAN, Frederick Gregory
Cook's attitude to Australia.
(Royal Australian Historical Society—*Journal and Proceedings*, vol.10, 1924. pp.121–30.)
Copies: NPL:M(991/R,Ref.Books); NPL:D(9/69); NPL:R(S991.06/1,Ref.Books).   2263

1924 CARRUTHERS, *Sir* Joseph Hector McNeil
Captain Cook in Hawaii.
(Newspaper cuttings, vol.165, pp.70–1, 1923–4.)
Sydney Morning Herald, Oct.10, 1924.
Copies: NPL:M(Q991/N).   2264

1924 WATSON, James Henry
Captain Cook.
Illus.
(*Navy League Journal*, Ap. 1924, pp.3–5.)
Copies: NPL:M(359.06/N).   2265

1925 COOK.
(Illustrated Chambers's Encyclopaedia. London, 1925. Vol.3, p.447.)
Copies: NPL:M(Q032/3H3); NPL:R(Q032/3A).   2266

1925 DORLING, Henry Taprell
Captain James Cook.
Illus. map.
(*In his* Sea venturers of Britain, by Taffrail, *pseud.* [i.e. H. Taprell Dorling]. Illus. by
C. King. London, Collins, 1925. pp.176–207.)
See also nos.2288, 2292.
Copies: NPL:M(Nichols Coll.); NPL:R(S909.8A/10).   2267

1925 DUNLOP, Norman John
James Cook and the Australian medical harbingers.
(*Medical Journal of Australia*, Sydney, Sept.1925, pp.362–73.)
Copies: NPL:M(Q610.5/M); NPL:R(DQ610.6/2); ANL:F(reprint).   2268

1925 WILLIAMSON, James Alexander
Captain James Cook, the pioneer of the Pacific Ocean.
Illus. maps, port.
(*In his* Builders of the Empire. Oxford, Clarendon Press, 1925. Chapter 4, pt. 2.)
See also no.2313.
Copies: ANL.   2269

1926 JONES, John A. Rupert
Captain James Cook as hydrographical surveyor.
(*Notes and Queries*, vol.151, 1926, Nov.6–27, pp.327–330, 345–7, 365–7, 384–6; Dec.11,
p.427.)
Copies: NPL:R(DS050/N911).   2270

1926 KITCHIN, Frederick Harcourt (Bennet Copplestone)
Some great moments.
(*In his* Dead men's tales. 1926. Chapter 3.)
Copies: ANL.   2271

1926 KUYKENDALL, Ralph Simpson
Captain Cook and the discovery of the Hawaiian Islands.
(*In his* A History of Hawaii. New York, Macmillan, 1926. pp.52–61.)
See also no.2298.
Copies: NPL:M(999.6/16A1); NPL:D(92/278); NPL:R(DS999.6A/9).   2272

[1926?] SCHULTZ-EWERTH, Erich
Erinnerungen an Samoa; [with bibl.]. Berlin, A. Scherl, [1926?].
Illus. port. pp.[ii], 171.
With references to Captain Cook.
Copies: NPL:M(989.4/S); ANL.   2273

1927 BAYLDON, Francis Joseph
Cook.
(Australian encyclopaedia. Sydney, A. & R., 1927. Vol.1, pp.304–9.)
Copies: NPL:M(Q039/A,Ref.Books); NPL:R(Q 990.1A/17).   2274

1927 BAYLDON, Francis Joseph
Dalrymple's relations with Cook.
(Royal Australian Historical Society—*Journal and Proceedings*, vol.13, 1927. pp.51–3.)
Copies: NPL:M(991/R,Ref.Books); NPL:D(9/69); NPL:R(S991.06/1,Ref.Books). 2275

1927 BERGER, Arthur
James Cook und die alte Königssage.
(*In his* Auf den Inseln des ewigen Frühlings; [no.]12, 1927.)
Copies: ANL.   2276

1927 WILLIAMS, William, *Bishop of Waiapu*
Cook's visit in light of Maori tradition.
Illus. map, port.
(*Gisborne Times*—Joint golden jubilees. Gisborne, N.Z., Gisborne Pub. Co., 1927. pp. 3–12.)
Copies: NPL:M(997.5/G).   2277

1927–8 PRICE, Archibald Grenfell
Captain James Cook, (bicentennial address).
(Royal Geographical Society of Australasia—South Australian Branch—*Proceedings*, vol.29, 1927–8, pp.22–9.)
Copies: NPL:M(980/R).   2278

1928 ANDERSON, Charles
Bicentenary of the birth of Captain James Cook.
Facs. illus. port.
(*Australian Museum Magazine*, Sydney, vol. 3, Oct./Dec. 1928, pp. 257–61.)
Copies: NPL:M(507/A); NPL:D(92/488); NPL:R(S590.6/17).   2279

1928 BAYLDON, Francis Joseph
Captain Cook, from a navigator's point of view. An address given to the Geographical Society of N.S.W. 11 Dec. 1928.
ff.9.
MS. carbon.
Copies: NPL:D(MS.Q144).   2280

1928 BICENTENARY of Captain Cook: [a short account of his life].
(*Nature*, Sept.29, 1928, pp.484–6.)
Copies: NPL:R(Q505/1).   2281

1928 DAVIDGE, J.L.
The Columbus of the Pacific: bicentenary of Captain Cook. [With port. and picture of the *Endeavour*.]
(*Advance Australia*, Sept.1, 1928, pp.5–9.)
Copies: NPL:M(Q059/A).   2282

1928 DAWSON, Warren Royal
Captain Cook: the bicentenary of a great navigator.
Facs. illus. port. pp.4.
Supplement to *Lloyd's List and Shipping Register*, Oct. 25, 1928.
Copies: NPL:M(Newscuttings File).   2283

1928 HANNAY, David
James Cook.
(*Blackwood's Magazine*, vol. 224, July–Dec., 1928, pp.483–504.)
Copies: NPL:R(DS050/B632).   2284

1928 HANNAY, David
'James Cook'.
ff.16, cm 23.5.
Extract from *Blackwood's Magazine* Oct.1928, pp.483–98.
Copies: NPL:D(MS.Q144).   2285

1928 PEEL, E.H. Hiley-
James Cook, Captain, R.N.
(Captain Cook Bi-centenary Celebrations, *Cleveland*, 1928—Souvenir, 1928. pp.9–13.)
Copies: NPL:M(Q923.9/C771.2/4A1); NPL:D(Q92/164); QOM; QU.   2286

1928 SOMERVILLE, Henry Boyle Townshend
[Captain Cook's family.]
(*In his* The Chart-makers. Edinburgh, W. Blackwood, 1928. pp.108–11.)
Copies: NPL:M(980/S).   2287

1929 DORLING, Henry Taprell
Captain James Cook.
(*In his* Sea venturers of Britain, by Taffrail, *pseud.* [i.e. H. Taprell Dorling]. London, P. Allan, 1929. pp.167–94.)
See also nos.2267, 2292.
Copies: NPL:M(Nichols Coll.).   2288

1929 NEWBOLT, *Sir* Henry
Captain James Cook and the Sandwich Islands.
(*In* Taylor, Albert Pierce—Sesquicentennial celebrations of Captain Cook's discovery of Hawaii, 1778–1928. Honolulu, Capt. Cook Sesquicentennial Commission, 1929. pp.58–61.)
Copies: NPL:M(Q980:Co4/T1A1).   2289

1929 NEWBOLT, *Sir* Henry
Captain James Cook and the Sandwich Islands; [with port. and discussion].
(*Geographical Journal*, vol.73, Feb. 1929, pp.97–101, 119–22.)
Paper contributed to the celebrations at Honolulu, Aug. 1928.
Copies: NPL:M(980:Co1/G1A1).   2290

1929 TAYLOR, Albert Pierce
Sesquicentennial celebrations of Captain Cook's discovery of Hawaii, 1778–1928. Honolulu, 1929.
Illus. pp.vii, 105.
(Hawaii—Board of Commissioners of Public Archives—*Archives of Hawaii*, pub. 4.)
Copies: NPL:M(Q980:Co4/T1A1); Captain Cook's Landing Place Trust; VSL.   2291

[193–?] DORLING, Henry Taprell
Captain James Cook.
(*In his* Sea venturers, [by] Taffrail, *pseud* . . . H. Taprell Dorling. London, Collins Clear-Type Press, [193–?]. pp.177–208.)
See also no.2267, 2288.
Copies: NPL:M(923.9/3C1).   2292

1930 STOKES, John F.G.
Origin of the condemnation of Captain Cook in Hawaii; [with bibl.]. Honolulu, 1930.
Reprint from Hawaiian Historical Society—*Annual report*, 39, 1930. pp.68–104.
Copies: NPL:M(923.9/C771.2/18A1); NPL:D(93/295); VSL.   2293

[1931] MACKENZIE, Donald Alexander
Worship of Captain Cook as white god.
(*In his* Myths and traditions of the South Sea islands. [1931.] Chapter 21.)
Copies: ANL.   2294

1931 MARGUET, Frédéric Philippe
James Cook.
(*In his* Histoire générale de la navigation. Paris, 1931. various pp.)
Copies: NPL:R(09:S909.9A/19).   2295

1932 DU PUY, William Atherton
[Cook's visit to Hawaii, 1778; with illus. of the monument to Captain Cook.]
(*In his* Hawaii and its race problem. Washington, U.S. Govt. Printing Office, 1932. pp.7–9.)
Copy: NPL:R(DS999.6A/11).   2296

1932 MUNDY, P.D.
Parents of Captain Cook: [entry of the marriage of James Cook and Grace Vace, in the parish register of Stainton-in-Cleveland, Oct.5, 1725].
(*Notes and Queries*, vol.162, Mar.5, 1932, p.175.)
Copies: NPL:R(DS050/N911).   2297

1933 KUYKENDALL, Ralph Simpson
Captain Cook and the discovery of the Hawaiian Islands.
(*In his* A History of Hawaii. New York, Macmillan, 1933. pp.52–61.)
See also no.2272.
Copies: NPL:M(999.6/16A2).   2298

1934 LONG, Charles Richard
Cook, the greatest of navigators.
(*In his* British worthies and other men of might. Melbourne, Robertson & Mullens, 1934. pp.87–96.)
Copies: NPL:M(920/10A1).   2299

1935 BLEDISLOE, Charles Bathurst, *1st Baron*
Captain James Cook, R.N.
Illus.
(*In his* Ideals of nationhood. New Plymouth, T. Avery, 1935. pp.119–24.)
See also no.2311.
Copies: NPL:M(A825/B646/1A1).   2300

1935 SEYDEWITZ, M.
James Cook.
(*In her* Eminent Englishmen, III: great explorers. Leipzig, Teubner, 1935.)
Copies: VSL.   2301

1936 CRESSWELL, M.
Captain James Cook, 1728–1779.
Illus. map, port.
(*Marine Observer*, London, 1936, Jan. pp.10–14; Feb. pp.51–3.)
Copies: NPL:R(Q551.506/4).   2302

[1936] ROBINSON, Gregory
Captain Cook.
(*In his* Ships that have made history. London, P. Davies & L. Dickson, [1936]. pp.137–53.)
Copies: NPL:M(656.509/R).   2303

1936 WOLLSCHLAEGER, Alfred (A.E. Johann, *pseud.*)
James Cook.
Map.
(*In his* Känguruhs, Kopra und Korallen. Berlin, Ullstein, 1936. pp.222–42.)
See also no.2309.
Copies: NPL:M(980/144A1). 2304

[1937] KEARTON, Cherry
Dedicated to Captain Cook; [with port.].
Illus.
(*In her* I visit the Antipodes. London, Jarrolds, [1937]. pp.11–18.)
Copies: NPL:M(980/K); ANL. 2305

1937 PERCY, W.S.
Yorkshire wool, and Captain Cook.
(*In his* The Empire comes home. London, Collins, 1937. pp.83–96.)
Copies: NPL:M(914.2/8A1). 2306

1937 PLOMER, William Charles Franklyn
Captain Cook.
(*In* Dobrée, Bonamy—From Anne to Victoria: essays by various hands. 1937. pp.290–300.)
Copies: ANL. 2307

1937 WAGNER, Henry Raup
The Voyage of Captain Cook, 1776–1780.
(*In his* The Cartography of the northwest coast of America to the year 1800, [by] H.R. Wagner; [with bibl. and descriptive lists of maps and place names still in use and obsolete place names]. Berkeley, Univ. Calif. Press, 1937. Vol.1, pp.183–90.)
Copies: NPL:R(Q970A/10). 2308

1937 WOLLSCHLAEGER, Alfred (A.E. Johann, *pseud.*)
James Cook; [with bibl. notes].
Map.
(*In his* Känguruhs, Kopra och Korallen. Stockholm, Lindqvists, 1937. pp.247–68.)
See also no.2304.
Copies: NPL:M(980/144B1). 2309

1938 KETTLEWELL, Robert Mountjoy
Cleveland village, being notes by R. Kettlewell on some of the records of the parish of Great Ayton, mainly the churchwarden's book, 1734–1844; to which is added a chapter by J. Fairfax-Blakeborough on village lore. Redcar, Yorks., Albert Cooper, 1938.
Illus. ports. pp.[vi], 118.
Includes biographical information on Cook.
Copies: NPL:M(942.74/1A1). 2310

1940 BLEDISLOE, Charles Bathurst, *1st Baron*
Captain James Cook.
(*In his* Ideals of nationhood. New Plymouth, T. Avery, 1940. pp.115–20.)
See also no.2300.
Copies: NPL:M(A825/B646/1B1).   2311

1942 WALTON, John
Captain Cook.
Map.
(*In his* Six explorers. London, O.U.P., 1942. pp.22–31.)
Living names.
Copies: NPL:M(910/W).   2312

1942 WILLIAMSON, James Alexander
Captain James Cook: the pioneer of the Pacific Ocean.
Illus. maps, port.
(*In his* Builders of the Empire. Oxford, Clarendon Press, 1942. pp.125–41.)
Reprint of 1925 edition, no.2269.
Copies: NPL:M(923.9/W).   2313

1948 GRIFFITHS, William Arthur
The Circumnavigators, Cook and Hunter.
(*In his* Pawns of history, pp.108–13.)
Typescript, 1948.
Copies: NPL:M(MSS Dept.A3098).   2314

1948 McCRAE, Hugh Raymond
James Cook: [biographical sketch, and account of a letter-weight made
from the timbers of the *Endeavour* and presented by him to Capt. Blair,
R.N.].
(*In his* Story-book only. Sydney, A. & R., 1948. pp.243–5.)
Copies: NPL:M(A828/M132.2/1A1).   2315

1949 JAMES COOK, 1728–79; [with reproduction in colour of painting
by E. Phillips Fox.]
(*National Geographical Magazine*, vol.95, pp.498–9, Ap.1949.)
Copies: NPL:R(S909.6A/6).   2316

1950 ACRES, W. Marston
Captain James Cook's family: [his mother and brother].
(*Notes and Queries*, vol.195, p.328, July 22, 1950.)
Copies: NPL:R(DS050/N911).   2317

1950 FYNMORE, A.H.W.
Captain James Cook's family: [his parents and brother].
(Notes and Queries, vol.195, Aug.5, 1950, p.349.)
Copies: NPL:R(DS050/N911). 2318

1950 HOLMES, *Sir* Maurice
Captain James Cook's family.
(Notes and Queries, vol.195, p.393, Sept.1950.)
Copies: NPL:R(DS050/N911). 2319

1951 DOBSON, E. Philip
The Boyhood of Captain Cook.
Illus.
(Geographical Magazine, London, vol.23, pp.512–20, Mar. 1951.)
Copies: NPL:R(S909.5A/5). 2320

1952 BOWEN, Frank Charles
Captain James Cook, 1728–1779; [with port.].
(In his Men of the wooden walls. London, Staples, 1952. pp.69–71, 76.)
Copies: NPL:M(359.0942/3A1). 2321

1952 LLOYD, Christopher
Captain Cook's wife.
(Mariner's Mirror, vol.38, pp.230–1, Aug. 1952.)
Copies: NPL:R(DS656.506/7). 2322

1953 SKELTON, Raleigh Ashlin
Captain Cook's wife.
(Mariner's Mirror, vol.39, pp.62–3, Feb. 1953.)
Copies: NPL:R(DS656.506/7). 2323

[1954] DIVINE, Arthur Durham
Captain James Cook.
(In his Six great explorers. [1954]. pp.46–84.)
Copies: ANL. 2324

1954 SKELTON, Raleigh Ashlin
Captain James Cook as a hydrographer: [lecture to Society for Nautical Research. With bibl.]
Plans, port.
(Mariner's Mirror, vol.40, pp.92–119, May 1954.)
Copies: NPL:R(DS656.506/7). 2325

1954 SKELTON, Raleigh Ashlin
Captain James Cook as a hydrographer.
Charts, diag. port. pp.92–119.
Author's presentation copy.
Reprint from *Mariner's Mirror*, vol.40, no.2, Nov. 1954.
Copies: NPL:M(980:Co1/52A1); NPL:D(9/72); NPL:R(DS656.506/7).   2326

1955 LEGGETT, George R.
Captain James Cook: [outline of a talk given at Cook's cottage on Australia Day 1955].
Illus.
(*Educational Magazine*, vol.12, no.3, pp.130–2, Ap.1955.)
Copies: NPL:M(371.306/2).   2327

1955 PIKE, L.H.
The Captain Cook story: facts and fictions.
Illus. port.
(*Australia and New Zealand Weekly*, vol.85, pp.4–5, 16, Oct.22, 1955.)
Copies: NPL:M(Q980.105/10).   2328

1956 BEAGLEHOLE, John Cawte
On the character of Captain James Cook.
Illus. port.
(*Geographical Journal*, London, vol.122, pp.417–29, Dec. 1956.)
Copies: NPL:R(DS909.6A/2).   2329

1956 SHARP, Charles Andrew
Captain Cook's forgotten theory.
(*In his* Ancient voyagers in the Pacific. Wellington, Polynesian Society, 1956. pp.1–15.)
See also no.2333.
Copies: NPL:M(572.999/2A1).   2330

1956 VILLIERS, Alan John
The Noblest of them all.
Illus.
(*In his* Pioneers of the seven seas. London, Routledge & Kegan Paul, 1956. pp.78–85.)
Copies: NPL:M(656.509/V).   2331

1957 SAMWELL, David
Some particulars concerning the life and character of Captain Cook. [With port. from painting by N. Dance, engraved by J.K. Sherwin.]
(*In his* Captain Cook and Hawaii: a narrative by D. Samwell. With an introduction by Sir Maurice Holmes. San Francisco, David Magee, 1957. pp.27–34.)
See also nos.2144–5, 2252.
Copies: NPL:M(923.9/C771.2/1D1).   2332

1957 SHARP, Charles Andrew
Captain Cook's forgotten theory.
(*In his* Ancient voyagers in the Pacific. Harmondsworth, Penguin, 1957. pp.11–31.)
See also no.2330.
Copies: NPL:M(572.999/2B1).   2333

1957 VILLIERS, Alan John
James Cook, seaman.
(*Quadrant*, vol.1, pp.7–16. Summer 1956.7.)
Copies: NPL:M(059/44).   2334

1957 WOOD, G. Bernard
Whitby recalls its past.
Illus.
(*Trident*, vol.19, pp.353–5, Aug.8, 1957.)
Copies: NPL:M(Q656.505/1).   2335

[1959] COX, Clarice
Captain Cook: the man history forgot.
Illus.
(*Paradise*, vol.71, pp.105–10 [Nov.1959] Holiday annual.)
Copies: NPL:M(Q989.605/1).   2336

1960 HALL, Willis and EVANS, I.O.
In Southern seas.
Illus.
(*In their* They found the world. London, Warne, 1960. pp.68–80.)
Copies: NPL:M(910.9/5A1).   2337

1961 WARNER, Oliver Martin Wilson
Cook.
Port.
(*In his* Great seamen. London, Bell, 1961. pp.82–115.)
Copies: NPL:M(926.56/1A1); NPL:R(920/1196).   2338

1962 LITTLE, C.H.
Captain Cook in Canada.
Illus. maps, port.
(*Canadian Geographical Journal*, vol.64, pp.188–97, June 1962.)
Copies: NPL:R(NQ910.6/1).   2339

1962 MAY, William Edward
The Sons of Captain Cook.
(*Mariner's Mirror*, vol.48, pp.308–309, Nov.1962.)
Copies: NPL:R(N387.06/2).   2340

1963 HOPKINS, R.W.
Captain Cook and St. Margaret's, Barking. [With bibl.].
(*Ancestor*, vol.3, p.21, Mar. 1963.)
Copies: NPL:M(Q929.106/2). 2341

1966 CURTIS, Caroline
Captain James Cook, 1728–1779.
Port.
(*In her* Builders of Hawaii. Honolulu, Kamehameha Schools Press, 1966. pp.5–16.)
Copies: NPL:M(999.6/48A1). 2342

1966 PEATTIE, Donald Culross
Captain Cook—discoverer supreme.
(*Australasian Manufacturer*, vol.51, pp.8–9, July 30, 1966.)
Copies: NPL:M(MDQ338.05/2); NPL:R(NF670.5/1); ANL. 2343

1966 PEATTIE, Donald Culross
Discoverer supreme: [Captain James Cook].
Illus. map, port.
(*In* Reader's Digest Association Pty. Ltd.—Great lives, great deeds. Sydney, the Association, 1966. pp.365–71.)
Copies: NPL:M(920.02/7A1). 2344

1968 GOURGEY, Brenda
Inspiration of Captain Cook.
Facs. illus. map, port.
(*Geographical Magazine*, London, vol.40, no.16, pp.1356–60, Aug. 1968.)
Copies: NPL:R(N910.5/1). 2345

1968 NAISH, George Prideaux Brabant
Cook as a navigator.
Illus. one in colour.
(*Endeavour*, vol.27, pp.38–41, Jan.1968.)
Copies: NPL:R(NQ505/7). 2346

1968 SKELTON, Raleigh Ashlin
Cook's contribution to marine survey.
Illus. maps.
(*Endeavour*, vol.27, pp.28–32, Jan.1968.)
Copies: NPL:R(NQ505/7). 2347

1968 TAYLOR, Eva Germaine Rimington
Navigation in the days of Captain Cook.
(Institute of Navigation, London—*Journal*. Vol.21, no.3, pp.256–76, July 1968.)
Copies: NPL:R(N623.8906/2). 2348

n.d. CAPTAIN COOK: cottage purchased for Victoria. [Newspaper cuttings.]

Copies: NPL:M(Q980:Co1/N2A1).

2349

CELEBRATIONS

See also the heading *Personal – Monuments.*

1868 DYER, Joseph

Proposal for a Grand International Exhibition to be held in Sydney in 1870, to celebrate the centenary of the discovery and taking possession of Australia in 1770, by Captain Cook. Sydney, 1868.

Extract from *Sydney Morning Herald*, Oct.1868.

Copies: NPL:M(042/P64).

2350

[187–?] WILSON, George Washington

A Trip to the paradise of the Pacific: the great Hawaiian volcano and the lepers' home. A reading, descriptive of a series of lantern slides; [by G.W. Wilson]. Aberdeen, J. Avery, pr., [187–?].

pp.28.

Copies: NPL:D(87/784, Pam.).

2351

1870 CHAPMAN'S centenary memorial of Captain Cook's description of New Zealand one hundred years ago. Auckland, Geo. T. Chapman, 1870.

Facs. illus. charts, pp.160, [iv].

A condensed account of Cook's three voyages, with a short biography and reprints of Cook's charts of New Zealand.

Copies: NPL:M(987/84A1); NPL:D(87/138); NPL:R(S997A/73); ANL; QOM; QU; VSL.

2352

1879 CAPTAIN COOK, [and the centenary of his death, by the Geographical Society of Paris].

(*Nature*, Feb.13, 1879, pp.334–5.)

Copies: NPL:M(Q505/N); NPL:R(DQ505/1).

2353

1879 GEOGRAPHICAL Society of Paris: (special meeting, centenary of the death of Captain Cook).

(Royal Geographical Society, London—*Proceedings*. Mar. 1879, pp.219–220.)

Copies: NPL:R(S909.6A/1).

2354

1879 HALLORAN, Henry

The Unveiling of the Captain Cook statue: an exultant ode. N.p., 1879.

pp.3.

Copies: NPL:D(87/263).

2355

1899 NEW SOUTH WALES—Department of Lands

Dedication of Captain Cook's landing place, Kurnell, Botany Bay . . . (May 6), 1899. Sydney, Govt. Pr., 1899.

Illus. map, port. pp.74.

Cover title: *Kurnell, the landing place of Captain Cook, 1770.*

Copies: NPL:M(991.1/N); NPL:D(89/1236); NPL:R(S920/C771/7); ANL.   2356

1899 [PROGRAMME]: dedication of Captain Cook's landing place, Saturday, 6th May, 1899. Sydney, Govt. Pr., 1899.

pp.4.

Copies: ANL:F.   2357

1899 YARRINGTON, *Rev.* William Henry Hazell

Kurnell, Botany Bay. A memento of the dedication, May 6th, 1899. [A poem.] Sydney, Turner & Henderson, 1899.

pp.7.

Copies: NPL:M(A821/Y).   2358

1899 YARRINGTON, *Rev.* William Henry Hazell

University prize poem: Captain Cook meditating on Australia's future . . . Memento of the dedication at Kurnell . . . Ap.28th, 1899, Cook Anniversary Day. Sydney, Turner & Henderson, 1899.

pp.7.

Copies: NPL:M(A821/Y); NPL:D; ANL:F.   2359

[19—?] YARRINGTON, *Rev.* William Henry Hazell

University prize poem: Captain Cook meditating on Australia's future.

(*In* Memento veteris aevi, 1859. Sydney, *A.C. World*, pr., [19—?]. pp.6–8.)

Copies: NPL:M(378.91/20A1).   2360

1901 BLADEN, Frank Murcott

The Landing of Lieutenant James Cook, R.N., at Botany Bay. Sydney, Govt.Pr., 1901.

Facs. illus. ports. pp.32.

Includes the landing of Captain Cook, R.N., Botany Bay, 1770, as produced in connection with the Commonwealth celebrations at Kurnell, Botany Bay . . . 7th January, 1901, by W.H.Yarrington.

Copies: ANL.   2361

1901 LANDING of Captain Cook, R.N., at Botany Bay: (official programme) [of the celebration] on Monday, 7th January, 1901. Sydney, Govt. Pr., [1901].

pp.4.

A feature of the Commonwealth celebrations, Sydney.

Copies: ANL:F.   2362

1901 NEW SOUTH WALES—Government Printing Office
The Landing of Lieutenant James Cook, R.N., at Botany Bay: [an account of Cook's landing in 1770, the dedication of Kurnell as a public park in 1899, and the Commonwealth celebrations there in 1901]. Sydney, Govt. Pr., 1901.
Illus. pp.32.
Copies: NPL:M(991.1/6A1); NPL:D(90/1497); NPL:R(S991/28); ANL; VSL.   2363

1901 YARRINGTON, *Rev.* William Henry Hazell
The Landing of Captain James Cook, R.N., Botany Bay, 1770: [a play in verse, by W.H.H. Yarrington. Composed for the Commonwealth celebrations at Kurnell, 7 Jan. 1901.]
(*In* N.S.W.—Government Printing Office—The Landing of Lieutenant James Cook. Sydney, Govt.Pr., 1901. pp.17–32.)
Copies: NPL:M(991.1/61A1); NPL:D(90/1497); NPL:R(S991/28); ANL; VSL.   2364

1905 BLADEN, Frank Murcott
Captain Cook's landing place at Botany Bay. [Extract from *Daily Telegraph*, Nov.4, 1905.]
(Newspaper cuttings, vol.113, pp.45–6.)
Copies: NPL:M(Q991/N).   2365

1905 CAPTAIN COOK: anniversary of his landing celebrated. [Extract from the *Australian Star*, Ap.28, 1905.]
(Newspaper cuttings, vol.4, pp.49–51.)
Copies: NPL:M(Q991/N).   2366

1905–6 [CAPTAIN COOK'S landing: anniversary celebrations, 1905–6. Extracts from Sydney newspapers.]
Illus.
(Watson, James Henry—Scrap-book, vol.3, 1905–9, pp.2–2A, 4–4A.)
Copies: NPL:M(F990.1/W).   2367

1907 CAPTAIN COOK'S landing: celebration of 137th anniversary. [Extract from the *Sydney Morning Herald*, Ap.29, 1907.]
(Newspaper cuttings, vol.7, pp.91–2.)
Copies: NPL:M(Q991/N).   2368

1907 YARRINGTON, *Rev.* William Henry Hazell
University prize poem: Captain Cook meditating on Australia's future . . . Kurnell, La Perouse and Commonwealth verses. Sydney, Turner & Henderson, 1907.
Illus. pp.16.
Copies: NPL:M(A821/Y).   2369

1908 138TH ANNIVERSARY of the landing of Captain Cook at Botany Bay, Tuesday, 28th April, 1908. Sydney, Govt. Pr., 1908.
pp.4.
Inserted is a card of invitation to the ceremony.
Copies: ANL:F.
2370

1908 YARRINGTON, *Rev.* William Henry Hazell
The Landing of Captain James Cook, R.N., Botany Bay, 1770. [A play in verse] as produced in connection with the Commonwealth celebrations at Kurnell . . . 7th Jan. 1901, by Rev. W.H.H. Yarrington. Sydney, Henderson, 1908.
Illus. ports. pp.14, [ii].
Copies: NPL:M(923.9/C771.2/15A1).
2371

[1908] YORKSHIRE SOCIETY OF NEW SOUTH WALES
[Handbook including Notes on Yorkshire, by E. Kilburn Scott, rules and regulations, 1907–8.] Sydney, S. D. Townsend, pr., [1908].
Illus. ff.[12].
One of the objects of the Society was to take part in the celebration of the anniversary of Cook's landing in Australia.
Copies: NPL:D(90/1510).
2372

1909 YARRINGTON, *Rev.* William Henry Hazell
The Landing of Captain James Cook, R.N., Botany Bay, 1770. [A play in verse] as produced in connection with the Commonwealth celebrations at Kurnell . . . 7th Jan. 1901, by Rev. W.H.H. Yarrington. Sydney, Turner & Henderson, 1909.
Illus. ports. pp.23.
Bound with 1908 edition.
Copies: NPL:M(923.9/C771.2/15A1).
2373

1916 YARRINGTON, *Rev.* William Henry Hazell
University prize poem: Captain Cook meditating on Australia's future. Delivered at the opening of the Great Hall of the Sydney University, July 18th, 1859. Sydney, *A. C. World*, 1916.
Illus. pp.8.
Includes reprint of article from *Sydney Morning Herald*, July 19, 1859.
Copies: NPL:M(A821/Y); ANL.
2374

[1920] 150TH ANNIVERSARY of the landing of Captain Cook at Botany Bay, Wednesday, 28th April, 1920: [programme. N.p., 1920.]
Illus. pp.[4].
Cover title.
Copies: NPL:M(991.1/15A1).
2375

1920 [PROGRAMME], State Conservatorium of Music, N.S.W. Concert [by] the Royal Sydney Apollo Club, in conjunction with the Conservatorium Orchestra . . . Town Hall, Sydney, Wednesday, 28th April, 1920. Sydney, Govt. Pr., 1920.

pp.14.

To commemorate the 150th anniversary of the landing of Captain Cook in New South Wales, the cantata *Captain Cook*, by the late J. A. Delany, with poem by P. E. Quinn, dealing with the life and death of the circumnavigator, was presented. The programme is accompanied by a ticket voucher for the performance, and a special notice relative to the celebration, issued by the Royal Australian Historical Society.

Copies: ANL:F. 2376

1921, 1923 [MENU CARD of dinners held Ap.28, 1921, and Ap.28, 1923, by the] National Club, Sydney, to commemorate the 151st [and] (153rd) anniversary of the landing of Captain Cook at Botany Bay, [also ticket for the 1921 function].

Copies: ANL:F. 2377

1923 MENU CARD, Ap.28, 1923.

See no.2377.

1927 HONORS TO CAPTAIN COOK: [the celebration to take place at Hawaii in 1928].

(*Outlook*, Aug. 1927, p.494.)

Copies: NPL:R(DF050/094). 2378

1927 RESTARICK, Henry Bond, *Bishop of Honolulu*

150th anniversary of the discovery of Hawaii by Captain Cook. By Bishop H. B. Restarick and A. P. Taylor.

(Hawaiian Historical Society—*Annual report*, 1927. pp.39–45.)

Copies: NPL:M(999.6/H). 2379

1927 [SPECIAL ARTICLES on Cook and the Sesquicentennial of Hawaii's discovery.]

(*Paradise of the Pacific*, Dec. 1927, vol.40, no.12.)

Copies: ANL:F. 2380

1927 WILLIAMS, William, *Bishop of Waiapu*

Cook's visit in light of Maori tradition.

Illus. map, port.

(*Gisborne Times*—Joint golden jubilees. Gisborne, N.Z., Gisborne Pub. Co., 1927. pp. 3–12.)

Copies: NPL:M(997.5/G). 2381

1928 AT THIS SPOT Captain Cook met death.

(*Honolulu Star-Bulletin*, p.7, Aug.20, 1928.)

Copies: NPL:M(MDQ079/340); ANL. 2382

1928 BICENTENARY Captain Cook Celebrations at Great Ayton, York-shire.

3 photographs on 1 mount. 2½″ x 4¼″.

Copies: NPL:M(Small Picture File: Cook-Celebrations, 1928/1).   2383

1928 BLAKEBOROUGH, J. Fairfax-

An Historical play to celebrate a great Yorkshireman and benefactor of the Empire; [produced at the Whitby celebration of the] (bi-centenary of Captain James Cook). Whitby, Horne and Son, 1928.

Facs. illus. port. pp.[ii], 48.

Copies: NPL:M(822.91/B); NPL:D(92/476); ANL; VSL.   2384

1928 CAPTAIN COOK BI-CENTENARY CELEBRATIONS, *Cleveland*

Souvenir of the . . . celebrations arranged in the Cleveland District . . . September 8th, 1928 to . . . 27th October, 1928. Middlesborough, Hood & Co., pr., 1928.

Facs. illus. map, port. pp.24.

Copies: NPL:M(Q923.9/C771.2/4A1); NPL:D(Q92/164); QOM; QU.   2385

1928 CAPTAIN COOK 150th anniversary celebrations, Hawaii 1 August 16th to 19th 1928.

2 albums of photographs.
Donated by the family of Sir Joseph Carruthers, 1968.

Copies: NPL:M(PXB24⁻¹⁻²).   2386

1928 CARRUTHERS, *Sir* Joseph Hector McNeil

Report . . . on the sesquicentennial celebrations of the discovery of the Hawaiian Islands by Captain Cook . . . at Hawaii, Aug. 1928. Sydney, Govt. Pr., 1928.

pp.6.

Copies: NPL:M(Q980:Co4/C1A1); ANL.   2387

1928 CELEBRATION of the bi-centenary of the birth of Captain Cook.

(*Victorian Historical Magazine*, vol.13, 1928, p.52.)

Copies: NPL:M(992/V).   2388

1928 [COLLECTION of leaflets, newscuttings etc., of the Cook Bicentenary, Whitby, 1928.]

Copies: NPL:M(Q980:Co1/W3A1).   2389

1928 DAWSON, Warren Royal

Captain Cook: the bicentenary of a great navigator.

Facs. illus. port. pp.4.
Supplement to *Lloyd's List and Shipping Register*, Oct.25, 1928.

Copies: NPL:M(Newscuttings File).   2390

1928 HALL, *photographer*
Opening of the Cook Bicentenary Exhibition at Whitby; with Captain Smith speaking and Lord Normanby standing on his right.
Photograph. 4½″ x 6″.
Copies: NPL:M(Small Picture File: Cook-Celebrations 1928/2).   2391

1928 HAWAII celebrates discovery of islands.
(*Honolulu Star-Bulletin*, p.10, Aug.17, 1928.)
Copies: NPL:M(MDQ079/340); ANL.   2392

1928 HOUSTON, Victor K.
Remarks of Hon. V. K. Houston of Hawaii in the [U.S.A.—Congress] House of Representatives [including speeches etc. at celebrations at Hawaii, Aug. 1928, in connection with Captain Cook].
pp.9.
(*Congressional Record*, Congress 70, Session 2.)
Copies: NPL:M(Q980:Co4/H1A1).   2393

1928 RESTARICK, Henry Bond, *Bishop of Honolulu*
Sesquicentennial celebration of Cook's discovery of Hawaii.
(*Hawaiian Annual*, 1928, pp.66–70.)
Copies: NPL:M(999.6/H).   2394

1928 [SESQUICENTENNIAL celebrations, Hawaiian Islands, Aug. 1928: photographs, press cuttings, programmes, etc.]
Copies of *Honolulu Star-Bulletin* Aug.15, 1928 sesquicentennial feature section and three photographs of jetty at Kealakekua Bay erected by Government of Australia are included.
Copies: NPL:M(F980:Co4/S1A1).   2395

1928 SOLEMN CEREMONIES at Kealakekua mark spot where Captain Cook died.
(*Honolulu Star-Bulletin*, p.1, Aug.18, 1928.)
Copies: NPL:M(MDQ079/340); ANL.   2396

1928 TRIBUTES PAID where Captain James Cook fell.
(*Honolulu Star-Bulletin*, p.5, Aug.20, 1928.)
Copies: NPL:M(MDQ079/340); ANL.   2397

1928 WAIMEA, KAUAI, honours Cook, Hawaii's discoverer.
(*Honolulu Star-Bulletin*, p.1, Aug.17, 1928.)
Copies: NPL:M(MDQ079/340); ANL.   2398

1928 WHITBY, *Eng.*—Urban Council
A Descriptive catalogue of the Cook Bi-Centenary Exhibition in the
Pannett Art Gallery, Whitby . . . 1928. [Organised by Whitby Urban
Council.] Whitby, Abbey Press, [1928].
Illus. pp.10.
The Dixson Library has another copy with MS. notes by F. M. Sutcliffe.
Copies: NPL:D(MS.Q149). 2399

1928 *WHITBY GAZETTE*, Eng.
Extracts, Sep.14, 1928, re Cook bi-centenary celebrations, Whitby, 1928.
Illus. pp.1–2, 7–8.
Copies: NPL:D(MS.Q149). 2400

1929 CARRUTHERS, *Sir* Joseph Hector McNeil
Bi-centenary of Captain Cook's birth . . . Oct.27, 1928. Address.
(Royal Australian Historical Society—*Journal and Proceedings*, vol.15, 1929, pp.292–7.)
Copies: NPL:M(991/R, Ref.Books); NPL:D(9/69); NPL:R(S991.06/1). 2401

1929 CRAMP, Karl Reginald
Bi-centenary of Captain Cook's birth: celebrations at the base of Captain
Cook statue, Hyde Park, Sydney. October 27, 1928.
(Royal Australian Historical Society—*Journal and Proceedings*, vol.15, 1929, pp.217–21.)
Copies: NPL:M(991/R, Ref.Books); NPL:D(9/69); NPL:R(S991.06/1). 2402

1929 RESTARICK, Henry Bond, *Bishop of Honolulu*
Cook sesquicentennial observance.
(*Hawaiian Annual*, 1929, pp.29–36.)
Copies: NPL:M(999.6/H). 2403

1929 TAYLOR, Albert Pierce
Sesquicentennial celebration of Captain Cook's discovery of Hawaii,
1778–1928. Honolulu, 1929.
Illus. pp.vii, 105.
(Hawaii—Board of Commissioners of Public Archives—*Archives of Hawaii*, pub.4.)
Copies: NPL:M(Q980:Co4/T1A1); ANL; Captain Cook's Landing Place Trust; VPL.
2404

1930 CARRUTHERS, *Sir* Joseph Hector McNeil
The Sesqui-centennial celebrations in the Hawaiian Islands in 1928:
[with app. of documents].
Illus.
(*In his* Captain James Cook, R.N. London, J. Murray, 1930. pp.203–305.)
See also no. 2406.
Copies: NPL:M(980:Co1/C2A1); NPL:D(93/37); NPL:R(S920/C771/2); Captain
Cook's Landing Place Trust; QParl; QU; VMoU; VSL. 2405

1930 CARRUTHERS, *Sir* Joseph Hector McNeil

The Sesqui-centennial celebrations in the Hawaiian Islands in 1928; [with app. of documents].

Illus.

(*In his* Captain James Cook, R.N. New York, E. P. Dutton, 1930. pp.203–305.)
See also no.2405.

Copies: NPL:M(980:Co1/C2B1); ANL. 2406

1930 TAYLOR, Albert Pierce

The Hawaiian Islands . . . papers read during the Captain Cook Sesqui-centennial Celebration, Honolulu, Aug.17, 1928. Edited by A. P. Taylor and R. S. Kuykendall. Published by Captain Cook Sesquicentennial Commission and the Archives of Hawaii Commission. Honolulu, The Printshop Co., 1930.

Frontisp. pp.93.

(Hawaii—Board of Commissioners of Public Archives—*Publication* no.5.)

Copies: NPL:M(999.6/T). 2407

1954 CONDE, Harold Graydon

Kurnell Trust: address by the President Mr. H. G. Conde, Oct.21, 1954.
ff.5.
Duplicated.

Copies: NPL:M(Pam.File QA923.9/C). 2408

1954–5 CAPTAIN COOK'S LANDING PLACE TRUST

Report of the Trustees of Captain Cook's Landing Place. [1954.]5, *to date*. Sydney, Govt. Pr.

Also published in N.S.W.—Parliament—Papers.

Copies: NPL:M(Q 711.06/2); NPL:R(NQ 919.4406/4); ANL. 2409

1956 NEW ZEALAND—High Commissioner in London

Cook and a hundred years after: catalogue of an exhibition of paintings, prints, documents, diaries, letters and other relics. Christchurch, Whitcombe & Tombs, 1956.

pp.16.

Printed in Great Britain. At head of title: *New Zealand House, London, June 1956.*

Copies: NPL:M; ANL. 2410

1960 ARTS COUNCIL OF AUSTRALIA

James Cook, 1904–60: [exhibition at the Macquarie Galleries, Sydney, sponsored by the Arts Council of Australia. Sydney, 1960.]

pp.6.

Copies: ANL. 2411

[1966] H.M.S. *ENDEAVOUR* TRUST
1770–1970: voyage into history. Sydney, Conpress pr., [1966].
Illus. one in colour, map, plan, ports. pp.8. Without title-page. Title from cover.
Copies: NPL:M(Q980:Col/H1A1); ANL.   2412

1967 LACK, Clem
The Bi-centenary of Captain Cook: his journey along the Queensland coast.
(*Local Government*, vol.62, Feb. 1967, pp.52+.)
Copies: NPL:M(Q352.094/1); ANL.   2413

1968 THE BRITISH MUSEUM—The King's Library
An Exhibition to commemorate the bi-centenary of Captain Cook's first voyage round the world: [catalogue. London, the Museum, 1968.]
ff.vi,35.
Photocopy.
Presentation copy to Mitchell Library from Map Room of British Museum.
Photographs and colour transparencies of the exhibition placed at M.L. Pic. Acc.1582.
Cased with the catalogue are two prospectuses of the exhibition.
Copies: NPL:M(Q980:Co2/B1).   2414

1968 [COLLECTION of articles published in *Australia & New Zealand Weekly* and *The Australian News*, July–Sep. 1968, to commemorate the bi-centenary of Captain Cook's first voyage round the world. London.]
Illus. 5 sheets.
Copies: NPL:M(Q980:Co2/C1).   2415

1968 [COLLECTION of pamphlets and newspaper articles issued to mark the celebrations held at Whitby, August 1968, to commemorate the bi-centenary of Captain Cook's first voyage round the world.]
12 articles.
CONTENTS:
Whitby Museum—Notes on exhibits.
Shell-Mex Ltd.—Yorkshire, East and North Ridings.
Captain Cook; biographical leaflet.
English, B.—The Rising tide: [prospectus about the play].
Leaflet giving programme of the bi-centenary celebrations.
Whitby Regatta—Souvenir programme.
St. Mary's Parish Church, *Whitby*—Captain James Cook bi-centenary service of thanksgiving . . . August 25, 1968.
Whitby, *parish*—Events during August 1968.
Captain James Cook, R.N., his Pacific explorations and circumnavigation of New Zealand [and] New Zealand today.
Whitby: [tourist guide].
Captain James Cook bicentenary: [souvenir programme].
Whitby Gazette, August 30, 1968.
Copies: NPL:M(Q980:Co2/C2).   2416

1968 EXHIBITION, 1968, at the British Museum, celebrating the bicentenary of Cook's first voyage.

17 photographs and 8 coloured slides.

Copies: NPL:M(Small Picture File: Cook-Celebrations 1968/1–17; FM5/511–18). 2417

1968 EXHIBITION, 1968, at the London Offices of the Agent General for N.S.W., celebrating the bicentenary Cook's first voyage.

2 photographs.

Copies: NPL:M(Small Picture File: Cook-Celebrations 1968/18–19). 2418

1968 LONDON BOROUGH OF TOWER HAMLETS—Libraries Department

Captain Cook: an exhibition and annual lecture at the Tower Hamlets Central Library. [Prospectus. London, the Department, 1968.]

pp.[4].

Cover title. Processed.

Undertaken to commemorate the bi-centenary of Cook's first voyage round the world.

Copies: NPL:M(923.9/C771.2/38A1). 2419

1968 PLYMOUTH CITY MUSEUM & ART GALLERY

Captain James Cook bi-centenary exhibition, 8th–28th August, 1968: [souvenir programme]. Plymouth, the Museum & Art Gallery, 1968.

Illus. port. pp.[12].

Copies: NPL:M(980:Co1/P3A1). 2420

1968 PUBLIC LIBRARY OF NEW SOUTH WALES—Library Liaison Officer, *London*

'Report on visit of the Library Liaison Officer to Whitby, Yorkshire, 24th to 27th August, 1968, in connection with Cook's bicentenary celebrations' made Sep. 4, 1968; with enclosures.

Typescript: xerox copy.

Original in Mitchell Library Correspondence 1377/1968.

Copies: NPL:M(Doc.1405). 2421

1968 ROSKILL, Stephen W., *Capt.*

Address given by Captain S.W.Roskill to open the Bicentenary Exhibition in memory of Captain James Cook, 1728–1779, at Great St. Andrew's Church, Cambridge, 18 Oct. 1968.

Typescript: xerox copy.

Copies: NPL:M(Doc.1406). 2422

1968 WIGGINS TEAPE LIMITED

Captain Cook on orbit round the world, 1768–1968: [collection of coloured facsimile documents in a folder]. London, Wiggins Teape, 1968.

CONTENTS:
Plan of the *Endeavour*.
A Letter from Cook to the Admiralty.
Part of the complement of the *Endeavour*.
Map of Tahiti.
Page from the ship's log.
Drawings of the dancer and the chief.
French map of the world.
Drawing of ship's officer.
Description of a kangaroo.

Issued to commemorate bi-centenary of Cook's first voyage.

Copies: NPL:M(Q980:Co1/W2A1).   2423

n.d. [COLLECTION of invitations, menus etc. to functions commemorating Captain Cook. Various dates.]

Copies: NPL:M(Vertical File).   2424

DEATH

1777–9 HOME, Alexander
Journals, 1777–1779.

ff.29, pp.61.
MS. 'Journal of the Account of Otaheite and our transactions there' (Sept. 1777–Jan. 1778), ff.28; also a page containing a chart of Trarabon. Typescript transcript of the same, pp.36.
MS. 'Journal of the Account of the Death of Capt. James Cook at Owhyee in the Sandwich Islands, January 1779' and 'Description of the Country of Kamtschatka from April 1779'. The journal ends abruptly. (pp.61. 4to.) Typescript transcript of the same, pp.7. Also an extract from sales catalogue printed c.1925. *See* Beaglehole, vol.3, pt.1, pp. cxcv–cxcvi.

Copies: ANL(MS.7).   2425

[1779–80] THOMSON, Charles
Commonplace-book. Late 18th century.

pp.c.170.
MS. Commonplace book of Charles Thomson, an American, containing transcripts of Cook's voyages with notes of letter from *Spanish Mercury*, 7 January 1780 concerning Cook's death. Also extract of a letter from Mr. Pallas, Professor at Petersburg to Mr. Busching, Counsellor at Berlin, dated 21 December 1779, re Cook's death and Capt. Clarke's (*sic*) call at Kamschatka.

Copies: ANL(Nan Kivell 4229).   2426

1779 ACCOUNT of the events at Karakakoa Bay, from 12th to 22nd February, 1779, containing a detailed account of the death of Captain Cook and the recovery of his body. *Anon.* Manuscript.

Fol. pp.21.
Follows fairly closely the details as given by Capt. King, but with several slight variations and additions. It is probably a transcript from a private diary or journal of some officer or seaman who accompanied Cook.

Copies: ANL.   2427

1779 CLERKE, Charles

Account of Cook's death. (Abstract of letter to Mr. Secretary Stephens, in the handwriting of Sir Joseph Banks, covering period Oct. 26, 1778, to Apr. 21, 1779.)

(Brabourne Papers.)

Copies: NPL:M(MS.A78⁻¹).   2428

1779 CLERKE, Charles

'Extract from Journal of Capt. Charles Clerke, R.N. from 14th Feb 1779, on which date he succeeded Captain Cook in command of H.M.S. "*Resolution*" until 13th March 1779'.

1 reel, positive microfilm.
Filmed by A.L. Faber, London, 1963 (Microfilm no.142 of A.L. Faber Microfilm Library). Original is in the Admiralty Library, London (Adm.MSS74/8).

Copies: NPL:M(FM3/641); ANL.   2429

1779 MS. ACCOUNT of the death of Cook, 9–20 July 1779, by an eyewitness.

1 vol.
(Miscellaneous papers relating to Cook.)

Copies: ANL(MS.8).   2430

1780 HARRIS, *Sir* James

[MS. copy of Letter to Sir Joseph Banks, from St. Petersburg, Jan. 7, 1780, referring to Cook's death.]

(Copies of documents relating to Captain James Cook, R.N., from originals in the Grey Collection, Auckland Public Library, ff.222–5.)

Copies: NPL:M(C697).   2431

1780 NACHRICHTEN von dem Leben und den Seereisen des berühmten Capitain Cook. Reval, Albrecht und Compagnie, 1780.

pp.48.
Photographic copy only in the State Library of Victoria.
A rare work published in Revel (*sic*, Tallinn) in Estonia. Jackson, item 91 is probably a record of it. Undoubtedly the first account of Cook's death to be printed in book form. The volume gives a short account of Cook's life, voyages and death, with many inaccuracies on his early career. Mainly taken from a letter, *Auszug des Briefes von Kensington den 4ten Febr. 1780 die Nachrichten von Kapitain Cook betreffend*. (Note from Nan Kivell copy.) *See also* Spence, p. 20, where he describes the pamphlet and records a French edition (no. 2433); possibly from the pen of J.R. or G. Forster.
Elegy on the death of Captain Cook, pp. 44–7.

Copies: ANL(Nan Kivell); VSL.   2432

1780 PRÉCIS de la vie & des voyages du Capitaine Cook. Ecrit de Kensington ce 4 Février 1780. Reval & Leipsic, Albrecht & Co., [1780?].

pp.47.
For note *see* no.2432, and *see also* Spence, p.20, who records another copy in the collection of J.B. Kroepelien, Oslo.

Copies: NPL:M(Safe 1/99); ANL.   2433

1780 SANDWICH, John Montagu, *4th Earl*

ALS dated Blackheath; Informs that Capt. Cook has been murdered by the natives of an island where he had had a more friendly reception than at Otaheite; the news comes from Capt. Clerke at Kamschatzcha where he has received very friendly treatment from the Russians; the voyage has been successful, only three men have died; Omai was left safely at Huaheine, but no particulars given in short letter from Cook by the same conveyance; horses, cattle and sheep were landed at Otaheita; Capt Gower (Gore) takes command of the *Discovery* and Clerke of the *Resolution*; Clerke means to make another attempt for the northern pasage.

f.1, cm 24.
Paginated 409.
Dealer's catalogue description in MS.Q159.

Copies: NPL:D(MS.Q158, pp.137–8).   2434

1780 SEWARD, Anna

Elegy on Captain Cook; to which is added An ode to the sun. London, J. Dodsley, 1780.

pp.23.
See also nos.2436, 2439–40, 2443, 2465–6.

Copies: NPL:M(C918); ANL.   2435

1780 SEWARD, Anna

Elegy on Captain Cook; to which is added An ode to the sun. 2nd ed. London, J. Dodsley, 1780.

pp.23.
See no.2435 for other editions.

Copies: NPL:M(C919); ANL:F; SPL; VSL.   2436

1781 Jan.23 ACCOUNT of part of the third voyage, describing discoveries in the North Pacific, the Sandwich Islands and the death of Captain Cook. *Anonymous.*

pp.20.
MS. copy of a letter written to Mrs. Strachan, dated Spithead, Jan.23, 1781. The writer was not an eyewitness of the death of Captain Cook, his being on board the *Discovery* at the time. The copy is unfinished, but gives a detailed statement concerning the conduct of Lieut. John Williamson.

Copies: NPL:M(Safe 1/67).   2437

1781 FORSTER, Johann Georg Adam

Strödde underrättelser om Capitaine Cooks sista resa och olyckeliga död i Söderhafwet, öfwersättning utur *Göthingisches Magazin* af A. Sparrman. Stockholm, P.A. Brodin, 1781.

Map, pp.47.

Copies: NPL:M(980:Co4/F1B1).   2438

1781 SEWARD, Anna

Elegy on Captain Cook; to which is added An ode to the sun. 3rd ed. London, J. Dodsley, 1781.

pp.23.

See no.2435 for other editions.

Copies: NPL:M(C920).

2439

1781 SEWARD, Anna

Elegy on his [Cook's] death.

(Succinct account of the life and voyages of Captain James Cook. *Universal Magazine*, 1781. p.285.)

See no.2435 for other editions.

Copies: NPL:M(910.4/122).

2440

[1783] THE BRITISH NAVIGATOR; containing Captain Cook's three voyages round the world. The first in the *Endeavour*, begun in the year 1768 and finished in 1771. The second in the *Resolution*, accompanied by the *Adventure*, commanded by Capt. Furneaux; begun in 1772 and finished in 1775. And the third in the *Resolution* and *Discovery*, the latter being commanded by Capt. Clerke; begun in 1776 and finished in 1780. Including every interesting particular in the course of those voyages and an account of the unfortunate death of Capt. Cook. Pt. 1–2. London, John Fielding, [1783].

Illus. 2 vols.

(*The Polite traveller and British navigator*, vol.5–6.)

Copies: NPL:M(910.8/43A5–6).

2441

1784 SAMWELL, David, *surgeon, Discovery*

'A Narrative of the death of Captain James Cook To which are added some Particulars concerning his Life and Character; also Observations respecting the introduction of the Venereal Disease into the Sandwich Islands. By David Samwell Surgeon of the *"Discovery"* 1784'.

ff.3, 1, 21; cm 33, 32.

Bound with modern title-page and foreword, and a leaf endorsed 'Manuscript Narrative of the Death of Captain Cook'. Included is a short vocabulary of native names used in Samwell's text, citing the alternative used in the official publication of the voyage. *See also* no. 2448.

Copies: NPL:D(MS.Q153).

2442

1784 SEWARD, Anna

Elegy on Captain Cook; to which is added An ode to the sun. 4th ed. With additions. Lichfield, printed and sold by J. Jackson and J. Dodsley, 1784.

With author's signature. *See* no.2435 for other editions.

Copies: NPL:M(C921); NPL:D(78/75).

2443

1784 TREVENEN, James

[Notes concerning paragraphs in the 1784 quarto edition of Cook's third voyage: photostat copy of the manuscript in the Provincial Library, British Columbia.]

ff.2.

See also no.2485.

Copies: NPL:M(C361).   2444

1785 BERÄTTELSE OM ENGELSKE Capit. Jac. Cooks wäldsamma Död är 1779, och hwad sedan hände Engländarne pä Öen Owhyhee.

(*Historiska Biblioteket*, vol.6–7, nos.46, 50, 52, 54, 56. Stockholm, 1785.)

Extracts only. A translation of an article on Cook's death from the weekly journal *Der Wissbegierige*, Wismar, nos.28–30, 1785.

See Du Rietz, Rolf— Captain James Cook: a bibliography. Upsala, 1960.

The journal was edited by Carl Christoffer Gjörwell, who presumably translated this article. The title of the journal was changed in 1786 to *Upfostrings-Sälskapets Historiska Bibliothek*. Almost the whole set was printed at Kumblinske Tryckeriet; in 1786 the printer was Johan A. Carlbohm; in 1787 And.J. Nordstron.

Copies: NPL:M(980:Col/H4A2).   2445

1786 SAMWELL, David

Détails nouveaux et circonstanciés sur la mort du Capitaine Cook; traduits de l'anglois. Paris, chez Née de la Rochelle, 1786.

pp.56 + [ii].

Published anonymously. *See also* no.2448.

Copies: NPL:M(C759).   2446

1786 SAMWELL, David

Interesting particulars respecting the death of Captain Cook. [From the Narrative of David Samwell, surgeon of the *Discovery*.]

Extract from the *New Annual Register* 1786, pp.198–202. *See also* no.2448.

Copies: ANL:F.   2447

1786 SAMWELL, David

A Narrative of the death of Captain James Cook; to which are added some particulars concerning his life and character, and observations respecting the introduction of the venereal disease into the Sandwich Islands. London, G.G.J. and J. Robinson, 1786.

pp.[iv], 34.

See also nos.2442, 2446–7, 2449, 2455, 2500, 2502, 2511, 2546, 2556.

Copies: NPL:M(C694); ANL; VSL.   2448

1786 SAMWELL, David

A Narrative of the death of Captain James Cook.

(*Weekly Entertainer*, Sherborne, Sept.25, 1786, pp.298–304.) Abridged, and with alterations. *See also* no.2448.

Copies: NPL:M(923.9/C771.2/1B1).   2449

1788 ARNOULD, Jean François Mussot

La Mort du Capitaine Cook, à son troisième voyage au nouveau monde: pantomime en quatre actes. Par M. Arnould. Répresentée pour la première fois sur le Théâtre de l'Ambigu-Comique, au mois d'Octobre 1788. Paris, chez Lagrange, 1788.

pp.36.

For a similar pantomime *see* The Death of Captain Cook, 1789, no.2452.

Copies: NPL:M(980:Co4/A1A1); ANL. 2450

1788 WILLIAMS, Helen Maria

Morai: an ode.

(*In* Kippis, *Rev.* Andrew—The Life of Captain James Cook. London, G. Nicol, G.G.J. & J. Robinson, 1788. App. 2, pp.520–7.)
Also appears in later editions.

Copies: NPL:M(Q980:Co1/K1A1); NPL:D(Q77/13, Q78/8,9); NPL:R(09:Q990A/49); SPL; VParl; VU(Baillieu). 2451

1789 DEATH OF CAPTAIN COOK: a grand serious-pantomimic ballet . . . as performed at the Theatre Royal, Covent Garden. *Anon.* London, printed for T. Cadell, 1789.

pp.19.

For a similar pantomime *see* no.2450.

Copies: NPL:M(782.9/2A1); ANL. 2452

1789 PORTLOCK, Nathaniel

[Death of Captain Cook described by an Hawaiian who was present.]

(*In his* Voyage round the world. London, John Stockdale, 1789. pp.308–9.)
Copies: NPL:M(Q910.4/1A1). 2453

[1789] THE REMARKABLE life and death of Captain Cook.

(*In* The History of Botany Bay in New Holland. Liverpool, printed by R. Ferguson [1789]. pp.16–31.)
See no.672 for full description of this item, and for other editions.

Copies: NPL:D(78/60). 2454

1789 SAMWELL, David

[Extract from Narrative of the death of Captain James Cook.]

(Kippis, *Rev.* Andrew—Biographia Britannica. 2nd ed. London, printed by Rivington and Marshall for J. Rivington and others, 1789. Vol.4, pp.230–34.)
See also no. 2448.

Copies: NPL:M(F920.042); NPL:R(C22Q20). 2455

1790 B., W.

Irregular ode on the death of Captain Cook.

(*Lady's Magazine*, 1790, p.100.)
Copies: NPL:M(052/L). 2456

1790 THEATRE ROYAL, *Richmond Green*

A Trip to Scarborough . . . To which will be added, not acted this season, a grand, serious, pantomimic ballet, in three parts, call'd The Death of Captain Cook. [Richmond, Eng., 1790.]

1 sheet.

Photograph of a Theatre Royal playbill for July 12, 1790.

Copies: NPL:M(792/7A1). 2457

1791 MORTIMER, George

Where Cook was killed.

(*In his* Observations and remarks made during a voyage . . . in the brig *Mercury*. London, the author, 1791. p.53.)

Copies: NPL:M(Q989.5/5A1). 2458

1794 A BRIEF ACCOUNT of the death of Captain James Cook: to accompany the print [engraved by S. Smith, I. Hall, and I. Thornthwaite after a painting by G. Carter]. London, Laurie and Whittle, 1794.

p.1.

The print is in the Dixson Collection, Drawer 7. An earlier edition published by G. Carter, Sayer and Bennet is in the Mitchell Library.

Copies: NPL:M(F923.9/C771.2/2B1). 2459

1796 TIMONEL, Leonardo

La Cokiada: tragedia nueva en tres actos por L. Timonel. La publica D. Angel Garcia Iñiguez. Malaga, por D. Luis de Carreras, 1796.

pp.94.

Listed in Spence, p.43.

Copies: NPL:M(980:Col/T1A1). 2460

[1801?] DIMSDELL, Joshua Lee, *quartermaster, Gunjara*

'Some Acct. of the Death & Remains of Capt. Cook—at Owhyhee recd from Joshua Lee Dimsdell Quarter Master of the *Gunjara* Capt. James Barber'. M.S. with extensive revision. 1801.

ff. 2, cm 32.

Watermark: 'C Wilmott 1798'. Dimsdell says that he received this account of Cook's death from Pihere, the native who fatally wounded Cook. A note explains that Dimsdell was resident on the island of Hawaii from July 1792 till the beginning of 1801. The MS. appears to be a rough draft.

Copies: NPL:D(MS.Q154). 2461

1801 RICHARD, Jerome F., *Abbé*

Dispositions des naturels des îles Sandwich: mort funeste de Cook. (Honneurs rendus à Cook . . . relation de la mort de Cook, etc.).

(*In his* Voyages chez les peuples sauvages. Paris, Laurens, aîné, 1801. Vol.2, pp.106–16, vol.3, pp.355–93.)

See also no.2463.

Copies: NPL:M(*989/R). 2462

1808 RICHARD, Jerome F., *Abbé*
Dispositions des naturels des îles Sandwich: mort funeste de Cook. (Honneurs rendus à Cook . . . relation de la mort de Cook, etc.).
(*In his* Voyages chez les peuples sauvages. 2nd ed. Paris, Laurens, ainé, 1808. Vol.2, pp.106–16, vol.3, pp.355–93.)
See also no.2462.
Copies: NPL:M(*989/R).   2463

1817 REAL CAUSE of the death of Captain Cook.
(*Naval Chronicle*, Jy–Dec., 1817, p.360.)
Copies: NPL:M(359.05/N).   2464

1817 SEWARD, Anna
Elegy on Captain Cook.
(*In her* Monody on Major André. 3rd ed. London, Longman, etc., 1817.)
See also nos.2435.
Copies: VSL.   2465

1817 SEWARD, Anna
Elegy on Captain Cook.
(*In her* Monody on Major André. 10th ed. London, Longman, etc., 1817. p.178.)
See also nos.2435.
Copies: NPL:M(821.79/S).   2466

1818 THEATRE ROYAL, *The Strand*
[Poster, Aug. 8, 1818, for Lionel and Clarissa and La Perouse, and advertising the pantomime ballet The Death of Captain Cook, to be produced Mon. 10th, in which the native Indian warriors will appear.]
Broadsheet.
Copies: NPL:M(Q980:Co1/T1A1).   2467

1818 THEATRE ROYAL, *The Strand*
Turnpike gate . . . To conclude with, 16th time in this theatre, the grand historical ballet, in two acts, called The Death of Captain Cook. London, Lowndes, pr., [1818].
1 sheet.
A Theatre Royal playbill for Sep.12, 1818.
Copies: NPL:M(Q980:Co1/T2A1).   2468

1822 THE VOYAGES of Captain James Cook round the world; with an account of his unfortunate death at Owhyhee, one of the Sandwich Islands. London, printed for T. Hughes, 1822.
Illus. pp.324.
Copies: NPL:M(980:Co1/25A1).   2469

1827 BROWN, William

[Letter written Feb. 12, 1827, by W. Brown, a gunner on board the *Resolution* during Cook's last voyage, describing the events which led to the death of Captain Cook.]

pp.3.
Typewritten copy.
Copies: NPL:M(F923.9/C771.2/1A1).   2470

1827 ELLIS, *Rev.* Williams

[Account of Captain Cook's death.]

(*In his* Narrative of a tour through Hawaii. London, H. Fisher, 1826. pp.110–12.)
See also no. 2472. Also published in Hamburg in 1827.
Copies: NPL:M(989.6/32A1); NPL:R(MD7Q12).   2471

1827 ELLIS, *Rev.* William

[Account of Captain Cook's death.]

(*In his* Narrative of a tour through Hawaii. 2nd ed. London, H. Fisher, 1827. pp.115–23.)
See also no.2471.
Copies: NPL:M(989.6/32C1).   2472

[1835 DEATH OF COOK.]

(Cook, James—Collected Voyages—Printed Accounts [1835. Fairburn's Edition]—
Voyages. London, J. Fairburn, [1835]. pp.292–7.)
Copies: NPL:M(980:Co1/32A1).   2473

1838 HOME, Alexander

The Death of Cook [described by Alexander Home, an officer on the *Discovery*].

(Home, George—Memoirs of an aristocrat. London, Whittaker, 1838. pp.302–9.)
This account of Cook's death conflicts with the generally accepted version, and the book was suppressed soon after its publication. Alexander Home, the author's father, was an eye-witness of the event. Page 301 refers to his journal having been confiscated by the Admiralty. This account of the death of Cook was given from memory.
Copies: NPL:M(923.9/H765/1A1); NPL:D(83/133); NPL:R(S920/H765).   2474

1839 DIBBLE, *Rev.* Sheldon

[Death of Captain Cook.]

(*In his* History and general views of the Sandwich Islands' mission. New York, Taylor & Dodd, 1839. pp.21–32.)
See also nos.2479, 2508.
Copies: NPL:M(279.96/D); NPL:D(83/316).   2475

1840 CAMPBELL, John

Death of Captain Cook, and summary of his discoveries.

(*In his* Maritime discovery and Christian missions. London, J. Snow, 1840. pp.136–44.)
Copies: NPL:M(989/C).   2476

1841 WELLESLEY, Richard, *1st Marquis*
In obitum viri eximi et celeberrimi navigatoris Jacobi Cook.
(*In his* Primitiæ et reliquiæ. London, W. Nicol, 1841. pp.53–8.)
Copies: NPL:M(821.79/W).   2477

1842 DEATH OF COOK: [extract from portion of an unknown memorandum book].
(*United Service Magazine* pt.2,1842, pp.45–50.)
Copies: NPL:R(DS355.05/1).   2478

1843 DIBBLE, *Rev.* Sheldon
[Death of Captain Cook.]
(*In his* History of the Sandwich Island. 2nd ed. Lahainaluna, Hawaiian Is., Press of the Missionary Seminary, 1843. pp.31–9.)
See also nos.2475, 2508.
Copies: NPL:M(279.96/D); NPL:D(84/335); VSL.   2479

1843 JARVES, James Jackson
[Death of Captain Cook.]
(*In his* History of the Hawaiian or Sandwich Islands. London, Moxon, 1843. pp.112–23.)
See also nos.2481, 2483, 2490.
Copies: NPL:M(999.6/J); NPL:D(84/248); VSL.   2480

1843 JARVES, James Jackson
[Death of Captain Cook.]
(*In his* History of the Hawaiian or Sandwich Islands. Boston, Tappan and Dennet, 1843. pp.124–36.)
See also nos.2480, 2483, 2490.
Copies: NPL:M(999.6/J); VSL.   2481

1846 LINDRIDGE, James
Death of Captain Cook.
Illus.
(*In his* Tales of shipwrecks. London, W.M. Clark, 1846. pp.309–11.)
Copies: NPL:M(910.4/L).   2482

1847 JARVES, James Jackson
[Death of Captain Cook.]
(*In his* History of the Hawaiian Islands. 3rd ed. Honolulu, Hitchcock, 1847. pp.66–71.)
See also nos. 2480–81, 2490.
Copies: NPL:M(999.6/J); VSL.   2483

1849 ROSS, Alexander
[Short description of state of place where Captain Cook was killed.]
(*In his* Adventures of the first settlers on the Oregon or Columbia river. London, Smith, Elder & Co., 1849. p.47.)
Copies: ANL.   2484

1850 TREVENEN, James
[Notes concerning paragraphs in the 1784 quarto edition of Cook's third voyage.]
(*In* Penrose, *Rev.* John—Lives of Vice-Admiral Charles Vinicombe Penrose . . . and Captain James Trevenen. London, J. Murray, 1850. pp.189–92.)
See also no.2444.
Copies: NPL:M(923.542/P); ANL; VSL.   2485

1862 HOPKINS, Manley
Early island discoveries . . . The tragedy in Kealakeakua Bay, etc.
(*In his* Hawaii. London, Longman, 1862. pp.77–111.)
See also no.2487.
Copies: NPL:M(999.6/40A1); NPL:D(86/261); NPL:R(S999.6/4).   2486

1866 HOPKINS, Manley
Early island discoveries . . . The tragedy in Kealakeakua Bay, etc.
(*In his* Hawaii. London, Longman, 1866. pp.83–118.)
See also no.2486.
Copies: NPL:M(999.6/40B1); NPL:D(86/262); NPL:R(S999.6/5).   2487

1868 LAST of the great navigator.
(*Overland Monthly*, Nov. 1868, pp.436–41.)
Copies: NPL:R(S050/0 96).   2488

[187–?] WHYMPER, Frederick
[Account of the death of Captain Cook.]
(*In his* The Sea. London, Cassell, [187–?]. Vol.3, pp.317–19.)
Copies: NPL:M(Q910.9/5A2).   2489

1872 JARVES, James Jackson
[Death of Captain Cook.]
(*In his* History of the Hawaiian Islands. 4th ed. Honolulu, Whitney, 1872. pp.59–64.)
See also nos.2480–81, 2483.
Copies: NPL:M(999.6/J); NPL:D(87/169); VSL.   2490

1873 STODDARD, Charles Warren
The Last of the great navigator.
(*In his* South-Sea idyls. Boston, James R. Osgood, 1873. pp.167–83.)
Later edition entitled *Summer cruising in the South Seas*, no.2493.
Copies: NPL:M(989/S).   2491

1873 TWAIN, Mark, *pseud.*
[Where Captain Cook died.]
(*In his* Innocents at home. Melbourne, George Robertson, 1873. pp.290–92.)
See also no.2496.
Copies: NPL:M(817.44); NPL:R(817.44/18).   2492

[1874] STODDARD, Charles Warren
The Last of the great navigator.
(*In his* Summer cruising in the South Seas. London, Chatto and Windus, [1874]. pp. 154–66.)
Earlier edition entitled *South Sea idyls*, no.2491.
Copies: NPL:M(989/S). 2493

1880 FORNANDER, Abraham
[Death of Captain Cook, and contributory events.]
(*In his* Account of the Polynesian race. London, Trübner, 1880. Vol.2, pp.157–200.)
An index was published by the Bishop Museum Press, Honolulu, 1909; copy in VSL.
Copies: NPL:M(572.99/F); NPL:D(88/284); VSL. 2494

1882 FRANCIS, B.
[Death of Captain Cook, and the monument at Kealakekua Bay; with woodcut showing the monument.]
(*In his* Isles of the Pacific. London, Cassell, 1882. pp.173–8.)
Copies: NPL:M(989/F). 2495

[1883?] TWAIN, Mark, *pseud.*
Roughing it; and The innocents at home. [New York, Chatto and Windus, 1883?]
Illus. pp.369–464.
Extract containing a description of the Sandwich Islands, and comments on the death of Cook. *See also* no.2492.
Copies: NPL:D(88/446). 2496

1884 BONWICK, James
Fate of Capt. Cook.
(*Athenaeum*, Aug. 1884, p.213.)
Copies: NPL:R(Q050/A867); Q Parl. 2497

1884 BROWNE, Robert Stewart
ALS to the Trustees of the Public Library of Victoria from West Melbourne, 11 Dec.1884, formally handing over to them a sketch of the bay where Captain James Cook was killed.
Copies: NPL:M(Doc.1301). 2498

[1891] BISHOP, *Rev.* Sereno Edwards
Cook's discovery of the Hawaiian Islands.
(Thurston, Lorrin A.—Vistas of Hawaii. Honolulu, W.F. Sesser, [1891]. pp.12–14.)
Copies: NPL:M(Q989.6/T). 2499

1893 SAMWELL, David
Some account of a voyage to South Seas in 1776, 1777, 1778: [extract, giving an account of Cook's death].
(Historical Records of New South Wales. Sydney, Govt. Pr., 1893. Vol.1, pt. 1, pp.450–78.)
See also no.2448.
Copies: NPL:M(991/N, Ref. Books); NPL:D(89/267); NPL:R(991/16).   2500

1896 EYKYN, *Rev.* Thomas
Cook's discovery of the [Hawaiian] Islands; [with account of his death].
(In his Parts of the Pacific, by a peripatetic parson. London, Swan Sonnenschein, 1896. pp.292–7.)
Copies: NPL:M(980/161A1).   2501

1899 SAMWELL, David
Extracts from the diary of Dr Samwell . . . [Sel. and with notes] by J. Edge Parkington.
(Polynesian Society—*Journal,* vol.8, Dec. 1899, pp.250–63.) *See also* no. 2448.
Copies: NPL:M(Q572.9/P); NPL:R(S572.99/2).   2502

[1907?] BLOXAM, *Rev.* Andrew
Extracts from journal of A. B. . . . general naturalist on H.M.S. *Blonde* at the Sandwich Islands . . . 1825. [1907?]
ff.52.
Multigraphed typescript.
Copies: NPL:M(Q989.6/B).   **2503**

1907 CHARLES, Samuel
The Death of Captain James Cook, being the narrative of the Honorable Captain Charles, M.L.C., who in the year 1850, made personal inquiries on the spot, and obtained the information from an eye-witness of the event. MS.
Copies: Captain Cook's Landing Place Trust.   2504

1907 DEATH of Captain Cook.
(Geographical Journal, Dec., 1907, pp.668–9.)
Copies: NPL:R(S909.6A/2).   2505

1907 [DESCRIPTION of the death of Cook, by a witness. Extract from the *Sydney Morning Herald,* June 25, 1907.]
(Newspaper cuttings, vol.7, p.137.)
Copies: NPL:M(Q991/N).   2506

1908 CAPTAIN Cook's last days. [Extract from *Brisbane Courier*, Feb.15, 1908.]

(Newspaper cuttings, vol.9, pp.104–5.)

Copies: NPL:M(Q991/N). 2507

1909 DIBBLE, *Rev.* Sheldon
[Death of Captain Cook.]

(*In his* A History of the Sandwich Islands. 3rd ed. Honolulu, T.H. Thrum, 1909. pp.20–7.)
See also nos.2475, 2479.

Copies: NPL:M(279.96/D); VSL. 2508

1912 SYNGE, Margaret Bertha
Cook's third voyage and death.

Illus. map.
(*In her* A Book of discovery. London, Jack, 1912. pp.330–8.)
See also nos.2514, 2550.

Copies: NPL:M(910.9/10A1). 2509

1914 PAYNE, Harold H.
Admiral Burney and the death of Captain Cook: some unpublished manuscripts. London, [1914].

(Captain Cook: newspaper cuttings, vol.2.)
Reprint from *Cornhill Magazine*, Nov. 1914, pp.677–91. The manuscripts comprise part of the Log of the *Discovery*, written by Burney, and a narrative, not in Burney's hand-writing, entitled An Account of the death of Captain Cook, etc. The manuscripts are now held in the Mitchell Library, *Safe 1/64,79.*

Copies: NPL:M(Q980:Co1/N1A2); NPL:R(S050/C817). 2510

[1916] SAMWELL, David
A Narrative of the death of Captain James Cook. [Ed. and indexed by B. Cartwright, Jr. Honolulu, 1916.]

pp.26.
(Hawaiian Historical Society—*Reprint* no.2.)
Edition limited to 500 copies. *See also* no.2448.

Copies: NPL:M(923.9/C771.2/1C1). 2511

[192–?] DIXSON, *Sir* William
'Notes re Captain Cook.' Compiled by Sir William Dixson.

pp.60.
With index. Includes copies of extracts from periodicals and manuscripts, of items concerning Cook and his associates, in particular accounts of Cook's death and the introduction of venereal disease to the Pacific Islands. Several press cuttings inserted.

Copies: NPL:D(WD3). 2512

1920 SEARLE, J.C.
A Hawaiian's version of Captain Cook's death.
(*Hawaiian Almanac*, 1920, pp.136–8.)
Copies: NPL:M(999.6/H). 2513

1920 SYNGE, Margaret Bertha
Cook's third voyage and death.
Illus. map.
(*In her* A Book of discovery. New York, Putnam, 1920. pp.330–8.)
See also nos.2509, 2550.
Copies: NPL:M(910.9/10B1). 2514

1922 TAYLOR, Albert Pierce
Tragedy of Captain James Cook.
Illus.
(*In his* Under Hawaiian skies. Honolulu, *Advertiser*, 1922. pp.48–67.)
See also no.2519.
Copies: NPL:M(999.6/25A1). 2515

1924 CAPTAIN Cook's death: romance of Hawaii. [Extract from the *Sydney Morning Herald*, Aug.28, 1924.]
(Newspaper cuttings, vol.165, pp.193–5. 1923–4.)
Copies: NPL:M(Q991/N). 2516

1926 FRESH NEWS of Captain Cook: a man who saw him die. [Extract from *World's News*, Sept.4, 1926.]
Illus.
(Captain Cook: newspaper cuttings, vol.1, p.115.)
Copies: NPL:M(Q980:Co1/N1A1). 2517

1926 GILBERT, George
Death of Captain James Cook . . . from . . . Narrative of Cook's last voyage, 1776–1780. Honolulu, Paradise of the Pacific Press, 1926.
pp.30.
(Hawaiian Historical Society—*Reprints*, no.5.)
Copies: NPL:M(923.9/C771.2/17A1). 2518

1926 TAYLOR, Albert Pierce
Tragedy of Captain James Cook, a notable historical figure.
Illus.
(*In his* Under Hawaiian skies. 2nd ed. Honolulu, *Advertiser*, 1926. pp.83–110.)
See also no.2515.
Copies: NPL:M(999.6/25B1). 2519

1926 THRUM, Thomas George
The Paehumu of Heiaus, non sacred, clearing an erroneous account as to the cause of Captain Cook's death.
(Hawaiian Historical Society—*Annual Report*, 1926. pp.56–7.)
Copies: NPL:M(999.6/H).   2520

1926 WILSON, W.F., *and* WALL, W.A.
Place of Captain Cook's death.
Illus. map.
(Hawaiian Historical Society—*Annual Report*, 1926. pp.58–63.)
Copies: NPL:M(999.6/H).   2521

1926 ZIMMERMANN, Heinrich
Captain Cook's death.
(*Living Age*, July 1926, pp.100–2.)
Copies: NPL:R(S050/L785).   2522

1926–7 CARRUTHERS, *Sir* Joseph Hector McNeil
Captain Cook, his last days and death.
Illus. port.
(*Federal Capital Pioneer Magazine*, Dec. 1926, pp.14–20; Jan. 1927, pp.10–15.)
Copies: NPL:M(Q059/F).   2523

1928 CARRUTHERS, *Sir* Joseph Hector McNeil
Report . . . on the sesqui-centennial celebrations of the discovery of the Hawaiian Islands by Captain Cook . . . at Hawaii, Aug. 1928. Sydney, Govt. Pr., 1928.
pp.6.
Copies: NPL:M(Q980:Co4/C1A1).   2524

1928 GOULD, Rupert Thomas
Bligh's notes on Cook's last voyage.
Illus.
(*Mariner's Mirror*, vol.14, Oct. 1928, pp.371–85.)
Copies: NPL:R(656.506/7); ANL.   2525

1928 GOULD, Rupert Thomas
Some unpublished accounts of Cook's death.
Illus. map.
(*Mariner's Mirror*, vol.14, Oct. 1928, pp.301–19.)
Copies: NPL:R(656.506/7); ANL.   2526

1928 THE MURDERER of Captain Cook: his confession.
(Pan-Pacific Union—*Bulletin*, Jan. 1928. p.7.)
Copies: NPL:M(Q059/6).   2527

1929 SPOT WHERE Captain Cook was killed: [extracts from statements of persons visiting the spot, 1804–37].

(Taylor, Albert Pierce—Sesquicentennial celebration of Captain Cook's discovery of Hawaii, 1778–1928. Honolulu, 1929. p.77.)

Copies: NPL:M(Q980:Co4/T1A1); Captain Cook's Landing Place Trust; VSL.   2528

1929 UNVEILING the bronze tablet [at Kealakekua Bay: speeches by J.C. Lane and Sir J.H. Carruthers].

Illus.
(Taylor, Albert Pierce—Sesquicentennial celebration of Captain Cook's discovery of Hawaii, 1778–1928. Honolulu, 1929. pp.42–6.)
Hawaii—Board of Commissioners of Public Archives—*Publication* 4.

Copies: NPL:M(Q980.Co4/T1A1); Captain Cook's Landing Place Trust; VSL.   2529

[1930] CARRUTHERS, *Sir* Joseph Hector McNeil
Captain James Cook, R.N. London, J. Murray, [1930].

Facs. illus. map, pp.xx, 316.
See also no.2531.

Copies: NPL:M(980:Co1/C2A1); NPL:D(93/37); NPL:R(S920/C771/2); Captain Cook's Landing Place Trust; QParl; QU; VMoU; VSL.   2530

1930 CARRUTHERS, *Sir* Joseph Hector McNeil
Captain James Cook, R.N. New York, E.P. Dutton, 1930.

Facs. illus. map, pp.xx, 316.
See also no.2530.
Copies: NPL:M(980:Co1/2B1); ANL.   2531

1930 EDGAR, Thomas
Thomas Edgar's story [of Cook's death. From Journal of Thos. Edgar, Feb. 14, 1779].

(*In* Godwin, George Stanley—Vancouver. London, Philip Allan, 1930. pp.289–96.)
Copies: NPL:M(923.9/V223/2A1); NPL:R(S909.8A/V223).   2532

[1930?] ROBERTS, Henry
Eye witness account of the death of Cook: facsimile from the log of H.R., mate of the *Resolution* and officer in charge of the pinnace in which Captain Cook went ashore for the last time. London, F. Edwards, [1930?]

50 copies only printed of this reproduction of 2 pages of an original manuscript of 144 pages, which are described in Francis Edwards' catalogue no.525, 1930, p.21.
Copies: NPL:M(F980:Co4/R1A1); ANL; VSL.   2533

1931 MANWARING, George Ernest
Cook's last voyage.

Illus.
(*In his* My friend the Admiral: the life, letters and journals of Rear-Admiral James Burney. London, Routledge, 1931. pp.133–42.)
Copies: NPL:M(A923.9/B); NPL:R(920/B965.4/1); ANL.   2534

[1935] ROSE, John Holland
Charges against Captain Cook in Hawaii; [with bibl. notes].
(*In his* Man and the sea. Cambridge, W. Heffer, [1935]. pp.270–72.)
Copies: NPL:M(910.4/R); NPL:R(S909.8A/32).   2535

1937 [DEATH of Captain Cook; with note by Charles Roberts Anderson.]
(Journal of a cruise to the Pacific Ocean, 1842–4, in the frigate *United States*. Durham,
North Carolina, Duke University Press, 1937. pp.50, 132.)
Copies: NPL:M(980/157A1).   2536

1938 TWAIN, Mark, *pseud.*
Story of Captain Cook.
(*In his* Letters from the Sandwich Islands. 2nd ed. Stanford, Calif., Stanford U.P.
1938. pp.150–64.)
See also nos.2557–8.
Copies: NPL:M(989.6/60B1).   2537

1939 MUNFORD, James Kenneth
Death of the Captain.
(*In his* John Ledyard: an American Marco Polo. Portland, Oregon, Binfords & Mort,
1939. pp.131–48.)
Copies: NPL:M(A923.9/L).   2538

1941 CHICKERING, William H.
Discovery and *Resolution.*
(*In his* Within the sound of these waves. New York, Harcourt, Brace, 1941. pp.113–202.)
Copies: NPL:M(999.6/C); ANL; VSL.   2539

1941 ZIMMERMANN, Heinrich
Extracts from Voyage round the world with Captain Cook, by Heinrich
Zimmermann, from Wisslock in the Palatinate. Mannheim, 1781. Trans.
by M.E. Webster.
(*Victorian Historical Magazine* vol.19, June 1941, pp.27–30.)
Copies: NPL:M(992/V); NPL:D(9/57).   2540

1944 DUMAS, Alexandre
Captain Cook: [an account of his murder, trans. into English by M.E.
Wilbur].
(*In his* Journal of Madame Giovanni. London, Hammond, Hammond & Co., 1944.
pp.205–11.)
See also no.2542.
Copies: NPL:M(843.76/D886/1A1).   2541

1944 DUMAS, Alexandre
Captain Cook: [an account of his murder, trans. into English by M.E. Wilbur].

(*In his* The Journal of Madame Giovanni. New York, Liveright, 1944. pp.249–57.)
See also no.2541.

Copies: NPL:M(843.76/D886/1B1).   2542

1949 MELLEN, Kathleen Dickenson
Death of Captain Cook.

(*In her* Lonely warrior. New York, Hastings House, 1949. pp.36–43.)

Copies: NPL:M(999.6/M).   2543

1957 CHEGARAY, Jacques
The Tragedy of Captain Cook.

(*In his* Hawaii: isles of dreams. London, Barker, 1957. pp.101–11.)
See also no.2545.

Copies: NPL:M(989.6/2A1).   2544

1957 CHEGARAY, Jacques
The Tragedy of Captain Cook.

(*In his* Hawaii: isles of dreams. New York, Sterling Pub. Co., 1957. pp.101–11.)
See also no.2544.

Copies: NPL:M(989.6/2B1).   2545

1957 SAMWELL, David
Captain Cook and Hawaii: a narrative by David Samwell. With an introduction by Sir Maurice Holmes. San Francisco, David Magee, 1957.

Illus. ports. pp.[xx], 42.
Limited edition, 750 copies. With portrait of author, and reproduction of The Death of Captain Cook, from a painting by Webber, engraved by Bartolozzi and Byrne. *See also* no.2448.

Copies: NPL:M(923.9/C771.2/1D1); ANL; WU.   2546

1959 BURNEY, James
The Last days of Captain Cook.

(*In* Day, Arthur Grove—A Hawaiian reader. New York, Appleton-Century-Crofts, 1959. pp.11–19.)

Copies: NPL:M(989.6/8A1).   2547

1959 LANGDON, Robert
The Last of Captain Cook.

(*In his* Island of love. London, Cassell, 1959. pp.42–6.)

Copies: NPL:M(989.5/2).   2548

Death – continued

1962 HOTIMSKY, Constantine Michael

The Death of Captain James Cook: a letter from Russia, 1779. [With bibl.] Sydney, Wentworth Books, 1962.

Illus. pp.16.

Copies: NPL:M(980:Co4/H2A1); ANL; QParl; QU; VMoU.   2549

1962 SYNGE, Margaret Bertha

Cook's third voyage and death.

Illus. map.
(*In her* A Book of discovery. New ed. Edinburgh, Nelson, 1962. pp.229–35.)
See also nos.2509, 2514.

Copies: NPL:M(910.9/10C1).   2550

1964 BEAGLEHOLE, John Cawte

The Death of Captain Cook. [Canberra, 1964.]

pp.14.
Processed. Presidential address to Section E, A.N.Z.A.A.S. 37th Congress, 1964. *See also* nos.2552–3.

Copies: ANL.   2551

1964 BEAGLEHOLE, John Cawte

The Death of Captain Cook: (presidential address to Section E, A.N.Z.A.A.S. 37th Congress, Canberra, 1964).

Port.
(*Australian Journal of Science* vol.26, pp.297–304, Ap. 1964.)
See also nos.2551, 2553.

Copies: NPL:M(506/28).   2552

1964 BEAGLEHOLE, John Cawte

The Death of Captain Cook.

(*Historical Studies: Australia and New Zealand*, vol.11, Oct. 1964, pp.289–305.)
Revised version.
See also nos.2551–2.

Copies: NPL:M(990.05/1); NPL:R(N994.006/1); ANL.   2553

1964 ELLIS, Malcolm Henry

The Killing of Captain Cook.

(*Bulletin*, vol.86, p.10, Feb.1, 1964.)
Copies: NPL:M(Q079/15); NPL:R(NQ050/B936).   2554

[1965] EDGAR, Thomas

An Eye witness report of the death of Captain Cook from the journal of Thomas Edgar, master of the *Discovery*.

p.1.
(*In* Cook, J.—Collected voyages—Printed Accounts [1965 Jackdaw ser.]—The Voyages of Captain Cook: a collection of contemporary documents. London, J. Cape, 1965. No.7.)

Copies· NPL:M(Q980:Co1/L1A1); NPL:R(NQ909.088/1); ANL.   2555

1966 SAMWELL, David
A Narrative of the death of Captain James Cook.
(*In* Day, Arthur Grove—True tales of the South Seas. New York, Appleton-Century, 1966. pp.304–20.)
See also no.2448.
Copies: NPL:M(808.83/2A1).   2556

1966 TWAIN, Mark, *pseud.*
Captain Cook's death-place; [and] (The Story of Captain Cook).
(*In his* Mark Twain's Letters from Hawaii; ed. . . . by A. Grove Day. New York, Appleton-Century, 1966. pp.214–21.)
See also nos.2537, 2558.
Copies: NPL:M(989.6/60C1).   2557

1967 TWAIN, Mark, *pseud.*
Captain Cook's death-place; [and] (The Story of Captain Cook).
(*In his* Mark Twain's Letters from Hawaii; ed. . . . by A. Grove Day. London, Chatto & Windus, 1967. pp.214–21.)
See also nos.2537, 2557.
Copies: NPL:M(989.6/60D1).   2558

1968 DAWS, Gavan
Kealakekua Bay revisited: a note on the death of Captain Cook.
(*Journal of Pacific History* vol.3, 1968, pp.21–3.)
Copies: NPL:M(998.05/1); NPL:R(N990.05/1); ANL.   2559

n.d. IN THE SOUTH SEAS: an old narrative. From a hitherto unpublished manuscript. [Description of shirt worn by Captain Cook at the time of his death.]
(Newspaper cuttings, vol.52, p.414.)
Copies: NPL:M(Q988).   2560

n.d. KINNEY, Henry Walsworth
[Island of Hawaii: extract describing the death of Cook. With view of Napoopoo, Kealakekua Bay.]
(Cook, James—Captain Cook's journals, memorials, etc.: newspaper cuttings. Vol.1, p.114.)
Copies: NPL:M(Q980:Co1/NA1).   2561

Illustrations

See also the subhead Third Voyage—Illustrations.

CARTER GROUP

Originals, Including Photocopies of Originals

CARTER, George
Death of Captain Cook.
1781. Oil painting. 59½″ x 84″. Untitled; signed.
Copies: ANL(Nan Kivell). 2562

CARTER, George
[Death of Captain James Cook]; probably by G. Carter.
Oil painting. 37″ x 47½″ inside frame. Unsigned; undated.
Copies: NPL:M(ML41). 2563

CARTER, George
Death of Captain Cook, possibly by Carter.
Photograph of oil painting. Meas. of original 24″ x 30″. Meas. of photo 5⅞″ x 7¼″.
Copies: NPL:M(Small Picture File: Cook– Death 4). 2564

CARTER, George
Death of Captain James Cook, by George Carter.
Photograph of oil painting. Meas. of original 16″ x 24″. Meas. of photo 4½″ x 5¼″.
Original in the possession of Donald Angus, London, 1938.
Copies: NPL:M(Small Picture File: Cook– Death 5). 2565

Reproductions

CARTER, George
Death of Captain James Cook by the Indians of O, Why, Ee, one of
the Sandwich Islands G. Carter pinxit. S. Smith engraved the landscape,
I. Hall engraved the portrait of Captain Cook, the figures by I. Thorn-
waite. London, Published . . . by G. Carter . . . and Messrs. Sayer and
Bennet . . . Jan.ʸ 1st, 1784.
Meas. of engraved surface 16¾″ x 23⅜″.
Plate has been clipped.
Copies: NPL:M(V*Cook 32). 2566

The Same; published . . . Feb.ʸ 1 1784.
Meas. of engraved surface 17″ x 23½″.
The edges are torn so that plate mark is not visible.
Copies: NPL:D(Pf64). 2567

Another print.

Meas. of engraved surface 16¾″ x 23¼″.
Edges are torn so that only part of plate mark is visible.
Copies: NPL:M(PXD60,f.5).   2568

The Same; publish'd 12 May 1794, by Laurie & Whittle . . . London.

Meas. of engraved surface 16¹⁵⁄₁₆″ x 23⁷⁄₁₆″.
Plate has been clipped so that plate mark does not show.
Copies: NPL:D(Pf65).   2569

The Same. Proof before letters.

Meas. of engraved surface 16¹⁵⁄₁₆″ x 23⁷⁄₁₆″.
Copies: NPL:D(Pf66).   2570

DEATH of Captain Cook.

Engraving.
(Young, *Rev.* George—The Life and voyages of Captain James Cook. London, Whittaker, Treacher, 1836. Opp. p.435.)
Copies: NPL:M(980:Col/Y1A1); NPL:D(83/194).   2571

DEATH of Captain Cook, from an engraving at the United Service Museum.

Process plate.
(Kitson, Arthur—Captain James Cook. London, J. Murray, 1907. Opp. p.474.)
Copies: NPL:M(923.9/C771.2/14A1); NPL:D(90/206); NPL:R(S920/C771/4).   2572

CLEVELEY GROUP

Originals, Including Photocopies of Originals

CLEVELEY, James

Owhyee—Sandwich Islands [Death of Cook].

Watercolour. 17⅜″ x 24″ meas. of view, on mount 24″ x 31¼″.
Unsigned; undated. Title lettered on mount. Probably after the aquatint by Jukes of the original painting by John Cleveley from the sketch by his brother James.
Copies: NPL:D(DGXV* Cook 15).   2573

Reproductions

CLEVELEY, James

Mort du Capitaine Cook.

See View of Owhyee, no.2579.

CLEVELEY, James

View of Owhyee one of the Sandwich Islands. Drawn on the spot by Ja.ˢ Cleveley. Painted by Jn.º Cleveley, London. F. Jukes Aquat.ᵗ

July 5 1788. London, T. Martyn. Aquatint. 17¼″ x 23¾″ meas. of view, on sheet 19½″ x 26⅛″ which seems to be cut on plate mark.
Title is taken from dedication.
For similar watercolours in the possession of Mrs. Upcher, 1958, and of S.F. Sabin, 1958 *see* notes and photographs filed at NPL:M PXn–163 and PXn–164, and *see also*

DG D27 and DG XV* Cook 12–15. The illustration filed at DG D27 differs from all the others as it shows Capt. Cook leaving his vessel for the shore, while the others show the attack on Cook. In each case the watercolour is part of a set, entries for which are filed under Cleveley, James—Drawings relating to Cook's 3rd Voyage. For a reproduction of the Sabin watercolour see *Geographical Magazine* Dec. 1956, p.385.

Copies: NPL:M(V*Cook 18).   2574

Another print.

Partly hand-coloured.

Copies: NPL:M(V* Cook 15).   2575

Another print.

Trimmed to edge of view, hand-coloured.

Copies: NPL:M(V* Cook 16).   2576

Another print.

Hand-coloured. No lettering visible below view. c.$16\frac{3}{4}''$ x $23\frac{1}{2}''$ meas. of view, on sheet 19'' x c.24''.

Copies: NPL:M(V* Cook 17).   2577

Another print.

Probably a very faint impression of the Jukes aquatint.

Hand-coloured. No dedication, aquatinter's or publisher's name visible. There is a very faint pencil inscription lower right which probably reads 'Ex^t. at Mr. Martyn's Academy Great Marlborough Street London 1788'.

(Cf. rest of set at DG XV* Cook 1–3).

Titled in ink below view 'Owhyee one of the Sandwich Islands (The Death of Capt Cook—'. 17'' x $23\frac{1}{8}''$ meas. of view, $19\frac{1}{4}''$ x $25\frac{1}{2}''$ meas. of plate mark, on slightly larger sheet.

Copies: NPL:D(DGXV* Cook 4).   2578

The Same; with title Mort du Capitaine Cook. Ja.^{s} Cleveley [del.]. Piringer [sc.]. Paris, Bance aîné.

Aquatint. $16\frac{7}{8}''$ x $23\frac{7}{8}''$ meas. of view, on sheet $19\frac{1}{8}''$ x $25\frac{3}{8}''$.

Title is followed by an explanatory note.

(Voyage du cap.^{e} Cook No.4.)

Copies: NPL:M(V* Cook 22).   2579

Another print.

Copies: NPL:M(V* Cook 20).   2580

Another print.

Copies: NPL:D(DG XV* Cook II).   2581

Another print.

Aquatint printed in two colours, with additional hand-colour.

Copies: NPL:M(V* Cook 19).   2582

The Same. Cleveley [del.] Piringer [sc.], in different style from above. Title as above. No explanatory note, imprint or series.

Aquatint. 16¾″ x 23⅝″ meas. of view, on sheet 19¾″ x 27⅛″.

Copies: NPL:M(V* Cook 21). 2583

DEATH of Captain Cook. [Reproduced from] . . . copy of an original oil-painting by Webber in the Alexander Turnbull Library.

(Zimmermann, Heinrich—Account of the third voyage of Captain Cook. Trans. by U. Tewsley. Wellington, N.Z., Govt. Pr., 1926. *Alexander Turnbull Library—Bulletin, no.2*).
Incorrectly attributed to Webber.

Copies: NPL:M(980:Co4/Z1E1); NPL:D(92/227). 2584

DODD GROUP

Reproductions

THE DEATH of Captain Cook.

Process plate.
(Story, Alfred Thomas—The Building of the Empire. London, Chapman & Hall, 1898. Vol.2, p.173.)

Copies: NPL:M(942/S); NPL:R(S909/62). 2585

DEATH of Captain Cook. (Dodd del. Birrell sculp.)

Pub. Jy. 20 1785 by I. Fielding.
(Cook, J.—Third Voyage—Printed Accounts [1785. Abridged.]—Third and last voyage. London, John Fielding and John Stockdale, [1785?]. Opp. p.261.)

Copies: NPL:M(980:Co4/4A1). 2586

THE DEATH of Captain Cook. S. Hill, Sc.

(Cook, J.—Collected Voyages—Printed Accounts [1797 ed.]—Captain Cook's three voyages to the Pacific Ocean. Boston, Thomas & Andrews and D. West, 1797. Vol.2, opp. p.256.)

Copies: NPL:M(980:Co1/13A2). 2587

THE DEATH of Captain James Cook. D. Lizars sculpt.

Published 1st April, 1785, by R. Morison and Son.
(Cook, J.—Third Voyage—Printed Accounts [1785. Perth ed.]—Voyage to the Pacific Ocean. Perth, R. Morison & Son, 1785. Vol.3, opp. p.130.)

Copies: NPL:M(980:Co4/5A3). 2588

THE DEATH of Captain James Cook, F.R.S. at Owhyhee in MDCCLXXIX. D. Lizars sculp.[t]

Published 1st. April 1785, by R. Morison & Son. Right-hand edge guillotined. Lettered at top: Cook's Voyages.
(Cook, J.—Third Voyage—Printed Accounts [1785. Perth ed.]—A Voyage to the Pacific Ocean. 3rd ed. Perth, R. Morison, 1789. Vol.3, opp. p.130.)

Copies: NPL:M(980:Co4/5B3). 2589

THE DEATH of Captain James Cook, F.R.S. at Owhyhee in 1779. D. Lizars sculpt.

Lettered at top of print: Cook's Voyages.
(Cook, J.—Collected Voyages—Printed Accounts [1790 ed.]—Captain Cook's voyages round the world. Newcastle, M. Brown, 1790. Vol.2, opp. p.646.)
Copies: NPL:M(980:Col/7A2). 2590

THE DEATH of Captain James Cook, F.R.S. at Owhyhee in MDCCLXXIX. (Drawn by D.P. Dodd & others who where (*sic*) on the spot. Engraved by T. Cook.)

Publish'd Nov.ʳ 20, 1784, by J. Fielding *and others*. At head of print: Captain Cook's Voyage Octavo Edition.
(Cook, J.—Third Voyage—Printed Accounts [1784 ed.]—Voyage to the Pacific Ocean. London, printed by W. & A. Strahan for Nicol and T. Cadell, 1784. Vol.3, opp. p.199.)
Copies: NPL:M(980:Co4/1A3). 2591

Another print.

(*Inserted in* Kippis, *Rev.* A.—The Life of Captain James Cook. Opp. p.467.)
Copies: NPL:D(Q78/9). 2592

THE DEATH of Captain James Cook FRS at Owhyhee in MDCCLXXIX. (Drawn by D.P.Dodd & others who where (*sic*) on the spot. Engraved by T. Cook.)

Without imprint.
(Cook, J.—Third Voyage—Printed Accounts [1793 English ed.]—A Voyage to the Pacific Ocean. London, printed for Champante and Whitrow, etc., 1793. Vol.3, opp. p.199.)
Copies: NPL:M(980:Co4/14A3). 2593

KAPTEIN COOK vermoord door de wilden te Owyhee.

Engraving.
(Cook, J.—Third Voyage—Printed Accounts [1787 Dutch ed.]—Reis naar den Stillen Oceaan. Rotterdam, A. Bothall en D. Vis, 1787. Frontisp.)
Copies: NPL:M(980:Co4/10A1). 2594

KAPTEIN COOK vermoord door de wilden te Owyhee.

Engraving.
(Cook, J.—Third Voyage—Printed Accounts [1787 Dutch ed.]—Reis naar den Stillen Oceaan. Rotterdam, A. Bothall en D. Vis, 1788. Frontisp.)
Copies: NPL:M(980:Co4/10A2). 2595

HODGES GROUP

Originals, Including Photocopies of Originals

DEATH of Cook, possibly by William Hodges.

Photograph 5½″ x 8″ of an oil painting 54″ x 79″ in Parliament House, Sydney.
Notes, 1966, on an attempt to verify the attribution to Hodges are filed with photograph.
Copies: NPL:M(PXn72). 2596

Originals, Including Photocopies of Originals

WEBBER, John
[Death of Cook], by J. Webber.

Oil. 33¼″ x 47″.
Unsigned; undated.
The scene is the same as in the Bartolozzi engravings.
Copies: NPL:D(DG26).   2597

WEBBER, John
[Death of Captain Cook]; by J. Webber.

Watercolour. 14″ x 21$\frac{1}{16}$″ pasted on mount.
Unsigned; undated.
The scene is the same as in the Bartolozzi engravings.
(*In* [Three voyages round the world], plate no. 1.)
Copies: NPL:M(PXD59—² f.1).   2598

ATTACK on a navigator, formerly attributed to Webber and said to be attack on Cook.

Watercolour. 15¼″ x 20½″ inside mount.
Presented by Sir William Dixson, 1929.
Govt. Pr. photo. (neg. no.51596) is at NPL:M PX B1675 no.14.
B.Smith suggests this may not be an incident on Cook's voyage and therefore not by Webber. He suggested Ibbetson.
Copies: NPL:D(DG21).   2599

The Same.
Photograph.
Copies: NPL:D(DL 679A).   2600

ATTACK on a navigator, formerly attributed to Webber and said to be attack on Cook.

Watercolour. 15¼″ x 20½″ inside mount.
Presented by Sir William Dixson, 1929.
Govt. Pr. photo. (neg. no.51595 is at NPL:M PX B1675 no.15.
B.Smith suggests that this may not be of Cook and probably not by Webber, possibly by Ibbetson.
Copies: NPL:D(DG30).   2601

The Same.
Photograph.
Copies: NPL:D(DL 679B).   2602

Reproductions

WEBBER, John
The Death of Captain Cook. Drawn by J. Webber. The figures engraved

by F. Bartolozzi. The landscape by W. Byrne. Published 1.Jany 1784 . . .
by J. Webber . . . and W. Byrne . . . London.

Meas. of engraved surface 16¾″ x 23″.
Meas. of plate mark, 19″ x 24″.
Copies: NPL:M(V* Cook 28). 2603

The Same.

Clipped.
Meas. of engraved surface 16¾″ x 22¾″.
Copies: NPL:M(V* Cook 29). 2604

The Same.

Meas. of engraved surface 16⅞″ x 23⅛″.
Meas. of plate mark 18¹⁵⁄₁₆″ x 24⁵⁄₁₆″.
Copies: NPL:D(Pf61). 2605

The Same.

Meas. of engraved surface 16⅛″ x 22⅞″.
This has been clipped closely so that no legend shows, and pasted on page.
(*In* [Three voyages round the world], plate no. 2.)
Copies: NPL:M(PXD59–¹). 2606

The Same.

Without dedication.
Meas. of engraved surface 16¾″ x 22¹⁵⁄₁₆″.
Meas. of plate mark 19⅛″ x 24″.
Copies: NPL:M(PXD60,f.2). 2607

The Same.

Final state of plate, proof before letters.
Meas. of engraved surface 16⅝″ x 22¾″.
Meas. of plate mark 18¾″ x 23⅞″.
Copies: NPL:M(PXD60,f.1.) 2608

Another print.

Copies: NPL:M(PXD60,f.4). 2609

The Same [entitled] Death of Captn Cook. Drawn by Jn° Webber. The
figures etched by Fra Bartolozzi. The landscape by Will Byrne. Published
. . . Jany 1: 1782 by J. Webber and W. Byrne, London.

Meas. of engraved surface 16¹¹⁄₁₆″ x 22¹¹⁄₁₆″.
Meas. of plate mark 18¹³⁄₁₆″ x 23¹³⁄₁₆″.
Without dedication. The plate is unfinished and so was apparently not published. It
appears to be an earlier state of the two plates following.
Copies: NPL:M(PXD60,f.3). 2610

The Same. A later state of the preceding plate.

Meas. of engraved surface 16¾″ x 22¾″.
Plate clipped so that title and imprint do not show.
(*In* [Three voyages round the world], plate no. 128.)
Copies: NPL:M(PXD59–²,f.4).   2611

The Same. Drawn by Jn.º Webber. The figures eng.ᵈ by Fra Bartolozzi. The landscape by Will Byrne.

Meas. of engraved surface 16¾″ x 22⅞″.
Plate clipped so that title and imprint do not show. This, despite the slight difference in the legend, is probably a later state than the two previous engravings. Cook's hat, which in the two previous engravings is of a different shape from the hat in the 1784 and 1785 engravings, has here been erased on the plate.
(*In* [Three voyages round the world], plate no. 129.)
Copies: NPL:M(PXD59–²,f.5).   2612

The Same [entitled] The Death of Captⁿ Cook. Drawn by J. Webber. The Figures engraved by F. Bartolozzi. The landscape by W. Byrne. Published . . . Janʸ 1st. 1785 by W. Byrne and J. Webber, London.

Meas. of engraved surface 9¾″ x 15⅞″.
Meas. of plate mark 11⅞″ x 15⅞″.
Lacks dedication.
(*In* [Three voyages round the world], plate no. 126.)
Copies: NPL:M(PXD59–²,f.3).   2613

The Same. A 'pull' taken to show an earlier state of the previous engraving.

Meas. of engraved surface 9 13/16″ x 14⅞″.
Meas. of plate mark 11 15/16″ x 16″.
(*In* [Three voyages round the world], plate no. 126.)
Copies: NPL:M(PXD59–²,f.2).   2614

The Same [entitled] Mort tragique du Capitaine Cook le 15. Février, 1779. J. Webber pinx. Fessard sculp. . . . Dédiée et presentée à Monsieur de Bougainville . . . par Isabey. Paris, chez Isabey.

Meas. of engraved surface 8⅝″ x 11 13/16″.
Meas. of plate mark 11½″ x 13 5/16″.
With letterpress giving a brief biography of Cook.
Copies: NPL:M(V* Cook 31).   2615

Another print.

Clipped so that plate mark does not show.
Copies: NPL:D(Pe 217).   2616

WEBBER, John

[The Death of Cook, drawn by Webber, engraved by Bartolozzi.]
Photograph.
Copies: Captain Cook's Landing Place Trust.   2617

WEBBER, John

Death of Captain Cook: [engraving]. Drawn by J. Webber, engraved by F. Bartolozzi . . . and W. Byrne.

Reduced facs. with notes.
(English, Thomas H.—Introduction to the collecting and history of Whitby prints. Whitby, Horne & Son, 1931. Vol.1, B15.)
Copies: NPL:M(Q942.7/E); NPL:D(Q93/118). 2618

[CARD CASE in tortoiseshell with representation "Mort du capitaine Cook le 16 février 1779". Morel F[ecit].]

In oxidised silver.
Picture meas. 1 $\frac{15}{16}$″ x 3 $\frac{1}{8}$″; case meas. 2 $\frac{3}{4}$″ x 4 $\frac{1}{4}$″.
Copies: NPL:D(DR19). 2619

COOKS ERMORDUNG in Hawaii, 1779 (zu S.24,25). Nach einem alten Stich.

Process plate.
(Schultz-Ewerth, Erich—Erinnerungen an Samoa. Berlin, A. Scherl, [1926?]. Opp. p.40.)
Copies: NPL:M(989.4/S). 2620

THE DEATH of Captain Cook.

Engraving, with five vignettes surrounding illus. John Tallis & Co., London & New York.
(Cook, J.—Collected Voyages—Printed Accounts [1842 ed. 1852.]—The Voyages of Captain James Cook round the world. London, John Tallis, [1852]. Vol.2, frontisp.)
Copies: NPL:M(Q980:Co1/4C2). 2621

DEATH of Captain Cook.

Photocopy, pasted in.
(Kippis, *Rev.* Andrew—A Narrative of the voyages round the world . . . by Captain James Cook. London, Bickers & Son, 1883. Frontisp.)
Copies: NPL:M(980:Co1/K2S1). 2622

DEATH of Captain Cook.

Process plate. Lettered: Plate XXIII, Cook's Voyages.
(Cook, J.—Collected Voyages—Printed Accounts [189-. Hawkesworth's ed.]—The Voyages of Captain James Cook. London, Ward, Lock, Bowden, [189-?]. Vol.2, p.1128.)
Copies: NPL:M(Q980:Co1/5A2). 2623

[DEATH of Captain Cook.]

Process plate, in colour. *Lettered at foot:* A Tall man struck him on the back with a long club.
(Kingston, William Henry Giles—Captain Cook. London, Religious Tract Society [1904]. Opp. p.270.)
Copies: NPL:M(980:Co1/K1A1). 2624

THE DEATH of Captain Cook at Owhyee, one of the Sandwich Islands, in the North Pacific Ocean. Grainger, del. et sculp.

Coloured engraving. Meas. within frame lines 4¾″ x 6⅞″. Meas. of plate mark 6⅜″ x 8⅜″.
Copies: NPL:D(DL Pd626).   2625

Another print.

(*Inserted in* Kippis, A.—The Life of Captain James Cook. Opp. p.468).
Copies: NPL:D(Q78/9).   2626

The Same, [entitled] The Death of Captain Cook by the Natives of Owhyhee. Grainger— delin et sculp.

Published . . . by C.Cooke . . . Oct.31, 1788 [London]. Engraving. Meas. of engraved surface 4⅝″ x 6⅞″.
Copies: NPL:M(SSV* Cook 11).   2627

DEATH of Capt.ⁿ Cook. T. Clerk sculp.ᵗ

Lettered at top of print: Cooks Voyages.
(Cook, J.—Third Voyage—A Voyage to the Pacific Ocean. Leith, pr. by W. Reid & Co. for A. Constable & Co., 1813. Frontisp.)
Copies: NPL:M(980:Co4/17A2).   2628

THE DEATH of Capt.ⁿ Cook, Feb.ʸ 14. 1779.

Engraving.
(Cook, J.—Collected Voyages—Illustrations—Illustrations to Captain Cook's voyages; in a series of one hundred and fifteen engravings from the original drawings. Cheapside, W. and S. Graves, pr., n.d.)
Copies: NPL:M(980:Col/I1A1).   2629

THE DEATH of Capt.ⁿ Cook, Feb.ʸ 14. 1779.

Engraving.
(Cook, J.—Collected Voyages—Printed Accounts [1790. Anderson, G.W.]—A Collection of voyages round the world. [Comp. by G.W. Anderson.] London, A. Millar, W. Law and R. Cater, 1790. Vol.6, opp. p.1969.)
Copies: NPL:M(980:Col/6A6).   2630

Another print.
Copies: NPL:D(DL Pd678).   2631

AN EXACT REPRESENTATION of the death of Capt.ⁿ James Cook, F.R.S. at Karakakooa Bay in Owhyhee, on Feb.ʸ 14. 1779.

London, Published by Alexʳ Hogg at the Kings Arms Nº 16 Paternoster Row.
(Cook, J.—Collected Voyages—A New, authentic and complete collection of voyages. London, Alex. Hogg, [1784–6]. Opp. p.587.)
Copies: NPL:M(A346).   2632

1785 AN EXACT REPRESENTATION of the death of Captn James Cook, F.R.S. at Karakakooa Bay in Owhyhee, on Feby 14. 1779. Accurately engraved from a drawing made on the spot purposely for this work by A. Hogg.

London, Published by Alex^r Hogg at the Kings Arms N° 16 Paternoster Row Mar. 12 1785.

(Cook, J.—Collected Voyages—Printed Accounts [1784. Anderson, G.W.]—A New, authentic and complete collection of voyages. London, Alex. Hogg, [1784–6]. Opp. p.587.)

Copies: NPL:M(F980/5A1). 2633

AN EXACT REPRESENTATION of the death of Captn James Cook, F.R.S. at Karakakooa Bay in Owhyhee, on Feby 14 1779. Accurately engraved from a drawing made on the spot purposely for this work by A. Hogg.

London. Published by Alex.^{r} Hogg at the Kings Arms N° 16 Paternoster Row Mar. 12 1785. Folded.

(Cook, J.—Collected Voyages—Printed Accounts [1785. Hogg's ed.]—A New authentic and complete collection of voyages. London, Alex. Hogg, [1785]. Vol.5, opp. p.1968.)

Copies: NPL:M(980/H). 2634

Another print.

Copies: NPL:M(SSV* Cook 10). 2635

EXACT REPRESENTATION of the Death of Captn. James Cook, F.R.S., at Karakooa (*sic*) Bay, in the Owhyhee, on Feb.14th. 1779 . . . from a drawing made on the spot . . . by A. Hogg: [process reproduction with notes].

(English, Thomas H.— Introduction to the collecting and history of Whitby prints. Whitby, Horne & Son, 1931. Vol.1, H14.)

Copies: NPL:M(Q942.7/E); NPL:D(Q93/118). 2636

MORT de Cook. Bernard direxit.

(Cook, James—Third Voyage—Printed Accounts [1785. French ed.]—Troisième voyage. Paris, Hôtel de Thou, 1785. Tome 1, p.1.)

Copies: NPL:M(Q980:Co4/2A1). 2637

MORT de Cook. Bernard direxit.

(Cook, J.—Third Voyage—Printed Accounts [1785. French ed.]—Cartes et figures du troisième voyage. Paris, Hôtel de Thou, 1785.)

Copies: NPL:M(Q980:Co4/2B1). 2638

MORT de Cook. Brion direxit.

(Cook, J.—Collected Voyages—Printed Accounts [1817. French ed.]—Atlas du troisième voyage. Paris, Lepetit, 1817.)
Bibliothèque Portative des Voyages. Traduite de l'anglois par MM Henry et Breton. Tome XXVIII, plate 1.

Copies: NPL:M(980:Co1/23A7). 2639

MORT du Capitaine Cook.

Engraving. Lettered below print: Tant qu'il regarda les naturels en face, aucun d'eux n'eut la hardiesse.
(Cook, J.—Collected Voyages—Printed Accounts [1811. French ed.]—Voyages du Capitaine Cook. Paris, Lerouge, 1811. Tome 6, p.112.)
Copies: NPL:M(980:Col/20A6). 2640

MORT du Capitaine Cook. Voyer sculp.

At head of print: Muerte del capitan Cook. Nlle. Bibliothèque des Voyages. Tome 5, plate 11.
(Cook, J.—Collected Voyages—Printed Accounts [1841? French ed.]—Voyages autour du monde. [Ed. by] . . . William Smith. Paris, Société Bibliophile, [1841?]. Tome 5, opp. p.251.)
Copies: NPL:M(910.4/253A5). 2641

MORTE del Capitano Cook. Dall'Acqua inc. Lazaretti colori.

Hand-coloured.
(Cook, J.—Collected Voyages—Printed Accounts [1816-17. Italian ed.]—Navigazioni di Cook. Milano, Sonzogno e Comp., 1817. Tomo 7, p.200.)
Copies: NPL:M(980:Col/22A7). 2642

OTHER ARTISTS

THE DEATH of Captain Cook.

Process plate.
(Captain Cook's voyages. [Ed.] by N.B.Synge. London, J. Nelson, 1903. p.509.)
Copies: NPL:M(980:Col/40A1). 2643

DEATH of Captain James Cook.C I W fec^t.

Pub. Jan.24, 1806, by James Cundee. London, Engraving. 5$\frac{3}{8}$" x 7$\frac{11}{16}$".
(*Inserted in* Kippis, *Rev.* A.—The Life of Captain James Cook. Opp. p.515.)
Copies: NPL:D(Q78/9). 2644

Another print.

Copies: NPL:M(Small Picture File: Cook— Death 1). 2645

Another print.

(Wilson, Robert—Voyages of discoveries round the world. London, James Cundee, 1806. Vol.3, frontisp.)
Copies: NPL:M(980/W). 2646

[DEATH of Cook.]

Engraving.
(Horn, W.O., *pseud.*—James Cook. Wiesbaden, J. Niedner, [1860?]. Opp. p.132.)
Copies: NPL:M(980:Col/H3B1). 2647

[DEATH of Cook.]

Engraving.
(Horn, W.O., *pseud.*—James Cook. Stockholm, Ebeling & Co., 1867. Opp. p.126.)
Copies: NPL:M(980:Col/H3A1).   2648

MORT du Capitaine Cook à Owhy-hée, Février 1779. Benard direxit.

Engraving. Lettered at top of print: au Frontispiece.
(Cook, J.—Third Voyage—Printed Accounts of Associatès—Rickman—Troisième
voyage de Cook. Paris, Belin, 1782. Frontisp.)
Copies: NPL:M(980:Co4/R1C1).   2649

REPRESENTATION of the death of Capt Cook: [engraving, possibly
after Webber]. Published . . . July 1, 1781; by S.A. Cumberlege, Paternoster Row.

Meas. of engraved surface 6″ x 7⅜″.
Copies: NPL:M(V* Cook 31).   2650

Another print.
Copies: NPL:D(DL Pd625).   2651

REPRESENTATION of the murder of Capt. Cook at O-why-ee.

Engraving.
(Cook, J.—Third Voyage—Printed Accounts of Associates—Rickman—Journal of
Captain Cook's last voyage. London, E. Newbury, 1781. Frontisp.)
Copies: NPL:M(980:Co4/R1A1); NPL:D(78/31).   2652

UNIVERSAL MAGAZINE

A succinct account of the life and voyages of Captain James Cook; with
an exact representation of the death of that celebrated navigator; communicated by respectable authority, and elegantly engraved copper.
London, 1781.

Illus. port.
Extract from the *Universal Magazine*, vol.68, no.476, June 1781, pp.281–5. *Bound with*
other magazine extracts. *Cover title* Magazine articles, Cook, Banks, Dalrymple, etc.
Copies: NPL:M(910.4/122).   2653

BROWNE, GORDON

DEATH of Captain Cook, [by Gordon Browne].

(Cook, J.—Collected Voyages—Printed Accounts [1876. Low's ed. 1895.]—Captain
Cook's three voyages round the world. Ed. by C.R. Low. London, George Routledge
& Sons, 1895. Opp. p.470.)
Copies: NPL:M(980:Col/37B1).   2654

CORNÈ, M. F.

DEATH of Captain James Cook. Oil on copper. 21″ x 29″. Attributed to M.F.Cornè. Copied from an engraving in Atlas to Cook's Voyages. [Reproduced, not in colour].

(*In* Brewington, Marion Vernon— The Marine paintings and drawings in the Peabody Museum, by M.V. and D.Brewington. Salem, Mass., the Museum, 1968. p.44.)

Copies: NPL:R(NQ758.2/2). 2655

HAMILTON

THE DEATH of Capt.[n] Cook at O-why-hee, near Kamschatka, whose discoveries in His Last Voyage, as well as those of his First and Second, will be included in this New & Improved System of Geography. Hamilton delin. Thornton sculp.

(Millar, George Henry—The New, complete authentic and universal system of geography. London, Alex. Hogg, [1782]. Facing p.216.)

Copies: NPL:R(09:F909.9A/1). 2656

Another print.

Meas. within frame line $6\frac{7}{8}$″ x $4\frac{5}{16}$″.
Meas. of plate mark $21\frac{1}{8}$″ x $7\frac{7}{8}$″.

Copies: NPL:D(DL Pe223). 2657

MACFARLANE, J.

THE DEATH of Captain Cook, [by] J.Macfarlane.

Process plate.
(Besant, *Sir* Walter—Captain Cook. London, Macmillan, 1903. Opp. p.154.)

Copies: NPL:M(923.9/C771.2/11D1); NPL:D(90/119). 2658

OZANNE

THE DEATH of Captain Cook.

Sepia drawing. $3\frac{3}{8}$″ x $5\frac{11}{16}$″, pasted on mount.
Unsigned, untitled and undated.
The main part of the view, meas. $2\frac{1}{2}$″ x $4\frac{1}{2}$″ has been superimposed on the lower right side of the view, and this part is discoloured, perhaps as a result of the paste used. It seems probable that this part was done first, and the background added later.
Pencil note on mount in an unknown hand "Sepia drawing by Ozanne".

Copies: NPL:D(DL Pf63). 2659

RAMBERT, J. H.

[DEATH of Captain James Cook.]
Oil, 40″ x 56½″ inside frame.
No signature or date visible.
Copies: NPL:D(DG211).   2660

ROBINSON, W.B.

[DEATH of Captain Cook. By] W.B.Robinson.
Process plate, in colour.
(Lang, John—Story of Captain Cook. London, Jack, [1906]. p.118.)
Copies: NPL:M(923.9/C771.2/13A1).   2661

SEARLE

VILLAGE of Kaileakula in the Island of Hawaii; on the left at the cluster of huts fell Captain Cook in the year 1779, [by Capt. Searle].
Coloured sketch.
Copies: VSL.   2662

WILLIAMSON, J.

DEATH of Captain Cook [by] J.Williamson.
Process plate, in colour.
(Cook, J.—Collected Voyages—Cook's Voyages of discovery; ed. by J. Barrow. London, Black, 1904. Opp. p.358.)
Copies: NPL:M(980:Co1/36G1).   2663

DEATH of Captain Cook [by] J.Williamson.
Process plate, in colour.
(Mitton, Geraldine Edith—Captain Cook. London, A. & C. Black, 1927. p.74. *Peeps at Great Explorers series.*)
Copies: NPL:M(980:Co1/M4A1).   2664

ZOFFANY, JOHN

DEATH of Captain Cook; [reproduction of the painting by J. Zoffany in the Greenwich Hospital Gallery].
Process plate.
(Manners, *Lady* Victoria *and* Williamson, George Charles—John Zoffany. London, John Lane, 1920. Opp. p.100.)
Derived from a drawing by Hodges, see pp.40, 202–3.
Copies: NPL:M(Q759.2/2).   2665

DEATH of Captain Cook.

Photograph of original painting. 5¾″ x 7½″.
Original in possession of the Greenwich Hospital Gallery.
Copies: NPL:M(Small Picture File: Cook—Death 11).   2666

Another 2 prints, with lettering "54. Death of Captain Cook" photographed in the lower left-hand corner.
Copies: NPL:M(Small Picture File: Cook—Death 10,12).   2666a

Articles, etc., about the Illustrations

1924 DIXSON, *Sir* William

Rare pictures relative to Australia (death of Captain Cook): notes of a lantern lecture.
(Royal Australian Historical Society—*Journal and Proceedings*. Vol.10, pp.205–7. 1924.)
Copies: NPL:M(991/R, Ref.Books); NPL:D(9/69); NPL:R(S991.06/1A, Ref.Books).
2667

1926 PHILLIPS, S.W.

Death of Captain Cook, some account of the contemporary illustrations of this incident.
(Hawaiian Historical Society—*Annual report* 1926, pp.64–8).
Copies: NPL:M(999.6/H).   2668

ILLUSTRATIONS, ETC.

This section includes works about places with which Cook was associated as well as illustrations of them.

THE APOTHEOSIS of Captain Cook, from a design by P.J. de Loutherbourg R.A. The view of Karakakooa Bay is from a drawing by John Webber, R.A. (the last he made) in the collection of M.ʳ G. Baker.
London. Pub.ᵈ Jan.ʸ 20. 1794 by J. Thane. Engraving. Meas. of plate mark 10½″ x 8⅝″.
Copies: NPL:D(DL Pf73).   2669

Another print.
Copies: NPL:M(SV*Cook 8).   2670

Another print.
Copies: NPL:M(V*Cook 33A).   2671

Another print.
Hand-coloured. Cut to omit plate mark.
Copies: NPL:D(DL Pe226).   2672

The Same.

Proof before letters.
Meas. of engraved surface $10\frac{7}{16}''$ x $8\frac{5}{8}''$.
Meas. of sheet $13''$ x $11\frac{1}{8}''$.
Copies: NPL:D(DL F78/5). 2673

NEPTUNE raising Captn Cook up to Immortality; a Genius crowning him with a Wreath of Oak, and Fame introducing him to History. In the Front Ground are the Four Quarters of the World presenting to Britannia their various Stores. (Designed by H. Ramberg. Engraved by J. Neagle and Ornamented by W. Grainger.)

Published as the Act directs by J.Cooke N°. 17 Paternoster Row.
At head of print: Frontispiece to Bankes's New System of Geography.
(*In* Bankes, *Rev.* Thomas, *and others*—A New, royal and authentic system of geography. London, C.Cooke, [1798]. Frontisp.)
Copies: NPL:M(X910/11A); VSL. 2674

[NINE PHOTOGRAPHS relating to Cook.]

Including photographs of:
Cook medallion, after Pingo.
Portrait, after Dance; copy of an American engraving, from the *Picturesque Atlas.*
Copley medal.
Resolution and *Adventure* medal.
Death of Cook, drawn by Webber, engraved by Bartolozzi.
Endeavour hull.

Copies: Captain Cook's Landing Place Trust. 2675

[PHILOSOPHY inviting Youth to the heights of Science: allegorical representation with bust of Cook, 3 Cupids playing around it, and a figure holding a scroll and pointing to a temple of Fame. With verse.] T. Stothard, del. T. Cook sculp.

[1789?] Engraving. $5\frac{7}{8}''$ x $3\frac{11}{16}''$. Plate mark cut.
Copies: NPL:D(DL Pd674). 2676

Another print.
Copies: NPL:D(DL Pd675). 2677

Another print.
(*Inserted in* Kippis, *Rev.* A.—Life of Captain Cook. Opp. p.518.)
Copies: NPL:D(Q78/8). 2678

PLAQUE commemorating Capt. Cook, inscribed with lines from W.C. Wentworth's poem *Australasia*, referring to Capt. Cook.

Negative.
(*In* Nicholls, E.D.Brooke—Collection of negatives, box 2.)
Plaque is attached to a wooden surface and is surrounded by a laurel wreath.
Copies: NPL:M(Orig.Negs.14). 2679

Coat of Arms, etc.

[1785] GRANT OF ARMS made to Mrs. Cook and to Cook's descendants in 1785.

Scroll meas. 15½″ x 20″, within 2 seals in metal cases attached to the bottom by ribbon. Coat of arms and crests in watercolour. In a leather covered case tooled with gold.

Copies: NPL:M(LR27). 2680

The Same, [entitled] Arms of Captain James Cook R.N. granted by King George III to his widow to be borne by his descendants and placed on any monument or otherwise to his memory.

Reproduction in watercolours of the original. Meas. of sheet 13″ x 9½″.

Copies: NPL:M(SSV*Cook 9). 2681

1785 [PORTION of Cook's coat-of-arms incorporated into publisher's decoration on title-page.]

(*In* Cook, J.—Third Voyage—Printed Accounts [1785 Abridged.]—Third and last voyage. London, John Fielding and J. Stockdale, 1785.)

Copies: NPL:M(980:Co4/4A1). 2682

1789 [AN ACCOUNT of Cook's coat of arms.]

(*In* Kippis, *Rev.* Andrew—Biographia Britannica. London, Rivington & Sons, 1789. Vol.4, p.245.)

Copies: NPL:M(F920.042); NPL:R(09:DF920/47). 2683

1797 [COAT OF ARMS of Captain James Cook.]

(*The Monthly Review*, vol.22, p.264. 1797.)

Copies: NPL:M(052/6); NPL:R(DS050/M789). 2684

[1912] CAPTAIN COOK'S coat-of-arms, as engraven on the Cook monument, [Whitby].

(*In* Captain Cook monument. Whitby, Horne & Son, pr., [1912]. p.10.)

Copies: NPL:M(923.9/C771.2/16A1); NPL:D(91/998). 2685

1930 [COAT-OF-ARMS of Captain Cook: engraved for a bookplate.]

(Australian Ex Libris Society, Sydney—*Journal*. No.1, 1930, p.27.)
See also no.2691.

Copies: NPL:M(097.06/A); NPL:D(93/673). 2686

1939 [SHIELD OF ARMS granted for Captain James Cook: plate with blazon.]

(Wagner, Anthony Richard—Historic heraldry of Britain. London, O.U.P., 1939. Plate 23, p.87.)

Copies: NPL:M(Q929.6/W); NPL:R(S929.6/4). 2687

1940 [ROUGH sketch of Capt. Cook's coat-of-arms; from a watercolour drawing previously in the Australian Museum, Sydney, and later transferred to the Mitchell Library.]
(*Australian Genealogist* vol.3, pt.8, p.154, Oct.1940.)
Copies: NPL:M(A929.05/A). 2688

n.d. ARMS of Captain James Cook, R.N., granted by King George III to his widow. [Reproduced in colour].
(*In* New South Wales—Government Printing Office—[Album of samples of the work. 1939?].)
Copies: NPL:M(Q655.3/1A1). 2689

Another print.
(*In* James Cook Papers—Biography and bibliography. p.349.)
Copies: NPL:D(MS.Q144). 2690

n.d. [BOOKPLATE of Captain Cook's coat-of-arms.]
(*In* Hobbes, Thomas—Philosophicall rudiments concerning government and society. London, R. Royston, 1651. Inside front cover.)
See also no.2686.
Copies: NPL:M(142/H). 2691

n.d. CAPT. COOK: [coat-of-arms. Reproduced in black and white].
(*In* James Cook Papers—Biography and bibliography. p.345.)
Copies: NPL:D(MS.Q144). 2692

n.d. ROBINS, J.F.
H.M.S. *Endeavour* and Cook's coat-of-arms.
Original sketch. Meas. inside frame 11½″ x 17″. Signed in lower right-hand corner.
Copies: Captain Cook's Landing Place Trust. 2693

Photograph.
(*In* James Cook Papers—Biography and bibliography. p.347.)
Copies: NPL:D(MS.Q144). 2694

London

See also the headings *Personal—Relics*, and *Personal—Monuments*.

1906 CAPTAIN COOK'S London residence.
(Newspaper cuttings, vol. 113, p. 47.)
Sydney Morning Herald, Aug. 9, 1906.
Copies: NPL:M(Q991/N). 2695

[1906] LONDON COUNTY COUNCIL

Captain James Cook, No.88 Mile End Road.

(*In its* Indications of houses of historical interest in London. London, [1906]. Pt.14, pp.12–16.)

Bound with other publications as London County Council—*Reports*, 1079–1168.

Copies: NPL:R(DQ352.0421/8). 2696

1907 MEMORIAL TABLET, terracotta in colour, which was fixed to Cook's house, 88 Mile End Rd., Oct.4, 1907.

Presented to the Trust by the London County Council.

Copies: Captain Cook's Landing Place Trust. 2697

1907 WHERE Captain Cook once lived: [at Clapham. Extract from *World's News*, 9.3.1907.]

(*In* Watson, James Henry— Scrap book, vol.3, p.2 (c).)

Copies: NPL:M(F990.1/W) 2698

1907–8 LONDON COUNTY COUNCIL—Architects Department

Photographs, exterior and interior, of 88 Mile End Rd., Stepney, 1907–8, 1950. With plans and architectural detail, 1958. Also, memorial tablet, terracotta in colour, which was fixed to the house, Oct.4, 1907; and chimney pot and wooden mantel-piece from the house. Presented to the Trust by the London County Council.

Copies: Captain Cook's Landing Place Trust. 2699

1917 BERTIE, Charles Henry

Captain Cook's house, no. 88 Mile End Road, E. [London].

Illus.

(Australian Historical Society—*Journal*. Vol.4, 1917. pp.24–5.)

Copies: NPL:M(991/R,Ref.Books); NPL:D(9/69); NPL:R(S991.06/1,Ref.Books). 2700

1926 COOK'S HOUSE . . . in Mile End Road, London. [Reproduction of a photograph. Extract from *Sydney Mail*, Ap.28, 1926.]

(Captain Cook: newspaper cuttings, p.98.)

Copies: NPL:M(Q980:Co1/N1A1). 2701

1926 THE HOUSE where Cook [lived] in Mile End Road, London. [Reproduction of a photograph. Extract from the *Daily Telegraph*, May 1, 1926.]

(Captain Cook: newspaper cuttings, p.94.)

Copies: NPL:M(Q980:Co1/N1A1). 2702

1929 FLETCHER, Hanslip

An East London sanctuary: [illustration].

Extract from the *Sunday Times* Mar.10, 1929. Shows the parish church at Barking where Captain Cook was married to Elizabeth Batts, Dec.21, 1762.

Copies: NPL:M(Small Picture File: Cook—Miscellanea 1). 2703

1933 QUEEN ANNE HOUSES doomed . . . at Clapham Common: [Cook's residence, no. 23 Church Row].
(*Observer*, London, Dec. 3, 1933, p.18.)
Copies: NPL:R(F079/O 14).   2704

1957 ROWSON, Cyril R.
Captain Cook's house. [With an illustration of 88 Mile End Road, London.]
(*Trident*, vol.19, p.89, Feb. 1957.)
Copies: NPL:M(Q656.505/1).   2705

Yorkshire

[190–?] CAPTAIN James Cook. Photographs of Yorkshire villages: Marton, Great Ayton, Staithes & Whitby. [190–?].
Album.
Copies: Captain Cook's Landing Place Trust.   2706

[1902] BALGARNIE, Florence
Captain Cook and Yorkshire.
(Old New South Wales; newspaper cuttings, vol.1, p.1.)
Copies: NPL:M(Q991/0).   2707

1924 CAPTAIN COOK'S birthplace.
Illus.
(Newspaper cuttings, vol.165, p.77. 1923–4.)
Letters from *Sydney Morning Herald*, Feb.12, 1924.
Copies: NPL:M(Q991/N).   2708

[1924?] CAPTAIN James Cook F.R.S.
c.1924. Postcard.
Shows Cook's portrait after Dance in medallion with facsimile of signature, and views of birth-place, etc.
Copies: NPL:M(Small Picture File: Cook-Birthplace 26).   2709

n.d. SCENES in Yorkshire, connected with the history of Captain Cook.
11 photographs.
Copies: Captain Cook's Landing Place Trust.   2710

Yorkshire

Easby

For references to the monument at Easby Hill *see* the heading ̰*Personal—Monuments—Great Britain—Easby.*

PERSONAL – ILLUSTRATIONS, ETC.

Yorkshire

Great Ayton

CAPTAIN COOK at Great Ayton.
(Newspaper cuttings, vol. 17, p. 21.)
Extract from *Sydney Morning Herald*, 18th June, 1910.
Copies: NPL:M(Q991/N).   2711

CAPTAIN COOK'S house, Great Ayton; and Back of Captain Cook's house, Great Ayton.
Two photographs. Each 4½″ x 6″.
Copies: NPL:M(Small Picture File: Cook—Birthplace 22a–b).   2712

CAPTAIN COOK'S school: [illustration. Extract from *Sunday Times*, Ap.25, 1909.]
(Newspaper cuttings, vol.13, p.26.)
Copies: NPL:M(Q991/N).   2713

GREAT AYTON, Yorks. Exterior and interior of schoolroom where Captain Cook was educated: [illustration].
(*In* Kingston, William Henry Giles—Captain Cook, his life, voyages and discoveries. London, Religious Tract Society, [1904]. p.22.)
Copies: NPL:M(980:Co1/K1A1).   2714

HOUSE at Great Ayton, where Captain Cook lived as a boy with his parents: [illustrations].
(*In* Kingston, William Henry Giles—Captain Cook, his life, voyages and discoveries. London, Religious Tract Society, [1904]. p.16.)
Copies: NPL:M(980:Co1/K1A1).   2715

PORCH AND SUNDIAL, Great Ayton Church, Yorkshire.
Photograph. 5″ x 4″.
Copies: NPL:M(Small Picture File: Cook—Birthplace 25).   2716

SCHOOLHOUSE of Captain Cook. [Extract from *Sydney Morning Herald*, 16 Feb.1924.]
(Newspaper cuttings: Captain Cook, p.51.)
Copies: NPL:M(Q980:Co1/N1A1).   2717

TINDALE, J., *photographer*
Captain Cook's school, Great Ayton, now converted into a museum.
1969. Two photographs. 6 15/16″ x 9⅝″.
Copies: NPL:M(Small Picture File: Cook—Birthplace 6–7).   2718

493

Yorkshire

Marton

For references to the Cook memorial urn at Marton *see* the heading *Personal—Monuments—Great Britain—Marton.*

BIRTHPLACE of Captn Cook, Marton in Cleveland.
Photograph by J. Tindale c.1968 of an old print. $6\frac{7}{8}''$ x $9\frac{5}{8}''$.
Copies: NPL:M(Small Picture File: Cook—Birthplace 8). 2719

The Same, an older photograph not showing handwritten title of old print. $7''$ x $11\frac{3}{4}''$.
Copies: NPL:M(Small Picture File: Cook—Birthplace 9). 2720

The Same, photograph c.1928.
$8\frac{1}{2}''$ x $6\frac{1}{2}''$.
Copies: NPL:M(Small Picture File: Cook—Birthplace 10). 2721

BIRTHPLACE of Captain Cook, Marton, Yorkshire: Enlarged and reproduced by heliotype from Rock & Co.'s Views and Scenery of Hull.
(*Historical Records of New South Wales.* Sydney, Govt. Pr., 1893. Vol.1, pt.1, p.299.)
Copies: NPL:M(991/N); NPL:D(89/267); NPL:R(994.4/44). 2722

BIRTHPLACE of Captain Cook, Marton, Yorkshire.
(*In* McFarland, Alfred—Captain Cook, his life and voyages, services to New Holland and to man. Sydney, Govt. Pr., 1899. p.7.)
Copies: NPL:M(923.9/C771.2/12A1); NPL:R(S920/C771/7). 2723

BOLCKOW, C.J.W., *Marton Hall, Yorks.*
ALS 13 Mar 1895 to E.A.Petherick, mentioning the cottage at Marton where Cook was born.
pp.3, 8vo; also TS copy.
(Miscellaneous papers relating to Cook.)
Copies: ANL(MS.108). 2724

CLIFFORD, R.C., *photographer*
Memoirs of the late Capt. Cook.
Photograph. $5\frac{1}{2}''$ x $7\frac{3}{4}''$ inside mount.
Shows Capt. Cook's monument and bronze tablet surrounded by views of church, school, house, etc., at Marton.
Copies: NPL:M(V*Cook 34B). 2725

COOK'S BIRTHPLACE: [illustration].
(*In* Chapman, George Thomson—Centenary memorial of Captain Cook's description of New Zealand one hundred years ago. Auckland, Chapman, 1870. pp.154.)
Copies: NPL:M(987/84A1); NPL:D(87/138); NPL:R(S997A/73). 2726

COOK'S BIRTHPLACE: [process plate].

(*In* Watts, Ebenezer John Moore—Stories from Australian history. Sydney, W. Brooks & Co., 1908. p.37.)

Copies: NPL:M(990.1/W); NPL:D(91/164). 2727

COOK'S BIRTHPLACE: [illustration].

(*In* Watts, Ebenezer John Moore—Stories from Australian history. 2nd ed. Sydney, W. Brooks & Co., 1914. p.39.)

Copies: NPL:M(990.1/W). 2728

COOK'S BIRTHPLACE in Yorkshire: [extract from the *Sydney Mail*, Ap.28, 1926].

(*In* Newspaper cuttings: Captain Cook, p.98.)

Copies: NPL:M(Q980:Col/N1A1). 2729

HORNE, W.N.

The Clay biggin, or cottage, where Marton Hall now is, where Captain Cook was born. Destroyed about 1786. [Reproduction of a sketch signed W.N. Horne.]

(Captain Cook bi-centenary celebrations, *Cleveland*, 1928—Souvenir. Middlesbrough, Hood & Co., pr., 1928. p.[8c].)

Copies: NPL:M(Q923.9/C771.2/4A1); NPL:D(Q92/164). 2730

KING, W.

Supposed cottage in which Captain Cook was born. Woodcut by W. King: [photographic reproduction, with notes].

(English, Thomas H.—Introduction to the collecting and history of Whitby prints. Whitby, Horne & Son, Ltd., 1931. Vol.1, K.7.)

Copies: NPL:M(Q942.7/E); NPL:D(Q93/118). 2731

NEW SOUTH WALES—Government Printer

Birthplace of Captain Cook: [a photograph].

(*In* Photographs illustrating the earliest times of New South Wales. Sydney, [n.d.]. p.80.)

Copies: NPL:M(F981/N). 2732

RUINS of the house Captain Cook was born in at Marton, Yorks.

Possibly head of a calendar with "December" inserted in title.
(*Inserted in* Kippis, A.—Life of Captain James Cook. Opp. p.3.)

Copies: NPL:D(Q78/9). 2733

VILLAGE OF MARTON, near Middlesborough, where Captain Cook was born: [illustration].

(*In* Kingston, William Henry Giles—Captain Cook, his life, voyages and discoveries. London, Religious Tract Society, 1904. p.12.)

Copies: NPL:M(980:Col/K1A1). 2734

Yorkshire

Marton Church

COOK'S BIRTH PLACE. Views of Marton Church.
(*Australian Town and Country Journal*, Mar.11, 1908.)
Copies: NPL:R(F079/A938).   2735

MARTON CHURCH where Captain Cook was baptised 1728: [view].
(*In* Kearton, Cherry—I visit the Antipodes. London, Jarrolds, [1937]. p.17.)
Copies: NPL:M(980/K); ANL.   2736

St CUTHBERT CHURCH, Marton in Cleveland.
Photograph. 3½″ x 5½″.
Copies: NPL:M(V*Cook 34C).   2737

The Same, newscutting illustration.
Copies: NPL:M(Small Picture File: Cook—Birthplace 5).   2738

TINDALE, J., *photographer*
St Cuthbert Church, Marton-in-Cleveland: exterior, memorial window, churchyard and Cook family tombstone.
c.1968. Four photographs. Each $9\frac{5}{16}$″ x $7\frac{11}{16}$″.
The window shows St Nicholas, the patron saint of sailors. The face of the Saint is supposed to be a likeness of Captain Cook.
Copies: NPL:M(Small Picture File: Cook—Birthplace 1–4).   2739

Yorkshire

Marton School

CAPT. COOK'S Memorial Schools, Marton.
Postcard photograph. 3½″ x 5½″.
Copies: NPL:M(V*Cook 34A).   2740

Yorkshire

Staithes

AERIAL VIEW of Staithes.
1952? Reproduction of photograph. 3¾″ x 5¼″.
Cut from the *Field*. Cutting includes letter to editor re view.
Copies: NPL:M(Small Picture File: Cook—Birthplace 24).   2741

THE SHOP at Straiths (*sic*), Yorkshire, where Captain Cook was apprenticed before he went to sea: [illustration].

(*In* Kingston, William Henry Giles— Captain Cook, his life, voyages and discoveries. London, Religious Tract Society, [1904]. p.50.)

Copies: NPL:M(980:Col/K1A1).   2742

STAITHES.

Photograph by J. Tindale c.1968 of oil painting. 6⅛″ x 9¾″.
The painting is in the possession of Whitby Urban District Council.

Copies: NPL:M(Small Picture File: Cook—Birthplace 19).   2743

STAITHS (*sic*): [wood engraving]. P. Starling, sc.

(*In* Young, Rev. George— Life and voyages of Captain James Cook. London, Whittaker, Treacher & Co., 1836. p.4.)

Copies: NPL:M(980:Col/Y1A1); NPL:D(83/194); ANL; Captain Cook's Landing Place Trust; VSL.   2744

STRAITHES (*sic*).

Photograph of old print. 3¾″ x 5½″.

Copies: NPL:M(Small Picture File: Cook—Birthplace 18).   2745

THORPE, Thomas

Staithes, dedicated to the Right Honorable the Earl of Pembroke. Sketched by Tho.ˢ Thorpe. Drawn on stone by John Jordison.

n.d. Lithograph. Hand-coloured. Meas. inside ruled frame lines 11⅛″ x 17⅛″.

Copies: NPL:D(DL Pf83).   2746

WALL, F.

Staithes, Yorkshire.

19-. Watercolour. 7″ x 10″ inside mount.
Signed "F.Wall". Untitled, undated.
Presented 1924.

Copies: NPL:M(V*Cook 34E).   2747

WILSON, G.W., *photographer*

Staithes & Cowbar—Nab, Yorkshire.

Photograph no.5450. 7⅜″ x 11¼″.

Copies: NPL:M(Small Picture File: Cook—Birthplace 23)   2748

Yorkshire

Whitby

For references to the statue at Whitby *see* the heading *Personal—Monuments—Great Britain—Whitby.*

THE "GHAUT". Whitby, now demolished, next to Cook's house in Grape Lane.

Photograph of a print. Meas. of photo. $9\frac{3}{4}''$ x $9\frac{5}{8}''$.
The print is in the possession of the Whitby Literary and Philosophical Society.

Copies: NPL:M(Small Picture File: Cook—Birthplace 12).   2749

TIN GHAUT, Whitby.

Postcard photograph $5\frac{1}{4}''$ x $3\frac{1}{4}''$.
With covering letter from H.L. Boyle, 1939.

Copies: NPL:M(Small Picture File: Cook—Birthplace 13).   2750

VIEWS of Whitby: (a) Harbour entrance, (b) Whitby from East Cliff, (c) West Cliff from East Cliff, (d) Whitby looking South, (e) East Cliff.

5 postcard photographs. Each $3\frac{1}{4}''$ x $5\frac{1}{4}''$.

Copies: NPL:M(V*Cook 34G–L).   2751

WHITBY: engraved by I. Walker from a drawing of Tayleure after Trueman. Pub. April 2nd 1798, by I. Walker. London.

(*Inserted in* Smith, E.—Life of Sir Joseph Banks. 1911. Vol.1, facing p.54.)

Copies: Australasian Pioneers' Club, Sydney.   2752

WHITBY, from the Angel Inn yard: [wood engraving] by P. Starling, sc.

(*In* Young, *Rev.* George—Life and voyages of Captain James Cook. London, Whittaker, Treacher & Co., 1836. p.8.)

Copies: NPL:M(980:Co1/Y1A1); NPL:D(83/194); ANL; Captain Cook's Landing Place Trust; VSL.   2753

WHITBY from west cliff.

Photograph. 7" x 11".

Copies: NPL:M(Small Picture File: Cook—Birthplace 11).   2754

WHITBY HARBOUR, c.1826.

Photograph c.1968 of old print. Meas. of photo. $6\frac{3}{4}''$ x $9\frac{3}{4}''$.
The print is in the possession of the Whitby Literary and Philosophical Society.

Copies: NPL:M(Small Picture File: Cook—Birthplace 20).   2755

Another print, date of view given in pencil on back as c.1750.

Copies: NPL:M(Small Picture File: Cook—Birthplace 21).   2756

BOYLE, H.L.

Site of residence near Grape Lane, Whitby. (H.L. Boyle to S. Wilcox, 25.6.1940).

(Ships: correspondence, etc. 1934–.)

Copies: NPL:M(MS.AS97).   2757

Yorkshire

Whitby House

CAPTAIN COOK'S house, Grape Lane, Whitby: [reproduction of a photograph].
(*In* Captain Cook monument. Whitby, [1912]. p.26.)
Copies: NPL:M(923.9/C771.2/16A1); NPL:D(91/998).   2758

CAPTAIN COOK'S house, Whitby.
Postcard photograph. $5\frac{1}{2}''$ x $3\frac{1}{2}''$.
Copies: NPL:M(V*Cook 34F).   2759

Another print.
Copies: NPL:M(Small Picture File: Cook—Birthplace 14).   2760

CRAWSHAW, Lionel T.
Capt. Cook's Attic, Whitby.
Etching. 7″ x 9″.
Signed 'Lionel T. Crawshaw'. Title scratched on plate.
Copies: NPL:M(V*Cook 35B).   2761

Reproduced, with notes, in English, T.H.—Introduction to the collecting and history of Whitby prints. Whitby, Horne & Son, 1931. Vol.1, C3.
Copies: NPL:M(Q942.7/E); NPL:D(Q93/118).   2762

CRAWSHAW, Lionel T.
Captn Cook's House [at Whitby].
Etching. $6\frac{7}{8}''$ x 5″.
Signed "Lionel T. Crawshaw" and titled in pencil below plate mark.
Copies: NPL:M(V*Cook 35A).   2763

HALL, E., *photographer*
Grape Lane, Whitby; Captain Cook's attic; stairs and other interior details.
7 photographs. Each $4\frac{1}{2}''$ x $6\frac{1}{4}''$.
Copies: NPL:M(Small Picture File: Cook—Birthplace 15–17).   2764

VIEW of Captain Cook's House from Whitby Harbour. [Reproduction of a photograph.]
(Captain Cook monument. Whitby, [1912]. p.33.)
Copies: NPL:M(923.9/C771.2/16A1); NPL:D(91/998).   2765

Melbourne, Victoria

Captain Cook's Cottage

1934 BRIERLEY, RUTHERFORD & SYME

Detailed plans for the removal of Cook's Cottage from Great Ayton to Melbourne. Prepared by Brierley, Rutherford & Syme, architects, York, Sept. 1933–Feb. 1934. Key to Cook's Cottage.

Copies: VSL. 2766

[1934?] CAPTAIN COOK'S Cottage, Melbourne.

1934+. Colour reproduction of photograph. 8½" x 12".
Captioned 'Captain Cook's cottage was built at Great Ayton, Yorkshire, by the parents Captain Cook and removed to the present site in the Fitzroy Gardens, Melbourne, in 1934'.

Copies: NPL:M(Small Picture File: Melbourne—Monuments—Cook's Cottage). 2767

1934 GILL, George Hermon

Captain Cook's cottage, by H. Gill; with drawings by E. Paterson. Melbourne, Lothian, 1934.

pp.32.
See also no. 2108.

Copies: NPL:M(923.9/C771.2/32A1); ANL; VSL. 2768

[1936?] PATTON, C.

Captain Cook's cottage, transferred from England to Fitzroy Gardens. Melbourne.

Reproduction of charcoal drawing, 7" x 9" pasted on mount.
The original is signed "C. Patton 1936" in lower right corner.

Copies: NPL:M(Small Picture File: Melbourne—Monuments—Cook's Cottage). 2769

1937 CAPTAIN COOK'S COTTAGE [in Fitzroy Gardens, Melbourne: a coloured reproduction from a photograph].

(*In* Howorth, Allison—Cooee England. Melbourne, G. Batchelor, 1937. Frontisp.)

Copies: NPL:M(914.2/H). 2770

1968 LAISHLEY, A.L.

The Cottage in the Fitzroy Gardens, [Melbourne].
Illus.
(*Yorkshire Life*, vol.22, no.8, Aug. 1968, pp.19 & 21.)

Copies: NPL:M(Q914·274/1). 2771

n.d. CAPTAIN COOK: cottage purchased for Victoria.

[Newspaper cuttings, various dates.]

Copies: NPL:M(Q980:Co1/N2A1). 2772

PERSONAL
MEDALS, MEDALLIONS, COINS AND POSTAGE STAMPS
Medals

The medals are here arranged in chronological order, the specimens of each medal being followed by illustrations of the medal. For references about the medals, *see forward—* Printed Books, Manuscripts, etc., about the Medals.

RESOLUTION AND *ADVENTURE* Medal, 1772. Brass medal. 44mm. *Obverse:* Head of George III. *Legend:* George III, King of Gr. Britain, France, and Ireland, etc. B:F *Reverse:* The *Resolution* and *Adventure*. *Exergue:* Sailed from England March MDCCLXXII.

With die crack across lower left corner of reverse side. Cast from first die, and shows anchor weighed.

Copies: NPL:M(R393).   2773

Another specimen.

Copies: NPL:D.   2774

The Same, in bronze, with die crack.

Copies: NPL:M(R394).   2775

Another specimen.

Copies: NPL:M(R395).   2776

Another specimen, with small loop inserted in top edge.

Copies: NPL:D.   2777

The Same, in silver.

Cast from second die, and shows anchors home.

Copies: NPL:M(R392).   2778

Another 2 specimens.

Copies: NPL:D.   2779

The authorship of this medal has been variously assigned. William Barnett, the gem engraver, and Edward Burch, R.A., have each been named as its designer, apparently because the medal bears the initials B:F. But a pamphlet published at Birmingham in 1926, entitled "Matthew Boulton's Otaheite medal" proves that Matthew Boulton, of Boulton and Fothergill, Birmingham, was the designer. The medal was struck to commemorate the departure of Cook's second voyage, and specimens of it were taken by Cook for distribution to the natives, as testimonies that he and his companions were the first discoverers. A second die was made for the medal as the first cracked and some of the specimens show this defect. There is also a slight difference in the angles of the anchors, the first die shows the anchor "weighed" and the second "home". The medal was struck in gold, silver, bronze and brass.

The Same. Photograph.

Copies: Captain Cook's Landing Place Trust.   2780

Reproduced in Clowes, W.L.—The Royal Navy. London, Sampson, Low, Marston and Co., 1899. Vol.4, p.117.

Copies: NPL:R(DQ359.0942/13).   2781

Reproduced in Kitson, Arthur—Captain James Cook. London, John Murray, 1907. Opp. p.499.

Copies: NPL:M(923.9/C771.2/14A1).   2782

Reproduced in McNab, R.—Murihiku: a history. Wellington, N.Z., W. & T., 1909. p.60.

Copies: NPL:M(997.9/M).   2783

Reproduced in The Hakluyt Society— Works, ser.2, vol.36, pt.2. The Quest and occupation of Tahiti. London, 1915. Opp. p.370.

Copies: NPL:R(S909.6/7).   2784

Reproduced in Gullick, W.A.—Australian medals and badges. Sydney, Govt. Pr., [1915]. p.1.

Copies: NPL:M(Q737.599/G).   2785

COPLEY MEDAL of the Royal Society, 1776. Rubbing from an electrotype of the Copley medal presented to Captain Cook (Australian Museum, N. 1189), original in British Museum. *Obverse:* Royal Society's coat of arms. *Legend:* Societas Reg. Londini; Nullius in verba. *Reverse:* Science seated, with attributes. *Legend:* G. Copley Bart. dignissimo; Jac. Cook. Arm. MDCCLXXVI.

The Copley gold medal was awarded to Cook for the best paper contributed to the Royal Society during the year 1776. This paper dealt with the methods employed to preserve the health of his ship's company on the second voyage. Though he knew before embarking on his last voyage that the medal had been awarded to him, it never actually came into his possession. It was presented to Mrs. Cook, and ultimately bequeathed by her to the British Museum.

Copies: NPL:M(Newscuttings File).   2786

The Same. Photograph of medal.

Copies: Captain Cook's Landing Place Trust.   2787

ROYAL SOCIETY'S MEDAL in commemoration of Captain Cook. Gold medal. 43.5mm. *Obverse:* Bust of Cook. *Legend:* Iac Cook oceani investigator acerrimus Reg. Soc. Lond. Socio suo. *Reverse:* Emblematical figure of Britannia. *Legend:* Nil intentatum nostri liquere. *Exergue:* Auspiciis Georgii III. L.P.f. (L.Pingo fecit).

Copies: NPL:M(R380).   2788

Another 2 specimens.

Copies: NPL:D.   2789

The Same, in silver.
Copies: NPL:M(R381).   2790

Another 2 specimens.
Copies: NPL:M(R382); ANL:F.   2791

Another 4 specimens.
Copies: NPL:D.   2792

Another specimen, incused on edge: Presented by His Grace Duke of
Northumberland to Henry Coll.^d Selby 21 Jany. 1785.
Copies: NPL:D.   2793

The Same, in pewter.
Copies: NPL:M(R383).   2794

The Same, in bronze.
Copies: NPL:M(R384); ANL(Nan Kivell 9528).   2795

Another 4 specimens.
Copies: NPL:M(R385–8).   2796

Another 3 specimens.
Copies: NPL:D.   2797

Another specimen.
Copies: ANL:F.   **2798**

This medal was struck in commemoration of Captain Cook by his fellow members of
the Royal Society. A voluntary subscription was opened, and to such fellows as contributed 20 guineas a gold medal was appropriated. Silver medals were assigned to
those who contributed a smaller sum, and to each of the other members one in bronze
was given. There were 20 of the gold medals, a number being presented to distinguished
personages.

Reproduction, engraved by I.Hogg; engraving of obverse only. Meas. of
engraved surface $1\frac{15}{16}$″ x $1\frac{1}{4}$″.
(Cook, J.—Third Voyage—Voyage to the Pacific. London, G. Nicol and T. Cadell,
1784. Vol.1, title-page.)
Copies: NPL:M(Q980:Co4/1B1).   2799

Another print.
(Cook, J.—Third Voyage—Voyage to the Pacific. 2nd ed. London, 1785. Vol.1,
title-page.)
Copies: NPL:M(Q980:Co4/1C1).   2800

Another print.

(Cook, J.—Third Voyage—Voyage to the Pacific. 3rd ed. London, 1785. Vol.1, title-page.)

Copies: NPL:M(Q980:Co4/1D1).   2801

Another print. Hand-coloured.

Copies: NPL:D(DL Pd672).   2802

The Same. Prevost sculp.

Engraving. Meas. of plate mark $2\frac{3}{16}$" x 4".
Shows obverse and reverse of medal joined by a short thick line.
(Cook, J.—Third Voyage—Printed Accounts—Troisième voyage de Cook: Cartes et figures. Paris, Hôtel de Thou, 1785. Title-page.)

Copies: NPL:M(Q980:Co4/2B1).   2803

The Same, engraver's name not on plate mark, but is the same as the Prevost.

(Cook, J.—Third Voyage—Printed Accounts. 1785—Troisième voyage de Cook. Paris, Hôtel de Thou, 1785. Tome 1, title-page.)

Copies: NPL:M(Q980:Co4/2A1).   2804

The Same, engrav'd from a medal of Mr. Pingo's by T. Trotter.

Publish'd . . . by G. Kearsley . . . July 27th 1784. Engraving.
Meas. of plate mark $3\frac{1}{4}$" x $5\frac{7}{8}$". Shows obverse and reverse medal joined by a thin line.
(Cook, J.—Third Voyage [1794.]—Abridgment of . . . last voyage. 7th ed. London, C. and G. Kearsley, 1794. Opp. p.1.)

Copies: NPL:M(980:Co4/3G1).   2805

Another print. Hand-coloured.

Copies: NPL:D(DL Pd671).   2806

The Same. London. Publish.[d] March 1st, 1785, by I. Sewell.

Engraving. Meas. of plate mark $6\frac{15}{16}$" x $4\frac{7}{16}$" Medal reversed.
Also has repro. of reverse side of medal of J.King. At head "European Magazine".
(Cook, J. *and others.* The Original astronomical observations . . . 1776–80. London, 1782. Frontisp.)

Copies: NPL:M(Q524/C).   2807

Another print. Hand-coloured.

Copies: NPL:D(DL Pd669).   2808

Another 3 prints.

Copies: NPL:M(P1/Cook—Pingo 5–7).   2809

Another print.

Copies: NPL:M(P3/41C).   2810

Reproduced in English, T.H.—Introduction to the collecting and history of Whitby prints. Whitby, Horne & Son, 1931. Vol.2, Ad.9.
Copies: NPL:M(Q942.7/E); NPL:D(Q93/118).   2811

The Same, proof before letters. Pencil inscription beneath "Médaille du Capitaine Cook."
Engraving. Meas. of plate mark 3½″ x 4″. This is the same as the Prevost engraving but the size of plate mark is bigger.
Copies: NPL:D(DL Pd670).   2812

The Same, 2 engravings of obverse only.
(Gianetti, M.— Elogio del Capitano Giacomo Cook. Florence, 1785. Title-page.)
Copies: NPL:M(Q923.9/C771.2/1A1).   2813

The Same. Engraving.
(Cook, J.—Third Voyage—Printed Accounts [1786]—Neueste Reisebeschreibungen. Nürnberg, Weigel und Schneider, 1786. Band 1, title-page.)
Copies: NPL:M(980.Co4/7A1).   2814

The Same. Engraving.
(Cook, J.—Collected Voyages—Printed Accounts [1837]—The Life, voyages and discoveries of Captain James Cook. London, John W. Parker, 1837. Title-page.)
Copies: NPL:M(980:Co1/34A1).   2815

The Same. Wood engraving, obverse only.
(Cook, J.—Collected Voyages—Printed Accounts [1852]—The Voyages of Captain James Cook round the world. London, John Tallis & Co., [1852. 2nd] title-page.)
Copies: NPL:M(Q980:Co1/4C1).   2816

Reproduced in Clowes, W.L.—The Royal Navy. London, Sampson Low, Marston and Co., 1899. Vol.4, p.139.)
Copies: NPL:R(DQ359.0942/13).   2817

Reproduced in Kitson, A.—Captain James Cook. London, John Murray, 1907. Opp. p.499.
Copies: NPL:M(923.9/C771.2/14A1).   2818

Reproduced in Gullick, W.A.—Australian medals and badges. Sydney, Govt. Pr., [1915]. p.141.
Copies: NPL:M(Q737.599/G).   2819

The Same, reproduction.
(N.S.W.—Govt. Pr.—Photographs illustrating the earliest times of New South Wales. Sydney, [n.d.] p.68.)
Copies: NPL:M(F981/N).   2820

The Same. Microfilm, positive and negative copies, of the medal in bronze.
(Papers, 1776–1926. Originals in the possession of R. Nan Kivell.)
Copies: NPL:M(FM4/1552,1707). 2821

CENTENARY of Death of Captain Cook. 1879. Silver. 23mm. *Obverse:*
Cook monument in Hyde Park, Sydney. *Legend:* Captain Cook killed at
Owhyhee 1779. McLean Sydney. *Reverse:* Sydney International Exhibi-
tion Building. *Legend:* International Exhibition Building. *Exergue:* Inner
Domain Sydney.
Copies: NPL:D. 2822

FIRST International Exhibition, Sydney, 1879. Medal. Pewter. 39mm.
Obverse: Bust of Cook. *Legend:* First International Exhibition: James Cook
discovered N.S.W. 1770. *Reverse:* Exhibition building. *Legend:* Commemoration medal. *Exergue:* N.S.Wales 1879.
Copies: NPL:M(R396). 2823

Reproduced in Gullick, W.A.—Australian medals and badges. Sydney, Govt. Pr., [1915]
p.32.
Copies: NPL:M(Q737.599/G). 2824

CENTENNIAL International Exhibition, Melbourne, 1888. Medal. Lead
and aluminium. 34mm. *Obverse:* Bust of Cook. *Legend:* Captain Cook.
Reverse Legend: Centennial International Exhibition. Melbourne 1888.
Opened the 1st of Aug. by His Excellency Sir H.B. Loch K.C.B.,
G.C.M.G. Governor of Victoria.
Copies: NPL:D. 2825

Reproduced in Gullick, W.A.—Australian medals and badges, Sydney, Govt. Pr., [1915.]
p.111.
Copies: NPL:M(Q737.599/G). 2826

CENTENARY Medal. 1888. Brass. 36 x 41mm. *Obverse:* Bust of Cook on
crossed flags. *Legend:* Centenary, 1888: Captain Cook. *Reverse:* Map of
Australia, bearing names of states except Tasmania.
Copies: NPL:M(R405). 2827

Another 2 specimens.
Copies: NPL:D. 2828

Reproduced in Gullick, W.A.—Australian medals and badges, Sydney, Govt. Pr., [1915.]
p.71.
Copies: NPL:M(Q737.599/G). 2829

COMMONWEALTH of Australia Medal. 1901. Bronze. 44mm. *Obverse:* Bust of Sir Henry Parkes. *Legend:* The Father of Australian federation, W.J. Amor Sydney. *Reverse:* Bust of Cook surrounded by a laurel wreath. *Legend:* To commemorate the establishment of the Commonwealth of Australia. 1901.

Copies: NPL:M(R191/K).   2830

The Same, in copper.

Copies: NPL:D.   2831

Reproduced in Gullick, W.A.—Australian medals and badges, Sydney, Govt. Pr., [1915.] p.111.

Copies: NPL:M(Q737.599/G).   2832

COURAGE and Perseverance Medal. n.d. Bronze. 38mm. *Obverse:* Bust of Cook. *Legend:* Capt James Cook. *Reverse: Legend:* Courage and perseverance. *Exergue:* Born 1728, died 1779.

Copies: NPL:M(R389).   2833

Another 2 specimens.

Copies: NPL:M(R390–91).   2834

Another 2 specimens.

Copies: NPL:D.   2835

Reproduced in Gullick, W.A.—Australian medals and badges. Sydney, Govt. Pr., [1915]. p.140.

Copies: NPL:M(Q737.599/G).   2836

Printed Books, Manuscripts, etc. about the Medals

1775 July 24 ROYAL SOCIETY, *London*

Printed announcement, with MS. particulars, signed J. Robertson Cl., requesting Banks' presence at a Council meeting to consider disposal of Sir Godfrey Copley's Medal. [On which is written, probably in Banks' hand, a list of native artifacts from the Pacific islands, with some of their native names.] Found loose inside Briscoe's journal, MS.96.

f.1, cm 33.

Copies: NPL:D(MS.Q158, pp.1–2).   2837

1776 July 10 COOK, James

ALS to Sir Joseph Banks, relating to descriptions of plants and engravings for his journal of the second voyage, and preparations for departure on the third voyage. He expresses gratification at being awarded a prize medal by the Royal Society.

pp.2.
(Letters of Capt. James Cook, R.N., p.11.)
This letter was part of the Brabourne Papers.
Facsimile filed at NPL:M(980:Co3/1A1). Neg. photostat filed at NPL:M(MS.A1713⁻²B, item vii).

Copies: NPL:M(Safe 1/68).   2838

1784 Aug.20 SANDWICH, John Montagu, *4th Earl*

ALS dated Hinchingbrook to Sir Joseph Banks: Requests Banks convey his thanks to the Council of the Royal Society for allotting him one of the medals struck to commemorate 'our great Navigator & much lamented friend'.

f.1, cm 23.5.
Paginated 403.
Typed transcript in MS.Q160, p.29.
Copies: NPL:D(MS.Q158, pp.169–70).   2839

1789 KIPPIS, *Rev.* Andrew

[Royal Society medals: account of Cook medals.]

(*In his* Biographia Britannica. 2nd ed. London, Rivington and Marshall, 1789. Vol.4, pp.189–90, 242–3.)
Copies: NPL:M(F920.042); NPL:R(09:DF920/47).   2840

1848 WELD, Charles Richard

[Resolution passed by the Royal Society, with reference to a medal to be struck in honour of Captain Cook, and an account of its distribution.]

(*In his* History of the Royal Society. London, John W.Parker, 1848. Vol.2, pp.137–44.)
This is the Royal Society's medal in commemoration of Captain Cook.
Copies: NPL:M(506/W); NPL:D(84/430); NPL:R(S506/100).   2841

1926 BIRMINGHAM—Assay Office

Matthew Boulton's "Otaheite" medal, distributed by Captain Cook on his second voyage to the Pacific Ocean, 1772. Birmingham, Assay Office, 1926.

Illus. pp.11.
Copies: NPL:M(Q980:Co3/B1A1); NPL:D(Q92/161); ANL.   2842

1931 ENGLISH, Thomas H.

[Medals struck in commemoration of Captain Cook.]

(*In his* Introduction to the collecting and history of Whitby prints. Whitby, Horne & Son, 1931. Vol.2, Ad.9.)
Copies: NPL:M(Q 942·7/E); NPL:D(Q93/119).   2843

1952 MACKANESS, George

Book collecting in Australia . . . The case of the Cook medals.

(*Amateur Book Collector*, Chicago, vol.2, p.3, Je 1952.)
Copies: NPL:M(Q010.9/M).   2844

PERSONAL

MEDALS, MEDALLIONS, COINS AND POSTAGE STAMPS

Medallions
Arranged by Artist After Whom They Were Designed

DANCE GROUP

CAPTAIN COOK: [a portrait medallion by Tassie after Dance's painting of 1776].

179–? White wax, on dull brown ground. Oval. $3\frac{5}{8}''$ x $2\frac{3}{8}''$ inside mat. Glazed in brown wooden frame.
Head and shoulders.
Unsigned. Artist and date of Dance portrait from Cook Bibliography, 1928 edition. Title from note on back in ink, continuing "hard enamelled paste / by Tassie / very fine / and in high relief."
Printed label reads "Cook, Captain James, Circumnavigator, 1779, $3\frac{3}{4}$ in (87)".
Copies: NPL:D(DL Pa94). 2845

[CAPTAIN COOK: medallion plaque portrait in alabaster, after portrait by Dance.]

n.d. Oval, in a gilt frame. $4\frac{7}{16}''$ x $3\frac{7}{16}''$ inside frame.
Head and shoulders.
Copies: NPL:M(P*28). 2846

HODGES

CAPT. COOK: [medallion plaque portrait by Wedgwood and Bentley, after Hodges].

c.1770. White on blue jasper. Oval. In a gilt and brown wooden frame. Meas. inside frame c.3" x c.$2\frac{1}{4}''$; framed $5\frac{3}{4}''$ x $4\frac{15}{16}''$.
Head and shoulders.
Title impressed below portrait. "Wedgwood & Bentley" impressed in back. Label on back of frame reads "Captn Cook (1728–1779) Old Wedgwood portrait Inscribed "Old 212". Wedgwood & Bentley 1770 period." Note in ink "From Rathbone's collection."
Copies: NPL:M(P*24). 2847

The Same, in slightly brighter blue, in gilt and wooden frame.

Cracked across lower part of portrait.
Copies: NPL:M(P*25). 2848

CAPT. COOK: [process plate reproduction of the medallion by Wedgwood after Hodges held by the Alexander Turnbull Library, Wellington, N.Z.].

Head only. With letterpress.
(*N.Z.L. Quarterly*, June, 1925, p.45.)
Copies: NPL:M(Q630.5/N). 2849

[CAPTAIN COOK: a Wedgwood portrait medallion designed before 1779, perhaps by John Flaxman, after Hodges.]

n.d. White on blue jasper. Oval, in gilt metal frame. Meas. inside frame $3\frac{3}{4}''$ x $2\frac{1}{2}''$; framed $4\frac{1}{4}''$ x 3".

Unsigned and untitled. "Wedgwood" impressed on back. Attribution to Flaxman from Rathbone's *Old Wedgwood and old Wedgwood ware*, p.48. With crack across ground, apparently mended.
Copies: NPL:D(DL Pa95).   2850

[CAPTAIN COOK: bust of Cook after Hodges.]

n.d. Intaglio process on clear brown gemstone. Oval. 16mm x 20mm. Initials "I.M.F.[ecit]" on back.
Initials "I.M." could stand for John Milton [*see* L. Forrer—*Biographical dictionary of medallists*, vol.iv, pp.82–5]. Traces of red sealing wax at top of oval on the back.
Head and shoulders.
Copies: NPL:D(DL Pa102).   2851

PINGO

[CAPTAIN COOK: a Wedgwood medallion from a model by John Flaxman, 1784, after Pingo.]

c.1784? White on green jasper. Oval. Meas. inside frame c.4½" x c.3¾"; framed 7½" x 6½". In frame of black wood and worn brown plush.
Head and shoulders.
Unsigned and untitled. Attribution to Flaxman and date from *The Explorations of Captain James Cook*, ed. by A. Grenville Price. Brown paper backing has inscription "5–V11/39/ This plaque is of french porcelain / was the property of Sir John Franklin (1786–1847) / when he was Governor of Tasmania 1837–1843. / On Lady Franklin's death many of Sir John's possessions passed to his sister Mrs Cracroft, who was Miss Lefroy's / grandmother / Captain Cook. / Given to me by Miss Jessie Lefroy of S.^t X / July 5–1939 / Gregory M. Mathews /"
Measurements also in same hand.
Copies: NPL:D(DL Pa96).   2852

[CAPTAIN COOK: photograph of medallion by L.Pingo.]

Oval. Meas. of port. 4⅜" x 3⅜".
Head and shoulders.
Copies: NPL:M(P3/11I).   2853

Another print.
Copies: NPL:M(P1/Cook—Pingo 4).   2854

CAPT. COOK: [medallion portrait plaque by Wedgwood after Pingo.]

n.d. White on blue jasper. Oval, in black wood and gilt frame. Meas. inside frame 4⅛" x 3¼", framed 6½" x 5½". Title impressed below portrait.
Head and shoulders in profile.
Transferred from the Australian Museum, Oct. 1955.
Copies: NPL:M(P*65).   2855

The Same without lettering and frame.

Meas. 4½″ x 3⅜″.
From the collection of Alfred Lee. Titled on back "Capt Cook".

Copies: NPL:M(P*26). 2856

The Same, in wooden frame.

Copies: NPL:M(P*53). 2857

The Same, in black basaltes.

Titled 'Capt Cook' on back.

Copies: NPL:M(P*27). 2858

The Same, coloured reproduction of white and blue Wedgwood medallion by Flaxman entitled 'Capt.[n] Cook', held in the British Museum.

(Cook, J.—Collected Voyages—Printed Accounts [1957. Price's ed.]—The Explorations of Captain James Cook. New York, Limited Editions Club, 1957. Frontisp.)

Copies: NPL:M(C956). 2859

[CAPTAIN COOK: Wedgwood portrait medallion after Pingo.]

n.d. White on green jasper ware. Medallion, meas. c.2⅝″ x c.2½″.
Head and shoulders in profile.
Inset on a Wedgwood blue and white vase which stands about 10½″ high. The names "Cook, Banks, Solander and Phillips [*sic*. i.e. A.Phillip] on white band surrounding vase. Inset on opposite side is replica of Webber's "Hope addressing Peace, Art and Labour" in white on green jasper ware.

Copies: NPL:D(DL DR1). 2860

[CAPTAIN COOK: Wedgwood portrait medallion.]

n.d. White on black jasper ware. c.5½″ x c.3½″.
Unframed. Untitled.
Three-quarter length.
Presented to the Trust by John B. Nelson, 1941.

Copies: Captain Cook's Landing Place Trust. 2861

CAPTAIN COOK: [Wedgwood portrait medallion, after Pingo].

1951. White on blue jasper, with white border on front of medallion. 4½″ x 3¼″.
Unframed.
Titled "Captain Cook". Impressed on back "Wedgwood 1951".
Head and shoulders.
Presented to the Trust by J.Wedgwood, Stoke-on-Trent, 1955.

Copies: Captain Cook's Landing Place Trust. 2862

ARTIST UNKNOWN

CAPTAIN COOK. 1728–1779: [process plate reproduction of the medallion held in the Underwriting Room at Lloyd's].

Head and shoulders in profile, but not after Pingo.

(Dawson, W.R.—Captain Cook, p.4, 1928. Supplement to *Lloyd's List & Shipping Register*, Oct. 25, 1928.)

Copies: NPL:M(Newscuttings File). 2863

Coins

HAWAIIAN CELEBRATIONS 1928. Half-dollar piece. Silver. 30mm.

Obverse: Bust of Cook. *Legend:* United States of America half-dollar. Capt. James Cook discoverer of Hawaii. In God we trust. *Reverse:* Figure of a native chief with view of the coastline. *Legend:* 1778-1928. E Pluribus unum.

This is a specimen of a coin struck to commemorate the 150th anniversary of the discovery of Hawaii by Captain Cook.

Copies: NPL:M(R397); Captain Cook's Landing Place Trust. 2864

Another 5 specimens.

Copies: NPL:M(R398–402). 2865

Reproduced in Taylor, A.P.—Sesquicentennial celebration of Captain Cook's discovery of Hawaii, 1778–1928. Honolulu, Captain Cook Sesquicentennial Commission and Archives of Hawaii Commission, 1929. Plate 28.

Copies: NPL:M(Q980:Co4/T1A1). 2866

Postage Stamps

[1928 HAWAIIAN STAMPS in commemoration of Captain Cook.]

CONTENTS:
1 sheet 5c blue (20 stamps)
1 sheet 2c red (25 stamps)
1 sheet 2c red (25 stamps)
1 pair 5c blue (2 stamps)
1 pair 2c red (2 stamps)
(Miscellaneous unused postage stamps, (b) 2c and 5c stamps commemorating Capt. Cook's Voyage.)

Copies: NPL:M(Safe3/40b). 2867

[1928 MEMORIAL STAMPS issued by the U.S. Government, in commemoration of the 150th anniversary of the discovery of the Hawaiian Islands, 18 Jan.1778.]

Copies: Captain Cook's Landing Place Trust. 2868

1929 TAYLOR, Albert Pierce
Captain Cook stamp issue.

(*In his* Sesquicentennial celebration of Captain Cook's discovery of Hawaii, 1778–1928. Honolulu, Captain Cook Sesquicentennial Commission and the Archives of Hawaii Commission, 1929. p.91.) *Hawaii—Board of Commissioners of Public Archives—Archives of Hawaii, Pub. no.4.*

Copies: NPL:M(Q980:Co4/T1A1).   2869

1945 POSTAGE STAMPS commemorate Captain James Cook.
Illus.
(*Walkabout*, vol.12, pp.34–36, November 1945.)
Copies: NPL:M(Q980/W).   2870

1961 ARGYLE, E.W.
[New Zealand postage stamp depicting Cook's *Endeavour:* illustration.]
(*Sea Breezes* n.s. vol.31, p.132, Feb. 1961.)
Copies: NPL:M(656.50905/1).   2871

MISCELLANEA

Manuscripts and Autograph Letters

172- —1959 MISCELLANEOUS PAPERS, 172- —1959.
3 vols. 2 boxes.
This collection was made up from manuscript material formerly kept at Ac 50, A1713⁻¹ and in Drawer 46.

CONTENTS:

Guide compiled in the Mitchell Library. ff.10. $A1713^{-1}$

a. Facsimiles and other copies of original manuscripts re voyages, 1768–1785. $A1713^{-2}$

b. Notes on Cook manuscripts and maps 1894–1954, held in the Mitchell Library and elsewhere. $A1713^{-3}$ item 1–2

c. Personal and biographical material, 1960, including primary and secondary source material.   item 2–4

d. Miscellaneous bibliographical material.   item 5

e. Papers re statue of Captain Cook erected in Hyde Park, Sydney, 1869–1874. Includes sketches and specifications, with letters by Sir A. Stephen and E.T. Blacket. Pictorial material filed at PX D6. $A1713^{-4}$

f. Correspondence and papers re editorship of the Cook Journal, 1890–1892, including letters to A.H. Bell from J. Corner and Elliot Stock. $A1713^{-5}$

g. Official correspondence to the Public Library of New South Wales, 1898–1957, re Cook and the acquisition of manuscripts, pictures and relics of Cook interest (*Restricted*). $A1713^{-6}$ item 1–3

Copies: NPL:M(A1713⁻¹⁻⁶).   2872

1765 Ap.11 GREAT BRITAIN—Admiralty Office

Copy of order addressed to Cook by Philip Stephens, for the discharge of Peter Cook of HMS *Grenville* due to illness; with corrections in Cook's hand.

Copies: NPL:D(MS.Q140,p.3).   2873

1765 GREAT BRITAIN—Victualling Office

MS. copies of three letters, Jan. 7, Feb. 27 & Ap. 10, 1765, re victualling the *Grenville*, Schooner, for the Newfoundland Expedition, of which Cook was in charge.

(Copies of documents relating to Captain James Cook, R.N., from originals in the Grey Collection, Auckland Public Library, ff.6–9.)

Copies: NPL:M(C697).   2874

1771–6 COOK, James

[Miscellaneous letters, 1771–6.]

pp.5.

CONTENTS:

MS7   ALS to John Harrison, Attorney, 24 Feb. 1776, concerning a charge against James Fleck (Cook's brother-in-law) of defrauding the Customs. (pp.2 negative photostat). Marriage certificate 21 Dec. 1772, of James Cook and Elizabeth Batts, at St. Margaret's Church, Barking, Essex.

MS7A   ALS to George Monkhouse, Mile End, 31 July 1771, concerning the wills of Monkhouse's sons, who died on the *Endeavour* (p.1 photographic copy of original, 1 photograph of TS copy).

NK33   ALS to George Perry, Victualling Officer, London, 11 July 1772, concerning corrections to charts, and supplies of wine. (p.1, photostat copy also held at MS 7A).

Copies: ANL(MS7,MS7A,Nan Kivell 33).   2875

1776 June 8 PHOTOGRAPHIC COPY of entry in ledger of catering firm of Ring and Brymer Ltd for dinner given by Captain Cooke (*sic*) on board the *Resolution* at Long Reach, 8 June 1776.

Copies: NPL:M(Doc.117).   2876

1784 May 30 HOWE, Richard Howe, *Earl*

ALS to Sir Joseph Banks, dated Admiralty, 30th May 1784: He called to tell Banks the King's sentiments re presentation of the History of Cook's last Voyage to the King of France & Empress of Russia, and about binding of the King's copies; asks to see Banks to discuss adjustments necessary, before seeing the King again.

pp.2, 24 cm.

(*Inserted in* Kippis, A.—Life of Captain James Cook, 1788.)

Copies: NPL:D(Q78/8).   2877

1830 Oct.8 SMITH, Isaac

ALS to E.H. Locker, Oct.8, 1830, stating that Mrs. Cook has no longer in her possession any papers in Capt. Cook's writing; she feels hurt by the idea that the Captain was severe, and has always found fault with the picture for its stern look. The writer, who was with him on his first two voyages, never thought him severe. He was loved and properly feared by the crew.

(Cook Documents from the Australian Museum, pp.3–4.)

Copies: NPL:M(Safe 1/83). 2878

1911 KITSON, Arthur

ALS to Edward Smith commenting on the portions of Smith's work which refer to Banks's connection with Cook and the voyages to the South Seas. Marton, Groombridge, Sussex, Sept.15, 1911.

pp.3.
(*Inserted in* Smith, E.—Life of Sir Joseph Banks, vol.1. 1911.)

Copies: Australasian Pioneers' Club, Sydney. 2879

[1965] LETTER from the Office of Sick and Hurt Seamen describing the effect of measures against scurvy.

pp.3.
(*In* Cook, J.—Collected Voyages—Printed Accounts [1965. Jackdaw ser.]—The Voyages of Captain Cook: a collection of contemporary documents. London, J. Cape, 1965. No.2.)

Copies: NPL:M(Q980:Col/L1A1); NPL:R(NQ909.088/1); ANL. 2880

Printed Books and Articles

1786 FLETCHER, Charles

A Maritime state considered as to the health of seamen, with effectual means for rendering the situation of that valuable class of people more comfortable; to which are annexed, some general observations on the diseases incident to seamen, and an appendix of additional notes and remarks in the order of the work. Dublin, printed for the Author by M. Mills, 1786.

pp.lvi, 342.
Cover title is Fletcher's Health of Seamen.
With references to Cook.

Copies: NPL:M(613.68/F). 2881

1807 BERNARDI, Oronzio

Arte de nadar; compendiado del que escribió en italiano. Madrid, imprenta de Alban, 1807.

Plates, pp.190.
Refers to Captain Cook and his observations on swimming and diving in the bay of Oaiti-piha, Tahiti, p.151–2, p.165, and in New Caledonia, p.137.

Copies: NPL:M(797.2/9A1). 2882

1847 FOWLER, Orson Squire
[Phrenological study of Captain Cook.]

Port. pp.71–2.

(*In his* Memory and intellectual improvement applied to self-education and juvenile instruction. 25th ed. New York, Fowler and Wells, 1847.)

Copies: NPL:M(139/1).   2883

[187?–1935   NEWSPAPER CUTTINGS relating to Captain Cook's voyages, journals, memorials, etc. 187?–1935.]

3 vols.

Copies: NPL:M(Q980:Col/N1A1–3).   2884

1902 KENNY, Alice A.
Captain Cook's tree.

Illus.

(*New Zealand Illustrated Magazine*, vol.6, April 1902, pp.60–62.)

Copies: NPL:M(059/N).   2885

1902 WHITE, T.
The Travelled goat: [a goat which accompanied Cook in his two voyages to New Zealand and round the world.]

(New Zealand Institute—*Transactions and proceedings*, 1902, pp.209–10.)

Copies: NPL:M(506/N); NPL:R(S506/8).   2886

1906 FRANKLIN, Benjamin
Passport for Captain Cook [allowing his ship in search of new countries in unknown seas to proceed without hindrance from United States armed vessels].

(*In his* Writings. New York, Macmillan, 1906. Vol.7, pp.242–3.)

At this period the United States was at war with Great Britain. In consideration of the generosity of Franklin, one of the gold medals struck in honour of Captain Cook was presented to him by the hand of Sir Joseph Banks, as well as a copy of Cook's Voyage, from the Admiralty Board.

Copies: NPL:R(S810/F831/7).   2887

1924, 1928 PURDY, John Smith
Captain Cook and the prevention of scurvy.

Extracts from *The Medical Officer*, London, July 12, 1924, also a type-written copy; and Dec.22, 1928.

Copies: NPL:M(MS.A1713⁻³, item 4).   2888

1925 IREDALE, Tom, *and* TROUGHTON, Ellis Le Geyt
Captain Cook's kangaroo.

Illus.

(*Australian Zoologist* vol.3, pp.311–16, Jan. 1925.)

Copies: NPL:M(Q590.5/A); NPL:D(MS.Q144, extract).   2889

[1928] McKILLOP, Catherine

Cook in a nutshell; comp. by C. McKillop, in commemoration of the bicentenary of the birth of Captain James Cook, R.N. Sydney, G. B. Philip, [1928].

pp.[13].
Cover title: Souvenir of Captain James Cook, R.N., 1728–1928.
An alphabet giving facts connected with Captain Cook.
Copies: NPL:M(980:Co1/M1A1); ANL.   2890

1950 SCOTT, T.C.S. Morrison-, *and* SAWYER, F.C.

Identity of Captain Cook's kangaroo. [With bibl.] London, 1950.

Facs. illus. pp.43–50, plates 3–5.
(British Museum, Natural History—*Bulletin, Zoology.* Vol.1, no.3, Mar. 1950.)
With account of the drawings by Sydney Parkinson and Sir Nathaniel Dance.
Copies: NPL:M(Q599.2/S).   2891

1954–5 MUSGRAVE, Anthony

Insects of Captain Cook's expedition.

Illus.
(*Australian Museum Magazine*, vol.11, September 1954—June 1955. *Various pp.*)
Copies: NPL:M(507/A).   2892

1957 LYSAGHT, Averil

Captain Cook's kangaroo.

Illus.
(*New Scientist* no.17, pp.17–19, March 14, 1957.)
Copies: NPL:R(DQ505/13).   2893

1957 LYSAGHT, Averil

The First specimens of Dacelo novae-guineae and D. leachii in European collections; [with] bibliography.

(*Emu*, vol.57, pp.209–10, July 1957.)
Copies: NPL:M(598.2901/E).   2894

1957 STONE, Walter William

Joseph Banks, Obarea, and the Rams Skull Press.

(*Biblionews*, vol.10, no.5, pp.16–18, May, 1957.)
Copies: NPL:M(Q010.5/3).   2895

1958 MILNE, Lorus *and* MILNE, Margery

[Note on Captain Cook's tortoise, Tui Nalila.]

Illus.
(*Natural History*, New York, vol.67, pp.190, 193, April, 1958.)
Copies: NPL:R(Q506/37).   2896

1962 CONRAD, M.
Captain Cook's coal ships.
(*Australasian Boating* Mar. 1962, pp.304.)
Copies: NPL:M(Q 797.205/3); ANL.   2897

n.d. WATSON, James Henry
Newspaper cuttings, etc. on Captain Cook; compiled and partly written by J. H. Watson.
Illus.
Copies: NPL:M(Q980:Co1/W1A1).   2898

Children's Books

See also the heading *Imaginative Literature on the Life of Cook—Children's Books.*

1784 AN AMERICAN, *pseud.*
New Holland and isles in the Pacific Ocean.
(*In* Geography epitomized; or, A tour round the world . . . description . . . in verse . . . for the use of schools. By an American. Philadelphia, J. Crukshank, 1784. pp.45–8.)
Copies: NPL:M(910.7/G).   2899

1786–90 CAMPE, Joachim Heinrich
Sammlung interessanter und durchgängig zweckmässig abgefasster Reisebeschreibungen für die Jugend. N.p., 1786–1790.
Map, 8 vols. in 4.
See also no.2902.
Copies: NPL:M(910.4/209A1–4).   2900

1803–4 CAMPE, Joachim Heinrich
Capitain James Cooks Reise omkring Jorden: en Láèsebog for Ungdommen, efter Campes Láèremaade . . . Oversat af H. C. Lund. Kiøbenhavn, Math. Joh. Sebbelom, 1803–4.
Illus. in colour, 3 vols. in 1.
Copies: NPL:M(980:Co4/C2A1).   2901

1808 CAMPE, Joachim Heinrich
Berättelse om en resa kring jorden, ifrån 1768 till 1771, af James Cook, Löjtant i Engelsk tjenst, samt H:r Banks och Solander, ryktbara Naturkännare. Stockholm, 1808.
Illus. pp.[ii], 180.
Series title: Geografikst bibliotek för ungdom [vol.11].
A Swedish translation by D. Krutmejer of J. H. Campe's German compilation for children on Cook's first voyage. Vols.11–13 of the series form the Cook abridgement.
See Du Rietz, R.—Captain James Cook: a bibliography. 1960, pp.25–6.
See also no.2900.
Copies: ANL.   2902

1808 LE COOK de la jeunesse; ou, Extrait des voyages les plus récens dans les régions les plus éloignées. Suivi de l'abrégé de la vie du Capitaine Cook par M. le Capitaine B * * [i.e. J.P. Bérenger]. Paris, 1808.

Illus. 2 vols.
Binder's title: Cook de la jeunes (*sic*).
See also nos. 54, 2904.

Copies: NPL:D(80/88–9).   2903

1814 LE COOK de la jeunesse; ou, Extrait des voyages les plus récens dans les régions éloignées. Paris, Giguet et Michaud, 1814.

Illus. 2 vols.
Taken from J.P. Bérenger's account.
See also nos. 54, 2903.

Copies: ANL.   2904

1818 BINGLEY, *Rev.* William
[Cook.]

(*In his* Biographical conversations on the most eminent voyagers. London, 1818. pp.239–348.)
See also nos. 2906, 2911.

Copies: NPL:R(MD3R36).   2905

1818 BINGLEY, *Rev.* William
[Cook.]

(*In his* Biographical conversations on the most eminent voyagers. 2nd ed. London, Sharpe, 1818.)
See also nos. 2905, 2911.

Copies: ANL; QU.   2906

1820 CAMPE, Joachim Heinrich

Des Capitäns James Cook Beschreibung seiner Reise um die Welt: ein nützliches Lesebuch für die Jugend. Nach Campe's [i.e. J. H. Campe's] Lehrart bearbeitet von F.W. von Schütz. New ed. Wien, B. Ph. Bauer, 1820.

Frontisp. 3 vols. in 1.
German version of Cook's voyages, translated by J. H. Campe, and re-told in dialogue form by F.W. von Schütz.

Copies: NPL:M(980:Col/49A1).   2907

1820 THE LIFE of Captain James Cook. Dublin, Richard Grace, 1820.

Illus. pp.179.
Published anonymously. Abridged for young readers, from the biography by A. Kippis.
Dixson Library copy lacks frontispiece.
See also nos. 2909–10, 2912–13, 2915–17.

Copies: NPL:M(923.9/C771.2/6A1); NPL:D(82/45); NPL:R(S920/C771/5).   2908

1821 THE LIFE of Captain James Cook. Dublin, Richard Grace, 1821.

Illus. pp.179.

Published anonymously. Abridged for young readers, from the biography by A. Kippis. *See also* nos. 2908, 2910, 2912–13, 2915–17.

Copies: NPL:M(923.9/C771.2/6B1); ANL. 2909

1824 THE LIFE of Captain James Cook. Dublin, printed by John Jones, 1824.

Frontisp. pp.179.

Published anonymously. Abridged for young readers from the biography by A. Kippis. *See also* nos. 2908–9, 2912–13, 2915–17.

Copies: ANL. 2910

1826 BINGLEY, *Rev.* William

[Cook.]

(*In his* Biographical conversations on the most eminent voyagers. 3rd ed. London, C. & J. Rivington, 1826. pp.248–365.)
See also nos. 2905–6.

Copies: NPL:M(A923.9/B). 2911

[183–?] THE LIFE of Captain James Cook. Stereotype ed. Belfast, printed by Joseph Smyth, [c.1830?].

pp.iv, 5–144.

Published anonymously. Abridged for young readers, from the biography by A. Kippis. Title repeated on wrapper, with imprint: Dublin, printed by C. M. Warren. Pp.143–4 are further condensed than the last pages of other editions of this title. No. 2917 is identical with this, except for addition of publication date.
See also nos. 2908–10, 2913, 2915–17.

Copies: NPL:M(923.9/C771.2/6D1); ANL. 2912

[1831] THE LIFE of Captain James Cook. New ed. London, W. Wetton, [1831].

Illus. pp.iv, 170, 6, 10.

Published anonymously. Abridged for young readers, from the biography by A. Kippis. The supplementary pages at the end of the volume are publishers' advertisements, of which the tenth last page is entitled *Superior books . . . published by C. F. Cock, Jan. 1831.* Pp.9–10 give an advertisement for the *National School Reader*. Stamped June 1832 inside front cover.
See also nos. 2908–10, 2912, 2915–17.

Copies: NPL:M(923.9/C771.2/6C1). 2913

1832 VERREAUX, Jules

L'Océanie en estampes; ou, Description géographique et historique de toutes les îles du Grand Océan et du continent de la Nouvelle Hollande. Notasie, Polynésie, Australie . . . Ouvrage destiné à l'instruction et à l'amusement de la jeunesse; orné d'une carte et de cent huit gravures . . . rédigé d'après les documens tant anciens que recens, et des notices inédites de voyageurs français et étrangers, M. M. Lesson, Sainson, Ellis, Marsden, etc. Par J. et E. Verreaux. Paris, Librairie Nepvue, 1832. pp.xvi, 437,[iii].

Copies: NPL:M(980/V). 2914

1834 THE LIFE of Captain James Cook. New ed. London, printed for the executrix of the late W. Wetton, 1834.

Frontisp. pp.iv, 170.
Published anonymously. Abridged for young readers, from the biography by A. Kippis.
See also nos. 2908–10, 2912–13, 2916–17.

Copies: ANL:F. 2915

1835 THE LIFE of Captain James Cook. New ed. London, printed for the executrix of the late W. Wetton, 1835.

Illus. pp.iv, 170.
Published anonymously. Abridged for young readers, from the biography by A. Kippis.
See also nos. 2908–10, 2912–13, 2915, 2917.

Copies: QOM. 2916

1835 THE LIFE of Captain James Cook. Stereotype ed. Belfast, printed by Joseph Smyth, 1835.

pp.iv, 5–144.
Wanting wrappers.
Published anonymously. Abridged for young readers, from the biography by A. Kippis.
Pp.143–4 are further condensed than the last pages of other editions of this title. No. 2912 is identical with this, except that it is undated.
See also nos. 2908–10, 2912–13, 2915–16.

Copies: NPL:R(S920/C771/6). 2917

1838 CHAMPAGNAC, Jean Baptiste Joseph de
Histoire du Capitaine Cook.

Illus.
(*In his* Le Petit matelot; ou, Voyage en Océanie . . . par C.–H. de Mirval. Paris, Lehuby, 1838. pp.220–36.)
See also nos. 2919, 2921.

Copies: NPL:M(989/34A1). 2918

[1842] CHAMPAGNAC, Jean Baptiste Joseph de
Histoire du Capitaine Cook.

Illus.
(*In his* Le Petit matelot . . . par E.–H. de Mirval. Paris, Lehuby, [1842]. pp.196–210.)
Bibliothèque Spéciale de la Jeunesse.
See also nos. 2918, 2921.

Copies: NPL:M(989/34B1). 2919

1849 THE LIFE of Captain James Cook, the celebrated navigator. London, Newman & Co., 1849.

pp.122.
Published anonymously. Adapted for young readers, from the biography by A. Kippis.
Listed in advertisement on verso of half title-page as being published by W. Tegg & Co.
Copies: NPL:M(923.9/C771.2/8A1). 2920

1853 CHAMPAGNAC, Jean Baptiste Joseph de
Histoire du Capitaine Cook.

(*In his* Le Petit matelot; ou, Voyage en Océanie. Chapter 12.)
See also nos. 2918–19.
Copies: ANL. 2921

[1871] KINGSTON, William Henry Giles
Captain Cook: his life, voyages, and discoveries. London, Religious Tract Society, [1871].

Listed in British Museum catalogue, which also lists [1890] and [1926] editions.
See also no. 2927.
Copies: VSL. 2922

[1886] MEISSNER, H.
James Cook; oder, Dreimal um die Erde. Ein Lebensbild für die reifere Jugend, von H. Meissner. Stuttgart, Gebrüder Kröner, [1886].

Illus. maps, pp.iv, 286.
Illustrations, by Fritz Bergen, include coloured plates. For Swedish edition *see* no. 2924.
Copies: NPL:M(980:Co1/M2A1). 2923

1894 MEISSNER, H.
James Cook, eller jorden rundt tre gånger; bearbetning från Tyskan [of H. Meissner] af D.S. Hector. Stockholm, P.A. Norstedt, 1894.

Illus. pp.296.
(*P.A. Norstedt & Söners Ungdomsböcker*, nr.18.)
Slightly abridged. Illustrations in black and white. For Stuttgart edition *see* no. 2923.
Copies: NPL:M(980:Co1/M2B1). 2924

[1899?] YATES, Matthew Thompson
Captain Cook.

Illus. port.
(*In his* Graphic stories of sailors. London, Collins' Clear-Type Press, [1899?]. pp.181–91.)
Copies: NPL:M(923.9/5B1). 2925

[19—?] WHITCOMBE AND TOMBS, LTD.
Under Cook's flag; [with chronology of Cook's life]. Auckland, W. & T., [19—?].

Illus. maps, port. pp.148.
(*Whitcombe's Historical Story Books*, no.533.)
Written for children, aged 10 to 12 years.
Copies: NPL:M(980:Co1/W2A1). 2926

[1904] KINGSTON, William Henry Giles
Captain Cook: his life, voyages and discoveries. London, Religious
Tract Society, [1904].
Illus. pp.319.
British Museum catalogue lists [1871], [1890], and [1926] editions.
See also no. 2922.
Copies: NPL:M(980:Co1/K1A1). 2927

[1905?] COOK der Weltumsegler. Leben, Reisen und Ende des Kapitäns
James Cook, für Jugend und Volk erzählt, von J. März. Zweite Aufl.
Leipzig, Otto Spamer, [1905?].
Illus. ports. pp.261, [xi].
Copies: NPL:M(980:Co1/50B1). 2928

[1906] LANG, John
The Story of Captain Cook . . . with pictures by W. B. Robinson. London,
T.C. and E.C. Jack, [1906].
pp.vii, 119.
(*Children's Heroes Series.*)
Copies: NPL:M(923.9/C771.2/13A1); ANL. 2929

[1908?] CAPTAIN COOK'S voyages of discovery. Leeds, E. J. Arnold,
[1908?].
Illus.
(*A. L. Bright Story Readers;* edited by A. Gardiner. No.146.)
Copies: QU. 2930

1908 WATTS, Ebenezer John Moore
Cook discovers New South Wales.
Illus. port.
(*In his* Stories from Australian history. Sydney, William Brooks, 1908. pp.36–47.)
Brooks's Australian School Series.
See also no. 2935.
Copies: NPL:M(990.1/W). 2931

1912 LONG, Charles Richard
Notable deeds of famous men and women, by C. R. Long and G. M.
Wallace. Melbourne, George Robertson, 1912.
pp.208.
Written for Grade III children attending Victorian schools.
Copies: NPL:M(904/12A1). 2932

1913 JOHNSTON, *Sir* Harry Hamilton
James Cook's first voyage; [and] (New South Wales).
Illus.
(*In his* Pioneers in Australasia, London, Blackie, 1913. pp.178–251.)
Pioneers of Empire.
Copies: NPL:M(980/J); NPL:R(S990/8). 2933

1913 JOHNSTON, *Sir* Harry Hamilton
Cook's second and third voyages.
Illus.
(*In his* Pioneers in Australasia. London, Blackie, 1913. pp.252–77.)
Pioneers of Empire.
Copies: NPL:M(980/J); NPL:R(S990/8).   2934

1914 WATTS, Ebenezer John Moore
Cook discovers New South Wales.
Illus. port.
(*In his* Stories from Australian history. 2nd ed. Sydney, William Brooks, 1914. pp.38–46.)
See also no. 2931.
Copies: NPL:M(990.1/W).   2935

1925 WOOD, George Arnold
The Voyage of the *Endeavour*. Melbourne, Macmillan, 1925.
Prepared for the use of schools.
See also nos. 730, 734, 736.
Copies: QU.   2936

1931 WADE, Mary Hazelton, *Mrs*
The Boy who loved the sea: the story of Captain James Cook. 1931.
Copies: ANL.   2937

1932 MAIDIÈRES, Pierre
Le Destin tragique de James Cook. Paris, Editions Jules Tallandier, 1932.
Illus. pp.124.
(*A travers l'univers. Collection illustrée pour la jeunesse.*)
Copies: NPL:M(923.9/C771.2/38A1).   2938

1934 LONG, Charles Richard
Cook, the greatest of navigators.
(*In his* British worthies, and other men of might. Melbourne, Robertson & Mullens, 1934. pp.87–96.)
Copies: NPL:M(920/10A1).   2939

1937 FOX, Lorene K.
[The First Antarctic expedition: Captain James Cook's expedition with *Resolution* and *Adventure*, 1772–5.]
(*In her* Antarctic icebreakers. New York, Double Day, Doran, 1937. pp.4–9.)
Junior Books.
Copies: NPL:M(989.8/F).   2940

[1939?] KUEHNWALD, Gerd

Unter den Kannibalen der Südsee: Tatsachenbericht über James Cooks Leben und Reisen von G. Kühnwald. Mit Bildern von M. Wulff. Berlin, A. Weichert, [1939?].

Frontisp. pp.112.
Written for children.

Copies: NPL:M(923.9/C771.2/20A1).   2941

1941 CURREY, Charles Herbert

James Cook . . . the voyage of the *Endeavour*.

Map, port.
(*In his* Notable pathfinders to new regions. Sydney, W. & T., 1941. pp.78–84.)
A book for schools.

Copies: NPL:M(910.9/C).   2942

1944 LOHSE, Charlotte

For James Cook.

Illus. map.
(*In* The Mysterious continent: the story of the adventurous sailors who discovered the south Pacific Islands. By C. Lohse and J. Seaton. Indianapolis, Bobbs-Merrill, 1944. pp.141–57.)

Copies: NPL:M(980/L); ANL.   2943

1947 WOOD, David

Cook, the explorer: [an account for children]. London, Peter Lunn, 1947.

Illus. maps, pp.217.

Copies: NPL:M(980:Col/W5A1); NPL:R(DS990A/208); ANL; VSL.   2944

1949 DE SELINCOURT, Aubrey

Mr. Oram's story, the adventures of Capt. James Cook; [written for children, by] (A. de Selincourt). Illus. by J. Baynes. London, Methuen, 1949.

Illus. port. pp.142.
With decorative maps as end-papers.

Copies: NPL:M(980:Col/D1A1); VSL.   2945

1952 SWENSON, Eric Pierson

The South Sea shilling: voyages of Captain Cook, R.N., by E. Swenson. Illus. by C. M. Daugherty. New York, Viking Press, 1952.

pp.224.
Written for children.
See also no. 2973.

Copies: NPL:M(980:Col/S3A1).   2946

1954 MERRETT, John
The True book about Captain Cook. London, Shakespeare Head Press, 1954.

Illus. maps, pp.142.
(*True Book Series.*)
See also nos. 2948, 2953.
Copies: NPL:M(923.9/C771.2/21A1).

2947

1954 MERRETT, John
True book about Captain James Cook; illustrated by F. Stocks May. London, Muller, [1954].

Illus. maps, pp.140.
See also nos. 2947, 2953.
Copies: ANL.

2948

1955 BUTCHER, T. K.
Captain Cook's voyages in the South Seas.

(*In his* Asia and Australasia. London, Dobson, [1955]. pp.83–98.)
Written for children.
Copies: NPL:M(910.8/B).

2949

1955 SPERRY, Armstrong
Captain Cook explores the South Seas. New York, Random House, 1955.

Illus. pp.184.
(*World Landmark Books.*)
See also nos. 2956, 2972.
Copies: NPL:M(980:Col/S2A1); ANL.

2950

1956 BROWN, Roderick Langmere Haig Haig-
Boy seaman; [with Cook on his second voyage].

(*In his* Captain of the *Discovery:* the story of Capt. George Vancouver. London, Macmillan, 1956. pp.1–17.)
Copies: NPL:M(910.4/B).

2951

[1956] WYMER, Norman George
Captain James Cook. London, O.U.P., [1956].

Illus. maps, port. pp.32.
(*Lives of Great Men & Women.*)
Copies: NPL:M(923.9/C771.2/22A1); ANL.

2952

1957 MERRETT, John
Captain James Cook; illus. by L. Hoffman. New York, Criterion Books, 1957.

Illus. map, pp.192.
(*Criterion Book for Young People.*)
See also nos. 2947–8.
Copies: ANL.

2953

1958 PEACH, Lawrence du Garde
The Story of Captain Cook: an adventure from history. Illustrated by
John Kenney. Loughborough, England, Wills & Hepworth, 1958.
Illus. in colour, pp.51.
(*Ladybird Book Series* 561.)
Copies: ANL. 2954

1959 GREENE, Carla
Captain Cook discovers the [Hawaiian] Islands.
(*In her* A Trip to Hawaii. New York, Lantern Press, 1959. pp.38–41.)
Copies: NPL:M(989.6/3A1). 2955

1960 SPERRY, Armstrong
All about Captain Cook. Rev. ed. London, W. H. Allen, 1960.
Illus., map as endpapers, pp.[iv], 147.
(*All About Books.*)
See also nos. 2950, 2972.
Copies: NPL:M(980:Col/S2B1); ANL. 2956

1960 SYME, Ronald
Captain Cook, Pacific explorer; [written for children], by R. Syme.
Illus. by W. Stobbs. New York, W. Morrow, 1960.
pp.96.
(*Morrow Junior Books.*)
Copies: NPL:M(980:Col/S4A1); ANL. 2957

1962 DANIELL, David Scott
James Cook: the discovery of New Zealand, 1768–71.
Illus. map.
(*In his* Explorers & explorations. London, Batsford, 1962. pp.72–90.)
Copies: NPL:M(910.8/27A1). 2958

1962 GROSSECK, Joyce, *Mrs*
Captain James Cook, 1728–1779.
Illus. map, port.
(*In her* Great explorers, [by] J. Grosseck [and] E. Attwood. Grand Rapids, Michigan,
Fideler, 1962. pp.110–20.)
Written for children.
Copies: NPL:M(Q910.9/4B1). 2959

[1962] LEYDEN, Peter
Capt. James Cook R.N. [Sydney, Australian Schools Press, 1962.]
Illus. part-coloured, pp.18.
(*Children's Australian Pictorial Biographies.*)
Copies: ANL. 2960

1963 DELEEUW, Adèle Louise

A World explorer, James Cook, by A. DeLeeuw. Illus. by N. Goldstein. Champaign, Illinois, Garrard Pub. Co., 1963.

Illus. in colour, maps as endpapers, pp.96.
(*World Explorer Books.*)
For children.
See also no. 2974.

Copies: NPL:M(923.9/C771.2/29A1); ANL.   2961

[1963] FRASER, Conon

With Captain Cook in New Zealand. Illus. by Harry Toothill. London, Muller, [1963].

Diag. illus. map, ports. pp. 144.
(*Adventures in Geography.*)

Copies: NPL:M(997/28A1); ANL.   2962

1963 WARNER, Oliver Martin Wilson

Captain Cook and the South Pacific, by the editors of *Horizon* Magazine; author, O. Warner, consultant . . . J. C. Beaglehole. New York, American Heritage Pub. Co., 1963.

Illus., some in colour, maps as endpapers, ports. pp.153.
(*Horizon Caravel Book.*)
See also no. 2968.

Copies: NPL:M(980:Col/W1A1); ANL.   2963

1964 DINGWELL, Alexander

The Great captain: the story of Captain Cook. London, Lutterworth Press, 1964.

Frontisp. in colour, map, pp.94.
(*Courage and Conquest ser.* no.9.)
For young readers.

Copies: NPL:M(923.9/C771.2/27A1); ANL.   2964

1964 KNIGHT, Frank

The Young Captain Cook, [by] F. Knight; illus. by J. Howell. London, Parrish, 1964.

Illus. pp.127.
(*Famous Childhoods.*)
For young readers.

Copies: NPL:M(923.9/C771.2/28A1); ANL.   2965

1964 KNIGHT, Frank

The Young Captain Cook, [by] F. Knight. Illus. by J. Howell. New York, Roy Pub., 1964.

pp.127.
For young readers.

Copies: NPL:M(923.9/C771.2/28B1); ANL.   2966

1964 LEYDEN, Peter

Life aboard the *Endeavour*. Sydney, Peter Leyden Publishing House, 1964

Illus. in colour, ports. pp.8.
(*Australian Visual Books, History*, no.3.)
For children. Cover title: *The Endeavour*.

Copies: NPL:M(Q990.1/10).   2967

1964 WARNER, Oliver Martin Wilson

Captain Cook and the South Pacific, by the editors of *Horizon* Magazine; author, O. Warner, consultant . . . J. C. Beaglehole. London, Cassell, 1964.

Illus., some in colour, maps as endpapers, ports. pp.153.
(*Cassell Caravel Book*, [no.] 6.)
First British edition. For New York edition *see* no. 2963.

Copies: NPL:M(980:Col/W1B1).   2968

1965 GREGORY, Olive Barnes

James Cook, by O.B. Gregory. Illus. by A. Oxenham. Exeter, Wheaton of Exeter, 1965.

Illus. in colour, pp.[24].
(*Read about it series*, book no.45.)

Copies: NPL:M(980:Col/G3A1).   2969

1965 RABLING, Harold

A New era dawns.

Illus.
(*In his* Pioneers of the Pacific: the story of the South Seas. Sydney, A. & R., 1965. pp.38–54.)
For young readers. Also published under title The Story of the Pacific, *see* no. 2971.

Copies: NPL:M(999/4B1).   2970

1965 RABLING, Harold

A New era dawns.

Illus.
(*In his* The Story of the Pacific. New York, Norton, 1965. pp.58–79.)
For young readers. Also published under title Pioneers of the South Seas, *see* no. 2970.

Copies: NPL:M(999/4A1).   2971

1965 SPERRY, Armstrong

Le Capitain Cook explore le Pacifique, [by] (A. Sperry); adapté [from the English] par J. Petrus. Paris, F. Nathan, 1965.

Illus. maps, ports. pp.157.
(*Histoire et Documents ser.*)
See also nos. 2950, 2956.

Copies: NPL:R(N920/C771/2).   2972

1965 SWENSON, Eric Pierson

The South Sea shilling: voyages of Captain Cook, R.N., by E. Swenson.
Illus. by C.M. Daugherty. New ed. Sydney, A. & R., 1965.

Maps as endpapers, pp.224.
Written for children.
See also no. 2946.
Copies: NPL:M(980:Co1/S3B1); ANL.   2973

1966 DELEEUW, Adèle Louise

A World explorer, James Cook, by A. Deleeuw. Illus. by N. Goldstein.
London, Muller, 1966.

Illus. in colour, maps as endpapers, pp.96.
(*World Explorer Books.*)
For children.
See also no. 2961.
Copies: NPL:M(923.9/C771.2/29B1).   2974

1967 MUSMAN, Richard

Captain Cook, [by] R. Musman. Illustrated by Biro, pseud. Maps by
K. Dance. [With bibl.] London, Hutchinson Educational, 1967.

Port. pp.[96].
(*Men of Mark.*)
For children.
Copies: NPL:M(980:Co1/M7A1).   2975

n.d. DISCOVERY of the Sandwich Islands.

(*National School Reader*. London, W. Wetton, n.d. pp.46–8.)
Copies: NPL:M(428/N).   **2976**

n.d. WHITCOMBE AND TOMBS, LTD.

Captain James Cook, for ages 12 to 14 years. Auckland, W. & T., n.d.

Illus. maps, port. as frontisp., pp.59.
(*Whitcombe's Story Books*, no.653.)
Copies: NPL:M(923.9/C771.2/31A1).   **2977**

MONUMENTS

References to statues and to memorials of Captain Cook are included here. References
to marble busts of Captain Cook are listed under the heading *Personal—Portraits.*
See also the heading *Personal—Celebrations.*

1915 WATSON, James Henry

Captain Cook: some monuments.

(Newspaper cuttings, vol.38, p.111.)
Extract from the *Sydney Morning Herald*, April 28, 1915.
Copies: NPL:M(Q990/N).   2978

1929 RESTARICK, Henry Bond, *Bishop of Honolulu*
List of monuments raised to Captain Cook.

(Taylor, Albert Pierce—Sesquicentennial celebration of Captain Cook's discovery of Hawaii, 1778–1928. Honolulu, 1929. pp.42–6.)
Hawaii—Board of Commissioners of Public Archives—*Publication* 4.

Copies: NPL:M(Q980:Co4/T1A1); Captain Cook's Landing Place Trust; VSL.   2979

1933 CRAMP, Karl Reginald
Some historical memorials and buildings.

Illus.
(Royal Australian Historical Society—*Journal and Proceedings*, vol.19, 1933, pp.1–39.)
Copies: NPL:M(991/R,Ref.Books); NPL:D(9/69); NPL:R(S991.06/1A,Ref.Books). 2980

1939 GORDON, M.
Captain Cook memorials.

Port.
(*N.Z. Railways Magazine*, May 1939, pp.51–3.)
Copies: NPL:M(Q656.205/N).   2981

n.d. [NEWSPAPER CUTTINGS, relating to Cook's voyages, journals, memorials, etc., 187- —1935.]
Illus. 3 vols.
Copies: NPL:M(Q980:Co1/N1A1–3).   2982

MONUMENTS IN AUSTRALIA

New South Wales

1872 CAMPBELL, Alexander
Letters from Alex. Campbell to Sir H. Parkes, Dec. 1, 24, 1872, and enclosure from Chas. Summers, Rome, undertaking to execute a statue of Captain Cook, 12 feet high, for £2000.

(Parkes correspondence, vol.9, pp.17–23.)
Copies: NPL:M(MSS.A879).   2983

1872 HILL, A.R., *Mrs*
Letter from Mrs A.R. Hill, Edinburgh, to Alex. Campbell, Sydney, May 3, 1872, describing model designed for her statue of Captain Cook to be erected in Sydney, and suggesting appointment of a local Committee for its assessment, states likeness of face is taken from the Dance portrait.

(Parkes correspondence, vol.10, pp.90–3.)
Copies: NPL:M(MSS.A880).   2984

1908 NATIONAL MEMORIAL to Captain Cook; proposed resumption of Cook's River and new botanical gardens.

(Newspaper cuttings, vol.12, p.66.)
Extract from *Daily Telegraph*, Sydney, 21st Nov. 1908. Proposal not carried out.
Copies: NPL:M(Q991/N). 2985

Botany Bay

n.d. PHOTOGRAPHS (2) of the marker buoy put up by the N.S.W. Maritime Services Board, to mark the approximate position where the *Endeavour* was moored in Botany Bay.

Copies: Captain Cook's Landing Place Trust. 2986

Hyde Park, Sydney

1867–74 BLACKET, Edmund Thomas
Proposed pedestal for Captain Cook's statue, Hyde Park.

1867–1874. 7 drawings and 1f. specifications. Var. sizes.
One of the drawings is dated 2.4.1867. Another, of the railing, incorporates the date 1874 in the design.
Further specifications, sketches and correspondence are filed at NPL:M A1713⁻⁴.
Copies: NPL:M(PX D6). 2987

1869–74 PAPERS re statue of Captain Cook to be erected in Hyde Park, 1869–1874.

Manuscript. Includes sketches and specifications, with letters by Sir Alfred Stephen and E.T. Blacket.
See also no.2987.
Copies: NPL:M(MSS.A1713⁻⁴). 2988

1869 H.R.H. THE DUKE OF EDINBURGH laying the foundation stone of the statue in memory of Captn. Cook, March 27, 1869, Sydney, N.S.W.

[Illustration.]
Copies: VSL. 2989

1869 STEPHEN, *Sir* Alfred
Letters from Sir Alfred Stephen to the Earl of Belmore, April 1869, thanking him for a donation of £50 for the Captain Cook column, and discussing the wording of the inscription.

(Belmore—Letters from his ministers and others, 1868–1872, vol.2, p.796–896.)
Copies: NPL:M(MSS.A2542⁻⁴). 2990

1872 COOK'S STATUE, pedestal, Hyde Park: [photograph].

(New South Wales—Colonial Architect—Photographs of public and other buildings &c., 1872. Pl. 154.)
Copies: NPL:M(X981.1/5). 2991

1875 NEW SOUTH WALES—Premier

Selection of sculptor of Cook's statue. Instructions [from the Premier] to Colonial Treasurer respecting. Sydney, Govt. Pr., 1875.

pp.3.

(Stephen, *Sir* Alfred—Public documents, vol.3.)

Copies: NPL:M(Q328.91/S).   2992

1876 COODE, KINGDON & COTTON

Letter from Coode, Kingdon & Cotton to N.S.W. Agent General in London, July 1, 1876, giving summary of correspondence between T. Woolner, sculptor, and N.S.W. Government, concerning execution of statue for erection on pedestal in Hyde Park; complains of delay in giving definite commission.

(Parkes correspondence, vol.9, pp.105–14.)

Copies: NPL:M(MSS.A879).   2993

[1878?] CAPTAIN COOK MONUMENT COMMITTEE

Captain Cook monument: [notice, with list of subscriptions, [1878?]].

pp.[4].

Copies: NPL:M(042/Pa255).   2994

[1878?] COOK'S STATUE, now in Hyde Park, Sydney, as it appeared in Waterloo Place, London, before its shipment to Australia.

Photograph. 8$\frac{11}{16}$" x 6$\frac{13}{16}$".

Copies: NPL:M(P3/41F).   2995

1878 STATUE of Captain Cook [by T. Woolner].

Illus.

(*Illustrated London News*, Aug., 1878, p.133.)

Mitchell Library copy in volume entitled Newspaper extracts relating to Australia.

Copies: NPL:M(F980.1/N); NPL:R(F050/129).   2996

1878 STATUE of Captain Cook [by T. Woolner].

Illus.

(Newspaper extracts relating to Australia.)

Extract from the *Sydney Mail*, Sept.14, 1878. Cover title: *Illustrations, volume 1.*

Copies: NPL:M(F980.1/N).   2997

[1879?] CAPTAIN COOK'S STATUE, presumably at time of erection.

1879? Photograph. 5$\frac{1}{2}$" x 3$\frac{3}{8}$".

Copies: NPL:M(Small Picture File: Sydney—Monuments—Cook—Hyde Park 1). 2998

1879 CEREMONY of unveiling the statue of Capt. Cook, Hyde Park, Sydney, Feb. 1879: [coloured woodcut].

(*Illustrated Sydney News*, Supp., Mar. 1879.)

Copies: NPL:M(NA108); NPL:R(F079/129).   2999

1879 COOK MEMORIAL, Sydney, 1879: [illustration].
(Newspaper extracts relating to Australia.)
Extract from the *Sydney Mail*, Supp., Mar.1, 1879. Cover title: *Illustrations, volume 1.*
Copies: NPL:M(F980.1/N).   3000

1879 LANDING of Captain Cook's statue.
Illus.
(*Illustrated Sydney News*, Jan. 1879. pp.7, 16.)
Copies: NPL:M(NA108); NPL:R(F079/129).   3001

1879 MACARTHUR, *Sir* William
Unveiling of Cook's statue, from Museum, 1879.
Photographs (2) probably taken by W. Macarthur.
(Macarthur, W.—Album of views etc., p.91.)
Macarthur Papers, part IV—Family and personal. Restricted issue.
Copies: NPL:M(PX A4358⁻¹).   3002

1879 MACLEOD, W.
Unveiling of the Captain Cook Statue, Hyde Park, 1879. W. Macleod
del. Litho. $8\frac{5}{8}''$ x $19\frac{1}{4}''$.
(Supplement to the *Sydney Mail*, Mar.8, 1879.)
Copies: NPL:M(V1/Mon Cook 1).   3003

The Same.
Reduced. Process plate.
(*Sydney Mail*, July 6, 1910, p.42.)
Copies: NPL:M(F991/S).   3004

1879 ROSMEAD, Hercules George Robert Robinson, *1st Baron*
Unveiling of statue of Captain Cook, Feb. 25, 1879.
(*In his* Speeches. Sydney, Gibbs, Shallard, 1879. pp.214–30.)
Copies: NPL:M(308); QParl.   3005

1879 STATUE to Captain Cook, [Hyde Park, Sydney].
(*Nature*, vol.20, May, 1879, pp.7–8.)
Copies: NPL:M(Q505/N); NPL:R(DQ505/1).   3006

[1879] UNVEILING of the Cook statue; procession and ceremony, Tuesday
   25 Feb., 1879. Order of procession and programme of proceedings.
   Sydney, Govt. Pr., [1879].
Illus. port. pp.16.
Large paper edition.
Two copies held in A.N.L., specially bound for the use of Princes George and Albert
Victor; presented by H.M. the King.
Copies: NPL:D(Q87/39); ANL; ANL:F; VSL.   3007

[1879] UNVEILING of the Captain Cook statue, Hyde Park, Sydney . . .
on Tuesday, 25th Feb., 1879; [with] (Order of procession [and] Pro-
gramme of proceedings). Sydney, Govt. Pr., [1879].
Illus. port. pp.7.
Title from p.1.
Copies: NPL:M(Q923.9/C771.2/3A1); NPL:R(S920/C771/8); ANL:F.   3008

1879 UNVEILING of Cook's statue.
1879. Photograph (4). c.4¾″ x 6⅜″.
Copies: NPL:M(Small Picture File:Sydney—Monuments—Cook—Hyde Park 8–11).
                                                                          3009

[1880?] ARMSTRONG, *Sir* A.
[Statue of Captain Cook in Hyde Park, Sydney, 1880?]
(*In his* [Photographs of New South Wales, 1880?] f.2.)
Copies: NPL:M(F981/A).   3010

1882 REID, J.A.
Cook's monument.
(*In his* The Australian reader. Melbourne, J. Whitelaw and Son, 1882. pp.82–4.)
Copies: NPL:M(990.1/R).   3011

1885 PLUMMER, John
Unveiling the Cook statue [in Hyde Park, Sydney].
(*In his* A Mayoral year. Sydney, Gibbs, Shallard & Co., 1885. pp. 73–4.)
Copies: NPL:M(394/P).   3012

1892 STATUE of Captain Cook at Sydney: [illustration].
(*In* Pratt, Mara L.—People and places. Boston, Educational Pub. Co., [1892]. Vol.1,
p.16.)
Copies: NPL:M(990/P).   3013

1893 MONUMENT to Captain Cook: [illustration].
(Tregarthen, Greville—Australian Commonwealth. London, T. Fisher Unwin, 1893.
p.176.)
Copies: NPL:M(990.1/100A1); NPL:R(MB1:Q35).   3014

1898 TAYLOR, John Michael
Captain Cook's statue, Hyde Park, Sydney: [illustration].
(*In his* Geography of New South Wales. Sydney, A. & R., 1898. p.6.)
Later editions published in [1902?], 1912, 1920, 1927.
Copies: NPL:M(981/1A).   3015

1906 MONUMENT to Captain Cook at Sydney: [process plate].

(*In* Marriott, Ida, *Mrs.*—Coming of the British to Australia. London, Longmans, Green and Co., 1906. Frontisp.)

Copies: NPL:M(991/28A1).   3016

1908 TRIBUTE from Yorkshireman in N.S.W. Tablet on statue in Hyde Park, Sydney.

(*Australian Town and Country Journal,* May 6, 1908.)

Copies: NPL:R(F079/A938).   3017

1917 WOOLNER, Thomas

[Captain Cook statue: letters, etc., and reproduction of photograph of the statue displayed in London in 1878.]

(*In* Woolner, Amy—Thomas Woolner. London, Chapman and Hall, 1917. pp.280, 295–7.)

Copies: NPL:M(927.3/W).   3018

1925 FORBES, G.

Captain Cook: Woolner's statue.

(Newspaper cuttings, vol.166, pp.167–8.)
Extract from the *Sydney Morning Herald,* Feb.2, 1925.

Copies: NPL:M(Q991.1/N).   3019

1928 TAYLOR, F.M. *Mrs*

Captain Cook's statue, Sydney.

Illus.
(*Commonwealth Home,* July 1928, p.14.)

Copies: NPL:M(MDQ059/10).   3020

1929 CRAMP, Karl Reginald

Bi-centenary of Captain Cook's birth: celebrations at the base of Captain Cook's statue, Hyde Park, Sydney, Oct.27, 1928.

(Royal Australian Historical Society—*Journal and Proceedings,* vol.15, 1929. pp.217–21.)

Copies: NPL:M(991/R,Ref.Books); NPL:D(9/69); NPL:R(S991.06/1A,Ref.Books).

     3021

n.d. CAPTAIN COOK'S STATUE, Hyde Park.

Various dates. 6 photographs, and 1 coloured reproduction. Var. sizes.

Copies: NPL:M(Small Picture File: Sydney—Monuments—Cook—Hyde Park 2–7, 12).

     3022

n.d. COOK'S STATUE, Hyde Park: [photograph].

(Photographic views in New South Wales, vol. II, p. 84. [n.d.].)

Copies: NPL:M(F981/P).   3023

n.d. COOK'S STATUE, Hyde Park, Sydney: [photograph].
(Photographic views of New South Wales, pl. 41.)
Copies: NPL:M(Q981/P).   3024

n.d. [STATUE.]
(Photographs of Sydney and N.S.W., p.44.)
Copies: NPL:M(F981/P).   3025

n.d. STATUE of Captain Cook in Hyde Park, Sydney.
Photograph. 11½″ x 10¼″.
Copies: NPL:M(P2/35).   3026

Kurnell

1821 FACSIMILE of tablet placed on the cliffs at Kurnell by the
Philosophical Society of Australasia in 1821.
Copper plate mounted on cedar.
Copies: NPL:M(LR35).   3027

Another, not mounted.
Found during the removal of New South Wales Government Printing Office from Bent
and Phillip Streets, Sydney, July 1961.
Copies: NPL:M(LR36).   3028

The Same.
Meas. inside frame 6¼″ x 6″.
Presented by Mrs. Thomas, Sep. 1961.
Copies: NPL:M(R305).   3029

[1821] PHOTOGRAPH of inscription placed on the face of the cliffs at
Kurnell, the landing place of Captn. Cook, 1770, in 1821.
Copies: VSL.   3030

[1821 REPRODUCTION of plate erected by the Philosophical Society of
New South Wales; with sonnets by Barron Field.]
Copies: Captain Cook's Landing Place Trust.   3031

[1821 TABLET to the memory of J. Cook and J. Banks, erected at Botany
Bay in 1821: photograph.]
(Miscellaneous photographs, etc., vol.1, no.11.)
Copies: SPL.   3032

1839 CAPTAIN COOK'S TABLET, Cape Solander. London, 1839.
Illus.
Extract from the *Literary World*, Nov.16, 1839, pp.97–9.
See also no.3039.
Copies: NPL:M(042/Pa152); ANL:F.   3033

1839 LESSON, René Primevère
[Tablet at Botany Bay inscribed to Cook's memory by the Philosophical
Society of Australasia 1822.]
(*In his* Voyage autour du monde. Paris, Pourrat, 1839. Vol.2, p.269.)
Copies: NPL:M(980/64A2).   3034

1839 LHOTSKY, John
Captain Cook's tablet at Cape Solander, Botany Bay, New South Wales.
Erected . . . on the spot where that great navigator first cast anchor in
New Holland, by Sir Thos. Brisbane, Bart. Governor of New South
Wales. Lithographed by G.E.Madeley . . . after a sketch taken on the
spot by Dr. Lhotsky.
Pub. by J. Lhotsky . . . 18 Sep. 1839. Litho. Meas. of view $9\frac{5}{8}''$ x $15\frac{1}{8}''$.
Copies: NPL:M(V*Cook 36).   3035

Another print.
Hand-coloured.
Copies: NPL:D(DG V*Cook 1).   3036

The Same, on India paper.
Copies: NPL:M(V*Cook 37).   3037

Photograph.
Copies: NPL:M(Small Picture File: Kurnell—Monuments—Cook tablet 1).   3038

The Same, [entitled] Captain Cook's tablet, Cape Solander, Botany Bay.
New South Wales.
1839. Wood engraving. $3\frac{7}{8}''$ x $6\frac{3}{8}''$.
(Australasian Scrap-book.)
Extract from *The Literary World*, vol.2, no.34, Nov.16, 1839, p.97.
Copies: NPL:M(F980/A).   3039

1840 HOLMAN, James
[Tablet to Cook, the navigator.]
(*In his* Travels in China, New Zealand, etc. 2nd ed. London, Routledge, 1840. p. 471.)
Copies: NPL:M(980/H).   3040

[185–?] GILL, Samuel Thomas
Landing place of Captn Cook, Botney (*sic*) Bay, N.S.W.
Watercolour touched with white. 7⅛″ x 10¼″.
Titled in pencil and signed "S.T.G.".
(*In his* Original sketches, f.15.)
Copies: NPL:M(PX*D383). 3041

[185–?] MASON, Walter G.
Curnell House. Captain Cook's landing place.
Watercolours. 3⅛″ x 4⅞″.
Titled "Curnell House". From woodcuts by W.G. Mason.
Copies: Captain Cook's Landing Place Trust. 3042

[185–?] TERRY, Frederick Charles
Landing place of Captain Cook.
Lithograph on tinted ground. c.3″ x 4½″.
(*In* Terry, F.C.—Views of Sydney Harbour no.3.)
Copies: NPL:M(SSV*Spec.Coll.Terry 14). 3043

[c.1870] STACK, John
Kurnell House. By John Stack, Surveyor-General's Office.
c.1870. Sepia drawing. Meas. inside mount 5⅝″ x 13⅜″.
Copies: Captain Cook's Landing Place Trust. 3044

1871 CAPTAIN COOK'S landing in Botany Bay, with fac-simile of Cook's chart and view of monument to Captain Cook. Sydney, Gibbs, Shallard, n.d.
Illus. pp.121.
Extract from the *Illustrated Sydney News* and *Sydney Morning Herald*. The monument, which consists of a stone column on a cube base, was erected in 1871.
Copies: NPL:M(991.1/C); NPL:R(MJ2:S3). 3045

1871 COOK'S LANDING in Botany Bay: monument erected by T. Holt.
Illus. map.
(*Illustrated Sydney News*, Ap. 17, 1871. pp. 49, 51.)
Copies: NPL:M(NA108); NPL:R(F079/129). 3046

1888 McLEOD, —
First landing place, Botany Bay, [1888]. From a recent sketch.
(*In* Forde, Joseph Michael—Albums of newspaper illustrations. Vol.5, p.118.)
Copies: NPL:M(Q991/F). 3047

[189–? NOTE on the resumption of Captain Cook's landing site at Kurnell
as a national monument, including a quotation from the *Sydney Gazette*
Mar. 22, 1822, describing the mounting of the memorial plaque at
Kurnell: newspaper cutting.]
Mounted.
Copies: NPL:M(981.1/54A1). 3048

1894 COOK'S MONUMENT, Botany Bay: [illustration].
(*In* Sutherland, Alexander and Sutherland, George—History of Australia and New
Zealand. London, Longmans Green and Co., 1894. p.24.)
New edition, 1922, also held in the Mitchell Library.
Copies: NPL:M(990/S). 3049

[1896?] MONUMENT à Botany Bay: [illustration].
(*In* Saint-Yves, Georges—L'Océanie. Tours, Alfred Mame, [1896?]. pp.12–13.)
Copies: NPL:M(Q980/S). 3050

1899 CAPTAIN COOK RESERVE dedicated to the public: (ceremony
at Kurnell).
(Newspaper cuttings, vol.145, pp.154–154B. [1896–9].)
Extract from the *Sydney Morning Herald*, May 8, 1899.
Copies: NPL:M(Q352.091/N). 3051

[1899?] MEMORIAL to mark the landing place of Captain Cook at
Kurnell, erected by Thomas Holt; [and] (Inscription on copper tablet
upon cliff at Kurnell). [Illustrations.]
(*In* McFarland, Alfred—Captain Cook. Sydney, Govt. Pr., [1899?]. pp.23, 31.)
Copies: NPL:M(923.9/C771.2/12A1). 3052

1899 NEW SOUTH WALES—Department of Lands
Dedication of Captain Cook's Landing Place, Kurnell, Botany Bay.
[Sydney, Govt. Pr., 1899.]
Illus. map, port. pp.74.
Copies: NPL:M(991.1/N); ANL; VSL. 3053

1899 NEW SOUTH WALES—Department of Lands
Plan of an area of 253 ac. . . . dedicated for public recreation at Cook's
landing place, Botany Bay. Sydney, 1899.
Scale 2 chains = 1".
Copies: NPL:M(F12/B2e). 3054

1900 NEW SOUTH WALES—Government Printer
Landing place of Captn Cook, Kurnell, Botany Bay.
1900. Photograph. 10¼" x 14⅛".
Copies: NPL:M(Small Picture File: Kurnell—Monuments—Cook Monument 1). 3055

Another print.
(New South Wales—Govt. Printer—Photographic views of New South Wales, p.41,
[1900].)
Copies: NPL:M(Beauchamp Collection 57,D231).   3056

[1904] FIRST LANDING-PLACE, Botany Bay: [illustration].
(*In* Kingston, William Henry Giles—Captain Cook. London, Religious Tract Society,
[1904]. p.89.)
Copies: NPL:M(980:Col/K1A1).   3057

[1906?] NEW SOUTH WALES—Immigration and Tourist Bureau
Kurnell, the birthplace of Australian history; [issued by the Govt.
Tourist Bureau]. Sydney, Govt. Pr., [1906?].
Illus. pp.20.
Cover title: *The Landing place of Captain Cook.*
See also nos.3059, 3061.
Copies: NPL:M(981.1/52A1); ANL:F.   3058

[1906?] NEW SOUTH WALES—Immigration and Tourist Bureau
Kurnell, the birthplace of Australian history; [issued by the Govt.
Tourist Bureau]. Sydney, Govt. Pr., [1906?].
Illus. pp.20.
Another printing. Cover title: *The Landing place of Captain Cook.*
See also nos.3058, 3061.
Copies: NPL:M(981.1/52A2).   3059

1907 COLLONS
Captain Cook's landing place.
1907. Watercolour. 5¾″ x 13½″.
Signed "Collons" lower left-hand side.
Titled "Kurnell" lower right.
Copies: Captain Cook's Landing Place Trust.   3060

1909 NEW SOUTH WALES—Immigration and Tourist Bureau
Kurnell, the birthplace of Australian history; issued by the Immigration
and Tourist Bureau. 2nd ed. Sydney, Govt. Pr., 1909.
Illus. port. pp.[33].
Cover title: *The Landing place of Captain Cook . . . issued by the Government Tourist Bureau.*
See also nos.3058-9.
Copies: NPL:M(981.1/52B1).   3061

1928 KURNELL, the birthplace of Australian history: James Cook, 1728–
1779.
Illus.
(*A.N.A.*, May, 1928, cover and pp.132–3.)
Copies: NPL:M(Q059/A).   3062

1928 MACDONALD, Walter Alexander
Forby Sutherland's grave at Kurnell.
Illus. map.
(Royal Australian Historical Society—*Journal and Proceedings*, vol.14, 1928, pp.281–98.)
Copies: NPL:M(991/R,Ref.Books); NPL:D(9/69); NPL:R(S991.06/1A,Ref.Books). 3063

[1933] ALANSON, A.G.
Kurnell, the birthplace of Australia. Sydney, G.B. Philip, [1933].
Illus. map, pp.95.
Copies: NPL:M(991.1/30A1); ANL; Captain Cook's Landing Place Trust. 3064

1948 CAPTAIN COOK'S LANDING PLACE TRUST
Royal visits to Captain Cook's landing place, Kurnell, Botany Bay . . .
1881–1946. Sydney, Govt. Pr., 1948.
Illus. map, port. pp.19.
Copies: NPL:M(Pam.File 991.1/C); Captain Cook's Landing Place Trust; VSL. 3065

1963 BROOKSBANK, Walter
Captain Cook's landing place.
Illus.
(*Walkabout*, vol.29, Sep. 1963, pp.15–17.)
Copies: NPL:M(Q980/W); NPL:R(NQ919.406/2); ANL. 3066

[1966?] CALTEX
Captain Cook's Memorial—Kurnell, Sydney, N.S.W.
Coloured illus. 8¾" x 11".
(Caltex—Historic scenic views no.3.)
Copies: NPL:M(Small Picture File: Kurnell—Monuments—Cook Monument 3). 3067

1967 RANDWICK HISTORICAL SOCIETY
Birth-place of Australia: historic Botany Bay. Randwick, N.S.W., the
Society, 1967.
Illus. map, pp.[8].
(Randwick Historical Society—*Pam*. no.4.)
Copies: NPL:M(991.1/64A1). 3068

n.d. BRASS TABLET in cliff, [and] (Curnell House): [2 small watercolours from woodcuts by W. Mason].
3⅛" x 5" each.
Copies: Captain Cook Landing Place Trust. 3069

n.d. CAPTAIN COOK'S MONUMENT at Kurnell.
Photograph. 6" x 8".
Copies: NPL:M(V*Cook 42D). 3070

n.d. CAPTAIN COOK'S MONUMENT, Kurnell.
Two photographs, c.6″ x 8″ and 5½″ x 7½″.
Copies: NPL:M(Small Picture File: Kurnell—Monuments—Cook Monument 2). 3071

n.d. CAPTAIN COOK'S MONUMENT, Kurnell, Botany: [photograph].
(Photographic views of Sydney, vol.1, p.94.)
Copies: NPL:M(Q981.1/P). 3072

n.d. COOK'S LANDING: [account of an excursion to Botany Bay].
Newspaper cutting, *bound with* Trip up George's River.
Copies: NPL:M(981.1/T). 3073

n.d. NEW SOUTH WALES—Government Printer
Tree planted by Miss Rawson, Kurnell.
Photograph no.9389. 6″ x 8″.
Copies: NPL:M(Small Picture File: Kurnell 1). 3074

n.d. NEW SOUTH WALES—Government Printer
Tree planted by Sir Henry Rawson, Kurnell.
Photograph no.9385. c.6″ x 8″.
Copies: NPL:M(Small Picture File: Kurnell 2). 3075

Liverpool

[c.191–] WATSON, James Henry
The Obelisk in Bigge Square, Liverpool.
Illus.
(*In his* Liverpool: [manuscript notes and newspaper cuttings]. 1907–1919.)
Describes a stone obelisk erected in 1854, primarily as a milestone, with engraved
inscription to Captain Cook.
Copies: NPL:M(Q991.8/W). 3076

Randwick

1874 CAPTAIN COOK STATUE at Randwick.
Illus.
(*Illustrated Sydney News*, Nov.14, 1874, pp.10, 21.)
Copies: NPL:M(NA108); NPL:R(F079/129). 3077

1876 GOODENOUGH, James Graham
[Unveiling of Cook's statue at Randwick, Oct.27th, 1874: report from
Sydney Morning Herald, Oct.28th of speech by Commodore Goodenough.]
(*In his* Journal. London, Henry S. King, 1876. pp.125–9.)
Copies: NPL:M(A923.542/G649.1/4A1). 3078

1878 GOODENOUGH, James Graham

[Unveiling of Captain Cook's statue at Randwick: speech, from the
Sydney Morning Herald, Oct.28th, 1874.]

(*In his* Memoir. London, C. Kegan Paul, 1878. pp.146–9.)

Copies: NPL:M(A923.542/G649.1/4C1).   3079

1879 CAPTAIN COOK: [illustration of monument erected by Captain T. Watson].

(*In* Blair, David—History of Australasia. Glasgow, McGready, Thomson and Niven, 1879. p. 72.)

Copies: NPL:M(Q990/B).   3080

[1909] CAPTAIN COOK'S STATUE, Randwick.

(*In* Cooper, D.M.—History of Randwick. Sydney, Randwick Municipal Council, [1909]. p.3.)
Illus.

Copies: NPL:M(991.1/C).   3081

n.d. CAPTAIN COOK'S MONUMENT, [erected by Capt. Watson at Randwick: photograph].

(Anglo-Australasian Photo Co.—Views of New South Wales, no.18, [n.d.].)

Copies: NPL:M(Q981/A).   3082

n.d. STATUE of Captain Cook standing in front of Captain Thomas Watson's home at Randwick, N.S.W.

Photograph. 9″ x 7⅛″.
Presented by W.H.Brown, 1931.
Shows statue and residence.

Copies: NPL:M(Small Picture File: Sydney—Monuments—Cook—Randwick 1). 3083

Queensland

Bustard Bay

1928 MONUMENT erected on Round Hill near Gladstone to commemorate the landing ashore on May 24, 1770 of Captain James Cook. O.Webb photo.

Half-tone reproduction. 11½″ x 9¼″.
Extract from *The Queenslander Pictorial*, May 24, 1928.

Copies: NPL:M(Small Picture File: Bustard Bay—Monuments—Cook 1).   3084

1928 STEWART, Francis William Sutton Cumbrae-

Memorial to Captain Cook at Bustard Bay [and at Possession Island].
Brisbane.

Illus.
(Historical Society of Queensland—*Journal*, vol.2, no.4, Mar. 1928. pp.[1], 159–91.)
Copies: NPL:M(994/H); NPL:D(92/248); NPL:R(S994.06/1). 3085

1955 CAPTAIN COOK Bustard Bay memorial.
(Historical Society of Queensland—*Bulletin* no.134, pp.1–2, Oct. 1955.)
Copies: NPL:M(Q994.06/2). 3086

1957 MUSGRAVE, Anthony
Captain Cook's Monument, Monument Point, inscribed 'Under the lee of this Point Lieutenant James Cook, R.N., landed on 24th May 1770'; with Views of the point.
1957. Four photographs. Each c.3" x 4".
(*In his* Album of photographs taken on a visit to Thirsty Sound, Qld., with G.P. Whitley, to observe fauna and flora recorded by James Cook in the same season of the year. Album 2, pp.11–15.)
Copies: NPL:M(PX A12). 3087

Cooktown

[19—] CONIGRAVE, Charles Price
Captain Cook Memorial, Cooktown.
Photograph. Titled in pencil on back, and signed 'CPC'.
(*In* Photographs of Papua, Australia, etc. taken by C.Price Conigrave, bet. 1907–1953, pt.8, no.12.)
Copies: NPL:M(PX A36). 3088

[19—] MONUMENT at Captain Cook's landing place, Cooktown.
Stereoscopic photograph.
From Alan R. McCullock's collection.
Presented by the Australian Museum, 1958.
Copies: NPL:M(Small Picture File: Cooktown—Monuments—Cook 1). 3089

1903 MONUMENT at Captain Cook's landing place, Cooktown: [illustration].
(*In* Burns, Philp & Co.—All about Burns, Philp & Co. Sydney, John Andrew, 1903. p.57.)
Copies: NPL:M(980/B). 3090

1906 CAPTAIN COOK'S MONUMENT, [Cooktown: illustration].
(*In* Lees, William—Picturesque Queensland. 4th ed. Brisbane, Gordon and Gotch, 1906. p.47.)
Copies: NPL:M(Q984/L). 3091

1907 BANFIELD, Edmund John
Captain Cook's monument, Cooktown.
Illus.
(*In his* Within the Barrier. Townsville, Willmett & Son, 1907. pp.83–4.)
Copies: NPL:M(Q984.6/B).   3092

1909–10 THOMSON, J.P.
[Captain Cook's monument, Cooktown.]
Illus.
(*Queensland Geographical Journal*, vol.25, 1909–10, pp.71–2.)
Copies: NPL:M(980/R).   3093

1925 COOK'S TREE AND CAIRN [at Cooktown].
Illus.
(Newspaper cuttings: Captain Cook. Vol.1, pp.90–91.)
Daily Mail, Oct.3, 1925.
Copies: NPL:M(Q980:Co1/N1A1).   3094

1957 MAY, L. Buchanan
Captain Cook's tree.
(*North Australian Monthly*, vol.3, p.17, Aug.1957.)
Copies: NPL:M(Q980.105/11).   3095

1960 THE TABLEAU on Cooktown's memorial in the main street of
Cooktown.
(*Queensland Geographical Journal*, vol.60, 1960–1, p.34.)
Copies: NPL:M(980/R).   3096

1969 QUEENSLAND—State Public Relations Bureau
Cook's Monument, Cooktown: [reproduction of a photograph].
(*In* Cook, James—First Voyage—Printed Accounts [1969 Reed's Edition]—Captain
Cook in Australia . . . Ed. by A.W.Reed. Wellington, N.Z., Reed, 1969. Between pp.96
and 97.)
Copies: NPL:M(980:Co2/11A1).   3097

n.d. MONUMENT to Captain Cook at Cooktown.
Photograph. $7\frac{5}{8}''$ x $5\frac{5}{8}''$.
Copies: NPL:M(Small Picture File: Cooktown—Monuments—Cook 2).   3098

Daydream Island

1945.6 PARKER, F.L.
Cook's discovery of Whitsunday passage; [with illus. of cairn erected on
Daydream Island].

(Royal Geographical Society of Australasia—South Australian Branch—*Proceedings*, vol.47, pp.78–9, 1945–46.)
Copies: NPL:M(980/R).   3099

Possession Island

1925.6 MEMORIALS to Captain James Cook, R.N. [on Point Hicks and Possession Island].
Illus.
(Royal Australian Historical Society—*Journal and Proceedings*, vol.11, 1925.6, pp.379–80.)
Copies: NPL:M(991/R,Ref.Books); NPL:D(9/69); NPL:R(S991.06/1A,Ref.Books). 3100

1928 MEMORIAL to Captain Cook at Possession Island.
Illus.
(Historical Society of Queensland—*Journal*, vol.2, no.4, March 1928, pp.187, 189–90.)
Copies: NPL:M(994/H); NPL:D(92/248); NPL:R(S994.06/1).   3101

1969 QUEENSLAND—State Public Relations Bureau
The Plaque on Cook's Monument, Possession Island: [reproduction of a photograph].
(*In* Cook, James—First Voyage—Printed Accounts [1969 Reed's Edition]—Captain Cook in Australia . . . Ed. by A.W.Reed. Wellington, N.Z., Reed, 1969. Between pp.96 and 97.)
Copies: NPL:M(980:Co2/11A1).   3102

Tasmania

Bruny Island

1968 SMITH, Patsy Adam
The Bounty of Bully Bligh.
Illus.
(*In her* Tiger country. Adelaide, Rigby, 1968. pp.124–34.)
Describes Captain Cook's tree, Bruny Island, and the Bligh Museum of Pacific History.
Copies: NPL:M(986/40A1).   3103

Victoria

Bendigo

1915 LONG, C.R.
[Monument to Cook, Bendigo, in the grounds of St. Paul's Church of England.]
(*Victorian Historical Magazine*, vol.4, 1914–15, p.155.)
Copies: NPL:M(992/V).   3104

[19—] GRIMWADE, W. Russell

[Cook monument at Point Hicks: two photographs by W. Russell Grimwade.]

(In case with map of coastline from Snowy River to Twofold Bay . . . with Lieutenant Cook's coast line and the track of H.M. Bark *Endeavour*.)

Copies: ANL. 3105

1925.26 MEMORIALS to Captain James Cook, R.N. [on Point Hicks and Possession Island].

Illus.

(Royal Australian Historical Society—*Journal and Proceedings*, vol.11, 1925.26, pp.379–80.)

Obelisk placed at Point Hicks at the request of the Royal Australian Historical Society. It was prepared by the Federal Government and placed in position by the Navigation Department.

Copies: NPL:M(991/R,Ref.Books); NPL:D(9/69); NPL:R(S991.06/1A,Ref.Books). 3106

n.d. [PHOTOGRAPH of Cook's landfall monument at Point Hicks.]

Copies: VSL. 3107

St. Kilda

1914 ALLAN, H.O.

The Captain Cook statue, St. Kilda beach . . . unveiling ceremony, Dec.7, 1914 . . . With a short memoir of the great circumnavigator. Melbourne, Osboldstone & Co., pr., [1914].

Copies: VSL. 3108

1915–17 BRONZE STATUE of Captain Cook; replica by J. Tweed of that by this sculptor at Whitby, Yorkshire: [illustration].

(*St. Kilda by the Sea Annual*, 1915–16, p.4, 1916–17, p.4.)

Copies: NPL:M(982.1/S). 3109

1931 COOPER, John Butler

Captain Cook's memorial.

Illus.

(*In his* History of St. Kilda. Melbourne, Printers Proprietary, 1931. Vol.2, pp.230–2.)

Copies: NPL:M(992.1/C). 3110

MONUMENTS IN NEW ZEALAND

1936 WRIGHT, W.H.

Sketch model for statue of Captain Cook [by W. H. Wright. Illustration.]

(*Art in New Zealand*, vol.9, no.1, Sept. 1936, p.35.)

Copies: NPL:M(Q709.905/A). 3111

1939 [PHOTOGRAPHS of the memorials at Marlborough Sounds and at Christchurch.]
(*N.Z. Railways Magazine*, May 1939, pp.51, 53.)
Copies: NPL:M(Q656.205/N).   3112

Christchurch

1936 COOK MEMORIAL: [view].
(*N.Z. Free Lance Annual*, 1936, p.49.)
Copies: NPL:M(F987.05/1).   3113

Gisborne

1906 MONUMENT recently erected at Gisborne to the memory of Captain Cook: [illustration].
Granite column, erected 1906.
Copies: NPL:M(Newscuttings File).   3114

1966 TURBOTT, H.A.
Spacious square to commemorate Cook.
(*In his* Turbott report on the development of the Gisborne foreshore. Gisborne, *Gisborne Herald*, pr., 1966. pp.34–9.)
Copies: NPL:M(711.558/1B1).   3115

1969 NATIONAL PUBLICITY STUDIOS
Memorial erected on the spot in Gisborne where Captain Cook first landed in New Zealand: [reproduction of a photograph].
(*In* Cook, James—Collected Voyages—Printed Accounts [1969 Reed's Edition]—Captain Cook in New Zealand . . . Ed. by A.H. & A.W. Reed. 2nd ed. Wellington, N.Z., Reed, 1969. Between pp.144 and 145.)
Copies: NPL:M(980:Co1/45B1).   3116

Ship Cove

1926 MONUMENT . . . at Ship Cove . . . Queen Charlotte Sound: [views].
(*New Zealand News and Views*, Mar. 1926, p.6.)
Copies: NPL:M(Q987.006/N).   3117

1935 COOK MEMORIAL, Ship Cove, Queen Charlotte Sound: [illustration].
(*In* Bledisloe, Charles Bathurst, 1st Baron—Ideals of nationhood. New Plymouth, Thomas Avery & Sons, 1935. p.120.)
Copies: NPL:M(A825/B646/1A1).   3118

1969 NATIONAL PUBLICITY STUDIOS

Cook Monument at Ship Cove, Queen Charlotte Sound; [with] (Inscription). [Reproductions of two photographs.]

(*In* Cook, James—Collected Voyages—Printed Accounts [1969 Reed's Edition]—
Captain Cook in New Zealand . . . Ed. by A.H. & A.W. Reed. 2nd ed. Wellington, N.Z.,
Reed, 1969. Between pp.144 and 145.)

Copies: NPL:M(980:Co1/45B1).   3119

MONUMENTS IN THE PACIFIC ISLANDS

Hawaiian Islands

1825 BYRON, George Anson Byron, *7th Baron*

Original manuscript log book of the voyage of H.M.S. *Blonde* to the
Sandwich Islands; from Sept.23, 1824 to Feb.6, 1826. Entry for Saturday,
July 16, 1825: "erected on shore a monument to the memory of Capt.
Cook."

The monument referred to was a cross of oak bearing the inscription on a copper plate.
It was placed about two miles distant from the spot where Cook fell.

Copies: ANL:F.   3120

1826 BYRON, George Anson Byron, *7th Baron*

Cross erected to Captain Cook's memory.

(*In his* Voyage of H.M.S. *Blonde* to Sandwich Islands, in the years 1824–1825. London,
John Murray, 1826. p.202.)

Copies: NPL:M(Q989.6/B).   3121

1845 WILKES, Charles

Monument to mark where Captain Cook was killed.

Illus.
(*In his* Narrative of the United States Exploring Expedition . . . 1838–42. Philadelphia,
Lea & Blanchard, 1845. Vol.4, pp.92–3.)

Copies: NPL:M(980/170A4).   3122

1863 A MONUMENT to Capt. Cook.

(*The Friend,* Ap. 1863, p.29.)

Copies: NPL:M(Q205/1).   3123

1877 COOK'S MONUMENT.

Illus.
(*The Friend,* Ap.1877, p.28.)

Copies: NPL:M(Q205/1).   3124

1882 FRANCIS, B.
[Death of Captain Cook and the monument at Kealakekua Bay; with woodcut showing the monument.]

(*In his* Isles of the Pacific. London, Cassell, 1882. pp.173–8.)
Copies: NPL:M(989/F).   3125

1885 MARTIN-CHABBIS, E.
Baie de Kerlakakira et monument du Capitaine Cook: [illustration].

(*In* Monnier, Marcel—Un Printemps sur le Pacifique; îles Hawai. Paris, Librairie Plon 1885. Plate opp. p.169.)
Contents lists plate opposite p.180.
Copies: NPL:M(989.6/39A1).   3126

1888 CAPTAIN COOK'S monument, Kaawoloa.
(*In* Chaney, George Leonard—Alo'ha. Boston, Roberts, 1888. Plate opp. p. 186.)
Copies: NPL:M(989.6/C).   3127

[189–?] CAPT. COOK'S MONUMENT, Kealakekua Bay: [reproduction of photograph].
(Glimpses of the Hawaiian Islands. N.p., n.d. Plate 13.)
Copies: NPL:M(989.6/G).   3128

[189–?] MONUMENT to Captain Cook, Kealakekua Bay: [engraving].
(*In* Cook, James—Collected Voyages—Printed Accounts [189?] Hawkesworth's ed.—Voyages of discovery . . . comp. . . . by Dr. Hawkesley (*sic*). London, Ward, Lock, Bowden & Co., [189?]. Vol.2, p.600.)
Copies: NPL:M(Q980:Co1/5A2).   3129

1890 WHITNEY, Henry M.
Cook's monument, Kealakekua Bay.

(*In his* Tourist's guide through the Hawaiian Islands. Honolulu, *Hawaiian Gazette*, 1890 pp.31–2.)
Copies: NPL:M(989.6/W).   3130

[1892] MONUMENT to Captain Cook: [illustration].
(*In* Pratt, Mara L.—People and places. Boston, Educational Pub. Co., [1892]. Vol.1, p.186.)
Copies: NPL:M(990/P).   3131

1894 NOTTAGE, Charles George
Captain Cook's monument [at Kealakekua Bay, Hawaii].
Illus.
(*In his* In search of a climate. London, Sampson Low, Marston & Co., 1894. pp.72–3.)
Copies: NPL:M(910.4/58A1).   3132

[1894?] STEVENS, John Leavitt
Captain Cook's monument [at Kealakekua Bay].

(*In his* Picturesque Hawaii . . . by J.L. Stevens . . . and W.B. Oleson. [N.p.] Edgewood
Pub. Co., [1894?]. Plate opp. p.10.)

It is incorrectly stated here that this was the monument erected by Lord Byron, Captain
of H.M.S. *Blonde*, in 1825.

Copies: NPL:M(Q989.6/S).   3133

1897 FROMHOLZ, Hugo
Cook-Denkmal.

(*In his* An den Küsten des Pacific. Berlin, Auguste Hoffmann, pr., 1897. p.72.)

Copies: NPL:M(Q910.4/34A1).   3134

1908 OBELISK and memorial plate at Hawaii.
(*Australian Town and Country Journal*, Ap.15, 1908.)

Copies: NPL:R(F079/A938).   3135

1908 [OBELISK erected at Kaawalo.]
Illus.

(*In* Baldwin, Charles W.—Geography of the Hawaiian Islands. New York, American
Book Company, 1908. pp.84–5.)

Obelisk of concrete erected 1874, under the direction of Major Wodehouse, the British
Commissioner, with the co-operation of Captain Cator of H.M.S. *Scout*.

Copies: NPL:M(989.6/B).   3136

1911 CAPTAIN COOK'S MONUMENT, Hawaii: [illustration].
(*In* Hallock, Leavitt H.—Hawaii under King Kalakaua. Portland, Smith and Sale, 1911.
pp.35–6.)

Copies: NPL:M(989.6/H).   3137

1912–13 COOK'S MONUMENT at Kealakekua; [with bibl.].
Illus.

(*Hawaiian Almanac*, 1912, pp.60–71; 1913, p.114.)

Copies: NPL:M(999.6/H).   3138

1921 HAMILTON, Claude N., *Lord*
Two early monuments to Captain Cook [erected in Hawaii].

Illus.

(*Geographical Journal*, London, Jan.1921, pp.34–6.)

The cross erected by the Captain of H.M.S. *Blonde*, and the stump of a coco-nut palm
(on the spot where Cook fell) on which three inscription plates were placed in 1837,
1839 and 1843 respectively. The third inscription plate is in the Bernice Pauahi Bishop
Museum, Honolulu.

Copies: NPL:R(DS909.6A/2).   3139

1924 CARRUTHERS, *Sir* Joseph Hector McNeil
Visit to Hawaiian monument.

Illus.
(Newspaper cuttings, vol.165, pp.72–3.)
Extract from the *Daily Telegraph*, Sydney, Oct.4, 1924.

Copies: NPL:M(Q991/N). 3140

1924 MONUMENT on the spot where Cook fell, Hawaii: [photograph, Sir Joseph Carruthers, 1924].

Copies: Captain Cook's Landing Place Trust. 3141

1924 PHOTOGRAPHS taken during the visit to Hawaii of Sir Joseph Carruthers, 1924.

6 framed photographs.
CONTENTS:
1. View of Capt. Cook's monument, Kewakekua Bay, Hawaii.
2. View of monument from the launch shewing landing canoe with Sir J.H.Carruthers, Dr. D. Carruthers and Mr. D. Hunter.
3. The inscription on the monument.
4. View of monument from the shore.
5. Cliff at "Kaawaloa" with grave caves. Monuments visible in background, also huts of the only two families there, one Hawaiian, the other Japanese.
6. Carruthers party before the monument.

Copies: Captain Cook's Landing Place Trust. 3142

1924 U.S.A.—Army
Kealakekua Bay and monument: aerial views. 1924. Two lantern slides.

One view from almost over the village of Napopo, facing the bay. The other is a close-up.
Presented by D.G. Stead, 1941.
Explanatory letter from donor filed at NPL:M PXn 185.

Copies: NPL:M(Slides 24/1–2). 3143

1927 COPPER TABLET erected by Lord Byron, Commander H.M.S. *Blonde*, 1825, on the hill above Kaawaloa.

Illus.
(Hawaiian Historical Society—*Annual report*, no.36, 1927, pp.36–7.)
Copies: NPL:M(999.6/H). 3144

1927 ONLY BRITISH SOIL in U.S.A. Territory, at Captain Cook's monument, Kealakekua Bay.

(Newspaper cuttings: Captain Cook, vol.1, p.125.)
Illustration, extracted from the *Sydney Morning Herald*, July 2, 1927.
Copies: NPL:M(Q980:Co1/N1A1). 3145

1929 TAYLOR, Albert Pierce
Australia's gift to Hawaii.

(*In his* Sesquicentennial celebration of Captain Cook's discovery of Hawaii, 1778–1928. Honolulu, 1929. p. 102.)

Copies: NPL:M(Q980:Co4/T1A1); Captain Cook's Landing Place Trust; VSL. 3146

1929 UNVEILING the bronze tablet [at Kealakekua Bay: speeches by J.C. Lane and Sir J.H. Carruthers].
Illus.

(*In* Taylor, Albert Pierce—Sesquicentennial celebration of Captain Cook's discovery of Hawaii, 1778–1928. Honolulu, 1929. pp. 42–6.)

Copies: NPL:M(Q980:Co4/T1A1); Captain Cook's Landing Place Trust; VSL. 3147

1932 DU PUY, William Atherton
[Cook's visit to Hawaii, 1778; with illus. of the monument to Captain Cook.]

(*In his* Hawaii and its race problem. Washington, 1932. pp.7–9.)

Copies: NPL:R(999.6A/11). 3148

n.d. COOK'S MONUMENT. Hawaii.
Photograph. 8″ x 6″.

Presented by A. Kitson to the Australian Museum and transferred in 1955.

Copies: NPL:M(Small Picture File: Cook—Monuments—Pac.Is.—Hawaii 2). 3149

n.d. MEMORIAL COPPER PLATE on tree stump near the spot in Kealakekua Bay where Cook died. Affixed October 17th 1837 by members of H.M.S. *Imogene.*
Photograph. 7″ x 3½″.

Copies: NPL:M(P3/41H). 3150

Another photograph.

8″ x 6″.

Presented by the Hon. J.S.McGowan to the Australian Museum 1911 and transferred in 1955.

Copies: NPL:M(Small Picture File: Cook—Monuments—Pac.Is.—Hawaii 1). 3151

n.d. MONUMENT at Kealakekua Bay and surrounding enclosure.
Photograph. 6½″ x 9″.

Copies: NPL:M(Small Picture File: Cook—Monuments—Pac.Is.—Hawaii 4). 3152

n.d. MONUMENT at Kealakekua Bay to the memory of Capt. Cook; and inscription.
Two photographs. Monument 9½″ x 5¾″, inscription 9″ x 9⅝″.

Presented by Lt. Col. C.B.Palmer, 1924.

Copies: NPL:M(V*Cook 38B–C). 3153

n.d. MONUMENT erected to the memory of Capt. James Cook at Kealakekua Bay, Hawaii, November 1874.

Photograph. $6\frac{1}{2}''$ x $4\frac{1}{2}''$.

Copies: NPL:M(P3/41G).   3154

n.d. MONUMENT of wood erected to the memory of Capt. Cook by Capt. Lord Byron, H.M.S. *Blonde*, 1825 at Kaawaloa.

Photograph.

Presented by Lt. Col. C.B. Palmer, 1924.

Copies: NPL:M(V*Cook 38A).   3155

n.d. MONUMENT set up in Kelakakua (*sic*) Bay, Hawaii.

Photograph. $5\frac{5}{16}''$ x $6\frac{11}{16}''$.

Pasted on back of photograph is a printed label with title as above, followed by "Lent by Rev. Canon Bennett, M.A., R.D." The label was probably cut from the catalogue of the Colonial and Indian Exhibition, 1886.

Transferred from the Australian Museum, 1955.

Copies: NPL:M(Small Picture File: Cook—Monuments—Pac.Is.—Hawaii 3).   3156

Norfolk Island

1953 Captain Cook Memorial, Norfolk Island: unveiling ceremony held on Friday, 24th July, 1953.

6 photographs. Each $4\frac{1}{2}''$ x $6\frac{1}{4}''$.

With list of contents and key to persons.

Copies: NPL:M(Small Picture File: Cook—Monuments—Pac.Is.—Norfolk Is. 1).   3157

1953 CONIGRAVE, Charles Price

Captain James Cook: memorial unveiled at Norfolk Island.

(Royal Australian Historical Society—*Journal and Proceedings*, vol.39, pp.215–16, 1953.)

Copies: NPL:M(991/R,Ref.Books); NPL:D(9/69); NPL:R(S991.06/1A,Ref.Books).   3158

1953 McCOMISH, Ida, *Mrs*

Address by Mrs. Ida McComish, F.R.G.S., on the occasion of her unveiling of the Captain Cook memorial, Norfolk Island, July 10, 1953.

Typescript.

(Miscellaneous primary and secondary source material re the life and voyages of Captain James Cook.)

Copies: NPL:M(MS.A1713^{-3} Item 4B,no.xvii).   3159

1953 WHERE COOK LANDED on Norfolk Island: [account of unveiling of memorial Jy 24, 1953].

Illus.

(*Pacific Islands Monthly*, vol.24, p.14, Sept. 1953.)

Copies: NPL:M(Q988.05/P).   3160

Tahiti

1883 COOK'S TREE—a tamarind tree planted by Capt.[n] Cook on Point Venus, Tahiti, to mark the spot from which he viewed the Transit of Venus in 1768.

1883. Photograph. c.10½″ x 8¼″.
Presented to the Australian Museum by C.T. Burfitt and transferred to the Mitchell Library in 1955.
Printed label of the Australian Museum corrects date on inset label as above to 1769.
Copies: NPL:M(SV*Cook 4).   3161

1906 WRAGGE, Clement Lindley
Captain Cook's memorial, Point Venus.
Illus.
(*In his* The Romance of the South Seas. London, Chatto & Windus, 1906. pp.206, 218, 220.)
The memorial is a pillar and ball erected by Captain Cook in 1769 to commemorate the observation of the transit of Venus, and was restored and surrounded by an iron railing by the local authorities. An inscribed plate was erected in 1901 by the Royal Society and the Royal Geographic Society.
Copies: NPL:M(988.7/W).   3162

1924 MEMORIAL to Captain Cook. Papeete, Tahiti.
Photograph. 1924.
Copies: Captain Cook's Landing Place Trust.   3163

1931 PHARE de la pointe de Vénus, et monument de Cook: [illustration].
(Exposition Coloniale Internationale de Paris—Commissariat des Etablissements Français de l'Océanie—Dans les eaux du Pacifique. Melun, 1931. opp. p.46.)
Copies: NPL:M(989.5/E).   3164

1937 C., G.R.
Cook Memorial at Point Venus, Tahiti.
Map.
(*Geographical Journal*, London. Jan.1937, pp.54–8.)
Copies: NPL:R(DS909.6A/2).   3165

n.d. COOK'S TAMARIND-TREE, Tahiti.
Wood engraving. c.6¾″ x 9¼″.
Cut possibly from the *Illustrated London News*. With paragraph entitled *Captain Cook's Tamarind-tree*.
Copies: NPL:M(Small Picture File: Cook—Monuments—Pac.Is.—Tahiti 1).   3166

MONUMENTS IN FRANCE

Méréville

[183–?] LA BORDE, Alexandre Louis Joseph de, *Comte*
Tombeau de Cook au parc de Méréville, près d'Estampes. [Designed by Pajou.]

(*In his* Description du parc de Méréville. N.p., [183–?]. pp.21–3.)
Copies: NPL:M(711/4A1).   3167

1913 MONUMENT to the memory of Captain Cook at Méréville: [illustration].

(*In* Triggs, H.Inigo—Garden craft in Europe. London, B.T.Batsford, [1913]. p.304.)
Copies: NPL:R(Q711/11).   3168

n.d. MONUMENT to the memory of Captain Cook by Pajou in the Parc de Méréville, France.

Photograph. 6″ x 4″.
For illustration of bust of Captain Cook, once part of this monument *see* the subheading *Personal—Portraits—Pajou.*

Copies: NPL:M(Small Picture File: Cook—Monuments—France 1).   3169

MONUMENTS IN GREAT BRITAIN

Buckinghamshire

1893 SIR HUGH PALLISER; [with copy of inscription on the monument to Cook erected by Palliser at Vache Park, Buckinghamshire].

(*Historical Records of New South Wales*. Sydney, Govt. Pr., 1893. Vol.1, pt.1, pp.479–84.)
This monument, consisting of a square block surmounted by a globe, was erected by Palliser when the news of Cook's death was received in England.

Copies: NPL:M(991/N,Ref.Books); NPL:D(89/267); NPL:R(994.4/44).   3170

1924 HAVIOL

Monument to Capt. Cook at Vache Park, Buckinghamshire. [Tracing by H. Fildes, 1924, of engraving by Haviol.]

Tracing.
A note by Fildes suggests the engraving is a cut from the *Illustrated London News.*

Copies: NPL:M(Small Picture File: Cook—Monuments—Eng.—Vache 1).   3171

1929 THE MONUMENT . . . erected by Sir Hugh Palliser at the Vache, Chalfont St. Giles: [photographic views, with explanatory note].

(*Geographical Journal*, vol.73, Feb. 1929, pp.100–101, 108–9.)
Copies: NPL:M(980:Col/G1A1); NPL:R(DS909.6A/2).   3172

1963 CAPTAIN COOK STAYS PUT: [note re memorial erected by Admiral Palliser at Chalfont St. Giles, Buckinghamshire].

(*Australia and New Zealand Weekly*, London, vol.93, p.16, Aug. 24, 1963.)
Copies: NPL:M(Q980.105/10).   3173

1963 MacSWEEN, Angus

An Unknown Captain Cook memorial [in Buckinghamshire, Chalfont St. Giles. With letter in reply by A. Bax.]

(Royal Australian Historical Society—*Journal and Proceedings*. Vol.49, pp.145–53, 224, July, November 1963.)

Copies: NPL:M(991/R, Ref.Books); NPL:D(9/69); NPL:R(S991.06/1).   3174

Cambridge

1836 COOK'S MONUMENT [in Great St. Andrew's Church, Cambridge; illustration and description].

(*Nautical Magazine*, Feb. 1836, p.73.)

Copies: NPL:R(S656.505/3).   3175

1910 MORGAN, *Rev.* James

Monument to Captain Cook.

Illus.

(*In his* A Short history of the Church of St. Andrew the Great, Cambridge. Cambridge, *Daily News*, 1910. pp.18–20, 46–7.)

Copies: NPL:M(283.42/M).   3176

1935 MURAL TABLET to the memory of Captain James Cook in the Church of St. Andrew the Great, Cambridge . . . [photograph, with] editorial notes.

(*United Empire*, June 1935, pp.308–9, 349.)

Copies: NPL:R(DS320.6/1).   3177

n.d. DESCRIPTION of a funeral tablet to Captain Cook in the chancel of St. Andrew's the Great Church, Cambridge.

(Bonwick Transcripts: Cook, case 3, no.224.)

Copies: NPL:M(B.T. ser.2, case 3).   3178

n.d. MONUMENT of the late Captain J. Cook, R.N. In Great St. Andrew's Church, Cambridge.

Engraving. 5½" x 3" inside frame. With text of inscription, entitled Sketch of monument erected at Cambridge, printed on separate sheet.

Transferred from the Australian Museum, Oct. 1955.

Copies: NPL:M(Small Picture File: Cook—Monuments—Eng.—Cambridge 1).   3179

Cleveland

1811 PROPOSAL for erecting a monument on Eaton-Nab, in Cleveland in memory of the celebrated navigator, Capt. James Cooke. Stockton-Upon-Tees, Christopher & Jennett, 1811.

Broadside.

With handwritten annotations.

Copies: ANL.   3180

1846 ORD, John Walker
[Account of an obelisk erected in 1827, on Easby Heights, by Robert Campion.]

(*In his* History and antiquities. London, Simpkin & Marshall, 1846. p.410.)

Copies: NPL:M(Q942.74/0); VSL.   3181

1909 CAPTAIN COOK'S MONUMENT, [Easby Hill, Yorkshire].
Illus.

(Newspaper cuttings, vol.13, p.26.)

Extract from the *Sunday Times*, Ap. 25, 1909.

Copies: NPL:M(Q991/N).   3182

1909 HEAVISIDES, Michael
[Career of Captain James Cook, and his monument on Easby Heights.]

Illus. port.

(*In his* Rambles in Cleveland, and peeps into the Dales. 3rd ed. Stockton-on-Tees, Heavisides & Son, 1909. pp.69–77.)

Copies: NPL:M(914.274/H); NPL:R(S942.74A/7).   3183

[1920?] EASBY HILL monument to Captain Cook.
c.1920. Photograph. 5⅞″ x 4⅛″.

Shows the Johnson family of Thirroul, N.S.W., at the monument.

Correspondence re gift of this photograph to the Library by George Johnson is filed at A1713⁻⁶. (*Restricted issue.*)

Copies: NPL:M(Small Picture File: Cook—Monuments—Eng.—Easby 3).   3184

1924 BLACKET, O.
Monument, [Easby Hill, Yorkshire: a letter].

(Newspaper cuttings, vol.165, p.111.)

Extract from the *Sydney Morning Herald*, Feb. 16, 1924.

Copies: NPL:M(Q991/N).   3185

[1968?] TINDALE, J.
Easby Hill monument to Captain Cook.

c.1968. Photograph. 9¾″ x 7½″.

Copies: NPL:M(Small Picture File: Cook—Monuments—Eng.—Easby 1).   3186

n.d. CAPTAIN COOK'S MONUMENT on Easby Hill.
Photograph. 6⅛″ x 4¼″.

Copies: NPL:M(Small Picture File: Cook—Monuments—Eng.—Easby 2).   3187

Greenwich

1937 COOK SECTION, National Maritime Museum.

(*Mariner's Mirror*, Jy. 1937, p.262.)

Copies: NPL:R(DS656.506/7). 3188

London

For views of the Woolner statue of Captain Cook in Waterloo Place, London, before its transhipment to Australia *see* the heading *Personal—Monuments in Australia—New South Wales—Hyde Park, Sydney*.

1910 CAPTAIN COOK MEMORIAL.

3 leaflets.

CONTENTS:

General Committee [list of members, Oct.1910].

Kitson, A.—James Cook, R.N., F.R.S.

First list of donations.

Copies: NPL:D. 3189

1914 CAPTAIN COOK MEMORIAL, (The Mall, London): the unveiling ceremony.

Illus. pp. 4.

Extract from *British Empire Review*, Aug. 1914.

Copies: NPL:M(Newspaper cuttings). 3190

1914 MEMORIAL STATUE of Captain Cook.

Illus.

(*Nature*, Jy. 9, 1914, pp.481–2.)

Copies: NPL:R(Q505/1). 3191

1914 STATUE of Capt James Cook by Brock, standing in the Mall near Admiralty Offices, London.

1914. Photograph. 27⅞″ x 16⅛″.

The photograph is signed 'Thos Brock, sculptor 1914'.

Copies: NPL:M(P4/Cook 1). 3192

1915 C., J.S.

Captain Cook's statue, [The Mall, London].

(Newspaper cuttings, vol.38, p.150.)

Extract from the *Sydney Morning Herald*, Sept.11, 1915.

Copies: NPL:M(Q990/N). 3193

1924 PHOTOGRAPH of Cook's monument at the Admiralty, London. 1924.

Copies: Captain Cook's Landing Place Trust. 3194

Marton

1805 RUDD, Bartholemew
Letter to Sir Joseph Banks, Apl.22, 1805, re James Fleck, nephew of Captain Cook, who is soliciting the position of Revenue Officer; also stating that the writer intends to erect a pillar on the site of Cook's birthplace.
MS. copy.
(Copies of documents relating to Captain James Cook, R.N., from the originals in the Grey Collection, Auckland Public Library, ff.287–91.)
Copies: NPL:M(C697). 3195

1928 GRANITE VASE in Stewart Park, Marton, on the site of Captain Cook's birthplace: [view with copy of inscription].
(*In* Captain Cook Bi-centenary Celebrations, Cleveland, 1928—Souvenir, p.[8ᵈ], 1928.)
Copies: NPL:M(Q923.9/C771.2/4A1). 3196

n.d. COOK MEMORIAL URN at Marton, England.
Photograph. 11½″ x 8¾″.
Copies: NPL:M(P3/16D). 3197

Whitby

[191–?] CAPTAIN COOK'S MONUMENT, Whitby: [photograph].
(*In* Souvenir of Whitby. Whitby, Horne & Son, [191–?].)
Without pagination.
Copies: NPL:M(Q914.274/S). 3198

[1912] CAPTAIN COOK MONUMENT [Whitby], with biographical sketch of the great circumnavigator and a short account of the unveiling ceremony, [Oct. 2, 1912]. Whitby, Horne and Son, Ye Abbey Press, [1912].
Illus. ports. pp.33.
Copies: NPL:M(923.9/C771.2/16A1); NPL:D(91/998); ANL:F; VSL. 3199

1912 PHOTOGRAPH of statue at Whitby. John Tweed, sculpt., Oct. 2, 1912.
Presented to the Trust by the Hon. Gervase Beckett.
Copies: Captain Cook's Landing Place Trust. 3200

1913 [STATUE AT WHITBY, and illustration of his death, with short account of Cook.]
(*In* Mee, Arthur—Popular science. London, 1913. Vol.7, opp. pp.4525–8.)
Harmsworth Popular Science.
Copies: NPL:R(S503/8). 3201

1932 COOK'S STATUE at Whitby: [illustration].

(*New Nation Magazine,* June 1932, p.34.)
Copies: NPL:M(Q630.5/N).   3202

1942 STATUE at Whitby: [view].

(*In* Mee, Arthur—Yorkshire, North Riding. London, Hodder and Stoughton, 1942.
Opp. p.257.)
Copies: NPL:R(DS942.74A/16).   3203

[1968?] CHADWICK STUDIO, *photographers*
Captain Cook's statue, Whitby.

c.1968. Postcard photograph. $5\frac{1}{16}$" x $3\frac{3}{16}$".
(*Chadwick Views.*)
Copies: NPL:M(P1/Cook—Statues—Whitby 1).   3204

n.d. CAPTAIN COOK'S STATUE, Whitby.

Photograph. $12\frac{1}{2}$" x $9\frac{3}{8}$".
Copies: NPL:M(P3/16C).   3205

Yorkshire

1966 WOOD, G. Bernard
Captain Cook's Yorkshire has many mementos of famous explorer.

Illus.
(*Pacific Islands Monthly,* vol.37, Mar. 1966, pp.85–7.)
Copies: NPL:M(Q988.05/P); ANL.   3206

PERSONAL

PORTRAITS

Originals cannot be reproduced without the permission of the owner.
Marble busts are included here. For statues *see back* the sub-head *Monuments.*
Arranged according to the artists in their alphabetical order: Beechey, Dance,
Fleischmann, Gainsborough, Hazelhurst, Hodges, Hudson, Le Vieux, Monnier, Van der
Myn, Pajou, Pingo, Reynolds, Romney, Webber, followed by unknown artists. Portraits
which closely resemble the work of any one of these are placed with his work, e.g. Dance
Group, Hodges Group, Webber Group. Sections are further divided into *Originals and
photocopies of originals*, and *Reproductions.* Where necessary the latter are arranged in two
groups: alphabetically by engraver, if any, or alphabetically by title of the reproduction.

BEECHEY

CAPTAIN JAMES COOK, Navigator, painted by Sir W. Beechey, R.A.
c.1763. [An alleged portrait of Cook.]

Photograph taken 1924 of oil painting on zinc. $9\frac{1}{4}''$ x $7\frac{1}{4}''$.
Beechey was born 1753. The sitter's general appearance and clothes would place him at a very much later date than Cook.
File of official Public Library of New South Wales correspondence, 1923–1928, concerning this portrait, is filed at NPL:M A1713⁻⁶ (*Restricted issue*).

Copies: NPL:M(PXn181).   3207

DANCE GROUP

Originals, Including Photocopies of Originals

Includes (a) copies of the Dance portrait, and (b) portraits closely resembling that by Dance.
The portrait by Nathaniel Dance, R.A., afterwards Sir N. Dance-Holland, one of the leading portrait painters of his day, was painted in May, 1776, between Cook's second and third voyages. Cook in a letter written in the third person to Mr. Banks, 24 May [1776] (*Letters to Capt. James Cook, R.N.*, p.9, M.L. Safe 1/68) expresses his willingness to sit to Mr. Dance for portrait on 25 May, 1776. The original oil painting is in the National Maritime Museum, Greenwich, and was formerly in the possession of Sir Joseph Banks. Mr. D. Samwell, one of the surgeons on the third voyage, says it is an excellent likeness and the only one he has seen that bears any resemblance to him. The portrait is reproduced in colour as frontispiece of the Hakluyt Society edition of the Journals of Capt. Cook, vol.1, 1955. A replica of this portrait, considered by London experts to be contemporary, is in the Library of the Parliament of the Commonwealth of Australia. Another replica is in Australia House, London, *see* no.3230.

DANCE, Nathaniel

Captain James Cook.

Oil painting. $37\frac{1}{2}''$ x 52″. Untitled; unsigned.
Contemporary copy by an unknown artist of the original portrait by Nathaniel Dance. *Reproduced in* Barrett,C.—Across the years. Melbourne, Seward, 1948. p.46.

Copies: ANL.   3208

DANCE, Nathaniel

Captain James Cook (printed [from the portrait by N. Dance in the National Maritime Museum, Greenwich,] to commemorate the Bicentenary of the birth of Captain James Cook, R.N. F.R.S. [etc]).

Pub. by I.Sutcliffe. Photogravure. $6\frac{1}{4}''$ x $4\frac{15}{16}''$.

Copies: NPL:D(DL Pd668).   3209

DANCE, Nathaniel

Captain James Cook, F.R.S. who was killed . . . Feb.ʸ 14ᵗʰ 1779.

Plumbago in black japanned and gilt frame. $11\frac{1}{4}''$ x $9\frac{3}{8}''$ inside mount.
Unsigned. Said to be by N. Dance. Title lettered below frame line. Old label inscribed 'B.T.Stow' pasted on backing board below S.Holden's framer's label. It was formerly the property of the Stow family of Devon, who also owned the log of the *Resolution*, kept by James King.
Presented by Sir Wm. Dixson, 1929.
Reproduced in Maggs Bros.—Engravings, etchings, and drawings: catalogue no.458. 1925. NPL:M(910.4/39).

Copies: NPL:D(DG31).   3210

DANCE, Nathaniel

Cook: [a portrait attributed to Dance].

Photograph of photograph of oil on canvas. Size of original 37½″ x 52½″.
Title lettered below portrait (it is not clear whether part of portrait or of frame).
Shows Cook seated with arm resting on map. Map, hat and book are on a bale. Another bale behind Cook. Seascape with ships on left.
The portrait was in the possession of Colnaghi & Abach c.1907, and the photograph from which this one was taken was supplied by them to the Library of Sir Robert Witt. Colnaghi in 1937 had no record of the whereabouts of the painting.
Copies: NPL:M(P1/Cook—Dance 58).   3211

Another print.
Copies: NPL:D(DL Pd667).   3212

DANCE, Nathaniel

Portrait of Captain Cook, by Nathaniel Dance, 1776. [Printed in colour, from the portrait in the National Maritime Museum, Greenwich.]

(Cook, J.—The Journals of Captain James Cook on his voyages of discovery . . . Ed. by J.C. Beaglehole. Cambridge, U.P., 1955. Vol.1, frontisp.)
Copies: NPL:M(980:Col/46A1).   3213

COPLEY, John Singleton, *the elder*

Captain James Cook [attributed to J.S. Copley the elder].

Miniature on ivory. Oval c.2¾″ x 2¼″.
Lettered on metal back of frame is "Captain/ James Cook/ 17 born 27/ murdered/ on S.ᵗ Valentines day/ at/ Owyhee./ 1779."
Purchased in 1887 from Rear-Admiral Henry M.C. Alexander who stated it had been obtained from a dealer in Cork to whom it was sold by Mrs. Cook, when she was in poor circumstances, and believed by Alexander to have been painted by John Singleton Copley the elder. The likeness is suggestive of the Dance portrait.
N.S.W. Colonial Secretary's correspondence re the purchase 1887 is filed at NPL:M A3935.
Reproduced in the *Australian Museum Magazine* vol.11, no.8, Dec. 1954, frontisp.
Copies: NPL:M(Min.116).   3214

Photograph.
Copies: NPL:M(P1/Cook—Dance 60).   3215

Photograph.
(Neg. held by Bird 1965 no.120–1).
Copies: NPL:M(P1/Cook—Dance 59).   3216

Coloured transparency.
Copies: NPL:M(FM2/183).   3217

COTES, Francis

James Cook, aged 40.

1768. Oil painting on wood. c.8¼″ x c.5¾″.
Signed "F Cotes fecit 1768". Title as above lettered above head.
Three-quarter length. Facial resemblance to Dance's Cook.
It has been suggested that the title was more recent than the portrait. Photograph shows that lower part of face and lapels have been retouched and that title has been altered. Letter from A.C. Murch, Melbourne, 13 Feb. 1899, unaddressed, with enclosed letter from a Joseph Banks, Wiltshire St, 24 Dec.1862, to his cousin George—stating "Uncle Joe sends with best love the picture of Capt. James Cook. Mr. Wilson offered to clean it free of cost or we should have sent before" is filed at NPL:M Doc 1302. Murch's letter makes it clear this refers to a portrait by Cotes, presumably this one.

Copies: NPL:M(ML122).   3218

Photograph.
(Govt. Pr. neg. no.49648.)
Copies: NPL:M(P1/Cook—Dance 62).   3219

Photograph.
Not showing title area. (Govt. Pr. neg. no.48021.)
Copies: NPL:M(P1/Cook—Dance 61).   3220

FOX, Emanuel Phillips

[Captain Cook. Portrait in oils, after Nathaniel Dance, R.A., copied by E.P. Fox.]
Felton Bequest, 1906.
Copies: VSL.   3221

NOBLE, John

Capt Cook: [a portrait] by Noble. 1775.

1775. Watercolour. Oval. 5⅛″ x 3⅞″ inside frame.
Signed 'J.N. 1775'. Title from paper label on frame. On back are two paper stickers reading 'Capt Cook *Miss Stuart*?' and '69'.
Half-length, three-quarter face, in naval uniform, with telescope under the left arm.
Dance group.
Copies: NPL:D(DL Pa11).   3222

S., R.

Captain Cook.

1813. Watercolour c.6⅞″ x 5½″ oval. Framed. Signed "R S 1813".
Mount covers part of picture including signature. Dance group.
Copies: NPL:M(121).   3223

[CAPTAIN COOK.]

Miniature in watercolours. Diam. 2¾″. In round wooden frame.
Artist unknown. Dance group.
Copies: NPL:M(Min.85).   3224

[CAPTAIN COOK.]

Miniature in watercolours, on silver snuff-box, surrounded by brilliants. $1\frac{3}{4}''$ x $1\frac{1}{4}''$ oval.
Artist unknown. Dance group.
Copies: NPL:M(Min.81).   3225

[CAPTAIN COOK.]

Miniature in watercolours, on wooden snuff-box. $2\frac{3}{16}''$ x $1\frac{1}{4}''$.
Artist unknown. Dance group.
Copies: NPL:M(Min.82).   3226

[CAPTAIN COOK.]

Miniature on ivory. $2\frac{3}{4}''$ x $2\frac{1}{4}''$. Glazed, in oval black wooden frame.
Artist unknown. Dance group.
Copies: NPL:D(DL Pa26).   3227

[CAPTAIN COOK.]

Portrait in oils.
Artist unidentified. Probably a copy of the Dance portrait, or of Fox's copy.
Copies: VSL.   3228

CAPTAIN COOK Royal Navy.

Oil painting on wood panel $9\frac{3}{4}''$ x $7\frac{1}{8}''$, extended over wooden frame $10\frac{5}{8}''$ x $8\frac{1}{8}''$.
Title written on back.
Artist unknown. Appears to be a poor copy of the engraving by Sherwin of the Dance
portrait.
Copies: NPL:D(DL38).   3229

[CAPTAIN JAMES COOK]: copy by Will Longstaff of Dance's portrait (Greenwich) purchased by Sir Joynton Smith and by him presented to Australia House, London, Jan.1928.

3230

CAPTN COOK.

Miniature on ivory. Oval. $3''$ x $2\frac{1}{4}''$ inside gilt frame.
Unsigned. Title from label on back.
Artist unknown. Dance group.
Copies: NPL:D(DL Pa24).   3231

CAPTn JAMES COOK, F.R.S.

Miniature on ivory. Oval. $2\frac{5}{8}''$ x $2\frac{1}{8}''$ inside gilt frame. Surrounded by gold tooling in
leaf design on blue crushed morocco, and the lettering 'LIFE.OF.CAPTAIN.COOK
KIPPIS'. Companion piece to Bligh volume at Q79/12.
Title from frontispiece portrait engraved by Heath, on which it is based.
Dance group.
(*Inset in* front cover of Andrew Kippis' The Life of Captain James Cook. 1788.)
Copies: NPL:D(Q78/8).   3232

CAPTⁿ JAMES COOK, F.R.S.

Miniature on ivory. Oval. 2⅜″ x 1⅞″ inside gilt frame. Surrounded by rope pattern tooled on green crushed morocco.
Title from frontispiece portrait engraved by Heath, on which it is based. Dance group.
(*Inset in* front cover of Andrew Kippis' The Life of Captain James Cook. 1788.)
Copies: NPL:D(Q78/9).   3233

MINIATURE of Captain Cook, F.R.S.

Process reproduction b./wh., from original in the possession of the Royal Society, London. The miniature was bought by the Royal Society in 1893, from G. Ellis, St. John's Wood, who acquired it in 1886 at Lord Brabourne's sale. It appears to be a copy from the original picture (by Heath) sometime in the possession of Sir Joseph Banks. *See* engraving in Kippis' Life of Cook.
(Muir, John Reid—The Life and achievements of Captain James Cook. London, Blackie, 1939. Opp. p.227.)
Copies: NPL:M(980:Col/M6A1); NPL:D(93/626); NPL:R(DS990A/195).   3234

[PORTRAIT of James Cook.]

Oil painting. 24½″ x 17¼″ inside frame.
Unsigned. Artist unknown.
Presented by Sir William Dixson, between June 1936 and Sep. 1938.
Copies: NPL:D(DG212).   3235

[PORTRAIT of James Cook.]

Photograph of painting. 9½″ x 7″.
Half-length, face turned somewhat to his right, left hand resting on a globe, and the right hand holding a pair of dividers.
Artist unknown. Dance group.
The portrait is in the Whitby Museum, Yorkshire.
Copies: NPL:M(P3/16A).   3236

Reproductions Arranged by Engraver

ADLARD

1822 Captain J. Cook. H. Adlard Sc.

London, publish'd June 1. 1882, by Wetton and Jarvis. Engraving, on India paper.
Meas. within frame lines 2⅞″ x 2⅛″. Meas. of plate mark 6″ x 4″.
Half-length.
(Portraits of illustrious persons, pub. by Wetton & Jarvis, London, 1820–1830. [Plate] 8.)
Copies: NPL:R(Q920/34).   3237

Another print.
Copies: NPL:M(P3/4E).   3238

The Same.
3 9/16″ x 2 1/16″ inside frame lines.
Copies: NPL:M(P1/Cook—Dance 22).   3239

ADLARD

1829 Jam^s. Cook. N. Dance delt. H. Adlard sculp.

London. Published by Thomas Kelly . . . June 1, 1829. Engraving. Meas. of port.
$3\frac{1}{8}''$ x $2\frac{3}{8}''$.
Half-length. Title is a facsimile of Cook's signature.
Copies: NPL:M(P3/4D). 3240

Another print.
(Australian Scrap-book p.3 [n.d.])
Copies: NPL:M(C336). 3241

Another print.
Copies: NPL:M(P3/4F). 3242

Another print.
Hand-coloured.
Copies: NPL:D(DL Pd567). 3243

ARMSTRONG

Captain James Cook. Painted by Sir Nath.[1] Dance. Engraved by Cosmo Armstrong.

London. Pub. for the proprietor, June, 1821. Engraving. Meas. within frame lines
$2\frac{9}{16}''$ x $1\frac{13}{16}''$.
Head and shoulders only.
Copies: NPL:D(DL Pd579). 3244

Another 3 prints.
Copies: NPL:M(P3/4B, P1/Cook—Dance 1–2). 3245

The Same.
Proof. 7" x 5".
(Scott-Waring, J.—Epistle from Oberea . . . to Banks. 4th ed. London, J. Almon, 1774.
Frontisp.)
Copies: NPL:M(C933d); NPL:D(Q77/50). 3246

Another print.
Hand-coloured.
Copies: NPL:D(DL Pd580). 3247

ARNDT

1789 Capit.^n James Cook: [engraving]. W. Arndt, sculpt.

(Kippis, *Rev.* Andrew—Leben des Capitain James Cook. Hamburg, B.G. Hoffmann,
1789. Band 1, frontisp.)
Copies: NPL:M(980:Co1/K2E1); NPL:D(78/7). 3248

BERGER

Captain, James Cook. N. Dance pinx: D. Berger sc:

Engraving. Meas. within frame lines 2⅜″ x 2⅜″. Cut to plate mark.
Head only, in medallion.
Copies: NPL:M(P3/4G).   3249

Another print.

Hand-coloured, cut to plate mark.
Copies: NPL:D(DL Pd588).   3250

Another print.

Cut.
(Australian Scrap-book, p.3, [n.d.])
Copies: NPL:M(C336).   3251

The Same.

Titled, but without painter's or engraver's name.
Meas. within frame lines 2⅜″ x 2⅜″. Meas. of plate mark 5¼″ x 3½″.
Copies: NPL:D(DL Pd596).   3252

The Same [entitled] 'Captain James Cook.'. 'de Mayr sc.' printed in reverse below frame lines.

Meas. within frame lines 2⅜″ x 2⅜″. Meas. of plate mark 5 15/16″ x 3 13/16″.
Copies: NPL:M(P3/10E).   3253

Another print.

Copies: NPL:M(P1/Cook—Dance 3).   3254

Another print.

Hand-coloured.
Copies: NPL:D(DL Pd584).   3255

The Same [entitled] 'Captain James Cook.' No other letters. Plate mark cut.

Copies: NPL:D(DL Pd643).   3256

Photograph of the portrait area only.

Copies: NPL:M(P1/Cook—Dance 4).   3257

BOLT

1788 James Cook, gemahlt von N. Dance, gestochen von I.F. Bolt, 1788.

Engraving. Meas. of port. 8⅞″ x 7¼″.
Three-quarter length.
Copies: NPL:M(P3/4H).   3258

Another print.

(Cook, J.—Geschichte der See-Reisen . . . Dritte Entdeckungs-Reise. Berlin, Haude und Spener, 1788. Band 2, frontisp.)

Copies: NPL:M(Q980:Co1/1A2). 3259

BOND

1821 Captain Cook: [drawn and engraved by W. Bond, from the large picture by George (*sic*) Dance.]

(Cook, J.—The Three voyages of Captain James Cook round the world. London, Longman, Hurst, Rees, Orme and Browne, 1821. Vol.1, frontisp.)

Copies: NPL:M(980:Co1/24A1); NPL:R(S990A/54). 3260

BONNEVILLE

Jacques Cook. F. Bonneville del sculps.

Paris. Engraving. Oval. Meas. within frame lines $4\frac{1}{4}''$ x $3\frac{3}{8}''$. Meas. of plate mark 8" x $4\frac{7}{8}''$. Three-quarter length. Closely resembles the engraving by Copia, listed below.

Copies: NPL:M(P3/5A). 3261

Another print.

Copies: NPL:M(P1/Cook—Dance 5). 3262

Another print.

(*Inserted in* Kippis, *Rev.* Andrew—Life of Captain James Cook. London, G. Nicol and G.G.J. and J. Robinson, 1788. Grangerized copy. Opp. p.391.)

Copies: NPL:D(Q78/8). 3263

CHAPMAN

1800 Captain Cook. J. Chapman sculpsit.

London. Published . . . Sep.20, 1800 by J. Wilkes. Engraving. Oval. Meas. within frame lines $4\frac{3}{8}''$ x $3\frac{3}{8}''$. Meas. of plate mark $6\frac{1}{2}''$ x $4\frac{1}{2}''$. Head only. Beneath portrait is a representation of the death of Cook.

Copies: NPL:M(P3/5B). 3264

Another print.

Copies: NPL:D(DL Pd554). 3265

Another 2 prints.

Copies: NPL:M(P1/Cook—Dance 6–7). 3266

Another 3 prints.

Cut.

Copies: NPL:M(P1/Cook—Dance 8–10). 3267

Another print.
Cut.
(Australian Scrap-book, p.4 [n.d.])
Copies: NPL:M(C336).   3268

Another print.
Hand-coloured.
Copies: NPL:D(DL Pd572).   3269

Another 2 prints.
Hand-coloured, cut.
Copies: NPL:D(DL Pd641–642).   3270

The Same.
Printed in colour.
Copies: NPL:M(P1/Cook—Dance 11).   3271

Another print.
Cut.
Copies: NPL:D(DL Pd558).   3272

Another print.
Cut.
Copies: NPL:M(P1/Cook—Dance 12).   3273

Reproduced, with notes, in English, Thomas H.—Introduction to the collecting and history
of Whitby prints. Whitby, Horne & Son, Ltd., 1931. Vol.1, C5.
Copies: NPL:M(Q942.7/E); NPL:D(Q93/118).   3274

CLERK
Capt. James Cook: [engraving]. T. Clerk sculp.[t]
(Cook, J.—Third Voyage—Printed Accounts—Voyage to the Pacific Ocean. Leith, pr.
by W. Reid & Co. for A. Constable & Co., Edinburgh, 1813. Frontisp.)
Copies: NPL:M(980:Co1/17A1).   3275

COLLYER
Capt: James Cook, F.R.S. From a Painting by M.[r] Dance in the
Possession of Joseph Banks Esq.[r] I. Collyer sc.
Published March 31st 1780 by J. Bew. Engraving. Meas. of engraved surface $5\frac{9}{16}''$ x $3\frac{1}{2}''$.
At head, "Engraved for Hervey's *Naval History* vol.V page 464." Plaque oval port.,
with telescope, anchor, fruit, scallop shell and other detail below. This seems to be the
same portrait as the engraving by Liebe listed below. Portrait is reversed.
Copies: NPL:M(P1/Cook—Dance 13).   3276

Another print.
Hand-coloured, cut to take short title and to omit Engraved for Hervey's *Naval History*.
Copies: NPL:D(DL Pd595).   3277

COOPER
Captain Cook: [wood engraving]. J. Cooper, sc.
(Mossman, S.—Heroes of discovery. Edinburgh, Edmonston and Douglas, 1868. p.67.)
Copies: NPL:M(A923.9/M).   3278

COOPER
Captain Cook: [wood engraving]. J. Cooper, sc.
(Mossman, S.—Heroes of discovery. New ed. Edinburgh, O. Anderson & Ferrier, n.d. p.215.)
Copies: NPL:M(A923.9/M).   3279

COPIA
Jacques Cook. Copia del et sc.
Engraving. Meas. of port. $4\frac{1}{8}''$ x $3\frac{1}{4}''$.
Three-quarter length, seated. Closely resembles the engraving by Bonneville listed above.
Copies: NPL:M(P3/11G).   3280

Another print.
Copies: NPL:M(P1/Cook—Dance 14).   3281

DALZIEL
J. Cook: [wood engraving]. G. Dalziel sc.
(Chambers's miscellany of useful and entertaining tracts. Edinburgh, W. and R. Chambers, 1845. [Vol.1,] no.40.)
Copies: NPL:M(923.9/C771.2/7A1).   3282

DANVIN
Cook: [engraving]. Danvin del.
(Domeny de Rienzi, Gregoire Louis—Océanie. Paris, Firmin Didot, 1836. Vol.1, p.8.)
Copies: NPL:M(980/115A1).   3283

FORMENTIN
Le Capitaine Cook. Imp. Litho. de Melle Formentin, Rue St André des Arts, N.º 59.
Lithograph. Meas. of lithographed surface c.$6\frac{1}{4}''$ x $6\frac{1}{4}''$.
Bust only.
Copies: NPL:D(DL Pd560).   3284

Photograph.
Copies: NPL:M(P1/Cook—Dance 15).   3285

The Same. Imp. Litho de Melle Formentin, chez Decronan ainé. Lith. Bernard.

Lithograph. Meas. within frame lines $9\frac{1}{2}''$ x $7''$. Meas. of lithographed surface c.$6\frac{1}{4}''$ x $6\frac{1}{4}''$. With decorated border.

Copies: NPL:M(P3/5E).   3286

FROSCH

James Cook. C Frosch sc.

Im Verlag van E. Fleischer in Leipzig.
Engraving. Meas. within frame lines $3\frac{1}{2}''$ x $3''$.
Head and shoulders only.

Copies: NPL:M(P3/5F).   3287

HALL

Jam.^s Cook. Engraved by H.B. Hall's Sons. New York.

Engraving. Meas. of port. $10''$ x $6\frac{15}{16}''$.
Head and shoulders only. Title is facsimile of Cook's signature

Copies: NPL:M(P2/25).   3288

Another 3 prints.

Cut.

Copies: NPL:M(P2/26–27,37).   3289

Photograph.

Copies: NPL:M(P1/Cook—Dance 17).   3290

Photograph.

(N.S.W.—Govt. Printer—Photographs illustrating the earliest times of New South Wales, p.79, [n.d.])

Copies: NPL:M(F981N).   3291

The Same.

Photo-litho reproduction.
(Public Library of N.S.W. Reproduction T1.)   3292

The Same.

Photograph of watercolour of the same portrait?

Copies: NPL:M(P3/11H).   3293

A reproduction of this portrait also appears on the commemorative poster, published c.1928 by Peacock Bros., Melbourne, (P3/40) and listed in this Bibliography as no.978. *See* First Voyage—Illustrations.

HALPIN

Captain James Cook: [engraving]. N. Dance pinxt., P. Halpin, sculpt.

(Cook, J.—Third Voyage—Voyage to the Pacific Ocean. Dublin, H. Chamberlaine, etc., 1784. Vol.1, frontisp.)

Copies: NPL:M(980:Co4/2A1). 3294

HALPIN

Captain James Cook: [engraving]. N. Dance pinxt., P. Halpin, sculpt.

(Kippis, *Rev.* Andrew—Life of Captain James Cook. Dublin, H. Chamberlaine, W. Colles *and others*, 1788. Frontisp.)

Copies: NPL:M(980:Co1/K2A1). 3295

HEATH

Captn James Cook, F.R.S.: [engraving]. Heath, sculp. From an original picture in the possession of Sir Joseph Banks, Bart.

[London,] published as the Act directs, June 12 1788, by G. Robinson and Co.
(Kippis, *Rev.* Andrew—Life of Captain James Cook. London, G. Nicol, G.G.J. & J. Robinson, 1788. Frontisp.)

Copies: NPL:M(Q980:Co1/K1A1); NPL:D(Q77/13); NPL:R(09:Q990A/49). 3296

HOLL

1829 Captain James Cook . . . Painted by N. Dance. Engraved by W. Holl.

London. Published by Thomas Kelly . . . 1829. Engraving. Meas. of port. $3\frac{3}{16}$″ x $2\frac{7}{8}$″. Meas. of plate mark $9\frac{13}{16}$″ x $6\frac{1}{2}$″.
Half-length. With facsimile of Cook's signature.

Copies: NPL:M(P3/6A). 3297

Another print.

Copies: NPL:M(P1/Cook—Dance 19). 3298

The Same, with decorated border around port.

Meas. of port. $3\frac{3}{16}$″ x $2\frac{7}{8}$″.
Plate mark cut.

Copies: NPL:M(P3/6B). 3299

Another print.

Imprint cut.

Copies: NPL:M(P1/Cook—Dance 20). 3300

Another 2 prints (one coloured) on India paper.

Meas. of plate mark $9\frac{13}{16}$″ x $6\frac{1}{2}$″.

Copies: NPL:D(DL Pd564; 592 coloured). 3301

HOLL

1831 Captain James Cook. Painted by N. Dance. Engraved by W. Holl
. . . Presented to Greenwich Hospital by the executors of Sir Joseph
Banks.

London. Published March 1, 1831, by Harding & Lepard. Engraving, hand-coloured.
Meas. within frame lines 4$\frac{15}{16}$″ x 3$\frac{7}{8}$″. Meas. of plate mark 9$\frac{3}{4}$″ x 7″.
Three-quarter length, seated.
Copies: NPL:D(DL Pd566).   3302

The Same.
Proof before letters, uncoloured.
Copies: NPL:M(P3/6C).   3303

The Same.
Proof, uncoloured.
Copies: NPL:M(P3/6D).   3304

Photograph.
Copies: NPL:M(P1/Cook—Dance 18).   3305

Reproduced, with notes, in English, Thomas H.—Introduction to the collecting and history
of Whitby prints. Whitby, Horne & Son, Ltd., 1931. Vol.1, H1.
Copies: NPL:M(Q942.7/E); NPL:D(Q93/118).   3306

The Same [entitled] Captain James Cook. Painted by N. Dance . . .
Engraved by W. Holl.
Fisher, Son & Co. London & Paris 1837. Engraving. Meas. of port. 4$\frac{7}{8}$″ x 4$\frac{7}{8}$″.
Three-quarter length, seated. With facsimile of Cook's signature.
(Australasian Scrap-book, p.69, [n.d.])
Copies: NPL:M(F980/A).   3307

Another print.
Copies: NPL:D(DL Pd650).   3308

Another print.
Imprint cut.
Copies: NPL:M(P1/Cook—Dance 54).   3309

The Same. Fisher, Son & Co. London & Paris [n.d.]
Copies: NPL:M(P3/7A).   3310

Another print.
Copies: NPL:M(P1/Cook—Dance 56).   3311

Another print.
Hand-coloured.
Copies: NPL:D(DL Pd571). 3312

HOLL
Captain Cook. Holl sculp.
Engraving. Oval. Meas. within frame lines $7\frac{7}{8}''$ x $1\frac{1}{2}''$.
Head only. With letterpress and section signature 5. Similar to the engraving by Thomson and with the same letterpress.
Copies: NPL:M(P3/7B). 3313

Another print.
(Australasian Scrap-book p.70, [n.d.])
Copies: NPL:M(F980/A). 3314

Another print.
Coloured.
Copies: NPL:D(DL Pd598). 3315

Reproduced, with notes, in English, Thomas H.—Introduction to the collecting and history of Whitby prints. Whitby, Horne & Son, 1931. Vol.1, H2.
Copies: NPL:M(Q942.7/E); NPL:D(Q93/118). 3316

HOLLOWAY
Capt: James Cook, F.R.S. From the original painting in the possession of Sir Joseph Banks, President of the Royal Society. Dance pinx.[t] T. Holloway del.[t] et sculp.[t]
Published . . . 1 Jan[y] 1790 by C. Forster. Engraving. Meas. of port. $5''$ x $4\frac{1}{16}''$.
At head "*Literary Magazine & British Review*".
Three-quarter length, seated.
Copies: NPL:M(P3/7C). 3317

Another print.
(Australasian Scrap-book, p.66, [n.d.])
Copies: NPL:M(F980/A). 3318

Another print.
Hand-coloured.
Copies: NPL:D(DL Pd576). 3319

Another print.
Imprint and heading cut.
Copies: NPL:M(P1/Cook—Dance 21). 3320

Another print.

Cut to edges of portrait but including title.
(Australian Scrap-book, p.6, [n.d.])
Copies: NPL:M(C336). 3321

Another 2 prints.

Hand-coloured, heading cut.
Copies: NPL:D(DL Pd574–575). 3322

HORSBURGH

[1836] Captain James Cook. N. Dance. [Engraved by] J. Horsburgh.

Published by Oliver & Boyd, Edinburgh. Engraving. $3\frac{1}{4}''$ x $2\frac{1}{2}''$.
(Historical account of the circumnavigation of the globe. Edinburgh, Oliver & Boyd, [1836]. Frontisp.)
Copies: NPL:M(910.4/H). 3323

The Same.

Photograph of engraving. $5\frac{5}{8}''$ x $4\frac{5}{16}''$ within frame lines.
Title etc. printed on mount.
With various cuttings relating to Cook pasted on mount, with some MS. notes.
Copies: NPL:M(P1/Cook—Dance 55). 3324

KLAUBER

James Cook. N. Dance pinxit . . . Sculpt. apud I.S. Klauber.

Augusta. 1793. Engraving. Meas. within frame lines 5″ x $4\frac{5}{8}''$.
Three-quarter length, seated.
Copies: NPL:M(P3/7D). 3325

Another print.

(*Inserted in* Cook, J.—Collected Voyages—Printed Accounts [1795 ed.]—Reizen rondom de waereld . . . Amsterdam & Leyden, Honkoop, Allart en van Cleef, 1795–1809. Atlas. Frontisp.)
Copies: NPL:M(F980:Col/1A1). 3326

LEGRAND

J. Cook, célèbre navigateur anglais. [Lithograph drawn by] Legrand; lith. de Ducarme.

Publiée par Blaisot. Meas. of lithographed surface c.4″ x 5″.
Dance group, but portrait reversed. Head and shoulders only.
Copies: NPL:D(DL Pd559). 3327

The Same, with added, "No 173".

Copies: NPL:M(P3/7E). 3328

LIEBE

Capit: James Cook. Dance pinx. Liebe sc.

Engraving. Meas. of engraved surface $4\frac{1}{2}''$ x $3\frac{1}{2}''$. Meas. of plate mark $6\frac{3}{8}''$ x $4''$.
This seems to be the same portrait as the engraving by Collyer, listed above, but portrait is reversed.

Copies: NPL:M(P3/7F). 3329

LIZARS

Captain Jam^s Cook F.R.S. Engraved by W. and D. Lizars, Edinburgh.

Engraving. Oval. Meas. within frame lines $3\frac{7}{8}''$ x $3\frac{3}{16}''$.
Title includes a facsimile of Cook's signature.
(*In* Young, *Rev.* George—History of Whitby. Whitby, Clark & Medd, 1817. Vol.2, p.861.)

Copies: NPL:M(942.7/Y); NPL:D(81/79). 3330

Another print.

Copies: NPL:M(P3/4A). 3331

MACKENZIE

Capt Cooke (*sic*). Mackenzie sc.

Pub. Oct.10, 1806, by James Cundee, London.
Oval. Meas. of port. $2\frac{7}{16}''$ x $1\frac{3}{4}''$.
Oval plaque bust facing slightly to the right, on anchor; globe, sextant, chart, telescope, surrounding; ship in background, palms and trees above.
(*In* Wilson, Robert—Voyages of discoveries. London, J. Cundee, 1806. Vol.2, frontisp.)

Copies: NPL:M(980/W). 3332

Another print.

Hand-coloured.

Copies: NPL:D(DL Pd585). 3333

MAURIN

Cook. A. Maurin. Lith. de Grégoire et Deneux.

Paris. Rosselin éditeur. Lithograph. Meas. of lithographed surface $3\frac{5}{8}''$ x $3\frac{5}{8}''$.
Head and shoulders only.

Copies: NPL:D(DL Pd561); VSL. 3334

MAYERS

James Cook. Stahlstich v. Carl Mayers. Kunstanstalt in Nürnberg. Verlag v. Julius Niedner in Wiesbaden.

Engraving.
(*In* Horn, W.O. von, *pseud.*—James Cook. Stockholm, Ebeling & Comp., 1867. Frontisp.)

Copies: NPL:M(980:Col/H3A1). 3335

The Same.
(*In* Horn, W.O. von, *pseud.*—James Cook. Wiesbaden, J. Niedner, [186–?]. Frontisp.)
Copies: NPL:M(980:Co1/H3B1).   3336

PAULI
J. Coock (*sic*). F. Pauli sc.
Engraving. Oval, $2\frac{3}{8}''$ x $1\frac{3}{4}''$. Meas. of plate mark $3\frac{7}{8}''$ x $2\frac{1}{8}''$.
Head and shoulders only.
Copies: NPL:M(P3/7G).   3337

PIGEOT
J. Cook. Pigeot sc.
Engraving. Meas. of port. $3\frac{1}{2}''$ x $3\frac{3}{4}''$.
Head and shoulders only.
Copies: NPL:M(P3/7H).   3338

Another print.
Hand-coloured.
Copies: NPL:D(DL Pd562).   3339

The Same.
Proof before title, on India paper.
Copies: NPL:D(DL Pd634).   3340

PORTMAN, L.
James Cook: [engraving]. L. Portman sc.
(Cook, J.—Collected Voyages. J. Cook's drie Reizen. Amsterdam, W. Holtrop en
Leeuwestyn, 1802. Deel 1, frontisp.)
Copies: NPL:M(980:Co1/15A1).   3341

PYE
Captain Cook: [engraving]. Pye sct.
(Cook, J.—Collected Voyages. Cook's voyages. Manchester, Sowler & Russell, 1799.
Frontisp.)
Copies: NPL:M(980:Co1/14A1).   3342

RÉMON
James Cook. Rémon sc.
Zwickau, b.d. Gebr. Schumann. Engraving. Meas. of port. $3\frac{7}{8}''$ x $2\frac{7}{8}''$, corners cut, meas.
of plate mark $7''$ x $4\frac{1}{2}''$.
Dance group, but portrait reversed. Head and shoulders only.
Copies: NPL:M(P1/Cook—Dance 24).   3343

RIDLEY

Captain James Cook. Engraved by Ridley from an original painting.

Pub. by G. Gold . . . Jan.31. 1803. Engraving, hand-coloured. Oval. Meas. within frame
lines 4″ x 3⅛″.
Head and shoulders only.
Copies: NPL:D(DL Pd570).   3344

Another 2 prints.

Hand-coloured, imprint cut.
Copies: NPL:D(DL Pd638–9).   3345

RIVERS

[Captain Cook.] N. Dance del. Rivers sculp.

London, J. Bumpus. Engraving. Meas. within frame lines 3$\frac{15}{16}$″ x 2$\frac{3}{16}$″. Meas. of plate
mark 6½″ x 5″.
Half-length. Underneath portrait is a representation of the death of Cook.
Copies: NPL:M(P3/8A).   3346

Another print.

Cut.
Copies: NPL:M(P1/Cook—Dance 25).   3347

ROBERTS

1825 Captain James Cook, F.R.S. From an original painting. R. Roberts
Sc$^\text{t}$

London, published by Jaques & Wright . . . 1825. Soft-ground etching. Meas. of
engraved surface c.4½″ x c.4¼″.
At head "Frontispiece".
Half-length, with hat & chart on table.
(Cook, J.—Collected Voyages. Voyages. London, Jaques & Wright, 1825. Vol.1, frontisp.)
Copies: NPL:M(980:Co1/27A1).   3348

Another print.

Heading cut.
Copies: NPL:M(P1/Cook—Dance 26).   3349

Another print.

Heading and imprint cut.
Copies: NPL:M(P1/Cook—Dance 28).   3350

The Same.

Published by W. Wright.
At head "Frontispiece".
(Cook, J.—Collected Voyages. Voyages. London, W. Wright, [1836?]. Vol.1, frontisp.)
Copies: NPL:M(980:Co1/27B1).   3351

Another print.

Copies: NPL:M(P1/Cook—Dance27).   3352

ROBERTS

n.d. Captn James Cook, R.N. Engraved from the original painting by
P. Roberts.

London. O. Hodgson. Engraving. Meas. within frame lines $5\frac{1}{2}'' \times 4\frac{1}{2}''$.
Three-quarter length, seated.

Copies: NPL:M(P3/8B).   3353

ROFFE

Captain Cook. Roffe Sc.

[London], Limbird. 1824. Engraving. Meas. of engraved surface $2\frac{3}{4}'' \times 2\frac{5}{8}''$.
(Cook, J.—Collected Voyages. Three voyages of Captain Cook round the world. New ed.
London, J. Limbird, 1824. Frontisp.)

Copies: NPL:M(980:Col/26A1).   3354

Another print.

(Australian Scrap-book, p.3 [n.d.].)

Copies: NPL:M(C336).   3355

ROGERS

Captain Cook: steel engraving. From the original picture by Dance in
the gallery of Greenwich Hospital. (Engraved by J. Rogers.)

London and New York, John Tallis & Co. [n.d.]. Engraving. $11'' \times 7\frac{1}{4}''$.

Copies: ANL:F.   3356

ROGERS

Captain Cook. Ob.1779. From the original picture by Dance in the
Gallery of Greenwich Hospital. Engraved by F. Rogers.

London & New York, John Tallis & Co. [n.d.]. Engraving. Hand-coloured. Meas. of
port. $4\frac{7}{8}'' \times 3\frac{7}{8}''$.
Half-length. Surrounding the portrait are vignettes. Above, a cocked hat, telescope,
sword, chart and flag; at sides and beneath, pictures of natives and island scenes.

Copies: NPL:D(DL Pd586).   3357

The Same.

Without engraver's name, entitled Captain James Cook.
London & New York, John Tallis & Co. [n.d.]. Engraving, uncoloured. Meas. of port.
$4'' \times 3''$.
Half-length.

Copies: NPL:D(DL Pd632).   3358

Another print.

Copies: NPL:D(DL Pd633).   3359

Another print.
Copies: NPL:M(P2/30).   3360

The Same.
Without engraver's name.
London Printing and Publishing Co., [n.d.] Engraving. Meas. of port. 4⅞" x 3⅞".
Half-length.
(Martin, Robert Montgomery—Australia. London, J. Tallis & Co., 1853.)
Copies: NPL:M(Q990.1/M): NPL:D(Q85/76); NPL:R(Q990.1/3).   3361

Another print.
Hand-coloured.
Copies: NPL:D(DL Pd565).   3362

SCRIVEN

Captain Cook. Engraved by E. Scriven. From an original Picture by
Dance in the Gallery of Greenwich Hospital.
Engraving. Meas. within frame lines 4$\frac{15}{16}$" x 3$\frac{15}{16}$".
Half-length. No imprint.
(Cook, J.—Collected voyages. Three voyages of Captain James Cook. London, W. Smith,
1842. Vol.1, frontisp.)
Copies: NPL:M(Q980:Co1/4A1).   3363

The Same.
Published by C. Knight.
Engraving. Meas. of port. 4⅞" x 3$\frac{15}{16}$".
Copies: NPL:M(P3/8C).   3364

Another print.
Imprint cut.
Copies: NPL:M(P1/Cook—Dance 29).   3365

The Same.
Published by Wm S. Orr & Co, London (under the superintendance of the Society for
the Diffusion of Useful Knowledge).
Engraving. Meas. of portrait 4$\frac{15}{16}$" x 3$\frac{15}{16}$".
Copies: NPL:D(DL Pd581).   3366

The Same.
Published by C. Knight . . . (under the superintendance of the Society for the Diffusion
of Useful Knowledge). London.
Engraving. Meas. inside ruled frame lines 5" x 4$\frac{1}{16}$".
Copies: NPL:M(P3/8D).   3367

Another 8 prints.
Copies: NPL:M(P1/Cook—Dance 30–36,57).   3368

Another print.
(Papers in the autograph of Capt. James Cook, 1728–1779. Frontisp.)
Copies: NPL:M(Safe 1/80).   3369

Another print.
Hand-coloured. Imprint cut.
Copies: NPL:D(DL Pd589).   3370

Another print.
Imprint cut.
Copies: NPL:M(P1/Cook—Dance 40).   3371

Reproduced, with notes, in English, Thomas H.—Introduction to the collecting and history
of Whitby prints. Whitby, Horne & Son, 1931. Vol.2, S1.
Copies: NPL:M(Q942.7/E); NPL:D(Q93/119).   3372

The Same.
Pub. by W. Mackenzie. Edinburgh.
Engraving. Meas. of port. $5\frac{1}{8}''$ x 4″.
Copies: NPL:M(P3/8E).   3373

Another 3 prints.
Copies: NPL:M(P1/Cook—Dance 37–39).   3374

Another print.
Copies: ANL:F.   3375

Another print.
Copies: NPL:D(DL Pd569).   3376

Reproduced in Carruthers, *Sir* Joseph—Captain James Cook, R.N. One hundred and
fifty years after. London, J. Murray, 1930. Frontisp.
Meas. of portrait $5\frac{3}{16}''$ x $3\frac{1}{2}''$.
Copies: NPL:M(980:Co1/2A1); NPL:D(93/37); NPL:R(S920/C771/2).   3377

SHERWIN
[Captain James Cook.] N. Dance [pinxit], J.K. Sherwin [sculpsit].
Proof of engraving. Meas. within frame lines $10\frac{1}{2}''$ x $8\frac{13}{16}''$.
Three-quarter length, seated.
(*In* [Three voyages round the world]. Plate 3.)
Copies: NPL:M(PXD59⁻¹).   3378

The Same.

Proof, with title. Meas. within frame lines $10\frac{1}{2}''$ x $8\frac{13}{16}''$.
(Webber, J.—Illustrations of Cook's voyages: original drawings f.1.)
Copies: NPL:D(DL PXX2).

3379

The Same [entitled] Captain James Cook. N. Dance pinx$\underline{^t}$ J.K. Sherwin sculp.

Published, April 20.th 1779, by J.K. Sherwin.
Engraving. Meas. within frame lines $10\frac{1}{2}''$ x $8\frac{13}{16}''$. Meas. of plate mark $11\frac{11}{16}''$ x $10\frac{3}{16}''$.
Three-quarter length seated.
Copies: NPL:M(P3/9A).

3380

Another print.

Hand-coloured.
Copies: NPL:D(DL Pe224).

3381

Another print.

With facs. signature of Cook pasted on mount.
Copies: NPL:M(P2/22).

3382

The Same. Engr$\underline{^d}$ by J.K. Sherwin Engraver to His Majesty & His Royal highn^{ss} Prince of Wales.

Publish'd [1779 Sh]erwin . . . & W. Hinton. Engraving.
Meas. of ruled frame lines $11''$ x $9\frac{1}{4}''$. Mounted so that plate mark does not show.
Three-quarter length, seated.
Part of the imprint is torn. 1779 added in pencil.
Copies: NPL:M(P3/10A).

3383

The Same. Publish'd Aug$\underline{^t}$ 1st 1784.

Engraving. Meas. inside ruled frame lines $10\frac{1}{2}''$ x $8\frac{3}{4}''$.
Three-quarter length, seated.
Copies: NPL:M(P2/21).

3384

Another print.

Copies: NPL:M(P2/31).

3385

The Same. N. Dance pinx$\underline{^t}$ J.K. Sherwin Sculp. Pub. . . . 1779 by J.K. Sherwin. Republished by John Sands of Sydney on the occasion of unveiling of the statue in Hyde Park. 1879.

Litho. Meas. within frame lines $11\frac{1}{8}''$ x $9''$.
Biog. notes below engraving.
Three-quarter length, seated.
Copies: NPL:M(P3/9B).

3386

Another print.

Copies: NPL:D(DL Pe225).

3387

The Same [entitled] James Cook, F.R.S., Captain, R.N. from the engraving
by J.K. Sherwin, after Dance Lemercier gravure. Printed in Paris.

London, [pub. by] Sampson Low, Marston and Co., [n.d.]. Engraving. Meas. of plate
mark 7⅞″ x 5⅜″.
Three-quarter length, seated.
(Clowes, W.L.—The Royal Navy. London, Sampson Low, Marston and Co., 1898.
Vol.3, opp. p.346.)
Copies: NPL:M(Bayldon Coll.); NPL:R(Q359.0942/12).   3388

The Same.

Reproduction, with extracts from the *Endeavour* Journal in facsimile and roman type.
Souvenir published by the Commonwealth Parliamentary Library to mark the acquisition
by the Library in 1923 of the *Endeavour* journal, and distributed to state schools.
Copies: NPL:M(P3/43).   3389

The Same, newspaper cutting from *Leader*, Melbourne, 29.12.23.
(Newspaper cuttings: Captain Cook, vol.1, p.43.)
Copies: NPL:M(Q980:Col/N1A1).   3390

The Same. Pub. Aug. 1st 1784 by J.K. Sherwin . . . and R. Williamson.
Reduced reproduction, 11¼″ x 9 5⁄16″, with notes.
(English, Thomas H.—Introduction to the collecting and history of Whitby prints.
Whitby, Horne & Son, 1931. Vol.2, S12.)
Copies: NPL:M(Q942.7/E); NPL:D(Q93/119).   3391

The Same. [Sherwin's engraving of Dance's portrait of Captain Cook. 1779.]
Engraving. 10¾″ x 9¼″.
Lower border removed. With a 20-line MS. note, signed by John M'Allister stating that
the engraving "is one of two copies which were presented to my mother at two different
times by the widow of Captain C."
Copies: ANL(Nan Kivell 9528); NPL:M(FM4/1552,1707, pos. and neg. microfilm).
                                                                                      3392

THOMSON
Capt. Cook. Dance pᵗ. Thomson sc.

Published by Harrison & Co., March 1794. Engraving. Oval, 1⅞″ x 1¾″, meas. of plate
mark 2⅞″ x 2⅜″.
Head and shoulders only.
With letterpress.
Similar to the engraving by Holl and with the same letterpress.
Copies: NPL:D(DL Pd640).   3933

Another print.
Hand-coloured.
Copies: NPL:D(DL Pd555).   3394

Another print.
Hand-coloured, cut to include title; without letterpress.
Copies: NPL:D(DL Pd649).   3395

Another print.
Copies: NPL:M(P3/10B).   3396

Another 2 prints.
Copies: NPL:M(P1/Cook—Dance 42–3).   3397

THOMSON
Captain Cook: [mezzotint]. Thomson, sculp.
$4\frac{7}{8}''$ x $3\frac{9}{16}''$.
Cut.
Copies: ANL:F.   3398

WALKER
Captain Cook. N. Dance, Pinx. Emery Walker, Ph. Sc.
Photogravure.
(Kitson, Arthur—Captain James Cook. London, John Murray, 1907. Frontisp.)
Copies: NPL:M(923.9/C771.2/14A1); NPL:D(90/206); NPL:R(S920/C771/4).   3399

WRIGHT
Capt. James Cook, F.R.S. Painted by N. Dance. Engraved by T. Wright.
Engraving. Meas. of port. $3\frac{1}{2}''$ x $2\frac{3}{4}''$.
Half-length.
Copies: NPL:M(P3/10C).   3400

Another print.
Copies: NPL:D(DL Pd568).   3401

Another print.
Hand-coloured.
Copies: NPL:D(DL Pd587).   3402

Another print.
Copies: NPL:D(DL Pd644).   3403

Another print.
Cut.
Copies: NPL:D(DL Pd645).   3404

Another 6 prints.
Copies: NPL:M(P1/Cook—Dance 44–9).   3405

Reproduced in Craik, George Lillie—Pursuit of knowledge. London, Charles Knight, 1831. Vol.1, opp. p.133.
Copies: NPL:R(DS374/18).   3406

Reproductions Arranged by Title of Reproduction

CAPT. COOK; [with autograph].
(Newspaper cuttings: Captain Cook, p.17.)
Extract from the *Adelaide Register*, Jan.23, 1923.
Copies: NPL:M(Q980:Co1/N1A1).   3407

CAPT. JAMES COOK, F.R.S. This celebrated circumnavigator was killed at Owhyhee, Feb.y 14th 1779. He was born at Marton, near Whitby, in Yorkshire, Oct.r 27th 1728.
London, William Darton . . . 1822. Engraving. Meas. of engraved surface c.4″ x 3″.
Meas. of plate mark 5″ x 3$\frac{1}{4}$″.
Head and shoulders only.
In background is a flag and part of the mast.
(Darton, William—A Cabinet of portraits. London, the author, 1823–30. Vol.1, no.14.)
Copies: NPL:R(DS769/20).   3408

Another print.
Copies: NPL:M(P3/5D).   3409

Another print.
Plate mark cut.
Copies: NPL:M(P1/Cook—Dance 50).   3410

CAPTAIN COOK.
Engraving. Meas. of port. 2$\frac{1}{4}$″ x 1$\frac{3}{8}$″.
Head and shoulders only.
Copies: NPL:M(P3/11D).   3411

[CAPTAIN COOK.]
Engraving. Oval. Meas. of port. 2$\frac{1}{2}$″ x 2″. Meas. of engraved surface 3$\frac{7}{8}$″ x 2$\frac{5}{8}$″.
Half-length.
Copies: NPL:M(P3/11E).   3412

[CAPTAIN COOK.]
Engraving. Proof before letters. Meas. of port. 2$\frac{1}{2}$″ x 1$\frac{3}{4}$″. Meas. of plate mark 6$\frac{5}{8}$″ x 4$\frac{1}{2}$″.
On India paper.
Half-length.
Copies: NPL:M(P3/4C).   3413

CAPTAIN COOK.

Process plate.
(*A.N.A.* Sydney, May 1928, p.132.)
Copies: NPL:M(Q059/A).   3414

[CAPTAIN COOK.]

Engraving. Oval. Meas. of port. $5\frac{1}{8}''$ x $4\frac{1}{2}''$. Meas. of engraved surface $10\frac{1}{16}''$ x $7\frac{1}{8}''$.
Head and shoulders only. Port. reversed.
(Australian Scrap-book, p.2 [n.d.].)
Copies: NPL:M(C336).   3415

CAPTAIN COOK.

(Besant, *Sir* Walter—Captain Cook. London, Macmillan, 1890. Frontisp.)
Copies: NPL:M(923.9/C771.2/11A1); NPL:D(89/128); NPL:R(S920/C771/1).   3416

CAPTAIN COOK.

Lithograph.
(Blair, David—History of Australasia. Glasgow, McGready, Thomson and Puien, 1878.
p.72.)
Copies: NPL:M(Q990/B); NPL:D(Q87/28).   3417

CAPTAIN COOK.

(Brady, Edwin James—Australia unlimited. Melbourne, Geo. Robertson & Co., [1918].
p.27.)
Copies: NPL:M(Q980.1/13A1); NPL:R(Q990.1A/26A).   3418

CAPTAIN COOK: [process plate, with autograph].

(Captain Cook monument. Whitby, Horne, 1912. Frontisp.)
Copies: NPL:M(923.9/C771.2/16A1); NPL:D(91/998).   3419

CAPTAIN COOK.

Process plate.
(Newspaper cuttings: Captain Cook, p.32.)
Extract from the *Sun*, Melbourne, June 16, 1923.
Copies: NPL:M(Q980:Col/N1A1).   3420

CAPTAIN COOK.

Process plate.
(Newspaper cuttings: Captain Cook, p.74.)
Extract from the *Evening Sun*, Melbourne, Mar.11, 1925.
Copies: NPL:M(Q980:Col/N1A1).   3421

CAPTAIN COOK.

(Newspaper cuttings: Captain Cook, p.80.)
Extract from the *Sunday News*, May 3, 1925.
Copies: NPL:M(Q980:Col/N1A1).   3422

CAPTAIN COOK.

(Cassell & Co.—Pictorial New Zealand. London, Cassell & Co., 1895. p.289.)
Copies: NPL:M(987/C).   3423

CAPTAIN COOK.

Process plate.
(Coad, Nelly Euphemia—History of the Pacific. Wellington, N.Z. Book Depot, [1926].
p.54.)
NPL:M(990/C).   3424

CAPTAIN COOK.

(Columbus and Cook. London, W. & R. Chambers, 1895. p.88.)
Copies: NPL:M(910.4/120A1).   3425

CAPTAIN COOK: [process plate], from a painting by N. Dance . . . in Greenwich Hospital.

(Fitchett, *Rev.* William Henry—New world of the south. London, G. Bell & Sons, 1913.
Vol.1, frontisp.)
Copies: NPL:M(990.1/F); NPL:R(DS990.1/3).   3426

CAPTAIN COOK.

Wood engraving.
(*Gibbs Shallard & Co.'s N.S.W. Weather Almanac.* Sydney, Gibbs Shallard & Co., 1872.
p.35.)
Copies: NPL:M(991.01/1).   3427

CAPTAIN COOK.

Process plate.
(Gillies, William—Stories in English history. Melbourne, Whitcombe & Tombs, 1910.
p.222.)
Austral History Readers.
Copies: NPL:M(942/G).   3428

[CAPTAIN COOK.]

Heliotype reproduction of engraving. Meas. of port. 4¾″ x 3¹¹⁄₁₆″.
Three-quarter length, seated. Port. reversed.
(*Historical Records of New South Wales.* Sydney, Govt.Pr., 1893. Vol.1, pt.1, frontisp.)
Copies: NPL:M(991/N,Ref.Books); NPL:D(89/267); NPL:R(994.4/44).   3429

The Same.

Proof.
Copies: NPL:M(P1/Cook—Dance 52).   3430

CAPTAIN COOK.

Process plate.
(Jose, Arthur Wilberforce—Short history of Australasia. Sydney, A. & R., 1899. p.9.)
Also published in other editions.
Copies: NPL:M(990/1A1); NPL:D(89/382). 3431

CAPTAIN COOK.

Process plate.
(Jose, Arthur Wilberforce, *and others*—New South Wales. Melbourne, Whitcombe & Tombs, 1912. p.17.)
Copies: NPL:M(981/J); NPL:R(E919.44/Jos). 3432

CAPTAIN COOK: [process plate], from a portrait in the Museum, Whitby. Artist unknown.

(Kitson, Arthur—Captain James Cook. London, John Murray, 1907. p.343.)
Copies: NPL:M(923.9/C771.2/4A1); NPL:D(90/206); NPL:R(S920/C771/4). 3433

CAPTAIN COOK. From the portrait by N. Dance R.A. in the Painted Hall, Greenwich Hospital.

Process plate.
(Kitson, Arthur—Life of Captain James Cook. London, John Murray, 1912. Frontisp.)
Copies: NPL:M(923.9/C771.2/14C1). 3434

CAPTAIN COOK.

Engraving.
(Life, voyages and discoveries of Captain James Cook. London, J.W. Parker, 1837. p.10.)
Copies: NPL:M(980:Col/34A1). 3435

CAPTAIN COOK.

Process plate.
(Marshall, Patrick—Geography of New Zealand. Christchurch, Whitcombe & Tombs, [1910]. p.25.)
Copies: NPL:M(987/M). 3436

CAPTAIN COOK.

Process plate.
(Martin, Arthur Patchett—True stories from Australasian history. London, Griffith Farran & Co., 1893. Frontisp.)
Copies: NPL:M(990/M). 3437

CAPTAIN COOK: [process plate], after the portrait by M. Dance.

(Mitton, Geraldine Edith—Captain Cook. London, A. & C. Black, Ltd., 1927. Frontisp.)
Copies: NPL:M(980:Col/M4A1). 3438

CAPTAIN COOK.

Process plate.
(N.S.W.—Immigration and Tourist Bureau—Kurnell. 2nd ed. Sydney, Govt.Pr., 1909. Frontisp.)
Copies: NPL:M(981.1/N). 3439

CAPTAIN COOK.

Engraving.
(Purves, David Laing—English circumnavigators. London, William P. Nimmo, 1874. Frontisp.)
Copies: NPL:M(910.4/P); NPL:R(D10Q47). 3440

CAPTAIN COOK.

Process plate.
(Royal Geographical Society of Australasia—Victorian Branch—Transactions and proceedings. Vol.14, 1896, p.20.)
Copies: NPL:M(980/R); NPL:D(9/226); NPL:R(DS992A/3). 3441

CAPTAIN COOK.

Process plate.
(Saunders, Alfred—History of New Zealand. Christchurch, Whitcombe & Tombs, etc., 1896. Vol.1, p.38.)
Copies: NPL:M(997/S); NPL:D(89/188). 3442

CAPTAIN COOK.

Process plate.
(Story, Alfred Thomas—Building of the Empire. London, Chapman & Hall, 1898. Vol.2, p.169.)
Copies: NPL:M(942/S); NPL:R(S909/62). 3443

CAPTAIN COOK.

Process plate.
(Sutherland, Alexander *and* Sutherland, George—History of Australia and New Zealand. London, Longmans Green & Co., 1894. Frontisp.)
Copies: NPL:M(990/S). 3444

CAPTAIN COOK.

Lithograph.
(Tregarthen, Greville—Australian Commonwealth. London, Unwin, 1893. Frontisp.)
Copies: NPL:M(990.1/100A1); NPL:D(89/630). 3445

CAPTAIN COOK, from an original sketch in the possession of Dr. M. Macdonald.

Process plate.
(Lowth, Alys—Emerald hours in New Zealand. Christchurch, Whitcombe & Tombs, [1907]. p.iv.)
Copies: NPL:M(Q987/L); NPL:R(S997A/19). 3446

CAPTAIN COOKE (*sic*).

Engraving. Meas. of engraved surface $2\frac{1}{4}''$ x $2\frac{3}{16}''$. Edges of sheet cut irregularly. Head and shoulders only.

Copies: NPL:D(DL Pd635).   3447

CAPTAIN JAMES COOK.

Engraving. Hand-coloured. Meas. inside ruled frame lines $2\frac{5}{8}''$ x $1\frac{15}{16}''$. Head and shoulders only.

Copies: NPL:D(DL Pd593).   3448

CAPTAIN, JAMES COOK.

Engraving. Meas. of plate mark $5\frac{1}{4}''$ x $3\frac{3}{4}''$. Head and shoulders only.

Copies: NPL:M(P3/10F).   3449

CAPTAIN JAMES COOK.

Engraving. Meas. inside frame lines $3\frac{3}{8}''$ x $2\frac{3}{4}''$. Half-length. Shows figure holding a compass in right hand. Decorative border of palms, flags and native implements. Corners cut.

Copies: NPL:M(P1/Cook—Dance 53).   3450

CAPTAIN JAMES COOK.

(Calvert, Albert Frederick—Exploration of Australia. London, G. Philip & Son, 1895. p.8.)

Copies: NPL:M(Q980.1/C); NPL:D(Q89/69).   3451

CAPTAIN JAMES COOK.

(Calvert, Albert Frederick—Exploration of Australia. London, G. Philip & Son, 1895. p.10.)

Copies: NPL:M(Q980.1/C); NPL:D(Q89/69).   3452

CAPTAIN JAMES COOK.

(Newspaper cuttings: Captain Cook, p.98.)
Extract from the *Sydney Mail*, Ap.28, 1926.

Copies: NPL:M(Q980:Col/N1A1).   3453

CAPTAIN JAMES COOK: [process plate]. From portrait by N. Dance; [with autograph].

(Newspaper cuttings: Captain Cook, p.119.)

Copies: NPL:M(Q980:Col/N1A1).   3454

CAPTAIN JAMES COOK: [process plate. From the original by Dance in the Greenwich Hospital].

(*Chautauquan*, Nov. 1902, p.135.)

Copies: NPL:R(DQ050/C499).   3455

CAPTAIN JAMES COOK.

Process plate.
(Heawood, Edward—History of geographical discovery. Cambridge, U.P., 1912. p.227.)
Copies: NPL:M(910.9/19A1); NPL:D(91/455); NPL:R(S909.9A/3).   3456

CAPTAIN JAMES COOK.

Process plate.
(Heawood, Edward—History of geographical discovery. N.Y., Otagon Books, 1965. p.227.)
Copies: NPL:M(910.9/19B1).   3457

CAPTAIN JAMES COOK.

Process plate.
(Long, Charles Richard—Stories of Australian exploration. Melbourne, Whitcombe & Tombs, [1910?]. p.41.)
Austral History Readers.
Copies: NPL:M(980/L).   3458

CAPTAIN JAMES COOK.

Process plate.
(McFarland, Alfred—Captain Cook. Sydney, Govt.Pr., 1899. Frontisp.)
Copies: NPL:M(923.9/C771.2/12A1); NPL:R(S920/C771/7).   3459

CAPTAIN JAMES COOK.

Process plate.
(McKillop, Catherine—Cook in a nutshell. Sydney, G.B. Philip & Son, 1928. Cover.)
Copies: NPL:M(980:Co1/M1A1).   3460

CAPTAIN JAMES COOK.

Lithograph.
(Morrison, W. Frederic—Aldine centennial history of New South Wales. Sydney, Aldine Pub. Co., 1888. Vol.1, frontisp.)
Copies: NPL:M(Q991/M); NPL:R(Q991E/12).   3461

CAPTAIN JAMES COOK.

Process plate.
(Synge, Margaret Bertha—Book of discovery. London, Jack, 1912. p.333.)
Copies: NPL:M(910.9/10A1).   3462

CAPTAIN JAMES COOK.

(Wakefield, Edward—New Zealand after fifty years. London, Cassell, [1889]. p.8.)
Copies: NPL:M(987/W); NPL:D(88/334).   3463

CAPTAIN JAMES COOK.

(Wakefield, Edward—New Zealand today. New York, Cassell, 1889.)
Copies: NPL:M(987/W).   3464

CAPTAIN JAMES COOK: [process plate], from the portrait by N. Dance in the Gallery of Greenwich Hospital.

(Wood, George Arnold—Discovery of Australia. London, Macmillan, 1922. Frontisp.)
Copies: NPL:M(980/125A1); NPL:D(92/153); NPL:R(DS990.1/19).   3465

CAPTAIN JAMES COOK: [process plate], from a portrait painted by N. Dance in 1776.

(Wood, George Arnold—Voyage of the *Endeavour*. Melbourne, Macmillan, 1926. p.44.)
Copies: NPL:M(980:Co2/W3A1); NPL:D(92/172); NPL:R(S990A/3).   3466

CAPTAIN JAMES COOK, born 1728—was killed 1779.

Engraving. Meas. within frame line $1\frac{7}{16}''$ x $1\frac{7}{16}''$.
Head and shoulders only.
Copies: NPL:M(P3/10J).   3467

CAPTAIN JAMES COOK, 1728–79.

Process plate.
(Murdoch, Walter Logie Forbes—Making of Australia. Melbourne, Whitcombe & Tombs, [1917]. p.37.)
Copies: NPL:M(990.1/M).   3468

CAPTAIN JAMES COOK: [process plate, by] J. McDonald, 1903.

(*Otago Daily Times and Witness*—Christmas Annual. Dunedin, Otago Daily Times & Witness Newspaper Co., 1904. p.13.)
Apparently McDonald's own conception in figure and pose. The face is copied from the Dance portrait.
Copies: NPL:M(F997/0).   3469

CAPTⁿ COOK.

Engraving. Meas. within frame lines $2\frac{3}{16}''$ x $1\frac{3}{16}''$.
Head and shoulders only.
Copies: NPL:M(P3/10G).   3470

Another print.
Copies: NPL:M(P3/10I).   3471

CAPTⁿ COOK.

Engraving. Meas. within frame lines $3\frac{1}{2}''$ x $2\frac{3}{4}''$.
Section signature 61 in lower right corner. Head and shoulders only.
Copies: NPL:M(P3/10H).   3472

CAPTN. JAMES COOK.

Process plate.
(Cramp, Karl Reginald—Story of the Australian people. Sydney, G.B. Philip & Son, 1927. Frontisp.)
Copies: NPL:M(990.1/C); NPL:R(DS990.1/13, Ref.Bks.).   3473

COOK.

Process plate.
(Watts, Ebenezer John Moore—Stories from Australian history. Sydney, W. Brooks, 1908. p.38.)
Copies: NPL:M(990.1/W); NPL:D(91/164).   3474

COOK.

Process plate.
(Watts, Ebenezer John Moore—Stories from Australian history. 2nd ed. Sydney, W. Brooks, 1914. p.40.)
Copies: NPL:M(990.1/W).   3475

INTREPID NAVIGATOR, Capt. James Cook.

(Newspaper cuttings: Captain Cook, p.94.)
Extract from the *Daily Telegraph*, Sydney, May 1, 1926.
Copies: NPL:M(Q980:Co1/N1A1).   3476

J. COOK.

Publié par Soetens & Fils à La Haye. Engraving. Meas. within frame lines 6″ x 4″.
Head and shoulders only.
Copies: NPL:M(P3/11F).   3477

J. COOK.

(Cook, J.—Collected Voyages [1864 Mueller's ed.]—Cook der Weltumsegler. Leipzig. Otto Spamer, 1864. p.1.)
Copies: NPL:M(980:Co1/M5A1).   3478

J. COOK.

(Roth, Theodor—Das Leben des Kapitän Cook. Stuttgart, Rieger & Sattler, [n.d.]. p.1.)
Copies: NPL:M(980:Co1/R2A1).   3479

JAMES COOK.

Wood engraving. Meas. of engraved surface $3\frac{1}{4}$″ x $2\frac{7}{8}$″.
Three-quarter length, seated.
Copies: NPL:M(P3/11A).   3480

JAMES COOK.

Wood engraving. Meas. of engraved surface 3¼" x 2⅞".
Three-quarter length, seated.
Copies: NPL:M(P3/11C).   3481

JAMES COOK: [process plate, with autograph].

(Newspaper cuttings: Captain Cook, p.47.)
Extract from the *Register*, Adelaide, Jan.26, 1924.
Copies: NPL:M(Q980:Co1/N1A1).   3482

JAMES COOK; [with autograph]. Waterloo and Sons, Ltd.

(Captain Cook's journal during his first voyage round the world . . . ed. by W.J.L.
Wharton. London, Elliot Stock, 1893. Frontisp.)
Copies: NPL:M(Q980:Co2/2A1); NPL:D(Q89/10); NPL:R(S990A/64).   3483

JAMES COOK: [process plate, with autograph].

(Cook, James—Captain Cook's voyages round the world. Ed. by M.B. Synge. London.
London, J. Nelson & Sons, 1903. Frontisp.)
Copies: NPL:M(980:Co1/40A1).   3484

JAMES COOK; [with autograph].

(Garran, Andrew—Picturesque atlas of Australasia. Sydney, Picturesque Atlas Pub. Co.,
1886. Vol.1, frontisp.)
Copies: NPL:M(F990/G); NPL:R(F990A/6).   3485

JAMES COOK. Meyer's Conv. Lex. N.372 Inst. Bibl. execud.

Engraving. Meas. within frame lines 3¾" x 2¾".
Head and shoulders only.
Copies: NPL:M(P3/10D).   3486

JAMES COOK. Né en 1728.

Engraving. Meas. of engraved surface 4¾" x 3".
Head and shoulders only.
Copies: NPL:M(P3/41C).   3487

JAMES COOK, 1772.

Process plate.
(Jack, Robert Logan—Northmost Australia. Melbourne, G. Robertson & Co., 1922.
Vol.1, p.65.)
Copies: NPL:M(984.6/13A); NPL:D(92/516); NPL:R(S994A/38).   3488

PORTRAIT of Captain Cook.

Wood engraving. Meas. of engraved surface 3¼" x 2¾".
Head and shoulders only.
Copies: NPL:M(P3/11B).   3490

[PORTRAIT of Cook, after Dance; photocopy of an American engraving, from the *Picturesque Atlas.*]

Copies: Captain Cook's Landing Place Trust.   3491

DODD

See no.3602.

FLEISCHMANN

PORTRAIT of Cook on the centre bronze entrance door to the Library of New South Wales, sculptured by Dr. Arthur Fleischmann.

c.14½″ x c.11¼″.

Copies: NPL(Front Doors).   3492

The Same, plaster cast.

c.18″ x c.15″. Damaged.

Copies: NPL:M(R351/C).   3493

GAINSBOROUGH

CAPT JAS. COOK. Painted by Gainsborough: [an alleged portrait].

Photograph of oval portrait on panel c.10″ x 8″, and of inscription on back.
Owned by the Leger Gallery, London 1934, who attributed it to Thomas Gainsborough and gave the inscription as post 1829.
Official correspondence of the P.L.N.S.W. relating to this is at NPL:M A1713⁻⁶.

Copies: NPL:M(P1/Cook—Gainsborough 1).   3494

HAZELHURST

CAPTAIN JAMES COOK, [by Thomas Hazelhurst].

Oil painting. 33½″ x 24″. Untitled; unsigned.

Copies: ANL.   3495

HODGES GROUP

Originals, Including Photocopies of Originals

HODGES, William

Captain James Cook.

Oil painting. 28⅝″ x 23″ inside frame.
Unsigned and undated. "C. Cook" in lower right-hand corner. Said to be of Cook and attributed to Hodges, because of its similarity to the engraving published as frontispiece to the 1777 edition of the account of the second voyage, but this identification seems uncertain. It has been suggested that it was by Zoffany.

A similar engraving by Thornton was published in G.W. Anderson—New, authentic and complete collection of voyages. 1784. The 1785 edition of this gives the original as in the possession of G.W. Anderson.

Purchased from the Leger Gallery, 1935. Presented by Sir William Dixson, 1935.

Extract from the report 1957 relating to the cleaning of the inscription which formerly read 'COOK', with detail photograph of it after cleaning are at NPL:M PXn183. Official correspondence of the P.L.N.S.W. re purchase, and cleaning of the inscription is at NPL:M A1713⁻⁶. (*Restricted issue.*)

Copies: NPL:D(DG213). 3496

Photographs (2) before cleaning.

One bears Charles Holmes' opinion on the attribution, in his hand.

Copies: NPL:M(P1/Cook—Hodges 9–10). 3497

Photograph taken after cleaning, 1957.

(N.S.W. Govt. Printer neg. no.48018.)

Copies: NPL:M(P1/Cook—Hodges 11). 3498

COPY of memo recording that Dr. James Mary Brydone visited the Mitchell Library May 1955 and stated that his grandfather, Surgeon-Superintendent of the convict ship *Eliza*, was a first cousin of Mungo Park, that Mungo Park and Captain James Cook were related and very alike and that the painting attributed to Hodges in the Dixson Galleries (DG 213) resembled them both.

Copies: NPL:M(PXn184). 3499

CAPTAIN JAMES COOK, from a portrait by Michaele-Felice Corné (1752–1832) in the Peabody Museum, Salem, U.S.A.

Half-tone reproduction.

Cut from Warner, Oliver—New light on Captain Cook's discoveries. (*The Listener* 28 Sep.1961.)

Copies: NPL:M(P1/Cook—Hodges 12). 3500

[CAPTAIN COOK.]

Miniature on ivory set in gold. 1⅞″ x 1½″ inside setting.

Very close to the engraving by Basire after Hodges.

Copies: NPL:M(Min.83). 3501

Reproductions Arranged by Engraver

BASIRE

Captain James Cook. F.R.S. Painted by Wᵐ Hodges. Engraved by J. Basire, 1777.

Pub . . . Febʸ 1ˢᵗ 1777, by Wᵐ Strahan . . . London. Engraving. Oval. Meas. of port. 6 5/16″ x 5 5/8″. Meas. of engraved surface 10¼″ x 7¾″.

Head and shoulders only.

(Cook, J.—Second Voyage. Voyage towards the South Pole. London, W. Strahan &
T. Cadell, 1777. Vol.1, frontisp.)
Copies: NPL:M(Q980:Co3/2A1); NPL:D(Q77/25); NPL:R(09:Q990A/15).　　　3502

Another print.
Copies: NPL:M(P2/28).　　　3503

Another print.
(Cook, J.—Second Voyage. [Plates to Cook's voyages.] London, 1777. Frontisp.)
Copies: NPL:M(F980:Co3/1A1).　　　3504

Another print.
Plate mark cut.
(*Inserted in* Kippis, A.—Life of James Cook. London, G. Nicol and G.G.J. and J. Robinson,
1778. Facing p.11.)
Copies: NPL:D(Q78/8).　　　3505

The Same.
Photograph. Meas. of port. $6\frac{9}{16}''$ x $5\frac{5}{16}''$.
Extract from Sydney past and present, vol.1, plate 30, [n.d.].
Copies: NPL:M(P1/Cook—Hodges 1).　　　3506

The Same.
Photo-lithograph. Executed at the Crown Lands Office, Melbourne.
Meas. of port. $6\frac{7}{8}''$ x $5\frac{1}{2}''$.
Copies: NPL:M(P1/Cook—Hodges 2).　　　3507

BERNARD

Le Cap^{ne} Jacques Cook, Membre de la Société Royale de Londres.
Bernard Direx.
Engraving. Oval. Meas. within frame lines $6\frac{1}{2}''$ x $5\frac{1}{2}''$. Meas. of plate mark $9\frac{1}{2}''$ x $7\frac{3}{16}''$.
At head within plate mark "P1 1". Head and shoulders.
(Cook, J.—Second Voyage. Voyage dans l'hémisphère austral. Paris, Hôtel de Thou,
1778. Tome 1, frontisp.)
Copies: NPL:M(Q980:Co3/3A1); NPL:R(Q990A/23.S.C.).　　　3508

Another print.
Copies: NPL:M(P3/13B).　　　3509

Another print.
(Cook, J.—Second Voyage. [Cartes des Voyages de Cook.] Lausanne, Hignou, 1796.
Plate 1.)
Copies: NPL:M(Q980:Co3/3B3).　　　3510

The Same.
Proof before letters.
Copies: NPL:M(P3/13A).   3511

The Same, [lettered].
Hand-coloured.
Plate mark cut except along lower edge.
Copies: NPL:D(DL Pd563).   3512

Photograph, [entitled] Le Cap^{ne} Jacques Cook.
Imprint omitted.
Copies: NPL:M(P1/Cook—Hodges 3).   3513

CATHELIN
Le Cap^{ne} Jacques Cook, membre de la Société Royale de Londres.
Gravé par L.J. Cathelin.
Engraving. Oval. Meas. of port. $3\frac{1}{2}''$ x $2\frac{1}{2}''$. Meas. of plate mark $7\frac{1}{4}''$ x $4\frac{5}{8}''$. Head and
shoulders.
Copies: NPL:M(P3/13F).   3514

The Same.
Proof before letters.
(Australian Scrap-book, p.4 [n.d.].)
Copies: NPL:M(C336).   3515

Another print.
Copies: NPL:M(P3/13E).   3516

Another print.
Hand-coloured.
Copies: NPL:D(DL Pd591).   3517

DALL'ACQUA
Capit.^{o} Giacomo Cook. Membro della Società Reale di Londra.
(Dall'Acqua inc.)
Engraving. Oval.
(Cook, J.—Collected Voyages. Navigazioni di Cook. Milano, Sonzogno e Comp.,
1816. Frontisp.)
Copies: NPL:M(980:Co1/22A1).   3518

FREEMAN
Captn James Cook. (Hodges delt., Freeman sculp^{t}.).
Published July 1 1809 by Richard Phillips, Bridge Street, Blackfriars, London. Engraving.
Oval.

(Cook, J.—Collected Voyages. The Voyages of Captain James Cook round the world. London, Richard Phillips, 1809. Vol.4, frontisp.)

Copies: NPL:M(980:Col/19A4); NPL:R(S990A/50). 3519

Another print.

(Cook, J.—Collected Voyages. The Voyages of Captain James Cook round the world. London, Sherwood, Neely & Jones, 1813. Vol.1, frontisp.)

Copies: NPL:M(980:Col/21A1). 3520

GABRIEL

Jacques Cook, né à Marton dans la province d'York le 27 8bre 1728, massacré dans la baie de Karakakooa le 14 fev^r 1779 Gabriel S^t

Engraving. Oval. Meas. of port. 5$\frac{13}{16}$″ x 3$\frac{11}{16}$″. At head "T8. Frontispiece." Port. reversed. Head and shoulders.

Copies: NPL:M(P3/13C). 3521

NOBLE

Captain James Cook, F.R.S. His first voyage performed in His Majesty's Ship the *Endeavour* . . . He was born at Marton in the North Riding of Yorkshire, and was unfortunately killed by the savages of the islands Owhyhee, aged 50 years & 3 months. Accurately drawn from an original painting & engraved by Mr. Noble.

London. Published by Alex^r Hogg at the King's Arms N° 16 Paternoster-Row.
At top of page: Frontispiece to Anderson's large folio edition of the whole of Captn Cook's voyages &c. complete.
(Cook, J.—Collected Voyages. A New, authentic and complete collection of voyages . . . [By] G.W. Anderson. London, printed for Alex. Hogg, [1784–6]. Frontisp.)

Copies: NPL:M(A346). 3522

PHILLIPS

Capt. Cook, F.R.S. Killed by the savages of Owhyhee. I. Phillips, sc.

Woodbridge, published by B. Smith & Co. 1815.
Oval. Lettering around port. Below port. is a scene.
(Cook, J.—Collected Voyages. Captain Cook's original voyages round the world. Woodbridge, B. Smith & Co., 1815. Frontisp.)

Copies: NPL:M(Q980:Col/2A1). 3523

STRUNCK

Captain James Cook. F.R.S. W.I. Strunck. Sculp. Amst.

Engraving. Oval. Meas. within frame lines 6$\frac{7}{16}$″ x 5″.
Head and shoulders.
(Cook, J.—Second Voyage. Reis naar de Zuidpool. [Trans. by] . . . P.L. Paris. 2nd ed. Utrecht, G.T. van Paddenburg en Zoon, 1793. p.72.)

Copies: NPL:M(980:Co3/7B1). 3524

Another print.
Copies: NPL:M(P3/13G). 3525

Another print.
(Australian Scrap-book, p.5, [n.d.].)
Copies: NPL:M(C336). 3526

TESTI

Giacomo Cook . . . G.M. Testi invento, Santi Soldaini disegno. A. Contardi inc. 1812. In Livorno presso la Società Menichelli e Beccari.

Engraving. Oval. Meas. within frame lines $8\frac{11}{16}''$ x $5\frac{5}{16}''$. Meas. of plate mark $19\frac{1}{4}''$ x $13''$.
Head and shoulders.
With poem and letterpress in Italian.
Copies: NPL:M(P3/15). 3527

THORNTON

A Striking likeness of the late Captain James Cook, F.R.S. His first voyage performed in the years 1768, 1769, 1770, 1771; —second voyage— 1772, 1773, 1774, 1775; —third voyage—1776, 1777, 1778, 1779, 1780. He was born at Marton in the North Riding of Yorkshire, Nov! 3ᵈ 1728 and unfortunately killed by the savages of the Island of Owhyee, Feb.ʸ 14ᵗʰ 1779. Accurately drawn from an original painting & engraved by Mr. Thornton.

London, pub. by Alexʳ Hogg . . . Sept! 11, 1784. Engraving. Oval. Meas. of port. $7''$ x $5\frac{3}{4}''$. Meas. inside ruled frame lines $15\frac{11}{16}''$ x $8\frac{1}{2}''$. At head "Frontispiece to Anderson's large folio edition of the whole of Capt.ⁿ Cook's voyages &c complete." Portrait reversed. Imprint cut.
Head and shoulders.
(Cook, J.—Collected Voyages. A New, authentic and complete collection of voyages round the world. London, A. Hogg, 1784. Frontisp.)
Copies: NPL:M(F980/5A1). 3528

Another print.
Cut to engraved surface.
Copies: NPL:M(P2/29). 3529

Another print.
Imprint cut.
(Australasian Scrap-book [1777–1866], p.1.)
Copies: NPL:M(F980/A). 3530

The Same [entitled] The Most striking likeness of the late Captain James Cook, F.R.S. His first voyage performed in the years 1768, 1769, 1770, 1771; —second voyage—1772, 1773, 1774, 1775; —third voyage—1776, 1777, 1778, 1779, 1780 . . . Accurately engraved by Mr Thornton from the original picture in the possession of G.W. Anderson Esq.

Published by Alex! Hogg . . . [London] Jan 22. 1785. Engraving. Oval. Meas. of port.
$3\frac{15}{16}''$ x $3\frac{1}{8}''$.
At head "Frontispiece to Hogg's cheap elegant octavo edition of Cook's Voyages etc
Complete."
(Cook, J.—Collected Voyages. A New and authentic collection of voyages round the
world . . . [revised] by Capt. J. Hogg. London, Alex. Hogg, [1785]. Vol.1, frontisp.)
Copies: NPL:M(980/H); NPL:D(78/25).   3531

The Same [entitled] The Most striking likeness of the late Captain James
Cook, F.R.S. He was born at Marton in the North Riding of Yorkshire
Nov 3 1728 and unfortunately killed by the savages of the Island of
Owhyhee, Feby 14. 1779. Accurately engraved by Mr Thornton from
the original picture in the possession of G.W. Anderson Esq.

Pub. by Alex! Hogg . . . [London] Jan 16, 1786. Engraving. Oval. Meas. of port. $3\frac{15}{16}''$ x
$3\frac{3}{16}''$. Meas. inside ruled frame lines $7\frac{1}{4}''$ x $4\frac{1}{2}''$. Cut to imprint.
(Cook. J.—Collected Voyages. Collection of voyages round the world. London, pr. for
A. Millar, W. Law and R. Cater, 1790. Vol.1, frontisp.)
Copies: NPL:M(980:Co1/6A1); NPL:D(79/37).   3532

Another print.
Cut to imprint.
From *Views in Australasia.*
Copies: NPL:D(DL Pd637).   3533

Another print.
Hand-coloured.
Copies: NPL:D(DL Pd578).   3534

Another print.
Uncoloured.
(Australasian Scrap-book, p.66.)
Copies: NPL:M(F980/A).   3535

Another print.
Copies: NPL:M(P1/Cook—Hodges 4).   3536

The Same.
Published by Alex! Hogg . . . [London, n.d.]
(Australian Scrap-book, p.5.)
Copies: NPL:M(C336).   3537

Photograph.
Most of title and imprint cut.
Copies: NPL:M(P1/Cook—Hodges 5).   3538

The Same.
Reproduction.
(*Australian Town and Country Journal*, Dec. 28, p.37, 1901.)
Copies: NPL:R(F079/A938).   3539

TOOKEY

Capt. James Cook, F.R.S. Hodges, pinxit. Tookey, Sculp.
Published . . . July 16, 1784 by W. Bent, [London]. Engraving. Oval. Meas. of port.
$3\frac{3}{4}''$ x $2\frac{7}{8}''$. Meas. of plate mark 7" x $3\frac{7}{8}''$.
Head and shoulders.
Copies: NPL:D(DL Pd647). 3540

Another print.
Copies: NPL:M(P1/Cook—Hodges 6); ANL. 3541

Another print.
Plate mark covered by mount.
Copies: NPL:M(P3/13H). 3542

Another 2 prints.
Hand-coloured.
Copies: NPL:D(DL Pd573,646). 3543

Another print.
Plate mark and imprint cut except for date.
Copies: NPL:D(DL Pd648). 3544

Another print.
Uncoloured.
(*Inserted in* Kippis, *Rev.* Andrew—Life of Captain James Cook. London, G. Nicol and
G.G.J. and J. Robinson, 1788. Opp. p.23.)
Copies: NPL:D(Q78/8). 3545

Reproductions Arranged by Title of Reproduction

CAP. GIACOMO COOK. Membro della Società Reale di Londra.

Engraving. Torino Appo Francesco Prato Librajo.
(Cook, J.—Collected Voyages. Storia dei viaggi . . . del Capitano G. Cook. Torino,
I. Soffietti e F. Prato, 1791. Tom.1, frontisp.)
Copies: NPL:M(980:Co1/8A1). 3546

LE CAPITAINE COOK.

Engraving. Hand-coloured. Oval. Meas. of port. within frame lines $3\frac{1}{4}''$ x $2\frac{5}{8}''$.
Beneath portrait is a representation of the death of Cook, with legend "Mort tragique du
Captaine Cook. à Owhy-hée, au mois de Février 1779". Portrait reversed. Half-length.
Copies: NPL:D(DL Pd557). 3547

CAPIT.º GIACOMO COOK. Mem.ʳº della Soc.ᵗᵃ Reale di Londra.

(Cook, J.—Collected Voyages. Navigazioni di Cook. Torino, Dalla Stamperia Alliana, 1830. Tom.1, frontisp.)

Copies: NPL:M(980:Col/31A1).   3548

CAPT. DAMPIER, 1686 [and] Capt Cook, 1770: [portraits in watermark on specially designed hand-made paper]. Manufactured by T.H. Saunders & Co.

[Pub. by J. Sands Ltd., 1878.] Oval. Meas. of sheet $23\frac{1}{2}''$ x $27\frac{1}{2}''$.
Hodges group. Head and shoulders.
3 sheets, with printed explanatory notes attached to back.

Copies: NPL:M(PXD61).   3549

CAPT: JAMES COOK.

Publish'd by G. Robinson Sep.ʳ 1; 1784. Engraving. Hand-coloured. Oval. Meas. of port. $2\frac{15}{16}''$ x $2\frac{7}{16}''$. Meas. of engraved surface within frame lines $6\frac{9}{16}''$ x $3\frac{5}{8}''$. Port. reversed. Head and shoulders.
Beneath portrait is a representation of the death of Cook.

Copies: NPL:D(DL Pd556).   3550

Reproduced, with notes in English, Thomas H.—Introduction to the collecting and history of Whitby prints. Whitby, Horne & Son, 1931. Vol.2, Ad 5.

Copies: NPL:M(Q942.7/E); NPL:D(Q93/119).   3551

CAPT. JAMES COOK, F.R.S. Was born at Marton in the North Riding of Yorkshire Nov.ʳ 3 1728.

Engraving.
(Cook, J.—Collected Voyages. A New, authentic collection of Captain Cook's voyages. Manchester, pr. by G. Swindells & Co., 1786. Frontisp.)

Copies: NPL:M(980:Col/4A1).   3552

CAPTAIN JAMES COOK.

Pub. by Fielding and Walker, 1780.
Engraving.
(Fitzgerald, W.—Ode to the memory of . . . Cook. London, G. Robinson, 1780. Frontisp.)

Copies: NPL:M(QA821/F).   3553

JACQUES COOK.

Engraving.
(Cook, J.—Collected Voyages. Voyages du Capitaine Cook. Paris, Lerouge, 1811. Tome 1, frontisp.)

Copies: NPL:M(980:Col/20A1).   3554

JACQUES COOK.

Engraving. Hand-coloured. Oval. Meas. of port. within frame lines $3\frac{7}{16}''$ x $2\frac{3}{8}''$. Meas. of plate mark $6\frac{1}{2}''$ x $4\frac{1}{4}''$.
Head and shoulders only.
Copies: NPL:D(DL Pd590).   3555

JAMES COOK.

Engraving.
(Cook, J.—Collected Voyages [1817] French Edition—Atlas du second voyage. Paris Lepetit, 1817. Plate 1.)
Bibliothèque Portative des Voyages, traduite de l'anglais par MM Henry et Breton. Tome XXIII.
Copies: NPL:M(980:Co1/23A7).   3556

JAMES COOK.

Engraving. Oval. Meas. within frame lines $2\frac{3}{16}''$ x $1\frac{13}{16}''$. Plate mark cut. Port. reversed.
Head and shoulders.
Copies: NPL:M(P3/13D).   3557

KAPITÄN JAMES COOK.

Process plate.
(Forster, Johann Georg Adam—James Cook. Leipzig, F.A. Brockhaus, 1922. Frontisp.)
Copies: (980/F).   3558

HUDSON

CAPTAIN COOK, painted by Thomas Hudson, 1701–1779, master of Sir Joshua Reynolds.

Photograph. $11\frac{3}{8}''$ x $9''$.
This portrait was discovered in 1922 in the possession of Mr. G.L. Beeforth, an art connoisseur and the founder of the Doré Gallery in Bond Street, who had picked it up in Scarborough 50 years before. The subject of the portrait is depicted in a red cutaway coat and white silk waistcoat. He wears his own hair, and carries a naval cocked hat under his arm. This information was supplied by John Sandes to the *Daily Telegraph* of 20th May, 1922. The portrait does not bear any resemblance to the Dance, Hodges or Webber portraits of Cook. It may be a portrait of another Captain Cook.
Copies: NPL:M(P3/16B).   3559

Another print.
$11\frac{1}{4}''$ x $9\frac{5}{8}''$.
Copies: NPL:M(P1/Cook—Hudson 1).   3560

Another print.
Framed, inscription cut away, and underneath the words "Reputed portrait of Captain Cook".
Copies: Captain Cook's Landing Place Trust.   3561

LE VIEUX

MARBLE BUST sculptured in 1790 by Le Vieux.

Photograph. Full-face.
(National Portrait Gallery—Photographs of portraits . . . of persons relating to Australia.
[1914. Plate 4].)
Copies: NPL:M(QA920/N). 3562

The Same.

Photograph, 1968. Profile.
Copies: NPL:M(P1/Cook—Le Vieux 1). 3563

Reproduced in Cust, *Sir* Lionel Henry—National Portrait Gallery. London, Cassell, 1901.
Vol.1, p.301.
Copies: NPL:R(DQ757/2). 3564

MONNIER

COLOURED PHOTOGRAPH from miniature ascribed to French artist Monnier.

Copies: Captain Cook's Landing Place Trust. 3565

MYN, VAN DER

ALLEGED PORTRAIT of Captain Cook by Van der Myn offered at Sotheby's, Dec. 1956.

Half-length, wearing naval uniform of Cook's period, gold embroidered blue coat, white
stock. Size 30″ x 25″ unframed.
Copies: NPL:M(MS.A1713⁻⁶ *Restricted issue*). 3566

PAJOU

POSTHUMOUS bust of Captain Cook by Augustin Pajou (1730–1809)

once part of a monument ordered from Pajou by the Comte de la Borde
in memory of his two sons, who died at sea, as well as of the English
navigator, Cook. The monument was erected in the reign of Louis XVI
in the grounds of the Chateau de Méréville. The bust was sold in 1887
and offered for sale by its owner in the 1930's.

Official correspondence of the P.L.N.S.W. is at A1713⁻⁶.
A photograph of the whole monument is Small Picture File under Cook, James—
Monuments—France 1.
Copies: NPL:M(MS.A1713⁻⁶; Small Picture File). 3567

Originals, Including Photocopies of Originals

Lewis Pingo (1743–1830) designed the medal which was struck for the Royal Society in commemoration of Captain Cook. This medal bears a profile portrait of Cook, which resembles the Dance portrait rather than those by Hodges and Webber. Pingo was chief engraver to the Royal Mint. He made exquisite drawings for the coins and medals which he struck, and his medals were of great merit and marked by much refinement.
For medallions by Pingo *see* the subheading *Personal—Medals etc.—Medallions*.

PINGO, Lewis

Capt.ⁿ James Cook F.R.S.

Miniature on ivory in ebony frame surmounted by a crest. $2\frac{1}{2}''$ x $2''$ inside frame, $5\frac{1}{4}''$ x $4\frac{3}{8}''$ framed.
Unsigned, undated. Title as above scratched on frame below portrait.
Very close to the engraving by T. Cook after Pingo.
Copies: NPL:M(Min.84).   3568

Reproductions Arranged by Engraver

COOK

Captᵗⁿ James Cook. F.R.S. T. Cook Sculp.

Publish'd Aug.ᵗ 13.ᵗʰ 1784 by J. Fielding, [London]. Engraving. Oval. Meas. of port. $3\frac{1}{4}''$ x $2\frac{5}{8}''$.
Head and shoulders.
(Cook, J.—Third Voyage—Printed Accounts [1784]. Voyage to the Pacific Ocean. London, J. Stockdale, Scatcherd and Whitaker, J. Fielding and J. Hardy, 1784. Vol.1, frontisp.)
Copies: NPL:M(980:Co4/1A1).   3569

Another print.
Copies: NPL:M(P3/41B).   3570

Another print.
(Cook, J.—Third Voyage—Printed Accounts [1785]. Voyage to the Pacific Ocean. London. J. Fielding, 1785. Vol.1, frontisp.)
Copies: NPL:D(78/33).   3571

Another print.
(Cook, J.—Third Voyage—Printed Accounts [1787]. Capitain Cooks dritte und letzte Reise. Anspach, J.L. Wetzel, 1787. Band 1, frontisp.)
Copies: NPL:M(980:Co4/9A1).   3572

Another print.
Hand-coloured.
Engraver's name and imprint cut.
Copies: NPL:D(DL Pd622).   3573

The Same. [Without publisher's imprint.]

(Cook, J.—Third Voyage—Printed Accounts [1793]. Voyage to the Pacific Ocean. London, Champante and Whitrow, 1793. Vol.1, frontisp.)

Copies: NPL:M(980:Co4/14A1).   3574

Photograph.

Copies: NPL:M(P1/Cook—Pingo 1).   3575

LIZARS

Captn James Cook F.R.S. . . . D Lizars sculp.

Published 1st April 1785 by R.M. Morison and Son. Engraving. Oval. Meas. of port. $2\frac{1}{2}''$ x $1\frac{15}{16}''$. At head "Cooks Voyages".
Head and shoulders.
(Cook, J.—Third Voyage—Printed Accounts [1785 Perth ed.]. Voyage to the Pacific Ocean. Perth, pr. by R. Morison, jun, for R. Morison and Son, 1789. Vol.1, frontisp.)

Copies: NPL:M(980:Co4/5B1).   3576

Another print.

Engraver's name cut.

Copies: NPL:M(P1/Cook—Pingo 2).   3577

SASSO

Giacomo Cook. Bosio dis. Sasso inc.

Engraving. Meas. within frame lines $6\frac{7}{8}''$ x $4\frac{1}{2}''$. Meas. of plate mark $8\frac{1}{2}''$ x 6''.
Full-length.
Shows Cook standing, facing to the left, leaning on a bale, chart below elbow, globe on bale, sea in background. Face is after Pingo.

Copies: NPL:D(DL Pd660).   3578

Photograph.

Copies: NPL:M(P1/Cook—Pingo 3).   3579

Reproductions Arranged by Title of Reproduction

CAPTN. JAMES COOK, F.R.S.

Engraving. Oval. Meas. of port. $3\frac{1}{4}''$ x $2\frac{5}{8}''$. At head "Engraved for the *Newcastle Magazine*".
Head and shoulders.

Copies: NPL:M(P2/24).   3580

Another print.

Bound with *Universal Magazine*—Succinct account of life and voyages of Captain James Cook, extract. [Plate 1] June 1781.

Copies: NPL:M(910.4/122).   3581

CAPTN JAMES COOK, F.R.S.

Engraving. Oval. Meas. of port. 3⅜″ x 2⅞″.
Head and shoulders.
Inserted in Kippis, A.—Life of Captain James Cook. London, G. Nicol [and others], 1788.
Opp. p.45.
Copies: NPL:D(Q78/8).   3582

REYNOLDS

Originals, Including Photocopies of Originals

REYNOLDS, *Sir* Joshua

Portrait of a young man.

Oil. 27″ x 21″.
Unsigned, undated and untitled.
Facing slightly to the left, left hand in vest. In civilian dress, dark coat, white stock and vest, vest gold-braided.
See Reynolds' "Notes and observations on pictures . . . with an appendix containing a transcript of Sir Joshua's account book, showing what pictures he painted and the prices paid for them"; ed. by W. Cotton. London, 1859, J.R. Smith. Entries for 23 April 1774 and May 1788 refer to payments by a Mrs. Cook.
A lithograph of this portrait was made in 1827 by A. Hoffay, and published by Dickinson. The title describes it as a "print of the celebrated circumnavigator, Captain James Cooke (*sic*) of the Royal Navy." However, it seems more likely to be the portrait of another Captain Cook.
Copies: NPL:D(DG20).   3583

Photograph.

(N.S.W. Govt.Pr.neg.no.48019).
Copies: NPL:M(P1/Cook—Reynolds 1).   3584

Reproductions

THE CELEBRATED circumnavigator, Captain James Cooke (*sic*) . . . Drawn on stone by Albert Hoffay from the original painting by Sir Joshua Reynolds. Printed by C. Hullmandel.

Published by Dickinson Oct.ʳ 1827. Engraving, proof. Meas. of port. 7″ x 5⅝″. Meas. of sheet inside mount 10⅞″ x 7″.
Copies: NPL:M(P3/14A).   3585

Another print.

Proof. Imprint covered by mount.
Presented by Sir William Dixson 1935.
Copies: NPL:D(DG287).   3586

PORTRAIT-STUDY, said to be of Captain Cook as a young man, by George Romney.

Photograph of oil painting.
Head and shoulders of a man aged about 30, with powdered wig and dressed in plain clothes. On a label on the back of the stretcher is written in ink 'Romney—Captn Cook'. The portrait is unsigned and does not resemble the Dance, Hodges or Webber portraits of Cook. It was offered at Sotheby's 12 January 1966 lot 164.
Notes relating to the portrait and to Romney, made when the portrait was offered are at NPL:M PXn 86.

Copies: NPL:M(Pl/Cook—Romney 1).   3587

WEBBER GROUP

Originals, Including Photocopies of Originals

Portraits by John Webber, R.A. artist with Cook's third voyage, are three in number.
(a) Original in National Portrait Gallery, painted at the Cape of Good Hope. Cook was there, Oct.–Nov. 1777, on his outward voyage, and that would be the date of the picture; unless, as Kitson suggests, it was painted from memory on the return journey in 1780.
(b) In Trinity House, Hull, full-length portrait.
(c) In the National Art Gallery Wellington, New Zealand. Dr. Beaglehole in the Hakluyt Society edition of the Journals of Capt Cook v.3, 1967 gives its history as follows: Mrs. Cook gave it to her nephew, Captain John Fleck, from whose daughter it passed through a dealer to H.W.F. Bolckow of Marton in 1864. After the death of the second H.W.F. Bolckow in 1934 it went by way of bequest and gift to Canon T. Harrison Park, of Marton, who sold it to the New Zealand Government in 1960.

WEBBER, John

Captain James Cook, R.N.

Photographic reproduction of oval portrait. Size of port. area $2\frac{1}{2}''$ x $3\frac{3}{16}''$.
(Cust, *Sir* Lionel Henry—National Portrait Gallery. London, 1901. Vol.1, p.301, no.26.)

Copies: NPL:R(DQ757/2).   3588

WEBBER, John

Captain James Cook, R.N.

Photograph of oval portrait. Photo of port. area $6\frac{11}{16}''$ x $5\frac{3}{16}''$.
Head and shoulders.
(National Portrait Gallery—Photographs of portraits . . . of persons relating to Australia. [1914. Plate 3.])
Copy of correspondence between Principal Librarian P.L.N.S.W. and Director N.P.G., 1928, re circumstances of acquisition of the portrait by N.P.G. are filed at NPL:M PXn 180.

Copies: NPL:M(QA920/N).   3589

Another print.

Copies: NPL:D(DL Pd594).   3590

The Same.

Photograph of the above photograph, reduced.

Copies: NPL:M(P1/Cook—Webber 3b).   3591

The Same.

Postcard photograph, 1965.

Copies: NPL:M(P1/Cook—Webber 3).   3592

A copy of this portrait was made by W.A. Moir c.July–Aug. 1907, *see* W.A. Moir— Prospectus of an exhibition of copies of historical paintings, Feb. 1908 (NPL:M. MS.Ad89).

WEBBER, John

Captain Cook.

Photograph, 1929, of oil painting. Size of original 43″ x 27⅛″.
Three-quarter length, hat in right hand on hip, telescope in left hand which is resting on a rock.
The original is in the National Art Gallery, Wellington, N.Z.
Reproduced in colour in the Institute of Navigation—*Journal* vol.21, no.3, July 1968, as frontispiece, *and in* the Hakluyt Society edition of the Journals of Captain Cook, vol.3 1967, as frontispiece.

Copies: NPL:M(P1/Cook—Webber 2).   3593

Another print.

Copies: NPL:D(DL Pd666).   3594

Reproductions Arranged by Engraver

AITKEN

Captain James Cook. (Painted by John Webber. Engraved on wood by Peter Aitken. In the National Portrait Gallery, London.)
(*The Century Illustrated Monthly Magazine*, vol.58, Sept.1899, p.756.)

Copies: NPL:R(DS050/C397).   3595

BARTOLOZZI

Captⁿ James Cook, F.R.S.

Painted at the Cape of Good Hope by J. Webber. F. Bartolozzi R.A. sculp.
Published . . . June 4th 1784, by J. Webber, [London]. Engraving. Oval. Meas. of port. 4½″ x 3¾″.
Head and shoulders.

Copies: NPL:M(P3/17A).   3596

Another 3 prints.

Copies: NPL:M(P2/36, P2/37); NPL:D(DL Pd597).   3597

Another print.

(*Inserted in* Kippis, A.—Life of Captain James Cook. London, G. Nicol & G.G.J. and
R. Robinson, 1788. Opp. p.ix.)
Copies: NPL:D(Q78/8).   3598

The Same.

Proof before letters.
(Webber, J.—Illustrations to Cook's voyages, original drawings, f.ii.)
Copies: NPL:D(DL PXX2).   3599

The Same.

Proof before title.
(Three voyages round the world . . . plates, no.4a.)
Copies: NPL:M(PXD59⁻¹).   3600

The Same.

Process reproduction. Meas. of port. $3\frac{3}{16}$″ x $2\frac{1}{2}$″.
(*Discovery*, vol.6, Sept. 1925, p.334.)
Copies: NPL:R(Q505/4).   3601

BIRRELL

Captain James Cook, F.R.S. Dodd del. Birrell sculp.

Published July 20, 1785 by J. Fielding, [London]. Engraving. Meas. of engraved surface
$5\frac{1}{8}$″ x $3\frac{1}{16}$″.
Full-length.
Shows Cook standing, musket in hand, with background of island scenery.
Copies: NPL:D(DL Pd636).   3602

Another print.

Imprint cut.
Copies: NPL:D(DL Pd577).   3603

Another print.

Copies: NPL:M(P3/41A).   3604

Another print.

(Cook, J.—Third Voyage—Printed Accounts [1785]. Third and last voyage. London,
John Fielding and John Stockdale, [1785]. Frontisp.)
Copies: NPL:M(980:Co4/4A1).   3605

The Same. S. Hill sc Boston.

Meas. of engraved surface 5″ x 3″.
(Cook, J.—Collected Voyages—Printed Accounts [1797]. Captain Cook's three voyages.
Boston, Thomas & Andrews and D. West. 1797. Vol.1, frontisp.)
Copies: NPL:M(980:Co1/13A1).   3606

The Same: [reproduction].

Meas. of port. 5⅛″ x 3″.
(*Magazine of American History*, Nov. 1890, p.349.)
Copies: NPL:R(S973.05/1).   3607

The Same: [reproduction, with notes].

(English, T.H.—Introduction to the collecting and history of Whitby prints. Whitby,
Horne & Son Ltd, 1931. Vol.1, B1.)
Copies: NPL:M(Q942.7/E); NPL:D(Q93/118).   3608

HAID

Capt.ⁿ James Cook, F.R.S. Painted at the Cape of Good Hope by J.
Webber.

Se vend chez Haid. Mezzotint. Round. Diameter 4¾″.
(*Inserted in* Kippis, A.—Life of Captain James Cook. London, G. Nicol and G.G.J. and
J. Robinson, 1788. Opp. p.1.)
Copies: NPL:D(Q78/8).   3609

Another print.
Copies: NPL:M(P3/17B).   3610

Reproductions Arranged by Title of Reproduction

LE CAPITAINE COOK.

Engraving. Meas. of oval plaque port. 4⅛″ x 3¼″.
No artist or engraver's name.
The portrait vaguely resembles those of the Webber group.
Copies: NPL:D(DL Pd582).   3611

Photograph.
Copies: NPL:M(P1/Cook—Webber 1).   3612

CAPT. JAMES COOK: engraving with representation beneath of the death of Cook.

6¾″ x 3⅞″.
This portrait is set in a mount with a sheet of MS. sailing directions for the coast of
Scotland from the Hill of Collin, Moray Firth, to Buchan Ness, Aberdeen, said to be in
the handwriting of Cook. The size of the whole inset is 14⅞″ x 9½″.
Copies: ANL.   3613

CAPTAIN COOK.

Oil painting. 39″ x 22½″ inside frame.
Unsigned, untitled and undated.
Full face. Coat and vest blue and gold-braided, white front.
Has been attributed to Webber but shows little resemblance to other portraits of Cook
by Webber.
Presented by Sir William Dixson 1929.

Copies: NPL:D(DG29).   3614

COOK: [a marble bust said to be a contemporary bust of Cook in the manner of Bacon].

20″ on short rectangular pedestal inscribed "Cook".
Nearly full face slightly turned to right, looking upward, hair *en queue* curling over the
ears, small turned down collar and lace cravat, vest with two vacant buttonholes, open
tunic and fur-lined cloak.
This bust was offered at Sotheby's 22 April 1937.
Official correspondence of P.L.N.S.W. relating to this bust is at A1713⁻⁶ (*Restricted issue*).

     3615

AN 18TH CENTURY painting on glass, showing a portly person in a green costume; with flowered waistcoat, in a landscape on the bank of a river, said to be a portrait of Captain Cook.

Photograph of painting. Size of original 26″ x 19½″.
With descriptive note by J. Leger & Son, 1929, stating that the portrait was obtained
by them direct from a descendant of Cook and that the family still owned the waistcoat.
Letter from Leger & Son, 20 Nov. 1929, is at NPL:M A1713⁻⁶ (*Restricted issue*).

Copies: NPL:M(PXn182).   3616

JAS COOK—Marine Surveyor.

1766 or 1767. Photograph of painting. Meas. of original 35½″ x 27″.
Inscription painted on back of portrait reads "This portrait of Jas. Cook—Marine
Surveyor was painted at Newfondland (*sic*) for Capt.ⁿ Groves the Governor in 1766".
Three-quarter length, facing three-quarters to the right, in uniform.
The portrait was bought by the National Portrait Gallery, London, in 1905. The catalogue
of the Gallery states the picture is dated 1766, but Kitson gives 1767 as the date. It seems
to represent a different person from that portrayed by Dance, Hodges or Webber.
A copy of this portrait by W.A. Moir was painted in 1907. (Prospectus of exhibition,
Feb.1908. NPL:M MS.Ad 89.)

Copies: NPL:M(P1/Cook—Unknown 2).   3617

Another 2 prints.

Copies: NPL:M(P1/Cook—Unknown 3); NPL:D(DL Pd623).   3618

Another print.

(National Portrait Gallery—Photographs of portraits . . . of persons relating to Australia.
[1914. Pl.2.])

Copies: NPL:M(QA920/N).   3619

Reproduced in Chatterton, E.K.—Britain's record. 1911. Facing p.124.
Copies: NPL:R(S942/166). 3620

MINIATURE said to be of Captain Cook, in the Whitby Museum, Yorkshire.

Photograph, 1965. 7⅞″ x 6⅜″.
Copies: NPL:M(P1/Cook—Unknown1). 3621

PORTRAIT of a young seaman of the period of Cook.

Oil painting. 12¼″ x 14¼″ stretched.
Unsigned, untitled, undated.
Full-length, in landscape.
Presented by A.E. Crome, Esq., 1948.
Copies: NPL:M(ML426). 3622

PORTRAITS

Collections

PAPERS re Capt. James Cook, Mrs Elizabeth Cook and the Cook Family, 1776–1926, once the property of King V. Hostick of Chicago.

R. Nan Kivell, London, 1962.
1 reel. Positive microfilm.
Filmed by Photographic Dept., Australia House, London, 1962. Detailed list at NPL:M A3923 (Microfilm Ref. Books). The papers include a collection of engraved portraits of Cook.
Copies: NPL:M(FM4/1552). 3623

PORTRAITS

Forgeries

ACCOUNT of trial of John Charles Lovell, John George Cousins and David Andrews on a charge of conspiracy to defraud in connection with Andrews' offering for sale a miniature of Capt. Cook recently painted by Constantino Celli and initialled M A S, as being by Sir Archer Shee, and a miniature of Banks and one of Phillip recently painted by Gladys Laycock of North Sydney, and initialled H R as being by Sir H. Raeburn. In the evidence Miss Laycock stated she had done other miniatures for Lovell and placed other initials on them by Lovell's order.
[Cuttings from *Daily Telegraph* and *Sydney Morning Herald*, etc., Nov. 1907, Feb. 1908.]

(Australian Museum—Newscuttings. pp.26–8, re Cook relics.)
Copies: NPL:M(MS.A3937). 3624

PERSONAL

Manuscripts, Articles, etc., about the Portraits

1776 May 24 COOK, James

AL written in the third person to Mr. Banks, in reference to an engraving of the New Zealand spruce, his sitting for Mr. Dance, *etc.*

pp.2.

(Letters of Capt. James Cook, R.N., p.9.)

This letter was part of the Brabourne Papers. Facsimile filed at NPL:M(980:Co3/1A1).

Copies: NPL:M(Safe 1/68).   3625

1899 MURCH, A.C.

ALS 18 Feb. 1899, enclosing a letter from Joseph Banks to his cousin, 24 Dec.1862, re a portrait of Captain James Cook by Francis Cotes; with carbon typescript biographical note on Cotes.

Copies: NPL:M(Doc.1302).   3626

[19– –] THORPE, William Walford

Notes on portraits, pictures and medallions of Cook by various artists.

Copies: NPL:D(MS.Q145).   3627

1924 DIXSON, *Sir* William

Rare pictures relative to Australasia: notes of a lantern slide lecture to the Royal Historical Society, 27 May 1924.

ff.15, cm 27.

Notes describing pictures of Cook and others.

Copies: NPL:D.   3628

For illustrations of the tree planted by Captain Cook to mark the spot from which he viewed the transit of Venus in 1769 *see* the subheading *Personal—Monuments in the Pacific Islands—Tahiti.*

For references to the Coat-of-Arms granted to Captain Cook *see* the subheading *Personal—Illustrations, etc.*

AMMUNITION BELT.

Leather belt, with separate pouches for carrying powder, shot and ball.

Col. Sec. Corres. filed at NPL:M A3935 gives source as J. Mackrell, and the belt is listed in the catalogue of Mackrell's exhibition.

Transferred from the Australian Museum, Oct. 1955.

Copies: NPL:M(R199).   3629

ATKINSON, James

Epitome of the art of navigation; or, A short, easy and methodical way to become a compleat navigator . . . revis'd and corrected . . . by W. Mountaine. London, printed for William Mount and Thomas Page, 1744.

Diags. 8 plates, tables, pp.448.
Said by the former owner Robert F. Philps to have been the copy used by Captain Cook on his voyages. Letter bound in from R.F. Philps to Sir Alfred Stephens, Je 23, 1893.
Copies: NPL:M(527/A). 3630

AUTOGRAPH ACCOUNT of a ship's day's work probably H.M.S. *Eagle*, for Wednesday, 3rd November, 1756.

ff.2. Framed beneath glass. 4″ x 8″.
Transferred from the Australian Museum, Oct. 1955. Col. Sec. Corres. re history and source of relics 1887–91, placed at NPL:M A3934–A3936.
Copies: NPL:M(R193). 3631

BIBLE—*Whole Bible*—English

The Holy Bible containing the Old and New Testaments. Oxford, M. Baskett, 1765.

Illus.
With Cook's bookplate.
On the authority of Mrs. Elizabeth Cook, this Bible is said to have been used by Captain Cook in conducting Divine service. Letter tipped in.
Copies: NPL:M(Q220/1A1). 3632

BOOK of Common Prayer. M. Baskett, 1763.

With the bookplate of Frances M'Allister and inscription on fly-leaf "presented by Capt. James Cook to Frances Wardale in the year 1769. John M'Allister and Frances Lieber were married August 28, 1783. Frances M'Allister died December 9, 1814."
Frances Wardale was a cousin of Captain Cook. In 1770 she married Mr. Lieber and settled in Philadelphia in 1773.
Copies: ANL(Nan Kivell 9528); NPL:M(FM41552,1707 pos. and neg. microfilm). 3633

BOSWELL, James

An Account of Corsica: the journal of a tour to that island, and memoirs of Pascal Paoli. 3rd ed. London, E. & C. Dilly, 1769.

Map, port. as frontisp., pp.400.
Author's presentation copy to Captain Cook. Has signature J. Cook on back of frontispiece. The volume is described by Camden Morrisby in his article entitled *Captain Cook, Boswell relic: Australian Museum treasure.* (*B.P. Magazine*, Mar.1, 1935, p.71. NPL:M Q059/B.)
Copies: NPL:M(945.95/1C1). 3634

CABIN TEA-CADDY, used on board the *Resolution*.

Wooden box, 4½″ high x 7⅝″ wide x 4¼″ deep, of cedar veneer on pine inlaid with walnut and other timbers. Two compartments inside with cedar lids and ivory knobs.
Transferred from the Australian Museum, Oct. 1955. Col. Sec. Corres. re history and source of the relic is filed at NPL:M A3934–A3936.
See also no.3651.
Copies: NPL:M(R196). 3635

CAPTAIN COOK'S azimuth compass [in the] National Maritime Museum, Greenwich: [photograph].

(*In* Muir, John Reid—Life and achievements of Captain James Cook. London, Blackie, 1939. p.272.)

Copies: NPL:M(980:Col/M6A1); NPL:D(93/626); NPL:R(DS990A/195); ANL; QParl; QU; VMoU; VSL. 3636

CAPTAIN COOK'S memorial ring, the design made from his hair.

With inscription 'Capt James Cook O.B. 14 Feb. 1779. AET:50 [in his 50th year]'. On an accompanying envelope is written in ink 'Worn by his widow' below title as above. Box has seal of Cook's coat of arms.
Presented 29/4/65 by Mrs. E. Hawker, whose great-grandmother was Jane Cragg, sister of Isaac Cragg Smith, nephew of Admiral Isaac Smith.

Copies: NPL:M(R363). 3637

CAPTAIN JAMES COOK Relics and MSS: [an album of manuscripts, relics and secondary material, by and about James Cook].

pp.148.
Contents list made and inserted, 1968. Three relics set inside front cover. The relics were bequeathed by Mrs. Cook to her servant Charles Doswell, Surrey. They passed to Ann Maria Sanford Arbery, great niece of his wife Sarah Doswell, and later into the possession of Dr. T.W. Shortridge, Honiton, Devon, c.1900.
CONTENTS:
Manuscript Items: Portion of the log book tables for HMS *Endeavour* 19 Oct., 1768; a fair copy of part of Cook's journal of HMS *Resolution* Dec. 18–28, 1774; the ships' husbands bill for HMS *Resolution* and HMS *Adventure* Aug. 1, 1772–Apr. 27, 1775, all in Cook's hand; a draft of the General Introduction for the published account of Cook's second voyages, partly in Cook's hand; a poem by Thomas Perry 'It is now my brave boys we are clear of the Ice . . .' written during the second voyage (?); two watercolour sketches of islands (one, of Bonavista), possibly by a member of one of the expeditions; A report on HMS *Perseverance*, 1783.
Other Material: (1) Printed maps—by Cook (NSW 1770), by Pierre Roger (Poictou, 1579) and by J. Boisseau (Sedan &c., 1642). (2) Relics—the Royal Society's commemorative medal of 1784, a tusk, and a gilt button. (3) Coats of arms of the Cook family. (4) Lunar tables. (5) A ledger sheet 1806–21. Letters, mainly to T.W. Shortridge, by Henry Adams, the British Museum, Royal Geographical Society, London, and Viscount Sidmouth; with notes and photos re Shortridge's collection.

Copies: NPL:D(MS.F1). 3638

CARVED DITTY BOX shaped like a coffin, on silver stand, containing a rough watercolour sketch of the death of Cook, with a lock of his hair and document of identification. With inscription 'Made of *Resolution* oak for Mrs Cook by crew'.

Inset in lid are two silver plates inscribed 'Quebec Newfoundland, Greenwich Australia' and 'Lono and the Seaman's Idol'. Inset in bottom is a third silver plate inscribed 'Captain James Cook slain at Owhyhee, 14 February, 1779'.
Enclosed in a glass box, silver mounted.
A sliding compartment in the bottom of the case contains a description by Thomas Hart of how the box was made, and a Statutory Declaration signed by C. Albert Maggs dated 19.8.12 stating that Thomas Hart was a relative of Mrs. Cook. There is also a roneoed sheet which says that Lono was the name of one of the four principal gods of Hawaii.
Ditty box meas. c.3$\frac{1}{2}$" x c.2$\frac{1}{2}$"; case meas. c.6$\frac{1}{2}$" x 9" x 5$\frac{7}{8}$".

Copies: NPL:D(DR2). 3639

A CATALOGUE of the different specimens of cloth collected in the three voyages of Captain Cook to the southern hemisphere; with a particular account of the manner of the manufacturing of the same in the various islands of the South Seas; partly extracted from Mr. Anderson and Reinhold Forster's observations, and the verbal account of some of the most knowing of the navigators; with some anecdotes that happened to them among the natives. Now properly arrainged and printed for Alexander Shaw, London, 1787.

pp.8 and 38 specimens.
The Mitchell Library holds three copies, and the Dixson Library holds two copies. The specimens differ in each copy.
Copies: NPL:M(C524; C525; C526); NPL:D(78/64; 78/65); ANL:F; SPL; VSL. 3640

CHIMNEY POT and wooden mantelpiece, from No.88 Mile End Rd., Stepney, London.
Presented to the Trust by the London County Council.
Copies: Captain Cook's Landing Place Trust. 3641

CLOCK which belonged to Captain Cook.
Dark wood and glass case with handle on the top; meas. c.19″ high. Clock face is plain, but has a gilt decoration around it. Inscription on brass reads "This clock belonged to Captain James Cook the navigator and made the voyage round the world with him in 1779".
Copies: NPL:M(LR33). 3642

A COLLECTION (50) of specimens of bark cloth (also feathers of small birds, hair of the natives, twine, plaited human hair, &c.), as collected in the different voyages of Capt. Cook to the South Sea.
The title-page is done by hand in ink, the parts in parentheses being interpolated in pencil. The specimens are mounted, with descriptions beneath in contemporary handwriting. Maggs Bros. stated in 1902, when offering the volume for sale, that only two other similar collections are said to have been made.
Copies: NPL:M(C523). 3643

COMMONPLACE BOOK c.1773–1780.
ff.108, cm 20.5.
Bound in vellum. Spine title 'T.H. v̄. Honert de STYLO N.T. GRAECO' in ink. The volume contains copies of poems by various authors, and a dialogue held in the Sheldonian Theatre 1773. '1773' is written on both covers in different styles, and on p.136 also. Inside the front cover are written 'R. Pusey' (ink) and 'W.J. Finne (?) Toot Balden' (pencil) both considerably erased. Inside the back cover is written 'This Book Sold to me by Mr. Smith Abingdon & Warranted to be Written by Captain Cook R. Pusey Abingdon Berks 1854' (ink). The volume seems to have been attributed to Cook on account of this note. The hand is not that of Cook. The poem on p.201, whose date (1780) is partly erased, was copied from the *Gentleman's Magazine* of June 1780; Cook died 1779. Further notes are filed in the Dixson Library at MS.93n.
Copies: NPL:D(MS.93). 3644

COMPASS incorporating protractor, ruler and spirit level, belonging to Alex Hood, master's mate, H.M.S. *Resolution* 1772–75. Made by J. Newman, 122 Regent St., London.

Boxwood and brass.

Copies: ANL(Nan Kivell). 3645

COOK, Elizabeth, *Mrs*

[Photograph of a chart of the Western Hemisphere, embroidered in silk by Mrs. James Cook, n.d.]

No scale given, ca16 cm in diam. on 1 sheet, cm 22 x 17, photograph, b./wh.
Shows tracks of Cook 1769–79.

Copies: NPL:M(M1 120/1769–79/1). 3646

CORDUROY made from native barks, to replace that worn on Captain Cook's voyage. 2″ x 6″. With leaf from Cook's log book of his second voyage on the *Resolution* containing his observations and remarks for Thursday 18th and Saturday 20th March 1773.

11″ x 7⅝″.

Copies: ANL. 3647

CUP, said to be the Communion Cup used by Captain Cook on his voyages, and its leather case.

Photograph. 7½″ x 9¼″.
The original is in the possession of the Dowager Viscountess Galway, Bawtry, Doncaster.

Copies: NPL:M(Small Picture File: Cook—Relics 1). 3648

The Same. Photograph of cup only; together with a copy of a letter from the Viscountess to the Library Liaison Officer, dated 1st December, 1962, with possible explanation of how the cup came into the possession of the family.

Copies: NPL:M(Small Picture File: Cook—Relics 2). 3649

DRESS SWORD belonging to Captain Cook.

Sword meas. 27″; has silver handle. Scabbard has silver trimmings and meas. 22⅝″.
Col. Sec. Corres. at NPL:M A3935 gives source of relic as J. Mackrell.
Transferred from the Australian Museum, Oct. 1955.

Copies: NPL:M(LR29). 3650

DRESSING CASE used by Cook.

Box of inlaid wood, 3″ x 6″ x 8⅜″. Inlay is similar in pattern to that on R196 (*see* no.3635).
Transferred from the Australian Museum, Oct. 1955. Col. Sec. Corres. filed at NPL:M A3935 gives source of relic as J. Mackrell and it is in the catalogue of Mackrell's exhibition.

Copies: NPL:M(R195). 3651

EPITOME of Voyages. 1497–1685. Captain Cook.

pp.94. cm 22.5.

Spine title. MS. summarises the early voyages to the South Pacific; with typescript index inserted at beginning. Typescript note inserted inside front cover states 'This MS. comes from the collection of Mr Bolckow . . . & it is said that this resumé of previous voyages to the South Seas was used by Capt. Cook & was probably written out for him.' Notes are filed at NPL:D, MS.97n.

Copies: NPL:D(MS.97). 3652

FIGURE HEAD of the *Resolution*.

Photograph. 7½″ x 9⅜″.

Original formerly in possession of Lord Galway, and presented by him to New Zealand after his term as Governor General in 1941.

Note in pencil on reverse of photograph by Mitchell Librarian 19.5.38 "There is sufficient similarity to the figure head shown in Holman's picture in the Dixson Gallery and in one of Webber's drawings to suggest that this relic is the genuine figurehead".

Copies: NPL:M(Ships File: Resolution). 3653

FOLDING TABLE of Spanish mahogany opening to 26″ x 27½″ with inscription: "This table was formerly the property of Captain Cook the circumnavigator, and was used by him during his three famous voyages. It was purchased by Dr Shortridge of Honiton from a grand niece of C. Doswell, Captain Cook's personal servant".

Copies: NPL:D(DR6). 3654

FRENCH CLOCK with decorative wooden carving, made by Leroy, Paris.

Reputedly owned by Captain Cook.

Copies: NPL:D(DR5). 3655

GANGWAY HAND-LINES (2), said to have been used on board H.M.S. *Discovery*, the companion ship during Captain Cook's third voyage, 1776–79.

Plaited rope, covered with canvas and varnished. c.44″ x 42″.

Presented to the Govt. of N.S.W. by E.N. Brown, 1891. Corres. re history and source of relics placed at NPL:M A3934–A3935.

Transferred from the Australian Museum, Oct. 1955.

Copies: NPL:M(R207). 3656

GILT BUTTON from Cook's field-dress uniform.

Inserted in Album of manuscripts, relics and secondary material by and about James Cook. Bequeathed by Mrs. Cook to her servant Charles Doswell, and later in the possession of Dr. T.W. Shortridge.

Copies: NPL:D(MS.F1/ii). 3657

GLASS STAR given by Captain Cook to the King of Aitutaki, in what is now the Cook Islands, together with MS. explanation by Rev. L.E. Threlkeld, dated at Sydney, February 22nd, 1854.

Frame meas. 14¼″ x 15″.

Copies: NPL:M(R226). 3658

GLASS TUMBLER used on the *Resolution*. Height 2⅜″; engraved '*Resolution/*
Capt Cook/ 1772'.

> Transferred from the Australian Museum, Oct. 1955. Col. Sec. Corres. re history and
> source of the relic placed at NPL:M A3934–A3936.
> Copies: NPL:M(R197). 3659

HEYLIN, Peter

Cosmographie in four books, containing the chorographie and historie
of the whole world and all the principal kingdoms, provinces, seas, and
isles . . . by P. Heylyn. 2nd ed. London, pr. for Henry Seile, 1657.

> pp.[9], 1098, [2].
> MS. note written on the title-page in 1787 by J. Thomas, purser of the *Resolution*, states
> that this volume was found in Cook's cabin after his death, and suggests it was the last
> book read by him.
> Copies: NPL:M(MS.A3058). 3660

INCLINOMETER, or gunner's quadrant, used for levelling in shore work.

> Instrument in brass, with marked rule 18¼″ long as base and a moveable spirit level with
> protractor which measures to 90°. Glass in level broken. Meas. of height 7⅛″.
> Maker's name engraved on one side "Spear 23 Chapel St. Ins maker to His Majesty's
> Ordnance".
> In wooden case.
> From Sir Joseph Banks Museum. Col. Sec. Corres. re relics placed at NPL:M A3936
> states that instrument was used by Cook on the *Endeavour*.
> Transferred from the Australian Museum, Oct. 1955.
> Copies: NPL:M(LR30). 3661

IVORY SCALE RULE.

> This relic goes with the sextant and pair of parallel rules placed at NPL:D DR 11 and
> DR 13. There is also a letter filed with DR 11 dated 29.4.1906 signed by E.A.A. Burney,
> stating that he believed that Captain Cook gave these relics to his grand-father, Dr.
> William Burney, the then head-master and founder of Royal Academy, Gasport (*sic*).
> Copies: NPL:D(DR12). 3662

LARGE FORKS used by Captain Cook.

> 6 forks with wooden handles with silver bands at each end. 9″.
> Transferred from the Australian Museum, Oct. 1955. Col. Sec. Corres. re history and
> source of the relics filed at NPL:M A3934–A3936.
> Copies: NPL:M(R210). 3663

LARGE KNIVES used by Captain Cook.

> 6 knives with wooden handles with silver bands at each end. 11¼″.
> Transferred from the Australian Museum, Oct. 1955. Col. Sec. Corres. re history and
> source of the relics is filed at NPL:M A3934–A3936.
> Copies: NPL:M(R208). 3664

LARGE KNIVES (2) with typed notes stating that they were used by
Cook on the *Endeavour*.

> Copies: NPL:D(DR16). 3665

NAUTICAL INSTRUMENT for chart work.

Brass instrument, T-shaped at one end and curved at the other. 15¼″ long.
Transferred from the Australian Museum, Oct. 1955. Col. Sec. Corres. on history and source of relics is filed at NPL:M A3935.
NPL:M(R216). 3666

NAUTICAL INSTRUMENT for chart work.

Brass ruler. 17¼″ x 1⅜″.
Arms which were placed at right angles at each end are missing.
Transferred from the Australian Museum, Oct. 1955. Col. Sec. Corres. on source and history of relics does not list source; Mitchell Library Corres. 408/1955 gives source as Govt. of N.S.W., but no further reference is given.
Copies: NPL:M(R217). 3667

NAUTICAL INSTRUMENT for chart work.

Instrument in brass, with swivel arm which moves along the curved surface of a protractor to 90°. Two sets of holes on the underside of this arm indicate that another part of the instrument may be missing. Meas. 16″ in length.
Col. Sec. Corres. on history and source of relics does not contain any information on this instrument. Mitchell Library Corres. 408/1955 gives source as Govt. of N.S.W., but no further reference is given.
Copies: NPL:M(LR32). 3668

NECKLET of Mrs. Cook's hair.

43″ long.
Small piece 2¾″ broken off.
Col. Sec. Corres. does not give source of relic. Mitchell Library Corres. 408/1955 gives source as Govt. of N.S.W., but no further reference is given.
Copies: NPL:M(R220). 3669

ORIENTAL BOX, said to have been the first present made by Cook to the lady he married.

Box meas. 4½″ x 13¼″ x 10″; curved lid and painted with red and gold Oriental designs. With a handle at each end.
Col. Sec. Corres. filed at NPL:M A3935 gives as source Mr. Mackrell's collection. Transferred from the Australian Museum, Oct. 1955. *See also* no.3756.
Copies: NPL:M(LR28). 3670

PARALLEL RULER.

17″ long. Dark wood with brass fittings. Inscribed 'W.B 1770'.
Copies: NPL:D(DR7). 3671

PASSAGES from the Bible and sacred hymns written and bound by one of the sailors of the *Resolution* during Captain Cook's third voyage.

MS. pp.205.
The writer lived in England from his return from the voyage until his death, after which his son gave the volume to Mr. William Taylor, who afterwards came to Australia and

settled in Geelong in 1849. At his death it came into the possession of Mr. F.W. Farmer of Caramut, Victoria, who presented it to the Warrnambool Museum. It was given by that institution in 1923 to the Commonwealth National Library.

Copies: ANL(MS.7A).   3672

PATTERNS of cloth made and worn by natives of the South Sea Islands, being part of the collection made by the celebrated circumnavigator Capt. James Cook in his first, second and third voyages.

3 pages of explanatory notes. 70 specimens in square quarto album. 63 numbered and 52 fully annotated.

Copies: ANL(Nan Kivell).   3673

PAYMENT RECEIPTS from the seamen of the ship *Brotherly Love*, the vessel on which it is erroneously said that Captain James Cook served his apprenticeship. Dated at Shields, England, March 18, 1749 and May 20, 1750.

ff.3 in MSS. Meas. inside frame $3\frac{7}{8}''$ x 6"; $3\frac{5}{8}''$ x $5\frac{3}{4}''$.

Copies: NPL:M(R224).   3674

PAYMENT RECEIPTS from seamen of the ship *Brotherly Love*, the vessel on which it is erroneously said that Captain James Cook served his apprenticeship. Dated at London, November 9 and October 14, 1754.

ff.3 in MSS. Meas. inside frame $3\frac{7}{8}''$ x 6"; $3\frac{1}{2}''$ x $5\frac{3}{4}''$.

Copies: NPL:M(R225).   3675

PIECE of cloth from the Sandwich Islands with a note: 'Given by Capt. Cook to my grandfather—R. Cory.'

9" x 7".

Copies: NPL:D(DR8).   3676

A PIECE of the rock from the scene of Capt. Cook's death in Kealakekua Bay, Hawaii, on Feb.14th, 1779.

Triangular-shaped rock, $1\frac{1}{8}''$ x $2\frac{1}{8}''$.
Label handwritten in ink on side 'A piece of the Coral rock on which Capt Cook was killed.'
Transferred from the Australian Museum, Oct. 1955. Col. Sec. Corres. re history and source of relics placed at NPL:M A3934–A3936.
See also no.3682.

Copies: NPL:M(R194).   3677

PIECE of the tree used by Captain Cook to moor his ship in Endeavour River, June 1770.

Wood meas. $12\frac{3}{4}''$ high.
A photograph of the whole tree is inset with a brass plate inscribed "Part of the tree shown in photo and used by Captain Cook to moor his ship in Endeavour River, June 1770. W.C. Thomson, S.S. *Aramac*".
See also no. 3679.

Copies: NPL:M(R181).   3678

PIECE of tree with photograph of the whole tree inset and ink inscription on base 'Part of Tree shown in photo and used by Capt Cook to moor his ship in Endeavour River June 1770''.

7¾" high.
See also no.3678.
Copies: NPL:D(DR9).   3679

PORTION of a beam compass.

Wooden ruler 14" long, with measurements for 12" marked. Further attachments missing. Metal plaque engraved 'H426'.
Transferred from the Australian Museum, Oct. 1955. Col. Sec. Corres. on history and source of relics does not contain any information on source, but in the Mitchell Library Corres. 408/1955 source is given as Govt. of N.S.W. No further reference is made.
Copies: NPL:M(R219).   3680

PORTION of inclinometer.

Brass instrument, c.13" long, consisting of a quadrant with three swivel arms attached. Transferred from the Australian Museum, Oct. 1955. Col. Sec. Corres. on history and source of relics does not contain any information on source, but in the Mitchell Library Corres. 408/1955 the source is given as Govt. of N.S.W. No further reference is made.
Copies: NPL:M(R218).   3681

PORTIONS of the rock on which Captain Cook stood when he was killed at Kaavaloa, 1779.

See also no.3677.
Copies: Captain Cook's Landing Place Trust.   3682

QUADRANT with a plumbline, which was used instead of a sextant.

Wooden instrument 9" high.
Transferred from the Australian Museum, Oct. 1955. Col. Sec. Corres. on source and history of relics does not contain any information on source, but in Mitchell Library Corres. 408/1955 source is given as Govt. of N.S.W. No further reference is made.
Copies: NPL:M(R214).   3683

RELICS of Captain Cook held in the Royal United Service Museum, Whitehall, London.

4 photographs mounted on 1 sheet.
CONTENTS:
A. Chronometer, originally the property of Capt. James Cook, R.N., F.R.S., the circumnavigator, and used by him on his voyages of discovery, 1772–79.
B. Punch bowl of J. Cook.
C. Sword or hanger belonging to Cook.
D. Telescope of Capt. J. Cook.
Copies: NPL:M(Small Picture File: Cook—Relics 3).   3684

RELICS of Captain Cook held in the Royal United Service Museum, Whitehall, London.

4 photographs mounted on 1 sheet.

CONTENTS:

A. Group of clubs and arms which were brought back by various members of Capt. James Cook's crew, which were obtained by them during the voyages of discovery, 1772–1779.
B. Club given to Capt. James Cook, by the King of Owhyhee.
C. A Tablet of portable desiccated soup, as used on Capt. James Cook's voyages.
D. Portion of the trunk of a coconut tree with two musket-ball holes in it, which were received at the time of the affray at Karakakooa Bay, Hawaii, when Capt. James Cook was killed.

Copies: NPL:M(V*Cook 39). 3685

SCALE of sines, etc. for navigation purposes, in ivory, reputed to have been given to William Burney by Captain Cook. 'W.B. 1770' cut into surface.

18″ long, folding.

Copies: NPL:D(DR18). 3686

SCARF presented by Capt Cook to the maternal ancestor of M.F. Morton, Esq., M.L.A.

Horse-shoe shaped embroidered scarf in red material. Letter from Commonwealth National Librarian dated 12.12.33 stating that he believes it to be of Peruvian workmanship and that it was acquired by Cook in 1768, is filed with it. Extensively damaged by moths.

Copies: NPL:M(R188). 3687

SET of pottery chessmen, said to have belonged to Captain Cook.

Photograph, with a letter dated 10.2.1917, describing the chessmen and their authenticity, sent by F. Rathbone to the Australian Museum.

Copies: NPL:M(Small Picture File: Cook—Relics 5). 3688

SEXTANT.

Brass instrument, c.5″ high and c.6½″ wide. In wooden box.
There is also a letter dated 29.4.1906 signed by E.A.A. Burney stating that he believed that Captain Cook gave the sextant and rulers (placed at NPL:D DR 12 & DR 13) to his grandfather, Dr. William Burney, head-master and founder of Royal Academy, Gosport. The authenticity of this relic has been questioned.

Copies: NPL:D(DR11). 3689

SHELL said to have been brought back from Australia by Cook, mounted in gold to form a snuff-box.

Pear-shaped box with squared ends meas. c.3¼″ x c.1¾″ at widest point. Lid is broken. Note by donor Mrs. J.E. Ferguson, née Connell, reads "Colonel J.C. Buxton of Bedgebrook Manor—Grantham England gave Lieu. H.C. Ferguson this shell snuff box of which he had several. The shells were brought from Aust'lia by Cap. Cook on The "*Endeavour*" early 1700—& given to the G.G. grand-father of the above made into snuff boxes . . ."

Copies: NPL:M(R231). 3690

SHIP'S COMPASS said to have been that of H.M.S. *Endeavour*.

Brass instrument in oak case. Engraving round edge of compass reads "G Adams Fleet Street London." Needle missing and glass broken. There is a sighting device across the top of the bowl. MS. note in ink on side of the lid "I hereby certify that I have examined this compass and that it appears to be rightly constructed. No 636. J.H. De Magalhaens". Correspondence re source and validity of this relic filed at NPL:M A3934 and NPL:M A3936⁻². Transferred from the Australian Museum, Oct. 1955.

Copies: NPL:M(R221). 3691

Heighway, William
Cook's compass: a note on its acquisition by the Mitchell Library.

Illus. (*Navigation* (Sydney), vol.2, Dec.1964, pp.167–73.)

Copies: NPL:M(527.06/1); NPL:R(N527.06/2); ANL. 3692

SHOE BUCKLES used by Cook for court wear.

Meas. c.2" x c.1¼"; surrounded with diamontés.
Col. Sec. Corres. at NPL:M A3935 lists source as J. Mackrell.
Transferred from the Australian Museum, Oct. 1955.

Copies: NPL:M(R206). 3693

SHOE BUCKLES used by Captain Cook for ordinary wear.

Meas. 3" x 3½", and covered in with leather.
Col. Sec. Corres. at NPL:M A3935 lists source as J. Mackrell, and buckles are listed in catalogue of Mackrell's exhibition.
Transferred from the Australian Museum, Oct. 1955.

Copies: NPL:M(R205). 3694

SHORE-BEARING PLATE.

Instrument in brass, with compass, protractor and swivelling arms with sights on ends. The supports of the compass are engraved with fish-like designs. Base of protractor engraved "T Pouilly Inventor Fecit Parisiis 1864."
The needle from compass missing, 2 sights broken. In wooden box.
Col. Sec. Corres. re history and source of relics placed at NPL:M A3936 states that instrument was used by Cook on the *Endeavour*.
Transferred from the Australian Museum, Oct. 1955.

NPL:M(LR31). 3695

SILVER CABIN SPOONS, engraved with the crest of Captain Cook.

12 spoons, 4 placed at R201(a); 4 at R201(b) and 4 at R201(c).
Transferred from the Australian Museum, Oct. 1955. Corres. of the Museum is placed at A3936⁻².

Copies: NPL:M(R201/A–C). 3696

SILVER CADDY SPOON to accompany tea caddy used by Cook.

Meas. c.1½" long.
Col. Sec. Corres. filed at NPL:M A3935 gives source as J. Mackrell, and the cutlery is listed in the catalogue of Mackrell's exhibition.
Transferred from the Australian Museum, Oct. 1955.

Copies: NPL:M(R204). 3697

SILVER DESSERT SPOONS (2), found in Captain Cook's sea chest.

Correspondence at NPL:M 408/1955 gives source as Govt. of N.S.W., and states that spoons were bequeathed by Mrs. E. Cook to Mrs. Sarah Doswell. Purchased from an aunt of Mrs. Doswell.
Transferred from the Australian Museum, Oct. 1955.
Copies: NPL:M(R223). 3698

SILVER GRAVY SPOON, engraved with crest of Captain Cook.

Meas. c.11½″ long.
Transferred from the Australian Museum, Oct. 1955. Corres. and history of relic filed at NPL:M A3935.
Copies: NPL:M(R202). 3699

SILVER KETTLE and spirit lamp.

Given by Queen Charlotte to Sir Joseph Banks, 1813.
Copies: ANL(Nan Kivell). 3700

SILVER TABLE SPOONS engraved with the crest of Captain Cook.

4 spoons, 8¾″ long.
The crests and the pattern up the handles are very worn.
Transferred from the Australian Museum, Oct. 1955. Corres. and history of the relics placed at NPL:M A3935.
Copies: NPL:M(R203). 3701

SMALL CELESTIAL GLOBE and Flamsteed's Celestial atlas, 1729.

Presented in 1882.
Copies: VSL. 3702

SMALL FORKS used by Captain Cook.

6 forks 7⅛″ long.
Transferred from the Australian Museum, Oct. 1955. Source was J.B. Smith *see* NPL:M A3936.
Copies: NPL:M(R211). 3703

SMALL KNIFE AND FORK, with typed notes stating that they were used on the *Endeavour*.

Copies: NPL:D(DR17). 3704

SMALL KNIVES used by Captain Cook.

6 knives with wooden handles with silver bands at each end. 8¼″.
Transferred from the Australian Museum, Oct. 1955. Col. Sec. Corres. re history and source of the relics filed at NPL:M A3934–A3936.
Copies: NPL:M(R209). 3705

SMALL METAL OBJECT found with small forks (Cook relics NPL:M R211. *See* no.3703.) It is 3⅛″ long with flat, sharp ends and a hole in one side. It does not seem to fit with any of the marine instruments or other Cook relics in the box.

Copies: NPL:M(R211/A). 3706

SMALL SPOON, with typed notes saying that it was used by Cook on the *Endeavour*.
Copies: NPL:D(DR18). 3707

STATION POINTER, used on the *Endeavour*.
Brass instrument in wooden box which is shaped like a violin.
Transferred from the Australian Museum, Oct. 1955. Information on the source and history is placed at NPL:M A3936.
Copies: NPL:M(R213). 3708

STERN PLATE of the *Resolution*.
Black wooden plate meas. c.40″ x c.22″, with portrait of Captain Cook in profile. Some of the edge is damaged.
Transfererd from the Australian Museum. Old label filed at NPL:M R226A.
Copies: NPL:M(XR12). 3709

TABLECLOTH with initials "E.C." with typed notes saying that it belonged to Cook's wife, Elizabeth.
Cloth meas. 33½″ x 28¾″.
Copies: NPL:D(DR15). 3710

TAPA CLOTH brought back by Alex Hood. Cloth 137″ x 25″. Double reed mat, plaited 60″ x 23¾″. Reed mat, plaited 58″ x 25½″.
Copies: ANL(Nan Kivell). 3711

TELESCOPE belonging to Captain Cook, in case.
34″ long.
Case has inscription 'Telescope—Capt. Cook, lent by R.J. Holden Christie, Pen Y Bryn, Saint Peter's Road, South Croydon'.
Copies: NPL:D(DR14). 3712

Christie Family
Cook's telescope: Christie family documents concerning its provenance and authenticity, 1891–1917.
ff.14.
Copies: NPL:D(MS.Q150). 3713

TELESCOPE, said to have been the property of Admiral Arthur Kemp, who served as a midshipman under Cook on board *Adventure*.
Barrel meas. 29″ when fully expanded. Leather covered, with brass fittings.
Copies: NPL:M(LR34). 3714

TRIANGULAR WOODEN SET SQUARE.

12″ x 9″.
Metal plaque nailed in centre, engraved 'H421'.
Transferred from the Australian Museum, Oct. 1955. Col. Sec. Corres. on history and source of relics does not contain any information on source, but in Mitchell Library Corres. 408/1955 source is given as Govt. of N.S.W., but no further reference is made.
Copies: NPL:M(R215).   3715

TWO FOOT RULE.

Ivory rule mounted with silver, with Cook's cipher. It folds into a box c.8″ long.
Col. Sec. Corres. filed at NPL:M A3935 gives source as Canon Bennett, and the rule is listed in the catalogue of J. Mackrell's exhibition.
Transferred from the Australian Museum, Oct. 1955.
Copies: NPL:M(R200).   3716

UNIVERSAL SUN-DIAL.

Brass instrument which stands about 5″ high. The initials "J.C." are incorporated in the design within the brass circle. Engraved on face "Made by Tho Wright Instrum^t maker to His Majesty". The bowl below the dial has a compass without a needle and a calendar engraved in the brass.
Col. Sec. Corres. filed at NPL:M A3936 states that instrument was purchased from James Bowen in 1887 and is supposed to have been designed by Cook. This could not be proved.
Transferred from the Australian Museum, Oct. 1955.
Copies: NPL:M(R212).   3717

WAIST COAT of Tahiti cloth embroidered by Mrs. Cook for him to wear at court, had he returned from 3rd voyage.

Col. Sec. Corres. filed at NPL:M A3935 gives source as Canon Bennett, and relic is listed in the catalogue of J. Mackrell's exhibition.
Copies: NPL:M(R198).   3718

WALKING CANE.

Inscribed on card: This walking cane was the property of Captain James Cook the great circumnavigator. It was given by his widow to Mr. John Fleck, whose mother was Captain Cook's sister. Mr. Fleck married my sister & at his death in 1836 this cane came into my possession.
Copies: ANL(Nan Kivell).   3719

WHITE WAISTCOAT, purchased in 1945 from the Hon. N.Diana Cook who was connected by marriage with Capt. Cook's family.

Copies: VSL.   3720

AUSTRALIAN MUSEUM, *Sydney*

[Cook relics in the Australian Museum, 1969.]

EXPLANATION OF ABBREVIATIONS USED IN THE FOLLOWING LIST:
Y. SINOTO   Locality of specimen checked by Dr. Sinoto.

PERSONAL – RELICS – *continued*

D.R.M.   Identification by D. R. Moore, Curator of Anthropology, Australian Museum.

Card Gallery Label—This information included as it sometimes varies from the register notation. Sometimes register shows no information at all.

CONTENTS:

MARQUESAS

1. *Register:* Carved Paddle. *Museum No.:* H.304. *Location:* Marquesas. *How obtained:* Sir J. Banks' Museum. Purchased from J. Calvert.

2. *Register:* Carved Paddle. *Museum No.:* H.310. *Location:* Marquesas. *How obtained:* Presented Government of N.S.W. Sir J. Banks' Museum. Purchased from J. Calvert.

3. *Register:* Carved Club. *Museum No.:* H.228. *Location:* Marquesas. *How obtained:* Presented Government of N.S.W. Sir J. Banks' Museum. Purchased from J. Calvert.

4. *Register:* Carved Paddle. *Museum No.:* H.305. *Location:* Marquesas. *How obtained:* Sir J. Banks' Museum. Purchased from J. Calvert.

5. *Register:* Carved Club—broad at one end. *Museum No.:* H.297. *Location:* Marquesas. *How obtained:* Sir J. Banks' Museum. Purchased from J. Calvert.

6. *Register:* Carved Club. *Museum No.:* H.286. *Location:* Marquesas.

7. *Register:* Tortoise shell ornament. *Museum No.:* H.338. *Location:* Marquesas. *How obtained:* Sir J. Banks' Museum. Purchased from J. Calvert. *Card Gallery Label:* (Forehead ornaments. Clam shell disc with cut turtle shell design. Marquesas). (D.R.M.)

8. *Register:* Straight carved club. *Museum No.:* H.290. *Location:* Marquesas.

8a.*Register:* Carved Paddle. *Museum No.:* H.303. *Location:* Marquesas.

9. *Register:* Carved Paddle. *Museum No.:* H.310. *Location:* Marquesas. *How obtained:* Presented Government of N.S.W. Sir J. Banks' Museum. Purchased J. Calvert.

10. *Register:* Small bowl. *Museum No.:* H.312. *Location:* Marquesas.

UNLOCALISED SPECIMENS

11. *Register:* Hook (bone pointed at one end and . . . barbed at other). *Museum No.:* H.139. *How obtained:* Presented Government of N.S.W. Purchased from John Mackrell.

12. *Register:* Necklace with a perforated gourd. *Museum No.:* H.118. *How obtained:* Presented Government of N.S.W. Purchased from (Rev. Canon F. Bennett, M.A.). *Card Gallery Label:* Musical Instrument?—Small gourd pierced with holes. (Rev. Canon F. Bennett, M.A.).

13. *Register:* Purse made with strung beads. *Museum No.:* H.157. *How obtained:* Presented Government of N.S.W. Acquired from Mrs. Thomas Langton. *Card Gallery Label:* Bead purse. Bag-shaped, of trade beads, with handle of coconut fibre. (Mrs. Thos. Langton.)

14. *Register:* Portion of Stone Axe. *Museum No.:* H.385. *How obtained:* Sir J. Banks' Museum. Purchased from J. Calvert.

15. *Register:* Stone Axe. *Museum No.:* H.379. *How obtained:* Sir J. Banks' Museum. Purchased from J. Calvert.

16. *Register:* Piece of red stone. *Museum No.:* H.378.

17. *Register:* Stone Axe without handle. *Museum No.:* H.349. *How obtained:* Presented Government of N.S.W.

18. *Register:* Scoop, of Horn. *Museum No.:* H.56. *How obtained:* Presented Government of N.S.W. Purchased from Rev. Canon Bennett.

19. *Register:* Carved Club? Marquesas. *Museum No.:* H.283. *Card Gallery Label:* Club—sapling of heavy hard wood, with the roots cut off, and handle carved. Fiji (probably obtained at Tonga, Friendly Is., S. Pacific).
20. *Register:* Matting with woven pattern. *Museum No.:* H.113. *How obtained:* Presented Government of N.S.W.
21. *Register:* Carved wooden implement (? horn). *Museum No.:* H.376. *How obtained:* Sir J. Banks' Museum. Purchased from J. Calvert.
22. *Register:* Small piece of coloured tapa (stuck on cardboard). *Museum No.:* H.204.
23. *Register:* Small piece of coloured tapa (stuck on cardboard). *Museum No.:* H.209.
24. *Register:* Small piece of coloured tapa (stuck on cardboard). *Museum No.:* H.206.
25. *Register:* Netting needle with fibre. *Museum No.:* H.153. *How obtained:* Purchased from John Mackrell.
26. *Register:* Small piece of coloured tapa (stuck on cardboard). *Museum No.:* H.202.
27. *Register:* Small piece of coloured tapa (stuck on cardboard). *Museum No.:* H.198.
28. *Register:* Small piece of coloured tapa (stuck on cardboard). *Museum No.:* H.196.
29. *Register:* Idol and charms (whale, turtles), carved ivory. *Museum No.:* H.151. *How obtained:* Acquired from Mrs. Thomas Langton.
30. *Register:* Shell. *Museum No.:* H.350. *How obtained:* Sir J. Banks' Museum. Purchased from J. Calvert. *Card Gallery Label:* (Breast ornament, golden cowrie. S.E. Pacific.) (D.R.M.)
31. *Register:* Small piece of coloured tapa (stuck on cardboard). *Museum No.:* H.211.
32. *Register:* Small piece of coloured tapa (stuck on cardboard). *Museum No.:* H.203.
33. *Register:* Small piece of coloured tapa (stuck on cardboard). *Museum No.:* H.205.
34. *Register:* 1 Wooden implement. *Museum No.:* H.368. *How obtained:* Presented Government of N.S.W.
35. *Register:* Large shell with string and hair attached. *Museum No.:* H.375. *How obtained:* Sir J. Banks' Museum. Purchased from J. Calvert.

NEW ZEALAND

36. *Register:* Fish Hook. *Museum No.:* H.386. *Location:* Pencil note in register—N.Z. Y. Sinoto. *How obtained:* Sir J. Banks' Museum. Purchased from J. Calvert. *Card Gallery Label:* (Boat shaped wooden shank with, reposing in it, a lure of iridescent Mutton shell (Haliotis Iris, Martyn); hook of bone, barbed—New Zealand).
37. *Register:* Fish Hook. *Museum No.:* H.326. *Location:* Pencil note in register—N.Z. Y. Sinoto. *How obtained:* Presented Government of N.S.W. Sir J. Banks' Museum. Purchased from J. Calvert. *Card Gallery Label:* (Piece of Mutton Shell (Haliotis Iris, Martyn) forming shank, with straight bone hook, New Zealand).
38. *Register:* Greenstone ear-ornament. *Museum No.:* H.334. *Location:* New Zealand. *How obtained:* Presented Government of N.S.W. Sir J. Banks' Museum. Purchased from J. Calvert.
39. *Register:* Fish Hook. *Museum No.:* H.138. *Location:* Register in pencil—N.Z. Y. Sinoto. *How obtained:* Presented Government of N.S.W. Purchased from John Mackrell. *Card Gallery Label:* (Fish Hook (Palu type). U-shaped pieces of wood, with a barbed bone point scarfed to the shorter arm of the shank. ? Tahitian Group, S. Pacific.)
40. *Register:* Fish Hook. *Museum No.:* H.137. *Location:* Register note in pencil—N.Z. Y. Sinoto. *Card Gallery Label:* (Fish Hook (Palu type). U-shaped pieces of wood, with a barbed bone point scarfed to the shorter arm of the shank. ? Tahitian Group, S. Pacific.)
41. *Register:* Jade Hatchet (unmounted). *Museum No.:* H.81. *How obtained:* Purchased

from John Mackrell. *Card Gallery Label:* (Adze Head. Stone with bevelled cutting edge New Zealand. J. Mackrell.)

42. *Register:* Greenstone ear-ornament (in fact, Nephrite—"N.Z. Jade"). *Museum No.:* H.332. *Location:* New Zealand. *How obtained:* Sir J. Banks' Museum. Purchased from J. Calvert.

43. *Register:* Greenstone ear-ornament (in fact, Nephrite—"N.Z. Jade"). *Museum No.:* H.333. *Location:* New Zealand. *How obtained:* Sir J. Banks' Museum. Purchased from J. Calvert.

44. *Register:* N.Z. Jade ear-ornament (in fact, Nephrite—"N.Z. Jade"). *Museum No.:* H.63. *Location:* New Zealand. *How obtained:* Purchased from Rev. Canon Bennett.

45. *Register:* Carved Paddle. *Museum No.:* H.302. *Location:* Marquesas ? locality from register. *How obtained:* Sir J. Banks' Museum. Purchased from J. Calvert. *Card Gallery Label:* (Paddle—carved with scroll-work on half the blade, the handle end is formed by a representation of a tattooed human head. New Zealand.)

46. *Register:* Jade ear-ornament. *Museum No.:* H.156. *Location:* New Zealand.

47. *Register:* Carved Wooden Mere. *Museum No.:* H.363. *Location:* New Zealand. *Card Gallery Label:* Mere, or Patou-Patou. Wood, cleaver-shaped.

48. *Register:* Greenstone axe. New Zealand. *Museum No.:* H.335. *Card Gallery Label:* "Axe-blade". Impure Nephrite or Jade. New Caledonia, S. Pacific.

49. *Register:* Axe-blade. *Museum No.:* H.383. *How obtained:* Sir J. Banks' Collection. *Card Gallery Label:* "Axe-blade." Black eruptive rock, bevelled on both faces. New Zealand.

50. *Register:* (Trnsf. to Mitchell Library. Greenstone Axe. N.Z.). *Museum No.:* H.82. *Card Gallery Label:* Adze or axe—Greenstone. Dusky Bay?, South Is., New Zealand. (J. Mackrell.)

51. *Register:* (Trnsf. to Mitchell Library). Axe (?) Adze. *Museum No.:* H.83. *Card Gallery Label:* Adze or Axe. Greenstone. Dusky Bay?, South Is., New Zealand. (J. Mackrell.)

52. *Register:* Old Collection. Cook Relics. Found unreg. when transferring "Cook" specimens to new building on date—1956 (?). *Museum No.:* H.612. *Card Gallery Label:* "Axe-blade." Dense, blackish-green Nephrite or Jade (?), bevelled on both faces. New Zealand.

53. *Register:* Stone Axe. *Museum No.:* H.384. *Location:* New Zealand. *How obtained:* Sir J. Banks' Collection. *Card Gallery Label:* Stone Axe "Toki". N.Z.

54. *Register:* Stone mere. *Museum No.:* H.319. *Location:* New Zealand.

55. *Register:* Stone mere. *Museum No.:* H.318. *Location:* New Zealand.

56. *Register:* Stone mere. *Museum No.:* H.317. *Location:* New Zealand.

57. *Register:* Whale's bone mere. N.Z. *Museum No.:* H.364. *Location:* New Zealand. *Card Gallery Label:* Handle (? Axe). Whale's bone, carved, & ornamented with Mutton shell. (Haliotis) discs. [No haliotis discs on specimen.]

SOCIETY ISLANDS

58. *Register:* Human bone. Pencil note—Society—Y. Sinoto. *Museum No.:* H.136. *How obtained:* Purchased from John Mackrell. *Card Gallery Label:* Fish Hook—Shank of white Mother-of-Pearl, and barbed hook of bone. Tahiti Group. S. Pacific.

59. *Museum No.:* H.327. *How obtained:* Presented Government of N.S.W. Sir J. Banks' Museum. Purchased from J. Calvert. *Card Gallery Label:* Fish Hook—Mother-of-Pearl shank and barb, with a bridle from the latter to proximal end of former. Tahiti Group Society Is., S. Pacific.

60. *Museum No.:* H.130. *How obtained:* Presented Government of N.S.W. Purchased from John Mackrell. *Card Gallery Label:* Fish Hook—Shank of Mother-of-Pearl, and unbarbed hook of Turtle Shell. Tahiti Group, S. Pacific.

61. *Register:* Pencil note in register—Society—Y. Sinoto. *Museum No.:* H.135. *How obtained:* Purchased from John Mackrell. *Card Gallery Label:* Fish Hook. Semi-circular-recurved, of thick white Mother-of-Pearl, with plain painted apex and proximal crutch-like termination, to which line is made fast. Tahiti Group, S. Pacific.

62. *Register:* Fish Hook & lines (Mother-of-Pearl & Tortoise-shell). Pencil note—Society—Y. Sinoto. *Museum No.:* H.133. *How obtained:* Purchased from John Mackrell. Presented Government of N.S.W. *Card Gallery Label:* Fish Hook. Mattou. Shank of Mother-of-Pearl, and unbarbed hook of black Mother-of-Pearl. Tahiti Group, S. Pacific.

63. *Register:* Fish Hook—Mattou.—Shank of Mother-of-Pearl, and unbarbed hook of Turtle Shell. Tahiti Group, S. Pacific. *Museum No.:* H.132. *Card Gallery Label:* Fish Hook—Mattou.—Shank of Mother-of-Pearl, and unbarbed hook of Turtle Shell. Tahiti Group, S. Pacific.

64. *Register:* Fish Hook—Mattou.—Shank of Mother-of-Pearl, and unbarbed hook of Turtle Shell. Tahiti Group, S. Pacific. *Museum No.:* H.134. *Card Gallery Label:* Fish Hook—Mattou.—Shank of Mother-of-Pearl, and unbarbed hook of Turtle Shell. Tahiti Group, S. Pacific.

65. *Register:* Coloured Tahiti Cloth. (Stuck on cardboard.) *Museum No.:* H.94. *How obtained:* Purchased from John Mackrell.

66. *Register:* Coloured Tahiti Cloth. (Stuck on cardboard.) *Museum No.:* H.95. *Location:* Could be from Sandwich Is. *How obtained:* Purchased from John Mackrell.

67. *Register:* Ordinary shoe buckle. *Museum No.:* H.191 (wrong number). *Location:* Could be from Sandwich Is. *How obtained:* Purchased from John Mackrell. *Card Gallery Label:* Specimen is actually a small piece of coloured Tapa stuck on cardboard.

68. *Register:* Small piece of coloured Tapa. Stuck on cardboard. *Museum No.:* H.201. *Location:* Could be from Sandwich Is.

69. *Register:* Small piece of coloured Tapa. Stuck on cardboard. *Museum No.:* H.199. *Location:* Could be from Sandwich Is.

70. *Register:* Jade Hatchet. *Museum No.:* H.146. *How obtained:* Purchased from John Mackrell. *Card Gallery Label:* Hafted adze. The stone head is bound on with coarse sinnet. ? Tahiti, Society Is., S. Pacific.

71. *Register:* Small Adze. *Museum No.:* H.315. *Location:* ? Australia (but specimen not Australian) likely Tahiti (?).

72. *Register:* Part of a chief mourner's dress; strung Mother-of-Pearl. *Museum No.:* H.149. *How obtained:* Purchased from John Mackrell. *Card Gallery Label:* (Pearl Shell pieces strung with trade bead pendants, possibly Tahiti, Soc. Is.). (D.R.M.)

73. *Register:* Large basket with shells interwoven. *Museum No.:* H.102. *Location:* ? Tonga. *How obtained:* Purchased from John Mackrell. *Card Gallery Label:* (Large bag, woven from coconut fibre (sinnet), decorated with cone shells and seed beads. Possibly Tahiti, Soc. Is.). (D.R.M.)

74. *Register:* Gorget, used to protect the neck and chest when fighting. (Cf Cook's First Voyage. Vol.II, pl. no.8, following page 184.) *Museum No.:* H.105. *How obtained:* Purchased from John Mackrell. *Card Gallery Label:* Woven chest plate used as protection in battle. Sinnet, Pigeon feathers, sharks teeth, pearl shell, Fringe—(?) dog hair. (?) Tahiti, Soc. Is. (D.R.M.)

75. *Register:* Mother-of-Pearl fish hook & line. *Museum No.:* H.140. *Location:* (possibly Tahiti Group). *How obtained:* Purchased from John Mackrell.

76. *Register:* Fish Hook & Line (Mother-of-Pearl & Tortoise-shell). *Museum No.:* H.131. *Location:* (possibly Tahiti Group). *How obtained:* Purchased from John Mackrell.

77. *Register:* Tortoise-shell fish hook. *Museum No.:* H.330. *Location:* (possibly Tahiti Group). *How obtained:* Sir J. Banks' Museum. Purchased from J. Calvert.

78. *Register:* Stone Adze. *Museum No.:* H.316. *Card Gallery Label:* Small adze. Head of dense black stone (volcanic), triangular in section, bound to handle-chock with fine two-ply coconut sinnet braid; the chock with two studs S.E. Pacific. (? Tahiti, Society Group). Specimen had no number or identification attached, but does seem to match up with cardboard description.

79. *Register:* Adze. (Cf Cook's First Voyage. Vol.II pl. no.9 (in pc.) 1773.) *Museum No.:* H.320. *Card Gallery Label:* Heavy adze. Head of dense black stone (volcanic), triangular in section, bound to handle-chock with coarse two-ply coconut sinnet braid; the chock long behind, and cleat-like. S.E. Pacific. (? Tahiti.)

80. *Register:* Court shoe buckle. *Museum No.:* H.192 (wrong number). *Location:* Could be from Sandwich Is. *How obtained:* Purchased from John Mackrell. *Card Gallery Label:* Specimen is small piece of coloured Tapa Cloth. Stuck on cardboard.

81. *Register:* Small piece of coloured Tapa. Stuck on cardboard. *Museum No.:* H.207. *Location:* Could be from Sandwich Is.

82. *Register:* Small piece of coloured Tapa. Stuck on cardboard. *Museum No.:* H.210. *Location:* Could be from Tahiti.

83. *Register:* Coloured Tahiti Cloth. Stuck on cardboard. *Museum No.:* H.95. *How obtained:* Purchased John Mackrell. *Card Gallery Label:* Coloured Tapa Cloth.

84. *Museum No.:* H.99. *How obtained:* Purchased J. Mackrell. *Card Gallery Label:* Tapa Cloth. Fine quality, without pattern. Tahiti, Society Is., S. Pacific.

85. *Register:* Cloak of matting, worn by Tahiti Chief. *Museum No.:* H.103. *How obtained:* Purchased from John Mackrell. *Card Gallery Label:* (Ink note sewn to specimen— bought by Capt. Cook from Otaheite. A mantle worn by one of the natives.)

86. *Register:* White Tapa cloth (strip stuck on cardboard). *Museum No.:* H.101. *Location:* Could be from Tahiti. *How obtained:* Purchased from John Mackrell.

87. *Register:* Pce. finely-woven tapa-white (strip stuck on cardboard). Note in register states trnsf. to Mitchell Library, 1955, but Museum still holds specimen.) *Museum No.:* H.215. *Location:* Could be from Tahiti.

88. *Register:* Pce. finely-woven tapa-white (strip stuck on cardboard). Note in register states trnsf. to Mitchell Library, 1955. *Museum No.:* H.216. *Location:* could be from Tahiti.

89. *Register:* Pce. finely-woven tapa-white. (Strip stuck on cardboard). Note in register states trnsf. to Mitchell Library, 1955. *Museum No.:* H.217. *Location:* Could be from Tahiti.

90. *Register:* Pce. finely-woven tapa-white. (Strip stuck on cardboard). Note in register states trnsf. to Mitchell Library, 1955. *Museum No.:* H.218. *Location:* Could be from Tahiti.

91. *Register:* Matting, worn in wet weather instead of cloth. *Museum No.:* H.98. *How obtained:* Presented Government of N.S.W. Purchased from John Mackrell. *Card Gallery Label:* (Ink note attached to specimen—bought by Capt. Cook from Otaheite. This mantle was worn by a chief of Otaheite.) (Cloak. Strips of Screw-Pine (Pandanus) leaves, with marginal fringe, and brown-stained ornamental border; used as a body covering or cloak in wet weather.)

92. *Museum No.:* H.97. *How obtained:* Purchased from John Mackrell. *Card Gallery Label:* Tapa cloth. Fine quality, with X-figure pattern. Tahiti, Society Is., S. Pacific.

93. *Register:* Idol and charms. *Museum No.:* H.151. *Location:* Hawaiian 20., N. Pacific. *How obtained:* Presented Government of N.S.W. acquired from Mrs. Thomas Langton. *Card Gallery Label:* Neck pendants—Human figure of ivory suspended round the neck by human hair string (King). Hawaiian 20., N. Pacific. (Mrs. Thomas Langton). Bird figure of ivory, suspended round the neck by human hair string.

94. *Museum No.:* H.150. *How obtained:* Presented Government of N.S.W. Purchased from Rev. Canon F. Bennett, M.A. *Card Gallery Label:* (Finger Ring. Turtle-shell with shark (*Carcharias lamia*, Risso) tooth attached. ? Tahiti, Society Is., S. Pacific. (Rev. Canon F. Bennett, M.A.)

95. *Museum No.:* H.114. *How obtained:* Presented Government of N.S.W. *Card Gallery Label:* Foundation for feather-cloak. Olona fibre (bark of *Touchardia latifolia*, Goudich), allied to the well-known Ramie fibre. The fine net, or nae, was formed with a netting needle, both the fineness and size of the thread varying in different, or even the same cloak; made in strips of eight to twelve inches, and joined together. (Brigham). Hawaii, Hawaiian Islands, N. Pacific.

96. *Register:* Feather Necklace. *Museum No.:* E.4403. *Location:* Hawaiian Is. *How obtained:* Exch. B.P. Bishop Museum. See catalogue of B.P.B. Museum, & papers relative to the exchange for further information about these necklaces. (4 bird feather necklets given to Capt. Cook.)

97. *Register:* Feather Necklace. *Museum No.:* E.4402. *Location:* Hawaiian Is. *How obtained:* Exch. B.P. Bishop Museum. See Catalogue of B.P.B. Museum, & papers relative to the exchange for further information about these necklaces. (4 bird feather necklets given to Capt. Cook.)

98. *Register:* Hawaiian helmet originally covered with feathers and presented by Halaviopuie, King of Hawaii, to Capt. Cook, Jan.26, 1779. *Museum No.:* H.141. *Location:* Hawaii.

99. *Register:* Shark's Tooth fitted as a knife. *Museum No.:* H.111. *Location:* Sandwich Is· *How obtained:* Purchased from Rev. Canon Bennett. *Card Gallery Label:* Figured· Cook's 3rd Voyage, vol.3, 2nd edition, pl.67, (near p.150) Fig. 2, A.M.Lib. 10769· "Instrument with which they cut up their prisoners." Plate penultimate to p.541, fig.6.

100. *Register:* Hawaiian Feather Cloak. *Museum No.:* H.104. *How obtained:* Purchased from Rev. Canon Bennett. *Card Gallery Label:* (Feather cape as worn by Chief. Honey eater and tropic frigate birds, Hawaii. Very rare). (D.R.M.)

101. *Register:* Shell fishing hooks (2). *Museum No.:* H.328–9. *How obtained:* Sir J. Banks' Museum. Purchased from J. Calvert. *Card Gallery Label:* (Pearl & turtle shell fish hook. Tahiti, Soc. Is.). (D.R.M.)

102. *Register:* Tapa. *Museum No.:* H.92. *Location:* Tahiti. *How obtained:* Purchased from John Mackrell.

103. *Register:* Tapa. *Museum No.:* H.93. *Location:* Tahiti. *How obtained:* Purchased from John Mackrell.

104. *Register:* Gorget—feathered. *Museum No.:* H.145. *Location:* Polynesia. *Card Gallery Label:* Stiff Gorget—Ta—omee. Donned in war as a protection to the chest. The base consists of highly finished four and five ply sinnet-braid plaited into one inch bands which overlap. The two cervical rows are bare, the others are ornamented with Pigeon feathers and edged with Shark's teeth, (*Carcharias lamia*, Risso.) with a circumferential edge of Dog's hair, and along the clavicular margins are three discs of pearl shell on each side. Tahiti, Society Is., S. Pacific. (H. Cook Smith.)

MISCELLANEOUS ITEMS

105. *Register:* Collecting bottle, said to be either Banks' or Solander's. Formed part of the Calvert Collection as it still bears traces of the MS. label of Sir Jos. Banks. *See* Cook's M.S.A.M.Lib. 10406. Letter dated at London 25 Sept., 1885. *Museum No.:* H.494. *Card Gallery Label:* (Collecting bottle—glass lined metal container—D.R.M.) Wm Adams, F.R.C.S. Engl. Pres. Government of N.S.W. in remarks column = Pres. by William Adams. *Card Gallery Label:* Commemorative Medal. Medal struck by the Royal Society of London, in 1784, in memory of Capt. James Cook, R.N., F.R.S. *Obverse:*—Bust of Cook to the left, and around margin—Jac. Cook

Oceani Investigator Acerimus, and on the exergue below—Reg.Soc.Lond./Socio Suo.

Reverse:—A figure of Britannia holding a spear in the left hand, the right holding a rudder resting on a globe; behind, a pedestal and shield; around margin is Nil intentatum nostri Liquere, and on the exergue—Auspiciis/Georgii/III/.

106. *Register*: Collecting bottle, said to be either Banks' or Solander's. Probably the flask referred to in the *Illustrated Sydney News*, 18.2.1871, and presented to Mr. Pittard, about 1860. *Museum No.*: H.495.

107. *Register*: Arrow stated to be partly made from the small leg bone of Capt. Cook. *Museum No.*: H.68. *How obtained*: Presented by William Adams.

108. *Register*: Statement of Rev. T.N. Staley, Bishop of Honolulu, as to the arrow with one of the supposed small leg-bones of Capt. Cook. *Museum No.*: H.70. *How obtained*: Presented. Wm Adams, F.R.C.S.

109. *Register*: Sheet Souvenir of Capt. Cook, bearing portrait and two journal extracts, as written in August, 1770. Presented by the Committee of the Commonwealth National Library, 1924. *Museum No.*: H.748.

110. *Register*: 2 Medals struck by Royal Soc. Has head George III on one side and one of "Resolution" & "Adventure" on the other. *Museum No.*: H.60. *How obtained*: Pres.

111. *Museum No.*: N.1189. *Card Gallery Label*: Copley Medal. The Sir Copley Medal of the Royal Society of London, presented by the Council in 1776 to Capt. James Cook, R.N., F.R.S., in recognition of a Paper read before the Society, March 7th, 1776, on "The Method taken for preserving the Health of the Crew of His Majesty's Ship the "Resolution" during her Late Voyage Round the World." The medal is the highest scientific distinction the Royal Society can bestow. The original is preserved in the British Museum, London. Pres. Trustees British Museum— (Electrotype).

112. *Register*: Dr. Green's statement—Statement by Mr. J.H. Green, D.C.L., F.R.S., President of the Royal College of Surgeons of England, and Senior Surgeon to St. Thomas' Hospital, London, as to the arrow with one of the supposed small leg-bones of Capt. Cook. *Museum No.*: H.69. *How obtained*: Presented Wm Adams, F.R.C.S. England.

113. *Register*: Oak timber said to be from S. "*Brotherly Love*" in which Capt. Cook was supposed to have served. *Museum No.*: H.493.

114. *Register*: "Note in register—probably the flask referred to in the *Illustrated Sydney News* 18.2.1871, and presented to Mr. Pittard, about 1860." *Museum No.*: H.495. *Card Gallery Label*: Collecting bottle. Oblong glass bottle encased in sheet iron, with bent over handle. Said to have belonged to Sir J. Banks and Dr. Solander, naturalists to Capt. Cook's First Expd., 1768–71 when the east coast of Australia was discovered.

AUSTRALIA

115. *Register*: Boomerang. *Museum No.*: H.313. *Location*: Australia. *How obtained*: Presented Government of N.S.W. Sir J. Banks' Museum. Purchased from J. Calvert.

116. *Register*: Boomerang. *Museum No.*: H.314. *Location*: Australia (prob. E. Australia). *How obtained*: Sir J. Banks' Museum. Purchased from J. Calvert.

117. *Register*: Plain club. *Museum No.*: H.294. *Location*: (prob. E. Australia). *How obtained*: Sir J. Banks' Museum. Purchased from J. Calvert.

NEW CALEDONIA

118. *Museum No.*: H.115. *How obtained*: Presented Government of N.S.W. Purchased from John Mackrell. *Card Gallery Label*: (Oblong Pouch. Finely knitted, of beaten

bark string with knitted string bags at ends, both for holding sling-stones used by slingers, and the whole worn as a belt. Balade, New Caledonia, S. Pacific).

119. *Museum No.:* H.119. *Card Gallery Label:* (Spear Gasket, or Throwing Cord.—Ounep. Plaited and decorated spear—throwing cord, with suspended ornaments of carved bone, and Kauri gum beads. The right fore-finger of the thrower is inserted in the loop at one end, and a turn of the knotted extremity taken round the spear. It enables the spearsman to throw with greater force and accuracy, and produces a rotary motion. Balade, N.E. New Caledonia, S. Pacific.)

120. *Register:* Comb for hair. Cf. Cook's 2nd Voyage. Vol.2, pl.20 (near p.121) fig.4. *Museum No.:* H.108. *Location:* N. Caledonia. (D.R.M.) *How obtained:* Acquired from Mrs. Thomas Langton. *Card Gallery Label:* (Hair pin or head scratchers. Wood.) (?)

121. *Register:* Comb for hair. *Museum No.:* H.109. *Location:* New Caledonia. (D.R.M.) *How obtained:* Purchased from John Mackrell. *Card Gallery Label:* (Hairpins or head scratchers (?) Wood. New Caledonia). (D.R.M.)

122. *Register:* Spear Gasket New Caledonia. Cf. Cook's 2nd Voyage. Vol.2, pl.20, (near p.121), figure 5. *Museum No.:* H.119. *Location:* New Caledonia.

FIJI

123. *Register:* Curved Club. *Museum No.:* H.284. *Location:* No locality given. *How obtained:* Sir J. Banks' Museum. *Card Gallery Label:* (Pineapple Club. Heavy dark wood; said to be used for killing the wounded after battle, and victims for the feast. Fiji (probably obtained at Tonga, Friendly Islands) (S. Pacific).)

TONGA

124. *Register:* Fish Hook. *Museum No.:* H.123. *Location:* Pencil note in register—Tonga. *How obtained:* Presented Government of N.S.W. *Card Gallery Label:* (Shank of bone, backed by Mother-of-Pearl, and a hook of Tortoise Shell bent on itself and barbed. Tahiti Grp., S. Pacific.)

125. *Museum No.:* H.127. *Location:* Pencil note in register—Tonga. *How obtained:* Presented Government of N.S.W. *Card Gallery Label:* (Fish Hook—Mattou—Shank of bone, backed by Mother-of-Pearl, and a hook of Tortoise shell bent on itself and barbed. Tahiti Group, S. Pacific . . . Tahiti crossed out in Pencil and "Tonga" written in.)

126. *Register:* Fish hook and line (Tortoise shell and bone). *Museum No.:* H.124. *Location:* Pencil note in register—Tonga. *How obtained:* Presented Government of N.S.W. Purchased from John Mackrell.

127. *Register:* Comb. *Museum No.:* H.351. *How obtained:* Sir J. Banks' Museum. Purchased from J. Calvert. *Card Gallery Label:* (Comb (portion). Fifteen palm-leaf midribs bound with grass or rush. ? Tonga (Tongatabu), Friendly Is., S. Pacific.)

128. *Register:* Fish hook and line. *Museum No.:* H.121. *Location:* Written in register in pencil—Tonga. *Card Gallery Label:* (Fish Hook—Mattou—Shank of bone, backed by Mother-of-Pearl, and a hook of tortoise shell bent on itself and barbed. Tahiti Grp., S. Pacific.)

129. *Register:* Fish Hook and line. Tortoise shell and bone. *Museum No.:* H.125. *Location:* Pencil note in register—Tonga. *How obtained:* Purchased from John Mackrell.

130. *Register:* Carved Club. Marquesas. *Museum No.:* H.285. *Gallery Label:* Pineapple club. Heavy dark wood; said to be used for killing the wounded after battle, and victims for the feast. Fiji. (Probably obtained at Tonga, Friendly Is., S. Pacific.)

131. *Register:* Carved Club. Marquesas. *Museum No.:* H.287. *Card Gallery Label:* Round Club. Heavy dark wood (*Casuaeina*) elaborately carved. Tonga (Tongatabu), Friendly Is., S. Pacific. (Fiji derived.)

132. *Register:* Fish Hook and line. *Museum No.:* H.126. *Location:* Tonga.

133. *Register:* Fish Hook and line. *Museum No.:* H.128. *Location:* Tonga.

SOUTH AFRICA

134. *Museum No.:* H.373. *Location:* South Africa. *How obtained:* Sir J. Banks' Museum. Purchased from J. Calvert. *Card Gallery Label:* (Castanets. Shell of Tortoise (Homopur areolatus. Thunb). with two wooden clappers and a plaited raw-hide holdfast. South Africa).

NEW HEBRIDES

135. *Register:* Paw Pipe. Cf. Journ. of Polyn. Soc., Vol.41, March 1932. Suppt. page 23. *Museum No.:* H.112. *How obtained:* Purchased from John Mackrell. *Card Gallery Label:* (Bamboo paw pipes—New Hebrides). (D.R.M.)

136. *Register:* Wooden Comb (carved). *Museum No.:* H.110. *Location:* (New Hebrides). (D.R.M.) *How obtained:* Purchased from John Mackrell.

AMERICAS

137. *Museum No.:* H.377 Specimen wrongly numbered—shows H.337 should be H.377. *Card Gallery Label:* Nose style. Bone, 5 inches long, roughly made. N.W. America (? Prince William Sound).

138. *Register:* Wood and bone fish hook. *Museum No.:* H.331. *How obtained:* Presented Government of N.S.W. Sir J. Banks' Museum. Purchased from J. Calvert. *Card Gallery Label:* Fish Hook? Sickle-shaped wooden shank, with straight bone hook, bound on with bark. ? North-East America.

139. *Register:* Grappling Implement—(bone harpoon head. Vancouver—written in register in pencil). *Museum No.:* H.106. *How obtained:* Purchased from John Mackrell. *Card Gallery Label:* (Harpoon Head. Bone head once barbed, split at base for reception of shaft plug; line of sinew eight feet long, terminating in a loop, whipped with plaited beaten bark string, and served over with cedar (?) bark, attached to head by-serving of the same and resin. Vancouver Is. N.E. America.)

140. *Register:* Fish hook and line (bone barb). *Museum No.:* H.122. *Location:* Vancouver (written in pencil). *How obtained:* Purchased from John Mackrell.

MELANESIA

141. *Register:* Shell armlet. *Museum No.:* H.337. *How obtained:* Sir J. Banks' Museum. Purchased from J. Calvert. *Card Gallery Label:* (Cone shell armlets—Melanesia (?) (D.R.M.)

3721

Printed Books, Articles, Manuscripts, etc., about the Relics

[1775?] BANKS, *Sir* Joseph
List of native artifacts probably from the voyage to the Pacific Islands, citing the native names of some items. Written, probably in Banks' hand, on the margin and verso of a letter from the Royal Society to Banks, 24 July 1775.

f.1, cm 33.
Found loose inside P. Briscoe's journal, NPL:D MS.96.
Copies: NPL:D(MS.Q158,pp.1–2). 3722

1776 PATERSON, Samuel

Catalogue of a curious collection of natural and artificial rarities, lately brought over from the new-discover'd islands in the South Seas, in His Majesty's ship *Resolution* . . . late the property of Mr. S. Jackson, deceased; which will be sold by auction . . . 14th March 1776, and the following day. [London, 1776.]

pp.12.

Copies: NPL:M(571/P). 3723

1785 DE CASTRIES

Copy of letter in French from de Castries to Sir Joseph Banks, May, 1785, re the loan to La Pérouse of two compasses used by Cook.

(Expédition de La Pérouse, 1785–8. pp.114–5.)

Transcripts of documents in the Service Hydrographique de la Marine, Paris.

Copies: NPL:M(MS.B1207). 3724

1790 LEVERIAN MUSEUM

A Companion to the Museum, late Sir Ashton Lever's, removed to Albion St. (Pt.1.) London, MDCCXC.

Illus. 2 vols.

The Museum contained items on Pacific Island, New Zealand, Australia, and some associated with Captain Cook. *See also* no. 3726.

Copies: NPL:M(060/L, pt.1 only); ANL. 3725

1806 LEVERIAN MUSEUM

Catalogue of the Leverian Museum [of Sir Ashton Lever] . . . The sale of the entire collection by Messrs. King and Lochee . . . 5th May 1806. London, Hayden Pr., [1806].

7pts. in 1, pp.296+17.

Wtg. appendix of last 5 days sale. Catalogue compiled by Edward Donovan. Part of *Every-day Book* Jy.18? with notes on the Museum bound with above. Many objects sold were collected by Captain Cook. *See also* no.3725.

Copies: NPL:M(570.7/L). 3726

1810 BULLOCK, William

Companion to Mr. Bullock's Museum, containing a brief description of upwards of seven thousand natural and foreign curiosities, antiquities and productions of the fine arts, etc. 8th ed. London, Henry Reynell and Son, pr., 1810.

Frontisp. pp.iv, 98.

Cover title: Descriptive catalogue of extensive museum of natural history, antiquities, etc. Many objects associated with Captain Cook and Sir Joseph Banks. *See also* nos. 3728–30.

Copies: NPL:M(507/B). 3727

1811 BULLOCK, William

Companion to Mr. Bullock's Museum, containing a brief description of upwards of ten thousand natural and foreign curiosities, antiquities and productions of the fine arts, etc. 10th ed. London, Henry Reynell pr., 1811.

Frontisp. pp.vi, 150.
Cover title: Descriptive catalogue of Mr. Bullock's extensive Museum. *See also* nos.3727, 3729–30.

Copies: NPL:M(507/B).   3728

1812 BULLOCK, William

Companion to Mr. Bullock's Museum, containing a brief description of upwards of fifteen thousand . . . curiosities etc. 12th ed. London, printed for the proprietor, 1812.

Illus. pp.xii, 136, pl.31.
Plates are hand-coloured engravings.
Cover title: Bullock's Museum. *See also* 3727–8, 3730.

Copies: NPL:M(507/B).   3729

1813 BULLOCK, William

Companion to the London Museum and Pantherion, containing a brief description of upwards of fifteen thousand national and foreign curiosities, etc. 15th ed. London, Whittingham & Rowland pr., 1813.

Frontisp. pp.xii, 151.
See also nos. 3727–9.

Copies: NPL:M(507/B).   3730

1813 PHILPOT, T.

Captain Cook's relics: [an article describing the advertisement in the *Western Luminary* Sept. 28, 1813 for auction sale of some possessions of Cook].

pp.4.
Bound with *Western Luminary* Sept.28, 1813.

Copies: NPL:M(Q923.9/C771.2/2A1).   3731

1813 *WESTERN LUMINARY:* the family newspaper . . . of the counties of Devon, Cornwall, Dorset & Somerset. Vol.1, no.30, Sept.28, 1813. Exeter, P. Flindell.

pp.8.
With advertisement on p.1, with heading *Museum*, which is a notice of an auction sale of c.300 lots previously in the possession of Captain Cook, at the White Horse, Lifton, 4th Oct., etc.

Copies: NPL:M(Q923.9/C771.2/2A1).   3732

1819 LONDON MUSEUM OF NATURAL HISTORY

Catalogue of the Roman Gallery of works of art and the London Museum of Natural History which will commence selling by auction . . . April 29, 1819 by Mr. Bullock. London, 1819.

Part 1–3, pp.114.
The British Museum holds five parts of this work. Contains Cook items *viz.* 31, 34, 44 of 6th day.
Copies: NPL:M(503/L). 3733

1849 KREEST, Christopher

ALS dated Billiter Sq., 4 Apr. 1849 to J.E. Taylor, Red Lion Court: re Molesworth Phillips' MS. of 'Capt. Cooke's last Voyage'; that he doesn't think it has anything about California; that he has Cook's powder horn & Phillips' gun; that the MS. was sent up to the Admiralty on the arrival of the Vessel and returned with other officer's private accounts after the official publication of the voyage.
Copies: NPL:D(MS.95). 3734

[1878–1913] NEWSPAPER cuttings, 1878–1913 relating to the log and relics connected with Captain Cook.

The log, relics and this volume were formerly in the Australian Museum, Sydney, and were transferred to the Mitchell Library, Oct. 1955.
Copies: NPL:M(MS.A3937). 3735

1879 HAMY, Ernest Théodore

Catalogue descriptif et méthodique de l'exposition organisée par la Société de Géographie à l'occasion du centenaire de la mort de Cook.
(Société de Géographie—Centenaire de la mort de Cook. Paris, Delagrave, 1879. pp.444–480.)
Extract from Société de Géographie—*Bulletin*, May, 1879.
Copies: NPL:M(923.9/C771.2/9A1). 3736

1879 HAMY, Ernest Théodore

Catalogue descriptif et méthodique de l'exposition organisée par la Société de Géographie à l'occasion du centenaire de la mort de Cook.
(Société de Géographie—Centenaire de la mort de Cook. Paris, the Society, 1879. pp.44–80.)
Extract from Société de Géographie—*Bulletin*, May, 1879.
Copies: NPL:M(923.9/C771.2/9B1); NPL:D(87/120); NPL:R(S920/C771/9). 3737

1879 MEYER, Adolf Bernhard

Cook's collections [in Vienna].
(*Nature*, vol.19, 1879, p.409.)
Copies: NPL:M(Q505/N); NPL:R(DQ505/1). 3738

1886 COLONIAL AND INDIAN EXHIBITION, *London*

Catalogue of the collection of relics of the late Captain James Cook . . .
exhibited by Mr. John Mackrell at the request of the Government of
New South Wales, in the court of that colony. N.p. 1886.

pp.7.

(Australian Museum—Papers re Cook relics, vol.2, 1887.)

With MS. annotations.

Copies: NPL:M(MS.A3935). 3739

1887 COPY of the statutory declaration made by Rev.F. Bennett and
J. Mackrell, July 26, 1887; previously held by the Australian Museum
in connection with their collection of Cook relics.

(Miscellaneous primary and secondary source material re the life and voyages of Captain
James Cook.)

Copies: NPL:M(MS.A1713⁻³ item 4, no.iv). 3740

1887–95 AUSTRALIAN MUSEUM, *Sydney*

Papers re Cook relics: [manuscript and typescript. 1887–95].

2 vols.

Copies: NPL:M(MS.A3935). 3741

1888 WHITE, Taylor

On the relics of Captain Cook's last voyage.

(New Zealand Institute—*Transactions and Proceedings*, vol.21, pp.397–8, 1888.)

Copies: NPL:M(506/N); NPL:D(9/93); NPL:R(DS506/8). 3742

1890–98 PARTINGTON, James Edge-

An Album of the weapons, tools, ornaments, articles of dress etc. of the
natives of the Pacific Islands; drawn and described from examples in
public and private collections in England (and Australasia) by J. Edge-
Partington. Issued for private circulation by J. Edge-Partington and
Charles Heape. Ser. 1–3. Manchester, various pubs., 1890–98.

Lithographs, 3 vols.

Copies: NPL:M(F572.99/P); NPL:R(F572.99/1–3, S.C.). 3743

1893–5 GIGLIOLI, Enrico Hillyer

Appunti intorno ad una collezione etnografica fatta durante il terzo
viaggio di Cook e conservata sin dalla fine del secolo scorso nel R. Museo
di Fisica, e Storia Naturale di Firenze. Firenze, 1893–5.

Illus.

Copies: NPL:M(Q572.99/G); ANL; VSL. 3744

1894 CAPTAIN COOK relics, interesting memorials now in Sydney
Museum.

Illus.

(Australian Town and Country Journal, Nov.10, 1894, pp.19–20.)

Copies: NPL:R(F079/A938).   3745

[19– –] THORPE, William Walford

Notes about ethnographical artifacts collected during Cook's voyages,
compiled by W.W. Thorpe, ethnologist. Includes notes on the Calvert
collection of artifacts.

Copies: NPL:D(MS.Q146).   3746

1900 PARTINGTON, James Edge-

Cook's voyages illustrated by specimens in the Cook collection in the
British Museum. London, 1900.

Photographs, with descriptions extracted from accounts of the voyages.

Copies: VSL.   3747

1901 MAIDEN, Joseph Henry

Two historical notes in regard to Captain Cook . . . 1. The club which
it is believed partly contributed to his death . . . 2. Inscription on a
mural tablet and gravestone commemorating some of Captain Cook's
family.

(Royal Society of New South Wales—*Journal and proceedings*, 1901, pp.47–52.)

Copies: NPL:M(506/R); NPL:D(90/213); NPL:R(DS506/9); ANL:F.   3748

1918 BRIGHAM, William Tufts

[Cook relics in Vienna, Petrograd, Sydney, etc.]

Illus.

(*In his* Additional notes on Hawaiian feather work, Honolulu, 1918. Supp.2, pp.1–15.)

Bernice Pauahi Bishop Museum—*Memoirs*, vol.7, no.1.

Copies: NPL:M(Q507/B); NPL:R(DQ572.999/4).   3749

1918–32 THORPE, William Walford

Notes relating to the Cook Relics. The property of W.W. Thorpe, being
a personal gift from the late Mr. Etheridge in 1918 with added notes
&c. by W.W. Thorpe. 1918–1932.

Illus. 2 vols.

Contents lists and subject keys made and inserted, 1968. The notes, mainly in the hand of
W.W. Thorpe, were compiled c.1918–1932 whilst he was working as ethnologist with the
Australian Museum, Sydney. The notes include photos and sketches, copies of correspon-
dence, and extracts from periodicals relating to the relics.

Copies: NPL:D(MS.Q145).   3750

1926 BARR, Flinders
Captain Cook's boomerang.

Illus.
(Newspaper cuttings: Captain Cook, 187––1935. Vol.1, p.111.)
Extract from the *Sydney Morning Herald*, July 3, 1926.

Copies: NPL:M(Q980:Col/N1A1). 3751

1928 ANDERSON, Charles
Bicentenary of the birth of Captain James Cook.

Facs. illus. port.
(*Australian Museum Magazine*, vol.3, Oct.–Dec. 1928, pp.257–61.)

Copies: NPL:M(507/A); NPL:D(92/462); NPL:R(S590.6/17). 3752

1928 COOK BI-CENTENARY CELEBRATIONS, 1928
List of articles loaned in connection with exhibition of relics and articles
of interest connected with Captain Cook. Marton-in-Cleveland, 8–15
Sep.1928.

ff.4.
Typescript with MS. note.
Includes lenders' names and insurance valuations.

Copies: NPL:D(MS.Q149). 3753

1928 R., W.A.
A Link with the Leverian Museum.

Illus.
(*Australian Museum Magazine*, vol.3, Oct.–Dec. 1928, pp.255–6.)

Copies: NPL:M(507/A); NPL:D(92/462); NPL:R(S590.6/17). 3754

1930 COOK RELICS: [illus. and notes re pendant including blue bead
used by Cook as trade in 1769; and cannon thrown overboard from the
Endeavour on Great Barrier Reef].

(Polynesian Society—*Journal*, vol.39, 1930, pp.388–9.)

Copies: NPL:M(Q572.9/P); NPL:D(9/159). 3755

1930 ERIKI, *pseud.*
James Cook . . . first gift to his sweetheart: an old lacquer box [later in
the Australian Museum].

Illus.
(*B.P. Magazine*, Sep.–Nov.1930, pp.41, 91.)
See also no.3670.

Copies: NPL/M(Q059/B). 3756

1942 MEE, Arthur
[Relics in the museum at Whitby.]

Illus.
(*In his* Yorkshire, North Riding. London, 1942. p.256.)

Copies: NPL:R(DS942.74A/16). 3757

[1946–8] AUSTRALIAN MUSEUM, *Sydney*

Copies of the Australian Museum's correspondence concerning the model of the *Endeavour*, 1947–8, and a ship's compass said to have been on the *Endeavour*, 1946–7; with further notes, cuttings, etc. on the Cook Relics transferred from the Australian Museum to the Mitchell Library.

List of contents is in the volume.

Copies: NPL:M(MS.A3936⁻²).   3758

1948 BUCK, *Sir* Peter Henry

[Note on known collections of Cook relics.]

(Bernice Pauahi Bishop Museum—*Report of the director*, 1948, p.39.)

Copies: NPL:M(Q507/B).   3759

1948 IREDALE, Tom

Bullock's Museum.

Illus.

(*The Australian Zoologist*, vol.2, pt.3, Feb.1948. Plates xvi–xviii, pp.233–7.)

One of the plates is portrait of William Bullock, after Rowley.

Copies: NPL:M(Q590.5/A).   3760

1948 McRAE, Hugh Raymond

James Cook: [biographical sketch, and an account of a letter-weight made from the timbers of the *Endeavour* and presented by him to Captain Blair, R.N.].

(*In his* Story book only. Sydney, Angus and Robertson, 1948. pp.243–5.)

Copies: NPL:M(A828/M132.2/1A1).   3761

1949 FREEMAN, John Derek

The Polynesian collection of Trinity College, Dublin, and the National Museum of Ireland; [with bibl.].

Illus.

(Polynesian Society—*Journal*, vol.58, pp.1–18, Mar.1949.)

Trinity College collection contains a number of pieces acquired on Cook's second and third voyages.

Copies: NPL:M(Q572.9/P); NPL:D(9/172).   3762

1950 RELIC of Cook's second voyage: medallion found in New Caledonia.

(*Pacific Islands Monthly*, vol.21, p.39, Nov.1950.)

Copies: NPL:M(Q988.05/P).   3763

1951 LLOYD, H. Alan

A Link with Captain Cook and H.M.S. *Endeavour*. [John Shelton's clock.]

Illus. map.

(*Endeavour*, vol.10, Oct. 1951, pp.200–204.)

Copies: NPL:R(Q506/38).   3764

1955 MOSCHNER, Irmgard

Die Wiener Cook-Sammlung, Südsee-Teil; [with bibl.]. Wien, Braumüller, 1955.

Illus. pp.135–253.

Reprinted from *Archiv für Völkerkunde*, Band 10, 1955. Describes the collection of artifacts of Pacific Islanders in the Museum für Völkerkunde, Vienna.

Copies: NPL:M(572.99/12A1); ANL. 3765

1957 CAPTAIN COOK relics exhibition at Greenwich.

Port.

(*Australia and New Zealand Weekly*, vol.87, p.5, Jan.19, 1957.)

Copies: NPL:M(Q980.105/10). 3766

1963 COOK RELICS leave cellar.

(*Sydney Morning Herald*, p.2, April 26, 1963.)

Copies: NPL:M(F079/S); NPL:R(F079/S982). 3767

[1966] LITTON INDUSTRIES NEWS BUREAU

Proposed press release on Cook's cannons: Aero Service may have located Captain Cook's lost cannons. [1966].

ff.4.

Typescript.

Copies: NPL:M(Q980:Co1/L 2A1). 3768

1968 PRICE, *Sir* Archibald Grenfell

Captain Cook: a remarkable record.

Illus. in colour, port.

(*International Nickel*, 1968, no.2, pp.12–17.)

Contains extracts from Cook's journal, and coloured illustrations of Cook's timekeeper.

Copies: NPL:M(Q673.73305/1). 3769

1969 THE RECOVERY of Captain Cook's cannons from Endeavour Reef near Cooktown, in January 1969: [illustrations].

(Cairns Chamber of Commerce—*Annual report*. 1968.9, pp.2–3.)

Copies: NPL:M(Q339.094/9). 3770

IMAGINATIVE LITERATURE ON THE LIFE OF COOK

CHILDREN'S BOOKS

[1840?] FOA, Eugenie, Mme, *pseud.*

Contes historiques pour la jeunesse. Paris, Desforges, [1840?].

Illus. pp.[vi], 349.

Includes a chapter on Captain James Cook.

Copies: NPL:M(920/6A1). 3771

IMAGINATIVE LITERATURE ON THE LIFE OF COOK –

CHILDREN'S BOOKS – *continued*

[1860?] FOA, Eugenie, Mme, *pseud.*
Le Capitaine Cook; ou, Le Schelling marqué. Paris, Simon Raçon. [1860?].

Frontisp. pp.27.
Pp.175–204 extracted from the author's Travail et celebrité contes historiques dédiés à la jeunesse.
Copies: NPL:M(980:Co1/F1A1).   3772

1906 HILL, Martha, *Mrs*
Captain Cook.

Map.
(*In* Happy hours for children, by M. Hill and friends. Ser.4. New ed. Hampstead, Sydney C. Mayle, 1906. pp.78–105.)
Copies: NPL:M(820.8/4B1).   3773

1952 BORDEN, Charles A.
He sailed with Captain Cook: [a novel for children by C. A. Borden]. Illus. by Ralph Ray. [With bibl.] New York, Crowell, [1952].

pp.[vii], 248.
See also no.3777.
Copies: ANL.   3774

[1952] KAMM, Josephine
He went with Captain Cook. London, Harrap, [1952].

Frontisp. in colour, illus. map, pp.176.
A story for children based on the life of Nicholas Young.
See also no.3776.
Copies: NPL:M(823.9/K); ANL.   3775

1955 KAMM, Josephine
He went with Captain Cook. London, Harrap, 1955.

Illus. map, pp.176.
A story for children based on the life of Nicholas Young. A reprint of no.3775.
Copies: QU.   3776

1968 BORDEN, Charles A.
He sailed with Captain Cook: [a novel for children, by] C.A. Borden. (Illus. by H. Tom Hall.) [With bibl.] Philadelphia, Macrae Smith, 1968.

pp.[205].
An account of the voyage of the *Endeavour*.
See also no.3774.
Copies: NPL:M(980:Co2/B1B1).   3777

IMAGINATIVE LITERATURE ON THE LIFE OF COOK –

FICTION

1781 Die GLÜCKLICHE Insel; oder, Beytrag zu des Capitain Cooks neuesten Entdeckungen in der Südsee aus dem verlohrnen Tagebuch eines Reisenden. Leipzig, Hertel, 1781.

pp.[8], 438.

Copies: ANL. 3778

[1930] SEIDEL, Ina

Das Labyrinth: roman. Berlin, Deutsche Verlags-Anstalt, [1930].

pp.627.
Reprint of 1922 edition. A novel based on the life of G. Forster.
See also no.3780.

Copies: NPL:M(A833/S). 3779

1932 SEIDEL, Ina

The Labyrinth: [a novel], by Ina Seidel. Translated [from the German] by O. Williams; with an introduction by I. Forbes-Mosse. London, John Lane, The Bodley Head, 1932.

pp.[xiv], 482.
A novel based on the life of G. Forster.
See also no.3779.

Copies: NPL:M(A833/S). 3780

1947 McGINNIS, Paul

Lost Eden: [an historical novel about Captain Cook's voyage in the South Pacific]. New York, McBride, 1947.

pp.287.

Copies: NPL:M(813.5/M). 3781

1948 BAUME, Eric

Devil Lord's daughter: [an historical novel. With bibl. note.] New York, Dodd, Mead & Co., 1948.

pp.272.
Describes the voyage of Captain Cook. *See also* no.3783.

Copies: NPL:M(A823/B). 3782

[1948?] BAUME, Eric

Devil Lord's daughter: [an historical novel. With bibl. note.] Sydney, Invincible Press, [1948?].

pp.245.
Describes the voyage of Captain Cook. *See also* no.3782.

Copies: NPL:M(A823/B). 3783

1954 ROBERTS, Lynette
The *Endeavour:* Captain Cook's first voyage to Australia. [With bibl.] London, Owen, 1954.

Facs. illus. ports. pp.280.

Copies: NPL:M(910.4/R); NPL:R(DS990A/213); ANL; QParl; QU.   3784

1956 BUSHNELL, Oswald Andrew
The Return of Lono: a novel of Captain Cook's last voyage. Boston, Little, Brown, 1956.

pp.290.
(An Atlantic Monthly Press Book.)
See also no.3786.

Copies: ANL.   3785

1957 BUSHNELL, Oswald Andrew
The Last days of Captain Cook: a novel. London, Chatto & Windus, 1957.

pp.272.
Originally published as Return of Lono: a novel of Captain Cook's last voyage. *See* no.3785.

Copies: NPL:M(813.5/B979/1B1); ANL; QParl; VSL; WU.   3786

1964 GOLĘBIOWSKI, Eugeniusz
Kapitan Cook; opowieść biograficzna. Warszawa, Czytelnik, 1964.

Facs. illus. map, pp.[296].

Copies: NPL:M(923.9/C771.2/36A1).   3787

1966 ENGLISH, Brenda H., *pseud.*
Into the north . . . A story of Whitby at the time of Captain Cook's first voyage of discovery. [A novel.] Whitby, Yorks., Horne & Son, 1966.

Plan, pp.235.

Copies: NPL:M(823.914/E58.1/1A1).   3788

1968 BLUNDEN, Godfrey
Charco Harbour: a novel of unknown seas and a fabled shore . . . The true story of the last of the great navigators, [Capt. Cook], his bark, and the men in her. London, Weidenfeld and Nicolson, 1968.

Map as endpapers, pp.401.
An account of the voyage of the *Endeavour. See also* no.3790.

Copies: NPL:M(A823/B658/5A1).   3789

1968 BLUNDEN, Godfrey
Charco Harbour: a novel of unknown seas and a fabled shore . . . The

true story of the last of the great navigators, [Capt. Cook], his bark, and the men in her. New York, Vanguard Press, 1968.

Map as endpapers, pp.401.
An account of the voyage of the *Endeavour*. *See also* no.3789.
Copies: NPL:M(A823/B658/5B1).   3790

FILMS

1947 NEW ZEALAND NATIONAL FILM UNIT
Moana Roa. 1947.

30 min. Less than one minute on Cook's discovery of the Cook Islands.
Copies: ANL.   3791

1963 AUSTRALIAN BROADCASTING COMMISSION
Remarkable occurrences. 1963.

30 min. A record of the life and journeys of Captain James Cook, illustrated from old engravings. Producer, K.L. Porteous; script, Lionel Hudson; commentators, Ron Haddrick, Gordon Scott.
Copies: ANL.   3792

MUSIC

[1965] ENGLISH, George Selwyn
Botany Bay 1770 . . . [full musical score] for large orchestra; [with a foreword from the journal of Captain James Cook]. Sydney, Southern Music Pub. Co., [1965].

pp.58.
Copies: NPL:M(Q782.15/1A1).   3793

1969 ELLIOTT, Malcolm
Captain Cook: [a song, with words and music].

(*In his* Songs of Australia. Sydney, J. Albert, 1969. p.3.)
Education Music. Cover title.
Copies: NPL:M(Music File).   3794

PLAYS

1785 O'KEEFE, John
A Short account of the new pantomime called Omai; or, A trip round the world. Performed at the Theatre Royal, Covent Garden. The pantomime and the whole of the scenery designed and invented by Mr. Southerbourg. The words written by Mr. O'Keefe, and the musick composed by Mr. Shields. New ed. London, T. Cadell, 1785.

pp.[2], 24.
First published 1785, the text of the new edition differs in several material aspects from that of the first (Holmes, no.52).
Copies: NPL:D(78/58).   3795

1785–6 THEATRE ROYAL, *Covent Garden*
Omai; or, A trip round the world. [A pantomime. Eleven playbills.] London, 1785–6.

For list of contents *see* no.4555.

1786 THEATRE ROYAL, *Covent Garden*
[Poster]: At the Theatre Royal in Covent Garden, this present Thursday, April 20, 1786, The Castle of Andalusia . . . to which will be added, for the 44th time, a new pantomime called Omai; or A trip round the world.

See also no.4558.

Copies: ANL:F. 3796

1788 ARNOULD, Jean François Mussot
La Mort du Capitaine Cook, à son troisième voyage au nouveau monde: pantomime en quatre actes. Par M. Arnould. Répresentée pour la première fois sur le Théâtre de l'Ambigu-Comique, au mois d'Octobre 1788. Paris, chez Lagrange, 1788.

pp.36.
For a similar pantomime *see* The Death of Captain Cook, 1789, no.2452.

Copies: NPL:M(980:Co4/A1A1); ANL. 3797

1790 THEATRE ROYAL, *Richmond Green*
A Trip to Scarborough . . . To which will be added, not acted this season, a grand, serious, pantomimic ballet, in three parts, call'd The Death of Captain Cook. [Richmond, Eng., 1790.]

1 sheet.
Photograph of a Theatre Royal playbill for Jy.12, 1790.

Copies: NPL:M(792/7A1). 3798

1796 TIMONEL, Leonardo
La Cokiada: tragedia nueva en tres actos por L. Timonel. La publica D. Angel Garcia Iñiguez. Malaga, por D. Luis de Carreras, 1796.

pp.94.
Listed in Spence, p.43.

Copies: NPL:M(980:Co4/T1A1). 3799

1818 THEATRE ROYAL, *Edinburgh*
Four playbills, advertising three performances of 'the Historical Ballet of Action, called Captain Cook', [with several other plays] in the Theatre Royal, Edinburgh, 30 Sep.–3 Oct. 1818.

ff.4.
Copies: NPL:D(W11,D59–62). 3800

1818 THEATRE ROYAL, *The Strand*

[Poster, Aug. 8, 1818, for Lionel and Clarissa and La Perouse, and advertising the pantomime ballet The Death of Captain Cook, to be produced Mon. 10th, in which the native Indian warriors will appear.]
Broadside.
Copies: NPL:M(Q980:Col/T1A1).   3801

1818 THEATRE ROYAL, *The Strand*

Turnpike gate . . . To conclude with, 16th time in this theatre, the grand historical ballet, in two acts, called the Death of Captain Cook. London, Lowndes, pr., [1818].
1 sheet.
A Theatre Royal playbill for Sep.12, 1818.
Copies: NPL:M(Q980:Col/T2A1).   3802

1901 YARRINGTON, *Rev.* William Henry Hazell

The Landing of Captain James Cook, R.N., Botany Bay 1770: [a play in verse, by W.H.H. Yarrington. Composed for the Commonwealth celebrations at Kurnell, 7 Jan. 1901.]
(*In* N.S.W.—Government Printing Office—The Landing of Lieutenant James Cook. Sydney, Govt.Pr., 1901. pp.17–32.)
Copies: NPL:M(991.1/61A1); NPL:D(90/1497); NPL:R(S991/28); ANL; VSL.   3803

1908 YARRINGTON, *Rev.* William Henry Hazell

The Landing of Captain James Cook, R.N., Botany Bay, 1770. [A play in verse] as produced in connection with the Commonwealth celebrations at Kurnell . . . 7th Jan. 1901, by Rev. W.H.H. Yarrington. Sydney, Turner & Henderson, 1908.
Illus. ports. pp.14, [ii].
Copies: NPL:M(923.9/C771.2/15A1).   3804

1909 YARRINGTON, *Rev.* William Henry Hazell

The Landing of Captain James Cook, R.N., Botany Bay, 1770. [A play in verse] as produced in connection with the Commonwealth celebrations at Kurnell . . . 7th Jan. 1901, by Rev. W.H.H. Yarrington. Sydney, Turner & Henderson, 1909.
Illus. ports. pp.23.
Bound with 1908 edition.
Copies: NPL:M(923.9/C771.2/15A1); ANL; VSL.   3805

1928 BLAKEBOROUGH, J. Fairfax-

An Historical play to celebrate a great Yorkshireman and benefactor of the Empire; [produced at the Whitby celebration of the] (bi-centenary of Captain James Cook). Whitby, Horne and Son, 1928.
Facs. illus. port. pp.[ii], 48.
Copies: NPL:M(822.91/B); NPL:D(92/476); ANL; VSL.   3806

1969 INGLIS, Robert Keith

95 men and a nanny-goat . . . a treatment for radio in story and song of the voyage of the *Endeavour*. [A prospectus of the programmes arranged by R. Inglis for the Australian Broadcasting Commission. Sydney?, the Commission, 1969.]

Facs. illus. maps, port.
Folded leaflet.
Based on the author's play entitled The Voyage of the *Endeavour*, commissioned for the Commonwealth Festival in London, 1965.

Copies: NPL:M(980:Co2/12A1).   3807

POEMS

[1775?] PERRY, Thomas

Song in commemoration of Captain Cook's voyage in the *Endeavour*. N.p., n.d.

(Cook Documents from Australian Museum, p.189.)
A broadsheet poem, without a title, having a vignette of a ship as headpiece. MS. copy of the poem on p.190. *See also* no.3809.

Copies: NPL:M(Safe 1/83).   3808

[1775?] PERRY, Thomas

Poem: 'It is now my brave boys we are clear of the Ice . . .'. 9 stanzas.

f.1. cm 30.
MS., perhaps contemporary copy; with note 'This Song was composed by Thomas Perry a Seaman on board the *Resolution* whilst returning from the second Voyage of discovery by Captain James Cook.' *See also* no.3808.

Copies: NPL:D(MS.F1, pp.71–2).   3809

1779 FITZ-GERALD, *Rev.* Gerald

The Injured islanders; or, The influence of art upon the happiness of nature. A poetical epistle from Oberea of Otaheite to Captain Wallis. By the author of the Academick sportsman. Dublin, T.T. Faulkner, pr., 1779.

pp.39.
Preface signed T.C.D., January 1st, 1779. *See also* nos.3811–12, 3823.

Copies: NPL:M(Q821.6/F553/1A1); NPL:D(77/28).   3810

1779 FITZ-GERALD, *Rev.* Gerald

The Injured islanders; or, The influence of art upon the happiness of nature. Dublin, T.T. Faulkner, pr., 1779.

pp.39.
Preface signed T.C.D. January 1st, 1779. Published anonymously. With engraving on title-page. *See also* nos.3810, 3812, 3823.

Copies: NPL:M(Q821.6/F553/1B1).   3811

1779 FITZ-GERALD, *Rev.* Gerald

The Injured islanders; or, The influence of art upon the happiness of nature. London, J. Murray, 1779.

pp.8, 28.

Preface signed T.C.D. January 1st, 1779. Published anonymously. With engraving on title-page. *See also* nos.3810–11, 3823.

Copies: NPL:M(Q821.6/F553/1C1).   3812

1780 FITZGERALD, W.

An Ode to the memory of the late Captain James Cook. London, printed for G. Robinson and others, 1780.

Port. pp.16.
See also no.3814.

Copies: NPL:M(QA821/F).   3813

1780 FITZGERALD, W.

An Ode to the memory of the late Captain James Cook. London, printed for G. Robinson and others, 1780.

pp.16.
Without portrait and half-title-page.
Bound with An Ode to the warlike genius of Great Britain. *See also* no.3813.

Copies: NPL:M(Q821.69/0); ANL.   3814

1780 SEWARD, Anna

Elegy on Captain Cook; to which is added An ode to the sun. London, J. Dodsley, 1780.

pp.23.
See also nos.6, 3816–18, 3820, 3828–9.
Reviewed in *Monthly Review*, vol.62, 1780, pp.458–61(NPL:M 052/6).

Copies: NPL:M(C918); ANL.   3815

1780 SEWARD, Anna

Elegy on Captain Cook; to which is added An ode to the sun. 2nd ed. London, J. Dodsley, 1780.

pp.23.
See no.3815 for other editions.

Copies: NPL:M(C919); ANL:F; SPL; VSL.   3816

1781 SEWARD, Anna

Elegy on Captain Cook; to which is added An ode to the sun. 3rd ed. London, J. Dodsley, 1781.

pp.23.
See no.3815 for other editions.

Copies: NPL:M(C920).   3817

1781 SEWARD, Anna

Elegy on his [Cook's] death.

(Succinct account of the life and voyages of Captain James Cook. *Universal Magazine*, 1781. p.285.)
See no.3815 for other editions.

Copies: NPL:M(910.4/122).   3818

1784 AN AMERICAN, *pseud.*

New Holland and isles in the Pacific Ocean.

(*In* Geography epitomized; or, A tour round the world . . . description . . . in verse . . . for the use of schools. By an American. Philadelphia, J. Crukshank, 1784. pp.45–8.)

Copies: NPL:M(910.7/G).   3819

1784 SEWARD, Anna

Elegy on Captain Cook; to which is added An ode to the sun. 4th ed. With additions. Lichfield, printed and sold by J. Jackson and J. Dodsley, 1784.

With author's signature. *See* no.3815 for other editions.

Copies: NPL:M(C921); NPL:D.   3820

1788 WILLIAMS, Helen Maria

Morai: an ode.

(*In* Kippis, *Rev.* Andrew—The Life of Captain James Cook. London, G. Nicol, G.G.J. & J. Robinson, 1788. App. 2, pp.520–7.)
Also appears in later editions.

Copies: NPL:M(Q980:Co1/K1A1); NPL:D(Q77/13,Q78/8,9); NPL:R(09:Q990A/49); SPL; VParl; VU(Baillieu).   3821

1790 B., W.

Irregular ode on the death of Captain Cook.

(*Lady's Magazine*, 1790, p.100.)

Copies: NPL:M(052/L).   3822

1797 FITZ-GERALD, *Rev.* Gerald

The Injured islanders; or, The influence of art upon the happiness of nature. A poetical epistle from Oberea of Otaheite to Captain Wallis.

(*In his* Poems. Dublin, Richard Edward Mercier and Co., pr., 1797. pp.25–50.)
See also nos.3810–12.

Copies: NPL:M(821.6/F553/1A1).   3823

1798 PYE, Henry James

Naucratia; or, Naval dominion. A poem. London, printed by W. Bulmer and Co. for George Nicol, 1798.

Frontisp. pp.[viii], 5–76.
Pt.3, lines 1–76 deal with the discoveries of Cook. Contains eight pages in manuscript, being additional lines copied from the second edition.

Copies: ANL. 3824

1806 ESMÉNARD, Joseph Étienne

Le Navigation: poëme (avec des notes historiques et géographiques). 2nde éd. Paris, Giguet et Michaud, 1806.

Illus. pp.[xv], 412.
Contains references to Cook in Chant sixième.
First published in 1805.

Copies: NPL:M(841.69/E). 3825

1810 WELLESLEY, Richard Colley Wellesley, *1st Marquis*
In mortem Jacobi Cook.

(*In* Posemata: praemiis Cancellarii academicis donata et in theatro sheldoniano recitata. Oxonii, Munday, 1810.)

Copies: ANL. 3826

1811 MITFORD, Mary Russell

Christina, the maid of the South Seas: a poem. London, printed by A.J. Valpy for F.C. and J. Rivington, 1811.

pp.[x], 332.
With errata slip. Pages following p.vi wrongly numbered ix–x.
Includes descriptive notes taken from the works of Bougainville, Cook, etc.

Copies: NPL:M(821.79/M); NPL:D(81/76). 3827

1817 SEWARD, Anna
Elegy on Captain Cook.

(*In her* Monody on Major André. 3rd ed. London, Longman, etc., 1817.)
See also no.3815.

Copies: VSL. 3828

1817 SEWARD, Anna
Elegy on Captain Cook.

(*In her* Monody on Major André. 10th ed. London, Longman, etc., 1817. p.178.)
See also no.3815.

Copies: NPL:M(821.79/S). 3829

1825 SONNET on visiting the spot where Captain Cook and Sir Joseph Banks first landed in Botany Bay; [and] (Sonnet on affixing a tablet to the memory of Captain Cook and Sir Joseph Banks, against the rock of their first landing in Botany-Bay).

(*In* Field, Barron—Geographical memoirs. London, John Murray, 1825. pp.497–8.)

Copies: NPL:M(981/F); NPL:D(82/55); NPL:R(09:L10/F). 3830

1833 HALLORAN, Henry

The Discovery of Eastern Australia: a poem . . . Incidents . . . taken from Cook's narrative.

(*Australian Almanack* . . . 1833. Sydney, E.W. O'Shaughnessey, 1833. pp.IX–XVIII.)
See also no.3837.

Copies: NPL:M(991.01/A); NPL:D(8/79); NPL:R(DS991.05A/3).   3831

1838 'CAPTAIN COOK'. A poem of 8 stanzas.

Extracted from *Drawing Room Scrapbook*, 1838, p.23.
Copies: NPL:D(MS.Q144, p.48a).   3832

1841 WELLESLEY, Richard Colley Wellesley, *1st Marquis*

'On the death of the distinguished man & famous navigator James Cook' and 'The Island of Tinian'. Translations of poems from Wellesley's 'Primatae et reliquiae' 1841; with corrections by Sir William Dixson.

ff.8, 3.
Manuscript and typescript.
Copies: NPL:D(MS.Q144).   3833

1867 FUERER, Carl Eduard

Cook und die Kanakas: [a poem].

(*In his* Hawaii-Nei. Barmen, W. Langewiesche's Verlagshandlung, 1867. pp.27–39.)
Copies: NPL:M(A831/F).   3834

1872 YARRINGTON, *Rev.* William Henry Hazell

University prize poem. Gold medal. Captain Cook meditating on Australia's future, [and other poems. Pub. by request, for bazaar in aid of St. Barnabas' Church, Balranald.] Sydney, Samuel E. Lees, pr., 1872.

pp.11.
(N.S.W. Pamphlets, vol.27.)
See also nos.3840, 3843–4, 3846–7, 3850.
Copies: NPL:M(042/Pa260).   3835

1873 McCRAE, George Gordon

Verses suggested by a letter-weight made from one of the timbers of Captain Cook's ship, the *Endeavour*, and long in the possession of the author's family.

(*The Critic*, Sydney. Vol.1, no.1, pp.8–9, Sept.20, 1873.)
Copies: NPL:M(Q059/22).   3836

1879 HALLORAN, Henry

The Discovery of Eastern Australia: a prize poem. Sydney, Govt. Pr., 1879.

pp.12.
See also no.3831.
Copies: NPL:M(A821/H); NPL:D(87/262).   3837

1879 HALLORAN, Henry
The Unveiling the Captain Cook statue: an exultant ode (*sic*). N.p., 1879.
pp.3.
Copies: NPL:D(87/263).   3838

1880 GILL, *Rev.* William Wyatt
Captain Cook's visit to Mangaia; The drama of Cook; Captain Cook's visit to Atiu.
(*In his* Historical sketches of savage life in Polynesia; with illustrative clan songs. Wellington, Govt.Pr., 1880. pp.174–90.)
See also no.3841.
Copies: NPL:M(398.1/G); ANL.   3839

1880 YARRINGTON, *Rev.* William Henry Hazell
University prize poem, and other verses. West Maitland, T. Dimmock, pr., 1880.
pp.48.
(Australian poems.)
See also no.3835.
Copies: NPL:M(A821/Pa5).   3840

1894 GILL, *Rev.* William Wyatt
Captain Cook's visit to Mangaia; The drama of Cook; Captain Cook's visit to Atiu.
(*In his* From darkness to light in Polynesia; with illustrative clan songs. London, Religious Tract Society, 1894. pp.243–64.)
See also no.3839.
Copies: NPL:M(398.1/G).   3841

1899 YARRINGTON, *Rev.* William Henry Hazell
Kurnell, Botany Bay. A memento of the dedication, May 6th, 1899. [A poem.] Sydney, Turner and Henderson, 1899.
pp.7.
Copies: NPL:M(A821/Y).   3842

1899 YARRINGTON, *Rev.* William Henry Hazell
University prize poem: Captain Cook meditating on Australia's future . . . Memento of the dedication at Kurnell . . . Ap.28th, 1899, Cook Anniversary Day. Sydney, Turner & Henderson, 1899.
pp.7.
See also no.3835.
Copies: NPL:M(A821/7); NPL:D(89/1412–13); ANL:F.   3843

1899 YARRINGTON, *Rev.* William Henry Hazell
University prize poem: Captain Cook meditating on Australia's future.

(*In* New South Wales—Department of Lands—Dedication of Captain Cook's landing place. Sydney, Govt.Pr., 1899. pp.71–4.)
See also no.3835.

Copies: NPL:M(991.1/N); NPL:D(89/1236); NPL:R(S920/C771/7); ANL:F.   3844

[19–?] T., W.
The Kurnell sketch: [four poems]. South Kensington, N.S.W., W. Henderson, pr., [19–?].

Illus. pp.[iv].

Copies: NPL:M(A821/T100).   3845

[19–?] YARRINGTON, *Rev.* William Henry Hazell
University prize poem: Captain Cook meditating on Australia's future.

(*In* Memento veteris aevi, 1859. Sydney, *A.C. World*, pr., [19–?]. pp.6–8.)
See also no.3835.

Copies: NPL:M(378.91/20A1).   3846

1907 YARRINGTON, *Rev.* William Henry Hazell
University prize poem: Captain Cook meditating on Australia's future . . . Kurnell, La Perouse and Commonwealth verses. Sydney, Turner & Henderson, 1907.

Illus. pp.16.
See also no.3835.

Copies: NPL:M(A821/Y).   3847

[1912] COWPER, William
Captain Cook: [a poem].

(*In* Long, Charles Richard *and* Wallace, Gilbert Murray—Notable deeds of famous men and women. Melbourne, Robertson, [1912]. p.135.)

Copies: NPL:M(920/12A1).   3848

1915 STRONG, *Sir* Archibald Thomas
James Cook: [a poem].

(*In his* Sonnets of the Empire. London, Macmillan, 1915. p.13.)

Copies: NPL:M(A821/S923/2A1).   3849

1916 YARRINGTON, *Rev.* William Henry Hazell
University prize poem: Captain Cook meditating on Australia's future. Delivered at the opening of the Great Hall of the Sydney University, July 18th, 1859. Sydney, *A.C. World*, 1916.

Illus. pp.8.
Includes reprint of article from *Sydney Morning Herald*, July 19, 1859. *See also* no.3835.

Copies: NPL:M(A821/Y); NPL:D(91/1745–7); ANL.   3850

1930 LAWLOR, Bob

Pink may, and other verse, by B. Lawlor. Illus. by H. Wiseman, R. Self and the author. Auckland, Chas. Davy, pr., 1930.

pp.[24].
Without pagination. 2nd impression.
Contains two poems about Captain Cook.
Sir Joseph Carruthers' copy, with author's inscription.
Copies: NPL:M(A821/L418.2/1A1).   3851

1931 SLESSOR, Kenneth

Five visions of Captain Cook.

Illus.
(*In* Slessor, K.—Trio: a book of poems, by K. Slessor [and others]. With drawings and designs by R. Lindsay, W.E. Pidgeon, J.E. Flett, G. Finey, and a map by J. Emery. Sydney, Sunnybrook Press, 1931. pp.[7–13].)
Copies: NPL:M(QA821/S).   3852

1951 INGAMELLS, Rex

The Great South Land: an epic poem. [With bibl. and notes.] Melbourne, Georgian House, 1951.

pp.227–66: Captain Cook.
Copies: NPL:M(A821/I).   3853

1957 BEARD, William

Humane conquistador; or, The early days of Captain James Cook and his epic adventures in the *Endeavour*. [A narrative poem], by W. Beard; [with foreword by G. Mackaness]. Sydney, priv. pr., 1957.

Port. pp.60.
Inscribed by the author to the Mitchell Library. Edition limited to 100 copies for sale and 25 for presentation.
Copies: NPL:M(A821/B368/8); ANL; QU; VSL.   3854

n.d. MORE, Hannah

[MS. on Captain Cook: extract from a poem entitled Slavery.]

(Bonwick Transcripts: Cook, case 3, no.210.)
Copies: NPL:M(B.T.ser.2, case 3a).   3855

ASSOCIATES OF COOK

Writings

TRACINGS on transparent linen of the handwriting of Pickersgill, Bootie, Clerke, Gore, Hickes (*sic*), Forwood and Wilkinson.

(Bonwick Transcripts: Cook, case 3, no.238.)
Copies: NPL:M(B.T. ser.2, case 3a).   3856

ASSOCIATES OF COOK
Biography

1832 PHILLIPS, Molesworth, *Lieut.-Col.*

ALS to Dr. Burney from West Square, London, Apr.27, 1832, re a dinner given by Sir Fletcher Norton to the officers of the *Resolution* and *Discovery* in 1776; with newspaper cutting re Phillips's death.

M. Phillips was an associate of Captain James Cook, and Dr. Burney was the nephew of Admiral James Burney.

Copies: NPL:M(Doc.1303).   3857

1914 WATSON, James Henry

Captain James Cook and his officers.

(Newspaper cuttings, vol.36, pp.14–15.)
Extract from the *Sydney Morning Herald*, Apr.25, 1914.

Copies: NPL:M(Q991/N); NPL:R(F079/S982).   3858

[192–?] DIXSON, *Sir* William

Notes re Cook and his associates.

pp.24.
MS.

Copies: NPL:D(WD4).   3859

1925 AARONS, F.

Cook's artists.

(Newspaper cuttings, vol.166, pp.170–2.)
Extract from the *Sydney Morning Herald*, May 16, 1925.

Copies: NPL:M(Q991/N); NPL:R(F079/S982).   3860

[193–?] DIXSON, *Sir* William

Lists of officers, crew and supernumeries, with record of deaths, for each of Cook's three Pacific voyages; compiled by Sir William Dixson.

ff.7; pp.9.

Copies: NPL:D(DL93/122; WD4).   3861

1932 DIXSON, *Sir* William

Notes on the crews on Captain Cook's voyages.

(Royal Australian Historical Society—*Journal and Proceedings*. Vol.18, 1932, pp.153–5.)
Copies: NPL:M(991/R, Ref.Books); NPL:D(93/129); NPL:R(S991.06/1A, Ref.Books).
    3862

1947 REYNOLDS, Graham

Captain Cook's draughtsmen; [with reproductions and map].

(*Geographical Magazine*, vol.19, pp.457–66, Feb.1947.)
Copies: NPL:R(S909.5A/5).   3863

1949 COOK, *Rev.* Arthur Malcolm
Men of Lincoln who sailed with Cook.
Illus.
(Royal Australian Historical Society—*Journal and Proceedings*. Vol.35, 1949, pp.116–30.)
Copies: NPL:M(991/R, Ref.Books); NPL:D(9/69); NPL:R(S991.06/1A, Ref.Books).
3864

1954 MERRILL, Elmer Drew
The Botany of Cook's voyages and its unexpected significance in relation to anthropology, biogeography and history. Waltham, Mass., Chronica Botanica Co., 1954.
Facs. illus. ports. pp.[iv, 224].
A cloth bound edition of *Chronica Botanica*, vol.14, no.5/6.
Copies: NPL:M(Q581.999/M); NPL:R(Q581.99/11); ANL; QU.   3865

1956 IREDALE, Tom
History of New South Wales shells, pt.1: Cook and his associates. Sydney, 1956.
Illus.
(Royal Zoological Society of New South Wales—*Proceedings*. 1954–5, pp.81–3.)
Copies: NPL:M(590.6/R).   3866

1959 LYSAGHT, Averil
Some eighteenth century bird paintings in the library of Sir Joseph Banks, 1743–1820; [with bibl.]. London, British Museum, 1959.
Plates, pp.[ii], 253, 371.
(British Museum, Natural History—*Bulletin* . . . hist. ser. vol.1, no.6.)
Copies: NPL:M(598.2/4A1); NPL:R(S506/163).   3867

1966 BEAGLEHOLE, John Cawte
The Wandering scholars: address at the opening of an exhibition from the Alströmer Collection of the Ethnographical Museum of Sweden, Stockholm, at the Dominion Museum, on 28 Oct. 1965 . . . Pub. by [the] Dominion Museum. Wellington, N.Z., 1966.
Ports. pp.15.
Brief account of the work of Linnaeus and the scientists on Cook's voyages.
Copies: NPL:M(509.8/2A1).   3868

1968 WHITEHEAD, Peter James Palmer
Forty drawings of fishes made by the artist who accompanied Captain James Cook on his three voyages to the Pacific, 1768–71, 1772–75, 1776–80, some being used by authors in the description of new species: [36 plates, some in colour. Comp. under the direction of and with] text by P.J.P. Whitehead . . . [Pub. by] the British Museum, Natural History; [with bibl.]. London, 1968.
Facs. ports. pp.xxviii, xxix–xxxi.
(British Museum, Natural History—*Publication* no.670.)
Includes information on the artists and naturalists.
Copies: NPL:M(F597.084/1A1); NPL:R(NF597.0022/1).   3869

ASSOCIATES OF COOK

ANDERSON, WILLIAM

Writings

1776 AN ACCOUNT of some poisonous fish in the South Seas, in a letter to Sir John Pringle, from W. Anderson, late surgeon's mate on board H.M.S. *Resolution*, now surgeon on that ship. London, 1776.

(Royal Society, London—*Philosophical transactions*, vol.LXVI, 1776, pp.544–76.)
Last page numbered 552–574.

Copies: NPL:M(615.94/A, extract); NPL:D(77/36, extract); NPL:R(N506/16).   3870

1801 AANMERKINGEN . . . over het land omtrent Koningin Charlotte Kanaal.

(*In* Cook, James—Collected Voyages—Printed Accounts, 1795. Reizen rondom de waereld. Leyden, Honkoop, Allart en Van Cleef, 1801. Vol.8, pp.222–54.)

Copies: NPL:M(980:Co1/12A8); ANL.   3871

1809 OBSERVATIONS on the natural productions of the country [i.e. Tasmania], on the inhabitants and their language.

(*In* Cook, James—Collected Voyages—Printed Accounts, 1809. The Voyages of Captain James Cook round the world. London, R. Phillips, 1809. Vol.5, pp.163–73.)

Copies: NPL:M(980:Co1/19A5).   3872

Biography

1790 BASTON, *Rev.* Guillaume André René
Quatrième narration, Anderson.

(*In his* Narrations d'Omai, insulaire de la Mer du Sud . . . Ouvrage traduit de l'O-Taïtien par M.K. *** & publié par le Capitaine L.A.B. [i.e. Abbé G.A.R. Baston]. Rouen, Le Boucher, le jeune, 1790. Tome 1, pp.211–48.)
An imaginary autobiography of Omai.

Copies: NPL:M(843.69/B); NPL:R(09:S843.69/B327/1); VSL.   3873

1916 BRITTEN, James
William Anderson, 1778, and the plants of Cook's third voyage. [With note.]

(*Journal of Botany*, vol.54, pp.345–52, Dec.1916; vol.55, p.54.)
Photographic copy.

Copies: NPL:M(980:Co4/B1A1).   3874

1921 MAIDEN, Joseph Henry
Records of Australian botanists.

(Royal Society of New South Wales—*Journal and Proceedings*. Vol.55, 1921, p.150.)

Copies: NPL:M(506/R); NPL:R(DS506/9).   3875

1938 IREDALE, Tom

William Anderson: ornithologist.

(*The Emu*, vol.38, pt.1, Jy 1938. pp.60–62.)

Copies: NPL:M(598.2901/E).   3876

BANKS, *Sir* JOSEPH

Writings and Correspondence

1773 JOURNAL kept by Sir Joseph Banks of a tour in Holland 1773. MS. in Banks' hand. 12 Feb.–22 Mar. 1773.

pp.79, cm 23.5.

Binder's title: *Journal of a tour in Holland 1773.* Bound in maroon half leather with maroon 'nonpareil' paper boards and end-papers.

Bookplate of Edward Stanhope. MS. title in another hand. MS. note by Sir William Dixson opposite p.1. Each page is headed and dated. On p.45 he makes reference to his voyage in the *Endeavour.*

Copies: NPL:D(MS.101).   3877

1773 THOUGHTS on the manners of [the women of] Otaheite, written in Holland for the amusement of the Prince of Orange.

pp.17, 4o.

Written at the request of Count Bentinck, in 1773.

Copies: ANL(MS.9,item4).   3878

[1774] AUTOGRAPH memoranda of expenses on account of Omai in 1774. N.p., n.d.

pp.3, 4o.

Banks' handwriting on outside only.

Copies: ANL(MS.9,item9).   3879

[1775] AUTOGRAPH memoranda of expenses incurred on account of Mr. Omai in the course of the year 1775. N.p., n.d.

pp.2, f.s., fo.

Copies: ANL(MS.9,item10).   3880

[1776] AUTOGRAPH memoranda of expenses incurred on account of Mr. Omai in the course of the year 1776. N.p., n.d.

pp.3, f.s., fo.

Copies: ANL(MS.9,item11).   3881

1780–96 AUTOGRAPH addresses to the Royal Society, London; [seven on the presentation of the Copley Medal, and one on being appointed to the Chair]. 1780–1796.

pp.77, fo.

Copies: ANL(MS.9,item15).   3882

1783 Jan.22 ALS to J.R. Forster in answer to Forster's letter of 6th July 1782, concerning the repayment of loans of money, Soho Square, Jan.22, 1783.

pp.2, 4o.

Copies: ANL(MS.9,item17). 3883

1787 May 1 ALS to David Scott, Manchester Sq., dated Soho Sq: He will forward Billings' instructions. He suspects an establishment is intended to follow upon the scientific expedition; discusses lime-burning experiments. P.S. requests Finest V . . . Cotton seeds.

ff.2, cm 23.5.

Copies: NPL:D(MS.Q158,pp.17–20). 3884

1791 Jy.8 BANKS to John Pitt, 2nd Earl of Chatham. Autograph draft: Understanding Capt. Molesworth Phillips is a candidate for the office of Agent of Royal Marines, he offers testimony in his favour. Phillips was present at the death of Capt. Cook, and though seriously wounded risked his life to save a comrade. Attests Phillips' honour, integrity and ability. Agrees to be Phillips' surety.

f.1, cm 23.
Written on verso of second leaf of ALS Burney to Banks, 6 July 1791.
Typed transcript in MS.Q159.

Copies: NPL:D(MS.Q158,p.124). 3885

1795 Aug.15 LETTER to Dr. Kippis, Aug.15, 1795, advising him to retract the erroneous statement that America would grant no protection to Cook's ships during the recent war.

MS. copy.
(Copies of documents relating to Captain James Cook, R.N., from originals in the Grey Collection, Auckland Public Library, ff.252–5.)

Copies: NPL:M(C697). 3886

[1801 +] 'A DESCRIPTION of a House in Terra del Fuego'; with 'Description of a New Zealand House' on verso. With 'Description of an Otaheite House'.

ff.2, cm 32.
Paper watermarked '1801'.
Found loose inside Briscoe journal MS.96.
Possibly in the same hand as other contemporary copies of Banks' correspondence.

Copies: NPL:D(MS.Q158, pp.79–82). 3887

1802 Jan.26 LETTER to Mr. Rudd, Jan.26, 1802, saying that he has stated Mrs. Fleck's case to the Admiralty, but they have refused to assist and suggesting raising a private subscription.

MS. copy.
(Copies of documents relating to Captain James Cook, R.N., from originals in the Grey Collection, Auckland Public Library, ff.272–5.)

Copies: NPL:M(C697). 3888

n.d. AUTOGRAPH account of presents for Omai.
pp.2, 4o.
Copies: ANL(MS.9,item13).   3889

n.d. AUTOGRAPH account of presents sent out with Omai.
pp.3, f.s., fo.
Copies: ANL(MS.9,item5).   3890

n.d. AUTOGRAPH account of the bills for Aedidee.
pp.2, 4o.
Copies: ANL(MS.9,item6).   3891

n.d. AUTOGRAPH account of the bills for Omai.
pp.2, 4o.
One of the items is a bill for Oedidee amounting to $46.16. 3.
Copies: ANL(MS.9,item8).   3892

n.d. AUTOGRAPH account of the presents intended to be sent to the
inhabitants of the South Sea Islands.
p.1, 4o.
Copies: ANL(MS.9,item7).   3893

n.d. AUTOGRAPH account of Things intended Omai; [and] Things
intended to be sent to Oedidee.
pp.2, f.s., fo.
Copies: ANL(MS.9,item14).   3894

n.d. AUTOGRAPH memoranda of [present which] Captain Cooke may
carry out for the benefit of the Society at large.
pp.2, f.s., fo.
Copies: ANL(MS.9,item12).   3895

1771–1808 AUTOGRAPH LETTERS signed to Sir Joseph Banks from
eight men (or their dependents) who claimed to have sailed in the
Endeavour under Captain Cook, asking for his assistance.
(Brabourne Papers, vol.2, 1771–1808.)
Copies: NPL:M(MS.A78⁻¹).   3896

1774–87 LETTERS RECEIVED, 1774–1787.
1 folder.
Photocopies.
Originals in possession of Mr. Kenneth Webster, 1962.
CONTENTS:
The correspondents include W. Anderson, 24 Nov. 1776; C. Clerke, 1 Aug. 1776; J.G.A.
Forster, 1 Sep. 1782; J.R. Forster, 6 Oct. 1779; J. King, 14 May 1781; A. Kippis, 21

Nov. 1785; J. Lind, 2 Mar. 1775; Baron Mulgrave, 6 Aug. 1774; Count von Rumford, 24 July 1784; Lord Sandwich, 9 Sep. 1782; D.C. Solander, 22 Aug. 1775; W. Wales, 8 Aug. 1787.

The letters contain many references to Captain James Cook.

Copies: NPL:M(MSS.1530). 3897

[1775? Jy.24] ROYAL SOCIETY, *London*

Printed announcement, with MS. particulars, signed J. Robertson Cl., requesting Banks' presence at a Council meeting to consider disposal of Sir Godfrey Copley's Medal. [On which is written, probably in Banks' hand, a list of native artifacts from the Pacific islands, with some of their native names.] Found loose inside Briscoe's journal, MS.96.

f.1, cm 33.

Copies: NPL:D(MS.Q158, pp.1–2). 3898

1801 RUDD, Bartholomew

MS. copies of four letters to Sir Joseph Banks, of application on behalf of Captain Cook's sister and nephews, 1801.

(Copies of documents relating to Captain James Cook, R.N., from originals in the Grey Collection, Auckland Public Library, ff.263–71.)

Copies: NPL:M(C697). 3899

1802 RUDD, Bartholomew

MS. copy of letter to Sir Joseph Banks, Jan.29, 1802, stating that Mrs. Fleck is now receiving £20 per annum from Mrs. Cook, so he thinks exertions on her behalf should cease.

(Copies of documents relating to Captain James Cook, R.N., from originals in the Grey Collection, Auckland Public Library, ff.281–5.)

Copies: NPL:M(C697). 3900

1805 RUDD, Bartholomew

Letter to Sir Joseph Banks, Apr.22, 1805, re James Fleck, nephew of Captain Cook, who is soliciting the position of Revenue Officer; also stating that the writer intends to erect a pillar on the site of Cook's birthplace.

MS. copy.

(Copies of documents relating to Captain James Cook, R.N., from originals in the Grey Collection, Auckland Public Library, ff.287–91.)

Copies: NPL:M(C697). 3901

1817 ARCHIMEDES, *pseud.*

[Open letter] To the Right Hon. Sir Joseph Banks; [urging the completion of the survey of New Holland. Signed Archimedes. Mar.8, 1817.]

(*Naval Chronicle*, vol.37, pp.211–12, Jan.–June 1817.)

Copies: NPL:M(359.05/N); NPL:D(80/56); NPL:R(DS359.0942/24). 3902

1796–1800 DRYANDER, Jonas

Catalogus bibliothecae historico-naturalis Josephi Banks . . . auctore Jona Dryander. Londini, Typis Gul. Bulmer et Soc., 1796–1800.

5 vols.

Copies: NPL:M(503/D); ANL. 3903

1886 THE BRABOURNE PAPERS, relating to the settlement and early history of the colony; purchased from Lord Brabourne by Sir Saul Samuel, Agent-General. A pamphlet containing a summary of the contents. Sydney, Govt. Pr., 1886.

pp.48.

See also nos.3905–6.

Copies: NPL:M(991/47A1); NPL:D(88/728); NPL:R(N994.02/63A). 3904

1886 THE BRABOURNE PAPERS, [relating to the settlement and early history of the colony; purchased from Lord Brabourne by Sir Saul Samuel, Agent-General. A pamphlet containing] a summary of the contents. Sydney, Govt. Pr., 1886.

pp.12.

Wanting title-page.

Reprinted from N.S.W.—Parliament—*Votes and Proceedings*, 1885–6. Vol.8, pp.1121–1132.

See also nos.3904, 3906.

Copies: NPL:M(Q991/14A1); NPL:D(Q88/1); NPL:R(Q342.91/3); ANL. 3905

1897 THE BRABOURNE PAPERS, relating to the settlement and early history of the colony; purchased from Lord Brabourne by Sir Saul Samuel, Agent-General. A pamphlet containing a summary of the contents. Sydney, Govt. Pr., 1897.

pp.48.

See also nos.3904–5.

Copies: NPL:M(991/47B1); NPL:R(N994.02/63A). 3906

1923 MAIDEN, Joseph Henry

Sir Joseph Banks, the father of Australia: [a bibliography].

(Royal Australian Historical Society—*Journal and Proceedings*, vol.9, 1923, pp.36–45.) Supplementary to the author's book published with the same title, 1909.

Copies: NPL:M(991/R, Ref.Books); NPL:D(9/69); NPL:R(S991.06/1A, Ref.Books). 3907

1924 DIXSON, *Sir* William

Rare pictures relative to Australasia: [notes about the different portraits of Banks and others].

(Royal Australian Historical Society—*Journal and Proceedings*, vol.10, 1924, pp.202–5.)

Copies: NPL:M(991/R, Ref.Books); NPL:D(9/169); NPL:R(S991.01/1A). 3908

1958 — DAWSON, Warren Royal

The Banks letters: a calendar of the manuscript correspondence of [i.e. addressed to] Sir Joseph Banks, preserved in the British Museum, the British Museum Natural History and other collections in Great Britain, [with Supplementary letters of Sir Joseph Banks, 1st–2nd Series]. Ed. by W.R. Dawson. London, British Museum, 1958–.

3 vols.
1st Supp. published as British Museum, Natural History—*Bulletin* . . . historical ser. vol.3, no.2, 1962. 2nd Supp. vol.3, no.3.

Copies: NPL:M(A925.8/B218/24A1–3). 3909

1963 NATIONAL LIBRARY OF AUSTRALIA—*Manuscript Branch*—Reference Division.

Sir Joseph Banks: a guide to his papers in the National Library of Australia. Canberra, the Library, 1963.

pp.20.
Duplicated.

Copies: NPL:M(Q A925.8/B218/6A1); ANL. 3910

Biography

[1773] AN EPISTLE from Mr. Banks, voyager, monster-hunter, and amoroso, to Oberea, Queen of Otaheite. Transfused by A.B.C., Esq., Second Professor of the Otaheite, and of every other unknown tongue. Enriched with the finest passages of the Queen's letter to Mr. Banks. Printed at Batavia, for Jacobus Opano, and sold in London by John Swan and Thomas Axtell, [1773].

pp.16.
With notes, mainly from Hawkesworth's Voyages. Date from Introduction. The author of this lampoon on Banks has never been discovered. *See also* no.3913.

Copies: NPL:M(C932). 3911

1774 COURTENAY, John

An Epistle, moral and philosophical, from an officer at Otaheite to Lady Gr*s**n*r; with notes, critical and historical, by the author of The rape of Pomona [i.e. J. Courtenay]. London, T. Evans, 1774.

pp.[ii], 31.
Published anonymously. Notes are mainly from Hawkesworth's Voyages.
For new edition *see* the author's *A Poetical epistle*, no.3920.

Copies: NPL:M(C934); NPL:D(77/31). 3912

[1774] AN EPISTLE from Mr. Banks, voyager, monster-hunter, and amoroso, to Oberea, Queen of Otaheite. Transfused by A.B.C., Esq., Second Professor of the Otaheite, and of every other unknown tongue. Enriched with the finest passages of the Queen's letter to Mr. Banks. 2nd ed. Printed at Batavia, for Jacobus Opano, and sold in London by John Swan and Thomas Axtell, [1774].

Frontisp. pp.16.
Dixson Library copy wanting frontispiece.
Introduction dated Dec.20, 1773. *See also* no.3911.

Copies: NPL:M(C932a); NPL:D(Q77/52). 3913

1774 SCOTT-WARING, John

An Epistle from Oberea, Queen of Otaheite, to Joseph Banks, Esq. [Attributed to J. Scott-Waring.] Translated by T.Q.Z., Esq., Professor of the Otaheite language in Dublin, and of all the languages of the undiscovered islands in the South Sea; and enriched with historical and explanatory notes. 2nd ed. London, J. Almon, 1774.

pp.15.

Formerly attributed to Richard Porson. According to Halkett and Laing this satire was written by Major John Scott (later Scott-Waring).
Attributed to Professor Fitzgerald by Spence (p.42).
See also nos.3915–18, 3935, 3974.

Copies: NPL:M(C933).   3914

1774 SCOTT-WARING, John

An Epistle from Oberea, Queen of Otaheite, to Joseph Banks, Esq. [Attributed to J. Scott-Waring.] Translated by T.Q.Z., Esq., Professor of the Otaheite language in Dublin, and of all the languages of the undiscovered islands in the South Sea; and enriched with historical and explanatory notes. 3rd ed. London, J. Almon, 1774.

pp.15.

See also nos.3914, 3916–18, 3935, 3974.

Copies: NPL:M(C933b); NPL:D(Q77/49); ANL.   3915

1774 SCOTT-WARING, John

An Epistle from Oberea, Queen of Otaheite, to Joseph Banks, Esq. [Attributed to J. Scott-Waring.] Translated by T.Q.Z., Esq., Professor of the Otaheite language in Dublin, and of all the languages of the undiscovered islands in the South Sea; and enriched with historical and explanatory notes. 4th ed. London, J. Almon, 1774.

pp.15.

Dixson Library copy grangerised; illustrations include portrait of Cook.
See also nos.3914–15, 3917–18, 3935, 3974.

Copies: NPL:M(C933d); NPL:D(Q77/50); ANL.   3916

1774 SCOTT-WARING, John

An Epistle from Oberea, Queen of Otaheite, to Joseph Banks, Esq. [Attributed to J. Scott-Waring.] Translated by T.Q.Z., Esq., Professor of the Otaheite language in Dublin, and of all the languages of the undiscovered islands in the South Sea; and enriched with historical and explanatory notes. 5th ed. London, J. Almon, 1774.

pp.15.

See also nos.3914–16, 3918, 3935, 3974.

Copies: NPL:M(C933e).   3917

1774 SCOTT-WARING, John

An Epistle from Oberea, Queen of Otaheite, to Joseph Banks, Esq. [Attributed to J. Scott-Waring.] Translated by T.Q.Z., Esq., Professor of the Otaheite language in Dublin, and of all the languages of the undiscovered islands in the South Sea; and enriched with historical and explanatory notes. 5th ed. Dublin, W. Wilson, 1774.

pp.17.

This edition is octavo in size. *See also* nos.3914–17, 3935, 3974.

Copies: NPL:M(C933f); NPL:D(77/29); ANL:F.   3918

1774 SCOTT-WARING, John

A Second letter from Oberea, Queen of Otaheite, to Joseph Banks, Esq. [Attributed to J. Scott-Waring.] Translated from the original, brought over by His Excellency Otaipairoo, Envoy Extraordinary and Plenipotentiary from the Queen of Otaheite, to the Court of Great Britain, lately arrived in His Majesty's Ship the *Adventure*, Capt. Furneaux. With some curious and entertaining anecdotes of this celebrated foreigner before and since his arrival in England. Together with explanatory notes from the Queen's former letter, and from Dr. Hawkesworth's Voyages. London, printed by T.J. Carnegy for E. Johnson, [1774].

pp.16.

With engraved vignette on title-page.

The Dixson Library holds another copy, (Q77/50), grangerised, bound with no.3916.

Copies: NPL:M(C933h); NPL:D(77/30).   3919

1775 COURTENAY, John

A Poetical epistle, moral and philosophical, from an officer at Otaheite to Lady Gr**v*n*r; with notes, critical and historical . . . Corrected and enlarged. New ed. London, T. Evans, 1775.

pp.[ii],33.

Published anonymously. Notes are mainly from Hawkesworth's Voyages.

For earlier edition *see* no.3912.

Copies: NPL:M(C934a).   3920

1778 BOWMAN, Hildebrand, *pseud.*

The Travels of Hildebrand Bowman, Esquire, into Carnovirria, Taupiniera, Olfactaria, and Auditante, in New Zealand, in the Island of Bonhommica, and in the powerful Kingdom of Luxo-Volupto on the great southern continent. Written by himself, etc. London, W. Strahan & T. Cadell, 1778.

Illus. pp.xv,400.

A satire addressed to Sir Joseph Banks and D.C. Solander.

Copies: NPL:M(910.43/B); NPL:D(77/17); NPL:R(SC).   3921

1779 MIMOSA; or, The sensitive plant. A poem dedicated to Mr. Banks and addressed to Kitt Frederick Dutchess of Queensberry elect. London, printed for W. Sandwich, 1779.

pp.vii,17.

Published anonymously.

Copies: NPL:M(Q827.6/M); ANL.   3922

[1780] A LETTER from Omai to the . . . Earl of ******** [Sandwich], late — Lord of the — . Trans. from the Ulaietean tongue. In which, amongst other things, is fairly and irrefragably stated the nature of original sin, together with a proposal for planting Christianity in the islands of the Pacific Ocean. London, J. Bell, [1780].

pp.[ii],35.
Date taken from p.[1].
Copies: NPL:M(C929).   3923

1783 SNIP, Simon, *pseud.*

The Philosophical puppet show; or, Snip's inauguration to the President's chair. Addressed to Sir J— B—, Βαρωγέτζos [i.e. baronet], a celebrated connoisseur in chickweed, caterpillars, black beetles, butterflies and cockle-sehlls (*sic*). By Simon Snip, F.R.S. [pseud. i.e. Charles Hutton]. London, W. Green, 1663 [i.e. 1783].

Frontisp. pp.[ii],37.
A satirical attack on Banks, attributed to C. Hutton, for a time Foreign Secretary to the Royal Society. In 1783–4 there was strong opposition to Banks from many members of the Royal Society, of which Banks was President.
Imprint taken from the copy in the Ferguson Collection. Part of the title-page has been cut away in the Mitchell Library copy. A note by Dawson Turner on the endpaper of the latter copy states that if this satire was ever published the copies were suppressed.
Copies: NPL:M(827.6/S); ANL:F.   3924

1784 AN HISTORY of the instances of exclusion from the Royal Society . . . with strictures of . . . the despotism of Sir Joseph Banks . . . by some members in the minority. London, J. Debrett, 1784.

pp.[2],27.
Inserted is portrait of Banks, T. Lawrence pinxt., Woolnoth sculp., published Apr. 1823 by Dean & Munday.
Copies: NPL:D(78/62).   3925

1788 WOLCOT, John [Peter Pindar, *pseud.*]

Peter's prophecy: or The President and poet; or, An important epistle to Sir J. Banks, on the approaching election of a President of the Royal Society. London, G. Kearsley, 1788.

Frontisp. pp.52.
See also nos.3927, 3931, 3938.
Copies: NPL:M(Q827.65/W).   3926

1788 WOLCOT, John [Peter Pindar, *pseud.*]

Peter's prophecy; or, The President and poet; or, An important epistle to Sir J. Banks, on the approaching election of a President of the Royal Society. 3rd ed. London, G. Kearsley, 1788.

Frontisp. pp.54.
Bound with his A Poetical . . . epistle to those literary colossuses, the reviewers. *See also* nos.3926, 3931, 3938.
Copies: NPL:R(DQ827.65/1).   3927

1788 WOLCOT, John [Peter Pindar, *pseud.*]
Sir Joseph Banks and the Emperor of Morocco: a tale. 3rd ed. London, G. Kearsley, 1788.

Frontisp. pp.27.
Bound with his A Poetical . . . epistle to those literary colossuses, the reviewers. *See also* nos.3929–30, 3933, 3940.

Copies: NPL:R(DQ827.65/1).   3928

1788 WOLCOT, John [Peter Pindar, *pseud.*]
Sir Joseph Banks and the Emperor of Morocco: a tale, by Peter Pindar Esq. 4th ed. London, G. Kearsley, 1788.

Frontisp. pp.27.
See also nos.3928, 3930, 3933, 3940.

Copies: NPL:M(C925).   3929

[1788] WOLCOT, John [Peter Pindar, *pseud.*]
Sir Joseph Banks and the Emperor of Morocco: a tale. N.p., [1788].

pp.15.
Half title-page only, without imprint. At foot of page is mentioned vol.2. *See also* nos.3928–9, 3933, 3930. 3940.

Copies: NPL:D(78/79).   3930

1794 WOLCOT, John [Peter Pindar, *pseud.*]
Peter's prophecy; or, The President and poet; or, An important epistle to Sir J. Banks on the approaching election of a President of the Royal Society.

(*In his* Works. London, John Walker, 1794. Vol.2, pp.103–43.)
See also nos. 3926–7, 3938.

Copies: NPL:R(S827.65/2, S.C.).   3931

1794 WOLCOT, John [Peter Pindar, *pseud.*]
Sir Joseph Banks and the boiled fleas: [a poem].

(*In his* Works. London, John Walker, 1794. Vol.2, pp.393–7.)
See also no.3939.

Copies: NPL:R(S827.65/2, S.C.).   3932

1794 WOLCOT, John [Peter Pindar, *pseud.*]
Sir Joseph Banks and the Emperor of Mroocco: a tale.

(*In his* Works. London, John Walker, 1794. Vol.2, pp.187–206.)
See also nos.3928–30, 3940.

Copies: NPL:R(S827.65/2, S.C.).   3933

1794 WOLCOT, John [Peter Pindar, *pseud.*]
Sir Joseph Banks and the thief-takers: [a poem].

(*In his* Works. London, John Walker, 1794. Vol.2, pp.283–7.)
See also no.3941.

Copies: NPL:R(S827.65/2, S.C.).   3934

1802 SCOTT-WARING, John

An Epistle from Oberea, Queen of Otaheite, to Joseph Banks, Esq., now the Rt. Hon. Sir Joseph Banks . . . [Attributed to J. Scott-Waring]. Translated by T.Q.Z., Esq., Professor of the Otaheite language in Dublin, and of all the languages of the undiscovered islands in the South Sea. Enriched with historical and explanatory notes. Pub. originally in the year 1774.

(*In* School for satire. London, Jaques & Co., 1802. pp.125–42.)
With MS. note, signed Mathias, attributing the work to Porson. According to Halkett and Laing it was written by Major John Scott (later Scott-Waring).
See also nos.3914–18, 3974.
Copies: NPL:M(827.69/S). 3935

1811 HOOKER, *Sir* William Jackson

Journal of a tour in Iceland in the summer of 1809. Yarmouth, J. Keymer, pr., 1811.

Frontisp. in colour, illus. pp.[lxii],503. Includes references to Sir Joseph Banks' visit to Iceland. *See also* no.3937.
Copies: NPL:R(DS949.1A/19). 3936

1813 HOOKER, *Sir* William Jackson

Journal of a tour in Iceland in the summer of 1809. 2nd ed. London, Longman, Hurst, Rees, Orme & Brown, 1813.

Frontisp. in colour, illus. maps, table, 2vols. Includes reference to Sir Joseph Banks' visit to Iceland. *See also* no.3936.
Copies: NPL:M(914.91/1B1–2). 3937

1816 WOLCOT, John [Peter Pindar, *pseud.*]

Peter's prophecy; or, The president and poet; or, An important epistle to Sir J. Banks, on the approaching election of a president of The Royal Society.

(*In his* Works. London, Walker and Edwards, 1816. Vol.1, pp.433–66.)
See also nos.3926–7, 3931.
Copies: NPL:M(827.65/W). 3938

1816 WOLCOT, John [Peter Pindar, *pseud.*]

Sir Joseph Banks and the boiled fleas: [a poem].

(*In his* Works. London, Walker and Edwards, 1816. Vol.2, pp.102–5.)
See also no.3932.
Copies: NPL:M(827.65/W). 3939

1816 WOLCOT, John [Peter Pindar, *pseud.*]

Sir Joseph Banks and the Emperor of Morocco: a tale.

(*In his* Works. London, Walker and Edwards, 1816. Vol.1, pp.467–83.)
See also nos.3928–30, 3933.
Copies: NPL:M(827.65/W). 3940

1816 WOLCOT, John [Peter Pindar, *pseud.*]

Sir Joseph Banks and the thief-takers: [a poem].

(*In his* Works. London, Walker and Edwards, 1816. Vol.2, pp.33–6.)
See also no.3934.

Copies: NPL:M(827.65/W).   3941

1817 BULLOCK, William

Concise and easy method of preserving subjects of natural history; intended for the use of sportsmen, travellers, &c. &c., to enable them to collect and prepare such curious and rare articles as they may wish to preserve, or to transmit in safety to any part of the world. London, printed for the proprietor, 1817.

Illus. pp.iv, 5–36.
As practised in Bullock's London Museum, containing collections made by Sir Joseph Banks on his voyage with Captain Cook.

Copies: NPL:M(590.7/B).   3942

1821 CUVIER, Georges Leopold Chrétien Frederic Dagobert, *Baron*

Eloge historique de M. Banks; lu à la séance publique de l'Académie Royale des Sciences, le 2 avril 1821. N.p., 1821.

pp.ii, 30.
Presentation copy from R. Brown to Alexander Macleay.
Also published in Suttor, George—Memoirs. 1855. pp.52–80. *See* no.3949.

Copies: ANL.   3943

1821 DUNCAN, Andrew

A short account of the life of the Right Honourable Sir Joseph Banks, K.B., President of the Royal Society of London. Read at the fortieth anniversary festival of the Harveian Society of Edinburgh, on the 12th of April, 1821. Edinburgh, printed by P. Neill, sold by Archibald Constable & Co., 1821.

pp.24.
ANL copy has autograph letter from the author inserted. One copy in Mitchell Library has p.22 wrongly numbered 23.

Copies: NPL:M(042/Pa418); NPL:D(82/81); ANL.   3944

1822 HOME, *Sir* Everard

The Hunterian oration in honour of surgery . . . delivered in the theatre of the [Royal] College [of Surgeons in London], Feb.14, 1822. London, Longman, Hurst, Rees, Orme and Brown, 1822.

pp.vii, 36.
Photographic copy only. ANL copy with typescript notes, and title-page for 1823 Oration inserted. Sir Joseph Banks was the subject of the Oration.
See also nos. 3972, 3985.

Copies: NPL:M(A925.8/B); ANL.   3945

1825 HAYWARD, Joseph

On the science of agriculture, comprising a commentary on and comparative investigation of the agricultural chemistry of Mr. Kirwan and Sir Humphry Davy, the code of agriculture of Sir John Sinclair, Sir Joseph Banks and other authors on the subject. London, Longman, Hurst, Rees, Orme, Brown and Green, 1825.

pp.4, xii, 220.

Copies: NPL:M(630/2A1). 3946

1829 SIR JOSEPH BANKS, Bart., P.R.S. London, Fisher, 1829.

Port. pp.8.
Title-page wanting.

Copies: NPL:M(QA925.8/B218/2A1); ANL(Pam.Vol.202, no.3900). 3947

1844 TOMLINSON, Charles

Sir Joseph Banks and the Royal Society: a popular biography, with an historical introduction and sequel. London, J.W. Parker, 1844.

pp.viii, 9–124.
Published anonymously. Charles Tomlinson's authorship was established in *Notes and Queries*, Oct.23, 1937, p.296.

Copies: NPL:M(A925.8/B218/18A1); NPL:D(84/465); ANL. 3948

1855 SUTTOR, George

Memoirs, historical and scientific, of the Right Honourable Sir Joseph Banks, Bart. Parramatta, N.S.W., E. Mason, 1855.

Frontisp. pp.80.
Frontispiece is portrait of Banks by E. Thomas. Eulogy, in French, pronounced on the death of Sir Joseph Banks, by Baron Cuvier, President of the National Institute of France, is printed on pp.52–80. A poem by W.C. Wentworth is printed on p.51.

Copies: NPL:M(A925.8/B218/3A1); NPL:D(85/278); NPL:R(S920/B218/2); ANL. 3949

[1880] SOTHEBY, WILKINSON & HODGE, *London*

Catalogue of a valuable collection of rare books and manuscripts; [the Sir Joseph Banks papers, sold by auction 15th June, 1880. London, Sotheby, 1880.]

pp.44.
Positive photocopy. Placed with this is prospectus of the sale.

Copies: NPL:M(FA925.8/B). 3950

[1886] SOTHEBY, WILKINSON & HODGE, *London*

Books and manuscript and printed topographical and heraldic collections relating to the County of Lincoln, from the library of Sir Joseph Banks: [extract from catalogue of auction, 13th March 1886. London, Sotheby, 1886.]

pp.48–61.
Photocopy.

Copies: NPL:M(A925.8/B218/4A1). 3951

[1886] SOTHEBY, WILKINSON & HODGE, *London*

Catalogue of the correspondence & letters of the Rt. Hon. Sir Joseph Banks . . . sold by order of his great nephew . . . Lord Brabourne, and other valuable autographs, which will be sold by auction, by Messrs. Sotheby, Wilkinson & Hodge . . . on Wednesday, the 14th April, 1886. London, [the Co., 1886].

pp.22.

Photoprint.

The catalogue, of 22 numbered pages, has been cut up and pasted in a ledger, which has the prices and the names of the purchasers at the side of the items. It is from the ledger that the photoprint has been made.

Copies: NPL:M(A925.8/B218/20B1). 3952

1889–96 COKE, *Lady* Mary

The Letters and journals of Lady Mary Coke. [Ed. by J.A. Home.] Edinburgh, D. Douglas, 1889–96.

Photoprints of pp.35, 153, 154, 192, 435, 437, 440, 442, 443 only, bearing references to Sir Joseph Banks and Dr. Solander.

Copies: NPL:M(QA920/Banks. *Pam.File*). 3953

[190–] SIR JOSEPH BANKS' MEMORIAL FUND
[Leaflets.]

CONTENTS:

1. Letter from J.H. Maiden on a statue for Banks reprinted from Sydney daily papers Feb.14, 1906.
2. Reproduction of portrait of Banks by Sir Joshua Reynolds, and engraving of Banksia ericifolia.
3. Advertisement of book entitled Sir Joseph Banks, the father of Australia, by J.H. Maiden. 1910.

Copies: NPL:M(A925.8/B218/5A1); NPL:D(90/1328, no.1, only). 3954

1909 MAIDEN, Joseph Henry

Sir Joseph Banks, the father of Australia. Sydney, Govt. Pr., 1909.

Facs. illus. maps, port. pp.xxiv, 244.

A volume of reviews extracted from newspapers is filed in the Mitchell Library at QA925.8/B218/5A1; the work is also reviewed in a letter from A. Kitson, dated 28 Mar. 1910, to J.H. Maiden (NPL:D, D.L.90/207). *See also* no.3907.

Copies: NPL:M(A925.8/B218/1A1); NPL:D(90/79); NPL:R(580.9/4); ANL. 3955

1911 LONDON—County Council

Indication of houses of historical interest in London, Pt.31; [with an account of the house of Sir Joseph Banks, no.32 Soho Square.] London, County Council, 1911.

pp.12.

Cover bears inscription to J.H. Maiden.

Copies: NPL:M(A925.8/B218/7A1). 3956

1911 SMITH, Edward

The Life of Sir Joseph Banks, President of the Royal Society; with some notices of his friends and contemporaries. London, John Lane, 1911.

Illus. pp.xvi, 348.
Reviewed in *Nation*, Nov.1911, p.450.

Copies: NPL:M(A925.8/B218/2A1); NPL:D(91/94); NPL:R(N920/B218/1); ANL; Australasian Pioneers' Club, Sydney. 3957

1918 HUXLEY, Leonard

Life and letters of Sir Joseph Dalton Hooker; based on materials collected and arranged by Lady Hooker. London, Murray, 1918.

Illus. map, ports. 2 vols.
Contains information about Banks, including an account of Lord Brabourne's connection with Banks' Journal.

Copies: NPL:M(925.8/H); NPL:R(S920/H783/1–2). 3958

[1918] SOTHEBY, WILKINSON & HODGE, *London*

The Property of the Lady Beryl Gilbert: [extract from catalogue, including papers relating to Sir Joseph Banks. Auctioned Oct.17th, 1918. London, Sotheby, 1918.]

pp.62–9.
Positive photocopy. Placed with this is prospectus of the sale.

Copies: NPL:M(FA925.8/B). 3959

1928 HERMANNSSON, Halldór

Sir Joseph Banks and Iceland; by H. Hermannsson. [With bibl. notes.] Ithaca, N.Y., Cornell Univ. Lib., 1928.

Illus. ports. pp.[8],99, pl.24.
(*Islandica* vol.18).

Copies: NPL:M(A925.8/B218/19A1); NPL:R(S949.103/1); ANL. 3960

1929 SOTHEBY AND CO., *London*

Catalogue of the Sir Joseph Banks papers: a . . . collection of letters addressed to Sir Joseph Banks, 1743–1820 . . . including . . . men famous in the early history of Australia . . . which will be sold . . . May, 1929. [With annotations.] London, J. Davy & Sons, pr., 1929.

Facs. pp.20.

Copies: NPL:M(A925.8/B218/16A1). 3961

[1929] SOTHEBY AND CO., *London*

[Extracts from catalogue of auction including papers of Sir Joseph Banks, held July 21st? and 22nd, 1929.]

pp.64, 106–108.
Positive photocopy.

Copies: NPL:M(FA925.8/B). 3962

[1930] MICHELMORE, G., and Co.

Sir Joseph Banks papers: [catalogue of a collection of papers offered for sale]. Edinburgh, Turnbull & Spears, pr., [1930].

pp.[i],19.

With typescript letter to Dr. G. Mackaness.

Copies: NPL:M(QA925.8/B218/4A1).   3963

1936 MACKANESS, George

Sir Joseph Banks, his relations with Australia. Sydney, A. & R., 1936.

Facs. ports. pp.[xiv], 146.

Copies: NPL:M(A925.8/B218/17A1); NPL:D(93/618); ANL.   3964

1937 GIRAUDOUX, Jean

Supplément au voyage de Cook: pièce en un acte . . . Illus. de M. Andreu. Paris, Librairie Bernard Grasset, 1937.

Illus. pp.[120].

Comedy was first performed in 1935.

Copies: NPL:M(842.9/G522/1A1).   3965

1939 DUVAL, Henri Auguste

Plantae succulentae, in Horto Alenconio. Auctore H.A. Duval, Parisiis apud Gabon et Socios, 1809. A facsimile, with an intro. [and bibl. notes] by William T. Stearn, [from the unique copy bequeathed to the British Museum by Sir Joseph Banks].

pp.105–9.

Reprinted from *The Cactus Journal* vol.7, June 1939.

Copies: NPL:M(Q583.475/D).   3966

1943 COOK, *Rev.* Arthur Malcolm, *Subdean of Lincoln Cathedral*

An Australian Boston: a forgotten chapter of local history. Boston, Eng., Church House, 1943.

Frontisp. map, ports. pp.[6],42.

An account of the men from Boston and its neighbourhood who took part in the discovery of Australia.

Copies: NPL:M(A923.9/C).   3967

1948 SUTTOR, George

Memoirs of George Suttor, F.L.S., Banksian collector, 1774–1859; ed. with notes and commentary by G. Mackaness. Sydney, D.S. Ford, pr., 1948.

Illus. port. pp.80.

(*Australian Historical Monographs*, no.17.)

From a copy of G. Suttor's original MS. memoirs, edited in 1906 by his grandson, Sir Francis Suttor, and prepared in typewritten form for members of the family. (Copy at NPL:M MS.A3072.)

Copies: NPL:M(A926.36/S); NPL:D(94/234).   3968

1951 COOK, *Rev.* Arthur Malcolm, *Subdean of Lincoln Cathedral*
Lincolnshire links with Australia. Lincoln, the Subdeanery, 1951.
Illus. maps, ports. pp.46.
See also no.3976.
Copies: NPL:M(990.1/37A1). 3969

1952 CAMERON, Hector Charles
Sir Joseph Banks, K.B., P.R.S.: the autocrat of the philosophers. [With bibl.] London, Batchworth Press, 1952.
Illus. ports. pp.xx,341.
See also no.3984.
Copies: NPL:M(A925.8/B218/21A1); NPL:R(N920/B218/3A); ANL. 3970

1952 HILL, James William Francis
The Letters and papers of the Banks Family of Revesby Abbey, 1704– 1760; ed. by J.W.F. Hill. Lincoln, Record Soc., 1952.
Frontisp. pp.[xxxi], 330.
(Lincoln Record Soc.—*Pubs.* vol.45.)
Contains genealogical and other references to Sir Joseph Banks.
Copies: NPL:R(N942.5306/1). 3971

1952 HOME, *Sir* Everard
The Hunterian oration in honour of surgery . . . delivered in the theatre of the [Royal] College [of Surgeons in London], Feb.14th, 1822.
(*In* Cameron, Hector Charles—Sir Joseph Banks. London, Batchworth Press, 1952. pp.297–307.)
See also nos. 3945, 3985.
Copies: NPL:M(A925.8/B218/21A1); NPL:R(N920/B218/3A); ANL. 3972

1954 MERRILL, Elmer Drew
The Botany of Cook's voyages and its unexpected significance in relation to anthropology, biogeography and history. Waltham, Mass., Chronica Botanica Co., 1954.
Facs. illus. ports. pp.[iv, 224].
A cloth bound edition of *Chronica Botanica*, vol.14, no.5/6.
Copies: NPL:M(Q581.999/M); NPL:R(Q581.99/11); ANL; QU. 3973

1955 SCOTT-WARING, John
An Epistle from Oberea, [Queen of Otaheite, to Joseph Banks, Esq.]; with decorations by R. Crooke. [Attributed to J. Scott-Waring.] Ferntree Gully, Vict., Rams Skull Press, 1955.
Facs. pp.21, [2].
Edition limited to 250 copies, of which this is no.38. Autographed by R.Crooke. Cover design and decorations printed by R. Crooke; medium used was silk screen. With facsimile of the 4th ed., 1774. This edition wrongly called 5th ed.
See also nos. 3914–18, 3935.
Copies: NPL:M(C993g). 3974

1955 WILKINS, Guy Lawrence

A Catalogue and historical account of the Banks shell collection; [with bibl.] London, British Museum, 1955.

Facs. illus. pp.[ii],71–119.
(British Museum, Natural History—*Bulletin* . . . history ser. vol.1, no.3.)
Copies: NPL:M(594/W); NPL:R(S506/163). 3975

1958 COOK, *Rev.* Arthur Malcolm, *Subdean of Lincoln Cathedral*

Lincolnshire links with Australia. 4th ed. Lincoln, Friends of Lincoln Cathedral, 1958.

Illus. maps, ports. pp.[vi],61.
See also no.3969.
Copies: NPL:M(990.1/37B1); NPL:R(N994.02/6). 3976

1961 WILLSON, Eleanor Joan

James Lee and the Vineyard Nursery, Hammersmith; [with bibl.] London, Hammersmith Local History Group, 1961.

Port. as frontisp. facs. map, pp.[xii],88.
Contains information on collecting in Australia and the introduction of Australian plants to England, and of Lee's association with Sir Joseph Banks and S.Parkinson.
Copies: NPL:M(580.9/2A1); NPL:R(N920/L478.3/1). 3977

1962 EVATT, Herbert Vere

Sir Joseph Banks Memorial . . . notes for an address. Sydney, Public Library of New South Wales, 1962.

ff.10.
Processed.
Copies: NPL:M(Q925.8/B218/1A1). 3978

1962 MACKANESS, George

Sir Joseph Banks, Bart. K.C.B., P.C., F.R.S.: an appreciation. [With bibl.] Sydney, the author, 1962.

pp.18.
Published to mark the publication by the Trustees of the Public Library of New South Wales of Banks' Journal during Captain Cook's first voyage. Edition limited to 250. The Mitchell Library holds another copy specially bound and identical with two other copies of this work presented to his Excellency, the Governor-General, Lord De L'Isle.
Copies: NPL:M(A925.8/218/23A1). 3979

1962 PUBLIC LIBRARY OF NEW SOUTH WALES

In celebration of the publication of the *Endeavour* Journal of Sir Joseph Banks, Thursday, 15th February, 1962; [programme]. Sydney, the Library, 1962.

Folder, pp.2.
Prospectus filed with this.
Copies: NPL:M(A925.8/B218/6A1). 3980

1963 RYDÉN, Stig

The Banks collection: an episode in 18th century Anglo-Swedish relations. [With bibl.] Stockholm, Almqvist & Wiksell, 1963.

Illus. map, ports. table, pp.131–34.
(Statens Etnografiska Museum—*Monograph ser., pub.* no.8.)

Copies: NPL:M(572.99/23A1); ANL. 3981

1964 CARTER, Harold Burnell

His Majesty's Spanish flocks: Sir Joseph Banks and the merinos of George III of England. [With bibl.] Sydney, A. & R., 1964.

Facs. illus., some in colour, graphs, maps, pp.xv, 520.

Copies: NPL:M(636.36/1A1); NPL:R(N636.36/1). 3982

1966 BEAGLEHOLE, John Cawte

The Wandering scholars: address at the opening of an exhibition from the Alströmer Collection of the Ethnographical Museum of Sweden, Stockholm, at the Dominion Museum, on 28 Oct.1965 . . . Pub. by [the] Dominion Museum. Wellington, N.Z., the Museum, 1966.

Ports. pp.15.

Copies: NPL:M(508.9/2A1). 3983

1966 CAMERON, Hector Charles

Sir Joseph Banks. [With bibl.] Sydney, A. & R., 1966.

Illus. ports. pp.xx, 341.
Reprint of no.3970.

Copies: NPL:M(A925.8/B218/21B1); NPL:R(920/B218/3B). 3984

1966 HOME, *Sir* Everard

The Hunterian oration in honour of surgery . . . delivered in the theatre of the [Royal] College [of Surgeons in London], Feb.14th, 1822.

(*In* Cameron, Hector Charles—Sir Joseph Banks. Sydney, A. & R., 1966. pp.297–307.)
Reprint of 1952 edition.
See also nos. 3945, 3972.

Copies: NPL:M(A925.8/B218/21B1); NPL:R(920/B218/3B). 3985

1968 LEMMON, Kenneth

The Golden age of plant hunters; [with bibl.] London, Phoenix House, 1968.

Facs. plan, plates, some in colour, ports. pp.x, 229.
Includes extensive discussion of Banks' work.

Copies: NPL:M(581.9/1A1); NPL:F(E581.9/Lem). 3986

1968 RAUSCHENBERG, Roy Anthony

Daniel Carl Solander, naturalist on the *Endeavour*. Philadelphia, 1968.

pp.66.
(American Philosophical Society—*Transactions*, n.s. vol.58, pt.8.)
With many references to Banks.

Copies: NPL:R(NQ506/5). 3987

ASSOCIATES OF COOK

BANKS, *Sir* JOSEPH

Biography
Articles, etc.

1772 SOME ACCOUNT of Dr. Solander and Mr. Banks, with an engraved head of the latter.
pp.[3].
Extract from the *London Magazine, or Gentleman's Monthly Intelligencer*, July, 1772, pp. 341–2.
Copies: NPL:M(A925.8/B218/13A1).   3988

1774 COURT of Apollo, being a selection of original and fugitive poetry, for the *Westminster Magazine*. An heroic epistle from the injured Harriot, mistress to Mr. Banks, to Oberea, Queen of Otaheite.
ff.2.
Published anonymously. Extracted from the *Westminster Magazine*, 1774, pp.42–3.
Copies: NPL:M(827.6/C).   3989

1789 [LIBERALITY to American making overland trip eastward to Philadelphia.]
(*Lady's Magazine*, 1789, p.53.)
Copies: NPL:M(052/L).   3990

[1802] SIR JOSEPH Banks, Bart., K.B.
Port.
Extract from the *European Magazine and London Review*, vol.42, Sept. 1802, pp.163–6.
Bound with Cook, James—Succinct account of life and voyages.
Copies: NPL:M(910.4/122); NPL:R(09:S050/E89).   3991

1819 MEMOIR of . . . Sir Joseph Banks.
Port.
(*Imperial Magazine*, vol.1, 1819, pp.1074–82.)
Copies: NPL:M(052/I).   3992

1820 BIOGRAPHICAL memoir of . . . Sir Joseph Banks.
(*Philosophical Magazine and Journal*, vol.56, Jy–Dec., 1820, pp.40–46.)
Copies: NPL:R(S505/6).   3993

1820 MEMOIR of Sir Joseph Banks.
Port.
(*New Monthly Magazine*, Aug., 1820, pp.185–94.)
Portrait bound between pp.120 and 121.
Copies: NPL:R(S050/N532).   3994

1820 OBITUARY . . . Sir Joseph Banks.

(*Gentleman's Magazine* June 1820, pp.637–8.)
Copies: NPL:R(S050/G338).   3995

1820 REVIEW of some leading points in the official character and proceedings of the late President of the Royal Society.

(*Philosophical Magazine and Journal*, vol.56, Jy–Dec., 1820, pp.161–74, 241–57.)
Copies: NPL:R(S505/6).   3996

1820 SIR JOSEPH Banks: [a memoir].

(*Gentleman's Magazine*, July, 1820, pp.86–8.)
Copies: NPL:R(S050/G338).   3997

1821 RIGHT HON. SIR Joseph Banks; [with silhouette].

(*Annual Biography and Obituary*, 1821, pp.97–120.)
Includes abstract of his will.
Copies: NPL:M(920/A); NPL:R(DS920/130).   3998

1830 COLMAN, George, *the younger*
[Visit of Omai and Sir Joseph Banks to Mulgrave Castle, near Whitby, 1775.]

(*In his* Random records. London 1830. Vol.1, pp.153–202.)
Copies: NPL:M(928.22/C); NPL:R(S920/C716.1/1); VSL.   3999

1832 LODGE, Edmund
Sir Joseph Banks.

Port.
(*In his* Portraits of illustrious personages of Great Britain. London, Harding and Lepard, 1832. Vol.II, pp.10.)
Portrait engraved by H. Robinson, from the original of Sir Thomas Lawrence in the British Museum. Pagination not continuous.
See also no.4003.
Copies: NPL:R(Q920/131).   4000

1833 BANKS; [with portrait].

(Gallery of portraits with memoirs. London, Charles Knight, 1833. Vol.1, pp.193–8.)
Copies: NPL:M(Q920/G); NPL:R(Q920/114).   4001

1835 JARDINE, *Sir* William
Natural history of fishes of the perch Family . . . with memoir and portrait of Sir Joseph Banks. Edinburgh, W.H. Lizars, and Stirling & Kennedy, 1835.

Port. pp.17–48.
(*Naturalist's Library—Ichthyology*, vol.1.)
Copies: NPL:R(S597.5/4).   4002

1835 LODGE, Edmund
Sir Joseph Banks.

Port.
(*In his* Portraits of illustrious personages of Great Britain. London, Harding and Lepard, 1835. Vol.12, p.10.)
Portrait engraved by H. Robinson, from the original of Sir Thomas Lawrence in the British Museum.
Pagination not continuous.
See also no.4000.
Copies: NPL:M(Q920.042/L).   4003

1837 CUNNINGHAM, George Godfrey
Sir Joseph Banks.

(*In his* Lives of eminent and illustrious Englishmen. Glasgow, 1837. Vol.8, pp.235–9.)
Copies: NPL:R(DS920/1022).   4004

1838 GARDINER, William
Visit to Banks.

(*In his* Music and friends. London, Longman, 1838. Vol.1, pp.116–23.)
Copies: NPL:M(927.83/G).   4005

1838 GORTON, John
Banks.

(*In his* General biographical dictionary. London, Whittaker, 1838. Vol.1.)
Copies: NPL:R(DS920/124).   4006

1843 PARISOT, V.
Banks.

(*In* Biographie universelle. Paris, Michand Frères, 1843. Tome 3, pp.13–19.)
Copies: NPL:R(DS920/601).   4007

1846 BROUGHAM AND VAUX, Henry Peter Brougham, *1st Baron*
Sir Joseph Banks.

Port.
(*In his* Lives of men of letters and science. London, 1846. Vol.2, pp.336–90, 502–6.)
Portrait is engraved on steel, by J. Brown. Mitchell Library copy dated 1847. *See also* no.4011.
Copies: NPL:M(Q920.02/B); NPL:R(DS920/784).   4008

1848 WELD, Charles Richard
[Memoir of Sir Joseph Banks; with some account of statue in the British Museum, and bibl.]

(*In his* History of the Royal Society. London, John W. Parker, 1848. Vol.2, pp.103–18, 302–5.)
Copies: NPL:M(506/W); NPL:D(84/430); NPL:R(S506/100).   4009

1849 BARROW, *Sir* John
Sir Joseph Banks.

(*In his* Sketches of the Royal Society. London, John Murray, 1849. pp.12–53.)
Copies: NPL:M(925/B). 4010

1855 BROUGHAM AND VAUX, Henry Peter Brougham, *1st Baron*
Sir Joseph Banks.

(*In his* Lives of philosophers of the time of George III. London, Griffin, 1855. pp.334–82.)
In his Works, vol.1. *See also* no.4008.
Copies: NPL:M(921.2/B); NPL:R(S320.8/5). 4011

1859 BANKS.
(*In* Nouvelle biographie générale. Paris, Didot Frères, 1859. Tome 4, pp.362–70.)
Copies: NPL:R(S920/699). 4012

1864 WALKER, William
Sir Joseph Banks.

(*In his* Memoirs of distinguished men of science of Great Britain living in the years
1807–8. 2nd ed. London, E. & F.N. Spon, 1864. pp.4–7.)
Copies: NPL:M(925/1B1). 4013

1870 EDWARDS, Edward
Founder of the Banksian Museum and Library.

(*In his* Lives of the founders of the British Museum. London, Trübner & Co., 1870.
Part 1, pp.487–510.)
Copies: NPL:M(027.5/E); NPL:R(S027.5/35). 4014

1876 SALVIN, Osbert
Banks' unpublished drawings, [made by S. Parkinson, during the voyage
of the Endeavour, 1768–9].

(*In* Rowley, G.D.—Ornithological miscellany. London, Trubner & Co., 1876. Vol.1,
pp.223–38.) These drawings are included in the Banks Collection in the British Museum.
Copies: NPL:R(Q598.2/10, S.C.). 4015

1876 SIR JOSEPH Banks
(*In* Eton portrait gallery . . . memoirs of the more eminent Eton men, by A Barrister of
the Inner Temple. With . . . steel engravings [mainly portraits] by C. Gabrielli. London,
1876. pp.503–12.)
Copies: NPL:R(DS920/1068). 4016

1885 BANKS; [with bibl.]
(*In* Dictionary of national biography. London, Smith, Elder, 1885. Vol.3, pp.129–33.)
Copies: NPL:M(920.042/1); NPL:R(920/3). 4017

1889 BARTON, George Burnett
Sir Joseph Banks, [by G.B. Barton and A. Britten].
Port.
(*In their* History of New South Wales. Sydney, Govt. Pr., 1889. Vol.1, pp.78–85.)
Copies: NPL:M(991/N); NPL:D(88/592); NPL:R(CD:994.4/52).   4018

1889–96 COKE, *Lady* Mary
The Letters and journals of Lady Mary Coke. [Ed. by J.A. Home.]
Edinburgh, D. Douglas, 1889–96.
Photoprints of pp.35, 153, 154, 192, 435, 437, 440, 442, 443, only, bearing references to
Sir Joseph Banks and Dr. Solander.
Copies: NPL:M(QA920/Banks. *Pam. File*).   4019

1890 COOPER, Thompson
Banks.
(*In his* Biographical dictionary. London, George Bell, 1890. Vol.1, p.132.)
Copies: NPL:R(DS920/924).   4020

1894 WILLIAMSON, George Charles
Sir Joseph Banks and his sister; [with portraits by Russell of Sir Joseph
Banks, Mrs. Banks, his mother, and Miss Sophia Banks.]
(*In his* John Russell, R.A. London, George Bell, 1894. pp.35–7.)
Copies: NPL:R(Q759.2/R964.2/1).   4021

1896 HOOKER, *Sir* Joseph Dalton
Sir Joseph Banks.
Port.
(*In* Banks, Sir Joseph—Journal. London, Macmillan, 1896. pp.xxiii–xxxviii.)
Copies: NPL:M(980/B); NPL:D(89/88); NPL:R(S990AE/21); ANL; QParl; VSL.
                     4022

1897 PIONEER of naturalist voyagers. Journal of Sir Joseph Banks, ed. by Sir J.D. Hooker: [a review].
(*Saturday Review* Jan.,1897, pp.44–5.)
Copies: NPL:R(Q050/S354).   4023

1898 MORRIS, Edward Ellis
Sir Joseph Banks.
(Library Association of Australasia—*Transactions and proceedings*, Oct.1898, pp.51–9.)
Copies: NPL:M(020.6/L); NPL:D(90/4); NPL:R(S020.6/5).   4024

1900 MORRIS, Edward Ellis
Botany of Cook's first voyage.
(*Victorian Naturalist* vol.17, 1900, pp.148–151.)
Copies: NPL:M(590.5/V); NPL:R(DS506/14).   4025

1903–5 MAIDEN, Joseph Henry
The Banksian plants: how they returned after 135 years.
(Old New South Wales, newspaper cuttings, vol.2, p.17, 1903–5.)
Copies: NPL:M(Q991/0).   4026

1904 BANKS.
(Encyclopaedia Americana. New York, The American Co., 1904. Vol.2.)
Copies: NPL:R(031/57).   4027

1904–5 MAIDEN, Joseph Henry
Work of Sir Joseph Banks: address by J.H. Maiden.
(Old New South Wales, newspaper cuttings, vol.2, p.12.)
Extract from the *Sydney Morning Herald*, 29th Mar. 1905.
Copies: NPL:M(Q991/0).   4028

1905 BROWN, E.
Sir Joseph Banks.
(*In his* What Australia lacks. Sydney, Eagle Printing House, pr., 1905. pp.23–30.)
Copies: NPL:M(A824/B).   4029

[1905] C., J.
Sir Joseph Banks, [by J.C. Extracted from the *Daily Telegraph*, Sydney,
June 17th, 1905.]
(Newspaper cuttings, vol.4, p.85.)
Copies: NPL:M(Q991/N).   4030

1905 MAIDEN, Joseph Henry
Observations on illustrations: Banks and Solander plants.
(Royal Society of New South Wales—*Journal*, 1905, pp.34–9.)
Copies: NPL:M(506/R); NPL:R(DS506/9).   4031

1905 SIR JOSEPH BANKS: [extract from *Sydney Morning Herald*, Jan.21,
Feb? 1905.]
(Newspaper cuttings, vol.116, pp.178–180, 186.)
Copies: NPL:M(F991.1/N).   4032

[1905–6 THE BANKS MEMORIAL. Extracts from the *Sydney Morning
Herald*, Apr.–May, 1905, Feb.14, 1906.]
(Newspaper cuttings, vol.131, pp.9–11.)
Copies: NPL:M(991.1/N).   4033

1905–6 SIR JOSEPH BANKS. [Extracts from the *Sydney Morning Herald, Daily Telegraph* and the *Evening News,* 1905–6.]
(Newspaper cuttings, vol.3, pp.157a, 162–163a; vol.4, p.85; vol.6, p.14.)
Copies: NPL:M(Q991/N).   4034

1906 MAIDEN, Joseph Henry
Sir Joseph Banks.
(Royal Australian Historical Society—*Journal and Proceedings,* vol.2, 1906, pp.22–3.)
Copies: NPL:M(991/R, Ref.Books); NPL:D(9/69); NPL:R(S991.06/1A, Ref.Books).
                                                                       4035

1908 MAIDEN, Joseph Henry
Records of Australian botanists.
(Royal Society of New South Wales—*Journal,* 1908, pp.63–4.)
Copies: NPL:M(506/R); NPL:R(DS506/9).   4036

1909 MAIDEN, Joseph Henry
Sir Joseph Banks, the father of Australia: [abstract of a lecture].
(Australasian Association for the Advancement of Science—*Report,* 12, 1909, pp.394–6.)
Copies: NPL:M(506/A); NPL:D(9/246); NPL:R(DS506/15).   4037

1914 BANKS: [short biographical sketch. With bibl.]
(New international encyclopaedia. New York, Dodd, Mead & Co., 1914. Vol.2, pp. 637–8.)
Copies: NPL:R(031/77).   4038

1917 BERTIE, Charles Henry
Notes from a lantern lecture, delivered Nov.11, 1913, with view of Banks's house, London.
(Australian Historical Society—*Journal and Proceedings,* 1917, pp.24–6.)
Copies: NPL:M(991/R, Ref.Books); NPL:D(9/69); NPL:R(S991.01/1A, Ref.Books).
                                                                       4039

1917 GEIKIE, *Sir* Archibald
Presidentship of Sir Joseph Banks, 1778–1789.
Port.
(*In his* Annals of the Royal Society Club. London, Macmillan, 1917. pp.144–267.)
Copies: NPL:M(506/G); NPL:D(91/473); NPL:R(S367.942/9).   4040

1919 BANKS.
(Encyclopaedia Britannica. Cambridge, U.P., 1910. Vol.3, p.333.)
Copies: NPL:D(Q91/3); NPL:R(DQ032/153).   4041

[1920] BANKS.

Port.

(Harmsworth's universal encyclopaedia. London, Amalgamated Press, [1920]. Vol.2, p.899.)

Copies: NPL:R(030/7). 4042

1920 CENTENARY of Sir Joseph Banks.

(*Science* Aug.1920, p.123.)

Copies: NPL:R(Q506/11). 4043

1920–21 [ARTICLES from the Linnean Society of London, *Proceedings* 133rd session, Nov. 1920–June 1921.]

Photographic copy.

CONTENTS:

Jackson, B. Daydon—Sir Joseph Banks as a traveller; [with bibl.]. pp.1–8.
Rendle, A.B.—Banks as a patron of science. pp.9–15.
Britten, James—Banks as botanist. pp.15–19.
Banks as Trustee of the British Museum. Appendix. pp.20–21.

Copies: NPL:M(A925.8/B218/15B1); NPL:R(S580.6/12). 4044

[1922] FARINGTON, Joseph

[Sir Joseph Banks mentioned in a contemporary diary; with port.]

(*In his* Farington diary. 2nd ed. London, Hutchinson, [1922]. Vol.1, various pp.)
See also no.4047.

Copies: NPL:M(927/F). 4045

1922 WOOD, George Arnold

Banks's manuscript journals.

(*In his* Discovery of Australia. London, Macmillan, 1922. pp.382–5.)

Copies: NPL:M(980/125A1); NPL:D(92/153); NPL:R(DS990.1/19). 4046

1923 FARINGTON, Joseph

[Sir Joseph Banks mentioned in a contemporary diary; with port.]

(*In his* Farington diary. 4th ed. London, Hutchinson, 1923. Vol.1, various pp.)
See also no.4045.

Copies: NPL:R(S920/F226/1). 4047

1923 FORSYTH, John

Biographical note [on Archibald Menzies; with reference to Sir Joseph Banks' instructions to him, etc.].

(*In* Menzies, Archibald—Journal of Vancouver's voyage. Victoria, B.C., William H. Cullin, pr., 1923. pp.vii–xii.)

Copies: NPL:M(917.11/M). 4048

1925 BANKS.

(*In* Illustrated Chambers's encyclopaedia. London, Chambers Ltd., 1925. Vol.1, pp. 719–20.)
Copies: NPL:M(Q032/341); NPL:R(Q032/1A, 1924 ed.).   4049

1926 SAUNDERS, Charles Francis

Of the eucalyptus and how Joseph Banks gave it one name and a Frenchman another.
(*In his* Trees and shrubs of California gardens. New York, 1926. pp.1–13.)
Copies: NPL:M(635.92/S); NPL:R(S635.92/10).   4050

1927 BEASLEY, H.G.

Metal mere, [with Sir Joseph Banks' coat of arms].
Illus.
(Polynesian Society—*Journal*, vol.36, Sept. 1927, pp.297–8.)
Copies: NPL:M(Q572.9/P); NPL:D(9/156); NPL:R(DS572.99/2).   4051

1928 SIR JOSEPH BANKS wears a Maori, not an Otahetian, cloak: [note].

(Polynesian Society—*Journal*, vol.37, 1928, p.93.)
Copies: NPL:M(Q572.9/P); NPL:D(9/157); NPL:R(DS572.99/2).   4052

1930 MACKANESS, George

Sir Joseph Banks and colonial currency; [with bibl.]
(Royal Australian Historical Society—*Journal and Proceedings*, vol.16, 1930, pp.263–7.)
Copies: NPL:M(991/R); NPL:D(9/69); NPL:R(S991.06/1A).   4053

1937 BIRTH-DATE of Sir Joseph Banks, [by J. Ardagh and R.S.B.].

(*Notes and Queries*, May 8, 1937, p.334, May 22, p.375.)
Quotes the Parish register and Banks' own statement.
Copies: NPL:R(DS050/N911).   4054

1939 ALLAN, H.H.

Banks and Solander: fathers of New Zealand botany.
Illus.
Extracted from the Royal New Zealand Institute of Horticulture—*Journal*, vol.8, no.4, pp.85–90, Mar.1939.
Copies: NPL:M(A920/Banks. *Pam. File*).   4055

1939 LEE, M.

Sir Joseph Banks.
(*Australian National Review*, Canberra, May 1938, pp.13–23.)
Copies: NPL:M(059/1).   4056

1939 MITCHELL, Rae Else–
George Caley: his life and work, [and association with Sir Joseph Banks.
With bibl.].

(Royal Australian Historical Society—*Journal and Proceedings*, vol.25, 1939, pp.437–542;
vol.26, 1940, pp.186–7.)

Copies: NPL:M(991/R); NPL:D(9/69); NPL:R(S991.06/1A).   4057

1943 DAVIES, John David Griffith
Sir Joseph Banks . . . 1743–1820.
(*Nature* Feb.13, 1943, pp.181–3.)
Copies: NPL:R(DQ505/1).   4058

1943 HUNKIN, Joseph Wellington, *Bishop of Truro*
Bicentenary of Sir Joseph Banks.
pp.6.
Extracted from *The Fortnightly*, Oct.1943, pp.271–5.
Copies: NPL:M(A925.8/B218/8A1); NPL:R(S050/F743).   4059

1945 ARBER, Agnes
Sir Joseph Banks and botany.
Reprinted from *Chronica Botanica* vol.9, pp.94–106, Autumn 1945.
Copies: NPL:M(QA925.8/B218/1A1).   4060

[1946] JARVIS, Henry Wood
[Banks and Australia.]
(*In his* Let the great story be told: the truth about British expansion. [With note on
sources and bibl.] London, Sampson Low, Marston, [1946]. pp.100–125.)
Copies: NPL:M(909/J); NPL:R(DS909/289); ANL.   4061

1946 O'DONNELL, John
Sir Joseph Banks and Australian science.
(*Australia's Progress*, Sydney. Vol.1, pp.24–7, Jan.1946.)
Copies: NPL:M(059/26).   4062

1949 CRONE, Gerald Roe
The Men behind modern geography: Sir Joseph Banks.
Port.
(*Geographical Magazine* vol.22, pp.142–4, Aug.1949.)
Copies: NPL:R(S909.5A/5).   4063

1950 CAMERON, Hector Charles
Failure of the philosophers to sail with Cook in the *Resolution;* [with
letters from Cook to Banks, and from Banks to the First Lord of the
Admiralty. With bibl. notes.] London, Clowes, 1950.

(*Geographical Journal* vol.116, pp.49–54, Sept.1950.)
Copies: NPL:M(980:Co3/C1A1, reprint); NPL:R(DS909.6A/2). 4064

1950 CRAMP, Karl Reginald
Kurnell and Sir Joseph Banks. [With illus. of memorials and inscriptions.]
(*Port of Sydney Journal* vol.3, pp.12–15, July, 1950.)
Copies: NPL:M(656.5/2). 4065

1950 DAWSON, Warren Royal
Sir Joseph Hooker and Dawson Turner.
pp.[5].
Extracted from *Journal of the Society for the Bibliography of Natural History*, vol.2, pt.6, 1950, pp.218–222.
Deals mainly with Hooker's and Dawson Turner's work on the Banks papers.
Copies: NPL:M(A925.8/B218/10A1); NPL:R(S570.306/1). 4066

[1950] GORDON, Mona Clifton
Banks, his island [i.e. New Zealand].
(*In her* Fame passes by, 1769–1885. Christchurch, Bascands Ltd., [1950]. pp.11–39.)
Copies: NPL:M(920/G); ANL. 4067

1950 SMITH, Bernard William
European vision and the South Pacific; [with bibl.].
Illus.
Reprinted from the *Journal of the Warburg and Courtauld Institutes*, vol.13, pp.65–100. 1950. Illustrations are reproductions from early artists' work.
Copies: NPL:M(Q759.09/2A1); NPL:D(95/121). 4068

1951 CAMERON, Hector Charles
Sir Joseph Banks.
(*In his* Samuel Crompton. London, Batchworth, 1951. pp.90–5.)
Copies: NPL:R(920/C945.5/1). 4069

1951 CRONE, Gerald Roe
Sir Joseph Banks and the first advance [in geography] in Britain.
pp.3–10.
(*In his* Modern geographers. London, Royal Geographical Society, 1951.)
Copies: NPL:R(S909.9A/154). 4070

1952 FINNIS, Harold J.
The MSS. of the York Gate Library.
Facs.
Royal Geographical Society of Australasia—South Australian Branch—*Proceedings*, 1951–52, vol.53, pp.29–45, Dec. 1952.)
Deals mainly with Banks' manuscripts.
Copies: NPL:M(980/R); NPL:R(DS993.06A/1). 4071

1953 ELLIS, Malcolm Henry
The Father of Australia.
(*Bulletin* vol.74, Apr.15, 1953, p.25.)
Copies: NPL:M(MDQ079/39); NPL:R(F079/B936).   4072

[1954] MADDISON, R.E.W.
Spring Grove, the country house of Sir Joseph Banks, Bart., P.R.S., by
R.E.W. Maddison and R.E. Maddison. [With bibl.]. London, Headley
Bros., pr., [1954].
Illus. plan, pp.[10].
Reprinted from Royal Society of London—*Notes and records*, vol.11, no.1, Jan.1954, pp.91–9.
Copies: NPL:M(A925.8/B218/9A1).   4073

1956 ANDERSON, Alexander Walter
Sir Joseph Banks.
(*In his* How we got our flowers. London, Benn, 1956. pp.124–30.)
First published 1950 as *The Coming of the Flowers*.
Copies: NPL:M(582/A); NPL:R(E635.909/And).   4074

1956 BISHOP, A.J.
The Courteous spirit.
Port.
(*Bank Notes* vol.39, pp.20–32, Dec.1956.)
Copies: NPL:M(Q332.1105/B).   4075

1956 KENNEDY, Keith
Sir Joseph Banks, naturalist.
(*Townsville Naturalist* vol.3, pp.6–8, June 1956.)
Copies: NPL:M(506/24).   4076

1957 ANDERSON, Bern
A Note on the Banks baton.
(*American Neptune* vol.17, p.67, Jan.1957.)
Copies: NPL:M(Q910.905/1).   4077

1957 STONE, Walter William
Joseph Banks, Obarea, & the Rams Skull Press.
(*Biblionews* vol.10, no.5, pp.16–18, May 1957.)
Copies: NPL:M(Q010.5/3).   4078

1959 LYSAGHT, Averil
Some eighteenth century bird paintings in the library of Sir Joseph
Banks, 1743–1820; [with bibl.] London, British Museum, 1959.

Plates, pp.[ii], 253, 371.
(British Museum, Natural History—*Bulletin . . . hist. ser.*, vol.1, no.6.)
Copies: NPL:M(598.2/4A1); NPL:R(S506/163). 4079

1960 CLARK, Charles Manning Hope
The Choice of Botany Bay. [With bibl.]
(*Historical Studies* vol.9, pp.221–32, Nov.1960.)
Copies: NPL:M(990.05/1); NPL:R(N994.006/1). 4080

1960 RYDEN, Stig
Unknown Cook collection identified. [With bibl.]
Illus. ports.
(*Ethnos* vol.25, pp.1–19, no.1–2, 1960.)
Copies: NPL:M(572.06/2). 4081

1962 DU RIETZ, Rolf
Three letters from James Burney to Sir Joseph Banks.
(*Ethnos* vol.27, pp.115–25, no.1–4, 1962.)
Copies: NPL:M(572.06/2). 4082

1962 LEE, J.E.
Notes on historic links between Lincolnshire and Australia, part 1.
(*Descent* vol.1, pp.21–4, pt.1, 1962.)
Copies: NPL:M(A929.106/1). 4083

1962 MACKANESS, George
Sir Joseph Banks, Bart. An appreciation.
(Royal Australian Historical Society—*Journal and Proceedings*, vol.48, pp.44–59, pt.1, 1962.)
Copies: NPL:M(991/R); NPL:D(9/69); NPL:R(S991.01A). 4084

1964 STRAUSS, W. Patrick
Paradoxical co-operation: Sir Joseph Banks and the London Missionary
Society. [With reply by W.N. Gunson.]
(*Historical Studies: Australian and New Zealand* vol.11, Ap.1964, pp.246–52; Ap.1965, pp.513–34.)
Copies: NPL:M(990.05/1); NPL:R(N994.006/1); ANL. 4085

1965 MACKANESS, George
Sir Joseph Banks, Bart: an appreciation.
(*In his* Bibliomania. Sydney, A. & R., 1965. pp.142–58.)
Copies: NPL:M(A824/M153.3/1A1); NPL:R(994.0016/1). 4086

COTES, Francis
Sir Joseph Banks by Cotes, 1770.

Photograph of framed port. in oils. Meas. within frame 6″ x 4⅝″. Meas. of original 36″ x 28″.

The original was offered at Christie's 3 June 1932. It shows a middle-aged man in light brown coat with green collar and white braid, white vest, leaning his arm on a pedestal. The portrait is possibly by Francis Cotes, but is most unlikely to be of Banks.
Further notes are filed with this photograph.

Copies: NPL:M(PXn170).   4087

CRAIG

CRAIG, W.M.
Sir Joseph Banks, Bart. &c. &c. &c.
W.M. Craig del., H. Robinson sc.

Published by Henry Fisher, Caxton, Liverpool. 1819. Engraving. Meas. of engraved surface, c.5″ x 4″.

Copies: NPL:M(P3/26G).   4088

Another print.
Copies: NPL:D(DL.Pd618).   4089

Another print.
Hand-coloured.
Copies: NPL:D(DL.Pd619).   4090

Photograph.
Uncoloured.
Copies: NPL:M(P1/Banks-Craig 1).   4091

DANCE

DANCE, George
Sir Joseph Banks.

Pencil drawing. 8″ x 7¼″, oval. Untitled; signed.
Copies: ANL.   4092

DANCE, George
The Right Honorable Sir Joseph Banks, K.B. President of the Royal Society. Geo. Dance del. June 27, 1803. W.ᵐ Daniell fecit.

Published by Will.ᵐ Daniell . . . London. June 1, 1811. Soft-ground etching. Meas. of plate mark 10¾″ x 8″.

Copies: NPL:M(P3/27A).   4093

Another print.
Copies: NPL:M(P3/35).   4094

Another print.
Copies: NPL:D(DL.Pe220).   4095

Another print, cut.
Copies: NPL:M(P1/Banks–Dance 1).   4096

Another print.
(*Inserted in* Smith, E.—Life of Sir Joseph Banks. 1911. Vol.2, facing p.227.)
Copies: Australasian Pioneers' Club, Sydney.   4097

EDRIDGE

EDRIDGE, Henry
Sir Joseph Banks: [pencil drawing by] Henry Edridge A.R.A. (1769–1821).

Size 12″ x 9″. Unsigned. Undated.
This excellent portrait was presented to the National Art Gallery of New South Wales by Mrs. John Lane, of London, widow of the publisher, in 1926.
Henry Edridge (1769–1821) was a genuine artist, but he owed much of his advancement to the friendly notice of Sir Joshua Reynolds, who permitted him to make copies of his portraits in miniature. Edridge's earliest works were painted on ivory, but his spirited drawings on paper with the figure slightly touched in, and the head carefully finished, are better known. He was made an A.R.A. in 1820.

Copies: Art Gallery of New South Wales.   4098

LAWRENCE

Originals, Including Photocopies of Originals

LAWRENCE, *Sir* Thomas
Sir Joseph Banks [by Sir Thomas Lawrence].

Photograph of pencil drawing.
(National Portrait Gallery—Photographs of portraits . . . of persons relating to Australia. [1914. Plate 5].)
Copies: NPL:M(QA920/N).   4099

Another print.
Copies: NPL:D(DL Pd665).   4100

The Same, photograph, 1965.
$5\frac{7}{8}″$ x $7\frac{7}{8}″$.
Copies: NPL:M(P1/Banks–Lawrence 5).   4101

Reproduced in Cust, Lionel Henry—National Portrait Gallery. London, 1902. Vol.2, p.87, no.853.

Copies: NPL:R(Q757/3). 4102

Reproductions Arranged by Engraver

CARDON

The Right Hon: Sir Joseph Banks, Bart. K.B. President of the Royal Society. From an original picture by T. Lawrence . . . in the possession of Samuel Lysons, Esq. Drawn by W. Evans. Engraved by A. Cardon.

Published Jan.1. 1810, by T. Cadell & W. Davies . . . London. Engraving. Meas. of plate mark $14\frac{3}{4}''$ x $10\frac{7}{8}''$.

Copies: NPL:M(P3/27B). 4103

Another print.
Copies: NPL:M(P3/36). 4104

Another 2 prints.
Copies: NPL:D(DL.Pe218,Pe228). 4105

Another print. Proof before letters.
(*Inserted in* Smith, E.—Life of Sir Joseph Banks. 1911. Vol.2, facing p.281.)
Copies: Australasian Pioneers' Club, Sydney. 4106

Another print.
Hand-coloured, cut.
Copies: NPL:D(DL Pe219). 4107

Another print.
Hand-coloured, cut to $5\frac{3}{4}''$ x $4\frac{1}{8}''$. Head and shoulders.
Pencil note on back in an unknown hand "1796".
Copies: NPL:D(DL Pd621). 4108

LIZARS

Sir Joseph Banks, Bart. K.B. (Lawrence del.[t], Lizars sc.) Engraved for the Naturalist's Library.

(Jardine, *Sir* William—Natural history of fishes of the perch family. Edinburgh, W.H. Lizars, 1835. Frontisp. *The Naturalist's Library*, vol.1.)
Copies: NPL:R(S597.5/4). 4109

McDONALD, J.

Portrait [after the picture by Thos. Lawrence, by J. McDonald, 1903.]
(*Otago Daily Times and Witness—Christmas Annual*, 1904. p.13.)
Copies: NPL:M(F997/0). 4110

McLEOD, W.

Sir Joseph Banks [portrait from a drawing by W. McLeod after Lawrence].

1886. Wood engraving. 4⅛″ x 3⅜″.

With frame of Australian native flowers. *Cut from* Garran, Andrew—Picturesque Atlas of Australasia. Sydney, 1886.

Copies: NPL:M(P1/Banks–Lawrence 4).   4111

PHILLIBROWN

Sir Joseph Banks. Bart. K.B: P.R.S. ob.1820. Lawrence pinx. Phillibrown sc.

Engraving. Meas. within frame lines 3⅞″ x 2 15/16″.

Copies: NPL:M(P3/28C).   4112

ROBINSON, H.

Sir Joseph Banks Bar.^t K.B., F.R.S.: [engraving] from the original of Sir Thomas Lawrence in the British Museum. Drawn by Wm Derby . . . and engraved by H. Robinson.

London. Published Jan.1, 1831, by Harding & Lepard. Meas. within frame lines 4 15/16″ x 3⅞″. Plate mark 15″ x 10⅜″.

Copies: NPL:M(P3/28B).   4113

Another print.

Copies: NPL:M(P2/23).   4114

The Same, photo-litho.

(Public Library of N.S.W. Reproduction T13.)   4115

The Same, [entitled] Sir Joseph Banks, Bar.^t K.B.: P.R.S. ob.1820. Engraved by H. Robinson from the original of Sir Thomas Lawrence in the British Museum.

London. Published July 1, 1831, by Harding & Lepard. Proof on India paper. Meas. within frame lines 4 15/16″ x 3⅞″. Plate mark 10″ x 7¾″.

Copies: NPL:D(DL Pd605).   4116

The Same. Published Decr.1. 1831.

(*Inserted in* Smith, E.—Life of Sir Joseph Banks. 1911. Vol.2, frontisp.)

Copies: Australasian Pioneers' Club, Sydney.   4117

The Same. Published April 1, 1832, by Harding & Lepard . . . London.

Meas. within frame lines 4 15/16″ x 3⅞″. Cut.

Copies: NPL:M(P3/28A).   4118

The Same. [Published by] John Tallis & Company, London & New York.

(Cook, J.—Collected Voyages. Voyages of Captain James Cook round the world. London, John Tallis, [1842]. Vol.2, frontisp.)

Copies: NPL:M(Q980:Co1/4C2).   4119

The Same. [Published by] John Tallis & Company, London & New York.

(Martin, Robert Montgomery—Australia. London, Tallis, 1853. Opp. p.59.)

Copies: NPL:M(Q990.1/M); NPL:D(Q85/76); NPL:R(Q990.1/3).   4120

Another print.

Copies: NPL:D(DL Pd606).   4121

Photograph

(N.S.W.—Govt. Printer—Photographs illustrating the earliest times of N.S.W.)

Copies: NPL:M(F981/N).   4122

The Same, heliotype, reproduced from *Martin's British Colonies.*

Copies: NPL:M(P1/Banks–Lawrence 1).   4123

Proof of the heliotype, before letters.

Copies: NPL:M(P1/Banks–Lawrence 3).   4124

Photograph of the heliotype.

Copies: NPL:M(P1/Banks–Lawrence 2).   4125

Reproduced in Tregarthen, Greville—Australian Commonwealth. London, Unwin, 1893. p.71.

Copies: NPL:M(990.1/100A1); NPL:D(89/630).   4126

Also reproduced in Brady, Edwn James — Australia unlimited. Melbourne, Geo. Robertson, [1918]. p.30.

Copies: NPL:M(Q980.1/13A1); NPL:R(Q990.1A26A).   4127

WOOLNOTH

Sir Joseph Banks, G.C.B. T. Lawrence R.A. Pinx.ᵗ I. Woolnoth Sculp.ᵗ

Pub. April 1, 1823 by Dean and Munday Threadneedle Street. $7\frac{1}{4}''$ x $4\frac{3}{8}''$ meas. of plate mark. Cut.

(*Inserted in* An History of the instances of exclusion from the Royal Society. London, J. Debrett, 1784.)

Copies: NPL:D(78/62).   4128

Reproductions Arranged by Title of the Reproduction

SIR JOSEPH BANKS, Pres. R.S., Sir T. Lawrence, pinx.

Soft ground etching. Meas. of plate mark $5\frac{7}{8}''$ x $4\frac{1}{2}''$.

(*Inserted in* Kippis, *Rev.* Andrew—Life of Captain James Cook. Opp. p.49.)

Copies: NPL:D(Q78/8).   4129

LIND, James
Banks and Solander.
Photograph of silhouette.
Copies: NPL:M(MS B1489⁻³ pt.5).   4130

Reproduced in Banks, *Sir* Joseph—*Endeavour* Journal. Sydney, P.L.N.S.W., 1962. Vol.1, facing p.84.
Copies: NPL:M(A925.8/B).   4131

MACINTOSH, W.P.

PLAQUE, by W.P. Macintosh.
c.189–. $22\frac{1}{4}''$ x $20\frac{1}{2}''$. Plaster. Brass-coloured.
Copies: Captain Cook's Landing Place Trust.   4132

PHILLIPS

Originals, Including Photocopies of Originals

There are several portraits of Banks by Phillips, four of which differ but little from each other. These four are in the possession respectively of the Dixson Galleries (The Library of N.S.W.), the Royal Society, the Royal Horticultural Society and the National Portrait Gallery. The engraving by Schiavonetti follows the portrait in the Dixson Galleries; those by Aitken, Brown, Fry, Herdwiller, Thomson and Wagstaff follow the Royal Society portrait, while Reynolds is after the Royal Horticultural Society portrait.

Notes on portrait of Banks by Phillips are filed at NPL:M PXn 171, 173 and 174.

PHILLIPS, Thomas
Sir Joseph Banks, 1743–1820.
c.1808–9. Oil painting. 55″ x 43″ inside frame. Unsigned. Undated. Title from frame label.
This portrait, purchased by William Dixson in 1929 from Capt. Knatchbull-Hugessen, was painted to the order of Don José de Mendoza y Rios, F.R.S., as a presentation to Banks. The engraving by Schiavonetti was made from this. After Lady Banks' death the portrait came into the possession of the Knatchbull-Hugessen family. A replica of the portrait was painted for Mendoza and by him bequeathed to the Royal Society. A copy of the portrait was made to the order of Capt. Knatchbull-Hugessen in 1929.

Notes on this portrait and other portraits by Phillips are at NPL:M PXn 171, 173 and 174.
Copies: NPL:D(DG25).   4133

Photographs (3)
Copies: NPL:M(P1/Banks–Phillips 2–4).   4134

PHILLIPS, Thomas
Sir Joseph Banks.

1810. Photograph of oil painting.
(National Portrait Gallery—Photographs of portraits . . . of persons relating to Australia.
[1914. Plate 6.])
Copies: NPL:M(QA920/N).   4135

Another 2 prints.
Copies: NPL:M(P1/Banks–Phillips 10); NPL:D(DL Pd651).   4136

The Same, photograph, 1965.
Copies: NPL:M(P1/Banks–Phillips 11).   4137

Reproduced with note in Cust, Lionel Henry—National Portrait Gallery. London, 1902.
Vol.2, p.87, no.885.
Copies: NPL:R(Q757/3).   4138

Also reproduced in Kitson, Arthur—Captain James Cook. London, John Murray, 1907.
Opp. p.100.
Copies: NPL:M(923.9/C771.2/14A1); NPL:D(90/206); NPL:R(S920/C771/4).   4139

PHILLIPS, Thomas
[Sir Joseph Banks.]

c.1814. Oil. 35″ x 27″ inside frame.
Unsigned. Undated.
Contemporary or near-contemporary copy of the portrait by Phillips which hangs in
the Guildhall Museum, Boston, Lincolnshire, and photographs of which are filed at
NPL:M P1/Banks–Phillips 5–7.
Copies: NPL:D(DG274).   4140

Photographs, (2) of head only in DG274.
Copies: NPL:M(P1/Banks–Phillips 8–9).   4141

The Same. [Process reproduction of the portrait in the Guildhall Museum,
Boston, Lincolnshire.]
(Royal Australian Historical Society—*Journal and Proceedings*. 1920, p.200.)
Copies: NPL:M(991/R); NPL:D(9/69); NPL:R(S991.06/1A).   4142

Reproductions Arranged by Engraver

AITKEN
Sir Joseph Banks. Engraved on wood by Peter Aitken, [from the] portrait
in the Royal Society, London.
(*Century Illustrated Monthly Magazine*, New York, Sept. 1899, p.757.)
Copies: NPL:R(DS050/C397).   4143

BOILLY

Banks. Alp. Boilly.

Engraving. Meas. of engraved surface c.3″ x 3$\frac{5}{16}$″.

Copies: NPL:M(P3/25A). 4144

BROWN

Sir Joseph Banks. Engraved by J. Brown [after Phillips].

London, Henry Colburn, 1846. Engraving. Meas. within frame lines 4$\frac{7}{8}$″ x 4″.

Copies: NPL:M(P3/25B). 4145

Another 3 prints.

Copies: NPL:D(DL Pd616, 617); ANL:F. 4146

FRY

Sir Jos.^{h} Banks . . . engraved with permission of Messrs Colnaghi, from their large print after Thos Phillips, R.A. by W.T. Fry.

Published June 1820 by T. Boys. Ludgate Hill.
Engraving. On India paper. Meas. within frame lines 2″ x 1$\frac{5}{8}$″. Plate mark 9$\frac{5}{8}$″ x 5$\frac{15}{16}$″.
With decorated border.

Copies: NPL:M(P3/25C). 4147

Another print.

Copies: NPL:D(DL Pe221). 4148

GREVEDON

Banks. N. Grevedon 1826. Lith. de C. Motte.

Meas. of lithographed surface c.10$\frac{1}{2}$″ x 10$\frac{3}{4}$″. On India paper mounted on leaf of folio volume size, with another leaf containing biography.

Copies: NPL:D(DL Pf67). 4149

Another print.

Hand-coloured.

Copies: NPL:D(DL Pf68). 4150

HERDWILLER

J. Banks. After T. Phillips. Herdwiller sc. 1835.

Engraving. Meas. of port. c.3$\frac{1}{4}$″ x 3$\frac{1}{4}$″.

Copies: NPL:M(P3/25D). 4151

Another print.

Copies: NPL:D(DL Pd620). 4152

The Same, proof before letters. On India paper.

Copies: NPL:D(DL Pd655). 4153

The Same, proof before letters but with engraver's name.

Meas. of sheet 9¾″ x 6½″.

Copies: NPL:D(DL Pd656).

4154

HOLL

Sir Joseph Banks, Bart., P.R.S. [Painted by] Tho.ˢ Phillips, R.A.; [engraved by] W. Holl.

Fisher, Son & Co, London 1829. Engraving. Meas. of port. 4$\frac{7}{16}$″ x 3½″. Meas. of plate mark 8$\frac{11}{16}$″ x 5¾″.

With facsimile of Banks' signature.

Copies: NPL:M(P3/21B).

4155

Another print.

Copies: NPL:D(DL Pd609); ANL:F.

4156

Another print, plate mark cut.

Copies: NPL:D(DL Pd607).

4157

Another print.

(*Inserted in* Smith, E.—Life of Sir Joseph Banks. 1911. Vol.2, facing p.313.)

Copies: Australasian Pioneers' Club, Sydney.

4158

Another print.

Hand-coloured, imprint and plate mark cut.

Copies: NPL:D(DL Pd608).

4159

The Same.

On India paper, mounted on sheet with plate mark.

Copies: NPL:M(P3/21A).

4160

Another print.

Copies: NPL:M(P1/Banks–Phillips 13).

4161

The Same, with letters but before imprint.

Meas. of sheet 10⅞″ x 7″.

(Australasian Scrap-book f.68.)

Copies: NPL:M(F980/A).

4162

The Same. 1832.

Meas. of port. 4$\frac{7}{16}$″ x 3½″.

Copies: NPL:M(P3/21C).

4163

Another print.

Copies: NPL:M(P1/Banks–Phillips 12).

4164

The Same. 1847.

Meas. of port. $4\frac{7}{16}''$ x $3\frac{1}{2}''$.

Copies: NPL:M(P3/21D). 4165

REYNOLDS

The R.^{t} Honble Sir Joseph Banks, Bar.^{t} G.C.B., President of the Royal Society of London, Honorary Member of the Horticultural Society of London. Painted by T. Phillips. Esq.^{e} R.A. Engraved by S.W. Reynolds . . . and S. Cousins . . . from the original picture in the possession of the Horticultural Society.

Pub.^{d} by S.W. Reynolds Augt 1822. Mezzotint.

Meas. of port. $17\frac{1}{8}''$ x 13″. Meas. of plate mark 20″ x $13\frac{3}{4}''$.

Copies: NPL:M(P3/20). 4166

Another print.

Copies: NPL:D(DL Pf71). 4167

Photograph.

Copies: NPL:D(DL Pd604). 4168

The Same.

London. Published Jany 1828 by M. Colnaghi. Mezzotint.

Meas. of port. $17\frac{1}{4}''$ x $13\frac{1}{8}''$. Meas. of plate mark 20″ x $13\frac{3}{4}''$.

Copies: NPL:M(P3/22). 4169

SCHIAVONETTI

Sir Joseph Banks, Bar.^{t} President of the Royal Society. Painted by T^{ho}.^{s} Phillips R.A. Engraved by N. Schiavonetti.

London . . . Published 1812 by N. Schiavonetti. Engraving.

Meas. of port. $17\frac{1}{8}''$ x $13\frac{1}{2}''$. Meas. of plate mark $20\frac{3}{16}''$ x $15\frac{3}{8}''$.

This is an engraving after the portrait in the Dixson Galleries (DG 25), listed in this Bibliography as no.4133.

Copies: NPL:D(DG P3/14). 4170

Another print, cut.

Copies: NPL:M(P3/34). 4171

Another print.

Hand-coloured, cut.

Copies: NPL:M(P3/46). 4172

The Same, proof with open letters on India paper.

Copies: NPL:M(P3/24). 4173

Another print.

Copies: NPL:M(P3/18).   4174

The Same, proof on India paper, fully lettered.

Copies: NPL:D(DL Pf72).   4175

Another print.

Copies: NPL:M(P3/45).   4176

Reproduced in Hooker, *Sir* Joseph Dalton—Journal of Sir Joseph Banks. London, Macmillan, 1896. Frontisp.

Copies: NPL:M(980/B); NPL:D(89/88); NPL:R(S990A/21).   4177

TARDIEU

Sir J.^{ph} Banks, voyageur—naturaliste. Président de la Societé royale de Londres. Né à Revesby dans le Comté de Lincoln, Angleterre, en 1743. Mort à Londres, le 9 Mai 1820 Dessiné d'après le tableau de Th. Phillips, et gravé par Ambroise Tardieu.

Meas. of oval port. 4″ x 3 $\frac{5}{16}$″.

Copies: NPL:D(DL Pd624).   4178

Photograph, cut.

Copies: NPL:M(P1/Banks–Phillips 17).   4179

The Same, proof before letters.

Meas. of plate mark 9 $\frac{3}{16}$″ x 5 $\frac{5}{16}$″.

Copies: NPL:D(DL Pd612).   4180

THOMSON

Sir Joseph Banks Bar.^{t} P.R.S. [Engraving after a picture by Phillips in the possession of the Royal Society] Thomson sc.

Published by H. Colburn & Co August 1.st 1820. Engraving.
Meas. of engraved surface c.5″ x 4½″. Meas. of plate mark 8¾″ x 5¾″.

Copies: NPL:M(P3/19A).   4181

Another 2 prints.

Copies: NPL:M(P3/19C); NPL:D(DL Pd614).   4182

Another print.

(Australasian Scrap-book p.47.)

Copies: NPL:M(F980/A).   4183

Another print.

Hand-coloured.

Copies: NPL:D(DL Pd615).   4184

The Same, on India paper mounted within frame line.
Meas. within frame line 8¼″ x 14 13/16″.
Copies: NPL:M(P3/19B).   4185

WAGSTAFF

Sir J. Banks. Engraved by C.E. Wagstaff. From a picture by T. Phillips,
in the possession of the Royal Society.
London. Published by Charles Knight. Engraving. Meas. within frame line 5¼″ x 4″.
Copies: NPL:M(P1/Banks–Phillips 14).   4186

Another print, cut.
Copies: NPL:M(P1/Banks–Phillips 15).   4187

The Same; [published by Knight], Under the Superintendance of the
Society for the Diffusion of Useful Knowledge.
Copies: NPL:M(P3/19E).   4188

Another 2 prints.
Copies: NPL:D(DL Pd611, 652).   4189

Another print.
(*Inserted in* Smith, E.—Life of Sir Joseph Banks. 1911. Vol. 1, facing p.58.)
Copies: Australasian Pioneers' Club, Sydney.   4190

Another print, cut.
Copies: NPL:M(P1/Banks–Phillips 16).   4191

Another print.
Hand-coloured.
Copies: NPL:D(DL Pd 610).   4192

The Same; [published] by Wm S. Orr & Co., London. Under the
Superintendance of the Society for the Diffusion of Useful Knowledge.
Copies: NPL:D(DL Pd653).   4193

The Same; entitled Sir J. Banks.
Engraved by Wagstaff from a picture by Phillips in possession of the Royal Society.
William Mackenzie, Glasgow. Engraving. Meas. of port. 5¼″ x 4″.
Copies: NPL:M(P3/19D).   4194

Another 2 prints.
Copies: NPL:D(DL Pd613); ANL:F.   4195

Another print.

Hand-coloured.

Copies: NPL:D(DL Pd654).   4196

Reproductions Arranged by Title of the Reproduction

THE R.^{t} HONBLE S.^{r} J BANKS B.^{t} &c &c &c T. Phillips R.A. 1816.

Dry-point. Meas. of engraved surface c.5$\frac{1}{2}$" x 5".
Meas. of sheet 9" x 5$\frac{3}{4}$".
Note in pencil at bottom of sheet. "Private plate, only 12 impressions made. [Signed]
Dawson Turner."

Copies: NPL:D(DL Pd603).   4197

Photograph.

Copies: NPL:M(P1/Banks–Phillips 18).   4198

REYNOLDS

Originals, Including Photocopies of Originals

REYNOLDS, *Sir* Joshua
Sir Joseph Banks, Bart. 1774–1820.

c.1773. Photograph of oil on canvas, 50" x 40".
Original is in possession of the Hon. Mrs. Clive Pearson, Parham Park, Sussex, England.
Glass neg. is at NPL:M GLASS NEG.(Copies) 29:11.
Coloured transparency is at NPL:M FM2/320.
Coloured slides (3) are at NPL:M FM5/116–118.

Copies: NPL:M(B1489^{-3} pt.5).   4199

Reproduced in colour in Banks, Sir Joseph—The *Endeavour* Journal. Sydney, 1962. Vol.1,
frontisp.

Copies: NPL:M(A925.8/B).   4200

CHODOWIECKI, Daniel
Joseph Banks: Esq; D. Chodowiecki: pinx; Berol.

Photograph of miniature portrait. Port. diam. 3$\frac{1}{2}$" x 3$\frac{1}{2}$".
The portrait, after Reynolds, is in the Deutsches Museum, Berlin (formerly the Kaiser-
Friedrich Museum).
Reproduced in Kaemmerer, L.—Chodowiecki, 1879.

Copies: NPL:M(P1/Banks-Reynolds 2).   4201

The Same, copy in oils by D. Kellner.

1933. On wood panel. Port. diam. 3$\frac{3}{4}$" x 3$\frac{3}{4}$".
Panel 8$\frac{3}{4}$" x 6$\frac{7}{8}$" inside frame.
On backing board 'D Kellner, Berlin, cop.1933'.

Copies: NPL:M(ML 120).   4202

Reproductions

SIR JOSEPH BANKS: painted by Sir Joshua Reynolds; engraved by W. Dickinson.

Pub. Jan.ʸ the 30.ᵗʰ 1774 by W. Dickinson. London. Mezzotint.
Meas. of port. 18″ x 14″. Meas. of plate mark 20″ x 13 15/16″.
Copies: NPL:M(P3/37).   4203

Another print.
Copies: NPL:M(P3/38).   4204

Another print, imprint cut.
Copies: NPL:M(P3/29A).   4205

Photograph of P3/29A.
Copies: NPL:M(P1/Banks–Reynolds 1).   4206

Reproduced in Phillips, *Sir* Claude—Sir Joshua Reynolds. London, 1894. Opp. p.162.
Copies: NPL:R(S920/R463/7).   4207

The Same; entitled Sir Joseph Banks. Bart. Sir Joshua Reynolds pinx.ᵗ S.W. Reynolds sculp.ᵗ

Mezzotint. Proof. Meas. of port. 5″ x 4″. Meas. of plate mark 8⅞″ x 6¾″.
Copies: NPL:M(P3/29B).   4208

Reproduced in Reynolds, *Sir* Joshua—Engravings. 1833. Vol.1, plate 39.
Copies: NPL:R(F759.2/R463/2 S.C.).   4209

RUSSELL

Originals, Including Photocopies of Originals

RUSSELL, John
Sir Joseph Banks, Bt

c.1778. Photograph of pastel lent by Lord Brabourne to the Royal Academy 1955. Size of original 24″ x 18″.
The original is signed "J. Russell". It was painted for the Knatchbull family and exhibited at the R.A. 1788.
Copies: NPL:M(P1/Banks–Russell 1).   4210

Reproductions

SIR JOSEPH BANKS Bar.ᵗ President of the Royal Society. Painted by J. Russell, R.A. . . . engraved by J. Collyer, A—

Published . . . May 16ᵗʰ 1789. Sold [by] Dickenson [and others]. Engraving. With open letters. Oval, meas. within frame lines 3⅞″ x 3″. Meas. of plate mark 6 15/16″ x 4⅜″.
Head and shoulders; holding map.
Copies: NPL:M(P3/26C).   4211

The Same. Published June 4th 1789. With full lettering, hand-coloured.
Imprint cut.
Copies: NPL:M(P3/26B).   4212

The Same, proof before letters, uncoloured.
Copies: NPL:D(DL Pd664).   4213

The Same, proof with painter's name & fully lettered title only, uncoloured.
Copies: NPL:D(DL Pd663).   4214

Another print.
Copies: NPL:M(P3/26A).   4215

The Same, entitled R.^{t} Honble Sr Joseph Banks K.B.
Engraved by Ridley [after the portrait by Russell].
Published by J. Sewell. Cornhill Oct 1. 1802. Engraving. Meas. within frame line
$3\frac{3}{8}''$ x $2\frac{13}{16}''$. Meas. of plate mark $3\frac{7}{8}''$ x $3''$.
At head *"European Magazine"*. Arm and map omitted.
Copies: NPL:M(P3/26E).   4216

Another 2 prints.
Copies: NPL:M(P1/Banks–Russell 2–3).   4217

Another print.
(*Inserted in* Smith, E.—Life of Sir Joseph Banks. 1911. Vol.2, facing p.164.)
Copies: Australasian Pioneers' Club, Sydney.   4218

Another 2 prints.
Hand-coloured.
Copies: NPL:D(DL Pd657, 662).   4219

Another print.
(*Inserted in* Kippis, *Rev.*—Life of Captain Cook, opp. p.130.)
Copies: NPL:D(Q78/8).   4220

The Same, entitled Sir Joseph Banks. F.R.S.
London. Published by Jacques & Wright. Soft-ground etching. Meas. of engraved surface
c.$4\frac{1}{4}''$ x $4''$. Arm resting on table, holding rolled paper.
(Cook, J.—The Voyages of Captain James Cook round the world. London, Jaques &
Wright, 1825. Vol.1, opp. p.12.)
Copies: NPL:M(980:Co1/27A1).   4221

The Same, entitled Joseph Banks Bar.^{t} Praesident der Königl.
Societaet der Wissenschaften zu London. Conrad Westemayr fecit.
Engraving. Meas. within frame lines $3\frac{3}{4}''$ x $2\frac{13}{16}''$.
The Collyer engraving, reversed.
Copies: NPL:M(P3/26H).   4222

The Same, entitled Bancks. Russel del. Laurens sc.

Zwickau, b.d. Gebr. Schumann. Engraving, corners cut. $3\frac{9}{16}''$ x $2\frac{3}{4}''$ plate mark $7\frac{1}{8}''$ x $3\frac{3}{4}''$.
Copies: NPL:D(DL Pd661). 4223

SERGENT-MARCEAU

SIR GUISEPPE BANKS. Sergent-Marceau dis. L. Rados inc.

Engraving. Meas. within frame lines $6\frac{1}{2}''$ x $4\frac{5}{8}''$. Meas. of plate mark $8\frac{3}{4}''$ x $5\frac{7}{8}''$.
Copies: NPL:D(DL Pd599). 4224

Another print.

Copies: NPL:D(DL Pd600). 4225

Photograph.

Copies: NPL:M(P1/Banks—Sergent–Marceau 1). 4226

WEST

WEST, Benjamin

Mr Banks. Painted by Benjamin West. Engrav'd by J.R. Smith.

Publish'd 15. April 1773 by S. Hooper N.º 25 Ludgate Hill, and J.R. Smith N.º 4 Exeter Court, Exeter Change, Strand. Mezzotint. Meas. of port. $22\frac{1}{4}''$ x $15''$.
Copies: NPL:D(DL Pf47). 4227

Another print, marked "Proof" in pencil.

Copies: NPL:D(DL Pf69). 4228

The Same, entitled Sir Joseph Banks B.^{t} Painted by Benjamin West. Engrav'd by J.R. Smith. London.

Pub. May 1. 1788 by Moltene, Colnaghi & Co. Mezzotint. Meas. of port. $22\frac{1}{2}''$ x $14\frac{7}{8}''$.
Copies: NPL:D(DL Pf70). 4229

The Same, entitled Sir Joseph Banks B.^{t} President, F.A.S. Trust.

Br. Mus. [etc.] Painted by Benjamin West. Engraved by J.R. Smith. Mezzotint. Meas. of port. $22\frac{1}{2}''$ x $14\frac{7}{8}''$. Imprint cut.
Copies: NPL:M(P3/30). 4230

Photographs (2).

Copies: NPL:M(P3/31–2). 4231

Photographs (2).

Copies: NPL:M(B1489^{-3} pt.5). 4232

ARTIST UNKNOWN

Originals, Including Photocopies of Originals

SIR JOSEPH BANKS as a young man.

35mm. coloured slides.
Artist unknown. Shows Banks seated at table with open folio, globe at his feet, large column with drapery and sky as background.
Original is in possession of the Hon. Mrs. Clive Pearson, Parham Park, Sussex, England, 1963.
NOT TO BE REPRODUCED WITHOUT THE PERMISSION OF THE HON. MRS. PEARSON.
Copies: NPL:M(FM5/121–2). 4233

SIR JOSEPH BANKES [*sic*. By an unknown artist.]

Photograph 1962 of oil painting. $6\frac{3}{4}''$ x $5\frac{3}{4}''$ inside frame.
The portrait, at Newby Hall, Yorkshire, shows the sitter in early middle age, half-length, three-quarter face to left. Title from label on frame.
The painting was at the Vyners' house in Gantby, Lincolnshire, before being brought to Newby Hall. One of the directors of Newby Hall (1962) is closely related to the Vyners.
Copies: NPL:M(P1/Banks—Unknown 1). 4234

Another 2 photographs.
Copies: NPL:M(P1/Banks—Unknown 2–3). 4235

Reproductions

THE CIRCUMNAVIGATOR.

In pencil beneath portrait: "Sr Joseph Banks". No.26, vol.1. On the same plate is No.25, "Miss Blosson".
(*Inserted in* Smith, E.—Life of Sir Joseph Banks. 1911. Vol.1, facing p.3.)
Copies: Australasian Pioneers' Club, Sydney. 4236

M.ʳ BANKES (*sic*).

Engraving. Round. Diameter within frame lines 3″ x 3″.
Meas. of plate mark $4\frac{1}{8}''$ x $4\frac{1}{16}''$.
Bust; in profile, looking right.
Copies: NPL:M(P3/26F). 4237

THE RIGHT HON.ᵇˡᵉ SIR JOSEPH BANKS Bar.ᵗ P.R.S. Eng.ᵈ by Mackenzie, from an original picture in the possession of M. Garthshore M.D., F.R.S.

Published Nov.1, 1801, by J.Walker, Paternoster Row.
Engraving. Oval. Meas. within frame lines $3\frac{3}{8}''$ x $2\frac{3}{16}''$.
(*Inserted in* Kippis, *Rev.* Andrew—Life of Captain James Cook. Facing p.xiv.)
Copies: NPL:D(Q78/8). 4238

Another print.

(*Inserted in* Smith, E.—Life of Sir Joseph Banks. 1911. Vol.1, facing p.156.)

Copies: Australasian Pioneers' Club, Sydney.   4239

Another print.

Hand-coloured.

Copies: NPL:D(DL Pd601).   4240

Another print, imprint cut.

Copies: NPL:D(DL Pd602).   4241

The Same, entitled The R.^t Honble Sir Joseph Banks Bar.^t President of the Royal Society, eng.^d by Mackenzie from an original picture in the possession of M. Garthshore M.D., F.R.S.

Pub. Oct.1, 1802, by M. Jones, Paternoster Row. Engraving, hand-coloured. Oval. Meas. within frame line $3\frac{3}{8}''$ x $2\frac{3}{16}''$.

Copies: NPL:M(P3/26D).   4242

BIBLIOGRAPHY

A LIST of portraits of Banks known to the National Portrait Gallery, London, 1932.

(*Enclosure to* Letter from N.S.W. Agent General's Office to Premier, N.S.W., 15 Sep. 1932.)

Copies: NPL:M(PXn172).   4243

Medallions

[BANKS: Wedgwood portrait medallion by James Tassie.]

1785. Wax. Oval, in brown wooden frame. Meas. inside frame c.$3\frac{5}{8}''$ x c.$2\frac{1}{2}''$; framed $5\frac{5}{8}''$ x $4\frac{1}{2}''$.

Handwritten label on back reads "Sir Joseph Banks K.B. 1743–1820. Original portrait in wax modelled by James Tassie 1785. Bought from the executors."

Copies: NPL:M(P*63).   4244

The Same [process plate reproduction, $4''$ x $2\frac{3}{4}''$].

(Maiden, J.H.—Sir Joseph Banks. Sydney, Govt.Pr. 1909. p.xxii.)

Copies: NPL:M(A923.8/B218/1A1).   4245

Photograph.

Copies: NPL:M(P1/Banks—Medallions 1).   4246

BANKS: [Wedgwood portrait medallion, said to have been modelled by John Flaxman, R.A.].

1789. White on blue jasper ware. Oval. c.3⅜″ x 2⅝″. In gilt frame. Title impressed below portrait.
Handwritten note in ink on discoloured paper stuck onto back "Old Wedgwood portrait of Sir Joseph Banks, designed by Flaxman and made 1789."
Head and shoulders, in profile.
Copies: NPL:M(P*61).   4247

The Same, without lettering. In gilt and wooden frame.

Meas. within frame 3″ x 2¾″. Cracked.
Copies: NPL:M(P*31).   4248

The Same, without lettering. In wooden frame.

c.4½″ x c.3″ inside frame; framed c.6¼″ x c.4¾″.
From the collection of Alfred Lee.
Copies: NPL:M(P*55).   4249

The Same, in white on lavender jasper. Oval, in gilt and wooden frame.

Meas. inside frame 3″ x 2⅜″; framed 6¼″ x 5½″.
Undated. "Wedgwood" impressed in back. No title impressed under portrait.
Copies: NPL:M(P*34).   4250

The Same, in white on blue jasper. Oval in brown wooden frame.

Meas. inside frame 2¾″ x 2¼″; framed 5⅛″ x 6″.
Undated. "Wedgwood & Bentley" impressed on back. No title impressed under portrait.
Slightly cracked. Blue jasper faded in places.
Copies: NPL:M(P*35).   4251

The Same, entitled Banks. Oval portrait medallion in black basaltes ware.

Meas. inside frame 3″ x 2¼″. In silver frame, with leather backing.
Unsigned. Dated bet. 1775–1780. Title impressed below portrait. "Wedgwood & Bentley" impressed on back.
Copies: NPL:D(DL Pa97).   4252

The Same, in black basaltes ware. Unframed.

4″ x 3¼″.
Copies: NPL:M(P*33).   4253

The Same, in black basaltes ware. In gilt wooden frame.

Meas. outside frame 6¼″ x 5⅜″.
Unsigned. Title impressed below portrait. Brown paper backing has been partly removed but nothing appears to have been impressed on medallion. Paper sticker on backing is stamped "347".
Copies: NPL:D(DL Pa98).   4254

The Same, entitled Joseph Banks Baronet 1781 by Flaxman in 1775.

1781? White on blue jasper ware. Oval. In gilt and wooden frame. Meas. outside frame
$6\frac{1}{4}''$ x $5\frac{1}{2}''$.
Unsigned. Title not impressed below portrait but written on paper label on back.
"Wedgwood" is impressed on back. Date of issue from title. Cracked.
Copies: NPL:D(DL Pa99).   4255

The Same, in white on blue jasper ware. Gilt frame.

Meas. outside frame $3\frac{1}{2}''$ x $2\frac{5}{8}''$.
Titled "Sir Joseph Banks/Flaxman" in pencil on back. "Wedgwood" impressed on
back. Jasper ware is a very bright blue.
Copies: NPL:D(DL Pa100).   4256

Photograph.
Titled "S.ʳ J: Banks" below portrait.
Copies: NPL:M(P1/Banks—Medallions 2).   4257

JOS.ˢʰ BANKS Esq.ʳ Dʳ Solander.

Published . . . by T. Wright 1 Apr. 1778. Engraving of oval portraits of Banks and
Solander taken from Wedgwood medallions. Meas. of each port. 2″ x $1\frac{5}{8}''$. Meas. of
plate mark $6\frac{5}{8}''$ x $4\frac{7}{16}''$.
Head and shoulders, in profile.
Titled as above at the head of each portrait. Portrait of Banks similar to medallion at
NPL:M P*61, without the name impression but profile is reversed.
Copies: NPL:M(P2/33).   4258

SIR JOSEPH BANKS: process plate reproduction of a medallion portrait
by Tassie.

The original is of glass, white on a black ground. Meas. of port. $2\frac{1}{4}''$ x $1\frac{3}{4}''$. Shows Banks
as an older man wearing loose clothing.
Head only; profile.
(Maiden, J.H.—Sir Joseph Banks. Sydney, Govt. Pr., 1909. p.164.)
Copies: NPL:M(A923.8/B218/1A1).   4259

Photograph.
Copies: NPL:M(P1/Banks—Medallions 3).   4260

SIR JOSEPH BANKS: [Wedgwood portrait medallion].

n.d. White on blue jasper ware. Oval. Unframed. $4\frac{1}{2}''$ x $3\frac{5}{8}''$.
Unsigned. Title and "Wedgwood" impressed on back. Shows Banks at a later age than
the medallions at NPL:M P*31, 34, 35. Has a drape round the base.
Copies: NPL:M(P*32).   4261

The Same, in brown wooden frame.
Meas. of frame 6″ x $4\frac{5}{8}''$. From the collection of Alfred Lee.
Copies: NPL:M(P*54).   4262

The Same, entitled Banks. Wedgwood portrait medallion in black basaltes ware. Oval, in a silver frame.

Meas. $4\frac{5}{8}''$ x $3\frac{5}{8}''$ framed.
Title impressed below portrait, but no impression made into back.
Copies: NPL:D(DL Pa101). 4263

[SIR JOSEPH BANKS: Wedgwood portrait medallion.]

n.d. White on black jasper ware. c.$5\frac{1}{2}''$ x c.$3\frac{1}{2}''$.
Unframed. Untitled.
With drape across base.
Presented to the Trust by John B. Nelson, 1941.

Copies: Captain Cook's Landing Place Trust. 4264

SIR JOSEPH BANKS: [Wedgwood portrait medallion, said to have been modelled by John Flaxman].

n.d. White on blue jasper ware. Oval. Unframed. $12\frac{7}{8}''$ x $9''$.
Unsigned and undated. Title and "Wedgwood" impressed on back. Shows Banks as a young man, dressed in a Roman toga.
Copies: NPL:M(P*4). 4265

WEDGWOOD medallion. Modelled by John Flaxman R.A. about 1770.

Old Wedgwood jasper, Wedgwood & Bentley period. Six portraits only made, Franklin, Priestley, Solander, Banks, Hamilton, Boyle. Portraits of this size are very rare, in all known collections only 15 portraits exist. F. Rathbone. Jan.29, 1891. No.H.223.
Copies: NAuM. 4266

Medals

ROYAL HORTICULTURAL Society medal. n.d. Silver. 37mm.

Obverse: Bust of Banks. *Legend:* Sir Joseph Banks Bt P:R:S: born 1743 died 1820. *Reverse:* *Legend:* The Royal Horticultural Society.
Copies: NPL:M(R272). 4267

Another specimen.
Copies: NPL:D. 4268

Statues and Busts

CHANTREY

THE RIGHT HON. Sir Joseph Banks Bar.^t G.C.B. [Mezzotint of statue in British Museum (Natural History)]; Francis Chantrey sculptor. Drawn by H. Corbould. Engraved by S. Cousins.

Cut. Meas. of sheet $14''$ x $12\frac{1}{2}''$.
Copies: NPL:M(P3/33). 4269

The Same. Proof before letters.

(*Inserted in* Smith, E.—Life of Sir Joseph Banks, 1911. Vol.2, facing p.331.)

Copies: Australasian Pioneers' Club, Sydney.   4270

[THE STATUE of Sir Joseph Banks by Chantrey in the British Museum (Natural History).]

3 photographs.

Taken after cleaning 1968, one shows the front of the statue including pedestal and inscription, the other is taken from the left, the third is the Latin inscription with translation. With notes on the statue 1968.

Copies: NPL:M(P1/Banks—Statues 3).   4271

[THE STATUE of Sir Joseph Banks by Chantrey in The British Museum (Natural History).]

Photograph. $5\frac{5}{16}''$ x 4''.

The photograph is taken from the right of the statue.

Copies: NPL:M(P3/261).   4272

The Same, enlarged to $11\frac{1}{4}''$ x $8\frac{1}{4}''$.

Copies: NPL:M(P2/39).   4273

STATUE of Sir Joseph Banks in the British Museum.

Illus.

(*Penny Magazine,* Aug., 1833, p.340.)

Copies: NPL:M(Q052/P); NPL:R(Q050/P416).   4274

RAITH, *Scotland*

[BUST of Sir Joseph Banks in the Museum at Raith, Scotland.]

Two photographs, full face and three-quarter face. Each $4\frac{7}{8}''$ x $3\frac{3}{4}''$.

Reproduced in Royal Australian Historical Society—*Journal and Proceedings,* 1920, p.199.

Copies: NPL:M(P1/Banks—Statues 1–2).   4275

Illustrations other than Portraits and Medallions

GILLRAY, James

The Great South Sea Caterpillar, transform'd into a Bath Butterfly J.ˢ Gʸ. des "et fecᵗ".

July 4th 1795. Published by H. Humphrey N.º 37 New Bond Street. Etching. $14\frac{1}{2}''$ x $10\frac{1}{2}''$ approx.

The Bath butterfly has the face of Sir Joseph Banks. Title is followed by: 'Description of the New Bath Butterfly—taken from the "Philosophical Transaction for 1795". "This Insect first crawl'd into notice from among the Weeds and Mud on the Banks of the South Sea; & being afterwards placed in a Warm Situation by the Royal Society, was changed by the heat of the Sun into its present form—it is notic'd & Valued Solely on account of the beautiful Red which encircles its Body, & the Shining Spot on its Breast; a Distinction which never fails to render Caterpillars valuable.'

Copies: NPL:M(P2/B).   4276

GILLRAY, James

The Great South Sea Caterpillar transformed into a Bath butterfly: [a cartoon].

(*In* Wright, Thomas—England under the House of Hanover. London, R. Bentley, 1848. Vol.2, p.380.)

Copies: NPL:M(942.07/W); NPL:R(S942.07/31).   4277

GILLRAY, James

The Great South Sea caterpillar transformed into a Bath butterfly: [a cartoon].

(*In his* Works of J. Gillray . . . collected. no.410. London? H.G. Bohn, 1851.)

Copies: NPL:M(X741.591/G483/1A1); NPL:R(09:RX741.5/3).   4278

GILLRAY, James

The Great South Sea caterpillar transformed into a Bath butterfly: [an explanation by T. Wright of the cartoon by J. Gillray.]

(*In* Wright, Thomas—Historical and descriptive account of the caricatures of J. Gillray. London, H.G. Bohn, 1851. pp.422–3.)

Copies: NPL:M(741/G); NPL:R(S741.5/13).   4279

MR. BANKS receiving a visit from the King of Duke of York's Island: [illustration].

(*In* Henry, David—Historical account of all the voyages round the world. London, F. Newbery, 1773. Vol.3, plate facing p.238.)

Copies: NPL:M(980/H); NPL:D(77/21); NPL:R(MD8R50); VU(Baillieu).   4280

REVESBY ABBEY: [copper engraving]. Drawn by T. Nash from a sketch by Wm. Brand, Esqr. Engraved by B. Howlett. Published July 1, 1803, by William Miller, London.

(*Inserted in* Smith, E.—Life of Sir Joseph Banks. 1911. Vol.2, facing p.306.)

Copies: Australasian Pioneers' Club, Sydney.   4281

SOHO SQUARE: [coloured lithograph] showing Banks' house with the glass front]. No. 46 of R. Ackermann's Repository of Arts, etc. Pub. Oct., 1812. London.

(*Inserted in* Smith, E.—Life of Sir Joseph Banks. 1911. Vol.2, facing p.295.)

Copies: Australasian Pioneers' Club, Sydney.   4282

ASSOCIATES OF COOK

BLIGH, WILLIAM

Writings

1791 July 26 BLIGH, William, to James Burney. ALS dated Providence at Spithead, to Burney, Norton St: Bligh is detained by strong westerlies; has left his log with Dalrymple; remarks concerning the *Bounty* mutiny; that Cook has erroneously charted part of Clerk's Isles as Anderson's Island; that charting of the Sandwich Isles & parts of east Asia coast, otherwise attributed, is Bligh's work; the American coast was surveyed by Cook till his death; Bligh's chart of the Sandwich Isles is deteriorated by Robert's miscopying of mountain sites; he leaves it to Sir Joseph & Burney to bring these remarks forward.

pp.4, cm 23.5.

Maggs Bros. catalogue description, typescript, also filed.

Copies: NPL:D(MS.Q163). 4283

Biography

1838 CHAMPAGNAC, Jean Baptiste Joseph de
Histoire de navigateur Bligh.
(*In his* Le Petit matelot; ou, voyage en Océanie. Paris, Lehuby, 1838. Chap.4.)
See also nos.4285–6.
Copies: NPL:M(989/34A1). 4284

[1842] CHAMPAGNAC, Jean Baptiste Joseph de
Histoire du navigateur Bligh.
(*In his* Le Petit matelot; ou, voyage en Océanie. Paris, Lehuby, [1842]. Chap.4.)
See also nos.4284, 4286.
Copies: NPL:M(989/34B1). 4285

1853 CHAMPAGNAC, Jean Baptiste Joseph de
Histoire du navigateur Bligh.
(*In his* Le Petit matelot; ou, voyage en Océanie. 1853, Chap.4.)
See also nos.4284–5.
Copies: ANL. 4286

1911 SMITH, Edward
Bligh's voyages.
(*In his* Life of Sir Joseph Banks. London, John Lane, 1911. pp.126–38.)
Copies: NPL:M(A925.8/B218/2A1); NPL:D(91/94); NPL:R(N920/B218/1); ANL;
Australasian Pioneers' Club, Sydney. 4287

1922 LORD, Clive Errol
Notes on Captain Bligh's visits to Tasmania in 1788 and 1792.
(Royal Society of Tasmania—*Papers and Proceedings*, 1922. pp.1–21.)
Copies: NPL:M(506/R); NPL:R(D5506/43); ANL. 4288

1928 GOULD, Rupert Thomas
Bligh's notes on Cook's last voyage.
Illus.
(*Mariner's Mirror* vol.14, Oct.1928. pp.371–85.)
Copies: NPL:D(9/72); NPL:R(DS656.506/7); ANL.   4289

1931 MACKANESS, George
The Life of Vice-Admiral William Bligh. Sydney, Angus & Robertson, 1931.
2 vols.
Copies: NPL:M(A923.59/B648.1/1A1–2); NPL:D(93/28–9); NPL:R(920/B648/1–2); ANL.   4290

1936 MACKANESS, George
Banks and Bligh.
(*In his* Sir Joseph Banks: his relations with Australia. Sydney, A. & R., 1936. Chap.6.)
Copies: NPL:M(A925.8/B218/17A1); NPL:D(93/618); ANL.   4291

1936 RUTTER, Owen
[Bligh as Master of the *Resolution*.]
(*In his* Turbulent journey. London, I. Nicholson and Watson Ltd., 1936. pp.30–60.)
Copies: NPL:M(A923.59/B648.1/3A1).   4292

1967 BEAGLEHOLE, John Cawte
Captain Cook and Captain Bligh. Wellington, New Zealand, Victoria University of Wellington, 1967.
pp.27.
The *Dr. W.E. Collins Lecture* delivered at the Victoria University of Wellington, 3 Aug. 1967.
Copies: NPL:M(923.9/C771.2/37A1).   4293

Portraits

BARKER

BARKER, Henry Ashton
William Bligh, 1805.
Process reproduction from a pencil drawing by H.A. Barker, in the possession of Capt. H. Littlehales Barker.
(Rutter, O.—Turbulent journey. London, Ivor Nicholson and Watson, 1936. Opp.p.216.)
Copies: NPL:M(A923.59/B648.1/3A1).   4294

DANCE, George
[Portrait.]

1794. Photograph of pencil drawing.
The original, signed 'Geo. Dance May 31.st 1794' is in the National Portrait Gallery.
Copies: NPL:M(P1/Bligh 2).   4295

DANCE, George
William Bligh: [tinted pencil drawing] copied by L. Skeats: original by G. Dance in National Portrait Gallery.
(*Inserted in* Smith, E.—Life of Sir Joseph Banks. 1911. Vol.1, facing p.132.)
Copies: Australasian Pioneers' Club, Sydney.   4296

MAY, Phil
Portrait of William Bligh.

Negative of a caricature.
(Foster collection, box 7, no.89.)
Copies: NPL:M(Glass Neg.,Copies 11).   4297

Originals, Including Photocopies of Originals

RUSSELL, J.
Portrait of Captain William Bligh.

Pre 1792. Photograph of original.
The original was exhibited at the Royal Academy. It was formerly in the possession of Mrs. Nutting of Warwick, Qld., and was sold to Wertheimer at the beginning of the century.
The photograph has a note on back in unknown hand about Bligh. Photos of a further inscription by Dr. Nutting are filed at NPL:M PXn 186.
Copies: NPL:M(P1/Bligh 4).   4298

Another print of the photograph.
Copies: NPL:M(P1/Bligh 5).   4299

Reproduced, entitled Captain Bligh.
(Historical Records of New South Wales. Vol.6.)
Copies: NPL:M(991/N Ref.Books).   4300

Another print of this reproduction.
Copies: NPL:M(P1/Bligh 6).   4301

Another print of this reproduction, entitled William Bligh, from a portrait by J.A. Russell, R.A., in the possession of W. Bligh Nutting Esq.

(Rutter, O.—Turbulent journey. London, Ivor Nicholson and Watson, 1936. Frontisp.)

Copies: NPL:M(A923.59/B648.1/3A1).   4302

CAP.ᵗ BLIGH.

Pre 1792. Miniature on ivory after Russell by unknown artist. Oval. $2\frac{3}{8}''$ x $1\frac{3}{4}''$ inside gilt frame. Surrounded by gold tooling in leaf design on blue crushed morocco, and the lettering "Voyage. to. the. South. Sea. Cap.ᵗ Bligh."
(*Inset in* front cover of his *Voyage to the South Sea*. London, G. Nicol, 1792.)

Copies: NPL:D(Q79/12).   4303

Reproductions Arranged by Engraver

ADLARD

Wm. Bligh. Drawn by J. Russell, R.A. Engraved by H. Adlard.

Engraving. Meas. inside frame lines $4\frac{3}{16}''$ x $3\frac{1}{4}''$. With facs. signature of Bligh. Half-length.

Copies: NPL:D(DL Pd659).   4304

Another print.

(*Inserted in* Murray, *Rev*. Thomas Boyles—Pitcairn. 3rd ed. London, Society for Promoting Christian Faith, 1854. Opp. p.34.)

Copies: NPL:M(999.7/2C1).   4305

The Same.

Engraving. Meas. inside frame lines $4\frac{3}{16}''$ x $3\frac{1}{4}''$.
Meas. of plate mark $6\frac{15}{16}''$ x $12\frac{3}{4}''$.
On sheet with engravings by Adlard of George H. Nobbs and John Adams.
Half-length.

Copies: NPL:M(P2/53).   4306

The Same. Photolithograph of engraving of Bligh only.

Pub. by Public Library of New South Wales.
Meas. inside frame lines $7\frac{5}{16}''$ x $5\frac{5}{8}''$.

(Public Library of New South Wales—Reproductions, T4.)   4307

CONDÉ

Cap.ᵗ Bligh. Painted from the life by J. Russell R.A. Crayon Painter to his Majesty . . . Engraved by J. Condé.

Engraving. Oval. Meas. within frame lines $5\frac{1}{16}''$ x $4''$.
Meas. of plate mark $8\frac{3}{16}''$ x $5''$.

Copies: NPL:M(P2/34).   4308

Another print, cut around frame lines but including artist's and engraver's names.
Copies: NPL:M(P1/Bligh 9). 4309

Another print.
Hand-coloured. Plate mark cut.
Copies: NPL:D(DL Pd658). 4310

Another print.
(*In* Bligh, W.—A Voyage to the South Sea. London, G. Nicol, 1792. Frontisp.)
Copies: NPL:M(Q988/9A1); NPL:D(Q79/12). 4311

Photograph.
(*In* Photographs illustrating the earliest times of New South Wales. p.11.)
Copies: NPL:M(F981/N). 4312

McLEOD

Governor William Bligh, by W. McLeod after Russell.
Wood engraving. Meas. of engraved surface c.$3\frac{1}{8}''$ x $2\frac{7}{8}''$.
Head and shoulders.
Cut; presumably from Garran's *Picturesque Atlas of Australasia.*
Copies: NPL:M(P1/Bligh 7). 4313

SMART

SMART, J.

Portrait of William Bligh.
Photograph of the original in possession of National Portrait Gallery, London.
This portrait was drawn for an engraving, in commemoration of the Battle of Camperdown which took place on October 11, 1797.
Copies: NPL:M(P1/Bligh 10). 4314

Reproduced in colour in Ingram, B.S.—Masters of maritime art: a second loan exhibition of drawings . . . Mar. 1937. Frontisp.
Copies: NPL:M(Q758/I). 4315

Also reproduced in colour in *Illustrated London News*, Mar.13, 1937, p.441.
Meas. inside ruled frame lines $4\frac{1}{8}''$ x $2\frac{7}{8}''$.
Copies: NPL:M(FA923.59/B648.1/2A1). 4316

Also reproduced in *Illustrated London News*, Mar.6, 1937.
Frontisp. Meas. inside frame lines $8\frac{1}{8}''$ x $5\frac{1}{2}''$.
Bound with the preceding, with cover title *Ill. London News*, Portrait of Bligh.
Copies: NPL:M(FA923.59/B648.1/2A1). 4317

[MINIATURE portrait.]

[1814?] Watercolour on ivory. 2⅜″ x 2″ in oval gilt frame with lock of hair and monogram 'WB' set in back.
The miniature came to the Mitchell Library from Mrs. H. Oakes, Bligh's great grand-daughter.
Copies: NPL:M(Min 53 Safe 1).

4318

Photograph.

(N.S.W. Govt.Pr. neg. no.49647.)
Copies: NPL:M(P1/Bligh 1).

4319

The Same. Copy on ivory over carbon base.
Meas. inside gold frame 2⅛″ x 2⅜″.
Copies: NPL:M(Min 239).

4320

Reproduced in colour in *Historical Records of New South Wales.* Sydney, Govt. Pr., 1898. Vol.6, frontisp.
The reproduction differs from the original, and has probably been badly retouched. The frame is also different, but matches reproduction of a miniature of Philip Gidley King opp. p.1.
Copies: NPL:M(991/N).

4321

Another copy.
Copies: NPL:M(P1/Bligh 8).

4322

Also reproduced in Rutter, O.—Turbulent journey. London, Ivor Nicholson and Watson, 1936. Opp. p.260. Uncoloured.
Copies: NPL:M(A923.59/B648.1/3A1).

4323

MINIATURE portrait.

1844? Photograph of oval portrait. Meas. of photo 5″ x 3⅞″.
The original is owned by Mrs. D.E.L. Oakes, 1961.
On back of miniature is written in faded ink "Bligh 1844" and on frame below portrait is written "Governor Bligh 1844". Shows a young man in civilian clothes, hair unpowdered.
Copies: NPL:M(P1/Bligh 3).

4324

Reproduced in Mackaness, G.—Life of Vice-Admiral William Bligh. Sydney, A. & R., 1931. Vol.2, frontisp.
Copies: NPL:M(A923.59/B648.1/1A2).

4325

[PORTRAIT.]

1814? Photograph of oil painting.
The original, owned by Mrs. D.E.L. Oakes, 1961, is very closely related to NPL:M Min 53.
Copies: NPL:M(P1/Bligh).

4326

Negative 35mm.

Copies: NPL:M(FM 1/B). 4327

PORTRAIT, possibly of William Bligh.

n.d. Oil. 11″ x 9″.

Unsigned and undated. Face is after Russell, but Bligh is shown seated in an armchair, his left hand extended to touch a telescope on a table beside him. There is a large sailing ship in the background.

Full-length.

Copies: NPL:M(ML337). 4328

BOULTON, MATTHEW

Portraits

MATTHEW BOULTON: [copper engraving]. Sir W. Beechey, pinxt., W. Evans, delt., A. Cardon, Sc.

(*Inserted in* Smith, E.—Life of Sir Joseph Banks. 1911. Vol.2, facing p.278.)

Matthew Boulton was the designer of the *Resolution* and *Adventure* medals distributed by Cook on his second voyage.

Copies: Australasian Pioneers' Club, Sydney. 4329

BURNEY, CHARLES

Writings

1791 Jy.6 ALS to Sir Joseph Banks dated Chelsea College: Seeking Banks' interest to assist his son-in-law Capt. Phillips to obtain the post of Agent of Marines, vacant by the death of Capt. Williams; Capt. Phillips accompanied Cook on his last voyage, his services were then recognised by promotion, he has a good reputation with his Commander and officers; hopes that Banks may support his candidature by a word in season to Lord Chatham or to Stephens. With draft of Banks' letter to Ld. Chatham, 8 July 1791, overleaf.

ff.2, cm 23.

Typed transcript made in Library, in NPL:D MS.Q159.

Copies: NPL:D(MS.Q158, pp.121–3). 4330

BURNEY, JAMES

Writings

1962 DU RIETZ, Rolf

Three letters from James Burney to Sir Joseph Banks.

(*Ethnos* vol.27, pp.115–25, no.1–4, 1962.)

Copies: NPL:M(572.06/2). 4331

Biography

1914 PAYNE, Harold H.

Admiral Burney and the death of Captain Cook: some unpublished manuscripts. London, [1914].

(Captain Cook: newspaper cuttings, vol.2.)

Reprint from *Cornhill Magazine* Nov.1914, pp.677–91. The manuscripts comprise part of the Log of the *Discovery*, written by Burney, and a narrative, not in Burney's handwriting, entitled *An Account of the death of Capt. Cook*, etc. Both the manuscripts are now in the Mitchell Library.

Copies: NPL:M(Q980:Col/N1A2); NPL:R(S050/C817).   4332

1922 FERGUSON, *Sir* John Alexander

Burney and his work: [extract from the *Sydney Morning Herald*, Feb.4, 1922].

(Newspaper cuttings, vol.166, pp.95–6.)

Copies: NPL:M(Q991.1/N); NPL:R(F079/S982).   4333

1931 MANWARING, George Ernest

Round the world with Captain Cook; (With Captain Cook in southern seas; [and] Cook's last voyage).

Illus.

(*In his* My friend the Admiral: the life, letters and journal of . . . James Burney. London, G. Routledge, 1931. pp.15–47, 64–154.)

Copies: NPL:M(A923.9/B); NPL:R(920/B965.4/1); ANL.   4334

CLERKE, CHARLES

Portraits

DANCE, Nathaniel

[Portrait of Captain Charles Clerke.]

1776? Photograph of oil painting in Government House, Wellington, New Zealand. Meas. of original $29\frac{5}{8}''$ x $24\frac{1}{2}''$. Meas. of photograph $7\frac{1}{4}''$ x 6''.

Copies: NPL:M(P1 Clerke 1).   4335

DANCE, Nathaniel

[Portrait, by Nathaniel Dance. Reproduced in black and white.]

(*In* Rienits, Rex—The Voyages of Captain Cook. London, Paul Hamlyn, 1968. p.81.)

Copies: NPL:M(Q980:Col/R1A1); NPL:R(NQ910.4/4).   4336

TAYLOR, John

Cha[s]: Clerk Esq.[r] drawn by John Taylor just before he sailed on his last voyage which he also painted in oil for Cha.[s] Ollie Esq.[r] &c.

Photograph. Meas. within frame line $12\frac{7}{8}''$ x $8\frac{3}{4}''$.
Half-length.
Title from inscription below frame line.
Original is in the possession of R. de C. Nan Kivell.
Copies: NPL:M(P2/47).   4337

TAYLOR, John
Captain Charles Clerke, R.N. [Reproduction from the drawing by
J. Taylor, in the collection of Sir Maurice Holmes.]
(*In* Muir, John Reid—Life and achievements of Captain James Cook. London, Blackie,
1939. p.234.)
Copies: NPL:M(980:Col/M6A1); NPL:D(93/626); NPL:R(DS990A/195); ANL;
QParl; QU; VMoU; VSL.   4338

CLEVELEY, JAMES
Biography

1934 ANDERSEN, Johannes Carl
Matavai Bay and Queen Charlotte Sound: [notes on Cleveley's picture
wrongly labelled Charlotte Sound in New Zealand].
Illus.
(*In his* Maori music with its Polynesian background. New Plymouth, N.Z., Avery, pr.,
1934. pp.i–ii.) Polynesian Society—*Memoir*, no.10.
Copies: NPL:M(572.997/A); NPL:D(93/58); ANL.   4339

1948 WARNER, Oliver Martin Wilson
[James Cleveley.]
Illus.
(*In his* Introduction to British marine painting. London, Batsford, 1948. p.15.)
Copies: NPL:M(758/W); NPL:R(S758/37).   4340

CLEVELEY, JOHN
Biography

1808 EDWARDS, Edward
John Clevely (*sic*).
(*In his* Anecdotes of painters. London, 1808. p.118.)
Copies: NPL:R(S759.2/23).   4341

1934 ANDERSEN, Johannes Carl
Matavai Bay and Queen Charlotte Sound: [notes on Cleveley's picture
wrongly labelled Charlotte Sound in New Zealand].
Illus.
(*In his* Maori music with its Polynesian background. New Plymouth, N.Z., Avery, pr.,
1934. pp.i–ii.) Polynesian Society—*Memoir*, no.10.
Copies: NPL:M(572.997/A); NPL:D(93/58); ANL.   4342

1948 WARNER, Oliver Martin Wilson
[John Cleveley.]

(*In his* Introduction to British marine painting. London, Batsford, 1948. pp.10, 15, 16, 18.)

Copies: NPL:M(758/W); NPL:R(S758/37).   4343

COOK, ELIZABETH, *Mrs.*

Writings

1782 ALS to her cousin Mrs. M'Allister in Philadelphia. Clapham, April 20, 1782.
pp.2.

Concerning Cook family affairs.

Copies: ANL(Nan Kivell 9528); NPL:M(FM4/1552,1707, pos. and neg. microfilm).
4344

Biography

See also the section *Personal—Biography*.

1776–1926 FAMILY PAPERS, 1776–1926.
24 items.

A collection of manuscript material relating to Captain Cook, his widow and his family. One letter, signed by James Cook, from the *Resolution* at Deptford, dated April 2, 1776, to the Commissioners of His Majesty's Navy asking for a supply of clothing to the ship. Eight letters to Mrs. F. McAllister, cousin of Captain Cook, including one from Elizabeth Cook, concerning Cook family affairs. Other letters of later date are those of John McAllister, Mrs. McAllister's son, who actively sought letters and relics of his famous cousin. Copies of letters from Cook to Sir Joseph Banks. Biographical note on Cook; newspaper cuttings concerning Cook, 1858–1926; extract from parish register relating to baptism of James Cook. Detailed contents list in ANL and NPL:M.

Copies: ANL(Nan Kivell 9528); NPL:M(FM4/1552,1707 pos. and neg. microfilm).
4345

1835 MRS. ELIZABETH COOK: [a notice of the death of Capt. Cook's widow].
(*Nautical Magazine*, London, Jy, 1835, p.431.)

Copies: NPL:R(DS656.505/3).   4346

1935 ROYAL EMPIRE SOCIETY
St. Andrew the Great, Cambridge: service in commemoration of Mrs. Elizabeth Cook, widow of Captain James Cook, R.N., on the one hundredth anniversary of her death, May 13th, 1935, 12 noon. London, 1935.

Folder.

Copies: NPL:M(920.7/C771.1/1A1).   4347

1952 LLOYD, Christopher
Captain Cook's wife.
(*Mariner's Mirror*, vol.38, pp.230–1, Aug.1952.)
Copies: NPL:R(DS656.506/7). 4348

1953 SKELTON, Raleigh Ashlin
Captain Cook's wife.
(*Mariner's Mirror*, vol.39, pp.62–3, Feb.1953.)
Copies: NPL:R(DS656.506/7). 4349

1961 ODEWAHN, Viv
Elizabeth Batts, widow of Captain James Cook.
(*Dawn*, Sydney, vol.10, p.13, Apr.1961.)
Copies: NPL:M(Q572.99106/2). 4350

1966 CANNON, Leslie
The Enigma of Elizabeth Batts. London, 1966.
Facs.
Photographic copy of *The Barking Record*, no.71, pp.13–15, Apr.1966.
Copies: NPL:M(923.9/C771.2/34A1). 4351

[1968] SMITH, Eric E.F.
Clapham: an historical tour. [Written and comp. by E.E.F. Smith.] London, Battley, [1968].
Facs. illus. pp.[ii],36.
Cover title. A description of Mrs. Cook's house in Clapham is given on p.24.
Copies: NPL:M(942.16/1A1). 4352

Portraits

HAZELHURST, James
Mrs. James Cook.
Oil painting. 33½″ x 24″. Untitled; unsigned.
Copies: ANL. 4353

HENDERSON, W.
Mrs Eliz[th] Cook. Aged 81 years.
1830. Oil painting. c.29¾″ x c.24¾″ inside frame.
Unsigned. On back of canvas is painted "Mrs Eliz[th] Cook. Aged 81 years. W: Henderson. Pinx:[t] 1830".
This portrait used to hang with eight others in the George St. show room of W. Chorley & Co., Sydney. Mr. Henry Chorley offered it on loan in 1938 as "apparently [that of]

the wife of Capt. Cook". The offer was not accepted as the authenticity of the portrait could not be proved. *See* Mitchell Library Corres. 1938/55 (in-letters) and 1938/70 and 148 (out-letters).

In Oct.1956 after Mr. Chorley's death the nine portraits were presented to the Mitchell Library by Mrs. H.J.A. Chorley. Six are of Yorkshire ancestors of F. Thornbury of Sydney called Dale and Reynolds; the seventh is of an unidentified boy, probably of the same family; the eighth is of Mr. Taylor, engineer, the connection with the Thornburys is not known. None of the names appears in Young's *History of Whitby*, but the Yorkshire marriage registers (for W. Riding) list a John Dale and Mary Reynolds, Oct.3, 1802.

Graves' Dictionary lists a William Henderson, Whitby, 1874–92, painter of figures; there is also a W.P.S. Henderson, domestic painter, London, 1836–74.

Other W. Hendersons do not seem to fit.

Possibly the portrait was painted by the Whitby Henderson from an earlier drawing or painting. For a description of Mrs. Cook *see* Muir, J.R.—Life and achievements of Captain James Cook, 1939.

Copies: NPL:M(ML430).   4354

Photograph, with frame.

(Neg. held by B. Bird 1965, no.120–2.)

Copies: NPL:M(P1/Cook, Elizabeth, *Mrs*.1).   4355

Photographs (2), without frame.

Copies: NPL:M(P1/Cook, Elizabeth, *Mrs*.2–3).   4356

The Same.

Photograph in colour.

Copies: Captain Cook's Landing Place Trust.   4357

COOK, JAMES, *Grandfather of Capt. J. Cook*

BIOGRAPHICAL extracts concerning James Cook, grandfather of Captain James Cook, 1692–1694, published 1853, 1863.

Typescript.

Copies: NPL:M(Doc.1408).   4358

DALRYMPLE, ALEXANDER

Writings

1773 A LETTER from Mr. Dalrymple to Dr. Hawkesworth, occasioned by some groundless and illiberal imputations in his account of the late voyages to the south. London, J. Nourse and others, 1773.

Folding chart, pp.iv, 35.

See Holmes, no.6. There are two issues of this rare pamphlet, the first on thick paper containing no chart, and the second on ordinary paper containing a *Chart of the South*

Pacifick Ocean. The Mitchell and Dixson copies both contain this chart. After Hawkesworth's reply in the preface to the second edition of his Voyages, Dalrymple prepared another pamphlet (*see* no.4360) which however was not published because of the death of Hawkesworth.

Copies: NPL:M(Q980/36A1); NPL:D(77/4).   4359

1773 MR. DALRYMPLE'S observations on Dr. Hawkesworth's Preface to the second edition. Sept.18, 1773.

(Bonwick transcripts: Cook, case 1, no.121.)
Transcript of a manuscript in the British Museum, this pamphlet is a spirited attack on Dr. Hawkesworth, whose death prevented its publication. Rare page-proofs exist in two states, the first ending on page 19, the second on page 20. (*See* Holmes, no.6.) For previous letter published by Dalrymple, *see* no.4359. *See also* no.4451. Microfilm of original also held in the Mitchell Library.

Copies: NPL:M(B.T.ser.2,box1).   4360

1783 ALS to Sir Joseph Banks concerning charts of the Sandwich Islands which he has had reduced for Webber. 12 Decr.,1783.

p.1.
Copies: ANL.   4361

1783 ALS to Sir Joseph Banks concerning plates of Kerguelen's Land, etc., with reductions for Webber, and reporting that he has found the longitude of Eimeo to be wrong. 13th Decr., 1783.

p.1.
Copies: ANL.   4362

1783 ALS to Sir Joseph Banks concerning views of Sulphur Island and Japan, with reductions for Webber, also referring to charts sent to him by Capt. King. 15th Decr., 1783.

p.1.
Copies: ANL.   4363

Biography

1773 HAWKESWORTH, John
[Reply to] A letter from Mr. Dalrymple to Dr. Hawkesworth, occasioned by some groundless and illiberal imputations in his Account of the late voyages to the South Seas.

(*In his* Account of the voyages undertaken . . . by . . . Byron . . . Wallis . . . Carteret . . . and Cook. London, W. Strahan and T. Cadell, 1773. Vol.1, Preface to 2nd ed.)
Copies: NPL:M(Q980/38B1).   4364

1849 BARROW, *Sir* John
Mr. Alexander Dalrymple, F.R.S.
(*In his* Sketches of the Royal Society. London, John Murray, 1849. pp.134–9.)
Copies: NPL:M(925/B).   4365

1852 EYRIÈS
Dalrymple.

(Biographie universelle. Nouvelle éd. Paris, 1852. Tome 10.)
Copies: NPL:R(DS920/660).   4366

1866 DALRYMPLE.
(Nouvelle biographie générale. Paris, 1866. Tome 12.)
Copies: NPL:R(S920/707).   4367

1879 HAMY, Ernest Theodore
Cook et Dalrymple: (discours prononcé devant la Société de Géographie,
à l'occasion du centenaire de la mort de Cook). Par . . . E.T. Hamy.
[With bibl. notes.] Paris, Librairie chez Delagrave, 1879.
pp.16.
Extract from the Société de Géographie—*Bulletin*, Mai, 1879.
Copies: NPL:M(923.9/C771.2/10A1); NPL:R(S990A/132).   4368

1893 RAINAUD, Armand
La Dernière controverse au sujet du continent austral: A. Dalrymple
et J. Cook.

(*In his* Le Continent austral: hypothèses et découvertes. Paris, Armand Colin, 1893.
pp.437–74.)
Copies: NPL:M(Q980/29A1).   4369

1922 JACK, Robert Logan
Vaugondy and Dalrymple maps.

(*In his* Northmost Australia. Melbourne, Robertson, 1922. Vol.1, pp.93–6.)
Copies: NPL:M(984.6/13A1); NPL:R(S994A/38); ANL.   4370

1927 BAYLDON, Francis Joseph
Alexander Dalrymple, the man who wished to command the *Endeavour*.
Map, port.
(Royal Australian Historical Society—*Journal and Proceedings*. Vol.13, 1927, pp.41–59.)
Copies: NPL:M(991/R, Ref.Books); NPL:D(9/69); NPL:R(S991.06/1A, Ref.Books).
                                                                         4371

1935 GOULD, Rupert Thomas
How the first voyage came about.

(*In his* Captain Cook. London, Duckworth, [1935]. pp.26–46.)
Great lives.

Copies: NPL:M(980:Col/G2A1); NPL:D(93/627); NPL:R(920/C771/3); ANL; VSL.
                                                                         4372

Portraits

BROWN

Reproductions Arranged by Engraver

BLOOD

Alexander Dalrymple Esqr late Hydrographer To the Admiralty. Engraved by Blood (with the Permission of Mr Asperne Proprietor of the *European Magazine*) from An Original Drawing by John Brown.

Engraving. Oval. Meas. within frame line $3\frac{1}{2}''$ x $2\frac{7}{8}''$. Cut. Half-length.

Copies: NPL:D(DL).   4373

Another copy.

(*Inserted in* Smith, E.—Life of Sir Joseph Banks. 1911. Vol.1, facing p.15.)

Copies: Australasian Pioneers' Club, Sydney.   4374

Reproduced in Clowes, W.L.—The Royal Navy. London, 1899. Vol.4, p.187.

Copies: NPL:R(Q359.0942/13).   4375

RIDLEY

A^r <u>Dalrymple</u> Son of Sir James Dalrymple Bar.^{t} born 24 July 1737. Engraved by Ridley, from an original drawing by John Brown.

Pub. by J.Sewell Cornhill Dec.1 1802. Engraving. Oval. Meas. within frame line $3\frac{3}{16}''$ x $2\frac{1}{2}''$. Meas. of plate mark $6\frac{3}{8}''$ x $4\frac{3}{8}''$.

Half-length.

With facsimile autograph. At head 'European Magazine.'

Copies: NPL:M(P1/Dalrymple 1A).   4376

Another print.

Copies: NPL:M(P1/Dalrymple 1B).   4377

Another print.

(*Inserted in* Kippis, *Rev.* A.—Life of Captain James Cook. Opp. p.15.)

Copies: NPL:D(Q78/9).   4378

Another print.

(*Inserted in* Kippis, *Rev.* A.—Life of Captain James Cook. Opp. p.15.)

Copies: NPL:D(Q78/8).   4379

Another print.

(*Inserted in* Bligh, W.—A Voyage to the South Seas. Opp. p.36.)

Copies: NPL:D(Q79/12).   4380

Reproduced in Mill, Hugh Robert—Siege of the South Pole. London, Rivers, 1905. Facing p.58.

Copies: NPL:M(989.8/M); NPL:R(DS999.8A/13); VSL.   4381

Originals, Including Photocopies of Originals

DANCE, George
Alexander Dalrymple.

1794. Pencil drawing. 10″ x 7½″. Untitled; signed.

Copies: ANL.   4382

Reproductions Arranged by Engraver

DANIELL
Alexander Dalrymple Esq.ʳ Geo. Dance del.ᵗ July 26, 1794. W.ᵐ Daniell Fecit.

Published . . . for Geo. Dance Esq.ʳ R.A. . . . April 10, 1802. Soft ground etching. Meas. of port. approx. 8″ x 6¼″. Meas. of plate mark 10½″ x 7¾″.
Half-length, profile.

Copies: NPL:M(P2/46).   4383

DOUGLAS, JOHN

Portraits

BROWN

GRAINGER
Dʳ. Douglas Bishop of Carlisle. Drawn from the Life by W.H. Brown. Engraved by W. Grainger.

Published . . . by C. Cooke, Nᵒ 17, Paternoster row, June 29ᵗʰ 1791. Engraving. Oval. 2¼″ x 1¹¹⁄₁₆″. Meas. of plate mark 5⅝″ x 3⁹⁄₁₆″.
At head: Engraved for the Senator.
(*Inserted in* Kippis, A.—The Life of Captain James Cook. Opp. p.494.)

Copies: NPL:D(Q78/8).   4384

MULLER

BOND
John Douglas: [steel engraving]. Muller, pinxt., W. Bond, sc.

(*Inserted in* Smith, E.—Life of Sir Joseph Banks. 1911. Vol.1, facing p.51.)

Copies: Australasian Pioneers' Club, Sydney.   4385

EDGAR, THOMAS

Biography

1939 SHENTON, J.T.
Thomas Edgar.

(*Mariner's Mirror*, vol.25, Jan.1939, p.115.)

Copies: NPL:R(DS656.506/7).   4386

Monuments

HEADSTONE to grave in Churchyard at Lydd, Kent, England.
Photograph. 7 3/16″ x 9″.
Copies: NPL:M(SV*Mon4).   4387

ELLIOTT, JOHN

Writings

MEMOIRS of the early life of John Elliott, of Elliott House, near Mission, Yorkshire, Esqr and Lieut^t of the Royal Navy, written by himself at the request of his wife for the use and amusement of his children only.

B.M.Add.MSS. 42714. *See* Beaglehole, vol.2, p.cxxxvi.
Typescript summary with extracts from the original are filed in the Mitchell Library in *Captain Cook Miscellanea*, vol.1, pp.21–4, at A1713⁻¹.

4388

FORSTER, JOHANN GEORG ADAM

Writings

1772–87 LETTERS from J.R. Forster and J.G.A. Forster, 23 June 1772, 19 Nov.1772, 5 Mar.1787, to Thomas Pennant re their association with Sir Joseph Banks; the appointment of J.R. Forster as naturalist aboard the *Resolution* in 1772 with Captain Cook, and of J.G.A. Forster, as illustrator.

(a) MS. (b) Typescript transcripts. Letters dated Nov.19, 1772 and Mar.5, 1787 by J.G.A. Forster.
Copies: NPL:M(ML Doc.489).   4389

1777 Mar.8 AUTOGRAPH NOTE to Mr. Banks accompanying the presentation of a copy of his *Voyage round the World*. Perry Street, March 18th, 1777.
p.1, 4o.
Copies: ANL(MS.9, item 67).   4390

1778 Jan.4 ALS to Sir Joseph Banks intimating that his father and he had been offered positions as teachers in an institution in Germany, and requesting Sir Joseph Banks to use his influence with Lord Sandwich to gain some recognition for the botanical work performed by his father and himself whilst with Cook on the *Resolution*. London, Jan.4, 1778.
pp. 4, 4o.
Copies: ANL(MS.9, item 68).   4391

1778 A LETTER to the Right Honourable the Earl of Sandwich, First
Lord Commissioner of the Board of Admiralty. London, G.Robinson,
1778.

pp.ii, 25, [6].
For note *see* no.4416.

Copies: NPL:M(Q980/35A1); NPL:D(Q77/58); VSL.   4392

[1789] LETTER of J.G.A. Forster to B.G. Hoffmann, bookseller, Hamburg,
May 9, [1789]. Requesting him to despatch three copies of Forster's
translation of the Account of the Pelew Islands [by G. Keate].

pp.2.
Original German MS., with English translation in typescript. Date from imprint of
German edition of Keate's Account.

Copies: NPL:M(MSS.Af34).   4393

Biography

1854 BRAINNE, Charles
Voyage de Cook et de Forster (1774).

(*In his* La Nouvelle-Calédonie. Paris, L. Hachette et Cie, 1854. pp.1–20.)
Copies: NPL:M(998.7/1A); ANL.   4394

1854 MOLESCHOTT, Jac.
Georg Forster, der Naturforscher des Volks; [pub.] zur Feier des 26.
November, 1854. Frankfurt a M., Meidinger, 1854.

pp.[viii], 295.
Copies: NPL:M(925.8/F733.1/7A1).   4395

1858 KOENIG, Heinrich
Georg Forster's Leben in Haus und Welt. 2nd ed. Leipzig, F.A. Brockhaus,
1858.

pp.xxiii, 309, 324.
Copies: NPL:M(925.8/F733.1/6B1).   4396

1863 KLEIN, Karl
Georg Forster in Mainz, 1788 bis 1793 . . . nebst Nachträgen zu seinen
Werken. [With bibliographical notes.] Gotha, Perthes, 1863.

pp.viii, 488.
Copies: NPL:M(925.8/F733.1/1A1).   4397

1925 IREDALE, Tom
Captain Cook's artists.

Illus.
(*Australian Museum Magazine,* July 1925, pp.224–30.)
Copies: NPL:M(507/A).   4398

1925 IREDALE, Tom
George Forster's paintings.
Illus.
(*Australian Zoologist*, vol.4, November 1925, pp.48–53.)
Copies: NPL:M(Q590.5/A).   4399

1925 JOSE, Arthur Wilberforce
The Forster paintings in the Australian Museum.
(Royal Australian Historical Society—*Journal and Proceedings*, vol.11, 1925, pp.155–7.)
Copies: NPL:M(991/R, Ref.Books); NPL:D(9/69); NPL:R(S991.06/1A).   4400

[1930] SEIDEL, Ina
Das Labyrinth: roman. Berlin, Deutsche Verlags-Anstalt, [1930].
pp.627.
Reprint of 1922 edition. A novel based on the life of G. Forster.
See also no.4402.
Copies: NPL:M(A833/S).   4401

1932 SEIDEL, Ina
The Labyrinth: [a novel,] by I. Seidel. Trans. [from the German] by
O. Williams; with an intro. by I. Forbes-Mosse. London, John Lane,
The Bodley Head, 1932.
pp.[xiv], 482.
A novel based on the life of G. Forster.
See also no.4401.
Copies: NPL:M(A833/S).   4402

1936 LEITZMANN, Albert
Georg und Therese Forster und die Brüder Humboldt: Urkunden und
Umrisse. Bonn, Ludwig Rohrscheid, 1936.
pp.x, 216.
Copies: NPL:M(923.9/4A1).   4403

1937 IREDALE, Tom
J.R. & G. Forster, naturalists.
(*The Emu*, vol.37, October 1937, pp.95–9.)
Copies: NPL:M(598.2901/E).   4404

1954 MERRILL, Elmer Drew
The Botany of Cook's voyages and its unexpected significance in relation
to anthropology, biogeography and history. Waltham, Mass., Chronica
Botanica Co., 1954.
Facs. illus. ports. pp.[iv, 224].
A cloth bound edition of *Chronica Botanica*, vol.14, no.5/6.
Copies: NPL:M(Q581.999/M); NPL:R(Q581.99/11); ANL; QU.   4405

1956 ANDERSON, Alexander Walter
The Two Forsters.

(*In his* How we got our flowers. London, Benn, 1956. pp.138–43.)
First published 1950 with title *The Coming of the flowers.*
Copies: NPL:M(582/A).   4406

1957 ASHER, J.A.
Georg Forster and Goethe.

(*A.U.M.L.A.* no.7, November 1957, pp.15–19.)
Copies: NPL:R(S806/8).   4407

1957 KERSTEN, Kurt
Der Weltumsegler, Johann Georg Adam Forster, 1754–1794. Bern, Francke, 1957.

Ports. pp.400.
Copies: NPL:M(925.8/F733.1/2A1).   4408

1958 DEUTSCHE AKADEMIE DER WISSENSCHAFTEN ZU BERLIN
Verzeichnis der Korrespondenten von Georg Forster; zusammengestellt von der Deutschen Akademie der Wissenschaften zu Berlin. Berlin, die Akademie, 1958.

pp.16.
(*Forsterausgabe.*)
Copies: NPL:M(925.8/F733.1/5A1).   4409

1965–66 HOARE, Michael Edward
Material relating to the Forsters, 1965–6.

1 box.
CONTENTS:
MS. draft and typescript papers on J.R. and J.G.A. Forster, by M.E. Hoare, Research Associate, Australian Academy of Science.
M.A. Thesis, T.S. pp.230. The Contribution of J.R. and G. Forster to the literature of Cook's second voyage, 1772–1775, by M.E. Hoare.
Unpublished bibliography of the Forsters by M.E. Hoare.
Photocopies of some letters in the British Museum.

Copies: Basser Library, Australian Academy of Science, 51.   4410

1966 BEGG, Alexander Charles
Dusky Bay: [in the steps of Captain Cook], by A.C. Begg and N.C. Begg. [With bibl.] Christchurch, N.Z., Whitcombe & Tombs, 1966.

Facs. illus., some in colour, maps, ports. pp.239.
Copies: NPL:M(987.6/23A1); ANL.   4411

Portraits

IOH. REINHOLD FORSTER und Georg Forster. Vater und Sohn. T.F.
Rigau pinx. D. Beïjel del. et sculp.

Photograph of print in the possession of R. de C. Nan Kivell, Esq., 1962. Size of print
10⅞" x 8⅝".

Copies: NPL:M(P2/40).   4412

JOHANN REINHOLD Forster/Johann Georg Forster. Von D.Berger
Geäti [sculp].

1782. Engraving. Round. Diam. within frame line 3¼". Meas. engraved surface 5⅞" x 3¾".
Head and shoulders in profile. Portrait of J.R. Forster taken from Wedgwood medallion
at NPL:MP*60.

Copies: NPL:M(P1/Forster 1).   4413

The Same entitled Reinhold und Georg Forster.

Process plate reproduction with letterpress.
Round. Meas. of diam. 6⅞".
From *Illustrierte Zeitung*, Leipzig, 31 Juli, 1875, p.77.

Copies NPL:M(P1/Forster 2).   4414

FORSTER, JOHANN REINHOLD

Writings

1772–87 LETTERS from J.R. Forster and J.G.A. Forster, 23 June, 1772,
19 Nov.1772, 5 Mar.1787 to Thomas Pennant re their association with
Sir Joseph Banks; the appointment of J.R. Forster as naturalist aboard
the *Resolution* in 1772 with Captain Cook, and of J.G.A. Forster, as
illustrator.

(a) MS. (b) Typescript transcripts.
Letter dated 23 June 1772 by J.R. Forster.

Copies: NPL:M(ML Doc.489).   4415

Biography

1778 FORSTER, Johann Georg Adam

A Letter to the Right Honourable the Earl of Sandwich . . . from George
Forster (i.e. J.G.A. Forster.] London, G. Robinson, 1778.

pp.[ii], ii, 25, 6.
Complaining that the author's father, J.R. Forster, had been prevented from writing
the official narrative of Captain Cook's second voyage around the world.
Bound as frontispiece in Mitchell Library copy is a sepia illustration entitled *The German
Doctor on his travels from England*, Doctor Faustus delt., Robinson. At foot of illustration:
The German Doctor with his family on his travels to England conducted by Mynheer Shinder Knecht.

Copies: NPL:M(Q980/35A1); NPL:D(Q77/58); VSL.   4416

1879 HET LOGBOEK van Cook gedurende zijn reis in 1772.

(Aardrijkskundig Genootschap—*Tijdschrift*, vol.3, p.315, 1879.)
Refers to the discovery of the copy of part of a log-book kept by J.R. Forster on the *Resolution*.
Copies: NPL:M(Q910.6/6).   4417

1908 MAIDEN, Joseph Henry
Records of Australian botanists.

(Royal Society of New South Wales—*Journal*, 1908. pp.67–8.)
Copies: NPL:M(506/R).   4418

1925 IREDALE, Tom
Captain Cook's artists.

Illus.
(*Australian Museum Magazine*, July 1925, pp.224–30.)
Copies: NPL:M(507/A).   4419

1937 IREDALE, Tom
J.R. & G. Forster, naturalists.

(*The Emu*, vol.37, Oct.1937, pp.95–9.)
Copies: NPL:M(598.2901/E).   4420

1954 MERRILL, Elmer Drew
The Botany of Cook's voyages and its unexpected significance in relation to anthropology, biogeography and history. Waltham, Mass., Chronica Botanica, 1954.

Facs. illus. ports. pp.[iv,224].
A cloth bound edition of *Chronica Botanica*, vol.14, no.5/6.
Copies: NPL:M(Q581.999/M); NPL:R(Q581.99/11); ANL; QU.   4421

1956 ANDERSON, Alexander Walter
The Two Forsters.

(*In his* How we got our flowers. London, Benn, 1956. pp.138–43.)
First published 1950 with title *The Coming of the flowers*.
Copies: NPL:M(582/A).   4422

1965–66 HOARE, Michael Edward
Material relating to the Forsters, 1965–6.

1 box.
CONTENTS:
MS. draft and typescript papers on J.R. and J.G.A. Forster, by M.E. Hoare, Research Associate, Australian Academy of Science.
M.A. Thesis, T.S. pp.230. The Contribution of J.R. and G. Forster to the literature of Cook's second voyage, 1772–1775, by M.E. Hoare.
Unpublished bibliography of the Forsters by M.E. Hoare.
Photocopies of some letters in the British Museum.

Copies: Basser Library, Australian Academy of Science, 51.   4423

1966 BEGG, Alexander Charles

Dusky Bay: [in the steps of Captain Cook], by A.C. Begg and N.C. Begg. [With bibl.] Christchurch, N.Z., Whitcombe & Tombs, 1966.

Facs. illus., some in colour, maps, ports. pp.239.

Copies: NPL:M(987.6/23A1); ANL. 4424

1967 HOARE, Michael Edward

Johann Reinhold Forster, the neglected philosopher of Cook's second voyage, 1772–1775.

(*Journal of Pacific History*, vol.2, 1967, pp.215–24.)

Copies: NPL:M(998.05/1); NPL:R(N990.05/1). 4425

Portraits

IOH. REINHOLD FORSTER und Georg Forster. Vater und Sohn. T.F. Rigau pinx. D. Beïjel del. et sculp.

Photograph of print in the possession of R.de C. Nan Kivell, Esq., 1962. Size of print 10⅞″ x 8⅜″.

Copies: NPL:M(P2/40). 4426

JOHANN REINHOLD Forste /Johann Georg Forster. Von D. Berger Geäti [sculp].

1782. Engraving. Round. Diam. within frame line 3⅛″. Meas. engraved surface 5⅞″ x 3¾″. Head and shoulders, in profile. Portrait of J.R. Forster taken from Wedgwood medallion at NPL:M P*60.

Copies: NPL:M(P1/Forster 1). 4427

The Same, entitled Reinhold und Georg Forster.

Process plate reproduction with letterpress. Round. Meas. of diam. 6⅞″. From *Illustrierte Zeitung*, Leipzig, 31 Juli, 1875, p.77.

Copies: NPL:M(P1/Forster 2). 4428

Medallions

[JOHANN REINHOLD FORSTER: Wedgwood portrait medallion, designed by Joachim Smith.]

1775. White on blue jasper ware. Oval in gilt and brown wooden frame. Leather backing. Meas. inside frame c.3″ x c.2½″; framed 4¾″ x 4⅛″. Head and shoulders, in profile. Signature "I S" impressed on base of arm. "Wedgwood and Bentley" impressed on back. Hand-written label on back "Johan (*sic*) Reinhold Forster, LL.D. Naturalist and traveller, born at Dirschan, Polish Prussia 1729. Professor of Natural History at Warrington Academy 1774. Accompanied Capt Cook

in his second voyage round the world as a naturalist . . . The portrait in fine old Wedgwood from a model by Joachim. 1775."
Transferred from the Australian Museum, Oct.1955.
Copies: NPL:M(P*60). 4429

Photograph.
(Neg. at FM1/F.)
Copies: NPL:M(P1/Forster 3). 4430

Reproduced in the *Australian Zoologist* vol.4, Nov.1925, p.53.
Copies: NPL:M(Q590.5/A); NPL:R(Q590.6/4). 4431

The Same, in white on green jasper ware. Oval in gilt metal frame.
Meas. inside frame $4\frac{5}{8}''$ x $3\frac{1}{2}''$; framed $5\frac{1}{8}''$ x $4''$.
Unsigned. Titled "Forster the botanist" in gold below portrait. "Wedgwood" impressed on back.
Copies: NPL:D(DL Pa92). 4432

[JOHANN REINHOLD FORSTER: Wedgwood portrait medallion.]
n.d. White on blue jasper ware. Oval in brown wooden frame. Leather backing. Meas. inside frame $3\frac{7}{8}''$ x $2\frac{3}{4}''$; framed $6\frac{1}{8}''$ x $4\frac{7}{8}''$.
Head and shoulders, in profile.
Unsigned; untitled. Similar plaque to that at NPL:M P*60, but lacks sprig of leaves on the right.
Back covered.
From the collection of Arthur Lee.
Copies: NPL:M(P*56). 4433

FURNEAUX, TOBIAS
Biography

1790 BASTON, Guillaume André René
Première narration, Furneaux.

(*In his* Narrations d'Omai, insulaire de la Mer du Sud . . . Ouvrage traduit de l'O-Taïtien par M. K*** & publié par le Capitaine L.A.B. [i.e. G.A.R. Baston]. Rouen, Le Boucher, le jeune, 1790. Tome 1, pp.3–67.)
An imaginary autobiography of Omai.
Copies: NPL:M(843.69/B); NPL:R(09:S843.69/B327/1); VSL. 4434

1791 LABORDE, Jean Benjamin de
Furneaux.

(*In his* Histoire abrégée de la Mer du Sud. Paris, P. Didot, l'ainé, 1791. Tome 2, pp. 404–12.)
Copies: NPL:M(980/L); NPL:R(09:Q990A/122); VSL. 4435

1881 BLAIR, David
Furneaux.

(*In his* Cyclopædia of Australasia. Melbourne, Fergusson and Moore, 1881. pp.142–3.)
Copies: NPL:M(Q990/B); NPL:R(Q990A/21A).   4436

1898 SHILLINGLAW, John Joseph
Notes on an original chart of the south and east coasts of Tasmania, supposed to have been constructed by . . . Furneaux . . . when associated with Cook on his second voyage.

(Royal Geographical Society of Australasia—Victorian Branch—*Transactions*, vol.16, 1898. pp.38–42.)
Copies: NPL:M(980/R); NPL:R(DS992A/3).   4437

[191–?] STRANG, Herbert, *pseud.*
The Voyage of Captain Furneaux.

(*In his* The Romance of Australia. London, H. Frowde, [191–?]. pp.119–23.)
Copies: NPL:M(980.1/S); NPL:R(S990.1/20).   4438

1931 MANWARING, George Ernest
My friend the Admiral: the life, letters and journal of . . . James Burney. London, G. Routledge, 1931.

Illus. port. pp.xvi, 313.
Contains references to Furneaux. The portrait facing p.30 is a reproduction of J. Northcote's portrait of Furneaux, *see also* no.4444.
Copies: NPL:M(A923.9/B); NPL:R(920/B965.4/1); ANL.   4439

[195–] BLIGHT, F.S.
Captain Tobias Furneaux, R.N., of Swilly, by F.S. Blight. Reprinted from the Transactions of the Plymouth Institution and Devon and Cornwall History Society, vol.22, 1952. Plymouth, Underhill, pr., [195–].

Illus. maps, port. pp.25.
See also no.4442.
Copies: NPL:M(923.9/F987/1A1).   4440

1952 EDWARDS, Gerald Hamilton-
Tobias Furneaux, 1735–1781; [with portrait from painting by James Northcote].

(*In his* Twelve men of Plymouth. Plymouth, the author, 1951. pp.33–8.)
See also no.4444.
Copies: NPL:M(920.042/E).   4441

[1956] BLIGHT, F.S.
Captain Tobias Furneaux, R.N., of Swilly, lecture by F.S. Blight. Delivered . . . 6th Mar. 1952.

Illus. maps, port.
(Plymouth Institution and Devon and Cornwall Natural History Society—*Annual reports and Transactions.* Vol.22, 1949.50–1955.6, pp.70–94.)
See also no.4440.
Copies: NPL:M(570.6/P).   4442

1960 FURNEAUX, Rupert

Tobias Furneaux, circumnavigator; [with bibl.]. London, Cassell, 1960.
Frontisp. illus. map, ports. pp.ix, 187.
Copies: NPL:M(923.9/F987/2A1); NPL:R(S909.4A/113); ANL.   4443

Portraits

NORTHCOTE, James

[Portrait, painted by James Northcote after Furneaux's return from Cook's second voyage. Reproduced in black and white.]
(*In* Rienits, Rex—The Voyages of Captain Cook. London, Paul Hamlyn, 1968. p.81.)
Original in possession of the Rt. Hon. The Earl of Birkenhead, Banbury. *See also* no.4439, 4441.
Copies: NPL:M(Q980:Co1/R1A1); NPL:R(NQ910.4/4).   4444

GORE, JOHN

Writings

1766–7 LOG BOOK of H.M.S. *Dolphin*, Aug.21, 1766–Oct.16, 1767, under the command of Captain Wallis.

2 vols.
The log is signed Jn. Gore, Master Hunter (he was engaged in hunting on the Island of Tinian), and this has led to the two volumes' being incorrectly described as the Log of the *Hunter.*
Wallis reported Tahiti as a favourable site for the observation of the transit of the planet Venus, due to take place in June 1769, and on this recommendation the Royal Society requested, through the Admiralty, that the *Endeavour* be sent to Tahiti.
Copies: ANL(MS.4); NPL:M(B1533–4, photostat copy).   4445

Biography

1828 SPARKS, Jared

[Biographical sketch of Gore.]
(*In his* Memoirs of the life and travels of John Ledyard. London, H. Colburn, 1828. pp.105–6.)
For other editions *see* no.4525.
Copies: NPL:M(A923.9/L); NPL:D(82/53, 82/54); NPL:R(S920/L476); ANL:F. 4446

Portraits

1780 WEBBER, John
Captain John Gore.

1780. Oil painting. 17″ x 12⅜″, oval. Untitled; signed.

Copies: ANL(Nan Kivell). 4447

Photograph.

11¾″ x 9″.

Copies: NPL:M(P1/Gore). 4448

HAMMOND, WILLIAM

Portraits

ABBOTT, L.F.
[Captain William Hammond.]

Photograph of painting. Meas. of original 50″ x 40″. Meas. of photograph 6⅜″ x 5¾″. Hammond was the owner of the *Resolution* and the *Adventure* before the Admiralty bought them for Cook's second voyage.

Copies: NPL:M(P1/Hammond 1). 4449

HAWKESWORTH, JOHN

Biography

1773 DALRYMPLE, Alexander
A Letter from Mr. Dalrymple to Dr. Hawkesworth, occasioned by some groundless and illiberal imputations in his account of the late voyages to the south. London, J. Nourse and others, 1773.

Folding chart, pp.[iv],35.

See Holmes, no.6. There are two issues of this rare pamphlet, the first on thick paper containing no chart, and the second on ordinary paper containing a *Chart of the South Pacifick Ocean*. The Mitchell and Dixson copies both contain this chart. After Hawkesworth's reply in the preface to the second edition of his Voyages, Dalrymple prepared another pamphlet (*see* nos.4360, 4451) which however was not published because of the death of Hawkesworth.

Copies: NPL:M(Q980/36A1); NPL:D(77/4). 4450

1773 DALRYMPLE, Alexander
'Mr. Dalrymple's Observations on Dr Hawkesworth's Preface to the Second Edition.' 12 Sep.1773.

ff.24, cm 26.

Typescript. MS. note 'Copy of MS. in British Museum never published.'

Copies: NPL:D(WD7). 4451

1810 DRAKE, Nathan

Literary Life of John Hawkesworth.

(*In his* Essays . . . illustrative of the *Rambler, Adventurer* and *Idler*. London, pr. by J. Seely, for W. Suttaby, 1810. Vol.2, pp.1–34.)

Copies: NPL:M(824.5/D). 4452

1900 MORRIS, Edward Ellis

Dr. John Hawkesworth, friend of Dr. Johnson and historian of Captain Cook's first voyage.

pp.218–38.

Extract from the *Gentleman's Magazine*, Sept.1900.

Copies: NPL:M(928.28/H); NPL:R(S050/G338). 4453

Portraits

REYNOLDS

Reproductions Arranged by Engraver

COOPER

John Hawkesworth, LLD. R. Cooper, sculp.[t]

London. Published by T. and J. Allman . . . 1823. Engraving. Meas. within frame line $3\frac{1}{4}''$ x $2\frac{1}{2}''$.

Head and shoulders.

Copies: NPL:M(P1/Hawkesworth 1). 4454

Another print.

Copies: NPL:M(P1/Hawkesworth 2). 4455

Another print, cut to omit imprint.

Copies: NPL:M(P1/Hawkesworth 3). 4456

The Same entitled Hawkesworth, L.L.D.

Copies: NPL:M(P1/Hawkesworth 4). 4457

HALL

John Hawksworth (*sic*) L.L.D. S.[r] Joshua Reynolds pinx. J. Hall sculp. Done from an Original Picture in the possession of the Hon.[ble] M.[r] Fitzmaurice.

Publish'd . . . Jan.1.st 1775, by T: Cadell in the Strand. Engraving. Oval. Meas. within frame line $2\frac{1}{4}''$ x $1\frac{3}{4}''$.

Head and shoulders.

Copies: NPL:M(P1/Hawkesworth 5). 4458

Another 3 prints.

Copies: NPL:M(P1/Hawkesworth 6–8). 4459

Another print, port. reversed.

Cut to omit imprint.

Copies: NPL:M(P1/Hawkesworth 9).   4460

HALPIN

John Hawkesworth, L.L.D. Engraved by M.ʳ Halpin from a painting by Sir Joshua Reynolds.

London. Published by Jones & C.º, April 9, 1825. Engraving. Meas. of engraved surface c.4½″ x 4″.
Head and shoulders.

Copies: NPL:M(P1/Hawkesworth 10).   4461

HOLL

Dr. Hawkesworth. [W.]Holl sculp.

Engraving. Oval. Meas. within frame line 2⅞″ x 1½″. With biographical letterpress.
Head and shoulders.

Copies: NPL:M(P1/Hawkesworth 11).   4462

Another print.

Copies: NPL:M(P1/Hawkesworth 12).   4463

HOPWOOD

John Hawksworth (*sic*), L.L.D. Engraved by J. Hopwood.

Engraving. Oval. Meas. within frame line 3⅝″ x 2¹⁵⁄₁₆″. Head and shoulders.

Copies: NPL:M(P1/Hawkesworth 13).   4464

MACKENZIE

J. Hawkesworth, L.L.D. Engrav'd by E. Mackenzie, from a Painting of Sir Joshua Reynolds R.A.

Printed for C. Cooke, Jan.ʸ 9.ᵗʰ 1808. Engraving. Oval. Meas. of port. 2⅞″ x 2¼″.
Head and shoulders.
(*Inserted in* Bligh, W.—A Voyage to the South Seas. Opp. p.11.)

Copies: NPL:D(Q79/12).   4465

SCHIAVONETTI

Hawkesworth. Painted by Sir Jos. Reynolds. Engraved by N. Schiavonetti.

Published 10.ᵗʰ Nov.ʳ 1806 by John Sharpe, Piccadilly. Engraving. Hand-coloured.
Meas. within frame line 2⅞″ x 2¹³⁄₁₆″.
Seated at a table.

Copies: NPL:D(DL Pd628).   4466

The Same. Uncoloured.

Cut to omit imprint.

Copies: NPL:M(P1/Hawkesworth 14).   4467

SMITH

Dr. Hawkesworth. Sir Jos. Reynolds Pin.^t A. Smith Sculp.

Publish'd by Harrison, & C.º Dec.ʳ 1 1794. Engraving. Oval. Meas. of port. 1 $\frac{15}{16}$ ″ x 1 $\frac{7}{16}$ ″.
Meas. of plate mark 2 $\frac{7}{8}$ ″ x 2 $\frac{5}{16}$ ″.
Head and shoulders.

Copies: NPL:M(P1/Hawkesworth 15). 4468

THORNTON

John Hawksworth (*sic*), L.L.D. One of the Editors of Cook's First Voyage.
[With port. of Captain James King]. Thornton sculp.

Published by Alex.ʳ Hogg at the King's Arms . . . [London]. Engraving. Oval. Meas.
within frame line 6 $\frac{3}{4}$ ″ x 5 $\frac{3}{8}$ ″. Meas. of plate mark 8 $\frac{15}{16}$ ″ x 13 $\frac{1}{2}$ ″.
Head and shoulders.
Plate from Anderson, G.W.—New authentic and complete collection of voyages, published
1784–6.

Copies: NPL:M(P2/32). 4469

Another print. Hand-coloured. Port. of Hawkesworth only.

Imprint erased.

Copies: NPL:D(DL Pd673). 4470

The Same entitled John Hawkesworth, L.L.D. one of the editors of Cook's
first voyage. Thornton sculp.

Published by Alex.ʳ Hogg at the King's Arms, no.16 Paternoster Row. Engraving. Oval.
Meas. within frame line 6 $\frac{11}{16}$ ″ x 5 $\frac{3}{8}$ ″.
(Anderson, G.W.—A New, authentic and complete collection of voyages round the
world. London, A. Hogg, [1784–6]. Opp. p.399.)

Copies: NPL:M(A346). 4471

Another print.

(Wilson, P.—A New, complete and universal collection of authentic and entertaining
voyages and travels. London, 1794. Opp. p.382.)

Copies: NPL:M(F980/W). 4472

The Same entitled John Hawkesworth, L.L.D. one of the Editors of
Cooks First Voyage.

Engraving. Oval. Meas. within frame line 4″ x 3 $\frac{1}{4}$ ″.

Copies: NPL:M(P1/Hawkesworth 16). 4473

Another print.

(Cook, J.—Illustrations to Captain Cook's voyages in a series of one hundred and fifteen
engravings from the original drawings. London, W. and S. Graves, n.d.)

Copies: NPL:M(980:Col/I1A1). 4474

WARREN

1802 John Hawkesworth, LL.D.: [steel engraving]. Warren sc., London,
pub. by Longman & Rees, Sept.1, 1802.

(*Inserted in* Smith, E.—Life of Sir Joseph Banks. 1911. Vol.1, facing p.31.)

Copies: Australasian Pioneers' Club, Sydney.   4475

WATSON

John Hawkesworth L.L.D. Sr Joshua Reynolds pinx.^{t} James Watson
fecit.

Publish'd . . . Decr 1.st 1773, by Ja.^{s} Watson . . . & B. Clowes . . . [London]. Mezzotint.
Meas. of engraved surface 12$\frac{1}{2}$" x 11".
Seated at a table.

Copies: NPL:M(P3/50A).   4476

The Same entitled John Hawkesworth, L.L.D.

Meas. within frame line 2$\frac{3}{8}$" x 2".

Copies: NPL:M(P3/50B).   4477

The Same entitled John Hawkesworth, L.L.D.

Meas. of port. 2$\frac{7}{16}$" x 2$\frac{1}{16}$".

Copies: NPL:D(DL Pd631).   4478

Photograph.

Copies: NPL:M(P1/Hawkesworth 18).   4479

UNKNOWN

John Hawkesworth, LLD. Engraved from an Original Picture.

Engraving. Oval. Meas. within frame line 3$\frac{1}{4}$" x 2$\frac{1}{2}$".
Head and shoulders.

Copies: NPL:M(P1/Hawkesworth 17).   4480

ARTIST UNKNOWN

DR. Hawkesworth, Æt. 43: [steel engraving].

(*Inserted in* Smith, E.—Life of Sir Joseph Banks. 1911. Vol.1, facing p.30.)

Copies: Australasian Pioneers' Club, Sydney.   4481

HODGES, WILLIAM

Biography

1808 EDWARDS, Edward
William Hodges, R.A.

(*In his* Anecdotes of painters. London, 1808. pp.241-51.)

Copies: NPL:R(S759.2/23).   4482

1924 FARINGTON, Joseph
[William Hodges: biographical sketch.]
(*In his* Farington diary. London, Hutchinson, 1924. Vol.4, pp.8–11.)
Copies: NPL:M(927/F).   4483

1925 IREDALE, Tom
Captain Cook's artists.
Illus.
(*Australian Museum Magazine*, July 1925, pp.224–30.)
Copies: NPL:M(507/A).   4484

1947 REYNOLDS, Graham
Captain Cook's draughtsmen; [with reproductions and map].
(*Geographical Magazine*, vol.19, pp.457–66, Feb.1947.)
Copies: NPL:R(S909.5A/5).   4485

1948 WARNER, Oliver Martin Wilson
[William Hodges.]
Illus.
(*In his* Introduction to British marine painting. London, Batsford, 1948. pp.31–2.)
Copies: NPL:M(758/W); NPL:R(S758/37).   4486

1959 GREAT BRITAIN—Admiralty
Oil paintings by William Hodges, R.A., draughtsman on Captain Cook's second voyage, 1772–1775. [Catalogue of paintings] exhibited in New Zealand, by courtesy of the Lords Commissioners of the Admiralty, June–Sept., 1959. [With biographical note and bibl., and] (Catalogue of additional material shown in the Alexander Turnbull Library, June–July, 1959). Wellington, N.Z., Govt.Pr., 1959.
Illus. pp.15, 9.
(*Alexander Turnbull Library Bulletin*, no.15 and supp.)
Copies: NPL:M(015.97/3).   4487

1965 ROYAL ACADEMY OF ARTS
Painting in England, 1700–1850, from the collection of Mr. & Mrs. P. Mellon. (Winter exhibition, 1964–5.) [Catalogue of an exhibition held by the] Royal Academy of Arts. London, 1965.
pp.x, 88.
Includes paintings by W. Hodges.
Copies: NPL:M(759.2/3A1).   4488

Portraits

DANCE, George
[Portrait. Reproduction of a pencil sketch by George Dance.]
(*In* Rienits, Rex—The Voyages of Captain Cook. London, Paul Hamlyn, 1968. p.81.)
Original in the Royal Academy of Arts, London.
Copies: NPL:M(Q980:Col/R1A1); NPL:R(NQ910.4/4).   4489

WESTALL, William
William Hodges, Esq., R.A., Landscape painter to the Prince of Wales:
[steel engraving by] Thorntwait, from an original painting by Mr. Westall,
published as the Act directs, 1 June, 1792, by C. Forster, [London].
(*Inserted in* Smith, E.—Life of Sir Joseph Banks. 1911. Vol.1, facing p.27.)
Copies: Australasian Pioneers' Club, Sydney.   4490

HOME, ALEXANDER

Biography

1838 HOME, George
Memoirs of an aristocrat, and reminiscences of the Emperor Napoleon;
by a midshipman of the *Bellerophon*. London, Whittaker & Co., 1838.
Copies: NPL:M(923.9/H765/1A1).   4491

HOOD, ALEXANDER

Biography

1801 WILLIAMS, John
Ode 20: To the memory of the brave Captain A. Hood . . . who was
mortally wounded in an action with the French . . . April 21 1798.
[With notes.]
(*In his* Nautical odes; or, Poetical sketches designed to commemorate the achievements
of the British Navy. London, E. and T. Williams, 1801. pp.74–7.)
Copies: NPL:M(Q821.79/W724/1).   4492

JACKSON, *Sir* GEORGE

Portraits

SIR GEORGE JACKSON-DUCKETT, Bart., M.P., Judge Advocate of
the Fleet.
Photograph of framed painting. $11\frac{1}{4}'' \times 9\frac{3}{16}''$.
On back of mount is inscription from the mural monument in the Chancel of the Church
of Bishop's Stortford, Herts., England.
Copies: NPL:M(P2/53).   4493

Another photograph.

8″ x 6″.

Copies: NPL:M(P1 Jackson, George 1).   4494

KING, JAMES
Biography

1785 MAVOR, *Rev.* William Fordyce
Elegy to the memory of Capt. James King. London, printed for the author, 1785.
pp.12.
Copies: NPL:M(C924).   4495

1874 KING, Alice
Captain Cook's companion.
(*In her* A Cluster of lives. 2nd ed. London, 1874. pp.137–59.)
Copies: NPL:M(920/K); NPL:R(DS920/945).   4496

Portraits

SHELLEY

Reproductions Arranged by Engraver

HOGG

Iac. King L.L.D F.R.S. Painted by S. Shelley. Engrav'd by I. Hogg.
Engraving. Medallion port. Meas. $1\frac{3}{4}$″ diam. Cut.
Head and shoulders, facing to the right.
Title-page vignette to *Voyage to the Pacific Ocean*. London, 1785. Vol.3.
Copies: NPL:M(P1/King 4).   4497

Another print.

(*In* Hammersley—Australia illustrated. Plate 24.)
Copies: NPL:M(D241).   4498

Another print.

(*Inserted in* Bligh, W.—A Voyage to the South Seas. Opp. p.13.)
Copies: NPL:D(Q79/12).   4499

THORNTON

Captain James King, LLD. F.R.S. Capt.[n] Cook's Co-adjutor in his Third and Last Voyage. [With port. of John Hawkesworth]. Thornton sculp.

Published by Alex.ʳ Hogg at the King's Arms . . . [London]. Engraving. Oval. Meas.
within frame line 6 11/16″ x 5 5/16″. Meas. of plate mark 8 15/16″ x 13 1/2″.
Head and shoulders.
Plate from Anderson, G.W.—New, authentic and complete collection of voyages published
1784–6.
Copies: NPL:M(P2/32).   4500

Another print.

(Anderson, G.W.—A New, authentic and complete collection of voyages round the
world. London, A. Hogg, [1784–6]. Opp. p.399.)
Copies: NPL:M(F980/5A1).   4501

Another print.

(Wilson, P.—A New, complete and universal collection of authentic and entertaining
voyages and travels. London, 1794. Opp. p.382.)
Copies: NPL:M(F980/W).   4502

Another print.

Hand-coloured. Portrait of King only. Imprint erased.
Copies: NPL:D(DL Pd676).   4503

UNKNOWN

Iac. King L.L.D F.R.S. [Painted by S. Shelley.]

London. Publish;ᵈ March, 1,ˢᵗ 1785 by I. Sewell Cornhill. Engraving. Medallion port.
1 5/8″ diam. Meas. of plate mark 6 15/16″ x 4 7/16″.
Head and shoulders, facing to the left.
At head: *European Magazine.*
Copies: NPL:M(P3/41C).   4504

Another 3 prints.

Copies: NPL:M(P1 Cook—Pingo 5–7).   4505

Another print.

(*Inserted in* Kippis, A.—Life of Captain James Cook. Opp. p.457.)
Copies: NPL:D(Q78/8).   4506

Another print.

(*Inserted in* Kippis, A.—Life of Captain James Cook. Opp. p.463.)
Copies: NPL:D(Q78/9).   4507

Another print.

Hand-coloured.
Copies: NPL:D(DL Pd669).   4508

Originals, Including Photocopies of Originals

WEBBER, John
Captain James King.
1782. Oil painting. 24″ x 20″. Untitled; signed.
Copies: ANL.   4509

Reproductions Arranged by Engraver

BARTOLOZZI
Captn James King L.L.D.—F.R.S. I. Webber pinxit. F. Bartolozzi R.A. sculp.
Publish'd . . . June 4th. 1784, by I. Webber . . . [London]. Engraving. Oval. Meas. within frame line $4\frac{5}{8}$″ x $3\frac{13}{16}$″. Cut.
Half-length.
Copies: NPL:D(DL Pd627).   4510

Another 3 prints.
Plate mark cut.
Copies: NPL:M(Pl/King1–3).   4511

Another print.
(*Inserted in* Webber, J.—Watercolours illustrating Captain Cook's last voyage. f.ii.)
Copies: NPL:D(DL PXX2).   4512

Another print.
(Australasian scrap-book.)
Copies: NPL:M(F980/A).   4513

Another print.
Cut.
(*Inserted in* Smith, E.—Life of Sir Joseph Banks. 1911. Vol.2, facing p.184.)
Copies: Australasian Pioneers' Club, Sydney.   4514

The Same. I. Webber pinxit. F. Bartolozzi R.A. sculp.
Proof before title. Oval. Meas. within frame line $4\frac{3}{8}$″ x $3\frac{5}{8}$″. ([Three voyages round the world.])
Copies: NPL:M(PXD59⁻¹).   4515

Another print.
(*Inserted in* Kippis, *Rev*. A.—The Life of Captain James Cook. Opp. p.450.)
Copies: NPL:D(Q78/8).   4516

Another print.
(*Inserted in* Kippis, *Rev*. A.—The Life of Captain James Cook. Opp. p.450.)
Copies: NPL:D(Q78/9).   4517

ASSOCIATES OF COOK

KIPPIS, *Rev.* ANDREW

Writings

1795 Aug.10 ALS to Sir Joseph Banks referring to the order of the United States Congress to seize Cook's vessel and stop explorations on the American coasts. Westminster, Aug.10, 1795.

pp.2, 4o.

Copies: ANL(MS.9, item 100).   4518

Portraits

ARTAUD

Reproductions Arranged by Engraver

BARTOLOZZI

Andrew Kippis, D.D. F.R.S. & S.A. W. Artaud, pinx.^{t} F. Bartolozzi, sculp.^{t}

London. Publish'd Octr 20.th 1792, by Thos Macklin . . . Engraving. $10\frac{7}{8}''$ x $8\frac{15}{16}''$. Meas. of plate mark $12\frac{7}{8}''$ x $9\frac{7}{8}''$.

Half-length.

Copies: NPL:M(P2/43).   4519

HAZLITT

Reproductions Arranged by Engraver

BAKER

Andrew Kippis, D.D., F.R.S. and S.A. Engraved by J. Baker, from a miniature picture by J. Hazlitt.

Published Feb.1796, by W. Bent. Engraving. Oval. Meas. within frame line $2\frac{5}{16}''$ x $1\frac{7}{8}''$. Meas. of plate mark $6\frac{7}{8}''$ x $4\frac{3}{8}''$.

Head and shoulders.

At head: '*Universal Magazine*'.

Copies: NPL:M(P1/Kippis 1).   4520

ARTIST UNKNOWN

ANDREW KIPPIS, D.D., F.R.S. & S.A.: [mezzotint]. Engraved by Ridley from an original picture in the possession of the Revd. Mr. Sumner. Published as the Act directs by Vernor & Hood . . . Sept.30, 1799.

(*Inserted in* Smith, E.—Life of Sir Joseph Banks. 1911. Vol.1, facing p.80.)

Copies: Australasian Pioneers' Club, Sydney.   4521

ANDREW KIPPIS.

London. William Darton . . . 1822. Engraving. Meas. of engraved surface c.3⅞" x 2⅝".
Meas. of plate mark 5" x 3¼". With obituary notice as letterpress.
(*Inserted in* Kippis, A.—The Life of Captain James Cook. Opp. p.viii.)

Copies: NPL:D(Q78/8).   4522

LEDYARD, JOHN

Biography

1790 AFRICAN ASSOCIATION

Proceedings of the Association for promoting the discovery of the interior
parts of Africa. London, pr. by C. Macrae, 1790.

Map, pp.xi, 236.
Sir Joseph Banks was one of the Association's Committee. The second chapter deals with
John Ledyard, Corporal of Marines on Cook's third voyage.

Copies: NPL:M(Q916/A).   4523

1828 SPARKS, Jared

The Life of John Ledyard, the American traveller; comprising selections
from his journals and correspondence. Cambridge, U.S.A., Hilliard and
Brown, 1828.

pp.xii, 325.
See also nos.4525–6, 4528–9.
Reviewed in the *North American Review* Oct.1828, pp.360–71 (NPL:R S050/N868).

Copies: NPL:M(A923.9/L).   4524

1828 SPARKS, Jared

Memoirs of the life and travels of John Ledyard, from his journals and
correspondence. London, H. Colburn, 1828.

pp.xii, 428.
See also nos.4524, 4526, 4528–9.
Reviewed in the *Quarterly Review*, July 1828, pp.85–113 (NPL:R S050/Q974).

Copies: NPL:M(A923.9/L); NPL:D(82/53,82/54); NPL:R(S920/L476); ANL.   4525

1829 SPARKS, Jared

Life of John Ledyard, the American traveller, comprising selections from
his journals and correspondence. 2nd ed. Cambridge, U.S.A., Hilliard
& Brown, 1829.

pp.xii, 310.
See also nos.4524–5, 4528–9.

Copies: ANL:F.   4526

1834 CRAIK, George Lillie
John Ledyard.

(*In his* Pursuit of knowledge. London, 1834. Vol.2, pp.373–87.)
Society for the Diffusion of Useful Knowledge—Library of Entertaining Knowledge.
See also no.4530.
Copies: NPL:R(DS374/19).   4527

1834 SPARKS, Jared
Travels and adventures of John Ledyard, comprising his voyage with
Capt. Cook's third and last expedition, his journey on foot 1300 miles
round the Gulf of Bothnia to St. Petersburgh, his adventures and residence
in Siberia, and his exploratory mission to Africa. London, pub. for
H. Colburn by R. Bentley, 1834.

pp.xii, 428.
Published anonymously. Half-title: *Life and travels of John Ledyard. See also* nos.4524–6,
4529.
Copies: NPL:M(A923.9/L).   4528

1834 SPARKS, Jared
Travels and adventures of John Ledyard, comprising his voyage with
Capt. Cook's third and last expedition, his journey on foot 1300 miles
round the Gulf of Bothnia to St. Petersburgh, his adventures and residence
in Siberia, and his exploratory mission to Africa. 2nd ed. London, pub.
for H. Colburn by R. Bentley, 1834.

pp.xii, 428.
Published anonymously. Half-title: *Life and travels of John Ledyard. See also* nos.4524–6,
4528.
Copies: NPL:M(A923.9/L); VSL.   4529

1876 CRAIK, George Lillie
[John Ledyard.]

(*In his* The Pursuit of knowledge under difficulties. New ed. London, George Bell, 1876.
pp.529–38.)
See also no.4527.
Copies: NPL:R(S374/25).   4530

1900 BANCROFT, Hubert Howe
[John Ledyard.]

(*In his* New Pacific. New York, 1900.)
See also no.4533.
Copies: NPL:R(S327.9/17).   4531

1905 LAUT, Agnes Christina
John Ledyard, the forerunner of Lewis and Clark.

(*In her* Vikings of the Pacific. New York, Macmillan, 1905. pp.242–62.)
Copies: NPL:M(910.4/110A1); ANL.   4532

1912 BANCROFT, Hubert Howe
[John Ledyard.]

(*In his* New Pacific. New York, The Bancroft Company, 1912. pp.346–8.)
See also no.4531.
Copies: NPL:M(980/B). 4533

1921 HOWAY, Frederic William
Authorship of the anonymous account of Captain Cook's last voyage. Seattle, Washington University State Historical Society, 1921.

Extract from *Washington Historical Quarterly*, vol.12, no.1, Jan.1921.
Copies: NPL:M(980:Co4/H1A1). 4534

1930 CARRUTHERS, *Sir* Joseph Hector McNeil
[Comments on Ledyard's journal, and the accuracy of his statements.]

(*In his* Captain James Cook, R.N. London, Murray, [1930]. pp.60–87.)
Copies: NPL:M(980:Co1/C2A1); NPL:D(93/37); NPL:R(S920/C771/2); Captain Cook's Landing Place Trust; QParl; QU; VMoU; VSL. 4535

1931 PALMER, H.
Captain James Cook, [by Sir J. Carruthers; with] (Note by the Editor).

(*Geographical Journal*, vol.77, May 1931, pp.491–6.)
A discussion of statements in the anonymous *Journal of Cook's last voyage*, 1781, and in Ledyard's *Narrative*.
anonymous *Journal of Cook's last voyage*, 1781, and in Ledyard's *Narrative*.
Copies: NPL:R(DS909.6A/2). 4536

1937 YANKEE Marco.
Facs. pp.185–8.
(*The Month of Goodspeed's Book Shop*, Boston. Vol.8, no.6, Feb. 1937.)
Copies: NPL:M(017.4/2). 4537

1939 MUNFORD, James Kenneth
Bound for the South Seas [and other chapters on Cook's third voyage].

(*In his* John Ledyard: an American Marco Polo. Portland, Oregon, Binsfords & Mort, 1939. pp.64–156.)
Copies: NPL:M(A923.9/L). 4538

1946 AUGUR, Helen
Passage to glory: John Ledyard's America. [A biography. With bibl.] New York, Doubleday, 1946.

Illus. ports. pp.[vii], 310.
An account of John Ledyard's experiences on the *Resolution* given on pp.58–111.
Copies: NPL:M(A923.9/L); ANL. 4539

1961 HALLIDAY, E.M.
Captain Cook's American.

Illus., some in colour, ports.
(*American Heritage*, vol.23, no.1, Dec. 1961, pp.60–72, 84–7.)
Copies: NPL:M(Q973.05/1). 4540

MASSON, FRANCIS

Biography

1956 ANDERSON, Alexander Walter
Pioneer plant-hunter

(*In his* How we got our flowers. London, Benn, 1956. pp.130–3.)
First published 1950 as *The Coming of the flowers.*
Copies: NPL:M(582/A). 4541

1968 LEMMON, Kenneth
Kew sends out its first hunter: [Francis Masson].

Port.
(*In his* The Golden age of plant hunters. London, Phoenix House, 1968. pp.42–73.)
Copies: NPL:M(581.9/1A1); NPL:R(E581.9/Lem). 4542

MONKHOUSE, GEORGE

1771 July 31   COOK, James
ALS to George Monkhouse, Mile End, 31 July 1771, concerning the wills of Monkhouse's sons, who died on the *Endeavour.*

Photographic copy of original, and photograph of TS copy.
Copies: ANL(MS.7A). 4543

NELSON, DAVID

Biography

1909 MAIDEN, Joseph Henry
The Banksian botanical collectors: David Nelson.

(*In his* Sir Joseph Banks, the Father of Australia. Sydney, Govt.Pr., 1909. pp.124–5.)
Copies: NPL:M(A925.8/B218/1A1). 4544

1916 BRITTEN, James
William Anderson, 1778, and the plants of Cook's third voyage; [with note].

(*Journal of Botany*, vol.54, Dec.1916, pp.345–52; vol.55, p.54.)
Photographic copy. Includes section on plants collected by Nelson.
Copies: NPL:M(980:Co4/B1A1). 4545

1921 MAIDEN, Joseph Henry
Records of Australian botanists.
(Royal Society of New South Wales—*Journal and Proceedings*. Vol.55, 1921, p.165.)
Copies: NPL:M(506/R).   4546

1956 ANDERSON, Alexander Walter
David Nelson.
(*In his* How we got our flowers. London, Benn, 1956. pp.143–9.)
First published 1950 as *The Coming of the flowers*.
Copies: NPL:M(582/A).   4547

1968 LEMMON, Kenneth
The Golden age of plant hunters; [with bibl.]. London, Phoenix House, 1968.
Facs. plan, plates, some in colour, ports. pp.x, 229.
Includes references to David Nelson, botanist on Cook's third voyage.
Copies: NPL:M(581.9/1A1); NPL:R(E581.9/Lem).   4548

OMAI

1774 GENUINE ACCOUNT of Omiah, a native of Otaheite . . . lately brought over to England by Capt. Fourneaux (*sic*) 1774: [extract from *London Magazine*, Aug., 1774].
Copies: ANL:F.   4549

1775 AN HISTORIC epistle from Omiah to the Queen of Otaheite, being his remarks on the English nation. With notes by the editor. London, T. Evans, 1775.
pp.iv, 44.
An anonymous satire.
Omiah, or Omai, was brought to England in 1773 by Captain Cook, and returned to Tahiti in 1776.
Copies: NPL:M(C930).   4550

1776 OMIAH'S FAREWELL; inscribed to the ladies of London. London, G. Kearsly, 1776.
pp.iv, 11.
Copies: NPL:M(C931); NPL:D(Q77/51).   4551

1777 PRESTON, William
Seventeen hundred and seventy-seven; or, A picture of the manners and character of the age, in a poetical epistle from a lady of quality [i.e. W. Preston]. London, T. Evans, 1777.
pp.[ii], 26.
Copies: NPL:M(Q821.6/P942.2/1A1).   4552

1780 A LETTER from Omai to the Right Honourable the Earl of ********,
late ——————— Lord of the ——————; trans. from the Ulaietean
tongue. In which among other things, is fairly and irrefragably stated
the nature of original sin, together with a proposal for planting
Christianity in the islands of the Pacific Ocean. London, J. Bell, 1780.

pp.[i], 35.

An anonymous satire. Date taken from p.[1].

Copies: NPL:M(C929). 4553

1785 O'KEEFE, John

A Short account of the new pantomime called Omai; or, A trip round
the world. Performed at the Theatre Royal, Covent Garden. The
pantomime and the whole of the scenery designed and invented by
Mr. Loutherbourg. The words written by Mr. O'Keefe, and the musick
composed by Mr. Shields. New ed. London, T. Cadell, 1785.

pp.[2], 24.

First published 1785, the text of the new edition differs in several material aspects from
that of the first (Holmes, no.52).

Copies: NPL:D(78/58). 4554

1785–6 THEATRE ROYAL, *Covent Garden*

Omai; or, A trip round the world. [A pantomime. Eleven playbills.]
London, 1785–6.

CONTENTS:

1785, Dec.27 She stoops to conquer . . . to which will be added, for the sixth time, a
new pantomime called Omai; or, A trip round the world.
1785, Dec.28 The Follies of a day . . . to which will be added Omai.
1786, Jan.5 The Grecian daughter . . . to which will be added Omai.
1786, Jan.9 The Roman father . . . to which will be added Omai.
1786, Jan.11 The Follies of a day . . . to which will be added Omai.
1786, Jan.19 The Orphan . . . to which will be added Omai.
1786, Jan.23 Romeo and Juliet . . . to which will be added Omai.
1786, Feb.14 The Grecian daughter . . . to which will be added Omai.
1786, Feb.24 The Comedy of errors . . . to which will be added Omai.
1786, March 13 The Duenna . . . to which will be added Omai.
1786, May 16 The Duenna . . . to which will be added Omai.

Copies: NPL:M(Q 792.5/T; F792/E May 16, 1786.) 4555

1786 SHARPE, Granville

An English alphabet for the use of foreigners, wherein the pronunciation
of the vowels or voice-letters is explained in twelve short general rules . . .
Abridged, for the instruction of Omai, from a larger work. [By G. Sharpe.]
London, pr. by J.W. Galabin for B. White and C. Dilly, 1786.

pp.76.

Published anonymously. *G. Sharpe's Tracts*, no.3, written on title-page.

Copies: NPL:M(421/S). 4556

1786 THEATRE ROYAL, *Covent Garden*
[Poster]: At the Theatre Royal in Covent Garden, this present Thursday, April 20, 1786, The Castle of Andulusia . . . to which will be added, for the 44th time, a new pantomime called Omai; or, A trip round the world . . . with a procession exactly representing the dresses, weapons and manners of the inhabitants of Otaheite, New Zealand . . . and the other countries visited by Captain Cook. [Also a notice of Omai's death.]
Copies: ANL:F.   4557

1786 May 8 THEATRE ROYAL, *Covent Garden*
The Duenna . . . To which will be added, for the 47th time, a new pantomime called Omai; or, A trip round the world. [London, 1786.]
1 sheet.
A Theatre Royal playbill for May 8, 1786.
Copies: NPL:M(Q792.5/T).   4558

[179–?] BANKS, Sarah, *sister of Sir Joseph*
Autograph Memorandums: [with coloured pencil sketch of an aboriginal]. N.p., n.d.
pp.24, 4o.
Gives list of those who sailed on board the *Endeavour*, and contains much re Omai.
Copies: ANL(MS.9,item 32).   4559

1790 BASTON, *Rev.* Guillaume André René
Narrations d'Omai, insulaire de la Mer du Sud, ami et compagnon de voyage du Capitan Cook. Ouvrage traduit de l'O-Taïtien par M. K*** & publié par le Capitaine L.A.B. [i.e. G.A.R. Baston]. Rouen, Le Boucher, le jeune, 1790.
Port. 4 vols.
An imaginary autobiography of Omai.
Copies: NPL:M(843.69/B); NPL:R(09:S843.69/B327/1–4); VSL.   4560

1792–3 BASTON, *Rev.* Guillaume André René
Omais, Freund und Reisegefährte des Kapitain Cook, Erzählungen und Berichte. Dresden, C.C. Richter, 1792–3.
3 vols. in 1.
Copies: VSL.   4561

1830 COLMAN, George, *the younger*
[Visit of Omai and Sir Joseph Banks to Mulgrave Castle, near Whitby, 1775.]
(*In his* Random records. London, Henry Colburn and Richard Bentley, 1830. Vol.1, pp.152–202.)
Copies: NPL:M(928.22/C); VSL.   4562

1832 COWPER, William

Civilized and savage life: [a sketch of Omai, who acted as interpreter to Captain Cook in his third voyage. With poem by W. Cowper and port. by Sir J. Reynolds.]

(*Penny Magazine* May 1832, p.69.)
See also no.4565.

Copies: NPL:R(DQ050/P416).   4563

1838 GARDINER, William

Music and friends. London, Longman, Orme, Brown and Longman, 1838.

Mention of Omai in vol.1, p.5.

Copies: NPL:M(927.83/G).   4564

[1847?] COWPER, William

Civilised and savage life: [a poem, by W.] Cowper, etc.

(*Spirit of Literature, Arts and Sciences*, [1847?], p.40.)
See also no.4563.

Copies: NPL:M(059/7).   4565

1883 MÉTENIER, J., *pseud.*

Embarquement d'Omai.

(*In his* Taïti, son présent, son passé et son avenir, par J. Métenier, [pseud. i.e. Joseph Bournichon]. Tours, Cattier, 1883. pp.189–92.)

Copies: NPL:M(Q989.5/M).   4566

1940 CLARK, Thomas Blake

Omai, first Polynesian ambassador to England: the true story of his voyage there in 1774 with Captain Cook, of how he was feted by Fanny Burney, approved by Samuel Johnson, entertained by Mrs. Thrale & Lord Sandwich and painted by Sir Joshua Reynolds; [with port. by Sir Joshua Reynolds]. San Francisco, The Colt Press, 1940.

pp.[iii], 115.
Edition limited to 500 copies.

Copies: NPL:M(A920/0).   4567

1968 RAUSCHENBERG, Roy Anthony

Omai.

(*In his* Daniel Carl Solander, naturalist on the *Endeavour*. Philadelphia, 1968. pp.53–4.)
American Philosophical Society—*Transactions*, n.s. vol.58, pt.8.

Copies: NPL:R(NQ506/5).   4568

Portraits

Reproductions Arranged by Engraver

BARTOLOZZI

Omai a Native of Ulaietea . . . N. Dance del. F. Bartolozzi sculp.

Publish'd . . . 25th Oct. 1774. Engraving. Meas. of port. 18″ x 11⅜″. Meas. of plate mark 21⅛″ x 12⅞″.
Full-length.
(*Inserted in* Three voyages round the world. Plate 56a.)
Copies: NPL:M(PX D59⁻¹).   4569

Another print.
Copies: NPL:M(P3/51).   4570

Another print.
Copies: NPL:D(DG P3/15).   4571

Another print.
Cut.
Copies: NPL:D(DG P3/16).   4572

Another print.
Plate mark cut.
Copies: NPL:D(DL Pf74).   4573

The Same. Proof after letters and before title.
(*Inserted in* Three voyages round the world. Plate 56b.)
Copies: NPL:M(PX D59⁻¹).   4574

Another print.
Copies: NPL:M(P3/52).   4575

Reproductions Arranged by Engraver

BERNARD

Omai. Bernard dir.

Engraving. Meas. of plate mark 9¼″ x 7⅛″.
(Cook, J.—Voyage dans l'hémisphère austral. Paris, Hôtel de Thou, 1778. Vol.1, plate 15.)
Copies: NPL:M(Q980:Co3/3A1); NPL:R(09:Q990A/28).   4576

CALDWALL

Omai. Drawn from the life by W. Hodges. Engraved by J^{as}. Caldwall 1777.

Engraving. Proof. Meas. of port. 8$\frac{7}{8}$″ x 6$\frac{15}{16}$″. Meas. of plate mark 11$\frac{7}{8}$″ x 9$\frac{13}{16}$″.
Head and shoulders.
(*Inserted in* Three voyages round the world. Plate 55.)
Copies: NPL:M(PX D59^{-1}). 4577

The Same. Omai. Drawn from Nature by W. Hodges. Engraved by J. Caldwall. N.º LVII.

Published Feby 1.st 1777, by Wm Strahan [and others]. London. Engraving 8$\frac{7}{8}$″ x 6$\frac{7}{8}$″.
Head and shoulders.
(*Inserted in* Kippis, A.—The Life of Captain James Cook. Opp. p.272.)
Copies: NPL:D(Q78/8). 4578

Another print.
(*Inserted in* Kippis, A.—The Life of Captain James Cook. Opp. p.395.)
Copies: NPL:D(Q78/9). 4579

Another print.
(Cook, J.—Voyage towards the South Pole. London, Strahan & Cadell, 1777. Vol.1, p.169.)
Copies: NPL:M(Q980:Co3/2A1); NPL:D(Q77/25); NPL:R(Q990A/15S.C.). 4580

PARRY, William

Omai—Sir Joseph Bankes (*sic*)—Dr. Solander.

1838. Watercolour painting, sepia. 15$\frac{1}{2}$″ x 14″. Titled; signed T.M.V.
From the original painting by William Parry.
Copies: ANL(Nan Kivell). 4581

Originals, Including Photocopies of Originals

REYNOLDS, *Sir* Joshua

[Omai.]

[1776.] Photograph of original painting. 9$\frac{1}{4}$″ x 5$\frac{7}{16}$″.
Full-length.
Original is in the possession of Mr. George Howard, Castle Howard, Yorkshire.
Copies: NPL:M(P1/Omai 3). 4582

REYNOLDS, *Sir* Joshua
[Omai. A study for a full-length portrait.]

Photograph of oil on canvas. Oval size of original 23¾" x 20¼". Size of photograph of port. 6⅛" x 5¾".
Head and shoulders.
Original is in the Yale University.
Copies: NPL:M(P1/Omai 1). 4583

Photograph.

10 7/16" x 9".
Inscription on back reads "Sir Joshua Reynolds P.R.A. Portrait of Omiah, the Otaheitan sight size. Oval 23½" x 20".
Copies: NPL:M(P1/Omai 2). 4584

Reproduced in Rienits, Rex—The Voyages of Captain Cook. London, Paul Hamlyn, 1968. p.97.
Copies: NPL:M(Q980:Co1/R1A1). 4585

REYNOLDS, *Sir* Joshua
Omai of the Friendly Isles.

Photograph of pencil drawing. 14¼" x 10½". Size of original 10½" x 7¾".
Titled below portrait.
Head and shoulders.
Original is in the Nan Kivell Collection.
Copies: NPL:M(P2/48). 4586

Reproductions Arranged by Engraver

JACOBI
Omai, A Native of the Island of Utietea (*sic*). Painted by Sir Joshua Reynolds. Engraved by John Jacobi.

London. Published August 15th 1777, by John Jacobi . . . Mezzotint. Meas. of port. 22¼" x 14⅞". Cut.
Full-length.
Copies: NPL:D(DL Pf75). 4587

The Same.

Published. Sep.ʳ 1ˢᵗ. 1780, by John Boydell. London. Mezzotint. Meas. of port. 22 5/16" x 14⅞". Meas. of plate mark 24 9/16" x 14⅞".
Copies: NPL:D(DL Pf76). 4588

Another print.

Copies: NPL:M(P3/39). 4589

LANGLOIS

Portrait d'Omai. Danvin, del. d'après J. Reynolds. Langlois Sc.

Engraving. Meas. within frame lines $5\frac{7}{16}$" x $3\frac{1}{2}$".
"Archipel de Tonga. 207" at head of print.
(Domeny de Rienzi, Gregoire Louis—Océanie. Paris, Firmin Didot, 1855. Tome 3.)
Copies: NPL:M(980/115A6).   4590

REYNOLDS, S.W.

Omai. A Native of the Island of Utietea (*sic*). Sir Joshua Reynolds, Pinx.^t S.W. Reynolds, Sculp.

Mezzotint. Meas. of port. $5\frac{15}{16}$" x $3\frac{13}{16}$". Meas. of plate mark $8\frac{7}{8}$" x $6\frac{7}{16}$".
Full-length.
Copies: NPL:D(DL Pe222).   4591

REYNOLDS, S.W.

Omai, a native of the Island of Utietea (*sic*). [Painted by] Sir Josh. Reynolds; [engraved by] S.W. Reynolds.

London, published 1834, by Hodgson, Boys & Graves, 6 Pall Mall. Meas. of engraved surface 6" x $3\frac{9}{16}$". Meas. of plate mark $8\frac{15}{16}$" x $6\frac{7}{16}$".
(Reynolds, *Sir* Joshua—Engravings. London, 1833. Vol.1, plate 48.)
Copies: NPL:R(F759.2/R463/2 S.C.).   4592

UNKNOWN

Omai.

Engraving. Oval. Meas. of plate mark $4\frac{13}{16}$" x $3\frac{11}{16}$".
Head and shoulders.
(Blummenbach, Johann Friedrich—Abbildungen naturhistorischer Gegenstände. Göttingen, H. Dieterich, 1810. No.4.)
Copies: NPL:M(590/B).   4593

ARTIST UNKNOWN

Reproductions

OMAI, amené en Angletere (*sic*) par le Cap.^ne Furneaux.

Engraving. Oval. Meas. of engraved surface $6\frac{9}{16}$" x $3\frac{3}{4}$". Meas. of plate mark $7\frac{1}{16}$" x $4\frac{1}{2}$".
"OMAI" in top of oval frame surrounding portrait, which is surrounded by books, etc. and with a scene depicted below. Resembles Hodges' portrait.
(Baston, *Rev.* Guillaume André René—Narrations d'Omai. Rouen, Le Boucher, le jeune, 1790. Tome 1, frontisp.)
Copies: NPL:M(843.69/B); NPL:R(S843.69/B327/1).   4594

PORTRAIT of Omai.

Engraving. Meas. within frame lines $8\frac{1}{16}$" x $6\frac{1}{4}$". Meas. of plate mark $9\frac{1}{4}$" x $13\frac{13}{16}$".
With "Portrait of Potatow". Profile. Similar to engraving by Noble.
(Anderson, G.W.—A New, authentic and complete collection of voyages round the world. London, Alex. Hogg, [1784–6]. Opp. p.481.)
Copies: NPL:M(F980/5A1).   4595

PORTRAIT of Omai. Noble, Sc.

Engraving. Meas. within frame lines $8\frac{1}{16}''$ x $6\frac{3}{16}''$. Meas. of plate mark $8\frac{13}{16}''$ x $13\frac{7}{8}''$.
Cut. With "Portrait of Potatow".
Profile.
(Wilson, Philip—A New, complete and universal collection of authentic and entertaining voyages. London, Alex. Hogg, [1794]. Between pp.480 and 481.)
Copies: NPL:M(F980/W).   4596

PALLISER, *Sir* HUGH

Biography

1844 HUNT, Robert M.

The Life of Sir Hugh Palliser, Bart., Admiral of the White, and Governor of Greenwich Hospital. London, Chapman and Hall, 1844.
Port. pp.xvi, 463.
Palliser's association with Cook is described on pp.62–123. Portrait is the engraving by Freeman from the Dance painting.
Copies: NPL:M(923.542/P); NPL:R(DS920/P168.4/1).   4597

Portraits

DANCE

Originals, Including Photocopies of Originals

[PORTRAIT: reproduction from the painting by Dance in the National Maritime Museum, Greenwich.]

(*In* Muir, John Reid—Life . . . of Captain James Cook. London, Blackie, 1939. Opp. p.23.)
Copies: NPL:M(980:Col/M6A1); NPL:D(93/626); NPL:R(DS990A/19S); ANL; QParl; QU; VMoU; VSL.   4598

Reproductions Arranged by Engraver

FREEMAN

Sir Hugh Palliser, Bart. Admiral of the White. Engraved by C. Freeman from a Painting by G. Dance R.A.
Engraving. Meas. within frame line $5\frac{1}{8}''$ x $4\frac{1}{8}''$.
Three-quarter length.
Quotation by Palliser below title.
(*Inserted in* Kippis, A.—The Life of Captain James Cook. Between pp.514–15.)
Reproduced in the *Historical Records of New South Wales*, vol.1, pt.1, opp. p.479; and as the frontispiece to R.M. Hunt's *Life of Sir Hugh Palliser, Bart.*
Copies: NPL:D(Q78/8).   4599

ORME

Reproductions Arranged by Engraver

ORME, E.

Sir Hugh Palliser Bar.^t Governor of the Royal Hospital for Seamen at Greenwich. D. Orme del. E^d. Orme sculp.

London. Published 1796 by I. Sewell. Engraving. Oval. Meas. within frame line $4\frac{1}{16}''$ x $3\frac{3}{16}''$.
Half-length.
At head: *European Magazine.*
(*Inserted in* Kippis, A.—The Life of Captain James Cook. Opp. p.4.)
Copies: NPL:D(Q78/9).   4600

PARKINSON, SYDNEY

Biography

[1878] COLENSO, *Rev.* William

Manibus Parkinsonibus sacrum: a brief memoir of the first artist who visited New Zealand. Together with several little known items of interest extracted from his journal. [With bibl.] Wellington, N.Z., Lyon and Blair, pr., [1878].

Extracted from the New Zealand Institute—*Transactions*, vol.10, 1877, pp.108–34.
Mitchell Library copy bound with the author's *On the day in which Captain Cook took formal possession of New Zealand.*
Copies: NPL:M(980:Co2/C1A1); NPL:R(DS506/8).   4601

1909 MAIDEN, Joseph Henry

The Banksian artists: Sydney Parkinson.

(*In his* Sir Joseph Banks: the Father of Australia. Sydney, Govt.Pr., 1909. pp.62–4.)
Copies: NPL:M(A925.8/B218/1A1); NPL:D(90/79); NPL:R(920/B218/2).   4602

1921 DIXSON, *Sir* William

Notes on Australian artists.

(Royal Australian Historical Society—*Journal and Proceedings*, vol.7, 1921, pp.100–101.)
Copies: NPL:M(991/R, Ref.Books); NPL:D(9/69); NPL:R(S991.06/1A, Ref.Books).   4603

1950 SAWYER, F.C.

Some natural history drawings made during Captain Cook's first voyage round the world: [a short survey of Parkinson's work].

Port.
(Society for the Bibliography of Natural History—*Journal*, vol.2, pt.6, Oct. 1950. pp.190–93.)
Copies: NPL:R(S570.306/1).   4604

1950 SCOTT, T.C.S. Morrison-

Identity of Captain Cook's kangaroo, by T.C.S. Morrison-Scott and F.C. Sawyer. [With bibl.] London, 1950.

Facs. illus. pp.43–50, plates 3–5.
(British Museum, Natural History—*Bulletin, Zoology*, vol.1, no.3, Mar.1950.)
With account of drawings by S. Parkinson and Sir N. Dance.

Copies: NPL:M(Q599.2/3); NPL:R(DS590.6/9). 4605

1954 MERRILL, Elmer Drew

The Botany of Cook's voyages, and its unexpected significance in relation to anthropology, biogeography and history. Waltham, Mass., Chronica Botanica Co., 1954.

Facs. illus. ports. pp.[iv, 224].
Includes: On the binomials appearing in Parkinson's Journal, The Linnean binomials used by Parkinson, and The New and mostly unlisted technical names in Parkinson's Journal.

Copies: NPL:M(Q581.999/M); NPL:R(Q581.99/11); ANL; QU. 4606

1961 WILLSON, Eleanor Joan

James Lee and the Vineyard Nursery, Hammersmith; [with bibl.]. London, Hammersmith Local History Group, 1961.

Port. as frontisp. facs. map, pp.[xii], 88.
Contains information on collecting in Australia and the introduction of Australian plants to England, and of Lee's association with Sir Joseph Banks and S. Parkinson.

Copies: NPL:M(580.9/2A1); NPL:R(N920/L478.3/1). 4607

1966 PALMER, G.

Duplication of folio numbers depicting fishes in Parkinson's unpublished drawings of animals from Cook's first voyage, 1768–1771.

(Society for the Bibliography of Natural History—*Journal*, vol.4, pt.5, pp.267–8, Feb. 1966.)

Copies: NPL:R(S570.306/1). 4608

Portraits

Originals, Including Photocopies of Originals

[SYDNEY PARKINSON by an unknown artist.]

Photograph of oil painting in the British Museum (Natural History). 7″ x 4½″. Taken before restoration.

Copies: NPL:M(P1/Parkinson 1). 4609

The Same. Photograph taken after restoration.

Copies: NPL:M(P1/Parkinson 2). 4610

Reproductions

SYDNEY PARKINSON. Jas. Newton, sculp.

Engraving. Oval. Meas. of plate mark $10\frac{11}{16}''$ x $8\frac{7}{8}''$.
(*In his* Journal of a voyage to the South Seas. London, Stanfield Parkinson, 1773. Frontisp.)
Artist unknown. The same portrait as no.4612. One copy, in the Mitchell Library, has plates reversed and hand-coloured.

Copies: NPL:M(Q980/P); NPL:D(Q77/54, 55); NPL:R(Q990A/41 S.C.).   4611

SYDNEY PARKINSON. Jas. Newton, sculp.

Engraving. Oval. Meas. of plate mark $10\frac{11}{16}''$ x $8\frac{7}{8}''$.
(*In his* Journal of a voyage to the South Seas. London, Charles Dilly, 1784. Frontisp.)
Artist unknown. The same portrait as no.4611. One Dixson Library copy is hand-coloured.

Copies: NPL:M(Q980/P); NPL:D(Q78/10,11,12); NPL:R(Q990A/42 S.C.).   4612

SYDNEY PARKINSON Ja.ˢ Newton sculp.

Photographs (2) of engraving. Oval. Meas. of port. $4\frac{3}{16}''$ x $3\frac{7}{16}''$.
Frontispiece to Parkinson's *Journal of a voyage to the South Seas*, 1773.

Copies: NPL:M(B1489⁻³ pt.5).   4613

The Same.

(*In* Banks, *Sir* Joseph—The *Endeavour* Journal. Sydney, A. & R., 1962. Vol.1, facing p.52.)
Copies: NPL:M(A925.8/B).   4614

1832 PHILLIPS, Molesworth, *Lieut.-Col.*

ALS to Dr. Burney from West Square, London, Apr.27, 1832, re a dinner given by Sir Fletcher Norton to the officers of the *Resolution* and *Discovery* in 1776; with newspaper cutting re Phillips's death.

M. Phillips was an associate of Captain James Cook and Dr. Burney was the nephew of Admiral James Burney.

Copies: NPL:M(Doc.1303).   4615

1875 [PORTRAIT, etched by A. Geddes; with biographical note.]

(*In* Wilkie, *Sir* David—Etchings by Sir D. Wilkie . . . and by A. Geddes . . . with biog. sketches by D. Laing. Edinburgh, 1875. Plate 11, p.31.)
Copies: NPL:R(Q759.22/W683/1).   4616

PRINGLE, *Sir* JOHN

1827 CRICHTON, *Rev.* Andrew
Sir John Pringle.

(*In his* Converts from infidelity. Edinburgh, Constable, 1827. Vol.1, pp.235–58.)
Copies: NPL:R(S284/10).   4617

1875 McCOSH, *Rev.* James
Sir John Pringle.
(*In his* Scottish philosophy. New York, Robert Carter, 1875. p.109.)
Copies: NPL:R(S142/3).　　　　　4618

1898 SIR JOHN PRINGLE . . . [reproduction of portrait] drawn by Kenneth H. Miller from old pictures.
(*Century Illustrated Monthly Magazine*, Dec.1898, p.292.)
Copies: NPL:R(DS050/C397).　　　　　4619

RICKMAN, JOHN

1921 HOWAY, Frederick William
Authorship of the anonymous account of Captain Cook's last voyage. Seattle, Washington University State Historical Society, 1921.
Extract from *Washington Historical Quarterly*, vol.12, no.1, Jan.1921, pp.51–8.)
Copies: NPL:M(980:Co4/H1A1).　　　　　4620

1930 HOWAY, Frederick William
[Introduction to] Zimmerman's Captain Cook. Toronto, Canada, Ryerson Press, 1930.
pp.1–15.
Copies: NPL:M(980:Co4/Z1F1); NPL:D(93/141).　　　　　4621

1931 PALMER, H.
Captain James Cook, [by Sir Joseph Carruthers. With] (Note by the editor).
(*Geographical Journal*, London, vol.77, May 1931, pp.491–6.)
A discussion of statements in the anonymous *Journal of Cook's last voyage*, 1781, and in Ledyard's narrative.
Copies: NPL:R(DS909.6A/2).　　　　　4622

SAMWELL, DAVID

1926–7 DAVIES, *Sir* William Llewelyn
David Samwell, 1751–1798, surgeon of the *Discovery*, London-Welshman and poet.
Facs. ports.
(Society of Cymmrodorion—*Transactions*, 1926–7, pp.70–133.)
Copies: NPL:M(A926.1/S; ANL.　　　　　4623

1939 JOUQUET

David Samwell: [reproduction of an engraving by Crétien in 1798 from a drawing by Jouquet].

(*In* Muir, John Reid—Life and achievements of Captain James Cook. London, Blackie, 1939. p.272.)

Copies: NPL:M(980:Col/M6A1); NPL:D(93/626); NPL:R(DS990A/195); ANL; QParl; QU; VMoU; VSL. 4624

SANDERSON, WILLIAM

1914 CROUCH, C.H.

Capt. Cook's old master: [William Sanderson, shopkeeper].
(*Notes and Queries*, Sept.5, 1914, pp.181–2.)
Copies: NPL:R(DS050/N911). 4625

SANDWICH, JOHN MONTAGU, *4th Earl*

Writings

1774 Aug.14 ALS dated Hinchingbrook, to Banks?: He is pleased that Omai is out of danger; thinks the terms for lodging Omai and Mr Andrews are reasonable, his (Omai's) being 'under your inspection' a great advantage; 20 gns. fee for Baron Dimsdale proper; welcomes correspondent's intended visit & suggests they go down together in Sandwich's coach to London where he has business, at a time to suit 'you & Dr. Solander'.

f.1, cm 23.
Paginated 217. Endorsed in pencil 'Sur J.B. went Oct.16 see Solander's letter of that date'. Photostat copy in MS.Q159. Typed transcript in MS.Q160, p.11.
Copies: NPL:D(MS.Q158, pp.135–6). 4626

1780 Jan.10 ALS dated Blackheath: Informs that Capt. Cook has been murdered by the natives of an island where he had had a more friendly reception than at Otaheite; the news comes from Capt. Clerke at Kamschatzcha where he has received very friendly treatment from the Russians; the voyage has been successful, only three men have died; Omai was left safely at Huaheine, but no particulars given in short letter from Cook by the same conveyance; horses, cattle and sheep were landed at Otaheita; Capt Gower [Gore] takes command of the *Discovery* and Clerke of the *Resolution*; Clerke means to make another attempt for the northern passage.

f.1, cm 24.
Paginated 409. Dealer's catalogue description in NPL:D MS.Q159.
Copies: NPL:D(MS.Q158, pp.137–8). 4627

1780 Oct.10   ALS dated Admiralty to Sir Joseph Banks: Informs Banks
that his gardener is discharged from *Resolution*; Capt. King & Webber
were presented to the King at Windsor, & the charts and drawings were
examined by HM with satisfaction; desires to consult Banks re publication
of the journals & drawings of Cook's third voyage, and the preservation
of such of the 200 drawings not selected for publication.

Paginated 411–12.

Copies: NPL:D(MS.Q158, pp.139–40; MS.Q160, p.13, typescript).   4628

1782 Sep.13   ALS dated Hertford St to Sir Joseph Banks: Enclosing letter
from Capt. King; he has seen Webber & it is clear unless a supply of the
proper paper for engraving is quickly obtained, the book will be much
delayed; Webber is willing to go to Paris to obtain it unless Banks knows
a better method; the sum of £1000 must be advanced for the paper;
should this be paid by the recipients of the profits of the work or by the
Admiralty?

Paginated 517–19.

Copies: NPL:D(MS.Q158, pp.141–4; MS.Q160, p.15, typescript).   4629

1782 Sep.16   ALS dated Hertford St to Sir Joseph Banks: He thinks no steps
can be taken to procure the paper until it is settled who is to pay for it;
suggests that Banks should write to Stephens, and he will meet him, but
does not wish to put himself forward; he is now deeply engaged in the
Rowleian controversy; thanks Banks on behalf of the Mayor of
Huntingdon for his intended gift of venison; hopes that Banks will visit
him at Hinchingbrook during the Mayor's feast.

Paginated 521–3.

Copies: NPL:D(MS.Q158, pp.145–8; MS.Q160, p.17, typescript).   4630

1782 Sep.21   ALS dated Hertford St to Sir Joseph Banks: He has forwarded
Banks' letter to Stephens requesting an interview with him; has just
returned from fishing at Shepperton; (postscript) he has no predeliction
for Cadel or any other printer & is willing to trust Banks' judgment,
expecting Banks will ascertain the Admiralty's particular wishes on the
subject.

Paginated 525–7.

Copies: NPL:D(MS.Q158, pp.149–52; MS.Q160, p.19, typescript).   4631

1782 Sep.23   ALS dated Hertford St to Sir Joseph Banks: Has had a satisfactory interview with Stephens who says Lord Keppel will continue the
publication along lines intended; the Admiralty will advance the money
for the paper, to be repaid from the profits; asks Banks' views how the
profits should be divided; King, Dalrymple & Roberts are speedily
making a general map on one sheet; Stephens is helpful & anxious to

promote the work & would endeavour to place the book in the hands of Nichols, but unfortunately Cadel had been employed to publish the advertisement.

Paginated 529–34.

Copies: NPL:D(MS.Q158, pp.153–8; MS.Q160, p.21, typescript).   4632

1782 Oct.6 ALS dated Hinchingbrook to Sir Joseph Banks: Has communicated the contents of Banks' letter to Dr. Douglas & will forward his answer immediately; though the Admiralty will advance the money for the paper, arrangements must be made to procure it; expects the division of the profits will be settled as soon as Banks returns to town; thinks Mr. Hodges received 2 yrs salary from the Admiralty in lieu of share of profits; conveys Mayor of Huntingdon's thanks for venison.

Paginated 535–7.

Copies: NPL:D(MS.Q158, pp.159–62; MS.Q160, p.23, typescript).   4633

1782 Oct.12 ALS dated Hertford St to Sir Joseph Banks: Wishes Banks to manage procurement of the paper; has no wish to send Webber but leaves it to Banks to employ any means he thinks proper; as Lord Keppel is likely to leave the Admiralty Board soon, it is desirable all arrangements be concluded before there is another change there.

Paginated 539 (339?)–542.

Copies: NPL:D(MS.Q158, pp.163–6; MS.Q160, p.25, typescript).   4634

1784 May 13 ALS dated Hinchingbrook to Sir Joseph Banks: He expects the paper mentioned by Banks by tonight's post from Dr Douglas, and will bring it with him on Monday (or could send it on Saturday); is happy to hear 'our publication will be made at the fixed time.'

Paginated 399 (499?)–60.

Copies: NPL:D(MS.Q158, pp.167–8; MS.Q160, p.27, typescript).   4635

1784 Aug.20 ALS to Sir Joseph Banks, dated Hinchingbrook: Requests Banks convey his thanks to the Council of the Royal Society for allotting him one of the medals struck to commemorate 'our great Navigator & much lamented friend.'

Paginated 403–4.

Copies: NPL:D(MS.Q158, pp.169–70; MS.Q160, p.29, typescript).   4636

1784 Aug.29 ALS dated Hinchingbrook to Sir Joseph Banks: He meant Wednesday evening for the meeting with Banks & Lord Howe, as he cannot be in town until then. Suggests Banks leave a message at Hertford St making an appointment.

f.1, cm 23.5.
Paginated 407.

Copies: NPL:D(MS.Q158, pp.171–2; MS.Q160, p.31, typescript).   4637

1932–8 THE PRIVATE PAPERS of John, Earl of Sandwich, First Lord of the Admiralty, 1771–1782. Ed. by G.R. Barnes and J.H. Owen. London, 1932–8.

Illus. ports. 4 vols.
(Navy Records Society—*Publications*, 69,71,75,78.)
Half-title: *The Sandwich papers.*
Copies: NPL:R(S359.06/2); ANL.   4638

Bibliography

[1954] ROUGH CALENDAR of the Sandwich Papers at Hinchingbrooke, compiled by R.A. Skelton c.1954; with copies of some of the papers relating to Cook and Banks.

ff.13,31.
Typescript.
Copies: NPL:M(MS.As172).   4639

Biography

[1770] LIFE, adventures, intrigues, and amours of the celebrated Jemmy Twitcher [i.e. John Montagu, Earl of Sandwich. 1770?].

Published anonymously.
Copies: ANL.   4640

[1780] A LETTER from Omai to the . . . Earl of ******** [Sandwich], late ——— Lord of the ———. Trans. from the Ulaietean tongue. In which, amongst other things, is fairly and irrefragably stated the nature of original sin, together with a proposal for planting Christianity in the islands of the Pacific Ocean. London, J. Bell, [1780].

pp.[ii], 35.
Date taken from p.[1].
Copies: NPL:M(C929).   4641

1925 CHANCELLOR, Edwin Beresford
The Earl of Sandwich.

(*In his* The Lives of the rakes. 1925. Vol.4, chapter 9.)
Copies: ANL.   4642

[1962] MARTELLI, George
Jemmy Twitcher: a life of the fourth Earl of Sandwich, 1718–1792. London, Cape, [1962].

Map as endpapers, ports. pp.292.
Copies: NPL:R(920/S221.3/4); ANL.   4643

ASSOCIATES OF COOK – SANDWICH, JOHN MONTAGU, *4th Earl*

Portraits

GAINSBOROUGH

Reproductions Arranged by Engraver

SHERWIN

John Earl of Sandwich. Painted by T. Gainsborough R.A. Engraved by
I.K. Sherwin . . .

London. Published January 1.ˢᵗ 1788, by I.K. Sherwin . . . Engraving. 21¾″ x 15″. Meas.
of plate mark 26⅞″ x 17⅞″.
Full-length.
Coat of arms below portrait.
Copies: NPL:M(P3/53).   4644

ARTIST UNKNOWN

JOHN, Earl of Sandwich: [steel engraving]. Engrav'd by I. Corner.

Cut. 6⅛″ x 4¼″.
(*Inserted in* Smith, E.—Life of Sir Joseph Banks. 1911. Vol.1, facing p.44.)
Copies: Australasian Pioneers' Club, Sydney.   4645

R.ᵗ HON. The Earl of Sandwich.

Publish'd by J. Walker, Pater-noster Row, January 1.ˢᵗ 1782. Engraving. Oval port.
above anchor, parchment and drape. Meas. of port. 2¾″ x 2⅜″. Meas. of engraved surface
6″ x 3⅝″.
Head and shoulders, in profile.
(*Inserted in* Kippis, A.—The Life of Captain James Cook. Opp. p.281.)
Copies: NPL:D(Q78/8).   4646

Another print.

(*Inserted in* Kippis, A.—The Life of Captain James Cook. Opp. p.186.)
Copies: NPL:D(Q78/9).   4647

SMITH, ISAAC

Biography

[1924] SELBY, Isaac

[Isaac Smith, the first of Cook's party to land in Australia.]
Port.
(*In his* Old pioneers' memorial history of Melbourne. Melbourne, The Old Pioneers'
Memorial Fund, [1924]. pp.41–2.)
Copies: NPL:M(992.1/S); NPL:D(92/315).   4648

Portraits

ADMIRAL ISAAC SMITH Capt Cooks Nephew from [collection of?] Dr. Hobill Cole.

n.d. Watercolour and wash drawing on cardboard. Meas. inside frame 6″ x 4¾″.
Unsigned, undated. Title from wooden backing in Sir William Dixson's hand.
Portrait is similar to the one at NPL:M(P1) no.4650, and could be a copy.

Copies: NPL:D(DL Pa5).   4649

PORTRAIT of Isaac Smith by an unknown artist.

Photograph of original oil. Meas. of photo 3¾″ x 2⅞″. Don. Mrs. Bairstow, W.E.A. Library, 4.8.1955.

Copies: NPL:M(P1/Smith, Isaac 1).   4650

Monuments

PIKE, Joseph

Monument erected at St. Mary the Virgin, Merton, by Mrs. Elizabeth Cook, widow of Captain James Cook, in memory of her relatives, Isaac Smith and other members of the Smith Family.

1933. Pencil sketch. 8½″ x 5⅝″ inside mount.
Signed 'Joseph Pike 1933' in pencil in lower right corner.
Presented by Colonel R.W. Murphy, 1951.

Copies: NPL:M(SV*Cook 1).   4651

The Same. Photograph of monument.

Copies: NPL:M(Small Picture File: Smith, Isaac 2).   4652

PIKE, Joseph

Tombstone of Admiral Isaac Smith and his family at Merton Parish Church.

1933. Pencil sketch. 8⅜″ x 6¼″ inside mount.
Unsigned and undated, but similar to signed and dated sketch of the monument erected by Mrs. Elizabeth Cook in memory of her relatives at Merton Church.
Presented by Colonel R.W. Murphy, Feb.1951.

Copies: NPL:M(SV*Cook 2).   4653

The Same. Photograph of tombstone.

Copies: NPL:M(Small Picture File: Smith, Isaac 1).   4654

SOLANDER, DANIEL CARL

Writings

1767 Oct.19 ALS to Messrs Collinson, dated British Museum: Accepts the Messrs Collinson invitation, & will arrange the day (probably Sat.) when he has seen Dr. Franklin, who is due in town tomorrow night.

p.1, cm 22.5.
(*Inserted in* Kippis, A.—Life of Captain James Cook. 1788. Opp. p.104.)
Copies: NPL:D(Q78/8).   4655

1773 Feb.16 ALS dated London to Sir Joseph Banks, Hague: Giving news of friends, and narrating the affair concerning Mr. Coleman, Benneck of the Museum, and an actress Miss Miller.
ff.2, cm 23.
Paginated 166, 167.
(*Inserted in* Kippis, A.—Life of Captain James Cook. 1778. Opp. p.152.)
Copies: NPL:D(Q78/9).   4656

1774 Nov.10 INCOMPLETE AL, dated CN Club to Sir Joseph Banks: His guns should arrive this week. Walsh feels England must display the Electric Eels to the world before Holland, so is buying some for John Hunter to dissect, Cavendish is amongst those subscribing to the cost. Walsh & Hunter are anxious to start dissection. The prints of Omai which Bartolozzi brought this morning have 'Ulaietee' spelt 'Utaietea' but only 70 copies have been taken so it will be corrected in the next. *Ends* 'The Duke of Athol, walked along . . .'.
ff.2, cm 22.
Paginated 227.
Copies: NPL:D(MS.Q158, pp.173–6).   4657

Biography

1772 SOME ACCOUNT of Dr. Solander and Mr. Banks.
pp.[3].
Extract from the *London Magazine; or, Gentleman's Monthly Intelligencer*, July, 1772, pp.341–2.
Copies: NPL:M(A925.8/B218/13A1).   4658

1778 BOWMAN, Hildebrand, *pseud.*
The Travels of Hildebrand Bowman, Esquire, into Carnovirria, Taupiniera, Olfactaria, and Auditante, in New Zealand, in the Island of Bonhommica, and in the powerful Kingdom of Luxo-Volupto on the great southern continent. Written by himself, etc. London, W. Strahan & T. Cadell, 1778.
Illus. pp.xv, 400.
A satire addressed to Sir Joseph Banks and D.C. Solander.
Copies: NPL:M(910.43/B); NPL:D(77/17); NPL:R(S.C.).   4659

1784 BANKS, *Sir* Joseph
[Letter, in Swedish, to J. Alströmer, 16 Nov., 1784, re Solander.]
(*Upfostrings-Salskapets Tidningar*, no.14, 21 Feb., 1785, pp.105–110.)
Negative microfilm; filmed by Yale University Photo. Services.
Copies: NPL:M(FM3/270).   4660

1786 SKINNER AND COMPANY

Catalogue of the Portland Museum, lately the property of the Duchess Dowager of Portland . . . sold by auction by Mr. Skinner and Co. . . . 24th April, 1786, and the thirty seven following days. London, Skinner, 1786.

Frontisp. pp.viii, 3–194.
Catalogue no.204. Dr. Solander was employed to catalogue the shells in the collection. Some prices added in manuscript.
Copies: NPL:M(507/S). 4661

1889–96 COKE, *Lady* Mary

The Letters and journals of Lady Mary Coke. [Ed. by J.A. Home.] Edinburgh, D. Douglas, 1889–96.

Photoprints of pp.35, 153, 154, 192, 435, 437, 440, 442, 443 only, bearing references to Sir Joseph Banks and Dr. Solander.
Copies: NPL:M(QA920/Banks. Pam. File). 4662

1896 HOOKER, *Sir* Joseph Dalton
Dr. Solander.

(*In* Banks, *Sir* Joseph—Journal. Ed. by J.D. Hooker. London, Macmillan, 1896. pp. xxxviii–xlii.)
Copies: NPL:M(980/B); NPL:D(89/88); NPL:R(S990A/21). 4663

1905 MAIDEN, Joseph Henry

Observations on illustrations: Banks and Solander plants.

(Royal Society of New South Wales—*Journal*, 1905, pp.34–9.)
Copies: NPL:M(506/R); NPL:R(DS506/9). 4664

1909 MAIDEN, Joseph Henry
Daniel Carl Solander (1733–1782).

facs. ports.
(*In his* Sir Joseph Banks, the Father of Australia. Sydney, Govt.Pr., 1909. pp.73–96.)
Copies: NPL:M(A925.8/B218/1A1); NPL:D(90/79); NPL:R(920/B218/2). 4665

1913 IREDALE, Tom
Solander as an ornithologist. N.p., 1913.

pp.127–35.
Reprinted from *The Ibis*, Jan.1913.
Copies: NPL:M(A925.8/S). 4666

1916 IREDALE, Tom
Solander as a conchologist. London, 1916.

pp.85–93.
Reprinted from the Malacological Society of London—*Proceedings*, vol.12, pts.2 and 3. *Bound as* Papers on mollusks.
Copies: NPL:M(594/I). 4667

1921 MAIDEN, Joseph Henry
Records of Australian botanists.
(Royal Society of New South Wales—*Journal*, vol.55, 1921, pp.166–7.)
Copies: NPL:M(506/R); NPL:R(DS506/9).   4668

1922–3 DR. SOLANDER: [reprinted from R. Chambers's Book of days].
(Royal Geographical Society of Australasia—South Australian Branch—*Proceedings*,
vol.24, 1922–3, pp.77–8.)
Copies: NPL:M(980/R); NPL:D(9/181); NPL:R(DS993.06A/1).   4669

1923 MAIDEN, Joseph Henry
Sir Joseph Banks, the Father of Australia: [a bibliography].
(Royal Australian Historical Society—*Journal and Proceedings*, vol.9, 1923, pp.36–45.)
Copies: NPL:M(991/R, Ref.Books); NPL:D(9/69); NPL:R(S991.06/1A, Ref.Books).
4670

1924 SIWERTZ, S.
[Memorials to Solander in Sydney, and his apparent disregard for his
Swedish nationality.]
(*In his* Lata Latituder. 1924. p.205.)
A translation of this paragraph by H. Josephi has been pasted in at back of volume.
Copies: NPL:M(980/S).   4671

1931 HOW the Solander monument was erected [at Kurnell].
Illus.
(*Swedish Australasian Trade Journal*, vol.18, June 1931, pp.375–6.)
Copies: NPL:M(Q339.0901/S).   4672

1939 ALLAN, H.H.
Banks and Solander: fathers of New Zealand botany.
Illus.
Extracted from the Royal New Zealand Institute of Horticulture—*Journal*, vol.8, no.4,
pp.85–90, Mar.1939.
Copies: NPL:M(A920/Banks. Pam. File).   4673

1940 FRIES, Rob.E.
Daniel Solander. Minnesteckning av Rob.E. Fries. [With bibl.] Stock-
holm, Almqvist & Wiksells, 1940.
Port. pp.23.
(*K. Svenska Vetenskapsakademiens Levnadst.* B7. Tavl 3.)
On cover: Levnadsteckningar över K. Svenska Vetenskapsakademiens ledamöter. 114.
Copies: Captain Cook's Landing Place Trust.   4674

1954 MERRILL, Elmer Drew

The Botany of Cook's voyages and its unexpected significance in relation to anthropology, biogeography and history. Waltham, Mass., Chronica Botanica Co., 1954.

Facs. illus. ports. pp. [iv, 224].
A cloth-bound edition of *Chronica Botanica*, vol.14, no.5–6.
Copies: NPL:M(Q581.999/M); NPL:R(Q581.99/11); ANL; QU.   4675

1960 RYDÉN, Stig

Unknown Cook collection identified: preliminary report [on the Alströmer Collection of the Ethnographical Museum, Stockholm].

Illus. ports. pp.1–19.
(*Ethnos*, vol.25, 1960.)
Copies: NPL:M(572.06/2).   4676

1962 BANKS, *Sir* Joseph

The *Endeavour* journal of Joseph Banks, 1768–1771; ed. by J.C. Beaglehole . . . [Pub. by] the Trustees of the Public Library of New South Wales, in association with Angus and Robertson. Sydney, 1962.

Facs. illus., some in colour, maps, ports. 2 vols.
Published from the original manuscript in the Mitchell Library. *See also* nos.704–706.
Copies: NPL:M(A925.8/B).   4677

1966 BEAGLEHOLE, John Cawte

The Wandering scholars: address at the opening of an exhibition from the Alströmer Collection of the Ethnographical Museum of Sweden, Stockholm, at the Dominion Museum. Wellington, N.Z., the Museum, 1966.

Ports. pp.15.
Copies: NPL:M(508.9/2A1).   4678

1968 RAUSCHENBERG, Roy Anthony

Daniel Carl Solander, naturalist on the *Endeavour*. Philadelphia, 1968.
pp.66.
(American Philosophical Society—*Transactions*, n.s. vol.58, pt.8.)
Copies: NPL:R(NQ506/5).   4679

Portraits

CHODOWIECKI, Daniel

Dr: Solander. D: Chodowiecki: pinx: Berol.

Photograph of miniature portrait. Port. diam. 3⅜" x 3⅜".
The portrait is in the Deutches Museum, Berlin, (formerly the Kaiser-Friedrich Museum).
Reproduced in Kaemmerer, L.—Chodowiecki, 1879.
Copies: NPL:M(P1/Solander 1).   4680

The Same; copy in oils by D. Kellner.

1933. On wood panel. Port. diam. $3\frac{5}{8}''$ x $3\frac{5}{8}''$.
Panel $8\frac{5}{8}''$ x $5\frac{7}{8}''$ inside frame.
On backing board 'D. Kellner, Berlin, Cop. 1933.'
Copies: NPL:M(ML119).   4681

LIND, James
Banks and Solander.
Photograph of silhouette.
Copies: NPL:M(MS.B1489⁻³ pt.5).   4682

Reproduced in Banks, *Sir* Joseph—*Endeavour* Journal. Sydney, A. & R., 1962. p.84.
Copies: NPL:M(A925.8/B).   4683

DR DANIEL Solander.
Photograph of a portrait.
Full-length, seated.
Original in possession of the Linnean Society, London.
Copies: NPL:D(DL Pd629).   4684

The Same [entitled] Dʳ. Daniel Solander, F.L.S. From a portrait in the possession of the Linnean Society of London, [engraved by] Swan Electric Engraving Company.

Engraving. Meas. of engraved surface $4\frac{1}{4}''$ x $3\frac{1}{8}''$. Meas. of plate mark $5\frac{1}{2}''$ x $3\frac{7}{8}''$.
Half-length, seated.
(Hooker, J.D.—Journal of the Right Hon. Sir Joseph Banks. London, Macmillan, 1896. Opp. p.xxxviii.)
Copies: NPL:M(980/B).   4685

The Same [entitled] Dr Solander, F.L.S.

Reproduction. Meas. of port. $4\frac{1}{8}''$ x $3\frac{1}{16}''$.
Half-length, seated.
Copies: NPL:M(P1/Solander 4).   4686

The Same [entitled] Daniel Carl Solander.

Process reproduction plate. Meas. of port. $3\frac{3}{4}''$ x $2\frac{3}{4}''$.
Half-length, seated.
(Maiden, J.H.—Sir Joseph Banks. Sydney, Govt.Pr., 1909. p.75.)
Copies: NPL:M(A925.8/B218/1A1).   4687

Photograph.
Copies: NPL:M(P1/Solander 5).   4688

The Same.
J. Graf, printer to the Queen. Lithograph. $8\frac{1}{4}''$ x $6\frac{3}{8}''$.
Copies: ANL.   4689

JOS.P.H BANKS Esq.ʳ Dʳ Solander.

Published ... by T. Wright 1 Apr.1788. Engraving of oval portraits of Banks and Solander taken from Wedgwood medallions. Meas. of each port. 2″ x 1⅝″. Meas. of plate mark 6⅞″ x 4 7⁄16″.
Head and shoulders, in profile.
Titled as above at the head of each portrait. Portrait of Solander similar to medallion at NPL:M P*29, without the name impression, but profile is reversed.
Copies: NPL:M(P2/33). 4690

Another print, cut to the Solander medallion.
Copies: NPL:D(DL Pd630). 4691

Dᴿ SOLANDER.

Engraving. Round. Diameter 3″ within frame lines.
Head and shoulders, in left profile.
Copies: NPL:M(P1/Solander 2). 4692

Another print.
Copies: NPL:M(P1/Solander 3). 4693

Medallions

WEDGWOOD medallion.

The portrait designed by Flaxman about 1770, is rare and one of the large series in high relief. The series only includes Franklin, Boyle, Solander, Newton, Priestley and Sir William Hamilton. Six examples were burnt at the Alexandra Palace fire in 1874. F. Rathbone. No.H.224.
Copies: NAuM. 4694

[SOLANDER: Wedgwood portrait medallion.]

n.d. White on blue jasper ware. Oval. 12⅞″ x 9″. Unframed.
Unsigned; untitled. "Wedgwood" impressed on back. Shows Solander in Roman toga. Head in profile.
Copies: NPL:M(P*5). 4695

The Same process plate reproduction.
Oval. Meas. of port. 3⅞″ x 2⅛″. "Solander" impressed on plaque below port.
(Maiden, J.H.—Sir Joseph Banks. Sydney, Govt.Pr., 1909. p.83.)
Copies: NPL:M(A923.8/B218/1A1). 4696

SOLANDER: [Wedgwood portrait medallion designed by John Flaxman, 1775].

n.d. White on blue jasper ware. Oval, in wood and gilt frame. Meas. inside frame 3⅛″ x 2½″; framed 6¼″ x 5½″.
Head and shoulders, in profile.

Unsigned. Title impressed below portrait and "Wedgwood & Bentley" impressed on back. Blue is slightly brighter than usual.
Copies: NPL:M(P*29).   4697

The Same.

Unframed. 4" x 3⅛". "Wedgwood & Bentley" impressed on back.
Copies: NPL:M(P*30).   4698

The Same.

White on blue jasper ware. In gilt frame. 3" x 2½" inside frame; 3½" x 3" framed. "Wedgwood" impressed on back.
Transferred from the Australian Museum, Oct.1955.
Copies: NPL:M(P*62).   4699

The Same.

Black basalt ware. Oval, in gilt wooden frame. Meas. inside frame 4" x 3⅛"; framed 6¼" x 5½".
Unsigned. Title impressed below portrait. Paper backing not removed. Cracked across centre.
Copies: NPL:D(DL Pa93).   4700

The Same.

Framed in wood. Meas. inside frame c.4" x 3⅛".
Copies: NPL:M(P*57).   4701

The Same process plate reproduction.

Oval. Meas. 4¼" x 3½". "Solander" impressed in plaque below portrait.
(Maiden, J.H.—Sir Joseph Banks. Sydney, Govt.Pr., 1909. p.79.)
Copies: NPL:M(A925.8/B218/1A1).   4702

The Same. Reproduction.

(Banks, *Sir* Joseph—*Endeavour* journal of Joseph Banks, 1768–1771; ed. by J.C. Beaglehole. Sydney, Trustees of the Public Library of N.S.W. in assoc. with A. & R., 1962. Vol.1, opp. p.36.)
Copies: NPL:M(A925.8/B).   4703

Photograph.
Copies: NPL:M(MS.B1489^{-3} pt.5).   4704

[SOLANDER: Wedgwood portrait medallion.]

n.d. White on black jasper ware. c.5½" x c.3½". Unframed; untitled.
Presented to the Trust by John B. Nelson, 1941.
Copies: Captain Cook's Landing Place Trust.   4705

JOS.PH BANKS Esq.r Dr Solander.

Published . . . by T. Wright 1 Apr. 1778. Engraving of oval portraits of Banks and Solander taken from Wedgwood medallions. Meas. of each port. 2″ x 1⅝″. Meas. of plate mark 6⅞″ x 4⅞″.
Head and shoulders, in profile.
Titled as above at head of each port. Portrait of Solander similar to medallion at NPL:M P*29, no.4697, without the name impression, but profile is reversed.
Copies: NPL:M(P2/33). 4706

Another print, cut to the Solander medallion.
Copies: NPL:D(DL Pd630). 4707

Medals

MEDAL to commemorate Daniel Carl Solander. Silver. 37mm.

Obverse: Head of Solander. *Legend:* Daniel Solander. *Legend on reverse:* Josepho Banks effigiem amici merito D.D.D. Cl. et Ioh. Alstroemer.
Copies: NPL:M(R403). 4708

Another 2 specimens.
Copies: NPL:D. 4709

MEDAL commemorating Dr. Daniel Carl Solander. Coined 1940, by the Royal Swedish Academy of Science. Silver.

Copies: Captain Cook's Landing Place Trust. 4710

SPARRMAN, ANDERS

Biography

1939 SÖDERSTRÖM, Jan Georg Karl

A. Sparrman's ethnographical collection from James Cook's 2nd expedition, 1772–1775; [with a short biography of Sparrman, bibl. and plates. Trans. from the Swedish by M. Leijer, and illus. by A. Hjelm.] Stockholm, Bokförlags Aktiebolaget Thule, 1939.

Diags. plates 24, pp.70.
(Statens Etnografiska Museum, Stockholm—*Publications,* n.s. no.6.)
Copies: NPL:M(Q572.99/S); ANL; VSL. 4711

1966 BEAGLEHOLE, John Cawte

The Wandering scholars: address at the opening of an exhibition from the Alströmer Collection of the Ethnographical Museum of Sweden, Stockholm, at the Dominion Museum, on 28 Oct., 1965 . . . Pub. by [the] Dominion Museum. Wellington, N.Z., the Museum, 1966.

Ports. pp.15.
Copies: NPL:M(508.9/2A1). 4712

ASSOCIATES OF COOK

Biography

1790 OBITUARY.
(*Gentleman's Magazine*, Aug.1790, p.765.)
Copies: NPL:R(DS050/G338).   4713

1850 PENROSE, *Rev.* John
From his [Trevenen's] birth to his return in 1780 from the voyage round the world with Captain Cook.
(*In his* Lives of Sir C.V. Penrose and Captain J. Trevenen. London, J. Murray, 1850. pp.182–202.)
Copies: NPL:M(923.542/P); ANL; VSL.   4714

Biography

1923 ANDERSON, G.H.
Early life and first voyage with Cook (1757–75); [and] (Second voyage with Cook, 1776–80).
(*In his* Vancouver and his great voyage . . . 1757–1798. King's Lynn, Thew & Son, 1923. Chap.1–2.)
Copies: NPL:M(923.9/V223/1A1); NPL:D(92/817).   4715

1930 GODWIN, George Stanley
Vancouver: a life, 1757–1798. [With app., historical notes, letters and other documents. Bibl.] London, Philip Allan, 1930.
Facs. illus. maps, port. pp.xi, 308.
Map in folder inside back cover.
Copies: NPL:M(923.9/V223/2A1); NPL:D(93/482); NPL:R(S909.8A/V223).   4716

1938 BARTLETT, N.
George Vancouver charting the south coast [of Western Australia].
Illus. port.
(*Early Days*, vol.1, Oct.1938, pp.39–48.)
Copies: NPL:M(Q995.06/E).   4717

1956 BROWN, Roderick Langmere Haig Haig-
Captain of the *Discovery*: the story of Captain George Vancouver. London, Macmillan, 1956.
Illus., some in colour, maps, pp.[vii], 181.
(*Great Stories of Canada*.)
Written for children.
Copies: NPL:M(910.4/B).   4718

1960 ANDERSON, Bern
Surveyor of the sea: the life and voyages of Captain George Vancouver.
[With bibl.] Seattle, Washington U.P., 1960.
Illus. maps, port. pp.xii, 274.
Copies: NPL:M(923.9/V223/3A1); NPL:R(N920/V223/1).   4719

WALKER, JOHN

1914 MAGGS BROS., *London*
Report, with extracts, of letters from James Cook to John Walker, Whitby,
dated 13 Sep.1771, 28 Nov.1772, 19 Aug.1775 & 14 Sep.1775. With
covering letter 25 Sep.1914, addressed to Angus & Robertson, Sydney.
Copies: NPL:D(MS.Q143, pp.79–114).   4720

WEBBER, JOHN
Bibliography

n.d. AUTOGRAPH catalogue of drawings and portraits in oil by Mr.
Webber. MS.
pp.12, fol.
Bears notes in pencil by Sir Joseph Banks.
Copies: ANL(MS.9,item 140).   4721

1965 ROYAL ACADEMY OF ARTS
Painting in England, 1700–1850, from the collection of Mr. & Mrs. P.
Mellon. (Winter exhibition, 1964–5.) [Catalogue of an exhibition held
by the] Royal Academy of Arts. London, 1965.
pp.x, 68.
Includes paintings by W. Hodges and J. Webber.
Copies: NPL:M(759.2/3A1).   4722

Biography

1785 MONNERON
Letters (3) from Monneron to La Pérouse, Ap.11, [12?], 14, 1785, re
the advice given him by Webber in his purchases for the voyage. Webber
is painting his portrait.
(Expédition de La Pérouse, 1785–8, pp.153–164.)
Transcripts of documents in the Service Hydrographique de la Marine, Paris.
Copies: NPL:M(MS.B1207).   4723

1789 ANECDOTE of Captain Cook and O'too [i.e. Pomaré. How Webber painted the portrait of the latter.]
(*In* Phillip, Arthur—Voyage . . . to Botany Bay. London, J. Stockdale, 1789. pp.292–4.)
Copies: NPL:M(Q 991/P); NPL:D(Q 78/26); NPL:R(09:Q 991A/7).   4724

1808 EDWARDS, Edward
John Webber, R.A.
(*In his* Anecdotes of painters. London, 1808. pp.218–19.)
Copies: NPL:R(S759.2/23).   4725

1919 CORNEY, Bolton Glanvill
[John Webber.]
(*In his* Quest and occupation of Tahiti . . . 1772–6. London, Hakluyt Society, 1919. Vol.3, pp.xlvii–xlviii.)
Copies: NPL:M(989.5/C); NPL:D(9/259); NPL:R(S909.6A/7).   4726

1923 [A COLLECTION of ethnographic objects from the South Seas, given by J. Wäber, i.e. J. Webber, to the Bernisches Historisches Museum, in 1791.]
Illus.
(*In* Zeller, R.—Führer durch die orientalische Sammlung . . . des Bernischen Historischen Museums. Bern, 1923. pp.1–2, 39–52.)
Copies: NPL:M(572/Z).   4727

1934 ANDERSEN, Johannes Carl
Matavai Bay and Queen Charlotte Sound: [explanatory note].
Illus.
(*In his* Maori music with its Polynesian background. New Plymouth, N.Z., Avery, pr., 1934. pp.i–ii.)
Polynesian Society—*Memoir* no.10.
Copies: NPL:M(Q572.997/A); NPL:D(93/58); ANL.   4728

1947 REYNOLDS, Graham
Captain Cook's draughtsmen; [with reproductions and map].
(*Geographical Magazine*, vol.19, Feb.1947, pp.457–66.)
Copies: NPL:R(S909.5A/5).   4729

1948 WARNER, Oliver Martin Wilson
[John Webber.]
Illus.
(*In his* Introduction to British marine painting. London, Batsford, 1948. pp.31–2.)
Copies: NPL:M(758/W); NPL:R(S758/37).   4730

MOTTET, J.D.
[John Webber.]

Photograph. Oval port. Meas. within frame $3\frac{7}{8}''$ x $3\frac{1}{8}''$. Original is in the Berne Historical Museum, Switzerland.

Copies: NPL:M(P1/Webber 1). 4731

Reproduced in Rienits, Rex—The Voyages of Captain Cook. London, Paul Hamlyn, 1968. p.114.

Copies: NPL:M(Q980:Co1/R1A1); NPL:R(NQ910.4/4). 4732

WEBBER, John

John Webber: a self-portrait. [Reproduction of original painting in the Public Library, Berne, Switzerland.]

(*In* Moore, William—Story of Australian art. Sydney, A. & R., 1934. Vol.1, p.6.)

Copies: NPL:M(Q709.901/M); NPL:D(Q93/85); NPL:R(DS759.29/3). 4733

SPILLER, J.

James Webber. J. Spiller, sculptor.

White marble bas-relief. 17″ x 17″.

Copies: ANL. 4734

WHATMAN, WILLIAM

1929 TAYLOR, Albert Pierce
Dedication of William Whatman tablet.

Illus.

(*In his* Sesquicentennial celebration of Captain Cook's discovery of Hawaii, 1778–1928. Honolulu, Captain Cook Sesquicentennial Commission, 1929. pp.47–8.)

Copies: NPL:M(Q980:Co4/T1A1). 4735

YOUNG, NICHOLAS

[1952] KAMM, Josephine
He went with Captain Cook. London, Harrap, [1952].

Frontisp. in colour, illus. map, pp.176.
A story for children based on the life of Nicholas Young.
See also no.4737.

Copies: NPL:M(823.9/K); ANL. 4736

1955 KAMM, Josephine
He went with Captain Cook. London, Harrap, 1955.

Illus. map, pp.176.
A story for children based on the life of Nicholas Young. A reprint of no.4736.

Copies: QU. 4737

1930 HOWAY, Frederick William
[Introduction to] Zimmermann's Captain Cook. Toronto, Canada, Ryerson Press, 1930.

pp.1–15.

Copies: NPL:M(980:Co4/Z1F1); NPL:D(93/141).   4738

BIBLIOGRAPHY

1868 PUTTICK AND SIMPSON
Catalogue of . . . books, including a selection from the library of . . . Samuel Rogers, the manuscript journals, log books, charts and papers, of the celebrated navigator, Captain James Cook . . . which will be sold by auction . . . March 10, [1868. London, 1868.]

pp.33–5.
Positive photostat.

Copies: NPL:M(Q980:Co1/P1A1).   4739

1879 JACKSON, James
Cartographie et bibliographie [relatives à Cook].

(Société de Géographie—Centenaire de la mort de Cook. Paris, Delagrave, 1879. pp.481–536.)
Société de Géographie—*Bulletin*, Mai, 1879.
See also nos.4741–2.

Copies: NPL:M(923.9/C771.2/9A1).   4740

1879 JACKSON, James
Cartographie et bibliographie [relatives à Cook].

(Société de Géographie—Centenaire de la mort de Cook. Paris, the Society, 1879. pp.81–136.)
Reprint. *See also* nos.4740, 4742.

Copies: NPL:M(923.9/C771.2/9B1); NPL:D(87/120); NPL:R(S920/C771/9); VSL.
                    4741

1879 JACKSON, James
James Cook, oct.27, 1728–fév.14, 1779: cartographie et bibliographie. Paris, 1879.

pp.43.
Reprint from the *Bulletin de la Société de Géographie*, Mai, 1879. *See also* nos. 4740–41.

Copies: NPL:M(980:Co1/J1A1).   4742

1886 COLONIAL AND INDIAN EXHIBITION
Catalogue of the collection of relics of the late Captain James Cook . . . exhibited by Mr. John Mackrell at the request of the Government of New South Wales, in the court of that colony. N.p., 1886.

pp.7.
(Australian Museum—Papers *re* Cook relics. Vol.2, 1887.)
With numerous MS. notes.
Copies: NPL:M(MS.A3935).   4743

[c.1910 LIST of Cook's logs, etc., in the possession of Mr. Bolckow. With transcript of a list of ships' logs, etc., relating to Cook's voyages 1768–1779, held in the Public Record Office, the British Museum, the Admiralty Library and in private collections; compiled by the Public Record Office, London, and annotated by Prof. W.J. Woodhouse.]
Copies: NPL:M(MS.A482A).   4744

1910 LIST of ship's logs relating to Cook's voyages, 1769–79, compiled in Public Record Office after some logs were transferred there from the Admiralty in 1910. [MS. copy in Mitchell Library; photographic copy and microfilm held in National Library.] Also a typescript *Catalogue of Illustrations of Cook's Voyages*, compiled by Bernard Smith (pp.28).

pp.3,28, ½ inch.
(Miscellaneous papers relating to Cook.)
Copies: ANL(MS.1080).   4745

[1914] SOTHEBY, WILKINSON & HODGE
Catalogue of . . . letters & manuscripts . . . consisting of letters from Capt. Cook . . . to James Walker . . . and diaries & letter-book of Lieutenant Ralph Clark written during his voyage to Botany Bay with the First Fleet . . . which will be sold by auction . . . 10th of July, 1914. [London], Dryden Press, [1914].

pp.12.
Copies: NPL:M(980:Co1/51A1); NPL:D(91/2004).   4746

1923 SOTHEBY, WILKINSON & HODGE
Catalogue of very important manuscripts by or relating to Captain James Cook, explorer, the property of H.W.F. Bolckow, Esq., M.P., deceased, Marton Hall, Marton-in-Cleveland, Yorkshire . . . sold by auction . . . 21st day of March, 1923. London, J. Davy and Sons, pr., 1923.

Facs. pp.16.
Mitchell Library copy with prices added. The Dixson Library holds another copy (WD6) bound with press cuttings and correspondence relating to the sale.
Copies: NPL:M(980:Co1/S1A1); NPL:D(92/495); VSL.   4747

1925 LIST of charts of Captain Cook at the British Museum . . . 1892; [and] List of manuscripts of and relating to . . . Cook, 1890, with additions to 1925.

(Captain Cook Miscellanea, vol.1, pp.3–8.)
Gives lists of original charts, illustrations, log books, journals, etc.
Copies: NPL:M(MS.A1713⁻¹).   4748

BIBLIOGRAPHY – *continued*

1926 PARTINGTON, James Edge-

Australasian prints, drawings, etc., in the collection of J. Edge-Partington, Esq. Beaconsfield, Eng., privately printed, 1926.

pp.[i], 41.
Dixson Library copy with notes by Sir William Dixson.
Copies: NPL:M(Q980/P); NPL:D(93/2).   4749

1927 MAGGS BROS., *London*

Australia and the South Seas: catalogue no.491. London, 1927.

Illus. pp.[ii], 281, [xi].
Copies: NPL:M(990/2A1); NPL:D(92/534).   4750

1928 LILLIE, W.

List of books & newspaper cuttings relating to Captain Cook, in Middlesbrough Public Library.

Illus.
(*In* Captain Cook Bi-centenary Celebrations, Cleveland, 1928—Souvenir. Middlesbrough, Hood & Co., pr., 1928. pp.16–19.)
Copies: NPL:M(Q923.9/C771.2/4A1); NPL:D(Q92/164); ANL.   4751

1928 MITCHELL LIBRARY, *Sydney*

Bibliography of Captain James Cook . . . comprising the collections in the Mitchell Library and General Reference Library [of New South Wales], the private collections of William Dixson . . . and J.A. Ferguson . . . and items of special interest in the National Library, Canberra. [Being a catalogue of the Cook Bicentenary Exhibition 1928; with] (Opening address . . . by the President of Trustees, Hon. D. Levy). Sydney, A.J. Kent, Govt.Pr., 1928.

pp.[xiv], 172.
Brief typed index at NPL:M 980:Col/M3A2.
Copies: NPL:M(980:Col/M3A1–2); NPL:D(92/215); NPL:R(S990A/137); ANL; SPL.
    4752

1928 MUSEUM BOOK STORE

Catalogue of rare maps of America: [catalogue no.110]. London, Robert Stockwell, pr., 1928.

pp.64.
Items include charts by James Cook.
Copies: NPL:M(980:Col/M8A1).   4753

1928 PANNETT ART GALLERY, *Whitby*

A Descriptive catalogue of the Cook Bi-Centenary Exhibition in the Pannett Art Gallery, Whitby, Oct.3rd to Nov.1st, 1928. Whitby, Horne & Son Ltd., Abbey Press, 1928.

Vignette, pp.10.
Cover-title. Illustrated cover.
Copies: NPL:M(980:Col/P2A1).   4754

1929 EDWARDS, FRANCIS, LTD.

Captain James Cook, 1728–1928: [a sale catalogue. London], R. Stockwell, pr., 1929.

Illus. ff.11.

Copies: NPL:D(MS.Q143, pp.115–36.)   4755

[193–?] WILLIAM F. WILSON'S POLYNESIANA COLLECTION

[Catalogue] index to section C. N.p., [193–?].

pp.54.

Lacks title-page and cover.

Chiefly lists pictorial items and relics connected with Captain Cook.

Copies: NPL:M(980:Col/W3A1).   4756

1936 CAMPBELL, Gordon

List of logs and journals.

(*In his* Captain James Cook. London, Hodder and Stoughton, 1936. pp.307–14.)

Dixson Library copy annotated by Sir William Dixson.

Copies: NPL:M(A923.9/C771.2/19A1); NPL:D(93/126); NPL:R(DS990A/128); ANL; QParl; VSL; WU.   4757

1936 HOLMES, *Sir* Maurice

An Introduction to the bibliography of Captain James Cook, R.N. London, F. Edwards Ltd., 1936.

pp.59.

Edition limited to 200 copies of which 150 are for sale. Printed by the Chiswick Press Ltd.; with inscription from the author.

Copies: NPL:M(980:Col/H2A1); NPL:D(93/122); NPL:R(S990A/158).   4758

[1947] ROBERTS, Stanley

Captain Cook's voyages: a bibliography of the French translations, 1772–1800. [With app. of works in French relating to Cook.] Oxford, U.P., pr., [1947].

pp.160–76.

With manuscript inscription from the author. Reprinted from *Journal of Documentation* vol.3, Dec.1947. A microfilm copy also held in the Mitchell Library at FM3/609.

Copies: NPL:M(980:Col/R1A1); NPL:R(S010.6/9); ANL.   4759

1950 GREAT BRITAIN—Hydrographic Department

Manuscript charts by Capt. Cook's assistants, of parts of Australia and New Zealand: [list].

(*In its* Summary of selected manuscript documents of historic importance preserved in the Archives of the Department. London, H.M.S.O., 1950. pp.43–48.)

Copies: NPL:M(Q980.01/G, Ref.Books).   4760

1952 HOLMES, *Sir* Maurice

Captain James Cook, R.N., F.R.S.: a bibliographical excursion. New ed. London, F. Edwards, 1952.

Facs. pp.103.
Edition limited to 500 copies, 425 for sale; with inscription by F. Edwards.

Copies: NPL:M(980:Col/H2B1); NPL:D(95/19).   4761

1955–68 Hakluyt Society Edition

The Journals of Captain James Cook on his voyages of discovery . . . Ed. [from the original MSS., with intro. notes and appendices] by J.C. Beaglehole, [and others. With] (Charts & views drawn by Cook and his officers, and reproduced from the original MSS.; ed. by R.A. Skelton). [And] (Addenda and corrigenda to vol.1) . . . Pub. for the Hakluyt Society. Cambridge, U.P., 1955–68.

Frontisp. in colour, illus. maps, ports. 3 vols. in 4, portfolio and addenda.
(Hakluyt Society—*Extra series* nos.34–6.)
CONTENTS:
[Vol.]1 The Voyage of the *Endeavour*, 1768–1771; with Addenda.
[Vol.]2 The Voyage of the *Resolution* and *Adventure*, 1772–1775.
[Vol.]3 The Voyage of the *Resolution* and *Discovery*, 1776–1780; pts.1–2.
Portfolio. Charts & views.

Vol. 4, still to be published, will contain a "series of essays on particular aspects of Cook's life and achievement and on the scientific results of the voyages, together with a bibliography and lists of the original charts, drawings and paintings made on the voyages." For further note and list of reviews, *see* no.227.

Copies: NPL:M(980:Col/46A1–4, X980/25); NPL:D(95/54–7, F95/1); NPL:R(S990A/ 215E, F990A/47); ANL; Captain Cook's Landing Place Trust; QOM; Q Parl; QU; VSL.
                                                                4762

1956 NEW ZEALAND—High Commissioner in London

Cook and a hundred years after: catalogue of an exhibition of paintings, prints, documents, diaries, letters and other relics. Christchurch, Whitcombe & Tombs, 1956.

pp.16.
Printed in Great Britain. At head of title: *New Zealand House, London, June 1956.*

Copies: NPL:M; ANL.   4763

1960 DU RIETZ, Rolf

Captain James Cook: a bibliography of literature printed in Sweden before 1819. Upsala, Almqvist & Wiksells, pr., 1960.

Illus. pp.28.
Edition limited to 300 interleaved copies, each numbered and signed by the author.

Copies: NPL:M(980:Col/D3A1); ANL; QU; SPL; VMoU.   4764

1960 PUBLIC LIBRARY OF VICTORIA—Research Department

Cook material in the Reference Library. Melbourne, the Library, 1960.

ff.[i,15].
Duplicated. Without title-page. Title taken from cover. Title on f.i reads *Material relating to Captain James Cook in the Reference Library.*

Copies: NPL:M;VSL.   4765

1960 SPENCE, Sydney Alfred

Captain James Cook, R.N., 1728–1779: a bibliography of his voyages, to which is added other works relating to his life, conduct & nautical achievements . . . Comp. by S.A. Spence. Mitcham, Sy., Eng., the Author, 1960.

Ports. pp.iv, 50.

Copies: NPL:M(Q980:Co1/S1A1, Ref.Books); NPL:D(Q96/1); NPL:R(NQ920/C771/1); ANL; QU; SPL; WU.   4766

1962 LEHIGH UNIVERSITY—*Library*—Rare Book Room

The Great South Sea: an exhibition of rare books and watercolours. Bethlehem, Pa., the Univ., 1962.

pp.12.
Cover-title.
Copies: NPL:M(910.4/106A1).   4767

1967 O'REILLY, Patrick

Voyages de Cook, (1769–1773–1776): bibliographie, [par] (P. O'Reilly [et] E. Reitman).

(*In their* Bibliographie de Tahiti et de la Polynésie française. Paris, Musée de l'Homme, 1967. Vol.1, pp.43–60.)

Copies: NPL:M(016.999/1A1).   4768

1967 SKELTON, Raleigh Ashlin

The Marine surveys of James Cook in North America, 1758–1768, particularly the survey of Newfoundland. A bibliography of printed charts and sailing-directions, by R.A. Skelton and R.V. Tooley. London, Map Collectors' Circle, 1967.

Facs. illus. maps, tables, pp.[34].
(Map Collectors' Circle—*Map collectors' ser.* vol.4, no.37.)
Plates not included in pagination.
Copies: NPL:M(917/2A1); NPL:R(N912.06/2).   4769

1968 THE BRITISH MUSEUM—The King's Library

An Exhibition to commemorate the bi-centenary of Captain Cook's first voyage round the world: [catalogue. London, the Museum, 1968.]

ff.vi,35.
Photocopy.
Presentation copy to Mitchell Library from Map Room of British Museum.
Photographs and colour transparencies of the exhibition placed at M.L. Pic. Acc. 1582.
Cased with the catalogue are two prospectuses of the exhibition.
Copies: NPL:M(Q980:Co1/B1).   4770

1968 EDWARDS, FRANCIS, LTD.

Captain James Cook . . . a catalogue of 200 books, charts, prints, etc., to mark the bi-centenary of his first voyage to the southern hemisphere in 1768; including books by and about his companions and associates, and on scurvy, health at sea and tropical diseases. London, Francis Edwards, Ltd., 1968.

Map, port. pp.29.
(Catalogue no.916.)

Copies: NPL:M(017.4/3A1).   4771

1773 DALRYMPLE, Alexander

A Letter from Mr. Dalrymple to Dr. Hawkesworth, occasioned by some groundless and illiberal imputations in his account of the late voyages to the south. London, J. Nourse [and others], 1773.

Folding map, pp.[iv],35.

Copies: NPL:M(Q980/36A1); NPL:D(77/4).   4772

1778 FORSTER, Johann Georg Adam

A Letter to the Right Honourable the Earl of Sandwich . . . from George Forster [i.e. J.G.A. Forster]. London, G. Robinson, 1778.

pp.[ii],ii,25,6.
Complaining that the author's father, J.R. Forster, had been prevented from writing the official narrative of Captain Cook's second voyage around the world.
Bound as frontispiece in Mitchell Library copy is a sepia illustration entitled *The German Doctor on his travels from England*. Doctor Faustus delt., Robinson. At foot of illus: *The German Doctor with his family on his travels to England conducted by Mynheer Shinder Knecht*.

Copies: NPL:M(Q980/35A1); NPL:D(Q77/58); VSL.   4773

1780 Jan.20   FORSTER, Johann Georg Adam

ALS to Sir Joseph Banks forwarding a printed account in German of the death of Cook. Cassell, 20th Jan.,1780.

pp.4, 4o.

Copies: ANL(MS.9,item 74).   4774

1780 Mar.27   FORSTER, Johann Georg Adam

ALS to Sir Joseph Banks intimating that Professor Lichtenberg had compiled, from material supplied by him [Forster] and his father, a little imperfect sketch of Cook's Life and Character. Cassell, 27th March, 1780.

pp.4, 4o.

Copies: ANL(MS.9,item 75).   4775

1780–90 FORSTER, Johann Georg Adam

Autograph letters [19] signed, to Sir Joseph Banks concerning various matters of science, and the translation of Cook's last voyage into German.

pp.72, 4o.
These letters cover the period 26th Nov.,1780, to Jan.10th,1790.

Copies: ANL(MS.9,item 77).   4776

[187– – 1935 NEWSPAPER CUTTINGS relating to Captain Cook's voyages, journals, memorials, etc. 187– – 1935.]

3 vols.

Copies: NPL:M(Q 980:Col/N1A1–3).   4777

[1878–1913] NEWSPAPER CUTTINGS, 1878–1913, relating to the log and relics connected with Captain Cook.

cm 33.

The log, relics and this volume were formerly in the Australian Museum, Sydney, and were transferred to the Mitchell Library, Oct.1955.

Copies: NPL:M(MS.A3937).   4778

[1890?] BONWICK, James

Captain Cook's logs compared. [MS. notes by Bonwick concerning statements and remarks in the official log of the *Endeavour*, and the private log in Cook's handwriting, placed side by side to show information in one omitted from the other.]

(Bonwick Transcripts: Cook, case 1, no.39.)

Copies: NPL:M(B.T. ser.2, case 1).   4779

1890 BONWICK, James

"Report on Cook's Logs . . . to James Backhouse Walker . . ." 13 Nov. 1890. MS., with covering letter.

ff.10.

Copies: NPL:D(MS.Q144,pp.193–312).   4780

1890 BONWICK, James

[Reports on the logs of the *Endeavour*, with special reference to the naming of Botany Bay, Port Jackson and New South Wales; with tracings of entries in the various logs and samples of Cook's handwriting.] 1890.

Copies: NPL:M(B.T. ser.2, Cook case 3a, no.228).   4781

1891 KING, Philip Gidley, *the younger*

Comments on Cook's log, H.M.S. *Endeavour*, 1770, with extracts, charts and sketches, April 1891. Sydney, Govt.Pr., 1891.

pp.30.

Another copy of the *Comments* is contained in *King Papers*, vol.5, and has MS. comments and corrections in pencil (NPL:MMS.A1980). *See also* no.4784. The log described is by C. Green and is held in the P.R.O., London. A MS. copy of the entries April–August 1770, is contained in *King Papers*, vol.2, and the same portion is printed in *Historical Records of New South Wales* vol.1, pt.1, pp.269–88. In a letter to Sir S. Griffith, Jan.4, 1892, King pointed out that some of the illustrations to the *Comments* were reproduced from sketches made by his father when surveying in 1818–21.

Copies: NPL:M(Q980.1/44A1); NPL:D(Q89/22); ANL:F.   4782

1891 KING, Philip Gidley, *the younger*

Publication of P.G. King's *Comments on Cook's Log* was authorized by Sir Henry Parkes to whom the first issue from the N.S.W. Government Printing Office was sent by King; distribution left to King. (P.G. King to Sir Henry Parkes, Nov.30, 1891.)

(Public Men of Australia, p.306.)

Copies: NPL:M(MS.A68).   4783

1892 KING, Philip Gidley, *the younger*

Comments on Cook's log, H.M.S. *Endeavour*, 1770, with extracts, charts and sketches, April 1891. New ed. Sydney, Govt.Pr., 1892.

pp.33.
See also no.4782.

Copies: NPL:M(Q980.1/44B1); NPL:R(Q990A/92).   4784

1892 KING, Philip Gidley, *the younger*

Letter to Capt. Wharton, June 15, 1892, in reference to the MS. log described in his *Comments on Cook's Log*; discusses method of hoisting boats in H.M.S. *Endeavour*.

(King Papers, vol.2, p.753.)

Copies: NPL:M(MS.A1977).   4785

1892 WHARTON, W.J.L.

Log kept by Molineaux as far as New Zealand, description and criticism. (Capt. Wharton to P.G. King, Oct.10, 1892.)

(King Papers, vol.2, p.771.)

Copies: NPL:M(MS.A1977).   4786

1898 MORRIS, Edward Ellis

[Original] log kept by Cook, on H.M.S. *Eagle*, was picked up by Professor Morris in a bookseller's shop in Bourke Street, Melbourne. (Prof. Morris to P.G. King, June 20, 1898.)

(King Papers, vol.2, p.824.)

Copies: NPL:M(MS.A1977).   4787

1899 MORRIS, Edward Ellis

Letters to A. Lee, Nov.20–Dec.12, 1899, reporting on a log of Cook's first voyage.

(*Letters to Alfred Lee.*)
The log described was later acquired by Alexander Turnbull.

Copies: NPL:M(MS.A1808).   4788

1901 BLADEN, Frank Murcott

Captain Cook and his logs; [with port.].

BIBLIOGRAPHY – *continued*

(Australian Town and Country Journal, Dec.28, 1901, pp.36–7.)
Compares the Royal, Museum, Admiralty, Palliser, and Corner copies of the Log of the *Endeavour.*
Copies: NPL:R(F079/A938).

4789

1901 BONWICK, James

Captain Cook in New South Wales; or, The Mystery of naming Botany Bay. [An examination of the Cook logs and journals.] London, Sampson Low, Marston & Co. Ltd., 1901.
pp.31.
Copies: NPL:M(991.1/B); NPL:D(90/127); NPL:R(S991.1A/12).

4790

1911 LETTER to the Editor, *Sydney Morning Herald*, re sale of two leaves from a journal of the first voyage.

(Sydney Morning Herald, Sept.15, 1911.)
Copies: NPL:R(F079/S982).

4791

1914 HISTORIC LETTERS to be sold: Captain Cook and Lieutenant Clark.

(Newspaper cuttings, vol.36, pp.51–3.)
Extract from *Sydney Morning Herald,* June 16, 1914.
Copies: NPL:M(Q991/N).

4792

1921 HOWAY, Frederic William

Authorship of the anonymous account of Captain Cook's last voyage. Seattle, Washington University State Historical Society, 1921.
Extract from *Washington Historical Quarterly,* vol.12, no.1, Jan.1921.
Copies: NPL:M(980:Co4/H1A1).

4793

1922 NOTES on sales: Captain Cook's manuscripts.

(The Times Literary Supplement, Dec.14, 1922, p.848.)
Copies: NPL:R(F079/T583/N).

4794

1923 PUBLIC LIBRARY OF NEW SOUTH WALES, *Sydney*

Report of the Trustees 1921/2. Syd., Govt.Pr., 1923.
ff.3.
Notes on recently acquired Cook items.
Copies: NPL:D(MS.Q144).

4795

1925 GARNSEY, E.R.

Cook's letterbook . . . second and third voyages.
(Newspaper cuttings, vol.166, pp.168–9, 170–1.)
Extracts from the *Sydney Morning Herald,* May 9 and 23, 1925.
Copies: NPL:M(Q991.1/N); NPL:R(F079/S982).

4796

1930 STOKES, John F.G.
Origin of the condemnation of Captain Cook in Hawaii; [with bibl.]. Honolulu, 1930.

pp.68–104.
Reprinted from the Hawaiian Historical Society—*Annual report*, 39, 1930.

Copies: NPL:M(923.9/C771.2/18A1); NPL:D(93/295); VSL.   4797

1931 PALMER, Howard
Captain James Cook [by Sir Joseph Carruthers; with] (Note by the Editor).

(*Geographical Journal* vol.77, May 1931, pp.491–6.)
A discussion of statements in the anonymous *Journal of Cook's last voyage*, 1781, and in Ledyard's narrative.

Copies: NPL:R(DS909.6A/2).   4798

1937 WOODHOUSE, A.
Some manuscript material relative to South Pacific exploration in the Alexander Turnbull Library: [typescript copy of a paper read at a meeting of the ANZAAS, Jan.1937].

ff.19.
The MSS. include a partial log, unsigned, of the voyage in the *Endeavour*, which was discussed in letters from Prof. E.E. Morris to Alfred Lee, Nov.–Dec.1899, and a copy of Banks' Journal.

Copies: NPL:M(MS.A2097).   4799

[194– –] FORSYTH, John Walter
Papers and card indexes.

38 boxes.
The collection consists of research material and indexes to it, and of manuscript notes and photocopies of documents, notes, correspondence etc. These are principally concerned with early navigators, their ships, the Dutch East India Company, maps.

Copies: NPL:M(MSS.979, FM3/674–5,678,700, 2FM4/2227,2229).   4800

1946 DILKE, O.A.W.
The English literature of exploration in the eighteenth century: [including a study of Cook's writings as literature].

(*The Mariner's Mirror*, vol.32, pp.225–30, Oct.1946.)

Copies: NPL:D(9/72); NPL:R(DS656.506/7).   4801

1951 TAYLOR, Clyde Romer Hughes
Note on the literature relating to Captain Cook's voyages.

(*In* Cook, James—Collected Voyages—Printed Accounts [1951 Reed's Edition]—Captain Cook in New Zealand. Wellington, N.Z., Reed, 1951. pp.27–30.)
See also no.4806.

Copies: NPL:M(980:Col/45A1); ANL; QParl; VSL.   4802

1953 COOK'S JOURNAL of the second voyage: a gift from Her Majesty [to the Alexander Turnbull Library, of photostat copy of original journal held in the National Maritime Museum, Greenwich].

(*Turnbull Library Record* no.11, pp.7–8, Nov.1953.)

Copies: NPL:M(027.405/1).   4803

1957 BEAGLEHOLE, John Cawte

Some problems of editing Cook's journals. [Paper read to ANZAAS, 1957.]

(*Historical Studies*, vol.8, pp.20–31, Nov.1957.)

Copies: NPL:M(990.05/1).   4804

1960 HISTORICAL TREASURE: Cook's log-book as auction prize. [Contemporary copy of log-book of the first voyage, by Orton and Hicks, and contemporary copy of journal of second voyage, both for auction at Christies.]

(*Australian Financial Review*, p.23, Nov.24, 1960.)

Copies: NPL:M(MDQ332.605/3); NPL:R(F079/A938); ANL.   4805

1969 COOK, JAMES—Collected Voyages—Printed Accounts. 1969 Reed's Edition

Captain Cook in New Zealand: extracts from the journals of Captain Cook giving a full account in his own words of his adventures and discoveries in New Zealand. Ed. [with intro., biog. and notes] by A.H. & A.W. Reed; [with note on the literature by C.R.H. Taylor, and bibl.]. 2nd ed. Wellington, N.Z., Reed, 1969.

Illus. maps, port. pp.262.
See also no.4802.

Copies: NPL:M(980:Co1/45B1).   4806

1969 TAYLOR, Clyde Romer Hughes

Going back to the manuscripts.

(*In* Cook, James—First Voyage—Printed Accounts [1969 Reed's Edition]—Captain Cook in Australia . . . Ed. by A.W. Reed. Wellington, N.Z., Reed, 1969. pp.12–15.) Article dated Tawa, 28 May 1968.

Copies: NPL:M(980:Co2/11A1).   4807

n.d. RELICS of ancient days: [Captain Cook pictures, maps, etc., in the Melbourne Public Library].

(Melbourne: newspaper cuttings, pp.27–8. [n.d.])

Copies: NPL:M(982.1/M).   4808

ERRATA
Not included in Index

No.89	for "viagens" read "viagems"; for "quarto" read "quatro"; for "mondo" read "mundo". *See also* no.678
No.114	for "Montemont" read "Montémont"
No.138	for "autour de" read "autour du"
No.162	entry should read "Narrative of the voyages round the world . . . with an account of his life . . . by A. Kippis. New York, 1858. pp.424.
No.165	ANL holds 1860 ed., Edinburgh, A. & C. Black
No.363	for "Markahm" read "Markham"
No.472	for "his" read "her"
No.565	for "Jeffrey" read "Jeffery"
No.586	for "verion" read "version"
No.633	for "June 5–9, 1766" read "June 5, 1766–June 9, 1768"
No.635	collation line, delete "40"
No.678	for "Capitano" read "Capitão". *See also* no.89
No.790	delete entry. *See* no.787
No.873	entry should read "Oestliche halb-Kugel verfasst von Herrn d'Anville Geographen des Königs von Frankreich nach den neuesten Entdeckungen verbessert herausgegeben von Herrn F.A. Schrämble. Gestochen von A. Amon. Wien, 1786"
No.1117	lines 7–11, read as follows: "The copy in the National Library of Australia is a bound photographic reproduction, originally prepared for presentation by Princess Elizabeth on behalf of King George VI, and bears the following inscription"
No.1120	for "improvements on" read "improvements of"
Nos.1218–19	delete "Dame Mabel Brookes' Collection"
No.1374	for "Palmestone's" read "Palmerstone's"
No.1440	for "40" read "4o"
No.1481	for "MS.7" read "MS.690"
No.1521	for "Dixson" read "Dixon"
No.1543	for "Jeffrey" read "Jeffery"
No.1705	ANL holds [1955] edition
No.1707	for "vol.23" read "vol.13"
No.1714 plate no.XXXVII	for "Mr.Smith" read "Mw. Smith"
No.1827	for "E.E. Petherick" read "E.A. Petherick"
No.1882	for "out" read "art"
No.1894	add call no."MS.9, item 16"
No.1912, no.4	"pp.4, folio" refers to no.4 only
No.1945	for "Cornbill" read "Cornhill"
No.2047	for "William" read "Walter"
No.2143	for "King, James C." read "King, James, *Capt.*"
No.2224	for "Jeffrey" read "Jeffery"
No.2316	for "Geographical" read "Geographic"
No.2425	for "MS.7" read "MS.690"
No.2427	entry should read: 1779 An account of the death of Captain Cook of the "*Resolution*" in making discoverys round the world in 1779, 9 February to 22 February, 1779. Anon. Manuscript. Follows fairly closely the details as given by Captain King, but with several slight variations and additions. It is probably a transcript from a private diary or journal of some officer or seaman who accompanied Cook. Copies: ANL(MS.8).
No.2430	delete entry
No.2724	for "MS.108" read "MS.524"

ERRATA – *Continued*

No.2852 for "Grenville" read "Grenfell"

No.2875 MS7 add (p.1, photographic copy of original)

No.3495 delete entry

No.3662 delete entry. *See below* no.3686

No.3671 Pair of parallel rules.
17″ long. Dark wood with brass fittings. Inscribed 'W.B. 1770'.
This relic goes with the sextant and ivory scale rule placed at DR 11 and DR 12. There is also a letter filed with DR 11 dated 29.4.1906 signed E.A.A. Burney stating that he believed that Captain Cook gave these relics to his grand-father Dr. William Burney, the then head-master and founder of the Royal Academy, Gosport.
Copies: NPL:D(DR 13).

No.3680 for "Metal plaque engraved" read "Australian Museum number"

No.3686 (3662) Scale of sines for navigation purposes.
Ivory rule 18″ long, folding. "W.B.1770" cut into surface. This relic goes with the sextant and pair of parallel rules placed at DR 11 and DR 13. There is also a letter filed with DR 11 dated 29.4.1906 signed by E.A.A. Burney stating that he believed that Captain Cook gave these relics to his grand-father, Dr. William Burney, the then head-master and founder of the Royal Academy, Gosport.
Copies: NPL:D(DR 12).

No.3715 for "Metal plaque nailed in centre, engraved" read "Australian Museum number"

No.3825 for "Le" read "La"

No.3910 for "*Manuscript Branch*—Reference Division" read "*Reference Division—*Manuscript Branch"

No.4006 for "Groton, John" read "Gorton, John G."

No.4018 for "A. Britten" read "A. Britton"

No.4056 for "1939" read "1938", and for "Lee, M." read "Lee, Minnie, *Mrs*"

No.4559 collation line, delete 40.

No.4567 for A920/0 read A920/O

ADDENDA

No.90a. [182–?] Robins' Edition
Voyages around the world, performed by Captain James Cook. London, J. Robins and Co., [182–?]
Illus. pp.798.
See also no.97.
Copies: ANL.

No.92a. 1820 La Harpe's Edition
Abrégé de l'histoire générale des voyages . . . Nouvelle éd., revue et corrigée. Paris, chez Etienne Ledoux, 1820.
24 vols.
With Atlas . . . dressé par Ambroise Tardieu, 1821. *See also* no.518.
Copies: ANL.

No.97a. 1824 KIPPIS, *Rev.* Andrew
A Narrative of the voyages round the world, performed by Captain James Cook. New York, 1824.
Copies: ANL.

No.113a. 1832 KIPPIS, *Rev.* Andrew
A Narrative of the voyages round the world, performed by Captain James Cook; with an account of his life during the previous and intervening periods. Boston, N.H. Whitaker, 1832.
Illus. 2 vols in 1.
Copies: ANL.

No.119a. 1836 La Harpe's Edition
Nouvel abrégé de l'histoire générale des voyages, par E.C. Piton. 2e éd., revue et . . . augmenté. Paris, Rignoux, 1836.
2 vols.
Copies: ANL.

No.741a. 1962 LEYDEN, Peter
Capt. James Cook, R.N. Sydney, Australian Schools Press, 1962.
Copies: ANL.

No.852a. 1968 *DAILY MIRROR.* No.8460, Aug.26, 1968. [With supp.] (*London Gazette*, no.118, Aug.26, 1768) [i.e. 1968]. Sydney.
Issue commemorates the departure of Captain Cook on his first voyage to the Pacific Ocean. This *London Gazette* is a composite newspaper in the style of 1768, bearing little resemblance to the official *London Gazette* of that time. Two editions of no.117, dated Aug.1768 and Aug.19, 1768 respectively, were issued by the *Daily Mirror* Aug.19th and 20th, 1968.
Copies: NPL:M(F980:Co2/D/1); NPL:R; ANL.

No.1003a. *See* no.1102a.

No.1102a. 1938–9 WARD, Edward
The Wooden world dissected in the character of a ship of war, as also the characters of all the officers . . . by the author of the London spy

[i.e. E. Ward]; reprinted from the 5th ed. of 1751, (with a foreword by G. Callender). [Interspersed with original MS and paintings by G.C. Ingleton, being a comparable account of the *Endeavour* and its personnel.] London, E. Chappell, pr., 1929.

Port. pp.xi,99.
(Society for Nautical Research—Occasional pubs., no.2.)
One of 50 copies on hand-made paper. This copy has been extended by 28ff. of MS and 25 original paintings made during 1938–9.
Copies: NPL:D(Q 92/59).

No.1383a. ELLIOTT, John, *A.B., Resolution*
Lepers Island.

Pen and indian ink wash drawing. $21\frac{3}{4}''$ x 14''.
Signed 'John Elliott' in ink, upper right corner. Titled in same hand in ink: 'Lepers Island when bearing from N70° W.^{t} to N20° W.^{t} Distant off shore 7 or 8 Miles' and below in pencil: 'Lepers Is. New Hebrides' in Capt. Fuller's hand. Pencil note by Capt. A.W.F. Fuller on back. Further notes filed.
Copies: NPL:D(DG SV8.3/6).

No.1383b. ELLIOTT, John, *A.B., Resolution*
Savage Island.

Pen and indian ink wash drawing. $21\frac{3}{4}''$ x $13\frac{1}{8}''$.
Signed 'John Elliott' upper right hand corner, in ink. Titled in same hand in pencil along lower edge: 'Savage Island West End bearing from E.N.E. to S. by W.^{t} Distant 2 Miles'. Pencil note by Capt. A.W.F. Fuller on back. Further notes filed.
Copies: NPL:D(DG SV8.1/3).

No.2705a. 1969 ST. MARGARET'S CHURCH, Barking, Essex, where Captain Cook was married.

1969. 6 photographs of interior.
Copies: ANL.

No.2862a. CAPTAIN COOK: [Wedgwood portrait medallion, after Pingo]. 1957. White on blue jasper, with white border on front. $4\frac{3}{8}''$ x $3\frac{1}{4}''$.

Unframed. Head and shoulders.
Impressed on back: Captain Cook / Hakluyt Society / Wedgwood / Made in / England / S7 / EC /
125 copies were restruck from the original mould by Wedgwood and distributed to the order of Hakluyt Society members.
Copies: ANL.

No.3707a. SNUFF BOX used by Isaac Smith.

Silver snuff box with ornamentation, engraved on bottom: Circa 1770. Believed to have belonged to Isaac Smith, the snuff box has a miniature portrait inset of a young man in a red uniform supposedly Isaac Smith. Inscribed on the inside rim are the words: 'Isaac Smith, the first man to have landed in Australia.'
Copies: ANL.

No.3807a. 1774 OTAHEITE: a poem. London, printed for the author, and sold by C. Bathurst, 1774.

pp.16.
Copies: NPL:D(77/27; Q 77/48); NPL:M(Q 821/O).

No.3814a. 1780 SCHOMBERG, *Sir* Alexander
An Ode to the memory of Captain James Cook of His Majesty's Navy, by A Sea officer [i.e. Sir A. Schomberg]. Dublin, W. Hallhead, pr., 1780. pp.23.
With inscription on half-title-page: "From the author, Sir Alexander Schomberg".
Copies: NPL:D(Q 78/35).

Please add the National Library of Australia to the holdings for the following items:
7, 13, 27–8, 32, 37–8, 40, 43, 45, 57, 70–71, 75, 76 (Nan Kivell), 88 (Nan Kivell), 90 (Nan Kivell), 100 (Nan Kivell), 114, 133, 138, 172, 184, 214, 231, 238, 245, 249, 252–4, 256–7, 264, 267, 291, 300, 307, 314, 319–22, 324–5, 334–5, 348, 357–8, 360–61, 364–5, 368 (ANL:F), 369–70, 372–3, 374 (Nan Kivell), 376–7, 379–88, 390, 399, 401, 403–4, 410–11, 418, 420, 426, 428, 430–31, 434, 436–8, 440–41, 444, 446–7, 450–51, 454, 456, 458, 461–2, 467, 470–71, 473, 475–6, 478–9, 481–4, 490–91, 502–3, 510, 511 (Nan Kivell), 530, 533–5, 537–40, 549, 551–3, 555, 557–62, 565–7, 614, 641, 653, 655, 657, 659, 665, 682, 685, 689–92, 701, 706–7, 712–14, 716–18, 720, 736, 740, 742–3, 746–9, 757–9, 761–2, 764–5, 769–74, 777–81, 783, 788–9, 791–4, 796, 798, 802–3, 806–10, 812, 814–16, 818, 820, 826, 828–9, 831–7, 840–42, 844–6, 848, 854, 868–9, 871, 873, 876 (Nan Kivell), 877–8, 880, 886–90, 894–9, 901–2, 904–5, 907–23, 926, 950, 955, 957, 960, 971, 979, 981, 986–7, 999–1001, 1019–20, 1036, 1039–40, 1045–6, 1050–51, 1058–9, 1061, 1064, 1066, 1068, 1073, 1077, 1081–2, 1090, 1092–3, 1095, 1099, 1102–3, 1106, 1211, 1220, 1244, 1248, 1261, 1263, 1266, 1268–9, 1274, 1276, 1280, 1284–5, 1288, 1292, 1297, 1299–1303, 1305–10, 1312, 1314–23, 1327–8, 1330, 1337, 1339, 1342–76, 1383, 1399, 1417–18, 1421–2, 1424–5, 1430, 1476, 1526–7, 1545, 1547, 1549, 1551–2, 1553 (Nan Kivell), 1559, 1567, 1581, 1585, 1591–8, 1601, 1603, 1605–6, 1609–10, 1612–13, 1615 (Nan Kivell), 1616–17, 1618 (Nan Kivell), 1623–5, 1630 (Nan Kivell), 1635–6, 1642, 1649, 1653, 1656, 1659, 1665–7, 1670, 1672–3, 1675–8, 1686, 1690–91, 1693, 1696–7, 1699–1704, 1707–10, 1716, 1720–41, 1784, 1867–8, 1878, 1880, 1882–4, 1930, 1962, 1965, 1966 (Nan Kivell), 1968, 1975, 2010, 2034, 2079, 2108, 2122, 2126, 2133–4, 2138, 2143, 2145–6, 2155, 2157–9, 2161–2, 2164–5, 2169, 2175–6, 2178, 2188, 2203, 2205, 2208–10, 2212–13, 2216, 2218, 2220, 2229–31, 2234, 2241, 2243, 2246–7, 2252–4, 2259–61, 2263, 2270, 2274–5, 2277–9, 2281–4, 2286–7, 2289–91, 2293, 2295–7, 2299–2300, 2302–4, 2308, 2315–23, 2325, 2329–35, 2339–41, 2344–8, 2350, 2353–4, 2358, 2369, 2373, 2379, 2381, 2385, 2388, 2390, 2393–4, 2401–3, 2405, 2407, 2423, 2439, 2441, 2443, 2446, 2451, 2453, 2458, 2462–4, 2469, 2471, 2476–7, 2480–81, 2483, 2486, 2488, 2490–91, 2494–5, 2497, 2500–2, 2505, 2508–9, 2511, 2513, 2515, 2518, 2520, 2522–4, 2527–30, 2532, 2535–6, 2538 2540–41, 2543–4, 2547–8, 2550, 2552, 2554, 2558, 2566 (Nan Kivell), 2571–2, 2574 (Nan Kivell), 2576, 2579 (Nan Kivell), 2584, 2591 (Nan Kivell), 2603 (Nan Kivell), 2604, 2615 (Nan Kivell), 2625, 2634 (Nan Kivell), 2650 (Nan Kivell), 2655–6, 2658, 2661, 2664, 2667–8, 2669 (Nan Kivell), 2684, 2687–9, 2695, 2700, 2722–3, 2726, 2730, 2735, 2761, 2767, 2770, 2773 (Nan Kivell), 2781–5, 2790, 2799, 2817–18, 2832, 2836, 2841, 2844, 2856, 2863, 2866, 2869–70, 2889, 2891–6, 2905, 2932–4, 2939–40, 2942, 2946, 2949, 2951, 2958, 2971, 2974–5, 2979–80, 2996–7, 3003–6, 3011–12, 3014, 3016, 3018, 3021, 3026, 3035–6, 3043, 3049, 3052, 3055, 3061, 3063, 3065, 3078, 3080–82, 3085–6, 3091, 3093, 3095–7, 3099–3104, 3106, 3110–11, 3116, 3118–19, 3121–3, 3125, 3132, 3138–9, 3147–8, 3158, 3160, 3162, 3165, 3169–70, 3172–4, 3177 (ANL:F), 3181, 3188, 3191, 3196, 3202–3, 3213, 3234, 3237, 3240, 3244 (Nan Kivell), 3261, 3264, 3269 (Nan Kivell), 3276 (Nan Kivell), 3287, 3296, 3297 (Nan Kivell), 3299 (Nan Kivell), 3307, 3316, 3317 (Nan Kivell), 3323, 3325, 3327 (Nan Kivell), 3329–30, 3334 (Nan Kivell), 3338, 3348 (Nan Kivell), 3353, 3357, 3358 (Nan Kivell), 3361, 3363, 3373, 3380, 3384 (Nan Kivell), 3388, 3398 (Nan Kivell), 3399, 3408, 3414, 3416–18, 3424, 3426, 3429, 3431–2, 3437–8, 3441–2, 3444–6, 3451–2, 3458–9, 3461–3, 3465–6, 3468, 3473, 3483, 3485, 3488, 3502, 3508, 3510, 3518, 3522–3, 3527–8, 3533, 3539, 3549, 3553, 3558, 3569, 3571–2, 3574, 3576, 3581, 3596 (Nan Kivell), 3599–3600 (Nan Kivell), 3738, 3742–3, 3745, 3749, 3752, 3754–7, 3760–4, 3766–7, 3769–70, 3777, 3782–3, 3789–90, 3804, 3812–13, 3825, 3827, 3829–30, 3837, 3840–42, 3848–9, 3852–3, 3862–4, 3866–7, 3869–70, 3902, 3907–9, 3921, 3925, 3932–4, 3936, 3950, 3958, 3965, 3967–9, 3971, 3974–6, 3979, 3982, 3984–5, 3987–8, 3992, 3995, 3997, 3999–4000, 4002–3, 4005, 4014–15, 4017–18, 4023–5, 4029, 4031, 4035–7, 4041, 4043, 4045–6, 4051–4, 4056–9, 4062–5, 4068, 4071–3, 4076–80, 4083–4, 4086, 4098 (Nan Kivell), 4102–3, 4108 (Nan Kivell), 4109, 4111, 4126–8, 4131, 4138–9, 4142–3, 4155, 4166, 4170, 4177, 4188, 4203 (Nan Kivell), 4208 (Nan Kivell), 4211 (Nan Kivell), 4227, 4230, 4245, 4265, 4269 (Nan Kivell), 4274, 4276, 4278, 4292, 4294, 4308 (Nan Kivell), 4313, 4321, 4323,

4336–7 (Nan Kivell), 4340, 4343, 4348–50, 4364, 4371, 4373 (Nan Kivell), 4376, 4380, 4383, 4398–4400, 4403–4, 4409, 4412 (Nan Kivell), 4418–20, 4425, 4426 (Nan Kivell), 4431, 4434, 4436–8, 4441, 4444, 4450–51, 4462, 4464, 4469, 4471, 4483–7, 4489, 4497, 4499–501, 4510 (Nan Kivell), 4515 (Nan Kivell), 4519 (Nan Kivell), 4524, 4531, 4535–7, 4540, 4542, 4544, 4546, 4548, 4550, 4560, 4562, 4564, 4566–7, 4569, 4574, 4585, 4586 (Nan Kivell), 4587, 4588 (Nan Kivell), 4591–2 (Nan Kivell), 4594–5, 4601–3, 4605, 4607, 4611–14, 4619, 4621–2, 4625, 4644 (Nan Kivell), 4648, 4658–9, 4661, 4663–6, 4668–70, 4672, 4677, 4679, 4685, 4687, 4692, 4696, 4702–3, 4713, 4716–19, 4724, 4726, 4729–30, 4732–3, 4735, 4738, 4743, 4747, 4749–50, 4758, 4761, 4767, 4769, 4771, 4773, 4789, 4791, 4794–5, 4797–9, 4801, 4803–4, 4806–7.

INDEX

THIS index mainly lists personal names and names of institutions, and titles of documents; *see also* the **List of Contents** on page v. Except for the instances noted below, each item has been indexed wherever it appears in the *Bibliography*, so that the item numbers listed under one heading in the index may refer to only one publication or document.

Dates in the index are printed in bold type, and precede the item number. They refer to the date of publication of an item, the date of the writing or the date of provenance, etc., of a document. If the date is enclosed in **square brackets** this indicates that the date of publication, etc., does not appear on the title-page; **n.d.** indicates that no date is apparent on the document.

Names include names of authors (other than Captain James Cook), editors, compilers, artists, engravers, printers, publishers, government departments and institutions, etc., mentioned in the description of the item indexed, and names of persons and institutions where their ownership of a document has been mentioned in a note in the *Bibliography*.

The **Subheading** *Journals* has been used under the names of persons who accompanied Cook on his voyages, to include *logbooks* as well as journals; *Publications* has been used to include an author's own publications as well as items in which the person's name appears in the title of a book or article which is other than biographical or relating to his work.

Under the heading for Captain James **Cook** entries have been indexed only if they would otherwise be difficult to find in the *Bibliography*.

Items listed in the section **Associates of Cook** in the *Bibliography* have not been indexed under the name of each associate. Only the references listed in the other sections of the *Bibliography* have been so indexed.

Illustrations, Charts and Maps, if published as plates in the official accounts of the three voyages, have also been indexed by title. In other instances title entries have been made selectively to assist the location of these items.

Names of **Places**, and of the **Ships** commissioned for Cook's three voyages to the Pacific Ocean, have been indexed only when they cannot be found easily from the List of Contents.

INDEX

C.I.W., *engraver* **1806** 2644–6

C.M., *illustrator* 218

CPC **[19– –]** 3088

C.v.d.B. 493

The Cabinet Cyclopaedia **1831** 112; **1834** 115

CABOT, THOMAS D. **1968** 2135

CADELL (Cadel) THOMAS, *publisher, London* **1773** 648, 650; **1775** 4458–60; **1776** 1385; **1776–7** 1404–7; **1777** 1216–17, 1291, 1336, 1381; **1778** 3921, 4659; **1779** 1226; **1784** 403, 1229, 1543–4, 1714; **1784–5** 1549; **1785** 665, 1552–3, 1743, 3795, 4554; **1787** 1640; **1789** 2452; **1803** 1642; **1810** 4103–8;

letter to **1784** 1904;

subject references **1782** 1897–8, 4631–2

CAILLOT, A. **1826** 104

CALAIS. Governor **1779** 1522

CALDWALL, JAMES, *engraver* **1777** 1381, *nos.25, 35, 47, 57,* 4577–80; **1785** 1743, *nos. 6–7*

Caledonia when at anchor in Ballarde Harbour: [coastal profile] 1376

CALIFORNIA. University, *Los Angeles.* Library **1965** 1946

CALPE, *publisher, Madrid* **1921–2** 684, 1243

CALTEX **[1966?]** 3067

CALVERT, *engraver* 957; **1865** 950–51

CALVERT, ALBERT FREDERICK **1892** 768

CALVERT, JOHN 3721

CAMBAGE, RICHARD HIND **1916** 797

CAMBIAGI, GAETANO, *publisher, Firenze* **1785** 1957

CAMBRIDGE, *England* 3175–9

CAMBRIDGE. Church of St. Andrew the Great *See* Church of St. Andrew the Great, *Cambridge*

Cambridge Geographical Series **1912** 392

CAMERON, HECTOR CHARLES **1950** 1204, 1318, 4064; **1951** 4069; **1952** 3970; **1966** 3984

CAMERON, IAN **1965** 475

CAMERON, RODERICK WILLIAM **1964** 306–7

CAMESINAISCHE BUCHHANDLUNG, *Wien* **1803** 65

CAMPBELL, ALEXANDER **1872** 2983–4

CAMPBELL, GORDON **1936** 287, 2093, 4757

CAMPBELL, JOHN **1779** 752, 1298; **1813** 753; **1817** 1656; **1840** 2476

CAMPE, JOACHIM HEINRICH **1786–90** 722, 2900–2; **1803–4** 1294; **1808** 724; **1820** 91, 2907

CAMPION, ROBERT **1846** 3181

CANADIAN GOVERNMENT ARCHIVES, *Ottawa* **1967** 1916

Canadian Historical Studies **1930** 1635

CANCRIN, J.A., *engraver* **1830** 526

The Cannibal Islands 264

CANNON, LESLIE **1966** 4351

CANNONS, from the *Endeavour* **1927** 1098; **1930** 3755; **1966** 3768

A Canoe of the Sandwich Islands: [illustration] **1785** 1743, *no.65*

Canoes of Oonalashka: [illustration] **1785** 1743, *no.50*

Canoes of Tahiti in 1773: [illustration] **1956** 1399

Canoes, Otaheite: [illustration] **[1774?]** 1379, *f.15a*

CAPE, JONATHAN, *publishers, London* **1958** 455; **[1962]** 4643; **[1965]** 236, 568, 1104, 1212, 2555

Cape of Good Hope, the *Adventure* inshore: [illustration] **1937** 1422

CAPE SOLANDER, *N.S.W. See* Kurnell, *N.S.W.*

Capitain Cooks dritte und letzte Reise **1787–1812** 1567

Capitain James Cooks Reise omkring Jorden **1803–4** 1294, 2901

Le Capitaine Cook et l'exploration de l'Océanie **1940** 290

Le Capitaine Cook explore le Pacifique **1965** 311, 2125, 2972

Le Capitaine Cook; ou, Le Schelling marqué **[1860?]** 3772

Caps of the natives of Oonalashka: [illustration] **1785** 1743, *no.56*

Capt. Cook landing at Botany Bay **1902** 940; **[1910?]** 941

Capt. Cook: the greatest of English navigators **[1928]** 280, 2078

Capt. Cooke's last voyage **1849** 3734

Capt. James Cook, R.N. (*Leyden*) **[1962]** 2114, 2960

Captain Cook
(*Besant*) **1890** 2045; **1895** 2047; **1903** 2062; **1904** 2064; **1914** 2073;
(*Gould*) **[1935]** 286, 2092;
(*Lloyd*) **1952** 296, 2101;
(*Mitton*) **1927** 279, 2077;
(*Musman*) **1967** 319, 2975

CHAMBERS, W. & R., *publishers, London*
1895 370, 2221

CHAMBERS, W.F. 1023

CHAMBERS, WILLIAM **1845** 2017; *see
also* Chambers, W. & R., *publishers,
London*

Chambers's Miscellany of Useful and
Entertaining Knowledge **1845** 2017

CHAMPAGNAC, JEAN BAPTISTE
JOSEPH DE **1836** 1997; **1838** 1663,
2918–19, 4284; **[1842]** 1664, 4285; **1853**
1668, 2921, 4286

CHAMPANTE, *publisher, London* **1793** 1575

CHANCELLOR, EDWIN BERESFORD
1925 4642

CHANTICLEER PRESS, *Paris* **1949** 222

CHANTREY, *Sir* FRANCIS 4269–73

CHAPMAN, CHARLES, *artist* **1777** 1381,
nos.17, 18, 20, 21

CHAPMAN, GEORGE THOMSON, *publisher, Auckland* **1870** 167, 2352, 2726

CHAPMAN, J., *engraver* **1800** 3264–74

CHAPMAN, WALKER **1965** 1244

CHAPMAN AND HALL, *publishers, London*
1844 4597; **1898** 375

Chapman's Centenary memorial of Captain
Cook's description of New Zealand **1870**
167, 2352

Characteres generum plantarum, quas in
itinere ad insulas Maris Australis **1776**
1385

Charco Harbour: a novel **1968** 3789–90

CHARLES, SAMUEL **1907** 2504

CHARLES SCRIBNER'S SONS, *publishers,
New York* **1967** 321, 2134

CHARLESTOWN: [chart] **1780** 1713

CHARLIAT, PIERRE-JACQUES **1959**
839, 1324, 1705

CHARLOTTE, *Queen* **1813** 3700

CHARLTON, WILLIAM **1776–9** 1462

A Chart of Captn. Carteret's discoveries at
New Britain **1773** 860

Chart of Cooks River in the N.W. part of
America **1784** 1714, *plate no.XLIV*

Chart of Cook's Strait in New Zealand **1773**
860

A Chart of Cooks Strait in New Zeland (*sic*)
894

Chart of Discoveries made in the South
Pacific Ocean . . . 1774 **1777** 1336, *plate
no.III*

[Chart of Kealakakua Bay, Hawaii] 1724

A Chart of New South Wales, or the East
Coast of New Holland **1773** 860

Chart of New-Zealand 925; **1772** 864; **1966**
924

Chart of New Zealand explored by Capt.
James Cook **1788** 877

Chart of New Zealand, explored in 1769
and 1770 **1773** 860

A Chart of New Zeland (*sic*) or the Islands
of Aeheinomouwe and Tovypoenammu
897

Chart of Norton Sound and of Bherings
Strait **1784** 1714, *plate no.LIII*

A Chart of part of New Zealand, or the
island of Aeheinomowe [i.e. North Island]
1770 857

A Chart of part of New Zealand or the island
of Tovypoenammu [i.e. South Island]
1770 858

Chart of part of the Coast of New South
Wales, from Cape Tribulation to Endeavour Straits **1773** 860

A Chart of part of the East Coast of New
Zeland (*sic*) 895

Chart of part of the N.W. Coast of America
1725

A Chart of part of the sea coast of New
South Wales **1891** 885–8

Chart of part of the South Sea **1773** 860

Chart of Polynesian islands drawn by Tupaia
for Cook, 1769 896

A Chart of the discoveries made by the late
Capt. Cook **1780** 1716

Chart of the Discoveries made in the South
Atlantic Ocean **1777** 1336, *plate no.IV*

Chart of the eastern coast of New Holland
1788 878

Chart of the Friendly Isles 1345; **1777** 1336,
plate no.XIV

A Chart of the Great South Sea or Pacific
Ocean **1955** 898

Chart of the Island Otaheite **1773** 860

A Chart of the Islands discover'd in the
Neighbourhood of Otaheite **1773** 860

Chart of the N.E. Coast of New Caledonia
1346

Chart of the N.E. Coast of the Island of
Desolation 1721

Chart of the N.W. Coast of America and
N.E. Coast of Asia **1784** 1714, *plate no.
XXXVI*

Chart of the Sandwich Islands 1726

A Chart of the sea coast of New South Wales
1770 859

INDEX

Cook's birthplace 3195–7

COOK'S COTTAGE, *Melbourne* 2766–72

Cook's debt to Torres **[1960?]** 741

Cooks dritter Entdeckungsreise **1789** 1571

Cooks Fahrten um die Welt **1963** 235; **1965** 237

Cooks Leben **1797** 1975

Cook's *Resolution* approaching Ship Cove, Queen Charlotte Sound, N.Z. **[195–]** 1417

COOK'S RIVER, N.S.W. **1908** 2985

COOK'S STRAIT, *N.Z.* Chart **1773** 860

COOK'S TAMARIND-TREE, *Tahiti* 3161, 3166

COOK'S TREE, *Bruny Island* **1968** 3103

COOK'S TREE, *Endeavour River (Cooktown)* **1770** 3678–9; **1893** 683; **1925** 3094; **1957** 3095

COOK'S TREE, *Hikutaia, N.Z.* **1902** 2885

COOK'S TREE, *Point Venus, Tahiti* 3161, 3166

Cook's voyage to the Pacific Ocean: [article] **1788** 1652

Cook's voyages **1894** 197, 2050

Cook's voyages: [questionnaire for children] **1968** 323

Cook's voyages and life **[182–?]** 1981; **1839** 128, 2005; **1842** 141, 2013

Cook's voyages and life . . . engraved for Dove's English classics **n.d.** 90

Cook's voyages of discovery **1865** 165; **1874** 168; **1879** 174; **1899** 200; **1904** 205; **1910** 211; **1930** 220

Cook's voyages round the world **n.d.** 108; **1799** 61; **1840** 132, 2009

COOKTOWN, *Queensland* 2088–98; *see also* Cook's Tree, *Endeavour River (Cooktown)*;

Museum **1969** 1082

COOLEY, WILLIAM DESBOROUGH **1831** 112; **1834** 115; **1874** 169

COOPER, J., *engraver* **1868** 3278–9

COOPER, JOHN BUTLER **1931** 3110

COOPER, ROBERT PALLISER **1771–4** 1142

COOPER, THOMPSON **1890** 2217, 4020

COPIA, *engraver* 3261–3, 3280–81

Copies of documents relating to Captain James Cook, R.N., from originals in the Grey Collection, Auckland Public Library 6, 593

Copies of instructions and correspondence between Cook and the Commissioners of the Victualling **1764–5** 1922

COPLEY, *Sir* GODFREY **1775** 2837; **1776** 2786–7; *see also* Copley Medal

COPLEY, JOHN SINGLETON, *the elder* 3208–11

COPLEY, ROGER **[1966]** 314

COPLEY MEDAL 3721, *no.111* **[1775?]** 3898 **1775** 2837; **1776** 1288–90, 2786–7; **1777** 1291; **1780–96** 3882

COPPLESTONE, BENNET, *pseud.* **1926** 2271

Copyright and piracy in eighteenth-century chart publication **1960** 540

LA COQUILLE QUI CHANTE, *Oslo* **1939** 1283

CORBOULD, H., *artist* **n.d.** 4269–70; **[182–?]** 966; **[183–?]** 967

CORDUROY 3647

CORNÈ, MICHELE FELICE **n.d.** 2655; **1961** 3500

CORNER, *Rev. Mr* **1894** 683

CORNER, I., *engraver* **n.d.** 4645

CORNER, JOHN 578, 1111, 2872

CORNER, SYLVIA **[195–?]** 737; **[1965]** 745, 2122

CORNEY, BOLTON GLANVILL **1919** 4726

Cornhill Magazine, London **1914** 1679, 2510

CORRALL, G., *publisher, London* **1777** 239

CORY, R. 3676

COSENS, F.W., *of Lewes* 578

Cosmographie in four books **1657** 3660

COTES, FRANCIS **n.d.** 4087; **1768** 3212–14; **1899** 3626

COTTA, I.G., *publisher, Tübingen* **1797** 1975

Cottage Library **1853** 153, 2021

COTTER, CHARLES H. **1967** 2133; **1968** 320

COTTON, W. **1859** 3583–4

Counties of England: History and topography of Yorkshire **[c.1822]** 2170

Country Journal **1923** 804

Courage and Conquest **1964** 2119, 2964

COURAGE AND PERSEVERANCE MEDAL 2833–6

Court of Apollo **1774** 3989

COURTENAY, JOHN **1774** 3912; **1775** 3920

COURTNEY, J.E. **[1918]** 2254

COURTNEY, WILLIAM LEONARD **[1918]** 2254

COUSINS, JOHN GEORGE **1907–8** 3624

INDEX

DE LATOUCHE-TRÉVILLE, LOUIS RENÉ MADELEINE LE VASSOR **1959** 461

DELATTRE, *engraver* **1785** 1743, *no.49*

DeLEEUW, ADELE LOUISE **1963** 2117, 2961; **1966** 2126, 2974

DELÉN, CARL, *publisher* **1802** 1274

DE L'ISLE, GUILLAUME **[177–?]** 861, 1932

DE L'ISLE, WILLIAM PHILIP SIDNEY, *Lord* **1962** 3979

de LOUTHERBOURG, P.J. **1795** 2669–73

DELPUECH DE COMEIRAS, V. **1825** 99

DE MAGALHAENS, J.H. **n.d.** 3691

DE MANNEVILLETTE, J.B.N.D. D'APRÈS **1803** 881

DE MAYR, *engraver* 3253–5

DE MENDOZA Y RIOS, *Don* JOSÉ **n.d.** 4133–4

DEMEUNIER, JEAN NICOLAS, *Comte* **1782** 1611–12; **1783** 1613–14; **1785** 1556–8; **1819** 1584

DE MIRVAL, C.-H. (E.-H.) *See* Champagnac, Jean Baptiste Joseph de

DE NAVA PALACIO, CESAREO **1795** 55, 1974

DENT, *publishers, London* **1906** 208; **[1911?]** 212; **1915** 215; **[1925]** 217; **1929** 219, 685; **[1954]** 226

DENT, *publishers, Toronto* **1924** 398

DENT, C. **[1911?]** 212

DENTON, V.L. **1924** 398

DÉPÔT GÉNÉRAL DES CARTES, PLANS & JOURNAUX DE LA MARINE, *Paris* **1784** 1940

DEPTFORD YARD, *England* **1768** 989–93

DERBY, WILLIAM, *artist* 4113–27

DER MYN, VAN **n.d.** 3566

Dernier voyage du Capitaine Cook autour du monde **1782** 1629; **1783** 1630

DER SPYK, L. VAN, *publisher, Leyden* **1791** 1632

Des Capitain Jacob Cook's dritte Entdeckungs-Reise **1788** 1569

Des Capitäns James Cook Beschreibung seiner Reise um die Welt **1820** 91, 2907

Des Hauptmanns Cook zweite Fahrt um die Welt **1778–80** 1225

Des Lieutenant Cook's Reise um die Welt in den Jahren, 1768, 1769, 1770 und 1771 **1774** 657

Des Lieutenants Georg Mortimer Bemerkungen auf seiner Reise in der Brigantine *Merkur* **1791** 251

DE SAINT-SAUVEUR, JACQUES GRASSET **1797** 258

DE S. VICENTE, CONDE **1795** 1293

DES BARRES, JOSEPH FREDERICK (FRIEDRICH) WALSH, *Capt.* **1781** 1939

[Description of the death of Cook, by a witness] **1907** 2506

Descriptiones animalium quae in itinere ad Maris Australis terras **1844** 1295

Descriptions for sailing in and out of ports **1758–62** 1912, *item 4*

Descriptions of the Harbour of Halifax & the Coast Adjacent **1768–79** 3

A Descriptive catalogue of the Cook Bicentenary Exhibition, *Whitby* **1928** 2399, 4754

DE SELINCOURT, AUBREY **1949** 2097, 2945

DESFORGES, *publisher, Paris* **[1840?]** 2008, 3771

DESILVER, ROBERT, *publisher, Philadelphia* **1818** 1583

DESPERRIÈRES, POISSONNIER **1780** 327, 1299

Le Destin tragique de James Cook **1932** 2089, 2938

Détails nouveaux et circonstanciés sur la mort du Capitaine Cook **1786** 1618, 2446

DEUTSCHE AKADEMIE DER WISSENSCHAFTEN, *Berlin* **1958** 4409; **1965–6** 1260

DEUTSCHE VERLAGS-ANSTALT, *Berlin* **[1930]** 3779, 4401

DEUTSCHES MUSEUM, *Berlin* 4201–2, 4680–81

Deuxième voyage du Capitaine Cook autour du monde **1880** 1240

Devil Lord's daughter: [a novel] **1948** 3782–3

DEWAR, ALEXANDER **1776** 1503

D'EXILES, ANTOINE FRANÇOIS PRÉVOST *See* Prévost d'Exiles, Antoine François, *Abbé*

Diagram of a double canoe seen at Amsterdam in the South Seas **[1774?]** 1379, *f.14b*

Diagram of a native canoe **[177–?]** 1379, *f.21a*

DIAL PRESS, *New York* **1947** 445; **1951** 295, 2099

DIBBLE, *Rev.* SHELDON **1839** 2475; **1843** 2479; **1909** 2508

DICKENSON, *bookseller* **1789** 4211

DICKINSON, *publisher* **1859** 3583–6

GAINSBOROUGH, THOMAS, *R.A.* 3494; **1788** 4644

GALABIN, J.W., *printer, London* **1786** 4556

GALES, J., *printer, Sheffield* 672

GALL & INGLIS, *publishers, London* **n.d.** 353

Gallery of portraits with memoirs **1833** 4001

GALLIMARD, *publisher, Paris* **1940** 290

GALT, JOHN **1820** 341, 2169; **1827** 343, 2174

GALWAY, *Dowager Viscountess, Bawtry, Doncaster* 3648–9

GALWAY, GEORGE VERE ARUNDELL MONCKTON-ARUNDELL, *8th Viscount* 1414, 3653

GANDY, BERN **1959** 928

GANGWAY HAND-LINES **1776–9** 3656

GARAT, (DOMINIQUE JOSEPH?) **1789** 1968

GARCIA IÑIGUEZ, *D.* ANGEL **1796** 2460, 3799

GARCIA ORTIZ, ELENA **[1957]** 229

GARDE, *M.* DE LA **n.d.** 1785, 1787

GARDINER, ALFONZO **n.d.** 275, 2930

GARDINER, WILLIAM **1838** 4005, 4564

GARNSEY, E.R. **1925** 4796

GARRAN, ANDREW **1886** 365, 4111, 4313

Garran's Picturesque atlas of Australasia **[1886]** 953

GARRARD PUB. CO., *Champaign, Illinois* **1963** 2117, 2961

GARRICK, DAVID **[177–]** 1107

GARTHSHORE, M., *M.D., F.R.S.* **1801–2** 4238–42

GASSET, M. ORTEGA Y *See* Ortega y Gasset, M.

GATHMAN, F., *seaman* **1765** 1922

GAUNT, MARY (Mrs Mary Miller, Mrs H. Lindsay) **1895** 372, 770

The Gazetteer, London **[177–]** 1206

GEDDES, A., *engraver* **1875** 4616

GEIBEL, *publisher, Altenburg* **1894** 271, 2048

GEIKIE, *Sir* ARCHIBALD **1917** 4040

Genera nova plantarum, 1776–1777 **1776–7** 1454

A General Chart: Exhibiting the Discoveries made by Captn James Cook **1784** 1714, *plate no.I*

A General collection of the best and most interesting voyages **1812** 77

A General collection of voyages and travels **1809–10** 74; **1813** 78, 79

A General history and collection of voyages **1814–15** 677, 1237, 1582; **1824** 679, 1238, 1586

Genesis of Queensland **1888** 682

Gentleman's Magazine, London **1771** 693; **1780** 3644; **1790** 4713; **1820** 3995, 3997; **1836** 1507

Genuine account of Omiah **1774** 4549

Geografikst bibliotek för ungdom **1808** 2902

Geographical Journal, London **1907** 2505

Geographical Magazine, London **1956** 1774

GEOGRAPHICAL SOCIETY OF NEW SOUTH WALES **1928** 2280

GEOGRAPHICAL SOCIETY OF PARIS *See* Société de Géographie, *Paris*

Geography epitomized **1784** 329, 2899, 3819

Georg Forster, der Naturforscher des Volks **1854** 4395

Georg Forster in Mainz **1863** 4397

Georg Forster's Leben in Haus und Welt **1858** 4396

GEORGE III, *King of Great Britain and Ireland* 1890; **1771** 627; **1780** 1891, 4628

GEORGE V, *King of Great Britain* 3007

GEORGE VI, *King of Great Britain* 1117

GEORGIAN HOUSE, *publishers, Melbourne* **1951** 3853; **1958** 231

GÉRIN, *engraver* **[1864]** 1943

The German Doctor on his travels from England **1778** 1439, 4773

The German Doctor with his family on his travels to England conducted by Mynheer Shinder Knecht **1778** 1439, 4773

Geschichte der neuesten Reisen um die Welt **1775** 662

Geschichte der neuesten Seereisen und Entdeckungen im Südmeer **1789** 1571

Geschichte der Reisen de Seit. Cook an der Nordwest- und Nordost-Kuste von Amerika **1791** 251

Geschichte der See-Reisen und Entdeckungen im Süd-Meer **1774** 657; **1778–80** 1249; **1784** 1253; **1788** 1569

THE GHAUT, *Whitby* 2749–50

GIANETTI, MICHELANGIOLO **1785** 1957

GIBBS, SHALLARD, *publishers, Sydney* **1870** 2031; **[1871?]** 3045; **1872** 3427; **1879** 361

GIBLIN, ROBERT W. **1928** 406

GIBSON, J., *engraver* **1773** 860

GIGLIOLI, ENRICO HILLYER **1893–5** 1643, 3744

GIGUET ET MICHAUD, *publishers, Paris* **1806** 3825; **1814** 80, 1979, 2904

GILBERT, DAVIES **n.d.** 615

GILBERT, GEORGE **1776–9** 1473; **1776–80** 1471–2; **1926** 708, 2518

GILBERT, JOSEPH
charts 1349–52, 1354–5;
coastal profiles 1353, 1356–9;
journal **1772–5** 1150;
manuscript notes **1771–4** 1116

GILFILLAN, JOHN ALEXANDER **n.d.** 949, 956–7; **1865** 950–5; **[1886]** 953; **[1899?]** 954; **1919** 952; **[1924]** 958; **1926** 955

GILFILLAN, T. (*sic*) A. **[1899?]** 954

GILL, GEORGE HERMON **1934** 2090, 2768; **1957** 2108

GILL, HERMON *See* Gill, George Hermon

GILL, SAMUEL THOMAS **n.d.** 3041

GILL, *Rev.* WILLIAM WYATT **1880** 1671, 3839; **1894** 1672, 3841

GILLI, MATHIEU BLANC **1787** 1959

GILLIES, WILLIAM **n.d.** 387, 1061

GILLRAY, JAMES **1795** 4276; **1848** 4277; **1851** 4278–9

GIRAUDOUX, JEAN **1937** 3965

GISBORNE, *N.Z.* 3114–16

Gisborne Times **1927** 2381

GJÖRWELL, CARL CHRISTOFFER **1785** 2445

GLASS STAR **n.d.** 3658

GLOBE, Celestial **1729** 3702

GLOUCESTERSHIRE, *England*. Records Office. Clerk of the Council's Department **1771** 627

GLOVER, D. 227

Die Glückliche Insel **1781** 3778

GOAT **1902** 2886

GODFREY, R.B., *engraver* 962

GODWIN, GEORGE STANLEY **1930** 413, 4716

GOEBIOWSKI, EUGENIUSZ **1964** 3787

GOLD, G., *publisher* **1803** 3344–5

The Golden age of plant hunters **1968** 3986, 4548

GOLDEN COCKEREL PRESS, *London* **1944** 1284; **1953** 1285

The Golden haze **1964** 306–7

GOLDSTEIN, NATHAN **1963** 2117, 2961; **1966** 2126, 2974

GOMELDON, JANE, *Mrs* **1784** 713

GOMEZ, BENJAMIN, *publisher, New York* **1796** 1579

GONDOLAT, *publisher, Budapest* **1962** 688

GONZALEZ, *printer* **1853** 155

GOODENOUGH, JAMES GRAHAM **1876** 3078–9

GOODRICH, FRANK BOOTT **n.d.** 353–5; **1859** 350

GORDON, M. **1939** 2981

GORDON, MONA CLIFTON **[1950]** 4067

GORE, JOHN
handwriting 3856;
journal (manuscript) **1768–9** 600; **1776–80** 1474–5;
publications **1781** 1609; **1784–90** 1543–6, 1550–54, 1556–7, 1559–60, 1562, 1569, 1572, 1574; **1793** 1575; **1796** 1579; **1813** 1581; **1818** 1583; **1819** 1584; **1824** 1586; **1831** 1587;
subject references **1780** 1538, 2434, 4627; **1782** 1898; **1827–8** 525;
illustration of 1785, 1787

GOS. IZD-VO GEOGRAFIC̄HESKOĬ LITERATURY, *Moskva* **1960–64** 233; **1963** 2118

GORTON, JOHN G. **1838** 2185, 4006

GOSLING, W. **1910** 2243

GOSPORT. Royal Academy 3662, 3689

Göthingisches Magazin **1781** 1639, 2438

GOULD, RUPERT THOMAS, *Lieut. Commander, R.N.* **1928** 1458, 1687–8, 2525–6, 4289; **[1935]** 286; **1935** 2092, 4372

GOURGEY, BRENDA **1968** 2345

GOURIET, J.B. **1811** 75

GOVERNMENT HOUSE, *Wellington, New Zealand* 4335

GOVERNMENT PRINTER, *Sydney* **1899** 2055, 2356–7, 2723; **1901** 2361, 2363; **[1904]** 1089; **1904** 1090; **1908** 2370; **1909** 3955; **1920** 2376; **1928** 2387; **[1965]** 745; **1965** 2122; *see also* New South Wales. Government Printing Office

GOVERNMENT PRINTER, *Wellington, N.Z.* **1914** 214; **1926** 1634

GOWEN, HERBERT HENRY **[1919]** 1682

GOWER, JOHN *See* Gore, John

GR*S**N*R, *Lady* **1774** 3912; **1775** 3920

GRABHORN PRESS, *San Francisco* **1965** 1946

GRACE, RICHARD, *publisher, Dublin* **1820** 1983, 2908–9; **1821** 1984

GRAF, J., *printer* **n.d.** 4689

GRAHAM, THOMAS **1815** 1949

GRAINGER, W., *engraver* 2625–7, 2674; **1791** 4384

GRANCHAIN, M. de, *translator* **1784** 1940

Les Grands navigateurs du dix-huitième siècle **1926** 278

GRANT OF ARMS (to Cook family) 2680–81

GRAPE LANE, *Whitby* 2749–50, 2757–8, 2764

Graphic stories of sailors **n.d.** 378, 2925

GRASSET, BERNARD, *publisher, Paris* **1937** 3965

GRASSET SAINT-SAUVEUR, JACQUES **1797** 258

GRASSO, GABRIELE **1903** 727

GRAVES, *Rev.* JOHN **1808** 2160

GRAVES, W. & S., *printers, London* **[177–]** 544

GREAT AYTON, *Yorkshire* 1949, 2087, 2257, 2310, 2706, 2711, 2713–15, 2717;
celebrations **1928** 2383;
church 2716;
residence 2712, 2766–7;
school 2718

GREAT BRITAIN. Admiralty
correspondence, etc. 7, 1083; **1764–79** 1; **1768–78** 616; **1771–8** 5; **1775–81** 1432;
letters from 1890; **1764** 1922; **1765** 2873; **1768–70** 603; **1780** 1891; **1784** 2877;
letters to 325, 1318, 2423, 4064; **1765** 1922; **1768** 621; **1770** 626; **1776** 4345;
instructions **1768–78** 616; **1928** 8;
(*first voyage*) **1930** 640; **1955** 641;
(*second voyage*) **1771–8** 1176; **1961** 1211; **1965** 1212;
(*third voyage*) **1771–8** 1500; **1776–7** 1524; **1777** 1525; **1953** 1526; **1967** 1527;
plans of H.M.S. *Endeavour* 1002, 1100;
publications **1760** 1927; **[1766?]** 1929; **1766** 1928; **1770** 1933–4; **1774** 1936; **1775** 1938; **1784–5** 1543–6, 1549, 1552–3;
statue of Capt. Cook 3189–94;
subject references 571, 1395, 1912, 3189–94, 4745; **1768** 994–5; **1771** 693; **1772** 1180; **1776** 1507; **1776–7** 1405; **1782** 1895, 1897–1900; **1821** 1911; **1838** 2474; **1906** 2887; **[c.1910]** 4744; **1930** 640; **1954** 1423; **1959** 4487

GREAT BRITAIN. Admiralty. Naval Intelligence Division **1945** 443

GREAT BRITAIN. Board of Longitude **1772–4** 1133; **1772–5** 1167–9, 1151; **1772–80** 1476; **1776** 1477; **1777** 1287; **1782** 1542; **1788** 718

GREAT BRITAIN. Hydrographic Department **1950** 537, 4760

GREAT BRITAIN. Ministry of Defence. Naval Historical Branch **1772–5** 1333

GREAT BRITAIN. Navy Board **1764–79** 1; **1765** 1922; **1893** 7

GREAT BRITAIN. Navy Commissioners **1768–78** 616; **1771–18** 5, 1176, 1500, 1503

GREAT BRITAIN. Navy Office 603

GREAT BRITAIN. Office of Sick and Hurt Seamen **1965** 236, 2880

GREAT BRITAIN. Prime Minister **1968** 2136–7

GREAT BRITAIN. Public Record Office 4745; **1891** 4782; **[c.1910]** 4744

GREAT BRITAIN. Treasury **1759** 1919; **1777** 1528

GREAT BRITAIN. Victualling Board 603; **1765** 1922, 2874; **1768** 617–20; **1768–78** 616; **1771–8** 5, 1176, 1500; **1772** 1181, 1183–90, 1192, 1194, 1196–7; **1776** 1505, 1509; **1777** 1528

The Great captain **1964** 2119, 2964

Great Lives **[1935]** 286, 2092

Great people in Australian history **[1966]** 314

Great sailor **1951** 295, 2099

GREAT ST. ANDREW'S CHURCH, *Cambridge See* Church of St. Andrew the Great, *Cambridge*

The Great South Land: an epic poem **1951** 3853

The Great South Sea **1962** 4767

The Great South Sea Caterpillar **1795** 4276; **1848** 4277; **1851** 4278–9

Great Stories of Canada **1956** 4718

GREEN, CHARLES
journal (manuscript) **1768–70** 586, 601;
publications **1788** 709–10, 718;
subject references **1891** 4782–3; **1892** 4784–5

GREEN, I. **[c.1786]** 1747

GREEN, J.H., *D.C.L., F.R.S., Pres., Royal College of Surgeons of England* 3721, *no.112*

GREEN, W., *publisher, London* **[1783]** 3924

GREENE, CARLA **1959** 1706, 2955

GREENWICH, *England* **1937** 3188, 3766; *see also* National Maritime Museum, *Greenwich*; Royal Hospital, *Greenwich*

GREENWICH HOSPITAL *See* Royal Hospital, *Greenwich*

GRÉGOIRE & DENEUX, *lithographers* **n.d.** 3334

INDEX

GREGORY, OLIVE BARNES **1965** 2123, 2969

GRENVILLE, H.M.S. 1, 603, 1912, 1922–3, 2873–4

GREVEDON, N., *engraver* **1826** 4149–50

GREY, *Sir* GEORGE **1854** 757; *see also* Grey Collection, *Auckland Public Library, N.Z.*

GREY COLLECTION, *Auckland Public Library, N.Z.* 6, 572, 593, 615, 644, 1522, 1533, 1901–2, 1907, 1910, 2431, 2874, 3899–3901, 3195

GRIBBLE, BERNARD 1042

GRIEG, *engraver* 984

GRIEVE, AVERIL MACKENZIE- **1939** 1283; **1944** 1284; **1953** 1285

GRIFFIN, WILLIAM **1776–80** 1478

GRIFFIN PRESS, *Adelaide* **1957** 228

GRIFFITH, GEORGE CHETWYND **1897** 2222

GRIFFITH, *Sir* SAMUEL **1891** 4782

GRIFFITHS, WILLIAM ARTHUR **1948** 2314

GRIGG, JOHN, *sailor* **1759** 1919

GRIGNION, G.(J.), *engraver* **1785** 1743, *nos.62, 65*

GRIMWADE, *Sir* WILFRID RUSSELL 2090, 2108, 3105

GROSKURD, CHRISTIAN HEINRICH **1784** 1275

Grosse Naturforscher **1952** 2100

GROSSECK, JOYCE, *Mrs* **1962** 472, 2959

GROVE DAY, ARTHUR *See* Day, Arthur Grove

GROVES, *Captain* 3617

GRUEBEN, A., *publisher, Dublin* **1791** 254

GUERNSEY, H.M.S. **[1764]** 1922

GUILDHALL MUSEUM, *Boston, Lincolnshire* **[c.1814]** 4140–42

GUNN, HUGH **[19– –]** 2255

GUNS (*Endeavour's*) *See* Cannons

GUNSON, W.N. **1964** 4085

GUTENBERG, *publisher, Hamburg* **1908** 210

GUTHRIE, WILLIAM **1785** 504; **[1820–30?]** 517

Guthries New system of geography **1785** 504; **[1820–30?]** 517

GWYTHER, JOHN **1954** 738; **1955** 740

GY, JS. **1795** 4276

GYLDENDALS FORLAG, *Kiøbenhavn* **1793** 674,1255

H., A.F. **1884** 269

H., W., *artist* **[c.1786]** 1747

H.B. HALL'S SONS, *engravers, New York* 3288–93

H.M. Bark *Endeavour*: a diagrammatic section of the interior **1965** 1000

H.M. Bark *Endeavour*: souvenir **1934** 820

H.M.S. *ENDEAVOUR* TRUST **[1966]** 1105, 2412

H.M.S. *Resolution*: [illustration] **1924–5** 1379, *f.34*

H.M.S. *Resolution* . . . and H.M.S. *Adventure* . . . in Matavay Bay, Tahiti, Au.26, 1773 **1954** 1423

H.M.S. *Resolution* taking in ice for water, in the Antarctic seas **1924–5** 1379, *f.26*

H.M.S. *Resolution* The Second Voyage 1772–1775 **1957** 1418

H.R. **1907–8** 3624

HAAS, HUGO **n.d.** 492

HACHETTE, *publisher, Paris* **1887** 187

HADDRICK, RON **1963** 541, 3792

HAGNER, F.R. **1842** 142

HAID, *engraver* **1788** 3609–10

HAIG-BROWN, RODERICK LANGMERE HAIG- **1956** 1322, 1704, 2951, 4718

HAILSTONE, E. **1869** 2199

HAKLUYT SOCIETY, *London* **1945** 291; **1955–68** 227, 641, 1211, 2106, 4762

HALAVIOPUIE, *King of Hawaii* 3721, *no.98*

HALE, ROBERT, *publisher, London* **1953** 1285

HALIFAX HOSPITAL **1759** 1919

HALL, *photographer* 1072, 1428, 2391, 2764

HALL, H.B., *engravers, New York* 3288–93

HALL, H. TOM **1968** 3777

HALL, J. (I.), *engraver* 978, 1810, 2566–70; **1775** 4458–60; **1777** 1381, *nos.36–8, 48, 56;* **1785** 1743, *nos.18, 22–3, 57, 60;* **1794** 2459

HALL, SIDNEY, *engraver* **1827** 520

HALL, WILLIS **1960** 2337

HALLIARD AND BROWN, *publishers, Cambridge, U.S.A.* **1828** 1660, 4524

HALLIDAY, E.M. **1961** 1707, 4540

HALLORAN, HENRY **1833** 3831; **1879** 2355, 3837–8

HALL'S SONS, (H.B. Hall), *engravers, New York* 3288–93

HALPIN, P., *engraver* **1784–8** 3294–5; **1825** 4461

HALSTEAD, MURAT **1898** 1674, 2223

INDEX

HAMILTON, *artist* 2656-7

HAMILTON, *publisher, London* **1966** 315

HAMILTON, CLAUDE N., *Lord* **1921** 3139

HAMILTON-EDWARDS, GERALD **1952** 4441

HAMLYN, PAUL, *publisher, London* **1968** 324, 552, 2138

HAMMERSMITH LOCAL HISTORY GROUP **1961** 3977, 4607

HAMMOND, T., *Colonel* **1772** 1180

HAMMOND, WILLIAM, *Capt.* 4449; **1772** 1180, 1193

HAMY, ERNEST THÉODORE **1879** 3736-7, 4368

HANNAY, DAVID **1928** 2284-5

HANSON, RAYMOND **1959** 928

HANSY, DE, *le jeune, publisher, Paris* **1774** 720

HARDING & LEPARD, *publishers, London* **1831** 3302-6; **1831-2** 4113-18; **1835** 4003

HARDY, JOHN, *publisher, London* **1784-6** 1545, 1551

HARGRAVE, LAWRENCE **[1910-11]** 786

HARLOW, VINCENT TODD **1929** 686; **1952** 450; **1953** 1526

HARMAR, T., *engraver* **1784** 1714, *plate no. II, V, XXXVI, LV*

HARMSWORTH, *Sir* LEICESTER 607

Harmsworth's Universal Encyclopaedia **[1920]** 2256, 4042

HARPE, JEAN FRANÇOIS DE LA *See* La Harpe, Jean François de

HARPER, *publisher, New York* **1839** 130, 2004

HARPER AND ROW, *publishers, New York* **1966** 316

HARRAP, *publishers, London* **1929** 407; **1940** 438; **1949** 449; **[1952]** 4736; **1955** 4737

HARRIOT, *"mistress to Mr. Banks"* **1774** 3989

HARRIS, J., *publisher, London* **1805** 67

HARRIS, *Sir* JAMES **1779** 1529-31

HARRISON, JOHN, *Attorney at Law, Guisbrough, Yorkshire* **1776** 1925, 2875

HARRISON, R.E. **1947** 445

HARRISON, W., *engraver* **1784** 1714, *plate no.XLIV*

HARRISON & CO., *publisher* **1794** 3393-8, 4468

HARRISSON, THOMAS HARNETT **1937** 1315

HART, THOMAS 3639

HARTLEBEN, A., *publisher, Wien* **1881** 268

HARVARD UNIVERSITY PRESS **1965** 476

HARVEIAN SOCIETY OF EDINBURGH **1821** 3944

HARVEY, WILLIAM **1771-5** 1152; **1776-7** 1479; **1777-9** 1480

HASWELL, BARRINGTON & HAS-WELL, *publishers, Philadelphia* **1841** 137, 2012

HASWHITLE, ROBERT **177-** 597

HASZARD, H.D.M. **1902** 382, 779

HAUDE & SPENER, *publishers, Berlin* **1772** 698; **1774** 657; **1775** 662; **1778-80** 1249-50; **1780** 1252; **1781** 1609; **1783** 1263; **1784** 1253, 1275; **1786** 248; **1788** 1569; **1789** 1571

Hauptmanns Cooks Fahrt um die Welt, von 1768 bis 1771 **1776** 664

The Haven-finding art **1956** 300

HAVIOL, *engraver* **1924** 3171

HAWAII **1968** 2135;
celebrations **1928** 2864-6; *see also* the section in the *Bibliography* headed *Personal—Celebrations*

HAWAII. Board of Commissioners of Public Archives **1929** 2291; **1930** 2407

HAWAII. King 3685

Hawaii celebrates discovery of islands **1928** 2392

HAWAIIAN HISTORICAL SOCIETY **[1916]** 1625, 2252; **1926** 2518

HAWAIIAN MISSION CHILDREN'S SOCIETY LIBRARY, *Honolulu* **1783** 1603

HAWAIIAN POSTAGE STAMPS **1928** 2867-9

HAWEIS, *Rev.* HUGH REGINALD **n.d.** 1589; **1886** 1590

HAWKER, E., *Mrs* 3637

HAWKESLEY, *Dr* **n.d.** 191

HAWKESWORTH, JOHN **n.d.** 189-91, 546, 1107, 1855; **1768-71** 575; **1773** 648-54, 712, 1108-9, 4359-60, 4364, 4451; **[1774]** 3919; **1774** 656-60; **1774-85** 498, 548; **1775** 661-2; **1778** 9, 1220; **1778-80** 1249; **1783** 245, 665; **1788** 1569; **1789** 670-71; **1795-1809** 52; **1796** 676; **1824** 679; **1956** 837

HAWKEY, WILLIAM **1772-4** 1153

HAYDEN, *printer, London* **1806** 3726

HAYWARD, JOSEPH **1825** 3946

HAZELHURST, JAMES **n.d.** 4353

HAZELHURST, THOMAS **n.d.** 3495

HAZLITT, J. **1796** 4520

INDEX

Historical account of the most celebrated voyages **1796** 57

An Historical account of the voyages of Captain James Cook **1805** 67

An Historical play to celebrate a great Yorkshireman **1928** 2384, 3806

Historical records of New South Wales 1, 7, 602, 614, 707, 716, 1024, 1112, 1177, 2500, 2722, 3429–30, 4300, 4321, 4599

Historical records of New South Wales: Cook, 1762–1780 **1893** 889

Historical records of New Zealand 214, 1134

HISTORICAL SOCIETY OF QUEENSLAND **1928** 812

Historischer Bericht von den sämmtlichen, durch Engländer geschehenen, Reisen um die Welt **1776** 664; **1778–80** 1225

Historiska Biblioteket **1785** 2445; **1785–7** 1264

The History of Botany Bay in New Holland **[1787?]** 668; **[1787]** 667; **[1789]** 672, 2149; **[1789?]** 2150

The History of Captain Cook's three voyages round the world **1784** 14

The History of Cook's cottage **1957** 2108

A History of geographical discovery in the seventeenth and eighteenth centuries **1912** 392; **1965** 477

History of maritime and inland discovery **1831** 112; **1834** 115

History of music **1775** 1516

History of New Holland **1787** 27, 28; **1790** 43; **1808** 71

An History of the instances of exclusion from the Royal Society **1784** 3925

History of the Royal Society **1848** 2018

History of the voyages and discoveries made in the north **1786** 249

HITCHINGS, SINCLAIR H. **1963** 1604

HJELM, A. **1939** 4711

HOARE, MICHAEL EDWARD **1965–6** 4410, 4423; **1967** 4425

Hobart Mercury **1904** 1091

HOBBES, THOMAS 2691

HODDER AND STOUGHTON, *publishers, London* **n.d.** 385; **1909** 383; **1936** 287, 2093; **1946** 292; **1948** 294; **1965** 475; **1967** 320, 2133

HODGES, WILLIAM **n.d.** 547, 1335, 1387–8, 1390–97, 1403, 1826, 1835, 2596, 2665–6, 3496–3558, 4594; **[c.1770]** 546, 1331, *f.3b*, 2847–51; **[1772?]** 1331, *ff.4–5, 7–8*; **1772** 1331, *ff.1–3, 3a, 6*, 1379, 1398; **1772–8** 1120; **1776–7** 1400–02, 1404–07; **1777** 1216–17, 1248, 1381, 4577–80; **1778**

4576; **1784** 1229; **1796** 1234; **1812** 1408; **[192–?]** 1242; **1937** 1422, 1424; **1954** 1423; **1956** 1399, 1425; **1965** 1409; subject references **1776** 1127; **1782** 1899, 4633

HODGES AND PAIN, *printers, London* **1784** 14

HODGSON, O., *publisher, London* **n.d.** 3353

HODGSON, BOYS & GRAVES, *publishers, London* **1834** 4592

HOFFAY, ALBERT, *engraver* **1859** 3583–6

HOFFMAN, LAWRENCE, *illustrator* **1957** 2109, 2953

HOFFMANN, B.G., *publisher and bookseller, Hamburg* **1789** 35, 1965, 4393

HOGG, *publishers, London* **[1859]** 350

HOGG, ALEXANDER, *publisher, London* **n.d.** 970–71, 979–80, 1048, 1389, 1402, 2634–6, 3522, 4469–74, 4500–3; **[177–]** 544; **1778** 751; **[1782]** 244; **1784** 1050, 3528–39; **[1784–6]** 17–19; **1785** 21, 2632–3; **1787** 26; **1793** 256; **[1794?]** 46; **[1794]** 49, 4596

HOGG, I., *engraver* **1784** 2799; **1785** 4497–9

HOGG, JOHN **[1785]** 21; **[1785–95]** 22

HOLDEN, S. **n.d.** 3217

HOLL, WILLIAM, *the elder, engraver* **n.d.** 4462–3; **1794** 3393–8; **1819** 2168; **1829–47** 3297–3316, 4155–65

HOLLAND, *Sir* NATHANIEL DANCE-*See* Dance, *Sir* Nathaniel

HOLLAND, S., *Major* **1781** 1939

HOLLIS & CARTER, *publishers, London* **1956** 300; **1967** 484

HOLLOWAY, T., *engraver* **1790** 3317–22

HOLMAN, FRANCIS **n.d.** 1415–16, 3653; **1952** 1435

HOLMAN, JAMES **1840** 3040

HOLMES, CHARLES **n.d.** 3497

HOLMES, *Sir* MAURICE **1936** 4758; **1939** 4338; **1949** 447; **1950** 2319; **1952** 4761; **1957** 1626, 2546

HOLSTEYN, P., *publisher, Rotterdam* **1778** 1221

HOLT, THOMAS 3052; **1871** 3045–6

HOLTROP, W., *publisher, Amsterdam* **1802** 64

THE HOLY BIBLE **1765** 3632

HOME (Hume), ALEXANDER journal (manuscript) **1777–9** 1481, 2425; publication **1838** 2474

HOME, *Sir* EVERARD **n.d.** 1924; **1822** 3945; **1952** 3972; **1966** 3985

HOME, GEORGE **1838** 2474, 4491

INDEX

HUNTER, D. **1924** 3142

HUNTER, FRANK **1964** 929

HUNTER, PERCY **1917** 2253

HUNTER, ship **1766–7** 4445

The Hunterian oration **1822** 3945; **1952** 3972; **1966** 3985

HUNTINGDON, *Mayor of* **1782** 4630, 4633

HUNTINGDON DRAFT LEAF **1770** 3, 583

HUNTINGTON, HENRY WILLIAM HEMSWORTH **1885** 364, 764

HURST AND CO., *publishers, New York* **n.d.** 1589

HUTCHINSON, JOHN **1768** 574

HUTCHINSON EDUCATIONAL, *London* **1967** 319, 2975

HUTTON, CHARLES **[1783]** 3924

HUXLEY, LEONARD **1918** 3958

HYDE PARK, *Sydney*
celebrations **1929** 2402;
monument 2822, 2872, 2987–3026, 3386–7

HYMNS 3672

I.E., *artist* **n.d.** 496

I.M. **n.d.** 2851

I.S. **1775** 4429–32

IBBETSON, *artist* 2599–2602

IBBETSON, JOHN, *Secretary to the Board of Longitude* 601, 1216

Ice Island, [with *Resolution*] **1773–4** 1379, *f.27a*

Ice Islands **1773–4** 1379, *f.29–30*; **1777** 1381, *no.30*

Ice Islands with the *Resolution* and the *Adventure* **1773–4** 1379, *f.28*

Ice Islands, with the *Resolution* in the foreground **1773–4** 1379, *f.27*

IFOULD, WILLIAM HERBERT **1944** 828

Illustrated Chambers's encyclopaedia **1925** 2266, 4049

Illustrated London News 3171; **1878** 2996; **1937** 4316–17

Illustrated Sydney News **[1870]** 2031; **1871** 3721, *nos.106, 114*; **1879** 2999, 3001

Illustrations of Australian plants collected in 1770 (*Banks and Solander*) **1901–5** 934

Illustrations of the botany of Captain Cook's voyage round the world in H.M.S. *Endeavour* in 1768–71 **1901–5** 934

Illustrations to Captain Cook's voyages **[177–]** 544

Illustrations to Cook's first voyage: British Museum **n.d.** 930

Illustrations to Cook's first voyage in the British Museum (Natural History) **n.d.** 931

[Illustrations to the voyages of Captain Cook] 545

Illustrierte Zeitung **1875** 4428

Immortals of History **1967** 318, 2131

IMOGENE, H.M.S. **n.d.** 3150–51

Imperial Magazine **1819** 3992

IMPRENTA REAL, *Madrid* **1795** 55, 1974

IMPRIMÉRIE DE GUILLAUME, *Paris* **1797** 715, 1594

IMPRIMÉRIE DE LA REPUBLIQUE, *Paris* **1798** 1653

L'IMPRIMÉRIE DE MOIROUX, *Macon* **1805** 334

IMPRIMÉRIE NATIONALE, *Paris* **1792** 1972

L'IMPRIMÉRIE ROYALE, *Paris* **1780** 327; **1784** 1940–41; **1836** 261

In Dusky Bay, New Zealand **1773** 1379, *f.31*

In the South Seas: an old narrative **n.d.** 2560

In the Steps of the Explorers Series **1959** 828

In the wake of Captain Cook **1895** 373

INCLINOMETER 3661, 3681

INGAMELLS, REX **1951** 3853

INGLETON, GEOFFREY CHAPMAN **1934** 820, 1078; **[1936–7?]** 1019; **[195–]** 1417, 1879; **1957** 228, 1020, 1418, 1880; **[1958?]** 232; **1958** 231; **1963** 532

INGLIS, ROBERT KEITH **1969** 3807

INGRAM, *Sir* BRUCE STIRLING **n.d.** 1835; **1937** 4315

Inhabitants of Northern Sound **1785** 1743, *no.54*

IÑIGUEZ, D. ANGEL GARCIA **1796** 2460, 3799

The Injured islanders **1779** 3810–12; **1797** 3823

An Inland view, in Atooi **1785** 1743, *no.35*

INSECTS **1954–5** 2892

The Inside of a hippah, in New Zeeland (*sic*) **1785** 1743, *no.10*

The Inside of a house, in Oonalashka **1785** 1743, *no.58*

The Inside of a house, Nootka Sound **1785** 1743, *no.42*

The Inside of a winter habitation, in Kamtschatka **1785** 1743, *no.78*

The Inside of the house, in the morai, in Atooi **1785** 1743, *no.34*

849

MILTON, JOHN **n.d.** 2851

Mimosa; or, The sensitive plant **1779** 3922

MINERVA, *publishers, Auckland* **1968** 490

MIRVAL, C.H. (E.H.) DE, *pseud.* *See* Champagnac, Jean Baptiste Joseph de

Mr. Dalrymple's observations on Dr. Hawkesworth's Preface to the second edition **1773** 4360, 4451

Mr. Oram's story **1949** 2097, 2945

MITCHEL (Mitchell), BOWLES **1772–5** 1161

MITCHELL, LORNA MARY MAL-TRAVERS **1962** 742; **1963** 743; **1966** 747

MITCHELL, MAIRIN **1949** 1701

MITCHELL, RAE ELSE- **1939** 4057

MITCHELL, THOMAS WALTER **1966** 2127–8; **1967** 2132; **1968** 2135–7

MITCHELL LIBRARY, *Sydney* **1928** 4752

MITFORD, MARY RUSSELL **1811** 3827

MITTON, GERALDINE EDITH (*Lady* Scott) **1927** 279, 2077

Moana, océan cruel **1966** 313

Moana Roa **1947** 3791

Modern, authentic and complete system of universal geography **[1800?]** 62

Modern traveller **1777** 240

Modern voyages **1790** 330, 331

MOERNER, CARL BIRGER, *Count* **[1923]** 2262

MOIR, W.A. **1907** 3592; **1908** 3617

MOLESCHOTT, JAC. **1854** 4395

MOLINEUX, ROBERT *See* Molyneux, Robert

MOLTENE, COLNAGHI & CO., *publishers, London* **1788** 4229

MOLYNEUX (Molineux), ROBERT **1768–9** 605; **1768–70** 604; **1769** 606; **1892** 4786

Monarchs of ocean, Columbus and Cook **1873** 760, 2204

MONCKTON-ARUNDELL, GEORGE VERE ARUNDELL, *8th Viscount Galway* 1414, 3653

MONKHOUSE, GEORGE **1771** 2875

MONKHOUSE, JONATHAN **1768–9** 607; **1769** 608

MONKHOUSE, WILLIAM BROUG-HAM **1769** 609

MONKHOUSE FAMILY **1771** 4543

MONNERON, — **1785** 4723

MONNIER, *artist* **n.d.** 3565

MONTAGU, EDWARD WORTLEY **1775** 1215

MONTAGU, JOHN, *4th Earl of Sandwich* *See* Sandwich, John Montagu, *4th Earl*

MONTÉMONT, ALBERT **1833–34** 114; **1835** 2183; **1835–7** 118; **1853** 154, 2192

The Month at Goodspeed's Book Shop **1937** 4537

Monthly Review, London **1772–9** 750; **1773** 653; **1776** 1245; **1780** 3815; **1784** 1543; **1797** 2684

MONUMENT POINT, *Bustard Bay, Queensland* **1957** 3087

Monuments in Easter Island: [illustration] **1777** 1381, *no.49*

Mooolelo Hawaii **1862** 1669

MOORE, ARTHUR **1913** 1094

MOORE, DAVID RAINSFORD 3721

MOORE, J., *publisher, Dublin* **1791** 254

MOORE, JOHN HAMILTON **1778** 751

MOORE, JOSEPH SHERIDAN **1863** 725, 2028

MOORE, WILLIAM **1934** 4733

MOOREHEAD, ALAN McCRAE **1966** 315–16; **1968** 322

MOORHOUSE, GEOFFREY **1968** 488

The Morai, an ode **1788** 1962, 2451, 3821

A Morai, in Atooi **1785** 1743, *no.33*

MORE, HANNAH **n.d.** 3855

MOREL, *artist* 2619

Moreplavatel' tumannogo Al'biona: Dzhems Kuk **1963** 2118

MORGAN, *Rev.* JAMES **1910** 2244, 3176

MORIN, *publisher, Amsterdam* **1787** 1959

MORISON, R., AND SON, *publishers, Perth* **1785** 1559, 2588–9, 3576–7; **1787** 1565; **1789** 670, 1281, 1572

MÖRNER, CARL BIRGER, *Count* *See* Moerner, Carl Birger, *Count*

Morning Chronicle **1773** 1108

MORRIS, EDWARD ELLIS **1897–1901** 1113; **1898** 4024, 4787; **[1899?]** 1087; **1899** 776, 1088, 1945, 4788; **1900** 380, 777, 4025, 4453; **1901–5** 934; **1937** 4799

MORRISBY, CAMDEN **1935** 3634

MORRISON-SCOTT, T.C.S. **1950** 987, 2891, 4605

MORROW, W., *publisher, N.Y.* **1960** 302, 2112, 2957

Morrow Junior Books **1960** 302

MORSKAGO SHLIAKHESHNAGO KELESHSKAGO **1796–1800** 1235

La Mort du Capitaine Cook: [pantomime] **1788** 2450, 3797

INDEX

Observations faites, pendant le second voyage de M. Cook **1778** 1223, 1261

Observations. Lunar and other observations made at places visited **n.d.** 1453

Observations made by Captain Cook and Captain King **1778** 1534

Observations made during a voyage round the world **1778** 1262

Observations on the diseases prevalent in the South Sea Islands **1783** 245

Observations on the transit of Venus in 1769 **[1836]** 119, 1998; **1837** 123, 2001

Observer, London **1933** 2704

Ocean scenes **[1847]** 347

L'Océanie en estampes **1832** 260, 2914

OCTAGON BOOKS, *New York* **1965** 477

An Ode to the memory of the late Captain James Cook **1780** 3812, 3814

Ode 20 **1801** 4492

ODEWAHN, VIV. **1961** 4350

O'DONNELL, JOHN **1946** 4062

OEDIDEE (Aedidee, O-Hedidee) 3891–2, 3894; **1777** 1381, *no.35*

OERTEL, WILHELM, *of Horn See* Horn, W.O. von, *pseud.*

An Offering before Capt. Cook: [illustration] **1784** 1743, *no.60*

AN OFFICER ON BOARD **1781** 1246

AN OFFICER RETURNED FROM THE VOYAGE **1780** 1651

Official guide to Whitby **1914** 2074

OHAMANENO HARBOUR. Chart **1773** 860

O-Hedidee: [portrait] **1777** 1381, *no.35; see also* Oedidee

O'KEEFE, JOHN **1785** 3795, 4554

AN OLD SAILOR, *pseud.* **1951** 1702

OLESON, W.B. **[1894?]** 3133

OLIVER, A. **1893** 927

OLIVER & BOYD, *publishers, Edinburgh and London* **[1836]** 119, 1998, 3323–4; **1837** 123, 2001; **1964** 474

OLLIE, CHARLES **n.d.** 4337

OLSEN, ÖRJAN **1935** 821

OMAI **n.d.** 3889–90, 3892, 3894; **1774** 1214, 3879, 4626, 4657; **1775** 1203, 1215, 1539, 3880; **1776** 3881; **1777** 1381, *no.57;* **1780** 1538, 2434, 4627; **1791** 252; **1830** 2175

Omai; or, a trip round the world **1785–6** 3796, 4554–5, 4557–8

Omai, first Polynesian ambassador to England **1940** 4567

Omais, Freund und Reisegefährte des Kapitain Cook **1792–3** 4561

Omiah's farewell **1776** 4551

On the science of agriculture **1825** 3946

150th anniversary of the discovery of Hawaii **1927** 2379; **1928** 2865

150th anniversary of the discovery of the Hawaiian Islands **1928** 2867–9

150th anniversary of the landing of Captain Cook in New South Wales **1920** 2376

138th anniversary of the landing of Captain Cook at Botany Bay **1908** 2370; **1920** 2375

OOPOA HARBOUR. Chart **1773** 860

OPANO, JACOBUS **[1773]** 3911; **[1774]** 3913

An Opossum of Van Diemen's Land: [illustration] **1785** 1743, *no.8*

ORANGE, *Prince of* **1773** 3878

ORD, JOHN WALKER **1846** 2188, 3181

Oregon State Monographs: Studies in history **1963** 1604

OREGON STATE UNIVERSITY PRESS **1963** 1604

O'REILLY, PATRICK **1967** 4768

ORELL FÜSSLI, *Zürich* **n.d.** 492

ORIENTAL BOX 3670

The Original astronomical observations made in the course of a voyage to the Northern Pacific Ocean **1782** 1542

The Original astronomical observations made in the course of a voyage towards the South Pole **1777** 1287

ORION BOOKSELLERS **1779** 1535

ORME, D., *artist* **1796** 4600

ORME, EDWARD, *engraver* **1796** 4600

ORMSBY, *Parish* **1780** 1953

Ornaments and weapons at the Marquesas: [illustration] **1777** 1381, *no.17*

Ornaments, utensils and weapons at the Friendly Isles: [illustration] **1777** 1381, *no.21*

Ornaments, weapons &c. at New Caledonia: [illustration] **1777** 1381, *no.20*

ORR, WM. S., & CO., *publishers, London* **n.d.** 3366, 4193

ORTEGA Y GASSET, M. **1921–2** 684, 1243

ORTIZ, ELENA GARCIA **[1957]** 229

ORTON, RICHARD, *clerk* 578, 617–19, 693, 4805

PERRY, GEORGE, *Victualling Officer, Lond.* **1772** 1197, 1875

PERRY, THOMAS **[17– –]** 3638; **[1775?]** 3808–9

PERRY, WILLIAM **n.d.** 579, 1441; **1771** 693

PERSEVERANCE, H.M.S. **n.d.** 1331, 1713, 1742; **1783** 3638

PERTHES, *publisher, Gotha* **1863** 4397

Pervoe krugosvetnoe plavanie kapitana Dzhemsa Kuka **1960–64** 233

PETER LEYDEN PUBLISHING HOUSE, *Sydney* **1964** 744, 2967

PETER PINDAR, *pseud. See* Wolcot, John

PETERMANN, A. **n.d.** 1377

Peter's prophecy **1788** 3926–7; **1794** 3931; **1816** 3938

PETHERICK, E.A. **1895** 2724

Le Petit matelot **1838** 1663; **1842** 1664; **1853** 1668

PETROGRAD, **[177–?]** 1932; **1918** 3749

PETRUS, J., *translator* **1965** 311, 2125, 2972

PHELIPEAU, *engraver* **n.d.** 557

PHILIP, *Prince, Duke of Edinburgh* **1952** 117

PHILIP, GEO. B., *publisher, Sydney* **1930** 1018; **1933** 732, 1933

PHILLIBROWN, *engraver* **n.d.** 4112

PHILLIP, ARTHUR, *Admiral* **n.d.** 3624; **1790** 43

PHILLIPS, *Sir* CLAUDE **1894** 4207

PHILLIPS, I., *engraver* **1815** 3523

PHILLIPS, JAMES, *publisher, London* **1784** 713–4

PHILLIPS, MOLESWORTH, *Lieut.-Col.* **1791** 3885, 4330; **1832** 3857, 4615

PHILLIPS, NANCY **1964** 929

PHILLIPS, *Sir* RICHARD, *publisher, London* **1800** 1977; **1809** 73, 3519–20; **1809–10** 74; **1820** 341; **1827** 343

PHILLIPS, S.W. **1926** 2668

PHILLIPS, THOMAS, *R.A.* 4133–98

PHILOSOPHICAL INSTITUTE OF VICTORIA *See* Royal Society of Victoria

Philosophical Magazine and Journal, London **1820** 3993, 3996

The Philosophical puppet show **[1783]** 3924

PHILOSOPHICAL SOCIETY OF AUSTRALASIA **1821** 3027–40, 3048, 3052

Philosophicall rudiments concerning government and society 2691

Philosophy inviting Youth to the heights of Science **[1789?]** 2676–8

PHILPOT, T. **1813** 3731

PHILPS, ROBERT F. **1893** 3630

PHIPPS, CONSTANTINE JOHN, *2nd Baron Mulgrave* **1768–71** 590; **1774** 3897

PHOENIX HOUSE, *London* **1968** 3986

The Phrenological Journal, London, **1831** 344

PICARD, E. **[1864]** 1943

PICKERSGILL, RICHARD
charts 863, 915–17; **1770** 862, **1893** 890;
handwriting **n.d.** 3856;
instructions to **1776** 1524;
journal (manuscript) **1768–70** 610–11; **1771–4** 1162–3;
journal (printed) **1893** 614, 716; **1907** 717; **1914** 718
publications **1907** 1606
subject references **1775** 1539

Picturesque atlas of Australasia **1886** 953, 2675, 3491

PICTURESQUE ATLAS PUB. CO., *Sydney* **1886** 365

PIDGEON, W.E. **1931** 3852

PIERONI, PIERO **1965** 310, 550

PIGEOT, *engraver* **n.d.** 3338–40

PIGUENIT, WILLIAM CHARLES 1021

PIHERE, *a native of the Hawaiian Is.* **[1801?]** 2461

PIKE, JOSEPH **1933** 4651–4

PIKE, L.H. **1955** 2328

PINDAR, PETER, *pseud. See* Wolcot, John

PINGO, LEWIS **n.d.** 2675, 2788–2821, 3568–82; **[c.1784]** 2852–62; **1784** 1547–8

Pink may: [poems] **1930** 3851

PINKERTON, JOHN **1812** 77

Pioneers of intellectual progress **[191–?]** 2240

PIRINGER, *engraver* **n.d.** 1772, 1747; **1787** 1764; **1788** 1757, 1779, 1783, 2579–83; *see also* Jukes and Piringer, *engravers*

PISSOT, *publisher and bookseller, Paris* **1772** 1272; **1782** 1611; **1788** 33, 1963

PITT, JOHN, *2nd Earl of Chatham* **1791** 3885, 4330

PITTARD, *Mr* 3721, *nos.106, 114*

Plan of a memorial to procure a pension for Captain Cooke (*sic*) **1780** 1955

Plan of Adventure Bay on Van Diemen's Land **1784** 1714, *plate no.IX*

Plan of Christmas Harbour on Kerguelen's Land **1784** 1714, *plate no.III*

A Plan of Christmas Island 1728

A Plan of Fort Venus in Royal Bay 920

[A Plan of Hippie Isles] 1729

[A Plan of Indian Cove, King Georges Sound] 1730

A Plan of King Georges Island or Otaheite 1769 902–3

A Plan of King Georges Island or Otaheite lying in the South Sea 1769 855–6

A Plan of Mercury Bay 918

[A Plan of Oaiti Peha Bay Otaheite Ete] 1731

A Plan of Queen Charlottes (sic) Sound 919

A Plan of Royal Matavie (sic) Bay 920

[A Plan of Ship Cove, King Georges Sound] 1732

A Plan of the Bay of A'watch'ka 1738

A Plan of the Harbour of Ohwarhe 921

[A Plan of the Harbours of Tah-row and Av, voi, ta Eimeo] 1733

[Plan of the Island of Anamocka] 1734

[A Plan of the Island of Otobui] 1735

A Plan of Tolaga Bay 922

A Plan of Whatdew and Mo-du 1736

Plant used at Otaheite to catch fish by intoxicating them 1777 1381, no.24

Plates to Cook's second voyage, comprising a portrait and 35 views 1776–7 1404–07

PLOMER, WILLIAM CHARLES FRANKLYN 1937 2307

PLUMMER, JOHN 1885 3012

PLYMOUTH CITY MUSEUM & ART GALLERY 1968 488, 2420

The Poa bird [177–] 546; 1776 1410–12; 1777 1381, no.52; 1784 1413

The Pocket Navigator [1808] 72

POCOCK, GUY NOEL [1954] 226; 1961 234

Poe-bird, New Zeeland (sic) 1777 1381, no.52; see also The Poa bird

POEDOOA, daughter of Orea, Society Islands [1785?] 1838–9

A Poetical epistle, moral and philosophical, from an officer at Otaheite 1775 3920

POINÇOT, publisher, Paris 1783 1614; 1788–90 50; 1795 1233, 1578

POINT HICKS, Victoria 3105–7

POINT VENUS, Tahiti 1883 3161; 1906 3162; 1931 3164; 1937 3165

Pôle sud ou austral: [a chart] 1911 1341

The Polite traveller and British navigator [1783] 11, 2441

POLYNESIAN SOCIETY, N.Z. 1928 4052 Memoirs 1932 417, 560; 1934 423, 1691

POMARÉ, King of Tahiti 1789 1381, no.38, 2146, 4724

PONZANO, J.T., publisher, Madrid 1861 163

Popular Library of Literary Treasures 1886 681

PORSON, RICHARD 1774 3914–18, 3935, 3974

Port Palliser: [sketch] 1776–9 1443

Port Praya in the Island of St. Jago, one of the Cape de Verds: [chart] 1777 1336, plate no.X

PORTEOUS, K.L. 1963 541, 3792

PORTLAND, Dowager Duchess 1786 4661

PORTLAND MUSEUM 1786 4661

PORTLOCK, NATHANIEL 1776–7 1447; 1777–8 1488; 1778–9 1489; 1789 2453

PORTLOCK, WILLIAM HENRY [1794?] 46; [1794] 49

PORTMAN, L., engraver 1802 3341

Portrait of a Maori [1773?] 1379, f.32b

Portrait of a native [177–?] 1379, f.19a

Posemata 1810 3826

Posliednee puteshestvie okolo svieta Kapitana Kuka s obstoiatelstvami o ego zhizni i smerti 1788 1570

Possession Bay in the Island of South Georgia: [illustration] 1777 1381, no.34

POSSESSION ISLAND, Queensland 3100–2

POST, VAN DER, publisher, Utrecht See Van der Post, publisher, Utrecht

POSTAGE STAMPS 1928 2876–9; 1945 2870

New Zealand 1961 2871

Potatau, chief of Punaauia n.d. 1379, f.17

POTATOW, chief [1773?] 1379, f.17; 1777 1381, no.56; 1791 252; see also Potatau

Potatow, the Otaheite admiral [1773?] 1379, f.17

POTEMKIN, Prince 1779 1529

POUILLY, T. 1684 3695

POULAHO, King of the Friendly Islands n.d. 1855, no.7; 1785 1743, nos.18, 20

POULTON, THOMAS H.M. 1888 1536

POUNCY, B.T., engraver 1777 1381, nos.30, 33; 1785 1743, nos.10, 54, 61, 74

POVERTY BAY, N.Z. 1769 582

POVERTY BAY-EAST COAST CENTENNIAL COUNCIL 1950 832

Sir Joseph Banks and the Emperor of Morocco **1788** 3928, 3929, 3930; **1794** 3933, 3934; **1816** 3940

Sir Joseph Banks and the Royal Society **1844** 3948

Sir Joseph Banks and the thief-takers **1816** 3941

SIR JOSEPH BANKS MEMORIAL **1962** 3978

SIR JOSEPH BANKS' MEMORIAL FUND **[190–?]** 3954

SIR JOSEPH BANKS MUSEUM 3721, 3661

SIWERTZ, S. **1924** 4671

SKEATS, L. **n.d.** 4296

SKELTON, RALEIGH ASHLIN **1953** 2323, 4349; **[c.1954]** 4639; **1954** 2104, 2325, 2326; **1955** 538; **1955–68** 227, 2106, 4762; **1956–7** 567; **1958** 539; **1965** 1946; **1967** 4769; **1968** 2347

Sketch of Dusky Bay in New Zealand; 1773 **1777** 1336, *plate no.XIII*

A Sketch of Kara'ka'kooah Bay in the Island of Hawhy'hee 1739

Sketch of Nootka Sound . . . 1778 **1784** 1714, *plate no.XXXVII*

A Sketch of part of the Bay of Rio de Janeiro 904

Sketch of Port Palliser **1784** 1714, *plate no. III*

A Sketch of the Harbour of St. Peter & St. Paul with Mount A'wautchka, as taken from the spit 1740

Sketch of the Harbour of Samganooda on the Island Oonalaska **1784** 1714, *plate no.LV*

Sketch of the Harbours on the North Side of Eimeo **1784** 1714, *plate no.XXX*

Sketch of the Marquesas de Mendoça **1777** 1336, *plate no.V*

Sketch of Van Diemen Land, Explored by Captn. Furneaux, in March 1773 **1777** 1336, *plate no.VIII*

Sketches and charts drawn on Cook: 2nd Voyage, by Fannin as Master of HMS Adventure (Captain T. Furneaux) **1772–5** 1384

Sketches of the Islands, Lagoon, Thrum-cap, Bow-Island, *etc.* 905–6

SKINNER AND COMPANY, *publishers, London* **1786** 4661

SKOTTOWE, THOMAS **1755** 1949

SLAUGHTER, WILLIAM **1854** 2022

Slavery: [poem] **n.d.** 3855

A Sledge of Kamtschatka **1785** 1743, *no.71*

SLESSOR, KENNETH **1931** 893, 3852

SMALES, *Rev.* GIDEON **1867** 2197; **1870** 2203

SMART, J. **n.d.** 4314–17

SMEETON, GEORGE **1824** 2172

SMIDT, NORMAN **1964** 929

SMITH, *Captain* **1928** 2391

SMITH, *of Abingdon, Eng.* **1854** 3644

SMITH, A., *engraver* **1794** 4468

SMITH, B., & CO., *publishers, Woodbridge* **[1815]** 83; **1815** 3523; **1822** 97

SMITH, BERNARD WILLIAM **1950** 562, 4068; **1955–68** 227; **1956** 1323; **[196–]** 4745; **1960** 549

SMITH, C.J. 579; **1773–5** 1121

SMITH, EDWARD **1911** 2879, 3957, 4287

SMITH, ERIC E.F. **1968** 4352

SMITH, ISAAC, *Admiral*
letters from **1821** 1911; **1830** 2878;
illustrations and charts **1769** 963–4; **1771–5** 1166;
Original sketches: [album] 497, 542, 1331, 1379, 1713, 1742
subject references **n.d.** 3637

SMITH, ISAAC CRAGG **n.d.** 3637

SMITH, J.B. **n.d.** 3703

SMITH, JOACHIM **1773–8** 4227–32; **1775** 4429–32

SMITH, JOSEPH R., *publisher, London* **n.d.** 108; **1840** 134; **1859** 3583–4

SMITH, *Sir* JOYNTON **1928** 3230

SMITH, MATTHEW **1778** 499; **1784** 1714, *plate no.XXXVII*

SMITH, PATSY ADAM **1968** 3103

SMITH, S., *engraver* 2566–70; **1777** 1381, *no.34*; **1785** 1743, *nos.41, 77*; **1794** 2459

SMITH, WILLIAM **[1841?]** 138, 140; **[1841]** 139; **1842** 142; **1846** 149; **1880** 1240

SMITH FAMILY **1933** 4651–4

Smith's Dock Journal **1929** 408

SMYTH, JOSEPH, *printer, Belfast* **n.d.** 1991; **[183–?]** 2912; **1835** 1996, 2917

SNIP, SIMON, *pseud.* **[1783]** 3924

SNUFF-BOX **n.d.** 3690

LA SOCIETÀ GEOGRAFICA ITALI-ANA, *publisher, Roma* **1903** 727

LA SOCIETÀ MENICHELLI E BECCARI, *Italy* **1812** 3527

SOCIÉTÉ BIBLIOPHILE, *Paris* **[1841?]** 138

INDEX

INDEX

WILLIS, THOMAS **1772-5** 1172-4

WILLS & HEPWORTH, *publishers, Loughborough, Eng.* **1958** 2110, 2954

WILLSON, ELEANOR JOAN **1961** 3977, 4607

WILMOTT, C. **1798** *watermark* 2461

Wilshire, H. **1926** 278

WILSON,— **1862** 3212

WILSON, G.W., *photographer* **n.d.** 2748

WILSON, GEORGE WASHINGTON **[187-?]** 2351

WILSON, HAROLD, *Prime Minister of Great Britain* **1968** 2136-7

WILSON, JAMES G. **[1939]** 436

WILSON, PHILIP **n.d.** 4472; **[1794]** 49, 4502, 4596

WILSON, ROBERT **1806** 68, 1052

WILSON, W., *publisher, Dublin* **1774** 3918

WILSON, WILLIAM F. **1926** 2521; **[193-?]** 4756

WINGE, PETER, *Nyköping* **1798** 259

Der Wissbegierige **1785** 2445

WISSENSCHAFTLICHE VERLAGS-GESELLSCHAFT, M.B.H., *Stuttgart* **1952** 2100

With Captain Cook in New Zealand **[1963]** 1648, 2962

WITT, *Sir* ROBERT **n.d.** 3218

WODEHOUSE, *Major* **1908** 3136

WOLCOT, JOHN **1788** 3926-30; **1794** 3931-4; **1816** 3938-41

WOLLSCHLAEGER, ALFRED **1936** 430, 2304; **1937** 433, 2309

WOLLSTON, *Rev.* FREDERICK **1784** 1904

WOLSKEL, AUGUSTUS **1941** 826

A Woman of Eaoo: [illustration] **1785** 1743, *no.23*

Woman of Easter Island: [illustration] **1777** 1381, *no.25*

A Woman of Kamtschatka: [illustration] **1785** 1743, *no.76*

Woman of New Caledonia: [illustration] **1777** 1381, *no.48*

Woman of New Zealand: [illustration] **1777** 1381, *no.58*

A Woman of Nootka sound: [illustration] **1785** 1743, *no.39*

A Woman of Oonalashka: [illustration] **1785** 1743, *no.49*

A Woman of Prince William's Sound: [illustration] **1785** 1743, *no.47*

Woman of Sta. Christina: [illustration] **1777** 1381, *no.37*

Woman of the Island of Tanna: [illustration] **1777** 1381, *no.45*

A Woman of Van Diemen's Land: [illustration] **1785** 1743, *no.7*

WOOD, *Rev.* Alfred Harold **1932** 419

WOOD, DAVID **1947** 293, 2944

WOOD, G. BERNARD **1957** 2335; **1966** 3206

WOOD, GEORGE ARNOLD 693; **1922** 802, 2259, 4046; **1925** 729, 2936; **1926** 730, 1029, 1096; **1933** 734; **1944** 736

WOODHOUSE, A. **1937** 4799

WOODHOUSE, W.J., *Professor* **[c.1910]** 4744

WOODING, J.G., *engraver* **[178-?]** 1049

WOODROW, W. **1905** 891

WOODWARK, T.H., *Whitby, retired solicitor* 1034

WOODYER, *engraver* **1785** 1743, *no.71*

WOOLF, HARRY **1959** 842

WOOLLETT, W., *engraver* **1773** 932, *nos. 5-6*; **1777** 1381, *nos.29, 44, 49, 61*; **1785** 1743, *no.25*

WOOLNER, THOMAS, *sculptor* 2987-3026; **1876** 2993; **1917** 3018

WOOLNOTH, I., *engraver* **1823** 4128

WOOLNOTH, T., *engraver* **1784** 3925

WOOLWICH YARD, *England* **1768** 989-93

The Works of the late Capt. James Cooke, R.N. **1888** 367

The World: tracks of H.M.S. *Resolution,* 1772-5 **1944** 1342

The World displayed **1815** 85

A World explorer, James Cook **1963** 2117, 2961; **1966** 2126, 2974

World Landmark Books **1955** 299, 2105, 2950

World on Mercator's projection: [map] **[1816?]** 1340

WORLD PUBLISHING CO., *Cleveland, U.S.A.* **1964** 307

World's News **1907** 2698; **1926** 2517

WORSFELD, W. BASIL **[19--]** 2255

WRAGGE, CLEMENT LINDLEY **1906** 3162

WRIGHT, *publisher, London* **n.d.** 109

WRIGHT, *Sir* JAMES **1775** 644